PTON

entr

# BUSINESS
# ECONOMICS

# ABOUT THE AUTHORS

**Mark Cook**, BA, MSc, is Principal Lecturer in Economics at the School of Business, Nene College of Higher Education in Northampton, and is a tutor on Henley Management College's distance learning MBA. He is the author of books on international business economics, supply-side economics and growth and structural change.

**Corri Farquharson**, BA(Hons), MBA, is Senior Lecturer in Economics at the School of Business, Nene College of Higher Education, and Course Director of BABS (BA Business Studies). She was previously Lecturer in Economics at the University of Sunderland Business School.

Both teach on a wide range of business economics courses at undergraduate, postgraduate and post-experience levels, and maintain close links with business and industry.

# BUSINESS ECONOMICS

## STRATEGY AND APPLICATIONS

Mark Cook and
Corri Farquharson

School of Business,
Nene College of Higher Education, Northampton

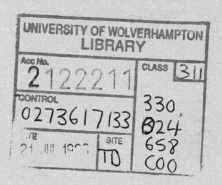

## PITMAN PUBLISHING

London · Hong Kong · Johannesburg · Melbourne · Singapore · Washington DC

PITMAN PUBLISHING
128 Long Acre, London WC2E 9AN
Tel: +44 (0)171 447 2000
Fax: +44 (0)171 240 5771

A Division of Pearson Professional Limited

**Visit the Pitman Publishing Website at
http://www.pitman.co.uk**

First published in Great Britain 1998

© Pearson Professional Limited 1998

The right of Mark Cook and Corri Farquharson to be identified
as authors of this work has been asserted by them in accordance
with the Copyright, Designs and Patents Act 1988.

ISBN 0 273 61713 3

*British Library Cataloguing in Publication Data*
A CIP catalogue record for this book can be obtained from the British Library

10  9  8  7  6  5  4  3  2  1

Typeset by Pantek Arts, Maidstone, Kent
Printed and bound in Great Britain by William Clowes Ltd, Beccles

*The Publishers' policy is to use paper manufactured from sustainable forests.*

# ABBREVIATED CONTENTS

# CONTENTS

# Part 2
# DEMAND, REVENUE AND COSTS

## Part 3
## MARKETING AND INVESTMENT DECISIONS

# PREFACE

*Business Economics* covers all the information found in a business economics course, but has the added benefit that this is related to corporate strategy. The aim of the book is to provide an international/European business economics text for students which is both rigorous and also applies theory to real business issues, using case studies and named company examples. The book attempts to bridge the gap between those texts which are traditionally theoretically focused and mainly US-based and the more applied texts on business economics. It is intended that the text should provide the reader with a better understanding of the business world and demonstrate the relevance of economics for business decisions.

In many universities, economics and corporate strategy are taught separately and the notion of producing a book on business economics and corporate strategy may appear odd. However, what this book shows is that there is no 'finishing point' to business economics; that it provides the foundation for, and the basis of the critical appraisal of corporate strategy. No student who has studied business economics should be without an appreciation of where business economics can support and inform other areas. Similarly, no student who is studying corporate strategy should do so without an understanding of the economic concepts, both theoretical and applied, that underpin strategy. Those who have previously taken other business-related courses will note the reference to concepts and topics already discussed in other areas of business. This also indicates that many areas of business are not discrete but are interrelated.

This book seeks to show the relevance of economics for the management of organisations. Economics should not be considered as simply theoretical modelling but as a necessary tool in business decision making. The text aims to illustrate to the business student more recent areas in economic thinking, such as transaction costs, while at the same time developing business environment issues which are likely to have most impact on organisations as they move into the next millennium. In particular, the text emphasises the increasing

globalisation and internationalisation of markets. Therefore, unlike many of the existing books on the subject, *Business Economics* has a distinct international flavour.

## The aims of this book

The primary aim of this book is to provide a clear, well structured, analytical and applied analysis of business economics and strategy. It sets the scene for the international environment in which organisations operate, discusses the important internal concepts and tools used by organisations, and then moves on to discuss strategic areas of business behaviour and to consider some of the most important international/European environmental issues facing organisations. These issues are reflected in the Part titles of the book.

More specifically, the text aims to be:

- *Comprehensive* in its coverage of the significant ideas and issues which are relevant to most types of business.
- *Strategic* in the way that economic concepts and ideas are developed to show how they can contribute to the organisation's long-term success.
- *International/European* in the manner in which applied examples are used to illustrate the concepts in the text. Moreover, this approach is reflected in the detailed consideration of international issues facing business organisations.
- *Practical* in its coverage of business issues and the way they relate to economic theory. The book considers many practical applications of the ways in which business undertakes decision making. It also provides over 100 practical case studies of business decision making in action, many drawing on articles from the *Financial Times*.
- *Theoretical* in the way it develops basic ideas and concepts in a logical manner, providing a clear exposition of the issues and underlying principles and allowing the more advanced student to develop these further.
- *Balanced* in the way it treats the various types of organisation. Thus, although there is a concentra-

tion on international and globalised industries, consideration is also given to small and medium-sized operations. In addition, the text discusses technological change, and the role of both service sector firms and the not-for-profit areas.

## Who should use this book

- This book is intended primarily for use by second-level and third-level business studies students, and for economics students for whom a course on business economics is available. On business studies degrees, business economics often makes up a significant part of the course, and the structure of the text makes it suitable for both those with and without a prior understanding of economics.
- Because of the text's development both into areas of business strategy and of internationalisation/Europeanisation, the text would also be appropriate for final-year business strategy courses, both on business studies and Euro-business studies degrees.
- MBA students should find that the practical discussions of business economics and business strategy will enhance their own experience and, because the text assumes no prior knowledge of business economics, it will be suitable for MBA courses.
- Postgraduate students on other specialist masters degree programmes should also find that this book provides them with a well grounded and critical approach to business economics. Even though some of them may not have received the theoretical underpinning for a course on business economics, this will be catered for in the background material within each chapter.
- The text, because of its great use of both international and specifically European case study material, will also be appropriate for English-speaking universities in continental Europe which include courses on business or managerial economics in their portfolios.
- In particular this text would be appropriate for those business economists who are seeking to focus on the applied rather than theoretical aspects of their subject.

## Key features of the book

### Structure
The text provides a clear and progressive structure to business economics, as the *plan of the book* (p xxii)

indicates. We have chosen to start by setting out the environment in which the organisation operates, considering the basic features of the organisation and its objectives. Then we move on to the development of demand, revenue and cost theories and applications. From here the text extends into areas of marketing and decision making, before turning to the links between business economic ideas and corporate strategy. Finally, in Part 5 on business issues consideration is given to some of the more pertinent areas facing organisations in the future.

### International/European focus
Each of the chapters focuses on providing as wide a perspective as possible in the discussion of business issues in terms of international and European examples. In this respect policy issues have a much greater European focus than in other texts.

### Strategic approaches
The book examines the development and use of business strategy from its foundations in business economics. Many texts do not cover strategic decision making but seek to develop business economics alone. Much of business strategy, however, has its foundations in business economics and this text indicates how business economics can be used in strategic decision making.

### Business issues
A number of business issues are considered which we believe to be most relevant for organisations, both over the past decade and in the future. These include the growth of 'green' economics, the globalisation of business activities, changes in the labour market and the arguments for the control of globalised businesses.

### Up-to-date developments
Each chapter includes new developments that have been taking place in business economics, and sometimes these developments are the subject of a whole chapter. There is an entire chapter on transaction cost economics, which provides the basis for the development of the organisation and the relationship between organisations. There are also up-to-date treatments of the methods of valuing environmental costs and benefits.

### Quantitative approaches
The use of quantitative methods has been undertaken sparingly. Where it is necessary to develop

the ideas further, the relevant quantitative approach is included in the main body of the chapter. Otherwise, the mathematical development appears in an Appendix at the end of the chapter. The mathematics has been specifically kept at a fairly basic level – algebra, calculus and basic geometry.

### Diagrams and tables

Where required, chapters have made use of diagrams and tables. These are supplements to the text and provide an alternative interpretation of the analysis in the chapter.

## Chapter features

### Objectives

Every chapter commences with a list of objectives, giving a structured outline to the ideas that will subsequently be developed.

### Business applications (cases)

These are short cases at the start of the chapter, introducing a practical business application of the theory to be discussed in the chapter. The chapters also include a wide range of cases based upon real companies, all of which can provide material for class discussion. There are over 120 cases in the book. After each case there are questions relating to the material in the case and these are followed by a discussion in the text of the salient issues to be brought out in the questions.

### Chapter summaries

Each chapter includes an extensive summary of the main points, which can act as a revision list for the reader.

### Review questions

Following the summary is a range of test questions associated with material in the chapter. The questions include both quantitative and qualitative problems and are suitable for student seminars and individual or group assignment work.

### Glossary of new terms

Every chapter contains a glossary defining the key new terms which were listed at the start of the chapter, together with other important definitions. Sometimes terms are repeated in other chapters, to save the reader from having to search the other chapters for the appropriate definition.

### Reading references and selected further reading

Not only details of references given in the main material in the chapter are included, but also a list of further reading which will either enable the student to explore the chapter topics in more depth or will more fully examine some important issues related to those considered in the chapter.

## How the book is structured

*The plan of the book* on page xxii, together with the diagram and explanation of the *key issues* (*see* pages xvii–xix), provide an overview of the connections between the various chapters and elements in the text. The text can be considered as being divisible into five Parts.

### Part 1 Introduction

After introducing the area of business economics, this section focuses on the organisation and its environment. Analysis is made of the different sizes of organisation in the UK and overseas and of the changes in industrial structure that have taken place. By concentrating on the organisation, the concept of business objectives is developed and comparison with other objectives is made of the profit maximising motive. In the light of the separation of ownership from control, the important areas of corporate governance and business ethics are explored.

### Part 2 Demand, revenue and costs

This initially considers the demand conditions faced by organisations. Starting from the more traditional view of demand theory, it explores the factors that affect the demand for an organisation's product or service, moving from individual demand to aggregate demand. The characteristics approach to demand is then developed, indicating the link between economics and marketing. Finally, behavioural theories of demand are investigated. One important aspect for organisations is the concept of elasticity and this is defined, showing how it can provide important information for the organisation in the pricing and advertising of its products. The third chapter in this section, Chapter 7, considers the estimation and forecasting of demand, and provides the reader with a whole range of estimation techniques that organisations might use. Finally, Chapter 8 considers the operational costs facing an organisation. Thus the section provides both an analysis of the revenue and cost features that impact on the organisation.

### Part 3 Marketing and investment decisions

This covers Chapters 9 to 13. First the section considers the theoretical and practical decisions relating to pricing. Drawing upon market structure analysis and the competitive nature of markets, the concepts of perfect competition, monopolistic competition, oligopoly and monopoly, are discussed, with consideration of how the structure of markets can influence pricing decisions. Often oligopolistic industries do not compete on price but use a whole raft of non-price methods. These are explored in Chapter 11, together with the marketing channels used by organisations. However, organisations are not only interested in maximising their objectives through pricing strategies. They are also concerned about staying within existing markets, as well as developing new markets and improving their performance through the correct investment decisions. Chapter 12 focuses critically on the area of investment appraisal and Chapter 13 develops this further in the discussion of risk and uncertainty in decision making.

### Part 4 Economics and corporate strategy

This is covered in Chapters 14 to 19 and opens with a discussion of strategy using Porter's approach. This approach is related back to the chapters on market structure in order to analyse organisational strategy's impact on the structure of competition. In the light of competitive strategy developed earlier, there is now a discussion of the competitive weapons that organisations can use to gain and protect market positions. Firms may seek to grow in size to protect their market and Chapter 17 develops this idea through the use of the transaction cost approach. Finally, the section investigates how an organisation can deter new entrants to its market, and how both reputation and quality can be used to enhance the organisation's position.

### Part 5 Business issues

Chapters 20 to 24 form the final section, which centres on areas that are most important in affecting the environment in which the organisation operates.

Chapter 20 turns attention to the organisation's relationship with the natural environment. During the 1980s and 1990s the growing importance of 'green' issues has resulted in the need for organisations to make changes in order to cope with the growing demands of environmental protection and green consumerism. At the same time some organisations have found that greater concern for environmental issues can confer competitive advantage.

Chapter 21 examines the globalisation of business. It discusses the growth in international trade and the development of trading blocs and the general theory behind the development of multinational organisations. As organisations have grown they have increased their market power, not only in domestic markets but also within Europe and internationally.

Chapter 22 covers the growth in government intervention in markets at both a domestic and an economic bloc level as a way of controlling market failure. There is a temptation in many business economics texts to consider the growth drivers behind organisations. During the 1990s we have witnessed the reverse. Organisations not only monitor their growth as a means of competitive advantage but also look to boundary shrinkage where necessary.

Chapter 23 considers the ways that the boundary of an organisation can alter through the process of demerger, down-sizing and the like.

Chapter 24 is the final chapter in this section and concerns labour market issues. This is an area which does not receive a great deal of analysis in many business economics texts. The chapter discusses the changes that have taken place in the labour market over the last 15 years, in particular focusing on the growth in female participation in the labour market, the ageing labour force, skill needs and the rise in levels of European unemployment.

This sectional approach to the text should not suggest that the reader is required to read earlier sections before moving on to later ones. The text may be used to dip into various chapters, according to course requirements, rather than read consecutively.

**FT** A key feature of the text is the selection of extracts from the *Financial Times*. These extracts are the copyright of the *Financial Times*, which has kindly given permission to reproduce them in this book. The extracts were all taken from the *Financial Times* CD-ROM edition.

## Instructor's manual

This is available to those lecturers adopting this textbook. It includes guidance on teaching from *Business Economics*, both in terms of level and of prerequisite knowledge, together with short commentaries on each chapter and comments on the cases. There is discussion on answering the question in the case studies and at the end of the chapters. Additional cases are provided for use as alternative or supplementary material for the majority of the chapters in the book. Overhead masters of many of the illustrations in *Business Economics* are also provided.

# KEY ISSUES

The key issues which are highlighted at the start of each chapter reflect the detailed diagram opposite. They demonstrate the links between business economics and strategy which are a distinguishing feature of this text. Business strategy, decision-making techniques and issues, economic concepts and business issues are all highly integrated with business economics. At the start of each chapter, the key issues covered are highlighted, with the shading indicating the most relevant areas that are considered in the chapter. Let us take as an example the international airline industry.

## Applying the key issues model

The key issues diagram shows how different areas, issues and concepts interlink. Each of the key issues may be discussed in depth by using the international airline industry as an example. Other, similarly 'rich' cases which may be found in the main body of the text include the telecommunications industry, the electricity supply industry and the supermarket industry in the UK and Europe. For example, 'pricing' links economic concepts with decision making, optimal outcomes, business strategy, and so on. Therefore, this illustrates how different industry observations are relevant to one or more given key issues.

## Management decision issues

The international airline industry has been undergoing a period of considerable change, which is likely to continue into the foreseeable future. One easily identifiable area of change is the increased trend for airline partnerships. Well-known airlines such as British Airways (BA) have entered into 'alliances' with other carriers around the world. In the USA their partner is USAir, and in Australia QANTAS. Examples of other alliances are KLM's venture with Northwest and the American airline Delta's agreements with both Swissair and Singapore Airlines.

There are three main reasons for this growth in cooperation between airlines: cost savings; the desire for increased access to domestic airports within destination countries; and the effects of regulation of the landing 'slots' (permission to land and take off) at airports. The cost savings are derived from airlines' ability to cut labour costs and other fixed costs by operating smaller, individual fleets more efficiently, while increasing the overall fleet size by entering into partnerships. These partnerships enable 'code sharing' – where an international flight is serviced by domestic aircraft and crew, thus removing the need for the international carrier to purchase additional capacity. At the same time, the passenger benefits from a 'straight through' service to the internal destination.

## Decision making

The decision to enter into a partnership with another airline requires certain competitive and market analyses and decision processes to be undertaken. The demand for seats on the identified routes needs to be forecast and potential partners identified. If there is not a preferred route, but the airline wishes to increase the scope of its service, then the alternatives must be identified and compared, looking at their advantages and disadvantages. Various statistical and non-statistical tools exist to facilitate this analysis. Passenger sensitivity to price on the chosen routes may also be modelled, using mathematical techniques, to predict reactions to price changes. On any one flight, passengers will have paid different prices for identical seats. Special offers, frequent flyer discounts and flexibility in changing tickets can all affect the price charged.

## Optimal outcomes to management issues

Once the alternatives have been identified and their various merits assessed, airline management will be in a position to make a rational decision regarding partner choice. The criteria could include the desire to partner a particular nation's airline, or to join an airline with an aggressive

# Key issues covered in this book

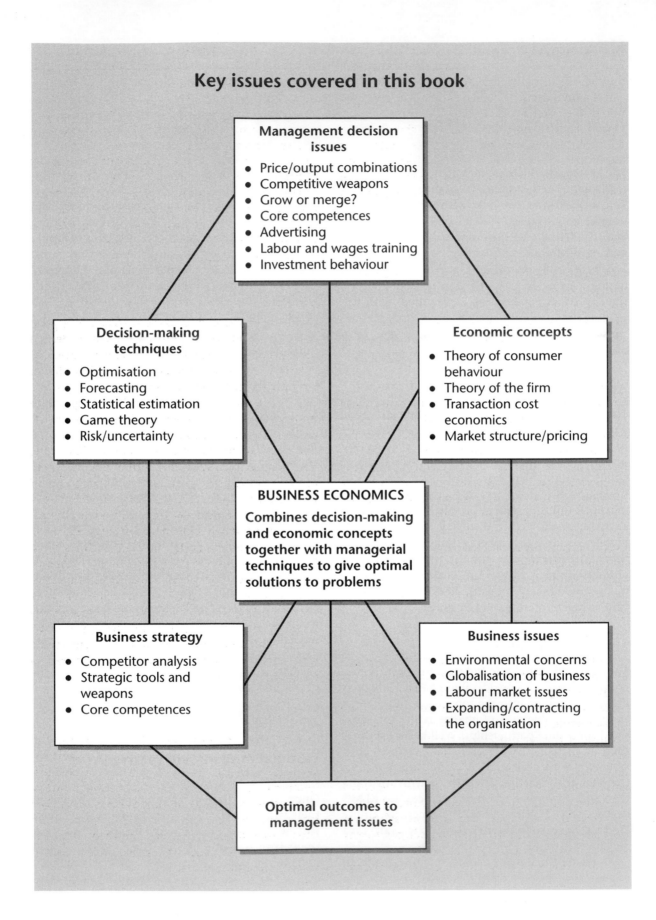

**Management decision issues**

- Price/output combinations
- Competitive weapons
- Grow or merge?
- Core competences
- Advertising
- Labour and wages training
- Investment behaviour

**Decision-making techniques**

- Optimisation
- Forecasting
- Statistical estimation
- Game theory
- Risk/uncertainty

**Economic concepts**

- Theory of consumer behaviour
- Theory of the firm
- Transaction cost economics
- Market structure/pricing

**BUSINESS ECONOMICS**

Combines decision-making and economic concepts together with managerial techniques to give optimal solutions to problems

**Business strategy**

- Competitor analysis
- Strategic tools and weapons
- Core competences

**Business issues**

- Environmental concerns
- Globalisation of business
- Labour market issues
- Expanding/contracting the organisation

**Optimal outcomes to management issues**

price-setting policy, or with very low fixed costs. Whatever the basis of the management's criteria, the 'bottom line' will always be a consideration, and the final decision will be based upon optimisation of the criteria, i.e. to minimise costs and maximise revenues, profits and market share, etc. In the airline industry, a specific measurement used is the revenue per passenger seat mile. Maximisation of this, while minimising costs, would be a rational strategy for an airline to adopt with respect to a chosen route.

## Economic concepts

Obviously, none of these decisions can be made without some reference to prices or costs. The theory of consumer demand is, therefore, a useful area of knowledge for the decision maker. The airline industry is not easy to classify into a single market structure; there are relatively few competitors in any domestic market, but many airlines worldwide. The competitive effect of such a structure is to intensify price competition and to increase attempts at non-price differentiation. Frequent flyer schemes and other loyalty programmes are popular, where the traveller is able to gain discounts or free upgrades. In addition, the airlines are always trying to stay ahead of competitors by offering extras to passengers, especially to those with the revenue-generating, more expensive tickets, such as business and first-class. Passengers can expect larger, more comfortable seats (which may fold out to become beds), personal video and audio services, on-board telephones, and other services designed to enhance comfort and standards.

## Business strategy

In order to gain success and maintain advantage over competitors, the airline must also be aware of what its competitors are doing. Transatlantic routes usually place the domestic European airline in competition with a North American one. This is because of the reciprocal manner in which 'slots' are auctioned off. For every slot sold to a foreign incoming airline, there is an expectation that a slot will be sold to the domestic airline in the corresponding destination airport. Knowledge of prices, non-price differentiation on-board and at the airport, or even in getting the passenger to the airport, can help guide the airline's decision to provide services such as express check-in facilities

for regular passengers, or executive lounges. By these methods, airlines can position themselves against their competitors in order to gain an advantage. Such environmental and competitive awareness can help to form the organisation's strategy and future direction. Techniques for analysis of competitors and the operating environment are described in the text. Identification of an airline's key competitors and the reason for their relative success can provide ideas for future developments, and awareness of the airline's own particular strengths and weaknesses can provide an important insight into its process of strategic analysis and development.

## Business issues

Once the airline knows where it wishes to go and what it wants to do, it must implement its desired strategy. There are limits to the number of alliances to which any single airline will be able to commit itself. Governmental permission will be required in order to engage in code sharing and to make alliances which might lead to monopoly situations. Passenger choice and competition in the market are important in most countries. Therefore, the final decision regarding airline alliances may actually lie with the government. Other forms of intervention which can affect the partnership decision include employment and labour problems. Airlines need to remain responsive to their employees' demands. In the USA, airlines have been severely affected financially by the demands of their air crew and pilots. Strikes are not uncommon and the losses in revenue over even a short period of time can wipe out profits. European airlines are not immune. British Airways and Air France staff went on strike in 1996. Agreements were hammered out very quickly with the staff to avert escalation of the action.

## Conclusion

Overall, then, it can be seen that each of the key issues within the diagram may be discussed with reference to the airline industry. There are obviously other links which may be made between the key issues, and there are also overlaps between the key issues and the different concepts introduced. By considering different concepts and theoretical perspectives, the links and overlaps would be different from those shown above.

# ACKNOWLEDGEMENTS

For all their help and encouragement, we would
like to thank:

John Mark, Senior Lecturer in Economics
of the Management Centre, King's College
London, University of London

Richard Welford, Professor of Business Economics
at Huddersfield University Business School

# HOW TO USE THIS BOOK

Many areas of business economics and strategy are interrelated, but to discuss the areas in detail requires a separation of the topics. For example, the discussion of government regulation and its effect on the organisation makes use of ideas of pricing behaviour and market structure as well as corporate governance and business ethics, yet for clarity the book has treated these topics separately.

Those readers following a more traditional business economics course will find that the chapters on business objectives through to techniques for decision making under risk and uncertainty (Chapters 3 to 13) cover the majority of the core areas they require.

Readers who already have a background in business economics and are now moving on to third-level courses on business strategy may like to review the above chapters and then study Chapters 14 through to 19, which cover economics and corporate strategy.

Those who wish to obtain a more applied approach to business issues and the business environment would be advised to consider Chapter 2 as an introduction to the environment, before turning to Chapters 20 to 24.

MBA courses can be very different in nature. The text would be most suitable for those courses where there is an explicit business economics module, and Chapters 3 to 13 will provide the major part of the information required. Where business economics courses encompass both internal and external factors, then Chapters 20 through to 24 should also be read. In addition, Chapters 14 to 19 on economics and corporate strategy should prove to be particularly useful in linking business economics to other disciplines.

Each of the chapters makes reference to material that either has been discussed earlier or will be developed in a later chapter. Therefore, study the chapters in whatever sequence is appropriate to your course or to your individual needs. Since all chapters have a list of objectives and well-developed summaries, you will be able to gain insight from these into the developments discussed in detail in each chapter.

The case studies in all chapters provide an opportunity for you to think further about the ideas discussed in the chapter. After each case study there is a series of discussion questions which can be used to test understanding of the material so far. The review questions at the end of each chapter require more thought and can be used to extend your knowledge further.

# PLAN OF THE BOOK

| PART 1 – INTRODUCTION | | | |
|---|---|---|---|
| Chapter 1<br>The scope of<br>business economics | Chapter 2<br>The organisation and<br>its environment | Chapter 3<br>Business objectives,<br>ethics and corporate<br>governance | Chapter 4<br>Alternative models<br>of the organisation |

| PART 2 – DEMAND, REVENUE AND COSTS | | | |
|---|---|---|---|
| Chapter 5<br>Consumer<br>behaviour | Chapter 6<br>Demand and<br>elasticity | Chapter 7<br>Estimating and<br>forecasting demand | Chapter 8<br>Determinants and<br>behaviour of costs |

| PART 3 – MARKETING AND INVESTMENT DECISIONS | | | | |
|---|---|---|---|---|
| Chapter 9<br>Pricing<br>decisions | Chapter 10<br>Pricing<br>practices | Chapter 11<br>Non-price<br>competition and<br>the marketing mix | Chapter 12<br>Investment<br>decisions and<br>the cost<br>of capital | Chapter 13<br>Techniques for<br>decision making<br>under conditions<br>of uncertainty<br>and risk |

| PART 4 – ECONOMICS AND CORPORATE STRATEGY | | | | | |
|---|---|---|---|---|---|
| Chapter 14<br>Elements of<br>business<br>strategy | Chapter 15<br>Analysing the<br>structure of<br>competition | Chapter 16<br>Competitive<br>weapons:<br>scale, scope<br>and core<br>competences | Chapter 17<br>Transaction<br>cost<br>economics | Chapter 18<br>Deterrence<br>and<br>reputation<br>as strategic<br>tools | Chapter 19<br>Quality<br>and the<br>economics<br>of the<br>organisation |

| PART 5 – BUSINESS ISSUES | | | | |
|---|---|---|---|---|
| Chapter 20<br>Business<br>issues<br>and the<br>environment | Chapter 21<br>The globalisation<br>of business<br>activities | Chapter 22<br>Government<br>intervention:<br>competition and<br>regulation | Chapter 23<br>The changing<br>boundaries<br>of the<br>organisation | Chapter 24<br>The labour<br>market |

# PART 1

# INTRODUCTION

CHAPTER 1

# THE SCOPE OF BUSINESS ECONOMICS

## OBJECTIVES

◆ To introduce and define 'business economics'.

◆ To illustrate the link between business economics, the management and decision sciences, and business strategy.

◆ To consider the link between business economics and mainstream economic theory.

◆ To introduce a selection of the tools and techniques which are covered elsewhere in the text.

## KEY TERMS

Balance of trade

Business economics

Business strategy

Decision sciences

Factor inputs

Globalisation

Optimisation

## CHAPTER OUTLINE

Business application

Introduction

The definition of business economics

Business strategy

The relationship to mainstream economic theory

The relationship to the decision sciences

The relationship to business and business strategy

Summary

Review questions

Glossary of new terms

Reading

## BUSINESS APPLICATION

# Management: drawing a line under corporate strategy

FT

If a scientist working in the new area of complexity theory were to tell the leader of a large company that the business world is complex and paradoxical, a likely response would be a weary 'tell me about it'. Managers know only too well that complexity and paradox are the stuff of modern management.

But if the scientist were to declare that complexity and paradox are attributes of non-linear systems – where the outcomes of any actions are unpredictable – that companies are such systems, and that strategic planning is not only useless but dangerous, the dialogue between science and commerce might end abruptly.

Most managers, after all, believe the conventional wisdom that planning is the main task of management. The growing complexity of business, they would say, makes strategic intent more important than ever. Not so, counter the growing number of complexity scientists and chaos theorists who are applying their ideas to business. Long-term business strategies can only be planned if each business action has a limited number of predictable outcomes. In a blatant bid to annexe management as a sub-set of their own discipline, the scientists claim that the increasing competitiveness of business and the explosive growth in communications have created a new situation that only they can make sense of. . .

Changeability is a much-prized quality in business these days but is usually desired to enable the company to achieve a better 'fit' with its environment. [Ralph] Stacey claims notions of 'fit' and long-term intent are recipes for stagnation and failure, and companies are only changeable when they achieve a state of creative tension on the edge of instability. 'The survivors and thrivers,' predict Stacey and David Parker,* will be organisations 'sustained far from equilibrium . . . (where) they are inherently changeable'.

They argue that we are entering an age in which companies will be organised by a process of self-organisation. Hierarchies and short-term planning are needed to run day-to-day operations, but the long-term future must be allowed to emerge from the self-organising activity of loose, informal, destabilising networks. The fatal weakness of intentional strategies is that they are relatively inflexible plans for wholly unknowable futures. Enlightened by the strange conclusions of complexity, adherents believe it is possible to imagine a company with an ambitious strategic intent being effortlessly out-performed by what appears to be a disorganised and aimless network of companies teetering on the edge of collapse. Indeed, they add, complexity theory suggests that even when the former wins, it will be by chance, not because of any merit.

*Chaos, Management and Economics. The Implications of Non-linear Thinking* (Institute of Economic Affairs, Hobart Paper 125, 1994).

Source: *Financial Times*, 8 September 1995. Reprinted with permission.

### Comment

Clearly, therefore, for the successful management of businesses in the 1990s it is not enough simply to be an expert in a single field. It is claimed in the above article that managers need to be able to make short-term strategic plans in order to maximise the performance of their organisation. They also need to remain flexible enough to allow the business to take its own best path in the future. Rather than make rigid plans for the future, they should build in enough flexibility for the organisation to be able to 'ride the waves' if the sea – the marketplace – becomes stormy.

### ◆ Exercise 1.1

Which disciplines do you think it is necessary for a successful manager in the 1990s to possess an understanding of (and why)?

## INTRODUCTION

Overall management success relies on knowledge of several different academic fields. Economics, business, decision making, statistics, production, advertising and accounting are just some of the areas which successful managers must take into account in their own planning processes. The ability to consider the 'big picture', to be able to predict the effects of different decisions on an organisation and its employees, is an important requirement of the manager. Obviously, nothing can make up for experience, but even experienced decision making can be enhanced by knowledge and the use of tools and techniques for analysing decisions.

Decision making and management ability can be further enhanced when other knowledge is possessed. Recognising the likely effects of changes in the business environment can allow the organisation to prepare more effectively for the eventual outcomes. Understanding presentations of numerical data and possessing the ability to manipulate data and analyse results are also important. The topics and areas mentioned above are representative of many different functional and specialist areas within business. However, an insight into these on a general level will help anyone interested in identifying the factors leading to the success of organisations. The study of **business economics** and **business strategy** brings them together in an integrated manner, as will be seen below.

## THE DEFINITION OF BUSINESS ECONOMICS

Business economics is concerned with the internal operations of the organisation from a decision maker's or manager's point of view. Business economics uses the concepts found within macro- and microeconomics and adapts them in an applied manner. Throughout this text, new concepts will be introduced to the reader. They will not be introduced because they are aesthetically pleasing from an economist's point of view, but because they will give an insight into operations and decision making within organisations.

An all-encompassing definition of business economics would be difficult to create. Although growing in popularity in the UK, it is only a young branch of the whole economics subject area. Rather than attempt to offer an overall definition, it is more appropriate to provide an overview of the concepts utilised and considered by business economics. These are:

- Utilisation of the technique of optimisation in order to analyse and improve organisational decisions.
- Consideration of individual consumer choice in order to gain an insight into both individual *and* market demand decisions and needs and to facilitate forecasting of that demand.
- Utilisation of analytical tools relating to the cost structures and supply structures of the organisation to understand supply decisions.
- Understanding of the effects that different factors can have on organisations and individuals; factors such as unemployment, increasing rates of inflation, the effect of increasing costs or increasing prices.

- Comprehending how changes in the objectives of an organisation, or in the strategic direction taken by the organisation, affect its behaviour and, ultimately, the behaviour of its rivals in the competitive marketplace.

## BUSINESS STRATEGY

By extending the ideas connected with business economics, it is possible to understand some of the basic concepts which are often linked with business strategy. The later chapters of this text will be concerned with bringing together business economics and business strategy. Business strategy looks at the manner in which organisations are operating and what their particular goals may be in the near and more distant future. Additionally, elements of business strategy provide frameworks for analysing the performance of organisations with reference to their chosen strategy or with reference to their potential performance against rivals in a new market area.

There are many similarities in the basic concepts included in the study of business economics and business strategy, for example the analysis of markets, analysis of competitors and the effects of different strategies in the marketplace. As a result, the two have been brought together within this single text.

## THE RELATIONSHIP TO MAINSTREAM ECONOMIC THEORY

Business economics is a specialist area within the subject of economics. Briefly, economics is concerned with the allocation of scarce resources and the manner in which markets, organisations and individuals interact when this takes place. Economists tend to specialise within different areas of economics as a whole subject, simply because there are so many branches of interest and focus. Perhaps the most simplistic division or area of focus occurs when economists consider themselves either 'macro' or 'micro' specialists.

Macroeconomics is the study and specialism concerned with the external (to businesses) environment. The causes and implications of the following are of particular interest to the macroeconomist:

- The rate of inflation in prices within the economy.
- The rate of unemployment within the economy.

- Interactions with other nations, which affect exchange rates, the **balance of trade** (is the nation a net importer or exporter?) and so on.

Microeconomists would tend to claim that they are interested in the internal decision-making environment of organisations; that is, at a more focused (and hence micro) level. Key concepts for the micro expert include:

- Pricing decisions within organisations.
- Understanding and forecasting demand for the organisation's product(s).
- Maximisation of profit levels and other objectives of the competitive organisation.
- The objectives of the organisation and the manner in which these are achieved within the competitive marketplace.

---

◆ **Exercise 1.2**

List the main areas of study for an economist specialising in:

- macroeconomics;
- microeconomics.

---

Note, however, that it is simplistic to assume that economics can simply be split into macro and micro. Certainly, there are concepts that are of particular and unique interest to one or the other, but there are also topics and concepts which overlap and which all economists and aspiring students of economics should understand in order to develop further. Examples would include the changing nature of industrial and economic structure, exchange rate changes and their implications, and the effects of developments in other aspects of business, such as strategic or technological developments.

An area on which some economists focus is that of industrial economics. Broadly speaking, this is the study of the structure of the economy and the manner in which organisations compete within those different identified structures; it combines macro and micro concepts as a result. The effects of different governmental policies and actions are also studied. Areas of specific interest to the industrial economist are:

- The competitive nature of markets and the classification of those markets into different market structures.
- The development of markets and the changes in markets over time as a result of governmental and other influences.

- Interactions between organisations and the development of theories to describe and predict future interactions.
- The effects of changes in the **factor inputs** (labour and capital – machinery) in markets as a result of innovation or technology. Such changes can spread at different rates through different markets and in different sectors of the economy.

These factors are also considered by the business economist. Obviously, industrial economists consider these in more depth and with a more specialist eye, while business economists use the more popular, interesting or adaptable concepts in order to carry out the analyses in which they are interested.

It is also too simplistic to assume that economics can exist in a vacuum. For example, the pricing practices of organisations may be biased by the business economist's advice, but decision makers or managers will also take into account the views and advice of the financial decision makers, or accountants, and those within the marketing department. Therefore, as well as looking at the relationship with economic theory, the relationship with **decision sciences** and business studies will also be considered below.

## THE RELATIONSHIP TO THE DECISION SCIENCES

Some of the more useful decision-making techniques and tools utilised within business economics are derived from the decision sciences. The basis for such techniques may be found in mathematics – quantitative decision making – and statistics – the analysis of risk and investment decisions. Such decision-making and analytical tools have been adapted by business economists over time to assist in their understanding and analysis. (This is also the case in terms of the relationship to economics: business economics uses ideas and adapts them for specific purposes.) It is therefore not necessary in the case of quantitative and statistical techniques to show their derivation from what mathematicians and statisticians would call 'first principles' (their theoretical development), but rather to show how these may be used for effective decision making.

Some commonly used mathematically and statistically based techniques included in this text are:

- **Optimisation** of the costs and revenues within an organisation to provide profit maximisation or even cost-minimisation production levels.

- Utilisation of regression analysis to assess the validity of demand-forecasting relationships or other predictions.
- Comparison and assessment of different projects in order to gauge the risk associated with them and ways in which the 'best' project may be chosen.
- Calculations of rates of return from projects and the value of those projects if stated in present-day terms in order to facilitate decision making and choice.

These have been adapted and adopted by economists and business economists over time. It is true to say that the study of economics relies on mathematics and has very close links with it. Indeed, many theories that have been developed and published have been proven using mathematical techniques. Currently, researchers and theorists attempt to prove their hypotheses via direct application of mathematics, or via the manipulation, analysis and evaluation of data collected empirically (from the world).

## THE RELATIONSHIP TO BUSINESS AND BUSINESS STRATEGY

It has already been pointed out that there are links between the insights offered by economists and those offered by business writers. These links are often built on by different theorists as they attempt to prove their hypotheses or to develop thinking yet further. One of the most popularly quoted and respected business strategy writers of the 1980s and 1990s is Michael Porter. His ability to outline his ideas and arguments won him popular acclaim; but his writing also stood up to academic criticism as a result of the fact that many of the new models he proposed were based on the neoclassical economic arguments of current economic thought.* Thus, on a variety of levels, Porter was able to influence contemporary business thought – especially with respect to the development of business strategies and the **globalisation** of business.

---

*Neoclassical economics is based on the thinking and teaching of eighteenth-century classical economists. It forms the foundation of much of the economics discussed in this text and, indeed, mainstream economics taught around the world.

Other business writers have contributed in similar ways and yet derived the basis of their arguments from economics. It seems appropriate, therefore, that economics and business can be brought together in this text. Aspects of business economics which are also of importance to business strategists and decision makers are:

■ The manner in which organisations decide which markets to develop and the methods they use in order to gain the positions and competitive advantages for which they strive.

■ Forecasting demand for products and services, as well as the manner in which prices are decided in the marketplace.

■ Interactions between competing organisations are difficult to predict, but there is now some understanding of the series of actions/reactions and the way in which 'false signals' may be sent out into the public domain in order to fool competitors.

■ Classification of markets and competitors within markets is an important analytical and decision-making tool on the part of both the business economist and business strategist.

Overall, then, it should be clear that there are many overlaps between business economics and business strategy. In the same way that it was argued that many of the decision-making tools of the decision sciences have been adopted by economists, it is proposed here that business strategists have adopted and adapted many of the concepts and tools used by economists.

## SUMMARY

◆ Business economics is a combination of several academic disciplines, including macroeconomics, microeconomics, management science, business strategy and the decision sciences.

◆ Economics is a complex subject. Individuals therefore tend to specialise in specific areas such as macro, micro, industrial or business economics.

◆ Business strategy has strong links with business economics. Concepts such as the analysis of markets and competitors and strategic development are common to both disciplines.

◆ There are several mathematical/statistical tools and techniques which may be used for decision-making purposes.

## REVIEW QUESTIONS

1  List the main subject areas from which business economics draws its concepts and ideas. How do these interrelate and what use are they to the business economist, or even the business manager?

2  What similarities between business economics and business strategy are claimed by the authors? Why are these significant to students and practitioners of business alike?

3  It is stated in the text that 'it is simplistic to assume that economics can exist in a vacuum'. Explain and discuss this phrase.

## GLOSSARY OF NEW TERMS

**Balance of trade:** The measure of imports versus exports within any economy in monetary terms. A balance of trade 'surplus' exists when the economy is a net exporter, a 'deficit' when the economy is a net importer.

**Business economics:** A discipline of economics concerned with the use and appropriation of resources within organisations. Also concerned with the competition faced by organisations and strategies required to be effective.

**Business strategy:** The operation of organisations with reference to a specific set of goals. Analysis of business strategy provides frameworks for the analysis of markets and competitors in given situations.

**Decision sciences:** The study, use and adaptation of mathematical techniques to assist decision making in business. Termed 'science' because the techniques are statistically rigorous.

**Factor inputs:** The 'factors of production' – land, labour, capital and enterprise (the combination of labour and capital) – which are the constituents of any economy.

**Globalisation:** The growth of organisations from their domestic context to competing in markets worldwide.

**Optimisation:** The most effective use of resources within the constraints of the organisation, for example balancing costs against benefits and doing the best within the limits of what is possible.

## READING

### Specialist texts from the areas introduced in the chapter

Minium, E M and Clarke, R B (1982) *Elements of Statistical Reasoning*, John Wiley, New York.
*Perhaps dated, but a reader-friendly background to some concepts introduced in this text. For example, Chapters 11 and 12 may be of interest to students wishing to know more once they have worked through Chapter 7 here on demand forecasting.*

Parkin, M and King, D (1997) *Economics*, European edn, 3rd edn, Addison Wesley Longman, Harlow.
*A well-illustrated text, using many real-life cases to explain concepts. This is a recommended text on many undergraduate students' first reading list.*

Nellis, J G and Parker, D (1997) *The Essence of Business Economics*, 2nd edn, Prentice Hall, Hemel Hempstead.

*From the 'Essence of...' series, a text aimed at part-time MBA students, but not beyond the level of a keen business student and offering insight into many of the areas within this text.*

Anderson, D R, Sweeney, D J and Williams, T A (1994) *Quantitative Methods for Business*, 6th edn, West, St Paul, Minneapolis.
*This book contains the chapters relevant to business students from the current authors' management science book.*

Johnson, G and Scholes, K (1997) *Exploring Corporate Strategy: Text and Cases*, 4th edn, Prentice Hall, Hemel Hempstead.
*The business strategy equivalent of Parkin and King – essential reading for undergraduate and postgraduate business students.*

CHAPTER **2**

# THE ORGANISATION AND ITS ENVIRONMENT

## OBJECTIVES

◆ To provide an overview of changes in the international environment facing organisations.

◆ To examine the changing nature of industrial structure in Europe.

◆ To discuss the changing pattern of export performance of European industry.

◆ To consider the process of deindustrialisation within European economies and the factors that are behind this process.

◆ To outline briefly the importance of large firms in the UK and Europe.

◆ To explore the reasons for the growing interest in the small firms sector within Europe.

## CHAPTER OUTLINE

## KEY TERMS

Deindustrialisation
GATT
Income elasticities
Outsourcing
Productivity
Sclerosis
Structural change
Trade balance

## BUSINESS APPLICATION

# European restructuring

**FT**

Will continental Europe's increased willingness to take potent economic medicine eventually provoke a backlash? From a purist perspective, the more commercial approach shown by European companies, such as Daimler-Benz, Philips and Alcatel-Alsthom, is welcome. So is the fact that some governments are gradually weaning their companies off state hand-outs and running tighter macroeconomic policies in an attempt to meet the Maastricht criteria for monetary union. Harsh measures are needed if European industry is to thrive in an increasingly competitive global market.

The snag is that, in the short term, such medicine leads to unemployment. So far in 1996, attention to the bottom line has led Daimler to pull the plug on Fokker and Philips to force large job cuts at Grundig. Equally, the drying up of state aid was a factor behind Bremer Vulkan's bankruptcy in February 1996. Meanwhile, tight macroeconomic policies have restrained economic growth and prevented some countries from bailing out their industries by devaluing their currencies. The result is that Germany's unemployment rate is at least 10 per cent and France's nearer 12 per cent.

So far, the backlash has been limited. Only in France, where last year's wave of unrest forced the government to dilute its pro-market policies, has it yet had much practical impact.

However, the drive to restructure European industry is accelerating. In the private sector, nostrums such as shareholder value are increasingly taking hold. Moreover, as state-owned groups are privatised, they will face market disciplines. Even France has not abandoned the restructuring process: in February 1996 the decision to privatise Thomson SA and merge the state-owned Aerospatiale with private-sector Dassault is a precursor to rationalising the defence industry.

Given such a trend, the possibility of a serious backlash cannot be dismissed. The main worry must be that politicians will respond to social disquiet by loosening macroeconomic policy or using other short-term palliatives. The transformation of European industry may yet be accomplished without major difficulties, but investors should not count on it.

*Source: Financial Times, 26 February 1996. Reprinted with permission.*

# INTRODUCTION

The market in which organisations find themselves is continually changing. On the one hand, trade and investment are growing more rapidly than world output and there is increasing integration of the international economy. At the same time, however, multilateralism is constantly threatening and regionalism is stronger in the Americas, Europe and Asia than ever before. Dramatic increases in the scale of technology, in terms of cost, risk and complexity, have rendered national markets too small to be meaningful economic units.

There has also been a growth in transnational strategic alliances which indicates a fundamental change in the mode of organisation of international economic transactions – trade and multinationals are being replaced by global networks. This global economy is integrated through information systems and information technology rather than organisation hierarchies. The result of all this change is an electronically networked world economy where national markets are losing meaning as separate units and geography is no longer the basis for the organisation of economic activity.

At the same time economic unions have developed which have a growing power over international trade. The three largest groups – the global triad, made up of the European Union (EU), the North American Free Trade Agreement (NAFTA) and the Asia Pacific Economic Co-operation group (APEC) – account for over 45 per cent of global trade. It is still open to question whether this move towards regionalism is an advancement to, or a movement away from, free trade. Moreover, it is also not clear whether managed economic interdependence will improve or constrain the potential of associated companies, sectors and economies.

Within Europe, the arrival of the Single European Market (SEM) in 1993, with its emphasis on the removal of physical, technical and fiscal barriers, also altered the behaviour of many organisations. For organisations outside the EU, there was greater emphasis on being inside what they called 'fortress Europe'. Thus there was a rise in extra-EU mergers with companies in the EU, while at the same time there was a growth in foreign direct investment to develop greenfield sites within Europe. At the same time the reduction in trade barriers between EU states led to organisations appraising their current plants which had traditionally served national markets. As a response to this there was a growth in cross-border mergers.

As the pieces of the SEM were being put into place there were two other important external events. The eighth round of trade talks – the General Agreement on Tariffs and Trade (GATT) Uruguay Round – was being finalised. This led to, among others items, a reduction in tariffs on manufactured goods, an agreement on agricultural protection, market access and support for agriculture, an agreement on technical barriers to trade, and an agreement on trade in services. At the same time the democratisation of the old communist Eastern European countries was taking place. The introduction of market reforms resulted in the privatisation of many state-owned industries and a rapid increase in the development of joint ventures and expansion of Western European companies into the East.

Privatisation was not the sole province of Eastern European countries. In the West the process of privatisation and contracting out of public-sector services had been going on from the early 1980s. This had switched previous monopolies from the public to the private sector where, free from the shackles of government control, many of them had become important and dominant industries. The success of privatisation, seen first in the US then in the UK, has been mirrored not only in Europe but also throughout the world. Given the size and dominance of such companies both in national economies and in Europe, this served to raise questions about anticompetitive behaviour and the 1980s and 1990s have seen the European Commission strengthen its hand in the area of competition policy.

Within Europe, as in the international community as a whole, the 1980s and 1990s have also seen a growth in the 'greening' of business. Prompted by various reports into the problems that might arise through deforestation, global warming and the increase in pollution, the international community began to examine ways in which pollution and environmental damage could be reduced. This has led to various pieces of legislation being passed aimed at controlling organisations. This encouraged some organisations to move quickly towards the production of 'environmentally friendly' products and there was a view that companies should behave more responsibly towards the environment.

Caring more for the environment was not the only area of corporate responsibility that arose during this time. There was also a rise in issues concerning corporate governance. The behaviour of companies, or their directors, came under the spotlight following payments to directors which some felt were not always related to company performance. Business ethics and ethical management were seen as areas where some organisations were not behaving responsibly. This kind of behaviour spilt over into environmental concerns where more footloose organisations sought to circumvent environmental controls which they perceived as being more costly, and moved to areas or regions where environmental legislation was less rigorously applied.

The 1980s and 1990s have seen, therefore, some large upheavals in the international environment facing organisations. The successful organisation is probably one which sees these as opportunities for growth rather than threats to its market position. The chapters that follow discuss many of these issues in detail, but at this stage we shall consider how these changes have affected the European business, starting with a discussion of the structural changes that have occurred in the international economy.

## STRUCTURAL CHANGE IN THE WORLD'S ECONOMIES

Economies can be divided up into three sectors: primary, secondary and tertiary. The primary sector includes all activities related to the extraction of natural resources, such as farming and mining. The secondary sector includes activities relating to the production of goods and the processing of materials. Manufacturing is the main constituent of this sector, although it also includes the construction sector and utilities such as gas, electricity and water. Finally, the tertiary sector includes both private and public services, such as insurance and banking, health and defence.

**Structural change** indicates variations in the relative size of these sectors which can be seen in terms of changes in output, employment and productivity. Thus 'restructuring' involves not only the changing composition of industries or of the labour force, but more generally changes in the terms and relations under which the process of capital accumulation for profit takes place.

Restructuring of the economy may take place suddenly, in response to an external or political factor, or the change can take place gradually. In the case of the former, economists of the Austrian school tend to see market adjustments as periodic

radical realignments of values necessitating sharp policy changes. On the other hand, it might be expected that the structure of an economy would change slowly over time as the pattern of demand changes, as a result of increases in income and changes in tastes. Thus these alterations will have knock-on effects on employment and output. One such example of this would be to consider products whose **income elasticities** of demand are high, such as cars, white goods and electronic goods, demand for which has increased over time compared with food and other basic necessities whose income elasticities of demand are much lower. An economy which produces a relatively high proportion of low-income-elastic products may well run into balance of payments problems, through low growth and low productivity, if it does not change the composition of its output. The pattern of demand is also responsive to changes in the age distribution of the population. Older people may demand different types of goods and services and different quality goods and services.

The supply side of the economy also has a role to play in any structural changes. The impact of technology has altered the pattern of goods and services that can be provided from the market as technical progress has reduced the cost of production. In doing so some workers have been displaced from the market, although at the same time the impact of technology has increased employment in those sectors or goods for which a country or region previously did not possess a comparative advantage. Changes in a country's exchange rate over the longer term can make its products less competitive and therefore structural changes will occur in the economy as it tries to produce other commodities which may give it greater competitiveness in the market. For example, the second major oil-price hike of 1980/81 posed particular problems for the UK economy. It was the only economy in the EU which was self-sufficient in oil. The pound sterling, therefore, acted as though it was a petro-currency – its value was related to the price of a barrel of oil. The rise in the value of a barrel of oil pushed the exchange rate of the pound from $1.55 to $2.38, so imports became relatively cheaper and exports relatively more expensive. Thus the shakeout in UK industry that was happening at that time was further hastened by the exchange-rate movement in the pound. Bean (1987) provides a good analysis of this situation.

The growth of international competition can also be viewed as one of the forces behind some of the structural changes that have taken place both in the UK and in Europe. The greater **productivity** in other countries, such as Japan and the South East Asian economies (Hong Kong, Singapore, Taiwan, and South Korea), has seen the EU countries losing market share, particularly in manufacturing; *see* Burda and Wyplosz (1993) and Cook and Healey (1995). Linked to this may be lower levels of investment, less research and development (R&D), poor management, restrictive practices by trade unions, pay settlements not linked to productivity and the consequences for some countries of having higher relative levels of inflation.

In other words, the amount of structural changes that affect a country can be the result of its own structural weaknesses when compared to the other members of its main trading bloc, for example the UK compared to Germany or France; or it may be the result of the general problems faced by a whole trading bloc in relation to other international trading blocs, for example the EU compared to the US and Japan. Overall for the EU, there has been a move sectorally out of agriculture. The move has been into the secondary sector to some degree, although the overall employment figure for manufacturing in the EU shows an appreciable decline, indicating the process of **deindustrialisation** which will be considered later in this chapter. The greatest move has been into the service sector of the economy, which now employs the majority of people in each of the member states of the EU. This process is not a singularly European one, since both the US and Japan show similar trends. For many people the changes in the manufacturing sector, which has historically provided the bulk of jobs, have given a great deal of concern. How has manufacturing changed over the last decade in the EU?

---

◆ **Exercise 2.1**

Why is it more difficult to undertake reforms in the labour market when an economy is undergoing structural change?

How can such reforms be helped, or hindered, by the different interest groups in an economy?

---

Structural changes not only affect the external sector of the economy through impact on trade, but have important consequences for employment. It is much more difficult to undertake labour-market reforms when an economy is undergoing a structural change which leads to increases in unemployment. However, there can be positive elements to structural change as an economy is expanding and on these occasions reforms can take place which apparently succeed in making no one worse off. These reforms can be to trade union legislation making it harder for groups of people to take strike action, or forcing groups to ballot their members before strikes take place.

## ◆ CASE STUDY 2.1

## The political economy of job creation

**FT**

The very high levels of European unemployment have spawned so many conferences, studies and books that they amount to a minor job creation effort in their own right. One more recent addition in April 1995 from the Centre of Economic Policy Research (CEPR) suggests that the rise in unemployment is not due to competition from developing countries, rapid technological change, or the generosity of welfare provisions (although the latter does help account for the 'persistence' of unemployment). Nor is high unemployment due to sclerotic labour markets or to labour market rigidities.

However, the document does suggest that any changes that need to take place to reduce unemployment do have to be well thought through. The problem for politicians is to assess who are the gainers and losers from any reforms. It is highly likely that the median voter in between the extreme losers and gainers does not have much stake either way in wholesale reforms. Because of the power of this group in voting terms, there has been little pressure to change the European system for greater flexibility or to change the US system for more security of income.

If there is going to be change or reform it may well be when an expanding economy is experiencing a high rate of structural change, implying a high rate of both job destruction and potential job creation. An example was Spain in the mid-1980s, which introduced large-scale temporary job contracts at well below union wage rates. Unfortunately a counterattack by the unions and government weakness have since undermined the reforms.

*Source*: Adapted from *Financial Times*, 20 April 1995. Reprinted with permission.

2 ◆ THE ORGANISATION AND ITS ENVIRONMENT

In any economy there are a number of interest groups which are linked to employment, including the government, employers, employees and shareholders. The balance between these interest groups may indicate the degree to which reforms can take place. Where employers are the most powerful group they may attempt to alter the labour market in favour of themselves. Conversely, where trade unions are in a powerful position they may be able to obtain a larger share of any returns that go to industry and prevent any major changes which might worsen their working conditions or reduce their salaries. Governments may be able to act in the interest of the nation and legislate for changes in the labour market.

## THE PERFORMANCE OF THE MANUFACTURING SECTOR

If the whole **trade balance** of the EU is considered, the Union's competitiveness does not appear to be a problem. The trade balance has permanently registered a surplus over the last decade. In 1994 it stood at 3.6 per cent of gross domestic product (GDP), which was even higher than the Japanese economy. However, the overall figures disguise was has been happening to particular areas or sectors of the economy. The trade balance for manufactured goods fell almost continuously between 1981 and 1992 when it barely remained positive. Since then it has recovered, but the sector as a whole is still fairly weak. Thus because of the strength of the service sector the improvement in the trade balance as a whole has hidden the problems for manufacturing.

For Japan there was a trade balance surplus over the whole of the period 1982–94. The US, in contrast, ran a continuous deficit which peaked at 3.3 per cent of GDP in 1986/87, reduced to 0.5 per cent of GDP in 1991 and widened again to 2 per cent of GDP in 1994. The changes in the trade balance in the US are matched almost equally by opposite changes in the trade balances in the EU and Japan (European Commission, 1995).

Compared with the US and Japan, the EU is less specialised in its exports. If those sectors which account for more than 3 per cent of total exports are added together, then they represent less than 30 per cent of total exports in the EU. The comparable figures are 51 per cent for the US and 62 per cent for Japan. For the EU, therefore, exports are spread more evenly across commodity areas. This may be a strength for the EU in that changes in the economic cycle or loss of comparative advantages in trade will upset its export potential the least. However, it can also be viewed as a weakness since EU sectors are not specialised enough to take advantage of economies of scale. In contrast to Japan and the US, the EU has little or no specialisation in electrical and electronics-related sectors. The sectors in which the Union specialises only include one high-technology sector – pharmaceuticals. It also appears to be the case that sectors in which the EU is doing well in terms of specialisation have been those in which it has been losing market share in domestic markets, thus the trade balance is relatively poor. These sectors would include textiles and jewellery. In terms of the destination of exports, each of the three areas dominates trade in its nearby export markets. The EU appears to have weaker trading links with some of the most dynamic and fastest growth economies, such as Latin America and the newly industrialised countries (NICs), although the latter area's growth in trade has improved quite dramatically since 1987.

Research and development is a key factor in the growth and competitiveness of the EU economy. There are a number of ways in which this can be measured, but two approaches tend to dominate. First, R&D activity can be based on input measures, that is, the amount of resources allocated to the research activity. Second, R&D can be based on output measures, that is, the outcome of the R&D process. Measured as a share of GDP, the EU has the lowest R&D spending of the US/Japan/EU triad, at 2.6, 2.9 and 2.0 per cent respectively (1991 figures, European Commission, 1995). A further weakness is a comparatively low contribution of business enterprises to total R&D. In relation to both R&D performed and R&D financed, EU companies appear to be less involved in R&D than are their US or Japanese contemporaries. Therefore the EU appears to suffer from a double handicap: a lower level of research spending combined with a less commercially oriented research effort. Two additional problems exist for the EU. It has more of its research geared towards military research and does not appear to be strong in linking this to commercial research; and compared with the US and Japan there is a costly duplication of research centres and activities which is related to the national basis on which technology has developed. It would be expected that the continued move towards stronger European integration would reduce this latter problem.

In terms of the sectoral aspects of technological competitiveness, the EU has only very few sectors with a strong research specialisation and a clear technological edge. The sectors in which research is concentrated are often medium-tech, while the EU is only weakly represented in information technology and electronics. Moreover, in the medium-tech mechanical engineering sector, the EU's largest exporting sector, R&D efforts are lower than those of Japan. Too often the European technological system appears to suffer from an overemphasis on fundamental research at the expense of commercial innovations. Although the EU has a relatively strong position in terms of new registered patents in the areas of aerospace, pharmaceuticals and general engineering, its share of new patents has been falling in all sectors apart from aerospace. Overall in terms of R&D the EU may be losing ground to the other triad members, and if this continues it will further change the structure of industry in the EU.

Therefore at present the EU's trade surplus hides some important changes that are occurring in its various sectors of production. Services appear to be flourishing and primary-sector trade appears to have improved during the early part of the 1990s. The main concern is with some sectors of manufacturing, and it is to this area that the chapter now turns.

# DEINDUSTRIALISATION

Earlier in this chapter it was shown that the industrial structures of the world's leading economies have been, and are, changing. There has been a gradual move from agriculturally based economies, to those based on manufacturing and then to more service-oriented economies. Manufacturing, because it employed a large section of the population and because it provided countries with tradeable products, has to some extent held a special place in the perceptions of both government and business. Thus much debate has occurred as to whether it matters if the manufacturing or secondary sector of the economy is declining. This process has been called deindustrialisation.

However, the process of deindustrialisation can be viewed in a number of ways:

- The decline in employment, in both absolute and relative terms, in the manufacturing sector of the economy.
- The decline in the share of national output contributed by the manufacturing sector of the economy.
- The decline in a country's share of world manufacturing output or world manufacturing exports.
- The failure, due to poor export performance and/or increased import penetration, to generate sufficient exports to finance a full-employment level of imports.

In addition to these viewpoints, the definition of deindustrialisation must be one which enables a comparison of one country with another and it should also be 'cause free': it should not predetermine its causes. The OECD (Organisation for Economic Co-operation and Development) definitions of deindustrialisation which are cause free and not time and place specific use one or both of the following to define deindustrialisation:

- a declining share of total employment in manufacturing; and
- an absolute decline in employment in manufacturing.

Tables 2.1 and 2.2 indicate that the developing economies generally and the UK economy in particular have experienced a declining share of civilian unemployment in manufacturing.

For the UK the fall in the demand for labour is associated with a reduction in output until 1987 and probably a rise in the wage level relative to the price of other factors. Some of the decline in manufacturing employment was to be expected, however, since the UK economy had passed the peak of production from North Sea oil and gas. Table 2.1 also indicates that there has been a change in the industrial structure of UK industry. In fact, by 1996 there were almost exactly the same number of employees in employment as there had been in 1971; however, employment in the manufacturing sector had shrunk by just over 4 million, while that in the service sector had increased by 3.8 million. Not all elements of the service sector have benefited from the growth in employment: it is the financial services sector – that is, banking and finance, insurance, business services and the like – which has been the major beneficiary of the boom in service employment. Areas such as transport and communications have shown a relative decline.

The absolute decline in manufacturing employment means that its share of total employment has also declined over time, especially if employment in other sectors is growing faster or contracting at a slower rate. To put this fact into perspective, the financial and business services sector were the fastest-growing sectors of the economy during the 1980s. Their output doubled, with an average real

**Table 2.1 Employees in employment by industry in the UK (thousands)[a]**

|  | 1971 | 1979 | 1981 | 1983 | 1986 | 1988[b] | 1993 | 1996 |
|---|---|---|---|---|---|---|---|---|
| **Manufacturing** | | | | | | | | |
| Extraction of minerals and ores other than fuels, manufacture of metal, mineral products, and chemicals | 1 282 | 1 147 | 939 | 817 | 729 | 688 | 599 | |
| Metal goods, engineering, and vehicle industries | 3 709 | 3 374 | 2 923 | 2 548 | 2 372 | 2 366 | 1 898 | 3 921 |
| Other | 3 074 | 2 732 | 2 360 | 2 159 | 2 126 | 2 168 | 1 693 | |
| Total manufacturing | 8 065 | 7 253 | 6 222 | 5 525 | 5 227 | 5 222 | 4 190 | |
| **Services** | | | | | | | | |
| Distribution, hotels, catering, and repairs | 3 686 | 4 257 | 4 172 | 4 118 | 4 298 | 4 442 | 4 549 | 4 878 |
| Transport and communication | 1 556 | 1 479 | 1 425 | 1 345 | 1 298 | 1 326 | 1 281 | 1 270 |
| Banking, finance, insurance, business services, and leasing | 1 336 | 1 647 | 1 739 | 1 875 | 2 166 | 2 475 | 2 629 | 3 361 |
| Other | 5 049 | 6 197 | 6 132 | 6 163 | 6 536 | 6 966 | 7 036 | 7 073 |
| Total services | 11 627 | 13 580 | 13 468 | 13 501 | 14 297 | 15 210 | 15 495 | 16 582 |
| Agriculture, forestry and fishing | 450 | 380 | 363 | 350 | 329 | 313 | 260 | 306 |
| Energy and water supply industries | 798 | 722 | 710 | 648 | 545 | 487 | 357 | 158 |
| Construction | 1 198 | 1 239 | 1 130 | 1 044 | 989 | 1 044 | 831 | 830 |
| All industries and services | 22 139 | 23 173 | 21 892 | 21 067 | 21 387 | 22 276 | 21 133 | 21 797 |

[a] As at June each year.
[b] The effect of revisions undertaken in 1991 impacted primarily on the 1989 and 1990 data.
*Sources: Social Trends*, No 21 (1991 edn), Table 4.11; *Employment Gazette*, April 1991; January 1994; *Labour Market Trends*, June 1996.

**Table 2.2 Changes in the labour force: selected countries (%)**

|  | France | Germany | Japan | UK | USA |
|---|---|---|---|---|---|
| *1950* | | | | | |
| Agriculture | 27.4 | 23.2 | 41.0 | 4.9 | 11.9 |
| Industry | 37.0 | 44.4 | 24.2 | 49.4 | 35.9 |
| Services | 35.6 | 32.4 | 34.8 | 45.7 | 52.2 |
| *1970* | | | | | |
| Agriculture | 13.9 | 8.6 | 17.4 | 3.2 | 4.5 |
| Industry | 39.7 | 48.5 | 35.7 | 44.8 | 34.4 |
| Services | 46.4 | 42.9 | 46.9 | 52.0 | 61.1 |
| *1994* | | | | | |
| Agriculture | 4.8 | 2.9 | 6.8 | 1.8 | 2.9 |
| Industry | 26.9 | 36.2 | 34.1 | 22.9 | 24.0 |
| Services | 68.4 | 60.8 | 59.1 | 75.3 | 73.1 |

*Sources*: Bairoch, P. (1968) *La population active et sa structure*, OECD, Brussels; Organisation for Economic Co-operation and Development (1991) *Labour Force Statistics*, OECD, Paris; OECD, *Country Reports (1995/6)*, OECD, Paris.

growth rate of over 7 per cent. One reason for this was the decline in other sectors of the economy, but this sector also benefited from changes in UK government policy which liberalised financial services. Employment in financial and business services rose from 7 to 13 per cent of total UK employment between 1979 and 1993, while at the same time employment in manufacturing fell from 31 to 20 per cent. It is doubtful whether the positive trend in the financial services sector can continue into the future since the liberalisation of financial services may have given just a 'one-off' boost. Thus, although financial and business services helped to raise the UK's GDP growth rate from 1.8 to 2.3 per cent in the 1980s, it cannot be relied on to do so in the 1990s. Therefore there is all the more reason to be concerned about deindustrialisation in the manufacturing sector; *see* Cook and Healey (1995).

Have the same deindustrialisation trends been found in the rest of the developed economies? In the 1980s the whole of the EU moved towards a postindustrial phase of economic development. By 1994, 55 million people were working in the private service sector (market services) compared with 46 million in manufacturing and mining, construction and agriculture, with an additional 28 million people employed in public services. Altogether 64 per cent of all those employed in the EU were working in service companies or institutions. According to EU figures, the gains and losses of employment between 1982 and 1994 were highly concentrated in a few sectors: *see* Figure 2.1.

**Figure 2.1 Employment by sector, 1982–94[1]**

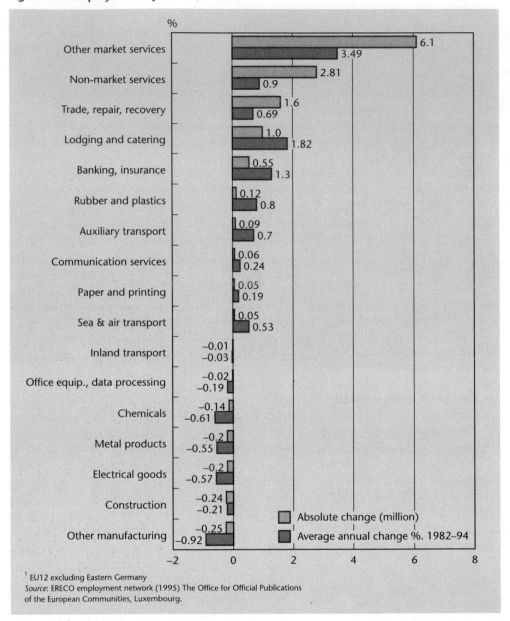

¹ EU12 excluding Eastern Germany

*Source*: ERECO employment network (1995) The Office for Official Publications of the European Communities, Luxembourg.

Service sectors, such as business and other private service ('other market services'), expanded most dynamically. The majority of manufacturing sectors stagnated, while metal production, mining, transport equipment and textiles and clothing shrank. The UK differs, therefore, from the rest of the EU since it has seen a large reduction in its manufacturing employment. Moreover, while the biggest unemployment loss within the EU occurred in agriculture, this was not the case for the UK since it has in recent years had a smaller proportion of its workforce involved with the agricultural sector.

Within the EU since 1982 almost 2 million jobs have been created in the business services sector, the equivalent of the whole of the chemical industry in Europe. Retail and wholesale distribution added an additional 1.6 million jobs and health and veterinary services another 1 million. A similar amount was added by lodging and catering services. Public services, including parts of health and education services, grew by more than 3 million. However, unlike what had happened in the UK, the contribution of banking and insurance, transport and communication services was much smaller.

The positive performance of services in relation to manufacturing is enhanced by the creation of part-time jobs in the service sector. The pattern of change, however, is not altered if labour input is measured in hours worked. The important technological branches, such as the electrical industry, chemical industry and office/data processing, did not provide any additional jobs. Between 1982 and 1994, significant job losses occurred in textiles and clothing industries, mining and metal production, and for manufacturing as a whole there was an overall loss of 3.7 million jobs. Part of this could be related to the world recession, but even removing this period a negative employment balance is still in evidence for the manufacturing sector.

Thus the decline in manufacturing is not a singularly UK phenomenon. However, the process does seem more marked in the UK than elsewhere. It may well be that the process of deindustrialisation started earlier in the UK, since it was the first industrialised nation, and that other EU countries will go through the same process. Such an argument appears to have some support if the shares of manufacturing in GDP are considered (*see* Table 2.3).

For all countries there appears to be a decline in manufacturing as a share of GDP. However, this proportional decline in output is not necessarily an indication of an ailing manufacturing sector, since part of the decline may be due to the fall in the price of manufactures relative to the prices of goods and services generally. Of more concern from a UK perspective is the general decline in its percentage of world manufacturing trade, a characteristic not shown generally by other trading nations, as Table 2.4 indicates.

## Table 2.3  Share of manufacturing in GDP

|  | 1960 | 1970 | 1975 | 1980 | 1986 | 1991 | 1994 |
|---|---|---|---|---|---|---|---|
| US | 28.6 | 25.7 | 23.4 | 22.5 | 19.9 | 19.6 | 17.9 |
| Japan | 33.9 | 35.9 | 29.9 | 30.4 | 29.3 | 29.7 | 25.8* |
| France | 29.1 | 28.7 | 27.4 | 26.3 | 22.2 | 21.3 | 21.1 |
| (West) Germany | 40.3 | 38.4 | 34.5 | 33.0 | 33.1 | 31.9 | 27.0 |
| Italy | 28.5 | 28.9 | 29.7 | 30.5 | 28.2 | 28.8 | 28.6 |
| UK | 32.1 | 28.1 | 26.3 | 23.1 | 21.8 | 20.9 | 20.9 |

*Sources*: Organisation for Economic Co-operation and Development (1988) *National Accounts of OECD Countries*, OECD, Paris; World Bank (1993) *Economic Outlook*, World Bank, New York; and OECD, *Economic Surveys (1995/96)*, OECD, Paris.

* 1993 data

## Table 2.4  World trade shares and deindustrialisation (%)

|  | Shares of world trade in manufactures | | | | | |
|---|---|---|---|---|---|---|
|  | 1950 | 1960 | 1970 | 1979 | 1990 | 1991 |
| France | 9.9 | 9.6 | 8.7 | 10.5 | 9.7 | 10 |
| (West) Germany | 7.3 | 19.3 | 19.8 | 20.9 | 20.2 | 20 |
| Japan | 3.4 | 6.9 | 11.7 | 13.7 | 15.9 | 17 |
| UK | 25.5 | 16.5 | 10.8 | 9.1 | 8.6 | 9 |
| USA | 27.3 | 21.6 | 18.6 | 16.0 | 16.0 | 18 |

*Sources*: Brown, C J F and Sheriff, T D (1979) 'De-industrialisation: A Background Paper' in Blockaby, F (ed) *De-industrialisation*, London: Heinemann; Office for National Statistics (1991) *Monthly Review of External Trade Statistics*, London: HMSO. Crown Copyright 1991. Reproduced by the permission of the Controller of HMSO and the Office for National Statistics.

It should not be concluded from the above that an absolute decline in employment in manufacturing is an indication of the continued downward slide of an economy. It is possible that technology in manufacturing is reducing employment in this sector while at the same time raising overall productivity. Moreover, technology could be market extending, as it creates new products, allows entry into new markets and generally makes an uncompetitive industry into a price-competitive one. The measures of deindustrialisation should also not be taken in isolation. For example, the output measure does not take into account changes in the population: industrial output per capita may show more or less deindustrialisation. Moreover, the measurement of services in particular is sensitive to the way in which they are defined and whether they are valued by volume or value etc. In addition, government statistics classify organisations according to their primary activity, so that if a manufacturing organisation '**outsources**' its accountancy or design function – tasks which it used to undertake in-house – then there will be a fall in manufacturing employment and a corresponding rise in service-sector employment. In fact, as an organisation grows the proportion of its workforce devoted to production may fall quite substantially. Thus, far from being a manufacturing company, it would be better designated as a service organisation.

But this is only part of the story. The decline of manufacturing activity and the rise of services are also due, both on a national basis and within the EU, to the limited competitiveness of traditional industrial production. They stem from the delay in the development of new technologies, the slow application of new organisational concepts such as total quality management, just-in-time management, value-chain management, benchmarking, reengineering and the like, and the problems of a high-price and high-quality strategy on product markets. Not only are EU companies facing reduced cost competitiveness, but they are also facing increasing technological competition from the South-East Asian and Eastern European economies based on a well-educated labour force and rapid economic transition. Complex types of industrial production can therefore be organised in developing countries and the advantages that EU workers previously held are being eroded. At the same time, since markets are becoming increasingly global then organisations are seeking to move their production processes to lower-cost areas. In many respects services are less affected since they tend to be more localised. Therefore, for the EU countries, labour is becoming increasingly specialised in skilled activities such as business management, research and development, technical and legal consulting, marketing, production management, design etc. The competitive advantage for the EU appears to be significantly higher in these fields than in the production of actual commodities.

So where does this leave the economies of the EU? Reducing barriers within the EU has opened up its internal market to greater competitive pressure. This has exacerbated the structural weaknesses of some of its member states. In the UK there are signs that the proportion of manufactured exports is beginning to rise. Some see this as a consequence of flexibility in the UK workforce; others see it as a result of the UK attracting a greater proportion of foreign direct investment (FDI) within the Union. This has forced inefficient UK firms out of the market and encouraged those which have remained to improve their efficiency, their patterns of work and productivity, while at the same time foreign-owned companies have begun increasingly to export their manufactured goods both to continental Europe and to South-East Asia. For the whole of the EU the problem may be whether it can export as many services to the rest of the world to replace those markets in industrial goods which it is losing.

Does the EU want its manufacturing sector to return or does it want to concentrate on services? If it wants the latter, then it needs to have access to foreign markets and to a limited extent this was achieved through the last **GATT** (General Agreement on Tariffs and Trade) round of trade talks. It also needs higher levels of skills and educa-

tion to provide these services. At the same time, the EU requires the decline in manufacturing to be 'managed' in such a way that the service sector grows to compensate for the loss of jobs.

On the other hand, if the EU still wants to be involved in mainstream manufacturing then it needs to consider a whole raft of policies. Such policies could include greater flexibility in the labour market; a larger amount of investment in industry, R&D and the diffusion of new technologies; greater levels of training both for employees and management in some countries, such as the UK; a move away from short-termism when projects are being evaluated and a greater involvement of banks with industry; the development of a vibrant small and medium-sized (SME) firms sector to compensate for the decline of traditional industries; consistency in macroeconomic policy, such as keeping inflation relatively low and reducing the volatility of interest rates; a reduction in government involvement in the economy because it tends to 'crowd out' private sector investment; and policies to overcome the **sclerosis** that has affected European stakeholders and decision makers.

Dealing with deindustrialisation on an EU-wide level does hide the weaknesses and problems that can still exist at a member state level. Some members may wish to go for flexible, low-wage sectors, which allows them to compete with other countries. In the UK's case this may also be associated with low skill levels. Unfortunately it is these same sectors which may be more prone to newly emerging competition. Other countries have tried to concentrate on higher skilled/high-value-added products, but the advantages in these are also being eroded. Can the EU survive by producing services? One estimate is that for each unit in value terms of manufactures exported the UK needs to export three units of services; *see* Cook and Healey (1995). If the same scenario exists in the EU, then a sustained comparative advantage in services is required.

The future for the EU is one where productivity needs to be raised, where products of higher quality need to be produced that cannot be currently produced by the emergent Asian 'tigers' and where the EU seeks to drive home its comparative advantage in services. The problem with the latter scenario is that deregulation in the service sector may lead to greater competition and job losses and it could thus experience many of the problems faced by manufacturing.

◆ **CASE STUDY 2.2**

# The ups and downs of services

*Does the split of output between manufacturing and service industries affect countries' economic cycles?*

Politicians in rich countries often fret about the shrinking share of manufacturing in the total output of their economics. One worry is that it is only manufacturing, not services, that can create 'real' wealth and 'proper' jobs. But there is a more intriguing question about manufacturing's diminishing share of GDP. What is its impact on the economic cycle?

Some economists argue that as services begin to account for a bigger share of output, economic cycles will become less bumpy, with shallower downswings. This, they say, is because the demand for services is less sensitive than that for manufactured goods to changes in income. They are in a way, more recession-proof.

One reason to think that this is the case is that services, unlike goods, cannot be stored.

Like individuals and haircuts, firms cannot stock up on services. In manufacturing, on the other hand, changes in the level of companies' stocks have a big influence on recessions. In America, they have accounted, on average, for more than half of the drop in GDP during recessions since the second world war. When a downturn begins, stocks pile up as firms are caught out by a slowdown in demand. They therefore have to cut output more sharply than the original fall in demand to bring their stock levels back to normal.

A third reason for thinking that services are more recession-proof than manufacturing is that they are much less capital-intensive. Since investment tends to be the first thing that firms chop when times are tough, big swings in capital spending by manufacturers tend to play an important role in economic cycles.

As in theory, so in practice? Employment in services has been less volatile than in manufacturing. A recent study* by Jaewoo Lee, an economist at the University of California at Irvine, provides strong evidence that as the share of American jobs accounted for by services has increased (from 50% at the start of the century to 80% today) the country's business cycle has become smoother, with smaller swings in unemployment and incomes. Moreover, states with a high share of service jobs, such as Hawaii, see the smallest rise in unemployment during recessions.

It would indeed be lovely to have smoother economic cycles. However, Andrew Wyckoff, an economist at the OECD, is less optimistic. In a recent article[†], he argues that, in the future, service businesses may well behave more like manufacturing ones and become more cyclical.

**Moving in tandem**

Mr Wyckoff argues that the spread of information technology (IT) through the service sector will encourage a blurring of the distinction between manufacturing and services. As advances in IT allow the 'codification' of knowledge, it will become increasingly easy to 'store' services in the form of software systems (e.g. telemedicine for medical diagnosis or expert systems for handling simple legal tasks, such as drafting wills).

In the past the only way to supply these services was through direct contact between producer and consumer. In the future, if services can be stored and thus in effect held as stocks by firms, then services too may become subject to stockpiling. And if production of these 'services' moves ahead of demand, downturns will be exacerbated as firms are forced to produce fewer of them.

Mr Wyckoff also points out that the argument that services are less capital-intensive than manufacturing is weaker than it looks. Four-fifths of the IT sold in America is now purchased by service providers. As these firms become increasingly capital-intensive, they are likely to become just as cyclical as manufacturing firms, slashing their investment plans as profits dip and therefore denting output and employment.

On top of this, Mr Wyckoff argues that deregulation in many countries has lately begun to expose previously sheltered service sectors – such as health care, telecommunications and transport – to much more open competition, both at home and abroad. This is forcing managers to keep a keener eye on costs and suggests that service-sector jobs will in future become increasingly vulnerable to economic contractions.

It is anyway easy to exaggerate the claim that services have been insulated from cyclical swings. Retailers, wholesalers, transport companies and some other service firms have always been affected by the economic cycle, albeit to a lesser extent than manufacturing firms. And there is some evidence that, if anything, services are playing a bigger role in downturns than in the past.

The biggest change has been in the fastest-growing service sector, the financial industry, which in most countries experienced a severe downturn in the early 1990s. This is also one of the businesses that has seen most of the barriers to entry that used to protect it swept away over the past decade or so. Until the next downturn, it will be impossible to tell whether this shake-out was a one-off adjustment to deregulation or the beginning of a long-term trend.

* 'Do Services Temper Business Cycles?', by Jaewoo Lee. University of California, Irvine, May 1996.
† 'The Growing Strength of Services', by Andrew Wyckoff *OECD Observer* No. 200, June 1996.
*Source*: © *The Economist*, London, 6 July 1996, p 104.

*Comment on the case study*

It has often been suggested that the restructuring of an economy towards services will have a detrimental impact on external trade. Case study 2.2 serves to add two more problems, those of a possible future shakeout from the service sector of the economy as deregulation is introduced and competition increases – a feature that can be seen in the banking/building society/insurance industry in the UK – and of the fact that the dampening effect on the cycles which an economy experiences from having a burgeoning service sector may be short lived. If this is the case, then it is not surprising that governments have sought to consider areas or sectors of the economy which will take up the growth in unemployed resources; the small firms sector is one of these.

## Definition and size of the SME sector

With the general rise in unemployment within the EU and the setting of a target by the European Commission for the creation of 15 million jobs by the year 2000 together with the halving of the current number unemployed, attention is being focused on the job-creating capacity of small and medium-sized enterprises (SMEs) within the Union. Moreover, in terms of employment growth for all the major economies, it is services that have contributed the most in the EU, the EFTA countries, Japan and the US. Since the SME sector accounts for much of the growth in the service sector of the EU, it is not surprising that the EU has turned its attention to the further job-creating ability of these companies.

There are a number of ways in which SMEs can be defined. It can be via the number of employees, turnover, number of vehicles, balance sheet total or the degree of financial autonomy. Since definitions could differ by member state, actions both at Union level and at national level can lead to different results. Thus in September 1994, the European Commission recommended to member states that a single set of definitions should apply to SMEs. These were:

- Micro-enterprises – less than 10 employees.
- Small enterprises – between 10 and 50 employees.
- Medium-sized enterprises – between 51 and 250 employees.
- Large enterprises – more than 250 employees.

This may provide a useful yardstick within the EU, but when making comparisons on an international level the problems with definitions still prevail. For example, a definition used in the US for a small firm is one with less than 1000 employees.

Within the EU in 1993 there were approximately 15 million enterprises employing 92 million individuals. Out of these enterprises, 99.9 per cent were SMEs, accounting for 80 per cent of employment, and 91.3 per cent were micro-enterprises, providing 31.8 per cent of total employment. Small enterprises accounted for 6.2 per cent of the total number of enterprises, but nonetheless supported 24.9 per cent of employment. Medium-sized enterprises were the least numerous of the SMEs at 0.5 per cent, but they generated 15.1 per cent of total employment. The large enterprises catered for just over 28 per cent of the workforce but only made up 0.1 per cent of the enterprises within the EU (European Commission, 1995).

## ◆ CASE STUDY 2.3

### Small firms follow after a slow start

'The first investors in Poland were the big US companies, the multinationals and companies from Britain, France and Italy, while the flagship German companies kept a low profile. This meant that foreign investment, seen by some suspicious Poles as sale of the national silver, was not also condemned as another German takeover', says Wojciech Kostrzewa, president of the Polish Development Bank. . . . 'Foreign companies have kept their promises, dealt fairly with the trade unions, created jobs, boosted exports and steered clear of scandals. This means that nobody really cares now where the invest-ment comes from, so long as it comes', he adds.

According to the official statistics, Germany has already moved into third place behind US-based com-panies and 'international' companies in the pecking order of foreign investments over $1 million.

The foreign investment agency PAIZ calculates that 61 German companies have invested $512 million over the past five years [1990–95], compared with the $1.7 billion invested by 56 US companies and $871 million by 13 multinational companies. Italy is in fourth place with $378 million but is second when future commitments are taken into account. Italian companies have pledged to invest a further $2.1 bil-lion, mainly connected with Fiat and related projects.

To date, German companies have pledged to invest a further $925 million in Poland, but this is expected to rise sharply as the Mittelstand [middle-sized] com-panies put down their roots.

In addition to the publicised investments by big companies such as Volkswagen or Siemens, however, there are large numbers of small but unrecorded investments of under $1 million by small private German companies which have already shifted plant and equipment or invested in outworking.

In some cases, German companies, including Mercedes-Benz, have kept a low profile, working through Polish partners rather than advertise to their German workforce that they are transferring work to cheaper locations abroad.

To date, investment by small German companies has been concentrated along the main Berlin–Warsaw highway and the Poznan area, while German traders have been making increasing use of the Baltic ports of Szczecin and Swinoujsci.

*Source*: *Financial Times*, 29 September 1995. Reprinted with permission.

---

◆ **Exercise 2.3**

1 What factors make it attractive for small firms to invest in Poland?

2 Why were German companies slower to seek entry into the Polish market?

3 Why are the middle-sized and small companies later in moving into the Polish market?

---

*Comment on the case study*

Case study 2.3 illustrates that small firms are not necessarily confined to their domestic markets. There has been increasing activity of small firms in foreign markets. Often they will be those mar-kets that are close by and the investment will be undertaken through a joint venture. The view that concentrating on SMEs as future generators of employment would reduce a country's potential for exporting may be erroneous.

Nonetheless, the case also indicates that German companies do not want to be seen as exporting jobs to low-cost Eastern European states. In many Eastern European countries the workforce can be adaptable to change and the education sys-tem provides a highly educated workforce. At the same time, wage rates are sufficiently low so that, with capital, Western European companies can produce good-quality output at lower wages but with the downside of lower levels of productivity in the first instance.

Because there are risks in moving into Eastern European economies, it is those organisations which are more likely to be in the position to bear the risks of failure that will be in the first wave of overseas investment. These are usually the larger organisations. Once the risks of trading are reduced, then middle-sized and small companies may look to invest in Eastern European markets.

## Measures to assist SMEs

The various national governments within the EU have their own domestic policies to aid and sup-port the SME sector, as Table 2.5 indicates.

Within the EU, Directorate General XXIII has responsibility for SMEs and the current pro-grammes, which run until 1996 and are costing ECU 112 million (£78 million), have the following main features:

■ To reduce the burdens on SMEs arising from EU legislation, and to improve the cash flow difficul-ties they face through the late payment of debts.

■ To improve the information flows to SMEs through a network of 200 European Information Centres.

■ To promote SME cooperation across borders through the Business Cooperation Network (BC-NET).

■ To promote a better structural and financial environment for SMEs during the 1990s.

The EU also provides financial support to SMEs through the European Investment Bank (EIB). One programme permits loans to be made avail-able at a 2 per cent rebate over 5 years, dependent on job creation.

## Table 2.5 Principal member state actions in SME policy

**Belgium**
- Introduction of an 'SME Barometer' to promote discussion on and generate ideas for SME policy.
- Increase in the availability and the amount of *'Overdracht Fonds'* which facilitate enterprise transfer.
- Social security reforms, e.g. reductions in employers' contributions.

**Denmark**
- Fiscal policy reforms – increase in public investment and tax reforms.
- Legislation on a state guarantee system available to private Development Companies (*Udviklingsselskaber*) investing in promising SMEs.
- Introduction of a 'rebate card' offering start-up grants and advice to entrepreneurs.

**Germany**
- New legislation (*Standortsicherungsgesetz*) for SMEs allowing a reduction in corporate tax on profits.
- Reduction in income tax on business earnings and a provision for inheritance tax allowance.
- '30-Points-Programme' set up to consider the recommendations of the White Paper and to relaunch the *'Eigenkapitalhilfe Programm'* to support start-ups.

**Greece**
- Privatisation, tax and competition policy reform.
- Establishment of regional institutes providing support for medium-sized enterprises.

**Spain**
- Reform of the 'Reciprocal Guarantee System' to reduce the cost of guarantees.
- Introduction of subsidised loans available for investment purposes.
- Setting up of a 'Joint Venture Capital fund' by the Instituto de Crédito Oficial for start-up firms.
- Easier SME access to the stock exchange, fiscal incentives and labour market reforms to increase flexibility.

**France**
- 'Plan Madelin' aimed at improving the economic environment of SMEs through fiscal reforms, easier access to credit, competition law reforms, easing of the burden of administrative procedures, promotion of inter-enterprise cooperation.
- Guarantee fund available to SMEs for investment purposes.

**Ireland**
- Network of 'County Enterprise Boards' established to support SMEs.
- Further development of the 'Business Expansion Scheme' to include tax relief on corporate gains.
- Introduction of a 'Seed Capital Scheme' to indirectly support start-ups with income tax advantages for entrepreneurs.

**Italy**
- Launch of *'Interventi per l'innovazione e lo sviluppo delle piccole imprese'* with tax allowances and direct subsidies for SMEs. The eight subprogrammes of this scheme provide support SMEs in such areas as R&D, loan guarantees etc.

**Netherlands**
- Creation of a plan *'Meer werk, weer werk'* to improve market flexibility.
- Improved access to subsidies for R&D costs.
- Development of apprenticeship schemes.
- Current investigation into the potential for easing taxation on SMEs.

**Portugal**
- 'Intercalary Programme' to facilitate SME access to finance, improve efficiency and foster growth.
- 'PEDIP II programme' – incorporates numerous aid measures for SMEs.
- Variety of support programmes to promote export and international trade.
- 'FRIE fund' to promote equity participation.

**United Kingdom**
- Establishment of 'Business Links' to foster cooperation and improve competitiveness.
- Improvement of the 'Small Enterprises Loan Guarantee Scheme' with an increase in the amount of loan available.
- Introduction of the 'Enterprises Investment Scheme' to improve access to equity funding.
- Provision for tax relief for those investing in unquoted companies.
- Creation of the 'Uniform Business Rate' which involves a reduction in the tax and social burden of SMEs.

Although the EU still faces a fragmented approach to the SME sector, its main problem may well lie with insufficient quality of data to understand this sector of the economy.

Although more attention has switched to small firms, the financial pages are still biased to the behaviour and actions of large organisations. We have seen how the international environment has changed for these organisations and one way in which they have reacted is to alter their size. This change in their boundaries is a response to the changing nature of international competition. Both in domestic and international markets, we have seen areas such as the aircraft industry (consider the proposed merger between Boeing and McDonnell-Douglas being discussed at the end of 1996) and electricity generating industry becoming less competitive. In other words, markets, both domestically and internationally, are becoming more oligopolistic and their control is becoming more concentrated in a few hands.

Markets are also becoming more difficult to separate, as Case Study 2.4 indicates.

◆ **CASE STUDY 2.4**

# Petrol stations pump it up: forecourts are attempting to lure customers with convenience shopping  **FT**

The European marketing arms of the big international oil companies can be excused for feeling under siege.

Just as cola and baked bean manufacturers are being forced to compete with cheaper own-label products on retailers' shelves, so discount petrol stations have become a common sight at British and Continental superstores in recent years. Their growing influence has put industry margins under pressure, nowhere more suddenly than in the UK, where supermarkets have captured a fifth of the retail petrol market.

Oil companies, though, are fighting back and much management time is being devoted first to persuading motorists of the advantages of buying a premium but more expensive make of petrol, and then capturing their loyalty to a particular brand. That is in spite of a general acceptance in the industry that consumers often find it hard to differentiate between the majors.

Industry executives speak of the shoelace test: 'If a customer standing on the forecourt of a petrol station bent down to tie his shoelace, would he be able to tell if he was on a Mobil, BP, Esso, Texaco or Shell site?'

Although the answer is almost invariably negative, that has not stopped the industry from launching ambitious projects that emphasise differentiation and encourage customer loyalty.

Last October Shell, with one of the UK's largest retail networks, introduced the first nationwide smart card incentive scheme for motorists.

David Pirret, the general manager of Shell UK's retail division, says more than 2m cards have so far been distributed, representing about 10 per cent of the UK driving public. The cards have allowed Shell to eliminate the paper vouchers and stamps that oil companies have traditionally given to customers to encourage brand loyalty – though at a price. Millions of pounds have been spent on installing 1,800 terminals at Shell sites.

Pirret, however, says the move to an electronic system has advantages other than its novelty value.

It gives the company detailed information on the buying patterns of individual consumers. And that, he adds, allows Shell to use 'micro-marketing techniques' to approach small groups of consumers through direct correspondence.

'For example, if we open a new station we can mail shot customers in the area,' he says.

Other companies agree that electronic loyalty schemes are more convenient to operate than the old paper-based ones. But the effectiveness of such schemes in securing brand loyalty is not wholly accepted in the industry.

Tony Rexburgh, head of marketing at BP Oil International, says motorists may simply wind up collecting all the cards issued by the various companies. There is also conflicting market research about whether customers like long-term incentive schemes. Simple give-aways of items such as glasses and mugs may seem old-fashioned, but they can be surprisingly effective.

Other companies worry about the 'glove box factor' with a long-term incentive scheme. That is the hard-to-compute level of payout that can arise at the end of such schemes.

One issue on which most companies do agree is that the transformation of petrol stations into broader retail outlets – effectively trying to turn the tables on supermarkets – has yet to run its course.

The introduction of concourse shops has revolutionised the economics of petrol marketing in recent years. Hundreds of low-volume rural stations slated for closure have been reprieved by the presence of a shop, say industry executives.

The shops were originally intended to draw motorists. But non-petrol buying traffic can account for 50–60 per cent of the turnover of some station shops.

Figures from Shell show that forecourt convenience stores in the UK account for £2 billion of the £31 billion convenience-shopping market in the country. But the company, which is converting five stations a week to full convenience store status, believes the market will grow rapidly as the number of old-style corner shops declines.

A good deal of experimentation is taking place across the industry, although 'a lot of people are simply fascinated by the latest wheeze,' says Pirret. Combining fast food outlets with petrol sales is the 'flavour of the month,' says Rexburgh. Texaco, which has Pizza Hut kiosks within several of its shops, says the results so far have been positive. . .

But there are signs of a small counter-revolution against the trend towards large, multi-service marketing operations.

Elf, one of the newest entrants in the UK, has added a back-to-basics element to its marketing strategy. It plans to introduce unmanned, fully automated mobile service stations for sites in which it would not be possible to build a permanent station. Such a strategy has proved successful for oil companies in several Continental countries.

*Source: Financial Times*, 12 January 1995. Reprinted with permission.

◆ **Exercise 2.4**

Consider the reasons why petrol retailing has altered during the 1990s.

Given that organisations are increasingly moving into other markets, is it still possible to talk about performance in single product markets?

*Comment on the case study*

The growing complexity and scale of competition are evident for the petrol retailers. The problems they face are also faced by organisations in other industries. The fact that the petrol retailers are competing with the supermarkets complicates matters yet further. An investigation of the food retail market would not necessarily show the increased competition from the petrol stations, but the threat is there nonetheless. Industry analysts, managers and other decision makers need to maintain an awareness of the whole economy and the potential opportunities and threats as well as investigating their own particular area of the market.

Add to this increased range of competition the implications and effects of improved technology, and such individuals would appear to have an impossible job. Tracking each consumer's unique purchasing habits via their EPOS (electronic point of sale) till receipts and their credit card accounts offers insight into what are popular items in given segments of the whole market. It is even better if the customer can be persuaded to take out a store account or loyalty card, because their habits can be tracked even more accurately and they may then be sent tailored publicity material by the organisation. Such technology makes the seller very powerful in terms of knowledge, but the seller must be large enough to make it feasible in terms of cost and, of course, must be able to use the information gathered effectively.

Some of the techniques which may be used to achieve such success are outlined in the remainder of this text.

This chapter has attempted to draw together a number of related strands within the area of the international environment faced by organisations. It has highlighted a number of important issues that will be discussed in detail in the forthcoming chapters and has considered in more detail the structural changes and challenges facing EU industry. The globalisation of business and the move towards free trade at the same time as the development of global trading blocs have resulted in increased pressures on both governments and organisations.

The chapter has outlined the structural changes that have occurred in the EU economy, and in particular considered the strengths and weaknesses in the EU's manufacturing base and its R&D record. It has also developed arguments for the growth in interest in the small firms sector and this sector's potential to provide many jobs for the future.

At the same time as these structural changes have been taking place through the greater internationalisation of markets, there has been, both at the domestic and the international level, a move towards the growth of oligopolistic markets. These markets, dominated by a few large companies, can yield greater market power to the organisations involved. Concentration ratios, at national and international levels, can indicate a measure of this market power, although the figures should be judged with caution.

Nothing is certain in business, but perhaps one thing is more certain in the future: the future will be different. The remaining chapters consider many of the important decisions that organisations will be required to make within the turbulent international framework and appraises the changes that have taken place in the international environment in which organisations operate.

## SUMMARY

◆ Organisations exist in a dynamic environment. This environment has been subject to increasingly rapid change and organisations have probably never faced such an uncertain world. There have been movements towards the globalisation of business activities, merger cycles, changes in the direction of multinational activity, the signing of the eighth GATT round on trade, the liberalisation of markets, the move towards privatisation and deregulation of markets, the development of regional trading blocs and increases in corporate responsibility, both in terms of the environment and in terms of company's own ethical behaviour.

◆ A main feature of the industrial economies of the world has been a shift in employment out of agriculture and manufacturing into the service sector. This has been a response to increased competition, changes in income and taste, supply-side factors and the impact of technology.

◆ There has been a persistent tendency for the industrialised countries to experience a decline in their manufacturing sectors. This process of deindustrialisation can be defined in a number of ways, but in the main it can be seen as a fall in manufactures as a proportion of GDP, the rise in the service sector of the economy, a fall in manufacturing employment and, for some countries, a decline in their percentage of total world exports.

◆ Within the EU the deindustrialisation process has been seen as a reflection of the Union's limited competitiveness in a number of areas, the delay in the development of new technologies, the slow application of new organisational concepts and the problems of a high-price and high-quality strategy in product markets. This is also coupled with the internationalisation of markets where producers are shifting their production platforms to lower-cost centres.

◆ The role of large national and multinational organisations has increased in the latter part of the twentieth century. All aspects of internal and external organisational thinking and systems have changed as a result of the role played by such organisations in both their local and the global economies.

◆ As unemployment has gradually risen in the EU there has been an increasing interest in small and medium-sized enterprises (SMEs). The very great majority of enterprises in the EU fall into this category, supporting most of the EU workforce and providing a large proportion of EU output.

◆ Each country recognises the importance of the SME sector and has responded in its own way towards helping these firms. The EU has sought to streamline this process through legislation and policies to encourage the sector overall and to prevent each country following a 'beggar-thy-neighbour' policy. EU policies have concentrated on improving cash flow to SMEs, improving information flows and encouraging cooperation across borders.

## REVIEW QUESTIONS

1 Why does structural change matter?

2 What factors have been put forward to explain deindustrialisation? Which are more appropriate to the UK economy and which are more relevant to the EU economies as a whole?

3 Why has there been a growing interest in SMEs when it is large organisations which continue to dominate world markets?

4 How has the pattern of trade changed within the EU?

5 The largest supermarket chains have developed beyond simply selling groceries in their stores. Many now provide services including banking, insurance and even dry cleaning. How does this diversification blur the distinction between markets?

## GLOSSARY OF NEW TERMS

**Deindustrialisation**: Often associated with a decline in the manufacturing sector output compared with other sectors of the economy or a decline in employment in manufacturing.

**GATT**: General Agreements on Tariffs and Trade.

**Income elasticities**: The percentage increase in quantity that arises when there is a percentage change in income.

**Outsourcing**: Contracting out of services and products which used to be done in-house.

**Productivity**: The increase in output per person.

**Sclerosis**: Structures that may exist in an economy, such as unions, power blocs or stakeholders, which are fairly rigid and slow down the process of change.

**Structural change**: The change in the structural make-up of an economy between primary, secondary and tertiary sectors.

**Trade balance**: The comparison of total exports of goods and services with imports of goods and services.

# READING

Brittan, S (1995) *Financial Times*, 'Economic Viewpoint: political economy of job creation', 20 April, p 24.

Cook, M and Healey, N (1995) *Growth and Structural Change*, Macmillan, Basingstoke.
*Although it considers deindustrialisation in a UK context, the book also provides valuable information on international comparisons.*

Corzine, R (1995) 'Petrol stations pump it up' Management (Marketing and Advertising), *Financial Times*, 12 January, p 10.

*The Economist* (1996) 'The ups and downs of services', 6 July, p 104.

Robinson, A (1995) *Financial Times*, Survey of Polish Foreign Trade and Finance (4) 'Small firms follow after a slow start', 29 September, p 32.

Storey, D J (1994) *Understanding the Small Business Sector*, Routledge, London.
*This book provides a comprehensive analysis of the research undertaken into small firms. It has a UK bias but contains important references to both the EU and US.*

Worthington, I and Britton, C (1997) *The Business Environment*, 2nd edn, Pitman Publishing , London.
*Of particular interest are Chapters 3–10, the 'Contexts' section.*

## Further reading

Bean, C (1987) 'The impact of North Sea oil' in Dornbusch, R and Layard, R, *The Performance of the UK Economy*, Oxford University Press, Oxford, pp 64–96.

Burda, M and Wyplosz, C (1993) *Macroeconomics: A European Text*, Oxford University Press, Oxford.

European Commission (1995) *Panorama of Europe*, The Office for Official Publications of the European Communities, Luxembourg.

European Network for SME Research (1995) *The European Observatory for SMEs*, 3rd Annual Report, European Network for SME Research, Zoetermeer, The Netherlands.

Gallagher, C, Daly, M and Thomason, J C (1990) 'The growth of UK companies 1985–1987 and their contribution to job creation', *Employment Gazette*, Feb, pp 92–8.

# BUSINESS OBJECTIVES, ETHICS AND CORPORATE GOVERNANCE

Business issues

Business strategy

Decision-making techniques

Economic concepts

Management decision issues

Optimal outcomes to management issues

## OBJECTIVES

◆ To outline the concept of profit maximisation as a business objective.

◆ To examine the shift away from profit maximisation by organisations as a result of their own growth and as a result of changes in the nature of markets generally.

◆ To outline the basic principles underpinning the concept of ethics and business ethics specifically.

◆ To discuss the implications for organisations of ethical behaviour.

◆ To highlight several contemporary issues regarding ethics which organisations face or have faced.

◆ To consider why corporate governance has grown increasingly important over the past two decades.

◆ To show how the principal agent problem can be related to the concept of corporate governance.

◆ To consider the role of corporate governance in Europe.

◆ To discuss the various methods by which corporate governance can be improved.

## KEY TERMS

Allocative efficiency

Corporate governance

Corporate social responsibility

Externalities

Morality

Neoclassical economics

Principal agent problem

Productive efficiency

Stakeholders

Stewardship theory

Two-tier board

## CHAPTER OUTLINE

Business application

The neoclassical model of the firm: the assumption of profit maximisation

The marginal revenue/marginal cost rule: measurement of profits

Separation of ownership and control: profit maximisation in practice

Introduction to the concept of ethical behaviour

Case study 3.1  Shell shocked by Greenpeace

Case study 3.2  Doing good boosts earnings per share: would businesses act ethically if it cost them money?

Particular actions and ethical systems

Worker safety and wage levels

Criticisms of a market economy

Social responsibility of firms

Shareholders and ethical investments

Case study 3.3  'Social cause marketing' has proved a powerful tool: but is it ethical?

The role of profits and business ethics

European issues

Introduction to corporate governance

The principal agent problem

Monitoring directors' behaviour

Independent directors

Audits

Directors' pay

Corporate governance in the public sector

Corporate governance in Europe

Summary

Review questions

Glossary of new terms

Reading

# Management: the ethical way to profitability

**FT**

German businessman Friedrich Schock recently cancelled a DM20m (£8.7m) contract with a US company because it was 'wanting to tie us into practices we could not accept'. The decision, he says, will put his family business of 1100 employees into the red next year by DM2m. But he insists his company's reputation for honesty must be maintained. 'You lose 10 per cent but you have to have the faith that you will gain 20 per cent in the long run.'

Schock is a member of the Caux Round Table, an informal group of European, American and Japanese business executives which has just held its 10th annual gathering in the Swiss village of Caux, near Montreux. The group has distributed 130 000 copies of its Principles for Business, an international code for good practice.

The world needs people 'with a strong frame of reference who are willing to change their ways', asserts CRT's chairman Jean-Loup Dherse, a former vice-president of the World Bank. He says the principles are 'a spur to the members themselves. Ethics are not the soap you want your neighbour to use to wash his face. They are your own deep desire to be clean'.

But Heidi von Weltzien Hoivik, head of business ethics at the Norwegian School of Management, warns against signing on to such codes simply to boost company image. Values have to be 'internalised' by individuals and then acted upon.

One CRT participant admits that his company felt compelled to pay bribes to set up factories in two Asian countries. Others like Schock, whose company manufactures kitchen and bathroom components, are more resolute. He refused payment 'in black money from Swiss bank accounts' for the sale of manufacturing licenses to Italy. He warns clients that all revenues, and their sources, will be declared for tax purposes.

Ryzaburo Kaku, chairman of the cameras-to-copiers corporation Canon, spoke about his personal commitment to environmental issues, as a survivor of the bombing of Nagasaki 50 years ago. Canon has a department of 300 people exclusively looking at ways of minimising damage to the ecosystem, 'for the sake of future generations', he says.

The company is committed to recycling and last year spent 12 per cent of gross earnings on research and development into high value added energy-saving products.

Many US corporations now have chief ethics officers as board members, points out Stephen Braswell, who fulfils the role at Prudential Insurance of America where he is also senior vice-president. Reginald Brack, chairman of Time Inc, publishers of Time Magazine and Time-Life Books, believes there is no conflict between ethical business practice and profitability.

'Many companies around the world have been highly profitable and highly responsible, with the most outstanding ethical practices imaginable,' he says.

Brack, a first-time CRT participant, is impressed by the experience of Reell, a small Minnesota manufacturer of clutches and hinges for notebook computers with 130 employees which is 'applying the acid litmus paper test to every decision they make by asking themselves: "Is this the right thing to do?"'.

The three founders run it on the principle of doing 'what is right even when it does not seem profitable', claims Robert Wahlstedt, its president. The company, which supplies Xerox and Compaq, has seen its share value rise from $250 (£156) to nearly $800.

CRT plans to survey leading corporations about their business principles, as well as seeking wider endorsement for its own code. Winston Wallin, chairman of the heart-pacemaker multinational Medtronic, and the CRT's chairman-elect, hopes the group will grow to have an impact on governments.

'It isn't beyond us to hope that we can make changes in the world as a result of what we are doing here,' he says.

*Source: Financial Times, 25 August 1995. Reprinted with permission.*

*Comment*

The case above illustrates the growing concern among organisations around the world with ethical behaviour. There are clearly situations above where less scrupulous organisations could have acted differently and made very large profits. The members of the Caux Round Table, on the other hand, are concerned with acting in either an ethical manner or with respect for the environment at all times. This may be expensive for them, even forcing losses at times, but the members believe that they will reap the benefits (and profits) of such good behaviour in the future. This chapter will consider some of the issues raised in this case. An outline of what ethical behaviour is commonly and legally accepted to be will also be outlined to give a basis for understanding.

# NEOCLASSICAL MODEL OF FIRM: THE ASSUMPTION OF PROFIT MAXIMISATION

Mainstream economic thought and teaching is based on what is known as the **neoclassical** model of the firm in the economy. The term neoclassical is used because its foundations lay in the theories and assumptions of the classical economists, such as Adam Smith. Smith was perhaps the most famous economist; he is frequently associated with the birth of economics and published the *Wealth of Nations* in 1776.

Adam Smith believed that markets, left to their own ends (or, as he termed it, the 'invisible hand'), would settle on a position of natural equilibrium. Equilibrium is a very important concept in economic theory. It allows economists to make analyses of markets (and organisations) in relation to a stable reference point, rather than attempting to analyse a situation where all factors are in flux.

In other words, 'equilibrium' is the situation where markets have settled on a given point without further likelihood of change. That is, at a given market price, the quantity of a product, such as spectacles, which suppliers (opticians) are willing to sell is the same quantity which the consuming public are willing to buy. There are no shortages or surpluses in the market, because both sides, supply and demand, are satisfied. Obviously, it will be easier to make an analysis of a market which has reached an equilibrium point and is therefore stable than to attempt to make an analysis of a market which has not settled and is constantly changing.

One of the assumptions which may be traced back to Smith and which has been adopted by economists as an undebatable truth is that organisations seek to maximise their profits within a given period. He made this assumption as a result of his belief in the invisible hand and also the fact that organisations will do all in their power to gain maximum benefit for themselves. In 1776, maximum benefit was very much measured in financial terms. There was little or no awareness in the eighteenth century of the negative effects of the exploitation of workers. Pollution and other environmental issues were of no major concern to either government, the general public or organisations. Therefore, industrial performance was measured purely by profit or earnings levels.

The concept of profit maximisation has survived for many as the major objective for an organisa-

tion until today. However, an awareness exists that organisations may strive for other objectives than profit maximisation and some economists even completely disregard profit maximisation. The assumptions and models of such economists are discussed in Chapter 4, where the behavioural theories and managerial discretion theories of the firm are compared and contrasted with the concept of profit maximisation. However, as was stated above, mainstream theory and teaching are based on the concept that organisations do attempt to maximise profits. Such a philosophy was acceptable and less open to debate in many countries in the developed world until the period between the world wars of 1914–19 and 1939–45.

Until this time, most organisations were managed and run on a day-to-day basis by their owners. Most were small, single-site operations which reflected the particular special skills of the craftsperson or salesperson. Obviously multinational organisations did exist (as early as the 1890s), but their numbers have increased considerably since 1945. The typical main or high street in towns and villages before this period included many different specialty shops and outlets. But the period of depression experienced between the wars sowed doubt on the merits of capitalism and the pursuit of profit for many small business owners. Many became victims of the depressed state of the economy and went out of business. Bakers and butchers still maintain a presence on the high street in many towns and countries. However, the growth of the larger organisations in manufacturing (and other) industries and the growth of the supermarket and out-of-town shopping have reduced the importance of the smaller organisation (*see* Chapter 2, page 15) in the economy. The reason for this decline will be investigated later in this chapter.

While there was a concentration of ownership and control of organisations within the hands of the small entrepreneur, there was considered to be more of a need for profits to be maximised. Owners depend on their businesses for their day-to-day survival (accommodation, food, heating and so on), which means that owners try to make the most money they are able to from their businesses. There is, and was, very little science involved in such a survival objective. Marketing, promotions and other activities *seemingly* detracted from the profits of the organisation. Therefore, the entrepreneur measured the effectiveness of activities by their effect on the 'bottom line', the profits stated at the end of the year.

# THE MARGINAL REVENUE/ MARGINAL COST RULE: MEASUREMENT OF PROFITS

The 'science' of measuring profit maximisation requires the analyst to have highly accurate information about the organisation's total costs and revenues, or marginal costs and revenues, or both.

Total costs and revenues are conceptually simple to understand. For each level of production achievable by the organisation, the associated level of total costs accrued and revenue gained may be plotted. This will give a diagram similar to that in Figure 3.1.

Total costs for a production level of zero will be greater than zero, due to the costs incurred in renting or buying accommodation and capital equipment, that is, the fixed costs of the organisation. Variable costs of production are added at each level of production. Total costs will increase throughout the range of production outputs considered. Total revenue, on the other hand, will increase steadily up to the maximum revenue level, given by $Q_{revmax}$. Total revenue will reach a maximum and then begin to decline as organisations attain less and less revenue for each unit sold. This decline is due to the discounts that the organisation is required to make to consumers to encourage them to purchase.

The quantity associated with the maximum profit level is $Q_{\pi max}$ which is the production quantity associated with the greatest distance between the revenue and cost curves – that is, the point at which the excess of earnings over expenditure is at its greatest. Such a point can be difficult to pinpoint accurately on a visual basis from a graph. For more accurate results, mathematical manipulation of the data is required.

A simpler visual confirmation of the quantity associated with profit maximisation is the point given by 'marginal' analysis. In economics, the **marginal** concept is used in many formats. Marginal means additional unit. Therefore, the marginal cost is the cost of producing an extra unit and the marginal revenue is the revenue gained by selling an extra unit. Marginal analysis is the analysis of the organisation's marginal cost/marginal revenue situation. The profit-maximising point occurs at the output at which marginal costs and revenues are equal (at the point at which marginal costs cut marginal revenue from below). Mathematically, this is derived in Chapter 4. The profit-maximising point may be seen clearly in Figure 3.2.

Assume that the profit associated with a production level of 101 units is £300. At this point, marginal revenues exceed marginal costs. Assume further that marginal revenue is constant and equal to the price of the product. Therefore, the marginal

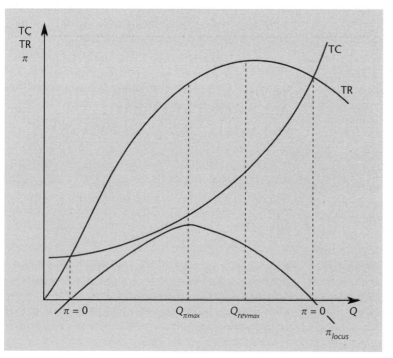

**Figure 3.1**

Total costs are given by TC. A production level of zero will have TC greater than zero, due to the organisation's fixed costs. Variable costs of production are added at each level of production and increase TC accordingly.

Total revenue, TR, increases up to the maximum revenue level, $Q_{revmax}$ – TR then declines as organisations attain less and less revenue for each unit sold as a result of discounts made to consumers to encourage them to purchase.

The quantity associated with the maximum profit level is $Q_{\pi max}$ – the production quantity associated with the greatest distance between the revenue and cost curves – that is, the point at which the excess of earnings over expenditure is at its greatest.

Profits are shown as a profit locus, $\pi_{locus}$ – showing the zero profit level, the maximum profit level and all intermediate points.

**Figure 3.2**

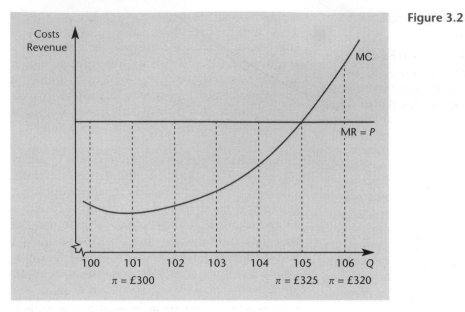

The profit associated with a production level of 101 units is £300. At this point, marginal revenues exceed marginal costs. Marginal revenue is constant and equal to the price of the product.

Any increase in production between 101 and 105 units will cause profits to increase yet further. Marginal revenues are greater than marginal costs at all points in this quantity range. If the additional revenues exceed additional costs by a total of £25, the total profit at 105 units produced is equal to £325.

At 105 units of production, marginal revenues equal marginal costs. This is the profit-maximising quantity of production. If the production quantity is increased to 106 units, marginal losses are made. If the level of marginal losses is equal to £5, then the total profit level will fall to £320. Further increases in production will incur further marginal losses. It may be concluded, therefore, that 105 units of production, generating profits of £325, is the profit-maximising point.

revenue curve is horizontal. This is assumed purely for ease of analysis.

Any increase in production between 101 and 105 units will cause profits to increase still further. This must be the case, since marginal revenues are greater than marginal costs at all points in this quantity range. Any additions to production therefore generate more revenue per additional unit than revenue. Assume that the additional revenues exceed additional costs by a total of £25. Thus, the total profit at 105 units produced is equal to £325.

At 105 units production, marginal revenues equal marginal costs. At this point, there are no additional profits to be made (marginal profit is equal to zero). This is the profit-maximising quantity of production. For proof, consider the production quantity 106 units. Here, marginal costs exceed marginal revenues; that is, marginal losses are made as a result of producing 106 units rather than 105. If the level of marginal losses is equal to £5, then the total profit level will thus fall to £320. Since £320 is obviously less than £325, further increases in production will

incur further marginal losses. It may be concluded, then, that 105 units of production, generating profits of £325, is the profit-maximising point.

## SEPARATION OF OWNERSHIP AND CONTROL: PROFIT MAXIMISATION IN PRACTICE

Although profit maximisation offers a neat and intuitive understanding of the financial operation of the organisation, several factors combine in the real world to mean that true profit maximisation is rarely aimed for, achieved or even measured accurately. The factors contributing to such problems are:

- There is a separation of ownership and control.
- Data relating to marginal costs and revenues are inherently inaccurate.
- Organisational objectives are rarely solely to maximise profits.

■ There is a choice between short-run and long-run profit maximisation.

Each of these factors will be developed briefly below. However, more detail and discussion are provided in subsequent chapters. The appropriate chapter numbers are given in brackets after the headings.

## There is a separation of ownership and control (*see also* Chapter 4) and organisational objectives are rarely solely to maximise profits

As was mentioned previously, the period between the wars marked a change in the manner in which organisations were run. 'Big business', the growth of the multinational, the era of mass communications and other popular clichés describe a period of massive growth for many organisations. They also describe some of the reasons for the growth of organisations.

The result of growth for most organisations is a loss of control by the owner as an individual. The owner has to delegate control to employed managers. Eventually, if the organisation is able to continue to grow, even to expand to other countries, then it may be the case that the owner sell rights to use and trade under the organisational name in those areas. Therefore, the owner becomes more and more detached from the day-to-day running of the organisation.

At the same time, the growth of any organisation requires funding: finance. One popular source of finance is to issue shares or to float the organisation on the stockmarket. Ownership is thus transferred from the entrepreneur to all those who buy, via shares, part ownership of the organisation. When ownership becomes diluted, decision making also becomes diluted. Decision making by consensus of the owners would make the organisation very slow to respond to events. Therefore, once share ownership is established within the organisation, it also usually follows that employed decision makers or managers are responsible for its day-to-day running.

The overall result of the separation of ownership and control is that managers frequently have different objectives to the shareholders or owners they represent. Their interests will be more focused on their own earnings, quality of working life, longevity in post and related factors than on the profit motive. A further factor supporting this is the fact that management salaries and performance success criteria are frequently based on sales levels and market share percentages. Such performance criteria therefore shift management focus away from the profit-making objective. This is particularly true in very turbulent times, because a profit maximiser will present a more volatile stream of maximum profits (or minimum losses) over time than an organisation which is concerned with sales revenues or market share. For a fuller explanation, *see* Chapter 4.

## Data relating to marginal costs and revenues are inherently inaccurate (*see* Chapter 8)

Accountants are constantly searching for ways in which to measure the costs and revenues within organisations accurately. Even for a one-product, small manufacturing organisation, it can be difficult to assign costs to given jobs and make the kind of analysis represented in Figure 3.2. A marginal revenue curve is unlikely to be horizontal. The marginal cost curve is also unlikely in reality to trace a neat U shape.

Once the organisation extends its interests beyond one product, or one site or to a large number of employees, it becomes increasingly difficult to assign costs accurately to given products or jobs. One issue which has not satisfactorily been resolved by accountants is the assignment of fixed costs between product or jobs. There are several methods which have been developed to do this. Current 'buzzwords' are ABC and ABM – activity based costing and activity based management.

ABC is essentially the tracing of costs back to their originating product or customer and charging them appropriately. This apportions costs to their source; as a result, fixed costs are split among the organisation's *activities* (products/customers) in relevant proportions. Variable costs are obviously directly charged to the activity concerned.

ABM uses the knowledge and information gained via ABC and applies it to manage organisational costs effectively. Financial management consultants, such as Coopers and Lybrand, are often contracted to assist organisations in reducing their costs. In these situations, appraisal using ABC will be carried out and then recommendations proposed based on an ABM framework.

## There is a choice between short-run and long-run profit maximisation

One of the arguments which economists have debated in the twentieth century is whether long-run profit maximisation can be achieved by following objectives other than short-run profit maximisation. It is argued that any activity which improves the short-term health of the organisation will necessarily add to its long-term prospects and hence its ability to earn profits.

Given the arguments outlined above, it can be seen that there is a correlation between the type of organisational ownership and its overall objectives. That is, the larger the organisation becomes the more likely it is to follow an alternative overall objective to that of profit maximisation. However, it is also intuitive that any organisation which survives, or is successful, within its competitive environment will earn greater revenues at a lower cost than an organisation which is not successful. Therefore, over time, the successful organisation will continue to improve on its previous successes (and enhanced revenues, reduced costs) and record long-term profit maximisation.

As the separation of ownership and control increases among organisations, shareholders are able to wield less and less power. Large organisations frequently have the individual's power diluted simply because there are so many shareholders. This reduction of shareholder power means that day-to-day and even more strategic decisions are made by the employed management. That is, management gain greater and greater power with reference to the operations of an organisation as the organisation grows.

As markets become more and more complex and the levels of competition in most markets increase, managers are pushed to take greater risks in order to make higher and higher returns. Indeed, as markets become more and more competitive, pressure is placed on all employees to improve productivity, cut costs and so on. The result in some cases is that 'corners are cut', or that improper means of some sort are used. Whatever the method, in all such events there will be a loss of welfare (the optimal distribution of income, quality of life and other similar measures, such as benefits) on the part of the consumer, the shareholder or society in general. When welfare losses occur, it may be claimed that ethics or ethical systems have been abused.

## INTRODUCTION TO THE CONCEPT OF ETHICAL BEHAVIOUR

All countries in Europe and the majority of countries around the world have markets which operate on a capitalist basis. The changes which have been observed in the traditionally socialist countries of the former Soviet Union have been relaxations of the planned, communist market systems. Western companies have been allowed into their markets and domestic organisations are now run with reference to management and shareholder decisions as opposed to the state-imposed decisions of the Soviet model. Competition and consumer choice have evolved as a result of capitalism.

Capitalist market systems require organisations to make four decisions, usually referred to as 'who, what, where and when?'. These may be summarised as follows:

- *Market* – which market to operate within.
- *Product* – what type and quantity of product or products to produce within that chosen market.
- *Price* – what price should be charged for that product within the market.
- *Time* – should the product be offered for sale in the market now, or at some stage in the future. Also, the question could be asked whether older products should be withdrawn from the market.

The combination of these four decisions is considered to be the market mechanism. Organisations in competitive markets must sell their products at competitive prices in order to survive. Within the same market, products which are overpriced compared with competitor's products will, *ceteris paribus* (other things being equal), not sell and the organisation will suffer losses as a result of the production costs incurred. Products which are underpriced will sell to maximum capacity very easily, but will not generate the income necessary to continue in the longer run. Thus, markets settle at a 'market' or 'equilibrium' price at which organisations cover their costs, earn sufficient profits to continue and availability to consumers is adequate.

The free or capitalist market mechanism is what Adam Smith termed the 'invisible hand of the market'. As was stated earlier, the market would, as a result of competitive systems, reach an equilibrium position. The market mechanism is considered to be an efficient market system. Perfectly competitive markets are said to be efficient. That is, perfectly competitive markets result in an optimal allocation of resources, and production of goods and services in a mix which benefits society. Markets 'clear' and settle at their own natural equilibrium positions. The question which arises with reference to ethics is whether or not capitalist market mechanisms are good, or moral. An efficient market may be optimal and provide benefits to society, but that benefit might not be equally distributed across all members of society. An efficient market need not be moral.

**Morality** implies that certain values are upheld and that the market operates in a manner which ensures that justice is done to all. However, capitalism leaves the decision about justice and values to individuals. As time passes, individual preferences change and so by their very nature do values. For example, consider the almost global change in values which has occurred with reference to the treatment of the environment. It used to be commonplace for waste to be dumped into the sea and for emissions into the air to be unrestricted. Preferences have changed in the second half of the twentieth century and both governments and individuals recognise that it is wrong and harmful to pollute the seas and the air to such an extent that clean-up is impossible. Attitudes have been further cemented by the realisation that the ozone layer has been damaged. Unless practices are changed, the damage will increase at such a rate that 'global warming' and the damage to the ozone layer are great enough to put the whole planet in danger. Preferences have changed in this case as a result of dramatic scientific findings; they change in other cases less dramatically as a result of shifts in taste and fashion.

## ◆ CASE STUDY 3.1

# Shell shocked by Greenpeace

**FT**

Shell's volte-face on the high seas is a disaster for the company, which no longer has an agreed means of disposal of the Brent Spar oil platform. It is damaging to all other companies subject to activist pressures. It is a setback for the British government, whose preferred policy for the disposal of some North Sea oil platforms seems to have become inoperable. Many argue that Shell's defeat is democracy's victory. . .

In hindsight, Shell failed either to detect the extent of public concern in continental Europe or to win adequate support for its argument that the best place for Brent Spar was in a deep trench in the Atlantic. But it had very strong arguments on its side: the residues from the Brent Spar tanks are likely to be far more damaging on land. Shell's naivety was to assume that science would win the day. As a result, years of careful cultivation of an environmentally friendly image have been thrown away.

If Shell had foreseen the strength of popular opinion, it could have steered a less damaging course, by dismantling some smaller rigs first. Brent Spar does pose unique problems, since most rigs do not possess a storage tank with toxic residues. Once committed to the policy of deep-sea disposal, however, Shell should have defended it far harder.

**Cool analysis**

With hindsight, the UK government also misjudged the hostility elsewhere in Europe to the scientific arguments. It was left in no doubt of that . . . at the conference of countries bordering the North Sea, which came after the boarding by Greenpeace had raised the public visibility of the planned disposal. The government stresses that the only sensible basis for environmental policy is cool analysis of costs and benefits. It is right. But it has failed to realise how little resonance this stance has with the public, not least in continental Europe. Accordingly, its assumption that it could rely on the letter of international marine pollution conventions turned out to be mistaken.

Meanwhile, Greenpeace has won one of the most dramatic victories in its 25-year history. The speed and impact of the exercise reflect its financial muscle, internal communications and sense for the public mood. . .

As for Shell, the Brent Spar is in danger of becoming a corporate albatross. First, it must find a berth, now expected to be in a Norwegian fiord. Then it must dispose of the redundant hulk. Last but not least, it must refurbish its battered image.

Most important of all, ways must be found to respond to these new pressures. The best policy cannot be to yield to every environmentalist demand, however irrational and costly. All governments should defend the conventions they have agreed; companies must be prepared to sell their decisions; and both must work harder to present the true costs and benefits of alternatives to the widest possible public, if necessary including publics abroad.

People no longer accept that the men from the ministry, let alone the multinational, know best. They are inclined to trust the man from Greenpeace instead. This is the battlefield in which companies and governments must be prepared to engage.

*Source: Financial Times*, 22 June 1995. Reprinted with permission.

*Comment on the case study*

Shell was planning to scrap its Brent Spar oil platform at sea. This contained unused oil, however, and environmentalists claimed that the act of sinking the Brent Spar would ruin the local sea environment if the oil were ever to leak out. Greenpeace, the international environmental pressure group, achieved a high level of publicity against the plans to sink the platform by occupying it uninvited. As a result, the UK government refused Shell permission to carry out its plans and demanded that the platform be disposed of on land. The media attention given this situation was huge. By its actions, Greenpeace succeeded, via the press, in embarrassing both Shell and the British government about their levels of respect for the environment.

What became clear as a result of the events surrounding the Brent Spar was that public concern for the environment cannot be ignored. Although there was scientific advice confirming that the environmental impact would be minimal, the general public was not convinced. During the period between the beginning of the occupation of the platform by Greenpeace and the climb-down by Shell, there were many demonstrations against Shell and even boycotts of its fuel stations across Europe. The public felt strongly enough about this

issue to take such direct action. Environmental activists from Greenpeace helped to highlight the intended actions and possible pollution by boarding and occupying the otherwise deserted rig, but 'ordinary' people took up the cause by making their own protests and boycotts.

Morality in this case dictated that the potential for any oil damage to the local sea environment was removed completely. Neither the British government nor Shell backed down immediately, believing that the scientific evidence would win over the protesters. Eventually, however, they succumbed to public opinion and removed the rig for onshore disposal.

## PARTICULAR ACTIONS AND ETHICAL SYSTEMS

There are clearly different opinions and cultural expectations which affect the moral and judicial base of states. There are also, just to confuse matters, subtle differences between what may be considered acceptable in one state compared to another. This section will consider specific examples of such subtleties.

◆ **CASE STUDY 3.2**

# Doing good boosts earnings per share: would businesses act ethically if it cost them money? [FT]

**A review of Elizabeth Vallance (1995) *Business Ethics at Work*, Cambridge University Press.**

As a recent survey of American business schools said: 'Greed is out, ethics is in'. Most companies now eagerly save whales and send their staff to divorce counsellors. No one seems to be heeding Milton Friedman, who wrote: 'Corporate officials (have no) social responsibility other than to make as much for their stockholders as possible.' Elizabeth Vallance's book is meant to help companies become even more ethical.

As she notes, businesses do good works not just because they are run by nice guys. To prosper today, they have to be seen to be doing good . . . Allied Dunbar discovered that a recruitment ad stressing the company's good works drew four times as many responses as other ads in the series. The recent customer boycott of Shell petrol stations made the point again.

'It's smart to be ethical,' as John Shad said on giving $10m to Harvard Business School for ethics teaching . . .

One could argue that if business ethics means anything, it means applying the values of one's personal life to one's company. Most chief executives in their personal life would do almost anything to avoid depriving a 50-year-old father of his income. 'Business ethics' might mean that the chief executive would sack such a man only if his company's survival depended on it. Few chief executives think like that. Vallance is right: business ethics means doing good only when this boosts profits. That is why, at a time when companies are becoming ever more 'ethical', employees are working longer hours for unchanged pay and are sacked more often. The difference is that they now get redundancy counselling.

*Source: Financial Times, 27 September 1995. Reprinted with permission.*

## Gifts and bribes

While it is acceptable to make a gift to a business contact, it is illegal to bribe him or her in order to gain unfair competitive advantage. Recipients as well as donors can be perceived as acting incorrectly if they accept a bribe. The problem here is what constitutes a gift and what constitutes a bribe.

There is no set rule to define a gift as opposed to a bribe. Additionally, it should be mentioned that 'entertainment' (paying for a contact's presence to do business in a social context) could also be construed as a bribe under certain circumstances.

Even in a particular country, the difference between a bribe or a gift will depend on the industry or market under consideration. Generally, however, it is accepted that there are certain circumstances and characteristics which will distinguish a gift from a bribe. These include:

- *Value* – Typically, a gift which is of little monetary value is indeed a gift. The actual value will vary from industry to industry and company to company. There may even be a corporate policy relating to the giving and receiving of gifts which defines their monetary value.
- *Timing/frequency* – A once-a-year gesture of goodwill, such as at Christmas or other culturally important occasions, is reasonably defined as a gift, whereas a continual stream of gifts is likely to be construed as something more than a gift.
- *Power of recipient* – If the recipient is in a position to make decisions which affect future contracts with the donor or unfairly to promote that donor internally, then gifts may be construed as bribes.
- *Accepted practice* – In some industries, it is common practice for sales executives and managers to give clients samples of their product for free and also to give away small novelties which bear the producer's name or the product name. Such gifts are unlikely to place the recipient in a position of scrutiny. However, this is not common practice in other markets and industries and would therefore cause problems for the recipient to explain away.
- *Policy and law* – Organisational policy and/or state legislation may overtly prohibit the giving of gifts to business contacts, government ministers or others. In such situations, it would be foolish to attempt to give a gift without the action giving rise to concern. The clearest example of this would be the fact that in most, if not all, of Europe, it is illegal to give gifts to police officers; the danger that such an action could be misconstrued as bribery is probably higher than in any other occupation.

As a rule of thumb, if a gift causes a conflict of interest for the recipient, then it may be construed as a bribe. If, however, no such conflict arises, then it is a gift. Obviously, policy and convention should also provide guidance in such cases. Generally, common sense and sensitivity to local customs can act as guides in such matters.

### ◆ Exercise 3.1

It has been seen above that the distinction between a gift and a bribe may be blurred. Similarly, are there occasions when an employee's leisure activities could discredit his or her employers? For example, protest rallies, membership of groups and so on. Is it morally right for employers to screen their employees' leisure activities?

There is no clear-cut answer to the question posed in Exercise 3.1. For example, in the UK, government and defence employment candidates are asked to complete a screening questionnaire when they apply for employment. A question asked in this is whether the candidate has been a member of, or involved in, any group whose intention was to destabilise the government. Obviously, in such cases it is important for national security that candidates are questioned with respect to their leisure, political or social activities.

However, a case which came to public attention in November 1996 related to the treatment of a candidate for employment (within the UK) by a US organisation. The candidate was asked to allow the employer to take a blood test, which would be analysed with respect to the candidate's use (or not) of alcohol and drugs. In the US, this is a common procedure for the employer. In the UK, it is not. The candidate claimed that he usually drank about 10 litres of beer per week. The test results showed that he had drunk many more litres in the week before the test was taken. The employer decided not to employ the candidate. He was obviously upset and explained that in the week before the test, he had been away at a conference and had been entertaining clients, causing an increase in his consumption. Public reaction was one of outrage. People firstly didn't think that the US employer should impose its rules on UK candidates for employment, on a cultural basis. Second, they were concerned that the employer should take a candidate's social/out-of-hours activities into account when deciding whether to employ or not.

## Other situations

Similar arguments and dilemmas arise with reference to employees who deal with the general public and are in a position to offer free gifts to certain clients. If the client happens to be a friend or a relative, could the action of donating a free gift or discount be misconstrued? Should there be a code of practice in such situations? Broadly, this could be defined as nepotism.

Although giving gifts and granting discounts may reflect a serious issue for employers, a potentially even more serious issue is employment nepotism, preferential treatment in employment for relatives. As was the case with reference to gifts and bribes, there may be a subtle difference between family favouritism and proper business behaviour.

A manager who employs a relative may do so in the express belief that the individual is the best person for the job. It would not be fair to exclude from consideration relatives of that manager just in case nepotism occurred. There are laws which protect candidates in such situations. Equal opportunities policies frequently exist, requiring that all candidates for employment are treated in the same way by prospective employers. Indeed, many larger organisations remove the possibility of any nepotism arising by carefully laying down the conditions and practices which must be met in order to select a future employee.

In smaller organisations, there may be a history of management by family members and therefore a positive policy of nepotism. Should such arrangements be prohibited by law? It would be difficult to do so. Sole proprietors and craftspeople who wish to pass on their skills and businesses to their offspring pose no ethical threat or immorality to society in wishing to do so.

## WORKER SAFETY AND WAGE LEVELS

European and domestic legislation requires that certain conditions concerning worker safety and conditions of work are met. For example, there are minimum temperatures to which an ordinary office, shopfloor or factory must normally be heat-ed. More significantly, there are also stringent safety requirements which must be met whenever an employee is using machinery. Within manufacturing industries, any equipment which could cause injury to an operator must have safety cut-off features. Presses, drills, lathes and other similar equipment are required to be operable only when two different finger controls are depressed or turned simultaneously. This is to prevent accidental injury to the hands.

Within offices where employees regularly work at computer screens, regulations require that antiglare screens are fitted and that the screen height and orientation within the office with reference to natural and artificial light are such that the employee does not suffer strain to the hands, neck or eyes. European legislation protects all employees in this respect. Legislation is sometimes unpopular; it increases the costs to the organisation. Imagine the cost of simply upgrading the personal computers in an office of ten people.

There is not yet a Europe-wide minimum wage. France and Belgium, among others, do have a minimum wage, but Britain does not. The argument against it is that costs would rise and that businesses would not be able to remain competitive on a domestic or international basis. This argument is particularly strongly supported by smaller businesses in Britain. Larger businesses also support it, but many know that, should a minimum wage be implemented, they would simply switch their manufacturing operations to other countries, probably in the Far East, where they could maintain a low wage bill.

## CRITICISMS OF A MARKET ECONOMY

There are various criticisms which may be levelled at a market economy with reference to ethical considerations. The basis for these criticisms rests with the fact that no market is completely free in its actions and that concentration of markets into the hands of larger organisations influences market mechanisms in favour of the organisation, rather than the consumer or employee.

In terms of the fairness, or equity, of the distribution of products within markets, it is frequently claimed that lower income earners are not able to purchase the basic necessities of life because their prices are too high. How does this arise?

**Figure 3.3**

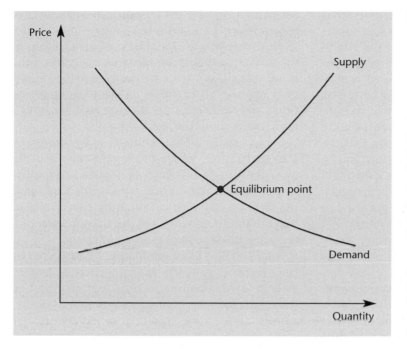

The higher the price, the greater the quantity which suppliers are willing to offer for sale in the market, hence the upward-sloping supply curve.

Conversely, the higher the price, the fewer units of the good or service consumers are willing (or able) to purchase and therefore the demand curve slopes downwards.

The point at which the supply and demand curves cross is the equilibrium point, denoting the market price and market quantity at which the market 'clears', that is, there is neither unsatisfied demand nor shortage of supply.

Where the market mechanism operates freely, supply satisfies demand at the market price and quantity. This may be clearly seen in Figure 3.3.

However, when organisations operate in markets which are not perfectly competitive, there are two possible points of production. These are:

■ **Allocative efficiency** – the organisation's average total costs and average total revenues are equal. When such a position is reached, all demand is satisfied. The organisation supplies goods or services to all those consumers wishing to purchase at the allocative efficiency level.

■ **Productive efficiency** – the organisation's marginal conditions are met: marginal cost equates to marginal revenue. The organisation is therefore acting so as to maximise its own profit levels.

The difference between these points may be seen in Figure 3.4. In some circumstances, governments

**Figure 3.4**

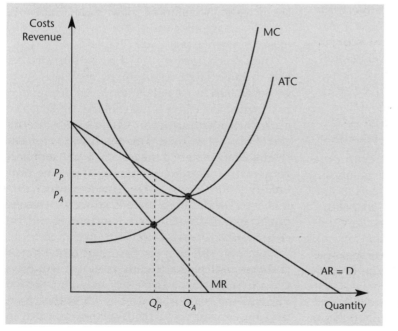

Since the organisation is operating under imperfect conditions, (total) average revenue (AR) slopes downwards and to the right. This equates to the organisation's demand curve. Marginal revenues (MR) are, at each quantity, less than AR. Average total costs (ATC) may be taken to be approximately equal to the firm's supply curve, while marginal costs (MC) cut ATC from below at the lowest level of ATC.

Allocative efficiency occurs at $P_A$, $Q_A$. Productive efficiency occurs at $P_P$, $Q_P$. It is clear that the allocative efficiency price level is lower than the productively efficient level, while quantity is greater. Thus, more units are available and consumers pay a lower price.

intervene to ensure that allocative efficiency is achieved. In these cases, a subsidy is paid to the producer to enable it to reach a position of allocative efficiency. This is usually the case where the producer is a government or stated-owned organisation. However, since these are rapidly becoming fewer in number in all countries of Europe via privatisation, more frequently price controls are placed on the organisation. These ensure that the rate of inflation is taken into account when implementing any price rises. The formula is called 'RPI minus $x$' where RPI is the retail price index (which details the percentage rate of inflation per annum) and $x$ is a constant value. The result of the RPI minus $x$ formula is a rate less than inflation which is the maximum percentage by which prices may rise in a given year.

Where monopolies exist, the case for government intervention in markets, as described above, can be even stronger. It is often argued that monopolies, as a result of their domination of the market, are able to exploit consumers. As a result of their position, they are able artificially to maintain a high price level and to restrict the quantity available in the marketplace. This means that they are able to earn supernormal levels of profits. A monopolist, as the dominant organisation in the marketplace, is able to continue with such behaviour and therefore exploit the consumer on a long-term basis. However, there are certain situations when this argument does not hold true. For example, nationalised industries, publicly held enterprises and even private monopolies do not always act to exploit the consumer. Frequently, utility supply is controlled by a monopolist in each market – electricity, gas, water – and the market equilibrium is at the allocative efficiency level.

## SOCIAL RESPONSIBILITY OF FIRMS

Organisations may be classified as economic agents. Primarily, it can be argued that the organisation operates to make a profit. Arguments to support this rely on the fact that without profits, organisations would not be able to generate funds for development and regeneration. Thus, overall, whatever the short-term objective of the organisation, it is claimed that in the long term profit maximisation is the only objective.

However, there is a counter argument: that organisations exist to perform other functions in addition to profit maximisation. It is further argued that organisations have responsibilities as a result of the power which they are able to gain in the marketplace. Such an argument is based on the belief that the complex nature of developed societies requires all agents – individuals, organisations, governments – to act in a manner which takes into account the needs of others.

Social responsibility is understood by some to be a social contract, where the organisation actually owes the society to which it offers a return. The nature of such returns are varied but usually take the form of a payment to the local community or support and sponsorship for the arts and local projects, donations to local groups and so on.

Additionally, throughout the 1990s there has been increasing awareness of the effect on society at large of the actions of organisations, that is, their **externalities**. Although some actions do not cost the organisation anything, society may invoke a cost as a result. Pollution would be an example of an externality. Consider the case of an organisation which dumps its waste into the local river. It may cost the organisation nothing to do this and it may be far cheaper than transporting the waste for 'safe' dumping, or making it safe on site. However, the local community suffers as a result of the pollution and has to pay to clear it up. In the past, the community would have borne much of the clear-up cost. But recently, with the growing awareness of environmental issues, organisations are expected to act in a responsible manner in order to avoid externalities in the first place. They are increasingly required by law to pay for clearing up the damage they cause. For further discussion of environmental issues, *see* Chapter 20.

The expectations of the organisation with respect to its corporate responsibility may be analysed with reference to its **stakeholders**. An organisation has internal and external stakeholders. (Stakeholders are investigated further in Chapter 15.) Internal stakeholders are management, employees and shareholders. External stakeholders are suppliers, consumers, financiers, government and the community. Although the weight of power which each is able to wield differs, there is growing awareness of the role of shareholders, consumers and the community. Organisations are expected to act responsibly with reference to their environment and they realise that failure to do so will place them in a position where they may be criticised. The criticism could lead to a boycott of their products by consumers, withdrawal of finance by financiers or failure to gain permission to locate elsewhere as a result of a local government or community decision.

## SHAREHOLDERS AND ETHICAL INVESTMENTS

Some organisations take their corporate responsibility further than the issues outlined above. They act in addition to ensure that any investments they make in supplier organisations or with reference to their own financial portfolios are 'ethical'. The UK's Cooperative Bank claims to have an ethical policy and so too does the Body Shop. The B&Q chain of do-it-yourself stores also attempts only to make contracts with environmentally friendly suppliers. This is particularly important since it sources hardwoods and softwoods for resale from these suppliers.

This means that organisations avoid involvement with others which may be seen to be acting in a morally or ethically suboptimal manner. Past examples of such behaviour include:

- Non-involvement with organisations operating in South Africa before apartheid was dismantled.
- Non-involvement with organisations which have poor records with reference to the misuse or abuse of animals, factory farming methods or laboratory experimentation.
- Non-involvement with organisations which have poor records with reference to pollution actions or poor environmental care.

However, a counter argument may be put forward. Where organisations have poor records with reference to the above, does withdrawal of involvement

actually harm them? In the short term and locally, there may be some effect. But the number of ethical investor organisations is so small as to make very little impact overall. Additionally, if less than ethical organisations are 'frozen out', they may not be able to afford to put right their wrongs and will therefore be permanently excluded. What is the 'correct' period of exclusion for an organisation claiming to have put right its wrongs?

Ethical investors have to consider carefully any links they may make with other organisations. An almost ubiquitous example of the adverse publicity which occurs when the media suspects unethical links is that of the Body Shop 'scandal' in the UK. The Body Shop, owned and built up by Anita Roddick since the 1970s, is a successful franchise selling environmentally friendly and ideologically sound bath, shower and other personal care products. Body Shop products are sourced from developing countries. They are based on natural ingredients and are not tested on animals. The company also sells products made by individuals for a 'fair wage' in developing countries.

However, in the mid 1990s, a media scandal arose because it was claimed that some of the Body Shop's investment portfolio was in non-ethical organisations. Anita Roddick fought back against the accusations and eventually proved them wrong. But the damage had already been done; some of the Body Shop's consumers had been lost due to lack of trust. Some of them will never be won back.

The Body Shop case is clearly outlined below. The argument being put forward is that 'social cause marketing', which can benefit organisations relying on putting forward an ideologically sound image to consumers, can backfire if there is any doubt with reference to their activities.

## ◆ CASE STUDY 3.3

### 'Social cause marketing' has proved a powerful tool: but is it ethical?   FT

Social cause marketing is riding high in the 1990s. Consumers support firms on the basis of their identification with preferred social causes. . .

Companies such as international cosmetics chain The Body Shop and ice cream producer Ben & Jerry's receive substantial free media publicity as a result of their identification with popular social issues. Consumers respond to the opportunity to purchase

products or services consistent with their social preferences, even paying a premium over competing products. Identification with popular causes is also good for employee morale and recruitment. Employees who feel a positive association with their employer's publicised values are more likely to be loyal and happy.

The Body Shop is a prime example. It has aligned itself with the 'green' and animal rights movements,

▶

Case study 3.3 *continued*

among others. Strategies include directly associating with organisations such as the Friends of the Earth and Greenpeace and prominently featuring displays and brochures supporting its preferred social causes in its outlets.

In addition, it has developed specific programmes such as Trade-Not-Aid to implement developing-world sourcing of ingredients. Anita Roddick, its flamboyant founder, rejects Friedmanism by proclaiming: 'I don't have any duty to shareholders at all', while vaunting the organisation's charitable contributions and social causes. The causes are presented as worthy and not merely as a merchandising strategy. Body Shop products are carefully positioned to be consistent with the company's social image – its 'natural' products sold in reusable containers.

The success of this approach contributed handsomely to the rapid growth of The Body Shop during its early years. Free publicity stemming from media coverage of the social issues substituted for advertising, while the marketplace reaction validated academic claims of consumer preferences for companies clearly identified with popular social causes.

Recently, though, this engine of success has been threatened as The Body Shop, Ben & Jerry's and other companies practising social cause marketing have come under attack in parts of the media for not living up to their own self-touted standards. Critics challenge claims that Body Shop products are genuinely 'natural' and allege that The Body Shop practises a double standard on its important issue of animal rights. Similar questions arise about the significance of developing-world sourcing for products and the levels of charitable contributions made by the company. . .

The reactions to these charges among the supporters of the corporate social responsibility movement have been mixed. Some have argued that higher standards should be imposed on companies that engage in social cause marketing. Companies that promote themselves as particularly socially responsible should, in the eyes of this group, have impeccable records to support their claims.

Others are concerned about the tendency to single out for criticism organisations that, in their view, are at least trying to do the right thing. The criticisms often seem picky (certainly there is a lot of leeway in the definition of 'natural' products). . . They fear that an intense 'hypocrisy inquisition' may have the perverse effect of driving out any semblance of the true social responsibility faith.

There is some merit to these concerns. One potential response to anticipated adverse publicity is for companies to become guarded about disclosing their efforts to implement ethics programmes or support popular social causes. If organisations become secretive about their ethics programmes out of fear of the hypocrisy watch, the programmes themselves may suffer. . .

Social representations engendered by companies as part of their marketing strategy should be evaluated in the same manner as other 'seller representations'. When coarse misrepresentations are made, for example that containers are recyclable when in fact they are not under the most common usage of the term, then the actions are clearly unethical. . .

Judgments pertaining to ethics are often bounded by informational and time constraints in the same manner as are economic judgments. Bounded moral rationality exists in the same manner as bounded economic rationality.

*Source*: © Thomas W Dunfee 1997. Reprinted with permission from *Financial Times Mastering Management*, Pitman Publishing.

## THE ROLE OF PROFITS AND BUSINESS ETHICS

The Body Shop example shows the trade-off decisions which organisations are required to make in order to balance their profits against their actions as ethical organisations. The Body Shop pays fair prices for goods produced in developing countries. It could, if it had different objectives, buy these at minimal cost and increase its profits. However, it would be exploiting its producers by not paying them a decent price. Additionally, it does not use animal testing at any stage of its production process. This can be an expensive alternative and involves investigation and awareness of the processes to ensure that animal testing does not occur.

The Body Shop would not claim to be a profit-maximising organisation. Its objectives are far more altruistic than that. However, in order to expand, funds must be raised. The Body Shop does therefore need to earn some profits in order to continue to expand and to continue with its search within less developed countries for natural personal-care ingredients and products.

## EUROPEAN ISSUES

There is no overall European approach or legislation regarding organisational ethics. It is not possible to force organisations or governments to be ethical. This was seen at the beginning of the chapter: individuals and organisations may act in a 'good' way but, as Kant argued, this is only moral if they believe in their action and they are not just acting in a manner which is likely to be acceptable. European legislation acts instead to encourage, to prohibit and to protect.

■ Subsidies are available to member governments and organisations which are willing to relocate into geographical areas within the European Union which require regeneration. Such subsidies serve to encourage relocation and may be used to reduce either the cost of relocation, running costs or both for a short period. The results of the encouragement will be reductions in unemployment and improvements in the local economy as a result of the jobs created.

■ Prohibiting legislation acts to discourage behaviour which is not socially acceptable, or which has an externality associated with it. Theft and murder are obvious examples; others include the legislation which exists to ensure that organisational management acts in a proper manner with reference to its responsibilities to shareholders and so on (such legislation will be discussed later in the chapter).

■ Legislation to prohibit exists in all aspects of governmental and organisational behaviour. Employment legislation dictates that certain conditions must be maintained for employees. There are laws which restrict the emissions which may be made into the atmosphere and the environment by manufacturing organisations. These protect both local residents and also the environment in general.

Overall, then, it is not possible to make someone act ethically if they don't wish to. Instead, legislation exists to ensure that actions which are not ethical are discouraged or that positive actions are encouraged.

# INTRODUCTION TO CORPORATE GOVERNANCE

**Corporate governance** is the sum of those activities which constitute the internal regulation of an organisation in compliance with the obligations placed on the firm by legislation, ownership and control. Given that there is often, in large organisations, a separation of ownership and control, corporate governance considers the responsibilities of the trustees and their care of assets which belong to another party.

This notion of separation of ownership and control is not new and has its foundations in the **'principal agent problem'** which will be considered later. However, the more recent concern about the ways in which large organisations have appeared to be managed, as some shareholders see it, not in their best interests has come about because of a number of areas which may have been open to abuse. Contemporary concerns would include the following:

■ The effect of changes in share ownership on the direction of the company. Here a predator company may purchase what it sees as an ailing company, which has been badly managed, replacing the management team and altering its strategy in its current markets. An example of this can be seen in the acquisition policy of the Hanson Group. Hanson purchased a number of companies which it perceived were weak, changed their levels of profitability and then sold them on at a profit. It was also suggested that Hanson altered the direction of some companies through a process of asset stripping, for example EverReady batteries.

■ The collapse of some large enterprises, when their company reports suggested a healthy balance sheet. A recent example of this 'problem' emerged in 1996 at Wicks, a do-it-yourself chain in the UK. Auditors have discovered that the previous management tended to overstate the company's level of profits, thereby enhancing its attractiveness to purchasers and shareholders. This has led to a number of the senior management team resigning or being suspended while auditors review the source of the enhanced profits.

■ The lack of transparency, accountability and disclosure of boards to shareholders.

■ Apprehension over the adequacy of board structures and processes.

■ Concern over the competence of directors.

■ The destabilising effect of the growth of some organisations through merger and takeover.

■ The short-term basis of corporate performance measures and decision making.

■ The high amount of executive compensation which appears not to relate to company performance.

■ The extent of business fraud.

■ The view that self-regulation is not working.

The extent to which these problems may occur within an organisation may be related to the organisation's previous history, how it has expanded, the organisation's economic environment, the quality of the organisation's administration, the legal environment, the strategies of the organisation, the character of the industry or community in which the organisation operates, and the expectations about the organisation and its governance.

Accountancy standards, commercial law and government policy are all struggling to make sense of the new corporate forms and activities that have burst through the boundaries of convention and well-understood practice. Today, organisations are a long way from those very large companies which had been seen to be in positions where they could not be challenged or overthrown.

Three factors in particular were seen as important in changing opinion about the behaviour of organisations. First, there has been a change in the relationship between the organisation and the state. External regulation has been seen as inferior to appropriate governance. Second, there has been a growing view stressing owners' and shareholders' rights over paid managers. Third, the behaviour of managers sometimes appears at odds with market needs. For example, the 1980s and 1990s have emphasised the role of entrepreneurial behaviour as individuals seek to react rapidly to changing situations, take risks, behave flexibly and use minimum overheads. This is in contrast to risk-avoidance, security-seeking and bureaucratic management styles of a number of large companies.

In addition, other factors have come into play in terms of the relationship between managers and owners. Shareholding has become more focused towards institutional investors and the latter have begun to exercise their potential power, influencing boards of directors and in so doing affect the rights of smaller shareholders. Changes in the barriers to trade, the growth of economies of scale, together with legislation such as the Single European Act, have resulted in a growth in merger and takeover activity. The changing nature of the environment in which organisations now find themselves has made many organisations open to possible takeover. This has resulted in incumbent management devising a whole range of activities to protect the company and developing suitable packages for themselves should the company be taken over. Often these actions appear to be at the expense of the shareholders.

There have been other occasions where company executives have been felt to be privileged to inside knowledge which they have used to their advantage to buy or sell company shares. Once again, this insider trading, as well as being illegal, may enhance the returns to company directors and be against the interests of shareholders.

There has also been a growth in litigation against companies and directors, particularly in the United States. Increasingly there have been calls for company boards to be more independent of company management, with proposals for a majority of independent external directors, an audit committee of independent external directors and similar board nomination and compensation committees. There have also been calls for more open disclosure of financial information.

Corporate governance problems have also been compounded with the growth of the newly privatised companies which have attached to them duties of accountability and regulation. In addition, there has been an increase during the 1980s and 1990s in different forms of companies, often going across international boundaries, such as international joint ventures. If organisations with complex cross-shareholding arrangements and other forms of risk sharing are included, then keeping control on these from a shareholder's perspective proves to be difficult.

## THE PRINCIPAL AGENT PROBLEM

One reason for the need for corporate governance is the principal agent problem. This occurs where the principal (a person or a group) appoints an agent (a single person or a group of persons) to act on their behalf. The agent, however, may have different objectives to those of the principal and the principal may not be in a position to monitor whether the agent is following their instructions or not. For small firms such an issue may not be a problem since the owners of the organisation may be heavily involved with running the business. For larger organisations where shares are sufficiently dispersed, owners may feel that they have lost control of the firm and that control lies with the management team.

For the principal agent problem to arise there has to be conflict between the objectives of owners and those of managers. Many shareholders are interested in both the size of the current dividend on their shares and its expected growth over time. From the manager's perspective it is quite possible that profit growth is also their objective, particularly where they are looking towards the successful running of one company as a springboard to moving to larger, more prestigious organisations. However, other concerns may take priority for management such as salary levels, their level of productivity or effort, job security and the size of the organisation. In large organisations such objectives may be possible to achieve since information can be more easily hidden and individual management performance can be harder to detect. The owners may be able to see the change in the performance of the company, but attributing which part of the performance is related to the actions of management can prove to be more difficult.

How can owners stop the management of companies acting opportunistically and against the wishes of shareholders? Certain factors have always been in place, such as the legal requirement to produce company accounts, external scrutiny where organisations wish to raise finance, and the share price. All might limit managers' opportunity to deviate far from the actions preferred by shareholders.

However, one proposed method by which the interests of managers can be brought more in line with the desires of shareholders is through the use of appropriate remuneration schemes. It may be possible for management to be given some fixed minimum level of reward with the remainder of their pay being related to the level of profits, such as the practice in the water industry, British Gas and the electricity generation business.

There are a number of alternative ways in which organisations can link payments to results:

- Bonus schemes which directly reward the performance of an individual. These would include piecework; output- and target-based bonuses; commission bonuses based on sales; and measured daywork.
- Collective bonus schemes based on output or productivity of the group/section/department or the whole company.
- Collective bonus schemes based on profits generated. Examples of these are profit-sharing schemes and employee share-option schemes.
- An individual's pay is determined by management's assessment of his or her performance, for example performance-related pay.

However, such approaches suggest that poor performance by management could still lead to the fixed amount being paid, while a very successful year would not lead to all the success being shown in the rewards to management. In other words, a payment scheme for management needs to be evolved that somehow links incentives to risk taking.

One approach to this problem and an issue that will be considered later is the notion of share options. These could give the manager the right to buy a fixed quantity of shares in the company at a future date. If the company is run so that the share price is enhanced, then the option may be taken up. A danger of such an approach is that the managers may seek to maximise short-term growth in share prices, take up their options to cash their shares and leave. Alternatively for middle management share-ownership plans may be advocated instead of share options.

Apart from agency theory (the principal agent problem), **stewardship theory** has also been put forward to explain the separation between shareholders and managers. This theory sees governance as having its foundation in company law. The expectation is that stewardship will be exercised by managers to whom the organisation has entrusted authority and responsibility, while requiring appropriate accountability. There is a view that managers act justly and responsibly for the good of the shareholders under the law.

On occasions shareholders may not trust executive managers to act responsibly and will lose confidence in their ability. This situation may lead to the requirement for more information, power and action. Thus there is a need for trust and confidence in the management.

## MONITORING DIRECTORS' BEHAVIOUR

There is a substantial amount of legislation which lays out national legal structures, policies and economic and social values. The ideas of unity and distinction have symbolised the way corporate governance is operated in both the UK and the US. This means that there is a single, unitary board which is made up of both executive and non-executive directors who have the same legal responsibilities. Shareholders have few responsibilities, but are able to move their funds from one company to another via the purchase and selling of shares based on the risks they perceive in the company and the level of profits they currently earn or expect to earn.

In both Europe and Japan there are important features that distinguish the operation of the organisation from that seen in the US and UK. It is quite common to have a **two-tier** board. This is the dominant system that operates in Germany. The supervisory board is kept separate from the executive board and the management of the organisation. In some European countries, this two-tier approach does not appear to be common. For example, in France less than 10 per cent of companies have supervisory boards. This can be explained, however, by the fact that over half the largest firms in France are either private or family owned and until recent privatisation almost 20 per cent were in state ownership. *See also* page 51 for further development of the two-tier approach.

In continental European countries the main difference in corporate governance is the separation of power. In Germany, for example, the main lenders and investors have much greater involvement and say in the development of the organisation. Conversely, in Japan it is the large financial institutions which hold the majority of the shares and there is a large degree of consultation and reciprocity which governs ownership and control.

This is very different from the UK's position. Various pieces of company legislation in the UK encourage the organisation to behave in a 'proper' manner. The main laws are the Companies Acts, regulation imposed by the Securities and Investments Board and voluntary codes such as the City Code on Take-overs and Mergers. In the UK shareholders receive returns once other groups or activities have been rewarded and, although holders of ordinary or voting shares have the right to vote on policies placed before them, their ability to influence the organisations depends on how widely the shares are dispersed and whether they can muster 50 per cent plus one of the shares in the organisation. Directors, on the other hand, are responsible for the governance of the organisation.

There has been a belief in the past that, through informal pressure, information and the power to remove support, there would be sufficient control in the system to prevent excesses or failure. However, there are many instances where shareholders have not been able to halt the slide of the company, prevent the managers behaving in an unethical manner or stop large payouts to directors when they leave the company. This highlights some of the weaknesses that have appeared in corporate governance, particularly during the 1980s and 1990s in the UK, and why shareholder groups are looking for new forms of control.

In the UK there are a series of statutory controls which regulate the activities of companies and their directors. The stock exchange codes cover areas such as:

- the responsibility for public documents
- mergers and acquisitions
- shareholdings and dealings
- loyalty and good faith
- skill and care.

These obligations are covered in acts such as the Company Securities (Insider Dealing) Act 1985, which makes it a criminal offence for any insider with unpublished, price-sensitive information to deal in the securities affected by this information. Directors are assumed to be insiders.

The Companies Act 1985 required complete and early disclosure by directors of any information on dealings in share options, shares or debentures. The Act requires that directors disclose all their interests, including those of their spouse or children. To ensure that the act is complied with the Department of Trade and Industry can investigate all books and papers pertaining to the company.

The City Code on Take-overs and Mergers is designed to make sure that each shareholder is treated equally during takeover bids. For example, if an offer is made to some shareholders at an early stage in a bid, one which they find acceptable, then it must be left open to all other shareholders. The Code also developed the rules for the conduct of organisations during a takeover, including once again the area of insider dealing.

The latest UK legislation on insider dealing came into force in 1994 with an extension of the Company Securities (Insider Dealing) Act 1985. Under the latest regulations it is illegal for an individual who has inside information to deal in price-affected securities or to encourage another person to deal. This new legislation expands the scope of the 1985 Act by widening the definition of who can be considered an insider and extending, for the first time, the definition of the securities covered to include derivative products. In addition, the definition of dealing has been widened to include subscribing for shares (as well as buying and selling).

## INDEPENDENT DIRECTORS

Under English law there is no distinction between the duties and liabilities of executive and independent (non-executive) directors. It is in the interest of both to ensure that the basic principles and practices of good governance are complied with. It is usual for executive directors to be responsible for the operation of the business, while non-executive directors should be able to stand back from the operations and provide a critical overview of the process. There may be occasions, however, where the expertise of non-executive directors means that they will become involved with the operations side of the business, notably where they possess some particular skill or expertise required by the organisation. In addition, beyond their normal role as non-executives, these individuals have a fiduciary obligation to those owners who cannot be represented on the board.

PRO-NED (Promotion of Non-Executive Directors) has distinguished four important features of the role of a non-executive director. These include giving an independent view on the operation of the company and the considerations of the board; monitoring and strengthening management; ensuring high standards of financial probity; and assisting executive directors in their leadership.

This requires a great deal from independent directors. It means that they must be kept well informed and that they should be truly independent of the executive directors. Questions have been raised as to where these independent directors should be found. If they are themselves executive directors of other companies then the relationship could be described as incestuous. In addition, this raises the problem of multiple independent directorships. Given the tasks that have been put forward for one independent directorship by PRO-NED, questions must be raised as to whether it is possible for these tasks to be accomplished fully by an individual who has a number of independent directorships.

## AUDITS

An audit is a report covering whether the books, records and internal controls of the company have been carried out properly during the year. It is not a certificate of worthiness or a guarantee. Auditors are expected to show that the financial records are a true and fair account. This does not mean that it should *be* the true and fair account, only that the correct procedures have been followed. It is the directors, not the auditors, who are responsible for the preparation and presentation of the company accounts. The auditors' duty lies to the shareholders, acting as 'watchdogs' on their behalf.

Concerns have been raised about the *role* of directors in preparing accounts. It has been suggested that sometimes these have been prepared in a way that is not in the interests of shareholders, perhaps in an attempt to hide some sensitive information. Although the shareholders elect the auditors, they are selected for election by the directors. Auditors need to establish a good working *relationship* with the directors, which may pose some issues as to who the auditors are working for. Finally, the auditors' role is to *report* and not to suggest whether problems exist.

The Cadbury Committee was set up to consider the three 'R's' (relationship, role and report) of auditing and the auditors' role in governance in response to a number of fraud cases in the UK.

### The Cadbury Committee

It is generally accepted that the Cadbury Committee had at least three objectives. First, to improve corporate governance and thereby limit the scope for a repetition of situations at BCCI, Polly Peck and Maxwell. Second, to preserve the unity board structure in the UK and not to move to the two-tier structure that is used in Germany. Third, to involve shareholders in UK companies more in the governance of their companies.

At the centre of the Cadbury Committee's deliberations was the need to strengthen the role of the audit committee, through greater involvement and development of the independent directors.

The Cadbury Committee suggested a number of ways to achieve these objectives:

- A division of power at the top of the company, with the suggestion that a non-executive chairperson should sit alongside a chief executive officer (CEO).
- The appointment of strong and independent non-executive directors to boards.
- The empowerment of audit committees, consisting largely of non-executive directors.
- The limitation of directors' contracts and full disclosure of their compensation packages through remuneration committees, consisting only of non-executive directors.

Although the Cadbury Committee has gone a long way in satisfying shareholders' concerns about the governance of organisations, many small shareholders still feel that they have very little influence on a board of directors. They sometimes feel that the large institutional shareholders still have some form of 'special relationship' with the directors. Finally, there is concern that Cadbury appeared to assume that governance was about checking, controlling and monitoring, rather than addressing the principal concern of a board: future strategy.

Nonetheless, the Cadbury Committee highlighted the strong view among shareholders and share-groups (groups of companies/people owing shares in a company as part of their overall portfolio) that the composition of the audit committees should be subject to shareholder approval and that shareholders should have the ability to put forward their own candidates for audit committees. Currently UK governance is being looked at further by Sir Ronald Hampel in a second Cadbury-type report.

## DIRECTORS' PAY

No sooner had the Cadbury Committee produced its deliberations than grave concern was raised about directors' remuneration. A number of private-sector firms were seen to be giving some of their directors large salary increases, particularly in terms of share options, and there appeared to be little relationship between directors' pay and the performance of the company. Of particular concern was the pay being received by managers of some of the newly privatised industries or directors in sectors which had been controlled by local authorities, such as higher education. Many of the newly privatised companies proved more difficult to control simply because of their size. In addition, government controls on top management wage increases, were relaxed as the industries entered the private sector without any effective substitute being in place. In the light of these high salary increases, Prime Minister John Major called for pay restraint by directors, particularly in recessionary periods when many employees were receiving cuts in their real wages. In addition, shareholders appeared to be particularly unhappy about some of the payments to directors, an area in which they perceived that they had little control. The growing concern about directors' pay could be seen in the fact that over 5000 shareholders turned up for the annual shareholders' meeting of British Gas in 1995 wanting some form of explanation for the extent of pay increases deemed necessary for some of the company's directors.

Such was the furore over directors' pay that the Confederation of British Industry (CBI) asked Sir Richard Greenbury, chairman of Marks & Spencer, to head an investigation into directors' pay. The committee's brief was to identify good practice in determining directors' remuneration and prepare a code of practice for use by UK public limited companies.

The Greenbury Report, produced in July 1995, has a central recommendation for companies to implement this code of best practice based on full disclosure of directors' pay, set by fully independent non-executive directors. These remuneration committees should report to shareholders on their pay policy for directors each year, through company annual reports. Directors' pay should be broken down into benefits in kind, basic salary, annual bonuses and long-term incentive schemes. Shareholders should be invited to approve all long-term incentive schemes, including share-option schemes, which could commit shareholders' funds over more than one year or dilute the equity.

If the company wishes to alter its remuneration scheme or where its policies have attracted controversy before, then the remuneration committee might put down a resolution on which shareholders can vote at the next annual meeting. The remuneration committee should also be sensitive to employment and pay elsewhere in the organisation.

Additionally, the Greenbury Committee recommended that one-year notice or contract periods for directors are best practice, but up to two years may be acceptable. Pay-offs to directors should avoid rewarding poor performance. Finally, and perhaps most controversial, was the recommendation that the government should act to tax profits on share options as income rather than capital gains.

## CORPORATE GOVERNANCE IN THE PUBLIC SECTOR

Many of the concerns about governance have been targeted at the private sector, yet there has been some concern, particularly during the 1990s, that the public sector is not free of the accusation of 'sleaze'. The public sector is quite diverse, however, and any set of governance procedures may need to be adapted to the different sectors. Moreover, although the Cadbury Report produced guidelines for private-sector firms, these may not always be appropriate for public-sector organisations which are not chiefly profit maximisers.

Included in the public sector here would be local government, health service authorities and trusts, grant-maintained schools, colleges and universities supported from public funds, and housing associations. These areas were one element investigated by the Nolan Committee, set up in 1994 to examine concerns about standards of conduct of all holders of public office, including arrangements relating to financial and commercial activities. The Nolan Committee sought to make recommendations about any changes which might be required to ensure the highest standards in public life.

The Nolan Committee, which produced its first report in May 1995, suggested a number of important principles that the public sector should follow:

- *Selflessness* – Holders of public office should take decisions solely in terms of the public interest. They should not make decisions in order to gain financial or other material benefits for themselves, their family or their friends.
- *Integrity* – Holders of public office should not place themselves under any financial or other obligation to outside individuals or organisations that might influence them in the performance of their official duties.
- *Objectivity* – In carrying out public business, including making public appointments, awarding contracts or recommending individuals for rewards and benefits, holders of public office should make choices on merit.
- *Accountability* – Holders of public office are accountable for their decisions and actions to the public and must submit themselves to whatever scrutiny is appropriate to their office.
- *Openness* – Holders of public office should be as open as possible about all the decisions and actions they take. They should give reasons for their decisions and restrict information only when the wider public interest clearly demands this.
- *Honesty* – Holders of public office have a duty to declare any private interests relating to their public duties and to take steps to resolve any conflicts arising in a way that protects the public interest.
- *Leadership* – Holders of public office should promote and support these principles by leadership and example.

## CORPORATE GOVERNANCE IN EUROPE

There have been attempts by the EU to develop a corporate governance framework which is common across the Union. Nonetheless, there are dif-

ferences between member states. For those countries where individual shareholders are more likely to be involved in the ownership of organisations, then the problems raised by the Anglo-Saxon (US/UK) model are more appropriate. However, in a number of countries such as Germany and Austria banks are more important, while in France, Greece, Spain and Portugal private or family ownership is of greater significance. In some countries the right of shareholders under their countries' legal arrangements are of secondary importance to the needs of employees or other stakeholders. Thus, although shareholders may have the same problems with management as they do, say, in the UK, this has not been given such a prominent place on the agenda.

From an EU perspective the main aim in terms of corporate governance is to develop a 'level playing field'. The Fifth Company Directive includes a number of provisions on the duties of directors, the rights of shareholders and how meetings should be conducted. Moreover, there are other statutes and directives which provide more overarching features of the corporate governance debate. For example, the EU has certain requirements for the disclosure of information: it requires organisations to produce company statutes and articles of association, details of ownership and any changes in status. In addition, the EU has proposals which include reducing the barriers to transfer of ownership and control; the introduction of two-tier boards; and compulsory employee participation in decision making. As can be gathered, such proposals may appear abhorrent to some member states and it is more likely that governance issues in the EU will address more international concerns such as the balance of power between management, institutions and individuals.

As for individual member countries, governance in Germany is controlled through the use of two-tier boards (the supervisory board and the executive board), the informal power of the banks and the representational system. The supervisory board is assembled from the main interest groups: employees, shareholders, professional advisers and bankers. The executive board uses the supervisory board to assess its plans, while the supervisory board will highlight its major concerns to the executive board. This interrelationship is important in assuring the stability of the industry and of particular countries during difficult economic conditions.

French corporate governance is related to the mix of both state ownership and private ownership that makes up the bulk of French enterprise. Between 60 and 70 per cent of organisations are owned by these two groups, with other shareholdings widely dispersed among the other parties. Thus institutions have little strength or authority. In the Netherlands some of the features of the UK/US approach can be seen. The Vereniging van Effectenbezitters shareholder group commented during the early 1990s on the poor performance of some of the large Dutch companies, especially Philips. As in France, family ownership is one of the main features of the large Italian companies, and therefore corporate governance has tended to take more of a back seat until recently. However, as in the Netherlands, some large Italian companies have not been performing well during the late 1980s and early 1990s and there has been growing criticism of some chief executive officers. The 1990 Amato Law, coupled with the reorganisation of financial markets following on from the Single European Act, has seen shareholders making greater demands on their corporate leaders.

## SUMMARY

◆ In the past, economists have assumed that organisations operate in order to earn maximum profits.

◆ As a result of the growth of organisations and the changes in the competitive nature of markets, it has been recognised for some time that organisations do strive for other objectives than profit maximisation.

◆ Moral or ethical behaviour implies that certain values are upheld. In capitalist societies ethical decisions are left to individuals and organisations.

◆ Increased consumer awareness of environmental and safety issues has meant that organisations have had to change in order to survive.

◆ Corporate governance is the sum of those activities which constitute the internal regulation of the organisation resulting from the obligations and legislation placed on it. The area has grown in importance since there has been increasing separation of the ownership of the organisation by its shareholders and the control of the organisation by its managers.

◆ The principal agent problem gives one reason for the need for corporate governance, although stewardship theory has also been put forward to explain the separation between shareholders and managers.

◆ There are a number of features which distinguish the operation of an organisation in the US/UK and Japan/continental Europe. Not least of these is the two-tier board in the latter areas. There are also differences in ownership. In France most organisations are controlled by the state or owned privately or by families. In the UK/US the majority of companies are owned by shareholders, although here they may be dominated by institutional holdings.

◆ In the UK there have been a number of reports considering corporate governance and directors' pay. The Cadbury report has looked at the former and the Greenbury report has considered the latter.

◆ Corporate governance issues, although initially raised in the behaviour of private-sector plcs. are also very relevant to public-sector organisations. Whereas shareholders want to know what companies in the private sector are doing, taxpayers have as much right to know what is happening to public bodies. An attempt to look at these in some detail can be found in the first report produced by the Nolan Committee.

## REVIEW QUESTIONS

1  There are often ambiguities in business where organisations or government attempt to prohibit certain actions, but cannot do so categorically because there are times when those actions have a 'good' or positive result. Discuss such examples.

2  In the light of the Body Shop's experience of bad publicity despite its attempts to act in an ethical manner, is it worth striving for recognition as a responsible organisation?

**3** Does the expansion of shareholders' rights conflict with improved business performance?

**4** Do the recommendations of the Cadbury and Greenbury reports go far enough in providing a framework for effective corporate governance?

**5** Why does the EU seek to have similar corporate governance regulations for all member states?

## GLOSSARY OF NEW TERMS

**Allocative efficiency:** The production situation in the market where all demand is satisfied at the given price.

**Corporate governance:** The structures and processes associated with production, decision making, control and so on within an organisation.

**Corporate social responsibility:** The acceptance by organisations that they have a responsibility to their local community, society and the environment.

**Externalities:** The costs associated with a given action which are not borne by the actor. For example, where a polluter does not pay the clean-up cost of its pollution, there exists an external cost of clean-up – an externality.

**Morality:** The adherence to given values to ensure that justice is done.

**Neoclassical economics:** Contemporary economic theory based on the concepts developed by the classical economics school of thought, which typically dates back to the eighteenth century.

**Principal agent problem:** Where a person or a group (the principal) appoints a single person or a group of persons (the agent) to act on their behalf. A mismatch in goals arises as a result of the fact that the principal (employer) is more emotionally and/or financially motivated to gain organisational success. The agent (employee) may be more concerned with their own aspirations and goals.

**Productive efficiency:** The production situation in the market where the organisation's marginal costs and revenues are equal (the profit-maximising position).

**Stakeholders:** Individuals and organisations with formal or informal links to an organisation. For example, an organisation's financial backers will be stakeholders, as will employees, suppliers and so on.

**Stewardship theory:** Governance is seen as having its foundation in company law with an agent being entrusted with the management of another's assets.

**Two-tier board:** The separation of the supervisory board of an organisation from the executive board and the management of the organisation.

## READING

Keasey, K and Wright, M (1993) 'Issues in corporate accountability and governance: an editorial', *Accounting and Business Research*, Vol 23, pp 291–303.
*This article provides an excellent overview of the development of corporate governance.*

Certo, S C (1992) *Modern Management: Quality, Ethics, and the Global Environment*, 5th edn, Allyn and Bacon, Needham Heights, Mass.
*Chapter 3 incorporates an overview of both corporate governance and business ethics.*

Cannon, T (1994) *Corporate Responsibility*, Pitman Publishing, London.
*A comprehensive text which is easy to read. The text includes a history of ethics, corporate responsibility and ethical issues such as the environment and inequity in society. Also provides an up-to-date treatment of ethics and governance issues, in the UK, US, Japan and continental Europe.*

Dunfee, T W (1997) 'Marketing an ethical stance' in *Financial Times, Mastering Management*, Pitman Publishing, London.

Financial Times (1995) 'Shell shocked by Greenpeace', 22 June, pXIV.

Shaw (1991) *Business Ethics*, Wadsworth, Belmont, CA.
*An American text which contains some key discussions in Chapters 2, 4, 8, 10 and 11.*

Smith, M (1995) 'Management: the ethical way to profitability', *Financial Times*, 25 August, p 10.

Suzman, M (1995) 'A fine act to follow', *Financial Times*, FT Guide to Business in the Community, 7 December, p IV.

**Further reading**
Charkham, J (1996) *Keeping Good Company*, Clarendon Press, Oxford.

Clarke, T (1995) 'Corporate governance', *Business Studies*, April, pp 9–12.

Demb, A and Neubauer, F F (1992) *The Corporate Board*, Oxford University Press, Oxford.

Donaldson, J (1992) *Business Ethics: A European Casebook*, Academic Press, London.

Ferguson, P R, Ferguson, G J and Rothschild, R (1993) *Business Economics*, Macmillan, Basingstoke.

Harvey, B (1994) *Business Ethics: A European Approach*, Prentice-Hall, Hemel Hempstead.

Mill, J S (ed M Warnock) (1962) *Utilitarianism*, Fontana, London.

CHAPTER **4**

# ALTERNATIVE MODELS OF THE ORGANISATION

## KEY ISSUES

Business issues

Business strategy

Decision-making techniques

Economic concepts

Management decision issues

Optimal outcomes to management issues

## OBJECTIVES

◆ To examine the criticisms which may be made of the 'accepted knowledge' of neoclassical economics, profit maximisation in particular.

◆ To introduce the concepts of imperfect information and 'bounded rationality' and their application in the understanding of the operation of organisations.

◆ To account for the factors and events leading to the decline in the number of owner-controlled organisations and the growth in shareholder-owned/employee-managed organisations.

◆ To discuss the alternatives to the neoclassical model and the assumptions underlying these.

◆ To outline, discuss and investigate the implications of the following alternative models: Baumol's sales revenue maximisation model; Marris's growth rate model of managerial enterprise; Williamson's managerial utility model; and Cyert and March's behavioural theory of the firm.

◆ To analyse critically the alternatives to profit maximisation.

## KEY TERMS

Bounded rationality

Behavioural theories

Discretion

(Profit) locus

Managerial discretion models

Managerial theories

Perfect knowledge

Satisficing

## CHAPTER OUTLINE

Business application

Criticisms of profit maximisation

Case study 4.1 Executive pay: a practical solution

Case study 4.2 Funding changes after the UK introduced the National Lottery

Alternatives to profit maximisation

Alternative managerial discretion models

Case study 4.3  More fuel needed for recovery

Case study 4.4  Shareholder value management: performance measure gains popularity

Concluding remarks

Summary

Review questions

Glossary of new terms

Reading

## Caterpillar plans to buy back 20m shares and raise dividend FT

Caterpillar, the US maker of construction equipment, said it would buy back 20m shares, or about 10 per cent of its stock, over the next three to five years, and also raised its quarterly dividend.

The decision to raise the company's quarterly pay-out to 35 cents a share, from 25 cents, puts the dividend slightly higher than where it was in early 1982, just prior to an industry downturn. It is the third dividend increase in the past 12 months.

Commenting on the share buy-back, Mr Donald Fites, Caterpillar's chairman, said: 'The strategic initiatives we have pursued in the past several years to modernise our plants, reduce costs, improve quality, invest in new products and expand into new markets have positioned us exceptionally well for the long-term.'

Analysts said the move reflected management's long-term confidence in the company's prospects. 'This is a signal that the company doesn't intend to squander cash on acquisitions or large capital expenditures,' said Mr Barry Bannister, a vice-president of equities research at SG Warburg in New York. He described the buy-back as a good use of the company's capital, noting that management was maximising profit margins by not embarking on an expansion programme at the top of a business cycle.

Caterpillar, which had $14.3bn in sales last year, has had five quarters of record earnings. Although members of the United Autoworkers Union walked out of its Midwestern factories 11 months ago, Caterpillar successfully weathered the strike using temporary workers.

*Source*: *Financial Times*, 8 June 1995. Reprinted with permission.

### Comment

It is commonly accepted among economists that the only goal of the organisation is to maximise profits in both the short and long run. As the Caterpillar case shows, profit margin maximisation may have been one objective, but other targets have also been in the sights of Caterpillar's management. Indeed, the profit-margin-maximisation goal has not been for the sake of profit maximisation alone, but in the hope that organisational longevity may result.

The fact that Caterpillar has increased its dividends will doubtless appeal to shareholders, who will receive 35¢ (US) per share in the payout. Such 'sweeteners' can sometimes have the effect of calming shareholders and giving them confidence in the controlling management team to whom, at the annual general meeting, they give their votes of confidence. With such a vote, the management team will have guaranteed their job stability and financial rewards for another year. Overall, they seem to be solidifying the position of Caterpillar in the marketplace and taking actions which will serve to maintain its position for a number of years to come.

Caterpillar is not alone among its competitors and rivals in pursuing objectives which are complements or alternatives to the profit-maximisation objective proposed by many economists. This chapter will examine the alternatives that may exist and will take the stance that it is blinkered to assume that profit maximisation is the only objective which organisations pursue. Indeed, in practice, many organisations would find it difficult to measure whether or not they are maximising profits, even if this were an objective.

## CRITICISMS OF PROFIT MAXIMISATION

The neoclassical assumption that organisations seek to maximise profits is often not observed among organisations in the real world. When economists make analyses of organisations, or work with them to improve performance, the neoclassical assumptions of the theory of the firm are (almost without exception) relaxed. For example,

the assumption of perfect information can be assumed inaccurate in any case you may wish to consider; there is no individual or organisation anywhere operating with perfect information.

Studies have been undertaken and have concluded that there are only small percentages of organisations in the real world aiming to attain profit maximisation. Indeed, Griffiths and Wall (1995) note Shipley's study, carried out in 1981 on 728 UK firms. The results given claim that only

15.9 per cent of firms can be considered true profit maximisers. The same study, however, reveals that 73 per cent of firms see profit as their principal goal in setting prices and 8 per cent include profit as a member of their goal set. Profit is not ignored in these firms, just not given the priority assumed by economists.

Profit maximisation is inherently difficult for organisations to track or measure. Perfect internal knowledge rarely exists and no organisation can claim to possess perfect external information with reference to the market and business environment in which they operate. They are therefore unlikely to possess accurate information about the organisation's total costs and/or total revenues.

## Imperfect information

It is very difficult for organisations to pinpoint exactly what their levels of marginal and total costs are at any one point in time. Marginal costs are not easy to define within any organisation. Management accountants – typically the source of any cost data – are only too aware that the definition and derivation of marginal costs are issues of debate worldwide. Likewise, total cost and revenue levels change with production levels and sales and thus change frequently. Each time that there is a price change or a change in the productive capacity of the organisation, the position of the profit-maximising quantity will alter. Therefore, the results of the analysis of total costs versus total revenues to pinpoint such a position would become outdated with every change, making it very difficult to derive the optimal, profit-maximising level of production as a result.

Consequently, cost and revenue situations are only used by organisations to guide policy decisions and to gauge performance trends. They are not used to gain a definitive value for the levels of maximum profit, or the production quantity required to gain this profit level. Such information is simply not available with the level of accuracy required and is likely to change on such a regular basis that its real strength will be merely for the analysis of trends and comparisons.

## Bounded rationality

One of the neoclassical assumptions is that of **perfect knowledge**. From the above, it is clear that this assumption is questionable in organisations operating in the real world, rather than in the economists'

theories. For many economists, this weakness in theory is a cause for concern. Austrian economists (such as Hayek, Menger, Mises and Schumpeter) in particular recognise the problem. Where knowledge is incomplete, uncertainty will therefore exist. The Austrians also further believe that organisations operating under conditions of uncertainty must be able to recognise what are their particular constraints (on production, trade and so on) before it is possible to measure them. This recognition on the part of the organisation leads to competition as each individual organisation attempts to gain its optimal position or situation.

Organisations which are able to recognise their particular constraints will eventually be able to define and measure them. Thus, they will be able to assess their own performance, to decide what performance measures are important to them and which are less so. Whichever they decide to concentrate on, they will be doing the same as all other organisations – they will be operating under conditions of '**bounded rationality**'.

That is, organisations are operating within the limits of their own knowledge, but as rational agents possessing that limited knowledge (rather than with perfect knowledge). Bounded rationality is a more realistic assumption on the part of the modern-day organisation than is perfect competition. Organisations take into account factors of which they are aware and/or may measure and take policy and strategy decisions to optimise their performance as a result. They are still operating under conditions of uncertainty, but this uncertainty may be reduced in some cases by their efforts to increase their knowledge.

Areas in which organisations are easily able to increase their knowledge are:

- *Competitors* – who they are, approximate market share, market prices, published future intentions, etc.
- *Market* – total market size, growth patterns, number of competitors, geographical spread of competitors and customers, etc.
- *Environment* – factors affecting the market, such as rates of interest, inflation, exchange, the overall influence of political parties, changes in legislation, etc.

Such information is readily available, via a number of sources, such as the financial press, company reports and public announcements made by organisations. More complex and individualised information is also available to all organisations as a result of their own interactions in the market and with competitors. Thus, under such circumstances, the bounded rationality of the organisation may be improved and the uncertainty reduced with relatively little effort. Other activities to reduce uncertainty require more effort, time and a greater cost on the part of the organisation. This is because the information required is more difficult to obtain, on a time or market-knowledge basis.

## Separation of ownership and control

In the early part of the twentieth century, particularly in Europe, the mainstay of the economy was the owner-managed organisation. Large, national and multinational organisations had not yet begun to proliferate; the 1950s and 1960s were the era of expansion and increases in organisational scope. As organisations grew, the number of owner-managed organisations fell. In order to finance the growth and expansion by raising funds, shares in organisations were sold to investors as a return for their willingness to take the investment risk. More and more businesses came to be owned by shareholders. These shareholders didn't even work at the organisations in which they held a stake. They increasingly put their trust in the employees and management of the organisation, only making their views known via the annual general meeting. In such organisations, owned by shareholders and

yet controlled by managers, there is a *separation of ownership and control.*

The phrase 'separation of ownership and control' is well known. It indicates that the owners of the organisation – the shareholders – possess no control over its day-to-day activities. The people with the real power are the employed management, who are often recognised as running organisations to satisfy their own needs or to protect their own welfare, rather than acting in the best interests of the owners.

Welfare for managers includes factors such as salary, non-monetary benefits, job security and perceived status within and outside the organisation. In many instances, it can be seen that these welfare factors are paid for at shareholders' expense. If profit is reduced as a result of management efforts to maximise welfare, then the available dividend payable is obviously reduced. The shareholders suffer for management gains. The separation of ownership from control thus means that the shareholders have less power over rectifying such situations than would be the case if they were personally involved with the organisation on a daily basis. The extent to which the separation of ownership and control exists varies across Europe. Although 'big business' exists in all countries, cultural differences and regulatory differences mean that there are larger numbers of smaller businesses in, say, France and Italy than elsewhere.

## ◆ CASE STUDY 4.1

## Executive pay: a practical solution  [FT]

Public disquiet in the UK over executive pay in privatised industries is justified because the system for fixing it is flawed. Indignation would increase if the public understood the full pension implications of big increases granted within a few years of retirement.

There is no such thing as a 'right' rate of remuneration, and arriving at one that satisfies all diverging interests is difficult. Striking a balance is a matter of judgment. Those who have to attempt it are often faced with the able but greedy. Most big companies have remuneration committees, but however hard they try to be objective, the results often look 'wrong'. There may be particular reasons for this, such as the influence of a member of the committee who has become used to such high pay himself that his judg-

ment is warped. Even where this is not so, all the pressures are in one direction – sharply upwards. . .

The logical solution is that remuneration should be decided by people who do not have a continuing relationship with the executives. There would then be a better chance (but no certainty) of achieving a better balance between the various conflicting interests.

How could this be done? By setting up a special executive remuneration advisory committee (Erac) to do the job.

The Erac would be elected by shareholders at the same time as they vote on the directors each year; its members would not be directors, but like directors would serve for set terms, say three years. . . Anyone could be nominated to the Erac. To eliminate cranks,

▶

Case study 4.1 *continued*

candidates would have to show on their nomination papers that they had the support of a proportion of the shareholders – say 3 per cent. . .

Although this proposal is offered in the context of the privatised industries, Eracs may be suitable for other companies above a market capitalisation of say £500m. They address the real problem in setting exec-

utive pay without cutting out the small shareholder. As important, they place the main burden where it ultimately belongs – on the large institutional shareholders, which have the interests of their beneficiaries to safeguard.

*Source*: *Financial Times*, 6 February 1995. Reprinted with permission.

### Comment on the case study

For UK privatised industries, the consumer is protected to an extent by a 'watchdog' set up specifically to oversee the pricing decisions and to deal with complaints about the service received. However, the case above shows that the small shareholder is not always protected; executive pay in such organisations is decided in many cases by the executives themselves. The proposal put forward here is that an independent panel of individuals decides what is, or is not, fair pay for the executives they are considering. Other large companies could also use the proposed committee format and also remove executive control over their own pay in such circumstances.

Although the proposal does not return full control in such cases to the shareholders, it does go some way towards removing power from the employed members of the organisation. The committee *would* be voted for by the shareholders; as such, it would be their decision to give the com-

mittee power to propose alternative remuneration packages for the shareholders to decide between. Where large numbers of shareholders are involved, a committee approach such as this would really be the only effective way of replacing some of their 'owner' decision-making power while maintaining systems which are workable and flexible.

## Profit maximisation is risky

It is commonly accepted that an organisation following the peaks and troughs in a market in order to gain profit maximisation will show greater fluctuations in its profit levels than an organisation following an alternative strategy.

Consider the case of Firm A, a profit maximiser, against Firm B, an organisation seeking to earn a profit (subject to a minimum constraint) but wishing also to achieve certain market share and revenue objectives.

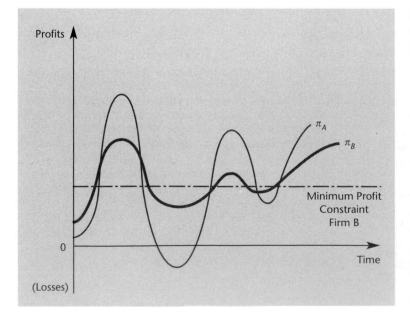

**Figure 4.1 Profit maximisation as an objective versus profit subject to a minimum constraint**

Firm A is the profit maximiser. Its stream of profits is volatile and subject to the whim of the market.

Firm B has a minimum profit constraint and other objectives to satisfy in addition. Its stream of profits is also subject to the whim of the market, but is less volatile. The fact that it 'only' needs to achieve the minimum constraint means that profits are more stable around the minimum profit constraint set.

In periods where the market is buoyant, Firm A will earn greater profits than Firm B. Firm A will be maximising, whereas Firm B will satisfy its minimum constraint and then concentrate on its other objectives.

In periods where the market is depressed, Firm A's profits will drop by a larger proportion than Firm B's. This is because Firm A is concentrating solely on profits, whereas Firm B's maximum achievable profits may drop to the minimum constraint. If not, Firm B will earn the minimum constraints and then concentrate on its other objectives.

Overall, as Figure 4.1 demonstrates, Firm A possesses a more volatile profit **locus** than Firm B. Firm B's profits are more concentrated around its minimum profit constraint, which makes it more stable than Firm A's locus. Firm A achieves very high profits at times, but also succumbs to very low profits (or even losses) at times when the maximum attainable profit level is reduced by market factors.

The relationship between profits and other objectives will be discussed in the remainder of this chapter. Before discussing the alternative objectives of the organisation, there is one more area of concern to be considered with reference to the profit-maximisation assumption.

## Not-for-profit organisations

Previously, economists have ignored or divorced their theories from the operations and objectives of not-for-profit organisations. Examples of such organisations are:

- *Charities* – Working to assist or improve circumstances for target groups via fundraising or direct action activities.
- *Public sector* – Services and agencies serving the public interest, funded by local or central government (for example, public services, emergency services).
- *Government funded* – In the UK, this includes universities and colleges, which receive income from a funding council. Examples of other such organisations include the radio and TV broadcaster the BBC, the Arts Council and national defence agencies.

These organisations have other objectives. They are run, in the main, for the public benefit. Retained earnings are a way of increasing the funds available for expansionary plans in future periods. However, declaring a profit at the end of the financial year would incite accusations of acting against the public interest. Therefore, the organisations discussed above are considered in many cases to be not for profit.

Various alternatives for not-for-profit organisational objectives exist. Overriding any objective in such cases would most probably be the objective to gain and improve efficiency with reference to a specified area of activity. These specific areas include:

- *Utility maximisation* – of either the administrators of the organisation or the contributors to the organisation. This creates an organisational culture of satisfaction and may well improve efficiency.

## ◆ CASE STUDY 4.2

# Funding changes after the UK introduced the National Lottery

A suitable example of the plight of not-for-profit organisations may be seen in the case of the UK's introduction of the National Lottery in November 1994.

Up to this point, charities had relied, quite successfully, on donations made by the public to high street shops, special public-awareness collection days and general donations.

The National Lottery changed things quite drastically, according to claims made by charities. They noticed a dramatic fall in donations made by the general public almost immediately. The feeling among the public, it was hypothesised, was that their conscience was clear because they were buying lottery tickets, money from which would eventually reach the charities. The chari-

ties, on the other hand, had to wait over a year before receiving anything from the National Lottery funds.

As a result of this time lag in payment, the charities were worse off in the short run; the public's donations had been diverted to the Lottery, on which the same amount (if not more) is being spent as was previously donated to charity. Therefore, the charities experienced a decline in their funds, as a result of a political and governmental act, nothing to do with their own activities. There is growing evidence after almost two years of Lottery operation to suggest that total monies are now increasing and that recipients of lottery funds will see an increase in their revenues.

*Source*: Authors.

■ *Quality maximisation* – with balanced costs and revenues. The organisation attempts continually to improve the service it offers to its customers or users within the given resource constraints.

■ *Maximising benefits* – to the customer or user. Minimising costs may also be an objective in such situations. The overriding concern, however, is to achieve maximum benefits. In such cases, losses may also be accrued in achieving the objective.

With reference to the above, it should be remembered also that there will be political factors which affect the choice of objective. It has already been mentioned that funding in many cases comes from local or central government. In making its funding decisions, the government may decide that there are given criteria for the organisation to fulfil before receiving monies. Thus, the not-for-profit organisation is relatively more vulnerable to changes in the political climate than are self-funding, for-profit organisations.

## ALTERNATIVES TO PROFIT MAXIMISATION

As a result of the issues raised above, a number of economists have published their own theories with reference to the objectives followed by organisations. These may be classified broadly into two categories:

■ **Managerial theories** – theories relating to organisations which operate on a 'non-owner-controlled' (Griffiths and Wall, 1995) basis. That is, the manager is an agent in the organisation, employed to work there.

■ **Behavioural theories** – theories relating to the actions and interactions between agents and principals within an organisation. Such theories have since been taken further by those interested in management theory, becoming a separate area of academic study in their own right.

The more commonly accepted managerial and behavioural models will be outlined in this section. They give alternative objectives for the organisation. There are also, in some cases, the authors' own criticisms of profit maximisation and their rationale for developing their theory.

## ALTERNATIVE MANAGERIAL DISCRETION MODELS

**Managerial discretion** describes the fact that the principal–agent relationship exists within the organisation. The agents with decision-making power, management, are responsible for decisions which affect the overall and day-to-day activities of the organisation. When making these decisions, managers have to use their own knowledge, experiences and understanding, that is, **discretion**.

### Baumol's sales revenue-maximisation model

W J Baumol's model of sales revenue maximisation was first published in 1959. It was proposed as an alternative to the (flawed) profit-maximisation objective of organisations, assumed by the neoclassical paradigm. Baumol proposed two types of model – static and dynamic. It is essential that the static model is developed and understood before the dynamic model can be considered.

Baumol put forward a number of justifications for the sales revenue-maximisation objective as opposed to profit maximisation. The more important ones are:

■ *Management priorities* – Managers are more likely to be concerned with utility maximisation on their part than profit maximisation on the organisation's part.

■ *Management rewards* – salary increases and 'slack earnings' (all perquisites and payments made to management in addition to salary payments) are more likely to be related to the level of sales earned by the organisation than to the level of profit.

■ *Financial institutions* – investors are more likely to be concerned with the level and trend in sales than in the level of profits. Thus, a clear upwards trend in sales will look more promising than a dip in profits, where they have been used internally to finance growth.

■ *Human relations* – it is easier to maintain a good relationship with employees when the organisation has rising levels of sales and a general feeling of buoyancy.

■ *Shareholders* – the imposition of a minimum profit constraint on management by shareholders ensures that their concerns are met, while it would be more difficult to set and measure a maximum requirement.

■ *Stability* – increasing levels of sales are usually associated with increasing market share. Therefore, the organisation may be considered to be improving its position in the market if its share is increasing.

The sales revenue-maximisation model proposed was based on the assumption that the organisation is operating in an oligopolistic market structure (that is, where there are only a few sellers in the market). In this respect, certain characteristics are identifiable about the internal and external processes involved for organisations within such markets.

Baumol recognises that, since it is large organisations that are most likely to be competitors within an oligopoly, then the chains of control and decision making are likely to be elongated. It is therefore considered more likely that it will take longer to arrive at and implement decisions within such organisations than within smaller competitors.

Within the market, it is claimed that there is tacit collusion between organisations to maintain the status quo. These incumbents, once the oligopoly has settled down into an equilibrium position, are able to enjoy a quiet life and split the profits between them. Additionally, there may be a general lack of interest on the part of organisations to compete in their market unless actions are undertaken by others to upset the current situation.

The oligopoly situation outlined above is assumed to operate in both the static and dynamic models of sales revenue maximisation outlined by Baumol.

## The static model

There are a number of assumptions associated specifically with the static model. These are:

■ A single time period, or horizon, for the organisation is assumed. There is therefore no interaction with other organisations or competition.
■ Sales revenue maximisation is the chosen objective of the organisation, subject to a minimum profit constraint, exogenously set by the shareholders. This profit constraint is set with reference to their own income and utility aspirations.
■ Traditional cost and revenue curves are assumed (that is, U-shaped costs and ∩-shaped revenue curves).

The model may therefore be derived from a simple diagram of total costs and total revenues, as seen in Figure 4.2.

In Figure 4.2, the profit-maximisation production quantity is given by the greatest gap between the total cost (TC) and total revenue (TR) curves. The quantities depicting zero (economic) profits are given by the points where TC and TR intersect. Continuing in a similar manner, the levels of profits earned may be plotted for each production quantity. This locus of profit is given by the profit locus, $\pi$.

The minimum profit constraint imposed by the shareholders is shown as a straight, horizontal line, $\pi_{min}$. This profit constraint is decided by the shareholders, regardless of the sales and other conditions of the organisation.

The quantity produced by the sales revenue maximiser will be the quantity which satisfies the minimum profit constraint and yet allows the greatest level of sales (quantity) to be achieved. This quantity is shown by $Q_{SRM}$. Alternatively, the profit maximiser's level of output is shown as $Q_{\pi max}$, the greatest gap between TC and TR.

It is clear, therefore, that the sales revenue maximiser will earn a lower profit, but produce a greater quantity than the profit maximiser. The sales revenue maximiser, then, is in a better position to capture market share than is the profit maximiser. In order to make more sense of the modern organisation, Baumol took the static model further, to include the role of advertising. However, there is no attempt to explain the effects on price, or even how the price is arrived at in either case.

## The static model with advertising

The additional assumptions made with respect to this development are:

■ Advertising is used by organisations as a policy decision by management to increase the number of sales in the market.
■ Sales revenue increases as increases in advertising expenditure are made. More fully, revenue increases positively in line with increases in advertising expenditure.
■ Total costs are independent of advertising, which is decided exogenously by management. Advertising expenditure does, however, increase as a factor of quantity produced.

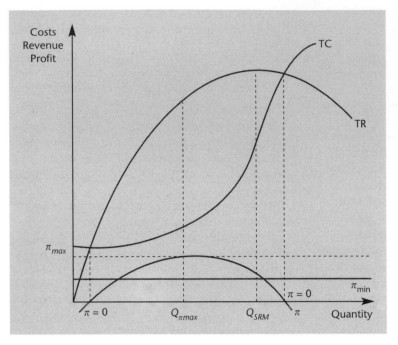

**Figure 4.2 Baumol's static sales revenue-maximisation model**

The profit-maximising production quantity is given by the greatest gap between the total cost (TC) and total revenue (TR) curves. The quantities depicting zero (economic) profits are given by the points where TC and TR intersect, that is, where they are equal. Continuing in a similar manner, the levels of profits earned may be plotted for each production quantity. This locus of profit is given by the profit locus, $\pi$.

The minimum profit constraint imposed by the shareholders is shown as a straight, horizontal line, $\pi_{min}$. This profit constraint is decided by the shareholders, regardless of sales and other conditions of the organisation.

The quantity produced by the sales revenue maximiser will be the quantity which satisfies the minimum profit constraint and yet allows the greatest level of sales (quantity) to be made. This quantity is shown by $Q_{SRM}$. Alternatively, the profit maximiser's level of output is shown as $Q_{\pi max}$: the greatest gap between TC and TR.

Thus, Figure 4.2 may be modified to include advertising expenditure. In Figure 4.3, total advertising expenditure is shown as a cost per unit. It rises as quantity rises, but never exceeds TC.

The profit constraint is given, as in Figure 4.2, by $\pi_{min}$. It is possible to derive the amount spent on advertising by the sales revenue maximiser and the profit maximiser. The sales revenue maximiser will advertise at the level where the minimum profit constraint is achieved, and yet maximum quantity is sold. This point is given by $A_{SRM}$. The quantity produced by the profit maximiser is given by $A_{\pi max}$ and less than that for the sales revenue maximiser.

The conclusions drawn are similar to those for the more simple static model. Additionally, Baumol claims that as well as increasing quantities sold, advertising, when undertaken on a *ceteris paribus* basis, does not increase price.

This claim reveals one criticism of the static model in general. At no point does Baumol make an attempt to analyse the relationship between price, advertising, total costs and quantity produced. His analysis and comments do not provide any apparent foundation for the claim that advertising does not increase price.

---

◆ **Exercise 4.1**

The assumption made by Baumol that advertising is linked to a per unit cost is flawed. Explain why.

---

The assumption that advertising can be linked to cost on a per unit basis is naïve. Any organisation undertaking advertising will not do so on a per unit basis, but initially as a 'sunk cost', to enable the organisation entering a market to compete against incumbent competitors on a more equal basis. Second, advertising is likely to be used on a 'lumpy' or sporadic basis to maintain an awareness of the organisation. Thus, advertising expenditure

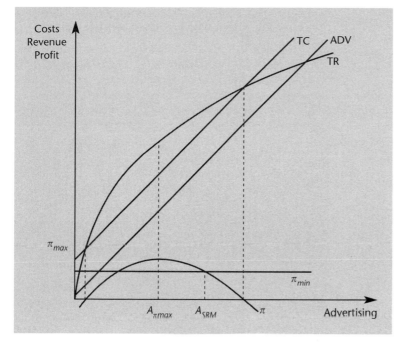

## Figure 4.3 Baumol's static sales revenue-maximisation model with advertising

The profit-maximising production quantity is given by the greatest gap between the total cost (TC) and total revenue (TR) curves. Advertising is assumed to be a constantly increasing expenditure and rises in parallel to TC. Different levels of profit are given by the profit locus, $\pi$.

The minimum profit constraint imposed by the shareholders is shown as a straight, horizontal line, $\pi_{min}$.

The advertising spend of the sales revenue maximiser will be the level which satisfies the minimum profit constraint and yet allows the greatest level of sales to be made. This level is shown by $A_{SRM}$. Alternatively, the profit maximiser's level of advertising is shown as $A_{\pi max}$, the greatest gap between TC and TR.

patterns will reveal peaks and troughs if related to quantities, rather than a constant increase as Baumol advocates.

## The dynamic model – the profit-optimising rate of growth model

Once the static model is developed, it may be extended and augmented to produce the dynamic model. The dynamic model has further assumptions. These are:

- The objective of the organisation is to continue to gain increases in sales revenue over its lifetime.
- Exogenously decided profits are used to finance growth and expansion of the organisation. These profits are retained for expansion, rather than paid out as dividends to the shareholders.
- Traditional cost and revenue curves exist.

If sales revenue increases over the lifetime of the organisation, it must therefore expand, or grow, in order to accommodate that increase. It is obvious that the greater the proportion of profits which are used to fund growth, the greater the growth will be. If more profits are distributed, the growth potential is reduced as a result.

Plotting growth versus revenue, as in Figure 4.4(a), it may be clearly seen that the maximum level of growth, $g_{max}$, is achieved at the level where retained profits are maximised, $R_{\pi max}$.

There will be a tradeoff between growth now and future earnings potential of the organisation if

retained profits are used to fund such growth. By plotting each set of growth versus revenue situations, the range of opportunities facing the organisation may be derived. However, it is not sufficient merely to plot each set of growth and revenue values in real terms, an iso-present value curve is required. This shows the discounted stream of revenues with reference to future earnings, that is, allowing for inflationary effects on the future value predicted, what its present-day value would be. (£1 sterling, held today, has a present value of £1, whereas £1 held in five years' time will be worth only a percentage of its current value if compared in terms of spending power – inflation will have taken its toll.) In order to be consistent, all revenues are compared in present value terms (see Chapter 12 for further explanation of present values). See Figure 4.4(b).

Figure 4.4(b) clearly shows that each iso-present value curve slopes downwards, from left to right between the growth and revenue axis. What each curve depicts is the tradeoff between growth and revenue in terms of future profit streams. The greater the growth, the greater the revenues and the greater the discounted stream of profits. It should be logical, therefore, that any rational organisation will aim to maximise its iso-profit levels, aspiring to earn the most rightward curve possible.

The optimal position for the organisation to balance growth and future profit streams is at the point of tangency between the growth locus and the iso-present value curves, see Figure 4.4(c). Any

## Figure 4.4 Baumol's dynamic sales revenue-maximisation model

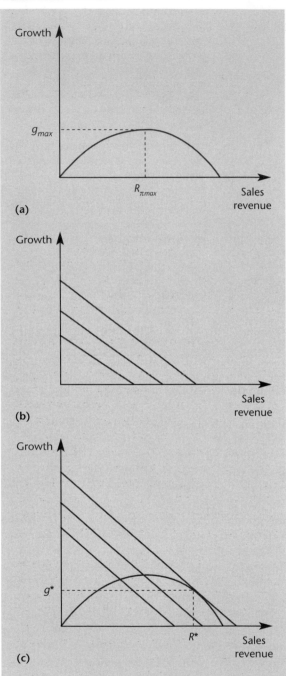

(a)

(b)

(c)

(a) Plotting sales revenue versus growth produces a growth locus given by $g$, when the tradeoff between revenue and growth is considered.

(b) Discounted, iso-present value curves which slope downwards, left to right, show the combinations of revenue and growth which give the same value of discount rate.

(c) Combining 4.4(a) and 4.4(b) gives an equilibrium, or optimum rate of growth $g^*$, with revenue optimised at $R^*$.

## Figure 4.5 Dynamic sales revenue maximisation – quantity output when revenue and growth are optimised

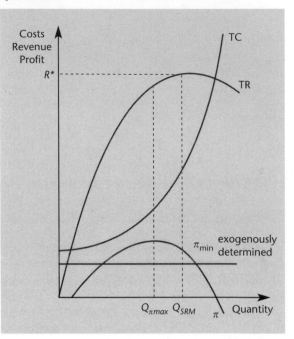

This diagram, similar to Figure 4.2, shows that the sales revenue maximiser produces $Q_{SRM}$ – derived with reference to $R^*$ in Figure 4.4(c) when $g^*$ is attained.

position below this point, that is, to the left, will be non-optimal since the organisation could move to a higher iso-present value curve and remain within the growth constraints of the locus. Any position beyond the point of tangency is unachievable to the organisation; the iso-present value curve is beyond the constraint of the growth locus. $R^*$ depicts the optimal rate of revenue, while $g^*$ is the optimal rate of growth.

Given the optimal rates of revenue and growth, the level of exogenously determined minimum profits may also be found. The minimum profit constraint, therefore, may be imposed on the management of the organisation. The minimum profit constraint may be superimposed on a 'snapshot', single-period costs and revenue diagram for the dynamic situation; see Figure 4.5.

Figure 4.5 may be analysed in much the same way as the simple static diagram (Figure 4.2). The minimum profit constraint, $\pi_{min}$, crosses the profit locus at the greatest level of production which it is possible for the sales revenue maximiser to achieve and still meet the constraint. This level, $Q_{SRM}$, is greater than the level of production for the profit maximiser (which produces at $Q_{\pi max}$).

Overall, then, Baumol's model of sales revenue maximisation offers an alternative to the profit-maximisation model. Although there is no indication given as to how the organisation reaches its market price, what affects its costs and revenues and how these are related to the production quan-tity, other conclusions may be drawn. Baumol clearly shows that the sales revenue maximiser will produce a greater quantity than the profit maximiser. The sales revenue maximiser is able to gain an optimal level of growth, taking into account the tradeoff between growth and revenue in the future. Also, advertising is claimed to increase levels of sales, more so for the sales revenue maximiser than the profit maximiser.

◆ **CASE STUDY 4.3**

# More fuel needed for recovery                    FT

It has been a hectic few weeks for Mr Christian Blanc, chairman of Air France. He has reshuffled senior management, faced a strike by cabin staff, launched an improved long-haul service and outlined plans to restructure Air Inter, Air France's domestic partner.

Mr Blanc's rescue plan for the ailing state-owned French carrier has reached a crucial phase. The fate of his latest initiatives for the airline, and the strength of opposition they encounter from the company's restive trade unions, will determine whether the lame duck he inherited in 1993 can be made to fly . . .

Air France has stopped flying on some unprofitable routes and introduced other cost-cutting measures aimed at raising staff productivity by 30 per cent between 1994 and 1997. By reducing the airline's financial charges, the capital injections have helped cut net losses from FFr8.5 bn in 1993 to FFr2.4 bn in the 15 months to the end of March, after exceptional items. In an attempt to revitalise the bureaucratic management at the airline, Mr Blanc has broken it into 11 profit centres, from cabin staff to maintenance, each responsible for its own results. To win back passengers, he has launched new products. This month, long-distance flights have been overhauled with new cabins and entertainment . . .

An additional problem is that Air France's competitors are not standing still. 'We set ourselves the goal of catching Lufthansa in terms of productivity and results,' says one senior executive. 'But other airlines started to restructure before we did, so they have built a lead.'

How big a lead is revealed in a study commissioned by Air France from Berger, the German consultancy group. It shows, for example, that administrative support costs are 40 per cent higher at Air France than at Lufthansa and that average salary costs for cabin staff are 27 per cent higher at the French carrier.

Mr Blanc is responding on several fronts. He has bought a software system from American Airlines to improve yield management – the maximisation of revenues per seat – which is due to start operating next summer.

He is also taking steps to strengthen his control over top management. At the end of last month, he replaced Mr Rodolphe Frantz, the airline's managing director who was known as 'Air Frantz' because of his long service. At the same time, Mr Blanc appointed Mr Jean-Pierre Courcol as managing director of Air Inter, the domestic carrier which is part of the Air France group. He will report directly to Mr Blanc . . .

Within Air France, Mr Blanc is also stepping up efficiency efforts. He is seeking to change the bureaucratic culture of employees and improve the quality of service. The clearest example concerns the cabin staff, described by one Air France official as demoralised and resistant to reform.

The solution, according to Mr Blanc, is to reorganise working practices and the terms of employment. According to Mr Blanc's proposals, flight attendants will be able to transfer to a new job within the company after a set period of time. New cabin staff will be hired at lower rates of pay, but will no longer face age restrictions concerning promotion. . .

'He has made progress, but competition is set to intensify,' says one airlines analyst, referring to the liberalisation of European air travel in 1997. 'He must accelerate restructuring, but this could harden opposition from the unions.' For Mr Blanc, the turbulence is not yet over.

*Source: Financial Times*, 18 September 1995. Reprinted with permission.

*Comment on the case study*

Air France can been seen to be combining a campaign for efficiency gains with a desire for revenue maximisation. Mr Blanc is concentrating on making the airline competitive with reference to others in the industry. He is also concerned that the revenue per seat is maximised; that is, that total revenue is maximised – sales revenue maximisation!

The case clearly points out that this is not the only activity being undertaken at Air France, but the restructuring and the change in air-crew pay and employment conditions will certainly help to reduce inefficiency and costs and also reduce total costs for the airline. The yield-management software purchased by Mr Blanc is used widely among North American airlines, which regularly monitor and amend passenger ticket prices in order to maximise revenue, passenger numbers per flight and so on. Yield management relates to the revenue gained per seat on an aircraft. Thus, maximising the yield on each seat is maximising the revenue gained on each seat. Yield management allows airlines to change the price of seats on given flights so as to ensure that the flight is optimally filled. Anecdotes abound about students paying cut prices for their tickets and sitting next to business travellers who have paid full fare. By balancing the numbers of seats available to each type of traveller (usually based on their urgency for travel and associated willingness to pay for it), airlines are able to optimise management of their revenues. *See* Chapters 9 and 10 for further analysis of organisational pricing decision making and policies.

It is pleasing to note that in this case, Air France is clearly following a revenue-maximisation model, albeit far more complex than that proposed by Baumol.

## Marris's growth rate model of managerial enterprise

The tradeoff between growth and profits was also investigated by Marris. His findings were first published in 1963 and link the growth in demand for the organisation's product with its growth in supply of capital. Once the link was established, Marris was able to show that for different combinations of growth in demand and supply there is a balanced level of growth for the organisation.

Marris assumes that the growth of the organisation depends on the utility functions of both management and owners. Each group has different factors which affect its utility, but both aim to maximise its utility. As a result of this friction between owners and management, a balance must be found – the 'balanced growth locus'. The basic assumption made by Marris is that there is a tradeoff between average profit rates and growth; the profit rate falls as (balanced) growth increases. The following sections show how the balanced growth locus is derived.

Marris contends that the utility of management in the organisation is dependent on factors that have been discussed previously: salaries, power, status, job security, perquisites and so on. Management will attempt to maximise these factors. The utility of the owners – the shareholders – is dependent on different factors: the profits earned, the quantity sold, levels of capital available to the organisation, market share and the public esteem gained.

### Growth in demand

Management decisions (delegated by owners) will affect the rate of growth in demand for the organisation's products. One constraining factor is the tradeoff between job security and the risk relating to projects undertaken to increase demand.

Growth in demand is achieved in two ways: diversification into new product areas and differentiation of current products. Marris does not distinguish between the different methods. What *is* important, however, is the fact that the percentage of new products succeeding in the marketplace is negatively linked to the rate of profits earned by the organisation. There is a tradeoff between funds for diversification and funds declared as profit, because funds declared as profit effectively decrease the amount of investment which may be made in research and development of new products. Investment into research and development of new products and the expenditure required to produce and launch these products form a cost which will obviously detract from the profits of the organisation in the period in which they accrue.

Management therefore needs to make a decision between the rate of diversification and the rate of profit it desires. The decision is, however, more complex than simply balancing diversification and profits. Managerial utility is very much determined by job security. Job security may be defined in financial terms as a combination of the following ratios and is known as the 'financial security constraint':

- *Leverage = total debt/total assets* – The greater the leverage, the more the organisation owes its financial backers, the more difficult it will be to borrow until the ratio is reduced.
- *Liquidity = liquid assets/assets* – The greater the liquidity, the more stock and other saleable assets the organisation has in proportion to its total assets. Lower liquidity indicates a capital intensity on the part of the organisation.
- *Retention ratio = retained profits/total profits* – The greater the retention ratio, the more the organisation is retaining for future projects. The lower the retention ratio, the higher the funds to pay dividends to shareholders.

The optimal combination of these ratios cannot categorically be stated for any set of managers or organisation, but will be dependent on the individuals involved and the environment in which their organisation is operating.

The effect on profits of the interaction between growth of demand and diversification may be shown for different levels of profit, subject to the financial security constraint. As has been previously stated, the greater the level of diversification, the lower the level of profits. The lower the level of profits, the lower the level of growth achievable. *See* Figure 4.6(a), where the levels of profit, $m_1$, $m_2$ and $m_3$, are shown with reference to diversification and growth in demand rates – $m_1$ is the lowest level of profits, $m_3$ the greatest.

### Growth in supply

Countering the growth in demand of the organisation is the growth in supply of capital. This depends on the owners of the organisation and their utility. Quite simply, the greater the level of retained profits, the lower the level of profits avail-

**Figure 4.6 Marris's growth rate model of managerial enterprise**

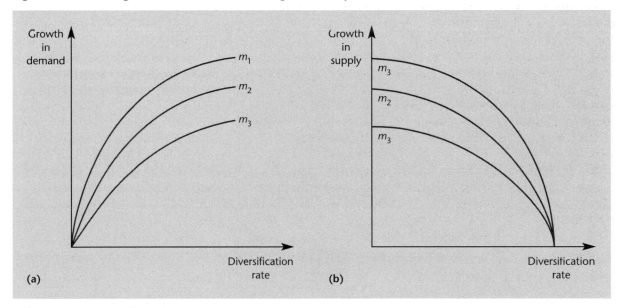

(a) *Growth in demand*. The effect on profits of the interaction between growth in demand and diversification is shown for different levels of profit, subject to the financial security constraint. The greater the level of diversification, the lower the level of profits. The lower the level of profits, the lower the level of growth achievable. *See* (b), growth in supply, where the levels of profits, $m_1$, $m_2$ and $m_3$, are shown with reference to diversification and growth in demand rates: $m_1$ is the lowest level of profits, $m_3$ the highest.

(b) *Growth in supply*. The higher the rate of retained profits, the greater the potential the organisation has for growth. If it is assumed that there is a limit to the level of diversification achievable by the organisation, Figure 4.6(b) may be derived. Here, the higher the rate of profits (rising from $m_1$ to $m_3$), the greater the rate of growth.

able for dividends. The owners must therefore decide whether to release funds for growth, or to take a 'cut' of the success to date. The higher the rate of retained profits, the greater potential for growth the organisation has. If it is assumed that there is a limit to the level of diversification achievable by the organisation, Figure 4.6(b) may be derived.

In Figure 4.6(b), the higher the rate of profits (rising from $m_1$ to $m_2$ to $m_3$), the greater the rate of growth. By combining Figures 4.6(a) and 4.6(b), the equilibrium positions for each level of profits may be found, that is, the levels of growth and diversification where the profit levels intersect. These equilibrium positions are the 'balanced growth' levels. This may be clearly seen in Figure 4.7.

The series of balanced growth levels may be seen for the intersections between growth in demand and supply for $m_1$, $m_2$ and $m_3$. Joining these balanced growth levels, or points, will give a balanced growth locus, as seen in the figure. The balanced growth locus shows the optimal levels of growth versus diversification attainable by the organisation for different levels of profits.

Overall, then, Marris brings together the utility objectives of the owners of the organisation with those of its managers. The result is a picture of the organisation's possibilities for growth and diversification. This is only a snapshot, however, due to the decisions made by management with reference to the financial security constraint and by the owners with reference to the retained profit levels. As with Baumol, a criticism of Marris's work exists because there is an assumption that the organisation is operating in a stable business environment and that decisions are made by those who implement them.

An additional criticism relates to the assumption made by Marris that research and development funds and advertising are lumped together. Obviously, product diversification cannot take place without research and development. Also, to be successful, developments usually need to be advertised. The lumping together of these is considered to be naïve by many commentators because research and development, and advertising require different processes and skills and take place at different times.

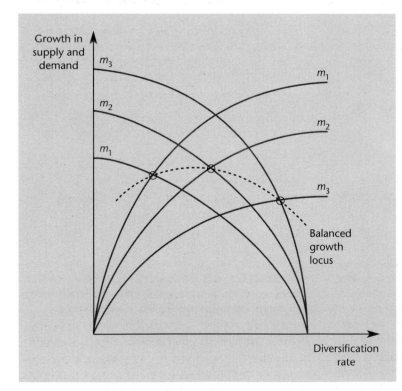

**Figure 4.7 Marris's growth rate model of managerial enterprise**

Combining the growth in demand and growth in supply figures given in Figures 4.6(a) and (b) provides Figure 4.7. A balanced growth locus may be plotted once the balance growth levels for each level of m ($m_1$, $m_2$ and $m_3$) are found.

## ◆ CASE STUDY 4.4

# Shareholder value management: performance measure gains popularity

**FT**

The stated goal of most quoted companies is to achieve the fastest possible growth in earnings per share. But according to a growing number of management consultants, companies are focusing on the wrong ambition.

Traditional accounting measures of performance can obscure the real economic impact of business decisions, they argue. Instead, cash-based measures are a far better guide to the business's ability to create value for shareholders. Moving the goalposts by switching to a cash-based measure – such as cash flow return on investment – can transform the way that companies analyse acquisitions, set performance measures, allocate resources and reward top executives.

The merits of this approach, known as shareholder value management, are being promoted by several consultancy firms, including Boston Consulting, McKinsey, PA Consulting, Marakon, Braxton, Harbridge House, Price Waterhouse and Coopers and Lybrand. . .

One of the most popular uses of shareholder value analysis is in assessing acquisitions and the allocation of resources. Consultants argue that many acquisitions fail to create value for the acquiring company's shareholders due to a misplaced emphasis on the impact of the deal on earnings per share. Instead, companies should analyse the impact on free cash flow.

Similar mistakes are made when companies plan expansion. Many companies have destroyed value by investing below the cost of capital. Mr Neil Monnery, vice-president of Boston Consultancy Group, believes that most companies do not know the cost and so can-

not build it into their investment decisions. There is a tendency to confine shareholder value analysis to strategic planning departments. But consultants argue that the greatest rewards stem from using the tool to create the discipline of external capital markets inside the company. This involves making an explicit link between operating decisions and their effect on shareholder returns.

Typically, the factors that influence shareholder returns are broken down into 'value drivers', such as sales growth, operating profit margin, cash tax rate, working capital, fixed assets, cost of capital and growth duration period. These can be subdivided into specific measures, such as cost per unit, cycle time or defect rate. . .

Establishing value-based performance measures throughout the company opens up the possibility of introducing widespread performance-linked incentives. 'If you have a method for measuring performance that is consistent with maximising shareholder value, what is wrong with trying to motivate people on the same basis to make sure that you align their interests with the shareholder?' asked Mr Joel Stern of Stern Stewart, a New York consultancy, at a recent Business Intelligence conference. . .

But, judging by the growth in its popularity in the US since the 1970s, consultants believe the adoption in Europe of shareholder value management is just a matter of time.

*Source: Financial Times*, 12 September 1995. Reprinted with permission.

---

*Comment on the case study*

Marris's balanced growth locus proposal would seem to have some worth if the case above is considered. A return to a focus on shareholders and shareholder value has shifted performance indicators to consider factors such as the profit margin, the minimum profit constraint (the operating profit margin), the rate of sales growth and similar measures which are not traditionally considered as performance measures with reference to accounting systems, but which could give some insight into the real worth of the organisation for shareholders.

Thus, an organisation with a steady sales growth and stable/controlled profit margin changes may fit into the Marris model of an organisation following a

balanced growth locus. Shareholder value measurement has been used in the United States for many years; its adoption in Europe would give greater emphasis to theoretical models such as Marris's.

## Williamson's managerial utility model

This model is also known as the model of managerial discretion. It concentrates on the conviction that the management of the organisation seeks to maximise its utility subject to the shareholders' minimum profit constraint. Job security is a major factor in the decision-making processes. Other factors affecting management utility are salary and the status associated with the constituents which make up the 'expense preference' of non-salary payments.

Williamson proposes that the more employees a manager is in charge of, the greater the budget and resources they will be responsible for. With this enhanced spending position comes increased status. Thus, overall, it can be claimed that management utility is a factor of staff expenditure, management perquisites and discretionary expenditure. The greater the value of each of these factors, the greater the utility of the manager. However, the greater the level of expenditure on these factors, the lower the level of profits can be in the same period.

A simple model to derive an equilibrium position in the tradeoff between managerial utility and profits is possible when considered in the context of profit and staff expenditure/discretionary investment. For the purposes of the simple model, assume that there is a zero level of perquisites. These are usually taxable and would therefore cause the model to be more complex than is required in order to make the analysis.

Consider managerial utility. For a given combination of profits and staff expenditure (for ease, including discretionary expenditure), a certain level of utility exists. Indifference curves may therefore be constructed for combinations of profit and staff expenditure which possess the same levels of utility. Any rationale manager will wish to move to the furthest right indifference curve possible. Such a relationship may be seen in Figure 4.8(a).

It is also possible to plot a profit locus for the relationship between profits and staff expenditure. As Figure 4.8(b) shows, the level of profit maximisation occurs at the level of expenditure $S_{\pi max}$. Also visible is the fact that zero profits occur at positive levels of staff expenditure. Between zero and $S_1$, increases in staff expenditure lead to reductions in the losses incurred by the organisation. Between $S_1$ and $S_{\pi max}$, profits are positive and continue to increase with staff expenditure. Between $S_{\pi max}$ and $S_2$, further increases in staff expenditure lead to reductions in the overall levels of profit. Beyond $S_2$, increases in staff expenditure lead to greater and greater losses. From this analysis, it should be obvious that there is an optimal level of staff expenditure with reference to the desire to maximise profits.

If Figures 4.8(a) and (b) are combined to produce Figure 4.8(c), it is possible to explain why organisations operating under a separation of ownership and control do not necessarily maximise

**Figure 4.8 Williamson's managerial utility model**

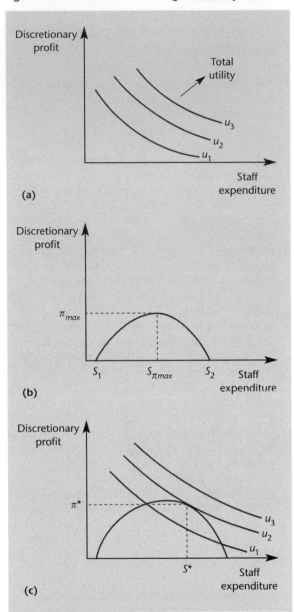

(a) Indifference curves showing utility levels of managers with reference to different levels of profits and staff expenditure. Utility increases with distance from the origin.

(b) Profit locus for the relationship between profits and staff expenditure.

(c) The satisficing 'equilibrium' position gained by the combination of (a) and (b).

profits. Management desire utility maximisation, at the furthest right indifference curve (Figure 4.8(a)). Profit maximisation occurs at the highest point on the profit locus (Figure 4.8(b)). However, the equilibrium position for the two is at the point of tangency of the furthest right indifference curve which still touches the profit locus. This is $S^*$, $\pi^*$ in Figure 4.8(c).

> ◆ **Exercise 4.2**
>
> Consider the effects that imposing a minimum profit constraint will have on this model. Use a profit constraint lower than $\pi^*$ and a profit constraint above $\pi^*$.

The simple model therefore demonstrates that, when managers seek to maximise their own utility rather than profits, profit levels are suboptimal. With reference to the profit locus, it could be argued that the level of staff expenditure is too high, that lower levels of staff expenditure would actually increase profits. The organisation may therefore be considered to be inefficient. However, in terms of managerial utility, which lies behind the higher level of staff expenditure, the situation could not be better, given the current constraints of the organisation.

A development of this model is to compare the situations when a tax is levied on profits. Obviously, a tax on stated profits results in a reduced level of after-tax profits. A profit maximiser will suffer a reduction in its after-tax profits equal to the amount of the tax. An organisation run for managerial utility maximisation, on the other hand, may not be liable for the full amount. If, in reaction to an increase in the level of tax, management decides to increase staff expenditure, the stated level of taxable profit will be reduced and thus also the tax burden on the organisation.

Overall, then, this model would seem to explain a number of identifiable phenomena, observed by analysts in the real world. Indeed, Williamson claims these to be the strengths of the model. They include:

- *Tax changes* – The model explains typical reactions to tax changes, such as diverting profits to prevent them being taxed by reinvesting them elsewhere and so on.
- *Staff cuts* – When organisations are taken over, or new management is appointed, staff cuts are possible without reductions in productivity.
- *Boom and bust behaviour* – Organisations typically reduce expenditure on staff perquisites and investment when the economy takes a downturn, while increasing these when matters improve.

However, a criticism of Williamson's model as well as the preceding ones is the lack of explanation with reference to how the oligopoly market's interdependence affects competitors' behaviour. The implications for price, quantity and other competitive factors are also ignored as a consequence.

## Weaknesses of managerial models

There are a number of generic criticisms which may be made of the managerial theories of the firm. These criticisms highlight the problems with the assumptions made in order to construct the models and also the difficulty faced by all economists in attempting to make provision for the cycle of action–reaction which occurs when any organisation changes its behaviour.

The managerial models are considered to be naïve in reference to their coverage of organisational behaviour within competitive markets such as oligopoly. Additionally, they offer no consideration of research and development activities which many organisations undertake as a matter of course.

The main criticisms are as follows:

- Profit is considered to be 'given', that is, exogenous to the model; this is particularly true of the minimum profit constraint included in many cases. Therefore there is no consideration of the manner in which desirable profit levels are obtained or decided on. The dynamic model is profit led; some further explanation of its derivation is required.
- It is assumed that profits are used to fund growth. There is no consideration of alternative ways in which growth may be funded, such as share issues or borrowing from financial institutions. However, Marris *does* consider the balance between internal and external finances in his work.
- Prices are assumed to be constant and organisations are assumed to be operating within stable oligopoly environments. Competitive markets and price competition are not covered.
- Quantities produced are related to revenues of the organisation, not to advertising or other factors.
- Research and development and product line extensions are ignored, except in the case of the Marris model which does include within the average profit margin an acknowledgement of product diversification and differentiation. Implicitly, this must include research and development.

Finally, it should be noted that the managerial models give insight into only a snapshot of the organisation's position. There is no explanation or outline of what future situations may be like. Therefore, the models provide only a one-off explanation of what organisations may look like and the manner in which they may act.

## Behavioural models of the organisation

Such models were developed in the 1950s and have not, on the whole, been updated in any depth since the 1970s and 1980s. More recent attempts to understand the theoretical behaviour of the firm have been made by experts in the field of management and organisational behaviour, rather than by economists.

Those credited with the development of the first, seminal works on the **behavioural theories** of the firm are H A Simon and the collaborative (research) pairing of R M Cyert and J G March.

Cyert and March's model is proposed within the context of an organisation where ownership and control have been separated. That is, the organisation is a large concern run by managers for shareholders. It is recognised that when such a situation exists, the organisation increases in complexity. Individuals all possess different aims and ambitions and therefore have multiple goals for the future. These multiple goals mean that there are, therefore, multiple decisions being made within the organisation and that there will inevitably, at some stage, be conflict. Thus the organisation is considered to be a coalition of workers operating within an uncertain and imperfect market.

The organisation is operating under conditions of uncertainty because its managers and decision makers possess limited knowledge about competitors and market conditions. Also, it is obviously impossible for them to be able to predict the future. They are assumed, as a result, to be rational decision makers, but with bounded rationality, a consequence of which is that they will learn from their experiences over time. Thus, the organisation's ability to react and grow will improve as managers become more adept in their understanding of their competitors and the business environment.

## CONCLUDING REMARKS

It has been argued by some economists that the alternatives to profit maximisation put forward in this chapter are merely short-run objectives. They claim that short-run objectives which maximise factors other than profits, such as growth or sales, or even satisficing models, merely place the organisation in a better position to maximise profits in the long run.

As a result of alternative activities, organisations gain a position of stability, or are able to consolidate a favourable market position which may then be used as a springboard for future gains.

It is also the case that each of the alternatives to profit maximisation outlined in this chapter has its own shortcomings. The lack of empirical testing, especially with reference to the managerial theories, does provide a cause for concern among some economists, as does the lack of explanation with reference to the market position of organisations which may be applied to all without fail. It is assumed that the organisation operates within an oligopolistic market structure; but the manner in which the market evolved, how prices are set and so on are not explained. Furthermore, other market structures are largely ignored. Finally, the assumption that minimum profit constraints of the firm are exogenously determined is less than satisfactory for many critics.

## SUMMARY

◆ In practice, very few organisations seek to maximise profits and none operates with perfect knowledge.

◆ Limited knowledge on the part of individuals and organisations, despite their desire to achieve maximum benefit, is known as 'bounded rationality'.

◆ A decline in owner-controlled organisations occurred in the 1950s and 1960s, with the growth of large, multinational organisations. Share issues to raise funds meant that ownership was distributed among many individuals, with the real power becoming delegated to employed managers.

◆ Alternatives to the neoclassical model have been published and may be classified into two categories: managerial discretion models and behavioural theories of the firm.

◆ Baumol's sales revenue-maximisation model emphasises the organisation's desire to maximise revenue rather than profits. The implication of this is a relatively more stable stream of profits in the long run.

◆ Marris's growth rate model of managerial enterprise addresses the conflict which arises between the desire to earn greater profits and that to reinvest in order to expand. The compromise put forward is the balanced growth locus.

◆ Williamson's managerial utility model recognises that managers in decision-making positions are often required to make difficult decisions. The overriding goal, however, is for optimum managerial welfare with reference to pay and job security; as a result, they satisfice in terms of the decisions they make which affect others.

◆ The alternatives to profit maximisation may also be criticised. There seems to be an overriding assumption that organisations are large and oligopolistic in nature, with the capacity to make decisions and implement changes which affect the market without invoking retaliation from fellow competitors.

## REVIEW QUESTIONS

1 Outline the possible conflicts in goals which may arise within an organisation where different groups have differing needs. Why is it that organisations are able to continue to operate despite the conflicts you have outlined?

2 Sales revenue maximisation offers an alternative to profit maximisation. Explain the criticisms which may be applied with reference to:
   - assumptions about cost and revenue information;
   - derivation of the minimum profit constraint;
   - the treatment of research and development and advertising.

3 The balanced growth locus provides an insight into resolution of the conflict between financial expansion and product expansion – does it stand up to the criticisms made of it?

4 Why does the separation of ownership and control cause problems for those attempting to understand the behaviour of the organisation with reference to the profit-maximisation objective?

5 Explain what is meant by 'satisficing' and how such a concept can aid analysis of the actions of managers within organisations.

6 Air France (see Case Study 4.3) is attempting to manage its yields (revenue per seat) effectively. This involves charging different prices to different passengers. How can such a policy possibly be successful?

## GLOSSARY OF NEW TERMS

**Bounded rationality**: When knowledge is incomplete, individuals and organisations make their best guesses or decisions with respect to the information which *is* known to them. The constraints on the information cause it to be termed 'bounded' and the fact that the organisation is attempting to make its best decision within that constraint indicates that it is acting rationally: hence 'bounded rationality'.

**Behavioural theories**: Theories developed to explain the interactions of the decision-making parties within an organisation. Behavioural theories take into account the preferences and (possibly) conflicting goals of the different decision makers.

**Discretion**: The combination of experience, knowledge and understanding used by managerial decision makers in order to gain the best possible result for the organisation in its present context.

**(Profit) locus**: On a graph, the line which traces the profit levels derived from the other values detailed on the graph;

in this case, the costs and revenues would be the other values. The difference between the cost and revenue at each quantity will be the profit level. (*See* Figure 4.2.)

**Managerial discretion models**: See 'managerial theories'.

**Managerial theories**: Theories which attempt to explain alternatives to the theory of profit maximisation where there has been a separation of ownership and control. Managerial theories provide an insight into other factors which management may attempt to maximise or satisfice.

**Perfect knowledge**: The neoclassical assumption that the individual or organisation has clear all-encompassing insight into the future. The implication of this is that there is never uncertainty or risk associated with any project since all outcomes are known.

**Satisficing**: An alternative to a maximising policy, where the individual or organisation attempts to satisfy the needs or requirements of different stakeholders in the best combination of required results.

## READING

Baumol, W J (1959) *Business Behaviour, Value and Growth*, Macmillan, New York.
*The first publication of Baumol's sales revenue-maximisation model.*

Charkham, J (1995) 'Executive pay – a practical solution', *Financial Times*, Personal view, 6 February, p 19.

Cyert, R M and March, J G (1963) *A Behavioural Theory of the Firm*, Prentice Hall, Upper Saddle River, NJ.

Fisher, A (1995) 'BMW reaffirms commitment to Rover', *Financial Times*, International Company News, 13 September, p 29.

Griffiths, A and Wall, S (1995) *Applied Economics*, 6th edn, Longman, Harlow.
*Chapter 3 provides an overview of the alternatives to profit maximisation, including details of the study by Shipley and consideration of not-for-profit organisations.*

Houlder, V (1995) 'Cash may be root of success', *Financial Times*, Survey of Management Consultancy (7), 12 September, p III.

Koutsoyannis, A (1993) *Microeconomics*, Macmillan, Basingstoke.
*Contains a complete section dedicated to the managerial and behavioural theories of the firm; very detailed in parts, but also very readable.*

March, J G and Simon, H A (1958) *Organisations*, Wiley, New York.

Marris, R (1963) 'A model of managerial enterprise', *Quarterly Journal of Economics*, Vol 77, May, pp 185–209.
*An exposition of the growth rate model.*

Morse, L (1995) 'Caterpillar plans to buy back 20m shares and raise dividend', *Financial Times*, International Company News, 8 June, p 33.

Reekie, W D, Allen, D E and Crook, J N (1993) *The Economics of Modern Business*, 2nd edn, Blackwell, Oxford.
*Chapter 1 includes a discussion of the profit-maximisation objective with reference to businesses operating in the real world.*

Ridding, R (1995) 'More fuel needed for recovery', *Financial Times*, 18 September, p 16.

Williamson, O E (1991) 'Strategizing, economising and economic organization', *Strategic Management Journal*, 12, pp 75–94.

**Further reading**
It is difficult to recommend general references which are specifically concerned with this topic. Those interested in further reading should consult the bibliographies and references in the texts and articles noted above.

# PART 2

# DEMAND, REVENUE AND COSTS

CHAPTER 5

# CONSUMER BEHAVIOUR

## OBJECTIVES

◆ To consider the various theories that have been put forward to explain consumer demand.

◆ To show how indifference curve analysis can explain the shape of consumer demand curves.

◆ To develop the theory of utility, showing its relationship to indifference curve analysis and to the shape of the demand curve.

◆ To examine the characteristics approach to demand showing its relationship to other theories of demand, as well as providing an alternative framework for the way consumers consider products.

◆ To understand the concept of diminishing marginal utility and its relationship to the marginal rate of substitution.

◆ To identify the arguments between neoclassical economists and behaviourists as the basis for consumer behaviour.

## BUSINESS APPLICATION

FT

# When it comes to the crunch

'That really annoys me! That's the third Walkers' truck I've seen in 35 minutes!' Truck-spotting is but a sideshow in the global strategic duel raging between United Biscuits (UB) and PepsiCo, Walkers Snack Foods' parent. PepsiCo wants to dominate the world's savoury snacks business; UB more modestly wants to make money in as many countries as possible.

Quite how UB makes a living in PepsiCo's shadow is a pressing issue. At the moment PepsiCo has caused UB to leave its home market, the US, and is intensifying pressure on UB across Europe, particularly in the UK.

Walkers is now the indisputable leader in UK standard crisps, it has become PepsiCo's largest foreign earner in food or soft drinks and has set its sights on the broader salty snack market.

Most crisp products have traditionally been sold on price. Yet Walkers, focusing on high quality and value-for-money, gives only a set volume discount and makes no own-label alternatives. It has poured cost savings into advertising and product development to stimulate consumer demand.

The strategy is hurting UB. The British owned company has tried to escape from the fray in standard crisps by moving upmarket into fancy flavours and textures with more expensive brands such as Phileas Fogg, McCoy's and Brannigans. Yet while Walkers' standard crisps are profitably growing volume at nearly 20 per cent a year, UB's upmarket crisp sales are flat.

Walkers has also improved the quality, particularly freshness – a fact noted by consumers – and this has helped increase sales. UB says others have closed the quality gap but admits the perception of Walkers' superiority lingers in some consumer minds.

Even though the prices are higher for Walkers' crisps, Walkers' goals for the next five years are to double its retail shelf space and output without adding another plant. It also intends to cut delivery times from 48 hours to eight. Taking sales from competitors will help build volume but most growth will come from expansion of the snack category through product innovation and a better value-for-money proposition for consumers.

*Source: Financial Times, 5 February 1996. Reprinted with permission.*

**Comment**

Often lying behind the desire to purchase one commodity or another lies price. In economics it is usually assumed that the greater the price the lower the quantity demanded. This relationship will be derived in this chapter. However, the crisp industry case indicates that Walkers are very successful even when its product is priced above that which is charged by its competitors. Moreover, PepsiCo/Walkers has noticed that it has a product whose characteristics appear to come closer to those demanded by the consumer, such as freshness. As we shall see later in this chapter, it is possible that consumers are more alert to the characteristics of the product and demand products which best fit their own preferred characteristics space.

# INTRODUCTION

The concept of demand seems very easy at first glance. Most businesspeople and consumers would recognise the fact that as prices are increased (lowered) quantity demanded will fall (rise). The theories developed in this chapter provide an understanding of why the relationship between price and quantity exists, and therefore a foundation for the development of demand theory in Chapter 6.

The theory of consumer behaviour flows directly from the idea of constrained maximisation. In other words, consumers often have insatiable desires for goods and services but are constrained in their purchasing behaviour by their income. Using the language of economics, the maximisation of consumer satisfaction is constrained by a budget constraint.

In developing this approach to consumer behaviour a number of tools need to be introduced. One of these is the **indifference curve**, which shows combinations of goods (bundles), each of which provides the consumer with the same level of satisfaction. Consumers can, and do, purchase a great many items and to pursue this analysis properly requires a diagram drawn in *n*-dimensional space. However, the main principles can be explained in a two-good (bundle) framework. Once an indifference curve has been constructed, a **budget line** can then be superimposed on the same diagram, from which a visual approach to the maximisation of satisfaction subject to a budget constraint can be developed.

It is sometimes assumed that individuals have insatiable wants, but is this the case? It is more likely that the consumer has a preferred bundle and the further away the consumer is from that bundle of goods the worse off he or she is. This preferred bundle is a satiation point or **bliss point**. That is, it is possible to have too little or too much of both goods. In this case too much of one of the goods takes individuals away from their bliss point and it is possible to return to the bliss point by reducing the consumption of that good. For example, suppose the products are cream cakes and chocolate. There may be some optimal bundle of the two goods that any individual would want to consume in each period. Any less than that would make the individual worse off, any more would also make the individual worse off.

The **characteristics approach** to consumer choice considers goods in terms of the characteristics they provide. For example, when purchasing a breakfast cereal consumers are not only considering the price, but also the characteristics of the product such as sweetness, healthiness, fibre content, amount of fruit etc. The characteristics approach provides an alternative insight into the development of consumer behaviour and provides managers with a tool which is much closer to the approach adopted from a marketing perspective. It also provides managers with information about where the gaps are in the market. Identifying where these gaps exist or which characteristics are most favoured encourages firms to brand their products, learn how to reposition their goods in the market and use other marketing tools to encourage consumer purchase.

The chapter finishes with a brief consideration of behaviourist views of consumer behaviour.

By the end of this chapter the reader should be in a position to understand why consumers make the decisions they do. Once this is known, the theory of demand can be developed further and sufficient information can then be provided to help managers in the forecasting of demand and their need for resources.

# THE THEORY BEHIND CONSUMER BEHAVIOUR

In Chapter 6 we develop the theory of demand, although many people seem to think the concept of demand is straightforward. At a particular price consumers are willing to purchase a certain quantity of a good (product). If the price of this commodity is reduced, all other factors remaining constant, then it would normally be expected that a greater quantity of the good would be purchased. This process can be seen in action many, many times during any day. So why is it that when the price of a commodity falls there is an increase in the quantity demanded, and is this always the case?

It is always possible to put forward the case that the relationship is self-evident and does not require any further investigation, yet such an approach would leave the investigator in the position of seeing – to use an alternative example – that when it is cloudy it often rains. The correlation between clouds and rain is likely to be high, but this does not provide the investigator with the answer: why does it rain when it is cloudy? If the relationship between price and quantity demanded is left to the obvious, then any relationship, in this case the demand curve, does not have any theoretical underpinnings. In fact, the discussion of the underpinnings to consumer theory throws up some of the most important concepts in economic analysis.

## INDIFFERENCE CURVE ANALYSIS

A useful starting point for indifference curve analysis is to consider the consumer or household and the way in which they distribute/allocate their income between commodities. Consumers are assumed to seek to maximise the level of satisfaction which they can secure from the consumption of goods and services. The maximisation of satisfaction is subject to an income constraint. In other words, the consumer or household cannot spend more than their income.

Initially it will be assumed that consumers are rational in their choice of commodities which give them particular levels of satisfaction. This means that they can decide between one collection (econ-omists call this a bundle) of goods compared with another and can also tell whether they are indifferent between one bundle of goods compared with another. A bundle is a group of commodities; each bundle can be made up from the same commodities but in different proportions.

Economists usually make a number of assumptions about the consistency of consumers' preferences. These assumptions or axioms, since they are so fundamental, include the axiom of 'completeness', that is, any two consumption bundles can be compared. Here given any two bundles – A and B – then either $(A_1, A_2) > (B_1, B_2)$ or $(B_1, B_2) > (A_1, A_2)$ or both, in which case the individual is indifferent between the two bundles. Secondly, there is the axiom of 'reflexivity'. That is, any bundle is at least as good as an identical bundle. Thirdly, there is the axiom of 'transitivity'. If the consumer prefers bundle A to bundle B, and bundle B is preferred to bundle C, then bundle A is preferred to bundle C. Without the idea of transitivity there would be no best bundle set.

Finally, for any bundle or good, consumers are assumed to prefer more of the bundle or good to less.

The bundles between which a consumer is choosing can be assembled from a range of commodities, but it is possible to undertake the same level of analysis by using a bundle that is made up of two commodities. Here different bundles will contain the two commodities but in different proportions. Suppose the two commodities are jeans and compact discs (CDs). If the consumer or household believes that three pairs of jeans and five CDs holds the same level of satisfaction as four pairs of jeans and four CDs, then the household is said to be indifferent between the two commodity bundles. In this case we could place both bundles on the same indifference curve. The indifference curve is a line on a graph which represents combinations of two products which give the same level of satisfaction to the consumer or household. Figure 5.1 shows indifference curve for jeans and CDs.

Why is the indifference curve this shape? Its shape is related first to the type of commodity which is in the consumption bundle. If it is assumed that both commodities, jeans and CDs, are 'goods' rather than 'bads', that is, the commodities are products from which the consumer gets satisfaction, then if the consumer has less of one good they would require more of the other

**Figure 5.1 An indifference curve**

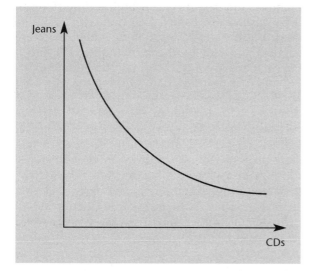

This shows an indifference curve for two commodities, jeans and CDs. The consumer is indifferent between all combinations of jeans and CDs. Each combination provides the consumer with the same level of satisfaction. The indifference curve is convex to the origin.

**Table 5.1 Total and marginal utility derived from the consumption of drinks**

| Number of drinks (D) | Total utility (TU) | Marginal utility = Change in total utility/Change in quantity of drinks = TU/D |
|---|---|---|
| 0 | 0 | – |
| 1 | 5 | 5 |
| 2 | 9 | 4 |
| 3 | 12 | 3 |
| 4 | 14 | 2 |
| 5 | 15 | 1 |
| 6 | 15 | 0 |

good to compensate for their loss. In this case the indifference curve would slope downwards from left to right.

Why does the indifference curve become flatter as the consumer or household moves along it from left to right? The explanation for this lies in the satisfaction or utility that a consumer gains from consuming an item. The more of an item consumed the greater the level of total satisfaction achieved by the consumer. Yet each extra unit of the commodity consumed, although increasing total satisfaction or utility, increases it at a diminishing rate. An example might make this clearer. On a hot day where an individual is thirsty, the first drink will give a great amount of satisfaction. The second drink may increase total consumer satisfaction, but when compared with the first drink does not provide the same level of satisfaction. The extra satisfaction (utility) that a consumer achieves by consuming an additional unit of the commodity is called **marginal utility**. Therefore, as extra units of a good are consumed *total utility may rise but at a diminishing rate*. That is, marginal utility falls as consumption increases; *see* Table 5.1. In terms of satisfaction the individual is more and more loath to give up one commodity in place of additional units of another.

Now go back to Figure 5.1. The movement around and down this indifference curve to the right means that the consumer is giving up jeans and consuming more CDs. That is, each bundle of jeans and CDs is made up of less jeans and more CDs as the consumer moves from left to right along the indifference curve. Continuing the movement to the right on this indifference curve, the consumer is being asked to give up more and more jeans and replace them in the consumption bundle by more and more CDs. However, as more CDs are consumed there is a diminishing **marginal rate of substitution** of jeans for CDs. Thus to give up jeans, for which the marginal utility must be rising as fewer are being consumed, requires a greater and greater quantity of CDs to be exchanged in the consumption bundle. This must be the case since the consumption of CDs is giving the consumer diminishing marginal utility. Therefore the indifference curve becomes very flat as the consumer moves down from left to right. It follows that, because there are fewer and fewer jeans being given up for additional units of CDs, there is a diminishing marginal rate of substitution of jeans for CDs. Similarly, the indifference curve becomes very steep as the consumer moves along it, upwards and to the left. An indifference curve as shown in Figure 5.1 is said to be convex to the origin.

The shape of the indifference curve in Figure 5.1 may be appropriate for many products, but for products such as cigarettes or alcohol there may be a sudden switch from positive to negative marginal utility.

Indifference curves have a number of other properties. Higher indifference curves are preferred to lower indifference curves since it has been assumed that the consumer, who is trying to maximise satisfaction or utility, will always prefer

**Figure 5.2 An indifference map**

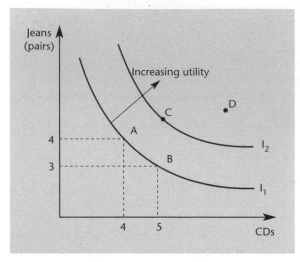

Here the consumer is indifferent between consuming a consumption bundle of four pairs of jeans and four CDs, and a bundle which consists of three pairs of jeans and five CDs. Indifference curves drawn further to the right provide consumer with greater satisfaction/utility. A series of difference curves is called an indifference map. Given the shape of the indifference curves, consumers would seek to be on the highest of these curves.

more of any consumption bundle to less. For example, in Figure 5.2 the original indifference curve has been constructed with the two combinations of jeans and CDs specified earlier, therefore points A and B lie on the same indifference curve. But what about point C? The consumption bundle, C, embodies more CDs and more jeans. It would obviously be preferred to points A and B and therefore will not lie on the same indifference curve as A and B. Thus point C must lie on a higher indifference curve, shown as $I_2$ in Figure 5.2. Using this argument, point D must lie on an indifference curve even further out to the right. Figure 5.2, therefore, shows a number of indifference curves, all of the same shape, moving out from left to right. Although there are gaps between the indifference curves drawn in Figure 5.2, in reality many other indifference curves lie between $I_1$ and $I_2$. In fact, if all these were drawn in they would fill in the space between $I_1$ and $I_2$. If a diagram is constructed with a number of indifference curves, it is called an **indifference map**.

All indifference curves slope downward from left to right and therefore have a negative slope. A further assumption of indifference curves is that they do not meet or intersect. Proof of this can be seen in Appendix 5.1.

## ◆ CASE STUDY 5.1

# The shape of trade union indifference curves

Many economists have begun to treat the preferences of trade unions between wages and employment in the same way as consumers choose between two commodities. Figure 5.3 illustrates the choice that trade unions need to make.

Lower wage levels will need to be compensated for by higher levels of employment. Combinations of employment and wages on indifference curve $I_2$ will be preferred to combinations on indifference curve $I_1$. The shape of these indifference curves will be dependent on the relative weight given by trade unions to wages and employment. A trade union whose dominant goal is higher wages will have a fairly flat indifference curve because compensating for a small reduction in wages would require a large increase in employment. Conversely, a trade union whose primary goal is employment would have indifference curves which were fairly steep. This may give economists some theoretical perspective on the shape of trade union indifference curves, but what shape do quantitative and qualitative data suggest? In a study by Clark and Oswald (1993), trade union leaders in the UK were asked about the primary goals of their trade

**Figure 5.3**

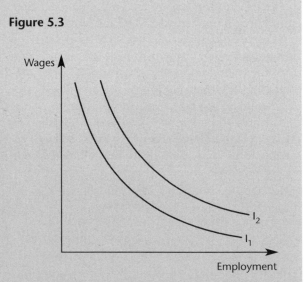

For trade unions lower wage levels need to be compensated for by higher levels of employment. Indifference curve $I_2$ is preferred to indifference curve $I_1$, since the former permits the trade union to obtain more of both wages and employment.

union. The results indicated that 60 per cent of trade union bosses felt that wage increases were preferred compared with 32 per cent who preferred increases in employment. If these results are to be believed, then the indifference curve that dominates trade union behaviour is fairly flat.

The results of the work by Clark and Oswald can be criticised, however. First, it has been developed from a study of the leaders of trade unions and these leaders could be somewhat detached about the behaviour of their own trade unions at branch level. Second, when responding to questions about their behaviour, trade union leaders may provide the answers that they believe the questioner wishes to elicit rather than giving a true picture of their behaviour. Finally, Clark and Oswald's study, undertaken in the late 1980s, may not be representative of trade union behaviour in the UK today.

*Source*: Authors.

---

### ◆ Exercise 5.1

Do you consider that achieving higher wages is still the goal of trade unions during the 1990s? Do you believe that the goals of trade unions differ between different European countries?

Construct the 'fairly flat' and 'fairly steep' indifference curves discussed in the case study. What might be the other goals of trade unions? What might be the shape of these indifference curves?

## The slope of the indifference curve

The indifference curves shown in Figure 5.2 have negative slopes. Figure 5.4 takes one of these indifference curves on which lie two consumption bundles, S and T. The slope of the indifference curve is called the **marginal rate of substitution (MRS)** between the two commodities. The MRS is, therefore, the amount of jeans that the consumer would have to give up in consuming an additional unit of CDs.

In Figure 5.4 the change in the quantity of jeans as the consumer moves round the indifference curve from S to T is shown by $\Delta J$. Similarly, the one-unit increase in CDs is shown by $\Delta C$. Mathematically this is written as:

$$MRS = -\Delta J / \Delta C$$

As the consumer moves down the indifference curve the MRS decreases. In other words, the consumer is willing to give up fewer and fewer units of jeans for a one-unit increase in CDs.

## The budget constraint

Consumers who are attempting to maximise their level of satisfaction or utility would like to consume

**Figure 5.4 The slope of the indifference curve – marginal rate of substitution (MRS)**

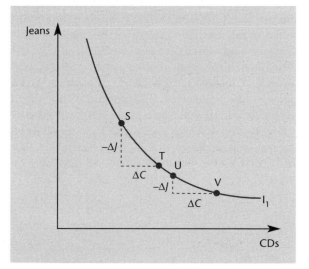

Moving round an indifference curve from S to T requires the substitution of CDs for jeans. We give up $\Delta J$ of jeans and consume more of $\Delta C$ of CDs. The slope of the line joining S to T is given by $-\Delta J/\Delta C$. This is called the marginal rate of substitution (MRS). If we move from U to V then the MRS declines the more we move to the right on the indifference curve.

more and more of the goods that make up their consumption bundles. In other words, they would like to be on the highest possible indifference curve. What prevents the consumer or household moving on to ever higher indifference curves is their income. Were it not for this constraint, the consumer or household could consume more and more goods for as long as the new bundle improved their utilities. In reality there is a limit in terms of human capacity to consume more and more of the goods in a consumption bundle – a feature noted earlier in the discussion of bliss points.

The income constraint is defined as the total income or wealth which the consumer or household is able to spend on goods and services in any one period. Mathematically the income constraint looks as follows:

$$Y = P_jJ + P_{cd}C \qquad (5.1)$$

where:   $Y$ = consumer's income
$P_j$ = price of jeans
$P_{cd}$ = price of CDs
$J$ = quantity of jeans
$C$ = quantity of CDs

Suppose in a given time period the consumer's income is £160, the price of jeans £40 per pair and the price of CDs £10 each. The budget constraint can now be used to determine the combinations that the consumer can just afford. It allows the consumer to spend all their income if they so wish on either jeans or CDs. Using the prices given above, the consumer could choose to spend all their income on jeans and in so doing would purchase 4 pairs of jeans and no CDs. Alternatively, the individual could spend all their income on CDs and in so doing would purchase 16 CDs and no jeans, Figure 5.5 shows this expenditure pattern.

**Figure 5.5  The budget line**

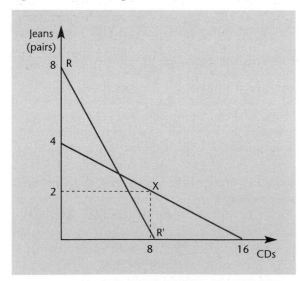

A budget line shows all the combinations of jeans and CDs which exhaust the consumer's income. When income is £160, the price of jeans £40 and price of CDs £10, then the consumer can spend all their income on jeans, purchasing 4 pairs of jeans or all on CDs, purchasing 16 CDs. Point X shows one combination of jeans and CDs which exhaust the consumer's income. Changes in the price of both goods alter the slope of the budget line, as shown by budget line RR'.

There will be other combinations of jeans and CDs which the consumer can buy which also exhausts income. In Figure 5.5, one such combination is X, which is a consumption bundle made up of 2 pairs of jeans and 8 CDs. By plotting all the possible combinations of jeans and CDs that can be purchased which just exhaust the consumer's income, the consumer's **budget line** can be constructed. Notice that if the prices of jeans and CDs are altered but the consumer's income remains constant, the budget line changes its slope. For example, suppose the price of jeans falls to £20 per pair and the price of CDs increases to £20: the new budget line is shown as RR' in Figure 5.5. The position of the budget line depends, therefore, on the relative prices of the two commodities and the level of income.

It is also possible to find the equation of the budget line. Equation 5.1 can be rewritten as:

$$P_jJ = Y - P_{cd}C$$

Dividing both sides by $P_j$ gives:

$$J = Y/P_j - (P_{cd}/P_j)C \qquad (5.2)$$

which is a straight-line equation of the form $Y = mX + C$ where $Y$ is the variable on the vertical axis, $X$ is the variable on the horizontal axis, $C$ is the intercept term and $m$ is the slope of the straight line that relates $Y$ to $X$.

In terms of Equation 5.2 and bearing in mind the budget line in Figure 5.5, $J$ is on the vertical axis, the intercept term on the vertical axis is $Y/P_j$, $C$ is the variable on the horizontal axis and the slope of the budget line is $-(P_{cd}/P_j)$.

The budget line shows the combinations of goods that the consumer could purchase with their monetary income. Its position depends on the prices of the two commodities and the total amount of income received by the consumer. The indifference curve developed earlier shows all the combinations of the two goods that give equal satisfaction to the consumer. In other words, the consumer who wishes to maximise their level of satisfaction will choose to be on the highest indifference curve possible in relation to their budget constraint. This is shown as Figure 5.6.

In Figure 5.6 there are also two other indifference curves, $I_0$ and $I_2$ with consumption bundles Y and Z attached to them, respectively. Given the assumptions made about indifference curves and consumer behaviour, consumers would not choose to be at point Y, even though it is available

**Figure 5.6 Consumer's equilibrium**

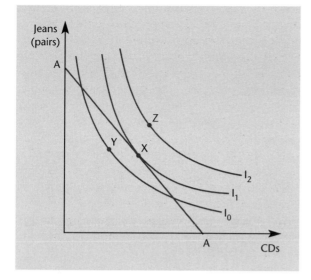

Given an initial budget, the consumer will seek to be on their highest indifference curve. This is shown as point *X* on indifference curve $I_1$. Although consumers may wish to be on indifference curve $I_2$, say at *Z*, they do not have the income to reach this difference curve.

to them with their current monetary income, since with budget line AA consumption bundle X is available on a higher indifference curve. Consumers may like to have consumption bundle Z since this is on an even higher indifference curve compared with X. However, given the current budget constraint faced by the consumer, indifference curve $I_2$ cannot be reached.

## Shifting the budget line

The equation of the budget line (Equation 5.2) indicates that if either the consumer's income, $Y$, or the price ratio, $P_{cd}/P_j$, changes, then the position of the budget line alters. The variable 'income' is in the intercept term of the budget line equation, thus changes in consumers' income will cause parallel shifts in the budget line but no change in its slope. If the price of CDs is altered, then only the slope of the budget line changes. However, Equation 5.2 indicates that a change in the price of jeans, $P_j$, will affect both the slope of the line and the intercept on the vertical axis of the budget line. These three cases can be viewed more easily with a simple example.

Suppose the consumer's budget (income) is £108, the price of a CD is £12 and the price of a pair of jeans is £27. If the consumer spends all their income on CDs, 9 CDs can be purchased. If the consumer spends all their income on purchasing jeans, 4 pairs can be purchased. In terms of Equation 5.2, $Y/P_j$ equals 108/27 or 4. The slope of the budget line, shown by $-(P_{cd}/P_j)$, equals $-(12/27)$ or $-(4/9)$. The slope and intercept obtained from these calculations are shown in Figure 5.7(a).

Suppose consumer's income is doubled to £216 while the prices of jeans and CDs remain constant. If the consumer wished to spend the whole of this income on jeans, then it is possible to purchase 8 pairs of jeans. If the whole of this income was spent on CDs, 18 CDs would be purchased. Therefore, doubling consumer income leads to a

**Figure 5.7 Shifting the budget line**

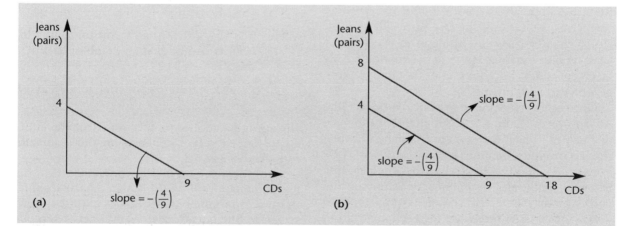

With a given income of £108 and price of jeans £27 and CDs £12, the slope of the budget line is $-(P_{CD}/P_j)$, or $-(4/9)$. Changes in income, therefore, do not affect the slope of the

budget line. An increase in income leads to a parallel outward shift of the budget line, as shown in **(b)**.

**Figure 5.8 Changing the slope of the budget line**

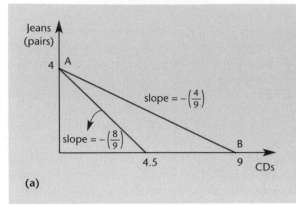

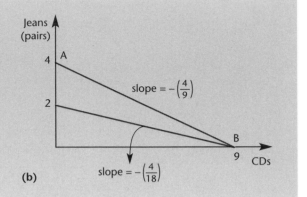

**(a)** An increase in the price of CDs from £12 to £24 causes the budget line to become steeper with respect to jeans, pivoting at A inwards towards the origin.

**(b)** An increase in the price of jeans leads to a pivoting of the budget line at B, inwards towards the origin. The slope changes from –(4.9) to –(4/18).

twofold increase in quantity of jeans purchased if all the income is spent on jeans, and a twofold increase in the amount of CDs that can be bought if all the income is spent on CDs. Since there has been no change in the price of either a pair of jeans or a CD, the price ratio remains constant and therefore so does the slope of the budget line. In this case, therefore, a doubling of consumer income leads to a parallel shift of the budget line out to the right, as Figure 5.7b indicates.

Instead of an increase in income, suppose the prices of the two goods alter. Returning to the example of jeans and CDs, if the consumer's income is £108, the price of a pair of jeans is £27 and the price of a CD is £12, suppose now that the price of CDs increases to £24 with the price of jeans remaining constant. Figure 5.8(a) indicates that the slope of the budget line has become steeper as the ratio of the two prices alters from –(4/9) to –(8/9). Because there is no $P_{cd}$ (price of CDs) term in the intercept term of Equation 5.2, its intercept does not alter and the budget line becomes steeper, pivoting at A.

Once again returning to the original budget line AB, shown in Figure 5.8(a), suppose that the price of a pair of jeans is increased to £54 per pair, while the consumer's income and the price of CDs remain constant. This time the budget line becomes flatter and the intercept changes on the vertical axis. The slope changes from –(4/9) to –(4/18), and the intercept term changes from (108/27) to (108/54). These two changes are shown in Figure 5.8(b).

Before proceeding with the analysis of indifference curves, it is worthwhile investigating the

concept of utility, which has been used interchangeably with the concept of consumer satisfaction earlier in this chapter.

## UTILITY THEORY

A useful starting point in the discussion of utility is the concept of the **utility function**. A utility function describes an individual's perception of the level of utility that can be attained from consuming every imaginable bundle of commodities available. Using the same approach adopted for indifference curve analysis, if there are assumed to be two commodities, S and R, the consumer's utility function would look like the following:

$$U = f(S,R)$$

where, $U$ is the utility that a consumer obtains from consuming each combination of $R$ and $S$

$S$ and $R$ are the amounts of goods $S$ and $R$ consumed

The utility function says, therefore, that the utility a consumer receives depends on the quantities consumed of $S$ and $R$.

Since there is a myriad of combinations of the two commodities, $S$ and $R$, assigning actual values to these is impossible. All that is required, however, is to find out whether a consumer prefers one bundle of goods over another. For example, the consumer may prefer 40$S$ and 30$R$ to 20$S$ and 35$R$. In this case the utility derived from the first combination is greater than the utility derived from the second. Here, it is not necessary to get actual figures for each of the utilities, it is sufficient to know that one utility value is greater than another.

If consumers are in a position to make judgements about the utility given by different bundles of the two commodities, then consumers must have complete information concerning their consumption decision. This means that the consumer must know the capacity of each good to provide utility, the price of each good and the income received by the consumer over the period in question. What is being hypothesised here is the concept of perfect information. Some people consider that this assumption is an abstraction from reality. Nonetheless, once a model is built under very rigid assumptions which aids the investigator in the understanding of a theoretical situation, it is possible to relax various assumptions to move closer to the 'real world' situation.

In addition to the assumption of perfect knowledge and perfect information, utility theory assumes that individuals are in a position to rank all conceivable bundles of commodities on the basis of the utility which each of these bundles provides.

## Marginal utility and the marginal rate of substitution

**Marginal utility** is defined as the increase in total utility that a consumer achieves by consuming one extra unit of a commodity while the amounts of all other goods remain constant. This concept was seen earlier in this chapter. In particular, the concept of diminishing marginal utility is important. Consuming more and more of one good while the amounts of other goods are held constant increases total utility but at a diminishing rate. That is, the marginal utility from consuming an additional unit of a commodity declines. In other words, the consumer faces diminishing marginal utility from consuming an additional item of the commodity.

While it is true that some economists contend that marginal utility theory serves no great purpose since total utility cannot be measured, others find the concept useful when used in conjunction with the marginal rate of substitution (MRS).

Going back to the example of jeans and CDs earlier in the chapter, it was noted that the slope of the indifference curve is called the MRS. From Figure 5.4 this is given as $-\Delta J/\Delta C$, that is:

$$MRS = -\Delta J/\Delta C = \text{the slope of the indifference curve}$$

As the consumer moves from point S to point T in Figure 5.4, they are reducing their consumption of jeans and increasing their consumption of CDs. Remember, too, that the total utility obtained from consuming these two different bundles of CDs and jeans must be the same, otherwise the two points would not lie on the same indifference curve.

The movement from S to T results in a loss in utility from consuming fewer pairs of jeans. This can be equal to the marginal utility of jeans, $MU_{jeans}$, multiplied by the change in the quantity of jeans, $J$. Mathematically this is shown as:

$$U = -(MU_{jeans} \times \Delta J)$$

Similarly, the gain in utility in consuming more CDs as the consumer moves from S to T is shown by:

$$U = MU_{CDs} \times \Delta C$$

Because S and T lie on the same indifference curve, there will be no change in utility as the consumer moves from S to T. If there were, S and T would not lie on the same indifference curve. Therefore, the loss in utility as the consumer reduces their consumption of jeans must be matched by the gain in utility that the consumer receives from consuming more CDs. Since the indifference curve is downward sloping to the right it has a negative slope or gradient, therefore in the movement from S to T, $\Delta J$ is negative while $\Delta C$ is positive. Along an indifference curve, therefore:

$$-(MU_{jeans} \times \Delta J) + (MU_{CDs} \times \Delta C) = 0$$

This can be rearranged to give:

$$(MU_{CDs}/MU_{jeans}) = + \Delta J/\Delta C$$

where $\Delta J$ is negative.

Since the marginal rate of substitution (MRS) is the slope of the indifference curve and has been shown earlier to equal $-\Delta J/\Delta C$, the ratio of the marginal utilities of the two commodities equals the MRS. That is:

$$-(MU_{CDs}/MU_{jeans}) = MRS$$

## Utility maximisation

The development of the concept of the marginal rate of substitution, market prices, budget constraints and marginal utility theory now provides business economists with the tools to investigate utility maximisation.

## Figure 5.9 Utility maximisation

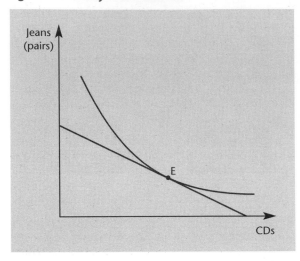

An individual will maximise their utility, subject to a budget constraint, at E. At this point, the slope of the budget line equals the slope of the indifference curve which also equals the ratio of the two goods' marginal utilities.

Figure 5.9 shows an equilibrium position for a consumer at point E. This is the highest indifference curve that the individual can reach given their current level of income. The budget line is said to be tangential to the indifference curve at E. At this point of tangency, the slope of the budget line will equal the slope of the indifference curve. It has already been established above that the slope of the indifference curve (MRS) equals the ratio of the two goods' marginal utilities. Thus at E:

> The slope of the = The slope of the
> indifference curve    budget line

or:

$$- (MU_{CDs}/MU_{jeans}) = -(P_{cd}/P_j)$$

This may be rewritten as:

$$MU_{CDs}/P_{cd} = MU_{jeans}/P_j$$

This last expression suggests that in equilibrium the marginal utility per pound spent on jeans must equal the marginal utility per pound spent on CDs.

Suppose this equilibrium condition is violated and that:

$$MU_{CDs}/P_{cd} < MU_{jeans}/P_j$$

Since the marginal utility per unit of currency from consuming pairs of jeans exceeds that of consuming CDs, the consumer could increase their utility by purchasing more pairs of jeans and fewer

CDs. As more pairs of jeans are purchased, the increase in total utility achieved rises but at a decreasing rate due to the law of diminishing marginal utility. That is, the marginal utility of jeans falls as more jeans are purchased. Similarly, as the consumer gives up consuming CDs, the marginal utility of CDs rises. Thus the inequality above eventually comes back into equilibrium, and no further changes in the consumption of CDs and jeans should be made.

This analysis has been conducted in the context of a two-unit consumption bundle. It is easily extended, however, to many commodities, although now a diagrammatic approach may not be possible. For N goods, $X_1$, $X_2$, $X_3$....$X_N$, the equilibrium condition would be:

$$MU_1/P_1 = MU_2/P_2 = MU_3/P_3 = .... = MU_N/P_N$$

It is now possible to use both indifference curve analysis and utility theory to derive the demand curve.

## Utility theory and the demand curve

Figure 5.10(a) shows a number of budget lines and indifference curves. Suppose the consumer has a level of income of £120 and the price of jeans per pair is £20 and the price of a CD is £15. If the consumer spends all their income on jeans, then 6 pairs of jeans can be purchased. Conversely, if all the income is spent on CDs then 8 CDs may be obtained. The budget line, given this income and the prices of CDs and jeans, is shown as AA. A utility-maximising consumer would choose to be at the point at which the budget line is tangential to the highest indifference curve and this is shown as point S. At S the consumer's demand is for 4 CDs and 3 pairs of jeans. In Figure 5.10(b) the relationship between the price of CDs and the quantity bought of CDs is shown. At S the consumer demand is 4 CDs at a price of £15 each: this is shown as S'.

Holding money income and the price of jeans constant, what will be the behaviour of the consumer as the price of CDs is reduced? Suppose the price of CDs is reduced to £10. There will be no change in the quantity of jeans that can be purchased if all the consumer's income is spent on jeans. Nonetheless, the slope of the budget line becomes smaller, that is flatter. It changes from –(15/20) to –(10/20). That is, the budget line pivots at A, giving a new budget line AB. B indicates the number of CDs that can be bought at the new lower

## Figure 5.10 Defining a demand curve for CDs

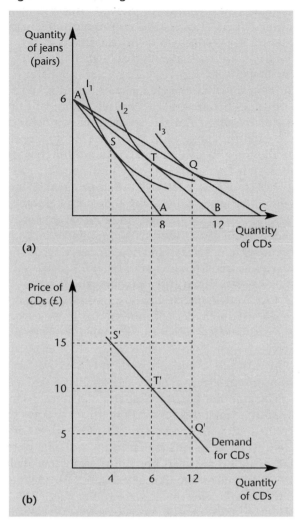

**(a)**

**(b)**

With an income level of £120, initial price of CDs £15 and price of jeans £20, the consumer faces budget line AA and chooses to be at S. Here 4 CDs are purchased at the price of £15 each, the remaining part of income being spent on jeans. This relationship between the price of CDs and the quantity of CDs purchased is shown as point S' in the lower diagram. A fall in the price of CDs leads to a pivoting of the budget line to AB and an increase in the quantity of CDs purchased to 6. This is shown as point T on the higher indifference curve $I_2$. The relationship between the price of CDs and the quantity purchased of CDs is once again, as shown in **(b)**, shown as T'. Similarly we can find point Q'. The relationship between the quantity purchased of CDs and the price gives us a demand curve for CDs.

price, assuming that money income remains constant and that no jeans are purchased: 12 CDs may now be purchased. With the new budget line AB, the consumer now maximises utility where AB is tangential to indifference curve $I_2$. This point is shown

as T, where 6 CDs are consumed. In Figure 5.10(b), the quantity of CDs of 6 units and the price £10 is shown as point T'.

It is possible to repeat the analysis for a further fall in the price of CDs, say to £5 each, and the new relationship between price and quantity of CDs consumed is shown as point Q' in Figure 5.10(b). In this diagram a relationship has been drawn which relates price of CDs to quantity demanded of CDs. This relationship is the demand curve for CDs and it has been drawn as downward sloping to the right. To draw this relationship, the level of income and the price of the other good have been held constant, an assumption that is required if a demand curve is to be constructed – *see* Chapter 6. Therefore, an individual's demand for a good can be derived from a series of utility-maximising points or points where an individual maximises satisfaction.

## Income and substitution effects

It is also possible to construct a demand curve from the substitution and income effects involved in indifference curve analysis. The substitution and income effects are based on the fact that, when the price of one good falls relative to another, consumers tend to substitute more of the cheaper good for the relatively more expensive one – the **substitution effect**.

However, if one good becomes relatively cheaper compared with other goods consumers can, if they wish, afford to buy not only more of the good whose price has been reduced but also more of the other goods in their consumption bundle. This is similar to a situation where the consumer has been given an increase in income while price levels remain constant. Therefore, a price reduction of a commodity also gives an **income effect**.

Consequently, when the price of a good changes there will be two effects, an income effect and a substitution effect. Figure 5.11 explains this in more detail.

In Figure 5.11 the consumer's initial budget constraint is shown as AA'. Given this budget constraint, the consumer attempts to reach their highest indifference curve shown as $I_1$. The point of tangency between the highest indifference curve and the consumer's budget line is shown as S. Suppose now that the price of good Y is reduced. This causes the budget line to pivot at A, giving a

### Figure 5.11 Income and substitution effects

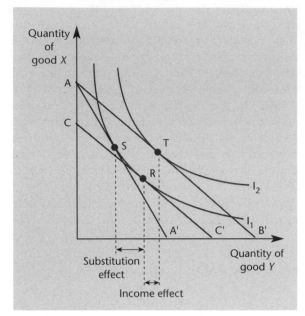

The consumer's initial budget line is AA' and, with indifference curve I₁, the consumer chooses to be at S. After a fall in the price of good Y, the consumer's budget line pivots at A to give a new budget line, AB'. The consumer can now reach a higher indifference curve, I₂, and chooses to be at T. The movement from S to T can be broken down into two effects. Moving from S to R is the substitution effect and the movement from R to T is the income effect. In Figure 5.11, both effects lead to the consumer purchasing more of good Y.

new budget line shown as AB'. This allows the consumer to move onto a higher indifference curve shown as I₂, and this higher indifference curve is tangential to the new budget line AB' at point T.

The move from S to T indicates that, after a fall in the price of Y, the consumer can purchase more of good Y and more of good X. In addition, the movement from S to T can be broken down into a substitution effect and an income effect. The way to separate these is as follows.

### Substitution effect

Starting at T, suppose just enough income is removed from the consumer to force them back to the original indifference curve I₁. Changing income leads to parallel shifts in the budget line – a fact that has been described earlier. In this case, taking income away from the consumer would lead to the consumer's budget line shifting to the left parallel to AB'. This new budget line is shown as CC'. It is tangential to indifference curve I₁ not

at S but at R. The movement from S to R around the same indifference curve is called the substitution effect. That is, the consumer substitutes towards the product whose price has fallen.

### Income effect

Suppose now that the income taken away from the consumer is restored. The budget line shifts outwards parallel from CC' to AB'. The consumer would move from R to T. This is the income effect, leading in this case to the consumer purchasing more of both X and Y.

In Figure 5.11 a fall in the price of good Y has led to consumers purchasing a greater quantity of Y, since T lies to the right of S. In other words, indifference curve analysis also provides an outcome which can lead to the construction of the demand curve. That is, a price fall leads to a greater quantity demanded of the product (good).

While the income and substitution effects described above are appropriate for most goods, the final position in which a consumer finds themselves compared with their initial position depends on the direction and size of both the income and substitution effects.

For inferior goods, as income increases the quantity demanded falls. Although these types of commodities are discussed in Chapter 6, it is sufficient to say at this stage that in the case of a price fall of an inferior good, the substitution effect will be to purchase more of that good, but the income effect is to reduce the quantity demanded. Thus, whether more of the good is demanded after a price fall depends on the relative sizes of these two effects. Figure 5.12 indicates this case.

Once again, as in Figure 5.11, it is possible to separate the movement from S to T into income and substitution effects following a fall in the price of good Y. The movement from S to R is the substitution effect found in Figure 5.11. This movement is around the same indifference curve I₁ towards consuming more of good Y. When the income is restored to the consumer, enabling them to move to budget line AB', the point at which the budget line AB' touches the highest indifference curve is shown as T. The movement from R to T is the income effect. In this case, when the income is restored to the consumer less of good Y is consumed. Good Y must be an inferior good. The substitution effect indicates a movement towards consuming more of the good for which the price has fallen relative to the other commodity. The

**Figure 5.12  Negative income effect less than substitution effect**

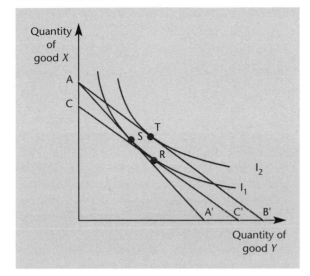

This shows the similar income and substitution effects considered in Figure 5.11. In this case the positive substitution effect towards consuming more of good Y following a fall in its price is partly reduced by a negative income effect, suggesting that good Y is an inferior good. Thus T lies between S and R.

income effect indicates a movement away from consuming good Y, since Y is an inferior good. The way these two effects have been drawn in Figure 5.12 indicates that the negative income effect does not completely outweigh the positive substitution effect towards consuming more Y. Thus a price fall still leads to more of the good being purchased.

A particular kind of inferior good is called a Giffen good, named after Sir Robert Giffen, who noted this effect with regard to the consumption pattern of potatoes during the Irish potato famine. Here a rise in the price of potatoes led to consumers purchasing more potatoes. Consequently, a fall in the price of a Giffen good leads to less of that good being purchased.

◆ **Exercise 5.2**

Using indifference curves, draw the case for a Giffen good where there is a price rise. What other goods might be termed Giffen goods? Why would knowledge of both income and substitution effects be important for producers?

◆ **CASE STUDY 5.2**

# Does cutting taxes improve the incentive to work?

During the 1980s a number of European countries cut income tax levels in response to the view that high levels of income tax acted as a disincentive to work hard. It was also felt that high tax levels acted as an incentive for some individuals not to declare their true income. In some countries the extent to which individuals fail to declare some, if not all, of their income to the tax authorities – the so-called underground economy – is quite considerable (*see* Table 5.2).

**Table 5.2  Estimates of the underground economy in Europe (% of gross domestic product)**

| France | Germany | Italy | Netherlands | Norway | Sweden | UK |
|--------|---------|-------|-------------|--------|--------|------|
| 4 | 4–24 | 6–26 | 5–22 | 6–16 | 4–17 | 2–15 |

*Source: Economie et Statistiques (1992) OECD, Paris.*

Did reductions in taxation encourage more people to offer themselves to the official labour market? Income and substitution effects may shed some light on this question.

The two commodities between which the individual is choosing are work and leisure. Figure 5.13 shows the budget line and indifference curve analysis for this aspect of the labour market.

**Figure 5.13  The income/leisure tradeoff**

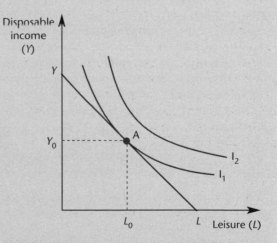

In the income/leisure model individuals trade off leisure time for income. An individual can choose to take all their hours for leisure (L) or work all hours (Y). Given this budget constraint, the individual seeks to be on their highest indifference curve. This point is shown as A on indifference curve $I_1$, where the individual takes $L_0$ amount of leisure and receives $Y_0$ income.

▶

Case study 5.2 *continued*

In Figure 5.13 the indifference curves $I_1$ and $I_2$ represent combinations of disposable income and leisure between which the individual is indifferent. The budget line represents the maximum hours of leisure, *L*, that the individual can take per period. If all the hours were worked instead, then disposable income would equal *Y*. Given this budget constraint, the individual will try to get onto their highest indifference curve and this is shown as point A.

If the government now reduces the tax rate the budget line will pivot at *L*, shifting out to the right. A lower tax rate increases the disposable income from any hours worked. But while a tax reduction unambiguously increases the income of a worker, does it lead to an increase in the number of hours worked?

To answer this question the substitution and income effects need to be considered. The tax reduction will have altered the relative price of leisure. For example, if before the tax reduction an hour of work earned the individual £7, then this is the amount of money that would be forgone if the individual took an hour of leisure. If the tax rate is reduced then an hour of leisure becomes more expensive in terms of the wages per hour of work forgone. Therefore, a reduction in the tax rate increases the price of leisure in terms of income forgone and the individual will tend to substitute away from the more expensive good, leisure. The income effect means that, with a higher disposable income following a tax reduction, the individual can effectively have more of both income and leisure than before, by working fewer hours (at a higher, post-tax rate) for a higher income (*see* Figure 5.14).

After the tax cut, the individual's budget line rotates to the right, pivoting at *L*. This is shown as budget line *LY'*. This enables the individual to move on to a higher indifference curve, shown as $I_2$. The point at which the new budget line *LY'* becomes tangential to the indifference curve $I_2$ is shown as point C. As before, the move from A to C can be broken down into a substitution effect, A to B, and an income effect, B to C. In Figure 5.14, the positive income effect for consuming

**Figure 5.14 Reduction in taxes and the income/leisure choice**

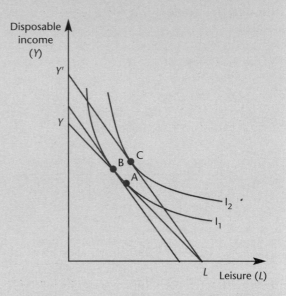

Given the original budget line *YL*, the individual maximises utility by choosing to be at *A* on indifference curve $I_1$. A reduction in tax shifts the budget line, pivoting at *L* to *LY'*. *A* to *B* is the substitution effect since the price of leisure has increased. *B* to *C* is the income effect following a reduction in taxes. Overall, the reduction in taxes in Figure 5.14 leads to an increase in leisure time taken.

more leisure outweighs the negative substitution effect away from leisure. It is theoretically possible that, far from improving the incentive to work, tax cuts may actually reduce the incentive to work. Early studies in the UK suggest that the income tax reductions of the 1980s did not lead to individuals supplying more of their hours to the labour market – *see* Cook and Healey (1995) and Brown (1988).

*Source*: Adapted from Cook, M and Healey, N M (1995), *Growth and Structural Change*, Macmillan, Basingstoke. Reprinted with permission of Macmillan Press Limited.

---

◆ **Exercise 5.3**

If income tax reductions do not lead to increases in hours worked in the labour market, why do they take place?

# REVEALED PREFERENCE THEORY

Although indifference curve analysis provides an alternative approach to the development of the demand curve to utility theory, both theories are formulated on fairly restrictive assumptions. For some people these assumptions are too confining and alternative theories have been sought to explain consumer behaviour. One of these is called the theory of revealed preference.

Once again there are a number of assumptions to consider, but some theorists argue that they are more suited to the way consumers behave in reality. The theory of revealed preference begins by looking at consumer choice. If an individual chooses alternative A over alternative B, then alternative B can never be classed above alternative A. Second, if alternative A is preferred to alternative B and alternative B is preferred to alternative C, then by iteration alternative A must be preferred to alternative C.

Given these assumptions, it is now possible to use the budget line analysis developed earlier to investigate revealed preference theory. Figure 5.15(a) shows a budget line AA' on which the consumer can select a bundle or combination of X and Y. Suppose the particular combination that is chosen is shown as W. If the price of good Y falls, then the consumer's budget line swivels outwards to the right, pivoting at A. This new budget line is shown as AB'. If the consumer now wishes to spend all their income, the new consumption bundle that will be chosen will lie somewhere

along the budget line AB'. But where along AB'? The individual could be at V, V' or some other point on AB'. In the earlier analysis of indifference curves the position of V or V' would have been developed from bringing together the income and substitution effects. However, in the case of revealed preference theory no indifference curves are present. Therefore, how can the position of V or V' be determined? Figure 5.15(b) may explain the new position of the consumer's consumption bundle.

Figure 5.15(b) reproduces the two budget lines of Figure 5.15(a), but the consumption bundle chosen by the consumer after the fall in price of good Y is taken to be V. Suppose the consumer loses sufficient income to shift the new budget line from AB' to CC'. Because CC' and AB' are parallel to one another, the ratio of the price of X to the price of Y is that which occurs after the fall in the price of good Y. As can be seen, the budget line CC' allows the original consumption bundle W to be chosen. So why will the consumer choose to be at U on budget line CC' rather than at W?

The new budget line CC' can be broken down in two sections, CW and WC' while the original budget line AA' can be divided into AW and WA'. Points on the section of the budget line AW are

## Figure 5.15  Revealed preference theory

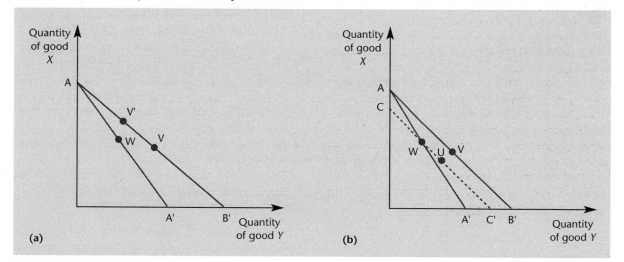

(a)

(b)

**(a)** On budget line *AA'* the individual chooses to be at *W*. A fall in the price of good *Y* leads to a rightward shift of the budget line to *AB'*, pivoting at *A*. The individual could choose to be anywhere on *AB'*, two possible points are shown, *V'* and *V*.

**(b)** This figure indicates that after a price fall in good *Y*, sufficient income is just removed so that a new budget line

CC' is obtained, drawn to go through the initial choice position of *W*. The consumer will not choose to be on *CW* of this line since originally *AW* was superior. The fall in the price of good *Y* will not lead to a fall in the consumption of good *Y*. Nonetheless, it could be at *W*. Restoring income to the consumer, and assuming *Y* to be a normal good, leads to a greater consumption of *Y*. Only if *Y* is an inferior good could *V* lie to the left of *W*.

superior to points on the section of the budget line CW. Since the consumer chose to be at point W initially, it must have been superior to all other points on AA'. In other words, W is superior to all the points on the section of the budget line AW. Since all the consumption bundles on AW are superior to all the consumption bundles on CW, it follows, therefore, that the consumption bundle *W* must be superior to all the consumption bundles on the section of the budget line CW. But what of the section WC' of the budget line CC'? Is W superior or inferior to all the points on this section of the budget line?

The consumer could have chosen point U to coincide with point W. In this case there would have been no substitution effect; the move from W(U) to V would have been an income effect only. If U lies to the right of W then there will be a combination of income and substitution effects, which are difficult to untangle. Since the price of *Y* has fallen there will be a substitution effect of the relative price fall in *Y*, and there will also be an income effect. However, there is a way forward which does not require disentangling the income and substitution effects. What is already known is that a fall in the price of *Y* will not lead to less *Y* being consumed. In this case, if *Y* is a normal good, then the income effect will be to increase the consumption of *Y*. So a fall in the price of *Y*, through the theory of revealed preference, will lead to more *Y* being consumed. In other words, the demand curve for *Y* will be downward sloping to the right. Only in the case where *Y* is an inferior good will V lie to the left of W in Figure 5.15(b).

At this stage, therefore, three theories have been developed to explain why the demand curve for most products will be downward sloping to the right. The theory of revealed preference does not require knowledge of utility maximisation, or the concept of indifference curves. Nonetheless, it does have the deficiency that the strength of the substitution effect cannot always be disentangled from the income effect.

# USING THE CHARACTERISTICS FOR DEMAND ANALYSIS

Lancaster's (1969) approach to demand concerned not only the choice consumers made between different quantities of jeans and CDs, given their current price, but the *characteristics embodied in the goods*. For example, some consumers may never consider purchasing British hi-fi equipment because it does not embody the characteristics they favour. These characteristics might be style, flexibility, quality of sound, after sales service and the like. In other words, price is an important factor in determining consumer purchases, but other characteristics of a product may be equally as important. In fact, once organisations discover which are the important characteristics favoured by the consumer, they may adapt their products to fit these and at the same time use non-price methods to bring them to the attention of the consumer. While continuing to use indifference curve analysis and utility maximisation, Lancaster developed the analysis further to claim that utility maximisation occurs not by purchasing the products themselves but from the characteristics or attributes derived from the products.

Lancaster's model is built on a number of assumptions:

- Each good will normally have more than one characteristic.
- Goods will have a mix of characteristics which will differ from one product to the next. Different products might be expected to contain similar if not identical characteristics.
- Goods which have similar characteristics, no matter how the goods are used, are possible substitutes for one another. For example, computer game consoles, home computers and compact disc players may have similar characteristics embodied in them and from a consumer's perspective the markets are not completely separate.
- Product characteristics can be measured. Car safety might be measured in terms of the number of pieces of safety equipment embodied in a car, for example air bags, door bars and anti-lock braking systems (ABS).
- Measurement of the characteristics is objective, not subjective.
- The number of products on the market exceeds the number of product characteristics allowing for competition between products.

Goods can consist of many characteristics, but it is not possible to construct diagrams which show all of these. Nonetheless, it is possible to develop the characteristics approach to demand by using products based on two characteristics.

## The two-characteristics approach to Lancaster's theory

Suppose the two main characteristics of a pair of running shoes are weight and durability. There are four pairs of running shoes which embody these characteristics, but not all in the same proportion. Figure 5.16 shows these four brands drawn in the characteristic space of weight against durability.

The four brands of running shoes are shown as $S_1$, $S_2$, ...$S_4$. Each of these running shoes embodies the characteristics of weight and durability in different proportions. For example, $S_1$ has more of the characteristic weight embodied in it than durability, while running shoe $S_4$ embodies more of durability than weight.

Within the characteristic space of Figure 5.16 there will be an indifference map, where each indifference curve shows combinations of weight and durability that give the consumer equal levels of utility or satisfaction. The consumer will attempt to reach their highest indifference curve. The constraint that is in operation once again is the consumer's income and the prices of the individual brands of running shoes. Suppose the price of each pair of running shoes is different, then with a given income the individual could purchase A of $S_1$, B of $S_2$, C of $S_3$ and D of $S_4$. These amounts are shown in relative terms along the rays for each of the running shoes in Figure 5.16. If the points A, B, C and D are joined together, then this acts as the income constraint line for the consumer. If the consumer's indifference map is now transposed onto Figure 5.16, the consumer will choose to be at B, which is the point on the highest indifference curve, $I_2$, given the current budget constraint.

## Figure 5.16 The two-characteristics space

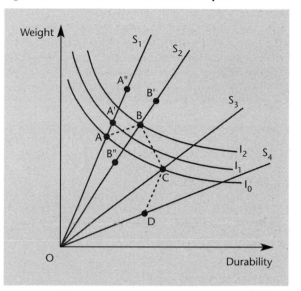

Four brands of running shoes each have different combinations of the two characteristics, weight and durability. $S_1$ has more of the characteristic weight than other shoes, while $S_4$ has more of the characteristic durability. At original price levels the consumer could purchase A of $S_1$, B of brand $S_2$, C of $S_3$ and D of brand $S_4$. The consumer will choose to have brand $S_2$ since B lies on the higher indifference curve, $I_2$. Price reductions in brands lead to movements out along any ray. The price reduction in brand $S_1$ allows the consumer to purchase A' of brand $S_1$. The consumer will still choose brand $S_2$ since B lies on the higher indifference curve. If the price of brand $S_1$ falls so that A" can be purchased, the consumer will shift from B to A".

## ◆ CASE STUDY 5.3

# The market for people carriers

There has been growing interest by manufacturers such as Renault and Mitsubishi in satisfying the demand for people carriers, cars with more than the normal five seats. In June 1995 there were ten different people carriers available to UK consumers. These people carriers, however, have different characteristics: some have a whole range of engine sizes while others are limited in the type of models that can be purchased. Others offer executive styling compared with some manufacturers who offer a more limited range of features. Pricing appears to be very competitive, thus people carriers are competing for sales more in terms of their characteristics and the way they fit the needs of the consumer. Table 5.3 indicates the range of models on offer to UK consumers.

**Table 5.3 People carriers in the UK**

| Vehicle | Price (£) | Seats | Engine (litres) |
| --- | --- | --- | --- |
| Renault Espace | 17 425–28 025 | 6 | 2.0–2.9 |
| Ford Galaxy | 15 995–21 500 | 7 | 2.0–2.8 |
| Volkswagen Sharan | 16 000–23 000 | 7 | 2.0–2.8 |
| Honda Shuttle | 22 995 | 6 | 2.2 |
| Peugeot 806 | 14 000–20 000 | 7 | 1.9–2.0 |
| Citroen Synergie | 14 000–20 000 | 8 | 1.9–2.0 |
| Fiat Ullysse | 14 000–20 000 | 7 | 1.9–2.0 |
| Toyota Previa | 18 060–26 313 | 8 | 2.4 |
| Mitsubishi Space Wagon | 15 799–16 499 | 7 | 2.0 |
| Nissan Serena | 13 415–15 995 | 8 | 1.6–2.3 |

*Source:* Sue Baker, *The Observer*, 25 June 1995, Business Section, p 12.

▶

Case study 5.3 *continued*

As one motoring journalist notes, the Ford Galaxy's larger windows give the driver the impression that they are sitting lower than in Renault's Espace. This would appeal to those drivers who do not like sitting up high when driving. Moreover, the Galaxy has style in addition to many of the characteristics of Renault's pioneering people carrier. However, the Volkswagen Sharan can easily be substituted for the Ford Galaxy. These two people carriers are clones, produced in the same Portuguese factory, but one of the Galaxy's strengths over its competitors is its wide variations of range and options. In total there are 14 versions and a range of extras including child seats, a bike rack, waterproof seat covers and a fridge. Contrast this with Honda's Shuttle. This has only a single version, but is aimed at the upper segment of the people-carrier market rather than at the wider market. Moreover, the Honda is available as an automatic only and its relatively poor range of features may not put it high on many people's characteristic lists. Thus in the people-carrier market the ten manufacturers are offering similar types of product which vary in their product characteristics.

On one level consumers have a series of demand characteristics which they are seeking. These may differ by income group, social class group, age and the like. Manufacturers supplying people carriers attempt to match their vehicle's characteristics with the different consumer focus groups.

*Source:* Authors.

◆ **Exercise 5.4**

What do you consider to be the important characteristics of people carriers? Would you expect these to differ by income/social class grouping? How could suppliers make sure that they match the characteristics of their people carriers with those demanded by consumers?

## Price changes in Lancaster's model

Returning to our example of running shoes, if the prices of each brand were to change by the same proportion, then the line ABCD in Figure 5.16 would lie either closer to the origin, for a price increase, or further away from the origin, for a price reduction – fewer units of each of the running shoes could be bought for a price increase and a larger number could be bought for a price decrease for any given level of budget. Suppose that only the price of running shoe $S_2$ decreases, allowing B' to be purchased with the current individual's income. The new budget constraint line shown in Figure 5.16 will be AB'CD and the individual will move up to B', since this must lie on a higher indifference curve.

Suppose that the price of B increases so that at the new price only B" can be purchased. Running shoe $S_2$ will now have priced itself out of the market, since both $S_1$ and $S_3$ will yield the consumer a greater level of utility. This example is not too far from the position in which running shoe manufacturers find themselves. There appear to be certain threshold prices, one of which is a price of £50 per pair. Nike's introduction of its new Air Pegasus range priced at £5 above the current market competition led to threats to the market for its best-selling running shoe as consumers switched to competitively priced shoes whose characteristics were seen to be very close substitutes for the Air Pegasus.

Returning to the budget line ABCD, suppose the price of running shoe $S_1$ decreases, allowing the consumer to purchase A' of running shoe $S_1$. A' is shown on indifference curve $I_1$. In this case the consumer will not switch from running shoe $S_2$ because B still lies on a higher indifference curve. Thus Lancaster's approach does appear to confirm the behaviour of consumers in that a price change may not lead them to switch brands. Consumers are seen, therefore, to be brand loyal in the short term. However, if prices were to continue to fall for running shoe $S_1$ so that A" was a possible consumption bundle, then the consumer would switch from running shoe $S_2$ to running shoe $S_1$. There may well be consumers who still purchase brand $S_2$ even after a subsequent fall in the price of brand $S_1$. These individuals, in their characteristics space, would still have A" on a lower indifference curve than $I_2$.

## Income changes in Lancaster's model

As with indifference curve analysis, an increase in income will shift the budget line outwards to the right and parallel to the original budget line. Conversely, a reduction in income will shift the budget line parallel inwards. If all four running shoes are viewed as normal goods, then as Figure 5.16 shows, if running shoe $S_2$ was chosen before the increase in income then running shoe $S_2$ will be chosen after the increase.

Suppose, however, that there are only three running shoes and running shoe $S_2$ is viewed as an inferior good by consumers. What is meant here is that, of the attributes that make up running shoe $S_2$, $S_2$ must contain more of the inferior attributes than at least one of the other (superior) brands. What will be the impact of an income increase now? Figure 5.17 shows the outcome.

Initially, given the individual's money income and the price of the shoes, the number of running shoes $S_1$, $S_2$, and $S_3$ that the consumer can purchase are shown as A, B, and C respectively. The consumer chooses to purchase brand $S_2$ since B lies on the highest indifference curve. After the income increase the consumer can purchase A' of brand $S_1$, B' of brand $S_2$ and C' of brand $S_3$. However, because brand $S_2$ is an inferior good the shape of the consumer's indifference curve alters to that shown in $I_1$. Here brand $S_3$ is now chosen because it lies on a higher indifference curve. The consumer must be nearing their saturation level for the attribute 'weight' and they maximise utility by reducing that in favour of an increase in the attribute 'durability'. Since $S_3$ has a higher ratio of durability to

weight, it is regarded as superior to running shoes $S_1$ and $S_2$ which are thus deemed to be inferior products.

## Gaps in the market

So far the point at which the consumer has been able to reach their highest indifference curve has been on one part of a ray for a brand. If you recall in Figure 5.16 this was at B. Suppose that a consumer reaches their highest indifference curve on the line that joins two brands at X; *see* Figure 5.18(a).

Here the consumer's indifference curve is tangential at a point on the line joining A to B. This does not correspond to any type of running shoe currently available. With running shoes there is no possibility of buying a certain amount of running shoe $S_2$ and combining it with another running shoe $S_1$! However, for commodities like soft drinks combining two commodities may be a possibility. Suppose that instead of running shoes the market in question is for soft drink, with the two characteristics being fizziness and sweetness. Figure 5.18b illustrates this case.

Once again, the highest indifference curve is reached at a point on the line that connects the two brands $B_1$ and $B_2$; this is shown as point A. In this case the consumer could obtain the product with characteristics that would make up A by combining brands $B_1$ and $B_2$ in different proportions. For example, the way in which a good with the characteristics of A could be obtained would be to combine ON of brand $B_2$ and then NA of brand $B_1$. Here, NA is parallel to OX. Alternatively, the product with characteristics that make up A can be obtained by combining OM of brand $B_1$ and MA of characteristic $B_2$. Since OMAN is a parallelogram, routes OMA and ONA offer equally attractive routes of obtaining good A which yields the highest level of satisfaction for the consumer. Of course, if producers find that such a combination yields a good with the characteristics which provide the greatest satisfaction for consumers, then they are likely to fill this gap in the market with a new product.

## Market segments

Under the characteristics approach in the soft drinks market, it is relatively easy to see that there will be some consumers who favour fizziness more than others, while other consumers will prefer sweetness. In other words, the market is becoming segmented. It is possible that a price change in

**Figure 5.17 An increase in income with an inferior attribute**

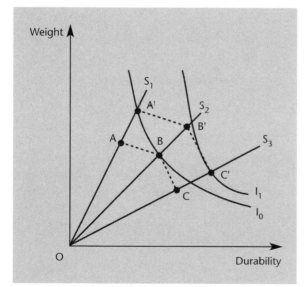

Suppose brand $S_3$ is a superior brand of running shoe compared with brands $S_1$, $S_2$. At the initial income and price levels, it is still possible that brand $S_2$ will be chosen since this lies on the highest indifference curve. An increase in income causes the shape of the indifference curve to change to $I_1$, and because $S_3$ is the superior product the consumer will switch towards consuming brand $S_3$, which now lies on the highest indifference curve $I_1$.

### Figure 5.18 Product gaps

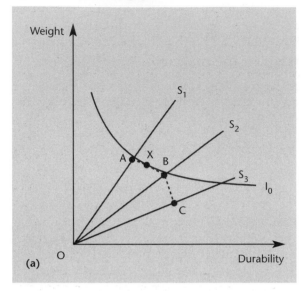

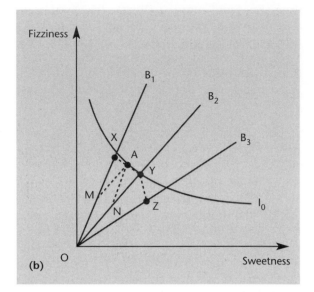

**(a)** With their current income and the prices of brands $S_1$, $S_2$ and $S_3$, the consumer's income constraint is shown as the dotted line A, B, C. It is possible that the budget (income) constraint touches the consumer's highest indifference curve, not on any of the rays but at a point between two of the rays. This point is shown as $X$ on line AB. Here there is currently a product gap in the market which would maximise consumer satisfaction.

**(b)** Point $A$, on income constraint line $XY$, is the position where the consumer would achieve greatest satisfaction. It is possible for organisations to make this brand by combining characteristics of brands $B_1$ and $B_2$. This could be ON of brand $B_2$ then NA of brand $B_1$, or OM of brand $B_1$ then MA of brand $B_2$.

brand $B_1$ in Figure 5.18b will have little effect on consumers whose preference is for products that are like brand $B_3$. If this is the case, how far can this segmentation go? The maximum number of market segments would not be expected to exceed the number of potential customers. But whether a new product will be developed depends on the distribution of consumers among the characteristics. If consumers are very close in their demands for the characteristics of a product, then market segmentation is more difficult. Conversely, if consumer preferences are widely distributed then market segmentation is possible. Market segmentation is most appealing where there are a number of clearly segmented markets, as Figure 5.19 indicates.

The market for soft drinks is clearly segmented and on this occasion the organisation needs to consider whether it should produce a range of products that satisfy all the market segments or opts for a limited range of segments.

The travel markets indicate elements of segmentation. Traditionally the market for UK citizens was primarily UK-based holidays. During the 1960s and 1970s, European holiday destinations such as France, Spain and Greece became popular. Within

### Figure 5.19 The scope for market segmentation

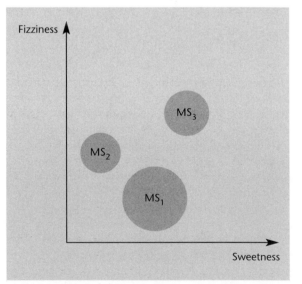

This shows a market segmented into three distinct segments. Where consumers demand very similar characteristics in their products, segmentation is more difficult. If distinct segmentation exists, then a price change in segment $MS_1$ will not cause a large shift of customers to other segments, since these do not contain the characteristics most sought by consumers in $MS_1$.

these markets there has been a further development of alternatives to beach holidays. Age plays an important part in market segmentation. Older age groups have tended to favour more cultural/non-beach holidays and higher income groups more secluded and specialist holidays, for example culinary holidays. Thus the holiday market can clearly be segmented by age, income and social class. By catering for these distinct groupings the overall holiday market has grown appreciably. However, travel firms do not often cater for all segments of the travel market, they tend to specialise in a few market areas.

This characteristics approach to demand takes demand closer to the area of marketing. The characteristics of a new product affect its rate of adoption. The speed with which a product is adopted may be related to:

- Its relative advantage over existing products.
- Its compatibility, that is, the degree to which a new product fits the values and experiences of potential customers.
- How difficult it is to understand and use.
- Its divisibility, that is, can the product be tried on a limited basis? For example, in the case of mini-discs the product requires a large investment outlay and, given the changes in technology in this area, the investment may soon become redundant.
- The degree to which the results of using a new product are communicated and described to others.

Although we know that products have different characteristics and consumers attach different degrees of importance to these characteristics, marketeers often distinguish between salient characteristics and secondary ones. The first type are those characteristics which easily come to mind, while secondary characteristics would be important if they were mentioned.

Consumers are likely to develop a set of beliefs about where each brand stands on each attribute. This set of beliefs is called the brand image. This brand image might be related to product quality, product features, product design and the like. For example, Mercedes as a brand and its attributes bring to mind characteristics such as 'well engineered', 'well built', 'durable' and 'high prestige'. Since consumers do not buy attributes but the benefits that flow from these, then the attribute, 'durable' could be translated into the benefit that a consumer will not have to buy another car for the next few years.

Figure 5.19 shows the different segments in a market. Producers need to be able to position themselves in the most attractive market. Positioning should take account of anticipated consumer preferences and the products that are offered by competitors. Producers may also wish to take account of anticipated ways in which consumer preferences might change. For example, suppose that there is expected to be a switch to consumers preferring better quality cars. Manufacturers such as BMW and Mercedes would be in a strong position to cater for this shift. In helping consumers determine the characteristics of their product, manufacturers have a whole raft of approaches. These would include the various forms of advertising, the use of appropriate distribution channels, sales promotions, packaging and design. Thus Lancaster's characteristics approach takes the concept of consumer behaviour closer to that adopted by marketers.

## Weaknesses of Lancaster's model

Some of the weaknesses that arise from Lancaster's characteristics approach to demand derive from the underlying assumptions made in developing the model. First, not all characteristics can be measured objectively, for example beauty, style etc. Second, different consumers may see the same product or brand as representing the same characteristics but in different ratios. Third, since goods have a whole range of characteristics it is important to understand how the various mixes of these lead to consumer satisfaction and how different combinations of the characteristics of a product yield more or less satisfaction.

In addition, Lancaster suggested that goods which have similar characteristics would be substitutes for one another. These goods may be different, for example cheese and beefburgers. Other experts suggest, however, that consumers make choices based on a utility tree approach, filtering out expenditure. Consumers start with the big purchases first, after which their income is divided up into different strands of expenditure. One of these strands will be food. This strand is further divided into the different types of food. Thus in the food sector there may be one strand for cheese, in which there is a choice between different types of cheese, but there will be a separate strand for the various types of beefburgers. Thus beefburgers and cheese are not really in competition with one another, even though the characteristics of the two food sectors are similar.

One further limitation is that Lancaster's approach focuses on the number of units of divisible products between which a consumer is choosing. Whereas this approach may be very suitable for non-durable goods, Lancaster's approach looks less satisfactory in explaining the choice between expensive consumer durables.

## BEHAVIOURAL PERSPECTIVES ON DECISION MAKING

The type of analysis that has been developed so far is called the neoclassical or general equilibrium approach. An alternative way to investigate consumer choice comes from behavioural economics. Here economics is combined with other disciplines such as psychology and management science. The starting point is that, before constructing simplifying models of consumer behaviour as the neoclassical approach does, analysts should study the kinds of problems that face decision makers and how they behave when confronted with them. In other words, get the facts then construct the theory. A problem with this approach is that the researcher is often armed with preconceived ideas about what facts to collect and what they should ignore.

Lying behind the behavioural perspectives of consumer behaviour is the view that minds work very much like computer programs. In other words, information is processed and followed by actions that result from working through procedures selected from menus of possible procedures, which are governed by the rules according to which the information processing has been done. Decision makers either implement their chosen procedure and then move on to further procedures for deciding what to do next, or if problems are encountered switch to other procedures.

The programs that people use for coping with decisions have various names, such as decision heuristics, rules of thumb, or recipes for success. For example, for a life insurance policy the program might be, 'get four quotes and choose the cheapest'. If the consumer's set of rules succeeds as a device for making decisions, they may fail to consider alternative decision procedures that could provide superior outcomes. As long as the approach adopted provides satisfactory results, there is no indication of a problem. In other words, in behavioural theory decision makers are satisficers.

But how do decision makers 'chunk through' the decision process? More recent work by Olshavsky and Granbois (1979) has shifted the focus from consumers using really complex decision processes to much simpler ways of choosing. In fact for really big decisions, they argue, there may be little in the way of decision processes involved because their sheer complexity may lead to severe information-processing problems. This is an extreme view of the behaviouralist approach since, at least in some areas of their life, consumers are able to express opinions about what they value or dislike and adjust these over time. In other words, they are able to make trade-offs between commodities. Here, indifference curves might be a reasonably good way of approximating consumers' attitudes towards various commodities. For the behaviouralist, indifference curves are also a possibility, but they would be drawn fairly close together, since the experience of consumers may be somewhat limited.

Normally, however, behaviouralists would try to avoid considering that consumers possess preference systems, but rather set out to obtain details of the person's system of rules that shape their satisficing activities. These behavioural theories are an interesting development of consumer choice behaviour and a useful outline of these can be found in the work of Earl (1988 and 1995).

## SUMMARY

◆ Understanding consumer behaviour, in particular in relation to changes in the price of a product, relies on more than intuition. This chapter has put forward a number of theories, such as indifference curve analysis, marginal utility theory and the characteristics approach to demand, to produce a demand curve which is downward sloping and to the right.

◆ An indifference curve represents bundles of commodities which yield the same level of satisfaction to the consumer. As indifference curves are drawn further out to the right, they give higher levels of satisfaction to the individual. A range of indifference curves is called an indifference map.

◆ Indifference curves are drawn convex to the origin and as they descend from left to right their slope becomes flatter. The slope of an indifference curve is called the marginal rate of substitution, which represents the change in quantity of one good necessary to offset a change in the consumption of another good while keeping the level of utility (satisfaction) constant.

◆ Although consumers seek to be on higher and higher indifference curves, their budget or income acts as a constraint on this process. This budget line represents all the combinations of products that can be bought with the consumer's monetary income. The consumer will therefore seek to be on the highest indifference curve which is just tangential to their budget constraint.

◆ Changes in the price of a commodity while all other prices and consumer income remain constant will lead to both an income effect and a substitution effect. When there is a reduction in the price of a commodity, the substitution effect leads to more of that product being purchased. The positive income effect leads to more of the same product being purchased so long as the product is a normal good. In the case of inferior goods, the income effect works in the opposite direction to the substitution effect.

◆ Utility theory is an alternative approach to the construction of the demand curve. A utility function describes the total utility received by the consumer from the consumption of a range of items. Utility theory relies on the fact that consumers can rank various bundles of commodities.

◆ Marginal utility theory is the change in total utility as one of the items in a consumer's consumption bundle is changed while the consumption of all other goods and services remains constant. As the consumer increases their consumption of a particular good, the marginal utility obtained from consuming the extra unit declines. This is known as the law of diminishing marginal utility.

◆ The attribute approach to consumer behaviour seeks to explain why some consumers in a given market prefer brand A to the other brands available. Some of the attributes are measurable, such as size or price, other attributes are sometimes in the eye of the beholder. Lancaster's characteristics approach, for all its weaknesses, still provides a framework for explaining the shape of the demand curve and also offers an explanation for spotting potential product gaps in the market.

## REVIEW QUESTIONS

1 Suppose that there are two individuals in Spain, one earning Pta75 000, the other not participating in the labour market. What will be the impact on the hours worked if the yearly wage is increased to Pta95 000? Use diagrams to outline your analysis.

2 Lancaster's characteristics approach to consumer theory yields results which are similar to those derived from indifference curve analysis and utility theory. Lancaster's approach can therefore be dispensed with. Discuss.

3 Consider new breakfast cereals which have been introduced over the past two years. To what extent do they fill a gap in consumer preferences?

4 You are considering taking a vacation. What characteristics or attributes do you consider to be most important? Did your last vacation fulfil these characteristics?

5 Using indifference curve analysis, show the impact of an increase in the price of a product when:
   a the product is a normal good; and
   b the product is an inferior good.

6 Construct a budget line for a consumer who has the choice between croissants and coffee, where the monetary income of the consumer is FF40, the price of croissants is FF5 and the price of coffee is FF10. In this diagram indicate the position where the budget line is just tangential to the highest indifference curve. What will be the impact on the consumer's consumption bundle of:

**a** an increase in income to FF60;

**b** an increase in the price of coffee to FF12; and

**c** a decrease in the price of croissants to FF2?

7 Assume that an individual consumes three goods, A, B and C. The marginal utility of each good is independent of the rate of consumption of the other two goods. The consumer's monetary income is £65 and the prices of the three goods, A, B and C, are £1, £3 and £5 respectively. The marginal utilities for each good are shown in Table 5.4.

**Table 5.4**

| Units | Marginal utility of A (units) | Marginal utility of B (units) | Marginal utility of C (units) |
|-------|-------------------------------|-------------------------------|-------------------------------|
| 1 | 12 | 60 | 70 |
| 2 | 11 | 55 | 60 |
| 3 | 10 | 48 | 50 |
| 4 | 9 | 40 | 40 |
| 5 | 8 | 32 | 30 |
| 6 | 7 | 24 | 25 |
| 7 | 6 | 21 | 18 |
| 8 | 5 | 18 | 10 |
| 9 | 4 | 15 | 3 |
| 10 | 3 | 12 | 1 |

**a** Given a monetary income of £65, how much of each good should the individual consume if they wish to maximise utility?

**b** Suppose that the consumer's income falls to £43 while the prices of the three goods remain constant. What combination of the three goods will the consumer choose?

# Appendix 5.1

## THE PROPERTIES OF INDIFFERENCE CURVES

Indifference curves do not intersect. Figure 5.20 indicates why this is the case. Because an indifference curve shows bundles of goods between which the consumer derives the same level of satisfaction, consumption bundle $S$ gives the individual the same level of satisfaction as consumption bundle $T$, since both lie on the same indifference curve. Consumption bundle $S$ also gives the consumer the same level of satisfaction as consumption bundle $Q$, since once again they lie on the same indifference curve. However, the consumer is indifferent between consumption bundle $Q$ and consumption bundle $R$, since they too lie on the same indifference curve, $I_0$. Nevertheless, consumption bundle $S$ is obviously superior to consumption bundle $R$, since the consumer can have more of both good $X$ and $Y$ at $S$. Thus $Q$ gives the same level of satisfaction as both $S$ and $R$, yet $S$ is superior to $R$. This cannot be the case. Therefore, indifference curves cannot intersect.

**Figure 5.20 Properties of indifference curves**

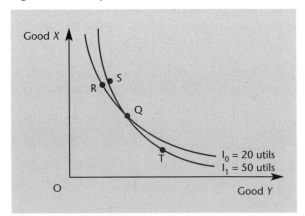

The consumer is indifferent between bundles $S$, $Q$ and $T$ since they all lie on indifference curve $I_1$. The consumer is also indifferent between bundles $R$ and $Q$. However, $S$ is preferred to $R$. Thus, how can $S$ be preferred to $R$ as well as being equal to $R$ since both $R$ and $S$ provide the same satisfaction as bundle $Q$? Indifference curves, therefore, cannot intersect.

## GLOSSARY OF NEW TERMS

**Bliss point:** The satiation point – a bundle of commodities that gives the consumer the greatest satisfaction.

**Budget line:** The different bundles of goods that can be purchased by a consumer while just exhausting their money income.

**Characteristics approach:** Instead of demanding products, consumers consider certain characteristics that a product provides when making their demand decision.

**Income effect:** The shift of a budget line following from a price change in one of the commodities that constitutes the individual's consumption bundle.

**Indifference curve:** A curve which represents different bundles of goods, all of which provide the same level of utility or satisfaction.

**Indifference map:** A set of indifference curves, which shows higher levels of satisfaction for the consumer as the indifference curves move from left to right.

**Law of demand:** This states that as the price of a product is reduced consumers usually tend to purchase a greater quantity of that product, all other factors remaining constant.

**Law of diminishing marginal utility:** As an extra unit of a good is consumed total utility rises but at a diminishing rate.

**Marginal rate of substitution:** The amount of one good that must be forgone for another good while keeping utility constant.

**Marginal utility:** The increase in total utility that arises from increasing the consumption of a good by one unit.

**Substitution effect:** The movement around the same indifference curve that follows from a price change in one of the goods.

**Utility function:** A relationship which connects total utility to the consumption of goods and services.

## READING

Baxter, J L (1993) *Behavioural Foundations of Economics*, Macmillan, Basingstoke.

Earl, P E (1988) *Lifestyle Economics*, Wheatsheaf, Brighton.

Earl, P E (1995) *Microeconomics for Business and Marketing*, Edward Elgar, Aldershot.
*These three texts illustrate many of the important discussion points about behavioural theories of consumer behaviour.*

Hicks, J D (1965) *Value and Capital*, 2nd edn, Oxford University Press, Oxford.
*This text, although probably for the more advanced student, is one of the seminal texts on consumer behaviour.*

Lancaster, K (1969) 'A new approach to consumer theory', *Journal of Political Economy*, Vol 74, pp 132–57.

Lancaster, K J (1971) *Consumer Demand: A New Approach*, Columbia University Press, New York.

Lancaster, K J (1974) *Introduction to Modern Microeconomics*, Vol 2, Rand McNally, Chicago.
*The works by Lancaster develop the characteristics approach to consumer demand in detail.*

Varian, H R (1991) *Intermediate Microeconomics: A Modern Approach*, 3rd edn, Norton, New York.

*This is one of the main theoretical texts for consumer theory, particularly Chapters 2, 3, 4, 7 and 8.*

**Further reading**

Brown, C V (1988) 'The 1988 tax cuts, work incentives and revenue', *Fiscal Studies*, Vol 9, 4, pp 93–107.

Clark, A and Oswald, A (1993) 'What shape are trade union indifference curves?', *The Economic Review*, November, pp 16–19.

Cook, M and Healey, N M (1995) *Growth and Structural Change*, Macmillan, Basingstoke.

Doyle, P and Fenwick, I (1975) 'Are goods goods?: some further evidence', *Applied Economics*, Vol 7, pp 93–8.

Firth, A (1991) 'The launch of Sky icecream', *Business Studies*, Vol 42, 3, pp 19–22.

Green, H A J (1976) *Consumer Theory*, Macmillan, London.

Olshavsky, R W and Granbois, D H (1979) 'Consumer decision making – fact or fiction?', *Journal of Consumer Research*, Vol 6, pp 93–100.

Oswald, A (1982) 'Wages, trade unions and unemployment: what can simple models tell us?', *Oxford Economic Papers*, November.

CHAPTER **6**

# DEMAND AND ELASTICITY

## KEY ISSUES

Business issues

Business strategy

Decision-making techniques

Economic concepts

Management decision issues

Optimal outcomes to management issues

## OBJECTIVES

◆ To explain the factors that affect the individual consumer's level of demand.

◆ To consider how the market demand curve can be assembled from individual demand curves.

◆ To identify the factors that affect the level of demand faced by the organisation.

◆ To understand how each of the individual independent variables in the demand function affects the quantity of demand for a good or service.

◆ To examine the ways in which the demand function can be developed in the demand equation.

◆ To consider the relationship between price, demand, marginal and total revenue.

◆ To outline the importance of demand sensitivity analysis (elasticity) to the behaviour of the organisation.

◆ To identify the factors that affect the price elasticity of demand.

◆ To develop and apply the concepts of advertising, cross-price and income elasticity to the behaviour of the organisation.

◆ To establish the arguments regarding whether there has been a global convergence of consumer tastes.

# CHAPTER OUTLINE

# KEY TERMS

Advertising elasticity

Arc elasticity of demand

Complementary goods

Cross-elasticity of demand

Cyclical normal goods

Demand function

Derived demand

Effective demand

Income elasticity of demand

Marginal revenue

Market demand curve

Non-cyclical normal goods

Price elasticity of demand

Shift in demand

# Demise of the Net Book Agreement

FT

In September 1995 the Publishers' Association decided it would no longer enforce the Net Book Agreement in the UK which for nearly 100 years had required booksellers to charge minimum retail prices for most books. Some within the book trade hoped retail price competition would stimulate demand in a market that had become relatively static. Consumer spending on books rose by only 17 per cent between 1990 and 1995, compared with an increase of 54 per cent on records, compact discs and video cassettes. The evidence on book sales since the demise of the agreement appears to give little support to such hopes. While sales of books have increased somewhat, they have not risen sufficiently to compensate for the cost of price-cutting.

The result is that three specialist bookselling chains – Books Etc, Dillons and Waterstone's – have reduced both the number of titles they are discounting and the average discount. However, the supermarket chains have become more aggressive in discounting, cutting the prices on more titles and by bigger percentages. The average list prices of the discounted titles show the supermarkets are focusing mainly on mass-market paperbacks while booksellers are cutting the prices of more expensive books.

There is little the independent booksellers can do to compete. Most have to pay more to obtain these books wholesale than the prices supermarkets are charging the customer. This might not matter if the abolition of the Net Book Agreement increased the total market. But figures published by the Office for National Statistics in March 1996 (Consumers'

Expenditure) suggest the reverse has happened. Spending on books in the first nine months of 1995 was 2.2 per cent higher (in nominal terms) than in the same period of 1994. But after the demise of the agreement, spending in the final quarter of 1995 was 6.8 per cent below the previous year. From this and other evidence, the conclusion is that the demand for books rose about 5 per cent in volume terms in the last quarter of 1995 compared with the last quarter of 1994. But the increase in volume failed to compensate for the average discount. In other words, demand was price-inelastic – a change in price has not produced a commensurate increase in sales.

This might have been expected in the short term. A study by Paul de Grauwe and Geert Gielens of Leuven University estimated price elasticity of demand in Belgium at –0.6: a 10 per cent fall in price would produce a 6 per cent increase in volume.

Studies in the UK, US and France suggest a higher figure might be expected in the longer term – price-elasticity of around –1. This would mean a 10 per cent fall in price would produce a 10 per cent increase in sales. But even this sort of elasticity may not improve profits since this would need an increase in volume greater than the reduction in prices and knowledge of the cost base. The figures so far from the book industry suggest that list prices will have to rise to make room for discounting. They also raise fears that the increased market share taken by discounters will reduce the range of titles it is profitable to publish.

*Source*: *Financial Times*, 18 June 1996. Reprinted with permission.

### Comment

Non-economists often discount economic theories as being irrelevant to solve real world problems. The case of the Net Book Agreement shows how accurate knowledge of both the price elasticity of demand and the other factors that affect demand could have alerted book suppliers and retailers to the possible consequences of abandoning the Net Book Agreement. In the light of these factors, this chapter seeks to explore both the theory of demand and the role of elasticity in decision making.

## INTRODUCTION

Knowledge of the level of demand is often central to the organising and planning of the business. If the current level of demand is not known, then making decisions on price, the use of existing resources and planning for future resource usage, the decision to undertake advertising and the eval-

uation of current advertising campaigns all become problematic and this can result in poor decision making. If demand, or its factors, can be understood, this provides managers with the chance to manipulate demand to the organisation's advantage. Since demand or quantity lies behind the calculation of revenue, demand therefore plays an important part in the determination of the level of profits once there is knowledge of the cost function faced by the organisation.

Information on demand aids short-term decision making and long-term strategic planning. Demand levels may indicate whether the organisation should continue with its current level of production and absorb any fluctuations in demand through the growth of or decline in stocks or inventories. However, demand which is seen to grow over the longer term may result in changes in the organisation's investment patterns. The level of market demand may also affect the level of competition in the market – the market structure. The existence of products for which demand is increasing and in markets for which the entry barriers are weak may well lead to other organisations entering such markets and thus changing the nature of the competition for the indigenous firms.

This chapter begins by investigating the factors that affect the individual consumer's demand for products. From this point it is possible to aggregate consumer demand to find the market demand curve for a product. Firms are particularly interested in factors important in affecting demand for their products. This chapter explores the most important factors, initially in terms of their aggregate effects by the use of a demand function, then by considering each factor individually. By examining the quantity demanded and each of the factors that affects demand separately, the assumption will be made that all other factors are held constant. This is something that is needed if the relationship between the dependent variable, quantity demanded and each of the independent variables is to be fully understood.

For an organisation it is not only important to appreciate how a dependent variable, say price, affects the quantity demanded, but also to know the magnitude of the effect. A measure of the responsiveness of one variable to another can be obtained through the concept of elasticity. The concept of elasticity is developed in the context of the impact of advertising, income and the price of related products and their effect on quantity demanded. With this knowledge at hand, organisations can have a much clearer set of guidelines about whether they should raise prices, respond to competitors' price variations or alter existing advertising campaigns.

Elasticity values also provide the organisation with information about different markets. Firms will seek out new markets where they have the chance to push up prices, achieve higher profit margins and do not face the problem of dealing with competitors. This suggests that markets are different or perhaps separate. The final part of this chapter deals with global markets and the degree to which there is convergence in tastes which therefore alters the elasticities of demand in these markets and in so doing reduces the boundaries between markets. The evidence that markets are becoming more global is not conclusive.

# FROM INDIVIDUAL TO MARKET DEMAND

In Chapter 5 extensive use was made of indifference curve analysis, revealed preference theory, marginal utility theory and the characteristics approach to demand to explain the theory behind the shape of the demand curve. These theories established that an individual's demand curve for a product is usually downward sloping to the right.

Consumer demand for a product (good) is shown as the amount of money customers are willing to pay during a specific period and under a given set of economic conditions. Therefore demand is different to need since it is possible that many individuals would like or need a car, but this is not turned into demand unless those individuals have the ability to pay. Demand which is backed up by the ability to pay, therefore, is called **effective demand**.

When making decisions to buy products consumers are believed to be rational. In this sense consumers consider the relative costs and benefits of any decision they have to make with their limited resources and purchase items that give them the greatest level of satisfaction in relation to their limited income. Sometimes individuals may behave irrationally, purchasing goods impulsively, paying little attention to price and quality; or perhaps because habit plays a part in consumer behaviour, the purchaser may not consider whether they really want the product or if there are alternatives available. Nonetheless, it is reasonable to assume that on the whole individuals do behave rationally. Rationality should not be confused with ignorance: the assumption of rationality does not necessarily mean that the consumer has perfect knowledge. Furthermore, rationality does not imply any moral approval. Economists may not approve of the purchasing behaviour of some individuals, but these individuals may still be behaving in a rational manner.

For an organisation, understanding the factors that affect demand and the level of demand itself is paramount if the organisation wishes to manage its resources well. For example, if market demand increases, what does this mean for stocks/inventories, the amount of labour and capital that might be required and the level of finance needed? There are other ways in which the level of market demand might also have an effect on the behaviour of the organisation, but it is sufficient at this stage to consider the three factors above as most important.

In the context of the firm or organisation, the concept of market demand is more useful than individual demand. How, therefore, can market demand be obtained from the individual demands of consumers? The move is fairly straightforward. The market demand curve is the sum of the individual consumers' demand curves. The shape of, or group of factors that affect, the market demand curve is thus related to the variables that affect an individual's demand for a product. In addition, unless the organisation is the sole firm in the market, the demand curve faced by an individual firm will not be the total market demand for a good or service. The two demand curves may differ. This issue is considered towards the end of this chapter.

To construct the **market demand curve** therefore means starting at the individual level. Suppose that there are two individuals, $A$ and $B$, whose demand for a product $x$ is related to the price of the product, $P_x$, the consumer's income,

$Y$, the price of alternative commodities, $P_{other}$, which may be either substitutes or complements to $x$, and the consumer's tastes, $T$. We can describe the relationship between the quantity demand of $x$ and these other factors in terms of a **demand function**.

For individual A, the demand function will be as follows:

$$Qd_{xA} = f(P_x, Y_A, P_{other}, T_A)$$

For individual B, the demand function is similarly:

$$Qd_{xB} = f(P_x, Y_B, P_{other}, T_B)$$

where $Qd_{xA}$ and $Qd_{xB}$ are the quantities demanded of good $x$ by individuals $A$ and $B$ respectively.

$Y_A$ and $Y_B$ are the incomes of individuals $A$ and $B$, and $T_A$ and $T_B$ are the respective tastes of the two individuals.

If all the factors on the right-hand side of these two demand functions are held constant apart from price, then most organisations will believe that if the price of $x$ is increased the quantity of $x$ demanded is likely to fall. Figures 6.1(a) and (b) indicate the relationship between the price of $x$ and the quantities demanded of $x$ for the two consumers $A$ and $B$.

In both (a) and (b), the two consumers are willing to buy a greater quantity of good $x$ at a lower price. There is no requirement that for both $A$ and $B$ the increase in quantity demanded expands at this lower price by the same amount, since although the consumers may be behaving ratio-

## Figure 6.1 Deriving the market demand curve

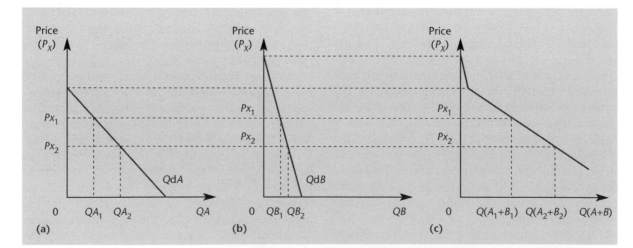

The market demand curve is the sum of all individual demand curves for a product. At price $Px_1$, demand is $QA_1$ in market $A$ and $QB_1$ in market $B$. Aggregate or market demand at price $Px_1$ is $Q(A_1 + B_1)$. Similarly, we can construct the aggregate or market demand for any other price levels.

nally, the relationship between the price of *x* and the quantity demanded of *x* can be different for the two consumers. Thus individual *A* moves to $QA_2$ following the fall in the price of *x* and for the same change in price individual *B* moves to $QB_2$. It is now possible to derive the market demand curve which is the horizontal summation of the individual consumers' demand curves. In the case where there are only two consumers, the market demand curve is shown in Figure 6.1(c). That is, it is the aggregate of the individual consumers' demand curves. In this case at price $PX_1$ the market demand is shown as $Q(A_1 + B_1)$.

## THE MARKET DEMAND CURVE

Before entering into a discussion of the factors that affect the demand for a product or service, it is important to distinguish between goods and services which are obtained for their direct consumption and those that are inputs into the manufacture and distribution of other products. The demand for these inputs will be related to the demand for the finished product. Thus the demand for this type of good is a **derived demand**. For example, the demand for computers leads to a derived demand for silicon chips; likewise the demand for leisure leads to a derived demand for sports clothing.

### ◆ Exercise 6.1

Consider two other products which have derived demands. How have the demands for these changed over the last five years?

How important are lag times in affecting the demand for products which have derived demand?

Regardless of whether a good or service is demanded for final consumption or is an input factor in providing other goods or services, the factors that affect the quantity demanded are likely to be fairly consistent. So what are the factors that could be suggested as being relevant in affecting the quantity demanded for a good or service?

Written in its functional form, a general demand function may look as follows:

$$Qd_x = f(P_x, O_x, A_x, St_x, P_z, O_z, A_z, St_z, Y, T, E, Cr, G, Pop, W, ..)$$

where,

$Qd_x$ = the quantity demanded of good *x* in a given time period

$P_x$ = the own price of the product or service *x*

$O_x$ = the number of outlets through which *x* is distributed

$A_x$ = the level of advertising or promotion for good *x*

## ◆ CASE STUDY 6.1

# Derived demand: the Japanese electronics industry          FT

With the rise in value of the yen and a downturn in economic activity, the early 1990s have not been good for Japan's electronics industry. However, by 1994 things had begun to look a lot better. In their 1994 results, many Japanese electronics companies, from consumer electronics firms to computer and semiconductor manufacturers, had been able to report a lift in profits and could foresee better times ahead.

The integrated electronics company Toshiba, for example, saw operating income quadruple in the first half of 1994, while the consumer electronics company Sharp managed to double its operating profits in the six months to September 1984.

The results provide evidence that many Japanese electronics companies still command a leading edge in key technologies which has enabled them to take advantage of buoyant demand overseas and thereby improve profits and future outlook.

The Japanese dominance of the memory chip market contributed significantly to the better results which electronics companies had reported in 1994. The growing sophistication of electronic equipment, from more powerful PCs and games machines to increasingly intelligent camcorders and communications tools, had boosted demand for memory and provided a bonanza for the leading Japanese manufacturers of dynamic random access memory chips. Likewise, the Japanese lead in liquid crystal display panels – in wide demand for lightweight, portable electronic tools – had contributed significantly to the recovery of many companies.

*Source: Financial Times*, 6 December 1994. Reprinted with permission.

$St_x$ = the style or design of product $x$

$P_z$ = the price of a related good (a substitute or complement)

$O_z$ = the number of outlets for a competitor product/service

$A_z$ = the level of advertising for the related good/service

$St_z$ = the style or design of the related good or service

$Y$ = the income of consumers or purchasers

$T$ = the tastes or preferences of consumers/purchasers

$E$ = the expectations of consumers/purchasers with regard to price etc.

$Cr$ = the cost and availability of credit

$G$ = government policy

$Pop$ = the change in the population

$W$ = weather conditions

The demand function shown above may well not include all the factors that you feel are important in affecting the quantity demanded of a product or service, yet it probably does include the main core factors.

---

◆ **Exercise 6.2**

1 Write down the demand function for skiing holidays in France.

2 Now construct the demand function for olives. Which variables are common to both demand functions?

---

It is possible to consider the variables on the right-hand side of the demand function as a number of distinct groups. The variables $P_x$, $O_x$, $A_x$ and $St_x$ could be considered as strategic variables under the control of the organisation. The variables $Y$, $T$ and $E$ are consumer variables, while the variables $P_z$, $O_z$, $A_z$ and $St_z$ are competitors' variables. The remaining variables, $W$, $Pop$, $G$ and $Cr$, could be considered as 'other' variables. These last three groups are exogenous, that is, outside of the control of the organisation.

## Understanding the relationship between the dependent and independent variables

The variable on the left-hand side of the demand function is called the dependent variable. Its value is related to the independent variables on the right-hand side of the function. Any change in one of the independent variables should not have an effect on any of the other variables on the right-hand side of the function if the variables are truly independent, and should lead only to changes in the dependent variable. In fact, many of the variables on the right-hand side of the function, in both theory and practice, may well be interrelated, the consequence of which will be discussed in Chapter 7.

---

◆ **Exercise 6.3**

Earlier in this chapter we constructed a general demand function. Suppose that the government raises income taxes: indicate why some of the variables are not truly independent.

---

The variables on the right-hand side of the equation all affect the quantity demanded; if they did not they would not be included in this demand function. If these variables are all changing together, it becomes increasingly difficult to look at the relationship which each of these is having on the quantity demanded. Therefore the way economists overcome this difficulty is to look at pairs of variables, that is, the relationship between the dependent variable and each of the independent variables separately, making the assumption that all the other variables on the right-hand side are held constant. Therefore, to look at the impact of price, $P_x$, on quantity, $Qd_x$, all the other variables in the demand function would be assumed to remain constant (*ceteris paribus*). The argument is that if the relationship between the dependent variable and each of the independent variables cannot be understood separately, it is not possible to understand the more complex picture of changes in a number of independent variables simultaneously and their subsequent effect on quantity demanded. The next section examines the important independent variables and their effect on the quantity demanded.

### Quantity demanded and own price

As was found in Chapter 5, there would normally be expected to be an inverse relationship between the quantity demanded of a product and changes in the product's price when all other variables remain constant. A relationship between the quantity demanded and price has already been seen in Figure 6.1 and is one of the most important relationships in consumer theory: the demand curve. If the relationship $Qd_x = f(P_x)$ is drawn from a mathematical perspective, the dependent variable, quantity, would be placed on the vertical axis, and the independent variable, price, on the horizontal axis. Historically, however, the relationship between the two from the economist's perspective has always been drawn in the opposite way, as Figure 6.2 indicates. The demand curve therefore slopes downwards from left to right and has a negative slope. Notice that the discussion here is about demand *curves*, yet many of the diagrams of demand curves are drawn as straight lines. The straight-line demand curve implies a constant slope which may not be appropriate for all products, a subject which will be returned to later, but it provides simplified analysis of the relationship between quantity and own price.

The demand curve therefore indicates that as the price of a product is reduced a greater quantity will be demanded. In Figure 6.2, as the price is reduced from $P_1$ to $P_2$ the quantity demanded extends from $Q_1$ to $Q_2$. This type of relationship between price and quantity would be appropriate for the majority of products, yet there are some products for which the demand curve slopes upward and to the right over part, if not all, of its range. Where price is an indicator of quality, we

**Figure 6.2 The demand curve**

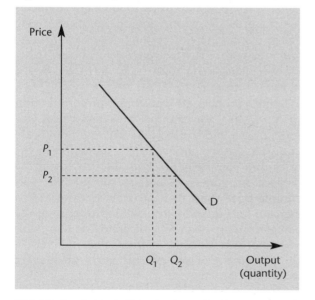

With all other factors held constant, at price $P_1$ consumers demand $Q_1$, at a lower price, $P_2$, consumers demand a greater quantity, $Q_2$. Therefore, for many products a fall in price is associated with an increased demand for the product.

might expect to find that as price increases consumers perceive the product as having superior qualities and therefore demand a greater quantity. For example, during the 1970s, one of two major tea retailers in the UK was forced to raise the price of its tea because of an increase in transportation costs. The other tea retailer, although not facing an increase in transportation costs, also raised the price of its tea. When asked to explain its pricing decision to the Department of Trade and Industry, the second tea retailer suggested that if it did not raise the price of its tea in line with its major competitor then consumers might perceive their tea as being of inferior quality. Because consumers do not possess perfect knowledge about all product characteristics, price is often used as some guideline reflecting the quality of the product. In the light of this argument, it will be interesting to see how consumers react to the purchase of Skoda cars after its takeover by Volkswagen. Skoda cars have historically been regarded as a reliable, 'no frills' means of transport which is relatively cheap to buy.

An upward sloping demand curve to the right may also be seen in the case of products which are perceived to have 'snob' value. One argument put forward as to why some products are purchased is that their price excludes a large proportion of the population. It is suggested that when the price of these commodities are reduced, thus allowing more consumers into the market, they lose their exclusive price tags and the original consumers abandon the products, to be replaced very quickly by the new consumers. It is possible, therefore, that a company which markets itself on exclusivity and quality sends conflicting signals to consumers if it produces a 'downmarket' product. Some people have questioned whether Gucci's tactic of using its name on products other than shoes for wider market appeal will damage consumers' perception of it as a high-quality producer. Finally, another example of a perverse demand curve can be seen in the case of Giffen goods. As discussed in Chapter 5, these are inferior goods but are commodities which take up a large proportion of consumers' income.

Whereas a change in the price of a commodity may lead to a change in the quantity demand – a movement along the demand curve (known as an extension or contraction) – it is possible that different quantities will be demanded but at the same price, as Figure 6.3 indicates. The next section considers the factors that can cause the whole of the demand curve to shift.

## Figure 6.3 A shift in the demand curve

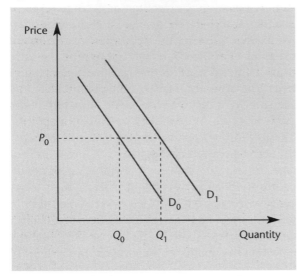

With demand curve $D_0$ at price level $P_0$, quantity $Q_0$ is demanded. If at the same price a different quantity is demanded, then this is associated with a shift in the demand curve. In Figure 6.3 a shift in the demand curve to $D_1$ leads to a greater quantity being demanded at the current price.

### Quantity demanded and the level of income

The relationship between a change in the level of income and its effect on the quantity demanded can be both positive and negative. For many products an increase (decrease) in income will lead to an increase (decrease) in the quantity demanded. These types of goods are called normal goods. One category of normal goods is luxury goods. For these products an increase in income leads to a large increase in quantity demanded; a good example of this type of product would be cars. However, not all goods are normal goods: there will be some commodities for which the demand declines as income increases, and these are called inferior goods. An example of an inferior good would be low-cost/quality food products. As income increases consumers tend to discontinue such purchases, substituting better-quality food products for the low-cost food brands. Since most goods could be thought of as normal goods, then as income increases we would see the demand curve in Figure 6.3 shifting to the right, from $D_0$ to $D_1$.

Knowledge of whether a commodity is perceived as normal, superior or inferior is obviously very important for producers. During upward swings in the economic cycle, producers of normal goods or superior goods will see sales rising, while producers of inferior goods will perhaps see a decline in sales. Conversely, during recessions when consumers trade down, producers of cyclical normal goods will see sales falling. It was noticed during the recession of the early 1990s that consumers traded down from superior food products produced by Marks & Spencer to perceived inferior producers such as those at Tesco, Safeway and Sainsbury's.

Apart from these short-term impacts of the economic cycle, because incomes have grown in real terms over the long run, producers of inferior goods will gradually see their sales fall. This may result in them leaving the market altogether or they may try to reposition their products as less inferior products. To return to the example of Skoda, which many people would view as an inferior product, it may benefit from being purchased by VW, whose image and products in certain car ranges are perceived as superior products.

### Quantity demanded and the price of related products

When purchasing items consumers often have a range of products from which to choose. In other words, there are often substitutes for a particular product. If the price of one of these substitutes falls then consumers may switch to the relatively cheaper product. Thus an organisation may see changes in the quantities purchased of its product not because it has changed the price of its product, but because there has been a change in the price of a competitor's product. For example, reducing the price of Levi's jeans may lead to a fall in the demand for Wrangler jeans so long as individuals see them as substitutes for one another. Using Figure 6.3, an increase in the price of a substitute good leads to a rightward shift in our organisation's demand curve to the right, as shown by the movement from $D_0$ to $D_1$.

Some products are consumed in conjunction with another, for example breakfast cereal and milk, or gin and tonic water. These products are **complementary goods**. Thus a reduction in the price of a complementary product increases the demand for that good; because our product is its complement there will also be an increase in demand for our good. This fall in the price of the complementary good will therefore lead to a rightward shift in our organisation's demand curve – the movement of the demand curve once again from $D_0$ to $D_1$.

### Quantity demanded and advertising

Advertising and other non-price methods of persuasion can be expected to influence the demand for an organisation's product. It would be expected that an increase in advertising might have a positive effect on the quantity demanded of a product. This would be seen as a shift in the demand curve to the right – again from $D_0$ to $D_1$. On the other hand, an increase in the level of advertising for a substitute product, *ceteris paribus*, would see a shift in the organisation's demand curve to the left. This would be shown by a movement of the demand curve in Figure 6.3 from $D_1$ to $D_0$. If a complementary product was to increase its level of advertising, then our organisation might see a rightward shift in its demand curve.

## Quantity demanded and consumer tastes
Consumer tastes are always changing and any movement or shift in tastes towards a firm's product or service will be seen in terms of a rightward shift in the demand curve. Since consumer tastes can change very rapidly, organisations must be prepared to consider the problems of consumers turning away from their products and causing high inventory levels. Therefore, some organisations will produce a large quantity of an item fairly quickly and when the market is satiated they will turn to the production of another item. Organisations will try to sustain any switch towards their product, via a change in tastes, by using non-price methods such as advertising to build up brand loyalty. For example, Levi's was the brand leader in jeans during the two decades after the Second World War. Other jeans manufacturers joined the market, so that by the 1970s consumer tastes had switched to Wrangler, Pepe and other manufacturers. An aggressive innovative marketing campaign by Levi's during the 1980s, especially for Levi 501s, resulted in Levi's once again dominating the jeans market.

The change in tastes towards customer service during the 1980s and 1990s also led to some organisations losing markets. The supermarket chains and British Telecom have responded well to changing tastes in this area.

## Quantity demanded and product quality/design
As was discussed in Chapter 5, consumers may purchase not only on the basis of price but on the characteristics which a good provides. Many organisations realise that being price competitive may not be sufficient to encourage consumers to buy their product(s) and that non-price factors such as design and quality are far more important. People often talk about Swedish design quality, Italian style or German engineering, and goods which possess these characteristics are often in great demand.

On a macroeconomic level, two National Economic Development Office (NEDO) studies undertaken in the UK suggested that quality is of greater importance than price in selling UK goods in foreign markets. There has been a large improvement in the quality and design of UK-produced goods since the 1980s, as exemplified by the cars produced by the Rover Group in the UK. An improvement in quality/design relative to its major competitors would be expected to lead to a rightward shift in the organisation's demand curve.

## Quantity demanded and consumer expectations
If consumers expect the price of a product to increase in the future, they may well attempt to purchase it in the current time period, thereby leading to a rightward shift in the current demand curve. This behaviour is seen most readily in the context of taxation changes in the Budget. If consumers expect the tax to increase on a product in the future, they may attempt to purchase the product now. In the context of the old Eastern European communist countries, because consumers felt that the availability of a product might become scarce in the future they often attempted to stockpile items. Conversely, if consumers have very optimistic views of the future in terms of availability, they may put off purchasing a commodity now, leading to a leftward shift in the current period's demand curve.

## Quantity demanded and number and quality of outlets
If an organisation has a limited number of outlets through which it can sell its product, then it may experience reduced demand. The same may apply if its outlets are regionally specific. The location of the outlets is also important. As an example of this, we have seen a move by the large food retailers to rationalise their outlets by moving towards lower-capital and maintenance cost, but more customer-friendly sites. European producers have often complained that the number of outlets through which they are permitted to sell their products in the Japanese market has been used as a form of non-tariff barrier to export sales. Organisations which face restrictions on the number of outlets through which they can sell their products will see their demand curve shifting to the left.

## Quantity demanded and other factors
Although the above factors may well be the most important in affecting the quantity demanded of a

product, there are others which may be more specific to industrial sectors. For example, environmental awareness and policies in Europe may have led to the demand curve shifting to the left for some products which are viewed to be 'bads'. Similarly, the demand curve for other products may have moved to the right because the commodities are seen as more environmentally friendly. In Germany, changes in packaging requirements may have led in the short term to some imports facing reduced demand.

The weather plays an important role in the demand for some products. During the hot European summers of 1991/2 beer sales increased appreciably; the cool summer weather of 1995 in the UK caused the demand curve for summer clothing to shift to the left compared with 1994.

Demographic trends also play a slow but significant part in shifting demand. In most European countries, apart from Sweden, the birth rate is falling. This has implications for the demand for nursery/primary school places and that for children's clothing and toys. Conversely, the growth in the number of older people within Europe will see a shift in demand towards the products that older people desire; this often involves branded products and those which have embodied in them a perception of quality.

◆ CASE STUDY 6.2

# The demand for consumer durables

Over time there has been a long-term underlying upward trend in the demand for consumer durables, although this has proved to be very volatile to short-run changes in income, much more so than the demand for non-durables. Table 6.1 shows how expenditure on consumer durables has changed over the last decade.

### Table 6.1 Consumer expenditure

|  | 1982 | 1985 | 1988 | 1991 | 1993 |
|---|---|---|---|---|---|
| Total consumer expenditure | 249 852 | 276 742 | 334 591 | 339 993 | 348 315 |
| Durable goods: | | | | | |
| Motor vehicles | 11 545 | 14 162 | 19 258 | 14 968 | 15 796 |
| Furniture and floor coverings | 4 975 | 5 145 | 6 864 | 6 115 | 6 983 |
| Other durable goods | 4 379 | 5 966 | 8 828 | 9 389 | 10 473 |
| Total | 20 652 | 25 192 | 34 950 | 30 472 | 33 252 |
| (% of total consumer expenditure) | 8.2% | 9.1% | 10.4% | 9.0% | 9.5% |
| Food (household) | 37 942 | 38 402 | 41 541 | 41 870 | 42 722 |

Source: *National Expenditure Accounts*, various editions. Crown Copyright. Reproduced by permission of the Controller of HMSO and the Office for National Statistics.

The demand for consumer durables depends on a number of factors, discussed below.

#### Consumer income

There would be expected to be a positive relationship between consumer income and the demand for consumer durables. Many durable goods which were classified as luxuries in the past, such as refrigerators or televisions, have now become necessities for most people. As a category, however, durables can be viewed as luxury items, the demand for which rises proportionately more as incomes rise. In the short run this effect can be related to the changes that occur in the economic cycle. Over the longer term, real incomes have tended to rise, giving a slow but increasing amount of income to be spent on durable good purchases.

#### Prices

As the price of consumer durables increases, it would be expected that the demand for these products would fall. However, over the long term the real price of durable goods has fallen as technological advances have made products cheaper in real terms. Moreover, there has been an increase in the level of competition in the market for the supply of consumer durables and this has also helped to reduce real prices. Since many durable products may also be viewed as 'mature' products, then there is also less scope to keep on increasing prices.

#### Product improvement and innovation

These two factors have helped bring new products to the market, for example microwave ovens. Product improvement and innovation have satisfied latent consumer demand and helped alter consumer tastes. In so doing, both factors have improved the demand for consumer durables.

#### Working patterns

The increased involvement of women in the labour market, and the reluctance of many men to share household jobs, has also led to opportunities for durable good manufacturers to produce labour-saving devices. In particular, the growth in households which possess two cars gives a clear indication of the move towards both adult members of dual-income households being involved in the labour market.

### Number of households

One feature of the housing market that has occurred over the last 30 years is the trend for individuals to live in their own dwellings prior to moving into family homes. In addition, there is evidence to suggest that older people remain as independent households for longer. A growing family that still remains in the current dwelling may not require many more consumer durables. The move towards separate households, however, often sees increased demand for fridges, freezers, washing machines etc. Of course, some of these newly formed households will not have the income to purchase many durable goods, yet there is still evidence that new household formation plays an important part in the long-term rise in the demand for consumer durables.

Many textbooks talk a great deal about household demand, yet organisations need to recognise that the household with 2.4 children is not the dominant one. There has been a growth in two-person, three-person and single-person households, which has implications for the total number of households that currently exist and therefore for the amount of income they have available to spend and for lifestyle needs. In the longer term, however, the fall in the birth rate may have implications for the number of new households that are set up.

*Source*: Authors.

---

◆ **Exercise 6.4**

1 Given the falling birth rate within Europe, what are the implications for the demand for consumer durables in both the short run and long run?

2 Would you expect the demand for consumer durables to differ between the countries in the EU?

◆ **Exercise 6.5**

1 What other factors would you include in the demand function for ice cream?

2 Who do you consider are the consumers of Scotch whisky? How would you attempt to increase the market for whisky?

---

## ◆ CASE STUDY 6.3

# Ice creams and frozen desserts

The UK ice-cream market has seen rapid growth over the last few years, but in relative terms consumption levels per capita are low when compared with the Scandinavian countries and the US (*see* Table 6.2).

### Table 6.2 European retail ice-cream consumption (per capita), 1990

| Country | Per capita consumption of ice cream (litres) |
|---|---|
| Sweden | 12 |
| Denmark | 7.9 |
| UK | 7.5 |
| Ireland | 7.4 |
| Switzerland | 6 |
| Netherlands | 5 |
| Belgium | 5 |
| Italy | 5 |
| Germany | 4.8 |
| France | 4.7 |

Source: Unilever/Wall's

The European countries' consumption of ice cream is dwarfed by that of the US, where consumers eat more than 21 litres per head each year.

The demand for ice cream shows the expected seasonal demand shifts, but aside from these short-run effects there have also been long-term increases in demand. Greater freezer ownership during the 1980s led to improved sales in the take-home sector, especially in multipacks, while the underlying trend upwards in convenience products and impulse snacks has benefited wrapped and hand-held products. However, of major significance is the refocusing of ice-cream marketing towards the adult market, which has offset falling birth rates and has led to a smoothing-out of ice-cream consumption throughout the year. Thus ice cream is no longer conceived of as a child-oriented product or one aimed at the dessert market, but one which is marketed to eat any time of the day or year.

*Source:* Adapted from *Keynote Report, Ice Creams and Frozen Desserts.* © Keynote Limited 1993. Reproduced with permission.

# FROM THE DEMAND FUNCTION TO THE DEMAND EQUATION

For an organisation, the demand function indicates the factors or variables which the organisation believes affects the quantity demanded. Not all factors are as important as others in affecting the demand for an organisation's output. However, the firm often requires more than just knowledge of the factors that affect its level of demand. What it would like to know is whether there is a specific form of the demand function which is applicable to itself. In other words, the relationship between the quantity demanded and each of the independent variables must be clearly specified.

Suppose that an organisation believes that the demand for its product is related to the product's price, the level of consumers' income, the level of advertising the organisation undertakes and the price of competitive products. If it is also expected that the association between these factors and the quantity demanded is best described by a linear relationship, then the demand function may be of the following form:

$$Qd_x = B_0P_x + B_1Y + B_2A_x + B_3P_{other} + E_t \qquad (6.1)$$

where,

$Qd_x$ = the quantity demanded of good $x$
$P_x$ = the price of good $x$
$Y$ = the level of consumers' income
$A_x$ = the level of advertising undertaken by the organisation
$P_{other}$ = the price of the competitive product
$E_t$ = a variable which takes account of all the other factors that can affect quantity demanded in the current time period
$B_0 \ldots B_3$ = the coefficients for each of the variables

The $B_0 \ldots B_3$ values could also be viewed as indicating the marginal impact of each independent variable on the quantity demanded. In fact, although the demand equation 6.1 has been constructed with all the coefficients having positive signs, we might expect some of them to be negative. Whether the coefficients are positive or negative depends on the relationship between the independent variable and the quantity demanded. For example, we would expect the coefficient $B_0$ to be negative, since as the price of the product increases for most goods the quantity demanded will fall. Equation 6.2 presents the demand equation again,

but on this occasion it has been constructed with numbers replacing the coefficients:

$$Qd_x = -2500P_x + 198A_x + 47Y + 345P_{other} + E_t \qquad (6.2)$$

Equation 6.2 also indicates that changes in advertising have a positive impact on the quantity demanded, that changes in income would have a positive impact on the quantity demanded, suggesting that good $x$ is a normal good, and that an increase in the price of a related product leads to an increase in the quantity demanded of $x$. Thus, good $x$ and the related product are substitutes. You may be wondering, how the numbers are obtained for each of the coefficients. These are usually calculated via regression analysis, a process that is outlined in Chapter 7.

The form in which we have written down the linear demand equation 6.1 resembles the mathematical form of $Y = mX$, where $Y$ is the dependent variable, $X$ the independent variable and $m$ the slope of the line that relates $Y$ and $X$. In terms of the demand equation, if it is believed that the only factor that affects quantity demanded is price then the equation would become:

$$Qd_x = B_0P_x$$

which is the same mathematical form as $Y = mX$. However, in Figure 6.1(a), when price equals zero quantity demanded is positive, therefore a more appropriate linear form for the demand equation would be $Y = mX + C$, where $C$ is a positive intercept term. Therefore, an equation such as $Y = 3X + 8$ has a slope of 3 and an intercept on the $Y$ axis of 8. Rewriting the demand equation, which includes only the independent variables $P_x$, $Y$, $A_x$ and $P_{other}$, into this alternative form of the linear equation gives:

$$Qd_x = A + B_0P_x + B_1Y + B_2A_x + B_3P_{other} \qquad (6.3)$$

where $A$ is the positive intercept coefficient.

The linear form is one way of writing down the demand function in terms of an equation. It is possible that two or more variables have a multiplicative influence on the quantity demanded. Such a form would be Equation 6.4.

$$Qd_x = AP_x^{B0}Y^{B1}A_x^{B2}P_{other}^{B3} \qquad (6.4)$$

By taking logarithms of both sides, Equation 6.4 would become:

$$\log Qd_x = \log A + B0\log P_x + B1\log Y + B2\log A_x + B3\log P_{other} \qquad (6.5)$$

See Appendix 6.3 for further explanation.

Equation 6.5 is now back in the linear form. However, the form in which the demand equation is written has implications for measuring the various elasticities of demand, as will be shown later; *see* Appendix 6.4.

## THE RELATIONSHIP BETWEEN PRICE, MARGINAL REVENUE AND TOTAL REVENUE

Figure 6.4 shows a demand curve. The demand curve indicates various combinations of price and quantity. One such combination is shown as price, £20, and quantity, 300. Suppose that the price of the product is reduced to £18. At this price the quantity demanded is 400 units. For both price/output combinations it is possible to calculate the total revenue received by the organisation. Since total revenue is given by:

Total Revenue (TR) = Price × Quantity

at price £20, the total revenue is £6000, whereas at price £18, total revenue is £7200. Thus for this organisation as price is reduced so total revenue increases. Will total revenue continue to increase as the price level is reduced? If this was the case firms would continue to reduce prices, and such a feature is not a scenario that many organisations follow. In fact, it might be expected that total revenue would fall after some point as the price level is reduced.

**Figure 6.4 Demand and total revenue**

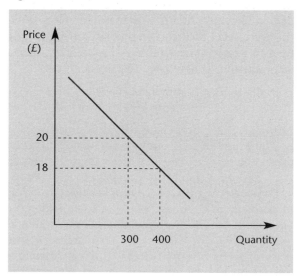

At price £20 300 units are demanded. Total revenue = price × quantity, therefore total revenue equals 20 × 300 = £6000. At price £18, total revenue is £7200. A demand curve can relate how total revenue changes as price changes.

This is because the more and more units of a product that a consumer purchases the smaller is the increase in the level of satisfaction that a consumer receives. This concept is called the law of diminishing marginal utility, discussed in Chapter 5. In other words, how can an organisation encourage greater consumption of a commodity for which individuals receive less and less satisfaction from consuming more and more of the product to entice consumers into purchasing the item. The way forward is to reduce the price of the product. At some stage the product's price might have to be reduced by a large amount to encourage further consumption. In this case it is highly likely that, although quantity demanded will increase, it will only do so by a small amount and the firm's total revenue will fall (*see* Table 6.3 below).

### Marginal revenue

Marginal revenue is defined as the change in total revenue that results from a one-unit change in the level of output (increase in demand) – *see* Appendix 6.1. Table 6.3 brings all these relationships together.

As Table 6.3 indicates, total revenue increases and then decreases. Since the demand curve faced by the organisation is downward sloping, the **marginal revenue** function lies below it. That is, marginal revenue is less than price for each unit of output. Moreover, marginal revenue is always declining. The table also indicates that the point at which marginal revenue reaches zero is the point at which total revenue is maximised. Any firm would therefore not be advised to expand its output beyond the point at which marginal revenue is zero. Figure 6.5 indicates graphically the relationships shown in Table 6.1.

**Table 6.3 The relationship between quantity demanded, total revenue and marginal revenue**

| Price (£) | Quantity demanded | Total revenue (£) | Marginal revenue (£ per unit) |
|---|---|---|---|
| 10 | 100 | 1000 | – |
| 9 | 200 | 1800 | 8 |
| 8 | 300 | 2400 | 6 |
| 7 | 400 | 2800 | 4 |
| 6 | 500 | 3000 | 2 |
| 5 | 600 | 3000 | 0 |
| 4 | 700 | 2800 | –2 |
| 3 | 800 | 2400 | –4 |
| 2 | 900 | 1800 | –6 |
| 1 | 1000 | 1000 | –8 |

It is also possible to establish further the relationship between demand, total revenue and marginal revenue by using one of the equations already established for demand. For example, suppose that the relationship between quantity demanded and price is shown by the following linear demand equation:

$$Qd_x = 1000 - 80P_x$$

This can be rewritten as:

$$P_x = 12.5 - 0.0125Qd_x$$

Since total revenue (TR) = Price × Quantity

$$TR = (12.5 - 0.0125Qd_x)Qd_x$$
or
$$TR = 12.5Qd_x - 0.0125Qd_x{}^2$$

Marginal revenue is the change in total revenue when output is changed by one unit. There are at least two methods for calculating the marginal revenue at any point. First, the total revenue equation could be differentiated with respect to $Qd_x$ to give:

$$dTR/dQd_x = \text{Marginal revenue (MR)}$$
$$= 12.5 - 0.025Qd_x$$

Here, marginal revenue will vary depending on the value that is substituted for $Qd_x$ in the equation. Moreover, as the quantity demanded increases marginal revenue falls. In fact, when $Qd_x$ equals 500, marginal revenue becomes zero and negative thereafter for higher values of output. If this is unclear, substitute the value $Qd_x$ equals 500 in the equation above.

The second approach to calculating the various values for marginal revenue is to substitute value $Qd_x$ into the total revenue equation. If the value of $Qd_x$ is then increased by one unit, a new $TR$ is calculated. The marginal revenue is now being obtained, since marginal revenue is the change in total revenue when output (quantity) is increased by one unit. Appendix 6.1 shows some of these calculations.

Whichever way we approach the calculation of MR, the equation is of the form $Y = mX + C$, that is, the equation of a straight line, with in this instance the intercept term on the vertical axis of 12.5 and a slope term of –0.025. The marginal revenue curve is therefore a straight line, downward sloping from left to right.

Figure 6.5 shows another important relationship between marginal revenue and total revenue. As marginal revenue falls so the slope of the total revenue, although still positive, is becoming flatter. In addition, the maximum point on the total revenue curve occurs when MR equals zero. So long as marginal revenue is positive total revenue is increasing, sometimes at a slower rate, but once marginal revenue becomes negative total revenue declines. An organisation would therefore never like to be in a position where marginal revenue is negative. Moreover, and perhaps more importantly, what the marginal revenue line is showing is the slope of the total revenue function (equation). In other words, when the equation of total revenue is differentiated with respect to quantity, the result is the slope of the total revenue equation or marginal revenue.

## DEMAND SENSITIVITY ANALYSIS

Figures 6.6(a) and 6.6(b) show two demand curves which indicate the most expected relationship between price and quantity. That is, when the price level falls (rises), the quantity demanded rises (falls). However, in Figure 6.6(a), the reduction in price leads to only a small increase in demand, while in Figure 6.6(b), the same reduction in price leads to a large increase in demand.

From an organisation's point of view, not only for revenue purposes but also for the planning and use of resources, it is important to recognise the degree to which quantity demanded alters when the price level changes. One measure that can be used to relate this information to the organisation is the concept of elasticity. This is defined as:

$$\text{Elasticity} = \text{Percentage change in } R/$$
$$\text{Percentage change in } T$$

Although the concept of elasticity is now going to be developed in the context of demand, it can be used elsewhere, to consider, for example, the sensitivity of output changes to changes in temperature.

By developing the concept of elasticity in terms of percentage changes, we can also consider the base from which the change in the variable is taking place. For example, a £5 increase in the price of a Euroshuttle ticket will have a different impact on Eurotunnel than a £5 increase in the price of Portuguese wine will have on wine producers in Portugal.

**Figure 6.5 The relationship between marginal revenue, total revenue and demand**

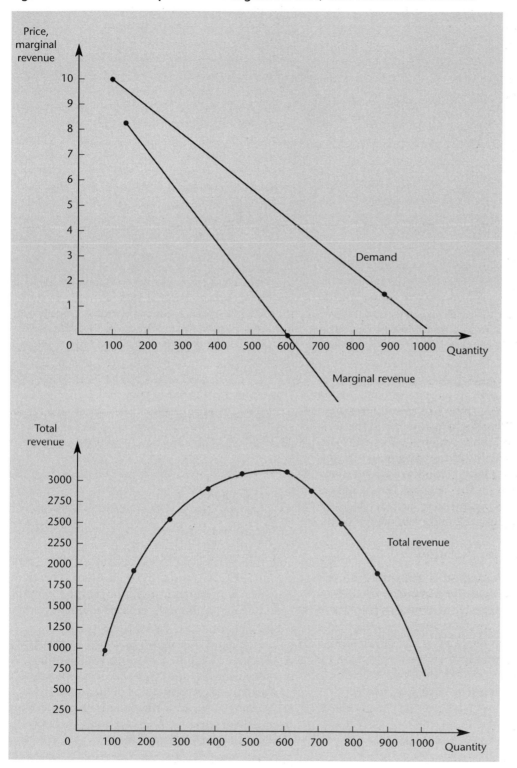

From Table 6.3, demand, marginal revenue and total revenue functions have been constructed.
Total revenue reaches its maximum when MR = 0.

**Figure 6.6  The sensitivity of quantity changes to price**

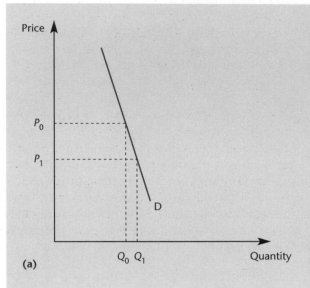

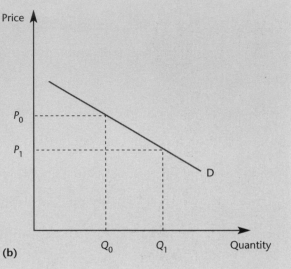

**(a)** A fall in price leads to a smaller proportionate increase in quantity demanded. Thus a price fall leads to a reduction in total revenue. A demand curve of this type is said to be inelastic.

**(b)** A reduction in price leads to a more than proportionate increase in quantity demanded. Total revenue rises after a price fall. This type of relationship is given by an elastic demand curve.

In considering elasticity in terms of demand and the demand function, there will be some variables under the control of the organisation – the endogenous factors – while others are outside the organisation's control – the exogenous factors. Understanding the effects of both endogenous and exogenous factors on the demand for its output should enable the organisation to react to these changes and help it make the appropriate responses.

## Price elasticity of demand

**Price elasticity of demand** is defined as the percentage change in quantity demanded divided by the percentage change in the product's price, i.e.:

$$E_d = \frac{\text{Percentage change in quantity demanded of good } x}{\text{Percentage change in price of good } x}$$

Mathematically this can be written as:

$$E_d = \frac{\Delta Q_x / Q_x \times 100}{\Delta P_x / P_x \times 100} \qquad (6.6)$$

where,  $E_d$ = the elasticity of demand
  $Q_x$ = the quantity demanded of good $x$
  $P_x$ = the price of good $x$
  $\Delta Q_x$ = change in quantity demanded of good $x$
  $\Delta P_x$ = change in price of good $x$

This can be rearranged to become:

$$E_d = \Delta Q_x / \Delta P_x \times P_x / Q_x$$

In terms of calculus this can be rewritten as:

$$E_d = dQ_x / dP_x \times P_x / Q_x$$

The term $\Delta Q_x / \Delta P_x$ ($dQ_x / dP_x$) is the reciprocal of the slope of the demand curve which is given by $dP_x / dQ_x$. Since the slope of the demand curve is constant, if the relationship between price and quantity is constructed as a straight line, then $\Delta Q_x / \Delta P_x$ ($dQ_x / dP_x$) will also be constant. Therefore, elasticity will depend, in a straight-line demand relationship, on the ratio of price to quantity, that is $P_x / Q_x$. For example, consider Figure 6.7.

The demand line shows that at price £5, quantity demanded will be 200 units, while at price £4, quantity demanded is 260 units. It is now possible to calculate the elasticity of demand. $\Delta P = 5 - 4$, $\Delta Q = 200 - 260$, and if the organisation is moving from A to B, then at A, $P = 5$ and $Q = 200$. The elasticity of demand is therefore:

$$E_d = -60/1 \times 5/200$$

$$E_d = -1.5$$

Suppose, however, that the organisation began at B and moved towards A, undertaking an increase

## Figure 6.7 Price elasticity of demand

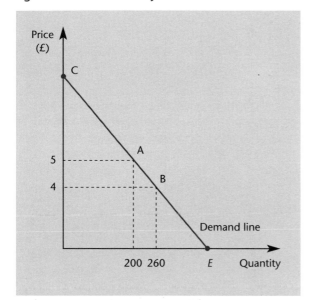

Moving from A to B gives a 1-unit fall in price (5 – 4) = 1 or $\Delta P$ and a 60-unit change in quantity demanded (200 – 260) = –60 or $\Delta Q$. $Ed = \Delta Q / \Delta P \times P/Q$. At A $Ed = -60/1 \times 5/200 = -1.5$. At B, however, $Ed = -60/1 \times 4/260 = -0.92$. Elasticity of demand alters as we move up and down a straight-line demand line and is dependent on the ratio of price to quantity, since the slope of the line is constant at both A and B.

in price. What would be the measurement of elasticity this time? Since $\Delta Q / \Delta P$, the reciprocal of the slope of the demand line, is constant, then there will be no alteration in the first term in the elasticity formula, however the ratio of price to quantity will be different if starting from B and moving to A, rather than starting from A and moving to B. Starting from B the elasticity of demand formula becomes:

$$Ed = 60/-1 \times 4/260$$

$$Ed = -0.92$$

What these calculations indicate is that when there is a straight-line demand function the elasticity varies along the demand curve. In fact, the elasticity of demand at point C in Figure 6.7 is infinite ($\infty$), since although price is positive, quantity demanded is zero and substituting this in the elasticity formula gives an infinite value for elasticity. Similarly, the elasticity of demand at point E can be shown to be zero.

Descending the demand curve from point C in Figure 6.7 to point E leads to the price elasticity

of demand varying from minus infinity to zero. It must pass, therefore, through the point at which elasticity equals –1. In fact, the point at which the elasticity of demand equals –1 is the midpoint on the demand curve. To establish this fact, consider the following equation for the demand curve:

$$Qd_x = A + BP_x \qquad (6.7)$$

Figure 6.8 describes this relationship between price and quantity, where B, the slope of the demand line, is negative. If quantity equals zero, then price equals –A/B from the equation above; on the other hand, if price equals zero, then quantity demanded equals A. The slope of the linear demand curve is given by $\Delta P / \Delta Q$, since B is the reciprocal of the slope of the demand line. Equation 6.7 can be rewritten as:

$$Qd_x = A + (\Delta Qd_x / \Delta P_x)P_x \qquad (6.8)$$

since the elasticity of demand shown earlier is:

$$Ed_x = \Delta Qd_x / \Delta P_x \times P_x / Qd_x$$

Then Equation 6.8 can be rewritten as:

$$Qd_x = A + Qd_x Ed_x \qquad (6.9)$$

## Figure 6.8 Elasticity of demand along a linear demand curve

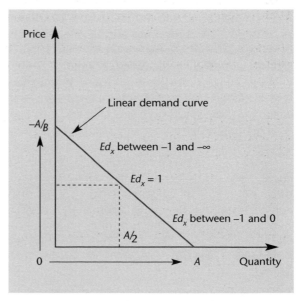

Since elasticity of demand alters as we move up or down a straight-line demand curve, it must go through the point of unitary elasticity, that is, where $Ed_x = 1$. This is the midpoint on the demand curve. To the left of $Ed_x = 1$, the demand curve is elastic, to the right it is inelastic.

If both sides of Equation 6.9 are divided by $Qd_x$ this gives:

$$1 = A/Qd_x + Ed_x \text{ or solving for } Ed_x$$
$$Ed_x = (Qd_x - A)/Qd_x \qquad (6.10)$$

Returning to Figure 6.8, the midpoint on the demand curve is where quantity equals $A/2$. Substituting this value for quantity in Equation 6.10 reveals that the elasticity of demand at the midpoint is equal to –1. If a value for quantity less than $A/2$ is substituted into Equation 6.10, then the elasticity value is a larger negative number and in the extreme case it has already been shown that if quantity equals zero then the elasticity of demand is equal to infinity. On the other hand, substituting a value for quantity greater than $A/2$ into Equation 6.10 gives a value for elasticity closer to zero. In fact, it has already been shown that if a value for quantity which equals $A$ is substituted into Equation 6.10, then the elasticity of demand becomes zero.

It is now possible to look at the three areas on the demand curve and use the conventional approach to elasticity, that is, when elasticity is in the range between –1 and –∞ (infinity), demand is elastic, where elasticity equals 1 there is unitary elasticity, and where elasticity lies between –1 and zero demand is inelastic.

Elasticity is quite often talked of in absolute terms, that is, without reference to its sign, and it has become acceptable to describe the elasticities as in Table 6.4. For example, a value of elasticity of demand $Ed = -3$, if taken in absolute terms, $|Ed| = 3$, indicates an elastic demand for the product.

With a downward-sloping linear demand curve the elasticity varies as we move along it. However, there are three special types of demand curve for which the elasticity does not change as price or quantity vary. Figure 6.9 shows these special cases.

Figure 6.9(a) shows a perfectly inelastic demand curve – a vertical demand curve. Here changes in price do not lead to any changes in quantity demanded. Using the elasticity formula, since $\Delta Q$ is zero, the elasticity for this type of demand curve is always equal to zero. Figure 6.9(b) indicates a perfectly elastic demand curve. Here the organisation

### Table 6.4 Elasticity ranges in absolute terms

| | |
|---|---|
| $|Ed| > 1$ | elastic demand curve |
| $|Ed| = 1$ | unit elastic demand curve |
| $|Ed| < 1$ | inelastic demand curve |

**Figure 6.9 Special cases of elasticity of demand**

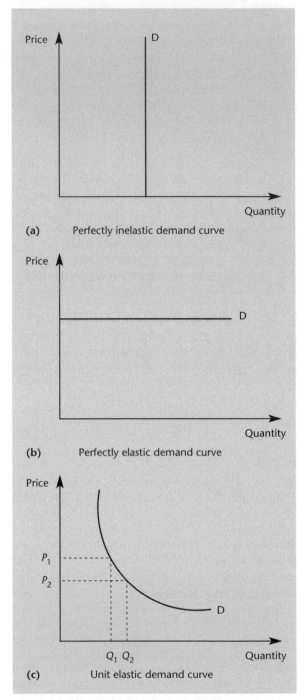

(a)  Perfectly inelastic demand curve

(b)  Perfectly elastic demand curve

(c)  Unit elastic demand curve

(a) This is a perfectly inelastic demand curve: changes in price lead to no changes in quantity and $Ed = 0$.

(b) This is a perfectly elastic demand curve: different quantities can be sold at the current price, $Ed = \infty$.

(c) This shows a demand curve drawn as a rectangular hyperbola. The characteristics of this curve are that total revenue remains constant at different price levels, thus its elasticity is equal to one.

can sell any quantity at the current price. This type of demand curve has already been discussed in Chapter 4. Because there is no change in price, the elasticity of demand is always equal to infinity. Finally, Figure 6.9(c) shows a unit elastic demand curve. The demand curve is of a particular type called a rectangular hyperbola which has the characteristic that a proportionate fall (increase) in price is matched by a similar proportionate increase (decrease) in quantity, thus total revenue stays the same and Ed = 1.

## Point and arc elasticity

The measurement of elasticity that has been developed so far is called 'point elasticity' – the elasticity of demand at a particular point on the demand curve. Once this has been calculated the organisation cannot rely on facing that particular estimate of elasticity of demand forever as it continues to change prices. In other words, point elasticity is best used when changes in price and quantity are fairly small, since such moves do not take the organisation too far away from its current measure of point elasticity. Where price changes are much larger, the use of point elasticity may lead to inaccuracies in the measurement of elasticity and an alternative measure may be required. This alternative approach is called **arc elasticity**. Arc elasticity is defined as the relative responsiveness of quantity demanded to a discrete change in price, and its intention is to provide a measure of the elasticity of demand over a range of prices. The arc elasticity formula was developed to provide average elasticity for incremental rather than marginal changes. Although the concept of arc elasticity is developed here in terms of the price elasticity of demand, it can be applied equally to the other elasticities that are developed later in this chapter. The formula for the arc elasticity of demand is:

$$Ed = \frac{(\text{Change in Quantity/Average quantity}) \times 100}{(\text{Change in price/Average price}) \times 100}$$

Using the notation developed earlier, this becomes:

$$Ed = \frac{(\Delta Q/(Q_1 + Q_2)/2) \times 100}{(\Delta P/(P_1 + P_2)/2 \times 100}$$

or:

$$Ed = \Delta Q/\Delta P \times (P_1 + P_2)/(Q_1 + Q_2)$$

Alternatively, arc elasticity can be expressed as:

$$Ed = (Q_1 - Q_2)/(P_1 - P_2) \times (P_1 + P_2)/(Q_1 + Q_2)$$

Returning to Figure 6.7, the point elasticity of demand at point A was –1.5, while the elasticity at point B was –0.92. If the arc elasticity is now calculated for these two points then:

$$Ed = (200 - 260)/(5 - 4) \times (5 + 4)/(200 + 260)$$
$$Ed = -60/1 \times 9/460$$
$$Ed = -1.17$$

The value of the arc elasticity lies between the two point elasticities calculated earlier. This result is to be expected, since the arc elasticity is simply a measure of the point elasticity at the midpoint of the arc that joins points A and B. If the arc, in other words the straight line between A and B, is drawn in Figure 6.7, then the point elasticities are the values at each end of the arc and the arc elasticity is the value midway along the arc.

## Elasticity, marginal and total revenue

An organisation is not only interested in the magnitude of the quantity change after a change in price, but also wishes to know the impact on total revenue. In Figure 6.5 the relationship between demand, marginal revenue and total revenue was established diagrammatically. When marginal revenue equals zero the maximum point on the total revenue curve was reached. It is now possible to expand on this earlier analysis.

Using the linear demand equation established earlier:

$$Q = A + BP$$

This can be rearranged to find the value for $P$:

$$P = Q/B - A/B$$

where B is negative.

Total revenue (TR) is Price × Quantity, or TR = $P \times Q$

Substituting in for $P$ yields:

$$TR = Q^2/B - Q(A/B)$$

Marginal revenue is the change in total revenue when output is changed by one unit, therefore differentiating the total revenue expression results in the expression for marginal revenue (MR):

$$MR = 2Q/B - A/B$$

When marginal revenue equals zero the above equation becomes:

$$0 = 2Q/B - A/B$$

$$2Q/B = A/B$$

or:

$$Q = A/2$$

When $Q = A/2$, this is the midpoint on the demand line. Thus when MR = 0, this is associated with the midpoint on the demand curve and at this point the elasticity of demand is equal to 1. Points to the left of $A/2$ have positive MRs. That is, a reduction in price leads to a greater quantity being demanded and would be associated with the elastic range of the demand curve, while points to the right of MR = 0 have negative values for MR and will be associated with the inelastic range of the demand curve.

In the elastic range of the demand curve, decreases in price will be associated with reductions in MR but increases in total revenue. Therefore, if an organisation realises that it is currently in the elastic range of its demand curve, a reduction in price will lead to an increase in total revenue. A summary of the effect which elasticity can have on total revenue is shown below.

**Table 6.5 The relationship between elasticity and total revenue**

| Elasticity | Price increases | Price decreases |
|---|---|---|
| $\|E\| > 1$ (elastic) | TR falls | TR rises |
| $\|E\| = 1$ (unit elastic) | TR constant | TR constant |
| $\|E\| < 1$ (inelastic) | TR rises | TR falls |

From an organisation's point of view, if it is faced with putting up its prices it would want its demand curve to be in the inelastic range. Similarly, if it is faced with a decision to reduce prices it would prefer the demand curve to be elastic.

Since both the value of elasticity and marginal revenue are saying something about how total revenue changes, it would not be too surprising to find that MR and elasticity can be related mathematically. Appendix 6.2 establishes this relationship, but here it is stated as:

$$MR = P(1 + [1/E])$$

The importance of this relationship in terms of pricing policy will be discussed in Chapter 9.

## Factors that affect elasticity of demand

Table 6.6 shows estimates of the elasticities of demand in the UK for a range of products.

Table 6.6 also gives an insight into some of the factors that may affect price elasticity of demand. Necessities tend to have inelastic demands, and for items such as bread, milk and sugar this appears to be the case. Consumers are more price sensitive to changes in the price of cheese and carcass meat, where the demand for such products is elastic. In the case of carcass meat, a 10 per cent increase in price would reduce demand by almost 14 per cent. Table 6.6 also indicates that the demand for frozen peas is relatively elastic. It might be expected, therefore, that if the price of frozen peas increases consumers will switch to cheaper substitute products.

Thus the data in Table 6.6 explain two of the factors that can be related to the elasticity of

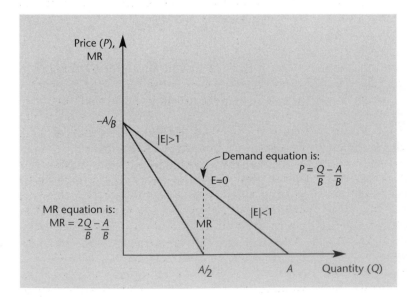

### Figure 6.10 Elasticity, marginal revenue and total revenue

The demand equation has an intercept on the vertical axis of $-A/B$ and a slope of $1/B$ where $B$ is negative. The marginal revenue equation has the same intercept on the vertical axis but has a slope twice the value of the demand equation. Where MR cuts the horizontal axis, MR = 0 and this is associated with quantity $A/2$. The demand equation cuts the horizontal axis at $Z = A$. Therefore the MR equation intersects the horizontal at the midpoint of the horizontal demand intercept. This is halfway along the demand line. Any quantity less than $A/2$ has a marginal revenue which is positive and this will be associated with increasing TR or where the elasticity of demand is in the elastic range.

**Table 6.6 Estimates of the price elasticity of demand for selected foodstuffs in the UK**

| Product | Price elasticity of demand |
|---|---|
| Bread | −0.09 |
| Milk | −0.18 |
| Sugar and preserves | −0.24 |
| Fresh potatoes | −0.21 |
| Other fresh vegetables | −0.25 |
| Processed vegetables | −0.54 |
| Frozen peas | −1.12 |
| Fruit juices | −0.80 |
| Cheese | −1.16 |
| Carcass meat | −1.37 |
| Other meat and meat products | −0.49 |
| Bacon and ham | −0.70 |
| Chicken (not free range) | −0.13 |
| Other poultry | −0.80 |
| Frozen convenience meat | −0.94 |

*Source*: *Annual Report of the National Food Survey Committee*, MAFF, 1995. The estimates are based on survey data between 1984, 1989 and 1995, HMSO. Crown Copyright 1995. Reproduced with the permission of the Controller of HMSO.

demand for a product. First, if the good is a necessity demand tends to be inelastic; and second, if there are substitutes for the product then the demand for the product will be elastic. What other factors affect the elasticity of demand?

The proportion of a consumer's income spent on a commodity may also affect the elasticity of demand. For example, the demand for products such as milk, tea and fast food may be relatively inelastic since they take up only a small proportion of average income. The demand for cars, holidays and housing may be much more sensitive to changes in price and it would be expected that the demand for these products would be relatively elastic.

The time period may also determine the measure of elasticity. When prices increase, consumers may take time to adjust their consumption patterns and find alternatives. The longer the time that consumers have to respond after a price change, the more inelastic the demand is likely to be. For example, large grocery multiples realise that consumers buy some products habitually, or their lifestyle is such that they do not have time to assess all the prices in their shopping basket. Thus these stores are able to raise the price of some products without seeing any major change in demand in the short term. After a time, however, consumers may realise that the price of their shopping has increased and begin to examine the prices of their purchases more closely; they may then substitute cheaper products for the more expensive ones. In other words, the

elasticity of demand for products may become more elastic in the long term.

Durable products tend to be more price elastic than are non-durable goods. This is probably due to the fact that not only are there often other durable goods which act as substitutes but it may also be possible to repair the durable good. Since durable goods often take up a larger proportion of income, consumers may wait until durable goods are discounted before entering the market. This may lead to a high degree of volatility in durable good sales.

Furthermore, the elasticity of demand for an individual firm may be different to that faced by the industry as a whole. The demand for petrol (gasoline/diesel) may be inelastic, but since there are a number of suppliers of petrol, an increase in the price of one supplier's petrol may lead to customers switching to competitive suppliers. Therefore the demand for petrol faced by an individual supplier may be thought of as elastic.

Before leaving this section on price elasticity of demand, it is worth developing the idea of how estimates of the price elasticities of demand are obtained. One method is to develop a regression model (*see* Chapter 7) based on the equation form chosen to represent the relationship between quantity demanded and its independent variables. Earlier in this chapter two alternative equation forms were developed, linear and multiplicative. From both of these forms we can obtain estimates of the elasticity of demand. In the linear form the elasticity is given by:

$$Ed_x = B_0 \times P_x / Q_x$$

while in the multiplicative form the elasticity of demand is equal to:

$$Ed_x = B_0$$

In the linear form the elasticity of demand is always the reciprocal of the slope of the straight-line demand relationship multiplied by price divided by quantity. This measure of elasticity rules out a demand relationship which is a curve. Here the slope changes at each point.

In the multiplicative form, the elasticity is always equal to $B_0$, the coefficient attached to the price of the product. This has advantages for the organisation, since no further mathematical calculations are required to find the own price elasticity of demand. However, the weakness with the multiplicative approach is that the elasticity value is constant and it has been argued earlier that the value for elasticity would be expected to vary as movements occur up and down the demand line. These ideas are further developed in Appendix 6.3.

Price is only one of the variables on the right-hand side of the demand function. It may be useful, therefore, to consider some of the other important measures of elasticity.

## Income elasticity of demand

**Income elasticity of demand** may be defined as the percentage change in quantity demanded of a good divided by the percentage change in income, all other factors remaining unchanged (*ceteris paribus*). Mathematically this definition can be written as:

$$E_Y = \Delta Qd_x/\Delta Y \times Y/Qd_x$$

or in terms of differentials:

$$E_Y = dQd_x/dY \times Y/Qd_x$$

This expression is similar to the price elasticity of demand formula seen earlier in this chapter, but here income ($Y$) has been substituted for own price.

For the majority of products it would be expected that as income increases (decreases) the quantity demanded would increase (decrease). These goods would be viewed as normal or superior goods. In this case the elasticity of demand would be positive. There are some goods for which demand decreases as the level of income rises and these are called inferior goods. Such goods have negative income elasticities.

As with price elasticity, it is possible to consider income elasticity over a range rather than at a point and the corresponding arc elasticity is given by:

$$E_Y = (Q_2 - Q_1)/(Y_2 - Y_1) \times (Y_2 + Y_1)/(Q_2 + Q_1)$$

Table 6.7 shows the income elasticities of demand for a variety of food products in the UK.

What Table 6.7 indicates is that certain products are inferior goods, such as margarine, potatoes and sugar, while foodstuffs, such as fruit juices, yoghurt and natural cheese, are superior products. It would not be possible to assume that these elasticities do not alter over time, since even more superior brands or goods can be brought to the market in the future. However, from an organisation's point of view, it is relevant to the way consumers perceive its products.

Generally, it is possible to categorise income elasticities of demand further. Goods for which $0<E_Y<1$ are normal goods, but can be described as **non-cyclical goods**. When income increases the demand for these products rises too, but the increase in demand is proportionately less than

### Table 6.7 Estimates of the income elasticities of demand for selected foodstuffs

| Product | Income elasticity |
| --- | --- |
| Margarine | −0.44 |
| Potatoes | −0.48 |
| Sugar and preserves | −0.54 |
| Bread | −0.25 |
| Cakes and biscuits | 0.02 |
| Tea | −0.56 |
| Instant coffee | 0.23 |
| Cheese, all | 0.19 |
| Natural cheese | 0.22 |
| Processed cheese | −0.12 |
| Fruit juices | 0.94 |
| Yoghurt | 0.58 |
| Fresh vegetables excluding potatoes | 0.35 |

*Source: Annual Report of the National Food Survey Committee*, MAFF, 1989. Crown Copyright 1989. Reproduced with the permission of the Controller of HMSO.

the increase in income. In Table 6.7 products that would fall into this category would be fresh vegetables, cheese and instant coffee.

Products which have $E_Y>1$ are also normal goods, but in addition they are products for which demand increases proportionately more when income rises. These are products whose demand is related closely to the economic cycle, thus they are called **cyclical normal goods**. The types of products that would fall into this category are those which have seen demand reduced during the recession in European economies during the early 1990s. These would be cars, capital expenditure, housing and white goods such as fridges, freezers etc.

## The importance of income elasticity

Knowledge of the various elasticities of demand is important for both organisations and government. A downturn in the economic cycle will be more harmful for organisations which produce normal cyclical goods. It may be possible, therefore, for governments to consider some form of aid package for these companies, particularly if they are located in specific regions. Agricultural products appear to have low income elasticities, thus in boom times there will be a switch in demand towards superior food products which can result in oversupply of staple products and reduced income for farmers.

From an organisation's point of view, companies which face negative income elasticities of demand for their products will see demand falling as real incomes increase. If they produce only a limited range of products, sales and profits may fall, perhaps leading to the closure of the business. The way forward for the organisation may be to diversify, producing cyclical and counter-cyclical products, merge or take over another company which produces products which are in a different cycle to those currently produced by the firm, or undertake a marketing campaign to alter consumers' image of the product. Such a campaign might be able to transfer perception of the product from inferior to normal or superior. On the other hand, if an organisation's product is normal but with an income elasticity of less than one, it is relatively recession proof and demand will not react in a volatile way as the economy moves through its trade cycles.

## Cross-elasticity of demand

It is very likely that a firm's products will be related to other products. Some of these related products will be substitutes, while others will be complementary. **Cross-elasticity** provides a measure of the degree of substitutability or complementarity between two products.

This is defined as the percentage change in quantity demanded of good $X$ divided by the percentage change in price of good $Y$:

$$E_{XY} = \frac{\text{Percentage change in quantity demanded of good } X}{\text{Percentage change in price of good } Y}$$

Using the formulae seen earlier, cross-elasticity may be written as:

$$E_{XY} = \Delta Q_X / \Delta P_Y \times P_Y / Q_X$$

In terms of differentials:

$$E_{XY} = dQ_X / dP_Y \times P_Y / Q_X$$

For arc cross-elasticity the formula is again similar to those developed before:

$$E_{XY} = (Q_{X2} - Q_{X1})/(P_{Y2} - P_{Y1}) \times (P_{Y1} + P_{Y2})/(Q_{X1} + Q_{X2})$$

If the products concerned are substitutes, then as the price of $Y$ increases, the demand for $Y$ will fall and the quantity demanded of the substitute good, $X$, will rise. The cross-elasticity of demand will be positive. For goods which are complements, the cross-elasticity of demand will be negative.

In the hi-fi industry, there would be expected to be a high positive cross-elasticity of demand between the compact disc players of Sony, Philips and Marantz, for example. In the same industry there would be expected to be a high negative cross-elasticity of demand for compact discs and compact disc players. Similarly, a high negative cross-elasticity exists for computer game software and computer game consoles.

Therefore, knowledge of the cross-elasticity of demand can tell an organisation how consumers view their rivals' products. This can therefore influence the pricing strategy that the organisation follows. Moreover, if the firm produces a range of products cross-elasticity can explain joint-product pricing; *see* Chapter 10. Of course, there are degrees of cross-elasticity. A small positive value for cross-elasticity suggests that, although the two products in question are substitutes, there is a weak relationship between them. The same type of analysis would be true for products where the cross-elasticity was a small negative number, but in this case the two products have a weak complementary relationship. Where the cross-elasticity equals zero there is no relationship between the two products.

The value of cross-elasticities of demand centres around whether the results are positive or negative. If the answer is positive, when do two products become strong substitutes? The answer to this question is really a matter of judgement. For some individuals a value of 1 for cross-elasticity of demand would represent a strong substitution effect, while for others it would imply a weak substitution effect. All that it is possible to say is that if the cross-elasticity of demand increases from 1 to 3 then the substitution effect is becoming stronger.

## ◆ CASE STUDY 6.4

## The UK newspaper industry: a case of cross-elasticity?

The price cut by the *Times* newspaper in July 1993 from 45 pence to 30 pence and the subsequent reduction to 20 pence at the end of June 1994 had a definite impact on the sales of the *Daily Telegraph* and other quality newspapers, as Table 6.8 indicates.

It is possible to calculate the cross-elasticity of demand for the *Daily Telegraph*, the *Independent* or any of the other quality newspapers. For example, taking the *Independent*, the cross-elasticity with the *Times* is 0.48. The cross-elasticity with the *Daily Telegraph* is 0.05. For both papers the cross-elasticity calculation makes the assumption that all other factors remain constant. In addition, both cross-elasticities are positive, suggesting that both the

▶

Case study 6.4 *continued*

**Table 6.8  Average daily broadsheet newspaper circulation**

|  | October 1992– March 1993 | October 1993– March 1994 |
|---|---|---|
| *Times* | 357 144 | 454 044 |
| *Daily Telegraph* | 1 033 573 | 1 016 468 |
| *Independent* | 358 102 | 300 849 |
| *Guardian* | 421 175 | 401 476 |
| Total | 2 187 994 | 2 172 837 |

*Source*: Audit Bureau of Circulation. Reprinted with permission.

*Independent* and the *Daily Telegraph* are substitutes for the *Times*, though in the *Daily Telegraph's* case it is only a weak substitute, which indicates strong brand loyalty.

By June 1994, the *Daily Telegraph* had seen sales fall below the 1 million mark, and the paper responded with a price cut from 48 pence to 30 pence. This was followed shortly thereafter by a cut in the price of the *Times* to 20 pence. By the middle of 1994, the sales of the *Daily Telegraph* had begun to rally; the sales of the *Times* continued to rise while those of the other quality newspapers continued to fall.

*Source*: Authors.

---

◆ **Exercise 6.6**

**1** Calculate the cross-elasticity of demand for the *Guardian* with the *Times*.
**2** Do you think that the price war in the newspaper industry can continue in the long term?
**3** Why has the *Guardian* not been involved in a price war?

## Advertising elasticity of demand

**Advertising elasticity** measures the responsiveness of sales to changes in advertising expenditure, and is defined as the percentage change in sales (output) of a product divided by the percentage change in advertising expenditure (A):

$$E_A = \frac{\text{Percentage change in output (sales)}}{\text{Percentage change in advertising expenditure}}$$

Mathematically, its definition is once again similar to the other elasticities discussed earlier:

$$E_A = \Delta Q_x/\Delta A_x \times A_x/Q_x$$

The arc advertising elasticity would be given by:

$$E_A = (Q_{x2} - Q_{x1})/(A_{x2} - A_{x1}) \times (A_{x1} + A_{x2})/(Q_{x1} + Q_{x2})$$

Advertising would normally be expected to have a positive effect on quantity demanded (output), but this effect might also be expected to decline as advertising expenditure continues to rise. It is possible that advertising elasticities are small positive numbers, which may be a reflection of the need to advertise just to hold on to market share. Thus the size of the advertising elasticity of demand may be influenced by the competitive nature of the market, an area that is further discussed in Chapters 11 and 18. However, if the advertising elasticity is small, it may be an indication that the current advertising campaign is not working, even though it is targeted at the 'right' audience, and an organisation may need to assess the various media through which advertising is being used. Advertising may, of course, not be getting through to the right audience. Finally, where the elasticity of demand is small, it may be the case that the organisation's products are cyclical and the downturn in the economic cycle cannot be compensated for by increased and improved advertising.

◆ **CASE STUDY 6.5**

# Advertising effects and effectiveness: it's not always that easy

Advertising represents an important means by which organisations communicate with their customers, both current and potential. The objectives of an advertising campaign are to:

■ Create awareness of a new product or brand.
■ Inform customers of the features and benefits of the product or brand.

■ Create the desired perceptions of the product or brand.
■ Create a preference for the product or brand.
■ Persuade customers to purchase the product or brand.

Whilst it is relatively simple to clarify what is to be measured when studying advertising effectiveness, the quantification of the relationship between advertising and sales seems to be fraught with problems.

There are several reasons that it is hard to detect advertising effects in mature markets. First, it is highly probable that in mature markets firms are operating on or next to the saturation point on their advertising response curves. Second, it is unlikely that new users exist, so most users will have had prior product experience and much brand choice will be based on inertia. Third, mature markets are competitive, so it is likely that there will be high levels of competitive advertising. Fourth, consumers' product-brand knowledge structures are likely to be well informed, so information needs are minimal.

In many cases advertising may be working simply to maintain the status quo, and the only way to detect the impact of advertising would be to eliminate it entirely to see if sales decline. This approach was taken by Maxwell House coffee during the late 1980s and sales declined appreciably.

Other factors also throw the link between advertising and sales into confusion. It is not usually the case that the other factors in the demand function are constant when advertising levels are changed. There is the possibility of reverse causality, with advertising affecting sales and the level of sales influencing the level of advertising expenditure. Advertising may be seen to be progressive in that sufficient levels of advertising may be needed before consumers change purchasing behaviour. Thus in the first instance advertising elasticities may be particularly small.

All these factors suggest, therefore, that the result of advertising elasticity calculations may not give an accurate picture in the short term of the success or failure of advertising campaigns.

*Source*: Adapted from D'Souza, G and Rau, R C (1995) 'Can repeating an advertisement more frequently than the competition affect brand preference in a mature market?', *Journal of Marketing*, April. Reprinted with permission of the *Journal of Marketing*.

◆ **Exercise 6.7**

1 Using a product of your choice, assess whether advertising has affected demand.

2 What other forms of non-price factors can be used to enhance product sales?

## Other elasticities of demand

At the beginning of this chapter a demand function was developed. In terms of the elasticities of demand that have subsequently been discussed, only four of the independent variables in the demand function have been utilised. It is possible, therefore, to consider other elasticities related to the other variables in the demand function. For example, cross-advertising elasticity of demand considers the change in the quantity demanded of good $X$ when the advertising expenditure on good $Y$ is altered. If $X$ and $Y$ are substitutes, then the cross-advertising elasticity of demand would be negative. For example, when a new video is released on to the market it is usually heavily advertised and the impact will be seen in declining sales of existing videos. For complementary products the cross-advertising elasticity would be positive. An organisation which produces a range of products which are complementary to one another, for example films and cameras, can heavily advertise one of the commodities and see an increase in sales of the complementary product.

Other elasticities which are of relevance are interest rate elasticities. Before the UK's entry into the European Exchange Rate Mechanism, interest rates had increased markedly, which reduced consumer demand for credit and subsequently reduced the demand for housing, cars and other durable goods. Knowledge of the interest rate elasticity of demand could enable organisations to ascertain the impact of these rate changes on demand. Finally, the weather elasticity of demand for products may be relevant for certain industries. Knowledge of this elasticity is important for the energy-generating industries. During warmer spells it has been noticed that there has been an upward shift in the demand for soft drinks and beer. If organisations know their weather elasticities of demand, then resource planning becomes much easier.

## Using elasticities in management decisions

The various elasticity values discussed previously allow managers of organisations to identify the relative importance of various factors in relation to the quantity demanded. The elasticity information, however, should be used with care. First, it may be point elasticity that has been calculated, thus the manager is not in a position to say that the elasticity calculated will remain at this level over the longer term. Second, in undertaking calculations for the various elasticities it has been assumed that all other factors remain constant;

often this is not the case. If many factors are changing simultaneously then there is an identification problem – see Chapter 7. Others argue that if the information is already available to calculate the elasticities of demand it could have been put to better use and the elasticity calculation is therefore unnecessary. However, there are many points in favour of elasticity calculations. Determining the sign and the size of the elasticity calculations provides a quick and easy method of assessing the relationship between an independent variable and its effect on the quantity demanded. It also allows the manager to rank the values of elasticity so that their relative effects can be compared.

Knowledge of price elasticity of demand can also help bridge the gap between pricing in theory and pricing in practice, since it permits the optimal markup to be applied to unit costs, thus allowing the profit-maximising prices of products to be determined.

Price elasticity of demand also plays a major role in the organisation's ability to discriminate between various markets, allowing the organisation to make larger profits than it would otherwise have if it had charged the same price in all markets. For example, because of the relationship between price elasticity and revenue, British Rail managers can determine whether price increases for rail commuters increases revenue from rail routes, or whether its policy of attempting to make rail lines pay is driving too many rail commuters away from rail and on to roads.

## THE DEMAND CURVE FOR THE INDIVIDUAL FIRM

Much of the analysis above has concentrated on the demand faced by the market. This market can be made up from a single firm, a few firms or many firms. Thus the competitive structure of the market may influence the shape of the demand curve faced by the individual firm. Moreover, even if there is a single producer of a commodity in the market, from a consumer's perspective this product may not be greatly differentiated from other products. For example, suppose that the apple industry only has one producer. If consumers see pears and other soft fruit as very close substitutes, then the demand curve faced by the apple producer is more elastic than might be expected under monopoly conditions. The nature of the product and the number of suppliers in a market may influence the elasticity of demand for the product. Where a market has a single provider it would be expected that the demand curve facing the individual firm would be fairly inelastic; where markets have a number of suppliers and the firms producing these products are in competition with one another, then the demand curve faced by an individual firm is more elastic. The nature of these markets is discussed in more detail later.

In addition to the numbers of suppliers in the market, the nature of the product itself may influence the elasticity of demand. Where a product is highly differentiated from its competitors then the demand curve may be fairly inelastic. One role of advertising, discussed in Chapter 11, is not only to push the demand curve for a product to the right but also to make it more inelastic. That is, the firm attempts to use advertising to enhance the difference between its product and those produced by its rivals.

Finally, the elasticity of demand for a firm's product may depend on the reaction to a price change by its rivals. If an organisation can alter its price without there being any change in the pricing behaviour used by its rivals, then the demand for its product may be fairly inelastic. If, however, rivals respond to the change in price by also changing their price, then demand may remain unaltered.

## ◆ CASE STUDY 6.6

### The demand for Mercedes-Benz cars

The factors that are believed to influence the current and future level of demand for Mercedes cars can be viewed under a number of headings: external threats, external opportunities and internal strengths. In Chapter 14 these are developed more fully in the context of business strategy, but here the emphasis is on demand-side factors.

There are a number of important competitors to Mercedes in the car market. In Europe and around the world the German BMW firm is the major competitor. Historically, BMW's strength was in the small car sector of the market, but with the development of its series 5 and 7 ranges it now competes directly with Mercedes' mid-range and luxury cars. The cooperation agreement between Renault (France) and Volvo (Sweden) in 1993 reduced these companies' car development costs and made their cars more competitive with Mercedes in the European market. In order to gain access to the Mercedes/BMW dominated luxury car market, Ford acquired the British company Jaguar. An even greater threat to Mercedes comes from the Japanese car makers, with the introduction of the Lexus and Infinity by Toyota and Nissan respectively. Thus the growth in the number of competitors and their pricing strategy has the potential to threaten the demand for Mercedes cars.

Another threat to Mercedes in particular comes from the laws and regulations governing emission requirements. Diesel engines, traditionally used by Mercedes, have come under criticism by environmentalists for their polluting effects. In addition, diesels are still seen to lack the power of petrol-driven engines and the switch in tastes to faster driving does not auger well for the diesel car.

Nonetheless, there are positive demand-side factors to consider for Mercedes. The high growth records of the Pacific Rim countries has seen an increased demand for quality luxury cars. The Single European Market is likely to enhance demand within the European Union and, while the improvement in the Eastern European economies will lead to an increase in demand for smaller/cheaper cars in the short term, the long-term scenario bodes well for Mercedes.

There must be a great temptation for Mercedes to try to lower its cost base by seeking suppliers in the new democratic Eastern European countries; however, the concern must be that its quality image would suffer. Currently, Mercedes is able to provide consumers with a picture of a high-priced quality product, which is technologically superior to many of its rivals.

One major problem that needs to be addressed is timing. Demand for even the best product may fail if the product is introduced to the market at the wrong time. Currently, it still takes Mercedes too long to get a new car to the market. Japanese companies have a much shorter product-development cycle and Mercedes has little choice but to speed up its development phase.

*Source*: Adapted from Weihrich, H (1993) 'Mercedes-Benz's move towards the next century', *European Business Review*, Vol 93, No 1. Reproduced by permission of MCB University Press.

### Comment on the case study

The Mercedes case indicates the importance to an organisation of changes in demand. Demand is not always going to be on an upward trend. Threats to demand may come about through the entry of new firms into a market which was previously thought to be safe. Demand may decline because consumer tastes change. Demand may also change because of the lifecycle of an organisation's products. Faced with a decline in demand firms may seek to buy out competitors, reposition its products in the market, undertake R&D to introduce new products on to the market or move into new markets. It is quite possible that decline in demand in the home market will lead to an organisation becoming more international.

# INTERNATIONAL CONVERGENCE OF TASTES

It has been established that the elasticity of demand an organisation faces for its product can be related to the number of competitors in the market, how well the product is differentiated from its competition and perhaps how well markets can be separated within a country.

On a national level organisations can benefit if markets can be separated geographically, since it is possible to charge different prices in different markets. In other words, the elasticities of demand are different in different markets.

Since the 1950s markets have tended to become more international. International finance, trading blocs, international media, international travel and multinational enterprises has meant that markets which used to be separated, both economically and culturally, have now drawn closer together. In many respects there has been a convergence of tastes between markets. This convergence has resulted in the elasticities of demand for products in different countries becoming closer. This can be seen in global products such as Fosters lager, McDonald's hamburgers, Nike and Reebok sportswear, the Ford Mondeo and Sony electrical/electronic equipment. If this process continues, then nationally based organisations will see future changes in their elasticities of demand as products previously not considered substitutes now become more acceptable as cultural and economic barriers are gradually eroded.

# SUMMARY

◆ Understanding demand and the factors that affect demand for an organisation's output are critical to resource planning. The relationship between the quantity demanded and the factors that affect this can easily be represented in a demand function.

◆ To understand how each of the variables on the right-hand side of the demand function is related to the quantity demanded requires the consideration of pairs of variables – the dependent variable and an independent variable, holding all of the other independent variables constant.

◆ If the dependent variable quantity and the independent variable price are considered, then the relationship is the demand curve. This is normally downward sloping to the right. In other words, as the price of a commodity is increased consumers demand less of the commodity.

◆ Changes in price are represented by a movement along a demand curve, whereas changes in the other factors on the right-hand side of the demand function lead to shifts in the demand curve. Changes in income, advertising or the price of substitute goods, for example, would lead to shifts in the demand curve.

◆ Some of the factors that cause shifts in the demand curve are under the control of the organisation. These would be the product's price, the organisation's level of advertising expenditure and product design. These are known as endogenous variables. Other variables in the demand function are outside the control of the organisation, such as consumers' income, competitors' advertising and changes in government policy. These are called exogenous variables.

◆ Elasticity is a measure of the responsiveness of one economic variable to another. In terms of demand theory, there are a number of measures of elasticity that are important for an organisation. Price elasticity of demand measures the responsiveness of demand to a change in the product's price. Cross-elasticity of demand measures the responsiveness of the quantity demanded of good $X$ to a price change in a related good. Income elasticity measures the responsiveness of a change in demand to changes in income. Advertising elasticity of demand measures the responsiveness of a change in quantity to a change in the organisation's level of advertising.

◆ Price elasticity can be elastic; that is, a change in price results in a larger proportionate change in the level of quantity and the price elasticity of demand will exceed 1. Goods can have unit elasticity; that is, a change in price results in a similar proportionate change in quantity that leaves total revenue unchanged. Finally goods can have inelastic demand, in that a change in price results in a smaller proportionate change in quantity. Here the elasticity of demand is indicated by $0<Ed<1$.

◆ Income elasticity can be positive, showing goods are normal, or negative, indicating that the good is inferior. Normal goods which have income elasticities greater than 1 are called cyclical normal goods. Normal goods which have an income elasticity, $0<E_Y<1$, are called non-cyclical normal goods.

◆ Cross-elasticities can be positive, indicating that the relationship between two commodities is one of substitution. Where the cross-elasticity of demand is negative the two commodities are complements.

◆ An understanding of the various elasticities of demand can prove to be very useful for the organisation in forecasting demand for its products, and these elasticities are easily calculated from statistical demand equations.

# REVIEW QUESTIONS

1  Explain what is meant by cross-elasticity of demand. Indicate how this might be measured and discuss how information about cross-elasticity of demand might be used by an Italian firm producing wine.

2  When is arc elasticity more useful for an organisation than the point elasticity concept?

3  The demand for holiday chalets in Normandy has been estimated to be $Q_d = 100\,000 - 45P$. If it is assumed that this relationship between price and quantity is valid in the future, calculate:

a The number of holiday chalets that would be demanded when the price is FF2000, FF4000, FF7000.

b The point price elasticity of demand at FF2000, FF4000, FF7000.

c The arc price elasticity between FF4000 and FF7000.

d Suppose that more British tourists wish to go on holiday to Normandy next year. What impact will this have on the demand for holiday chalets?

4 Would you consider the price elasticity of demand for the following products to be high or low?

    a Levi's jeans.

    b Fiat Puntos.

    c Coca-Cola.

    d Sainsbury's cola.

    e Snickers bars.

5 Explain how you would derive a demand curve for a particular product Z, given the following information: $P_z = Dm5$, $Q_z = 30$ and the price elasticity of demand is –1.2.

6 You have been given the following information about your products' income elasticities:

**Table 6.9**

| Product | Income elasticity |
|---------|-------------------|
| Shoes | –0.5 |
| Trousers | +0.3 |
| Shirts | +2.4 |
| Ties | +0.1 |
| Jackets | –0.3 |

Explain to your managing director the impact of the economic cycle on the demand for your organisation's products.

7 The Oslo Furniture Company has calculated that its demand equation for tables looks like the following:

$$Q_d = 3000 + 38P - 92A + 9Y + 19P_{other}$$

where,

    $Q_d$ = quantity demanded of tables
    $P$ = price of tables
    $A$ = advertising expenditure on tables
    $Y$ = consumers' income
    $P_{other}$ = price of competitors' tables

Would you consider the demand equation calculated above to be an appropriate one for the Oslo Furniture Company? Explain your answer.

8 An organisation has calculated the following elasticities for its product:

    Own price elasticity of demand = –0.3

    Advertising elasticity of demand = 0.2

    Cross-elasticity of demand = 0.01

What do these elasticities of demand imply for the organisation's pricing and advertising policy?

9 The demand equation for Luxembourg Ales is given by the following:

$$Q_d = 1273 - 4P + 11A - 8P_{other}$$

where,

$Q_d$ = the quantity demanded of lager
$P$ = the price of Luxembourg Ales' lager
$A$ = the level of advertising on lager undertaken by Luxembourg Ales
$P_{other}$ = the price of a related product

Suppose that Luxembourg Ales has the following information:

$P$ = Lf2000
$A$ = Lf10 000
$P_{other}$ = Lf3000

Calculate:

a The point own price elasticity of demand for lager.

b The point advertising elasticity of demand for lager.

c The point cross-elasticity of demand for lager.

# Appendix 6.1

## THE ALTERNATIVE APPROACH TO CALCULATING MARGINAL REVENUE

Earlier in this chapter marginal revenue was obtained by differentiating the total revenue function with respect to quantity. Since marginal revenue is defined as the change in total revenue as output (quantity) is varied by one unit, an alternative approach to calculating marginal revenue is to take the total revenue function and substitute into it a value for quantity. If quantity is now increased by one unit, then total revenue can again be calculated. The difference between the two total revenue values will give the value for marginal revenue.

Using the equation seen earlier:

$$TR = 12.5Qd_x - 0.0125Qd_x^2$$

suppose $Qd_x = 1$

$$TR = 12.5 - 0.0125 = 12.4875$$

Suppose the value of $Qd_x$ is increased to 2.

Total revenue now becomes:

$$TR = (12.5)2 - (0.0125)4$$

$$TR = 25 - 0.05 = 24.95$$

$$\text{Marginal Revenue (MR)} = \frac{\text{Change in Total revenue}}{\text{Change in quantity by one unit}}$$

$$MR = \frac{24.95 - 12.4875}{2 - 1}$$

$$MR = 12.4625$$

If the marginal revenue equation earlier is used to calculate marginal revenue, then:

$$MR = 12.5 - 0.025Qd_x$$

Substituting the value $Qd_x = 1$ in the above equation yields:

$$MR = 12.475$$

Substituting the value $Qd_x = 2$ gives:

$$MR = 12.45$$

The midpoint between these two values for MR is 12.4625, which is the same as the value of MR calculated by using the difference in the total revenue equation. This latter calculation is based on calculating MR at the midpoint between two levels of output.

# Appendix 6.2

## THE RELATIONSHIP BETWEEN MARGINAL REVENUE AND ELASTICITY

Total revenue (TR) = Price × Quantity

Marginal revenue (MR) = $\dfrac{\text{Change in TR}}{\text{Change in output by one unit}}$

Suppose that when the price level is $P_1$ the quantity demanded is $Q_1$, TR = $P_1Q_1$. Similarly, when the price level changes to $P_2$ the level of quantity changes to $Q_2$, TR = $P_2Q_2$.

The change in TR = $P_2Q_2 - P_1Q_1$.

The price level $P_2$ is made up from the original price $P_1$ plus the change in the price, that is:

$P_2 = (P_1 + \Delta P)$

Similarly, $Q_2 = (Q_1 + \Delta Q)$.

If there is a price fall from $P_1$ to $P_2$, then $\Delta P$ is negative and $\Delta Q$ will be positive.

The change in total revenue (TR) = $(P_1 + \Delta P)(Q_1 + \Delta Q) - P_1Q_1$.

Multiplying and removing the brackets gives:

$\Delta TR = P_1Q_1 + P_1 \Delta Q + Q_1 \Delta P + \Delta P \Delta Q - P_1Q_1$

This simplifies to:

$\Delta TR = P_1 \Delta Q + Q_1 \Delta P + \Delta P \Delta Q$

Since only small adjustments in price are being considered, the last term in the above equation can be ignored.

Now, MR = $\Delta TR/ \Delta Q$, therefore from above MR = $P_1 + Q_1\Delta P/\Delta Q$ (1)

For price $P_1$ and quantity $Q_1$, the point elasticity of demand is shown by:

$Ed = \Delta Q/\Delta P \times P_1/Q_1$

This can be rearranged to:

$Ed/P_1 = \Delta Q/\Delta P \times 1/Q_1$

The right-hand side of the above equation is the reciprocal of the final term in the marginal revenue equation, (1), above. Therefore, the marginal revenue equation can be rewritten as:

MR = $P_1 + P_1/Ed$, or MR = $P_1(1 + [1/Ed])$

# Appendix 6.3

## LOGS AND DIFFERENTIATION

With any equation the first differential gives us the slope of the line of curve. Suppose that we have the equation $Y = 3x^2$. The only two unknowns here are $Y$ and $x$. It is possible to draw this equation and if we did it would be a curve; you should try this. To find the slope of this curve, which we would expect to be different at each point since curves do not have constant slopes, we need to differentiate the above equation. That is, we need to answer the question, 'By how much will $Y$ change when we alter $x$?'. In mathematical terms this is shown as the differential of $Y$ with respect to $x$, or $dY/dx$.

There are many rules of differentiation, but the power function rule is the one needed here.

The power function rule is as follows. Given an equation of $Y = x^n$, then $dY/dx$ = power.coefficient.variable$^{power-1}$. Thus for equation $Y = 3x^2$ above, $dY/dx = 2.3.x^{2-1}$ or $dY/dx = 6x$. Since this is the slope term, we can see that the slope will alter for different values of $x$, which is what we would expect for a curve.

For an equation such as $Y = 8x$, $dY/dx = 1.8.x^{1-1}$. So $dY/dx = 8$. There are two important things to note here. First, when we write down an equation $Y = 8x$, it is really $Y = 8x^1$. Second, in mathematics anything to the power of 0 is equal to 1. As we can see from above, $dY/dx = 8x^0$. Since $x^0$ equals 1, then $dY/dx = 8$.

There are a number of rules of logarithms that are relevant for Equation 6.4. These are the log of a product rule and log of a power rule.

The log of a product rule states that:

$\log(wv) = \log w + \log v$ ($w,v > 0$)

so:

$\log(x^4.y^6) = \log x^4 + \log y^6$.

The log of a power rule states that:

$\log x^a = a.\log x$

so if $Y = x^3$, then taking logs of each side yields:

$\log Y = 3.\log x$

## Appendix 6.4

# CALCULATING ELASTICITIES FROM DEMAND EQUATIONS

Suppose that the organisation faces a linear demand equation of the form:

$$Q_x = A + B_0 P_x \qquad (6.11)$$

The point price elasticity of demand is given by:

$$Ed_x = dQ_x/dP_x \times P_x/Q_x$$

Equation 6.11 may be differentiated to find $dQ_x/dP_x$, which equals $B_0$. Substituting this into the elasticity formula gives:

$$Ed_x = B_0 \times P_x/Q_x$$

Suppose, however, that the demand equation is better described by the multiplicative form:

$$Q_x = AP_x^{B0} \qquad (6.12)$$

Then once again referring to the elasticity formula:

$$Ed_x = dQ_x/dP_x \times P_x/Q_x$$

is it possible to substitute for $dQ_x/dP_x$?

Differentiating Equation 6.12 with respect to price results in:

$$dQ_x/dP_x = (B0)AP_x^{B0-1}$$

The right-hand side of this equation can be re-written as:

$$dQ_x/dP_x = (B0)AP_x^{B0}/P_x \qquad (6.13)$$

Since $AP_x^{B0} = Q_x$ from Equation 6.12, then Equation 6.13 becomes:

$$dQ_x/dP_x = (B0)Q_x/P_x \qquad (6.14)$$

Equation 6.14 can now be rewritten as $B0 = dQ_x/dP_x \times P_x/Q_x$.

The right-hand side of this is the elasticity of demand, $Ed_x$. Therefore, $B0 = Ed_x$.

The power of the price variable is its elasticity.

## GLOSSARY OF NEW TERMS

**Advertising elasticity**: The percentage change in quantity demanded of a product divided by the percentage change in advertising of the commodity, all other factors remaining constant.

**Arc elasticity of demand**: The average elasticity over a particular range of a function.

**Complementary goods**: Where a consumer, when demanding one good, will also be likely to demand another good. For example, where an increase in the price of good $X$ leads to a fall in the demand for good $X$, and where $X$ and $Y$ are complementary goods, there will also be a fall in the demand for good $Y$.

**Cross-elasticity of demand**: The percentage change in quantity demanded of good $X$ divided by the percentage change in price of good $Y$, all other factors remaining constant (*ceteris paribus*).

**Cyclical normal goods**: Products for which demand rises powerfully when the level of income is increased.

**Demand function**: The relationship between the dependent variable, quantity demanded, and the variables that influence quantity demanded, the independent variables. These independent variables may include the level of advertising, own price and level of income.

**Derived demand**: The demand for all inputs used in the production of another commodity.

**Effective demand**: The level of desire or need for a product with the ability to pay for this need.

**Income elasticity of demand**: The ratio of the percentage change in quantity demanded of a good, divided by the percentage change in income, all other factors remaining constant.

**Marginal revenue**: The change in total revenue that arises when output is changed by one unit.

**Market demand curve**: The horizontal sum of individual consumers' demand curves.

**Non-cyclical normal goods**: Goods for which the demand increases weakly when the level of income increases.

**Price elasticity of demand**: The percentage change in quantity demanded of a good divided by the percentage change in price of the good, all other factors remaining constant.

**Shift in demand**: A movement of the demand curve either to the left or to the right that results from a change in one of the non-own-price factors in the demand function.

## READING

Baumol, W J (1981) 'On empirical determination of demand relationships', in Wagner, L (ed) *Readings in Applied Microeconomics*, Oxford University Press, Oxford.

Earl, P E (1995) *Microeconomics for Business and Marketing*, Edward Elgar, Aldershot.

*Financial Times*, 6 December 1994. Nakamoto, M, 'Survey of Jananese Industry (2)'.

Green, H A J (1971) *Consumer Theory*, Penguin Modern Economics, London.

Varian, H R (1991) *Intermediate Microeconomics: A Modern Approach*, 3rd edn, Norton, New York.

*There are many texts which provide the background to demand and elasticity. The above four books provide extensive information on this area and should be considered in detail if the student wishes to pursue further study.*

### Further reading

Herriges, J A and King, K K (1994) 'Residential demand for electricity under inverted block rates: evidence from a controlled experiment', *Journal of Business and Economic Statistics*, Vol 12, No 4, pp 419–30.

Jong-Ying, L (1994) 'Fresh fruit consumption in Japan', *Agribusiness*, Vol 10, No 6, pp 513–20.

CHAPTER 7

# ESTIMATING AND FORECASTING DEMAND

## KEY ISSUES

Business issues

Business strategy

Decision-making
techniques

Economic concepts

Management
decision issues

Optimal outcomes to
management issues

## OBJECTIVES

◆ To explain and discuss the implications of the
identification problem in estimating demand.

◆ To introduce and discuss a selection of techniques for
estimating and forecasting demand.

◆ To outline and discuss the advantages and disadvantages
of:

– Interviews and questionnaires, used to gauge initial
reactions to a proposed new or modified product.

– Consumer clinics and laboratory experiments, which
give guidance to producers about consumers' likes and
dislikes in relation to a number of alternatives for
characteristics of the new product or its packaging.

– Live market studies, used to gain reactions to the actual
products launched on to a market.

◆ To examine the appropriateness of the above techniques,
with reference to different situations.

◆ To explain the analysis of the results of an OLS regression
used to estimate demand and to highlight some of the
problems which arise when a model contains inaccuracies.

## CHAPTER OUTLINE

## KEY TERMS

## BUSINESS APPLICATION

# Porsche sees sharp expansion in output

FT

Porsche, the German sports car group which saw sales plummet in the early 1990s, expects to boost output to 18 500 units in the 1995–96 financial year, from 17 268 in 1994–95 and lift that to about 30 000 in 1996–97. The sharp expansion will come from the group's new two-seater Boxster convertible due to be launched in September.

Mr Hans Riedel, Porsche's head of sales and marketing, said more than 10 000 customers had made down-payments on Boxsters. Scotching fears that many would be trading down from Porsche's dearer 911 range, he said research into 2500 potential customers had shown that 80 per cent were first-time buyers. Porsche expects output to be divided equally between the 911 and the Boxster once the newcomer is in full production. Mr Wendelin Wiedeking, Porsche's chief executive, revealed the car, with a mid-mounted six-cylinder engine, would cost DM76 500 ($52 000) in Germany.

That is well below the 911 range and should help Porsche recapture some sales lost when it discontinued its cheaper four-cylinder range.

Market research had also shown the Boxster would appeal to female buyers, helping Porsche towards its target of having 30 per cent of its customers as female.

The company, which made net profits of DM10m in the first half of the current year, declined to give a full-year forecast beyond saying it should be 'clearly better'.

Sales to the end of January 1996 jumped 17 per cent to 9570, compared with the same period last year. Mr Wiedeking said recent figures 'continued the positive trend', confirming that 'Porsche has succeeded in making a turnround'.

Mr Wiedeking said the company, which reported a DM2.1m net profit in 1994–95, would focus on developing sales in new markets and reinforcing its presence in established regions.

*Source: Financial Times, 6 March 1996. Reprinted with permission.*

▶

*Comment*

What is market research? How does Porsche know that 30 per cent of the customers for its new Boxster car will be females? How does this help them to predict profit levels for the year? These types of questions will be answered much more fully in this chapter. Basically, however, Porsche has used data it already possesses and also surveyed customers and probably also dealers to gain new data in order to predict, or forecast, sales for the Boxster.

Existing data Porsche will already possess will be numbers of cars sold, the different prices charged for the cars, the locations of the sales and extras purchased by consumers. It may also know how frequently its loyal customers purchase new cars, whether they use Porsche-administrated finance agreements or other ways of paying for the cars and so on.

Dealers can provide the information discussed above. They will also be able to feed back typical consumer questions and comments about the cars. Market research literally means finding more out about the consumers. To do this, Porsche will have had to identify prospective consumers (perhaps via dealers) and gain information from them about their likes and dislikes, their income, the amount they would be willing to pay for a car, facts about their lifestyle and so on. Sometimes specialist agencies are contracted to undertake such projects; they have experience and ability not possessed by the commissioning organisation.

Once information has been collected, it must be processed, using the techniques given in this chapter. The results will allow organisations such as Porsche to forecast the levels of sales in the coming period and then, using the sales forecast in parallel with price and cost data, profits may also be forecast. Porsche has obviously taken a great deal of effort in order to undertake its market research; it even knows the likely proportion of female consumers. Such analysis would require the collection of more in-depth data than simply the potential levels of sales. As depth or quality of analysis increases, so too does cost. Organisations are aware of this and plan their market research with reference to their own budgets.

# INTRODUCTION

This chapter will introduce some of the basic techniques which are used when making estimates and forecasts of demand for different products and services. Qualitative methods will be introduced and discussed; this is where data relating to consumer preferences and attitudes are collected and analysed in order to estimate and forecast demand. Quantitative methods will also be explained. These utilise and manipulate existing data, about sales for example, to provide estimates or forecasts of future levels of sales.

# DEMAND ESTIMATION AND DEMAND FORECASTING

All organisations require information relating to the likely future demand for their product(s). If this information is available, they will then be able to plan stocks, production and so on so that they may best meet this demand. The better the estimates or forecasts of future demand, the more effective the organisation will be in making these plans, and there will be less waste, fewer stockouts and a reduced risk of launching new or modified products which fail to sell well in the marketplace.

Actual methods of demand estimation and forecasting vary from organisation to organisation. The possible techniques range from simple 'same as before' calculations to the use of complex computer models. Whichever is chosen, to be effective an organisation should be constantly reviewing and updating its forecasts in order to take account of the changes which occur in its chosen marketplace and within the economy. Thus, the forecasting cycle is a series of constantly changing and continually updated forecasts of demand for an organisation's product(s). This may be seen in Figure 7.1.

The forecasting cycle represents an ongoing improvement to existing forecasts or estimates. Before this point is reached, however, an initial forecast has to be made. The stages in making any forecast may be outlined as:

- Identify the relevant relationships (affecting demand).
- Measure the relationships identified.
- Simulate the identified relationship (that is, test the relationship on previous or historical data) and modify as appropriate to gain accuracy.
- Forecast future values using the modified relationship.

## Figure 7.1  The forecasting cycle

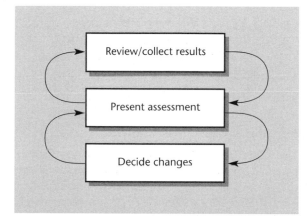

The forecasting cycle requires the organisation to use previous results to test its current model. If the model is no longer an accurate predictor of likely future values, due to changes in the market situation or economy, the model should be changed to take these into account. Any additional factors which need to be included as a result of changes in the market situation or economy should be incorporated. The organisation may then use its model to predict future values. In time, these results may be reviewed and the cycle will begin again.

# IDENTIFYING THE RELEVANT RELATIONSHIPS

In order for the organisation to be able to estimate or forecast demand for its product(s), it must first understand which factors affect that demand. These were introduced in Chapter 6 and should now be clear. An organisation may know that over different time periods, demand for its products changed with price. It would be tempting to tabulate and plot this relationship and to assume that the resultant table and graph were the demand schedule for the product. Consider Figure 7.2.

Assume that demand for the Erehwon Company's product over the last three time periods was known to have been quantities $Q_A$, $Q_B$ and $Q_C$, where the prices charged were $P_A$, $P_B$ and $P_C$. A denotes time period 1, B denotes time period 2 and C denotes time period 3. Plotting these points on the same price and quantity axes gives a downward-sloping relationship which looks like a standard demand curve.

This is not the case, however. Over the different time periods, how could the organisation be sure that other factors apart from price did not also change? This is the **identification problem**. Other factors which could also cause such a demand curve are competitors changing their prices, changes in fashions or tastes and also changes in the conditions of supply. The organisation therefore faces the identification problem: which factors change and affect demand for its product?

## Figure 7.2

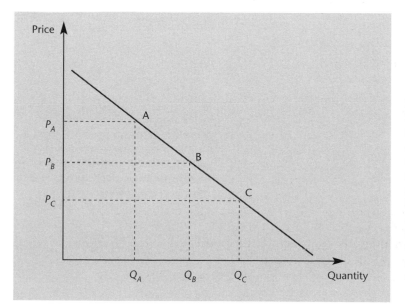

If demand over the last three time periods is known to have been quantities $Q_A$, $Q_B$ and $Q_C$, where the prices charged were $P_A$, $P_B$ and $P_C$, the relationship could be plotted as shown. However, plotting these points on the same price and quantity axes gives a downward-sloping relationship which looks like a standard demand curve. Further information, such as supply levels, is required in order to determine whether this is in fact a demand curve or not. (A denotes time period 1, B time period 2 and C time period 3.)

## SIMULTANEOUS RELATIONS

A complicating factor in attempting to identify the factors affecting demand is the interrelationship between supply and demand. Shifts of the supply curve will cause movements along the demand curve for a product and vice versa. These interrelationships between the curves are known as **simultaneous relations**. In order to estimate demand effectively for its product, an organisation needs to be able to analyse the interactions between its supply and demand functions and then isolate the effects of these changes. Thus, although the Erehwon Company's supply curves for each time period in the example given above can be superimposed on its demand curves, resulting in Figure 7.3, the problem of simultaneous relations and identification still exists.

In Figure 7.3, the relationship between supply and demand in each time period may clearly be seen. Each of the points $P$ and $Q$ is derived from the separate demand and supply curves. $D_A$ and $S_A$ are the curves corresponding to period 1 ($P_1$ and $Q_A$), $D_B$ and $S_B$ ($P_B$ and $Q_B$) the curves for period 2, and $D_C$ and $S_C$ ($P_C$ and $Q_C$) the curves for period 3. It should now be obvious that the graph plotted in Figure 7.2 is not a demand curve, merely a plot of the different periods' equilibria positions on the same axes. To estimate demand for the Erehwon Company's product, the changes in supply and demand need to be analysed, decomposed and stated individually. If this is possible, then statistical analysis of the data, such as **ordinary least squares (OLS)**, may be undertaken (*see* later in this chapter).

In cases where the identification problem may not be resolved, or where price and quantity data are not sufficient to make meaningful analysis, additional data relating to demand are required. This may be gathered by qualitative methods such as those discussed below.

## ESTIMATING DEMAND VIA QUALITATIVE METHODS

There are a number of qualitative methods by which demand may be estimated:

- Interviews and questionnaires.
- Laboratory experiments/consumer clinics.
- Market studies.

These methods are frequently used for the purposes of market research. Organisations are always searching for sources of **competitive advantage** over their competitors. If they can gain insight into consumer reactions to their products and those of competitors, future products can encompass appropriate modifications. Additionally, as a result of market research, organisations are able to identify the product attributes which are important to the consumer. Such information may then be used in future product development *and* also in advertising campaigns. Therefore, advertisements may direct consumers' attention to the key attributes identified, with a view to increasing sales.

**Figure 7.3**

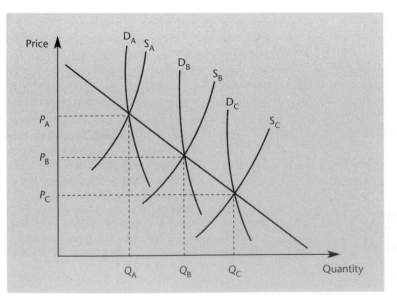

The relationships between supply and demand in each time period, 1, 2 and 3, are shown on the same axes. Each of the points $P$ and $Q$ are derived from these separate demand and supply curves. $D_A$ and $S_A$ are the curves corresponding to period 1 ($P_A$ and $Q_A$), $D_B$ and $S_B$ ($P_B$ and $Q_B$) the curves for period 2 and $D_C$ and $S_C$ ($P_C$ and $Q_C$) the curves for period 3.

The line joining the different equilibria is not a demand curve, merely a plot of the different periods' equilibria positions on the same axes.

# Interviews

Interviews and questionnaires can be as simple as an individual randomly soliciting consumer views when standing in the town centre on a Saturday morning, or as precise as identifying a target population and then contacting and interviewing each member of that population. What is important in this respect is the fact that the organisation is out in the marketplace and asking people's opinions about changes to products and new products which may be made available. When interviews or questionnaires are analysed, a number of inaccuracies may arise. If these are not accounted for (or the analyst is not aware of them) demand may be inaccurately estimated. Common problems arising are as follows.

## Sample bias (who is asked)

If the interview is intended to investigate the 'general public's' reaction to a new car product, it would bias the sample if the interviewer stood outside the local car accessories shop. The sample population in this respect would include a larger number of informed consumers than exist in the general population as a whole.

Another common bias which the interviewer (and interview designer) need to be aware of is the fact that, *typically*, the higher an individual's income, the less likely they are to be willing to spend time responding to interviews or questionnaires. Therefore, such techniques may be a poor vehicle for investigating higher income earners' attitudes to the issue/concept/product under consideration.

## Validity (honesty)

Validity could be summarised as follows:

■ Are the respondents telling the truth?
■ Are the respondents telling you what they think you want to hear?

These are common problems to be overcome. Repeating questions in a slightly different way throughout the interview or questionnaire can verify the consistency of a respondent's replies.

A common problem with both interviews and questionnaires is that the respondents tend to understate their age and overstate their income. A strategy used to get around these issues is to ask respondents to place their age (or income) within a band. For example, the income bands used by organisations specialising in collecting consumer opinion are usually similar to those given below:

Income: in which band does your gross (before deductions) annual salary fall?

> £0–£4 999
> £5 000–£9 999
> £10 000–£14 999
> £15 000–£19 999
> £20 000–£24 999
> £25 000–£29 999
> £30 000–£39 999
> £40 000–£49 999
> £50 000–£74 999
> £75 000–£99 999
> £100 000+

The respondent can then reply, in the case of a questionnaire, by marking the appropriate band, rather than needing to state their exact income. The higher the income, the larger the band; this reduces accuracy but also increases the likelihood of a higher income earner responding at all.

Even if the respondent is not deliberately trying to mislead, an interview or questionnaire presents inherent problems in terms of investigating attitudes to and estimating demand. As was discussed in Chapter 6, economists frequently make the assumption that individuals are **rational** and **utility maximising**. This is not necessarily the case. Consumers do not always act in a rational manner. It is asking a lot of consumers to be able to predict their (assumed rational) actions accurately when they are in the artificial situation of being questioned about their future purchasing habits.

Awareness of these factors will affect the validity of demand estimates.

## Reliability (accuracy)

Obviously, the data collected is of no use if it is not accurate. The better the understanding of the present market and consumers, the more effectively the organisation will be able to supply them in the future. To ensure and improve accuracy, larger samples of responses are collected. Increased sample size will decrease the effect of a 'freak' respondent's replies. The larger the sample size, the more acceptable the results will be, according to statistical theory.

Unfortunately, the larger the sample size, the greater the cost involved. Organisations undertaking such research must balance the cost against the level of accuracy required.

## Cost

Interviews are more costly than questionnaires as a way of investigating opinions and attitudes to obtain an estimate of demand. Interviews are usually more in-depth than questionnaires and may be used to seek clarification or more detail in areas of particular interest highlighted by questionnaire results.

Processing the information collected from interviews is more complicated, and hence costs more, than processing questionnaire results. This is especially true of situations where the interview includes questions demanding a 'free form' reply as opposed to asking which of a number of bands the appropriate answer falls into (*see* above). More interviewer training is required and fewer interviews can be completed in a given period.

Any organisation will be keen to reduce costs to as low a level as possible. Implementation costs may be managed more effectively by carefully considering the following:

- Accurate identification of the target sample population.
- Training the researchers about the nature of the interview/questionnaire being undertaken and also about identifying and approaching appropriate research subjects (i.e. making sure that they are able to recognise and identify people from the targeted sample population).
- Investigating the effectiveness of the interview or questionnaire by analysing the results of a pilot study before launching into full-scale implementation. Thus any problems arising from the wording of questions, lack of understanding on the part of the researcher etc. may be ironed out before major investment is made.

## Laboratory experiments/consumer clinics

Laboratory experiments are sometimes known as consumer clinics. These may be used to expose consumers to changes to a product which is already on the market and to gauge reactions to these changes, or to investigate reactions to new products. Consumer clinics are more expensive than interviews or questionnaires. As such, it can be in the organisation's interests to test the market via these less expensive methods and to use the consumer clinic as a way of confirming results, or for fine-tuning understanding of the market.

Consumer clinics take place in controlled environments, hence the alternative name 'laboratory experiments'. As many conditions as possible are maintained constant, while consumers' reactions to the new or changed product are observed. In consumer clinics consumers are invited to enter a mockup of a shop, designed to emulate the conditions under which the consumer usually makes a purchase decision. The consumer is given a budget or cash and asked to shop as they would do normally.

The organisation's product is placed next to competitors' products on the shelves in the mockup shop. The position on the shelf may be changed in order to ascertain the optimum position to bid for in the supermarkets. The packaging, pack size and so on may be changed. Prices are also changed in an attempt to ascertain the best price for the new product with reference to the market prices of competitors' products.

A number of problems/inaccuracies arise, however:

- Consumer reaction is difficult to gauge. Preconceptions and assumptions about consumer attitudes have to be made in order to gain an initial position from which to begin observations.
- Consumers are not spending their own money and may therefore not act as they would in a real shop.
- The controlled nature of the experiment may have an effect on the consumers' actions and the results.
- The consumer is aware that they are in a controlled environment and may try to act as they think they should, rather than how they would in real life.

Consumer clinics are nonetheless an important stage in the process of striving to understand and estimate consumers' demand for an organisation's product(s). Consumer clinics allow an insight into the manner in which consumers behave or are affected by changes. It is believed that a carefully controlled and analysed consumer clinic will mirror the manner in which the market will act once the product reaches it. Attention does need to be paid to selecting consumers for the clinic to ensure that they are representative of the market the product will enter.

## Market studies

Market studies are the most expensive way of estimating demand. Here, the product is released on to a given part or section of the market in order to gain final verification of likely total demand for the product(s). Market studies may precede a staged rollout of the product across the whole national or international market over time, or a full launch of the product across the market at once.

A market study involves changing certain variables, such as price, within a **test site/group**. Thus, reactions to the new or changed product/service may be gauged. Similar test sites or groups are used, with control groups being maintained throughout the period of the study.

Packaging materials, packaging colours and size can all be changed in a market study. Advertising for the product may also be undertaken. The Tyne Tees television region in the North East of England is often used as its geographical position provides a distinct control area for the purpose of such studies.

Within the Tyne Tees area, three rivers provide the population focus for the three major conurbations which exist around Middlesborough (Tees), Newcastle-upon-Tyne (Tyne) and Sunderland (Wear). These conurbations are surrounded by networks of villages and smaller towns. To the south the North Yorks Moors, to the west the Yorkshire Dales and to the north the Cheviots make a natural geological boundary to the area. Few, if any, other areas in the UK possess such characteristics.

Additionally, Newcastle-upon-Tyne is often seen as a microcosm of London; it is keen to be seen as such and several local development agency advertising initiatives have included this message. Fashions and trends often reach Newcastle at the same time as they reach London. It is therefore cheaper and easier to take reactions there as an indication of the likely reactions of the population as a whole than to mount campaigns in London and the South East. For example:

■ Cadbury's Twirl chocolate bar was tested in the Tyne Tees area before gaining national promotion and release.

■ Brylcreem tested its complete range of hair products in the area before national release.

Market studies are therefore effective vehicles for testing reactions to changes in product attributes. However, it is only *reactions* and not *habits* which are being monitored. A decrease in price may well induce more purchases of a product, but for how long? Consumers could lose interest in the product over time, or it could be superseded by a competitor's product. Increased purchase as a reaction to price decreases may also only signify that consumers are stockpiling the product.

## Summary of qualitative demand estimation methods

Overall, then, the difficulties involved in estimating demand via any of the methods discussed above are related by some common factors. The overriding worry is that the respondent is not acting or reacting as they would normally when exposed to the test. This may manifest itself as over- or understatement of quantitative data or acting or responding as the observer might wish, rather than honestly. There is nothing that can be done about these inaccuracies. Various methods exist to detect and minimise the effects of such behaviour; those outlined above were increased sample size, repeating questions in a slightly different way and so on.

The major problem faced by any organisation attempting to estimate demand is identification of the correct sample population. The subsequent piloting of any test will act to validate or disprove the assumptions made, allowing adjustments before the whole target sample is researched. Once piloting has been undertaken, the organisation will be in a more informed and confident position regarding the accuracy of the final results.

## ♦ CASE STUDY 7.1

## Furnishing the world

For managers the only thing harder than rescuing a failing business is reinventing a successful one. Nobody knows this principle better than retailers who venture overseas. As store chains strike out beyond their home markets, they often have to change the formula that had previously guaranteed success. This happens to many types of business, but retailers are particularly close to customers. They must therefore move especially fast to adapt to local peculiarities. The trick is to do so without destroying the very thing that made them successful in the first place.

As the world's most competitive retail market, the United States has a well-deserved reputation as a graveyard for foreign retailers – and especially for Europe's non-food retailers. Even Britain's Marks and Spencer has struggled to make a success of its acquisition of

▶

Case study 7.1 *continued*

Brooks Brothers. Four years ago it looked as if IKEA might suffer a similar fate.

Today, however, this Swedish firm is going from success to success in America. Its secret seems to be a classic example of the difficult art of 'change management'. IKEA has draped itself in the stars and stripes by adapting but not destroying its original formula. Meanwhile, its experience in America has persuaded it to remix its recipe elsewhere.

### In the beginning, hubris
It is not hard to see why IKEA was initially so confident about America. In the decade after it opened its first non-Scandinavian outlet, in Switzerland in 1973, the furnishing chain's vast out-of-town warehouse stores decked out in Sweden's blue and yellow colours had marched triumphantly across much of Western Europe.

Its formula was based on reinventing the furniture-retailing business. Traditionally, selling furniture was a fragmented affair, shared between department stores and small, family-owned shops. All sold expensive products for delivery up to two months after a customer's order.

IKEA's approach trims costs to a minimum while still offering service. It starts with a global sourcing network, which now stretches to 2300 suppliers in 67 countries.

IKEA displays its enormous range of more than 10 000 products in cheap out-of-town stores. It sells most of its furniture as knocked-down kits, for customers to take home and assemble themselves. The firm reaps huge economies of scale from the size of each store and the big production runs made possible by selling the same furniture all around the world.

This allows the firm to match rivals on quality, while undercutting them by up to 30% on price. An IKEA store, with its free crèche and Scandinavian café, is supposed to be a 'complete shopping destination' for value conscious, car-borne consumers. In the *Harvard Business Review* last year Richard Norman and Rafael Ramirez gushed that IKEA had forced both customers and suppliers to think about value in a new way 'in which customers are also suppliers (of time, labour, information and transportation), suppliers are also customers (of IKEA's business and technical services), and IKEA itself is not so much a retailer as the central star in a constellation of services'.

### Americans think bigger
Why, then, did this successful and apparently flexible system hit problems in America? In 1985, IKEA opened a 15 700 square metre (169 000 sq ft) warehouse store outside Philadelphia. At first, with the dollar at around SKr8.6, it was quite easy to make money, says

Anders Moberg, IKEA's chief executive. Six more shops (five on the east coast and one in Los Angeles) followed in as many years.

But things had started to go wrong. By 1989 the American operation looked to be in deep trouble. In each new European country it entered, the company had normally broken into profit after two or three years with its third or fourth store. In America it was still losing money. And this could not be blamed wholly on a slowdown in the economy and a weak furniture market.

Many people visited the stores, looked at the furniture, and left empty handed. Customers complained of long queues and constant non-availability of stock. Imitators were benefiting from the marketing effort IKEA had made in introducing Americans to Scandinavian design. Worst of all, since it was still making many of its products in Sweden, IKEA's cherished reputation for low-cost furniture was threatened as the dollar's value dropped to SKr5.8 by 1991.

### Use your eyes
To achieve this IKEA had to revise several of its central tenets. The most basic was that it could sell the same product in the same way in Houston as it could in Helsingborg. IKEA took this approach to such extremes that its advertising deliberately stressed not only its clean Scandinavian design, but its blue-and-yellow Swedishness.

IKEA had cheerfully broken several of the rules of international retailing: enter a market only after exhaustive study; cater for local tastes as much as possible; gain local expertise through acquisition, joint ventures or franchising. 'We don't spend much money or time on studies. We use our eyes and go out and look, and say it will probably do quite well here. Then we may adapt, but quite often we stick to our opinions,' says Mr Moberg.

This iconoclasm had paid off in Europe, but it helped to get the firm into trouble in America. In 1989 and 1990 Mr Moberg himself spent much time in the American stores, talking to customers. 'We were behaving like all Europeans, as exporters, which meant we were not really in the country,' he says. 'It took us time to learn this.'

Unapologetically European products jarred with American tastes and sometimes physiques. Swedish beds were narrow and measured in centimetres. IKEA did not sell the matching bedroom suites that Americans liked. Its kitchen cupboards were too narrow for the large dinner plates needed for pizza. Its glasses were too small for a nation that piles them high with ice: Mr Carstedt noticed that Americans were buying the firm's flower vases as glasses.

So IKEA's managers decided to adapt. The firm now sells king and queen-sized beds, in inches, as part of complete suites. After noticing that customers were inspecting IKEA's bedroom chest, and then walking away without buying, Mr Carstedt worked out that because Americans use them to store sweaters in, they wanted the drawers in the chests to be an inch or two deeper. Sales of the chests immediately increased by 30–40%. In all, IKEA has redesigned around a fifth of its product range in America; its kitchen units are next on the list.

The firm has changed its American operations in other ways, too. 'When we went in, we hadn't planned a clear strategy of how to supply the American market at low cost,' Mr Moberg admits. That meant, for example, that it was shipping sofas from Europe, adding to costs and problems of stock availability.

### Soul searching

Successful though the outcome has been, IKEA's American experience posed wider questions for the whole firm's future. Could it adapt its retailing concept to local peculiarities without compromising the Swedish identity at the heart of its marketing and brand image? Could it continue to control costs if it was forced to dilute the uniformity of its product range? And as the firm's operations became ever more global, could IKEA retain the intimate corporate culture that was an important part of its success?

In many ways, IKEA is still seeking answers. The search became urgent when, hard on the heels of its American difficulties, overall sales growth slackened thanks to slower than expected growth in Eastern Europe and recession in Sweden and Germany, IKEA's two largest markets. The firm reacted with intense soul-searching. In 1992–93, it opened only six new stores, compared with 16 the previous year.

Another problem imposed by growth was the management of an increasingly complex global supply chain, one that led to glitches in quality control and stock availability. The firm has begun random checks on goods as soon as it receives them; it has also taken equity stakes in some East European suppliers to help improve quality.

### And your lesson today

IKEA's contortions should frighten all would-be globalists. They show how even an adaptable system based on what Mr Moberg calls 'permanent evolution' could not prevent teething troubles in a major market. But unlike many foreign venturers, IKEA started with the advantages of being both unconventional and rich. As Vanessa Cohen, a retailing consultant at Coopers & Lybrand, points out, IKEA did comply with at least one of the rules of international retailing: its strong balance sheet in Europe enabled it to absorb its initial American losses.

So far the results of IKEA's reorganisation are encouraging. At 8.35 billion guilders ($4.5 billion), its sales for the year to August grew by 6%. IKEA does not reveal its profits, but outsiders estimate its 1993 net profit margin at 6.7%, a creditable figure given recession in core European markets. The firm claims that in the year to August, 116m customers – equivalent to 2% of the world's population – visited its 108 wholly owned stores, spread across 18 countries (another 15 stores, mainly in the Middle East, Hong Kong and Spain, are franchised).

*Source*: © *The Economist*, London, 19 November 1994. Reprinted with permission.

### ◆ Exercise 7.1

Why is it important for organisations to investigate thoroughly the level of likely demand for their new product(s) or within new markets which they wish to enter?

### Comment on the case study

An example of the importance of taking into account the views of the consumer may be seen in the case of the Swedish furnishing firm IKEA's attempt to break into the United States market.

IKEA, a Swedish furnishing retailer, opened its first US store near Philadelphia in 1985. Several others were opened in following years on the West Coast, close to Los Angeles. By 1989, it was obvious that people were visiting the stores, but were not purchasing. IKEA was not experiencing the usual stream of profits which had previously followed after two or three years of opening its third or fourth stores in a country. Something had gone wrong in the transition from European to global retailer.

Case study 7.1 claims that IKEA had failed to take account of the 'local peculiarities' presented by the US market. The strategy which had worked in Europe – selling furniture for home assembly, supplied by global suppliers with exclusive contracts from out-of-town stores – had failed in the US. All these factors kept costs down and prices up to 30 per cent lower than competitors. What had not been successfully transferred to the US market, however, was the product range and the shopping experience.

The problems with the shopping experience were that queues were longer than US customers were accustomed to and products were frequently out of stock, at least those which gained favour with the US market. At the time IKEA prided itself on supplying the same products worldwide (hence it was a low-cost global supplier). This was the problem. US consumers were obviously interested – they were looking but not buying. After investigation by some leading IKEA managers, including Anders Morberg, the chief executive, the problems were identified.

IKEA had not researched the US market prior to entry. It had followed its usual strategy of stepping into the market, believing that there were opportunities to be exploited. Indeed there were. However, had IKEA made use of qualitative methods to forecast demand and investigate reactions to its products, the initial problems would not have arisen. A study of the market would have highlighted the following:

■ The beds were too small for US tastes, and were in metric as opposed to imperial measurements.
■ The kitchen cupboards were not wide enough to take typical US plates, which were large enough for pizza.
■ The glasses on sale were not large enough to include the generous quantities of ice served in many beverages.
■ The drawers in chests of drawers would not be deep enough to store sweaters in, as many consumers required.

Thus IKEA's policy of entering a market without wide-ranging market study cost it dear in the initial years. Mr Morberg commented that IKEA 'don't spend much money or time on studies'. Later, he realised that the company was acting more like an exporter to the US than an integral part of its retailing population, as was desired.

As a result, in 1989 and 1990, 20 per cent of products were redesigned to cater for the US market. Also, 45 per cent of production was transferred to local suppliers. Additionally, in order to cater for local cultural expectations, the number of cash registers in each store was increased, thus improving throughput by 20 per cent.

By becoming flexible and catering for local tastes, IKEA began to show success in the US market in 1991/2. Other management techniques and policies had also changed, including aspects of stock control, budgeting and planning. Of interest here, however, is the lesson learned in an expensive manner by IKEA with reference to its product policy. Despite this, company management still claim that it will 'continue to jump into big new markets feet first' because it is easier to adapt and make changes once the company is established.

# QUANTITATIVE ANALYSIS AND INTERPRETATION OF DATA

When the organisation has collected data on consumer reactions, it must analyse the results. It may be that there is already information available within the organisation which can be used: sales data for other products, results of previous surveys and so on. Whatever the source of the information, it needs to be analysed and used in a manner which will produce a meaningful estimate or forecast of future demand.

## Time series and cross-sectional data

Organisations which possess data relating to demand for products will usually be able to classify it in two ways. The data will be arranged in either a 'time series' or a 'cross-sectional' manner.

Time series data is a series of observations of a variable over time. For example, an electrical goods company with monthly sales figures for its food mixer over a five-year period possesses time series data. Analysis of trends in demand over time are therefore possible when an organisation possesses this kind of data.

Cross-sectional data is collected within a period or at the same time and is subgrouped into appropriate sections of the population under consideration. Continuing with the food-mixer example, if the electrical goods firm, for each of its monthly sales, also knows what proportions were bought by those aged 18–24, 25–29, 30–34 etc., then it possesses cross-sectional data with reference to the purchasers. This information can assist organisations wishing to evaluate which segments of the buying population to target with respect to appropriate advertising campaigns or new products etc.

## Time series analysis/estimation

Where an organisation possesses historical time series data with reference to its product(s), it may use it to estimate future demand. In order to be able to do this, it must recognise the trends in the data, or the relationship between sets of data. This analysis can be simplistic or complex, as was the case for qualitative analysis. As also stated previously, the cost and accuracy of the estimate increase with the level of complexity of the technique utilised. However, although cost is obviously an important factor for an organisation to consider, it must also attempt to use the appropriate methods to analyse and interpret the data it has collected. Otherwise, the data and subsequent estimates will be worthless, no matter how carefully they have been collected.

The simplest technique for interpretation of data is a scattergram analysis with a 'line of best fit'. More complicated techniques include 'smoothing' of the trend, to reduce the effect of random events by moving averages and weighted moving averages. Moving averages may be calculated manually or by use of a computer spreadsheet program. More complex techniques, such as regression analysis (see later), can be performed using spreadsheets such as *Lotus 1-2-3* and *Excel*. However, fuller sets of results are available when dedicated computer programs such as *4Profit* and *MicroFit* are used to analyse the data collected.

## Analysis of trends

The simplest way in which a trend in demand may be analysed is to plot the data accurately on a graph. On the *X* axis will be the independent variable, for example price of the product or consumer income in each of several different time periods. On the *Y* axis will be the dependent variable, demand in this case, in each of those time periods.

Plotting a scattergram may thus give some indication of trends in demand over time, particularly if a 'line of best fit' is superimposed on it.

Consider the scattergram given in Figure 7.4. With the line of best fit superimposed as A–A, it is clear that, over time, quantity demanded of videocassette recorders by French households has shown a steady increase.

The trend in demand is not usually as simplistic as a steady upward or downward trend. More frequently, trends follow identifiable, perhaps repeating, patterns which may be categorised into the four main groups given below:

- secular
- cyclical
- seasonal
- random.

### Secular trends

Generally speaking, trends which exhibit long-run changes in an area under consideration are known as secular. For the purposes of estimating demand, the concern is to identify long-run changes in consumer behaviour. In such a series of observations, a definite upward, downward or constant trend may be seen. That is, secular trends are a general movement of an increasing or decreasing nature in, say, demand.

### Cyclical trends

Cyclical variations may be observed and tied in to changes in the economy. These are usually accepted as those changes which take longer than one year in terms of the complete cycle. Any set of

**Figure 7.4**

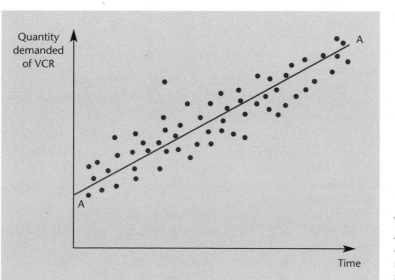

With the line of best fit superimposed as A–A, it is clear that over time, quantity demanded of videocassette recorders by French households has shown a steady increase.

data under analysis may exhibit a cyclical trend; however, for the purposes of demand estimation the concern is to identify a cyclical trend in demand for the organisation's product.

Perhaps the most famous cyclical trend which has been observed in Europe is the 'business cycle'. This concept is disputed among different groups of economists. Assuming that there is validity in the claims of those who believe they have identified it, the discussion below applies.

The business cycle completes one full cycle approximately every 8–10 years. At various stages in the business cycle, certain characteristics may be observed. These observations have implications for overall demand in the economy.

Confidence of business owners is known to improve as the cycle begins an upswing. This improvement in confidence often means that business owners invest more heavily in their businesses, or that they expand production operations by increasing overtime opportunities or by employing additional staff. With extra income from their employment, staff will be in a position to spend or save. If they choose to spend, demand for goods in general increases and a **multiplier effect** begins. The economy steadily expands (or, more properly, experiences growth); thus, the owners' improved confidence leads to growth, which will lead to further growth etc. The improvements in the cycle continue until business owners begin to feel uneasy about the level of activity in the economy, believing that it cannot continue indefinitely. At this point, growth will slow down, workers will be laid off or have their working hours cut. This means that they will be more prudent with their income, reducing their level of purchases, and thus the level of demand in the economy will begin to fall.

Note that there is evidence to suggest that the multiplier effect is not that strong. Certain sectors of the economy respond to the upward and downward pressures on the economy more than do other sectors.

### Seasonal trends

Seasonal trends relate to regular annual cycles of events. Typical examples of demand for products which exhibit seasonal trends are the demand for Christmas products, Easter eggs, skiing equipment etc. Other seasonal trends also exist, not necessarily connected with demand. An example of this could be the increase in seasonally adjusted unemployment in the UK each September as school and college leavers are counted within the unemployment figures for the first time.

### Random trends

A random event which cannot be predicted would cause fluctuations in demand. Examples include major events such as the economic effects of war, earthquakes etc. Less drastic events such as a government wage and price freeze could also cause unpredicted and unpredictable effects on the economy. Changes and shocks which occur in the London, New York and Hong Kong stock exchanges often have implications for economies in Europe.

## Barometric forecasting

Barometric forecasts take into consideration changes in various **indicators**. Barometric forecasts predict *when* changes are likely to occur, rather than predicting values. Four categories of indicators may be identified:

**Long leading** – changes occur which suggest that the rest of the economy is likely to improve/worsen in the medium to long term.

**Leading** – changes occur which suggest that the rest of the economy is likely to improve/worsen in the short term.

Typical long leading and leading indicators are:

- Average weekly hours worked (manufacturing).
- Average number of new claims for unemployment benefit.
- Numbers of new orders for consumer goods and materials.
- Numbers of orders for new plant and equipment.

**Coincidental** – changes which occur at the same time as other changes in the economy.

Typical coincident indicators are:

- Personal income minus transfer payments.
- Index of industrial production (total).
- Manufacturing and trade sales.

**Lagged** – changes can be identified as having occurred which confirm that the economy has moved in a given direction.

Typical lagged indicators are:

- Average duration of unemployment.
- Changes in labour costs per unit output (manufacturing).
- Commercial and industrial loans outstanding.
- Change in consumer price index for services.

◆ **Exercise 7.2**

Consider the list of leading and lagged indicators given. Why do you think that they precede or follow changes in the economy? Give reasons.

---

If organisations are aware that certain changes have occurred, or are likely to, they will be in a stronger position to adapt and change policies accordingly and at the appropriate time.

Rather than rely on the estimated time periods applicable to a lagged or leading indicator, it is more usual to consider a set of indices grouped together as a **composite index**. The rationale for this is that, when a group, as opposed to an individual indicator, is considered, the effect of random fluctuations which affect a single indicator will be smoothed or averaged out across the group and thus the overview given will be more balanced. Composite indices are combinations of leading, coincidental and lagged indicators which are then weighted.

An alternative to the composite index approach is the **diffusion index**. This is used to investigate the strength of changes in the economy at any time. For example, a diffusion index usually contains (only) leading indicators and is expressed in terms of the percentage of individual indices which are rising. Thus, the diffusion index will range in value between 0 and 1 (or 0 per cent and 100 per cent). The closer to zero, the fewer indices in the economy which are rising. The nearer to 1 (or 100 per cent), the more indices which are rising or growing.

An extension of barometric forecasting is the scenario planning approach (developed by Royal Dutch/Shell in the 1970s) where possible outcomes are considered and *subjective additions* are made to existing, conventionally attained forecasts. Pierre Wack was involved in the development of scenario planning. In *Scenarios: uncharted waters ahead* (1985), he describes the technique.

Briefly, scenario planning evolved because conventional forecast techniques were recognised as being based on certain assumptions relating to the current economic climate and understanding. Therefore, there is a lack of ability to foresee and account for any major changes which may occur within the forecast period.

Scenario planning embraces uncertainty to the extent that several decision scenarios are written with respect to any situation under consideration. There are a number of stages before the final scenarios are released to management:

- Initial scenarios are written in a descriptive manner which encompasses a variety of future events.
- Management and specialist input is then gleaned in order to understand and explain the uncertainties which are presented by the scenarios.
- Further scenarios are written, using data which illustrate potential changes in the market and also in associated markets for the product(s).
- The array of possible outcomes are assigned to two 'families': A and B. Family A contains likely outcomes, whereas Family B contains outcomes which pose a challenge to accepted (and Family A) assumptions.
- Family A and Family B are presented to management for consideration and decision making.

The scenario planning approach emphasises the evolutionary and varied nature of outcomes. The scenarios are flexible and open to change and are derived through consultation with management and experts, thus improving their ability to provide understanding and the validity of the process. Additionally, this 'building block' approach assists in filtering out any outcomes or scenarios which do not make sense.

## Moving average smoothing

Smoothing is a technique used to reduce the effects of random events and thus to allow a reliable estimation of demand to be made. The simplest form of smoothing is 'moving average' smoothing. Here, the average of a number of time series observations is calculated, in preference to simply making an estimate of the next period's results.

The data given in Table 7.1 relate to the total sales of compact discs (CDs) per week over a 26-week period in a music store.

The mathematical formula for a moving average may be given by:

$$\text{Moving Average} = \Sigma(\text{Data for most recent } N \text{ periods})/N$$

where,

$N$ = the chosen value for the moving average period

As $N$ changes, the description of the moving average calculated changes. If $N = 3$, it would be called a 'three-period moving average'; if $N = 4$, it would be called a 'four-period moving average' and so on.

**Table 7.1**

| Week | Sales of CDs per week |
|------|------|
| 1 | 1223 |
| 2 | 2324 |
| 3 | 1245 |
| 4 | 1236 |
| 5 | 1258 |
| 6 | 1232 |
| 7 | 1240 |
| 8 | 1238 |
| 9 | 1246 |
| 10 | 1465 |
| 11 | 1006 |
| 12 | 1018 |
| 13 | 1020 |
| 14 | 956 |
| 15 | 968 |
| 16 | 1111 |
| 17 | 1007 |
| 18 | 984 |
| 19 | 1056 |
| 20 | 1032 |
| 21 | 1028 |
| 22 | 1022 |
| 23 | 1012 |
| 24 | 1017 |
| 25 | 1040 |
| 26 | 1023 |

**Table 7.2**

| Week | Sales of CDs per week | Three-week moving average |
|------|------|------|
| 1 | 1223 | |
| 2 | 2324 | 1597.33 |
| 3 | 1245 | 1601.67 |
| 4 | 1236 | 1246.33 |
| 5 | 1258 | 1242.00 |
| 6 | 1232 | 1243.33 |
| 7 | 1240 | 1236.67 |
| 8 | 1238 | 1241.33 |
| 9 | 1246 | 1316.33 |
| 10 | 1465 | 1239.00 |
| 11 | 1006 | 1163.00 |
| 12 | 1018 | 1014.67 |
| 13 | 1020 | 998.00 |
| 14 | 956 | 981.33 |
| 15 | 968 | 1011.67 |
| 16 | 1111 | 1028.67 |
| 17 | 1007 | 1034.00 |
| 18 | 984 | 1015.67 |
| 19 | 1056 | 1024.00 |
| 20 | 1032 | 1038.67 |
| 21 | 1028 | 1027.33 |
| 22 | 1022 | 1020.67 |
| 23 | 1012 | 1017.00 |
| 24 | 1017 | 1023.00 |
| 25 | 1040 | 1026.67 |
| 26 | 1023 | |

Given the data in Table 7.1, it is possible to calculate a three-week moving average in the following manner.

First, calculate the moving average for the first three weeks to gain the moving average for demand in week 2, $MA_2$, that is, the middle week of the series:

$$MA_2 = (1223+2324+1245)/3$$
$$MA_2 = (4792)/3$$
$$MA_2 = 1597.33$$

Then calculate the moving average for weeks 2–4 to gain the moving average for demand in week 3, $MA_3$, the middle week of that series:

$$MA_3 = (2324+1245+1236)/3$$
$$MA_3 = (4805)/3$$
$$MA_3 = 1601.67$$

Continue in the above manner until all possible averages have been calculated.

Once all the moving averages have been calculated, insert them in the appropriate position on the data table (*see* Table 7.2).

Figure 7.5 plots raw data relating to sales against the three-week moving average for sales in the 26-week period. It can clearly be seen that the three-week moving average fluctuates less than the raw sales data. That is, the moving average technique smooths out the fluctuations in the raw sales data. A projection or forecast for the next period in the series can be added to Figure 7.5. This is extrapolated from the previous trends and is shown by the broken line on the $MA_3$ series.

The more observations used, the better the moving average forecast can be. Also, the slower the rate of change within the economic or sales environment as a whole, the greater the accuracy of the estimates derived by this technique. Overall, it is generally accepted that as a technique for estimation of demand the moving average is best used in a simple, well-recorded situation which is not undergoing rapid change.

## Weighted moving averages

Where the economic situation is highly volatile, a simple moving average is less reliable as an estimator of demand than is a **weighted moving average**. Here the most recent data is given greater significance, or weighting, than data relating to earlier time periods.

**Figure 7.5  Sales of CDs per month**

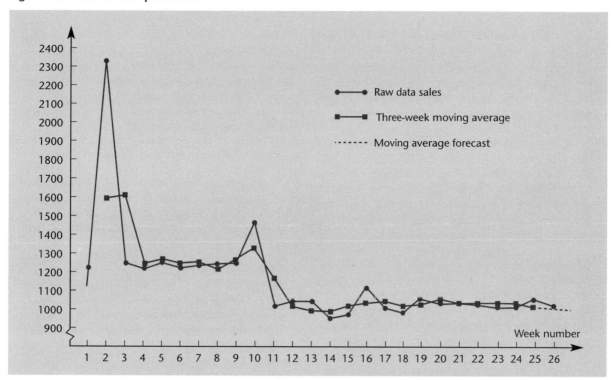

In the case of the data already considered in Table 7.1, typical weightings for the three-week moving average might be 0.6 for the most recent period (say $t$), 0.3 for the period preceding $t$ (that is, $t$–1) and 0.1 for the period preceding $t$–1 (that is, $t$–2). A further way of looking at weighted moving averages is exponential smoothing, where the weights decline geometrically, going backwards over time. (*See* Appendix 7.1.)

Thus, using these weightings, the calculation of the weighted moving average for the first three weeks would be:

$$WMA_2 = 0.6(1245)+0.3(2324)+0.1(1223)$$
$$WMA_2 = 747.0 + 697.2 + 122.3$$
$$WMA_2 = 1566.5$$

Similarly, the weighted moving average for weeks 2–4 to gain the value for the third week will be:

$$WMA_3 = 0.6(1236)+0.3(1245)+0.1(2324)$$
$$WMA_3 = 741.6 + 373.5 + 232.4$$
$$WMA_3 = 1345.5$$

◆ **Exercise 7.3**

Calculate the weighted moving averages for the remainder of the observations in Table 7.1. Check these against Table 7.3.

**Table 7.3**

| Week | Sales of CDs per week | Three-week moving average | Three-week weighted moving average |
|---|---|---|---|
| 1 | 1223 | | |
| 2 | 2324 | 1597.33 | 1566.50 |
| 3 | 1245 | 1601.67 | 1347.50 |
| 4 | 1236 | 1246.33 | 1250.10 |
| 5 | 1258 | 1242.00 | 1240.20 |
| 6 | 1232 | 1243.33 | 1239.40 |
| 7 | 1240 | 1236.67 | 1238.00 |
| 8 | 1238 | 1241.33 | 1243.00 |
| 9 | 1246 | 1316.33 | 1376.60 |
| 10 | 1465 | 1239.00 | 1167.70 |
| 11 | 1006 | 1163.00 | 1059.10 |
| 12 | 1018 | 1014.67 | 1018.00 |
| 13 | 1020 | 998.00 | 981.40 |
| 14 | 956 | 981.33 | 969.60 |
| 15 | 968 | 1011.67 | 1052.60 |
| 16 | 1111 | 1028.67 | 1034.30 |
| 17 | 1007 | 1034.00 | 1003.60 |
| 18 | 984 | 1015.67 | 1029.50 |
| 19 | 1056 | 1024.00 | 1034.40 |
| 20 | 1032 | 1038.67 | 1032.00 |
| 21 | 1028 | 1027.33 | 1024.80 |
| 22 | 1022 | 1020.67 | 1016.60 |
| 23 | 1012 | 1017.00 | 1016.00 |
| 24 | 1017 | 1023.00 | 1030.30 |
| 25 | 1040 | 1026.67 | 1027.50 |
| 26 | 1023 | | |

◆ **CASE STUDY 7.2**

# Moving faster to stay with the pack

FT

Ever popular and urbane, Mr Louis Schweitzer, chairman of France's state-controlled Renault vehicles group, let his mask slip a little yesterday after aggressive questioning from both sides of the Channel on the group's poor 1995 results. . .

Mr Schweitzer repeated his view that Renault's 41 per cent drop in net profits to FF2.14bn (£278m), announced on Tuesday, stemmed largely from factors beyond its control. However, he could not hide the fact that the figures have set back hopes that the French government – which still owns 53 per cent of Renault – might dispose of more shares in the near future.

'It is not often fund managers tell you they won't buy a share at virtually any price,' says one analyst. 'But that's almost the case at Renault.' Even an upturn in the market, good first-half results and signs that the crucial new Mégane mid-sized range is selling well may not be enough to convince hardened investors.

Renault blamed weak European demand, currency depreciations and the Mégane's introduction for the swing to a FF1.7bn operating loss at its core car division after profits of FF289m in 1994. West European car sales rose just 0.6 per cent last year, while demand in France, Renault's home market, was hit by December's strikes.

The company, like other north European carmakers, also suffered a competitive disadvantage compared with counterparts, such as Fiat, based in countries with weaker currencies. And Renault was hit by the replacement of the well-regarded R19, which competes in Europe's biggest car segment, with the Mégane.

'But all that is not enough to explain last year's results,' says Ms Sabine Blumel, an analyst at IMI in London. Like many counterparts, she is disappointed Renault did not signal how its results were deteriorating last year. Most analysts were forecasting a loss of about half the size. Some were also dissatisfied that the company did not hint at earnings this year.

In an interview, Mr Schweitzer said Renault had been taken by surprise by the severity of the downturn last year – explaining why analysts may have felt ill-informed. The unpredictable market is why he says it is 'not fair' to make forecasts for 1996. . .

The improvement in Renault's models has not always been reflected in their pricing and profit margins, in spite of the fact that current models are unrecognisable from the bland and poorly-built cars of the 1980s. Although praised in the media, the Laguna is often sold at a discount, whereas Peugeot's direct competitor, the new 406, is likely to sell without heavy price cuts.

Mr Schweitzer admits there is a pricing problem, stemming from the fact that Renault's image remains weaker outside France. That affects pricing policy and makes its margins even more reliant on domestic sales.

Renault faces a fundamental structural problem as a single brand company, with a relatively small range of models, compared with multi-brand rivals. With only one brand, an important model change leaves the group relatively vulnerable.

All carmakers face risks with big model changes. Old stock has to be cleared, often at low prices, while launch costs can be staggering. But a manufacturer with more than one brand can often time model changes to cause the least disruption.

Mr Schweitzer denies single branding is a 'major handicap' and says Renault has no plans to change. He admits, however, the company has a problem with executive cars, where margins are usually biggest.

The combination of these factors explains why analysts are bearish about Renault this year. Many expect the cars side to stay in loss. Nor do they think Renault's resurgent commercial vehicles side, which increased its operating profits fivefold last year to FF978m, is big or strong enough to fill the gap in the long term.

*Source: Financial Times, 21 March 1996. Reprinted with permission.*

### Comment on the case study

Renault is clearly facing problems in making accurate profit forecasts. It may be that the public's attitude towards its cars is poor, despite the fact that some of its more recent models are different to typical Renault models of the past. It would be difficult to make allowances for attitudes when making a trend analysis and forecast of sales by Renault. However, regression analysis, as outlined in the next section, would allow inclusion of an attitude factor by giving it a numerical value and including it within the equation used to estimate demand. The attitude factor could be changed as consumers' attitudes are perceived to change; forecasts would therefore change accordingly. It would also be possible to make an allowance for the discounting behaviour which has been experienced with sales of the Laguna, further improving the accuracy of the results.

# ECONOMETRIC TECHNIQUES: REGRESSION ANALYSIS

**The development of regression analysis**

In 1886 Francis Galton observed that there seemed to be some (positive) correlation between tall parents and the height of their children and also shorter parents and the height of their children. He also noted that the children's height, however, tended towards the population average. He termed this 'regression towards mediocrity'. Galton set up a model to predict the height of children based on knowledge of their parents' height. The model was simple: he used two independent, exogenous variables (height of mother, height of father) to estimate/predict the dependent variable – the height of their offspring.

Over the last 100 years, regression analysis has progressed from predicting simple factors such as the height of children to the more complex problems of looking at the dependence of one variable on others with a view to estimating levels of demand, inflation, unemployment etc. However, the basic principle remains.

**Regression analysis** uses data already collected and provides an estimate of demand in a standardised or equation form. If the estimated equation can be verified as accurate, then by substituting the next time period's values, a forecast of future values may be made.

Assume that a music store wishes to gain an estimation of demand for its CDs in an equation form similar to that seen in Chapter 6. The store has considered various factors affecting demand for its CDs and it seems likely that demand is affected by the price of the CDs and the price of music cassettes (which are substitutes for CDs). That is:

$$QD = f(P_{CD}, P_{cassette})$$

where,

$QD$ = demand for CDs
f = 'a function of'
$P_{CD}$ = price of CDs
$P_{cassette}$ = price of cassette tapes

In this example, demand for CDs is what is known as the dependent variable. That is, the level of demand is dependent on the levels of the other variables in the equation. These other variables are known as independent variables. The independent variables are not affected by other constituents of the equation. However, the levels of these in each time period combine to affect the level of the dependent variable: demand.

With knowledge of the estimated equation, the music store will be in a position to substitute expected values for the price of CDs and music cassettes in the next time period into the equation to gain a forecast for demand for CDs in that next period.

Whenever regression analysis is undertaken, there are three main factors to be taken into account:

■ The choice of factors affecting the dependent variable is important. For example, is it realistic to assume that demand is affected (for instance) by price and the price of a substitute? Also, is it possible to collect accurate data relating to each of the factors chosen?

■ Identification of factors can be difficult and can lead to the grouping together of a number of unidentified factors as an 'error term'. For example, an equation may be found to be 98 per cent accurate for predicting demand for a product using only the variables price and price of substitute. This accuracy may be adversely affected if further variables are included in the equation. Thus, the 2 per cent inaccuracy should be attributed to the 'error term' unless other factors can be identified and included to the extent that the accuracy of the estimated equation is improved beyond 98 per cent. This is the basis of the correlation coefficient $R^2$ (discussed later in this chapter).

■ The form of the estimated equation is also an important consideration. The equation could take many forms, the most common being either linear or exponential (otherwise known as multiplicative).

Thus, with reference to the demand for CDs, the linear and exponential forms are:

Linear form $\quad D = a + bP_{CD} + cP_{cassette}$

Exponential form $\quad D = aP_{CD}{}^b Y^c{}_{cassette}$

In order to make an interpretation of the exponential form, it can be reduced to a linear form. In this case by taking logarithms to both sides:

$$lnQ = lna + blnP_{CD} + clnP_{cassette}$$

Further, if:

$lnQ = Q^*$, then:
$Q^* = a^* + bP^*{}_{CD} + cP^*{}_{cassette}$

Once the variables and the form of the equation have been decided, the software discussed previously may be used to estimate the values of the coefficients and to provide statistical results to assist the verification of the equation. In these cases, past data values with reference to each of the variables within a given time period are input, the program executed and estimates gained for the values of these variables. The difference between actual and estimated values is analysed. The smaller the gap between actual and estimated, the better the estimates are taken to be. That is, the better the *fit*.

## Verifying the accuracy of the estimated regression equation

Regression analysis, whether performed manually or with computer support, can be classified as either 'simple regression' or 'multiple regression'. Simple regression is concerned with the effect of changes in one independent variable on the dependent variable, that is, a simple linear relationship. For most purposes simple regression is not sufficient; multiple regression is required. In multiple regression, the effects of changes in more than one independent variable on the dependent variable are estimated. A type of regression called ordinary least squares (OLS) will be outlined here. It is sometimes used by econometricans, although OLS is a basic technique on which more popularly used techniques are founded. Explanation of the more specialist techniques may be found in the reading references noted at the end of the chapter.

It should be clear that for estimating equations such as that for the demand for CDs discussed previously multiple regression techniques are required. There are two independent variables in the estimated demand for CDs equation: price and price of cassettes.

Whichever method is used, a number of steps must be followed in order to verify the accuracy of the estimated regression equation. The steps are easily broken down into three categories: economic, statistical and econometric.

The steps will be described on the following pages. In order to aid understanding, reference will be made to the example of the estimated demand equation for CDs. When the data relating to demand for CDs, price of CDs and price of cassettes for the period Week 1 to Week 26 (Table 7.4) was used to run a regression on *4Profit* educational software, the results in Table 7.5 were obtained.

**Table 7.4**

| Week | Sales of CDs per week | Price of CDs (£) | Price of music cassettes (£) |
|------|------|------|------|
| 1 | 1223 | 10.50 | 8.99 |
| 2 | 2324 | 8.50 | 8.99 |
| 3 | 1245 | 10.50 | 8.99 |
| 4 | 1236 | 10.50 | 8.99 |
| 5 | 1258 | 10.50 | 8.99 |
| 6 | 1232 | 10.50 | 8.99 |
| 7 | 1240 | 10.50 | 8.99 |
| 8 | 1238 | 10.50 | 8.99 |
| 9 | 1246 | 10.50 | 8.99 |
| 10 | 1465 | 9.99 | 8.99 |
| 11 | 1006 | 10.99 | 8.99 |
| 12 | 1018 | 10.99 | 8.99 |
| 13 | 1020 | 10.99 | 8.99 |
| 14 | 956 | 10.99 | 6.99 |
| 15 | 968 | 10.99 | 6.99 |
| 16 | 1111 | 9.99 | 8.99 |
| 17 | 1007 | 10.99 | 8.99 |
| 18 | 984 | 10.99 | 8.99 |
| 19 | 1056 | 10.99 | 8.99 |
| 20 | 1032 | 10.99 | 8.99 |
| 21 | 1028 | 10.99 | 8.99 |
| 22 | 1022 | 10.99 | 8.99 |
| 23 | 1012 | 10.99 | 8.99 |
| 24 | 1017 | 10.99 | 8.99 |
| 25 | 1040 | 10.99 | 8.99 |
| 26 | 1023 | 10.99 | 8.99 |

**Table 7.5 Ordinary least squares estimation**

| 26 Observations Dependent variable is quantity demanded of CDs | Period used Week 1 – Week 26 | | |
|------|------|------|------|
| Regressor | Coefficient | | t Statistic |
| Intercept | 6310.828 | | 34.769 |
| Price CDs | −503.609 | | −40.958 |
| Price cassettes | 25.540 | | 2.213 |
| $R^2$ | 0.9871 | Durbin-Watson stat | 1.895 |
| Adjusted $R^2$ | 0.9859 | F statistic (2,23) | 876.731 |

From this it is possible to derive the estimated equation. The dependent variable, demand will be on the left-hand side. The independent variables, price and price of cassettes, will be on the right-hand side. There is also a constant or autonomous level of demand. This is given in Table 7.5 as the 'intercept'. The values for these variables are given in Table 7.5 as the coefficients, the values which precede the variables in the estimated equation.

Thus, in this case, the estimated equation is:

$$QD = 6370.828 - 503.609P_{CD} + 26.540P_{cassette}$$

References to this equation and the other results given in the table will be made as the accuracy of the estimated relationship is verified on the following pages.

## Economic verification

There are two steps to be taken to verify the economic validity of the estimated equation. These steps are concerned with the estimated coefficient presented in the equation.

### Sign
Is the sign given before the estimated coefficient correct? For example, in the estimated demand equation for CDs, the sign of the price coefficient is negative and the sign of the price of cassettes coefficient is positive. In basic economic theory, under normal circumstances, these are 'correct' relationships. It would be expected that there would be a negative relationship between demand for a product and price of a product. Similarly, there would be expected to be a positive relationship between demand for a product and price of a substitute good.

Had the sign relating to the price coefficient been positive, the model would not necessarily have been rejected. Economists recognise that types of goods exist which possess an upward-sloping demand curve. These are Giffen and Veblen goods. Veblen goods are also known as goods with 'snob value' – such as diamonds and caviare – where the quantities demanded increase as price increases (hence the possibility of a positive price coefficient).

### Magnitude
Is the estimated coefficient to the correct order of magnitude? That is, given historical knowledge of relationships, are the estimated coefficients within expected limits? This can be gauged by considering the estimates with reference to data or previously accepted estimated equations. (Obviously, this is not possible in the example followed, as there are no previously estimated equations.)

If the estimated equation passes these two steps, then it would seem logical to carry on with the statistical and econometric tests. If the estimated equation does not pass these steps, it may be the case that the underlying assumptions and data which have contributed to the estimated relation contain an error of some sort. Thus, it may be necessary to redefine the equation.

## Statistical verification

The statistical tests for verification of the likely accuracy of the estimated equation will be explained here only as tools to assist the procedure. The statistical theory and first principles for these tests will not be discussed. The tests which should be undertaken relate to the following:

- Testing whether each estimated coefficient, individually, is related to and able to explain variations in the dependent variable (the '$t$' test).
- Testing whether the estimated coefficients as a group are related to and able to explain variations in the dependent variable (the $F$ test).
- The overall validity of the equation in terms of explaining variations in demand (consideration of $R^2$ and adjusted $R^2$).

### The '$t$' test
The '$t$' test is based on the null hypothesis ($H_0$) that there is no significant statistical relationship between the dependent variable and each of the independent variables. If this null hypothesis can be proved incorrect, then each of the estimated coefficients may be independently accepted as being significantly statistically related to the dependent variable.

The test relies on a comparison between the $t$ values for each of the estimated coefficients given in the results table and a value for $t$ (critical value of $t$ or $t^*$) as derived from $t$ distribution tables (Table 7.6).

If $t_{results} > t^*$, then $H_0$ is rejected; there *is* a significant statistical relationship between the independent variable under consideration and the dependent variable.

> $H_0$: there is not a significant statistical relationship between demand and each of the independent variables.

To derive the critical $t$ value ($t^*$) from the '$t$' tables, the following steps should be undertaken:

## Table 7.6 Areas under the tails of the *t* distribution

| Degrees of freedom | Probabilities | | | | | | | |
|---|---|---|---|---|---|---|---|---|
| | .80 | .60 | .20 | .30 | .10 | .05 | .02 | .01 |
| 1 | 0.325 | 0.727 | 1.376 | 3.078 | 6.314 | 12.706 | 31.821 | 63.657 |
| 2 | 0.289 | 0.617 | 1.061 | 1.886 | 2.920 | 4.303 | 6.965 | 9.925 |
| 3 | 0.277 | 0.584 | 0.978 | 1.638 | 2.353 | 3.182 | 4.541 | 5.841 |
| 4 | 0.271 | 0.569 | 0.941 | 1.533 | 2.132 | 2.776 | 3.747 | 4.604 |
| 5 | 0.267 | 0.559 | 0.920 | 1.476 | 2.015 | 2.571 | 3.365 | 4.032 |
| 6 | 0.265 | 0.553 | 0.906 | 1.440 | 1.943 | 2.447 | 3.143 | 3.707 |
| 7 | 0.263 | 0.549 | 0.896 | 1.415 | 1.895 | 2.365 | 2.998 | 3.499 |
| 8 | 0.262 | 0.546 | 0.889 | 1.397 | 1.860 | 2.306 | 2.896 | 3.355 |
| 9 | 0.261 | 0.543 | 0.883 | 1.383 | 1.833 | 2.262 | 2.821 | 3.250 |
| 10 | 0.260 | 0.542 | 0.879 | 1.372 | 1.812 | 2.228 | 2.764 | 3.169 |
| 11 | 0.260 | 0.540 | 0.876 | 1.363 | 1.796 | 2.201 | 2.718 | 3.106 |
| 12 | 0.259 | 0.539 | 0.873 | 1.356 | 1.782 | 2.179 | 2.681 | 3.055 |
| 13 | 0.259 | 0.538 | 0.870 | 1.350 | 1.771 | 2.160 | 2.650 | 3.012 |
| 14 | 0.258 | 0.537 | 0.868 | 1.345 | 1.761 | 2.145 | 2.624 | 2.977 |
| 15 | 0.258 | 0.536 | 0.866 | 1.341 | 1.753 | 2.131 | 2.602 | 2.947 |
| 16 | 0.258 | 0.535 | 0.865 | 1.337 | 1.746 | 2.120 | 2.583 | 2.921 |
| 17 | 0.257 | 0.534 | 0.863 | 1.333 | 1.740 | 2.110 | 2.567 | 2.898 |
| 18 | 0.257 | 0.534 | 0.862 | 1.330 | 1.734 | 2.101 | 2.552 | 2.878 |
| 19 | 0.257 | 0.533 | 0.861 | 1.328 | 1.729 | 2.093 | 2.539 | 2.861 |
| 20 | 0.257 | 0.533 | 0.860 | 1.325 | 1.725 | 2.086 | 2.528 | 2.845 |
| 21 | 0.257 | 0.532 | 0.859 | 1.323 | 1.721 | 2.080 | 2.518 | 2.831 |
| 22 | 0.256 | 0.532 | 0.858 | 1.321 | 1.717 | 2.074 | 2.508 | 2.819 |
| 23 | 0.256 | 0.532 | 0.858 | 1.319 | 1.714 | 2.069 | 2.500 | 2.807 |
| 24 | 0.256 | 0.531 | 0.857 | 1.318 | 1.711 | 2.064 | 2.492 | 2.797 |
| 25 | 0.256 | 0.531 | 0.856 | 1.316 | 1.708 | 2.060 | 2.485 | 2.787 |
| 26 | 0.256 | 0.531 | 0.856 | 1.315 | 1.706 | 2.056 | 2.479 | 2.779 |
| 27 | 0.256 | 0.531 | 0.855 | 1.314 | 1.703 | 2.052 | 2.473 | 2.771 |
| 28 | 0.256 | 0.530 | 0.855 | 1.313 | 1.701 | 2.048 | 2.467 | 2.763 |
| 29 | 0.256 | 0.530 | 0.854 | 1.311 | 1.699 | 2.045 | 2.462 | 2.756 |
| 30 | 0.256 | 0.530 | 0.854 | 1.310 | 1.697 | 2.042 | 2.457 | 2.750 |
| 40 | 0.255 | 0.529 | 0.851 | 1.303 | 1.684 | 2.021 | 2.423 | 2.704 |
| 60 | 0.254 | 0.527 | 0.848 | 1.296 | 1.671 | 2.000 | 2.390 | 2.660 |
| 120 | 0.254 | 0.526 | 0.845 | 1.289 | 1.658 | 1.980 | 2.358 | 2.617 |
| x | 0.253 | 0.524 | 0.842 | 1.282 | 1.645 | 1.960 | 2.326 | 2.576 |

*Note*: The probabilities given in the table are two-tailed tests. Thus, a probability of 0.05 allows for 0.025 in each tail. For example, for a probability of 0.05 and 21 degrees of freedom, *t* = 2.080. This means that 2.5 per cent of the area under the *t* distribution lies to the right of *t* = 2.080 and 2.5 per cent to the left of *t* = −2.080.

*Source*: From Table III of R A Fisher and F Yates, *Statistical Tables for Biological, Agricultural and Medical Research*, 6th edn, Harlow: Longman Group Ltd, 1974; previously by Oliver & Boyd, Edinburgh, by permission of the authors and publishers.

- Identify the appropriate number of 'degrees of freedom' as a result of including a constant term and independent variables within the regression. Subtract this value from the number of observations included in the regression.
- Identify the appropriate level of significance to be used for the '$t$' tests. It is usual for a 5 per cent level of significance to be used. This may be broadly taken to imply a 95 per cent confidence interval within which actual values of the estimated coefficient will lie.

In the case of demand for CDs, there is one constant term and two independent variables (price and price of cassettes). Thus this total of three variables should be subtracted from the number of observations included in the regression (26). The degrees of freedom for this regression are $26 - 3 = 23$.

Therefore, the $t^*$ for 23 degrees of freedom and 5 per cent significance level, $t^{0.05}_{23}$, may be looked up in the tables. *For these purposes, it is usual to use a two-tailed test and to consider only the magnitude and not the sign of the estimated t values.*

From the tables, $t^{0.05}_{23}$ can be seen to be 2.069. Thus $t^* = 2.069$.

Comparing this value to the estimated values for $t$ for the independent variables from the results tables allows acceptance or rejection of the null hypothesis $H_0$.

The '$t$' test and therefore the null hypothesis must be applied independently to each of the $t$ values for the estimated coefficients. The '$t$' test is applied to the $t$ values for the independent variables *only* in this case (not the constant term), because the null hypothesis relates to the independent variables.

The '$t$' tests for the example of demand for CDs give the following results.

### Price

H$_0$: there is not a significant statistical relationship between price and quantity demanded.

Given that $t^* = 2.069$ and $t_{price} = 40.958$ (remember that the sign of the estimated $t$ is usually ignored) and since $t^* < t_{price}$, H$_0$ is rejected. Thus, it is accepted that there is a significant statistical relationship between price and quantity demanded.

It may therefore be assumed that changes in price of CDs do have an effect on the demand for CDs.

### Price of cassettes

H$_0$: there is not a significant statistical relationship between price of cassettes and quantity demanded.

Given that $t^* = 2.069$ and $t_{cassette} = 2.213$ and since $t^* < t_{cassette}$, H$_0$ is rejected. Thus, it is accepted that there is a significant statistical relationship between price of cassettes and quantity demanded.

It may therefore be assumed that changes in the price of cassettes do have an effect on the demand for CDs.

Overall, then, both '$t$' tests have shown that there are significant statistical relationships between price of CDs, demand and price of cassettes and demand for CDs.

### The $F$ test

The $F$ test is based on the null hypothesis that there is not a significant statistical relationship between the dependent variable and the group of independent variables. If this null hypothesis can be proved incorrect, then the estimated coefficients as a group may be accepted as being significantly statistically related to the dependent variable.

The test relies on a comparison between the $F$ value given in the results table and a value for $F$ (critical value of $F$ or $F^*$) as derived from $F$ distribution tables (Table 7.7).

If $F_{results} > F^*$, then H$_0$ is rejected; there *is* a significant statistical relationship between the independent variables as a group and the dependent variable.

H$_0$: there is not a significant statistical relationship between demand and the group of independent variables.

To derive the critical $F$ value from the $F$ tables ($F^*$), the following steps should be undertaken:

- Identify the appropriate number of 'degrees of freedom' as a result of including a constant term and independent variables within the regression.
- To gain the appropriate degrees of freedom for the numerator, identify the number of independent variables. In this case there are two (price and income).
- The appropriate degrees of freedom for the denominator are gained by identifying the total number of constant and independent variables included in the regression. This number should then be subtracted from the number of observations included in the regression.

In this case, there are one constant term and two independent variables (price and price of cassettes). Since there are two independent variables, the degrees of freedom for the numerator are 2. The total of three variables should be subtracted from the number of observations included in the regression (26). The degrees of freedom for the denominator in this case are $26 - 3 = 23$.

**Table 7.7 F distribution for 5% significance**

| | | \multicolumn{19}{c}{Degrees of freedom for numerator} |
|---|---|---|---|---|---|---|---|---|---|---|---|---|---|---|---|---|---|---|---|
| | | 1 | 2 | 3 | 4 | 5 | 6 | 7 | 8 | 9 | 10 | 12 | 15 | 20 | 24 | 30 | 40 | 60 | 120 | ∞ |
| | 1 | 161 | 200 | 216 | 225 | 230 | 234 | 237 | 239 | 241 | 242 | 244 | 246 | 248 | 249 | 250 | 251 | 252 | 253 | 254 |
| | 2 | 18.5 | 19.0 | 19.2 | 19.2 | 19.3 | 19.3 | 19.4 | 19.4 | 19.4 | 19.4 | 19.4 | 19.4 | 19.5 | 19.5 | 19.5 | 19.5 | 19.5 | 19.5 | 19.5 |
| | 3 | 10.1 | 9.55 | 9.28 | 9.12 | 9.01 | 8.94 | 8.89 | 8.85 | 8.81 | 8.79 | 8.74 | 8.70 | 8.66 | 8.64 | 8.62 | 8.59 | 8.57 | 8.55 | 8.53 |
| | 4 | 7.71 | 6.94 | 6.59 | 6.39 | 6.26 | 6.16 | 6.09 | 6.04 | 6.00 | 5.96 | 5.91 | 5.86 | 5.80 | 5.77 | 5.75 | 5.72 | 5.69 | 5.66 | 5.63 |
| | 5 | 6.61 | 5.79 | 5.41 | 5.19 | 5.05 | 4.95 | 4.88 | 4.82 | 4.77 | 4.74 | 4.68 | 4.62 | 4.56 | 4.53 | 4.50 | 4.46 | 4.43 | 4.40 | 4.37 |
| | 6 | 5.99 | 5.14 | 4.76 | 4.53 | 4.39 | 4.28 | 4.21 | 4.15 | 4.10 | 4.06 | 4.00 | 3.94 | 3.87 | 3.84 | 3.81 | 3.77 | 3.74 | 3.70 | 3.67 |
| | 7 | 5.59 | 4.74 | 4.35 | 4.12 | 3.97 | 3.87 | 3.79 | 3.73 | 3.68 | 3.64 | 3.57 | 3.51 | 3.44 | 3.41 | 3.38 | 3.34 | 3.30 | 3.27 | 3.23 |
| | 8 | 5.32 | 4.46 | 4.07 | 3.84 | 3.69 | 3.58 | 3.50 | 3.44 | 3.39 | 3.35 | 3.28 | 3.22 | 3.15 | 3.12 | 3.08 | 3.04 | 3.01 | 2.97 | 2.93 |
| | 9 | 5.12 | 4.26 | 3.86 | 3.63 | 3.48 | 3.37 | 3.29 | 3.23 | 3.18 | 3.14 | 3.07 | 3.01 | 2.94 | 2.90 | 2.86 | 2.83 | 2.79 | 2.75 | 2.71 |
| | 10 | 4.96 | 4.10 | 3.71 | 3.48 | 3.33 | 3.22 | 3.14 | 3.07 | 3.02 | 2.98 | 2.91 | 2.85 | 2.77 | 2.74 | 2.70 | 2.66 | 2.62 | 2.58 | 2.54 |
| | 11 | 4.84 | 3.98 | 3.59 | 3.36 | 3.20 | 3.09 | 3.01 | 2.95 | 2.90 | 2.85 | 2.79 | 2.72 | 2.65 | 2.61 | 2.57 | 2.53 | 2.49 | 2.45 | 2.40 |
| | 12 | 4.75 | 3.89 | 3.49 | 3.26 | 3.11 | 3.00 | 2.91 | 2.85 | 2.80 | 2.75 | 2.69 | 2.62 | 2.54 | 2.51 | 2.47 | 2.43 | 2.38 | 2.34 | 2.30 |
| | 13 | 4.67 | 3.81 | 3.41 | 3.18 | 3.03 | 2.92 | 2.83 | 2.77 | 2.71 | 2.67 | 2.60 | 2.53 | 2.46 | 2.42 | 2.38 | 2.34 | 2.30 | 2.25 | 2.21 |
| | 14 | 4.60 | 3.74 | 3.34 | 3.11 | 2.96 | 2.85 | 2.76 | 2.70 | 2.65 | 2.60 | 2.53 | 2.46 | 2.39 | 2.35 | 2.31 | 2.27 | 2.22 | 2.18 | 2.13 |
| | 15 | 4.54 | 3.68 | 3.29 | 3.06 | 2.90 | 2.79 | 2.71 | 2.64 | 2.59 | 2.54 | 2.48 | 2.40 | 2.33 | 2.29 | 2.25 | 2.20 | 2.16 | 2.11 | 2.07 |
| | 16 | 4.49 | 3.36 | 3.24 | 3.01 | 2.85 | 2.74 | 2.66 | 2.59 | 2.54 | 2.49 | 2.42 | 2.35 | 2.28 | 2.24 | 2.19 | 2.15 | 2.11 | 2.06 | 2.01 |
| | 17 | 4.45 | 3.59 | 3.20 | 2.96 | 2.81 | 2.70 | 2.61 | 2.55 | 2.48 | 2.45 | 2.38 | 2.31 | 2.23 | 2.19 | 2.15 | 2.10 | 2.06 | 2.01 | 1.96 |
| | 18 | 4.41 | 3.55 | 3.16 | 2.93 | 2.77 | 2.66 | 2.58 | 2.51 | 2.46 | 2.41 | 2.34 | 2.27 | 2.19 | 2.15 | 2.11 | 2.06 | 2.02 | 1.97 | 1.92 |
| | 19 | 4.38 | 3.52 | 3.13 | 2.90 | 2.74 | 2.63 | 2.54 | 2.48 | 2.42 | 2.39 | 2.31 | 2.23 | 2.16 | 2.11 | 2.07 | 2.03 | 1.98 | 1.93 | 1.88 |
| | 20 | 4.35 | 3.49 | 3.10 | 2.87 | 2.71 | 2.60 | 2.51 | 2.45 | 2.39 | 2.35 | 2.28 | 2.20 | 2.12 | 2.08 | 2.04 | 1.99 | 1.95 | 1.90 | 1.84 |
| | 21 | 4.32 | 3.47 | 3.07 | 2.84 | 2.68 | 2.57 | 2.49 | 2.42 | 2.37 | 2.32 | 2.25 | 2.18 | 2.10 | 2.05 | 2.01 | 1.96 | 1.92 | 1.87 | 1.81 |
| | 22 | 4.30 | 3.44 | 3.05 | 2.82 | 2.66 | 2.55 | 2.46 | 2.40 | 2.34 | 2.30 | 2.23 | 2.15 | 2.07 | 2.03 | 1.98 | 1.94 | 1.89 | 1.84 | 1.78 |
| | 23 | 4.28 | 3.42 | 3.03 | 2.80 | 2.64 | 2.53 | 2.44 | 2.37 | 2.32 | 2.27 | 2.20 | 2.13 | 2.05 | 2.01 | 1.96 | 1.91 | 1.86 | 1.81 | 1.76 |
| | 24 | 4.26 | 3.40 | 3.01 | 2.78 | 2.62 | 2.51 | 2.42 | 2.36 | 2.30 | 2.25 | 2.18 | 2.11 | 2.03 | 1.98 | 1.94 | 1.89 | 1.84 | 1.79 | 1.73 |
| | 25 | 4.42 | 3.39 | 2.99 | 2.76 | 2.60 | 2.49 | 2.40 | 2.34 | 2.28 | 2.24 | 2.16 | 2.09 | 2.01 | 1.96 | 1.92 | 1.87 | 1.82 | 1.77 | 1.71 |
| | 30 | 4.17 | 3.32 | 2.92 | 2.69 | 2.53 | 2.42 | 2.33 | 2.27 | 2.21 | 2.16 | 2.09 | 2.01 | 1.93 | 1.89 | 1.84 | 1.79 | 1.74 | 1.68 | 1.62 |
| | 40 | 4.08 | 3.23 | 2.84 | 2.61 | 2.45 | 2.34 | 2.25 | 2.18 | 2.12 | 2.08 | 2.00 | 1.92 | 1.84 | 1.79 | 1.74 | 1.69 | 1.64 | 1.58 | 1.51 |
| | 60 | 4.00 | 3.15 | 2.76 | 2.53 | 2.37 | 2.25 | 2.17 | 2.10 | 2.04 | 1.99 | 1.92 | 1.84 | 1.75 | 1.70 | 1.65 | 1.59 | 1.53 | 1.47 | 1.39 |
| | 120 | 3.92 | 3.07 | 2.68 | 2.45 | 2.29 | 2.18 | 2.09 | 2.02 | 1.96 | 1.91 | 1.83 | 1.75 | 1.66 | 1.61 | 1.55 | 1.50 | 1.43 | 1.35 | 1.25 |
| | ∞ | 3.84 | 3.00 | 2.60 | 2.37 | 2.21 | 2.10 | 2.01 | 1.94 | 1.88 | 1.83 | 1.75 | 1.67 | 1.57 | 1.52 | 1.46 | 1.39 | 1.32 | 1.22 | 1.00 |

*(Left margin label: Degrees of freedom for denominator)*

*Source*: M Merrington and C M Thompson, 'Tables of Percentage Points of the Inverted Beta (F) Distribution', *Biometrika*, vol 33, 1943, p 73. Reprinted with the permission of the authors and trustees of *Biometrika*.

The appropriate level of significance to be used for the $F$ tests must be decided. As with the '$t$' test, it is usual for a 5 per cent level of significance to be used.

Thus the $F^*$ for (2,23) degrees of freedom and 5 per cent significance level, $F^{0.05}_{(2,23)}$, may be looked up in the tables.

From the tables, $F^{0.05}_{(2,23)}$ can be seen to be 3.45. Thus $F^* = 3.45$.

Comparing this value to the value of $F$ from the results table allows acceptance or rejection of the null hypothesis $H_0$.

The $F$ test for the example of demand for CDs gives the following results:

$H_0$: there is not a significant statistical relationship between the independent variables as a group and quantity demanded.

Given that $F^* = 3.45$ and $F_{results} = 876.731$, and since $F^* < F_{results}$, $H_0$ is rejected. Thus, it is accepted that

there is a significant statistical relationship between the independent variables as a group and quantity demanded of CDs.

It may therefore be assumed that changes in price of CDs and also changes in price of cassettes do jointly have an effect on the demand for CDs.

### $R^2$ and adjusted $R^2$

$R^2$ is the coefficient of determination: the goodness of fit for a multiple regression model.

$$R^2 = \frac{\text{Variation explained by regression}}{\text{Total variation of dependent variable}} \times 100$$

The $R^2$ values give an impression of the overall validity of the equation in terms of the completeness of the independent variables in explaining variations in demand. $R^2$ is a 'raw' or unadjusted value, while the adjusted $R^2$ value is adjusted to take into account degrees of freedom, that is, the inclusion of several independent variables.

It is important to consider the adjusted $R^2$ value, since the $R^2$ value may be increased by simply increasing the number of independent variables in the model being used for estimation. Accounting for degrees of freedom recognises this and provides a more realistic figure.

The $R^2$ values in the results table show a probability. When expressed as a percentage (i.e. multiplied by 100), the $R^2$ values give the percentage of variations in the dependent variable explained by the regression. The $R^2$ values are actually a ratio of the explained (by the regression) variations in demand to the unexplained (or random) variations in demand in the estimated equation.

In the example of demand for CDs, the $R^2$ values show the probability (percentage) of the estimated equation explaining variations in demand when price and income are included. Thus it can be seen from the $R^2$ value that the estimated equation $QD = 6370.828 - 503.609P_{CD} + 26.540P_{cassette}$ explains 98.71 per cent of variations in demand for CDs. Even when adjusted for degrees of freedom, the equation can be seen to explain 98.59 per cent of variations in demand for CDs.

$R^2$ and adjusted $R^2$ values are sometimes also called the goodness of fit values. This relates to how well the estimated, or sample, regression line fits the observed data. Obviously, there will very rarely be a perfect fit (giving an $R^2$ value of 1 or 100 per cent) between the estimated line and the observed data line. Therefore, the $R^2$ or goodness of fit values give an indication of how well the model describes the actual data.

As a general rule, a 'very good' $R^2$ value would be in excess of 0.90. A 'good' $R^2$ value would lie between 0.80 and 0.89 and a 'reasonable' $R^2$ value would lie between 0.70 and 0.79. For an estimated regression equation to be acceptable, the $R^2$ value should be in excess of 0.70. Anything below that would indicate that there may be an identification or specification error in the model used. If the $R^2$ value falls below 0.70, it would be prudent to respecify the form for the estimate and repeat the regression.

Due to the manner in which regression analysis is sometimes taught, the tendency is to inspect the $R^2$ values first. Given some of the hazards that can arise with statistical modelling, it may be better to inspect for deficiencies with the model before accepting a high $R^2$.

There is further discussion of the implications of statistical tests for the validity of the estimated equation in the next section on econometric tests.

# Econometric verification

## Multicollinearity

Whenever independent variables are included in an estimated relationship, the problem of **multicollinearity** exists. What is of importance is the extent to which it exists. Strictly speaking, multicollinearity is a linear relationship between the independent variables in a regression model. Concern should arise where there is a high level of multicollinearity, interrelationship between the independent variables, even if it is not a perfect interrelationship.

High levels of multicollinearity will have an effect on the accuracy or validity of the estimated coefficients. Remember, however, that multicollinearity always exists, to a degree.

As a guideline, multicollinearity may be detected by investigation of the estimated $t$ and $R^2$ values.

Multicollinearity may give rise to insignificant, or 'smaller than normal', $t$ values. Additionally, when the level of multicollinearity is high, two or more of the $t$ values will be not significant even though the $R^2$ value is high ('high' usually being 0.8 or greater). It is possible that the low significance of a $t$ value indicates not that multicollinearity exists, but that the variable is not significant. Many computer printouts produce correlations for one independent variable on another, which may give an indication of the level of correlation.

Therefore, it is for the analyst to consider the overall validity or accuracy of the estimated values as a whole and to decide whether action needs to be taken or not.

If multicollinearity is considered to be a problem, a number of corrective measures may be taken. If both variables appear to be moving in the same direction, one option is to 'drop' a variable and run the regression without including what might be considered to be a less significant variable (by '$t$' test or previous experience). However, dropping a variable may give rise to specification error.

Alternatively, if it is considered best not to drop a variable, the model can be transformed, by subtracting a one-time-period lagged relation from the original relation and running the regression with respect to the subsequent relation. This reduces the problematic relationship between the terms. Two other problems may be created as a result, however. First, lagging the model causes the loss of one set of observations; this means that the degrees of freedom are reduced. Second, the error terms may become correlated; thus reducing multicollinearity but giving rise to autocorrelation (*see* next section).

In the original model, the relationship was:

$$QD_t = \text{ß}_1 + \text{ß}_2 P_{CD_t} + \text{ß}_3 P_{CAS_t} + U_t$$

where,

$\text{ß}_1$ = constant term
$\text{ß}_2$ = price coefficient
$P_{CD_t}$ = price of CDs observation in each period ($t$)
$\text{ß}_3$ = price of cassette coefficient
$P_{CAS_t}$ = price of cassette observation in each period ($t$)
$U_t$ = 'disturbance term'

The disturbance term is included in the model to acknowledge the fact that there will be unexplained variations in demand in each time period.

This relationship, when lagged, becomes:

$$QD_{t-1} = \text{ß}_1 + \text{ß}_2 P_{CD_{t-1}} + \text{ß}_3 P_{CAS_{t-1}} + U_{t-1}$$

Subtracting the lagged relation from the original gives:

$$QD_t - QD_{t-1} = \text{ß}_2(P_{CD_t} - P_{CD_{t-1}}) + \text{ß}_3(P_{CAS_t} - P_{CAS_{t-1}}) + U_t - U_{t-1}$$

The transformed model can be seen in the linear form by letting:

$$QD_t - QD_{t-1} = QD^T, \ P_{CD_t} - P_{CD_{t-1}} = P_{CD}{}^T,$$
$$P_{CAS_t} - P_{CAS_{t-1}} = P_{CAS}{}^T \text{ and } U_t - U_{t-1} = U^T$$

Thus,

$$QD^T = \text{ß}_2 P_{CD}{}^T + \text{ß}_3 P_{CAS}{}^T + U^T$$

Transformation of models for these purposes is possible manually. However, most forecasting software packages usually contain an option or command to do this as required.

### Autocorrelation

**Autocorrelation** occurs when the error terms ($U_t$) within a regression equation are serially correlated. That is, there is an identifiable pattern which arises between successive error terms. Theoretically, without autocorrelation, the error terms would be normally distributed and therefore a random pattern between successive error terms is expected.

Autocorrelation presents a problem because it will cause the unexplained variations (error terms) to be consistently over- or underestimated. Two situations which can lead to autocorrelation are economic cycle inertia and specification bias, in the case of an excluded variable. If autocorrelation is positive, the trend exhibited by plotting these unexplained variations over time is either an upward or a downward trend as a result of the interlinkages between the residuals; *see* Figure 7.6(a).

**Figure 7.6**

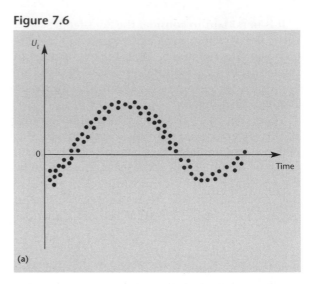

(a)

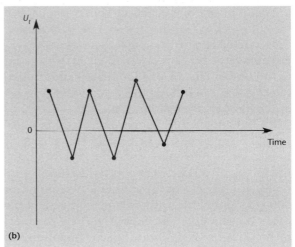

(b)

**(a)** Positive autocorrelation exhibits either an upward or a downward trend as a result of the interlinkages between the residuals.

**(b)** Negative autocorrelation causes the trend in unexplained variations to break down and exhibit a 'saw tooth' pattern. This is caused when the alternate unexplained variations are of the same sign.

Note also that autocorrelation may be negative as well as positive. It may cause the expected trend in unexplained variations to break down and exhibit a 'saw tooth' pattern where alternate unexplained variations are of the same sign; *see* Figure 7.6(b).

Autocorrelation may exist in time series or cross-sectional data, as described in the example below.

It would be unacceptable if the spending habits of Family A affected the spending habits of Family B to such an extent that, if Family A received an increase in net income and consequently spent that extra amount on home improvements such as double glazing, Family B, without an increase, followed suit.

◆ **CASE STUDY 7.3**

# The feel-bad factor

Candid as ever, Kenneth Clarke caused a political storm on March 15th when he said that it may be years before voters feel good about the economic recovery. He is probably too pessimistic. True, they are currently growing more miserable by the day. Consumer spending growth is slowing sharply. Retail sales rose by only 0.1% in the three months to February, compared with the previous three months. The Confederation of British Industry's distributive-trades survey, published on March 14th, showed that trading conditions for retailers in February were the worst for two years.

The reasons seem obvious. While booming exports have boosted manufacturers, consumers have faced higher taxes and rising interest rates. The housing market shows no sign of picking up, and the growth in average earnings actually slowed slightly during January. So no wonder consumers are tightening their belts.

Yet there are plenty of reasons for expecting consumer spending to rebound strongly. The role of house prices is easily exaggerated: though they have been flat during the current upturn, consumer spending has grown as rapidly during this recovery as it did at the same stage in the last one. Nor did last April's tax increase prevent consumption from rising. That is hardly surprising, as disposable (post-tax) incomes actually rose on average last year by 3.4% (0.8% in real terms).

David Mackie, an economist in the London office of JP Morgan, an American investment bank, expects personal disposable income to rise sharply in 1995, by a nominal 5.3% and by 2.6% in real terms. According to Mr Mackie, though higher taxes will eat up 0.8% more of personal income this year than last, and higher interest rates will account for 1.1% more than in 1994, this will be outweighed by a 6.1% jump in personal incomes.

This will come, firstly, from more people finding work. Unemployment continues to fall steadily – by 27,400 in February – and, unlike the early months of the recovery, the majority of new jobs created are now full-time ones. Earnings growth will rise as the jobs market tightens (January's fall was a statistical quirk reflecting hefty bonuses paid to City workers last January). More overtime will be worked (overtime was 4.5% higher in January than a year earlier).

Many workers will also share in the growing fortunes of their employers. Often ignored by economists, the use of profit-related pay has soared during the past decade; it is now paid to 16% of private-sector workers. Mr Mackie estimates that last year's total payout was a hefty £2.5 billion; with profits continuing to soar, 1995's total will be higher. So, by summer, consumers will probably feel better. The real question for Mr Clarke is this: will they thank the government?

*Source*: © *The Economist*, London, 18 March 1995. Reprinted with permission.

---

The effect of this irrational expenditure would be an underestimation on the part of any model of expenditure for Family B, that is, larger than expected variations in demand. If the copycat spending spread to other families in the street, it is not difficult to understand that the validity of the original model would be severely affected.

### Comment on the case study

Consumers are known to act with hindsight to the extent that, in an economic recovery, it can take a long time before they have enough confidence in the recovery to increase their personal expenditure. This phenomenon is widely documented and accepted. The case study points out that consumer expenditure in the UK is soon going to pick up as consumers slowly realise that their increased earnings are not a short-term trend, but are likely to last for a considerable period of time. This is known as the 'feel-good factor': the increases in various areas of the economy which combine to give employers and consumers confidence in the economy as a whole. Kenneth Clarke (then UK Chancellor of the Exchequer) claimed that the recovery would take a long time. But the economists quoted claim that the combination of increasing disposable income and increasing levels of full-time employment will assist the recovery in consumer expenditure.

Whether the economy's recovery is slow or the upswing is more dynamic, one thing to be expected is that autocorrelation will exist. The momentum built into any upswing – whether fast or slow – will cause successive observations which are likely to be interdependent. In this case estimates of future levels of demand will be biased.

The implication of the existence of autocorrelation is that the $R^2$ value will be high while the $t$ and $F$ statistics will be overestimated. Thus, the estimated equation may seem to be acceptable statistically, as a result of the linkages between the sequential error terms.

The test for autocorrelation relies on a comparison between the Durbin-Watson statistic given in the data results table and an upper and lower Durbin-Watson statistic ($d_u$ and $d_L$) as derived from Durbin-Watson statistic tables (Table 7.8). The Durbin-Watson test is based on the null hypothesis that there is no autocorrelation present. If this null hypothesis can be proved correct, then the estimated equation may be accepted as correct.

### Table 7.8  Durbin-Watson statistic for 5% significance points of $d_L$ and $d_u$

| | $k' = 1$ | | $k' = 2$ | | $k' = 3$ | | $k' = 4$ | | $k' = 5$ | |
| | $d_L$ | $d_u$ | $d_L$ | $d_u$ | $d_L$ | $d_u$ | $d_L$ | $d_u$ | $d_L$ | $d_u$ |
| $n$ | | | | | | | | | | |
|---|---|---|---|---|---|---|---|---|---|---|
| 15 | 1.08 | 1.36 | 0.95 | 1.54 | 0.82 | 1.75 | 0.69 | 1.97 | 0.56 | 2.21 |
| 16 | 1.10 | 1.37 | 0.98 | 1.54 | 0.86 | 1.73 | 0.74 | 1.93 | 0.62 | 2.15 |
| 17 | 1.13 | 1.38 | 1.02 | 1.54 | 0.90 | 1.71 | 0.78 | 1.90 | 0.67 | 2.10 |
| 18 | 1.16 | 1.39 | 1.05 | 1.53 | 0.93 | 1.69 | 0.82 | 1.87 | 0.71 | 2.06 |
| 19 | 1.18 | 1.40 | 1.08 | 1.53 | 0.97 | 1.68 | 0.86 | 1.85 | 0.75 | 2.02 |
| 20 | 1.20 | 1.41 | 1.10 | 1.54 | 1.00 | 1.68 | 0.90 | 1.83 | 0.79 | 1.99 |
| 21 | 1.22 | 1.42 | 1.13 | 1.54 | 1.03 | 1.67 | 0.93 | 1.81 | 0.83 | 1.96 |
| 22 | 1.24 | 1.43 | 1.15 | 1.54 | 1.06 | 1.66 | 0.96 | 1.80 | 0.86 | 1.94 |
| 23 | 1.26 | 1.44 | 1.17 | 1.54 | 1.08 | 1.66 | 0.99 | 1.79 | 0.90 | 1.92 |
| 24 | 1.27 | 1.45 | 1.19 | 1.55 | 1.10 | 1.66 | 1.01 | 1.78 | 0.93 | 1.90 |
| 25 | 1.29 | 1.45 | 1.21 | 1.55 | 1.12 | 1.66 | 1.04 | 1.77 | 0.95 | 1.89 |
| 26 | 1.30 | 1.46 | 1.22 | 1.55 | 1.14 | 1.65 | 1.06 | 1.76 | 0.98 | 1.88 |
| 27 | 1.32 | 1.47 | 1.24 | 1.56 | 1.16 | 1.65 | 1.08 | 1.76 | 1.01 | 1.86 |
| 28 | 1.33 | 1.48 | 1.26 | 1.56 | 1.18 | 1.65 | 1.10 | 1.75 | 1.03 | 1.85 |
| 29 | 1.34 | 1.48 | 1.27 | 1.56 | 1.20 | 1.65 | 1.12 | 1.74 | 1.05 | 1.84 |
| 30 | 1.35 | 1.49 | 1.28 | 1.57 | 1.21 | 1.65 | 1.14 | 1.74 | 1.07 | 1.83 |
| 31 | 1.36 | 1.50 | 1.30 | 1.57 | 1.23 | 1.65 | 1.16 | 1.74 | 1.09 | 1.83 |
| 32 | 1.37 | 1.50 | 1.31 | 1.57 | 1.24 | 1.65 | 1.18 | 1.73 | 1.11 | 1.82 |
| 33 | 1.38 | 1.51 | 1.32 | 1.58 | 1.26 | 1.65 | 1.19 | 1.73 | 1.13 | 1.81 |
| 34 | 1.39 | 1.51 | 1.33 | 1.58 | 1.27 | 1.65 | 1.21 | 1.73 | 1.15 | 1.81 |
| 35 | 1.40 | 1.52 | 1.34 | 1.58 | 1.28 | 1.65 | 1.22 | 1.73 | 1.16 | 1.80 |
| 36 | 1.41 | 1.52 | 1.35 | 1.59 | 1.29 | 1.65 | 1.24 | 1.73 | 1.18 | 1.80 |
| 37 | 1.42 | 1.53 | 1.36 | 1.59 | 1.31 | 1.66 | 1.25 | 1.72 | 1.19 | 1.80 |
| 38 | 1.43 | 1.54 | 1.37 | 1.59 | 1.32 | 1.66 | 1.26 | 1.72 | 1.21 | 1.79 |
| 39 | 1.43 | 1.54 | 1.38 | 1.60 | 1.33 | 1.66 | 1.27 | 1.72 | 1.22 | 1.79 |
| 40 | 1.44 | 1.54 | 1.39 | 1.60 | 1.34 | 1.66 | 1.29 | 1.72 | 1.23 | 1.79 |
| 45 | 1.48 | 1.57 | 1.43 | 1.62 | 1.38 | 1.67 | 1.34 | 1.72 | 1.29 | 1.78 |
| 50 | 1.50 | 1.59 | 1.46 | 1.63 | 1.42 | 1.67 | 1.38 | 1.72 | 1.34 | 1.77 |
| 55 | 1.53 | 1.60 | 1.49 | 1.64 | 1.45 | 1.68 | 1.41 | 1.72 | 1.38 | 1.77 |
| 60 | 1.55 | 1.62 | 1.51 | 1.65 | 1.48 | 1.69 | 1.44 | 1.73 | 1.41 | 1.77 |
| 65 | 1.57 | 1.63 | 1.54 | 1.66 | 1.50 | 1.70 | 1.47 | 1.73 | 1.44 | 1.77 |
| 70 | 1.58 | 1.64 | 1.55 | 1.67 | 1.52 | 1.70 | 1.49 | 1.74 | 1.46 | 1.77 |
| 75 | 1.60 | 1.65 | 1.57 | 1.68 | 1.54 | 1.71 | 1.51 | 1.74 | 1.49 | 1.77 |
| 80 | 1.61 | 1.66 | 1.59 | 1.69 | 1.56 | 1.72 | 1.53 | 1.74 | 1.51 | 1.77 |
| 85 | 1.62 | 1.67 | 1.60 | 1.70 | 1.57 | 1.72 | 1.55 | 1.75 | 1.52 | 1.77 |
| 90 | 1.63 | 1.68 | 1.61 | 1.70 | 1.59 | 1.73 | 1.57 | 1.75 | 1.54 | 1.78 |
| 95 | 1.64 | 1.69 | 1.62 | 1.71 | 1.60 | 1.73 | 1.58 | 1.75 | 1.56 | 1.78 |
| 100 | 1.65 | 1.69 | 1.63 | 1.72 | 1.61 | 1.74 | 1.59 | 1.76 | 1.57 | 1.78 |

*Note*: $n$ = number of observations; $k'$ = number of independent variables.

*Source*: J Durbin and G S Watson, 'Testing for a serial Correlation in Least Squares Regression,' *Biometrika*, vol 38, 1951, pp 159–177. Reprinted with the permission of the authors and trustees of *Biometrika*.

$H_0$: there is no autocorrelation present.

A set of decision criteria which can be transferred to a number line is used in order to inform the decision-making process. The number line is given in Figure 7.7.

The $DW_{results}$ statistic must be placed on the number line to ascertain the appropriate accept/reject decision to be applied. $H_0$ is then either accepted or rejected. To place the $DW_{results}$ statistic onto the line, $d_L$ and $d_u$ must be gained from the Durbin-Watson statistics table. Once $d_L$ and $d_u$ are known, they may be placed on the number line in the appropriate place. The value for $4-d_u$ and $4-d_L$ should also be calculated and placed on the number line. With these values in place, it will be clear which zone the $DW_{results}$ statistic falls into as it too is placed on the line. Subtracting $d_L$ and $d_u$ from 4 (the maximum possible DW statistic) gives values for $4-d_u$ and $4-d_L$. These also need to be placed on the number line.

One drawback of the Durbin-Watson test is that a zone of indecision exists where the presence of autocorrelation cannot clearly be accepted or rejected. More complex tests do exist to assist decision making where such situations arise, but they will not be discussed here.

To derive the upper and lower Durbin-Watson values ($d_L$, $d_u$) from the Durbin-Watson statistics tables, the following steps should be undertaken:

- Identify the appropriate number of independent variables ($k'$) within the estimated equation.
- Identify the number of observations ($n$) used in the regression.
- In the case of demand for CDs, there are two independent variables (price and price of cassettes) and 26 observations. Thus, $k' = 2$ and $n = 26$.
- Identify the appropriate level of significance to be used for the Durbin-Watson test. As with the $t$ and $F$ tests, it is usual for a 5 per cent level of significance to be used.

Thus $d_u$ (for $k' = 2$, $n = 26$) for 5 per cent significance level may be found to be 1.55 from the tables. Similarly, $d_L$ may be found to be 1.22.

Superimposing these values on the number line, along with the $DW_{results}$ statistic of 1.895, the results may be seen in Figure 7.8.

Thus it can clearly be seen that the $DW_{results}$ statistic falls into the zone to accept the $H_0$: no autocorrelation.

It may therefore be assumed that there is no autocorrelation in the data relating to the price of CDs and also in the data relating to the price of cassettes.

If it is found that autocorrelation does exist, steps must obviously be taken to correct the model. There are several methods available to do this. Briefly, since as already discussed consumers tend to make autocorrelated consumption decisions, the best way to solve for autocorrelation is to redefine the model. This should be done to include changes

**Figure 7.7**

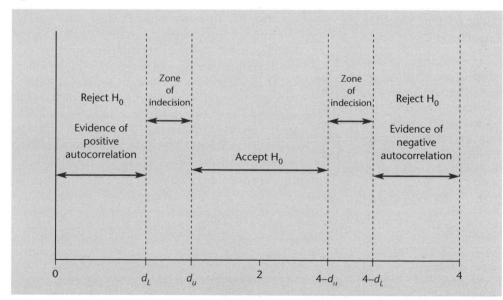

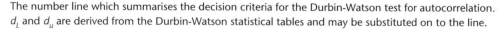

The number line which summarises the decision criteria for the Durbin-Watson test for autocorrelation. $d_L$ and $d_u$ are derived from the Durbin-Watson statistical tables and may be substituted on to the line.

**Figure 7.8**

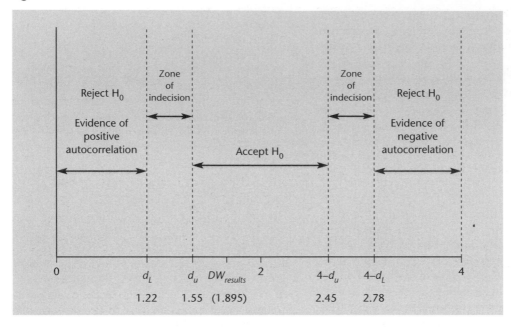

The Durbin-Watson decision criteria, showing the appropriate results from the estimated relationship for CD sales. Since $DW_{results}$ lies between $d_u$ and $4 - d_u$, the negative hypothesis is rejected: there is no evidence of autocorrelation.

in independent variables with respect to sequential time periods rather than using the raw data; technically speaking, using 'first-order differences', that is, looking at the rate of change rather than absolute values. Equally valid for these purposes is the inclusion of an additional variable in the model, or inclusion of a time variable.

## Overall verification of the validity of the estimated equation

Once the three stages of verification have been followed – economic, statistical and econometric – it should be obvious whether or not the model is acceptable. If it is acceptable, then the model may be used to forecast demand for forthcoming time periods. This is done by substituting in to the equation expected values for the independent variables which are likely to occur in that period.

If the model is not acceptable, then remedial measures to correct the common faults recognised above should be followed.

It should be remembered, however, that all forecasts, no matter how impressively accurate they may seem, are after all only forecasts. Economic and technological changes and so on can result in the model being based on invalid assumptions. Its accuracy will therefore be affected.

From the discussion, it can be seen that regression analysis involves a complex process and detailed understanding of the market under analysis. Organisations which use the technique tend to be large manufacturing firms wishing to forecast demand for their product or range of products. Such organisations possess the resources and data to perform such analyses effectively and with varying levels of accuracy.

## ◆ CASE STUDY 7.4

# Future imperfect

While Albert Einstein is queuing to enter heaven, he meets three men. He asks about their IQs. The first replies 190. 'Wonderful,' exclaims Einstein. 'We can discuss my theory of relativity'. The second answers 150. 'Good,' says Einstein. 'I look forward to discussing the prospects for world peace'. The third mumbles 50. Einstein pauses. 'So what is your forecast for GDP growth next year?'

This old joke sums up most people's view of economic forecasters. Their reputation has been severely dented of late, not least because they failed to predict the strength of the world economic boom in the late 1980s and then, worse still, failed to warn of the consequent recession.

Are forecasts becoming less accurate? Financial deregulation and globalisation have made it harder to track the economy, so you might expect the answer to be yes. The facts, however, suggest otherwise.

Table 7.9 judges the forecasting record of Britain's Treasury over the past 13 years. It shows the mean absolute error (i.e. adding up the differences between forecast and outturn each year and ignoring its sign) of forecasts made each March for growth, inflation and the current account in the year ahead. During 1985–91 the average error for growth was 0.7 of a percentage point, compared with 1.2 points in the previous six years. The Treasury's forecasts of inflation and the current account also seem to have improved.

But such tests depend upon the time horizon. Looking at the forecasts which the Treasury made in the previous November of each year, its GDP forecasts for the period since 1985 seem to be more off beam than before, though it has got better at predicting inflation.

Victor Zarnowitz, an economist at the University of Chicago, has studied a large number of American forecasts over the past 30 years. Taking the mean absolute error of predictions made at the end of each year for the year ahead, he finds that the accuracy of growth forecasts has hardly changed (see Table 7.10). Inflation forecasts have become less accurate since the 1960s – but that is not surprising, given the surge in inflation in the 1970s.

Mr Zarnowitz also compared the average error of these forecasts with the error from forecasts using a crude extrapolation of four-year moving averages of output and inflation. Professional forecasters will be relieved to know that the extrapolations proved much less accurate.

### Table 7.9  British economic forecasts

Mean absolute error of forecasts, % points

| Treasury forecasts* made in: | 1979–84 | 1985–91 |
|---|---|---|
| **March** | | |
| GDP | 1.2 | 0.7 |
| Inflation | 1.4 | 1.2 |
| Current account† | 1.0 | 0.9 |
| **November** | | |
| GDP | 0.5 | 1.4 |
| Inflation | 2.7 | 1.4 |
| Current account | 1.0 | 1.2 |

*for year ahead  † as % of GDP
Source: S G Warburg, updated by The Economist

### Table 7.10  American economic forecasts

Mean absolute error of forecasts*, % points

| | 1959–67 | 1962–76 | 1969–89 |
|---|---|---|---|
| GDP | 1.2 | 1.2 | 1.1 |
| Inflation | 0.6 | 1.0 | 1.1 |

*Selection of private and government forecasts
Source: Zarnowitz

Further evidence that American forecasters have improved their aim comes from *Blue Chip*, an American newsletter, which polls about 50 economists each month. The mean absolute error of October forecasters for GDP growth in the following year fell from 1.1 percentage points in 1977–83 to 0.9 of a point in 1984–91.

Forecasters may be no worse than they used to be, but that is still not good enough. In particular, their biggest blunders tend to be at turning points, when the economy dips into recession – the very time when forecasts are most needed.

Conventional forecasting relies upon a computer model built from the economist's favourite theory about how the economy works. Using past data, he tries to get the best fit for hundreds of equations that attempt to explain the relationships between economic variables. Assumptions about such things as tax rates, which cannot be forecast because they are decided by governments, are then plugged in and the computer cranks out an economic forecast.

Disappointment with such models has encouraged some economists to test different kinds of crystal balls. Two developments pursued in America over the past decade have attracted growing interest.

■ The first is **vector auto-regressive models** (VARS). These are much simpler, with far fewer variables than standard macroeconomic models. The process makes virtually no use of economic theory to establish casual links. Each variable is 'explained' largely by detecting patterns in its own statistical history; to make a prediction, the forecaster extrapolates this history into the future. Experience in America suggests that VAR models may be helpful in predicting turning points.
■ A second development is the use of **financial-spread variables** (e.g. the gap between short- and long-term interest rates and **business-confidence surveys** as leading indicators of activity. Past experience suggests that financial indicators are also good at spotting turning points. For example, if short-term interest rates rise relative to long-term rates, this typically heralds an economic slowdown.

More recently, several British economists have gone down the same road. Gavyn Davies, an economist at

Case study 7.4 *continued*

the London branch of Goldman Sachs, has attempted to incorporate both of these techniques into forecasts for the British economy. Almost all standard economic models completely missed Britain's latest recession. But, claims Mr Davies, his new model, which uses both VAR and financial-spread indicators, would have given at least 12 months' warning of recession, if it had been available. It would also have predicted each of the previous two recessions and would have given no false alarms of recession during the past two decades.

Only time will tell whether VAR methods will continue to beat standard models. Their weakness is that they work only for as long as statistical relationships hold true, and in the past such models have often broken down almost as soon as they were used. In fact, this is just an extreme case of a general difficulty with all models based on past experience: they cannot cope with structural changes in the economy. Unprecedentedly high levels of debt in America and Britain, for instance, may have weakened the benefits of lower interest rates, which may explain why recovery has taken longer to happen than most economists predicted.

It is probably best to see VAR models and financial indicators not as alternatives to macroeconomic models, but as complementary, above all in helping to spot turning points. Economic forecasting will never be 100% accurate, except by luck. But armed with every tool available, an economic forecaster just might earn his keep.

*Source*: © *The Economist*, London, 13 June 1992. Reprinted with permission.

### Comment on the case study

Although this chapter has concentrated on forecasting demand, it should be remembered that other forecasts are also made on a regular basis. In the case study a comparison is made between UK and US economic forecasts. These were forecasts relating to the macroeconomy: GDP, inflation and the current account.

The point is clearly made that forecasts are far from accurate and the difficulty involved in producing accurate forecasts is discussed. The economist making the comparison, Victor Zarnowitz, claims that the accuracy of forecasts improved very little in the period between 1960 and 1991. This is despite improved computer technology and backup. The problem, Zarnowitz claims (like Wack with reference to scenario planning analysis, discussed earlier), is due to the inclusion in models of subjective judgements about the likely future tax rate etc., that is, exogenous shocks which will threaten the validity of the assumptions made.

## SUMMARY

◆ This chapter has explained the difficulties in identifying variables to be included in models for estimating or forecasting demand.

◆ An introduction was given to several frequently used qualitative techniques for estimating and forecasting demand in the marketplace, and their advantages and disadvantages were discussed.

◆ Quantitative techniques used for estimating and forecasting demand based on analysis of trends were explained. The moving average technique used to smooth trends was developed, via an example to show the manner in which forecasts can be made.

◆ Barometric forecasting and scenario planning analysis were put forward as alternatives to conventional forecasting techniques.

◆ Via a practical example, the validity of an estimated relationship given by an OLS regression analysis was tested. Economic, statistical and econometric criteria for verification of the model's accuracy were tested step by step.

◆ The problems of multicollinearity and autocorrelation were introduced, associated with regression analysis. Tests for their detection were outlined and steps suggested which may be taken to rectify problems.

# REVIEW QUESTIONS

**1** Using the data given in Table 7.1:

   **a** Calculate the weighted moving average estimates for weeks 4–16. The weightings to be used are:

$$\text{Week}_t = 0.65$$
$$\text{Week}_{t-1} = 0.25$$
$$\text{Week}_{t-2} = 0.1$$

   **b** Plot the weighted moving averages gained in (a) and the simple moving averages given in the text on the same axes. Make a comparison of the two. Why do differences arise?

**2** Under which circumstances would it be most appropriate to use the following:

   **a** A simple forecast from raw data?

   **b** A moving average forecast?

   **c** An estimated relation equation (regression analysis)?

**3** Within your own economy, estimate the lead or lag relevant to indicators discussed in the chapter. Compare the values you derive with those for two and five years ago, or with another economy for which you are able to gain data.

**4** With reference to the OLS regression results in Table 7.11:

   **a** State the estimated equation.

   **b** Explain the tests which may be undertaken to verify the validity of the model given.

   **c** Undertake the tests you outline in (b) above. Be sure to comment on and discuss the results you derive.

**Table 7.11 Ordinary least squares estimation**

| 25 Observations Dependent variable is quantity demanded | (Period used: 1971–1995) | | |
|---|---|---|---|
| Regressor | Coefficient | | $t$ Statistic |
| Intercept | 99.182 | | 21.2310 |
| Price | −0.0305 | | −0.0735 |
| Income | 0.0031561 | | 2.4736 |
| $R^2$ | 0.9228 | Durbin-Watson statistic | 1.6927 |
| Adjusted $R^2$ | 0.8809 | $F$ statistic (2,22) | 14.8619 |

**5** What are the main features of the following different qualitative analysis techniques:

   **a** Questionnaire/interview.

   **b** Laboratory experiments/consumer clinics.

   **c** Test sites.

Compare and contrast the different techniques with reference to cost, complexity and quality of information resulting.

6 How would you test the validity of the following estimated relationship:

$$Q_D = 4255.09 - 354.67P + 47.92Y + 12.45C$$

where,

$Q_D$ = Quantity of cinema tickets purchased
$P$ = price of cinema tickets
$Y$ = income of head of household
$C$ = number of children in family

The equation relates to the estimated sales of cinema tickets by a major cinema chain. The chain has gained data on a quarterly basis for the past five years with reference to the independent and dependent variables given above.

What further information would you, as an analyst attempting to forecast demand, require in order to make the forecast?

7 What problems might be encountered in attempting to identify the factors affecting demand for a product (such as in (6) above) and in defining the estimated relationship

# Appendix 7.1

## EXPONENTIAL SMOOTHING

Smoothing techniques require that the weights given to observations decline as time passes. When exponential smoothing is used, the weights decline *geometrically*. Therefore, the weight given to the most recent event will be the largest, that to the most distant (in time) event the smallest. Consider Equation 7.1 which relates to the data for a single time period, *t*, and provides a forecast for sales in period *t+1*:

$$S_{t+1} = eS_t + (1 - e)\hat{S}_t \qquad (7.1)$$

where,

$S_{t+1}$ = Sales forecast in *t+1*
$e$ = weighting ($0 <= w =< 1$)
$S_t$ = sales data for time period *t*
$\hat{S}_t$ = sales *estimate* time period *t*

But,

$$S_t = eS_{t-1} + (1 - e)\hat{S}_{t-2} \qquad (7.2)$$

Therefore, substituting 7.2 into 7.1 gives:

$$S_{t+1} = eS_t + e(1 - e)S_{t-1} + (1 - e)^2\hat{S}_{t-2}$$

If this equation were extended to include sales data, rather than estimates, the equation would be:

$$S_{t+1} = eS_t + e(1 - e)S_{t-1} + e(1 - e)^2S_{t-2} + e(1 - e)^3S_{t-3} + \ldots$$

This is derived from the general form of the geometric progression, which is:

$$e, e(1 - e), e(1 - e)^2, e(1 - e)^3, e(1 - e)^4 \ldots$$

Thus, when $e = 0.7$, the series of weights will be:

$e$ = 0.7
$e(1 - e)$ = 0.21
$e(1 - e)^2$ = 0.063
$e(1 - e)^3$ = 0.0189
$e(1 - e)^4$ = 0.00567

It may be seen that the weights decrease rapidly in just a few time periods, placing greater emphasis on the most recent figures.

# GLOSSARY OF NEW TERMS

**Autocorrelation:** Lack of independence between sequential error terms within a model.

**Competitive advantage:** The manner in which the organisation is able to gain superiority over competitors. If the organisation is able to identify its source of competitive advantage, it acts to ensure that its activities include that source.

**Composite index:** An index value calculated using a combination of leading, lagged and coincidental indicators (see below).

**Cross-sectional data:** Data collected for the same period of time which is split into certain groupings based on characteristics such as age, income etc.

**Diffusion index:** A composite index containing only leading indices which is expressed in percentage terms to reflect the proportion of indices which are rising or growing (improving).

**Identification problem:** The difficulty encountered in trying to identify other variables which affect demand when it is inextricably linked to supply.

**Indicator:** A key measurable factor within the economy which has been proven to precede changes in the economy (leading indicator), to coincide with changes in the economy (coincidental indicator) or to follow changes (lagged indicator). Changes in the values of indicators (for example, new orders for goods) signify that the economy has changed. Knowledge of the lead or lag time once change is identified allows organisations to react accordingly.

**Multicollinearity:** The interrelationship between independent variables within an estimated model.

**Multiplier effect:** The positive or negative effects of a change in the economy which have a spiralling effect on other areas of the economy. The overall change is greater than the original change as a result.

**Ordinary least squares (OLS):** The regression analysis technique used in this chapter, which is a basic technique on which more complex methods are based.

**Regression analysis:** The technique used to verify the accuracy of an estimated relationship where data exist for each of the variables included within the model.

**Simultaneous relations:** The interplay between supply and demand, which needs to be isolated in order to resolve the identification problem.

**Test site/group:** A defined geographical area or sample of the population used by an organisation to test reactions to its product. The results of the test site/group tests are used to inform the final decisions about product attributes, price, packaging and so on.

**Time series data:** Data collected over a period of time with respect to a given variable.

# READING

Anderson, D R, Sweeney, D J and Williams, T A (1994) *Quantitative Methods for Business*, 6th edn, West Publishing Co, St Paul, Minneapolis.
*Text especially written for business students. Includes many examples and worked examples. Chapter 6 is of particular interest, it deals with forecasting techniques.*

Hill, S (1993) *Managerial Economics: The Analysis of Business Decisions*, Macmillan, Basingstoke.
*Chapter 5 provides an overview of the qualitative techniques discussed here and also the identification problem.*

Douglas, E U (1992) *Managerial Economics*: International Students edn, Prentice-Hall, Upper Saddle River, NJ.
*Chapters 4 and 5 outline and discuss in some depth the techniques used here. Examples are given, but the level of mathematics required to understand the arguments can be quite high at times.*

Gujarati, D (1988) *Basic Econometrics*, 2nd edn, McGraw-Hill International, New York.
*The following chapters may be of interest to more mathematically competent students – OLS Chapter 3, Autocorrelation Chapter 12, Multicollinearity Chapter 10.*

Wack, P (1985) 'Scenarios: uncharted waters ahead' in *Harvard Business Review – Strategy*, Harvard Business School Press, Boston, MA.

CHAPTER **8**

# DETERMINANTS AND BEHAVIOUR OF COSTS

## OBJECTIVES

- ◆ To introduce and discuss the nature of costs.

- ◆ To outline the main types of costs constituting short-run cost curves.

- ◆ To examine cost–volume analysis with reference to the break-even point.

- ◆ To understand the process of constructing a long run average total cost curve.

- ◆ To outline how and why costs change in the long run.

- ◆ To indicate methods by which the long-run average total cost curve can be established.

- ◆ To examine the importance of cost to the organisation.

## CHAPTER OUTLINE

## KEY TERMS

# Guessing the cost

FT

Bosses may repeatedly call for lower interest rates – but they are far more likely to know the price of a pint of lager than the base rate.

A survey of 600 executives conducted by NOP for British Telecommunications shows that while fewer than one in 10 of them know the current 6.25 per cent base rate (March 1996), nine out of ten can accurately state the price of a pint.

Given that few businesses are lucky enough to be charged only base rates on corporate loans, their ignorance on the cost of loan finance might be excusable. But the BT survey shows that lack of knowledge about business costs in general – even among owners, partners and directors – extends much further.

BT, which is running an advertising campaign based on the cost of its calls, says that more than half of UK executives cannot even guess their office rent.

The prices of photocopiers and laptop computers were significantly underestimated, while only one quarter of the executives came close to estimating the cost of a ream of paper.

There were large regional variations. Only half of London executives guessed the price of a photocopier correctly, compared with 99 per cent in Northern Ireland. While 9 per cent nationally knew the base rate, no Scottish bosses identified the correct figure.

However, everyone of them correctly costed a pint of lager, compared with only 78 per cent in London.

BT said its annual survey showed many bosses were 'clueless when it comes to key business costs'. It said that, while women were no more in touch with prices than men, they were more prepared to admit ignorance.

*Source*: *Financial Times*, 4 March, 1996. Reprinted with permission.

### Comment

The survey undertaken by BT might be regarded as not really fair. Bosses may not know the details of some costs since cost centres are managed by someone else and it is the bosses' role, along with their board, to undertake strategic management. Moreover, accurate knowledge of some costs may be costly to obtain and the organisation may be following a satisficing objective rather than one of profit maximisation. Nonetheless, greater knowledge of costs and how they behave as output changes can be argued to be important factors in highly competitive markets, and it is to the examination of costs that we now turn.

# INTRODUCTION

In markets where organisations seek to maximise profits or have other business objectives, it is important for organisations to understand how their costs are behaving. Information on costs is not always as accurate as the economist would like, the data often being obtained through accounting means. This accounting interpretation of costs is often based on historic costs and does not usually take account of opportunity costs, thus the link between accounting views of cost and economists' views of cost is sometimes vague.

Nonetheless, costs play an important part in decision making in managerial economics. **Short-run cost curves** provide data for making operating decisions. Here we are often looking at the outcome of changing the variable factor – labour – and its impact on the marginal revenue and cost curves of the organisation. In the long run all fac-

tors of production can be varied and consideration is made of the least cost solution for the organisation in terms of its long-range planning process. This knowledge of whether the firm experiences **economies of scale** or **diseconomies of scale** is paramount in the decision whether or not to expand. If a firm can achieve lower long-run average costs as it expands output, then production may be met by increasing the firm size; if diseconomies occur as output expands, then the decision for the organisation may be to decentralise, putting production in a number of smaller plants. Estimating the shape of these cost curves is, therefore, important and this chapter considers the various means by which this can occur.

The chapter also looks at the minimum efficient scales of industries and, in the light of these results, suggests whether these have an impact on merger and acquisition activity. Finally, we examine not the advantages to the firm as it grows but the advantages to firms in a regional locality as the whole industry grows – the external economies of scale.

# THE NATURE OF COSTS

The economist's use of information relating to costs is usually with reference to a decision-making process related to choice between projects. Economists are frequently interested in the difference between such projects in terms of the opportunity cost which may arise. This is in contrast to the typical accountant's use of cost information for reporting and budgeting purposes. There are thus identifiable differences in the approaches taken by economists and accountants in their use of cost information and the manner in which each group expects it to be presented. Both uses of cost information are valid in their relevant spheres.

# TIME PERIODS

Before discussing the different types of costs, it is important to make the distinction between periods in time, as accepted by economists. Differentiating between time periods in such a manner is extremely important to the economist as an aid to the understanding of costs, revenues and the behaviour of firms. The distinction between time periods is made with reference to the organisation's ability to vary factor inputs. There are four factors of production: land, labour, capital and entrepreneurship (enterprise). When considering time periods, it is common to think in terms of two factors of production – labour and capital. Discussion of time periods with regard to land and enterprise is less common, and this is the case with the approach taken here.

## The short run

In the short run, not all factor inputs are variable; at least one input is fixed. For example, while it may be relatively easy for an organisation to vary, say, the level of labour it employs, in the short term capital inputs are not so easily varied.

## The long run

In the long run, all factor inputs are variable. An organisation is able to change the level of labour, capital and the other factors of production which it employs.

It should be noted that the period of time encompassed within both the short and long run will vary for different organisations and is not related to calendar time. For example, the long run for a manufacturing company is likely to be much shorter than the long run experienced by a farm, which is dependent on the length of the growing and harvesting cycles which exist in the agricultural industry.

# FIXED COSTS AND VARIABLE COSTS

A distinction must be made between types of costs in order to make the best use of information. For the economist, a very important distinction to be made is the difference between fixed costs and variable costs.

The total cost level of any organisation is given by the sum of fixed and variable costs.

That is:

Total costs = Total fixed costs + Total variable costs

or:

$$TC = TFC + TVC$$

## Short-run fixed costs

**Fixed costs** are those costs incurred which do not vary whether the level of production is 0 or 1000 or any other level, hence the name 'fixed'. Organisations must pay them regardless of their production level. The fixed cost curve is therefore a horizontal line which denotes a constant level of costs; *see* Figure 8.1.

Examples of costs and payments which organisations make which may be considered as fixed costs are:

- Payments relating to the purchase or rental of business premises, including interest and depreciation charges.
- Payments relating to the purchase or rental of machinery, including interest and depreciation charges.
- Salaries and allowances paid to staff on a regular basis, regardless of the productive situation of the organisation.
- Energy costs incurred in maintaining heat and light supplies to the organisation's premises.

**Figure 8.1**

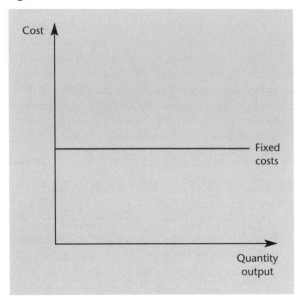

Fixed costs are those costs which do not vary with output. They can be depicted by a horizontal line.

In the short run, it is possible for costs to be fixed. In the long run, however, all costs are variable. Thus, in the long run, fixed costs tend towards zero.

## Semi-fixed costs/semi-variable costs

Recognition of the fact that fixed costs become variable in the long run does cause problems for the economist attempting to analyse 'real world' examples. The theory is widely accepted, but makes no allowance for the fact that, when attempting to apply it, the economist encounters 'fuzzy' areas of costs, neither fixed or variable. Examples of such fuzzy areas are:

- Salary payments made to staff which include production-related payments or bonuses.
- The fact that, as production increases, it may be necessary to purchase additional factor inputs. For instance, an organisation may have no choice but to employ extra labour as production reaches capacity for the existing labour force.

In cases where an organisation experiences **semi-fixed/semi-variable** costs, although the average variable cost curve trend will continue to decline, the point where the additional labour is employed may be seen on the cost curve as a vertical line. Subsequent additions to the labour force, or other factor inputs, will also cause such a phenomenon. The overall effect will be one of a jagged, or saw-tooth, profile to the cost curve; *see* Figure 8.2.

**Figure 8.2**

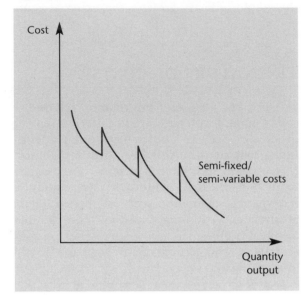

Although short-run variable costs are usually drawn as smooth cost curves, changes in the variable factors are not always constant. These discrete changes, say in the quantity of labour, result in a jagged or saw-tooth profile for the short-run cost curve.

## Short-run variable costs

**Variable costs** are the costs associated with production. Therefore, they are the costs which vary as output changes. In the short run with a variable quantity of labour (L) but fixed quantity of capital (K), as production increases total variable costs increase but average variable costs may be observed to fall, up to a certain level of production, after which they begin to rise. This relationship between average variable costs and the level of production may be considered to be increasing returns to the variable input so long as average variable costs are falling. This would mean that the marginal productivity of inputs is rising within this range. However, the marginal productivity of the variable input, although rising, does so at a decreasing rate due to the law of diminishing returns (*see* Figure 8.3). Table 8.1 may explain the situation better.

Table 8.1 indicates that for the first five units of labour there are increasing returns to the variable factor. After the fifth unit of labour is added the organisation experiences diminishing returns. Although total product is still rising, it is doing so at a diminishing rate. The increases in marginal productivity will eventually fall to zero and then begin to decline as variable input increases. Suppose the organisation is paying each unit of

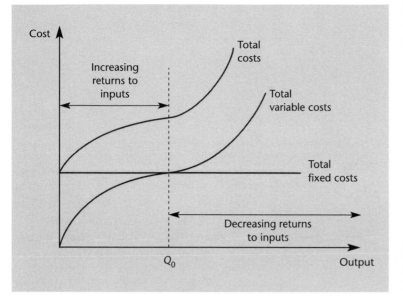

**Figure 8.3  Total fixed costs, total variable costs and total costs in the short run**

Total costs are the sum of total fixed costs plus total variable costs. Up to output $Q_0$ there are increasing returns to the variable factor in the short run, thereafter decreasing returns.

**Table 8.1  Relationship between marginal, average and total product**

| Number of workers (capital is fixed at 10 units) | Total product (TP) | Average product (AP), or TP/amount of labour | Marginal product (MP) or $\Delta TP/\Delta L$ |
|---|---|---|---|
| 1 | 4 | 4 | 4 |
| 2 | 14 | 7 | 10 |
| 3 | 25.5 | 8.5 | 11.5 |
| 4 | 40 | 10 | 14.5 |
| 5 | 60 | 12 | 20 |
| 6 | 72 | 12 | 12 |
| 7 | 77 | 11 | 5 |
| 8 | 80 | 10 | 3 |
| 9 | 81 | 9 | 1 |
| 10 | 75 | 7.5 | –6 |

labour the same salary. After the fifth unit of labour is added each additional unit of labour is less and less productive due to the law of diminishing returns. Thus it is becoming more and more expensive to produce each unit of output. It may therefore be seen that the average variable cost curve falls up to five units of labour input because the organisation is experiencing increasing returns and rises thereafter. The short-run average variable cost curve is drawn as U-shaped; *see* Figure 8.4.

Examples of costs and payments which organisations make which may be considered as variable costs are:

■ Wages and payments made to staff whose employment terms vary in relation to the production levels of the organisation.
■ Energy costs related to the productive process. That is, additional electricity etc. which is used

to fuel the production process: running machinery, heating factory space etc.
■ Raw materials costs incurred so that the production process may take place.

Once again, in the long run, all costs are variable. There are no fixed costs.

## SHORT-RUN COSTS

Mention has already been made in this chapter of the short run and the long run. The important distinction to note is that in the short run some factors of production and the costs subsequently associated with these are variable, while some costs are fixed. In the long run, all factors of production are variable (as are the associated costs), thus in the long run there are no costs which are fixed.

**Figure 8.4**

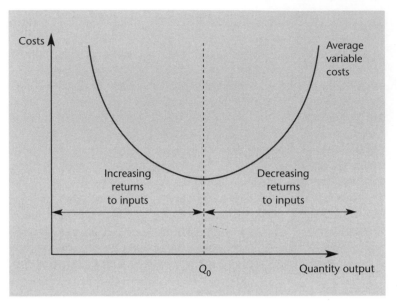

Because of increasing returns to the variable factor, short-run average variable costs decline up to output level $Q_0$. Decreasing returns to the variable factor cause average variable costs to rise after $Q_0$.

Due to the variable nature of the factors of production, short-run costs usually relate to a given plant size and variable quantities of labour. Movements along short-run cost curves are caused by changes in production levels as the variable factor is changed, whereas shifts in short-run cost curves are caused by changes in the factor inputs, such as an improvement in technology which results in increased productivity, or changes in the level of capital.

## Total, fixed, variable and marginal costs in the short run

As has already been discussed, short-run total costs are equal to the sum of fixed and variable costs. This relationship is illustrated by Figure 8.5. When considering cost levels, it is usually more informative to consider average costs. Average costs are the costs *per unit of production*. These are calculated by dividing total cost levels by the number of units produced. That is:

$$TC = TFC + TVC$$

where,  TC = total costs
  TFC = total fixed costs
  TVC = total variable costs

Thus, to calculate the average cost levels:

$$AFC = TFC/Q$$
$$AVC = TVC/Q$$

and:

$$ATC = TC/Q = AFC + AVC$$

where, AFC = average fixed costs
  AVC = average variable costs
  ATC = average total costs

Also of use is knowledge of the marginal cost level of production. The concept of 'Marginality' is widely used by economists in relation to a variety of quantitative situations. 'Marginal' shows the effects on costs, or revenue, of producing one extra unit. Thus, marginal cost is the additional cost incurred as a result of producing one extra unit; marginal revenue is the additional revenue gained as a result of selling one extra unit etc. In the short run therefore, where labour is the only variable factor, the increased cost of producing the extra unit will be equal to the marginal variable cost (MVC).

To calculate marginal cost, the difference between total costs of production of subsequent units is found. That is, the marginal cost of the first unit is equal to the difference between producing zero units and producing one unit. The marginal cost of the second unit is equal to the difference between producing the first unit and the second unit etc.

In the case of Table 8.2, the marginal costs of the second unit would be equal to the difference between costs of 107.00 and 126.00, that is 19.00. Therefore the marginal cost of the second unit is 19.00.

The marginal cost of the third unit is equal to the additional total cost incurred as a result of producing a third unit, in this case, the difference between 126.00 and 143.00, which equals 17.00. The marginal cost of the third unit is equal to 17.00.

**Figure 8.5  Costs in the short run**

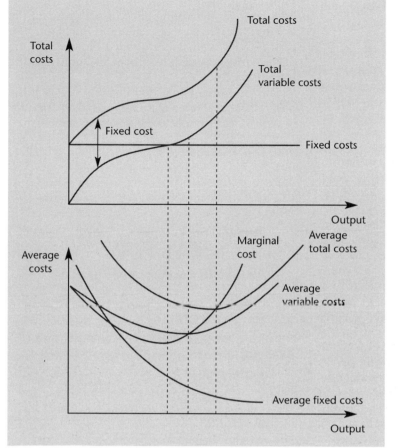

This shows the relationship between total and average cost curves. The lower figure indicates the important relationship between marginal cost and average costs, in that marginal cost cuts average variable costs and average total costs from below through their minimum points.

**Table 8.2**

| Q | TC<br>TFC+TVC | TFC | TVC | ATC<br>AFC+AVC | AFC<br>TFC/Q | AVC<br>TVC/Q | MC<br>ΔTC/ΔQ |
|---|---|---|---|---|---|---|---|
| 1 | 107.00 | 85 | 22 | 107.00 | 85.00 | 22.00 | 21.38 |
| 2 | 126.00 | 85 | 41 | 63.00 | 42.50 | 20.04 | 38.00 |
| 3 | 143.00 | 85 | 58 | 47.66 | 28.33 | 19.33 | 17.00 |
| 4 | 159.00 | 85 | 74 | 39.75 | 21.25 | 18.50 | 16.00 |
| 5 | 174.00 | 85 | 89 | 34.80 | 17.00 | 17.80 | 15.00 |
| 6 | 189.00 | 85 | 104 | 31.50 | 14.17 | 17.33 | 15.00 |
| 7 | 205.00 | 85 | 120 | 29.28 | 12.14 | 17.14 | 16.00 |
| 8 | 223.00 | 85 | 138 | 27.88 | 10.63 | 17.25 | 18.00 |
| 9 | 243.00 | 85 | 158 | 27.00 | 9.44 | 17.56 | 20.00 |
| 10 | 266.00 | 85 | 181 | 26.60 | 8.50 | 18.10 | 23.00 |
| 11 | 293.00 | 85 | 208 | 26.64 | 7.73 | 18.91 | 27.00 |
| 12 | 325.00 | 85 | 240 | 27.08 | 7.08 | 20.00 | 32.00 |
| 13 | 363.00 | 85 | 278 | 27.92 | 6.54 | 21.38 | 38.00 |
| 14 | 408.00 | 85 | 323 | 29.14 | 6.07 | 23.07 | 45.00 |
| 15 | 461.00 | 85 | 376 | 30.74 | 5.67 | 25.07 | 53.00 |

The marginal cost of the eighth unit in Table 8.2 is equal to the additional cost incurred as a result of producing the eighth unit, that is, the difference between total costs of 205.00 and 223.00. Thus, the marginal cost of the eighth unit is equal to 18.00.

In the example given by Table 8.2, the marginal costs of the first five units are declining, or diminishing. This is as a result of increasing returns to inputs. The marginal cost of the fifth and sixth units are equal, at 15.00. The marginal costs for the seventh to fifteenth units exhibit an increasing trend. This is due to diminishing returns to inputs. The full relationship between different types of costs may be seen in Figure 8.5. Note also that marginal costs always cut the average total cost curve from below at the lowest average total cost level.

# THE ACCOUNTANT'S VERSUS THE ECONOMIST'S VIEW: COST–VOLUME ANALYSIS

Accountants would also call this type of analysis break-even analysis. However, in terms of economic theory this represents a misnomer because it disregards the fact that economists include an allowance for normal profits within the total cost function. Thus, the accountant's point of no profits, the break-even point, equates to the economist's point of no supernormal (abnormal) profits. For ease, this section will be discussed in the context of the break-even point.

Break-even occurs at the production level where total revenue is equal to total costs. Consider Figure 8.6. Total revenue rises more quickly than total costs as production increases. Fixed costs are constant along the production range shown. Variable costs may be derived by measuring the vertical difference between the fixed cost curve and the total cost curve at any level of production.

The vertical difference at any level of production between the total cost and total revenue curves denotes the profit earned by that unit of production. This marginal profit is more commonly known as the marginal contribution to fixed costs and profits, or **profit contribution** $(\pi_c)$. Algebraically:

$$\pi_c = P - AVC$$

where,

$$P = \text{price}$$
$$AVC = \text{average variable cost}$$

Thus, the profit contribution is equal to the difference between the selling price of the unit and the average variable cost of producing that unit. The contribution is therefore divided between paying off a percentage of fixed costs and contributing towards profits.

The break-even production quantity occurs at the point where total revenue equals total costs. This may be derived algebraically in the following manner:

$$TR = TC \tag{8.1}$$

But,

$$TR = P \times Q \tag{8.2}$$

And,

$$TC = TFC + (AVC \times Q) \tag{8.3}$$

Substituting (8.2) and (8.3) into (8.1):

$$P \times Q = TFC + (AVC \times Q)$$

Rearranging:

$$(P - AVC)Q = TFC$$

Substitute for $Q^*$ = break-even quantity and $(P - AVC) = \pi_c$:

$$\pi_c Q^* = TFC$$

Therefore:

$$Q^* = TFC/\pi_c$$

The equation may also be rearranged to derive the quantity required to earn a given level of profit.

Thus, a wide range of information may be derived via break-even analysis. The weaknesses in this approach relate to the underlying assumptions made:

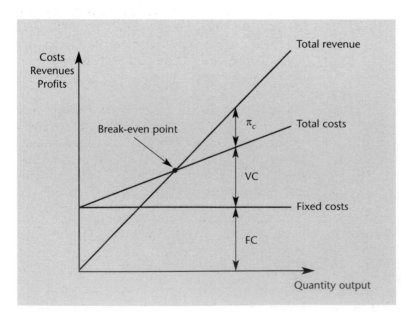

**Figure 8.6**

Break-even points from the accountant's perspective occur where straight-line total revenue and total cost functions intersect. At this point profit is zero.

- Perhaps the greatest constraint is the fact that break-even analysis assumes that the price level is constant. Changing the price level means that the calculations need to be reworked and the graph redrawn.
- The mix of products is also assumed to remain constant, that is, the ratio of products A : B across the whole range of production is the same.
- Semi-variable/semi-fixed costs do not exist in this approach. Costs are either fixed or variable. (This problem was discussed earlier in the chapter.)
- The 'curves' are straight lines in this example. Break-even analysis is frequently discussed in terms of straight-line curves. However, economists recognise that the total cost and total revenue relationships are in fact non-linear, giving rise to curves!

## OPERATING LEVERAGE

One way in which different cost–volume situations may be compared is by considering **operating leverage**, which describes the ratio of fixed costs to variable costs. Consideration of operating leverage therefore gives information about the extent to which the organisation uses or is bound to use fixed compared to variable factors of production.

Operating leverage is essentially an elasticity concept. It shows the proportionate reaction of profits to a proportionate change in quantity of output:

$$OL = \% \text{ change } \pi / \% \text{ change } Q$$

That is:

$$OL = \Delta\pi/\pi/\Delta Q/Q$$

Or, rearranging:

$$OL = \Delta\pi/Q * Q/\pi$$

where:

        $OL$ = operating leverage
        $\pi$ = profits
        $Q$ = quantity output

Operating leverage is greatest at the production quantity just beyond the break-even point. Operating leverage decreases as quantity produced increases beyond this level.

Comparison of the operating leverages for two or more organisations should be done at the same level of output for both. The nearer the value is to zero, the lower the leverage and the greater the emphasis of the organisation's production process on fixed factors of production. The higher the operating leverage, the more the leverage and the greater the organisation's production process relies on variable factors of production.

Additionally, the greater the leverage, the more quickly the organisation's profits will rise as production is increased from its current level. Remember, however, that operating leverage is a comparative value. As production increases, operating leverage for successive levels decreases. Thus, to make an effective comparison, production levels used for organisations under consideration should always be the same.

## LONG-RUN COST CURVES

In the short run the only factor of production that is usually variable is labour. However, in the long run all the factors of production, land, labour, and capital, may be varied. In the long run, therefore, the problem with the diminishing returns to the variable factor that was discussed with reference to the short run can be overcome by changing one or more of the fixed factors of production. Recall that the short-run average total cost curve is U-shaped because of diminishing returns to the variable factor, labour.

Figure 8.7 shows a typical short-run cost curve with the organisation producing output $Q_1$ with a short-run average cost of $C_1$. Each short-run cost curve is associated with a given level of capital (machines), that is, it shows how short-run average costs behave when labour is varied while the level of capital stock is held constant. If the level of capital is altered, or the organisation alters its level of capital, then there is a movement to a different short-run cost curve.

Suppose that, given the initial average total cost curve of $ATC_1$, the organisation experiences an increase in the demand for its product/output, shown by the point $Q_2$. Initially, the organisation may not believe that this new, higher level of demand is going to remain at this level for the foreseeable future, and it may well respond by attempting to satisfy this new level of demand, $Q_2$, by using its existing labour force more intensively, that is, by offering them overtime pay or by employing more labour. The former will increase the per unit cost of the new level of output, the latter, because of the law of diminishing returns, will also lead to increased average costs

**Figure 8.7 From short-run to long-run average costs**

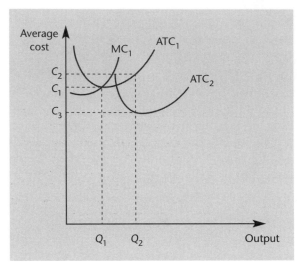

Each ATC curve is associated with one level of fixed capital and varying quantities of labour. Producing more output in the short run means shifting around a short-run set of cost curves. Output $Q_2$ can be produced at cost $C_2$ with cost curve $ATC_1$. This may not be the least-cost solution since by varying the quantity of capital (shifting to a new set of short-run cost curves) output $Q_2$ can be produced more cheaply at cost $C_3$.

**Figure 8.8 Short-run cost curves for four scales of plant**

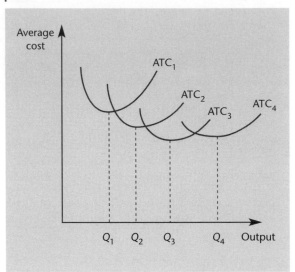

Each quantity of capital, fixed in the short run, leads to a different short-run cost curve as labour is varied. By moving, in the long run, to greater quantities of capital, the short-run cost curves fall – $ATC_1 \rightarrow ATC_4$.

per unit of output. However, it may be possible to produce output $Q_2$ with lower average costs than $C_2$, that is, by producing it more capital intensively rather than more labour intensively. If this is the case, then we cannot be on the average total cost curve $ATC_1$, since changing the level of capital implies that we are on a different short-run average total cost curve. The organisation will only move to this new short-run average total cost curve, which involves a change in the level of capital stock, if the new, higher level of demand is seen as permanent. If the new, higher level of demand is not viewed as permanent, then the organisation could find that it has invested in capital stock that will lie idle in the future. Therefore, two conditions are important in the move to invest in a greater amount of capital stock, first that the change in demand is viewed as a lasting change, and second that producing output $Q_2$ more capital intensively is cheaper than the current procedure of using more labour. If these two conditions are met then, as Figure 8.7 indicates, the organisation can produce $Q_2$ at average cost $C_3$ on its new short-run average total cost curve $ATC_2$.

It is now possible to repeat the analysis above to show how we could move to $ATC_3$. A series of these short-run cost curves is shown in Figure 8.8, which illustrates a series of outputs produced by plants which have embodied in them different levels of capital stock, that is, different scales of plant, and $Q_1$, $Q_2$, $Q_3$, and $Q_4$ indicate the minimum costs of production with four given plant sizes.

Of course, in reality, there are many more short-run average total cost curves that lie in between these curves and further to the right. What has been happening in moving from $Q_1$ through to $Q_4$ is the change in both the level of the labour input and the level of capital, in other words the organisation must be concerned now with the long run. Figure 8.9 shows the **long-run average total cost curve (LRATC curve)** and indicates that this consists of the lower boundary or envelope of all the short-run average total cost curves.

The LRATC curve indicates that no other combination of inputs exists that can produce each level of output $Q$ at an average cost below that which is exhibited by the LRATC curve. Figure 8.9 also shows that cost of producing any level of output does not necessarily occur at the minimum point on a short-run average total cost curve; only on $ATC_3$ is this the case.

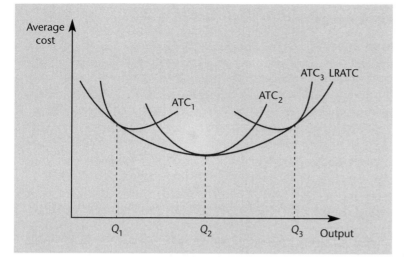

**Figure 8.9 The long-run average total cost curve**

Since each short-run cost curve requires a different amount of capital, a long-run average total cost curve indicates the minimum possible average cost of producing any level of output on the assumption that all factors are variable. Up to output $Q_3$ we have increasing returns to scale, after $Q_3$ diseconomies of scale.

## ◆ CASE STUDY 8.1

# Come fly the unfriendly skies

Increased competition in the airline industry in the United States has caused the competitors to reexamine their costs. Any reduction in costs means that they are able to reduce prices whilst still maintaining a profit margin.

The domestic US market is actually dominated by low-cost and therefore low-priced operators who are now beginning to worry the larger airlines. The cut-price airlines are successful due to the current economic climate which sees company bosses cutting back upon their employees' expense accounts and requiring them to purchase cheaper tickets, without the extra 'frills'.

The cut-price airlines are able to operate on a lower fixed costs and variable cost basis than their competitors for a number of reasons:

- They fly into and out of less congested airports; thus paying less for the privilege of landing and take-off 'slots' in the airport's timetable.
- Their pilots are paid up to 50% less than those working for the larger airlines *and* they work up to 40% longer each month.

- In the case of Southwest airlines, the fleet is made up of the same aircraft: Boeing 737s. This therefore reduces the costs incurred in servicing and repairs; tools, maintenance training and substitutability of planes and parts are all specific and simplified.

Overall, then, the smaller airlines are managing to compete in a very competitive industry against much larger airlines and surviving. This is at a time when the industry is static in terms of passenger numbers and where the competitive advantage comes from offering lower-priced seats to those passengers. The larger airlines, despite their better in-flight service offers, cannot compete on fare prices because their costs are too high. As a result, a number have decided to follow the pattern devised by the low-cost airlines and give the traveller what they want: cheap, no-frills flights.

*Source*: © *The Economist*, London, 5 November 1994. Reprinted with permission.

---

### ◆ Exercise 8.1

Although larger airlines might be able to achieve economies of scale, how have the smaller airlines proved to be so successful?

Why might the larger airlines have higher costs?

# LEARNING CURVES

As individuals become more experienced in the tasks they undertake, it has been noticed that the average costs per unit tend to decline over time as the factors of production learn the production process and therefore become more adept or efficient at what they are doing. Arrow (1962) called this relationship 'learning by doing'.

This **learning curve** or experience curve has been studied and empirical work appears to confirm the fact that unit costs tend to decline by a relatively stable percentage each time total output is doubled. At all levels of the labour force we may get this learning curve effect. Managers may learn how to get the best out of their employees; operations managers may learn to improve the way the organisation functions. It is not only labour which can experience the learning curve effect: savings may be made in raw materials as the organisation learns to reduce scrap and recycles waste parts and energy.

The learning curve was originally applied to aircraft manufacturing during the 1930s but has subsequently been applied to many other manufacturing processes, including shipbuilding and white goods manufacturing.

With regard to production and cost theory, the learning curve can be seen in terms of the improvement in the productivity of the variable inputs, given constant factor prices – for example improvements in labour productivity while the average pay per worker is kept constant. If this learning effect does occur, then what we should see is that the improvement in labour productivity shifts up labour's marginal productivity curve; in other words a reduction in the marginal cost curve. This shift downwards in the marginal cost curve will lead to an associated reduction in both the average variable cost and average total cost curves. This 'learning by doing' effect can be seen in Figure 8.10 and indicates one other important effect of the learning process: that the learning effect is greatest when the production process starts, and then diminishes thereafter. Therefore for many mature processes there may be little or no further learning effect to experience. As Figure 8.10 indicates, the cost of producing 2 units of output is £800 while the cost of producing 4 units of output is £650. It is often assumed that in the

## Figure 8.10 The learning curve

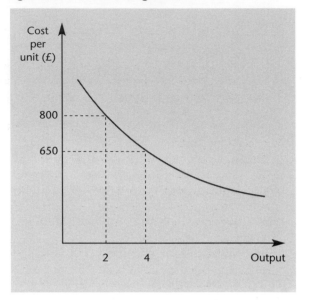

The learning curve indicates that the learning effect is greatest when the production process starts. Thus it costs £800 to produce the first two units and only £650 to produce 4.

learning curve process a given percentage change in output will produce a constant percentage decrease in the cost of the last unit produced, although this has not always been the case.

There are several provisos that we must bear in mind when using this learning curve analysis. First, if between two units of output costs fall by 30 per cent, we cannot assume that by doubling output again we should see costs fall by a further 30 per cent. The advantages that appear to lie behind the learning curve are sometimes (wrongly) assumed to extrapolate into the future, particularly where individuals might want to give a more than optimistic set of long-run cost or price decisions for appraisal purposes.

Moreover, we must not confuse the cost savings of the learning curve effect with the economies of scale outlined earlier. Figure 8.9 indicates what we would expect to see happen to long-run average total costs as output increases. In the long run all factors of production are variable; however there is still one constant, the level of technology. If there are technological breakthroughs then we might expect to see cost savings per unit of output and this would be associated with a shift downwards in the long-run average total cost curve.

◆ CASE STUDY 8.2

## The privatisation of Deutsche Telekom

On January 1st 1995, Deutsche Telekom became an Aktiengesellschaft (AG) – a joint stock company – and from some time in early 1996 the privatisation process proper will be launched with a first share issue. That will raise, it is hoped, between DM15 billion (£6 billion) and DM20 billion.

Some observers feel that this move will prove to be problematic. The company will be coming to the market encumbered with massive debts and a host of burdens from its public sector past, which could make it decidedly unattractive for private investors.

Turnover, however, has been growing rapidly, thanks not least to an explosion of new users in East Germany. It was up 9.3 per cent in 1993 to DM59 billion, and in East Germany up from DM3.5 billion to DM4.5 billion.

Its investment programme in the east has transformed the former communist state from a telecommunications backwater. The cumulative cost of modernisation will have been DM60 billion by 1997. Ironically it is the scale of that investment which has many observers worried. Telekom has had three huge projects running simultaneously: the eastern investment, the construction of a television cable network, and the establishment of mobile phone networks. The company are also positioning themselves as a global player in the telecommunications market with recent deals with France Telecom, and the purchase of a 20 per cent stake in Sprint, the US telecommunications company.

On the down-side the company has a huge debt burden, now standing at DM107 billion, or almost 70 per cent of its balance sheet. Although this expansion programme is due to slow in the next few years, there is still a view that the new German state will need to take over some of Deutsche Telekom's debt in the future to make it an attractive proposition for investors. Meanwhile there has also been an explosion of potential competitors from the private sector, getting ready to compete with the monopoly once the EU enforces competition in voice telephone services from 1998. As the telecommunications market place starts to look crowded, for Telekom, the real question is to assess the level to which they are becoming customer orientated which means recognising the fact that they are a customer service industry. The prospect of privatisation is certainly having a galvanising effect on the company but they still have a long way to go up their learning curve if they are not to lose market share very rapidly to companies which are more customer focused.

*Source: Financial Times, 6 July 1994. Reprinted with permission.*

◆ Exercise 8.2

How might the learning curve effect result in Deutsche Telekom not being one of the major players in the telecoms market in the short term?

Why are learning effects less for companies which are not pioneers in a market?

## THE SHAPE OF THE LONG-RUN AVERAGE TOTAL COST CURVE – ECONOMIES OF SCALE

Figure 8.9 indicated what is known as the U-shaped LRATC curve. This curve shows increasing returns to scale (economies of scale) up to $Q_3$ and decreasing returns (diseconomies of scale) thereafter. But are LRATC curves always U-shaped? Figure 8.11 (*see* p 188) shows three other possibilities for the LRATC curve.

Figure 8.11(a) indicates an LRATC curve which is always declining as output increases, in other words, economies of scale are never exhausted and it is economic for a single company to satisfy the entire market. One company can provide the whole of the market at a lower cost than two or more companies. Here one company can still experience further economies of scale even though it is currently meeting market demand. There may also be major barriers to entry into these industries. When only one company comes to dominate the domestic market simply because it can continue to face lower average costs, this is

**Figure 8.11 The shape of the long-run average total cost curve (LRATC)**

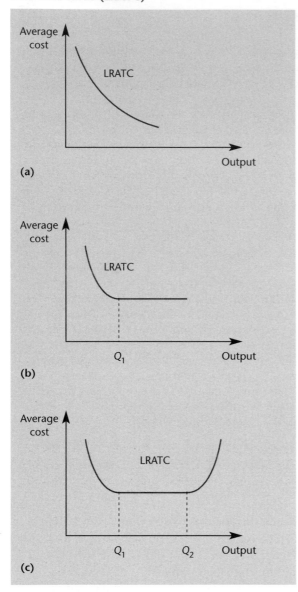

(a) A long-run average total cost curve which is continually declining.

(b) A long-run average total cost curve which exhibits economies of scale up to $Q_1$ and no further falls in average total cost.

(c) A long-run average total cost curve with economies of scale up to output level $Q_1$ and diseconomies of scale after output $Q_2$.

a natural monopoly. Many public utilities such as electricity generation, the gas industry and perhaps telecommunications would fit this category if left without government intervention. Figure 8.11(b) shows an LRATC curve which shows economies of scale up to point $Q_1$, beyond which there are no further economies of scale. In fact, it is possible to argue that for points to the right of $Q_1$ further economies of scale are merely offset by an equal amount of diseconomies of scale. Figure 8.11(c), on the other hand, displays an LRATC curve which shows increasing returns to scale up to $Q_1$, constant returns to scale between $Q_1$ and $Q_2$ and diseconomies of scale thereafter.

It is important for an organisation to know the shape of its LRATC curve. For example, suppose an organisation knows that its LRATC curve is of the type shown in Figure 8.9, but it also knows that this minimum point on the LRATC curve is reached when it possesses only a small proportion of the total market. In this case the market will support a number of firms at the minimum points on their LRATC curves, perhaps even hundreds, and the market could be a highly competitive one with a large number of small or medium-sized firms. In the case of an LRATC curve shown in Figure 8.11(b), $Q_1$ shows the position of the '**minimum efficient scale' (MES)** of production. This is the scale of the plant beyond which the unit costs of production are constant. Knowledge of the output level at which an organisation reaches this MES point is again important because this will enable the organisation to know whether its home market alone can support sufficient sales for the organisation to reach the MES point; if not it may have to look for sales abroad. Further discussion of the MES occurs later.

The three LRATC curves in Figure 8.11 exhibit decreasing, constant and increasing returns to scale, and in Appendix 8.1 a mathematical explanation of these is given. Before turning to the various methods used to estimate the shape of the LRATC curve, it is worth considering the issue of social and private costs.

◆ CASE STUDY 8.3

## Banana exporters and EU access

Caribbean banana exporters are relieved at the European Court's rejection of a German Challenge to the European Union's controversial banana import regime, but they remain concerned about possible attacks on their preferential access to the lucrative EU market (October 1994). The EU's banana import regime, which was implemented in 1993, imposes the quota for Latin America fruit. Suppliers from the Caribbean, Africa and the Pacific region have access to the remainder of the EU's needs of about 1.5 million tonnes per year, tariff-free. Caribbean producers are particularly worried about the support that Latin American producers are getting from the Americans.

Caribbean producers feel most threatened, however, by the planned changes in the way complaints about trade will be treated when the World Trade Organisation (WTO) is established. Caribbean banana exporters are aware that the new trade rules will force them to compete with other producers on the same terms. The necessity to cut production costs is accepted, but difficult to implement, according to the industry's administrators. Small producers on the islands cannot hope to enjoy the economies of scale of the Latin American multinationals and thus their production will decline as they are squeezed out of markets.

*Source: Financial Times, 19 October 1994. Reprinted with permission.*

---

◆ **Exercise 8.3**

How do banana quotas into the EU affect economies of scale?

How could Caribbean countries be helped if Latin American countries obtain preferential treatment in market access?

---

◆ CASE STUDY 8.4

## The European lager market

Brewing of the most popular type of beer – known to the British as lager – is ideally suited to economies of scale and mass-market production. Quite early in the production of lager oligopolies of large brewers were established around the world, particularly in smaller, easily dominated markets, although the Japanese and American markets were also not immune from this process. Heineken came to dominate its small Dutch home market, as did Carlsberg in Denmark. In France the food group BSN also made large gains in lager production and market share, although it should be noted that the per capita consumption of lager in France is low.

The world's largest beer company is Anheuser-Busch International Limited, producer of Budweiser, which has reached this stage because of its huge market in the US. It is twice the size of its second major US competitor, but as Table 8.3 indicates, these two companies are separated by Heineken in the world league. It is interesting to note that only 13 per cent of Heineken's output takes place in its home market.

Most countries have one, two or three brewing groups whose concentration ratio exceeds 75 per cent of beer sales in their home markets. However, the German and British brewing industries, the two largest in Europe, are exceptions to this pattern of production. In Germany,

regional fragmentation is one of the main reasons put forward to explain why German producers have not been heavily involved in other European markets.

**Table 8.3 The largest international brewing groups (million hectolitres), 1991**

| Brewer | Country | Output (million hectolitres) |
|---|---|---|
| Anheuser-Busch | US | 101.4 |
| Heineken | Netherlands | 52.7 |
| Miller-Brewing | US | 52.0 |
| Kirin | Japan | 34.0 |
| Foster's | Australia | 26.2 |
| Brahama | Brazil | 25.3 |
| BSN | France | 23.9 |
| Adolf Coors | US | 22.8 |
| South African Breweries | South Africa | 22.4 |
| Carlsberg | Denmark | 21.4 |
| Modelo | Mexico | 21.1 |
| FEMSA | Mexico | 20.0 |
| Antartica Paulista | Brazil | 20.0 |
| Stroh | US | 18.5 |
| Asahi | Japan | 16.4 |
| Guinness | UK | 14.0 |

*Source: Brewers and Licensed Retailers Association.*

Case study 8.3 *continued*

In 1991 there were almost 1300 separate brewers in Germany, around 60 per cent of these in Bavaria. Although there has been some move towards mergers and economies of scale, local loyalties and family controls have not helped this process.

In the UK, although the market is dominated by six brewing companies, regional brands have survived better than in other countries. This is mainly due to the tied system that has operated between the brewers and the pubs and this has meant that national and international brands have faced barriers to entry in the UK.

*Source*: Authors.

◆ **Exercise 8.4**

Why are economies of scale less in the German beer market?

How far do cultural differences determine an organisation's economies of scale?

*Comment on the case studies*

These case studies show the importance of economies of scale for a wide range of organisations in different sectors of the economy. It is important to note that the desire for economies of scale is only one of a number of motives for an organisation's success and growth. It is also possible to improve profits and reduce costs by shrinking the organisation, particularly where the organisation is on the upward section of its long-run average total cost curve.

## Social and private costs

In our discussion so far there has been no distinction between private and social costs. In other words, costs to producers have been assumed to be the same as costs to society and costs to society have been assumed to be the same as costs to producers. In fact there are many occasions when these assumptions do not hold and producers act in a manner which harms others without having to pay the full costs. For example, a coal-fired power station imposes a cost on society – in the form of environmental damage caused by acid rain – over and above the private opportunity costs (i.e. the costs of land, labour, capital equipment and the like) which fall on the producer. The additional social cost is known as an externality or spillover effect and, being a cost, is negative. Although the costs of pollution are examined in Chapter 20, some of the basic ideas can be developed here.

Figure 8.12 shows that marginal pollution costs rise with output beyond a certain level, $Q_1$. Up to this level of output the level of pollution can be absorbed by the economy. Pollution is seen here as providing a negative externality imposing costs on society which are not borne by the organisation. Marginal net private benefit (MNPB) is the additional benefit which organisations receive from selling an extra unit of output, minus the organisation's private costs of producing the extra unit of output.

**Figure 8.12 Social and private costs**

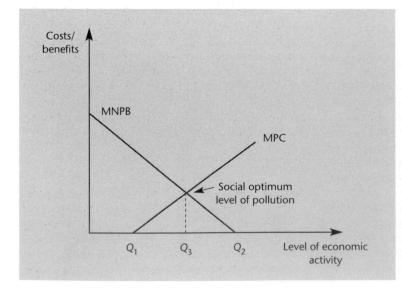

Organisations would like to produce more output as long as MNPB>0. Their optimum level of production is $Q_2$. After output level $Q_1$ the environment cannot absorb the cost of pollution and any additional units of output lead to rising marginal pollution costs. The social optimum level of pollution is at the intersection of MNPB and MPC, that is, $Q_3$.

If no notice was taken of the externality produced by pollution, then organisations would like to produce at the point at which MNPB is zero, that is, at $Q_2$. The social optimum level of output is, however, at $Q_3$, the point at which MNPB equals marginal pollution costs. Once we go beyond $Q_3$ each additional unit of output adds more to pollution costs than it does to net private benefit, therefore there is a loss to society. Similarly, at output levels below $Q_3$ society would also lose, since each unit of output adds more to private benefit than it does to pollution costs. Chapter 20 indicates a number of ways in which organisations may be encouraged to produce at the socially efficient level, these include tradeable permits, environmental taxes and the like. One method of pollution control put forward is a carbon tax. This proposed tax by the EU would have a number of effects on consumers and producers, but in the context of the organisation's private costs, it would raise these costs by internalising more of the costs of production, thus reducing the supply of 'bads' to the market.

The issue about social and private costs has highlighted the importance of the actual position of cost curves. However, at this stage, how can we find out the shape of the LRATC curve and how important is its shape for the behaviour of organisations?

One approach would be to turn to empirical evidence of LRATC curves, but accurate data are difficult to come by. Often only the organisation possesses relevant, and not always accurate, cost information. Three approaches to measuring the shape of the LRATC curve have become popular:

- Regression or statistical estimation.
- The engineering approach.
- The survivor technique.

## Regression or statistical measures of scale economies

As we have seen, in the long run all factors of production are variable, in other words, all costs are variable and the task we face is to determine the shape of the least-cost production curve for different sizes of plant. The most obvious way to conduct a statistical analysis is to take one plant over a period of time, say 20 years, and then by using monthly or quarterly data (either 240 or 80 observations) look at how output and costs vary. The equation would have total cost as the dependent variable and the independent variables would include output and any other exogenous or endogenous variable that we considered to be important influences on total cost. So long as the exogenous and endogenous factors are held constant, then we would be able to estimate the effect of output on total costs. Herein lies the problem. It is unlikely that over a 20-year period these other factors are going to remain constant, and any changes in them will result in an impact on costs. If these exogenous and endogenous factors are not taken into account fully then the relationship between total cost and output can only be an approximation. Moreover, when it comes to the measurement of costs, are these a true reflection of actual costs? From an economist's perspective, are an accountant's views of costs appropriate? These will not take into account opportunity costs; moreover, how is depreciation apportioned to the cost of producing an item and how are overhead costs allocated to the production of a particular commodity?

Since time series observations cannot be used with any degree of accuracy to derive estimates of the long-run cost function, an alternative approach would be to use data or observations from various plants at a particular point in time – cross-sectional regression analysis. As with time series analysis, cross-sectional studies compare different-sized firms at a particular point in time, with total costs as the dependent variable against a range of appropriate independent variables. Once again, there are problems with this approach. Total costs at any point in time in the various plants will be related to the costs of inputs, but factor costs can vary for the various plants given localised demand and supply conditions. Thus, unless all the plants are located in the same area or region, some will be facing higher input costs and this could lead to a misinterpretation of the results. In addition, it is possible that the different plants operate different procedures for capital depreciation, costing methods and the manner in which they reward labour. For example, the cost of labour may be distorted if some receive only salaries while others receive lower salaries but are compensated for this by profit-sharing schemes or benefits in kind. Moreover, the way labour is rewarded in terms of its wages, that is, whether they are linked to output or not, may also influence the productivity of the workforce.

## The survivor technique

Because of the difficulties in obtaining satisfactory estimates of long-run cost/output relationships via regression analysis, alternative methods of assessing the shape of the LRATC curve have been developed. The first of these is the survivor technique, developed initially by Stigler (1958). Stigler believed that more efficient firms, those with lower average costs, would survive and grow, taking increasing market share from less efficient firms, which in the long run would leave the market. The procedure is to rank an industry's plants by their size on two different dates, grouping them into size classes and noting which classes have increased or decreased their percentages of industry capacity. It can then be deduced that those size classes whose industry shares are growing are relatively efficient and those whose shares are contracting are relatively inefficient, that is, have higher average costs. The results of studies suggest the following:

■ The smallest classes will display decreasing percentages. These plants will either cease to exist in the long run or, because of economies of scale, will grow into larger plants.

■ A range of larger plants will show increasing percentages indicating constant returns to scale, that is, the horizontal portion of the LRATC curve.

■ The very large plants will probably show slightly decreasing percentages, consistent with decreasing returns to scale.

Stigler used this analysis to conclude exactly this type of relationship for the car industry in the US and it has subsequently been used to examine the economies of scale in banking, cement and the steel industries, to name but three.

The advantage of the survivor technique is that it can prove to be very useful when individual firms are averse to giving information on costs. Nonetheless, there are a number of problems:

■ The approach assumes that survival is linked to the minimisation of long-run costs.

■ It makes the assumption that firms are faced by highly competitive markets. It is possible that, where there are sufficiently high barriers to entry into a market, inefficient firms can survive over the longer term. Moreover, where general macroeconomic demand is high inefficient firms can survive, especially if the more efficient firms do not have the capacity to satisfy the market fully.

■ Where markets are separated for geographical reasons, behind tariff barriers or where there are high transportation costs, it is possible for strategically located firms to survive even though they are relatively inefficient.

■ The survival of many small firms over time may be due to the fact that they offer specialised or personalised services which outweigh their inherent inefficiencies.

■ The survivor technique requires us to examine plants over a long time period and in this case we cannot assume that the level of technology remains constant. In fact, it is possible that particular kinds of technology are more easily taken up by different sizes of firms, thus what we are seeing is a downward shift in the LRATC curve rather than a movement along this curve.

■ The survivor technique does not differentiate between plants that are newly constructed and those that have improved their productivity via various management techniques, such as just-in-time management, leading to higher productivity. From a statistical viewpoint the survivor technique may tell us which plant size is more efficient, but not how much more.

■ Given the problems with this approach, let us look at a more practical technique to measure the shape of the LRATC curve – the engineering approach.

## The engineering approach

This approach starts from the point of the existing plant and involves asking production engineers to design a plant or a set of plants for different levels of output. Because the approach is experimental, engineers assume that the costs of inputs stay the same, as will the level of technology. The engineering approach is therefore closer than any other estimation technique to considering the timeless nature of theoretical cost functions.

As with the other techniques, there are a number of problems to consider:

■ Extending engineering production functions further than the range of existing plants or moving from the pilot plant to the full-scale operation can prove to be difficult.

■ Unanticipated production delays or problems with the supply of inputs as the production process grows can lead to estimation errors in the engineering approach.

■ There is still the problem of harmonising accounting views of costs with those of the economist and the problem of apportioning fixed costs among a number of projects.

Bearing in mind these issues, what does the engineering approach tell us in general about the shape of the LRATC curve? The L-shaped LRATC curve appears to be the most prevalent, suggesting that LRATCs fall as output increases to the minimum efficient scale and are constant thereafter.

As we have seen, economists draw many of their cost functions as smooth curves. This would lead us to make many calculations of the long-run cost curve at varying output levels. This approach would be far too expensive and the alternative approach is to estimate as few points as possible, with the minimum efficient scale (MES) point being one and an output level of some proportion of MES as one of the other points.

If the engineering approach can be used it should be possible for us to find the MES points for a range of industries.

## MES estimates

Tables 8.4 and 8.5 indicate MESs calculated for industries in the EU and the UK. Although the information in these is a little dated, it does provide evidence of the similarity between MES in the UK and EU. The MES is the level of output at which scale economies are exhausted, that is, where the LRATC curve is at its minimum. The MES represents the production unit (plant or establishment) which has reached its optimal size in terms of gathering all the technical economies available. There may still be non-technical economies, such as financial economies and those from bulk buying, which remain available at the industrial unit, that is, the firm or enterprise level.

**Table 8.5 Minimum efficient scale in selected UK and EU markets**

| Product | MES as a percentage of UK production | MES as a percentage of EU production |
|---|---|---|
| Books | na | na |
| Bricks | 1 | 0.2 |
| Dyes | >100 | na |
| Aircraft | >100 | na |
| Titanium oxide | 63 | 50 |
| Cement | 10 | 1 |
| Synthetic rubber | 24 | 3.5 |
| Electric motors | 60 | 6 |
| Kraft paper | 11 | 1.4 |
| Petrochemicals | 23 | 3 |
| Nylon | 4 | 1 |
| Cylinder block castings | 3 | 0.3 |
| Small cast-iron castings | 0.7 | 0.1 |
| Carpets | 0.3 | 0.04 |
| Diesel engines | >100 | na |

Source: European Economy (1988) 'The Economics of 1992', No 35, March, The European Commission, Brussels.

Table 8.4 shows some broad trends in economies of scale. They appear larger in transport equipment, chemicals and machinery, but in contrast appear to be much smaller in food, drink, tobacco, textiles and clothing. These sectors are characterised by relatively flat demand and contain products where

**Table 8.4 Branches of manufacturing and their economies of scale**

| Branch | Economies of scale |
|---|---|
| Motor vehicles | Very substantial economies of scale in both production and development costs. |
| Other transport | Variable economies of scale: small for cycles and shipbuilding but very substantial in aircraft production. |
| Chemical industry | Substantial economies of scale in production processes. For some products such as pharmaceuticals, R&D provides an important source of economies of scale. |
| Metals | Large economies of scale for production processes. |
| Electrical engineering | Substantial economies of scale at both the product level and for development costs. |
| Paper, printing and publishing | Substantial economies of scale in paper mills and in particular in the printing area. |
| Rubber and plastics | Moderate economies of scale in tyre manufacturing. Small economies of scale in factories making rubber and moulded plastic articles. |
| Drink and tobacco | Moderate economies of scale in breweries, small economies of scale in cigarette factories. In marketing, economies of scale are substantial. |
| Food | The main source of economies of scale is the individual plant. Economies of scale are available at the marketing and distribution level. |
| Timber and wood | No economies of scale for plants in these sectors. Possible to have economies of scale from specialisation and longer production runs. |
| Footwear and clothing | Small economies of scale at the plant level but some economies of scale from specialisation and longer production runs. |

Source: European Economy (1988) 'The Economics of 1992', No 35, March, The European Commission, Brussels.

the technological content is fairly low. In contrast, in sectors where there are economies of scale markets face much more buoyant demand and products tend to have a higher technological content. Clearly, those sectors which have high MES figures in their national markets are those more likely to have gained from the development of the Single Market within Europe. In the UK's case, these sectors would include dyes, aircraft, titanium oxide, electric motors, diesel engines and to a slightly lesser degree rubber and petrochemicals.

Over time the MES might be expected to alter due to the impact of technological change. Nonetheless, if it is assumed that technical knowledge is fairly mobile, other countries in Europe may well experience similar effects for the MESs in their countries. Therefore, if we take aircraft, in Table 8.5, for the UK to reach its MES it would like to sell in overseas markets. A similar argument could be made for the German and French aircraft industries. If everyone is trying to sell into their domestic markets as well as into other European markets, then none of the country's aircraft industries will reach their MES unless they have substantial sales outside of Europe. US aircraft builders, on the other hand, may well be in a position to reach their MES point by selling only into their own domestic market. Thus when the Americans and each of the individual European countries compete in a third market, it is highly likely that US aircraft manufacturers will have a distinct cost advantage. One way to overcome the relative disadvantage which the European aircraft builders face is for them to form a partnership where each of the European countries makes part of a plane and then sell the completed plane in each of their domestic markets and externally outside of the EU. This may well have been the reason for setting up Airbus Industrie and the economies of scale which have followed have seen it grow into the second largest aircraft manufacturer, becoming a real threat to Boeing of the US.

Table 8.5 shows the technical economies of scale. There are further non-technical economies to be gained, such as cost savings on finance, sales and promotion, marketing and the like. For example, the removal of some trade barriers after the establishment of the Single Market in the EU could allow a member country to sell its products in a wider range of markets, reducing cultural differences and leading the organisation to benefit from a larger audience over which some of these costs can be shared.

Although this section has concentrated on scale economies and their existence, these provide only one of a number of factors behind the desire for organisational growth. Factors such as making higher levels of profits, growth to protect market share, growth to enhance salaries and growth as mere survival are just a few of the other reasons that are important factors in changes in the size of the organisation. Conversely, for other organisations the growth motive is neither important nor achievable. The reason that some firms stay relatively small is that the demand for their products is not sufficient to enable them to move down their long-run cost curve, or that they fill a narrow niche in the market. In addition, it is possible that diseconomies of scale occur when the level of output is small so that the market consists of a number of smaller firms.

Some firms do not have the objective of growth. Work by Storey (1994) and others suggests that these are more likely to be the firms that exit the market. Other firms wish to grow, perhaps to achieve economies of scale, yet are constrained in their growth through the lack of finance or labour market restrictions. Thus in an economy we are likely to see a range of firms, not all of which are at the most efficient size, and not all of which have economies of scale as the prime motive for growth.

Conversely, as Chapter 23 notes, it may well be that many firms now consider themselves to be beyond the minimum point on their long-run average total cost curve, and are attempting to reduce output and save costs. This may be achieved through downsizing, which may involve demerging, and changing the management structure of the organisation by switching to flatter hierarchies and removing layers of middle management.

# SUMMARY

◆ This chapter has developed the concept of time periods and in particular has concentrated on cost curves, both in the short run and the long run. Short-run cost functions are used for current operating decisions. Long-run cost functions are utilised more in long-range planning.

◆ In the short run only one factor of production is variable and this is usually labour. In other words, to increase output in the short run we can vary the labour input. Varying one factor while holding other factors constant leads to diminishing returns to the variable factor and explains why the short-run cost curves are drawn as U-shaped.

◆ While the short-run cost curve shows the minimum cost for a particular level of plant, the long-run cost curve shows the minimum cost for the optimal plant size, given the current level of technology. Changes in technology, which are usually assumed to be positive, lead to a downward shift in the long-run average total cost curve.

◆ Downward-sloping long-run average total cost curves show increasing returns to scale. LRATC curves which are flat exhibit constant returns to scale and upward-sloping LRATC curves exhibit diseconomies of scale.

◆ The shape of the LRATC curve is important in establishing the output level at which LRATC are minimised – the minimum efficient scale (MES) of production. This result is important to the growth of the organisation as well as to the decision to sell overseas or not.

◆ As the organisation grows or continues to produce, it would be expected to learn from this process. Thus it is possible that succeeding units of output are produced at lower cost because of this process of learning. This reduction in average total costs is related to the organisation's learning curve or experience curve.

◆ This chapter has also investigated the methods by which the shape of the LRATC curve can be estimated. Three approaches were put forward: statistical methods, the survivor technique and the engineering approach. In the first approach a regression model is developed but over time the assumption that all the other variables are constant apart from output is violated. In the case of the survivor technique, the weaknesses lie with the assumption that firms that survive are those that seek to minimise costs. Moreover, it fails to take into account barriers to entry and the strategic location of firms. Engineering studies provide the 'best' method by which to estimate the shape of the LRATC curve, being based on calculations of the expected cost of production that can result from estimates of larger-sized plants based on the costs of current smaller plants which may or may not be currently in operation. But once again, there are still problems with unanticipated production delays and the difference between accountants' view of costs compared with those of economists.

◆ Cost–volume profit analysis or break-even analysis was introduced, comparing the economist's view of profit to the accountant's. It was seen that the break-even quantity is actually the point which the economist would define as the normal profit point. The contribution to fixed costs and profits was discussed in terms of the (marginal) profit contribution. Mathematically, it was seen that the break-even point and other production levels may be calculated if the level of average variable costs and profit contribution required are known.

## REVIEW QUESTIONS

1  To what extent does the survivor technique, as a method for estimating the shape of the LRATC curve, overcome the problem of technological change?

2  Using the Cobb-Douglas production function discussed in Appendix 8.1, show the case for constant returns to scale and diseconomies of scale.

3  Does the minimum efficient scale (MES) tell us anything about international merger and acquisition activity?

4  What are the implications for organisations which do not learn from their behaviour?

5  Indicate the possible changes in the LRATC curve that result from the following:

   a  A fall in the wage rate.

   b  Improved productivity by the workforce.

   c  A reduction in the cost of capital faced by the organisation.

   d  The development of a new technological process applicable to the organisation.

   e  Improvement in worker and management training.

   f  An increase in the learning experience.

6  With reference to Table 8.1, divide a piece of graph paper into two and draw two sets of axes. The $x$ axis label should be 'quantity', the $y$ axis label should be 'cost'.

   a  On the first set of axes, plot the ATC, AVC and MC for the production range given.

   b  Indicate on the graph the regions of:

   – decreasing returns to factor inputs;

   – Increasing returns to factor inputs.

   c  On the second set of axes, plot the TC, TVC and TFC for the production range given.

   d  What is distinctive about the point where marginal costs are at a minimum?

# Appendix 8.1

## RETURNS TO SCALE

To estimate the various returns to scale, one approach is to use a production function which relates output to the various inputs. One fairly common form of the production function is the Cobb-Douglas production function. This is shown as follows:

$$Q = AK^a L^b$$

where,

   $A$ = a constant representing the technical properties of the production system

   $a$ and $b$ = the output elasticity of demand for capital and labour

$Q$, $K$ and $L$ = the quantities of output, capital and labour respectively.

The concept of elasticity has already been defined in Chapter 6 but, as a reminder, the elasticity of demand is shown as:

$$E_d = \frac{dq}{dp} \times \frac{p}{q}$$

If we differentiate the Cobb-Douglas production function with respect to labour (L) the following results:

$$\frac{dQ}{dL} = AbK^a L^{b-1}$$

This can be rearranged to:

$$\frac{dQ}{dL} = AK^aL^b \times \frac{b}{L}$$

Since $AK^aL^b = Q$, our formula becomes:

$$\frac{dQ}{dL} = Q \times \frac{b}{L}$$

This can now be rearranged to find the value for $b$:

$$b = \frac{dQ}{dL} \times \frac{L}{Q}$$

The right-hand side of the above equation looks very similar to the formula for the elasticity of demand. Because it is a relationship between output ($Q$) and labour ($L$), it is called the output elasticity of labour. Similarly, we could undertake the same mathematical reasoning to show that $a$ equals the output elasticity of capital.

We are now in a position to look at the economies of scale. If $a + b = 1$ we have constant returns to scale, if $a + b > 1$ we have increasing returns to scale, and if $a + b < 1$ we have decreasing returns to scale.

Suppose that we now increase the labour and capital inputs into the production function by a multiple, $S$, which exceeds one. The Cobb-Douglas production function now becomes:

$$Q = A(SK)^a(SL)^b$$

This can be rearranged to:

$$AK^aL^b \times (S)^{a+b}$$

which reduces to:

$$Q \times (S)^{a+b}$$

So if $S = 2$ and $a+b > 1$, then $Q$ increases by more than 2. In other words, we have increasing returns to scale, a movement down the LRATC curve.

## GLOSSARY OF NEW TERMS

**Diseconomies of scale:** Increasing long-run average total costs as output is increased.

**Economies of scale:** Lower long-run average total costs as output is increased.

**Engineering approach:** A method by which production engineers can assess the shape of the LRATC curve.

**Fixed costs:** A cost that does not vary as output changes.

**Learning curve:** Sometimes called the 'experience curve', the average cost reduction over time due to the production experience.

**Long-run average total cost curve (LRATC):** the way average costs behave when all the factors of production are variable.

**Marginal cost:** The change in total cost as output is altered by one unit.

**Minimum efficient scale (MES):** the point on the LRATC curve at which costs are minimised.

**Operating leverage:** The proportionate reaction of profits to the proportionate change in quantity of output.

**Profit contribution:** The marginal contribution to fixed costs and profits.

**Semi-fixed/semi-variable costs:** Costs which over their whole range do not alter smoothly but are subject to discrete changes.

**Short-run cost curve:** The shape of the cost curve when only one factor of production is altered while other factors of production remain constant.

**Survivor technique:** A method of assessing the shape of the LRATC curve of plants based on the idea that relatively efficient plants experience a growing share of the market over time.

**Variable cost:** A cost that varies as output changes.

## READING

Arrow, K J (1962) 'The economic implications of learning by doing', *Review of Economic Studies*, Vol 29, No 2.
*This text provides some of the seminal work on the aspect of learning curves.*

Ferguson, P R, Ferguson, G J and Rothschild, R (1993), *Business Economics*, Macmillan, Basingstoke.
*Most of the ideas regarding economies and diseconomies of scale are dealt with here.*

Griffiths, A and Wall, S (1996) *Intermediate Microeconomics: Theory and Applications*, Addison-Wesley Longman, Harlow.
*The text provides an easier introduction to the theory of costs with some useful applications.*

Begg, D, Fischer, S and Dornbusch, R (1994) *Economics*, 4th edn, McGraw-Hill, Maidenhead.

Parkin, M and King, D (1997) *Economics*, 3rd edn, Addison-Wesley Longman, Harlow.
*Both the above texts provide good introductions to the theory of costs.*

**Further reading**

Dobson, S, Maddala, G S and Miller, E (1995) *Microeconomics*, McGraw-Hill, Maidenhead.

Gold, B (1981) 'Changing perspectives on size, scale and returns: an interpretive survey', *Journal of Economic Literature*, Vol 19, No 1, March, pp 5–33.

Haldi, J and Whitcomb, D (1967) 'Economies of scale in industrial plants', *Journal of Political Economy*, Vol 75, pp 373–85.

Jackson, D (1982) *Introduction to Economics, Theory and Data*, Macmillan, Basingstoke.

Salvatore, D (1986) *Microeconomic Theory and Applications*, Macmillan, Basingstoke.

Stigler, G J (1958) 'The economies of scale', *Journal of Law and Economics*, Vol 1, No 1, pp 54–71.

Storey, D J (1994) *Understanding the Small Business Sector*, Routledge, London.

Varian, H (1993) *Intermediate Microeconomics*, 3rd edn, Norton, New York.

Wengle, J (1995) 'International trade in banking services', *Journal of International Money and Finance*, February, pp 47–64.

PART 3

# MARKETING AND INVESTMENT DECISIONS

CHAPTER 9

# PRICING DECISIONS

## OBJECTIVES

◆ To consider the different market situations of perfect competition, monopolistic competition, oligopoly and monopoly, and to consider the implications of these on market price and quantity sold.

◆ To develop the concepts of 'price taker', 'price maker' and 'price discrimination'.

◆ To consider the characteristics of a mutually dependent (interdependent) oligopoly and to investigate the conditions and reactions of such mutuality.

◆ To examine types of price leadership and non-collusive oligopoly.

◆ To introduce and discuss pricing policies and objectives for organisations operating under various market conditions, such as non-profit maximisation, limit pricing, transfer pricing and organisations in the public sector.

## KEY TERMS

Cartel

Conjectural variation

Delivered price

Limit price

Monopolistic
competition

Monopoly

Oligopoly

Perfect competition

Reaction function

Transfer price

## CHAPTER OUTLINE

Business application

Introduction

Market structures/types of competition

Pricing under monopoly conditions

Case study 9.1 The kingdom of power

Oligopoly

Cartels and collusion: collusive oligopoly

Case study 9.2 Dutch cartel appeal rejected

Case study 9.3 OPEC

Case study 9.4 The rise and fall of the Net Book Agreement

Delivered pricing

Limit pricing

Pricing for other objectives

Price discrimination

Case study 9.5 Anglian Water car parks

Transfer pricing

Summary

Review questions

Glossary of new terms

Reading

# Nintendo and Sega attacked by MMC for 'inflated prices'

Nintendo and Sega, the Japanese companies which dominate the video games market, inflate their UK prices by monopolistic practices, the Monopolies and Mergers Commission ruled yesterday. In a strong attack on the business practices of the companies' UK subsidiaries, the commission said Nintendo UK and Sega Europe operated against the public interest. Monopolistic practices in the industry had adverse effects on the prices and availability of video games, it said. The report suggests a Sega Mega Drive console with software selling for £87.82 in the US would cost £132.39 in the UK, £116.62 in Germany and £112.64 in France. Games cartridges typically cost £15–£30 in the UK.

Mr Jonathan Evans, corporate affairs minister, said he would draw the commission's findings to the attention of competition authorities in the EU, the US and Japan. It was not clear last night what action, if any, those authorities might take. The report follows an investigation initiated by Sir Bryan Carsberg, director-general of fair trading, in January 1994. Sega is best known for its 'Sonic the Hedgehog' while Nintendo has a range of games featuring the 'Mario Brothers'. Cartridges – which are loaded with games software by Sega, Nintendo or a third party – are designed to work only with a particular manufacturer's console.

The commission said the two companies had: Established a discriminatory price structure resulting in games software prices that were excessive compared with the consoles on which they were played. Controlled the supply of third party games software through licensing conditions which left them as sole suppliers of games cartridges. Restricted the rental and part exchange of games software. It recommends changes in the licensing conditions operated by the two companies, arguing in particular they should no longer arrange or control the manufacture of the games cartridges. Mr Evans said the government accepted the report. There would now be a three-month period for consultation.

Sega Europe said last night it was disappointed by the report and remained confident the success of its consoles and games was a consequence of their quality and competitive pricing. The commission had failed fully to appreciate the nature of the technology involved and the speed of change in the market, it said. Nintendo said it rejected any idea pricing was excessive or against the public interest. All its products faced the test of consumer demand and satisfaction.

*Source: Financial Times, 10 March 1995. Reprinted with permission.*

### Comment

It is often the case that government agencies, such as the MMC, are asked to investigate the pricing practices in markets which may be against the public interest. The public interest is judged to have been abused if an organisation, or group of organisations, is able to maintain artificially high prices or to restrict quantities of the product available in the marketplace.

By comparing the price of video game consoles in the UK with those in the USA, Germany and France, the MMC concluded that Sega and Nintendo *were* in fact acting against the public interest by charging higher prices than elsewhere in Europe. Additionally, it was claimed that these two organisations were also operating a price-discrimination mechanism with respect to the games sold for the consoles. Because they are the sole suppliers of compatible games in the UK, they are able to charge higher prices to retailers; they are also able to impose restrictions on the hire and rental of games. These factors, according to the MMC, give Sega and Nintendo considerable market power. They are thus exploiting their consumers.

The fact that the two main manufacturers of video consoles and games in the UK have both been investigated might suggest that they have entered into (illegal) collusion to set and maintain prices. This is not mentioned in the case study. However, if this were to be proven, it could be termed a 'cartel' arrangement. On the other hand, it could be the case that these two organisations have competitively acted and reacted to each other's pricing strategies and that the best results for each of them is gained via price levels which are similar to each other. That is, the situation may have arisen through collusion or through competition.

Such competitive and non-competitive interactions between organisations will be investigated in this chapter. The conditions required for successful price discrimination will be outlined and discussed. Other pricing decisions required on the part of the organisation will also be introduced and examined.

# INTRODUCTION

Any organisation which provides goods or services to fee-paying customers *must*, by its very nature, charge a price for that good or service. Economists are fond of the expression that 'there is no such thing as a free lunch'. That is, for everything which we receive, there is some form of price to pay for it.

This chapter will investigate the difference between those organisations in the market which are 'price takers' and those which are 'price makers' and will consider the implications for pricing of the different market structures within which organisations operate.

The neoclassical assumption that organisations seek to maximise profits (or minimise losses) will form the basis for most of the analysis within this chapter. Where revenue from sales exceeds costs of production, profits are made. However, where costs exceed revenues, a loss is accrued. As will be seen in a variety of situations throughout the chapter, a short-term loss is not necessarily a bad thing.

Interactions between and within firms have implications for the pricing of products and services. Here too, time will be spent considering a variety of situations where prices are affected by such interactions. For instance, where a firm owns several plants or stages of production, internal transfer sales of production units between these stages occur. Such sales require a price.

There will also be discussion and explanation with respect to the mechanisms and market conditions which allow private-sector and public-sector monopolists to charge artificially high prices in their product markets. The fact that they are able to charge different customers different prices will also be investigated. In competitive markets, prices are not always set at the level which will earn normal profits for firms; they are sometimes set higher, generating supernormal profits for the incumbents and yet there is no flood of new entrants to such markets. Such a situation may be explained by the theory of limit pricing. This theory and its effect on markets is discussed in this chapter.

When a group of firms operating within an oligopoly market make agreements with reference to the price of their products or the quantity of their products to be sold in the marketplace, a cartel is said to have been formed. Several models of cartel exist which have been observed empirically. Two will be outlined here, along with a discussion of the problems faced in maintaining a successful cartel.

Finally, the pricing decisions of the various departments within an organisation are discussed in the context of internal sales of intermediate products. The advantages of transfer pricing are discussed, particularly with reference to the international context.

## MARKET STRUCTURES/TYPES OF COMPETITION

Within the neoclassical paradigm, a number of market structures exist. Each is discrete and different to the others in a defined manner. The underlying assumption and linking similarity between these structures are that the firm is operating so as to maximise its profits (or to minimise its losses). Figure 9.1 shows the distinct categories recognised by economists within the neoclassical framework. Most simply, a distinction is made between perfect and imperfect competition. Within the imperfect category, economists identify monopolistic competition, oligopoly and monopoly structures.

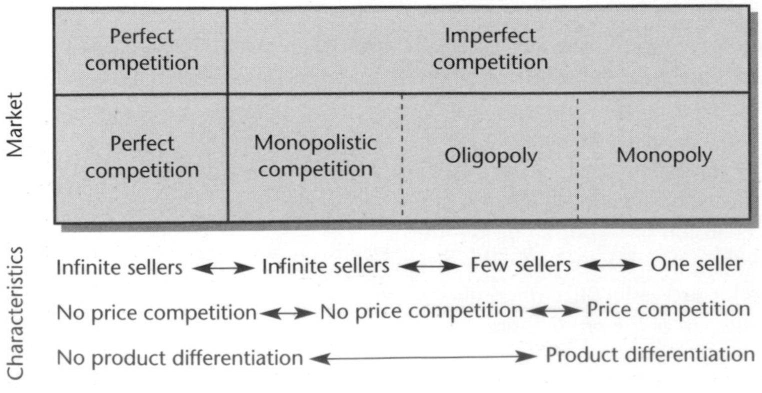

**Figure 9.1**

The distinct market structures, as recognised by economists. Perfect competition is the benchmark by which others are measured. A feature of monopolistic competition is the lack of price competition and an infinite number of buyers and sellers. The oligopoly structure has only a few sellers; competition is on either a price or non-price basis, or both. There is only one seller in a monopoly market; market prices and quantities offered for sale are controlled by the monopoly organisation.

## Perfect competition

**Perfect competition** is widely accepted *not* to exist. So, why bother with it? This is a question asked by many students encountering the concept for the first time.

Most simply, perfect competition provides a 'controlled environment' for analysis. Because of the assumptions made, the model allows economists to investigate and observe changes in markets without having to separate out any complicating factors. Thus, the observations made under conditions of perfect competition provide a benchmark for analysis. When the same changes are made in different market conditions, the analyst has some idea of the expected results; deviations from this are likely to be caused by other factors.

The basis for comparison arises because perfect competition provides the economist with an analogy to the scientists' laboratory conditions. One factor is changed at a time and the effect noted. The model may then be returned to its original position before another factor is changed and that effect noted. A clear understanding of the effects of all factors is built up.

So, to return to the question of 'why bother?', once perfect competition is understood, assumptions may be relaxed, various changes repeated, noted and understood more easily in the context of the real world.

## Assumptions of perfect competition

There are a number of assumptions made in constructing a perfectly competitive model:

- There are infinite buyers and sellers; no one buyer or seller has greater power in the market than others.
- There is perfect knowledge or perfect information in the market, possessed by all participants.
- There are no transaction costs – for transportation, for setting up supply agreements etc.
- Each firm acts to maximise its profits/minimise its losses.
- The product offered by all firms is identical (homogenous).
- There are no barriers to firms wishing to enter or exit the market.

## Implications of perfect competition

Given the assumptions of perfect competition, it becomes obvious that no one buyer or seller is able

**Figure 9.2**

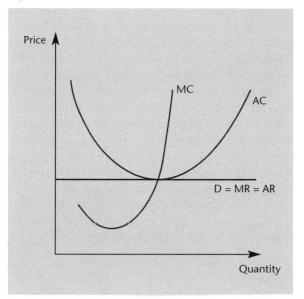

Under conditions of perfect competition, no one buyer or seller is able to influence price by acting alone. Thus, all parties within such a market are price takers. Furthermore, because there are infinite buyers and sellers, no individual party acting alone is able to control the quantity they sell. Thus, the demand curve for a perfectly competitive organisation is horizontal (reflecting the price-taking nature of any individual organisation). Marginal costs, MC, cut average costs, AC, from below at the lowest level of AC. In equilibrium, this is also the point of tangency with the D = MR = AR curve (D = demand, MR = marginal revenue, AR = average revenue).

to influence price by acting alone. Thus, all parties within such a market are **price takers**. Furthermore, because there is an infinite number of buyers and sellers, no individual party acting alone is able to control the quantity it sells. Figure 9.2 gives the demand curve for a perfectly competitive firm. It can clearly be seen that the demand curve is horizontal (reflecting the price-taking nature of any individual organisation).

## Monopolistic competition

Under **monopolistic competition**, product differentiation exists based on non-price characteristics, the product's brand name, for instance. Otherwise, the perfect competition assumptions are maintained. The price elasticity of demand for each organisation's product is relatively elastic with respect to price as a result of the fact that there are many (alternative) suppliers in the industry. Each firm is able to affect demand for its product to some extent, as a result of its product-differentiation activities. Some economists even claim that each form holds a very small, localised monopoly even though it is operating in a larger, competitive market in a broader sense – hence the term monopolistic competition.

Consider Figure 9.3, which shows the relationship between costs, revenues and demand. The demand curve slopes because the organisation faces a finite demand for its differentiated product. However, consideration must still be made of the MC = MR intersection to derive the profit-maximising quantity produced and of the demand curve in order to derive price. Profit (or loss) levels can be found by looking at the AC level at the market price and quantity levels.

## Monopoly

Strictly speaking, **monopoly** refers to the case where there is only one seller in the market. Indeed, there are many cases where there is only one seller in the market and the definition is not questioned. However, economists, fitting in with government definitions, usually regard any one organisation with greater than 25 per cent of market share as a monopolist. Thus, officially, a

monopoly market may consist of more than one organisation. However, one of those organisations will wield considerable market power. A monopoly in strictest terms *is* the industry, and economists frequently use such a concept for ease of analysis.

## PRICING UNDER MONOPOLY CONDITIONS

Under monopoly conditions, the efficiency of the market is potentially reduced. By contrast, a perfectly competitive market will clear at the point of allocative and productive efficiency; that is, where MC = MR and AC = AR. Under conditions of monopoly, the monopolist will maximise profits at MC = MR and thus be productively efficient. It should be noted that a common criticism against monopolies is that, due to their market power, prices are held artificially high; consumers wishing to buy the product have no choice but to purchase from the monopolist and must therefore pay the monopolist's price. An implication of the high price level charged by the monopolist is that the quantity of its product available on the market will be lower than the market-clearing level which would be seen under conditions of competition.

**Figure 9.3**

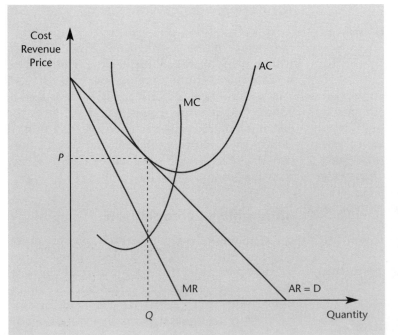

The demand curve slopes because the organisation faces a finite demand for its differentiated product. The MC = MR intersection denotes the profit-maximising quantity produced; trace this up to the demand curve in order to derive price. Normal profits are gained in this case because AC = AR at the equilibrium price and quantity.

'Deadweight loss' measures the allocative inefficiency of such a restriction on output. This may be quantified as the reduction in consumer surplus and producer surplus which arises as a result of the restriction to output in a given industry or sector. It would be difficult to measure the deadweight loss empirically, but as a theoretical concept it is attractive. In principle, if the market quantity is restricted, then not all consumers will be able to purchase all that they desire of the product at the stated price – for some the price will be too high. This means that a welfare loss to society is incurred. For a more technical explanation, see the next paragraph.

Monopoly conditions mean that the monopolist is able to charge an inflated price for restricted quantities of its product. To see this, compare the following. Under conditions of competition, the organisations' (within the industry) MC curves can be combined (or summed) to show the industry supply curve. This will meet the demand curve at the equilibrium point. However, if that same industry were taken over by a monopoly, then the monopolist's MC equals MR at the point of profit maximisation. This point is different and less efficient than the competitive industry's equilibrium. The monopolist's equilibrium will be at the point where price is higher and quantity lower than the free-market equilibrium. Thus, the monopoly incurs a cost to society of the magnitude of the deadweight loss induced plus a cost to the consumer of the magnitude equal to the loss in consumer surplus/gain in organisation's revenue. *See* Figure 9.4.

## Natural monopolies

Natural monopolies exist or arise where the market is more effectively served by a single organisation, even if some other market form had existed initially. Historically, natural monopolies have been supported by central governments since they have existed in markets which supply public goods. These goods, it was argued, would not even be supplied if left to the free movements of the market mechanism. Thinking in this area has changed since the early 1980s as a result of the privatisation programmes enacted by governments, especially in Europe. The sales of publicly owned utilities and other nationally owned assets, as well as the liberalisation of markets, has resulted in increased competition in many of the relevant markets. That is, other organisations have joined the market with a view to gaining market share.

**Figure 9.4**

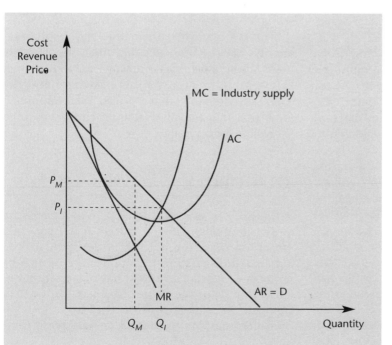

The monopolist achieves productive efficiency and equilibrium at $P_M Q_M$. By comparison, the competitive industry equilibrium will be at the point of allocative efficiency (supply meets demand) at $P_I Q_I$ – a lower market price and greater market quantity.

◆ **CASE STUDY 9.1**

# The kingdom of power

To German consumers paying well over the European average for electricity the riches of VEBA and RWE look ill-gotten. The German Industry Association reckons that the country's power cartel, which accommodates nearly 1,000 generators and distributors of electricity, adds DM15 billion ($11 billion) to companies' electricity bills. Coal subsidies and strict environmental rules account for some of that, but genuine competition is still years away.

At the summit of the hierarchy are the nine interconnected utilities, of which RWE and PreussenElektra, VEBA'S electricity subsidiary, are the biggest. Market-sharing agreements give each a territory in which it can generate and distribute electricity without fear of competition from others. RWE, for example, dominates North Rhine-Westphalia, the most populous and industrialised state; PreussenElektra has the run of northern Germany. Below the big nine are hundreds of regional and local distributors, some of them partly owned by the inter-connected utilities.

The economics ministry would like to end electricity's exemption from cartel rules, and to outlaw market-sharing agreements and concessions that give distributors exclusive rights to use the local grids of most cities. But the utilities have the political clout to block any liberalisation that does not include the rest of Europe. And the European Commission's proposals for deregulation are being held up by diplomatic wrangling, mainly between France and Britain.

The Berlin-based cartel office, which wants the utilities to open their grids to competing generators, has pressed ahead with lawsuits alleging that the concession- and market-sharing pacts contradict European law. But a more serious threat to the cartel may be their customers. Even though big consumers get special discounts, some businesses in energy-intensive industries, such as aluminium, have shifted production abroad. Two glass factories near Aachen recently stopped buying electricity from RWE and hooked up to a regional Dutch utility instead.

The utilities are girding themselves for a fight. Where possible they are buying stakes in the city-owned distributors, strengthening their grip on local markets. PreussenElektra, for example, hopes to buy a minority share in Bremen's local utility (if it can overcome the likely opposition of the cartel office). The big utilities are also investing heavily in cheaper energy sources, such as hydroelectric power from Scandinavia. When deregulation finally comes, they could use their clout to buy up smaller competitors – heedless of customers' interests.

*Source:* © *The Economist*, London, 8 July 1995. Reprinted with permission.

## Comment on the case study

The German electricity industry is an example of a natural monopolist, actually a duopolist, running a cartel which owns the generators responsible for the generation and distribution of electricity. However, what this strangely formed natural monopoly has discovered is that it is unable to maintain its market power.

The generating companies previously owned the means of distribution and generation in Germany without question or competition. This gave them the power to exploit customers and to charge prices which exceeded the European average. Customers were obviously not content with this state of affairs. Improvements in technology and the fact that European policy makers would like to see the German cartel disbanded have added a new dimension to the choice available to discontented customers.

Indeed, two industrial customers of electricity in Germany have changed their suppliers. They now buy cheaper electricity from a regional Dutch electricity supplier instead.

This is a case where the natural monopoly argument, that the market could not support more than one supplier, breaks down. The infrastructure is available to supply from elsewhere and the German companies have priced their supply so high that it is actually viable for customers to go elsewhere more cheaply.

## OLIGOPOLY

**Oligopoly** means 'few sellers'. When there are only a few sellers in the market it is frequently observed that competition is fierce. Also, the organisations within oligopolies are said to be *interdependent* – the actions of one organisation will affect and shape the actions of others. Rather than compete on price, oligopolists tend to compete on non-price factors to protect and increase their market share. Within oligopoly, economists accept two situations, one where mutual dependence is recognised and one where it is not.

## Pricing under oligopoly: mutual dependence recognised

Where mutual dependence is recognised, a price cut by one of the organisations will be matched by the others. The reaction of the other organisations to any change in the price of a product may be guessed at by any organisation in the oligopoly. This guess, or expectation, is known as **conjectural variation** (CV). Conjectural variation is defined as 'The expected percentage change in rivals' strategic variable divided by the contemplated change in the organisation's strategic variable.'

Thus, conjectural variation is equal to zero where no reaction is expected. Unity occurs where the rival is expected to exactly match the action taken. The conjectural variation value will be less than (greater than) one when the rivals fail to (more than) match the proposed change. This concept can be developed in the context of the kinked demand curve.

### Kinked demand curve

Developed by Hall and Hitch (1939) and also independently by Sweezy the same year, the kinked demand curve may be used to explain why prices become 'sticky' in oligopolistic markets. Thus, it is possible to extrapolate that organisations may resort to competition on non-price factors/behaviour.

In Figure 9.5, the region above the market price shows demand as relatively elastic. In the region below, demand is relatively inelastic. The organisation does not wish to change price as long as the marginal cost curve passes through the gap in the marginal revenue curve (that is, through the profit-maximising equilibrium level). Marginal costs may vary from any level between $MC_1$ and $MC_2$.

There are two aspects to any organisation's conjectural variation when looking at the kinked demand curve. In the price region above the equilibrium, any price change will not be matched by rival organisations; thus CV is equal to zero. In the price region below the equilibrium price, any price reduction *will* be matched by rivals, CV therefore being equal to one. Thus, following any price reduction, each organisation will maintain its original market share, but at the expense of profits, which will be reduced due to the lower price paid for the product and the inelastic nature of that section of the demand curve.

A criticism put forward by many is that the theory is incomplete in assuming that the equilibrium position is achieved without explanation. However, it does provide an explanation of the theory of sticky prices. The fact that organisations set prices at the point where MC = MR in accordance with profit-maximising theory shows that it is possible for large variations in the marginal revenue curve to exist before a new price level becomes appropriate. Again, *see* Figure 9.5. In this case, the gap between $MC_1$ and $MC_2$ is relatively large. As a

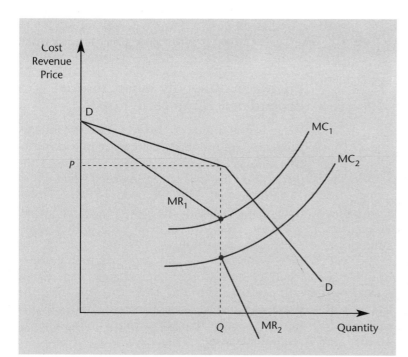

**Figure 9.5**

The section of the demand curve above *P* is relatively elastic. Price increases from *P* to greater than *P* will not be matched due to the revenue losses associated with such a move. The section of the demand curve below *P* is relatively inelastic. Price reductions from *P* to below *P* will be matched; an increased quantity will be sold, but total revenue will be reduced. The gap between $MC_1$ and $MC_2$ is relatively large. As a result, marginal costs may vary between $MC_1$ and $MC_2$ before the market price and quantity associated with the original equilibrium position are caused to move.

result, marginal costs may vary between $MC_1$ and $MC_2$ before the market price and quantity associated with the original equilibrium position are caused to move.

### Conscious parallelism

There may be situations where a price rise is matched by rivals in the market. The CV would therefore be equal to one. If production costs were to rise *across the board*, for all organisations, then it is not inconceivable that all organisations would increase prices. Such a price rise, if simultaneous and tacitly agreed by all rival organisations, is known as conscious parallelism.

### Price leadership models

Under price leadership models, one organisation tends to lead in implementing price changes, followed quickly by its rivals. The price leader takes a risk by changing its price. There is a danger that its lead will not be followed by the others. Thus the price leader may encounter revenue losses before it is able to adjust its price back to the original level. Price leadership models assume that there is agreement among organisations with reference to the leader in their particular situation. The fact that the accepted organisation is able to maintain its leadership status is also assumed.

Note, however, that Koutsoyiannis (1993, pp 247–8) outlines as a criticism of price leadership models (such as those given below) the fact that the leader organisation is often both the low-cost leader *and* the dominant organisation, one condition being the prerequisite for the other. She is arguing, therefore, that it is simplistic to identify low cost and dominant as two distinct categories of price leader. However, for the purposes of exposition, assume that there are three types of leader: barometric, low-cost and dominant firm.

### *Barometric leader*

Barometric price leaders predict and react to the appropriate point in time and economic climate to make a price change. For instance, after an industry/sector-wide cost increase (or similar event) a price rise would be appropriate. If the rival organisations trust the leader's judgement then they will also change their prices. If they feel that the change has been too severe, then they will adjust to a lesser degree, leaving the leader in a position where it will have to readjust its prices. If no individual organisation has the absolute trust of the others, it is not

inconceivable that the leadership responsibility is shared by all of the organisations in rotation in the industry/sector over a period of time.

### *Low-cost leader*

The low-cost leader has significant cost advantages over its rivals. As such, it is therefore in a position to dictate price. Its rivals will be concerned that any price war instigated will incur the wrath of the leader, which will be easily able to engage in it and win(!). This is not the type of exercise the rivals would like to be involved in and so they tend to wait for signals from the low-cost price leader. In the event of a price war, the rival organisations would incur greater losses than the leader. Thus, the rivals tacitly agree to follow the price adjustments of the low-cost leader.

### *Dominant firm leader*

The dominant firm is larger, relative to its rivals. It therefore dictates prices to the other organisations in the industry/sector. In this case, the rival organisations are effectively price takers. By considering the position of the rival organisations with respect to quantity produced at given prices, the dominant firm is able to ascertain where its own profit-maximisation position will be at those different prices and therefore command the industry/sector price level in accordance with this judgement. Other firms may not achieve profit maximisation at these price levels.

As has already been stated, there is an argument accepted by some economists that the low-cost leader is also likely to be the dominant firm.

## Pricing in oligopoly where mutual dependence is not recognised

When organisations do not recognise the interdependencies in the market, they act in a competitive manner. Augustin Cournot was one of the first economists to postulate on such situations in 1838. He modelled the behaviour of two organisations operating from the same well at (assumed) zero cost within the mineral water industry. For these two organisations, Cournot assumed that they would be naïve enough to assume that there would be no reaction to any change made by the competitor. There is therefore no learning through experience by either competitor. Cournot further assumed that the organisations would be profit maximising.

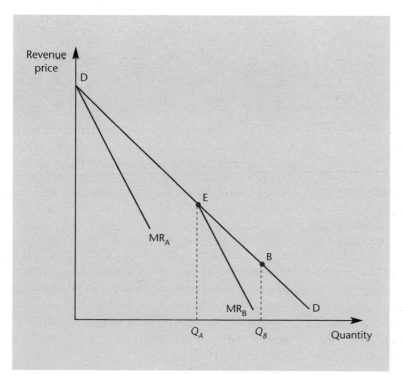

Consider Figure 9.6. If organisation A, given demand curve DD, initially maximises profit at quantity $Q_A$ (half the market), the demand curve for the second organisation will be given by ED. Organisation B will therefore profit maximise at quantity $Q_B$. Given that there is no learning, organisation A will look at the market and believe that it will maximise profit by producing less than its original position, because organisation B's production has to be taken into account. Organisation A will therefore contract its profit-maximising quantity. Organisation B, at the same time, will believe that its profit-maximising quantity is larger than originally anticipated. Thus, over time, organisation A will contract and organisation B will expand their respective profit-maximising quantities. It is the case that the market will eventually settle at an equilibrium level where the two organisations produce one-third each of the purely competitive quantity. A will have contracted to this level and B will have expanded to it. Neither firm has an incentive to change from this level; there is a stable equilibrium at this point. Total production is only two-thirds of the competitive level, but more than the monopoly situation (which is half of the competitive level).

Stackelberg developed this analysis, isolating and mapping the organisation's behaviour possibilities as **reaction functions**. These are plotted within a single product space, based on quantity produced and iso-profit levels. The reaction functions for each firm are derived by plotting the individual purely competitive output, the monopoly output (and, on a straight-line mapping, all combinations in between) to give the **best response** for each, given the output of the other. Reaction functions are plotted on the same axes to give the competitive equilibrium position. This point is known as the Nash equilibrium and depicts the point where neither organisation has an incentive to change behaviour (*see* Figure 9.7).

It is clear in Figure 9.7 that the best profits attainable by each organisation when a competitor exists are at the point where the organisations share the market and produce one-third each of the competitive level. This is the same level as the Cournot equilibrium, hence the term 'Cournot–Nash' equilibrium.

## Game theory: non-collusive oligopoly

Game theory is the name given to the situation where competition exists between the organisations in an interdependent (oligopoly) situation. Theories relating to games exist for two players (two-person games) or more than two players (*n*-person games). The Cournot–Nash-type analysis is derived from a two-person game.

**Figure 9.6**

Firm A has a demand curve DD, initially maximising profits at quantity $Q_A$ (half the market). The demand curve for Firm B is given by ED. Firm B will therefore maximise profits at quantity $Q_B$. Since there is no learning, Firm A will look at the market and believe that it will maximise profits by producing less than its original position, because Firm B's production has to be taken into account. Firm A will therefore contract its profit-maximising quantity. Firm B, at the same time, will believe that its profit-maximising quantity is larger than originally anticipated. Thus, over time, Firm A will contract and Firm B will expand their respective profit-maximising quantities. The market will eventually settle at an equilibrium level where the two firms each produce one-third of the purely competitive quantity. Neither firm has an incentive to change from this level; there is a stable equilibrium at this point. Total production is only two-thirds of the competitive level.

**Figure 9.7**

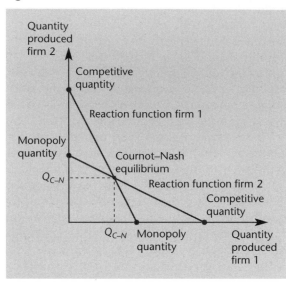

The two firms' reaction functions are plotted on the same axes. Their intersection gives the competitive equilibrium position. This point is the Cournot–Nash equilibrium and depicts the point where neither firm has an incentive to change behaviour. The Cournot–Nash equilibrium quantity is two-thirds of the competitive quantity.

There can be cooperative and non-cooperative games. The games where players are striving for the same goals and there will therefore be a loser are known as zero-sum games. This is because the players have exactly opposite interests and thus one will win, one will lose. Games also exist where each player has a different, achievable goal, known as non-zero-sum games. However, the starting point for all such analysis is the Prisoner's Dilemma game.

### Prisoner's Dilemma

Prisoner's Dilemma is a non-cooperative game which illustrates the real-world conflicts which exist for decision makers. The dilemma which arises is whether to strive for the security of a basic payoff, or to trust the other player and earn an enhanced payoff. The model was originally written in the context of two prisoners, under questioning for the same crime, trying to decide whether to confess or deny their part in the crime. The payoffs for the prisoners were given in terms of the length of the custodial sentence with which they would be punished.

If both confess, then each will receive a three-year sentence. If both deny, then each will receive a five-year sentence. It would seem, therefore, that the best strategy for either prisoner is to confess to the crime. However, this is only if both confess. If A confesses and B denies, then A will be punished by a ten-year sentence, while B will walk free (and vice versa, if B confesses). Thus, although the confession strategy gives the shortest sentence if the prisoners cooperate and act to minimise their combined sentences, there is the possibility of walking free if one confesses while the other denies. There is therefore an incentive for cheating on any agreement which may have been made prior to arrest. Hence the dilemma! (*See* Figure 9.8.)

In this case, as in any other case, an equilibrium position will occur, the Nash equilibrium. While not necessarily gaining the greatest payoff for either player, it arises from the dominant strategy of each player. The dominant strategy is that which will provide the player concerned with the best payoff given the worst action of the other player. That is, the **maximin** solution (*see* Chapter 13). In this case: deny, deny (5,5).

**Figure 9.8  The Prisoner's Dilemma**

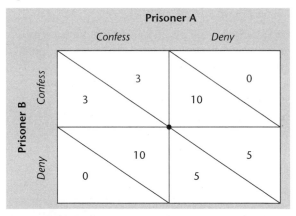

The sentences which Prisoners A and B will suffer, given the different possible scenarios, are shown in the payoff matrix, above. If A confesses and B denies, A will be sentenced to 10 years, while B will go free. The Nash equilibrium is 5,5: deny, deny.

Prisoner's Dilemma can be likened to the duopoly situation where each of the firms has a temptation to cheat on a collusive agreement because it will generate greater profits for them, despite the fact that the possibility of an even worse payoff exists if both firms were to cheat on the agreement.

For the profits payoff table given in Figure 9.9 for the alternative strategies of advertising on TV (TV) versus no TV advertising (noTV), identify the Nash equilibrium position.

**Figure 9.9**

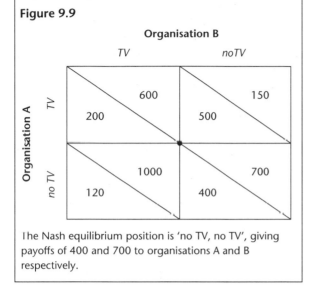

The Nash equilibrium position is 'no TV, no TV', giving payoffs of 400 and 700 to organisations A and B respectively.

# CARTELS AND COLLUSION: COLLUSIVE OLIGOPOLY

When organisations join together to set prices or quantities which will operate in the marketplace, their objective is to reduce the risk involved for member parties and therefore stabilise the income expectations of those involved in the collusion. Groups of organisations which formally agree to collude are known as a **cartel**.

Collusion and cartels are illegal in most forms. There *are* some exceptions, for example where collusion between organisations is permitted in order to maintain production or to ensure standards. Cartels take many forms. Organisations may pool their total revenue, they may ensure that each member takes its turn to secure a contract, they may spread across an industry, or split the industry into sectors based on production needs or geographically with reference to the position of customers etc. Many cartels set their members' quotas; these restrict total cartel output and therefore maintain an artificially high price within the industry.

## Joint profit-maximising cartel

Here, the price is set by a central agency, agreed on by all parties to regulate the cartel. A joint profit-maximising cartel acts in a similar manner to a multiplant monopolist. *See* Figure 9.10: in this two-firm cartel, the overall cartel situation is given by Figure 9.10(c). The cartel marginal cost curve is the sum of firm A and firm B's individual levels. The cartel demand and marginal revenues are found similarly. Firm A's situation is given in Figure 9.10(a) and firm B's in Figure 9.10(b).

The overall cartel quantity and price are set by the central agency, with reference to the cartel's marginal cost and revenue equilibrium position. The cartel will therefore earn maximum profits. This price is then adopted by firm A and firm B. Their individual quantities are derived by tracing the $\Sigma MC_{cartel} = MR_{cartel}$ level back to each individual firm's $MC_{firm}$ curve. At this intersection, quantity is derived with reference to the horizontal distance of the intersection beyond the origin along the quantity axis. The level of profit or loss relevant to each firm is then found by superimposing their own AC curves onto the appropriate axis.

## Market-sharing cartel

In a market-sharing cartel, there is general agreement on the price level to be charged. This may be set by a dominant member, or by bargaining between each of the members. Members are then free to sell their product to consumers in the marketplace, although they agree not to undercut the cartel price. Product differentiation may come from product differences, or from perceived differences. That is, the organisations compete on non-price factors. This type of cartel is obviously very relaxed in terms of its operation. Unless each firm in the cartel has equal costs and price can be set at monopoly level, the cartel will be more unstable than a joint profit-maximising cartel. Lower-cost firms are more likely to be in a position to undercut rivals and to cheat on the agreement(s).

Market-sharing cartels are sometimes arranged on a quota basis. Here, the price is decided by the cartel members and then limited quantities of production are allocated for sale to each member. The allocative split may be made in a variety of ways, for instance according to the geographical location

**Figure 9.10 Joint profit-maximising cartel**

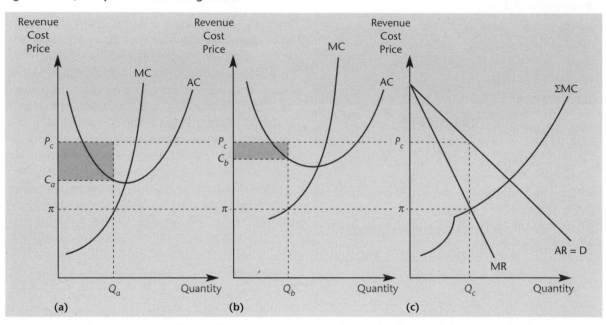

(a) Firm A in the cartel produces at the cartel's profit-maximising cost level. Since $P_c>C_a$, profits of the shaded area are made.

(b) Firm B in the cartel produces at the cartel's profit-maximising cost level. $P_c>C_b$, profits are made, but these are smaller than Firm A's.

(c) The cartel finds its profit-maximising level at the point where $\Sigma MC = MR$. Thus the cartel price level, $P_c$, may be derived for members to use. Firms produce where their individual $MC = \Sigma MC = MR$.

▪ Profits

of consumers. A more complicated method of splitting the market into quotas is a pro-rata cost-differential method based on the differences in members'

levels of costs. Obviously, again, unless the member organisations have very similar cost structures, the cartel will be unstable and members liable to cheat.

## ◆ CASE STUDY 9.2

### Dutch cartel appeal rejected

An appeal by a cartel of Dutch building contractors against a heavy European Union fine for fixing prices was rejected by the EU's Court of First Instance yesterday.

The European Commission fined the network of Dutch and other building companies called SPO Ecu22.5m ($27.7m) in February 1992, telling them after a four-year probe to disband the cartel they ran to share out business and dictate prices for over a decade, depriving the market of competition. The cartel started

in 1973 but had been operating at full strength since 1980. Various rules were applied, such as a Code of Honour and in 1986 a set of price-regulating rules.

The SPO represents 4,000 larger contractors and 3,000 other building companies. The Commission concluded at the time that the contract sums had been 3 per cent too high on average since 1989 when the industry introduced a countrywide uniform code.

*Source: Reuters,* 23 February 1995. Reprinted with permission.

#### Comment on the case study

This Dutch cartel of building contractors managed to set prices and split the market into agreed shares for over 15 years. Its longevity was protected by an internal 'code of honour,' among other rules. The prices set by the cartel were higher than the competitive market would have been by 3 per cent, according to the EU court which rejected the

appeal against a fine for the restrictive practices.

The cartel members were all part of a network, representing thousands of individual companies. That the cartel was able to establish itself and succeed is remarkable, because, as the discussion below illustrates, the greater the number of members, the more unstable a cartel is likely to be.

## Problems within cartels

Economists, including Fellner (1950), have identified a number of problems inherent within cartels. These problems apply to all cartels, including the joint profit-maximising cartel.

- *Cost disclosure and accuracy* – members have an incentive to understate their level of costs where the price may be affected by the bargaining process and where profits are divided among members in a cost-differential manner. Even if the cartel is able to collect information with reference to its members' costs, it is unlikely to be able accurately to calculate the cartel/market levels appropriately.
- *Market demand* is another factor which the cartel is likely to find it difficult to calculate accurately. The market must be identified, the effect of any close substitutes taken into account and economic changes considered.
- *Negotiation lag* – the time it takes to organise even a few firms, to gain agreement about appropriate price levels, quotas and so on, can make binding agreements difficult to achieve. If there are then any changes in the market situa-

tion, renegotiation becomes necessary and the whole process begins again.

- The fact that a negotiation lag exists and that it is difficult to communicate market changes between members means that any agreements tend to lead to *stickiness*. In the context of the joint profit-maximising cartel, this means sticky prices and thus a movement away from the profit-maximising position in the event of any market changes.
- *'Free-riding'* is an identifiable problem in the context of any cartel. Where organisations have higher cost bases than their fellow members, but gain from the profit-sharing nature of the cartel, they are classed as free-riders.
- Although cartels attempt to control the markets in which they are operating, there is always a danger that there will be a *market entry* by another organisation or even group of organisations. This would obviously undermine the power of the cartel and cause it to have to dissolve.
- Of course, except under exceptional circumstances, cartels are *illegal*. Therefore, there are pressures to keep agreements covert, to prevent cheating and generally to maintain the operation of the cartel without bringing its existence under investigation.

## ◆ CASE STUDY 9.3

# OPEC

OPEC (Organisation of Petroleum Exporting Countries) is one of the most famous cartels in the world. It was formed in 1960, by five major oil exporters, Iraq, Iran, Kuwait, Saudi Arabia and Venezuela. This rose to 13 member countries very quickly. In terms of activity and standing in the International Community, OPEC was most prominent in the 1970s. The price of oil and quantity of oil available on the international markets were dictated by OPEC throughout this period. Saudi Arabia is considered to have the greatest supply capacity within OPEC. The implication and indeed effect of this was that the Saudis were often involved in negotiations regarding overall production and price throughout the 1970s and 1980s. OPEC has taken a lower profile in terms of publicity in the 1990s.

There are various theories surrounding the success and longevity of the OPEC cartel, given the dynamic and volatile market within which it is operating. Two of the more popular theories are:

- OPEC is a joint profit-maximising cartel.
- Saudi Arabia is a dominant producer and price

leader within the cartel, with the ability to affect the quantities of oil available in the market.

The joint profit-maximising theory is based on the fact that OPEC has a large share of the world market. Whereas other oil producing countries have very little excess capacity, OPEC has the capability to vary its production by very large amounts. Tracing the rise and fall of prices, OPEC fits the pricing model applicable to any non-renewable resource, that is, that market prices are initially set at a relatively high level, due to the fact that supply is finite. This price is maintained at an artificially high level, as would be the case if the industry is under monopoly power. Over the period 1973–4, the price of oil rose. It was constant between 1975 and 1978 and rose again in 1979–80. In the period 1981–2, the price fell again. The changes in price can be attributed to changes in the quantity of oil sold. Overall, however, it is contended that the OPEC countries were maximising profits and restricting supply to the markets when prices fell.

▶

Case study 9.3 *continued*

Saudi Arabia, as has already been mentioned, is considered to be a dominant member of the cartel, with the ability to set prices. Other members of the cartel are therefore price takers, unable on their own to affect that market price. Over time, various writers have observed that prices follow a cyclical pattern. However, within this pattern, it can be seen that when the price of oil is high, the cartel tends to cut the price and increase the quantity sold. When this occurs, Saudi Arabia has reduced the quantity it sells and therefore forced the price back up again, hence the contention that Saudi Arabia is the dominant member.

Saudi Arabian changes in output, as a percentage of world market share, and OPEC percentage changes in price may be seen in Table 9.1.

It is clear that when the price falls, output is increased by Saudi Arabia in the period beforehand. Conversely, when price increases, Saudi Arabia has been restricting its output in the period(s) beforehand. Thus, Saudi Arabia is acting as a dominant member of the cartel. Overall, however, its power and OPEC's power have both been decreasing steadily over the period shown, thus reducing their ability to manipulate prices later on as effectively as was the case in the 1970s. This reduction in power may be seen in terms of the constant decreases in market share observed.

*Source*: Authors.

**Table 9.1**

| Year | Share of non-communist World output OPEC | Share of non-communist World output Saudi Arabia | Price of OPEC crude oil (% change) |
|------|------|------|------|
| 1970 | 58.4 | 9.3 | – |
| 1971 | 62.9 | 11.3 | 29.6 |
| 1972 | 63.7 | 13.7 | 8.6 |
| 1973 | 67.5 | 16.0 | 38.9 |
| 1974 | 67.8 | 18.0 | 262.1 |
| 1975 | 65.4 | 16.4 | 9.4 |
| 1976 | 67.5 | 18.4 | 10.0 |
| 1977 | 67.0 | 19.2 | 11.9 |
| 1978 | 64.5 | 18.1 | 0.4 |
| 1979 | 63.2 | 18.9 | 44.4 |
| 1980 | 63.2 | 21.3 | 65.3 |
| 1981 | 59.5 | 23.1 | 11.8 |
| 1982 | 48.6 | 16.3 | −2.5 |
| 1983 | 45.7 | 13.0 | −12.8 |
| 1984 | 44.3 | 11.6 | −2.1 |
| 1985 | 41.7 | 8.5 | −4.3 |
| 1986 | 44.9 | 11.7 | −14.5 |
| 1987 | 45.0 | 10.2 | −23.8 |
| 1988 | 47.3 | 11.6 | −1.6 |
| 1989 | 49.7 | 11.2 | 0.0 |
| 1990 | 50.7 | 13.7 | 23.5 |
| 1991 | 59.7 | 20.3 | −14.6 |

*Source*: Adapted from Carlton, D W and Perloff, J M (1994) *Modern Industrial Organisation*, 2nd edn, HarperCollins, New York.

## ◆ CASE STUDY 9.4

# The rise and fall of the Net Book Agreement

Refer to the Business Application case study on p 108 of Chapter 6. In a competitive market, supporters of the Net Book Agreement argued, esoteric and specialised books would be priced too high for readers be able to buy and these would thus not continue to be published. Only mainstream, high-volume books with low price elasticity of demand would generate profits for the publishers. The Net Book Agreement protected the publishers of such material because it required that the publishers' price for books be maintained in all outlets. There was therefore no price competition allowed on the part of retailers.

### ◆ Exercise 9.2

Explain the view that the Net Book Agreement set up a cartel which keeps the price of books artificially high and claims that it would be better to 'pile 'em high and sell 'em cheap'.

Answer with reference to the price elasticity of demand for various types of books and the total level of revenue gained by retailers in each area.

## DELIVERED PRICING

The concept of **delivered pricing** is relatively simple. Where organisations are geographically dispersed but in competition with each other, the price quoted to customers is likely to be the 'door' (or factory) price plus transport costs. Thus, customers receive a quote related to receiving the product at their own door. Delivered pricing is more likely to be experienced in industry-to-industry business, rather than in retail business.

Where a number of organisations are competing on delivered prices, the price they would charge a given customer will rise at a diminishing rate with distance (and hence transport cost). The fact that organisations are competing on such a basis is sometimes termed 'spatial competition'. Haddock (1982) makes the point that all organisations involved in spatial competition are likely to use 'basing-point' pricing to set their door price; *see* Figure 9.11. All door prices are likely to be similar as a result of the homogenous nature of the product. Thus, price differentials are caused by different transport costs. However, within the same region, prices are still likely to be similar. Haddock questions the door-price similarity. Is it due to the fact that organisations are colluding on the door price, or is it due to the fact that there is non-collusive behaviour, perhaps following the price changes of a price leader of some sort?

# LIMIT PRICING

**Limit pricing** occurs when a dominant organisation or group of organisations in an industry reduce the market price of the product to such an extent that potential entrants are deterred. The concept of limit pricing was developed by Bain (1956). His main argument was that, by maintaining a price above the competitive price, the incumbent(s) can deter potential entrants, or potential entrants are deterred from the industry via barriers to entry. Thus, Bain was attempting to explain why prices could be set above the market's theoretically competitive level and yet no entry occurred.

In this model, the LAC (long run average cost) curve is assumed to be L-shaped and to remain constant beyond the minimum cost level. The quantity at which the minimum cost level is reached is the optimal scale of production (the optimal plant size within the industry) and is denoted by $\bar{x}$. The minimum cost level is also the competitive price level: price cannot fall below LAC in the long run. *See*

**Figure 9.11**

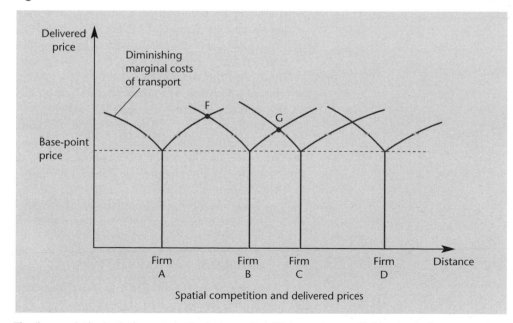

Spatial competition and delivered prices

The 'base-point' price is the organisation's door price. All door prices are likely to be similar as a result of the homogenous nature of the product. Price differentials are caused by different transport costs. However, within the same region, prices are still likely to be similar. Firms A and B's delivered prices are the same at the point of intersection between their marginal costs of transport lines, point F. This is greater than the price level at the intersection between Firms B and C's marginal transport costs, because B and C are closer together. The *x* axis shows distance between firms.

Figure 9.12. Total industry demand is given by DD and the competitive market size, if it were to exist, may be found at the intersection of the demand curve and the LAC curve.

Bain argued that, in pure competition, the market price would be equal to the level of LAC and LMC. In a monopolistically competitive market, the price would be equal to the LAC at a point of tangency, but greater than LMC (excess capacity exists because costs are not minimised). Any entrant assumes that the entry price will be charged after their entry. They are thus drawn to the market by the earnings potential of the limit price. Incumbents attempt to maintain a limit price which is not attractive to newcomers. The limit price is greater than the competitive price; the limit price $P_L$ therefore includes a margin above that competitive price. This margin is called the **condition of entry** and denotes the amount by which incumbents may raise the price above the competitive level without attracting entrants. Mathematically:

$$E = \frac{P_L - P_C}{P_C}$$

**Figure 9.12**

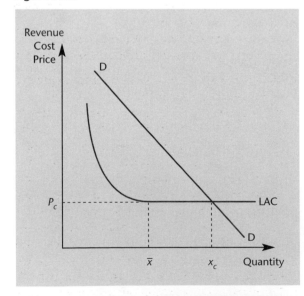

The quantity at which the minimum cost level is reached is the optimal scale of production (the optimal plant size within the industry), $\bar{x}$. The minimum cost level is also the competitive price level, $P_c$ – price cannot fall below LAC in the long run. Total industry demand is given by DD and the competitive market size, if it were to exist, would be found at the intersection of the demand curve and the LAC curve: $x_c$.

where,

E = condition of entry
$P_L$ = limit price
$P_C$ = competitive price (where $P_C$ = LAC)

By rearranging, it is possible to separate out the limit price:

$$P_L = P_C(1+E)$$

While the price level in itself does not act as a deterrent to entry, there are barriers to entry which cause a time lag or financial burden on the potential entrant. These barriers, according to Bain, may act as deterrents. The barriers to entry are:

■ Product differentiation.
■ The absolute cost advantage of established organisations.
■ Economies of scale earned by incumbents.
■ Initial capital requirements for entrants.

The limit price can vary, according to a variety of factors. If it is assumed that the limit price *is* maintained once the entrant has joined the market, the following observations apply:

■ Market share of the entrant. If this is greater than $\bar{x}$ there is no barrier. If, however, the market share falls below $\bar{x}$, LAC are greater and the limit price (and E) will be greater than $P_C$. The smaller the entrant's market share, the greater the $P_L$ and the greater the E.
■ The number of firms as incumbents. The greater the number of firms, the smaller each individual's market share and thus the higher the limit price (and the entry gap) may be.
■ The steepness of the LAC curve also has an effect on $P_L$: the steeper the curve, the higher the limit price.
■ The more elastic the demand curve, the higher limit price can be.

---

◆ **Exercise 9.3**

1 Vary the steepness of the LAC to show how the limit price will vary.

2 On the same axes, show the difference in limit price between a relatively elastic market demand curve and a relatively inelastic curve.

---

The Bain model of limit pricing thus puts forward the case that, at the limit price, incumbent firms can enter the industry, but that there are other barriers to entry. This model has been criticised for assuming that the limit price is maintained after entry has occurred. The Sylos postulate provides the alternative view that the pre-entry quantity is maintained by incumbent firms, but that total production will rise and, therefore, that price will tend towards the competitive level.

## PRICING FOR OTHER OBJECTIVES

Baumol's sales revenue-maximisation model (*see* Chapter 3) outlines the situation where, due to a minimum profit constraint, the sales revenue maximiser has reason to reduce price from a profit-maximising level to that which will stimulate extra sales for the organisation. The rationale for this may be factors such as stability of income, increasing market share etc.; all objectives which tend to suggest a longer-term perspective on the part of the firm.

## PRICE DISCRIMINATION

Price discrimination is usually practised by a monopolist, or a group of organisations acting together as a monopolist would. It occurs when the organisation charges some customers a higher price than others for an identical product, or charges a customer a higher average price on a smaller quantity/volume purchase than on a larger one.

As a definition, Parkin and King (1997) propose that price discrimination is '*an attempt by a monopoly to capture the consumer surplus (or as much of the surplus as possible) for itself*', that is, to charge as closely as possible to each individual consumer's preferred price for a product or service, therefore reducing their consumer surplus and capturing it as profit for the organisation. If, in Figure 9.13, the organisation is able to charge every price between *P* and *C*, thus satisfying the needs of all customers exactly, then the area *PEC* is revenue for the firm. Had only one price, *P*, been in effect, the area *PEC* would have been consumer surplus: the amount above the market price which some consumers are willing to pay.

Examples of price discrimination include the act of charging students and retired citizens a reduced fee for public transport, dental care etc. Price distinctions are also commonly made between business and domestic consumers of a range of goods

**Figure 9.13**

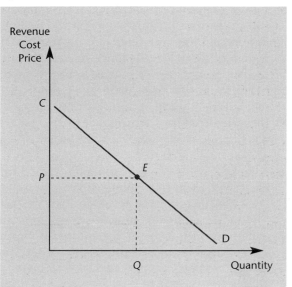

If the organisation is able to charge every price between *P* and *C*, thus satisfying the needs of all customers exactly, area *PEC* is total revenue for the organisation. Had only one price, *P*, been in effect, the area *PEC* would have been consumer surplus: the amount above the market price which some consumers are willing to pay. Thus, charging different prices allows the organisation to gain consumer surplus for itself.

and services: from energy and water consumption to stationery and office furniture.

There are three major conditions which must be satisfied in order to achieve successful discrimination:

■ Separable markets: it must be possible to prevent arbitrage selling from the lower-price buyer to the higher-price buyer in different markets. Separating markets is easiest where the criteria for separation is easily checked. Price discrimination based on gender or age is easily observed and usually easy for people to prove. As a result, service providers find it easier than others to discriminate on price. Instant-consumption products and direct services (for example dental care) can only be 'consumed' by the individual. It is not possible for someone who pays less for the same service to have dental care on your behalf!

■ The markets must exhibit differing price elasticities so that price discrimination is profitable. The level of marginal revenue in each of the markets must be equal in order for profits to be maximised. This level of marginal revenue is equal to the value where the organisation's MC are equal to the combined (summed) markets'

MR. *See* Figure 9.14. ΣMR is derived from the sum of $MR_A$ and $MR_B$ (that is, $MR_A + MR_B$). At the profit-maximising point ΣMR = MC, the appropriate quantity in each market may be found ($Q_A$ and $Q_B$). Tracing upwards to the demand curve in each market from the appropriate quantity to be sold gives the profit-maximising price in each market. By comparing the price level in each market to the general AVC curve, profit/loss levels in the individual markets may be derived.

■ A lack of price competition from rival firms must exist to prevent price competition eroding the profit-maximising levels in each market. Therefore, successful price discriminators are usually monopolists or a cartelised group of firms. There is an exception here: where the level of service is important and customers are willing to pay extra to gain the services of a particular individual or organisation, even though price competition exists, the perceived value to customers of gaining the higher quality service will be worth the extra charge.

Depending on the level to which organisations are able successfully to discriminate on price, there are three categories, or degrees, of price discrimination.

## First-degree/perfect price discrimination

The organisation is able to charge each consumer the maximum they are willing to pay for the product. Thus the producer is able to capture the entire consumer surplus from the consuming public. Each consumer pays a different, individual price – which is related to their consumption decisions, income etc.

An example here would be highly skilled professionals who are able to charge what they think each consumer is willing to pay for their services: lawyers, doctors and dentists could fall into this category.

## Second-degree/imperfect price discrimination

Discrimination between buyers is based on a time or urgency basis, or on a quantity/volume basis. In the case of a time basis, those willing to pay a higher price will receive the product or service immediately, while those prepared to wait for a longer period will pay a lower price to gain the same product output. In this case, the discrimination is imperfect because the producer does not

**Figure 9.14**

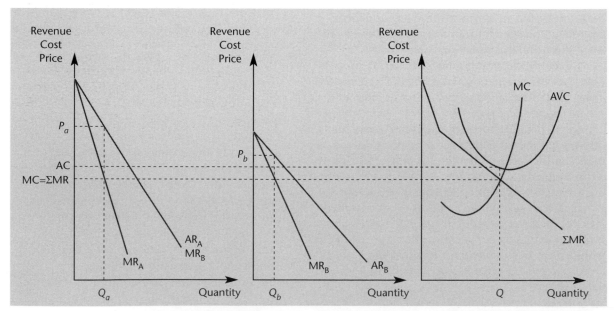

ΣMR is derived from the sum of $MR_A$ and $MR_B$. At the profit-maximising point, ΣMR = MC, the appropriate quantity in each market may be found ($Q_A$ and $Q_B$), using each organisation's MR curve individually. Tracing upwards to the demand curve in each market from the appropriate quantity to be sold gives the profit-maximising price in each market. By comparing the price level in each market to the general AVC curve, profit/loss levels in the individual markets may be derived.

**Table 9.2 Block pricing example: prices charged for 5-litre tins of domestic-quality paint to professional decorators**

| Price (per 5-litre tin) | Quantity bought |
|---|---|
| £15 | First 10 |
| £12.50 | Next 10 |
| £11.00 | Next 10 |
| £10.00 | All over 30 |

necessarily capture all of the consumer surplus. There will be some consumers who maintain their consumer surplus despite the discrimination.

An example of the time/urgency basis would be choosing between an expensive, express photographic film-processing service versus waiting longer for the return of the photographs, but at a reduced price compared to the express price.

An example of the quantity/volume basis would be offering discounts to consumers according to the amount of output they consume. A sliding-scale approach may be used, where progressive units in an order are cheaper. Or units may be 'blocked' into several distinct pricing blocks (*see* Table 9.2).

## Third-degree (imperfect price discrimination)

This occurs when firms differentiate between consumers in two or more ways for a given product/service at a given point in time. For example, consumers may be separated according to type (small business, household, industrial) and by the time of day at which they consume the product or service.

In much of Europe, telephone and electricity charges are based on the time of day *and* day of week *and* type of customer. This is third-degree price discrimination: more than one set of discrimination criteria are being used at any one time.

The difficulty for the price discriminator is in deciding what its optimal output is and distributing that output among the different markets so that the revenue received will be optimised/maximised.

It is mathematically possible to derive the relative prices to be charged in two different markets in order to achieve profit maximisation:

Given that,

$$MR = P(1 + 1/E_d)$$

If the marginal revenues are the same in each market, then,

$$MR_1 = MR_2$$

However,

$$MR_1 = P_1(1 + 1/E_{d1}) \quad \text{and} \quad MR_2 = P_2(1 + 1/E_{d2})$$

Thus,

$$P_1(1 + 1/E_{d1}) = P_2(1 + 1/E_{d2})$$

Therefore, it is possible to determine the relative prices in the given markets:

$$P_1/P_2 = (1 + 1/E_{d2}) / (1 + 1/E_{d1})$$

## ◆ CASE STUDY 9.5

### Anglian Water car parks

Around the perimeter of Rutland Water, a reservoir in the UK, the owners, Anglian Water, operate several car parks. These are positioned very close to purpose-built cafés, restaurants, boat and cycle-hire centres. Access to the area surrounding the reservoir is free of charge and thousands of visitors each year spend a day enjoying the countryside, fishing or cycling around the reservoir.

While there is no charge for access, Anglian Water does charge for car parking. The charges are modest, but exhibit an element of second-degree price discrimination, based on the time/urgency criterion. During the week and on Saturdays, the charge is £1 per day (transferable to all other car parks throughout the day). On the busiest day in terms of visitor numbers, Sunday, the daily charge rises to £2 per day (still transferable).

Anglian Water is therefore attempting to gain extra revenue on a Sunday. It knows that more people visit on a Sunday. Although the price is double, it is still very modest and so people are still willing to pay. Thus, Anglian Water is capturing consumer surplus for itself as revenue.

*Source*: Authors

## ◆ Exercise 9.4

1  List five examples of price discrimination of which you are aware, either through personal experience or general knowledge.

2  How are the markets separated?

3  How many markets are there?

4  Is the separation effective? How is it controlled by the supplier?

# TRANSFER PRICING

Large firms such as ICI, Coopers and Lybrand and other multinational corporations (MNCs) are often split (decentralised) into profit and/or cost centres (divisions) in order to create efficiency within each of the divisions and within the organisation as a whole. The rationale behind cost and profit centres is that individual managers are more easily able to monitor and control costs than is a centralised function set up for that purpose.

If the systems and processes within the organisation are such that divisions are passing their intermediate products to other divisions, then a transaction must take place between divisions. Then each is able to account for its receipt of production units and its production of a finished (in its context) product to be sold on. Remember, these transactions are internal to the organisation as a whole. However, prices must be set and sales recorded. The prices which are used in the sale from division to division are **transfer prices**.

## Transfer pricing with no external market

When a division (A) of the organisation is merely supplying another division (B) with a product where there is no external demand for the intermediate product, what are the organisation's and the divisions' optimal output decisions?

Assume that the organisation has a profit-maximising objective. Each division will need to be induced to produce and sell a quantity of the (intermediate) product which will generate maximum overall profits. The decision-making process will follow the logic laid out below.

The overall MC curve will be equal to the sum of the two parts, i.e.:

$$MC_t = MC_a + MC_b$$

The organisation's MR and demand positions will be known, therefore it is possible to determine the overall profit-maximising price and quantity. Knowledge of the optimal transfer price is required such that Division A will produce an optimal quantity of the intermediate product, Division B will produce an optimal finished quantity of products and also the market price set will be at profit-maximising levels.

Assuming that the organisation produces an optimal quantity ($Q$) overall, Division A will also produce this quantity such that:

$$Q = Q_a$$

The transfer price ($P_{tr}$) should be set at the level of MC generated by A in production of $Q$ units. Therefore:

$$P_{tr} = MC_a$$

At this level, the demand for the intermediate product will be perfectly elastic; it will be able to sell as many units as it wishes at this price. It will not sell greater than $Q$, however, because any quantity would not generate maximum profits for Division A. Thus:

$$P_{tr} = MC_a = MR_a$$

For Division B, the net marginal revenue (NMR) for its finished product will be:

$$NMR = MR_t - MC_b$$

This level will be exactly the same as $MC_a$ (since $MC_t - MC_b = MC_a$ when $MR_t = MC_t$). Thus, the profit-maximising quantity for Division B to produce will be $Q$, while the profit-maximising price for Division B will be derived when:

$$NMR = MC_a \text{ and therefore } NMR = MR_a$$

which implies a production/sales level of $Q$ and price $P$: the profit-maximising level. *See* Figure 9.15.

## International transfer pricing

Larger organisations and multinational corporations which have divisions or subsidiaries in different countries have an added dimension to their transfer pricing decisions. It will be necessary for them to adhere to the local legislation, tax and duty regulations etc. The opportunity exists to increase the profits of the organisation by manipulation of the transfer prices between countries. These exist in several areas.

### Tax and import duty savings

If the intermediate product is to be transferred between countries with different tax rates on corporate profits, then it can be in the organisation's interest to manipulate the transfer price accordingly. Obviously, the demand conditions need to be right; this is easiest to ensure when the markets are internally linked.

■ If the intermediate product is being transferred to a country with high taxes on corporate profits, then it is in its interests to keep the transfer price high so that earnings are suppressed in the destination country.

**Figure 9.15**

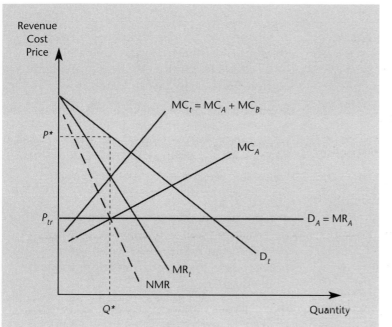

When there is no external market for intermediate products, the profit-maximising transfer for A's product will be at the level given by $MC_A = MR_A$. This is at the optimum market quantity for the finished product, $Q^*$, but the profit-maximising price for the finished product is $P^*$, at the *net* marginal revenue point, $NMR = MC_A$.

■ If the intermediate product is being transferred from a country where the corporate taxes are higher than in the destination country, it is in the organisation's interests to keep the transfer price low so that the majority of the profits are stated in the country where the tax rate is not as great.

■ If the intermediate product is being moved onto a country where the ad valorem import duty is high, then it will be in the organisation's interest to keep the transfer price (and therefore the duty payable) as low as is practicable.

### Repatriation of dividends
Where the repatriation of dividends is restricted, it is possible to move potential earnings out of the country by keeping the transfer price low and therefore transferring potential earnings to another division.

### Finance of new subsidiaries
In order to make the best of new company credit arrangements etc., an organisation may find it in its interests to keep transfer prices to the new subsidiary low so that it generates a healthy (and therefore attractive) balance sheet and is therefore in a position to attract new credit from the locality.

### Labour and public relations
In some situations, a high level of stated profits for a division will cause customers to demand lower prices, or for the labour force to demand higher wage rates. Charging higher transfer prices can alleviate this problem by causing the local profits to be understated.

## SUMMARY

◆ This chapter has introduced and examined a number of decisions which firms may have to make as they price their products.

◆ It was seen that the market structure in which the firm is operating is an important factor for the firm's pricing decision. Monopolists are 'price makers' and firms operating in perfectly competitive markets are 'price takers'. Oligopolists may either make or take prices.

◆ Oligopolists operate in markets where there are few sellers. Competition in oligopolistic markets tends to concentrate on non-price factors. Promotional activities and advertising are important to the oligopoly firm.

◆ Where a group of organisations join together for common interest, a cartel is formed. Cartels are usually illegal, due to their detrimental effects on the levels of welfare in the market. Cartels may be joint profit maximising or market sharing.

◆ The price level in a monopoly is likely to be higher and with a restricted quantity available compared to competitive situations.

◆ Monopolists are able to choose which price to charge their customers. By discriminating, on price, consumer surplus may be converted into revenue for the price discriminator.

◆ Natural monopolies exist when the market conditions are such that one producer owns the factors of production, or that economies of scale arising from a monopoly situation are not achievable when more than one organisation operates within the market/industry.

◆ Limit pricing is used by organisations wishing protect their position in a market. The limit price is the greatest price which they can possibly charge without attracting entrants from elsewhere.

◆ If divisions within organisations sell intermediate products between themselves, a transfer price is charged. There can be financial benefits from setting the correct transfer price. Where an external market also exists for the intermediate product, price discrimination may take place.

## REVIEW QUESTIONS

1  If an organisation manufacturing and selling video computer games in different countries    wishes to discriminate on price, advise on the conditions necessary for successful implementation.

2  Given that the marginal cost in market A ($MC_A$) is equal to 35 ECUs while price elasticity of demand ($E^P_d$) has been estimated at –1.6, while the marginal cost in market B ($MC_B$) is 40 ECUs, with an estimated price elasticity of demand ($E^P_d$) of –2.5, determine the profit-maximising price levels to be charged in each market.

3  In the summer of 1995, a sign on the Confiroute-owned French autoroute gave the prices of various types of fuel available at the next five service stations. The operators of the service stations were also displayed. One of the signs showed the prices for unleaded fuel, per litre. The prices were as shown in Table 9.3.

**Table 9.3**

| Distance | Operator | Price |
|----------|----------|-------|
| 2 km | Esso | 6.11 |
| 28 km | Shell | 6.11 |
| 55 km | Mobil | 6.09 |
| 89 km | BP | 6.02 |
| 141 km | Total | 6.02 |

Account for the differences in price displayed. What factors are likely to affect the pricing decisions of the sellers?

4  Outline the considerations for an organisation wishing to set internal (transfer) prices for its intermediate products.

5 Identify the dominant strategy equilibrium for the prisoner's dilemma given in Figure 9.16. The payoffs shown are for the two organisations in a duopoly market situation. These two are the only operators of rural bus services along the same routes. The dilemma is whether or not to increase the frequency of services. Overall, between the two, more frequent services will mean that fewer passengers travel on each bus, thus reducing the revenue received per bus. The number of passengers carried in total will be increased. If both bus operators increase the frequency of services, the extra cost of provision will exceed the additional revenue. If only one operator increases frequency, it will more than cover its additional costs, earning greater profits, while the other operator will suffer lost passengers and see its earnings fall.

**Figure 9.16**

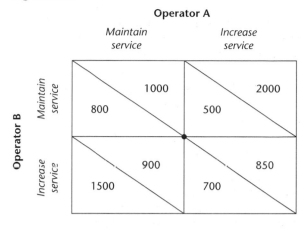

## GLOSSARY OF NEW TERMS

**Cartel:** A group of organisations which makes restrictive agreements with respect to quantities and hence prices for the mutual gain of the cartel members.

**Conjectural variation:** The expected change in a rival organisation's strategic variable as a ratio of a change in the strategic variable of the (own) organisation under consideration. For example, a price rise by Firm A may have a likelihood of reaction by Firm B of 0.6 (or 60 per cent).

**Delivered price:** The price charged by a seller to deliver the product to the door of the customer. Delivered prices include the transport costs charged by the seller.

**Limit price:** The highest price level which may be charged in a market without attracting potential entrants to that market.

**Monopolistic competition:** There is some distinction between products on a brand basis and so each one of the many sellers is able to dictate its own selling price and thus influence quantity sold.

**Monopoly:** One seller exists in the market. Therefore it has complete influence over selling price or quantity sold.

**Oligopoly:** (Literally, few sellers.) The few firms operating within an oligopolistic market are mutually dependent (interdependent) on each other with reference to the selling price and quantity sold. Non-price competition is important; this is a common feature of oligopolistic behaviour.

**Perfect competition:** A market situation where the firm is one of an infinite number within its market. Each firm is thus unable to influence price or quantity sold of the homogenous product.

**Reaction function:** The 'best response' or 'maximum payoff' function for a firm in an oligopoly, given knowledge of other firms' behaviour.

**Transfer price:** Internal prices charged by organisations when intermediate products are sold on by divisions within the organisation.

## READING

Adelman, M A (1982) 'OPEC as a cartel' in Griffin, J M and Teece, D J (eds) *OPEC Behaviour and World Oil Prices*, George Allen & Unwin, London.

American study and Belgian study, University of Leuven, on price elasticity in demand for books reported in *Financial Times*, 'Profits left on the shelf' by Frances Fishwick, 18 June 1996.

Bain, J S (1956) *Barriers to New Competition*, Harvard University Press, Cambridge, Mass.

Chamberlin, E (1993) *Theory of Monopolistic Competition*, Harvard University Press, Cambridge, Mass.

Cohen, K J and Cyert, R M (1965) *Theory of the Firm*, Prentice-Hall, Upper Saddle River, NJ.

Cournot, A (1838) *Rechèrches sur les Principes Mathématiques de la Theorie des Richesses*, Paris.

Fellner, W (1950) 'Collusion and its limits under oligopoly', *AER Papers and Proceedings*.
*Outlines some of the problems facing a cartel operating within oligopoly market conditions.*

Haddock, D D (1982) 'Basing-point pricing: competitive versus collusive theories', *American Economic Review*, Vol 72, June, pp 289–306.
*A discussion of spatial pricing, with the 'door price' as the base or reference price.*

Hall, R L and Hitch, C I (1939) 'Price theory and business behaviour', *Oxford Economic Papers*, May, pp 12–45. *Provides an analysis of the manner in which prices are determined in oligopoly markets using the kinked demand curve as a tool.*

Hnyilcza, E and Pindyk, R S (1976) 'Pricing policies for a two part exhaustible resource cartel: the case of OPEC', *European Economic Review*, no 8, pp 139–54.

Pindyk, R S (1978) 'Gains to producers from the cartelization of exhaustible resources', *Review of Economic Statistics*, no 60, pp 238–51.

Stackelberg, H von (1952) *The Theory of the Market Economy*, Hodge, London.

Sweezy, P (1939) 'Demand under conditions of oligopoly', *Journal of Political Economy*, Vol 47, August, pp 568–73. *Introduces the kinked demand curve as a tool to determine the equilibrium position in oligopoly markets.*

**Further reading**
Koutsoyiannis, A (1993) *Modern Microeconomics*, 2nd edn, Macmillan, London. *An intermediate-level economics text. A mathematical approach is used and there is some useful insight into the theoretical concepts relating to pricing.*

Miller, R L and Meiners R E (1986) *Intermediate Microeconomics*, 3rd edn, McGraw-Hill, New York. *Less technical and mathematical than Koutsoyiannis, but still offers some useful explanations.*

Ferguson, P R and Ferguson, G J (1994) *Industrial Economics: Issues and Perspectives*, 2nd edn, Macmillan, Basingstoke. *Comprehensive with respect to the welfare losses under conditions of monopoly.*

Carlton, D W and Perloff, J M (1994) *Modern Industrial Organisation*, 2nd edn, HarperCollins, New York. *Includes a detailed analysis of OPEC as a case study.*

Parkin, M and King, D (1997) *Economics*, 3rd edn, Addison Wesley Longman, Harlow. *An introductory economics text providing basic explanations of concepts such as price discrimination.*

CHAPTER **10**

# PRICING PRACTICES

## OBJECTIVES

◆ To consider the pricing strategies that are actually used by organisations.

◆ To investigate the pricing strategies which organisations use under conditions of incomplete information.

◆ To examine the approach of markup pricing within organisations and show how it is related to marginalist approaches to pricing.

◆ To develop the methods that organisations use to price their products in established markets.

◆ To establish the main methods which organisations use to set new product prices.

◆ To identify how product prices change, as competition, learning effects and the product lifecycle affect the price of the product.

◆ To outline the empirical evidence on pricing behaviour.

## KEY TERMS

Markup pricing

Penetration pricing

Predatory pricing

Prestige pricing

Price fixing

Price lining

Price positioning

Price tendering

Product bundle pricing

Product lifecycle

Promotional pricing

Skimming price

## CHAPTER OUTLINE

Business application

Introduction

Pricing with incomplete information

Search costs and pricing methods

Pricing objectives

Markup pricing

Case study 10.1 Profit margins in action

Case study 10.2 Built from the bargain basement

Case study 10.3 The travel industry

Pricing in existing markets

Price positioning

Prestige pricing

Case study 10.4 Executive cars

Price lining

Promotional pricing

Product bundle pricing

Predatory pricing

Price fixing

Price tendering

New product pricing

Skimming price strategy

Penetration pricing

Determining price and quality jointly

Impact of learning curves

Pricing and the product lifecycle

Empirical evidence on pricing

Case study 10.5 New car prices: don't be taken for a ride

Summary

Review questions

Appendix 10.1 The relationship between demand and marginal revenue

Appendix 10.2 Non-smooth marginal revenue curves

Appendix 10.3 The relationship between marginal variable cost and marginal cost

Glossary of new terms

Reading

## Drug companies face anti-trust review

**FT**

Anti-trust authorities in the US have launched what could become a wide-ranging investigation into the way drugs companies set their prices. A number of the 22 drugs makers in the Federal Trade Commission's (FTC's) order authorising the inquiry maintained – in March 1996 – that they did not collude in setting prices. Schering Plough, for instance, repeated earlier assertions that its prices are arrived at 'entirely legally' and are 'determined in response to market forces'.

Companies being reviewed include big non-US manufacturers such as Glaxo Wellcome, as well as big US manufacturers such as Merck and American Home Products.

The Federal investigation comes at a time when pharmaceutical companies have begun to raise their prices in the US again, after a period in which most had held them level. Political pressure on the drugs makers from the early years of the Clinton presidency has receded, following the failure of the administration's healthcare reform plans.

The FTC's review follows an agreement by a group of large drugs companies to settle a claim from retail pharmacists that they had colluded in charging higher prices to pharmacists than they did to other, larger customers. A settlement that cost the drugs companies $400m.

In an order authorising the inquiry, however, the agency's commissioners said its terms of reference covered whether the manufacturers were 'engaging in unlawful concerted activities to raise, fix, maintain or stabilise the prices of pharmaceutical products in the United States'. Even if the FTC's investigation focuses primarily on prices charged to small pharmacists, it could prove more damaging to the drugs makers than the settlement they recently agreed. That settlement did not require the manufacturers to change their pricing practices in any way. Any action by Federal regulators, on the other hand, would almost certainly require a change in practice.

*Source: Financial Times, 28 March 1996. Reprinted with permission.*

## INTRODUCTION

In Chapter 9 a variety of pricing models were put forward covering a range of competitive conditions, objectives and entry conditions. This chapter seeks to discuss the pricing practices actually adopted by organisations and the consequences which these have not only for the organisation's output but also for its profits. The case study on pharmaceutical manufacturers suggests one approach to pricing in practice – price fixing. There is, however, no single approach to the way organisations develop the prices for their products and empirical studies give conflicting views. There may also be differences between what business decision makers say they are doing and what they are actually doing. It might be expected that the pricing decision will depend on the type of product, the level of competition organisations face in their markets, the age of their products, whether they are existing or new products, the nature of production, i.e. whether the products are produced singly or in joint production, and whether or not the organisation is using its full capacity. Thus if an organisation faces some, if not all, of these different factors in its market alternative pricing formulations are possible. It would appear that,

because management knowledge and expertise differ, this too may influence pricing approaches. Some may have knowledge of marginal concepts, others may not. Moreover, it could be argued that too much attention has been given to price and that this is only one factor in a raft of attributes that concern the consumer in their decision to purchase a product/service.

It is also important to consider what is meant by price. The published price for a commodity may differ from the actual price paid, since the purchaser may be able to negotiate a range of discounts. Prices may also differ if the product is to be sold to a consumer or another organisation. In addition, some prices may not be known with certainty since the negotiated price is kept secret.

Prices also tend to be dynamic and this chapter considers some of the factors behind the change in prices over time. In addition, when considering actual pricing practices, organisations often find themselves considering their pricing under conditions of uncertainty. Often organisations find themselves uncertain about future demand, future costs and future competition. These factors influence the pricing strategy chosen. This chapter therefore examines the pricing of products/services under conditions of uncertainty, a situation far removed from the theories of pricing behaviour analysed in Chapter 9.

This chapter has not adopted a lifecycle approach to pricing, beginning with new product pricing before moving on to the pricing of existing products, but considers the more mature markets first before exploring in detail the additional uncertainties of bringing a new product to the market.

## PRICING WITH INCOMPLETE INFORMATION

In Chapter 9 the pricing models developed were analysed under conditions of certainty. Here the organisation was clear about its level of competition, had an objective of maximising profits, knew sufficient information to construct its marginal revenue and marginal cost curves and could estimate its demand conditions with certainty. In practice, even if some of the information is known with accuracy, firms rarely know all the information they would like. In Chapter 3 the question was raised as to whether firms actually seek to maximise profits at all. Lester's (1946) work further raised the question of the practical difficulties that organisations might face in trying to determine what their marginal costs were by experimentation, particularly in the case of multiplant processes. In fact, as already discussed regarding the work by Hall and Hitch (1939), there are shortcomings with the marginalist approach to pricing. In particular, there is a great deal of uncertainty in oligopolistic markets which tends to encourage firms to set prices well in advance of production, planning to maintain them over a period of time. Prices determined in this way differ from the conventional wisdom of market-clearing prices set up through the interaction of supply and demand.

It may be possible, however, to adapt marginalist pricing analysis under conditions of uncertainty. Assuming that an organisation has some estimate of its demand curve, it is now possible to derive some estimation of its marginal revenue equation. If you are unsure about the relationship between demand and marginal revenue, see Chapter 6 or Appendix 10.1. If an organisation can now find its marginal cost function, then placing marginal revenue equal to marginal cost gives the profit-maximising level of output. If you now turn to Appendix 10.1 once again, when the profit-maximising level of output is known it is possible to find the profit-maximising price level.

An alternative route to the marginalist pricing strategy outlined in Chapter 9 can be found from the starting point of elasticity. Suppose that the organisation has an estimate of the current elasticity of demand for its product. The own price elasticity of demand is given by:

$$E_d = \Delta Q/\Delta P \times P/Q \text{ or } dQ/dP \times P/Q$$

To find the optimal price we can proceed in one of two ways. First, in Chapter 6 a relationship between marginal cost and elasticity was developed. This relationship was:

$$MC = P(1 + 1/E_d)$$

Therefore, if the organisation knows its elasticity of demand and an estimate of its current marginal costs, then the optimal price can be found by substituting into the above equation for marginal cost.

Alternatively, given the estimate for own point price elasticity of demand, what must be known is at least one pair of price (P) and quantity (Q). Therefore, from the elasticity formula above it is possible to determine $\Delta Q/\Delta P$ or $dQ/dP$. If the organisation believes that it faces a linear demand function of the form $P = a - bQ$, where $a$ is the intercept term and $b$ the slope of the demand curve, then it is possible to relate the slope of the demand curve to part of the elasticity equation above. The slope of the demand curve, $b$, shows the relationship between the change in price and the change in quantity and can also be written as $\Delta P/\Delta Q$ or $dP/dQ$. Therefore, the term $dQ/dP$ obtained from the elasticity formula is the reciprocal of the slope of the demand curve. Thus in the demand equation we can now write down a number or expression for the slope term in the demand equation. With regard to the demand equation, the organisation would now know the slope of the demand equation, and because it knows at least one value for price and quantity – these were used to calculate $\Delta Q/\Delta P$ in the elasticity formula – then it can substitute these values into its demand equation to determine the value of the intercept term. Because the organisation now knows both $a$ and $b$, it is possible to write down the straight-line equation for demand. Once the demand equation is known, it is possible to deduce the equation for total revenue and calculate the marginal revenue equation. We can now determine the optimal price using the procedure outlined earlier and shown in Appendix 10.1. Although this may look tortuous, a simple example might help at this stage.

Suppose that the elasticity of demand $E_d = -2$, and price $P = 15$ and quantity $Q = 10$. Using the elasticity formula $E_d = \Delta Q/\Delta P \times P/Q$ we can calculate $\Delta Q/\Delta P$. That is:

$$-2 = \Delta Q/\Delta P \times 15/10, \text{ or } \Delta Q/\Delta P = -20/15$$

Since the slope of the demand equation is given by $\Delta P/\Delta Q$, which is the reciprocal of $\Delta Q/\Delta P$, then:

$$\Delta P/\Delta Q = -15/20$$

In the linear form of the demand equation, $P = a - bQ$, and the slope of the demand equation is $\Delta P/\Delta Q = -b$. Therefore:

$$-b = -15/20, \text{ or } b = 15/20$$

Our demand equation now becomes:

$$P = a - 15/20 \times Q$$

Since we know one price/quantity pairing, $Q = 10$ when $P = 15$, our demand equation becomes for this pair of price and quantity:

$$15 = a - 15/20 \times 10$$

Solving for $a$ gives the following: $a = 15/2$.

The general linear demand equation for any pair of price and quantity becomes:

$$P = 15/2 - 15/20 \times Q$$

It is now possible to follow the procedure outlined in Appendix 10.1.

One feature of the construction of both the marginal revenue and marginal cost equations (functions) is that they are based on one-unit changes in the level of output. Suppose that demand, the equation of which lies behind the construction of the total revenue equation, cannot be divided into single units of output, for example batches may come by the 100, 2000 and so on, or the organisation does not wish to, or have the ability to, compute one-unit changes in output – then the total revenue curve will be discontinuous. This discontinuity in the total revenue curve means that it is not possible to construct a smooth marginal revenue curve (see Appendix 10.2), therefore the optimal price for the product cannot be found. In this case the organisation is faced with comparing incremental costs and incremental revenues and choosing the price at which the maximum contribution is made.

## SEARCH COSTS AND PRICING METHODS

From the consumer's point of view, with a homogenous product it would be rational for consumers to search for the product with the lowest price, up to the point at which the costs of searching match any further reduction in price of the commodity as the products are sampled. So long as search costs are smaller than any reductions in price of the product achieved through searching, consumers will continue to search for the commodity. The process of search by the consumer means that if search costs are low organisations which offer lower-priced products will see high levels of consumer demand, while those which set their prices high will see low levels of demand. This confirms the earlier views of demand and price. If search costs are high, however, then those firms which have set higher prices may well see relatively high levels of demand.

In addition, there are two further factors to consider. Consumers, having searched for the commodity, may find it available at different prices. If after some point in their search process they wish to return to products which earlier they had rejected since they had anticipated finding a cheaper product, will these still be available? Second, do consumers know the range of prices of the commodities for which they are searching? It may also be argued that consumers will have different search costs. Some may have greater knowledge about the market through the various forms of advertising, personal contacts and the like; others might be constrained in their search process because of the lack of mobility and financial support. All these factors provide the opportunity, therefore, for the organisations to offer different prices even for a very similar product.

Search costs play their part in many items, such as running shoes or trainers. In many consumer catalogues consumers are asked to pay the full price for the most favoured brands. Nike Air Max Triax retail at £89 in consumer catalogues such as Family Album. Increasing the search for these trainers would indicate that at many sports shops they could be purchased for £69, while the purchase of a running magazine for £2.20 would show that these same trainers could be bought for £62. At each stage it can be argued that consumers trade off the increased costs of search for an additional price reduction.

From the organisation's viewpoint, the search costs are related to the information about costs and revenues. Obtaining information about marginal cost and marginal revenue may not be inexpensive and the extra costs incurred in finding more information may not be recouped in improvements in profits. It could well be that the current information about the way in which costs and revenues behave may be sufficient for an organisation to determine a price which is good enough for what they want. Of course, this is always presupposing that the organisation knows the terms marginal revenue and marginal costs. Thus it may be not too surprising that the decision makers in organisations choose a method to price their products which may not involve the marginalist approach outlined in Chapter 9. This is not to say that some organisations do not use the marginalist approach, but many small and medium-sized enterprises may be led to use different approaches because of the costs of finding out more precise information about costs and revenues measured against the benefits to be seen in terms of market share and improved levels of profits.

If the marginalist approach is not to be adopted, although organisations may be satisfied with other approaches to setting prices, then in theory there may be occasions when the optimal level of profits is not reached. In practice, however, the search costs which enable the firm to price at the optimal point may be greater than any gain in additional profits, thus these non-marginalist pricing strategies may be more optimal than they appear on first inspection. Nonetheless, organisations cannot always be sure that the pricing strategies they have adopted are better than those under marginalist pricing, particularly if they have no knowledge of the optimal price. Thus it could be argued that the organisation should regularly attempt to calculate the prices it would charge under marginalist methods.

Before discussing the various pricing strategies that organisations use, it may be worthwhile considering the organisation's pricing objectives.

the US and the UK sought a target rate of return. On first inspection this target rate of return appears to be in conflict with the goal of profit maximisation, yet if the target is set as a means to deter entry into the market it might be associated with the notion of long-term profit maximisation. Conversely, if the target market return is believed to be the maximum that can be obtained, this could be identified with short-run profit maximisation. However, it could be argued that the use of a target market return implies that a particular price is used to achieve this target and this price could be very different from the profit-maximising level.

Target market share, on the other hand, may not be compatible with profit maximisation, since the target market share may be linked to managerial decisions. It is possible that other business objectives may also move the organisation away from the profit-maximising price. For example, for planning purposes an organisation may set its price so that it can achieve consistent levels of sales over time, which may guarantee customers and reduce the stresses on management who may have to alter prices frequently to take account of changes in demand conditions. Although this procedure may not appear to be close to the marginalist approach, a consistent pricing strategy may help deter new entrants into the market and thus help towards long-term profit maximisation. Conversely, a new entrant which knows that the existing organisation is price inflexible can use the lags in its decision making to gain rapid market entry, leading to the incumbent firm facing much reduced profits.

Thus the pricing objectives or strategies of the organisation may influence how close or how far the organisation moves away from the marginalist approaches discussed earlier and in Chapter 9. Indeed, the question which we seek to ask and answer is, precisely what approaches do firms use in setting prices?

The remaining part of this chapter seeks to discuss the pricing methods that organisations use, both for new and existing products, commencing with markup pricing.

## PRICING OBJECTIVES

An organisation which seeks to maximise profits may well be operating a different pricing strategy to one which is trying to increase its market share. Work by Lanzillotti (1958) and Shipley (1981) suggested that the majority of organisations in both

## MARKUP PRICING

**Markup pricing** or cost-plus pricing (full cost pricing) is where an organisation sets the price of product to cover all direct costs plus a percentage markup as a contribution towards profits. The most common approach is for the firm to estimate, first, its average variable cost for producing and marketing an item for a normal or standard level of output. On to these variable costs the organisation adds an assessment of the overhead costs incurred in the production of the product. This overhead charge is usually expressed as a percentage of average variable costs. This provides the organisation with an estimated value for its average variable costs. On top of this figure for the estimated average variable cost is added a markup for profits.

Suppose that the variable costs in the production of an item are Kr10 million and the total overhead costs are Kr26 million, then overhead costs are apportioned to the product at 260 per cent of variable costs. Suppose further that the average variable cost of producing each item is Kr10, then the organisation adds to this Kr26 for overhead costs. Therefore the estimated value for average variable costs is Kr36. If on to this is added a markup of 20 per cent, then the total cost of the product will be Kr43.2. In terms of a mathematical expression, the markup pricing rule could be written as:

$$P = FAC + X\%(FAC)$$

where,

FAC = fully allocated costs per unit

Where there are no fixed costs, then the expression becomes:

$$P = AVC + X\%(AVC) \quad (10.1)$$

This can be simplified to:

$$P = AVC(1 + X\%) \quad (10.2)$$

From the organisation's point of view, it would be hoped that when considering the total sales of the product, the markup would be large enough to cover at least all of the overhead costs and variable costs. But how large can this markup be? Demand conditions or the level of competition in the market place may be very influential on the degree to which the firm can set its markup. A higher markup may be expected to reduce demand. However, the degree to which this reduction in demand affects the organisation's revenue and profits depends on the elasticity of demand for the product. Therefore, it is quite possible that profits could be increased by selling the product at a lower price.

Since it is based on average variable costs, rather than the interaction of marginal revenue and marginal cost, does this mean that the marginalist approach to pricing is distinct from the approach taken under markup pricing? It is

possible to establish a relationship between the two pricing mechanisms.

## Relationship between markup pricing and marginalist pricing

In Chapter 6 a relationship was established between marginal revenue (MR) and elasticity of demand. This relationship is shown below:

$$MR = P(1 + 1/E_d) \quad (10.3)$$

where $E_d$ is usually negative.

If the organisation is a profit seeker, the decision makers will set marginal revenue equal to marginal cost (MC). Equation 10.3 can now be rewritten as:

$$MC = P(1 + 1/E_d) \quad (10.4)$$

Rearranging Equation 10.4 to obtain the expression for price (P) gives.

$$P = MC \times 1/(1 + 1/E_d) \quad (10.5)$$

Taking the expression in brackets, $(1 + 1/E_d)$, then this can be rewritten as:

$$[E_d + 1]/E_d$$

$1/[E_d + 1]/E_d$ can now be rewritten as $E_d/(E_d + 1)$. Equation 10.5 now becomes:

$$P = MC \times E_d/(E_d + 1) \quad (10.6)$$

In the case where total variable cost is linear and goes through the origin, then marginal cost will equal average variable cost (see Appendix 10.3) and Equation 10.6 becomes:

$$P = AVC \times E_d/(E_d + 1) \quad (10.7)$$

Multiplying this expression out gives:

$$P = AVC(E_d)/(E_d + 1) \quad (10.8)$$

Although the next line seems to complicate matters, Equation 10.8 could be written as:

$$P = [AVC(E_d) + AVC - AVC]/(E_d + 1) \quad (10.9)$$

If the first two terms in the numerator are collected together, then Equation 10.9 becomes:

$$P = [AVC(E_d + 1) - AVC]/(E_d + 1) \quad (10.10)$$

Separating the terms out on the right-hand side of Equation 10.10 leads to the following:

$$P = AVC(E_d + 1)/(E_d + 1) - AVC/(E_d + 1) \quad (10.11)$$

Because there are common factors in the numerator and denominator of the first term on the right-hand side, Equation 10.11 becomes:

$$P = \text{AVC} + (-1)\text{AVC}/(E_d + 1) \quad (10.12)$$

At this stage recall equation 10.1, $P = \text{AVC} + X\%(\text{AVC})$. This is the same as Equation 10.12, where the markup term is given by:

$$X\% = -1/(E_d + 1).$$

Therefore, the optimal markup on costs is given by $-1/(E_d + 1)$.

Suppose that the elasticity of demand for the organisation's product is $E_d = -3$, by substituting this into Equation 10.12 it is possible to calculate the percentage markup used by the organisation:

$$P = \text{AVC} + (-1)\text{AVC}/(-3 + 1) \quad (10.13)$$

or,

$$P = \text{AVC} + \text{AVC}(1/2) \quad (10.14)$$
$$P = \text{AVC} + 50\%\text{AVC} \quad (10.15)$$

A 50 per cent markup on average variable cost is the profit-maximising percentage if the elasticity value is equal to $-3$. What has been calculated here is the optimal markup or the profit margin on a product as a percentage of unit costs.

Profit margins or markups can be calculated not only in terms of costs but also in terms of price. Whereas the markup on costs could be expressed as:

Markup on cost = (Price − AVC)/AVC

the markup on price is:

Markup on price = (Price − AVC)/Price

The two formulae are very similar and are expressing the idea of a markup, one in terms of cost and the other in terms of price. In terms of Equation 10.15, expressed in terms of the markup on costs, it is possible to write a similar expression for the optimal markup on price. Starting from the same expression, Equation 10.3, that is:

$$\text{MR} = P(1 + 1/E_d)$$

If it is again assumed that the organisation seeks to maximise profits, MR can be replaced by marginal cost to give:

$$\text{MC} = P(1 + 1/E_d)$$

Dividing both sides of this equation by price ($P$) leads to the following:

$$\text{MC}/P = 1 + 1/E_d \quad (10.16)$$

Rearranging Equation 10.16 gives:

$$-1/E_d = 1 - \text{MC}/P$$

or,

$$-1/E_d = (P - \text{MC})/P \quad (10.17)$$

In Equation 10.7, it was argued that for a straight-line total variable cost line which went through the origin MC could be replaced by AVC. This procedure can be repeated for Equation 10.17:

$$-1/E_d = (P - \text{AVC})/P \quad (10.18)$$

The right-hand side of this equation is the optimal markup on price, as we have seen earlier. The optimal markup on price is therefore $-1/E_d$.

Suppose that the elasticity of demand was $-2$, then the optimal markup on price would be $-1/-2$, or 50 per cent. Table 10.1 shows the optimal markups for cost and price for various elasticity measurements.

As Table 10.1 shows, products with higher elasticities, that is, the products with more elastic demands, would be expected to have lower markups. Products which have higher elasticities were found, in Chapter 6, to be those for which there were a high number of perceived substitutes. Thus in a market which is highly competitive, the markups achieved by an organisation will be fairly low. However, for some products which are necessities, where $0 < E_d < 1$ then a high level of markup may be achievable, especially if there are few competitors producing similar products and where there are few direct substitutes. Table 10.2 shows the markups on selected grocery items.

Table 10.2 indicates that the more price sensitive the item, the smaller the markup will be. Staple products, such as milk, bread and coffee, have very low markups. Products which have higher markups are those where demand is less sensi-

**Table 10.1 Profit-maximising markups at various elasticity levels**

| Price elasticity | Optimal markup on cost (%) | Optimal markup on price (%) |
|---|---|---|
| −1 | | 100 |
| −2 | 100 | 50 |
| −3 | 50 | 33.3 |
| −4 | 33.3 | 25 |
| −5 | 25 | 20 |
| −6 | 20 | 16.7 |
| −7 | 16.7 | 14.3 |
| −8 | 14.3 | 12.5 |
| −9 | 12.5 | 11.1 |
| −10 | 11.1 | 10 |

**Table 10.2 Markups on selected grocery items**

| Item | Markup on cost (%) | Markup on price (%) |
|---|---|---|
| Bread – own label | 0–5 | 0–5 |
| Bread – brand name | 30–40 | 23–30 |
| Coffee | 0–10 | 0–9 |
| Biscuits | 20–30 | 17–23 |
| Fresh fruit – in season | 40–45 | 29–33 |
| Fresh fruit – out of season | 15–20 | 13–17 |
| Milk | 0–5 | 0–5 |
| Non-prescription drugs | 35–55 | 26–35 |
| Snack foods | 20–25 | 17–20 |
| Soft drinks | 0–10 | 0–9 |
| Toothpaste | 15–20 | 13–17 |

tive to price changes. There are also different markups for related products, such as bread, perhaps suggesting the different income groups of the purchasers. For fresh fruit, supermarkets are able to make higher markups on the product when fruit is in season. Once the season has passed consumer demand may move away from these products, leading supermarkets to reduce their margins.

## Is elasticity that important?

One factor that is important from the above discussion is that markup pricing strategies and marginalist pricing strategies, far from being different, can be shown to produce optimal prices in a convincing way. The markup procedures can also reduce search costs, since often the decision maker in an organisation will have to weigh the cost of obtaining marginal improvements in information against the revenues that may accrue to the organisation.

However, with regard to demand, do organisations really make use of elasticity values in order to set prices, and if so, how certain can they be of their estimates of price elasticity? There is some evidence that organisations do not use elasticity to determine their markups but ascertain them through trial and error, perhaps choosing a markup which they perceive other firms are using in their market. But as Table 10.1 indicates, smaller markups would be used when the elasticities of demand are greater, that is, when markets are more competitive. Therefore, the actions of organisations in the way they set their markups may be mimicking the elasticity approach.

However, suppose that the organisation can obtain an estimate of its price elasticity of demand at the current output level. It has already been shown in the case of a linear demand curve that the elasticity of demand will change as the organisation moves up and down its demand line. In other words, to determine the value of elasticity at any other point on the demand curve, we need to know the point on the demand curve at which we started and the point at which we currently are on the demand curve. However, any change in the level of output cannot be determined unless the organisation knows the price it wishes to charge for the product. In Equation 10.15, the price or the optimal markup on costs depends on the value of the elasticity. Thus we have a circular argument. Elasticity depends on price, and output and price are related to elasticity. Even if the elasticity value is constant, markup pricing requires knowledge of marginal or average costs, the precise value of which depends on the level of output. Since the level of output depends on price, which is based on a markup of average or marginal costs, this poses another problem.

What is being suggested here is that markup pricing, although providing an alternative to, and sometimes an equivalence with, marginalist methods of pricing, has its problems. But to the extent to which business decision makers learn from markup pricing about how much the market will bear, then markup pricing may provide a good approximation to marginalist pricing. However, for true optimal pricing, marginalist theories may be the better approach.

## Markup pricing and demand changes

Using either elasticity or market experience to determine the profit margin, how will the markup set by the organisation respond to changes in the level of demand? Figure 10.1 may supply an answer to this problem. Initially the demand curve is shown as $D_1$ and, because this is downward sloping to the right, its associated marginal revenue lies below it, shown as $MR_1$. The profit-maximising price is shown as $P_1$, obtained from the point at which MR intersects MC. The percentage markup used by the organisation is the difference between AVC (MC) and the price, and this is shown, for example, as 45 per cent.

Suppose that the demand for the product increases. There are a number of ways in which this may be interpreted. First, it is possible that the demand for the product increases by the same proportion at each price level, and that is the approach adopted in Figure 10.1. This swivelling of the demand curve from $D_1$ to $D_2$ is called an

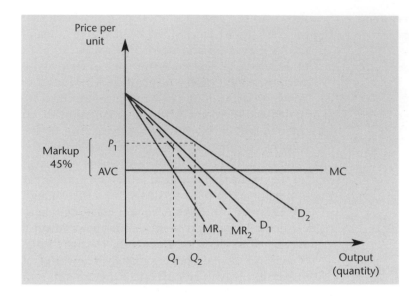

**Figure 10.1  Changes in demand and the impact on markup pricing**

Initial demand curve $D_1$ with associated marginal revenue curve $MR_1$. Profit-maximising point is at $P_1Q_1$. After the iso-elastic demand curve shifts to $D_2$, with its associated marginal revenue line $MR_2$, the price stays at $P_1$ but the profit-maximising organisation will product output $Q_2$.

iso-elastic demand curve shift, since the elasticity of demand is the same on the new demand curve as it was on demand curve $D_1$ at each price level. To show this, look at the following calculations of elasticity. In Chapter 6 the formula for price elasticity of demand was shown to be:

$$E_d = (\text{Change in quantity})/(\text{Change in price}) \times P/Q$$

Suppose that two price and quantity combinations are known on the demand curve $D_1$. That is, when the price of the product is $P_1 = £3$, $Q_1 = 8$ units, and when $P_2 = £2$, $Q_2 = 10$ units. Substituting these pieces of data into the elasticity formula:

$$E_d = (8 - 10)/(3 - 2) \times 3/8$$

This gives an elasticity of demand:

$$E_d = -3/4$$

If quantity increases by the same proportion at each price level, say 10 per cent, then at the price $P_1 = £3$, quantity equals 8.8 units, and when $P_2 = £2$, $Q_2 = 11$. If the elasticity of demand is once again calculated at the price level $P_1 = £3$, but this time on demand curve $D_2$, then:

$$E_d = (8.8 - 11)/(3 - 2) \times 3/8.8$$

This gives an elasticity of demand:

$$E_d = 6.6/-8.8 = -3/4$$

Since the elasticity value determines the optimal markup for the organisation, the markup after a shift in the demand curve following an equal percentage increase in quantity at each price level must be the same as the markup before the equal percentage increase in price, because the elasticities

of demand are the same. In Figure 10.1, this equal markup is shown with the new optimal price found from the intersection of MC and $MR_2$. But are shifts in the demand curve likely to be iso-elastic shifts? If the demand curve shift is not an iso-elastic shift, then continuing to operate the existing markups will lead the organisation to move away from the 'correct' markup, but it may not be worthwhile to correct the error because of the search costs required to improve the cost information.

However, if the organisation realises that demand elasticities have changed markedly, e.g. due to changes in the competitive nature of its markets, then it may respond by varying the markup. So, for example, it would be expected that a new product for which there are few substitutes may have a high degree of markup; where markets are separated, price discrimination may ensue with different product markups. Staple products or necessities will often have low levels of markup, while higher-quality products or those aimed at higher income groups may have higher markups. Seasonality factors also play their part in markup policies. When products come into season, their quantity, quality, taste, etc often improve and consumers are willing to pay higher markups for these seasonal products. As the season continues quality may fall and the markup on the product is also reduced. Markups can be considered also in terms of profit margins, the markup being the percentage which a wholesaler or retailer adds to their buying-in price, and the profit margin being the percentage difference between the buying price and selling price. Case study 10.1 shows the size of the profit margins in a variety of European markets.

◆ CASE STUDY 10.1

# Profit margins in action

### Toys and games in Italy
Profit margins are relatively high in the toys and games market in Italy, with the final price often being recommended by the producer or importer. The wholesaler usually takes a margin of around 10 per cent of this final price and the retailer a margin in the region of 30–40 per cent. Department stores and hypermarkets take lower margins on these products at around 25–30 per cent of the final price, giving some idea that the product is used as one to entice customers to purchase there as well as perhaps suggesting a higher throughput of customers. The relatively high profit margins on toys and games are related to the fact that many of these products have high risks attached to them, due to the 'faddiness' of some products, and retailers do not want to be involved in holding stocks of the items once the season has passed.

### Cooking appliances in France
The market for cooking appliances is extremely competitive and prices vary widely according to the product and the type of outlet. The overall retail price index for cooking appliances fell by 2–3 per cent in 1994 as a result of fierce competition in this market. It is normal for wholesalers to operate with a margin of around 12–16 per cent on their selling prices, excluding value-added tax.

Retailers' margins vary markedly, anywhere from 15–30 per cent depending on the type of outlet, with hypermarkets taking smaller margins and the specialist shops larger ones (up to 30 per cent).

### Men's and women's outerwear in the Netherlands
The retail trade in outerwear is very competitive, with special offers, sales and 'permanent' price reductions often in evidence. Some retailers see the need for codes of practice in the industry since some outlets are able to offer outerwear at extremely low prices due to dealings with illegal manufacturers.

In general, specialist outerwear shops have the highest profit margins at around 39 per cent, while women's outerwear shops have an average profit margin of around 37 per cent. The highest profit margins are achieved by specialist shops in the best areas of the cities and towns.

*Sources*: Economist Intelligence Reports, *Marketing in Europe*: Vol 369, August 1993; Vol 388, March 1995; and Vol 381, August 1994. Reprinted by permission of Corporate Intelligence on Retailing, London.

◆ **Exercise 10.1**

1 List the major factors which you consider to be important in influencing markup rates or profit margins.

2 To what extent will the Single European Market affect markup rates or profit margins in each of the countries within the European market?

3 Would you expect the profit margins for toys and games, kitchen appliances and outerwear to alter over the year and over the economic cycle?

### Comment on the case study
In Table 10.2 we noted the varying markups that could occur on grocery items. The three areas noted in case study 10.1 indicate something that we have seen earlier, that is, that the markup/profit margin depends on the level of competition. It also varies depending on the quality of the outlet, with better-quality outlets able to achieve higher markups or margins. It is worth noting also that these changes depend on the level of economic activity. During downturns in economic activity markups/profit margins appear to be reduced.

## Markup pricing and inflation

Suppose that an organisation experiences an increase in its cost base due to the influence of inflation. What impact will this have on prices? A useful way of approaching the answer to this question is with an example. Suppose that an organisation has a 20 per cent markup over average variable costs which are currently at £5. The organisation now faces a 15 per cent increase in average variable costs due to the effects of inflation. Table 10.3 indicates what might happen to the price of the organisation's product.

Because the average variable costs and the markup have increased by 15 per cent, the market

**Table 10.3**
**The effects of inflation on markup prices**

| | Before inflation of 15% | After inflation of 15% | Change (%) |
|---|---|---|---|
| Average variable costs | £5 | £5.75 | 15 |
| 20% markup | £1 | £1.15 | 15 |
| Market price | £6 | £6.90 | 15 |

price has also increased by a similar amount. In other words, the impact of an inflation rate of 15 per cent leads to the increase in costs being passed on fully to the market price. In Table 10.3 the markup price also increased by 15 per cent and this suffices to keep the real value of the contribution to the organisation's overheads and profits constant. Whether the consumer will pay the increased costs of inflation really depends on the elasticity of demand for the commodity and whether consumers' income has kept in line with inflation. If their income has also increased by 15 per cent, there is no reason to expect that there will be any reduction in the quantity of the good demanded. However, if consumer income rises by less than 15 per cent, then by using a constant markup rate the organisation may see sales fall. In other words, the markup rate will need to respond to the change in real consumer income.

## ◆ CASE STUDY 10.2

### Built from the bargain basement

**FT**

If you were a skirt-wearing, meat-eating shopper with a penchant for electrical appliances, then 1994 was a good year. All these commodities have fallen in price. Why were consumers able to get such good deals? The answer was twofold: the state of the UK and world economy; and the retail sector's problems. The world recession has caused firms to cut their profit margins, in addition the entrance of new companies into some of these markets has kept prices low as has the introduction of new commodities into existing markets, such as own-label cola. Moreover, some companies have finished their re-structuring processes and are now in a position to use their new strength to price cut and attempt to improve their market share.

In the clothing market the chief executive of Austin Reed believes the market is splitting into two: consumers look to certain retailers which offer good value and twice yearly sales, whilst others are offering virtually continuous discounts and promotions. The problem with this latter group is that customer perceptions of their goods have changed. For the former companies, buying more in bulk has helped reduce costs and by improving efficiency, profit margins can remain healthy.

But as a Bank of England inflation report noted (June 1994), on average, profit margins are much reduced in the retail sector. What retailers would like is a bout of general inflation which would allow them to put prices up as wage levels also rise. This is not a likely scenario as long as the UK economy is being managed more closely along a path of steady growth, since following this approach is likely to keep inflationary pressures under control. In this case firms may have to continue facing lower profit margins for some time to come.

*Source: Financial Times, 20 August 1994. Reprinted with permission.*

### ◆ Exercise 10.2

1 In what ways can an organisation increase its profit margins under conditions of low inflation?

2 What is the likely impact on profit margins of lowering trade barriers?

*Comment on the case study*

During conditions of relatively high inflation, organisations can expect to adjust their markups and margins with inflation. This may be possible where wage inflation keeps in line with price inflation. A danger for domestic producers is that by adopting this approach they will price themselves out of their own domestic markets as consumers perceive that imported goods have smaller markups/margins. Conversely, it is possible for foreign producers to take advantage of relatively higher domestic inflation to push up their own markups/margins, so as to keep their products in line with domestic producers.

## Markup pricing and market structure

In oligopoly market conditions organisations are often reluctant to compete on price. If one organisation lowers its price there may well be the opinion that all other organisations will also lower their prices. If, on the other hand, organisations raise their prices, there may be a belief that competitors will not raise theirs, leading to a fall in quantity demanded. Even if all the organisations in an oligopoly market structure agree to raise their prices but one organisation raises theirs by a greater amount, then once again this organisation can expect to lose sales. In many oligopolies, therefore, the conditions exist for price stability.

In such a model, once a markup level is established any changes that occur in the cost base of one organisation are likely to be felt by the remaining organisations and therefore all costs and associated markups will move together. It follows that the relative prices of all organisations will remain the same at the new price level. Since one organisation will expect all others to operate similar markups and alter their prices by the same amount whenever there is a change in the cost base, there will be a predictable level of prices in operation. This process of constant parallelism means that all firms have a high degree of certainty about prices and markups in oligopoly markets.

An example of this process can be seen in the car industry, where changes in the cost base that arise through changes in the cost of raw materials often feed through into different car manufacturers, who respond by altering prices by similar amounts.

Because there are similar markups this provides a useful signal to potential competitors who are looking to enter the market. These new entrants may look in the short term to reduce their own markup to gain entry. Even for existing firms, this is not to say that price wars do not break out under oligopoly conditions, as they manipulate prices further to gain an advantage in the market.

## ◆ CASE STUDY 10.3

# The travel industry

The three largest chains of travel agents in the UK have introduced penalty charges on holidays and flights booked by credit card. Lunn Poly and Going Places, which had introduced charges of £1 for each holiday or flight booked on a credit card early in the summer of 1995, were followed by Thomas Cook in July 1995. The fees provide a new source of income for the travel agents in a market where profit margins are worryingly slim. In 1995 four travel companies went out of business: Blenheim Travel, Euro Northern Travel, Skyway Travel and Avco Travel.

The argument put forward for the charge on holiday makers who use their credit cards comes from a European Union directive which has ensured that any company selling package holidays must have a bond or similar arrangement to protect consumers' payments. Consumers have long realised that paying for their holidays by credit card has enabled them to have an additional safety net should anything go wrong with their travel firm. Although the charge looks minimal, for a family costs can add up. Tour operators see the charge as a means to cover their costs, but others see it as a mechanism by which all the operators can improve their profit margins in a market that is becoming increasingly competitive and one where the current profit margins appear to be diminishing.

*Source*: Authors.

## ◆ Exercise 10.3

1 With the closure of many of the smaller travel firms, how will the change in competition affect the margins used by travel agents?

2 Are changes in the business cycle likely to have an impact on profit margins in the travel industry?

### Comment on the case study

The competitive structure of the travel industry is changing. There are many small, specialist providers, but the main bulk of holidays is increasingly coming under the auspices of a few large providers. Until the market has settled down its highly competitive nature will see tour operators cutting their margins as a means to attract customers and thereby weaken their competitors'

positions. The annual charge outlined in the case study is one way in which the tour operators can cover their lower markups elsewhere in the holiday business.

## PRICING IN EXISTING MARKETS

Where a market is already in existence the current price level may have been influenced by a number of factors. Governments may have intervened in the market in the past and therefore influenced prices. The market may have been subject to rationing, thus shifting the price from its free-market level. Organisations may have adopted different approaches to price setting: some may have followed the marginalist approach, others may have used markup pricing. The nature of competition may also have influenced prices, as might the objectives of the organisations which make up this market. In other words, where a market has been in existence for some time there are a range of historic and current factors which influence the price of a product. Where a new firm seeks to enter this type of market or an existing firm seeks to increase its presence in the market, a whole range of pricing approaches can be used.

## PRICE POSITIONING

Given the existence of current products on the market, the new product may be priced higher or lower than those already in the market, depending on the new product's attributes. We have seen in Chapter 6 Lancaster's approach to product demand based on the attributes of products. Thus a new organisation might position its product in a market not only in terms of price but also in terms of the product's attributes. For example, hi-fi amplifiers appear at different prices. Some UK manufacturers who are trying to provide the consumer with the idea that their products are not mass-produced commodities like those of some of their South-East Asian competitors will price their products at premium prices, indicating the degree of craftsmanship that is involved with the product. Price differentials will also exist according to whether amplifiers have different levels of power (watts), the number of filters and so on.

Given that an organisation perceives its product as different from those which currently exist in the market, how does it find its price? There must be a maximum that consumers are willing to pay for a product with certain attributes. For example, if we return to our running shoes example in Chapter 6, where the two attributes were weight and durability, a consumer might be willing to pay £80 for a highly durable running shoe in the current market and no more. This threshold price is in the mind of the consumer and, from the consumer's perspective, if the market price is below the threshold price then they may be willing to buy the product. If organisations only knew what consumers' threshold prices were, then they would set their prices accordingly. Market research may give the organisation information about consumers' threshold price. But in any case, if a product enters a market and subsequently changes its price over time, it is quite possible that this will give organi-sations sufficient information about the nature of the consumers' threshold price.

Overall, a producer which enters an established market would expect to see similar products but all priced at different prices depending on their attributes. A market such as this exists for automatic washing machines. Washing machines have different spin speeds: some have dual spin speeds while others are single spin speed. Some are only cold water-fill, others have the facility of both hot and cold fill. Some automatic washing machines have over 30 possible programmes for washing different types of garments, while others have a limited range of programme options. In addition, some have timers allowing the machine to be set to use cheap-rate electricity during the night, while others do not have this facility and require the purchase of a time switch. A new automatic washing machine, therefore, needs to consider the attributes of existing washing machines and to be priced accordingly.

Within the automatic washing machine market manufacturers such as Hotpoint, Indesit, AEG and Zanussi do not usually produce a single machine but a range catering for different segments of the washing machine market. Here the washing machines are substitutes for one another but have embodied in them different levels of quality. A washing machine manufacturer may also introduce products/services which are complementary to the other goods in its product/service portfolio, such as tumble driers and repair/maintenance servicing. In other words, organisations often provide a product line – a range of interrelated products.

## PRESTIGE PRICING

When an organisation produces a range of products, there will obviously be a product which sits at the top of its product portfolio. These products may well have attributes which exceed those for other products further down the product range, but organisations may enhance these by putting a high price on the product to increase the perceived value to potential customers. This process of **prestige pricing** gives signals to the consumer that they are expecting to receive a commodity which is of high quality. This, however, is not always the case and price is not always a good indicator of quality. Prestige pricing can lead to a limited customer base, but conversely it may augment the 'snob value' effect.

Many car firms use prestige pricing to good effect. Mercedes, BMW and Jaguar all produce expensive cars aimed at the top end of the market. These cars exude certain characteristics of lifestyle, high income, reliability, quality and the like. It took some time before Japanese manufacturers such as Toyota, Honda and Mazda realised that, although their products had many, if not more, of the attributes found in other European-manufactured cars such as reliability, total customer satisfaction and quality fittings, their pricing structures had been set too low. Consumers therefore perceived them as lower-quality products. Honda began advertising heavily, comparing its products with the then class leaders such as Mercedes, Volvo and BMW. At the same time it began pricing more highly than ever before. The result was that by 1988, Honda was selling 70 770 Acuras (its equivalent of the Mercedes) in the US, 80 per cent more than Mercedes which had been the class leader.

In the case of prestige pricing consumers rely to a greater extent on judging the quality of a product in relation to its price. It is often assumed that consumers have perfect knowledge, but this is not usually the case. Consumer knowledge of a product can be improved by asking friends and colleagues about the products they purchase, by the acquisition of specialist magazines or consumer reports, and by consulting adverts and the like. However, there is some doubt in the consumer's mind whether some of their information sources are giving a truly unbiased opinion. In the case of consumer reports, a less biased view may be per-

ceived but it is sometimes difficult to relate the products in question with the consumer's own lifestyle needs. Using either approach involves time and sometimes money and therefore increases the search costs for the consumer. It would be expected that the greater the price of the product the more search time would be involved in assessing its merits. It may also be thought that the more technical a product the more consumers link price with quality.

Where a product has been available on the market for some time, consumers could be expected to have greater knowledge of its performance and characteristics and use these along with price to judge its merits. Where a product is new to the market, price may be the paramount factor in providing quality signals to the consumer.

### ◆ Exercise 10.1

1 Below are listed a number of the main attributes of cars. How are these addressed by:

a European luxury car makers?
b Japanese luxury car makers?

Style, colour choice, delivery, reduced environmental damage, speed, resale value, reliability, lifestyle needs, optional extras as standard, self-image.

2 What strategies could Japanese car manufacturers use to improve their position in the luxury car market?

## ◆ CASE STUDY 10.4

# Executive cars

Life used to be straightforward for Japan's luxury car makers. Merely by making highly reliable cars that exuded wealth they could keep their wealthy customers happy and eager to order replacements every few years. But as the Japanese car market has matured, and economic and social changes have affected customer tastes and market conditions, the environment for the country's executive car makers has become considerably more demanding. It used to be that people who wanted executive cars just wanted the very best and would buy the most expensive car from the catalogue even without seeing it. But today consumers appear to be more demanding, looking for qualities such as safety, comfort and ease of driving.

This is forcing Japanese car manufacturers to review their pricing strategies. Moreover, the Japanese home markets are facing greater competition as the rise in the value of the yen means that foreign imports are becoming even more price competitive.

The problem for the Japanese is how to respond. Should they produce cars with the same attributes as their major rivals, when quantity and quality of attributes have been the main plank for successful sales in the past, or should they reduce prices? If the latter strategy is pursued, how will consumers respond to Japanese executive cars that are below the prices of their main competitors such as Mercedes and BMW?

*Source: Financial Times, 30 June 1994. Reprinted with permission.*

## Comment on the case study

Case study 10.4 shows once again how Japanese executive car makers have learnt from the market leaders and been able to change their pricing strategies so that consumers feel that they are buying quality cars. One result has been for the major European car makers to adopt similar production processes to the Japanese, thus their cars are now equally as reliable. Producers are now examining means other than pricing to keep ahead of their rivals.

# PRICE LINING

Under this pricing strategy the organisation sets the price for a product and then develops the product which allows the firm to maximise profits at this price. Car manufacturers and electronics manufacturers are two of a number of sectors which use this approach. At first glance, **price lining** appears to be the reverse of earlier methods of setting price. In these costs were found and this influenced the price on the market. But for many products – for example, cars – consumers have in mind the approximate price they are willing to pay. A similar phenomenon can be seen with the market for CD players, speakers and other hi-fi equipment. Confectionery manufacturers may also use price-lining approaches for crisps and chocolate bars.

# PROMOTIONAL PRICING

Organisations use **promotional pricing**, under which they reduce the price of the product over a short period to attract sales. There are a number of reasons why promotional pricing might take place. The organisation might want to increase its market share and so use promotional pricing as a loss-leader approach. It may be responding to promotional pricing or non-price competition from its rivals. The organisation may find that its current market is saturated or that it has high inventory levels. The organisation may have received a reduction in its cost base through lower-cost raw materials from suppliers or a favourable move in the exchange rate and wish to pass some of these lower costs on to the consumer. In addition, it may wish to continue with an earlier pricing strategy of low price competition in which it perceives the consumer rates as one of its major assets. These are just a few of the many possible influences on this type of pricing strategy. There may also be times of the year when promotional pricing is more in evidence. For example, in January many department stores use promotional pricing for their crockery or linens to attract back tired Christmas customers. Car retailers use cash rebates, low-interest-rate finance or longer warranties to attract sales in the months when their sales are relatively flat.

Sometimes organisations are forced into this pricing regime in the short term in response to a competitor's behaviour, the result of which may lead to a reduction in profits. The same outcome may occur if the organisation underestimates the elasticity of demand for the product. With an inelastic demand, a price reduction will see an increase in the quantity demanded but at the expense of a deterioration in revenue. A promotional pricing strategy may also provoke a promotional pricing war from the organisation's main competitors. Where consumers are able to store the product easily, they may stop buying the product at its normal price and stock up during the promotional pricing periods. It is also possible that promotional pricing alerts the consumer to the importance of pricing for a product and alters the way they behave in the future when the price is returned to normal. A good which is often used for promotional pricing may suffer from being viewed as inferior by the consumer and thus its long-term sales may fall as consumers move towards perceived superior products.

Goods which are often used in promotional pricing are those with more elastic demands, so that when the price is reduced total revenue will increase. Commodities which would fit this category are foodstuffs and detergents. Similarly, durable products which are only bought infrequently would fall in this category, such as video recorders and hi-fi equipment. These commodities take up a relatively high proportion of consumers' income and therefore have elastic demands.

It has been considered on a number of earlier occasions whether the consumer has perfect knowledge. For a person studying a particular market sector, the knowledge may cover all possible products and suggests evidence of consumer omniscience. But is this the way consumers behave? Consumers often do not know all the products that are available and finding this information out may require high search costs. If the search costs are high it would be expected that the consumer is less well informed about the availability of substitutes. It has been suggested by Nelson

(1970), among others, that for some goods the consumer has a fairly good idea of their attributes prior to buying them. These attributes are easily classified. Examples of products which are evaluated in terms of their search attributes are clothing and food. Other goods, however, cannot be truly assessed until the item has been purchased: these are said to contain experience attributes. Examples of items that would fit this category are the quality of paint and the effectiveness of deodorants. Some items' attributes may only be partially evaluated even after repeated purchase and these have been called credence goods; here the consumer tends to rely on the assigned brand image or name. Professional services fall into this category, such as financial services, as does the quality of products such as photographic film for many consumers. In terms of search costs, credence goods will tend to be more search costly than experience goods, which are themselves more search costly than search products. It would be expected, therefore, that promotional pricing would be more often used when the consumer evaluates the product in terms of search costs, where a price reduction is more likely to lead to a more elastic demand for the product.

## PRODUCT BUNDLE PRICING

Sometimes instead of selling two products separately an organisation will sell two products together as a **product bundle**. Examples of this can be seen in the computer games market. Buying a Sega Mega Drive not only provides the customer with the games console but one or two games for the machine are often supplied at the same time. Restaurants offer set menus often covering three courses. For example, the cost of a starter, main course and dessert may be £12 when purchased as a product bundle, but if the three courses are purchased separately the starter may be £2.50, the main course £10.00 and the dessert £3.00. Some in-town supermarkets use this pricing strategy by offering free parking if the customer redeems their car-parking ticket at the checkout. Other examples can be found in the sports and entertainment arena, where theatres and sports teams sell season tickets at less than the cost of single tickets and hotels sell specially priced packages that include room, meals and entertainment. With all these examples it is possible for all the products or items to be bought separately.

As a pricing strategy the organisation will set the price of the product bundle at less than the sum of the items if they were purchased separately. It may set the price of the individual items at a level above their normal markups so that customers are encouraged to purchase the product bundle and in doing so end up with an item which they would not have purchased if they could only obtain the items separately. Some consumers may not wish to buy the whole product bundle but may wish to purchase one of the items separately, and in doing so will pay a price higher than they otherwise would have for the privilege. Other consumers will switch to the product bundle because it offers a cheaper way of purchasing the items that they were going to buy separately anyway. Since the organisation realises that pushing up the price of the individual items is likely to damage its revenue, it requires the price of the product bundle to be set at such a level that the revenue from sales exceeds any loss incurred by the reduction in the sales of the individual items.

## PREDATORY PRICING

Many markets are oligopolistic, that is, they are dominated by a few large organisations. It is quite possible that all the organisations in an oligopoly are not of equal size, and therefore one organisation at least could be in a position to lower prices, because, being large, it may have a lower cost base. Here the organisation with the lowest cost base can prey on its rivals by lowering prices and so force its competitors out of the market. When faced with this action by the lowest-cost organisation, competitors may be forced to lower their prices also, but they may not be in a position to match the market leader's price over the long term. Alternatively, the other organisations may decide not to reduce their prices and may suffer a loss in market sales to the more aggressive market leader. Either way, these other organisations are forced to leave the market, putting the low-cost firm in a monopolistic situation.

**Predatory pricing** can also be used to damage the position of a new entrant. The lower price may mean that the new entrant cannot compete on economies of scale. In addition, promotional activity can be increased by the existing organisation(s) to make it even harder for the new entrant to pick up market share, other than by also increasing its own marketing activity. In other words, oligopolies differentiate their products through advertising as a means of providing barriers to entry. A new entrant may not be able, in the short run, to match the incumbent organisations' level of advertising and at the same time push its prices down far enough to gain an initial foothold in the market.

Predatory pricing does not always require the dominant organisation in a market to push its prices below that of its competitors. It may be possible for the dominant organisation, because of its high level of advertising, to brand its product quite extensively, giving its products an even greater perception of quality. Thus, before any predatory pricing takes place the dominant organisation may be in a position to offer its product to the market at a slightly higher price than its competitors. For example, suppose the price differential is 15 pence. If the dominant organisation lowers its prices by 10 pence, they will still be above the prices charged by the other organisations in the industry, but they may see sales falling as consumers switch towards the products produced by the dominant organisation, which are now relatively cheaper. To restore their differentials, the other organisations may be forced to reduce prices below costs, forcing them out of the market in the long term.

An example of predatory pricing is said to have been in effect in transatlantic air routes. Both in the 1970s in response to Laker Airways and in the 1980s in response to Virgin Atlantic and Peoples Express, the existing transatlantic suppliers, British Airways, Pan Am and TWA, reduced fares. In the 1970s Laker Airways began to offer cheap North Atlantic air fares to the US selling at £99 return: this undercut the major players on these routes by at least £200. British Airways did not counteract immediately, realising that Laker Airways had borrowed heavily. When Laker was faced with high levels of debt and interest payments, then like other major carriers on the North Atlantic route BA reduced fares to match those of Laker Airways. These larger carriers were also able to bear the cost of the predatory pricing regime by cross-subsidising their transatlantic provisions from other profitable worldwide routes. The result was the exit of Laker Airways from the North Atlantic route.

## PRICE FIXING

A feature that is often noticeable in an oligopolistic market structure is that organisations do not appear to compete on price but on non-price factors. An organisation may believe that if it pushes the price up other organisations will not follow and the price leader will lose market share. Suppose, however, all the organisations agree to set the price; that is, when one organisation puts up its price all the other organisations do follow. Although demand may be reduced after the price rise, all organisations may benefit from increased revenue if the market demand for the product is price inelastic. **Price fixing**, or the collusion of organisations in setting prices, enables them to increase profits but is to the detriment of customers who are really facing supply from a monopoly position. During the 1990s there was evidence of price fixing within the European Union by steel manufacturers and ready-mix concrete producers. Price fixing is probably also more prevalent in sectors such as steel and cement where there are high fixed costs to be covered. It is sometimes difficult to distinguish price fixing from price leadership under oligopoly. Even without a price leader, it is possible that organisations closely follow any changes in price. This process of conscience parallelism, that is, all organisations changing their prices in line with one another due to changes in raw material prices or increases in sectoral wage costs, should not be thought of as price fixing if there is no evidence of collusion taking place.

## PRICE TENDERING

**Price tendering** has often been used to gain public-sector contracts and has become more and more prevalent in the UK as previous public-sector arrangements have been put out to the private sector through a process of contracting out. The procedure involves the purchaser advertising the contract and specification to encourage possible suppliers to put forward a price at which the contract could take place. Often the process is undertaken under sealed bids to prevent collusion and it would be thought that the organisation making the lowest bid would receive the contract. However, price is only one aspect of the contractual arrangement. There may be a need to look at the length of time to undertake the service, whether the purchaser believes that the potential supplier can actually deliver on the contract, and the quality of the service or good provided by the supplier. Given all these factors, the contract may be awarded not to the lowest tender price but to the organisation which best fits all the criteria set out by the purchaser.

It is possible for suppliers to use a loss-leader approach to win the first contract, thereby building up a strong relationship with the purchaser which enables them to win further contracts but this time at more 'reasonable' prices. There have also been cases where suppliers have colluded in setting the prices for contracts. Here all suppliers set prices higher than the actual cost of the work, but one supplier may set its inflated price slightly lower to win the contract. Suppliers may take it in turns to use this approach, sharing out contracts among themselves. A similar type of price fixing can occur in the antiques trade through auction rings. Here, a number of buyers of antiques agree how a particular series of lots will be split between them. They then agree not to put excessive bids in against one another and are able to purchase the various lots at very competitive prices.

## NEW PRODUCT PRICING

The pricing techniques discussed so far have been for existing products or for products which are duplicating, in many respects, those that are already in existence. Can the same pricing strategies be used for new products? First, what is meant by the word new? Is this a new product to the organisation which is simply a new version of existing products? For example, a toaster manufacturer may introduce a new toaster which allows for variations in the size of the slice of bread. The market for toasters is already in existence and the toaster manufacturer can price its new toaster within the framework of existing markets.

However, suppose that the product is completely new to the market, for example an interactive television and media package which allows the consumer to accept or reject current programmes, substituting alternative programmes. In this case there is no benchmark. It may be possible to learn from the way in which other new innovations were brought to the market, such as electronic calculators and satellite television, but the producer may only be able to learn so much from these because of the product's uniqueness. The next section considers some of the pricing strategies that can be used for new products.

## SKIMMING PRICE STRATEGY

Using this pricing strategy the organisation sets a high price initially for its product with the inten-

tion of offering the product to a select group of customers. Some would see this as 'skimming the cream' off the top of the market. These customers must be willing to pay a high premium for this new product and in doing so are making a large contribution towards the overheads and profit of the organisation.

Intel often uses a **skimming price strategy** when it introduces a new computer chip. The price is set at such a level that only a few segments will adopt the new, improved chip, then as sales fall the price is lowered as a means of drawing in the next price-sensitive level of customers. For example, when Intel produced its Pentium chips they were priced at $1000 each. This only attracted business and other serious users to purchase them. After a while Intel reduced the price of Pentium chips by 30 per cent per year and this led the price of Pentium PCs to fall, putting them in the price range of many home owners. Thus Intel was able to skim the cream off a number of markets and enhance its revenue.

It has been argued that the skimming price strategy is equivalent to short-run profit maximisation where the organisation is attempting to get as much profit as possible over the short term. However, skimming price methods can also be linked to long-run profit maximisation. The length of time over which an organisation can obtain high levels of profits using a skimming price strategy can be related to the barriers to entry into this market. Where the barriers to entry are high, the innovative firm can achieve high levels of profits even over the long run. Where price is being used as an indicator of quality in the consumers' perceptions, then a skimming price strategy may also be a long-term strategy. If the price is reduced over the life of the product it is possible for this to alter consumers' perceptions of the product, damaging sales to such an extent that the product loses profitability.

For some organisations there may be little to distinguish the short term from the long term. This would be the case if the product was seen as having only seasonal interest. Examples of products that would fit this category are toys associated with current popular films, skateboards and some types of fashion wear. Here, because of the short time-frame, organisations see the long run as a short period of calendar time. In 1996 two of the most popular Christmas toys were Buzz Lightyear and Woody from the film *Toy Story*. They were likely to have high levels of popularity until the next major children's film arrived and thus the products were set at premium prices, at around £20–35.

For many products a skimming price strategy is often used in the introductory or growth phase of a product lifecycle, then, as interest in the product fades, prices are lowered. In other words, when a product is introduced it may have an inelastic demand and a skimming price strategy may be deemed appropriate. As demand wanes and the product becomes more elastic in demand, prices will fall. Depending on the barriers to entry, over time new firms will enter this highly profitable market producing similar products and this too causes the elasticity of demand for the product to change.

In Figure 10.2, the initial demand curve faced by the organisation after the introduction of the product is shown as $D_1$. The organisation operates a skimming price strategy, pricing its product at $P_1$ and selling quantity $Q_1$. The organisation's revenue is shown as the rectangle $0P_1AQ_1$. Once the product has been on the market for some time, interest may wane and new organisations enter the market. The demand curve shifts to $D_2$. Notice that if the organisation stayed with its original price, there would be no demand for its product. The organisation is forced, therefore, to reduce its price and in doing so can achieve revenue $0P_2BQ_2$.

**Figure 10.2 Price and the product lifecycle**

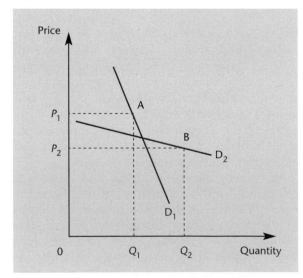

Using a skimming price strategy in the growth phase of the product lifecycle, the organisation's demand curve is shown as $D_1$ and at a skimming price $P_1$, $Q_1$ is demanded. Total revenue is $0P_1AQ_1$. During the maturity phase of the product lifecycle, demand becomes more elastic, the demand curve also shifts to the left and the organisation is forced to reduce its price to $P_2$. Total revenue is now $0P_2BQ_2$.

A skimming price strategy is particularly useful where the organisation has limited production capacity. In this scenario it is better for the organisation to sell its limited output at the highest price it can possibly achieve. If demand remains high in the future, then the organisation may expand capacity and reduce the price of the product. Skimming prices are also more appropriate where an organisation does not know the level of demand. If this has been assessed incorrectly, the organisation can lower the skimming price without harming the relationship between supplier and consumer.

Such a pricing strategy clearly identifies customer market segments and enables the organisation to move down towards higher-elasticity groups over the product lifecycle. This appears to be a strategy adopted by a number of electronics and computer manufacturers. Originally digital audiotape was priced at a premium rate with the anticipation of reducing its prices to a wider market over time. However, the audio industry was reticent to move into this medium given the simultaneous development of compact disc players. Thus digital audiotape machines are still very expensive and associated mainly with the recording industry. A similar example can be seen in the computer games market when the introduction of the Sega Saturn machine, costing a little under £400, catered for the top end of the market. The machine came down in price within a year, partly reflecting a move away from a skimming price strategy but more as a response to Sony's Playstation, which was brought onto the market later on in 1995 at around £100 cheaper.

A market-skimming strategy requires a number of important conditions to be in play. First, the product's quality and image must support its higher price and at that price enough customers must want to buy the product. Second, because the number of items sold may be small, the increased costs faced by the organisation should not absorb the high revenue possible by following a skimming price strategy. Finally, in the short run competitors should not be able to enter the market easily and undercut the high price.

## PENETRATION PRICING

**Penetration pricing** is a strategy of setting a relatively low price when the product is first put on the market to enable the organisation to obtain a large market share. This may require the organisation to forgo high levels of profits in the short term, but it may enable it to achieve long-run profit maximisation. This strategy is very useful where the demand for the product is anticipated as being elastic and where the organisation is anticipating that rivals will enter the market. Penetration pricing may also be the appropriate strategy where the organisation has underutilised capacity or where it can achieve significant economies of scale from producing a larger output.

There are many examples of penetration pricing strategy. For example, the Bank of Scotland used its Direct Line, Privilege and Churchill subsidiaries to improve its profits and market share in the car insurance market by selling direct to consumers at market-penetrating prices. Its success in this field has allowed it to lower costs, which further enables it to keep prices low. The computer firm Dell used penetration pricing to sell high-quality computer products through lower-cost mail-order channels. The other competitors, such as IBM and Apple, were unable to match its prices through normal retail outlets.

For a penetration pricing strategy to work the market must be highly price sensitive, so that a low price leads to a high demand for the organisation's products. Costs must fall as sales increase and the low price must keep out competition, otherwise profits will only be a short-term phenomenon. In the case of Dell above, its penetration pricing strategy was short term, as both IBM and Compaq developed their own direct distribution channels.

## DETERMINING PRICE AND QUALITY JOINTLY

Whenever a new car model is introduced it comes in a number of price ranges. The prices reflect the quality of the product. At the bottom of the range there may be mock leather seats and most of the fascia will be plastic; as you move up the range, seat coverings become fabric and the plastic may imitate real wood. At the top of the range you find real leather upholstery and real wood as part of the fascia and door panels. What the organisation must do is to assess how these attributes are valued in the eye of the consumer and price accordingly to maximise the level of profits. It is almost like a whole set of new products that have been introduced and the organisation needs to assess the price for each model in the range. Therefore, for some products quality and price are entwined so closely that both are considered at the same time.

This approach to consumer demand can be likened to Lancaster's attributes approach, but here we are comparing products with better-quality attributes and then pricing accordingly.

## THE IMPACT OF LEARNING CURVES

The concept of the learning curve has already been discussed in Chapter 8. There it was noted that the organisation's costs per unit fall over time as it becomes more efficient at producing each item. This reduction in per unit costs is not related to the costs of inputs, which are assumed to remain constant, but is due to the reductions in per unit costs as the firm learns about its production process. Cost reductions through learning effects are likely to be greater at the beginning of a production run and, even though subsequent units of production provide a learning effect, this becomes smaller as the number of units increases. In terms of a new product, the learning curve effect can be seen in downward shifts in both the average cost and marginal cost curves.

**Figure 10.3 The learning curve effect and product prices**

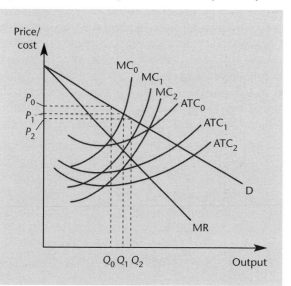

A profit maximising organisation will seek to produce in circumstances where MR = MC, with average total cost (ATC$_0$), marginal cost is MC$_0$ and the organisation produces output $Q_0$ at price $P_0$. As the organisation learns about its production processes, ATC falls and so will MC. Initially the fall in ATC is large, showing large learning curve effects. The movement from ATC$_1$ to ATC$_2$ is smaller than that from ACT$_0$ to ATC$_1$ – indicating smaller learning curve effects as output continues to rise.

Initially, in Figure 10.3, with average total cost $ATC_0$ and its associated marginal cost curve $MC_0$, the profit-maximising organisation produces at output level $Q_0$, obtained from the intersection of the marginal revenue and marginal cost curves. The price is then found from the demand curve and is shown as $P_0$. With no other changes in either plant size or demand, the initial learning curve effect is seen by a downward shift in both the marginal and average total cost curves, to $MC_1$ and $ATC_1$ respectively. The profit-maximising organisation will now produce a greater level of output, shown as $Q_1$, and set a lower price, $P_1$. Subsequent learning effects will be smaller and one such effect is shown by the average total cost curve, $ATC_2$, and marginal cost, $MC_2$.

## PRICING AND THE PRODUCT LIFECYCLE

The **product lifecycle** theory maintains that products have limited lives and through the course of their life they pass through a number of distinct phases.

- At the beginning of a product's life, the *introductory phase*, consumers have a low awareness of it. There is potential for the organisation to charge a premium price for the product, since the demand for it is likely to be inelastic, although the emphasis may be more on the promotion of the product as an attempt to expand consumer awareness.
- In the *growth phase*, buyers become increasingly aware of the product and sales grow. Competitors

gain knowledge of the product and if entry barriers are low they may begin to enter this market, causing the demand for the product to become more elastic.

- Once the product enters the *maturity phase*, consumers are well aware of it, its price and its attributes. A number of rival organisations may have entered the market, causing a high degree of price competitiveness. This may reduce prices down towards the marginal cost of production. In the maturity phase the growth in sales will have begun to slow and may even have levelled off.
- Finally, the product enters the *decline phase* of its cycle. This may be due to changes in the tastes of consumers or a superior product arriving in the market. Organisations may attempt to stimulate sales through non-price methods such as advertising and money-off vouchers, and some organisations may attempt to boost sales by further reducing the margin between costs and prices.

We can look at a number of products to see how they fit this product lifecycle model. In the opening growth phase, market leaders may be forced to consider either a skimming price strategy or a penetration price strategy. Polaroid often uses the former. It charges as high a price as possible for a new camera, then after the initial slowdown in sales the price is cut to attract the next price-sensitive sector of the market. IBM uses a similar pricing approach. Amstrad, on the other hand, uses a penetration pricing strategy. In 1986 it placed its wordprocessors on the market at 25 per cent of the price of competitors'. Similarly, companies introducing domestic satellite television into the

**Figure 10.4  The product lifecycle**

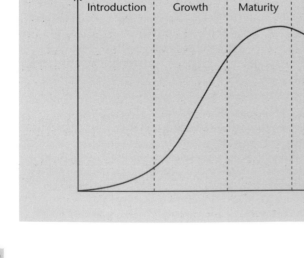

The product lifecycle has four distinct phases: introduction where sales growth is slow; the growth phase, where there is a period of rapid market acceptance; maturity, where there is a slowdown in sales growth; and decline, where sales drop off and profits decline.

UK used a penetration pricing strategy. Set-up costs were high but the satellite manufacturers needed to sell to a large proportion of the market.

When we enter the maturity phase we are probably dealing with the phase reached by most products. This phase tends to be longer than other periods in the product lifecycle. The slowdown in sales growth leads to many producers with many products to sell. This overcapacity leads to greater competition. Competitors begin to lower their prices, increase their advertising spend and increase their R&D to try to find better versions of the product. For example, Johnson & Johnson began to target the adult market with its baby shampoo and powder. Lucozade began to aim its products at younger, sportier people rather than older convalescents.

As the product falls into decline, due to changing social habits or technological innovation, market leaders will try to retain their high price relying on brand loyalty. This decline phase may be relatively slow, as in the case of oatmeal cereal, or more rapid, as in the case of gramophone records. Carrying weak products can be very costly to the organisation in terms of managing the declining product and keeping a weak product may prevent resources from being used more profitably elsewhere. However, an organisation may remain in the sector in the hope that competitors leave first. Procter & Gamble made some useful profits from its liquid soap business as other companies withdrew.

If the product lifecycle is to be believed, business decision makers can adjust prices accordingly once they have knowledge of the phase in the lifecycle which their product has reached. However, while some studies such as that by Rogers (1962) have supported the shape of the product lifecycle, others by Swan and Rink (1982) have suggested that the product lifecycle does not follow the S-shaped curve shown in Figure 10.4. Their study suggested that the shape of the product lifecycle may be influenced by the actions of the organisation itself. For example, an organisation which sets high entry barriers may see its own sales rises for very long periods. It may influence the shape of the product lifecycle by the extent to which it promotes the product. An innovator may also be able to achieve large learning curve effects which allow it to stay ahead of its rivals over the long term. Therefore, although the product lifecycle provides a neat solution to the ways in which an organisation might adapt its prices over time, in reality it is not independent of the behaviour of the organisation, and in this sense there is no guarantee that prices will behave in the way prescribed by the theory.

# EMPIRICAL EVIDENCE ON PRICING

Hall and Hitch's study in the 1930s was probably the first to consider how organisations actually attempted to derive the market price for their products. The results indicated that organisations used a cost-plus approach and further studies have suggested that a number of variants on this practice are most commonly used. Empirical work suggests that, where organisations base their prices on the costs of production, the separation of costs into fixed and variable costs is often arbitrary. Furthermore, where the organisation is a multi-product producer the allocation of costs among the various products varies greatly. In addition, organisations appear to use a number of methods for obtaining unit costs.

Nevertheless, studies by Andrews (1949) and others appeared to suggest that many organisations were using average or full cost pricing methods. Studies in the 1960s and 1970s also appeared to confirm this; *see* Fog (1960). Of course, there were organisations which appeared not to use this method of pricing but used some of the approaches outlined earlier, such as price lining and penetration pricing. However, a pricing approach based on average costs appeared to be most prevalent. With the reliance on average costs to set prices, were organisations paying too little attention to demand-side factors? This did not appear to be the case. When organisations were questioned about their markups a large proportion suggested that the markup reflected changes in demand conditions, although a shift in demand conditions could lead to different responses in terms of markups. Both Hazeldine (1980) and Hawkins (1973) concluded that demand-side factors were influential in setting prices. Hawkins concluded that markups were higher when demand is inelastic, when there are barriers to entry and when the economy is more buoyant. Eichner (1987) also supports this view.

Dean (1978) argued that costs played only a minor part in determining price. Costs provided a lower floor to which price could fall but, once above the floor, the price could vary markedly. Cunningham and Hornby (1993) support this view in their analysis of pricing practices in small firms.

What the empirical evidence suggests is that both supply- and demand-side factors affect the pricing of products, but that it would be hazardous to infer consistency in organisations' pricing strategies.

◆ **CASE STUDY 10.5**

# New car prices: don't be taken for a ride

August is traditionally the month in the UK when the new prefix begins on car registration plates. What has always been of interest for the consumer is the price of a new car in the UK when compared with those in the rest of Europe. A UK report (by the Monopolies and Mergers Commission (*New Motor Cars*, HMSO, 1992) shows that new cars can cost as much as a third more in the UK than they do in Italy, one of the cheapest countries. Moreover, it makes no difference where the car has been made.

One explanation for the differentials in prices has been blamed on currency volatility, but some consumers believe that markups differ between countries. For example, a Ford Fiesta assembled in the UK is 33 per cent more expensive to buy in the UK than in Italy. Conversely, a Ford Mondeo built in Belgium is more expensive in Belgium than that in the UK, and its UK price is only 5 per cent dearer than in Italy. Interestingly, French motorists pay more for a Renault 19 and Laguna, Citroen ZX or Peugeot 106 than does anyone else in Europe. British-built Rovers suffer from similar fluctuations in price throughout Europe. The price of a Rover 214 differs by 50 per cent between the lowest and highest prices, in Italy and Germany. It costs 40 per cent more in the UK than Italy, while a Rover 416 is 25 per cent more expensive in the UK than in Italy.

The report takes account of differences before and after tax and different specifications for each market. Even after this the differentials between countries are quite marked, as Table 10.4 shows.

The Consumers' Association in the UK suggests that the price differentials show evidence that the car manufacturers are 'working the market'. Currency alterations do account for some of the differential, but not all. In fact, there is evidence that in the UK small cars are overpriced while bigger cars are much more competitive. One explanation for the higher price paid by UK consumers is that driving in the UK occurs on the left-hand side, but the Consumers' Association feels that, even with this factor taken account, it is still difficult to conclude that currency fluctuations are the main issue. It is very difficult to track down these currency factors in any case, since different parts of the car are made in different countries whose currencies may or may not have appreciated against sterling.

The conclusion could be drawn that the level of demand and the degree of competition are major factors in determining the markups on the ranges of cars. The fact that there is no pan-European pricing policy for cars could be explained by the following:

■ *Consumers* – car ownership in the EU is related to consumer wealth, the availability of public transport, car sales tax and the possibility of obtaining a car through a remuneration package.
■ *Dealer arrangements* – there are often specific factors which restrict dealer freedom, such as the EU block-exemption regulation.
■ *Other factors* – items which are standard in some cars, such as electric windows and in-car stereo systems, are not standard in others.

**Table 10.4  Prices for selected cars across Europe (£)**

|  | UK | France | Belgium | Italy | Germany | Spain |
|---|---|---|---|---|---|---|
| Fiat Cinquecento (with tax) | 5110 | 5676 | 5518 | 4839 | 5778 | 5288 |
| Fiat Cinquecento (without tax) | 4349 | 4786 | 4580 | 4067 | 5025 | 4025 |
| Nissan Micra (with tax) | 7775 | 7979 | 8566 | 6982 | 8542 | 7919 |
| Nissan Micra (without tax) | 6617 | 6727 | 7108 | 5867 | 7427 | 6186 |
| Ford Fiesta 1.1L (with tax) | 8131 | 8735 | 7972 | 6546 | 8806 | 8265 |
| Ford Fiesta 1.1L (without tax) | 9920 | 7365 | 6616 | 5501 | 7657 | 6457 |
| Volkswagen Golf (with tax) | 9316 | 9189 | 10366 | 8689 | 9857 | 9847 |
| Volkswagen Golf (without tax) | 7928 | 7748 | 8603 | 7081 | 8571 | 7693 |
| Rover 214 (with tax) | 11795 | N/A | 12877 | 9111 | 12625 | 10818 |
| Rover 214 (without tax) | 10038 | N/A | 10686 | 7656 | 10978 | 8451 |
| BMW 316i (with tax) | 15479 | 17129 | 17792 | 14734 | 17179 | 17851 |
| BMW 316i (without tax) | 13174 | 14141 | 14765 | 12381 | 14938 | 13944 |
| Vauxhall Omega (with tax) | 18430 | 20771 | 21694 | 16730 | 21127 | 21743 |
| Vauxhall Omega (without tax) | 15685 | 17513 | 17638 | 13889 | 18371 | 16987 |

Source: Monopolies and Mergers Commission (1992) *New Motor Cars*, HMSO, London. Crown Copyright 1992. Reproduced with the permission of the Controller of HMSO.

◆ **Exercise 10.5**

**1** Can the European Commission reduce the level of price differentiation between the different makes of cars in the European Union, or can market forces be relied on to reduce price discrepancies?

**2** There is no current pan-European pricing policy for cars in Europe, but should there be? Should car companies continue with essentially national pricing policies?

### Comment on the case study

Launching a new car on to the market is more likely to follow a penetration strategy for mass-market cars, while for more exclusive cars, such as Ferrari or Lotus, a skimming price approach may be more appropriate. However, if a penetration pricing approach is used Case study 10.5 indicates that this price can vary between markets. Some of this variation will be due to differences in national markets, although at other times it may be the organisation which develops different pricing policies in differ-ent markets. For example, Airbus sells its aeroplanes at about the same price everywhere, but other companies have different prices in separate markets, the price being set to allow for differences in economic conditions, competitive situations, laws and regulations and higher costs. A pair of Levi's jeans costs approximately $30 in the United States yet sells for $63 in Japan and $88 in Paris.

Some of the reasons for the price differential are higher shipping and insurance costs, import tariffs, costs associated with exchange-rate fluctuations and the like. Moreover, distribution costs can vary since retailers in one country may prefer to buy in smaller quantities. For example, Campbell found that, whereas its domestic (US) retailers ordered soup in boxes of 48 of the same variety, UK retailers preferred to order boxes of 24 cans of different varieties. Thus Campbell's distribution costs were higher in the UK and led to higher prices for its soups. In other words, organisations face a whole raft of possible ways to price their products in the domestic market and these are further complicated when selling into separate geographical markets.

## SUMMARY

◆ This chapter has examined a number of the most widely used pricing practices in actual market situations.

◆ Whereas in Chapter 9 pricing was considered under conditions of certainty, typically organisations do not possess full information concerning their cost and revenue functions, therefore pricing decisions are made under conditions of uncertainty. It is possible, however, to adapt marginalist pricing analysis when uncertainty exists, either using an estimate of the organisation's demand curve or starting from some knowledge of the price elasticity of demand.

◆ Where information is uncertain, decision makers need to balance the costs of searching for more accurate information against the benefits which such information brings in terms of improved profit performance. Where search costs are small, the organisation can be expected to undertake sufficient information-gathering activity, producing an output close to the profit-maximising level. If, however, search costs are in excess of any gain in profit, then alternative pricing strategies to the marginalist approach may be pursued.

◆ Empirical research suggests that many organisations secure an optimal pricing strategy through markup pricing, where prices are established to cover all direct costs plus a markup for profit. Markup pricing can be the same as marginalist pricing if the markup chosen is related to the elasticity of demand. There is some debate as to whether organisations do in fact use elasticities of demand to derive their markups. Nonetheless, markets which are more competitive will have more elastic demands and the elasticity approach suggests that these markups will be smaller.

◆ Markup pricing indicates that with iso-demand curve shifts an organisation will not alter its percentage markup. However, in the case of inflationary conditions which affect the cost base, the organisation will pass all of these on to the consumer. Markup pricing also acts as a coordinating device in oligopolistic markets.

◆ Where markets have been in existence for a length of time, the current pricing regime is already in place and the organisation has a range of pricing techniques available to it. It may use price positioning, establishing the price of the commodity in relation to the attributes of the product compared with the competitors in the market. Higher prices can be linked to products which possess more attributes in relation to other products on the market.

◆ Where an organisation wishes to give the appearance that the product is of high quality, a prestige pricing strategy may be used. Sometimes, however, an organisation may be producing a product for which there is a 'going price' in the market. In this case the company attempts to produce a product which allows it to maximise profits at this price. Such an approach is called price lining.

◆ The chapter has discussed other pricing strategies used by organisations in existing markets. Promotional pricing can be used to attract a customer to the product. Product bundle pricing is used to sell two products together instead of separately, at a price which is less that of the two products if they were bought separately. Predatory pricing, that is, deliberately setting a price low, can be used to deter new entrants into a market as well as driving out some, if not all, of the existing competition. Organisations may attempt to fix the price of the product by agreeing on a price through collusion.

◆ When the products are new to the market, alternative pricing strategies may have to be pursued since the demand curves for the products will be even less certain. This chapter investigates two approaches to the pricing of new products, skimming pricing and penetration pricing. In the former, the organisation sets a relatively high price for the product in order to obtain high short-term profits. Such a pricing strategy may be appropriate where the demand for the product is not expected to extend very much beyond the short run or where there are sufficiently high barriers to entry. Penetration pricing, however, is more appropriate where the organisation's expectations of demand stretch further than the short run. The price is set relatively low in an attempt to obtain a large share of the market, where the organisation expects the barriers to entry into the market to be low.

◆ Whichever pricing strategy is chosen for a new product, it would be expected that over time price modifications would be made. These revisions in price may be due to the impact of learning curves lowering the cost base of the organisation, changes in the level of competition and the role of the product lifecycle, which may alter the elasticity of demand for the product over time.

◆ Prices for the same product may differ between countries. Part of the reason comes from differences in national markets in terms of the level of competition, legislation and so on. In addition, price differentials exist because of the nature of retailing, the role and impact of exchange rate differentials, the impact of tariffs and higher shipping and insurance costs.

◆ This chapter has therefore shown that in practice organisations do not follow a single pricing regime. They appear to be quite happy to adapt their pricing structures to changes in their circumstances. Nonetheless, some of these approximate to the marginalist approach seen in Chapter 9.

## REVIEW QUESTIONS

1  An Italian clothing company sells its shirts to retailers for L30 000 each, approximately 25 per cent over the wholesaler's average variable costs, which is constant at L22 500 per shirt.

   Calculate the price elasticity of demand.

   If the organisation was looking for a 40 per cent markup, what value would be appropriate for elasticity of demand?

2  Consider the markups on different items sold through a supermarket. Which items would you consider to have the highest markups? Why?

3  What are the major issues in:
   a  Product bundle pricing?
   b  Prestige pricing?

4 Why do organisation price items as loss leaders? What are the problems with this approach? Are there specific items which are best used as loss leaders? Which groups of consumers respond best to loss-leader pricing?

5 A German beer company cut the prices of its beer by 4 per cent during the second quarter of 1995 and in response there was an 8 per cent increase in beer sales over that period compared with a year earlier.

   a Calculate the point price elasticity of demand for German beer.

   b Calculate the company's optimal beer price if the marginal cost is DM10.

6 What are the disadvantages of using the product lifecycle to determine the price of a product?

7 Using examples, consider products where a skimming price strategy has been used. Has this strategy worked?

8 Penetration pricing strategies are the same as loss-leader strategies. Discuss.

# Appendix 10.1

## THE RELATIONSHIP BETWEEN DEMAND AND MARGINAL REVENUE

Suppose that a firm's demand curve has been estimated to be:

$$Q = 100 - 5P$$

where,

    $Q$ = Quantity demanded
    $P$ = Own price

This demand curve can be rearranged in terms of price to give:

$$5P = 100 - Q$$

or,

$$P = 20 - Q/5$$

In this relationship price ($P$) will be on the vertical axis of a diagram of price against quantity ($Q$). $Q$ will be on the horizontal axis, the intercept term is 20 and the slope of the demand equation is $-1/5$.

Finding the organisation's marginal revenue equation requires the construction of its total revenue equation. Total revenue is price multiplied by quantity. This is shown below:

    Total Revenue (TR) = Price ($P$) × Quantity ($Q$)

Using the demand equation from above:

$$TR = (20 - Q/5)Q$$

or,

$$TR = 20Q - Q2/5$$

Marginal revenue (MR) is the change in total revenue as the output of the organisation is altered by one unit. Mathematically this can be obtained from differentiating the total revenue equation with respect to quantity:

$$MR = dTR/dQ = 20 - 2Q/5$$

The marginal revenue equation indicates that there is an intercept term of 20 on the vertical axis – the same as the demand equation – and a slope of $-2/5$, that is, a slope or gradient twice as steep as that for the demand curve.

Suppose that the intersection of marginal revenue and marginal cost indicates that the profit-maximising level of output is $Q = 20$. This can be substituted into the demand equation to determine the profit-maximising price:

$$P = 20 - 20/5, \text{ or } P = 16.$$

## Appendix 10.2

# NON-SMOOTH MARGINAL REVENUE CURVES

Suppose that the total revenue curve is of the type shown in Figure 10.5.

Over the horizontal stretches of the total revenue curve there is no change in total revenue as output increases. Marginal revenue is defined as the change in total revenue when output is altered by one unit. Over the flat stretches of the total revenue curve, therefore, the marginal revenue is zero. Since this happens on a number of occasions, marginal revenue will not be drawn as a smooth curve and it does not enable the organisation to estimate the particular point at which profits will be maximised.

**Figure 10.5  Discontinuity in the total revenue curve**

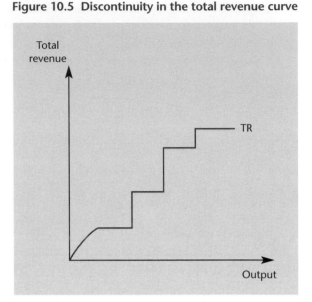

Where total revenue is a stepped function, marginal revenue is zero over the horizontal parts of the total revenue function.

## Appendix 10.3

# THE RELATIONSHIP BETWEEN MARGINAL VARIABLE COST AND MARGINAL COST

Figure 10.6 shows a linear total variable cost curve (TVC) which goes through the origin and two levels of output with their associated total variable costs. As the figure shows, when the level of output is 10 units the total variable cost is £550 and when the output increases to 15 units the total variable cost is £825.

Average variable cost is defined as total variable cost divided by the number of units of output. Therefore, when the level of output is 10 units, the average variable cost (AVC) equals 550/10, or 55. Similarly, the average variable cost when 15 units of output are produced is 825/15, which again equals 55. Therefore, one of the characteristics of a total cost curve that goes through the origin and is a straight line is that the average cost is always constant.

It is also possible to calculate the slope of the TVC line. This can be obtained in a number of ways, but the approach adopted here is to use the formula:

$$\text{Slope (gradient)} = \frac{\text{The vertical distance between two points on a line}}{\text{The horizontal distance between two points on a line}}$$

In the case of the TVC line in Figure 10.6, the gradient or slope is equal to:

$$\text{Slope} = (825 - 550)/(15 - 10) = 275/5 = 55$$

The slope of this line equals the average variable costs calculated earlier. Therefore, one conclusion that can be reached about a linear line that goes through the origin is that the average term equals the slope or the marginal term.

Earlier it has been established that in economics economists call the slope or the gradient of the total cost curve marginal cost. It follows, therefore, that the slope of the TVC line is called the marginal variable cost (MVC).

Figure 10.7 reproduces a diagram seen earlier in Chapter 8 (Figure 8.3), but this time the cost

**Figure 10.6 The relationship between total variable cost, marginal cost and average variable cost**

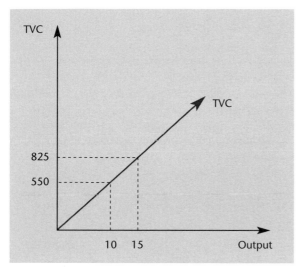

The slope of the TVC curve is called marginal variable cost.

**Figure 10.7 Total, variable and fixed cost curves**

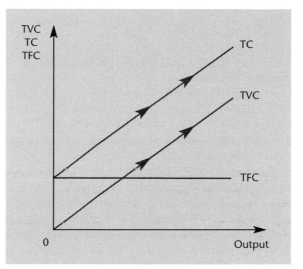

Since TC and TVC are parallel, the slope of TVC (MVC) and the slope of TC (MC) are equal. It is possible to replace the term MVC with MC.

curves have been drawn as straight lines. Since TC is the sum of TVC and TFC, and because TFCs are constant as output changes, then TC is parallel to TVC, the distance between the two being TFC. Since TC is parallel to TVC their two slopes or gradients are the same. The slope of the TVC curve,

marginal variable cost (MVC), equals the slope of the TC curve, marginal cost (MC). Therefore, in discussing the relationship between AVC and MVC in Figure 10.7, it is possible to replace MVC with MC. It follows that, with a linear TVC line that goes through the origin, AVC equals MC.

## GLOSSARY OF NEW TERMS

**Markup pricing:** A pricing strategy where the market price is determined by adding a percentage markup to the direct cost ( average variable cost) of the product.

**Penetration pricing:** The price of a new product is set deliberately low to enable the organisation to obtain a large customer base.

**Predatory pricing:** Setting the price of a product at a deliberately low level to destroy or eliminate the competition.

**Prestige pricing:** The process of deliberately setting a high price for the product to attract prestige-minded consumers.

**Price fixing:** A procedure by which organisations within a market agree on a price to sell their products enhancing their profits and thereby removing price competitiveness.

**Price lining:** The organisation sets a price and then develops a product which allows it to maximise profits at this price.

**Price positioning:** Pricing a product in relation to competing products.

**Price tendering:** A situation where a contract is offered to the market and organisations put in prices (bids) for the contract.

**Product bundle pricing:** The strategy of pricing two or more products together as a parcel for a single price.

**Product lifecycle:** The assertion that products have limited lives and go through distinct phases of growth, maturity, saturation and decline.

**Promotional pricing:** The reduction of the price of a product over the short term to attract customer sales.

**Skimming price:** A price strategy of setting a high price initially for the product to 'skim the cream off the market' before subsequently reducing the price.

# READING

Griffiths, A and Wall, S (1997) *Applied Economics: An Introductory Course*, 7th edn, Addison Wesley Longman, Harlow.
*This text includes a chapter on pricing practices in a European context.*

Hirschey, M, Pappas, J L and Whigham, D (1995) *Managerial Economics: European Edition*, Dryden Press, London.
*The text includes some useful theory and practical illustrations of pricing.*

Kotler, P, Armstrong, G, Saunders, J and Wong, V (1996) *Principles of Marketing: European Edition*, Prentice Hall, Hemel Hempstead.
*This text covers a wide range of marketing issues, but chapters 16 and 17 provide some good illustrative material on pricing practices.*

Nagel, T T and Holen, R K (1995) *The Strategy and Tactics of Pricing*, 2nd edn, Prentice Hall, Hemel Hempstead.
*This text provides a comprehensive discussion of a wide range of pricing strategies.*

## Further reading

Andrews, P W S (1949) *Manufacturing Business*, Macmillan, London.

Cunningham, D and Hornby, W (1993) 'Pricing decisions in small firms', *Management Decisions*, Vol 31, No 7, pp 46–55.

Dean, J (1978) 'Techniques for pricing new products and services' in Britt, S H and Boyd, H W (eds) *Marketing and Administrative Action*, 4th edn, McGraw-Hill, Maidenhead.

Dorward, N M (1987) *The Pricing Decision: Economic Theory and Business Practice*, Harper and Row, London.

Eichner, A S (1987) 'Prices and Pricing', *Journal of Economic Issues*, December, Vol 21, No 4, pp 1555–84.

Fog, B (1960) *Industrial Pricing Policies*, North-Holland, London.

Hall, R L and Hitch, C J (1939) 'Price Theory and Business Behaviour', *Oxford Economic Papers*, Vol 2, pp 12–45.

Hawkins, C J (1973) *Theory of the Firm*, Macmillan, Basingstoke.

Hazeldine, T (1980) 'Testing two models of pricing and protection with Canada/US data', *Journal of Industrial Economics,* Vol 29, No 2, December.

Lanzillotti, R (1958) 'Pricing objectives in large companies', *American Economic Review*, December, Vol 48, No 5, pp 921–40.

Lester, R A (1946) 'Shortcomings of Marginal Analysis for Wage-Employment Problems', *American Economic Review*, Vol 36, No 2, pp 63–82.

Nelson, P (1970) 'Information and Consumer Behaviour', *Journal of Political Economy*, Vol 78, No 3, pp 311–29.

Odajiri, H and Yamashita, T (1987) 'Price markups, market structure and business fluctuations in Japanese manufacturing industries', *Journal of Industrial Economics*, Vol 35, No 34, pp 317–32.

Rogers, E M (1962) *Diffusion of Innovations*, Free Press, New York.

Shipley, D D (1981) 'Pricing objectives in British manufacturing industry', *Journal of Industrial Economics*, Vol 29, No 4, pp 429–43.

Swan, J E and Rink, D R (1982) 'Fitting marketing strategy to varying product life cycles', *Business Horizons*, Vol 25, No 1, pp 72–6.

CHAPTER $11$

# NON-PRICE COMPETITION AND THE MARKETING MIX

## OBJECTIVES

◆ To introduce the concept of the marketing mix – the four Ps.

◆ To investigate the manner in which the marketing mix can be manipulated.

◆ To consider the economist's view of advertising within oligopolistic markets.

◆ To look at the role of the product as a strategic tool to be used by organisations within the marketplace.

◆ To consider the empirical effect of advertising on industrial structure, conduct and performance.

## KEY TERMS

4Ps

Channels

(Consumer) durable good

Generic product

Horizontal differentiation

Jobber

Marketing mix

Non-durable good

Own brand/private label

Portfolio analysis

Quality differentiation

Strategic business area (SBA)

Vertical differentiation

## CHAPTER OUTLINE

Business application

Introduction

The marketing mix

Case study 11.1 Video console computer games and PC compatible games

Product decisions: Ansoff's portfolio analysis

Product variations and organisational conduct and performance

Product quality and competition

Advertising and market structure

Case study 11.2 Fall-out from a product flop

Case study 11.3 MMC lifts price controls on condoms

Concluding remarks

Summary

Review questions

Glossary of new terms

Reading

# Europe reaches for its cereal

The French are abandoning their croissants, Belgians their rolls and Italians their habit of nothing but espresso. Across Europe, people are swapping their traditional breakfasts for a bowl of processed grain and cold milk. The European market for breakfast cereals has grown in recent years to be worth some £1bn annually.

Even during recession, most countries have increased consumption. For example, sales in France, the second largest European market for cereal after the UK, increased by 21 per cent in the year to May 1993.

Europe has become an increasingly competitive market for cereal manufacturers. The recent acquisition of two cereal companies by the Dutch food and drinks company BolsWessanen, giving it almost 10 per cent of the European cereal market overnight, has brought into the open what industry insiders have known for some time.

To compete seriously, companies must have the market share and financial muscle to back new products with heavy advertising. This year, Kellogg is estimated to be spending £6m in the UK alone to support its Corn Pops brand.

Harrison & Crosfield, the UK conglomerate which sold the companies to BolsWessanen, admitted it would not compete in this league by shedding what had been for it a successful, but peripheral, business.

The European breakfast cereals market is controlled by a few large companies. According to the *Food Industry Bulletin*, Kellogg dominates with more than 50 per cent, followed by Weetabix at 9.5 per cent and Cereal Partners Worldwide, a joint venture between Nestlé and General Mills, with 6 per cent.

The arrival of CP in 1989 is widely credited with setting off the real explosion in the market. Within three years, through aggressive marketing and new product launches, it had won sales of some $348m (£225m). Naturally, Kellogg fought back. When CP launched its Golden Grahams, Kellogg came back a few weeks later with its own Golden Crackers. When CP introduced Clusters, Kellogg responded with Nutfeast.

The battle even threatened a veteran campaigner, Tony the Tiger, of Frosties fame. CP lit upon Huey, Dewey and Louie, Donald Duck's nephews, as the cartoon warriors, for its Trio cereal in France.

But the biggest beneficiaries of the battle between the cereal giants appear to have been the manufacturers of own label products. Own labels claim 11.5 per cent of total European cereal sales, second only to Kellogg. The European market for private label products is widely acknowledged to be growing at a faster rate than the branded sector.

It is partly due to the increasing number of adults who are turning to cereal as a healthier breakfast option. In the UK, for example, the own label market is largely an adult market, focusing on mueslis and bran products.

*Source: Financial Times, 4 October 1994. Reprinted with permission.*

## Comment

The tastes of the European citizen at breakfast time appear to be changing. More and more are switching to a cereal-and-cold-milk start to the day, as opposed to their traditional fare. Such a change represents a huge opportunity for cereal manufacturers and supermarkets.

This opportunity is the reason for the increasing expenditure on advertising breakfast cereals by the largest competitors. Kellogg holds the largest market share, with over 50 per cent, but Weetabix and Cereal Partners Worldwide also hold relatively large market shares. As a result, in protecting these shares and in their attempts to increase the cereal-buying population, the advertising budgets for these organisations add up to millions of pounds sterling per annum.

The market is considered to be lucrative and the competitors are keen to exploit their current positions. An additional problem for the well-known brands is the increasing share of the market being taken by the own-label, supermarket brands. In Europe 50 per cent of these are manufactured by BolsWessanen, a Dutch company. The implication as own-label cereals take off, however, is that the recognised brands will have to spend even more on advertising to maintain their position. New brands were also being developed by the organisations mentioned. The hope in such cases is that consumers will buy the newly launched products as well as the established products because they recognise the manufacturer's brand name.

How are the advertising campaigns put together? Who decides whether they should be on television, radio or posters? How can the impact of advertising be increased? Do money-off coupons tempt the consumer to try, or are they a waste of money? Should another product be added to the range, to sell under the name already recognised by customers?

# INTRODUCTION

This chapter will consider the role of advertising and other forms of non-price competition in the marketplace. It has previously been noted that, where organisations are operating in an oligopolistic market structure, they will often compete on a non-price basis. Economists argue that there are measurable effects of advertising in all market structures. These effects will be looked at both theoretically and in terms of the application of advertising in appropriate markets, for example the effect that advertising and new product development have on the competitive nature of markets.

The concept of the product will be introduced and investigated, with reference to both the economists' and the marketers' definitions. This will enable and inform a discussion and exposition of the various marketing decisions which any organisation has to take. Within the discussion of the product, the ideas of horizontal and vertical product differentiation will be introduced and discussed.

Throughout the chapter, the context of organisations selling to individual consumers will be emphasised, although business-to-business marketing will also be considered briefly.

Advertising and other forms of promotion have previously been cited as the manner in which non-price competition takes place. The implications of advertising and other forms of non-price competition will be discussed here, not just in the context of the oligopolist. The use of research and development and new product placement also gives organisations a competitive edge in their market(s). The effect of invention, innovation and diffusion of the product on to the general marketplace will be discussed in this context.

Finally, the role of people as contributors to the success of organisations on a non-price basis will be introduced. The effect that loyalty, service and training, as well as customer focus, have on sales, market share and profit will be outlined.

# THE MARKETING MIX

The **marketing mix** consists of *'the marketing manager's controllable factors, the marketing actions of product, price, promotion and place that he or she can take to solve a marketing problem'*, according to Berkowitz *et al* (1992). The marketing mix therefore contains the tools that marketers use to construct and manipulate a product's brand identity. Different combinations of these factors can contribute to a product's (continued) success or demise.

The marketing mix is also known as the **4Ps**: product, price, promotion and place. Evolution in marketing theory and practice and changes in the business environment have meant that strict application of the 4Ps will no longer guarantee a product's success. Despite the changes in marketing philosophy, however, many marketers still recognise that the 4Ps provide the basic framework for marketing in the late stages of the twentieth century.

## Product

Of the 4Ps, the concept of product and the ensuing debate relating to what constitutes a product have perhaps attracted the attention of most critics. According to Kotler *et al* (1996), the basic definition of the product is: *'anything offered to a market for attention, acquisition, use or consumption that might satisfy a want or need'*. This definition means that a product could be anything from an actual, physical entity (for example, a pencil) offered for sale to the provision of an instantly consumed service (for example, a telephone number enquiry service).

There are various ways in which products may be classified. The most simple is between type of buyer: consumer or industry. For the purposes of this chapter, the more interesting category is that of consumer products – this will form the basis for discussion and analysis. In the previous paragraph, the products (the pencil and the telephone number enquiry service) may be classified by their nature, that is, by what they provide for the consumer. This classification mechanism may be broken down into a number of categories:

- *Pure tangible* – an actual physical product, such as a pencil which has no after-sales service associated with it.
- *Tangible* – a physical product sold primarily for what it is, or what it does, such as a car which is bought for its transportation properties. Added to this, the product comes with some after-sales service provision.
- *Service with accompanying goods and services* – where a product is sold on the strength of the reputation accorded to it. For example, the difference between airline seat tickets is not the piece of paper upon which they are printed, but the quality of the service received by the consumer as a result of their purchase.
- *Pure service* – a service offered for sale, such as telephone number enquiries. The product in the case of a pure service is non-tangible.

◆ **Exercise 11.1**

For each of the categories given above, provide three further examples of products which fit the definitions given.

It may be difficult to assign a product solely to one category. For example, is dental care a service with accompanying goods and services, or is it a pure service? Which category would a meal at McDonald's or Burger King fall into? These categories classify the items by comparing the level of tangible product to level of service associated with it. Such a classification system can become onerous to use.

An alternative system is one where product categories are more broadly defined as **consumer non-durables**, **consumer durables** and service. Consumer non-durables are one of several use products which are purchased relatively frequently by consumers with quite a large amount of market knowledge. Consumer durables are less frequently purchased, as they are designed to last for long time periods, or for many uses. Less market knowledge may exist here, although consumers will shop around to find the best product offering. The relationship between these categorisation alternatives is given in Table 11.1.

An alternative way of classifying consumer products is with reference to three criteria:

- Frequency of purchase.
- Attributes used in purchase.
- Effort expended by the consumer with reference to their purchase decision.

When these criteria are used, the following categories exist:

- *Convenience* – Frequently purchased, easily substituted for and easy to obtain.
- *Shopping products* – Infrequently purchased, based on an informed purchase decision (by

comparing product attributes) and reasonably widely available.

- *Speciality products* – Infrequently purchased, based on strict criteria arising from substantial research with limited availability.
- *Unsought products* – Very infrequently purchased, consumers are likely unwillingly or accidentally to find themselves in the position of demand, rather than shopping around in advance. Some research is undertaken, but with limited availability. An example of an unsought product might be a life assurance policy relating to a mortgage.

Obviously, the category into which any product falls is partially decided by individual experience and opinion. Over time, as markets develop or decline, the category into which a product falls may change. For example, in the 1970s a computer would have fallen into the speciality product category. Only very large or specialist businesses and government departments had any use for computers. In the 1990s, the personal computer has become almost a shopping product for many households.

◆ **Exercise 11.2**

Name five products which have changed category in the last five to ten years (in your opinion). Be prepared to justify this list with fellow students.

**Product branding**

An important part of the product, historically, has been the concept of the brand. The brand serves as an identification system for the consumer. The brand name, brand mark and trademarks associated with products are used to convey to the consumer certain quality standards and characteristics about a product. To illustrate this point, consider Coca-Cola. In terms of its ingredients, Coca-Cola is simply carbonated, flavoured water. What makes it unique is the fact that Coca-Cola as a brand has been associated, via marketing and especially advertising, with young people, a certain, fun, way of life etc. So Coca-Cola, the carbonated, flavoured water, has become a formidable brand name as a result of the fact that consumers identify with the marketing that has been offered and therefore identify with the product. Other producers of carbonated, flavoured water wishing to compete with Coca-Cola have to compete on flavour – a small part of the product – and more so with the brand itself. As a result, in the global soft drinks industry,

**Table 11.1**

| Product categories | Broad product categories |
|---|---|
| Pure tangible | Consumer non-durables \| Consumer durables \| Service |
| Tangible | |
| Product with good or service | |
| Pure service | |

Coca-Cola has few competitors because of the financial resources required to establish and maintain efficient market share; although there are many relatively small competitors in many of the distinct geographical markets worldwide.

Other aspects of product branding which should be mentioned are brand extension and multibrands. If a brand is doing particularly well, other products may be launched under the same family name to capitalise on its success. This is brand extension. The other products may be modifications to the original, or completely new products. There are advantages associated with making a brand extension. Although the product is not necessarily known, the brand will be and therefore will more easily attract consumers. For example, think of 3M's entry into the computer disk market. 3M is already well known in its traditional marketplace for its range of sticky tapes and its patent of Post-it™ notes, sticky-backed pads of paper which are used widely in offices to stick messages to desks, PCs and so on. The entry into the computer disk market uses some of the tapes' technology and expertise, but is also more likely to be successful because the 3M name is already known and associated with successful products. The budget required to advertise a product within a brand extension will be lower than that required to launch a completely new brand.

Multibrands exist when a producer launches two or more products under the same brand name. The products within a multibrand will fall into the same product category and will therefore be in competition with each other. This means that the products are substitute goods. Most soap powder and detergents manufacturers possess such portfolios. There is a sound rationale for an organisation to want to launch products which will be competing with each other:

- More products mean that the producer can demand more shelf space and therefore gains a better chance of 'crowding out' competitors' products, and attracting the marginal consumer to one of its own products.
- If the launch of products is spread over time, then the producer can advertise, promote and generate interest in each of the multibrand products while maintaining the brand name at the forefront of consumer interest for a long period. Here again, marginal consumers may be attracted by the new product.

## Generic and own-label brands

An interesting phenomenon of the late 1980s and early 1990s has been the growth in popularity of **generic products** and **own-label brands**. Previously, particularly in terms of consumer nondurables, consumer preference had been for branded goods. That is, until 'Marlboro Friday' in the United States, consumers and producers had previously believed that own-label products were inferior goods (*see* Chapter 5) compared to branded goods. Marlboro Friday refers to the day when Philip Morris (owners of Marlboro) cut the price of the brand in order to compete with the supermarkets' cheap, own-label, unbranded bestselling cigarettes. Now many supermarkets are selling their own products to compete with branded products. The question to be asked is whether private label products are actually becoming a brand in their own right.

## Augmented products

So far, the product has been discussed and categorised in the context of its use to the consumer. Theodore Levitt (1972) was the first to identify that it is not enough to produce and sell a perfect physical product. Increasingly, consumers are attracted by advertising, packaging, warranties, after-sales service etc. In fact, he claimed:

> The new competition is not based upon what companies produce in their factories, but between what they add to their factory output in the form of packaging, services, advertising, customer advice, financing, delivery arrangements, warehousing and other things that people value.

Essentially, Levitt was looking beyond the product as it had been conceived by marketing experts and was more concerned with the complete consumption package. To illustrate this thinking, the ideas of the core product, tangible product and augmented product were developed. These three elements combine to make the product, as considered by today's marketers.

Figure 11.1 illustrates the relationship between the core, tangible and augmented product. It can be seen that the core product is the item that has been previously considered in this chapter as the product, that is, the physical unit or the service which is being offered to the public for consumption. Added to this are the factors which combine to constitute the tangible product: the product's packaging, brand (where applicable), style and any features

**Figure 11.1**

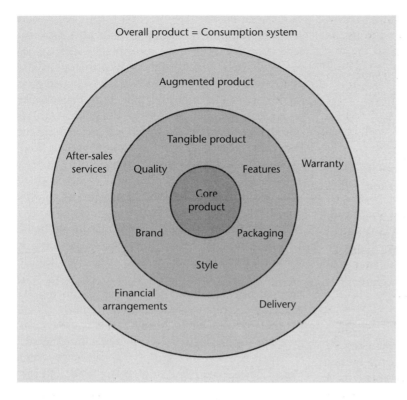

Levitt's 'augmented product' consists of the core product, the thing that is being sold, along with all its packaging, brand and other features which make up the tangible product. Levitt contends that consumers make purchase decisions based on more than this. They also consider the additional services and attributes in the product offering: the augmented product. As consumers become more sophisticated, the pressure on producers to supply better-quality augmented products increases.

which make it different from the competitor's version. Finally, the product is augmented by the offer and delivery of after-sales service, delivery, warranty etc. These all combine to provide the augmented product, or the complete consumption package.

Product is obviously a very important factor within the marketing mix. Without product, the other Ps would be pointless. Whether the product is of high or low quality, offers little or comprehensive levels of after-sales service, are decisions which the producer must make with reference not only to their own but also to the market position. Little mention has been made here of the importance of making the correct packaging and service decisions with reference to the product. These can combine to contribute to its success. There is not enough space to enter into discussion of how these decisions might be made, what the factors affecting the decision are and so on. If the reader is interested in these aspects, see the reading references at the end of this chapter. Each of the marketing textbooks listed will provide further insight.

## Promotion

Promotion is the activity which takes the product to the marketplace. Any activity which heightens the public's awareness of a product is promotion. There are three main ways in which promotion can eventually raise the awareness of the general public about a product: promotion aimed at the consumer, promotion aimed at the trade and promotion aimed at the salesforce.

Consumer promotion takes a variety of different forms. These are constantly being developed and honed. It would be difficult to give a comprehensive list here, so the more common and effective ones will briefly be described:

- *Samples* – given to the consumer free of charge to test the product prior to purchase. Sample-sized products might also be sold to the consumer, where the sample is a small version of the actual product to give a taste of the real thing.
- *Coupons* – distributed to homes or available at the point of sale to offer discounts or free products to consumers, to attract them to try the product.
- *Price packs* – specially low-priced product packages designed to attract trial of the product.
- *Premiums* – usually gifts which are offered free to consumers after purchase of the product. The consumer may have to send off for the gift, or may be given it at the point of purchase.
- *Displays* – used at the point of sale to heighten interest in the product.

With reference to promotion aimed at trade, the overall objective is slightly different, since the producer is attempting to convince the retailer to stock and sell its product. The promotional activities used here include:

- *Conventions and shows* – Attendance at specialist conventions where the appropriate traders will be can be very effective. They will be able to see the product, possibly try it for themselves and generally gain more understanding of it. Additionally, the retailer may be able to negotiate special terms for delivery, payment etc.
- *Competitions* – retailers are offered the opportunity to enter competitions, lotteries and other events sponsored by the producers.
- *Merchandise* – free gifts, pens, mugs, clocks, calculators; anything in fact, which bears the producer's or the brand name are given to retailers by the producer. This may be on receipt of an order, or simply as an inducement to make an order.

When targeting the salesforce, the techniques used are similar to those used to attract trade interest:

- *Bonuses* – Where a salesperson exceeds a certain volume of sales they may qualify for a bonus. This type of promotion is likely to occur on a producer-owned, or run, sales outlet where the producer wishes to sell more of a given product or range.
- *Gifts* – similar to the idea of bonuses, salespeople are rewarded for achieving sales targets by earning free gifts from the producer.

---

◆ **Exercise 11.3**

What types of promotional activity are you aware of? Describe the activity involved in promoting the following:

1 convenience products
2 consumer non-durables
3 consumer durables
4 shopping products
5 speciality products
6 unsought products.

---

Although promotional activity is important, there are other aspects to promotion which also require attention.

### Publicity

Any new product, or product wishing to maintain or increase market share, will require ongoing publicity. Otherwise, imitations and competitors will find it easier to steal customers away. Various forms of publicity will be associated with a product.

If the product is likely to cause a stir, goes against public opinion or requires a level of after-sales service, the producer may set up a public relations team to deal with enquiries, set the record straight and generally ensure that the product receives good press reporting etc. The public relations team may also try to gain editorials and air time for the product. This is effectively, for them, a form of free advertising; the newspaper, television or radio highlights their product and they don't have to pay for it.

The fact that the product has received press attention is likely to be good for the producer if the attention has been handled well. Someone once said that there is no such thing as bad publicity. You may disagree, but on the whole, attention by the press leads to public attention and can lead to sales. Consider the 1994 case of Sainsbury's cola versus Coca-Cola (*see* Case study 18.5 on p 434). Although Sainsbury was threatened with legal action by Coca-Cola because its labels were considered too similar, its sales of its own cola increased. 'The result was a blizzard of free publicity which Coca-Cola needed like a hole in the head; and sure enough, by the week, trade rumour had it that Sainsbury was selling more of its own version of Coke than it was of the original.' (*Financial Times*, 23 April 1994.) By the end of March 1995, claimed *The Economist* (1 July 1995, p 79) Cott-produced cola (Sainsbury, Safeway and Virgin) had gained 27 per cent of overall market share and Coca-Cola's share had fallen from 44 per cent to 32 per cent.

### Advertising

Apart from the free advertising mentioned above, producers also pay to advertise their product. The debate about what function advertising serves will be covered later in this chapter. Does advertising serve to inform the consumer about the product or to persuade consumers to buy it? For now, discussion will be limited to the decisions faced by the organisation as it embarks on an advertising campaign as part of its promotional activity.

Advertising is promotional activity which is non-personal communication, designed to reach the maximum number of people within the target segment. The message is delivered by paid media and is designed and published/released by the organisation responsible for the product in question.

The first decision to be made is whether to use 'in-house' advertising or to contract that function out to a specialist advertising agency. There are pros and cons relating to each decision. For instance, in-house advertising is likely to be cheaper, but those responsible may lack up-to-date knowledge that is only gained by being active in a number of different markets at the same time. On the other hand, there is an argument that an advertising agency will not have such specialist knowledge of the particular market segment for the product in question.

Next the producer, in conjunction with the advertising department or agency, must agree four factors:

- *Budget* – The amount to be spent on the advertising campaign will dictate the other three factors.
- *Message* – The message must be *desirable, exclusive* and *believable*. In its execution, the message may reflect a lifestyle, fantasy, mood/image, or give technical or scientific information about the product.
- *Medium* – The message must be delivered via the medium or media which will maximise *reach, frequency* and *impact*. To maximise these factors, it is important to plan the timing of the advertising and to plan the advertising carefully so that the target audience is reached. For example, if the target audience is young people aged 18–30, it would be a waste of money to advertise in a magazine aimed at retired citizens, or to advertise on TV during a programme aimed at children.
- *Evaluation* – To assess the success of the advertising campaign, a variety of techniques may be used: for example, asking people in the street to recall the message, or if they are able to recognise the product from a selection.

Promotion is obviously an important aspect of the 4Ps. There are many aspects to promotion. Perhaps the most important thing to remember is that careful planning, targeting and evaluation can increase the effectiveness of promotion and also make it more cost-effective.

The combination of the product and promoting it are obviously important. Equally essential is that the product is available to the consumer; that it, is in the right place.

## Place

Where the product is placed is an important factor for the producer to consider. The greater the number of intermediaries between the producer and the market, the lower the profit made by each. Obviously, high levels of vertical integration will increase the profit for the producer. The manner in which the producer gets its product to the market is known as the **channel**. Given in Table 11.2 is a comparison between different recognised channels. The level of control that the producer has over the channel is also shown.

The table clearly shows that there are various routes, or channels, between the producer and the consumer. The most direct, the zero-level channel, occurs when the producer sells directly to the consumer. This may be by door-to-door sales, from producer's warehouse or producer's showroom to the consumer. An example of a zero-level channel would be an organisation such as a kitchen manufacturer with its own showrooms, design and installation service. A one-level channel involves a retailer between the producer and the consumer. An example of a one-level channel would be an insurance broker, holding details of hundreds of insurance policies and searching through these for the consumer.

Most consumer channels, however, are two-level channels, where producers sell their products on to a wholesaler, who then assembles orders for, say, local convenience stores, who are then able to receive a full range of goods without having to

**Table 11.2 Different levels of marketing channel**

| Level of control | Channel type | Channel details |
|---|---|---|
| High | Zero-level | Producer → Consumer |
| | One-level | Producer → Retailer → Consumer |
| | Two-level | Producer → Wholesaler → Retailer → Consumer |
| Low | Three-level | Producer → Wholesaler → Jobber* → Retailer → Consumer |

* Jobbers – usually intervene in the market to serve smaller retailers who would not normally be served by wholesalers.

*Source*: Adapted from Kotler, P, Armstrong, G, Sanders, J and Wong, V (1996) *Principles of Marketing*, European edn, Prentice Hall, Hemel Hempstead.

negotiate and deal with numerous producers. Smaller retailers are sometimes not large enough to qualify for larger wholesalers' minimum order quantities. In cases like this, a **jobber** will act as an intermediary between the wholesaler and retailer.

In cases where the producer, wholesaler and retailer are totally unified, or vertically integrated, a vertical marketing system exists. This may be on a corporate basis, as a result of complete vertical integration. Equally, contractual arrangements – franchise, sponsorship or manipulation of market power – may give rise to such a system.

The usual channel to consumers is via some sort of wholesaler/retailer combination. From a consumer's point of view, there is likely to be no perceivable difference between the wholesalers that a retailer uses. The consumer will usually not be aware whether the wholesaler is a broker, merchant (stocking a variety of products within a discrete product range) or a cash and carry. Where the difference arises for the consumer is in terms of the type of retailer they visit and buy from.

Retailers are differentiated by the availability of their own product mix, not only the place, but also the prices they charge for products and the extent of personal attention they give to the consumer. If retailers are classified in terms of the service they offer to consumers, a distinction is easily made, which can be extended to incorporate prices charged and place:

■ *Self-service* – The consumer is free to walk around the store, viewing and selecting the product(s) which they wish to purchase for themselves. Usually convenience and grocery-type shopping.
■ *Self-selection* – The consumer makes a product choice by viewing the range of products available for themselves. A salesperson is then required to compile the consumer's order and to complete the transaction. The salesperson may also offer advice if required by the consumer. Electrical goods and cosmetics may be sold by this method.
■ *Limited service* – Larger department stores may offer limited service to the consumer. Advice and service are available. Sales staff compile the consumer's order and complete the transaction. High street department stores offer a limited service to customers. Some small, old-fashioned grocery stores also operate in this manner.
■ *Full service* – The consumer is fully attended to by sales staff in a full service retailer. Advice,

compilation of the order and probably financial services are available to consumers. Some department stores offer a full service to consumers. The quality and price of products sold are likely to appeal to higher income groups.

To generalise, the more the consumer does for themselves, the greater the range they are likely to find available and the cheaper the products available. Self-service is the norm in supermarkets across the Western world. Limited service is also a concept with which most consumers are familiar. For both these types of retailer, costs are low and therefore the retailer is able to charge lower prices to achieve the same margin as higher-cost retailers. The range of products is likely to be relatively large in such retailers. The income elasticity of products sold by these outlets is likely to be lower than for full-service outlets. That is, the fuller the service, the higher-quality and more luxurious the products offered are likely to be.

## Price

Pricing has already been dealt with in Chapters 9 and 10. The aspects of pricing which require a decision with respect to the marketing mix are those strategies outlined in Chapter 10.

There are various strategies, as you are aware, that an organisation may utilise at different stages in a product's lifecycle. The objective of the organisation will also affect its pricing decisions. It has already been noted that many aspire towards profit maximisation, but in practice, it is almost impossible to make the analyses required to determine whether this is being achieved.

This section will be used to simply outline the possible pricing strategies that an organisation may use as a part of the marketing mix. For explanations, revisit Chapter 10.

The pricing of the product is perhaps the most sensitive aspect of the 4Ps. If a product is priced too high relative to competing products, it is unlikely to sell. If it is priced lower, it will gain extra market share for the producer. Unless, that is, the price is so low that it gives an impression of poor quality. At the new product launch stage, the producer needs to decide on the pricing strategy to be used. This should be done in the context of the 4Ps.

If a penetration strategy is to be used (pricing below current market price, gaining market share and brand loyalty, then increasing the price), the promotional activity should reflect this. A way of

◆ **CASE STUDY 11.1**

## Video console computer games and PC compatible games

In the first quarter of 1993, video console computer games were experiencing massive sales in the UK. Retail outlets appeared in the shopping streets of many towns. The Sega MegaDrive, Game Gear, Nintendo NES and Gameboy were selling in excess of one million per year for the handheld versions alone (*Financial Times*, 29 April 1993). Space in the retail outlets was almost solely devoted to these formats of games. PC-compatible games were available, but the selection was limited and the shelf space given to them in stores was minimal. At this time, the average price of games as they were released was £40 (MegaDrive), £30 (Game Gear), £30 (NES) and £20 (Gameboy).

As a result of the improvements in PC technology and increased sales of PCs for the home in the UK, particularly from Christmas 1994 onwards, the dedicated video console games have experienced a reduced level of sales. The retail outlets have changed to reflect this. Shelf space is predominantly given to PC-compatible games. The Sega and Nintendo games are available at the rear of the stores, with a limited selection available on the shelves. Also, the prices of these games have been cut. When it was first released, *Cool Spot*™ was priced at around £37.99. During the summer of 1994, the price fell to between £10.99 and £17.99, as the game was available in many outlets on sale, special offer etc. During the summer of 1995, it was repackaged as a 'classic game', with a different box cover, and the selling price rose slightly to £20.

Thus the pricing decisions for *Cool Spot*™ are clearly observable in terms of its lifecycle even to the extent that a 'lifecycle extension' was attempted during 1995.

*Source*: Authors.

doing this is to offer for sale 'trial-size' units of the product at a relatively low average price to entice consumers to try rather than to buy their usual product. Alternatively, a new, lower-priced product may be offered as an extension to an already known brand.

If skimming is the chosen strategy, beginning at a higher market price and gradually reducing it until the equilibrium level is reached, the advertising and promotional campaign will have to be slightly different. Initially, consumers need to feel that they are paying for something special: quality, limited edition etc. At the later stages, the promotion will reflect mass appeal and the lower price tag.

As has already been discussed in Chapter 10, pricing decisions are not made only at the new product (or birth) stage. Prices need to be constantly monitored and changed to maintain position in the marketplace. As competition increases, price usually falls. As a product ages, particularly in the decline stages of its lifecycle, prices are frequently reduced to maintain market share and revenue.

### New developments to the 4Ps

At the beginning of this section, it was stated that the 4Ps model continues to provide a fundamental framework for the study and practice of marketing. However, there have been dramatic changes in markets and marketing in the 1990s alone.

The producer has a harder time surviving in the marketplace unless there is something distinctive or unique about their product offering. Additionally, the changing focus of organisations from their product to the needs of their consumers is seen as a technique for gaining and maintaining *competitive advantage* (something which will be discussed in greater depth in Part 4). Certainly, however, this customer focus is more and more evident in many markets, as producers and suppliers battle to gain sales.

For example, UK supermarkets are currently battling to gain consumer loyalty by offering loyalty cards to their customers. The supermarkets analyse the list of purchases made each time the consumer presents their loyalty card at the electronic-point-of-sale cash desk. Then purchasing trends are identified: does the customer buy petfood, are they vegetarian, do they buy babycare products? Appropriate vouchers and offers are posted to the customer. Thus, the supermarkets are using sophisticated technology to individualise the service they are able to offer to customers.

It is the service attributed to the product and therefore included in the augmented product which Christopher (1992) identified as the way forward for organisations to succeed in the marketplace. Christopher takes Levitt's (1972) point that *'people don't buy products, they buy benefits'* and builds a convincing argument for organisations to pay attention to the complete product offering.

The framework discussed provides a checklist of the methods which should be used to identify the aspects of service which are important to the consumer, which are most cost-effective and which will result in the greatest customer retention.

# PRODUCT DECISIONS: ANSOFF'S PORTFOLIO ANALYSIS

Igor Ansoff (1987) is attributed with the development of a framework for analysing a portfolio of products within a strategic, developmental and manageable context. Within the framework, the organisation's products are placed in the appropriate position on a grid which represents market growth and new market opportunities for existing and new products.

Where there is an existing product within an existing market, the decision maker must decide whether the product can achieve further market penetration. If the existing product is successful, can its benefits be sold to members of other (say, demographic) markets? This would entail market development and strategies appropriate to such a goal.

Where the producer has a new product, it must decide whether it should be offered to existing consumers, that is, to follow a product development strategy. This may involve a brand extension, or a completely new product; both are product development strategies. Finally, where the producer wishes to place a new product in a new market, strategically, diversification is to be considered.

Diversification is the most risky of the strategies within Ansoff's product/market opportunities matrix. It can be used to move into a market where the organisation has no previous experience or if products present a steep learning curve which the organisation must go up very quickly in order to be successful.

This **portfolio analysis** idea was developed further by Bruce Henderson of the Boston Consulting Group and was concerned with the attractiveness of strategic business areas (that is, product ranges or market areas) within a given competitive posture. It was taken further by the McKinsey Consulting Company to provide the matrix given in Figure 11.2.

In this McKinsey model, the prospects of different **SBAs** (strategic business areas) are classified as one of two categories according to their attractiveness – good or poor. Similarly, the expected competitive positions of the organisation are classified into the categories of good or poor. From this, SBAs may be seen as any one of four strategic positions:

**Figure 11.2**

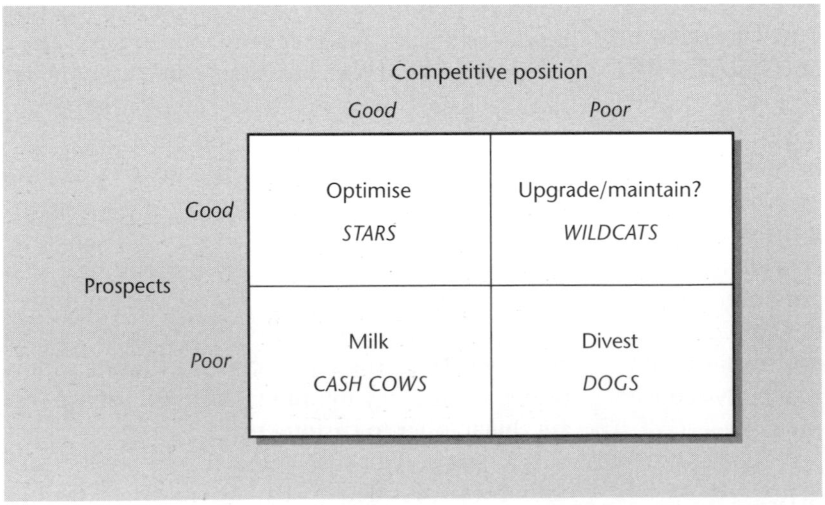

An extension of Ansoff's portfolio analysis, the McKinsey Consulting Company matrix. In this model, the prospects of different SBAs (strategic business areas) are classified as one of two categories according to their attractiveness – good or poor. Similarly, the expected competitive positions of the organisation are classified into the categories of good or poor. From this, SBAs may be seen as any one of four strategic positions: stars, cash cows, wildcats and dogs.

- *Stars* – Attractiveness is good and so too is the expected competitive position. Stars should be optimised on; resources should be directed towards Stars, as they have been historically.
- *Dogs* – The opposite of Stars, attractiveness is poor, so too is the expected competitive position. The organisation should divest itself of Dogs.
- *Cash cows* – Can be milked to support Stars and Wildcats. These have poor prospects, but a good expected competitive position. Cash cows should be maintained until their competitive position begins to slip.
- *Wildcats* – Represent a decision to be made by the organisation. Prospects are good, but the expected competitive position is poor. If the organisation has the resources to catch up with the competition and gain a market position, these resources should be directed towards Wildcats. Earnings from the other categories should be directed towards Wildcats.

Overall, the McKinsey matrix provides the organisation with information relating to the future prospects of the business areas in which it is operating. It will therefore be able to make both product and portfolio decisions as a result.

That the Ansoff, BCG and McKinsey matrices exist is enough to suggest that there has been much academic debate and advice about the manner in which the product portfolio should be managed by the organisation. What these frameworks omit is an analysis of what might be an appropriate number of products to hold in the portfolio and what might be an acceptable level of risk for producers wishing to make investments in new products.

The authors of these models were attempting to put forward suggestions and checklists for decision making, rather than prescriptive decision methodologies. As they stand, the models may be applied to many and (almost) any industry. However, a fault that the authors put forward is that many managers look to them to solve their problems immediately (as a 'quick fix') and with little thought from themselves.

# PRODUCT VARIATIONS AND ORGANISATIONAL CONDUCT AND PERFORMANCE

Economists looking at the competitive nature of markets have noticed that there are certain changes which occur in accordance with different product strategies.

## Imitation

When a product is imitated by competitors, increased units of the product will be released on to the market. This is termed 'product inflation'. When such imitation occurs, a detrimental effect is noticed by the original producer: loss of market share. Increased competition also has an effect on the pricing strategies used by producers. Where the market has expanded and there are a larger number of competitors offering substitute products, the original producer can find itself in a loss-making situation if its prices are maintained. In such a market, the competitive forces and the increased supply of the product will force the market price down. Thus, the original producer has to move with the market to maintain position.

It is also observed that the quality of products will deteriorate in markets where heavy competition and imitation occurs. In such cases, the producer has to reduce the price of its original product and thus suffer lower profit margins, or reduce the costs of production, reduce quality and compete at a lower level in the market.

## Product diversity

In an attempt to regain the market share lost as a result of competition, producers will often engage in additional research and development activity. Therefore, from a consumer's point of view, the market becomes increasingly saturated with similar models. On the other hand, some economists agree with Galbraith's (1958) view that increased product diversity encourages excessive consumption on the part of the consumer. As society becomes more and more affluent, product diversity is used to satisfy less important needs and thus welfare losses are suffered as a result of increasing wealth on the part of higher income groups.

There is an argument that product diversity and competition can work to change the composition of markets. If there is intense competition in a market, the weaker competitors will exit and leave slack to be taken up by the remaining competitors. This will give them the opportunity to exploit monopoly situations eventually. Such an argument is influenced by the definition of entry barriers and the existence of contestable markets. Although it may seem attractive initially, there are more complex arguments to be considered. (*See* Chapter 9 for an explanation of limit pricing, one of the arguments presented.)

# PRODUCT QUALITY AND COMPETITION

Where product diversity or imitation exists, the producer must position its product in the market with reference to the quality of others. There are three ways in which products may be **differentiated with respect to quality**: vertically, horizontally and innovational differentiation.

## Vertical quality

Where there are real product differences across a range of products, they are differentiated vertically. Usually, **vertical product differentiation** occurs as more and more attributes are added to increasingly more technical or complex products. Cars, stereo systems, coffee makers and pens may all be differentiated on a vertical quality basis.

The Sony Walkman range provides an illustration of such a vertical differentiation strategy. The range consists of a basic personal stereo cassette player, a more sophisticated player which also has a radio receiver and, at the top of the range, portable compact disc-playing capacity, Dolby noise reduction, anti-roll mechanism and so on.

If an organisation is considering offering products within a range, its average costs will obviously increase as those products are offered. For a range of products, it is possible to derive the optimal product offering for an organisation with reference to the demand and cost conditions for those different products.

Consider Figure 11.3(a). Prices are assumed to remain constant as more and more products are offered. The initial, one-product equilibrium position is given by price $\bar{P}$, quantity $x_1$ (from demand curve $d_1$). The average costs incurred at this point are $AC_1$ (see Figure 11.3(b)). If another, better-quality product is added to the producer's portfolio, demand curve $D_2$ may be derived. Price is still $\bar{P}$ and quantity sold $x_2$ at average cost level $AC_2$. Additional products of increasing quality may be added in a similar manner until the situation given in Figure 11.3(c) is gained. Here, there are four products on offer, the price is constant and, as products are added to the portfolio, average costs are seen to rise. The producer can find an optimal mix of products to offer by deriving their $AC_{option}$ curve – the curve broadly tracing the producer's supply curve for different quantities of products at various levels of quality. Between the fourth and the fifth units, the producer will be earning normal

**Figure 11.3**

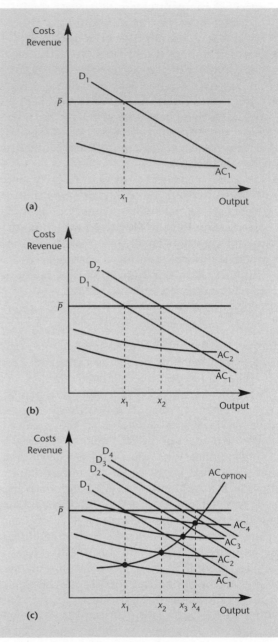

(a) Prices are assumed to remain constant as more products are offered. The initial one-product equilibrium position is $\bar{P}$, $x_1$ (demand curve $D_1$). Average costs incurred are $AC_1$.

(b) If another, better-quality product is added to the producer's portfolio, demand curve $D_2$ may be derived. Price is still $\bar{P}$, quantity sold $x_2$, at average cost level $AC_2$.

(c) Additional products of increasing quality may be added in a similar manner to (b). The producer can find an optimal mix of products to offer by deriving its $AC_{option}$ curve – the producer's supply curve. Between the fourth and fifth units, the producer will be earning normal profits and should add no further products to the portfolio.

profits and should add no further products to the portfolio. Note that the incremental demand curves are closer and closer to each other. This is because consumers become saturated with quality and do not strive for further quality improvements.

## Horizontal quality

Where there is **horizontal quality differentiation**, product differences are based not on the number of attributes a product possesses, but on the manner in which the attributes are mixed within each product. Many consumer goods are differentiated on a horizontal quality basis. For example, branded breakfast cereals are all very different. The attributes on offer are flavour, appeal to children, added vitamins and minerals etc. Different mixes of these combine to produce different products.

For example, the Kellogg range of breakfast cereals is of equal quality throughout. Kellogg considers its quality to be high (remember that it does not produce private-label cereals). However, the range

includes Cornflakes, Bran Flakes, Honey Nut Cornflakes, Rice Crispies and so on. Each of the above possesses different characteristics compared to the next in terms of flavour and ingredients. Kellogg even produces cereals aimed at children, with chocolate flavouring, banana flavouring and different shapes. But the entire range is of the same high quality.

For a given quality level, the relationship between products within the same horizontal quality range may be seen in Figure 11.4.

The maximum quality level is given by $Q_{max}$. Products A, B and C possess different mixes of attributes. If the attributes are given in terms of a variety scale, then products A and B can be seen to share some attributes because there is a crossover between them on the variety scale axes. Similarly, products B and C possess some similar attributes. Product B will achieve sales given by the shaded area (B,B,B). Sales are lost to products A and C as a result of the similarities between A and B and B and C. Thus, an organisation wishing to increase its sales should seek to mix the attributes of its

**Figure 11.4**

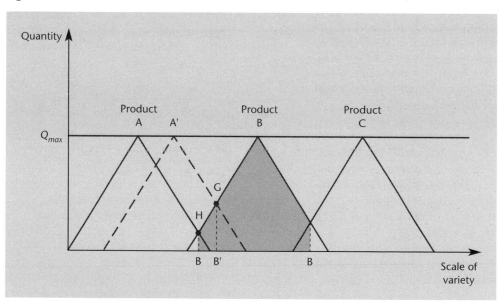

The relationship between products within the same horizontal quality range. The maximum quality level is $Q_{max}$. Products A, B and C possess different mixes of attributes. On a variety scale of attributes, products A and B share some attributes because there is a crossover between them on the variety scale axes. Similarly, products B and C possess some similar attributes. Product B will achieve sales given by the shaded area (B,B,B).

Sales are lost to products A and C as a result of the similarities between A and B and B and C. To increase its sales an organisation should mix the attributes of its products so that there is no overlap, as seen here. To increase sales of A at the expense of B, A's producer should shift the mix of attributes so that A contains more of the attributes of product B; A's position will then be shifted to A' and reduce B's sales by (B,B',G,H).

products so that there is no overlap, as is seen in the figure. An organisation wishing to increase sales at the expense of a competitor (say, for A to steal sales from B) may shift the mix of attributes so that A contains more of the attributes of product B; A's position will then be shifted to A' and reduce B's sales by (B,B',G,H).

## Innovational quality

When innovational quality differentiation exists, the producers are seeking to add attributes to an existing product. Alternatively, new products are being launched on to the market. Thus, product improvements and modifications are made which effectively bring a new offering to the market.

# ADVERTISING AND MARKET STRUCTURE

Broadly speaking, there is a two-way *cause-and-effect* relationship between advertising and market structure.

Where a market is perfectly competitive, there is no need for advertising and certainly no case for an individual within the industry to advertise. Since products are homogenous, any advertising will improve the consumer's knowledge of all products. This will not necessarily benefit the advertising producer.

In the case of monopolistic competition, advertising will serve to increase market share for the advertising producer's product. Brand identity and consumer loyalty will also be strengthened as a result of such efforts. This may cause more inefficient producers to lose market share and exit the industry in the longer run. Thus there will be increased concentration over time.

Such a situation may lead to an oligopolistically competitive market. Non-price competition is the single most important aspect of such a market. Thus advertising may cause an oligopoly to evolve and is a necessary activity to maintain the status quo. Further discussion of the role of advertising in an oligopoly market is given later.

Where the market is dominated by a monopoly producer, the role of advertising differs. Consumers do not need to be persuaded to purchase the product at the expense of other products. The monopo-list must convince consumers that they require the product on offer, but are not competing against clear substitute products. The monopolist must therefore advertise to maintain a market for the product. The objective will be to maintain and increase awareness and price elasticity of demand for the product. Thus advertising is necessary for the longevity of the success of the product, but the likely expenditure requirements are lower than would be the case if the market were competitive.

## Advertising in oligopoly where mutual dependence is recognised

Where organisations are in imperfect competition and products are being advertised, there will be an ongoing battle between competitors to maintain market share. As advertising decisions are changed, it becomes difficult to analyse the effects. The *ceteris paribus* criterion cannot be adhered to, since changes made will also affect the decisions made by competitors. Thus it is not possible to tell whether the change in advertising has increased the volume of sales, or whether increased sales are a result of the same market share in a larger market.

Instead, when making decisions organisations look for effectiveness in terms of payback. They are effectively operating in a prisoner's dilemma (*see* Chapter 9). The payback matrix would have to be constructed with the decisions 'maintain advertising' and 'increase advertising'.

---

◆ **Exercise 11.4**

Construct a hypothetical prisoner's dilemma matrix for the advertising decisions discussed above.

---

Coordination of changes in advertising expenditure is unlikely to occur in practice. Organisations competing for market share will not necessarily trust each other to coordinate such activities. Even if there were an effort to coordinate activities, organisations would not be able to make allowances for the individual levels of advertising skill, creativity and success of the efforts of their marketing departments or agencies.

◆ **CASE STUDY 11.2**

## Fall-out from a product flop

A high-profile flop is the nightmare of every consumer goods company. If customers shun your hotly promoted new product and competitors deride it, how do you rebuild esteem and market share?

Unilever is starting to find out. Having lost a damaging nine-month battle against Procter & Gamble to establish a high-technology detergent in Europe, Unilever is applying the lessons learnt to a new flagship product and marketing strategy.

Unilever's original problem remains: it lost leadership of the £6bn a year European detergent market to P&G more than a decade ago. The US group was developing products faster and was more effective at pan-European marketing than the Anglo-Dutch group.

The first attempt to crack the problem was the launch last spring of Persil Power in the UK and Omo Power on the continent using a manganese catalyst, the 'Accelerator'. P&G discovered the catalyst damaged a handful of dark colours on thin cotton fabrics and exploited the flaw to great effect with, for example, pictures of tattered boxer shorts.

The fall-out was widespread. Consumers lost confidence in the product and to a small extent in the brand; they became confused about which product they should use on which clothes; and Power's qualities – even P&G admitted it was the best in the market on some stains – were lost in the deluge of bad publicity.

Four of the key lessons learnt were: test products even more extensively to catch any flaws which could be used against it; do not neglect the brand while heavily promoting a new product; cater to differences between national markets while drawing on any pan-European efficiencies in manufacturing or marketing; communicate more effectively about the company to the press, customers and bodies like consumer associations rather than rely on product promotion.

The second attempt is the launch of New Generation Persil as the flagship product in the UK and on the continent under different names such as Omo Total. 'We have to get back on to the front foot in the market,' a Unilever executive said. . .

After some consumers had used Power too indiscriminately and exacerbated its flaw, Unilever is paying more attention to sloppy washers this time. The breadth of New Generation will help them, as will packaging and promotion more tightly geared to national markets.

Yet, the new product is not meant for fine fabrics such as wool and silks so Persil is launching yet another detergent, Persil Finesse, for them. In reality, detergent makers are no nearer the consumer ideal of one-product-does-all. Brand segmentation – varieties of Persil are rising from six to eight products – is still seen by manufacturers as a useful way to build market share.

On the communications front, Unilever is developing an advertising campaign for New Generation which will hark back to old themes such as Persil being the trusty, caring helper in the kitchen.

For direct consumer contact, Unilever is building a database of some 10m UK people it can send samples or information. Plucking benefit from adversity, it has added to that list all those who called its 'customer care lines' about Power.

When it announced the new product last week, it also took care to handle the press better than it did during the soap war. Although officials of Lever Brothers, its detergent subsidiary, made the running, corporate press officers were on hand for broader questions.

But for all their speed in bringing a new, hopefully, fault-free product to market on a sea of soothing advertising, Unilever officials acknowledge that their biggest challenge lies ahead: turning around public perceptions. Market share figures and consumer polling will plot their progress in agonising detail in the months ahead.

*Source: Financial Times,* 19 January 1995. Reprinted with permission.

**Table 11.3 UK laundry detergent market share**

| | 1994 | | |
| | Apr 30 | Jun 11 | Dec 24 |
|---|---|---|---|
| Procter & Gamble (e.g. Ariel) | 50.6% | 50.0% | 52.8% |
| Unilever total of which | 32.6% | 33.2% | 31.0% |
| Persil brand total of which | 26.5% | 28.9% | 26.0% |
| Persil Power | 0.8% | 4.5% | 2.3% |
| | At Power's launch | At Power's peak | Unilever decides to replace Power as flagship detergent |

*Source: Neilson.*

### Comment on the case study

An oligopolistic market situation can result in spiralling advertising expenditure by the competing organisations. Sometimes the organisations use weaknesses (perceived or real) in their competitors' products to increase demand for their own products. This was clearly seen in the case of Unilever's launch of Omo Power (Persil Power in the UK) in 1994. The detergent contained an added ingredient which was claimed to improve cleaning power. What actually happened, as the competitor Procter & Gamble discovered, was that the added ingredient damaged the fibres in a small number of clothes. P&G capitalised on this fault and modified its advertisements to include pictures of clothes ruined by the new Unilever product.

The detergent market in Europe is highly concentrated and highly competitive. This error cost Unilever in its attempt to regain a market share leadership position. In order to recover some of the market share lost, another product, 'New Generation Omo (Persil)', was launched. This had been developed in parallel with Power initially and gave Unilever a quick fallback. However, the damage had been done. Market share was down, consumer trust was adversely affected and consumers were also becoming confused about which product in the range was appropriate for which clothing.

Unilever, as the case points out, had made four errors in launching Power in Spring 1994. Most importantly, it had not thoroughly tested the product before launch. Second, it had relied on the success of the product and had ignored the fact that it would be an addition to an existing range of products – the Omo (Persil) brand. Additionally, the differences between national markets had not been catered for (*see* Chapter 21). Finally, the promotional activity had relied heavily on advertising and had ignored the role of good PR, which communication with the press could have provided.

The implications of these errors may clearly be seen in Table 11.3. Market share was rapidly lost in the UK, clearly picked up by Procter & Gamble at the same time.

## The persuasion/information debate

A debate exists about the nature of, or rationale for, advertising. One school of thought contends that the role of advertising is to persuade the consumer to purchase, the other that the role of advertising is to provide information about products to consumers.

### Advertising as persuasion

The advertising as persuasion view has, as its advocates, economists such as Bain, Comanor and Wilson. For them, persuasion is used to alter consumers' preferences for products, thus increasing the levels of brand loyalty exhibited. As advertising increases brand loyalty, it will also increase the entry barriers for potential competitors.

In order to become a competitive rival, entrants will also have to advertise their product and overcome the strength of the brand identity already gained by the incumbent. On the other hand, the incumbent will be in a position to increase the price of its product, if it so wishes, because it will have created a situation through its advertising where the price elasticity of demand for the product is tending towards zero. That is, the price elasticity of demand is becoming more inelastic. As consumers become loyal to the product, they will become less sensitive to price changes. As was seen in Chapter 6, where price elasticity of demand for a product is relatively inelastic, the effect on revenue of a price increase will be an increase in revenue. Thus, it is in the interests of the producer to advertise to gain consumer loyalty and then to increase the price of the product.

The argument above, where demand becomes more and more inelastic, is argued to represent exploitation of the consumer. The fact that consumers' preference has been altered means that they will disregard other products. Thus, by their own myopia, created by the producer's advertising, it is argued that consumers' welfare is reduced. The lack of choice means that there may be consumers who are forced to make second-best decisions. Also, there may be social costs involved, as consumption of consumer goods increases as a result of a successful advertising campaign which instils derived demand in consumers, rather than a need.

### Advertising for information

As an alternative view, economists such as Stigler, Telser and Nelson claim that the role of advertising is to provide information for the consumer. If there is an advertising campaign, consumer ignorance will be reduced and thus the public will be more aware of the product attributes.

Following this line of argument, consumer welfare is said to be increased by advertising, rather than reduced. Consumers become aware of the product, its attributes and its availability. This increased information will result in a reduction in transaction costs and search costs for the consumer.

This analysis may be taken further. If marginal costs (MC) of the search may be measured and matched against marginal benefits (MB) for the consumer (as in Figure 11.5), a hypothetical equilibrium position for the optimal level of search (Q*) may be derived.

As can be seen from the figure, the optimal level of search for a consumer durable is greater than that required for a non-durable. This is logical, since consumers will take more time and gain more information before purchasing a product which is more expensive and which will be around longer than a non-durable.

The argument may be developed further to investigate the effect of advertising as information on prices, barriers to entry and competition. Prices will fall as a result of the increased competition which arises after a product has become known to the consumer. As a result of increased competition, entry barriers will fall. Additionally, as a result of the increased competition, lower prices and better knowledge that the consumers have about the products, price inelasticity of demand will rise. Consumers will be more and more sensitive to price changes.

A critique of this view is that the above arguments are relevant, but limited. Where consumers are given information, they can reduce their level of search and gain welfare benefits. However, where the consumer is completely ignorant with

reference to the existence of a product, they cannot demand more information, they will not be in a position to change their level of search, search costs etc. That is, the level of search in such a case of absolute ignorance will go from zero to something. Once some product knowledge is possessed by consumers, the argument for reducing costs and increasing welfare stands, but not until . . .

Overall, the debate about advertising as a source of information versus a tool for persuasion is inconclusive. There are arguments and empirical evidence to support both views. It should be noted here, however, that to classify advertising as either one or the other is dangerous. More commonly, advertising can contain a mixture of information and persuasive images/words. The mix of these will allow advertising to fall predominantly into one camp or the other, although sometimes it may be impossible to argue either way (*see* Exercise 11.5).

---

◆ **Exercise 11.5**

1  Do TV advertisements for detergent (for clothes) persuade or inform?

2  Do magazine advertisements placed by auto manufacturers persuade or inform?

3  Are there any products or services which fall completely into either the persuade or inform category?

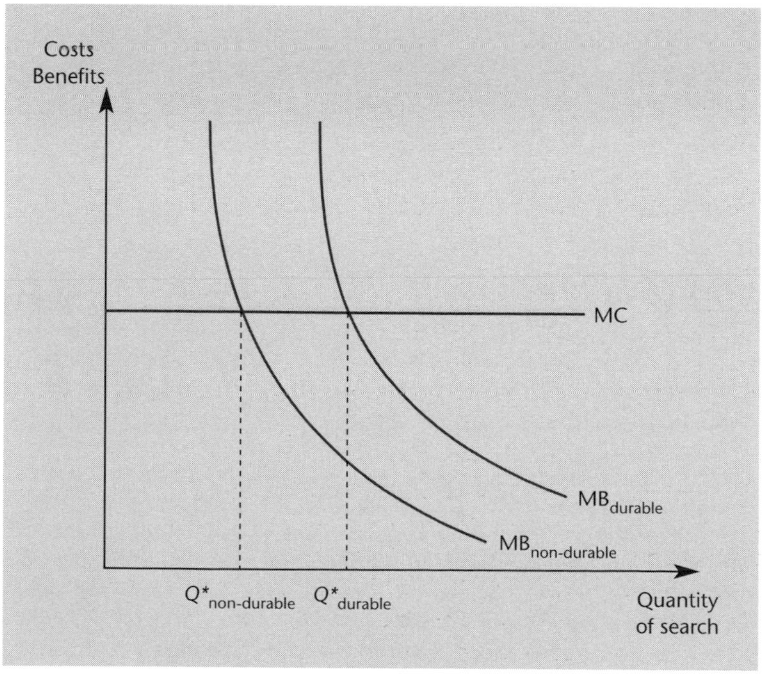

---

**Figure 11.5**

Advertising can increase the welfare of the consumer by reducing search costs and increasing their knowledge of the product. Plotting marginal costs (MC) of search against marginal benefits (MB) for the consumer, the equilibrium position for the optimal level of search (Q*) may be derived.

The optimal level of search for a consumer durable is greater than that required for a non-durable. Consumers will take more time and gain more information before purchasing a product which is more expensive and which will be around longer than a non-durable.

## Advertising and the effect on retail sales and retailers

Mixed effects have been observed on retailers as a result of manufacturers' advertising. Two distinctions may be made: where the manufacturer advertises and where it does not.

Where the manufacturer does not bother to advertise, there are limits to the market share which it may gain. This is as a result of the brand competition which arises. It is likely that no manufacturer holds a substantial part of the market and therefore the brand competition is high. Consequently, retailers are not forced to enter into high levels of competition for the right to sell a manufacturer's product. The manufacturers' prices are low and the retailers' high. Therefore, the level of profits made by the retailers is also high.

If manufacturers advertise, the analysis changes. Their power increases, as consumers recognise and demand their product. The power attributed to the brand increases and the negotiating position of the retailer is less strong. The retailer is likely to be less able to demand discounts for carrying the product(s) on offer; the price which they are charged will be higher, as a result of the inflated power of the manufacturer. A consequence of the advertising and greater power is that the manufacturers' profits increase at the expense of the retailers.

## Benefits of advertising

The arguments put forward above give contradictory results and analysis about both the benefit of advertising and also its effect on welfare. Although the argument that advertising merely increases prices and restricts consumer choice is an appealing one, there

**Table 11.4  Prices of spectacles ($US) – comparison of countries where advertising is allowed and not allowed**

| Advertising allowed | | Advertising not allowed | |
|---|---|---|---|
| United Kingdom | 19.80 | Ireland | 34.50 |
| Belgium | 20.10 | New Zealand | 44.50 |
| Japan | 22.10 | | |
| USA | 23.40 | | |
| (West) Germany | 23.50 | | |
| France | 26.10 | | |

*Source*: © *The Economist*, London, 15 March 1985.

are advertising decisions which have been observed to provide more benefit more than they cost.

For some reason, advertising of spectacles has been chosen by a long list of economists as a case study or research area. In the United States, there are some states which permit spectacle advertising and some which don't. In Europe, too, there are some countries which permit spectacle advertising and some which don't. There is therefore a full range of structures for investigation; perhaps this is why so many studies have been performed!

The results of the studies show conclusively that where advertising is restricted (so as not to mention price, for example) or banned, prices are higher than where advertising is permitted (*see* Table 11.4). Thus, the conclusion may be reached that advertising benefits the consumer and that the costs of advertising are outweighed by the benefits. However, a question raised by a number of observers is whether the quality of the product is reduced as well as the price. There are no conclusive studies either way which also consider the potential changes in product quality.

## ◆ CASE STUDY 11.3

## MMC lifts price controls on condoms

**FT**

The government yesterday lifted price controls on condoms supplied by LRC Products, manufacturers of the Durex brand, after the Monopolies and Mergers Commission said concern about Aids had created an increasingly competitive market.

However Mr Neil Hamilton, corporate affairs minister, said LRC, a subsidiary of London International Group, would have to undertake not to enter into agreements under which wholesalers or retailers stocked only its condoms. Mr Hamilton said he had written to Sir Bryan Carsberg, director-general of fair

trading, asking him to negotiate such an undertaking with LRC. Sir Bryan asked the commission to investigate the condom market in March last year.

Controls on LRC's prices were introduced in 1982 after an earlier inquiry. LRC, which has about 75 per cent of the UK market, told the current inquiry that it would over time raise its prices to average European levels if the controls were lifted.

The commission said, however, that changes in the market meant other suppliers would challenge LRC if it raised prices. It said the easing of condom advertising restrictions and government publicity campaigns had resulted in a sharp increase in demand in 1987–88. Although growth later slowed, the commission said it appeared to have picked up again in the past two years.

Mates condoms, owned by Pacific Dunlop of Australia, were launched in 1987 and have a UK market share of 14 per cent.

The commission said condoms were now stocked in an increasingly wide range of outlets, including supermarkets. Last year Superdrug Stores started the first condom price war by cutting its prices by a third. The commission said greater competition between retailers meant that an increase in LRC trade prices would not necessarily be reflected fully in retail prices.

Mr Hamilton said he had considered the position of the National Health Service, which purchased 23 per cent of UK condom supplies for free distribution. He said the commission felt there would be sufficient competition to protect the NHS. The NHS was in a position to look for quality suppliers worldwide, he said.

London International Group said: 'Competition, supported by advertising and marketing, could substantially increase the number of condom users, helping further to reduce the number of unplanned pregnancies and to combat the spread of HIV/Aids and other sexually transmitted diseases.'

*Source: Financial Times, 31 March 1994. Reprinted with permission*

### Comment on the case study

There seems to be a strong argument in Case study 11.3 for the advertising as information view leading to an increase in consumer welfare and decreases in prices. The UK government removed controls on prices of condoms on 30 March 1994. The expected result of this ruling was further decreases in prices; despite the London Rubber Company's (LRC) claims that it would increase its prices to bring them up to the average European level.

The result of previous slackening of price controls and the removal of advertising restrictions was a condom price war, instigated by the Superdrug chain of stores. Sharp increases in demand were also observed after the changes were made.

The UK's government is very much of the opinion that further reducing restrictions would increase competition and demand in the UK market. The government further hopes that these changes are likely to be followed by reductions in the cases of Aids, sexually transmitted diseases and unplanned pregnancies. Thus, as a result of the change in legislation, the argument may be proposed that reduced restrictions on advertising and price lead to increased consumer welfare.

## CONCLUDING REMARKS

One of the major points that should be made here is that it is very difficult to measure the effects of advertising. This has been touched on earlier in the chapter. However, as Ferguson and Ferguson (1994) state:

More often than not economists have tended to ignore the fact that different promotional activities overlap. Mostly, this reflects the problems associated with collecting data on forms of promotional activity other than advertising. If (as seems likely) the effects of advertising and other promotional activity are similar, then empirical work which considers only advertising will give misleading results.

Additionally, remember that the 4Ps form a framework for finding the optimum marketing mix for marketing experts. Economists are actually interested in other issues as well. For example, the fact that products may be differentiated on a quality basis, either horizontally or vertically, has produced numerous theoretical arguments. The debate about the role of advertising as information or persuasion is also an aspect in which economists have particular interest.

Overall, it should be noted that there has been a change in the perspective of organisations. The product is no longer their most important asset. Many now realise that the consumer is important and that consumer satisfaction will help the longevity of a product and an organisation. This is to the extent that a number of larger organisations are developing augmented products which focus entirely on the needs of the consumer at all stages of the supply chain.

Overall, then, the nature of the 4Ps has changed in line with the increasing sophistication of consumers and increased standards of living. The economist is concerned with more than the 4Ps, although there is validity in using the framework as a starting point for analysis.

# SUMMARY

◆ The marketing mix comprises the 4Ps: product, price, place and promotion. Although the nature of the 4Ps has changed, the concept remains valid.

◆ In terms of product classification, numerous systems exist. The most basic distinction is between product or service, or alternatively durable goods and non-durables. More complex systems differentiate between convenience goods, shopping goods, specialty goods and unsought goods.

◆ The importance of generic or own-label goods is increasing in the retail sector, especially for super-markets in the area of consumer non-durables.

◆ Economists debate the role of advertising. There is debate about whether it serves to inform or persuade. Additionally, the effects on market structure, profits and price elasticity of demand are dependent on which of these views is believed.

◆ Economists believe that there exist optimal levels of search for the consumer which are based on marginal analysis of advertising.

◆ The success of products may be predicted, or decided with reference to Ansoff's or McKinsey Consulting Group's portfolio matrices.

# REVIEW QUESTIONS

1 Use the concepts of product mix, product range and product item to explain the behaviour of the Coca-Cola company worldwide.

2 Discuss the elements constituting the core, tangible and augmented products for a durable and non-durable product of your choice.

3 Distinguish between levels of service provided for three products of your choice from distinct product categories.

4 Outline the possible actions which may be taken once a product reaches the 'decline' stage of the lifecycle.

5 It is a fact advertised by Kellogg that it *never* makes breakfast cereal for anyone else. Explain why it may have chosen to follow such a strategy.

6 Examine the possible differences influencing pricing decisions in different European markets.

7 Under which circumstances might an organisation wish to increase the price of its product? What marketing is required to do this successfully?

8 Give examples of one-channel, two-channel and three-channel systems with reference to particular products or product ranges.

9 With reference to the information versus persuasion debate, analyse the role of advertising for:
   – passenger cars
   – chocolate confectionery
   – pharmaceuticals.

10 Compare and contrast the types of promotion seen in supermarkets, record stores and clothes stores.

11 Give examples of horizontal and vertical product quality differentiation. Are there any markets which are particularly suited to either vertical or horizontal differentiation?

12 Make an Ansoff or McKinsey-type analysis of the Compaq computer company's product portfolio.

13 Account for the growth of generic/own-label product sales at the expense of branded products in supermarkets.

# GLOSSARY OF NEW TERMS

**4Ps:** The constituents of the optimum way in which a good or service is offered on the market (product, place, price, promotion).

**Channels:** The routes taken by products from manufacturer to marketplace. One-, two- and three-level channels exist. A one-level channel is where the manufacturer *is* the retailer, a three-level channel where the manufacturer sells the product to a wholesaler, who sells to a jobber (*see* below), who sells to a retailer.

**(Consumer) durable good:** A good which is not consumed *per se:* its usefulness extends beyond a single consumption period, for example washing machines and televisions.

**Generic product:** *See* own label/private label.

**Horizontal differentiation:** Product differences which are based on different mixes of attributes for products of a similar quality are horizontal differentiators (*see* quality differentiation).

**Jobber:** A company which purchases stocks of consumer products for resale to small retailers at lower prices than wholesalers are able to offer.

**Marketing mix:** The combination of the 4Ps.

**Non-durable good:** A good which is consumed within the time period in which it was bought, for example groceries and elements of the typical weekly shop.

**Own brand/private label:** The terms used to describe products sold by supermarkets and other retailers which carry their brand name, rather than a manufacturer's brand name.

**Portfolio analysis:** A tool used to analyse the future potential of products within an organisation's complete set of offerings.

**Quality differentiation:** This can be horizontal or vertical. Products are differentiated with respect to their range of attributes and additional features (vertical), or on the manner in which attributes are mixed at a given level of vertical quality (horizontal).

**Strategic business area (SBA):** A defined product market or submarkets in which an organisation has decided to concentrate its activities.

**Vertical differentiation:** Product differentiation based on differences in quality or attributes possessed by products (*see* quality differentiation).

# READING

Ansoff, I (1987) *Corporate Strategy*, revised edn, Penguin Business, Harmondsworth.
*A wide-ranging text which includes discussion of concepts such as portfolio analysis.*

Berkowitz, E N, Kerin, R A, Hartley, S W, Rudelius, W (1992) *Marketing*, 3rd edn, Irwin, Homewood, Il.

Brassington, F and Pettitt, S (1997) *Principles of Marketing*, Pitman Publishing, London.

Christopher, M (1992) *Logistics and Supply Chain Management: Strategies for Reducing Costs and Improving Service*, Pitman Publishing, London.
*Also considers the augmented product, but from a supply chain perspective, where all of the organisation's activities are built around providing service to the consumer.*

Ferguson, P R and Ferguson, G J (1994) *Industrial Economics: Issues and Perspectives*, 2nd edn, Macmillan, Basingstoke.
*Specialist industrial economics text. Some interesting theories and empirical evidence are given with respect to the effects of advertising on price elasticities and the power of manufacturers and retailers as a result.*

Galbraith, J K (1958) *The Affluent Society*, Houghton Mifflin, Boston.
*Very readable and non-technical in many respects. Includes some valuable insights into the implications of increasing standards of living in Western economies.*

Kotler, P, Armstrong, G, Sanders, J and Wong, V (1996) *Principles of Marketing*, European edn, Prentice Hall, Hemel Hempstead.

Koutsoyiannis, A (1993) *Modern Microeconomics*, 2nd edn, Macmillan, Basingstoke.
*Specialist economics text, including some technical and mathematical illustrations of the theories relating to advertising and non-price competition.*

Levitt, T (1972) 'Production line approach to service', *Harvard Business Review*, Sept – Oct, pp 41–2.
*Provides discussion of the augmented product concept.*

CHAPTER $12$

# INVESTMENT DECISIONS AND THE COST OF CAPITAL

## KEY ISSUES

Business issues

Business strategy

Decision-making techniques

Economic concepts

Management decision issues

Optimal outcomes to management issues

## OBJECTIVES

◆ To consider the ways in which organisations assess the performance of investment projects.

◆ To understand how the process of discounting cash flows can be used by organisations to compare current costs with future cash flows.

◆ To compare and contrast the various forms of investment appraisal.

◆ To appreciate how discounted cash flow techniques can be used to accommodate changes in discount rates and different levels of inflation.

◆ To examine other non-discounting forms of investment appraisal and compare them to the discounting approaches.

◆ To consider whether the capital structure of an organisation affects its investment behaviour and the approaches taken by organisations to the risks and costs of debt and equity financing.

◆ To understand the benefits which the organisation can obtain from the process of post-auditing.

## CHAPTER OUTLINE

Business application

Introduction

The capital budgeting process

Estimating cash flows

Estimating the discount rate

Calculating net present value

Case study 12.1 Alcan profits from the pit and the pendulum

Case study 12.2 Nuclear Electric 'has negative value'

Scenario analysis

Internal rate of return

Case study 12.3 Energy mission out to woo Beijing

Comparison of NPV and IRR

Payback method

Case study 12.4 Consortium to dig $680 million Denmark–Sweden tunnel

Case study 12.5 Good reason to be cautious

Return on capital employed

Alternative investment criteria

General problems associated with investment appraisal

Cost of capital

Cost of debt

Risk-free rate plus premium

Dividend evaluation model

Capital asset pricing model

Weighted cost of capital

The Modigliani–Miller view of the cost of capital

Reviewing past investment projects

Summary

Review questions

Glossary of new terms

Reading

## KEY TERMS

Beta coefficient

Capital asset pricing model

Capital budgeting

Cost of capital

Cost of debt

Cost of equity

Dividend valuation model

Internal rate of return

Net present value

Payback period

Post-audit

Risk-free rate of return

Risk premium

Weighted average cost of capital

**BUSINESS APPLICATION**

## Tunnel vision

FT

It is painfully obvious that, in building the Channel Tunnel, Eurotunnel has faced circumstances completely beyond the control of its company and contractors. These include base levels of real interest rates, a supply of buoyant equity capital, variations in British and French rail policy, developments in the ferry industry and competitive responses of the port and ferry operators.

Many of the above have broken badly for the Eurotunnel shareholders, compounding the cost overruns of about 100 per cent and construction delays, entailing further capitalised interest additions to the senior debt burden. While one can feel for the investors (and inevitably the lenders) now nursing their losses, the initial projections for the project estimated internal rates of return far in excess of the return on safer government securities. That anticipated equity return was probably insufficient compensation for the very real risks, given the leveraged capital structure and the likelihood of cost overruns. It certainly has proved so with 20–20 hindsight.

In any event much of the social benefit from a private Eurotunnel is likely to arise from the greater market-driven competition and innovation now more likely for cross-Channel traffic.

Eurotunnel may well have driven home the risks of leverage equity investment in long-lived infrastructure investments with rear-end load profitability. Nevertheless, it is likely that the capital of Eurotunnel will at some point in the future perform reasonably well.

*Source*: Adapted from *Financial Times*, 22 September, 1995. Reprinted with permission.

### Comment

The above scenario shows how difficult it sometimes proves to assess accurately the future expected returns of an investment project and the cost of the project. In the case of the Tunnel the project opened one year late in 1994, at a cost more than twice the original estimate of £5 billion.

This chapter does not investigate the problems surrounding the risks and uncertainty associated with expected returns, since this area is discussed in Chapter 13; nor does it consider non-monetary or social benefits that can arise from such a project. This chapter concentrates, however, on how businesses assess long-term capital investments and appraises the manner in which organisations assess the profitability of investment projects and the uncertainty of cash flows, before moving on to discuss how investment projects can be financed.

It is, therefore, a chapter which concentrates on the time value of money, but the reader should appreciate that appraising investment projects can be viewed in a much wider sense.

## INTRODUCTION

In earlier chapters the emphasis was placed on how firms organise their production in terms of pricing (Chapters 9 and 10), the organisation's costs (Chapter 8) and business objectives (Chapters 3 and 4), all approached during fairly narrow time horizons. This chapter examines decisions made by organisations which will have implications for their performances over a number of years.

Investment decisions are not made lightly. They are often associated with a large capital outlay at the start of the project and will bring in returns over many years. Investment in new capital can be a response to a number of stimuli. It can be to replace worn-out equipment, it can be to expand the output of existing products or to move into new markets, it may be to introduce more technologically sophisticated equipment which will improve the productivity of the organisation, or a response to changes in the competitive environment.

Because investment projects give returns into the future, an organisation needs to compare current outlay with future returns. Since a pound in the future is not the same as a pound in the current time period, this chapter reviews the process of discounting for investment projects. In addition, returns in the future are expected returns: these are not often known accurately and it might be expected that changes in the organisation's environment, both politically and in economic terms, can lead to inaccuracies in the predicted cash flows from the project and organisations can find that they have invested in a project which does not prove to be profitable.

In the light of these problems, this chapter begins by examining the capital budgeting process and then moves on to consider the methods used by organisations to assess the profitability of investment projects. It finishes by examining the process of post-audits, that is, comparing the expected performance of a project with its actual performance, and the role of cost-of-capital variations in different countries.

## THE CAPITAL BUDGETING PROCESS

In one sense the **capital budgeting** process is straightforward: an organisation invests up to the point at which the marginal returns from the project match the marginal costs of the project. As has been noted earlier, however, the cost of the investment project will be in the current time period, but the returns are likely to be over a number of time periods. Therefore, the value of future returns in the current time period will have to be considered so that tradeoff can be made between the current outlay and the current value of all future returns. In the first instance the organisation needs to assess the cost of the project. Next, it needs to estimate the expected returns over the whole time period for which the project will be in existence. Included here may also be an estimate of the value of the machinery (investment) at a specified termination date and an appreciation that many investment projects (e.g. the Channel Tunnel) will have negative cash flows for the opening years of their life. Since future returns are expected returns, these will be associated with a certain degree of risk and this risk must be estimated. Here, management requires an estimate of the probability distribution associated with the expected return. To convert a future income stream into its value at the current time period requires knowledge of a discount (interest) rate. This process is shown below.

Suppose that an individual is the beneficiary of a will and is granted a sum of money equivalent to £10 000 per annum. The individual has received the £10 000 for the current year but still wishes to undertake further expenditures in the current year. They make a request to have now the £10 000 which is due next year. If the current risk-free rate of interest (the discount rate) is 10 per cent, how much should the individual receive?

The individual should not receive £10 000 in the current time period, since they could invest this at the current rate of interest of 10 per cent and have £11 000 next year. In other words, a mathematical formula can be developed which shows the size of the sum of money this year that when invested at the current rate of interest of 10 per cent just gives £10 000 next year.

What is known is the following:

$$\text{Sum this year} \times (1 + r) = \text{Sum next year} \quad (12.1)$$

where,

$$r = \text{the interest (discount) rate}$$

In terms of our individual, the formula becomes:

$$£10\,000 \times (1 + 0.1) = £11\,000$$

Equation 12.1 also indicates how much a sum next year would be worth in the current time period. By rearranging 12.1 the following is obtained:

$$\text{Sum this year} = \text{Sum next year}/(1 + r) \quad (12.2)$$

Using our individual once again:

$$\text{Sum this year} = £10\,000/(1 + 0.1)$$
$$\text{Sum this year} = £9090.90$$

It follows that if the sum of money is £9090.90 in the current time period then, at a rate of interest of 10 per cent, the sum next year will be worth £10 000.

Suppose that we are interested in the current value of a sum more than one time period away. The formula for a sum two time periods away is:

$$\text{Sum this year} = \text{Sum in two time periods}/(1 + r)^2$$

For other time periods the general formula is:

$$\text{Sum this year} = \text{Sum in time period } n/(1 + r)^n$$

What has been determined above is the time value of money.

Returning to the idea of organisations undertaking investment plans, since it is now possible to convert a future income stream into its value in the current time period, the sum of these future income streams discounted to the present date can be compared with the cost of the investment project. This gives the present value of an investment project. If the **present value** of a future income stream exceeds the cost of the investment, it may be deduced that the project is worth undertaking since the present value of the project will be positive.

It is possible, however, that the organisation can undertake a number of investment projects which all give positive present value income streams in excess of the capital cost of each of the projects. The organisation, in this case, can rank the projects, starting with the project that gives it the greatest present value (discounted stream of future income from the project minus the cost of the project).

Before proceeding any further, it is worth considering a number of issues in the process outlined above. First, from where is the project financed? Is it from external borrowing or from internal sources? Second, what is the appropriate discount rate? This should reflect the time value and risk of the project. Third, a net present value needs to be calculated. Finally, once the various net present values have been obtained, a decision needs to be made as to whether the project should take place or not. For example, larger organisations which are producing a range of products may be in a much better position to bear the negative cash flows that might occur in the early years of a project. A similar project for a smaller organisation or one which produces a limited range of products may be rejected because the risks are too large.

In addition, the management must be aware that the flows produced from the project(s) are estimates and need to be assessed as accurately as possible. All individuals or groups who are inputting into the capital budgeting process must therefore be working to a consistent set of policies.

## ESTIMATING CASH FLOWS

Cash flows from a project occur in future time periods – and therein lies the uncertainty. The importance of building in an allowance for inflation will be considered later, but at this stage it is vital to consider cash flows on an incremental basis. That is, the cash flow for any project should be measured by the difference in the income stream with and without the project. The cash flow will not include any previous costs incurred – sunk costs – but only costs relating to the current investment project. If the current project influences expenditures and receipts in other divisions, this must be included. For example, if division A is thinking of introducing a new product which will act as a substitute for a product made by division B, any loss in cash receipts for other divisions must be taken into account.

It is also necessary to take into account opportunity costs. If an organisation uses its internal funds for one investment project, it loses the opportunity of using these funds elsewhere, such as in purchasing equities or bonds. Thus this loss of opportunity should be charged against the current project.

What of the cash flows themselves? Earlier in this chapter the cash flow (in this case the annual sum of £10 000 per year) occurred all at once. In reality, cash flows may well occur throughout the year and not in the same amounts at different time periods. In other words, the cash flows themselves may be 'lumpy'. It may be better to look at cash flows on a daily basis for some organisations, or if this is not possible on a monthly or quarterly basis. Nonetheless, some organisations may have to accept that all cash flows occur at a particular time point in the year.

Any cash flows that arise from an investment project are likely to be subject to tax, thus the cash flows from a project which are to be discounted at a suitable interest rate should be cash flows on an after-tax basis. This may be a problem, since tax regulations are often subject to change throughout the lifetime of a project. This will be the case particularly where the project is expected to have a long lifespan. In addition, depreciation can be expected to affect the organisation's cash flow, in the sense that the investment will have a market value at the end of its life. Often the difference between the salvage value of the investment project and the depreciated book value is treated as ordinary income and taxed at the organisation's marginal tax rate.

## ESTIMATING THE DISCOUNT RATE

The present value of a future income stream can be obtained if we have the appropriate discount rate. Where the project is risky, it would be anticipated that a high discount rate would be used. In the case where the money for the investment project is obtained internally, then the discount rate, or cost of capital, needs to compensate shareholders for the return they could have obtained by investing in a risk-free asset in the capital market. In addition, the cost of capital should also compensate them for the risk they are facing by not investing in a risk-free project but in the more risky investment project. It follows, therefore, that the discount rate used in a project is that which is offered in the market for financial assets which have the same level of risk. Since there are many traded financial assets which include varying degrees of risk, the appropriate discount rate is not too hard to obtain.

## CALCULATING NET PRESENT VALUE

Calculating the **net present value** of a project requires a comparison of the expected returns discounted at the appropriate rate of interest with the cost of the investment. The following equation shows the process:

$$\text{Net present value (NPV)} = -C_0 + R_0 + R_1/(1 + r) + R_2/(1 + r)^2 + \ldots$$
$$R_n/(1 + r)^n$$

where,

$C_0$ = The cost of the investment
$R_0$–$R_n$ = The expected returns in each time period
$r$ = The discount rate

Using the above criterion, if the NPV is greater than zero then the organisation should consider making the investment. Notice in the above that the same discount rate, $r$, is used for each time period. This assumption may be too restrictive and it is possible to modify the NPV formula so that different rates of interest appear in different time periods. In addition, the expected returns in each time period do not have to be positive, and the formula can easily be adapted to accommodate these as well.

A simple example might indicate how the NPV formula works. Suppose that an organisation has estimated the following cash flow proceeds in the various time periods for an investment project that costs DM1 million and faces a discount rate of 10 per cent:

$$\text{NPV} = -1\,000\,000 + 30\,000 + 125\,000/(1 + 0.1) + 450\,000/(1 + 0.1)^2$$
$$+ 885\,000/(1 + 0.1)^3$$
$$= -1\,000\,000 + 30\,000 + 113\,636.4 + 371\,900.8 + 665\,413.5$$
$$= -1\,000\,000 + 1\,180\,950.7$$
$$= 180\,950.7$$

This project would therefore add DM180 950.70 to the organisation and it should be undertaken. At higher discount rates the present values of the positive cash inflows from the project will become smaller, and at a discount rate of 20 per cent the project would be rejected, as the cost of the project exceeds the discounted value of future income streams, that is, the NPV is negative. This case is shown below:

$$\text{NPV} = -1\,000\,000 + 30\,000 + 125\,000/(1 + 0.2) + 450\,000/(1 + 0.2)^2 + 885\,000/(1 + 0.2)^3$$
$$= -1\,000\,000 + 30\,000 + 125\,000(0.8383) + 450\,000(0.6944) + 885\,000(0.5787)$$
$$= -1\,000\,000 + 30\,000 + 104\,162.5 + 312\,480 + 512\,149.5$$
$$= -41\,208$$

The process of discounting the future income streams to the current value can be quite labour intensive; however, tables are available, *see* Table 12.1. Thus $1/(1 + 0.2)_2$, which signifies discounting a future sum two periods away using a discount rate of 20 per cent, can be obtained from Table 12.1 by taking the column under 20 per cent and selecting the second row.

The decision criteria for investment are, therefore, for the organisation to accept investment projects which have positive NPVs, especially where the organisation has unlimited access to capital. Where capital is rationed, however, a separate set of decisions rules are required which will be considered later in this chapter.

## Table 12.1  Present value of $1: $PVIF_{i,n} = 1(1 + i)^n = 1/FVIF_{i,n}$

| Period | 1% | 2% | 3% | 4% | 5% | 6% | 7% | 8% | 9% | 10% | 12% | 14% | 15% | 16% | 18% | 20% | 24% | 28% | 32% | 36% |
|---|---|---|---|---|---|---|---|---|---|---|---|---|---|---|---|---|---|---|---|---|
| 1 | .9901 | .9804 | .9709 | .9615 | .9524 | .9434 | .9346 | .9259 | .9174 | .9091 | .8929 | .8772 | .8696 | .8621 | .8475 | .8333 | .8065 | .7813 | .7576 | .7353 |
| 2 | .9803 | .9612 | .9426 | .9246 | .9070 | .8900 | .8734 | .8573 | .8417 | .8264 | .7972 | .7695 | .7561 | .7432 | .7182 | .6944 | .6504 | .6104 | .5739 | .5407 |
| 3 | .9706 | .9423 | .9151 | .8890 | .8638 | .8396 | .8163 | .7938 | .7722 | .7513 | .7118 | .6750 | .6575 | .6407 | .6086 | .5787 | .5245 | .4768 | .4348 | .3975 |
| 4 | .9610 | .9238 | .8885 | .8548 | .8227 | .7921 | .7629 | .7350 | .7084 | .6830 | .6355 | .5921 | .5718 | .5523 | .5158 | .4823 | .4230 | .3725 | .3294 | .2923 |
| 5 | .9515 | .9057 | .8626 | .8219 | .7835 | .7473 | .7130 | .6806 | .6499 | .6209 | .5674 | .5194 | .4972 | .4761 | .4371 | .4019 | .3411 | .2910 | .2495 | .2149 |
| 6 | .9420 | .8880 | .8375 | .7903 | .7462 | .7050 | .6663 | .6302 | .5963 | .5645 | .5066 | .4556 | .4323 | .4104 | .3704 | .3349 | .2751 | .2274 | .1890 | .1580 |
| 7 | .9327 | .8706 | .8131 | .7599 | .7107 | .6651 | .6227 | .5835 | .5470 | .5132 | .4523 | .3996 | .3759 | .3538 | .3139 | .2791 | .2218 | .1776 | .1432 | .1162 |
| 8 | .9235 | .8535 | .7894 | .7307 | .6768 | .6274 | .5820 | .5403 | .5019 | .4665 | .4039 | .3506 | .3269 | .3050 | .2660 | .2326 | .1789 | .1388 | .1085 | .0854 |
| 9 | .9143 | .8368 | .7664 | .7026 | .6446 | .5919 | .5439 | .5002 | .4604 | .4241 | .3606 | .3075 | .2843 | .2630 | .2255 | .1938 | .1443 | .1084 | .0822 | .0628 |
| 10 | .9053 | .8203 | .7441 | .6756 | .6139 | .5584 | .5083 | .4632 | .4224 | .3855 | .3220 | .2697 | .2472 | .2267 | .1911 | .1615 | .1164 | .0847 | .0623 | .0462 |
| 11 | .8963 | .8043 | .7224 | .6496 | .5847 | .5268 | .4751 | .4289 | .3875 | .3505 | .2875 | .2366 | .2149 | .1954 | .1619 | .1346 | .0938 | .0662 | .0472 | .0340 |
| 12 | .8874 | .7885 | .7014 | .6246 | .5568 | .4970 | .4440 | .3971 | .3555 | .3186 | .2567 | .2076 | .1869 | .1685 | .1372 | .1122 | .0757 | .0517 | .0357 | .0250 |
| 13 | .8787 | .7730 | .6810 | .6006 | .5303 | .4688 | .4150 | .3677 | .3262 | .2897 | .2292 | .1821 | .1625 | .1452 | .1163 | .0935 | .0610 | .0404 | .0271 | .0184 |
| 14 | .8700 | .7579 | .6611 | .5775 | .5051 | .4423 | .3878 | .3405 | .2992 | .2633 | .2046 | .1597 | .1413 | .1252 | .0985 | .0779 | .0492 | .0316 | .0205 | .0135 |
| 15 | .8613 | .7430 | .6419 | .5553 | .4810 | .4173 | .3624 | .3152 | .2745 | .2394 | .1827 | .1401 | .1229 | .1079 | .0835 | .0649 | .0397 | .0247 | .0155 | .0099 |
| 16 | .8528 | .7284 | .6232 | .5339 | .4581 | .3936 | .3387 | .2919 | .2519 | .2176 | .1631 | .1229 | .1069 | .0930 | .0708 | .0541 | .0320 | .0193 | .0118 | .0073 |
| 17 | .8444 | .7142 | .6050 | .5134 | .4363 | .3714 | .3166 | .2703 | .2311 | .1978 | .1456 | .1078 | .0929 | .0802 | .0600 | .0451 | .0258 | .0150 | .0089 | .0054 |
| 18 | .8360 | .7002 | .5874 | .4936 | .4155 | .3503 | .2959 | .2502 | .2120 | .1799 | .1300 | .0946 | .0808 | .0691 | .0508 | .0376 | .0208 | .0118 | .0068 | .0039 |
| 19 | .8277 | .6864 | .5703 | .4746 | .3957 | .3305 | .2765 | .2317 | .1945 | .1635 | .1161 | .0829 | .0703 | .0596 | .0431 | .0313 | .0168 | .0092 | .0051 | .0029 |
| 20 | .8195 | .6730 | .5537 | .4564 | .3769 | .3118 | .2584 | .2145 | .1784 | .1486 | .1037 | .0728 | .0611 | .0514 | .0365 | .0261 | .0135 | .0072 | .0039 | .0021 |
| 21 | .8114 | .6598 | .5375 | .4388 | .3589 | .2942 | .2415 | .1987 | .1637 | .1351 | .0926 | .0638 | .0531 | .0443 | .0309 | .0217 | .0109 | .0056 | .0029 | .0016 |
| 22 | .8034 | .6468 | .5219 | .4220 | .3418 | .2775 | .2257 | .1839 | .1502 | .1228 | .0826 | .0560 | .0462 | .0382 | .0262 | .0181 | .0088 | .0044 | .0022 | .0012 |
| 23 | .7954 | .6342 | .5067 | .4057 | .3256 | .2618 | .2109 | .1703 | .1378 | .1117 | .0738 | .0491 | .0402 | .0329 | .0222 | .0151 | .0071 | .0034 | .0017 | .0008 |
| 24 | .7876 | .6217 | .4919 | .3901 | .3101 | .2470 | .1971 | .1577 | .1264 | .1015 | .0659 | .0431 | .0349 | .0284 | .0188 | .0126 | .0057 | .0027 | .0013 | .0006 |
| 25 | .7798 | .6095 | .4776 | .3751 | .2953 | .2330 | .1842 | .1460 | .1160 | .0923 | .0588 | .0378 | .0304 | .0245 | .0160 | .0105 | .0046 | .0021 | .0010 | .0005 |
| 26 | .7720 | .5976 | .4637 | .3607 | .2812 | .2198 | .1722 | .1352 | .1064 | .0839 | .0525 | .0331 | .0264 | .0211 | .0135 | .0087 | .0037 | .0016 | .0007 | .0003 |
| 27 | .7644 | .5859 | .4502 | .3468 | .2678 | .2074 | .1609 | .1252 | .0976 | .0763 | .0469 | .0291 | .0230 | .0182 | .0115 | .0073 | .0030 | .0013 | .0006 | .0002 |
| 28 | .7568 | .5744 | .4371 | .3335 | .2551 | .1956 | .1504 | .1159 | .0895 | .0693 | .0419 | .0255 | .0200 | .0157 | .0097 | .0061 | .0024 | .0010 | .0004 | .0002 |
| 29 | .7493 | .5631 | .4243 | .3207 | .2429 | .1846 | .1406 | .1073 | .0822 | .0630 | .0374 | .0224 | .0174 | .0135 | .0082 | .0051 | .0020 | .0008 | .0003 | .0001 |
| 30 | .7419 | .5521 | .4120 | .3083 | .2314 | .1741 | .1314 | .0994 | .0754 | .0573 | .0334 | .0196 | .0151 | .0116 | .0070 | .0042 | .0016 | .0006 | .0002 | .0001 |
| 35 | .7059 | .5000 | .3554 | .2534 | .1813 | .1301 | .0937 | .0676 | .0490 | .0356 | .0189 | .0102 | .0075 | .0055 | .0030 | .0017 | .0005 | .0002 | .0001 | * |
| 40 | .6717 | .4529 | .3066 | .2083 | .1420 | .0972 | .0668 | .0460 | .0318 | .0221 | .0107 | .0053 | .0037 | .0026 | .0013 | .0007 | .0002 | .0001 | * | * |
| 45 | .6391 | .4102 | .2644 | .1712 | .1113 | .0727 | .0476 | .0313 | .0207 | .0137 | .0061 | .0027 | .0019 | .0013 | .0006 | .0003 | .0001 | * | * | * |
| 50 | .6080 | .3715 | .2281 | .1407 | .0872 | .0543 | .0339 | .0213 | .0134 | .0085 | .0035 | .0014 | .0009 | .0006 | .0003 | .0001 | * | * | * | * |
| 55 | .5785 | .3365 | .1968 | .1157 | .0683 | .0406 | .0242 | .0145 | .0087 | .0053 | .0020 | .0007 | .0005 | .0003 | .0001 | * | * | * | * | * |

*The factor is zero to four decimal places.

## ◆ CASE STUDY 12.1

# Alcan profits from the pit and the pendulum    FT

Mr Jacques Bougie, Alcan's president, describes the past 10 years as a 'swinging decade' for his company. That does not mean Alcan executives were 'jet-setting away in the fast lane' but that profits were 'swinging like a pendulum as we went from being Canada's most profitable company in 1988 to three years of losses – from 1991 to 1993.'

As the aluminium industry's most international company – it was then producing the metal in Australia, Brazil, the UK as well as Canada – Alcan was hurt more than most by the collapse of the Soviet Union. As local demand neared zero, an extra 2m tonnes of Russian aluminium poured into western markets, driving prices down. By 1993 prices had dropped to unprecedented levels.

Mr Bougie recalls that Alcan made effective cuts in production costs. Between 1990 and 1993, sales volumes rose by 5 per cent and annual costs were cut by $1bn (£600m), mainly because of direct management action. The pain was considerable. More than 10,000 jobs were cut ot 18 per cent of the global total. 'Unfortunately,' says Mr Bougie, 'this was not enough to offset the reduction in sales revenues, which fell by $1.5bn between the two years.'

More had to be done. Last year Alcan sold about $500m-worth of assets to cut its debts. Sales included its 73.3 per cent shareholding in Alcan Australia for US$245m, its North American building products operations for an estimated $120m, its North American extrusions businesses for an undisclosed sum, and smaller operations in North America, Brazil and the UK.

A similar level of asset sales seems likely this year. The group recently agreed in principle to sell its metal distribution chain in the US. This week it announced it hoped to sell most of its 'downstream' operations in the UK in one package to one buyer. That package includes 12 British businesses with combined sales of more that £400m ($635m), 4,200 employees and a book value of about £200m.

This is by no means a desperate company selling the family silver to survive. Mr Bougie, a slight, intense man, would not set out on any journey without a good reason and clear idea of the best route. The restructuring of Alcan has all his hallmarks.

Now 48, Mr Bougie – a graduate in law from Université de Montréal and in business administration from Ecole des Hautes Etudes Commerciales – joined Alcan in 1979. Ten years later he was appointed president. Colleagues describe him as a very logical thinker and as persistent.

That logical approach was clear when, in 1992, Alcan undertook a study of the market outlook for aluminium.

It looked at every product in every country and then at the viability of its 125 businesses. That was decided, says Mr Bougie, by comparing the net present value of forward earnings for each business with the capital employed in that business. 'That gave us an objective indicator of businesses that were potentially wealth creating, those that were wealth diluting, and those which were actually wealth destroying.'

The study concluded aluminium was a good, growing business, if a company was a low-cost producer. And that Alcan had the assets, technology, and position to succeed. Mr Bougie suggests the world may face a 'protracted period of disinflation, if not deflation, and, in common with other raw materials producers, we will have to live with world prices that will still be cyclical but fluctuating about a lower average level than in the past.'

Alcan reorganised its structure from a geographical to a global product-line one. That cut management and staff, and gave economies of scale to the commodity-type businesses that Alcan decided were to be its principal operations: producing new aluminium and rolling.

In the late 1980s and early 1990s Alcan's capital expenditure peaked at more that $1bn a year as it modernised its smelters and expanded its rolling capacity in the US and Germany.

Alcan's study also showed the aluminium business was likely to see high growth rates in the use of the metal by the automotive industry and in Asia. Growth in the car business, if it comes, will be beyond the year 2000 when manufacturers may use aluminium for car structures. Alcan has developed techniques to allow 'all-aluminium' cars to be produced in big volumes. Last year, it acquired a substantial plant in eastern Germany capable of being converted to produce aluminium body sheet for cars.

In Asia, Alcan has a long association with Nippon Light Metal, Japan's biggest aluminium group, and has been operating in China for 31 years.

Mr Bougie says Alcan is now more that halfway through a disposal programme expected to take between 18 months and two years. 'We are in no hurry, this is no fire sale. We want to get the best value for shareholders and . . . we have to think about the employees.' Alcan will emerge as a streamlined organisation, concentrating on doing fewer things well, able to remain profitable in the cyclical troughs. Streamlined does not mean smaller, Mr Bougie insists. 'We will have a bigger bottom line.'

*Source: Financial Times*, 23 March 1995. Reprinted with permission.

## ◆ CASE STUDY 12.2

### Nuclear Electric 'has negative value'     **FT**

Nuclear Electric would have a negative net present value of about £600m if it was privatised under proposals being studied by the government, says a report published yesterday by an anti-nuclear group.

The Consortium of Opposing Local Authorities has conducted a financial valuation of Nuclear Electric's assets which concludes that the older Magnox stations are not able to be privatised, the advance gas-cooled reactors have a net present value of close to minus £1bn, and that Sizewell B, the recently opened pressurised water reactor, has a net value of £400m.

*Source: Financial Times*, 10 February 1995. Reprinted with permission.

### ◆ Exercise 12.1

1  What other types of investment are likely to have costs at both the beginning and the end of their lifetimes?

2  In the case of Nuclear Electric, suppose its income stream for the Magnox reactor is the following:

Initial outlay, C = £2bn

Returns in periods 1,2,3,4 are £300m, £600m, £900m and £1.5bn respectively.

The rate of return is 15%

There will be a decommissioning charge of £1bn in five years time.

Calculate the NPV for the Nuclear Electric Magnox Reactor.

How could the government convert the negative net present value into a positive one?

### Comment on the case studies

These two case studies highlight the relevance of calculating the net present value for the two organisations.

Case study 12.1 suggests that the technique was used to focus on ascertaining which segments of the market showed profitable investment returns. A positive net present value could be obtained if Alcan was a low-cost producer. This might suggest that organisations, even where they have a negative NPV, may wish to examine once again the returns and cost element of their businesses to consider ways of reducing their cost base before making a final decision on whether to invest or not.

Case study 12.2 indicates the problems for organisations which have an asset which is going to require large levels of expenditure at the end of the project, during its decommissioning phase. Thus for the Magnox reactor there is an initial cost followed by a stream of returns and then high levels of cost once again. After nuclear reactors have been closed they require many years of supervision so that harmful radiation is reduced slowly over time.

## SCENARIO ANALYSIS

When considering NPV calculations, great store is placed on the future expected returns from an investment project. It is possible for organisations to find that changes in market conditions could result in a change in a number of the key variables in the investment calculation. For example, the entry of a new organisation into the market could lead to a fall in market share and have an impact on price.

Scenario analysis permits management to consider the effect of potential future scenarios or events. These can then be transferred into the NPV or discounted cash flow model and a new NPV can be calculated.

For example, suppose an organisation is considering investing in the following project: capital outlay, £5000, current discount rate, 15 per cent and returns of £2000, £2000 and £2000 in years one, two and three. The NPV calculation is:

$$NPV = -5000 + 2000 + 2000/(1 + 0.15) + 2000/(1 + 0.15)^2$$

or,

$$NPV = 254.28$$

On the basis of these expected returns the project would be acceptable, since NPV>0.

Suppose that the decision makers are more pessimistic about future returns, with these expected to be £2000, £1750 and £1750 for the three years. All other factors are constant. Under this pessimistic scenario the NPV is –£152.58. The project would therefore be rejected.

Alternatively, it is possible that decision makers are more optimistic about future returns, perhaps expecting a boom in consumer demand. The three expected returns are £2000, £2500 and £2500 for years one, two and three. All other factors remaining constant, the NPV can be shown to equal £1067.80. The project is therefore acceptable.

There are limits to this sensitivity analysis, however. First, what exactly does optimistic or pessimistic mean? The factors that may be altered in the optimistic/pessimistic scenario may be sometimes more related to the marketing department, while on other occasions that may be connected to the production department. How can we be sure that optimistic in the marketing department is the same as optimistic in the production department? In other words, predictions are subjective.

Second, in the above analysis our optimistic/pessimistic outlook only affected expected returns. It is possible that a change expected in the future affects a number of variables. For example, suppose that the government tightens its fiscal policy by pushing up interest rates; this may also affect future sales. Therefore, both the interest rate and expected returns would alter.

Finally, scenario analysis provides no rules to guide the decision maker as to whether the initial appraisal advice should or should not be amended in the light of the sensitivity data.

# INTERNAL RATE OF RETURN

Another method which uses the discounted cash flow technique to ascertain the profitability of an investment is the **internal rate of return** (IRR). The IRR is the discount rate which just makes the present value of an investment project equal to zero. Thus the present value formula becomes:

$$0 = -C_0 + R_0 + R_1/(1 + K) + R_2/(1 + K)^2 \ldots R_n/(1 + K)^n$$

The equation is solved for $K$, the internal rate of return, that is, the discount rate that just makes the present value of the income stream minus the cost of the investment equal to zero. When the value of $K$ has been found, it is compared with the cost of capital or risk-adjusted discount rate that the organisation uses, and if $K$ exceeds this rate the project is accepted. As with the NPV method, the organisation can rank its various projects in terms of their IRRs, selecting those with the highest IRRs first.

## ◆ CASE STUDY 12.3

# Energy mission out to woo Beijing                                    FT

Mrs Hazel O'Leary, US energy secretary, arrives in Beijing today heading a specialist mission whose main purpose will be to advance US power and environmental sector interests in what could become a huge Chinese market, writes Tony Walker.

The delegation, which includes representatives of some of the biggest US power companies, engineering firms, and investment banks, is expected to sign a series of agreements with the Chinese. But, in the light of the continuing row over copyright issues, US officials have been retreating from earlier predictions of $4bn to $8bn (£2.5bn to £5bn) in deals.

Mrs O'Leary's arrival coincides with a threatened trade war between China and the US, but she has been at pains to separate her mission from the copyrights issue.

The composition of the energy mission underlines the fact that the power sector will dominate the agenda this week – in private sessions with Chinese officials and at a seminar on Wednesday sponsored by China's state planning commission and the US energy department. In the delegation are representatives of General Electric, the Wing Group, Energy Power Corporation and CEA (Community Energy Alternatives Incorporated), all of which are in power project negotiations.

Discussions will also focus on coal-washing technology, efficient energy usage, oil and gas, petrochemicals, coal slurry techniques and gasification.

US and other international power companies have been pressing China for greater flexibility over returns on equity investments, but a lingering dispute among Chinese leaders over the internal rate of return (IRR) on investment and other issues has stymied progress.

Of some 50 projects pending, negotiations on about a dozen large investments are well advanced, but could not proceed until China had clarified its policy on BOT-type (build–operate–transfer) schemes, according to a Western official who specialises in the energy sector.

'Power plant approvals are moving very slowly,' he said. 'The question is: does the Chinese government begin to give preliminary approval to large projects and thus send a reassuring signal that, while it might be in cautionary mode, it is still proceeding.'

Power companies had expected China last year to specify priority projects as part of its deliberations on planning targets for the coming year. But silence from the authorities has indicated continuing differences over how they should structure deals with foreign partners.

*Source: Financial Times, 20 February 1995. Reprinted with permission.*

*Comment of the case study*

It is clear from Case study 12.3 that the developed nations wish to gain entry and production facilities in one of the last untapped markets, China. Any capital investment which uses the IRR technique of appraisal requires, for acceptance, that its IRR is more than the organisation's discount rate or cost of credit. In the case of the developments in the Chinese market, the Chinese authorities may want Western knowledge and expertise but do not want large proportions of the profits or returns on the investment to accrue to Western companies. Thus, if a substantial proportion of the returns from these investment projects are to remain in China, the cash flow to the companies would need to be reduced and this lowers the IRR. If the IRR falls below the organisation's discount rate, then no investment takes place and China's development could slow down.

---

◆ **Exercise 12.2**

Suppose that the Chinese government sets the returns so low that the IRR is less than the US power companies' cost of capital. Under what circumstances would the US power companies still wish to undertake the investment projects?

---

## COMPARISON OF NPV AND IRR

Both IRR and NPV methods of assessing investment projects use the process of discounted cash flows. The purpose of any technique for assessing investment projects is that they provide the organisation with accurate signals of which projects they should invest in. It is possible that the NPV and IRR methods provide contradictory signals as to which project is the better. It is possible to show that, say, for two projects, A and B, A could have the higher NPV but B could have the higher IRR. With this lack of consistency, how can an organisation be sure that it is investing in the correct project? Table 12.2 may help with the explanation.

Table 12.2 indicates that Project X has the higher NPV at a discount rate of 12 per cent, while Project Y has the higher IRR. The reason for the difference is that the positive net cash flows from a project over its lifetime are implicitly assumed to be reinvested at the organisation's cost of capital or discount rate. In the IRR method these positive net flows are reinvested at the IRR. Since there is

**Table 12.2 Net present value and internal rate of return on two mutually exclusive investment projects**

|  | Project X | Project Y |
|---|---|---|
| Initial outlay | Fr1 000 000 | Fr1 000 000 |
| Net expected returns |  |  |
| Year 1 | 100 000 | 350 000 |
| Year 2 | 0 | 350 000 |
| Year 3 | 500 000 | 350 000 |
| Year 4 | 500 000 | 350 000 |
| Year 5 | 1 400 000 | 350 000 |
| NPV @ discount rate of 12% | Fr1 378 720 | Fr1 261 680 |
| IRR | 20.3% | 22.1% |

no certainty that the organisation can reinvest these net cash flows at the same higher IRR, it is generally better to use the NPV approach. In particular, when the IRR is very high the idea that the positive cash flows can be invested at rather high levels of IRR is erroneous.

A problem that may occur in the comparison of IRR and NPV is what happens if we use different discount rates. It is possible that project A is better than project B when the discount rate of 10 per cent is used, but as higher and higher discount rates are used project B could be favoured over project A. The reason is to do with the timing of the capital inflows from the project. Projects which have larger returns further in the future will find that these become smaller and smaller figures in present value terms as the discount rate grows. Figure 12.1 shows the case for two investment projects, A and B, and their relationship to the discount rate. A reversal of project rankings occurs at the crossover discount rate. This reversal may not be as big an issue as it first appears, since many alternative investment projects do not involve a crossover discount rate. Moreover, if a crossover discount rate does occur it is often too high or too low to affect the project rankings.

Suppose that the project has both positive and negative inflows, as shown in Table 12.3.

This type of cash flow may seem odd at first sight, but in gravel workings it is possible that a

**Table 12.3 IRR with positive and negative cash flows**

| Project | Cash flow in £ | | | IRR % | NPV at 10% |
|---|---|---|---|---|---|
|  | $C_0$ | $C_1$ | $C_2$ |  |  |
| F | –4 000 | 25 000 | –25 000 | 25 and 400 | –1934 |

**Figure 12.1 Present value and the market rate of interest**

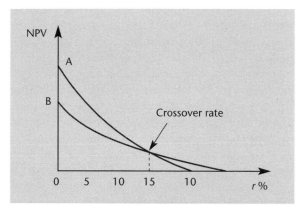

The NPVs for two investment projects, A and B, are plotted here as a function of the market rate of interest or discount rate. At lower discount rates project A is preferred, while at higher discount rates project B is preferred. At one discount rate, 15 per cent, the decision makers are indifferent between project A and project B. This discount rate is called the crossover rate.

project which costs £4000 in the first year brings in £25 000 in the second and, because the mining company has to restore the land, it may have to invest substantial sums at the termination date. Calculation of the NPV and IRR is as follows:

$$NPV = -4000 + 25\,000/(1 + 0.1)$$
$$- 25\,000/(1 + 0.1)^2$$
$$= -4000 + 22\,727.27 - 20\,661.1$$
$$NPV = -1933.8$$

The internal rate of return is:

$$0 = -4000 + 25\,000/(1 + K) - 25\,000/(1 + K)^2$$

where $K$ is the discount rate (internal rate of return) to be calculated.

Therefore, multiplying both sides by $(1 + K)^2$ gives:

$$0 = -4000(1 + K)^2 + 25\,000(1 + K) - 25\,000$$
$$0 = -4000(1 + K^2 + 2K) + 25\,000 + 25\,000K$$
$$- 25\,000$$

This reduces to:

$$0 = -4000K^2 + 17\,000K - 4000$$

Dividing all terms by 1000 and solving the quadratic yields the following:

$$0 = (4K - 1)(K - 4)$$

Therefore, either $K = 0.25$ (25%), or $K = 4$ (400%).

Here there are two discount rates which make NPV = 0. The reason for this is the double change in the cash flows. It is possible to adapt the IRR rule to take into account the case of two IRRs, but such adaptations are not necessary for the NPV method. A further issue with the IRR rule is that the internal rate of return needs to be compared with a hurdle rate. Suppose that the IRR is greater than the hurdle rate in some periods but not for others. In such circumstances a single-figure IRR is not really valid. Another problem for the IRR rule is where there is only a single value for the IRR but the project does not yield a positive NPV. Finally, a further difficulty is that the IRR evaluates projects on the basis of their percentage rate of return rather than in absolute terms. Thus if project A, with an outlay of £5000, is calculated to have an IRR of 20 per cent and project B, with an outlay of £50 000, has an internal rate of return of 18 per cent, and they both clear the hurdle rate of 15 per cent, then investment project A will be favoured over B. Yet the organisation would receive a much higher return (profit) from project B. It follows, therefore, that although both NPV and IRR use discounted cash flow techniques of investment appraisal, the difficulties that have been encountered with IRR, although they can sometimes be adapted for, suggest that NPV is a more consistent approach.

NPV and IRR are not the only two ways in which an investment project can be appraised, and some of the alternatives are considered briefly below.

## PAYBACK METHOD

Companies often require the initial outlay on the project to be recoverable before a specified cut-off point, as illustrated in Table 12.4.

Project A takes one year to recover the initial outlay, while Project B takes two years. If the organisation used the **payback** rule with a one-year cut-off period, it would accept only Project A. If it used the payback rule with a cut-off period of two years,

**Table 12.4 Payback as an investment appraisal technique**

| Project | Cash flows, lira | | | | Payback period, years | NPV at 10% |
| | $C_0$ | $C_1$ | $C_2$ | $C_3$ | | |
| --- | --- | --- | --- | --- | --- | --- |
| A | -2000 | 2000 | 0 | 0 | 1 | -182 |
| B | -2000 | 1000 | 1000 | 5000 | 2 | 3492 |

both projects are acceptable. On inspection of the two income streams, Project B appears superior to Project A. Thus the payback approach has some difficulty in ranking investment projects consistently.

The problem arises because the payback approach gives equal weight to all cash flows before the payback period and no weight to subsequent flows. It therefore prefers projects which have large returns in the early years and nothing later to projects which give small returns in the early years but large returns later. This may provide an explanation of the disappointing growth performance of the UK economy since the Second World War, in that UK companies have sought investment projects which give them a high return early on in their lifecycle, while Japanese and German companies have been willing to wait longer for returns which have proved to be much larger in the future; see Cook and Healey (1995). In addition, the payback approach fails to recognise the time value of money. Suppose that an investment project which costs Lr300 today just gives a return of Lr300 in one year's time. An investor would not be happy with such a capital flow.

However, there are some advantages to the payback approach. Payback is quick and simple to calculate and is most easily understood by management. It is also said that the payback approach leads to the selection of less risky projects where the organisation faces mutually exclusive investment decisions. An example of mutually exclusive investment projects occurs where an organisation has two subsidiaries with two separate cost centres, each undertaking separate investment programmes. However, it is highly unlikely that any project is truly independent. At one extreme we could consider an oil-refining company which produces both gases for commercial use and fertiliser. In this case,

investing in improving fertiliser production may affect future investment in the commercial gas plant.

An advantage of the payback approach is that, because future cash flows are more uncertain, an investment appraisal technique that relies on speed of return may well reduce these risks.

Furthermore, the payback approach saves management time, in that the expected returns after the payback period do not have to be calculated. Finally, the payback method may be seen as an appropriate approach when capital is scarce, in that the quicker the money comes in from one investment project the quicker it can be used for another. Lumby (1994) notes that, 'Between 60% and 90% of firms experience capital rationing in that they have found it necessary to reject some acceptable projects. The causes of the capital rationing were that some projects were rejected in order to maintain earnings per share or a particular dividend policy, as well as a constraint being imposed by management on the amount of borrowings.' However, more recent work (Barwise (1996)) suggests that most well-managed companies are not constrained by a lack of capital – the exceptions being small businesses, companies in less-developed capital markets and companies in distress – and the rationing of capital is used as a device to encourage disciplined thinking. However, it could be argued that capital rationing was in evidence in British Aerospace during the early 1990s, after its expansion plans during the 1980s into land and commercial development and the Rover Group led to it not having sufficient funding to develop Rover further as well as undertaking new investments in its aerospace division. Thus the Rover Group was sold to BMW, enabling British Aerospace to use its new capital to finance other areas of its business.

## ◆ CASE STUDY 12.4

### Consortium to dig $680 million Denmark–Sweden tunnel

A DKr3.8bn ($680m) contract to build the tunnel section of the first direct road and rail link to connect Sweden and Denmark has been awarded to companies from Scandinavia, Britain, France and the Netherlands.

The DKr14.4bn Oresund crossing connecting the cities of Malmo and Copenhagen is the second of two large bridge and tunnel projects which will provide Sweden with its first land link to Denmark through to Germany and the rest of western and central Europe.

A consortium of NCC (from Sweden), John Laing (UK), Dumez-GTM (France), E. Phil & Son (Denmark), and Boskalis Westminster Dredging (Netherlands) yesterday won the contract to build the 3.7km tunnel section of the 16km crossing. Symonds Travers Morgan of the UK will be responsible for designing the tunnel section.

A separate contract worth DKr1.4bn went to a consortium of Per Aaesleff (Denmark), Ballast Nedam (Netherlands) and The Great Lakes Dredge and Dock Co (US).

Separate contracts to build two bridges, including a 1.09km cable-stayed elevated bridge that will cross the shipping lanes have still to be awarded and are likely to cost a further DKr5.4bn.

The crossing from Sweden to Zealand island will link with the DKr20bn Storebaelt bridge-tunnel project which is largely built, connecting Zealand and neighbouring Funen island to the Danish mainland, A third project, the Fehmern Belt, linking the southern Danish Island of Lolland with Germany has still to receive backing from the two governments.

The two Danish/Swedish crossings have attracted wide international interest. Five consortia, of 23 companies from six European countries and the US, bid for the Oresund tunnel contract. The closest rival to the winner was a consortium which included Tarmac (UK), SAE (France), Strabag (Germany), Christiani & Nielsen (Denmark) and Kraftbyggarna (Sweden). Twenty 175m-long, prefabricated concrete tunnel sections, each weighing about 50,000 tonnes, are to be lowered into a massive trench dug in the seabed. The tunnel,

claimed to be the largest immersed tube tunnel in the world, will contain a two-lane motorway in each direction as well as a railway track in each direction.

It will stretch from an artificial peninsula near Copenhagen airport to an artificial island in the Oresund channel, where it will connect to the bridge sections of the project.

The crossing, now forecast to open in 2000, was held up by objections from environmentalists in Sweden who forced the two governments to impose tough specifications on the link to ensure water flows in and out of the polluted Baltic sea were not impeded. The project as a result is expected to cost more than its present budget of DKr14.4bn.

The project is being financed by international borrowing, backed by guarantees from the two governments. Payback is scheduled to take 24 years from opening, based on revenues from the Danish and Swedish state railways and vehicle tariffs.

*Source: Financial Times, 18 July 1995. Reprinted with permission.*

## ◆ CASE STUDY 12.5

# Good reason to be cautious

Earlier this month, the Department of Trade and Industry encouraged companies to adopt a longer-term view when deciding whether to make an investment.

'Successful companies make both short-term (two to three years) and long-term investments,' the DTI says in *Money & Machines*, its free guide to successful capital investment in manufacturing. 'Long-term investments are vital for sustained advantage over the competition.'

The DTI guide follows an address last November by Michael Heseltine, the trade and industry secretary, to the Confederation of British Industry conference, when he accused UK industry of not investing enough.

Publicly-owned companies arguably have good reason for not taking a longer-term view. Projects with long-term paybacks are often earnings diluting in the short term. Managers fear that shareholders, seeing this, might sell the shares.

But are private companies with fewer external financial pressures acting irrationally by not taking a longer-term investment view?

Not at all, according to David Storey, head of the SME centre at Warwick University.

Storey sums up the attitudes of the companies his unit surveys in the Midlands: 'They say "We are having a good patch now, but when is the next recession coming along? The answer is three years time, isn't

it?".' He observes: 'Businesses are cautious – and they have every right to be.'

Take two hypothetical managing directors, Storey says. Drop one in a national economy growing at a stable rate of more than 3 per cent per annum for 20 years. Drop the other in a country where annual GDP growth has again and again swung up 4 per cent and then down 2 per cent during the same period.

Ask them what would be a comfortable playback period on an investment. The first would not be worried to wait longer than three years before seeing a return. The second is unlikely to commit capital to a project unless be can see the return on a four-year horizon, Storey says.

A CBI survey last year indicated that British managers fell into the second, anxious bracket. In spite of strong growth forecasts and falling inflation, the report showed that two companies in five were still targeting 20 per cent rates of return.

A measure of the low level of British investment comes from Japan's Ministry of Finance: the ratio of plant investment to GDP shows British investment falling from 3.2 per cent in 1973 to 2.8 per cent in 1990, compared with a rise from 6.4 per cent to 7.7 per cent during the same period in Japan.

Case study 12.5 *continued*

Much as the UK government would like to see more longer-term investment, neither business nor government believes the other is willing to make long-term commitments. While the government is pressing business to improve its handling of investment opportunities – most recently in the DTI handbook – companies doubt the government's ability to deliver the stability it promises.

Sudhir Junankar, associate director for economic analysis at the CBI, tends to agree with Storey – companies are being rational in erring on the side of caution bearing in mind past volatility in inflation and interest rates, he says.

The government has targeted inflation to be between 1 and 4 per cent. But companies Junankar spoke to tended to factor an annual rate of 5 per cent into their investments.

Small and medium-sized companies have a strong case for caution, he concludes: 'Companies would be short-termist indeed if they thought that low inflation would be sustained over a long period of time, as we have not yet had one complete cycle of low inflation.'

*Source: Financial Times, 28 February 1995. Reprinted with permission.*

### Comment on the case studies

The two case studies show two aspects of the payback approach to investment appraisal. For large capital investments the payback may not occur for many years and in this respect there are likely to be greater uncertainties about the future cash flows from the project. In addition, as the opening business application pointed out, the estimates of costs and discount rates may be inappropriate. Case study 12.5, however, highlights the importance of consistency in government policy. One view of the UK's macroeconomic record is that it has been subject to much larger elements of stop–go policies which have encouraged its organisations to think in a 'short-term' way. In this respect investment projects which have short payback periods are preferred.

◆ **Exercise 12.3**

1 In Case study 12.5, to what extent do share-holders dictate the payback period?
2 Do you consider that large investment projects require more government involvement and cannot be left to the private sector alone? Give examples to justify your answer.

### The discounted payback rule

To overcome the problem with the time value of money that exists with the normal payback approach, companies often use the discounted payback rule. This rule asks, 'How many years does it take the project by discounting the future returns for the project just to cover its initial outlay?' Suppose Project A has a cash flow of £6500 which lasts seven years and Project B has a cash flow of

£6000 which lasts ten years. Both projects have a capital outlay of £20 000 and the discount rate is 10 per cent. It should be fairly obvious by now that Project B will have the higher present value. Project A, however, has a higher return in all periods of its life than Project B, so it will have the shorter discounted payback. That is, if we use the discounted approach to investment appraisal it will take just under four years for the discounted cash flows from Project A to match the original outlay. The discounted payback for Project B is just over four years.

Thus the discounted payback approach is a superior investment appraisal technique than the simple payback approach in that it attempts to account for the time value of money. That is, money at the early stage of a project is worth more than the same money at a later stage in the returns from a project. There is still, however, the issue that the discounted payback approach depends on the choice of the arbitrary cut-off date. This approach may therefore be suitable for projects which have similar cash flow profiles, such as in the property sector where investments are expected to produce a more even, long-term flow of returns.

## RETURN ON CAPITAL EMPLOYED

This is an accounting approach to the assessment of an investment project. To calculate the return on capital employed (ROCE), or the average return on book value, it is necessary to divide the average forecasted profits of a project after depreciation and taxes by the average book value of the investment. This ratio is then assessed against the book rate of return for the organisation as a whole or against some other external yardstick, such as the average book rate of return for the industry.

In Table 12.5 the average book rate of return for an investment project is 44 per cent. This is based on an investment project which costs £9000, runs for three years and depreciates at a constant rate of £3000 per year. Notice also for simplicity that there are no taxes. The criterion for selection is that if the ROCE exceeds the going rate of return for the company overall, the investment is acceptable.

There are a number of advantages with using the ROCE approach. Evaluating a project in terms of a percentage rate of return is using a concept with which many areas of management are familiar. A project which is described as having a five- or six-year payback period may not convey much to management, but being told that the project has a return on capital of 44 per cent may be effective. Second, the ROCE evaluates a project in terms of its profitability, which, rightly or wrongly, is considered by some as the real focus of investment appraisal. Finally, shareholders often assess the company on its overall return on capital employed and there may be some logic in doing the same for each investment project.

Against these perceived advantages must be set a number of deficiencies with the approach. There are many ways in which the ROCE can be calculated and, because there is no accepted manner, the appraiser can choose the approach which shows the potential investment project in the best light. Second, since ROCE measures the return on the investment in percentage terms, it fails to take into account the financial size of the project. For example, if investment A has an ROCE of 30 per cent and investment B has an ROCE of 25 per cent, the ROCE criterion suggests that project A should be chosen so long as it exceeds the organisation's average cost of capital. However, suppose that the 30 per cent return for investment A is £350 000, while the 25 per cent return for project B (which is larger) is £1 million. Then it might be suggested that the ROCE approach has chosen the wrong project.

In addition to these two problems, the ROCE ignores the time value of money. It gives no allowance for the fact that immediate receipts are more valuable than distant ones. Here, two projects which have the same ROCE may have very different income streams, with one bringing in more money early in its lifetime than the other. The ROCE appears to ignore this fact, quite the reverse of the payback approach which ignores the fact of income that comes in later in the project's life.

A further problem with the ROCE approach is that it depends on accounting income rather than on a project's cash flows. These are often very different. The accountant classifies some cash outflows as capital investment and others as operating expenses. These operating expenses are deducted immediately from each year's income. The capital expenditures are depreciated over the lifetime of the project at a rate set by the accountant. Then the depreciation charge is deducted from each year's income. Thus the ROCE approach depends on which items the accountant treats as capital investment and on the level of depreciation. These procedures are used for reporting purposes, and the accountant's decisions should not affect the overall decision whether to accept or reject an investment project.

## Table 12.5 Computing the average book value of an investment

| Project A | Cash flow, £ | | |
| --- | --- | --- | --- |
| | Year 1 | Year 2 | Year 3 |
| Revenue | 12 000 | 10 000 | 8 000 |
| Other costs | 6 000 | 5 000 | 4 000 |
| Cash flow | **6 000** | **5 000** | **4 000** |
| Depreciation | 3 000 | 3 000 | 3 000 |
| Net income | **3 000** | **2 000** | **1 000** |

The average annual income is (3000 + 2000 + 1000)/3 = 2000

| | Year 0 | Year 1 | Year 2 | Year 3 |
| --- | --- | --- | --- | --- |
| Gross book value of the investment | 9000 | 9000 | 9000 | 9000 |
| Accumulated depreciation | 0 | 3000 | 6000 | 9000 |
| Net book value of the investment | 9000 | 6000 | 3000 | 0 |

The average net book value is (9000 + 6000 + 3000 + 0)/4 = 4500.

The average book rate of return = (Average annual income)/(Average annual investment) = 2000/4500 = 0.44 or 44 per cent.

## ALTERNATIVE INVESTMENT CRITERIA

Scenario analysis, as outlined earlier, considers the main underlying variables that may affect future demand and therefore expected cash flows. To each factor that is believed to affect the future demand for the product is attached a probability, although an optimistic/pessimistic scenario can be adopted. The change in the factor is considered in terms of its effect on the cash flows and therefore the present value of the project. Some of the factors that may be considered responsible for changes in future cash flows may be outside the control of the organisation, such as political changes, but others may be more under the direct control of the organisation, such as perceptions of the product or quality issues. Control of these last two factors, for example, can improve the expected cash flow.

Break-even analysis considers the critical value at which the project's NPV is zero. For example, the organisation may have a critical market share at which it is aiming or a pivotal level of costs. If there is any deviation from these points, the organisation may begin to lose money on the project.

## EXTENSIONS AND PROBLEMS ASSOCIATED WITH INVESTMENT APPRAISAL

In all the techniques discussed there has been a general assumption that management has the necessary information to enable it to make the 'correct' investment decision. This may not be so. It has been mentioned before that, because the investment gives future returns, these cannot be known with complete accuracy.

Both costs and revenues should be considered in real terms, that is, taking account of inflation, rather than in nominal terms. To incorporate the effects of inflation into the discounted cash flow analysis used earlier, we can use the Fisher relationship. That is:

$$(1 + \text{Real rate of interest})(1 + \text{Rate of inflation}) = (1 + \text{market rate of interest})$$

Thus if the rate of inflation is 5 per cent, and the market rate of interest 15.5 per cent, the real rate of interest is:

$$\text{Real rate of interest} = (1 + \text{market rate of interest})/(1 + \text{Rate of inflation}) - 1$$

Using the numbers from above:

$$\text{Real rate of interest} = (1 + 0.155)/(1 + 0.05) - 1$$

or,

$$\text{Real rate of interest} = 10\%$$

The techniques described above make great use of data, financial or otherwise. This suggests that many management techniques of investment appraisal are quantitative. However, there should also be room for subjective, qualitative data.

Although the organisation may consider that the project has a particular lifetime related to when the management believes the project or investment wears out, this period can be abruptly curtailed if there are changes in technology which render the existing project obsolete. Changes in areas of the organisation's economic environment should also be considered. What could be the implications on the organisation's cash flow of a government signing a trade agreement with another country? Will environmental or health and safety regulations affect project receipts and, in addition, will this dramatically alter the project's lifetime?

For larger corporations there may be a need to evaluate a range of investment proposals from the different divisions from a whole organisation perspective. The separate divisions may have analysed the investment proposal from their own division's experience and this parochial view could have repercussions for the whole organisation.

Training can be one of the most important elements in the ability of an organisation to sustain its position in the market and grow. It can have slow but longer-term effects on the organisation and, unlike investment in a capital project, may not give the necessary high short-term rewards.

Therefore, in terms of the investment decision training has two important features. Training may enhance the profitability of the organisation by improving productivity, enriching its skills base and thus improving its competitiveness. In this respect, training can lead to higher expected returns in the future and thereby improve the flows from an investment project. The British system of training and education has often been regarded as one of the root causes of the UK economy's poor productivity record; *see* Healey and Cook (1996).

Training can be viewed in terms of the investment appraisal techniques outlined earlier for capital projects. This investment in training – the investment in human capital – can be seen from two perspectives. From the individual's point of view, periods of training may be associated with lower income during training which is compensated for by higher income once the training is completed. From the organisation's point of view, training an individual can be costly (the capital outlay), but the organisation hopes to improve the returns in terms of productivity after training over the employee's whole working life. Thus current cost needs to be assessed against improved future returns from the employee. This is the familiar discounted cash flow argument restated, but this time in terms of human capital investment.

Assessing actual returns to investment in human capital has its difficulties, not least of which is the separation of individual ability and the influence of family background on expected future returns. It may well be that investment in training is simply used as a screening device to separate out those who have particular skills and qualifications from those that do not.

In many respects investment in new technology has features in common with the decision to invest in training. Although it may be reasonably easy to estimate the cost of the new technology, organisations often underestimate the costs of training that go with it to execute the technology. Changes in information technology can vastly reduce the cost of inventories, can be used to supply a just-in-time ordering process, can enable organisations to be in a better position to meet customer needs, and generally improve customer service. However, they may require consideration of the organisation's culture and general operations if the full impact of the change in information technology is to be seen. From the appraisal of an investment project it is much easier to introduce new levels of technology into an existing production process which has little effect on the way the organisation works, although from a strategic perspective the ability of managers to think and organise differently may give them strategic advantages in the marketplace. Thus when considering the impact of new technology on production processes, managers might benefit from using some form of tradition appraisal technique, but then should consider further the wider implications of the project. Thus if investment appraisal only considers the traditional approaches projects may be dismissed as unprofitable, when a wider consideration of the increased competitiveness, long-term strategic value and possible changes in the organisation itself may render the project highly profitable, although perhaps a more risky investment.

In this context of risk, although Chapter 13 will consider it in more detail, it is useful to note at this stage that because an investment project is to give returns in the future, these cannot be known with certainty and the view of the expected return may depend on the manager's attitude to risk. A risk-taking manager may give a more optimistic view of expected future returns. In this case the manager is attaching a probability to the expected return.

Suppose, however, that probabilities cannot be accurately established: managers will then face a situation of uncertainty. One way of adapting to this is to adjust the cost of capital upwards by a risk premium, or to use sensitivity analysis, outlined earlier in this chapter.

## COST OF CAPITAL

In previous sections the relevance of the cost of the investment project has been developed. But from where does the finance for an investment project come? The organisation could raise investment funds internally via undistributed profits, depreciation and tax provisions, or externally from a mixture of debt and share issue (equity financing) where it seeks long-term finance or bank loans and trade credit for short-term finance. Where the investment is financed internally there is an opportunity cost or forgone return on these funds to take into account. The cost of external funding is the lowest rate of interest that lenders and stockholders require if they loan to, or invest their monies in the organisation. Given that external funding comes primarily from a mix of debt and equity, how are the costs and mix of these determined?

## COST OF DEBT

The **cost of debt** is the return the investors require to lend their money to the organisation. Since the interest payments made by organisations on borrowed funds are tax deductible, it is necessary to compute the after-tax debt. For example, suppose that an organisation borrows DM200 000 at an interest rate of 10 per cent. The interest charges before tax are DM20 000. Since these interest charges are tax deductible, part of the interest charge paid out to investors is going to be made by the tax authorities. Thus the cost of the borrowed money to the organisation is given by:

$$k_d = r(1 - t) \qquad (12.2)$$

where,

$k_d$ = cost of borrowed funds to the organisation
$r$ = interest rate paid
$t$ = marginal tax rate

If, for example, the marginal tax rate in the UK is 24 per cent and the interest rate at which the organisation borrows is 7 per cent, the after-tax cost of the debt is:

$$k_d = 7\%(1 - 0.24)$$

or,

$$k_d = 0.07\ (0.76)$$

so,

$$k_d = 0.0532$$

This rate is applicable only to the new debt or the marginal debt. It makes no difference whether the organisation borrowed at higher or lower interest rates for previous investments.

Where the investment project is financed via equity, there are a number of methods by which the **cost of equity** can be measured. These are the risk-free rate plus a premium, the dividend evaluation model and the capital asset pricing model (CAPM). In the next section each of these is examined in turn.

## RISK-FREE RATE PLUS PREMIUM

When a lender purchases stock in a company it requires a return to compensate for its opportunity cost of reducing its expenditure (consumption) elsewhere, together with a return to compensate for risk taking. One procedure that can be used to estimate the cost of equity capital ($k_e$) is to note that it consists of a **risk-free rate of return** ($R_f$) plus a **risk premium** ($R_p$):

$$k_e = R_f + R_p$$

The risk-free rate of return can be estimated from the short-term interest rate charged on government securities. In the UK this would consist of the six-month UK Treasury Bill rate, which in June 1996 was 5.75 per cent. These short-term interest rates are easily obtained by looking at the financial press. The risk premium is made up of two components. First, there is greater risk in investing in an organisation's securities as opposed to investing in the safer government securities. Second, if individuals buy common stock rather than bonds, there is a greater risk of payment since the interest and principal payments to bondholders is paid first with payments to stockholders following behind. Therefore the formula above becomes:

$$k_e = R_f + S_1 + S_2$$

where,

$S_1$ = the excess interest rate of the organisation's bonds over the rate of return on government bonds ($R_f$)

$S_2$ = the additional risk in purchasing the organisation's stocks rather than bonds

On average this rate has been seen to be around 4 per cent. Thus if the rate on government securities is 7 per cent (the risk-free rate) and the rate on the organisation's bonds is 12 per cent, then:

$$k_e = 7 + 5 + 4 = 16\%$$

## DIVIDEND EVALUATION MODEL

In the **dividend evaluation model**, if a situation of perfect information is assumed, the value of a share of common stock in an organisation should be equal to the present value of all future dividends expected to be paid on the stock, which are then discounted by the relevant rate of return of the investor ($K_i$). Suppose that the dividend per share is $D$, and this is expected to remain constant over time. The present value of this income stream from the common stock is given by:

$$PV = \sum_{t=1}^{n} D/(1 + K_i)^t$$

where $t$ = the time period over which the dividends are paid, running from time period 1 to time period $n$.

For example, in June 1996, the dividend per share for Associated Dairies (ASDA) was 2.65 pence. If these values were expected to be constant over a two-year period, and the relevant rate of return over this period was 5 per cent, then the present value of the income stream is:

$$PV = 2.65/(1 + 0.05) + 2.65(1 + 0.05)^2$$
$$= 2.52 + 2.4$$
$$= 4.92 \text{ pence}$$

Where the dividend is paid out in perpetuity, $n$ equals infinity. If something is paid out in perpetuity, the above equation is the equation for an annuity, which can be written as:

$$PV = D/K_i$$

This equation can be derived as follows.

If $PV = \sum_{t=1}^{n} D/(1 + K_i)^t$

then $PV = D/(1 + K_i) + D/(1 + K_i)^2 + D/(1 + K_i)^3 \ldots$

Suppose we let $D/(1 + K_i) = y$

and $1/(1 + K_i) = x$

then,

$$PV = y + yx + yx^2 + \ldots \text{ or}$$
$$PV = y(1 + x + x^2 + \ldots) \qquad (12.3)$$

Multiplying Equation 12.3 by $x$ gives:

$$(PV)x = y(x + x^2 + x^3 + \ldots) \qquad (12.4)$$

Subtracting equation 12.4 from equation 12.3 gives:

$$PV - (PV)x = y$$

or,

$$PV(1 - x) = y$$

Substituting back into this equation for $x$ and $y$ gives:

$$PV(1 - 1/(1 + K_i)) = D/(1 + K_i)$$

Multiplying both sides of the above by $(1 + K_i)$:

$$PV([1 + K_i] - 1) = D$$

or,

$$PV(K_i) = D$$

so,

$$PV = D/K_i$$

This model is fine so long as the dividend is expected to be constant over its lifetime. Suppose, however, that the dividend is believed to increase by a constant amount (h) each year. The equation developed above for the annuity can be modified to give:

$$PV = D/(K_i - h)$$

Solving this equation for $K_i$, gives:

$$K_i = D/PV + h$$

This equation suggests that the investor's required rate of return is the ratio of the dividend paid on the share to the price of the share plus the expected growth rate of the dividend payments of the organisation (h).

## CAPITAL ASSET PRICING MODEL

At this stage, where an investment project is riskless for discounting purposes the risk-free rate of interest can be used. But as has been developed in the preceding sections, many investments are not risk free and in this respect what is needed is a method to estimate the riskiness of an investment. The **capital asset pricing model (CAPM)** was formulated to show how the expected return on an asset could be related to its risk, while at the same time providing a precise definition of the meaning of risk.

What would be expected in terms of risk is that a portfolio made up of one share is likely to be more volatile than a portfolio made up of a range of shares (a diversified portfolio). Individuals could therefore lower their risks, in particular company-specific risks, by purchasing a diversified portfolio of shares. This approach may reduce company risk, but if the portfolio is made wider and wider, matching the general spread of shares in the market, the overall equity market risk still exists. Therefore, every share is made up of two elements of risk, one related to the market and the other related to the company. Of these two risks, one cannot be avoided, the market risk. Investors desire a higher return for exposure to market risk.

In the CAPM model the market risk is measured by **beta**. When an individual organisation's stock moves in line with the returns on all stocks, this beta value is equal to one. When the return on the stock varies more than the return on all stocks, the beta value exceeds one and, conversely, when the return on the stock varies less than the return on all stocks, the beta value is less than one. In other words, an organisation which has a beta value of 1.5 would see that its shares outperform the market as the general share market grows, but would fall back more when the share market declines. The majority of companies have beta value close to one, but the latest estimate for the Rank Organisation is that its beta value is 1.5, while Manchester United's beta value is 0.4; Dimson (1995).

Using the approach developed earlier, the cost of capital to an organisation estimated by the CAPM model is:

$$K_e = R_f + B(K_m - R_f)$$

where,

$K_e$ = the cost of equity to the organisation
$R_f$ = risk-free rate of return
$B$ = the stock-market risk for the organisation
$K_m$ = the average rate of return on the stock of all organisations

Therefore $(K_m - R_f)$ is the market risk premium or the risk premium on the average stock.

Suppose that $R_f = 10\%$, $K_m = 15\%$, $B = 0.6$. It is possible to calculate the cost of equity to the organisation:

$$K_e = 10 + 0.6(15 - 10)$$
$$K_e = 10 + 3 = 13\%$$

Notice that if the value of beta is increased so that the company's stock becomes riskier, then the equity cost of capital to the organisation would rise. We can see this below. Suppose that the value of beta is increased from 0.6 to 1.2. $K_e$ now becomes:

$$K_e = 10 + 1.2(15 - 10) = 10 + 6 = 16$$

It follows that the greater the market risk for an organisation, measured in terms of its beta value, the greater the equity cost of capital to that organisation.

However, although it is possible to find out the company's beta value, does the project which is being considered by the organisation have the same beta value? Many projects have a beta value different to that of the company because the company itself is financed with debt, which increases the riskiness of its shares. The appropriate beta value for the project is therefore the company's beta value with the effect of borrowing removed from the company's shares. For example, suppose that a company has a beta value of 0.8. If this company is financed by 75 per cent equity and 25 per cent debt, the beta of the underlying company would be obtained by multiplying the beta of the company by the proportion of equity. The company's underlying beta would be 0.8 × 0.75, which equals 0.6. Thus to estimate the cost of equity capital for a company the beta of its shares can be used, but to estimate the cost of capital for the underlying business, its underlying beta should be used.

# WEIGHTED COST OF CAPITAL

An organisation is likely to raise capital from a variety of sources. Some of it will be undistributed profit, some will be from borrowing, some will come through the sale of debt and equity. The marginal cost of this capital is, therefore, a weighted average of the cost of raising the different types of capital. How the various combinations of debt and equity finance are arrived at depends on the optimal capital structure for the organisation. The organisation will choose the combination of debt and equity financing which minimises the overall **weighted average cost of capital**.

Different forms of financing have different advantages for the organisation. If it borrows money the interest is tax deductible, but will need

to be paid out. This gives the organisation a bias towards using borrowing as a source of finance. However, interest must be paid on borrowed funds, while the dividends on stocks come much lower down a company's payment list. Thus for the company the risk is higher for funds which are borrowed rather than for stock which is sold, because as it raises a greater proportion of its finance through borrowing it runs an increased risk that it will not be able to pay the interest on the funds borrowed. Often the interest rate on borrowing is lower than that on stocks, therefore the company may attempt to reduce its costs of finance by using more borrowing. However, more borrowing means more financial risk, since the organisation may be placed in a position where it would find it difficult to meet its interest payments. Therefore, the weighted cost of capital declines at first as the organisation moves from zero debt to a certain level of debt, but thereafter, as the amount of debt financing increases, it has increased risk associated with it which may offset the reduced cost of the debt financing.

For example, suppose that the total cost of capital for the organisation is $K_t$ and this is made up of the cost of debt, $K_d$, and the cost of equity, $K_e$.

$$K_e = W_d K_d + W_e K_e$$

where $W_d$ and $W_e$ are respectively the proportions of debt and equity capital that make up the organisation's capital structure.

If the organisation wants a debt:equity ratio of 70:30, while the cost of equity capital is 12 per cent and the cost of debt (after tax) is 8 per cent, then the total cost of capital is:

$$K_e = 0.7(8) + 0.3(12) = 5.6 + 3.6 = 9.2\%$$

$K_e$ is the composite marginal cost of capital that can now be used to evaluate all investment projects. It would be expected that the marginal cost of capital would rise since, as the organisation raises additional amounts of capital by borrowing and selling stocks, its organisation's debt:equity ratio rises and this poses a higher risk for lenders and investors.

As Lumby (1994) notes, the evidence is that many companies experience so many difficulties in calculating the WACC that they don't bother. Instead they substitute a management-determined figure as an estimate. This is the case both for the cost of equity and the cost of debt capital.

In the case of equity capital, the first problem is which share valuation model to use – the dividend evaluation model or the CAPM? The problem with the former is the tax on dividends, since the model uses a net-of-tax dividend figure. An assumption is often made that the investor is a basic-rate taxpayer, but this may not be the case. Moreover, it has sometimes proved difficult to derive a suitable estimate for the future rate of growth of dividends.

In the case of CAPM, the beta value is estimated on the basis of the past relationship between a company's return and the market's return. However, what is really required is an estimate of future betas. Second, there are data-input problems with all three of CAPM's variables.

In the case of debt, tax regimes in the real world are very complex and it is often difficult to estimate accurately the impact of tax on debt capital. Because some debt capital is unquoted and is issued in complex forms, this further compounds the problems of allowing adequately for the impact of tax and imputing the values for unquoted debt.

## THE MODIGLIANI–MILLER VIEW OF THE COST OF CAPITAL

In the discussion of the weighted cost of capital model above, it was suggested that the weighted average cost of capital will fall initially with the substitution of cheaper debt for more expensive equity. After this point, holders of both equity and debt are likely to demand higher returns to compensate them for their exposure to an increased risk of failure by the organisation. However, the Modigliani–Miller proposition is that the capital structure of the company does not matter. That is, it is the cash flows that are of most importance to the organisation and it does not matter how these cash flows are divided up among the various claimants. Such a statement may seem odd, since it suggests that an organisation in Sweden, which has access to more debt financing (borrowing) as a proportion to equity financing than another company in Spain which has borrowed the same amount through the more expensive equity financing, does not have any advantages in the marketplace. If the Modigliani–Miller theorem is correct, both organisations should face the same weighted **cost of capital**. The only way this can occur is if the Swedish company faces higher costs of equity finance to offset its lower costs of debt financing. It is possible to suggest that such a situa-

tion exists since as the debt:equity ratio rises in the Swedish company (since it is borrowing through debt), equity holders may want higher returns to compensate for the higher risk associated with a company which is more debt ridden.

What the Modigliani–Miller theorem postulates is that companies will become heavily geared (that is, they will be financed by a high proportion of debt). But when actual companies are examined this is just not the case. Thus the real-world conditions suggest that organisations do not want high levels of gearing; Habib (1995). Why is this so?

First, we need to examine the tax advantages, not only for the organisation but also for the individual investor, of using debt or equity finance. It may be to the advantage of the organisation to try to finance borrowings from debt, since interest payments are tax deductible, but from the investor's point of view personal taxes are often lower on equity than on debt and the risk of bankruptcy favours equity financing rather than debt financing. The principal agent theory (*see* Chapter 3) also provides an explanation of why the capital structure matters. As the gearing of a company alters so might the behaviour of the manager(s). A manager who has a small equity stake in the company may be less involved in its activities. An outside investor might therefore consider a company in which the manager has a small equity stake as a less attractive investment. It might also be argued that an entrepreneur is more likely to take a reckless gamble with other people's money rather than their own. Conversely, if the managers hold a very large proportion of the equity, any profits will accrue more to the managers. They might therefore disregard the risk element in some projects. If these succeed, the managers receive a large reward; if they don't, the cost is borne mostly by the debtholders. In addition to these arguments, debt – which requires interest payments, unlike equity where the dividends are subject to the discretion of the managers – may encourage managers to make more conservative decisions on investments, or encourage the organisation to hold on to more liquid assets than is normal.

What these arguments suggest is that the ratio of debt to equity does matter and companies which are highly geared will be doing something about this, or are likely to be in the throes of exiting the market, or are companies heavily involved with acquisitions and mergers, such as Hanson.

# REVIEWING PAST INVESTMENT PROJECTS

Whichever way is chosen to appraise an investment project, it is important to review the project at the end of the capital budgeting process. This enables the decision makers to assess the actual cash flow from the project against the expected or projected cash flow, and perhaps enable the decision makers to learn why any discrepancies exist. In doing so they will be able to build these unexpected changes into future cash flows from other, similar investments. It is highly likely that there will be differences in expected and actual cash flows, since the world is subject to dynamic, unforeseen changes. But the differences between actual and expected cash flow could be divided into those factors that are completely outside the control of the organisation and those which the organisation may be able to influence.

This process can also be extremely important for the organisation and its approach to investment appraisal. If the decision makers realise that the investment project will undergo a **post-audit**, they may make more careful estimates of future cash flows and strive harder to hit their predicted targets. The process of post-auditing has its downside, however, in that risky but profitable investment projects may be shelved since there would be a great deal of explaining to do if the expected cash flows fell very short of actual cash flows. It should also be borne in mind that sometimes the cash flow that actually occurs from a project will be far different to that which was expected, simply because of unexpected factors in the organisation's macroeconomic environment, such as exchange-rate fluctuations, strikes and the like. Nonetheless, it has been generally observed that the best-run companies are those which place the greatest emphasis on the post-audit approach.

# SUMMARY

◆ This chapter has examined the capital budgeting decisions of organisation. These are one of the most important decisions made by managers, committing funds in the current time period in the hope of achieving expected returns in the future which more than compensate for this capital outlay.

◆ Investment projects can be undertaken for a variety of reasons: to replace worn-out capital stock, to expand production of the existing product and expand into new markets, as a response to government directives on health and safety grounds, or as a means to reduce the organisation's costs.

◆ Given that the organisation is making a capital outlay in the current time period for the investment project, it needs to compare this with the current value of future returns. That is, the future returns, which are expected returns, need to be discounted at the appropriate discount rate for the organisation.

◆ There are a number of methods which the organisation can use to assess the profitability of an investment project. The net present value (NPV) and internal rate of return (IRR) both use a variation on the discounted cash flow method of investment appraisal. Under the NPV method, projects are acceptable if their NPV>0. If the discount rate under the IRR method exceeds the market rate of interest, the project is acceptable.

◆ There are other methods by which investment projects can be appraised which do not include a discounted cash flow technique. Here would be included the payback method and return on capital employed (ROCE).

◆ An organisation can raise funds internally and/or externally. The cost of raising funds internally is the opportunity cost of not being able to invest that money elsewhere. For external funds organisations use a combination of debt and equity. The cost of debt is the interest charge on borrowed money adjusted for tax. The cost of equity can be broken down into two elements: a risk-free rate of return which is to compensate investors for deferring their consumption, and a risk premium to compensate investors for the risk they are taking.

◆ There are a number of ways in which organisations can estimate the cost of equity capital and this chapter has considered the CAPM approach, the WACC method, the dividend evaluation model and the risk-free rate plus premium approach.

◆ The Modigliani–Miller theorem postulates that it does not matter what the debt:equity ratio of an organisation is. Yet in reality organisations are rarely highly geared, that is, they do not have a high debt:equity ratio. There appears to be too much risk if the organisation is highly geared and organisations which find themselves in such positions often do so for short periods when they may be facing financial difficulties, or may find that they exit the market shortly after.

◆ It is very important to review the investment project after it has been implemented. This may provide the organisation with a set of learning criteria for future investment plans, reduce over-optimistic expected return forecasts, and encourage managers to reach targets set.

## REVIEW QUESTIONS

1 Consider an investment project costing £175 000 that is expected to generate net cash flows of £200 000 in each of two years.
   a Calculate the expected NPV for this project using discount rates of 10, 15 and 20 per cent.
   b Sketch the expected NPV profile for this project.
   c What is the IRR for this project?

2 An organisation is considering a capital outlay on an investment project of £10 000. In the current year the expected return is £5000, with expected returns of £4000 and £3000 in years two and three. Suppose that the market rate of interest is 14 per cent and the rate of inflation is 6 per cent. Should the organisation undertake the investment project?

3 What is the cost of equity for an organisation, if the beta value of its stock is 0.8, the risk-free rate of return is 9 per cent and the rate of return on the average stock is 15 per cent?
   If the beta value had been 1.7 rather than 0.8, what would have been the cost of internal equity capital?

4 Your organisation has a target rate of return on investment of 35 per cent. Using this criterion, evaluate the following two projects, both of which have a capital outlay of DM20.5 million and a lifespan of four years. The net cash flows from the two projects are shown in Table 12.6:

Table 12.6 Net cash flows (DM millions)

| Year | Project A | Project B |
|------|-----------|-----------|
| 1 | 10 | 4 |
| 2 | 8 | 6 |
| 3 | 6 | 9 |
| 4 | 4 | 11 |

   a Which of the projects would be acceptable using the IRR criterion?
   b Which of the projects would be acceptable using the NPV method of investment appraisal with a discount rate of 15 per cent?
   c Compare the two recommendations. Which investment appraisal technique do you consider to be better?

5 Can education be viewed in the same light as investment in capital? How would you evaluate whether further education was worth undertaking?

6 You have been asked by your organisation to assess whether an investment project which lasts for 10 years is worth undertaking. Your calculations indicate that it has a positive NPV. What would be the impact on your calculations of:
   a A rise in interest rates?
   b An increase in taxation, both consumer and corporation?

CHAPTER **13**

# TECHNIQUES FOR DECISION MAKING UNDER CONDITIONS OF UNCERTAINTY AND RISK

## KEY ISSUES

Business issues

Business strategy

Decision-making techniques

Economic concepts

Management decision issues

Optimal outcomes to management issues

## OBJECTIVES

◆ To differentiate between conditions of uncertainty and risk.

◆ To highlight and discuss the different attitudes to risk which have been categorised by economists.

◆ To show the use of decision criteria under conditions of uncertainty.

◆ To examine the Hurwicz Alpha decision criteria under conditions of uncertainty.

◆ To illustrate the choices which exist between projects under conditions of risk via decision trees.

◆ To differentiate between projects under conditions of uncertainty, using the Expected Value method.

◆ To show that probability distributions may be used to differentiate between projects under conditions of risk.

◆ To examine the use of more complicated decision methods under conditions of risk, when the nature of different projects means that simple methods cannot be used.

◆ To discuss the evaluation of decisions made with reference to the quality of information and data utilised.

## CHAPTER OUTLINE

Business application

Uncertainty and risk

Attitudes to risk

Making decisions under conditions of uncertainty

Case study 13.1 Apocalypse maybe

Case study 13.2 Protest in the pipeline

Decision making under conditions of risk

Case study 13.3 Taking shelter in an unpredictable world

Evaluating decisions

Concluding remarks

Summary

Review questions

Glossary of new terms

Reading

## KEY TERMS

Attitude to risk

Coefficient of optimism

Decision tree

Expected value

Marginal utility of money

Maximax decision criterion

Maximin decision criterion

Minimax regret decision criterion

Probability distribution

Risk

Risk-adjusted net present values

States of nature

Uncertainty

## BUSINESS APPLICATION

# Switch without a timetable – digital terrestial television

FT

Sometime in 1997 the UK government hopes that broadcasters will be able to add considerably to the choice available to viewers by launching as many as 30 channels of digital terrestrial television across the country.

If it goes ahead on schedule it will probably be the first service in the world to broadcast digital, as opposed to the existing analogue, television from land-based transmitters on a large scale.

Both the US and Australia are also well down the road of drawing up regulations for the launch of digital terrestrial television. The US envisages existing broadcasters such as ABC and CBS vacating their present frequencies and moving entirely to digital in 15 years. This would free huge spectrum capacity to auction off for mobile communication use. . .

Convergent Decisions Group, consultants specialising in digital issues, believes that if the vacated analogue capacity were auctioned off in the UK, it could bring in £2bn a year for the government.

For viewers digital terrestrial offers high quality, multi-channel television without the need for satellite dishes or connection to cable networks. Robust pictures that do not have ghosting like analogue pictures can be picked up on ordinary wire set-top aerials. But a 'black box' decoder is needed.

The UK government approach is to divide the available digital capacity into six blocks of frequencies or 'multiplexes', each capable of broadcasting a minimum of three high-quality digital television channels to between 60 and 90 per cent of the UK population. There are similar plans for digital radio. In fact, it becomes almost meaningless to talk of separate channels at all as opposed to streams of bits in the world of digital terrestrial.

Fast-moving sport on a wide screen, for instance, would require 6 Megabits of capacity, whereas a studio discussion featuring talking heads might need only 2–3 Megabits. A controller can match capacity to the pictures being shown and move from three to six or even more channels depending on the schedule.

All existing broadcasters will be guaranteed the equivalent of one high-quality digital channel although they will have to broadcast at 80 per cent of the schedule they are offering their existing viewers.

▶

Business application *continued*

No money will change hands directly in the bids for 12-year digital terrestrial licences which will be awarded by the Independent Television Commission, the regulatory body. Instead, the licences will go to those prepared to make the greatest commitment to developing the technology by offering a diversity of programmes and the greatest subsidy to reduce the price of decoder boxes. . .

The fact that no final date has been set for the transfer from analogue to digital has also been criticised on the grounds that there is very little incentive to move to digital unless there is a timetable and therefore a compelling reason to make the large investments needed.

The existing broadcasters are also unhappy that they are being given so little digital capacity as of right – they can always apply for more in consortia bidding for multiplexes – when they will be the providers of the programmes so vital to the success of the venture.

'The government should end consumer and investor uncertainty and settle on a timetable for the switch,' (to digital) Mr John Birt, director general of the BBC,

said recently. He argued that broadcasters should operate the multiplex, 'imaginatively focusing on viewer need and taking the prime commercial risk' wherever they can attract sufficient revenues to fund their programme services. . .

Serious questions remain mainly about the financial viability of digital terrestrial in an intensely competitive world of digital satellite. If 150 channels are available from satellite will enough people be prepared to pay to buy the equipment to see 20–30 channels?

Even more important is the question of whether digital terrestrial channels will have enough on offer – apart perhaps from wide-screen format – to persuade consumers to buy the new equipment. . .

BSkyB is looking at the viability of creating a black box able to receive both digital satellite and digital terrestrial channels. If one could be produced at reasonable cost, it could be the key to drive forward the two new ways of distributing channels and increasing the reach of multi-channel television in the UK.

*Source*: *Financial Times*, 7 November 1995, Survey on new broadcast and communication media (3). Reprinted with permission.

*Comment*

How do organisations decide whether or not to invest in projects such as digital television? Obviously, there is potential for huge gains in revenue for successful participants. However, there is also potential for losses if the project changes shape, say as a result of political pressures, or the economic environment changes.

Developing technology and investing in the hardware required for digital television demand large financial inputs. How does an organisation decide whether or not to get involved, or when to get involved? From the number of organisations participating in research and development for digital television technology, it would seem that the prospects are good for this area of the television industry. There are dangers, however, and the race to create a decoding 'black box' for consumers at home will result in potential losses for some organisations who are currently spending huge amounts on such development. At an earlier stage, each of the organisations working in this area will have made a decision to become involved in the industry. How these decisions may have been made is the basis of this chapter.

There are many techniques which may have been used by these organisations in order to decide whether they wish to invest in the technology: expected returns, risk-adjusted net present values or other project analyses. These and others will be outlined and discussed in the sections which follow. The decision-making techniques which assist in differentiating between choices will be outlined and then worked through, in order to illustrate their use. First, however, it is important to differentiate between the economist's definitions of uncertainty and risk.

# UNCERTAINTY AND RISK

Individuals and organisations face decision-making situations every day. In some cases, the decision to be made is a simple one – the results and implications of the alternatives are known and there is no penalty for making the wrong decision. Under different circumstances, there may be some doubt as to the exact outcome of a given project. It could be that an alternative will yield either a great profit or a massive loss, depending on what reaction competitors make to the implications and results of the decision maker's choice to implement one of the projects under consideration compared to other choices. Another time, it may not be possible to decide in a simple manner between alternatives because the timespans and paybacks of the various alternatives differ so significantly. This chapter will outline some of the tools and techniques which may be used in the situations outlined above.

Before progressing any further, a distinction needs to be made between **uncertainty** and **risk**:

■ **Uncertainty** – the values of the possible alternative outcomes are known, but the likelihood or probability of any of the given outcomes occurring is not known. For example, an organisation may know that its sales of a new product are likely to be 1000 units per week. What the organisation does not know, however, is the likelihood of the product being successful – it may be 50 per cent, 60 per cent, or the product may be unlikely to succeed, in which case it may only be 10 per cent assured of success.

■ **Risk** – the values of the possible alternative outcomes are known and so too are the likelihoods of the given outcomes occurring. To continue with the new product example from above, under conditions of risk, the organisation knows that the level of sales will be 1000 units per week *and* that the likelihood of the product being successful is 60 per cent.

Therefore, an organisation faced with a condition of risk is in a more informed position than an organisation faced with a condition of uncertainty. It is possible to convert uncertainty into risk by making estimates of the likelihoods of outcomes occurring on a subjective basis. It should be noted that the estimates of the likelihood of outcomes occurring under different conditions should be made as accurately as possible. The more information and data which can be taken into account when attempting to assign such probabilities/estimates of the different situations occurring, the more accurate the final result will be. Overall, the result is only ever as good as the information used to derive it.

# ATTITUDES TO RISK

A word of warning – depending on the decision maker's **attitude to risk** (and uncertainty), various decision criteria will be invoked. Decision makers always blur the *science* of their mathematical methods because of their attitude to risk. It should

always be remembered that mathematical methods, no matter how attractive the resulting figures may be, are based on someone's attitude to taking risks. This is the case even if the results are given to two or three significant figures or more!

Economists recognise that different individuals and organisations will have different attitudes to taking risks. For simplicity, these are split into three types: risk averse, risk neutral and risk seeking. Attitudes to risk are considered in terms of the individual's valuation of their **marginal utility of money** (MUM).

This refers to the additional utility (satisfaction) which an individual derives by receiving one extra unit of money (a pound, sterling, a franc, an escudo, a guilder and so on). In all cases, it is assumed that an individual's total utility will increase as long as additional units of money are given to that individual. However, the amount of the increase will differ with each individual's attitude, or valuation of money.

Offered the choice of £500 with certainty or the chance of £2000 with a probability of 0.5 or £0 with a probability of 0.5 (as a result, say, of the toss of a coin), different attitudes to risk will determine whether or not the risk is taken. Some individuals would opt to take the £500 and receive a certain value with no risk at all. Other individuals would opt to gamble their potential receipt of the £2000 on the toss of a coin. That is to say, some individuals are gamblers, some prefer not to gamble and will accept a lower payoff as a result of that lack of willingness to gamble.

## Risk averse

The individual's marginal utility of money increases more slowly than income. That is, the individual gains less and less additional utility from additional units of wealth. The individual will therefore favour an assured income, or an income with little associated risk, compared to a potentially large income from a risky project or venture.

Risk-averse individuals could also be called conservative with respect to their attitude to decision making.

In the example outlined above, the risk-averse individual would choose to take £500 with certainty. The additional utility associated with the £2000 (or £0) gamble is not sufficient to satisfy the individual that it is worth the risk of gaining nothing – £0.

## Risk neutral

The individual has a constant marginal utility of money. Thus, there is indifference between an assured income level with no or little associated risk and a larger income level from a riskier project or venture.

In the £500 with certainty versus £2000/£0 gamble, the risk-neutral individual would not be able to decide what to do. The additional utility associated with the additional income does not decrease as the sum increases.

## Risk seeking

The individual has a marginal utility of money which increases more quickly than income. The individual therefore gains increasing levels of additional utility from extra units of wealth. Thus, a project with relatively higher levels of associated risk and a higher income is preferred to a low-risk project which has a guaranteed (albeit lower) income associated with it.

In the example outlined above, the individual would choose to make the gamble, that is, choose the £2000/£0 option. The fact that the utility associated with higher levels of wealth increases means that a 50/50 chance of gaining £2000 is more attractive in terms of utility than the option of £500 with certainty. The fact that there is a chance of gaining £2000 far outweighs the fact that the individual may not gain anything at all.

A graphical summary of the attitudes to risk outlined may be seen in Figure 13.1. The marginal utility of money (MUM) on the *y* axis is plotted against monetary values on the *x* axis. Clearly, for Individual A (risk averse), the increases in utility as value increases are smaller than those for Individuals N (risk neutral) and S (risk seeking).

Similarly, the increases in utility for Individual N are constant and smaller at all levels than the increases for Individual S as monetary values rise. Increases in utility for Individual S grow as monetary value increases.

Obviously, the attitudes to risk outlined above relate to individuals. The attitudes are also relevant with reference to organisations. That is, the decision makers within the organisation make the decisions required of them for its operation and these are tainted by individual attitudes to risk and perhaps also swayed by organisational strategy.

It has already been stated that uncertainty exists when there is a lack of knowledge of the actual probability or probabilities of a known outcome occurring. Even if the outcome values of alterna-

### Figure 13.1 Attitudes to risk: marginal utilities of money

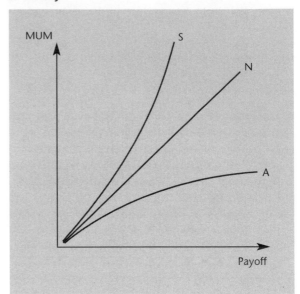

The marginal utility of money (MUM) for the risk-seeking individual (S) is greater than the mum for the risk-neutral individual (N). Therefore S's curve slopes upwards, as monetary values increase. N's MUM curve is linear because constant increases in monetary value result in constant increases in utility. The risk-averse individual's (A) curve shows that as monetary values increase, there are smaller and smaller increases in utility.

tive projects are known, there is still a condition of uncertainty because there is no knowledge of the probabilities associated with these outcomes.

## MAKING DECISIONS UNDER CONDITIONS OF UNCERTAINTY

There are two possible approaches which may be adopted with reference to decision making under uncertainty.

■ Decision makers use their knowledge and experience to assign subjective probabilities to the occurrence of given outcomes and then estimate the likely payoff for alternative projects. Thus the condition of uncertainty is effectively converted into a condition of risk and the decision made with reference to conditions of risk (*see* later section).

■ Decision makers prefer not to make assumptions about probabilities of outcomes occurring and therefore take decisions under the existing conditions of uncertainty.

Given the attitudes to risk outlined above, it is possible to analyse an individual's decisions relating to uncertainty in the same manner. This section will provide a variety of decision criteria which may be utilised in order to choose between projects when uncertainty exists. These may also be classified with reference to attitudes to risk.

In each case, the possible outcomes associated with different projects which could be adopted are presented. Additionally, the effect of different 'states of nature' are also shown. States of nature are the different possible conditions under which a project may be run. For example, different levels of economic activity, or different levels of optimism about the likely success of the project for other reasons, may be taken into account as states of nature. This means that it is possible to compare the outcomes associated with the given projects under different conditions. The conditions used here are economic states – recession, normal or boom economy. It is also possible to use other classifications for the states of nature such as poor, average, good or pessimistic, neutral, optimistic and so on. Overall, then, the project decision takes into account the attitude to risk of the decision maker, or the different identified environmental conditions which could affect the project's success.

## Maximin decision criterion

When using the **maximin** method, a conservative (risk-averse) decision criterion is being utilised. The worst possible payoff for each project is found. The best value of these is then chosen as the project to undertake. The decision maker is therefore making the best of the worst scenarios presented. Thus, the decision maker is able to avoid undertaking a project which will induce large losses if the worst possible scenario of the portfolio occurred. This is because the worst possible scenario is considered for each project and the best of those worst outcomes within the scenarios considered is chosen.

In the example in Table 13.1, the maximin decision-making criterion would require a decision between the lowest payoffs for each of the projects. This payoff occurs for each project in a recession (*see* Table 13.2).

## Maximax decision criterion

The **maximax decision criterion** is the least conservative (risk-seeking) behaviour. The best payoff from each of the projects is found, then the project with the largest payoff is chosen as the pro-

**Table 13.1**

| Project | State of nature | | |
| | Recession payoff £ | Normal payoff £ | Boom payoff £ |
| --- | --- | --- | --- |
| A | 60 | 80 | 100 |
| B | 65 | 70 | 75 |
| C | 55 | 80 | 105 |

**Table 13.2**

| Project | Minimum payoff |
| --- | --- |
| A | £60 |
| B | £65 |
| C | £55 |

The largest minimum payoff, or maximum minimum, or maximin, is from Project B: £65 in this case.

**Table 13.3**

| Project | Maximum payoff |
| --- | --- |
| A | £100 |
| B | £75 |
| C | £105 |

The largest maximum payoff, or maximum maximum, or maximax, is from Project C: £105 in this case.

ject to undertake. In terms of the example in Table 13.1, the Maximax project would be project B (*see* Table 13.3).

Maximin and maximax are decision criteria which are simplistic, but useful. In deciding on which of the criteria to consider, individuals/organisations need to be aware of their attitude to risk. Risk aversity in the decision maker will favour the use of the maximin criterion, while risk-seeking behaviour and attitudes will lead the decision maker to choose the maximax decision-making criteria.

## Minimax regret decision criterion

The **minimax regret decision criterion** introduces the concept of **regret**, or the 'opportunity cost' of an incorrect decision. Thus, it allows the decision maker to analyse the gains and losses which may be associated with a correct or incorrect decision when a given state of nature occurs. It is possible, therefore, for decision makers to minimise their potential losses should an undesirable state of nature arise. The regret between projects is calculated for each state of nature. Thus, in a recession, the project with the largest payoff will have no regret; the others' regret will be the difference between the largest (no-regret) payoff and the payoff for the project under consideration.

A regret matrix may be drawn up for the projects under consideration and the maximum regret may then be identified and noted. The optimal project under the conditions of the minimax regret decision criterion will be the project which has the smallest maximum regret (i.e. the minimum maximum regret, or the minimax regret).

In terms of the example considered above, the regret matrix would be as in Table 13.4. Therefore, Project A would be undertaken in this case since it has the smallest maximum regret, at £5, as opposed to B's £30 and C's £10.

From the three decision criteria discussed above, three different project choices have been made. The maximax criterion favoured Project C, the maximin Project B and the minimax regret criterion found in favour of Project A. Can they *all* be correct? How do three different approaches giving three different answers provide any guidance at all?

The answer to this lies in the attitudes to risk and the manner in which individuals' attitudes to risk

**Table 13.4**

| Project | State of nature | | | Maximum regret for each project £ |
|---|---|---|---|---|
| | Recession regret £ | Normal regret £ | Boom regret £ | |
| A | 5 | 0 | 5 | 5 |
| B | 0 | 10 | 30 | 30 |
| C | 10 | 0 | 0 | 10 |

shape their decision-making processes. Thus, for any one individual, only one project would have been preferred; there would have been only one answer. But since there were different attitudes to risk being considered, different solutions were forthcoming.

A further method of dealing with decision making under conditions of uncertainty *and* which takes into account the decision maker's attitude to risk is the Hurwicz Alpha decision criterion.

## ◆ CASE STUDY 13.1

## Apocalypse maybe

Britain is preoccupied with the possibility of an outbreak of Creutzfeld-Jakob disease caused by exposure to beef infected with BSE. It is too late for policy to affect the outcome for those already exposed to the infection, but not too late to affect the rate of future exposure. In the debate about what needs to be done, economists (true to form) have so far concentrated on macro-matters such as public borrowing and the external deficit. They have been silent on a far more important question of microeconomics: how should Britain weigh the cost of attempting to eradicate BSE against the benefits of fewer exposures in future?

On the face of it, economics offers a way to think about this: cost–benefit analysis. The trouble is, although it deals with risk tolerably well, cost–benefit analysis is bad at dealing with uncertainty. To an economist, these are very different. If you know that there is a 30% chance of rain tomorrow and a 70% chance that it will stay fine, your decision about whether to carry an umbrella is subject to risk; if you have no idea whether it will rain, you face not risk but uncertainty.

The difference matters. Known probabilities allow weights to be attached to the cost of, say, getting wet in the rain. Weighted costs and benefits can be added up, and suitably discounted according to how far in the future they lie, to yield a single number: net present benefit. In theory, this allows different policies, such as carrying an umbrella, to be compared with others, such as not carrying one.

Without probabilities, such comparisons are impossible. Britain's BSE scare is a case of decision-making under uncertainty. If BSE were eradicated in a spare-no-expense way (by destroying all cattle), the possibility of further exposure would be greatly reduced. If BSE were eradicated more slowly, a greater possibility of human infection would remain. How much greater is unknown. Given this, how is the right policy to be discovered?

Decision theory has some ideas. First, write down a 'cost matrix'. The upper part of Table 13.5 shows how this might look, using arbitrary units for illustration. Across the top are assumptions about the ability of BSE to infect humans: zero, low, medium and high.

**Table 13.5**

| | Assumptions about infectivity | | | |
|---|---|---|---|---|
| | Zero | Low | Medium | High |
| **Cost Matrix** | | | | |
| Do nothing | 0 | 20 | 50 | 100 |
| Mild intervention | 10 | 20 | 35 | 60 |
| Strong intervention | 40 | 42 | 45 | 50 |
| **Regret Matrix** | | | | |
| Do nothing | 0 | 0 | 15 | 50 |
| Mild intervention | 10 | 0 | 0 | 10 |
| Strong intervention | 40 | 22 | 10 | 0 |

Reading down, the matrix considers three policies: do nothing, intervene mildly (selective culling) and intervene strongly (destroy all cattle).

If BSE does not infect humans and the government does nothing, the cost is zero. Assume that the gross cost of selective culling is 10, and that total destruction costs 40. That completes the first column of the matrix. Assuming no government action, suppose a low rate of infection costs 20, a medium rate 50 and a high rate 100. That completes the first row. To fill in the other cells, assume that selective culling reduces the rate of infection by 50% and that total destruction reduces it by 90%.

In principle, the real thing could be done for BSE, based on known or discoverable facts. It would need lots more cells, and would show pounds not 'units'. When you have got it (the matrix, that is), how do you use it? You can apply one of several rules. Gamblers might favour 'minimin' – the minimum of minimums. This says, be lucky: go for the policy that puts the lowest cost within reach. In the pretend matrix shown here, that is 'doing nothing'. It offers a net cost of zero (the lowest in the matrix) so long as luck holds and infectivity is zero.

At the other extreme, a hypercautious government would prefer 'minimax' – the minimum of maximums. For each policy, this asks what the worst result would be, and then chooses the policy that offers the best of these bad outcomes. It puts a floor, as it were, under disaster. The worst result for 'do nothing' is 100, for mild intervention it is 60 and for strong intervention it is 50. Minimax chooses strong intervention.

A third rule seems more appealing than either of these, though it may not be obvious at first sight. It is called 'minimax regret'. First you derive a regret matrix from the cost matrix. To do this you ask, for each

assumption about infectivity in turn, which policy produces the best result. Then you compare the results of the other two policies with that best result, and regard the difference in cost as a measure of regret. Consider medium infectivity, for instance. The best policy is mild intervention, at a cost of 35. In the regret matrix, set that cell to zero. The cost of doing nothing, given medium infectivity, is 50, so if you chose that policy you would be 50 minus 35 worse off than under the best policy. Score 15 in the matrix. The cost of strong intervention is 45, which is 10 more than the best outcome: score 10.

Once the regret matrix is complete, apply the minimax rule as before. For each policy, what is the outcome you would regret most? For 'do nothing' it is a regret of 50 (if infectivity turns out to be high); for mild intervention it is 10 (if infectivity is either zero of high); for strong intervention it is 40 (if infectivity is zero). Minimax regret chooses the policy that gives the lowest of these results. It puts a floor not under disaster, but under how bad you are going to feel if things go wrong. In this case, the rule would lead you to choose mild intervention.

Three rules, three different choices, and no firm basis for preferring one rule over another: each expresses an attitude to danger as valid as the others. But it is not quite a dead-end. Decision theory cannot create certainty where none exists, but it offers a way to organise one's thoughts, crystallise one's prejudices about caution and highlight the kinds of information that are needed to do better. British ministers should have their regret matrix worked out. It may be inconclusive – but it beats staring into space and thinking about mortality.

*Source:* © *The Economist*, London, 30 March 1996.

### Comment on the case study

The 'beef crisis' in the UK in 1996 may be clearly illustrated with reference to different attitudes to risk and the use of the regret matrix. Laid out in Case study 13.1 is an identification of the costs of three different levels of activity associated with UK government actions. These levels of activity are analogous to the different projects, A, B and C, in the example in Table 13.1. The different states of nature are given by the levels of infectivity – there are four in the case, as opposed to the three used in the previous example. As the case points out, the three decision criteria lead to three different solutions – none of which is 'correct', since different attitudes to risk are used.

## Hurwicz Alpha decision criterion

The Hurwicz Alpha decision criterion utilises a weighted average approach to the decision-making

process. The maximum payoff has an appropriate **coefficient of optimism** applied to it; so too does the minimum payoff. The weighted average of these values is then calculated in order to find the value of a given project or strategy. The process is repeated for each project or strategy under consideration. The optimal or chosen project/strategy will be the one with the lowest value once the weighted average has been calculated.

The value of each project/strategy is :

$$H_i = \alpha M_i + (1 - \alpha)m_i \ldots \tag{13.1}$$

where:

$H_i$ = Hurwicz Alpha value for each project/strategy from $i = 1$ to $i = n$

$\alpha$ = coefficient of optimism ($0 < \alpha < 1$) – a subjective valuation of the likely success of the project by the decision maker.

$M_i$ = maximum payoff from project

$m_i$ = minimum payoff from project

The Hurwicz Alpha criterion therefore takes into account the decision maker's attitude to risk, or even intuition about the likely success of a given project or projects. Hurwicz Alpha allows complete flexibility because the process may be repeated each time an environmental change causes the coefficient of optimism to change. It allows the decision maker to consider both the best and the worst possible payoffs from a particular project and to make a balanced decision having taken these into account.

There is no consideration made of the average or neutral outcome value. In many cases this may be considered positive, or an advantage of the decision criterion, since it can be argued that decision makers and organisations are rarely aware of the average value of the projects they are considering, even if they are aware of the best and worst scenarios. The drawback of this decision methodology is that the decision maker is required subjectively to decide the coefficient of optimism.

The coefficient of optimism decided on will be affected by the individual decision maker's attitude to risk. Therefore, the possibility exists for undue optimism to blur the decision-making process. Caution is therefore required.

The Hurwicz Alpha decision criterion may be used to calculate values for the example given in Table 13.1. Assume that the coefficient of optimism for a maximum payoff is positive/optimistic: that it is believed that there is a 65 per cent chance of a successful outcome occurring. This would translate to a 0.65 probability of a successful outcome occurring. Using equation 13.1, the following values for Projects A and B in Table 13.1 may be found:

Project A :

$$H_A = \alpha M_A + (1-\alpha)m_A \ldots \qquad (13.1)$$

where,

$\alpha = 0.65$
$H_A = 0.65(£100) + (1 - 0.65)(£60)$
$H_A = £65 + (0.35)(£60)$
$H_A = £65 + £21$
$H_A = £86$

Project B :

$$H_B = \alpha M_B + (1 - \alpha)m_B \ldots \qquad (13.1)$$

where,

$\alpha = 0.65$
$H_B = 0.65(£75) + (1 - 0.65)(£65)$
$H_B = £48.75 + (0.35)(£65)$
$H_B = £48.75 + £22.75$
$H_B = £71.5$

Thus, with reference to the values forthcoming for $H_A$ and $H_B$, the chosen project would be Project B, with a value of £71.5, compared to Project A's value of £86. Project B's Hurwicz Alpha value is closer to zero and indicates a safer choice for the risk-averse decision maker.

---

◆ **Exercise 13.1**

Calculate the Hurwicz Alpha value for Project C (Table 13.1) using the coefficient of optimism of 0.65.

Compare this value to the values for Projects A and B and state which should be the chosen project of the three.

---

When Project C is also considered, with its Hurwicz Alpha value of £87.5, it may be seen that Project B would still be optimal – it is still the lowest value, or value closest to zero of the three. If the decision maker were to choose a risk-seeking strategy, the preferred project would be the project with the greatest Hurwicz Alpha value; in this example Project C, with a value of £87.5. Thus, the attitude to risk affects both the choice of projects once Equation 13.1 has been applied and also the coefficient of optimism which is used to calculate the Hurwicz Alpha value.

The Hurwicz Alpha decision criterion is a method which may be used to make decisions under conditions of uncertainty. It *is* subjective, requiring decision makers to state their coefficient of optimism. Strictly speaking, it could be argued that the Hurwicz Alpha decision criterion is actually a method for decision making under conditions of risk. The coefficient of optimism could be argued to be analogous to assignment of probabilities of success. Once probabilities relating to the success of, or likelihood of, an outcome occurring are assigned, a condition of risk and not uncertainty exists. Decision making under conditions of risk will be considered after Case study 13.2.

◆ **CASE STUDY 13.2**

# Protest in the pipeline

FT

In the next few months numerous offshore drilling rigs will materialise in the exposed waters west of the Shetland and Orkney Islands to take advantage of the warmer weather in the UK's newest oil province.

Their task will be to assess the potential of the 'Atlantic Frontier', a vast area bordering on open ocean which the government and oil industry hope will boost Britain's oil reserves.

Early forecasts suggest the area could contain about 3.5bn barrels of oil. That is small by North Sea standards, but the possibility that it may contain the last of the big UK fields has set off a rush by oil companies to drill existing exploration blocks and to acquire new ones.

The harsh weather, complex ocean currents and deep water of the area pose technical challenges. The tough operating conditions have also raised questions about environmental risks to the nearby islands from large-scale development of the area.

Local officials say the present environmental debate is more muted than in the 1970s, when the first North Sea oil fields were established. But there are worries about the way in which Atlantic Frontier fields may be developed.

The main concern among island residents is whether an offshore pipeline network will be built to link the fields to one of the existing oil terminals at Sullom Voe on Shetland or Flotta on Orkney.

The alternative, offshore loading of shuttle tankers, is viewed with suspicion by many islanders. All the main islands are home to various seabird populations, and the Faeroe Shetland Channel is an important migrating route for mackerel, one of the region's valuable fish species. The initial development of British Petroleum's Foinaven field, the first commercial project, will be based on a floating production vessel. The oil will then be loaded on to shuttle tankers which will call at Flotta to unload.

Martin Hall, director of environmental services in the Shetland Islands, says: 'We've had tanker incidents, such as the Braer disaster in 1992, but we haven't had any problems with the (North Sea) pipelines.'

Some officials worry that offshore tanker loading could be the first step in bypassing the islands altogether. 'The worst scenario,' according to Hugh Halcro-Johnston, convener of the Orkney Islands Council, 'is that both islands would be bypassed. We would then have the constant (environmental) risk with no (economic) benefit at all.'

Uncertainty surrounding the area's potential has complicated the issue of whether to build a pipeline. The big pipeline systems in the North Sea were built to serve a handful of giant fields.

None of the Atlantic Frontier fields discovered so far is of a size to justify a dedicated pipeline. Oil companies say total output would have to reach 400 000 to 500 000 barrels a day before they would consider a common pipeline system.

Most discoveries are therefore likely to involve offshore tanker loading, at least in their initial development stages. But are such techniques more dangerous than a pipeline?

Tom Ffye, deputy manager of BP's Atlantic Frontier programme, says offshore spillage is rare, even in bad weather: 'Most offshore loading spills tend to be small, less than 10 barrels.' He claims the potential for disaster is much greater with a pipeline.

Most local officials now say many of their fears about the offshore operations have been assuaged. 'The big worry is the tankers,' says Cliff Johnston, director of the IOE Group of consultants at Herriot Watt University in Edinburgh, which has undertaken environmental studies of the area. 'The simple fact is that one could have a large number of tankers going past the islands.' This increases the risk of another Braer-type accident and a large-scale spill.

The effects of a spill would vary according to the type of oil involved, says Johnston. The Foinaven oil, for example, is 'heavy and waxy but not very toxic'. Very little would evaporate, as in the case of the Braer, and it would tend to collect in floating lumps that would be much like mini-icebergs. 'It would not kill much but it would create quite a mess,' says Johnston.

But even a spill which did not do much harm to fish and birds could cause lasting damage to the image of the islands, according to Halcro-Johnston. To ease islanders' fears the oil companies have undertaken a rare co-operative study of the potential environmental impact of large-scale development of the area. BP is also preparing a detailed oil spill response plan for its Foinaven project that should be completed in the next few months.

The attention the companies have so far paid to the environment has been noted by local officials. 'The oil companies are reasonably upfront at the moment,' says Hall. But officials say relations could sour if offshore loading emerges as the industry's favoured long-term transport solution. Johnston believes local sentiment in favour of a pipeline is so strong that both Shetland and Orkney residents would favour it, even if it meant the closure of one of the two island terminals and the loss of hundreds of jobs.

*Source: Financial Times, 10 May 1995. Reprinted with permission.*

### Comment on the case study

Case study 13.2 illustrates the variety of scenarios which face decision makers. It is not always easy to identify the different states of nature and the numerical differences between projects. In this case, the choice is clearly between the construction of a pipeline, or the ferrying of oil via tankers. Locals would prefer the pipeline because the chance of spillage is reduced, but the oil companies will not invest unless the production of oil is great enough to justify the expense. The forecast for the area's oil reserves are 3.5 billion barrels of oil, possibly one of the last of the large North Sea oil fields. The pipeline will be expensive to build, even if it does simply link to an existing line bringing oil in from the North Sea. Tankers will be cheaper, but carry an increased risk of large-scale spillage. Additionally, the decision makers must take into account the cost to them of clear-up and fines if they do spill oil. Thus, in order to include all factors, the costs and benefits of the decision whether or not to invest in a pipeline must somehow be accounted for and presented as a matrix for decision makers.

# DECISION MAKING UNDER CONDITIONS OF RISK

Remember that a condition of risk exists when additional information is available to that in the condition of uncertainty. Under conditions of risk, knowledge exists of the probabilities of outcomes of a project occurring in addition to the outcome values of the project (the 'known' when dealing with uncertainty).

## Measuring risk

When measuring risk and making decisions under conditions of risk individuals usually utilise a mathematical process involving the calculation of certain financial values, such as the **expected value**, the **risk-adjusted net present value** and the coefficient of variation. Each of these will be discussed and outlined at the appropriate point in this section. However, briefly, the definitions of each are as follows:

- *Expected value* – the weighted average value of a project when the various payoffs and states of nature are taken into account.
- *Risk-adjusted net present value* – a value for a project which is calculated by taking the

individual's attitude to risk into account. This value also allows comparison of projects with different durations, because all expected values are stated in 'present values' – the effects of inflation, for example, are taken into account to give a net present value.

- *Coefficient of variation* – a tool for the comparison of projects which could not otherwise be made. Projects with different expected values and other conditions may be compared in order to find which is the least risky and which the most risky.

All of the concepts mentioned above are subjective in that they take account of the individual's, or the individual organisation's, attitude to risk and likelihoods of outcomes occurring. *Thus, the calculations, although complicated, cannot be regarded as entirely accurate due to the vacillations of the individual (and organisation) with reference to the economic and other conditions with which they are continually interacting and the **estimated** risk associated with them.* Although the methods outlined below offer attractive and persuasive solutions to the question of which project to choose, because they allow the decision maker to calculate values to many decimal places, it should be remembered that these values are based on the subjective estimates of probabilities of payoffs occurring.

For the methods outlined below, the example given in Table 13.1 (*see* page 311) will be expanded. Each of the methods outlined below builds on the previous one. The complexity and analysis possible improve and increase accordingly.

## Decision trees

**Decision trees** provide a graphical or diagrammatic representation of the decision-making process. In Table 13.1, there is a three-way decision to be made: to implement project A, B or C. Such a decision is represented as in Figure 13.2(a). Here, the lines represent the choices. These are the different branches (hence decision trees). To highlight the fact that a decision must be made, convention requires that a 'node' is drawn at the beginning of the branches. The decision node is usually represented by a square.

If there are different states of nature to be taken into account, these may be represented as in Figure 13.2(b).

Thus, decision trees show, at a glance, the choices and different scenarios facing the decision maker. The results of the different scenarios are

**Figure 13.2 Decision trees**

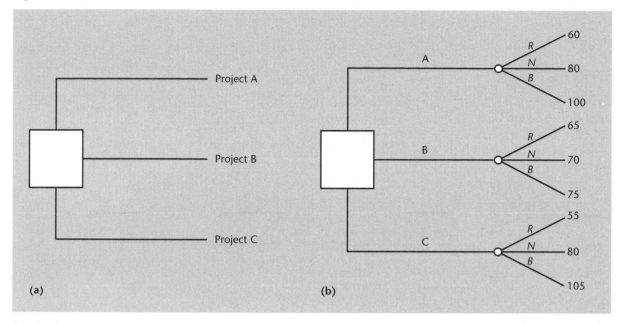

**(a)** The choice between projects A, B and C is represented by the square 'decision node' which leads to the branches showing the expected values for each of the projects.

**(b)** Each project's outcomes are affected by the state of nature. This is clearly shown on each of the project branches by a state of nature node, usually a circle, which shows the three possible outcomes on separate branches.

shown on the appropriate branches, providing a representation of Table 13.1, with the points where decisions are required or awareness of the effects of different states of nature highlighted by the decision and state-of-nature nodes. While it is an advantage that it is intuitively simple to construct a decision tree, it is a disadvantage that they very quickly become complicated and take up a lot of space.

## Probability distribution(s)

**Probability distributions** show the range of possible outcomes of a project which are considered likely to occur. It is usual to state the probabilities of these outcomes occurring as a decimal (i.e. a value between zero and one). Probability distributions are a graphical representation of the payoff tables in Table 13.6. Assume that the probability assigned to the occurrance of a recession is 0.2, the probability of a normal economy occurring 0.6 and the occurrence of a boom occurring 0.2. Thus, Table 13.1 may be restated as Table 13.6.

In Table 13.6, the original values are retained, but the additional information relating to the probabilities is also included.

**Table 13.6**

| Probability of state of nature occurring | 0.2 | 0.6 | 0.2 |
|---|---|---|---|
| | State of nature | | |
| Project | Recession payoff £ | Normal payoff £ | Boom payoff £ |
| A | 60 | 80 | 100 |
| B | 65 | 70 | 75 |
| C | 55 | 80 | 105 |

### Simple probability distribution

The crudest way in which risk may be considered is in terms of the simple probability distribution. Here all possible outcomes and the probability of each occurring are listed in a payoff matrix and may also be shown graphically.

### Discrete probability distribution

The payoff values and probabilities may be depicted graphically as a discrete probability distribution (*see* Figure 13.3(a)). Bars are used to show the probability of each the three possible payoffs occurring for each of projects A, B and C.

PART 3 ◆ MARKETING AND INVESTMENT DECISIONS

**Figure 13.3 Probability distributions**

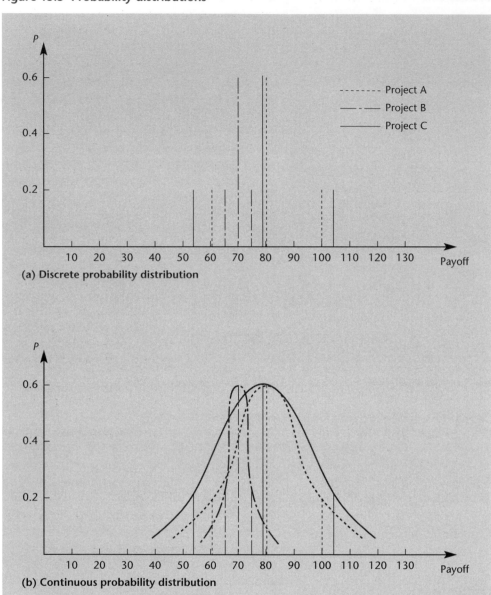

**(a)** On the *Y* axis, the probability is plotted, on the *X* axis, the payoff values. Thus, for each project, it is possible to depict each of the cells in the payoff table (Table 13.6).

**(b)** The discrete probability distribution is extended to show that there is a full range of payoffs and probabilities which affect the projects under consideration.

However, the simple probability distribution is limited; only the states identified are plotted. Obviously, in most cases there are 'in-between' situations where the economy is somewhere between a recession and normal state. The payoff values will change accordingly (rise in this case to somewhere between the recession value and the normal value). To show that there is the possibility of the in-between states of nature occurring, the continuous probability distribution is used.

**Continuous probability distribution**
The continuous probability distribution takes into consideration the possibility of intermediate/in-between payoffs existing in addition to those discretely listed in the payoff matrix.

Thus, any value within the range stated may theoretically occur.

The fact that some payoffs are more likely to occur than others is not ignored. The probabilities stated with reference to the discrete/simple distribution are a guide to the likelihood of values in between occurring. This is shown graphically by joining the bars of the discrete distribution to trace a continuous curve. Such a situation may be seen in Figure 13.3(b).

The continuous probability distribution curve may be a normal/symmetrical (bell-shaped) distribution, or a skewed distribution. Skewed distributions are obviously more difficult to deal with and will not be considered in this chapter. The assumption for the remainder of the chapter is that the projects under consideration will result in a payoff matrix and probability distribution which is symmetrical. In statistics terminology, this is known as a 'normal curve'.

From Figure 13.3, it is clear that Project A and Project C have the same normal economy payoff values, £80, and that these are equally likely to occur – for both there is a 0.6 probability. Project B has a normal economy payoff of only £70, but this also has a probability of 0.6 occurring.

Remember that the decision maker is attempting to discriminate between the projects given in Table 13.6. It would seem on first investigation that Project B is not as good as Projects A and C. This is because the highest probability payoff is lower in Project B than in A or C. How could this be proved?

## Expected values – the weighted outcome value of a project

An important analysis which needs to be made when considering conditions of risk is the average or weighted payoff for a given project (the **expected value**) and also the range of payoffs which the project may produce. The expected value (EV) takes into account the different payoffs for a project when different states of nature are quoted. EV also takes into account the probabilities that the different states of nature may occur. This is why the EV is a weighted average value. The probabilities of different states of nature occurring are the weights assigned to the payoffs. The weighting technique will be clarified below with reference to the project examples in Table 13.6.

The expected value combines the probability of an outcome occurring and the predicted payoff

from the project if the outcome *does* occur. To calculate the expected value, the outcome value or payoff is multiplied by the appropriate probability for each state of nature. The individual expected values of the project for each state of nature are added together to calculate the overall expected value of the project. This overall, summed expected value takes into account the weighted probabilities of the outcomes occurring. The equation describing this method is given by:

$$EV = \Sigma \, [(Vi) * (Pi)] \text{ for states of nature from } i \text{ to } N \dots \qquad (13.2)$$

where,

  EV = Weighted probability of outcomes
  $i$ = states of the economy up to $N$ states
  $V$ = value of the predicted outcome, or payoff
  $P$ = probability of state of nature occurring

The EV is thus an *averaged* value, giving the (weighted) mean overall value of outcomes for a given project under different states of nature.

From Table 13.6, the expected value of Project A ($EV_A$) is:

  $EV_A = \Sigma \, [(Vi) * (Pi)]$ for each of the 3 states of nature (R − B)
  $EV_A = [(60 * 0.2) + (80 * 0.6) + (100 * 0.2)]$
  $EV_A = 12 + 48 + 20$
  $EV_A = £80$

Expected value of Project B ($EV_B$) is:

  $EV_B = \Sigma \, [(Vi) * (Pi)]$ for each of the 3 states of nature (R − B)
  $EV_B = [(65 * 0.2) + (70 * 0.6) + (75 * 0.2)]$
  $EV_B = 13 + 42 + 15$
  $EV_B = £70$

From the above, then, it is clear that for Project A, once the predicted outcomes, the payoffs and the states of nature have been weighted, the expected value is £80. This means that the overall expected value of Project A is equal to £80 when the different states of nature and the possible payoffs are taken into account. This may be compared to the expected value of Project B – £70.

In terms of the decision-making process, the expected value allows comparison between projects with reference to the magnitude of the weighted value. Therefore, since Project A has a greater expected value than Project B, Project A should be chosen from the two.

---

◆ **Exercise 13.2**

Calculate the expected value for Project C, Table 13.6.

Compare this value to the expected values for Projects A and B. Which project is most attractive now?

---

The expected value of Project C is equal to £80. Therefore Project C is also preferable to Project B since C's expected value is greater. However, it should be noted that there is no difference between the expected values of Projects A and C. That is, the expected values of both projects are £80. There is no way of deciding between the two projects with only the expected value information.

In order to decide between Projects A and C, further analysis is required. One method is to consider the standard deviations of the projects. First, however, consider the case of Swiss Re, an organisation using risk management to protect itself in the short term to gain longer-term success.

◆ **CASE STUDY 13.3**

## Taking shelter in an unpredictable world

The cigar puffing, Harvard-trained management consultant has been let loose. Since taking over as chief executive of Swiss Re last September Lukas Muhlemann has made all the moves expected of a former employee of McKinsey & Co.

In this period Muhlemann has shaken up the world's second largest reinsurer by selling off its peripheral businesses, a move which has resulted in a halving of the group's premium income. He has set an earnings target double that achieved in recent years, and he is devoting management energy to an ambitious new strategy of partnership and product innovation.

Only a pair of red braces would be required to complete the picture of a hard-nosed, profit-orientated practitian in the conservative, if not gnomic, world of Swiss insurance and reinsurance. It is an image which Muhlemann – who at 44 is a youngster among the insurance industry's leaders – prefers not to cultivate.

He emphasises Swiss Re's team approach to decision making: 'There are some areas where probably the training of McKinsey & Co helps you to short cut some things a little bit. And there are other areas where I'm glad that I have colleagues who have been 30 years in the business.' Nor is he the only reformer in the business: Munich Re, the world's largest reinsurance company, is embarking on a low-key internal reorganisation intended to streamline chains of command.

But the strategy Swiss Re has adopted under Muhlemann is undeniably bold, a response to changes affecting all Europe's insurers and reinsurers. (Reinsurers limit insurers' exposure to losses by sharing their risks.) As deregulation spreads across the continent – affecting Switzerland despite its position outside the EU and forcing insurers to concentrate on their strengths and cut costs – Swiss Re's tactics could prove a model for others. 'Swiss Re has got a lot of solid fundamentals but it really did need someone who was going to take the organisation into the 21st century,' says Heidi Hutter, ex-Swiss Re employee and now head of Lloyd's of London Equitas' 'old-years' liabilities project. . .

Natural catastrophes have resulted in unprecedented losses, he says. But even a Kobe-sized earthquake could have been worse. A strategy based on reinsurance alone has dangers, however. The sector is not immune from volatility in insurance premium rates – and the evidence that world prices are softening has grown.

The unpredictability of natural disasters and uncertainty about global warming could make the industry prone to larger swings in profits and make insurance deals offering the best risk/reward ratio harder to spot. Market entrants, particularly in the fast-growing Bermuda market, are attempting to shake established reinsurers' grip on the market with more aggressive deal making. . .

For instance, by trading options on a 'catastrophe futures' index, which varies according to the incidence of natural disasters, insurance companies can hedge against catastrophes or carry more risk in the hope of boosting profits. Muhlemann admits such products are at the experimental stage: 'There are some people who have actually designed products and sell them but I don't think that we have an established market.' But Swiss Re aims to 'have the maximum array of tools, of product and product combinations, to find the most efficient and attractive ways of meeting our clients' problems. I think that is the philosophy.'

With the dangers of derivatives apparent from the Baring bank collapse, Muhlemann is quick to refute suggestions that derivatives might be used in a speculative fashion, making profits swings more pronounced. 'We think of it as another technology to manage risks and to pass on the risks to other investors. So we don't see this as something that will increase our volatility. We see this as an additional way of managing our risk.'

Muhlemann has set a target return on equity of 15 per cent – approximately double the rate achieved by Swiss Re in the past few years. Part of the improvement is likely to come from investment gains. But he is also determined that conservative Swiss underwriting

traditions should not be abandoned, even if world premium rates soften.

'The way that we work with our clients is that we take a very long-term perspective. We focus on quality and not so much on year-to-year results. Swiss Re has been here for 130 years and it has paid dividends every year since 1869.'

*Source: Financial Times, 6 March 1995. Reprinted with permission.*

### *Comment on the case study*

Even Swiss Re refers to, and attempts to manage, the risk which it accrues as a result of its insurance dealings. Risk in this case refers to the amounts which Swiss Re is able to cover as a result of its activities – that is, the amounts it sets aside as potential losses, but which may be revenues if the events insured against do not occur. The tools and techniques used by Swiss Re are far more complex than any of those outlined in this chapter. However, the foundations of all such techniques are in the basics outlined here.

Swiss Re trades on a 'catastrophe futures index', which takes into account the likelihood of a natural disaster occurring and the cost if it did occur. The portfolio offered is then a combination of these two factors. Additionally, the decision could be taken to limit the amount of risk to which the portfolio is exposed if there has previously been a decision made with reference to a maximum level of exposure. Greater risk in the portfolio could bring greater levels of profit, but also losses. Thus, Swiss Re is using a risk-management strategy that allows it some say over what it is willing to lose if the market moves in the wrong direction. At the same time, it will have some idea about the level of profits if the market moves in its favour. The more risk it is willing to take, the greater the gap between the greatest potential profits and losses. The gap between these values could be termed the earnings range. A way in which the earnings range could be measured for different projects is by the standard deviation.

## Standard deviation (σ)

The standard deviation of the expected profit levels for any project guides the decision-making process further than consideration of the expected

values alone. The standard deviation of a project shows the spread of the risk involved in undertaking it. The standard deviation method quantifies the range of outcomes/payoffs of a given project with reference to the different states of nature. The greater the standard deviation, the greater the range of possible values for the project.

The greater the spread of possible payoff or income values a project may generate, the less desirable/attractive it becomes as a viable project. This is because the greater the range of values, the less likely the expected value amount is to occur. The expected value would be accurate if the economy were normal, but if the state of nature were recessionary, or in boom, then it would seriously mislead the decision maker.

Additionally, even though the expected value for two projects may be the same, the standard deviations for the two projects are likely to be different and therefore allow a decision to be made between the two. The standard deviation method may thus be used to make a choice between Projects A and C.

The mathematical function describing the standard deviation is given by:

$$\sigma = \sqrt{(\Sigma\ [(Vi - EV]^2 * Pi}\ \text{for types of outcome}$$
$$\text{from } i \text{ to } N) \dots \qquad (13.3)$$

As the value of the standard deviation increases, so too does the risk involved in undertaking the project. Thus, when considering or comparing projects in terms of the risk involved, the project with the lowest standard deviation will be the project with the least risk associated with it. *Comparing standard deviations in this manner may only be done when the expected values of the projects under consideration are equal.* Thus, in the case of Table 13.6, only Projects A and C may be compared. The standard deviation measures the dispersion around the mean value (or expected value) for the project.

Standard deviation of Project A:

$$\sigma_A = \sqrt{\sum ([Vi - EV]^2 * Pi \text{ for states of nature from } R \text{ to } B)}$$

$$\sigma_A = \sqrt{\begin{array}{c}(([V_R - EV]^2 * P_R) + ([V_N - EV]^2 * P_N) + \\ ([V_B - EV]^2 * P_B))\end{array}}$$

$$\sigma_A = \sqrt{\begin{array}{c}(([60 - 80]^2 * 0.2) + ([80 - 80]^2 * 0.6) + \\ ([100 - 80]^2 * 0.2))\end{array}}$$

$$\sigma_A = \sqrt{\begin{array}{c}(([-20]^2 * 0.2) + ([0]^2 * 0.6) + ([20]^2 * \\ 0.2))\end{array}}$$

$$\sigma_A = \sqrt{((400 * 0.2) + (0 * 0.6) + (400 * 0.2))}$$

$$\sigma_A = \sqrt{(80 + 0 + 80)}$$

$$\sigma_A = \sqrt{160}$$

$$\sigma_A = \text{£}12.65$$

---

### ◆ Exercise 13.3

Calculate the standard deviation of Project C (Table 13.6). Compare this to the standard deviation for Project A and state which is preferred.

---

The standard deviation for Project C is equal to £15.81. This value is larger than that for Project A (£12.65). Therefore, according to the argument previously proposed, Project A has a smaller range of payoffs than Project C. Project A has less risk associated with it as a result. Project A will be preferred in this case.

The standard deviation value acts as a constant unit of measurement of the range (or spread of risk) of the payoffs for a given project. Comparisons of the value of the constant (the standard deviation) provides analysis of the risk associated with different projects. By adding one standard deviation to *and* subtracting one standard deviation from the **expected value**, the range of incomes for **68.26 per cent** of possible outcomes may be found. That is, whenever the standard deviation range around the expected value is found, the decision maker will *always* know where 68.26 per cent of outcomes are likely to lie. This may be seen in Figure 13.4.

Intuitively, the smaller the standard deviation, the smaller the range of possible outcomes and hence the lower the risk associated with the project under consideration.

Adding and subtracting two standard deviations to and from the weighted probability expected value will give the range of income for 95.45 per cent of possibilities. This is very attractive; adding and subtracting two standard deviations to the expected value provides a high degree of certainty with reference to the likely range of values within

**Figure 13.4  Using standard deviations to differentiate between projects**

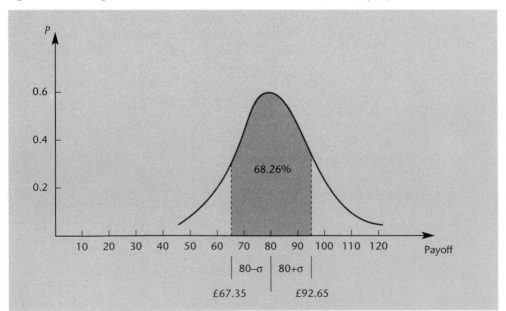

The continuous probability distribution for Project A is shown. The expected value for Project A is £80. The standard deviation value is £12.65. By adding £12.65 to £80, and subtracting £12.65 from £80, the range of values highlighted is calculated (£67.35 to £92.65); 68.26 per cent of outcomes will be within this range.

which any project is likely to fall. For Project A, 95.45 per cent of the time the outcomes will lie between £54.70 and £105.30.

---

◆ **Exercise 13.4**

Calculate the range of values for 68.26 per cent of outcomes for Project C.

Compare this to Project A and state which is the least risky project to undertake.

---

Project C has a Standard Deviation of £15.81. Calculating the range of values within which Project C will lie 68.26 per cent of the time gives £64.19 to £95.81. (Two standard deviations, or 95.45 per cent of the time, the range is £48.38 to £111.62.) Superimposing the results for Project C onto Figure 13.4 gives Figure 13.5.

It is clear on examination of Figure 13.5 that Project A has a smaller range of outcomes. Project A is therefore less risky than Project C. Project A is the more desirable project to undertake.

However, Project B is still unaccounted for. Even though Project A is preferable to Project C, it is not possible to compare the standard deviations of projects with different expected values. A further tool for analysis is required which allows compari-

son of projects with different expected values and different standard deviations.

## Coefficient of variation

Where projects have differing standard deviations and differing expected values, it is useful to be aware of the **coefficient of variation**. It is simple to calculate and merely a tool for comparison. The coefficient of variation is given by:

$$CV = \sigma / EV \ldots \tag{13.4}$$

where,

$CV$ = coefficient of variation
$\sigma$ = standard deviation
$EV$ = weighted probability outcome value

The coefficient of variation for any project will lie between zero and one. The closer to zero the value of the coefficient, the less risk there is associated with the project.

The coefficient of variation for Projects A and B is shown below.

Project A:

$$CV_A = \sigma_A / EV_A$$
$$CV_A = 12.65/80$$
$$CV_A = 0.158$$

**Figure 13.5 Differentiating between Projects A and C**

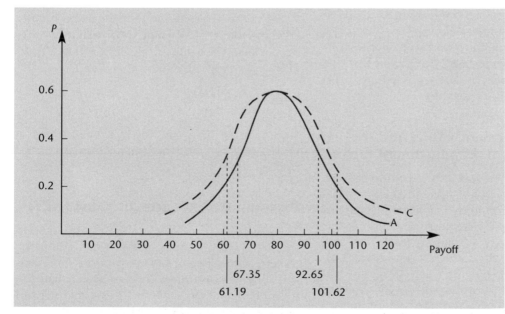

Project A's outcome will lie between £67.35 and £92.65 68.26 per cent of the time, while Project C's will be between £64.19 and £101.62. Project A has the smaller risk associated with it and this is clearly identifiable in the figure.

Project B:

$$CV_B = \sigma_B/EV_B$$
$$CV_B = 7.07/70$$
$$CV_B = 0.101$$

Thus, Project B has the smaller/closer to zero co-efficient of variation. Project B is the less risky of Projects A and B as a result.

---

◆ **Exercise 13.5**

Calculate the coefficient of variation for Project C.

Compare this to the coefficients of variation for Projects A and B. Which is the most attractive project to undertake?

---

Project C's coefficient of variation is 0.198. This value is greater than those for both Projects A and B. So, even though Project C has a greater expected value than Project B, it is a more risky proposition. Overall, Project B is the least risky project to undertake. The coefficient of variation is smallest, the standard deviation is smallest too. However, it would have been possible to overlook Project B if the analysis had stopped simply at the comparison of expected values, where Project B was lowest.

The preceding arguments in the risk section have all assumed that the decision maker is averse to risk. The references to the standard deviation and the coefficient of variation both assumed that the decision maker would be looking for the least risky alternative or project.

When the attitude to risk differs from risk aversity, or indeed needs to take into account the level of risk aversion, a different analysis is required. This is considered in the next section.

## Certainty equivalent values and the certainty equivalent adjustment factor

For any individual, there will be a point where the guaranteed level of payoff from a risk-free project and the level of payoff from a project which has risk associated with it will generate indifference. At this point, the level of payoff from the risk-free income becomes known as the 'certainty equivalent' (CE), that is, the level of income where the individual does not distinguish between projects. This relationship may be given for each of the types of individual attitudes to risk by the following functions which relate CE to the expected value of a project:

CE < EV – risk aversity
CE = EV – risk neutrality
CE > EV – risk seeking

where,

CE = certainty equivalent
EV = expected value of a risky project

For example, an individual is unable to choose between a project with a certain sum of £4000 and a project which does have risk associated with it, but which, if successful, will generate a payoff of £7600. In such a case, the individual has a risk-averse attitude to risk (CE < EV) and the value of the certainty equivalent is £4000.

The above may be reconciled into an adjustment factor which can be used when calculating the **risk-adjusted net present value** (*see* next section) of any project. The certainty equivalent adjustment factor (ß) is calculated as follows:

$$ß = CE/EV \ldots \tag{13.5}$$

where,

CE = certainty equivalent
EV = expected value of a risky project

if,

ß < 1 – risk aversity
ß = 1 – risk neutrality
ß > 1 – risk seeking

For example, where the individual was indifferent between a £4000 sum with certainty and a risky £7600, the value of the CE is £4000. The EV of the risky project is £7600. Therefore:

$$ß = 4000/7600$$
$$ß = 0.657$$

Since ß is less than one, the individual is seen to be risk averse; confirmation of the conclusion reached above.

## Risk-adjusted net present value (NPV)

The risk-adjusted net present value will allow for the individual's attitude to risk when comparing projects with different capital costs (discount rates) and different cash flows. It may be calculated by multiplying the NPV, found in the manner outlined in Chapter 12, by the CE adjustment factor:

$$\text{risk-adjusted NPV} = (ß * NPV) - C_0 \ldots \tag{13.6}$$

For information, from Chapter 12:

$$NPV = -C_0 + R_0 + R_1/(1 + r) + R_2/(1 + r)^2 + \ldots + R_n/(1 + r)^n$$

where,

$$C_0 = \text{cost of the investment}$$
$$R_0 \rightarrow R_n = \text{expected returns in each period (1 to } n\text{)}$$
$$r = \text{the discount rate}$$

For example, assume that a 'certain return' project generates a net cash flow of £12 000 per annum over three years with a 10 per cent rate of return (10 per cent discount rate). This is compared to a risky project which generates a net cash flow of £16 300 over four years with a 14 per cent rate of return at the end of each year. Both projects have an initial outlay of £6000 (in year 0) and the individual is risk averse with ß = 0.657.

$$NPV_{certain} = (12\,000 * 2.4868)$$
$$NPV_{certain} = £29\,841.60$$
$$\text{Risk-adjusted } NPV_{certain} = (29\,841.60 * 0.657)$$
$$\text{Risk-adjusted } NPV_{certain} = £19\,605.93$$

Accounting for the £6000 outlay, the risk-adjusted stream of funds generated is:

$$R.A.NPV_{certain} = 19\,605.93 - 6000$$
$$R.A.NPV_{certain} = £13\,605$$

---

◆ **Exercise 13.6**

Calculate the NPV, risk-adjusted NPV and payoff (accounting for the initial outlay of £6000) for the risky project.

Compare the result to the certain sum project and state which is the more attractive project for the decision maker to choose.

---

The NPV for the risky project is £47 493.31, the risk-adjusted NPV £31 203.11 and the final payoff £25 203.11. Thus, the risky project is the more attractive, since it generates a larger final payoff compared to the certain sum payoff when both projects have been adjusted for risk.

The risk-adjusted NPV is a useful tool for the comparison of projects which generate different cash flows, run for different periods of time and could otherwise not be compared.

# EVALUATING DECISIONS

It was pointed out earlier in the chapter that the worth of any decision-making criterion could be affected by the subjective nature of the attitudes to risk of the decision maker involved. It is also true that the worth of any decision undertaken is affected by the inputs, that is, the information and data used to formulate the possible payoffs (and to decide on the probabilities of states occurring, where appropriate).

Thus, the quality of the decision maker's choice depends on several factors. These may be summarised as follows.

## Optimal search costs

There comes a point in the collection of information where the cost of improving the information available is greater than the benefit which may be gained by such improvements. Therefore, the decision maker needs to be aware of the point at which it would be prudent to stop information search and begin to process the information/data collected.

## Data interpretation

Even when the data has been collected, there is a danger that the interpretation may not be appropriate. Decision makers should attempt to ensure that their use of data is appropriate and that subsequent interpretation is accurate.

For example, it may not be appropriate to use data relating to the payoffs from other, historical projects which were similar to those under consideration for the future if it is known that the product of the projects is now obsolete, or entering the decline stage of its lifecycle.

Historical data relating to production and sales of a monochrome television set for mass purchase would not be of any use in the 1990s because most consumers now purchase colour televisions.

## Decision criteria

The decision maker should always attempt to use the appropriate decision criteria. If information is available which would allow the decision maker to utilise, or to assign probabilities to, different states of nature, then it would be naïve, if not foolish, to attempt to make an analysis using decision criteria for dealing with uncertainty rather than risk.

## Attitude to risk and other factors

The appropriateness of the decision maker's attitude to risk and other factors which may bias or blur the ability to make an optimal or objective decision should be considered throughout the decision-making process. For example, if decision makers are aware that they are typically risk seeking and that the economy is entering a downturn, they may wish to hold back on their enthusiasm more than usual in order to make a more appropriate decision.

Furthermore, decision makers should attempt to remain flexible in approach and be ready to make use of or take into account additional factors which may come to light after the main decision analysis has taken place. It can be difficult sometimes to decide whether to adopt new information arising in full, or to attempt to predict how it might affect the decisions already made.

## CONCLUDING REMARKS

Obviously, there are merits associated with the use of each of the decision-making techniques outlined in this chapter. The techniques for making decisions under conditions of uncertainty may be categorised with reference to the manner in which they deal with attitudes to risk. The maximin decision criterion is a conservative or risk-averse criterion. The maximax decision criterion, on the other hand, favours a risk seeker's attitude. The Hurwicz Alpha decision criterion, with its coefficient of optimism, allows decision makers to declare their own expectations with reference to the likely success of the project.

The techniques which allow decision makers to differentiate between projects under conditions of risk also have their relative advantages and disadvantages. The decision tree approach is an illustrative method, which allows decision makers to see the results associated with all outcomes and which also shows the manner in which these are derived and related. There is no opportunity, however, to weight the outcomes for attitudes to risk, beyond that provided with reference to the probabilities assigned to the 'states of nature'. Another illustrative approach is probability distribution. This, too, is an unweighted method for attitudes to risk. It does have the advantage, nevertheless, of highlighting clearly where means (expected values) differ between projects and how large the range of earnings is. The continuous probability distribution shows the in-between states-of-nature possibilities. The disadvantage is that the probability distribution is only really of any use where the expected values of the projects are the same; there is no insight where the expected values differ.

The standard deviation for the earnings of a given project with reference to the different states of nature gives information about the dispersal of the earnings and thus the attractiveness of the project may be gauged. If projects have different expected values, the standard deviation method is not sufficient. However, the ratio of the standard deviation to the expected value provides the coefficient of variation. This permits comparison of projects with different standard deviations and expected values. The approaches based on the standard deviation values highlight the better project to choose when all known factors are taken into account, but they do not give any hint as to what the actual earnings might be. Where information relating to the cash flows for different projects is known and the decision maker's attitude to risk is available, the likely earnings for projects may be calculated using the risk-adjusted NPV (net present value). But no account is taken here of the different possible states of nature, except in deciding on the discount rate.

## SUMMARY

◆ Uncertainty exists when the payoffs, or outcomes, of different projects are known for different states of nature (the economy) but not the probability that these payoffs will occur.

◆ Risk exists when both the payoffs of different states of nature and also the probabilities of these states of nature occurring are known.

◆ Three categories for attitudes to risk exist: risk averse, risk neutral and risk seeking. These are classified with reference to marginal utility of money – mum.

◆ Under conditions of uncertainty, the maximax, maximin and minimax regret criteria may be used.

◆ The Hurwicz Alpha decision criterion can be used to make decisions under conditions of uncertainty, but requires decision makers to state their coefficient of optimism – analogous to the probabilities used for decision making under conditions of risk.

◆ The choices which exist between projects under conditions of risk may be illustrated using decision trees.

◆ The expected value method is a simple yet useful method which may be used to differentiate between projects.

◆ Probability distributions are a graphical representation of the expected values of given projects.

◆ More complicated decision methods under conditions of risk may be used when the nature of different projects means that simple methods cannot be used. These include standard deviation, coefficient of variation and the risk-adjusted net present value method.

◆ The quality of decisions made depends on the accuracy of data, which must be balanced against the cost of ensuring accuracy.

◆ It is important to use the appropriate decision criterion at the appropriate time.

◆ Individual and organisational attitudes to risk can bias the decision maker.

## REVIEW QUESTIONS

1 Suppose that a firm is considering investment in a new product. The firm estimates that the costs of production and marketing the product are equal to £6000. Three possible outcomes can result from this investment:
   ◆ The product can be extremely successful and yield a net profit of £30 000.
   ◆ The product can be moderately successful and yield a net profit of £8000.
   ◆ The product can be unsuccessful, in which case the loss incurred will be equal to the cost of producing and marketing the product, i.e. £6000.
   Also assume that if the person does not invest in the new product, the £6000 can be invested elsewhere and that this is certain to yield a net profit of £1000.
   The decision maker possesses no knowledge of the probabilities of the product being extremely successful, moderately successful or unsuccessful.

   a Based on the maximin decision criterion, which alternative should be selected?

   b Based on the minimax regret decision criterion, which alternative should be selected?

   c Based on the maximax decision criterion, which alternative should be selected?

2 For the following payoff table (Table 13.7) which relates states of the economy and project payoffs for three different retail projects, find the following:

   a Maximax decision criterion solution.

   b Maximin decision criterion solution.

   c Minimax regret decision criterion solution.

**Table 13.7**

| Project | State of nature | | |
| | Recession payoff £ | Normal payoff £ | Boom payoff £ |
| --- | --- | --- | --- |
| A | 250 | 400 | 550 |
| B | 400 | 450 | 500 |
| C | 320 | 400 | 480 |

3 Compare the following projects in Table 13.8.

**Table 13.8**

| State of the economy | Project A | Project B | Project C |
|---|---|---|---|
| Recession | 200 | 600 | 500 |
| Normal | 1000 | 1000 | 1000 |
| Boom | 1800 | 1400 | 1500 |

Where $P(R) = 0.3$, $P(N) = 0.4$ and $P(B) = 0.3$.

  a  Construct a continuous probability distribution and calculate the standard deviation for the three projects.

  b  Which is the better project to undertake in terms of minimum risk?

  c  If a project were also under consideration which had an EV of £1500 and standard deviation of £465, which of the four projects would in your view carry the greatest chance of success?

4 Suppose that a decision maker is indifferent between a 8 per cent rate of return on a risk-free investment and a 15 per cent rate of return on an investment with risk. The projects under consideration are expected to generate a net cash flow of £15 000 per annum for the next three years.

  a  Using the present value method, which project would you as a manager be most likely to undertake?

  b  If there were an initial outlay in Year 1 of the project of £45 000, would your decision be affected?

  c  Consider the case where the manager regards a certain sum of £16 000 as equivalent to the risky net flow of £20 000.

    i  What is the value of the certainty equivalent?

    ii  What does this imply about the manager's attitude to risk?

    iii  Using the certainty equivalent adjustment factor (ß), compare the two projects explicitly in terms of risk. That is, do the present values still suggest that one investment will be superior?

5 The manager of a service station must decide which of two vending machines to install on the garage forecourt. Both machines will initially cost £20 000. The manager anticipates that Machine 1 will generate a net cash flow of £24 000 for each of the next five years, while Machine 2 will generate a net cash flow of £30 000 in each of the next four years. Which of the machines will the manager install if:

  a  The risk-adjusted discount rate is 8 per cent?

  b  The risk-adjusted discount rate is 16 per cent?

  c  The certainty equivalent coefficient ß = 0.70 for Machine 1 and ß = 0.75 for Machine 2, when the risk-free discount rate is 9 per cent?

6 Compare Projects A, B and C in Question 3, where the decision maker's coefficient of optimism is 0.80 and the decision maker is a risk-averse individual.

7 What advantages does the standard deviation method for choosing between projects hold over the expected value method?

**8** What effects are different attitudes to risk likely to have on the decision maker under conditions of both risk and uncertainty? How might the attitude to risk be accounted for under these different conditions?

**9** Swiss Re (*see* Case study 13.3) is spreading its risk by investing in a 'catastrophes futures index' to manage the exposure within its portfolio. How does managing a portfolio in such a manner work?

**10** When dealing with decisions under conditions of uncertainty, the regret matrix is frequently used. How, though, can it guide decision making when it sometimes generates no 'correct' solution?

## GLOSSARY OF NEW TERMS

**Attitude to risk:** Individuals are classified as being risk averse, risk neutral or risk seeking. Their decision making will be affected by their attitude to risk, since it will bias their willingness to take a chance that a project will succeed.

**Coefficient of optimism ($\alpha$):** Decision makers state their belief that a project will be successful as a decimal between 0 and 1. This is the coefficient of optimism.

**Decision tree:** A graphical representation of the decision-making process. A decision tree illustrates the possibilities which the decision maker assesses when choosing between different projects.

**Expected value:** The weighted average of a project, given the different payoffs for different states of nature and the probability of those states occurring.

**Marginal utility of money (mum):** Used to classify attitudes to risk. Marginal utility of money shows the decision makers' additional satisfaction gained from receiving an additional unit of wealth.

**Maximax decision criterion:** A risk-seeking criterion. The best of the best possible payoffs from each project is chosen.

**Maximin decision criterion:** A risk-averse criterion. The best of the worst possible payoffs from the different projects is chosen.

**Minimax regret decision criterion:** This takes into account the regret associated with making the wrong decision, should a better project payoff exist for the state of nature which occurs.

**Probability distribution:** All possible project outcomes are listed against the appropriate probabilities of different states of nature occurring. Graphically, the probability distribution may also be used to show the different outcomes.

**Risk:** The values of different payoffs for a project under different states of the economy/states of nature are known, so too are the probabilities that each of the different states will occur.

**Risk-adjusted net present value:** NPVs were covered in Chapter 12. The risk-adjusted NPV makes an allowance for the decision maker's attitude to risk so that different projects may be compared in present-day values.

**States of nature:** Projects have different payoffs according to the different conditions under which they may run. These different conditions may relate to the economy, or to different levels of optimism about the success of the projects. Whichever system of classification is used, the different conditions are individually known as states of nature.

**Uncertainty:** The values of different payoffs for a project are known, with reference to different states of the economy/states of nature (*see* above).

## READING

Anderson, D R, Sweeney, D J and Williams, T A (1994) *An Introduction to Management Science: Quantitative Approaches to Decision Making*, 7th edn, West, St Paul, MN.
*Chapter 14 provides an overview of the main concepts covered in this chapter.*

Hill, S (1993) *Managerial Economics: The Analysis of Business Decisions*, Macmillan, Basingstoke.
*Chapter 4 provides a general framework and also some alternatives not covered here for decision making under uncertainty.*

Koutsoyiannis, A (1991) *Non-Price Decisions: The Firm in a Modern Context*, Macmillan, London.
*Chapter 11 gives comprehensive coverage of the concepts in this chapter. This is particularly detailed and may be of benefit to the more mathematical reader.*

CHAPTER **14**

# ELEMENTS OF BUSINESS STRATEGY

## KEY ISSUES

Business issues

Business strategy

Decision-making techniques

Economic concepts

Management decision issues

Optimal outcomes to management issues

## OBJECTIVES

◆ To introduce, explain and discuss a variety of introductory aspects of strategy and strategic management, and to give a brief overview of the development of strategy as a discipline.

◆ To outline the strategic process of analysis, choice and implementation.

◆ To introduce techniques of strategic analysis for both internal and external analysis and to discuss the advantages and disadvantages of different techniques/ approaches.

◆ To analyse the alternatives for making strategic choices: generic strategies, and portfolio analysis in particular.

◆ To highlight the problems arising in strategic implementation and offer some techniques to assist.

## KEY TERMS

Business strategy

Competitive advantage

Mission

Strategic business unit (SBU)

Stakeholders

SWOT anaylsis

Value chain

## CHAPTER OUTLINE

Business application

Introduction

The development of business strategy

Levels of strategy

The process of strategy

Strategic context

Incremental versus fundamental strategy and strategic change

Strategic analysis

Case study 14.1  Quiet revolution at Bata Shoe: the paternalistic model

Strategic capability

Strategic choice

Case study 14.2 Bus exports keep growing: the IMF would approve

Case study 14.3 Brand name of the hotel game: creation of a strong brand image is vital

Case study 14.4 The odd couple

Strategic implementation

Summary

Review questions

Appendix 14.1  Ratio analysis

Glossary of new terms

Reading

# Ford: Jac the Knife

Its cars dominate the best-seller lists in both North America and Europe. Its market share is growing in the rest of the world. Is it Ford's goal, as some of Detroit's analysts believe, to overhaul General Motors (GM) as the motor industry's market leader? Alex Trotman, the car maker's boss, denies this. Besides, he has a more pressing problem. Consumers may love Ford's cars, but the firm is not making much money from them.

In the second quarter of this year, Ford made net profits of $1.6 billion on sales of $36.4 billion, well behind GM (Whose net profits were $2.3 billion sales of $44 billion). After a slack September, Ford's third-quarter profits, to be announced next week, are expected to fall sharply compared with the same period last year; some analysts predict a loss from its North American operations. Last year, Ford earned only $667 per vehicle sold in North America; Chrysler, says Harbour and Associates, a Detroit consultancy, earned $1,259.

The culprits are no longer trade unions or padded manufacturing plants. After a decade of cost-cutting and job losses, Ford's factories are now among the most efficient in North America, using fewer workers than Chrysler or GM to build its cars and trucks. So Ford is now shifting its cost-cutting efforts to two other areas: new product development, and its component suppliers.

Two years ago, when Ford launched its Mondeo car, it bragged that it had cost $6.5 billion to develop. The car was the first designed for all the firm's main markets, and has sold well. But Ford is no longer proud of the Mondeo's massive cost. In return for its investment, Ford got three new models, a new engine and some rebuilt component plants. But Chrysler's new line of small cars, code named JA, has cost barely $1 billion to develop. Similarly, Ford's new Windstar minivan, sold only in North America, has cost $100m less for its new NS minivan range, which includes a new engine and a choice of wheelbases, and is made in Europe as well.

Since the Mondeo, Ford has clammed up about its investment costs, but industry insiders reckon it is spending up to twice as much as its rivals for every new product.

'We're not satisfied with our current performance,' admits Jac Nasser, Ford's boss of product development. Known as 'Jac the Knife' because of his previous cost-cutting efforts in Ford's Australian and European operations, Mr Nasser is heading an effort to shave 12 months off the three years or more it now takes Ford to develop new models. As part of a wider reorganisation begun in January (called 'Ford 2000'), worldwide design and engineering operations have been spilt between five separate 'vehicle centres', each focused on a particular market segment. The system involves forming teams from the market planners, designers, engineers and manufacturing experts who used to work separately.

Ford is also moving to standardise components, particularly the parts customers do not notice, such as windscreen wipers and window motors. By 2000 the firm plans to have only 16 different vechicle platforms (chassis), down from today's 25. That will not mean fewer models – the average platform would have eight variations, compared with five now – but it will simplify design, engineering and manufacturing. It will also allow Ford to build a greater variety of models on each assembly line, and so respond more flexibly to demand.

At the same time, the company is squeezing suppliers. Earlier this year Ford told 100 of its main component makers that it wants to cut the cost of parts by 20% over the next four years through a mixture of supplier price cuts and more efficient purchasing. It is asking suppliers to take on engineering duties that the firm used to perform in-house. And suppliers will have to hand back to Ford any windfall profits they might make from shifting currencies.

Unsurprisingly, the component makers are dismayed. At recent meetings with the car maker's managers, 'many said they would rather lose Ford's business than continue under the current circumstances,' according to one participant. Nevertheless, Ford will probably get its way: it is cutting its roster of 1,600 suppliers by about half; malcontents will simply fall off the list.

Mr Nasser says that Ford has identified ways to trim costs by an average of $700 per car over the next few years; bigger savings could follow.

*Source*: © *The Economist*, London, 14 October 1995, p 106. Reprinted with permission.

## Comment

Ford, the internationally-known automobile manufacturer, has found success in volume of sales, but not in turning these into profits.

Is Ford's goal to be the most successful motor manufacturer in the world worth it if lower profits are part of the bargain? Or is Ford looking further into the future, seeing the reduced profits now as a worthwhile price to pay for future success?

▶

Business application comment *continued*

Although Ford's production costs are lower than those of other manufacturers, its product development and component-supply costs are higher than its competitors. With this in mind, Ford is turning its attention to the way in which it operates across the world. The company is attempting to change its operations from an *ad hoc* system based in each selling country to an all-encompassing design and manufacturing operation which will span the world.

Ford's strategy, it would seem, is to reduce its costs to as low a level as possible and to use this low cost base to improve its performance worldwide. Its longer-term strategy shows a desire to globalise the company while rationalising the range of products it offers.

Ford can be observed here as following the basic ideas of business strategy. It is seeking *competitive advantage* through *lowest-cost production* and *globalisation* of its operations to capitalise further on its success. These concepts, among others, will be introduced, discussed and developed in this chapter.

## INTRODUCTION

This chapter will introduce the basic concepts of business strategy. The unique vocabulary of the strategist will be the first area to be introduced. Each writer on strategy, it seems, coins a new phrase or term to describe the concept they are introducing or analysing. These concepts typically deal with the manner in which organisations analyse, choose and implement strategy. Strategy details the manner in which organisations will achieve their goals. Also relevant is the range of products which the organisation will manufacture or supply to gain success. Additionally, therefore, a variety of analytical tools, models and frameworks which are available in deciding on the portfolio of products or business interests to maintain or from which to divest will be discussed in some depth.

Finally, improvements in technology, leading to better communications, production methods and a better standard of living, have contributed to a desire on the part of many organisations to operate in markets farther afield. At its ultimate, this is termed globalisation. Two seminal works relating to the manner in which globalisation may be achieved will be outlined and discussed in the final section of the chapter.

## THE DEVELOPMENT OF BUSINESS STRATEGY

**Business strategy** as an academic discipline is relatively new, although economists have been aware of and discussing the main issues for many years. The recognition of the need for strategic business awareness on a popular basis dates back only to the 1950s. This was the era of the growth of the multinational organisation, improved global communications and better standards of living in the Western world, leading to better sales opportunities for organisations.

The chronology of business strategy may be plotted as an increasingly complex and all-encompassing discipline. In the 1950s, the strategic emphasis was on the financial analysis and management of organisations. This was extended in the 1960s to include and develop the planning of organisational finance and overall development. It was at this stage that Igor Ansoff began to publish articles and books about business strategy. His model of portfolio analysis (*see* Chapter 11) was more fully accepted in the 1970s. Indeed, this type of analysis was developed further in the 1970s by other writers and theorists *and* by organisations. The Boston Consulting Group and General Electric Company product development matrices both grew out of Ansoff's original work. This type of analysis was eclipsed in the 1980s by frameworks which attempted to analyse the whole business *and* the industry in which it was operating. Such a context brought the name Michael Porter to the public arena. At the same time, and well into the 1990s, growing numbers of management and strategy gurus published their views and models for gaining and maintaining competitive advantage in markets. Successful writers such as Tom Peters, Charles Handy, Kenichi Ohmae, C K Prahalad and Gary Hamel have all published works propounding different ways of achieving dominance and longevity in the competitive marketplace.

Many strategy textbooks trace the rationale for the origin of business strategy back to the phrase associated with Darwin 'the survival of the fittest'. An alternative development which is often quoted is that of the origins of strategy coming from the military. Competition in business has been likened to a battlefield by many writers. As a justification for his belief in logistics and supply chain analysis, Christopher (1992) cites the claim that the failure of the British army in the American War of Independence was its lack of ability to organise, while the Second World War and the more recent Gulf War were in themselves exercises in strategy and logistics management and, indeed, case studies in successful management.

## LEVELS OF STRATEGY

As mentioned previously, there are various levels at which strategy may be formulated and implemented. There are debates about whether strategy should be strictly prescribed by the organisation's chief executive, or whether there should be interaction between top-level executives and the workforce (thus empowering and involving the workforce). Even though there is such a debate, what is not disputed is that the organisation and all its employees should be aware of where it is going and how it intends to get there – its **mission**. One way in which this was communicated in the late 1980s and early 1990s was via a **mission statement**.

Mission statements were less fashionable in the mid-1990s than they were even five years previously. The idea of any mission statement is to motivate the workforce in line with the organisation's vision, or overall goal. Traditionally, the vision of an organisation shows where or what a charismatic leader(s) sees the organisation achieving in the longer term. The mission statement should be simple, easy to understand and memorable. It should also provide a balance between what management, owners and workforce perceive to be important. Although this is difficult to achieve, the mission statement should therefore stimulate and inspire those with an interest in the organisation, without alienating any of the subgroups. Mission statements which are emotive and engender active participation are more likely to be accepted by those involved. Once the mission statement has been defined, the organisation must design and implement a strategy which will allow its achievement. There are commonly two levels of strategy: the corporate level and the business (operating unit) level. Corporate-level strategy is more concerned with which business (that is, its products or markets) the organisation wishes to be in, what it will achieve within that business and how to maintain its position or objectives within that business. Thus, corporate-level strategy defines the activities for the organisation for the longer term. It is concerned with the broad definition of the organisation's direction and scope, that is, the level to which activities will be pursued and the resources which will be utilised in order to succeed. Corporate strategy should not be too prescriptive or definite in its outcomes, although a time parameter and other guiding principles for the measurement of levels of success (or failure) provide benchmarks for the organisation.

Corporate-level strategy may be developed by top-level executives or by a specific planning group or department. It will then be communicated to the rest of the organisation for implementation. In fiercely hierarchical organisations, the methods of implementation will also be communicated. There will be no interaction: the leaders of the organisation will dictate to all extents the corporate strategy, its implementation and measurement.

Other organisations employ a more interactive approach to strategy formulation and implementation. In these cases, a broad strategic direction will be communicated to the workforce, who may then be asked for their input into the manner in which it will be implemented and its success measured. Alternatively, the workforce may be left to react to the day-to-day changes in the marketplace, thus *crafting strategy*, as proposed by Mintzberg (1987), to fit in with the environment in which the organisation is operating. This approach to strategy is termed emergent.

There are several schools of thought with reference to the manner in which strategy should be formulated. The debate between these was most fierce in the late 1980s. One aspect of the debate revolves around whether strategy should be mechanistically planned, communicated and implemented, or whether more of a two-way, emergent and empowered process should be used. This debate will be discussed later in this chapter when the different types of strategy are discussed.

Business-unit-level strategy is more concerned with how the organisation (or a section of it) is going to compete in its chosen market. The strategy and decisions made at a business unit level are concerned with how to compete and what the competitive strategy is. The jargon of strategy uses the term of the business unit, or the **strategic business** unit (SBU), to describe a variety of situations. Ansoff differentiated between the strategic business area and the strategic business unit when introducing the concept of competitive posture analysis/portfolio analysis (*see* Chapter 11).

By identifying the nature and range of businesses in which it is operating, the organisation (or analyst) is able to identify distinctive segments of the environment in which it does business (or wishes to do business). The strategic business area should not be looked at in terms of product or market share, but in terms of growth prospects, profitability prospects and the degree of uncertainty associated with the business area (the expected turbulence in the environment); that is, the lifecycle effects in terms of the growth and length of the entry stage of the lifecycle, the likely growth and length of the future stage(s) of the lifecycle and the associated profitabilities.

Ansoff claimed that 'if the firm is to maintain growth, management must be continually concerned with adding new SBAs to the firm and divesting from SBAs which no longer meet growth objectives'. Therefore, the process of strategic analysis, choice and implementation are ongoing and continuous. For a successful organisation, the process of strategy is of utmost importance and reviews and changes are being made at all levels on a continuous basis (*see* Figure 14.1).

## THE PROCESS OF STRATEGY

Strategy is a continuous process. Once up and running, the process of strategy becomes circular *and* coincidental. In business schools in the UK in the late 1980s and early 1990s, one of the most popular diagrams to explain this was the analysis–choice–implementation triangle, as published by Johnson and Scholes (1993). Indeed, this diagram illustrated the front cover of the second edition of their text. It is reproduced in Figure 14.2.

Organisations are aware that, as the environment and their market(s) change, strategies become out-

**Figure 14.1 Strategic business areas, strategic business units and operating units**

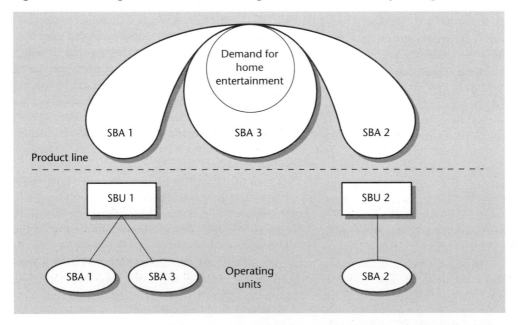

As can be seen here, the organisation is operating to satisfy demand in the home entertainment market. Strategic business area 1 (technology 1) is the video recorder market. Strategic business area 2 (technology 2) is the market for photographic equipment, and strategic business area 3 (technology 3) is the blank computer disk market. Thus the organisation's product portfolio includes video recorders, computer disks, camera and lenses.

Strategic business unit 1 is responsible for SBAs 1 and 3, whereas SBU 2 is responsible for SBA 2. Once the products have been developed and marketed, the organisation's operating units will be responsible for the day-to-day activities relating to the products.

**Figure 14.2 The process of strategy: the process triangle**

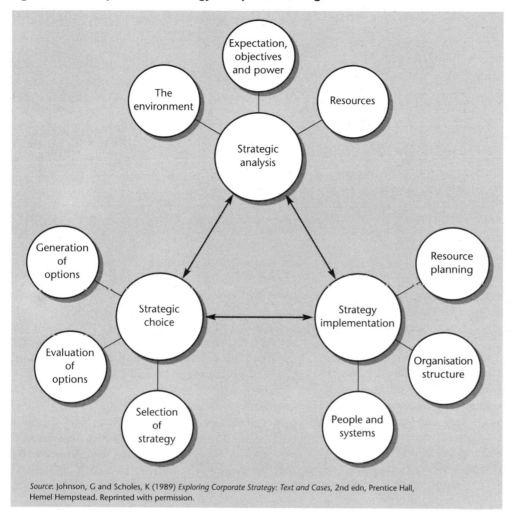

Source: Johnson, G and Scholes, K (1989) *Exploring Corporate Strategy: Text and Cases*, 2nd edn, Prentice Hall, Hemel Hempstead. Reprinted with permission.

The figure shows that there is no start and finish for the process of strategy. Instead, organisations should be continually analysing and reviewing their strategies and implementing these, along with any changes. There is not a one-way cause-and-effect relationship between analysis, choice and implementation. As the figure shows, the three constituents of the process are contemporaneous and interlinked.

dated and require alteration. Historically, in the period up to the 1970s, organisations were able to achieve success via rigid planning and strategy-implementation programmes and processes. In the period since the mid-1970s, the process of strategy and strategic management has become more emergent. Organisations may begin with an idea of the manner in which they intend to achieve their goals, but are much more flexible about how they will get there. Some organisations are even willing for members of the workforce to have an input into what the goals should be, as these are the people who are more 'in tune' with the marketplace and the environment. (This is in line with Mintzberg's approach.)

Strategic change and the management of change have developed as a subject in their own right. There

are many texts dedicated to this alone. By way of an introduction, it may be useful to outline some of the more important aspects of strategic management, using the strategic process triangle outlined above. By considering this in more depth, aspects of strategic management will become clearer.

## STRATEGIC CONTEXT

An important aspect of the process of strategy is the strategic context in which the organisation is operating. Strategists claim that small businesses have different objectives and management needs to larger organisations. These in turn are different to the context of charity and public-sector

**Table 14.1**

| Type | Strategic objectives | Typical business environment | Main internal stakeholders |
|---|---|---|---|
| Small business | Growth, survival | Localised competition, dynamic | Management (who are owners) |
| Professional partnership | Maximum revenue, growth | Localised competition, low organisation (brand) identity | Partners |
| Multinational corporation | Profits, sales, market share | Complex and very competitive | Owners, management, employees |
| Charity | Maximum monetary Donations or revenue | Increasingly, competitive | Paid employees, volunteers |
| Public-sector department | Dependent on government policy | Fluid | Government |

*Source*: Adapted with permission from Johnson, G and Scholes, K (1993) *Exploring Corporate Strategy: Text and Cases*, 3rd edn, Prentice Hall.

organisations. Table 14.1 shows the different aspects of different organisations' contexts.

Table 14.1 shows that there are differences between the typical strategic objectives of different types of organisation. For example, the small business is likely to be striving for growth or survival in a locally competitive and dynamic operating environment. The main internal **stakeholder** in this case will be the owner(s) who also manages the organisation. A conflict can often arise in a successful small business when it grows to a size that requires the owner to become a dedicated manager, rather than participating in the day-to-day production or delivery of its product. At this point, small business owners sometimes face a dichotomy, where they perceive that they have no time (or, perhaps, the capacity) to learn about management instead of production, but where they recognise that they need to change role. Reactions to this dilemma frequently result in the owner working even harder and trying to perform two or more roles to maintain success.

Compare this to the multinational organisation, where there may be a multiplicity of strategic objectives, even though management and employees are specialised in their roles, thus giving rise to a complex and possible conflictual environment. The main stakeholders in this case are management, the owners of the organisation (the shareholders) and the employees. It is obvious here, then, that the strategic process is very complex for the multinational, especially where there are cultural differences to consider.

Charities are facing a changing market. Their overall objective is to maximise revenues or monetary donations. As a result of the increasing number of charities and the state of the economy in many European countries, charities face fierce competition for funds. This is particularly true in the UK, where charities are claiming a reduction in donations made to them directly, as a result of the introduction in 1994 of a new National Lottery. The charities claimed in 1995 that their direct donations had fallen and that monies raised by the National Lottery had not yet been handed over to them. They were therefore temporarily starved of funds.

Increasingly, charities are employing paid workers with private-sector business experience to change the way in which they operate. Charities have realised that in order to survive and compete effectively, they need to take on a more businesslike attitude to all aspects of their operations. There can be problems with such change, especially if the charities rely on a volunteer workforce. These people typically volunteer to work for their chosen charities as a result of a sense of benevolence or vocation. Paid employees working with volunteers tread a fine line between extracting maximum performance and professionalism from volunteers and these same volunteers wishing to help in their own special way. Paid employees therefore require high levels of human resource management and communication skills, on top of their ability to do their assigned jobs.

## INCREMENTAL VERSUS FUNDAMENTAL STRATEGY AND STRATEGIC CHANGE

Another facet which forms the foundation of strategic management is the difference between incremental and fundamental change. An organisation may decide that its strategy should be all-encompassing and involve all areas of the organisation at the same time. Fundamental change occurs when the organisation decides completely to reorganise its activities and internal operations. All employees are involved and affected. Fundamental change requires a shift in focus, direction or other major change for the organisation. By definition, the effects of fundamental change are wide ranging and have a great impact.

Incremental change, on the other hand, represents a softer approach to the process and effects of change. Incremental change may be executed over time, or between different departments. It still has an overall aim or goal and will therefore move the organisation onwards. The effects may be no less drastic than where fundamental change occurs, only more measured.

The following sections will provide a fuller discussion of the elements of the strategic process. Aspects of analysis, choice and implementation will be investigated further to illustrate the activities which accompany the process in more depth.

# STRATEGIC ANALYSIS

To make a strategic analysis of the organisation, all aspects must be investigated. The organisation must go through the painful process of identifying its weaknesses as well as its strengths. Threats from competitors and other aspects of the environment must be identified as well as the opportunities that may arise. Strategic analysis may be carried out by an internal member of the organisation, or by person(s) specialising in such activity and external to the organisation. There are advantages and disadvantages in both.

Internal analysts stand to be influenced by their own personal biases and agendas. They may also be too close to the organisation to make any useful analysis. They may be so close that they are unable to see the whole picture. Theodore Levitt (1960) called this 'marketing myopia'. The advantage of using internal analysts is that they know the organisation's business and understand it. Some of the larger and more complex industries and market sectors are so vast and so complex that it would take too long for any individual to learn their intricacies before they can be effective in analysis of those markets.

External analysts may be contracted to investigate and make recommendations with reference to an organisation's strategy, management of strategic change or even strategic direction. Such external analysts are known as management consultants. The structure of the management consulting industry reflects that of other industries. There are small, medium and large, even multinational organisations. Some specialise in specific areas, such as human resource management, production management, financial management and so on. Others, such as Coopers and Lybrand, Andersen Consulting and KPMG, have international operations and can provide consultancy in a variety of areas additional to those mentioned above.

That external analysts are less specifically informed about the businesses, markets and industries in which an organisation is operating can be an advantage, however. External analysts may be able to see more clearly by looking in than those who are attempting to look out. Some businesspeople claim that external analysts are free to ask naïve questions that change people's perspectives on their business as they attempt to answer them. Additionally, external analysts are frequently brought in to confirm what organisations already know. Subsequent job or budget cuts, especially if contentious, may then be blamed on the analysts, rather than on internal management. This means that management have someone else to blame and may be able to maintain better relations with their workforce as changes are implemented.

## Internal analysis

Strategic analysis may be divided into two broad categories: internal and external. Internal analysis is concerned with looking at the resources, the systems and processes utilised within the organisation. Additionally, it is concerned with the organisation's strategic capability, that is, what it will be able to do in the future. There are various ways in which an internal analysis may be made. Basically, however, the analyst is concerned with the resources which the organisation owns or manages and the manner in which it utilises and deploys them.

Internal analysis may take the form of pure quantitative analysis. Although shortsighted as an analytical framework, this does provide a beginning for a more complete internal analysis. Quantitative analysis is usually concerned with the financial health of the organisation and in generating statistical data with reference to statements of resources and stocks owned or produced. Ratio analysis can be employed to do this and will give a snapshot look at the financial health of the organisation.

Calculation of ratios in order to perform analysis

is relatively easy. The action of comparing the organisation's ratios to industry norms and previous organisational performance is more important. The balance given by the financial health check should be considered carefully, as should likely future results and performances. What is also important here are the trends which may be identified with reference to the organisation. The effect of additional finance requirements, revenue and expenditure may also be considered by the analyst. Details of basic financial ratios for ratio analysis are given in Appendix 14.1.

A more balanced method of undertaking an internal analysis is the resource audit. When performing a full resource audit, the analyst will look at the resources available to the organisation, the manner in which they are interlinked and therefore where *synergies* are derived, and also where systems work against the organisation. The analyst will also consider the past and current industry situation and *benchmark* (or compare and measure) the organisation against those norms. Then, the analyst will consider these resources with reference to what the organisation produces or supplies and match these up against the key issues facing the organisation from within. That is, the analyst will identify the organisation's key strengths and weaknesses. Such an analysis will lead to an understanding of the organisation's strategic capability.

The analyst is able to consider the synergies within the organisation using Porter's (1985) **value-chain** analysis. Value-chain analysis allows the analyst to look at the infrastructure of the organisation with reference to the activities which it supports. Therefore, every aspect of the organisation is considered with reference to the value it adds to the organisation. The rationale for such analysis is that, if an area or activity does not actually add value to the organisation, it should be reorganised or dropped. Porter differentiates between primary activities and support activities. *See* Figure 14.3, which gives an illustration of the value-chain model.

The flow of activity through the organisation may be clearly seen in the value chain. Raw materials enter, are made into products by the manufacturing process and then packaged ready for shipping. The finished goods are sold to customers and delivered, with appropriate levels of after-sales service. Underlying these primary activities are the support activities. The overall infrastructure of the organisation, the manner in which resources are purchased and processed are all part of the support activities. The term resources is used in this context to range from capital assets to human resources.

The efficient flow of materials through an organisation is important, but equally so is the manner in which they are processed and converted into finished products. Revolutionary equipment,

**Figure 14.3 Value-chain analysis**

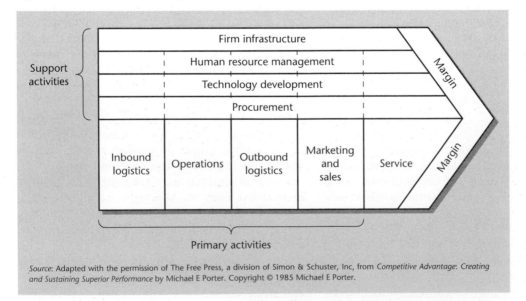

*Source*: Adapted with the permission of The Free Press, a division of Simon & Schuster, Inc, from *Competitive Advantage: Creating and Sustaining Superior Performance* by Michael E Porter. Copyright © 1985 Michael E Porter.

The framework depicts the support and primary activities which link to form an organisation's value chain. By considering these activities and departments as part of a greater whole, rather than in isolation, linkages and synergies may be identified and strengthened (or detracting aspects realigned).

or a highly capable workforce, are of no use independently. Coordination and management of these resources are required in order to produce and sell products successfully. Additionally, the internal layout of the organisation, its actual physical flow, must be carefully designed in order to ensure that the minimum waste of resources occurs through the inbound, production, marketing and sales processes of the primary activities.

The organisational culture and management style are also important. Handy (1993) makes a useful introductory analysis of these. If culture and management style are not in line with the organisation's aspirations, the mismatch will ultimately lead to breakdown or failure of some sort. Thus, internal analysis must include consideration of the 'people factors'. A management style which is highly autocratic, for example, would be entirely out of place in an organisation where the workers are encouraged to maintain high levels of communication and cooperation and are empowered to make production decisions of their own. At some point, such a setup will inevitably lead to breakdown of some sort. Additionally, the mix of employees within the organisation is important. Many tests exist to assess personalities and working styles. Briefly, these identify different types of personalities and their different skills in terms of being introverted, extroverted, project initiators, project finishers, team workers, innovators etc. The optimum outcome of such an analysis is that there is a mix of skills and working styles that best suits the organisation in line with its mission and strategy.

## ◆ CASE STUDY 14.1

# Quiet revolution at Bata Shoe: the paternalistic mould is being broken

FT

Mr Stanley Heath summoned about 40 of his top managers from around the world to Miami last month to relay a polite but firm message: it was time to start pulling together as a team.

Both the meeting and the message marked a break from the past at Bata Shoe Organisation, the hitherto secretive, family-owned company which is the world's biggest footwear manufacturer.

Mr Heath, aged 56, has launched a quiet but determined revolution since last September, when he became the first outsider to move into the chief executive's office at Bata's headquarters in suburban Toronto. Bata owes its growth over the past five decades largely to Mr Tom Bata, who transplanted the family shoe business from Czechoslovakia to Canada in the early 1930s before the Nazi occupation.

Since then, it has expanded into 60 countries. Bata claims to sell more than 1m shoes a day from 65 factories and 6300 retail stores. Its businesses range from the franchise for Nike sneakers in Chile to the distribution of Adidas shoes in India, where it has operated for more than 50 years and now owns more than 1200 shops.

But Bata still bears many hallmarks of a family business. In keeping with its low profile, it has never disclosed revenues or profits. Even senior managers are kept in the dark about many aspects of the company's performance.

A paternalistic management style has permeated the company for decades. The Bata family demanded the absolute loyalty of trusted local managers, many of whom were plucked from Bata operations, initially in Czechoslovakia, and later from the Netherlands, the UK and Italy.

According to Mr Heath, 'they were encouraged to run their own show, and the level of commitment and loyalty was so huge that the family could always depend on them'. In many cases, the most rugged individualists still run the strongest subsidiaries.

Mr Heath, however, wants managers at all levels to broaden their view of the business by sharing more of their ideas and information with colleagues in other parts of the world.

If he has his way, products will cross national boundaries and Bata will take its place among such brand-name powerhouses as Procter & Gamble and Unilever.

Mr Heath's appointment last September coincided with Mr Bata's 80th birthday. The family patriarch still travels the world as the company's chief ambassador. He was in South Africa recently, looking at the feasibility of Bata rebuilding the sizeable business it distanced itself from during the years when sanctions were in place.

He also spends a good deal of time in the Czech Republic, where Bata has reclaimed some of the family assets – including its flagship shoe store on Wenceslas Square in Prague – which were confiscated by the communists. Bata has also opened a factory not far from the family's home town of Zlin. Mr Bata's son, Tom Bata Jr, who was educated at Harvard but has a reputation as a less forceful manager than his father, also relinquished most of his executive duties last year to step into a more ambassadorial role. The Batas have distanced themselves from the business in other ways

▶

Case study 14.1 *continued*

too. Mr Heath reports to the board of the main holding company, which is dominated by outsiders. The chairman is Mr Frans van den Hoven, former chairman of Unilever, and its members include Mr Carl Hahn, retired head of Volkswagen.

Mr Heath, a UK-born Canadian who previously headed the Latin American food operations of RJR Nabisco, the US tobacco and consumer products group, says he is now 'trying to create an environment in which at least the top 30–40 people around the world begin to buy into a sense of teamwork'. He adds that 'I'm not looking for violent change,' but rather seeking to 'massage' the organisation.

Ms Georgina Wyman, Bata country manager in the Czech Republic, says that her new boss has made an impression in the past seven months with his 'diplomatic toughness'.

Mr Heath has begun his quiet revolution by giving regional executives in Paris, Mexico City, Toronto, Singapore, Harare and Calcutta greater authority to take products or retailing concepts across national boundaries. Bata has already had some success with Bubblegummers, a children's shoe brand. But Mr Heath says he wants 'to push that a little bit harder to see whether Bata, as well as being in manufacturing and a first-class retailer, could create some distinctive brands that we could sell to third parties'. Since his arrival, Mr Heath has also made a handful of key head-office appointments. He recruited a chief financial officer with a retailing background.

A marketing expert has been brought in from Levi Strauss, the US jeans maker, to spearhead development of new brands, expand consumer research and stay abreast of retailing concepts.

Mr Heath also plans to strengthen the head office team with a vice-president of technical services, charged with improving the quality, service and innovative flair of Bata's manufacturing operations around the world. Again, the idea is that breakthroughs at one factory will be a catalyst for others. With demand for shoes in Western Europe and North America levelling off, Mr Heath expects that much of Bata's growth will come from countries such as India, Indonesia, Thailand, Malaysia and the bigger countries of Latin America.

The rapid modernisation of shopping malls in Spain, Portugal and Italy has created opportunities for expansion on the retailing side. Mr Heath also hopes to make inroads in Poland, where many older people still remember the Bata name.

'The countries where we're getting most of the growth right now are capable of a lot more,' he says. But hopes of sharply rising consumption in the Soviet Union have been eclipsed by political turmoil there and more attractive opportunities elsewhere.

The task of bringing fresh thinking to an organisation with 65 000 employees scattered across the world, including many remote factories and shops, is likely to test Mr Heath's reputed toughness as well as his diplomatic skills.

He appears to be girding himself for more vigorous massaging. 'We've kicked off this process of team building,' he says.

'What happens next is going to be very important.'

*Source*: *Financial Times*, 28 March 1995. Reprinted with permission.

*Comment on the case study*

This case clearly outlines how the management style of the organisation is changing. The new management, under the leadership of Stanley Heath, is becoming less paternalistic and is encouraging communication and cooperation by its regional executives. This communication, it is hoped, will transform the organisation's operations across the world.

Instead of dictating strategy from above, Bata top management is now looking for input from its local-level managers. The organisation has, since the 1930s, demanded huge loyalty from its employees and seen them rewarded with the role of managing the best subsidiaries. After the change, there will still be a demand for loyalty and motivation, but employees will also be given the opportunity to communicate with each other and share successful ideas.

The organisation is moving into the competitive environment of 1990s shoe manufacture and retail by attempting to create and develop brands which can be sold in the newly developing European and Latin American markets. Manufacturing techniques will also be updated to support the expected growth.

Bata can easily be observed as an organisation in change. The change in management style reflects the changes desired by Stanley Heath with regard to the organisation as a whole. Here it can be seen that the changes are seemingly consistent. Not only has Heath attempted to open up the geographical boundaries within which the organisation operates, he is augmenting this with an attempt to open up communications inside the organisation. Thus, as operations broaden, regional managers will be able to share with and support each other.

## Cost savings in linkages

Under internal analysis, the manner in which the linkages between primary activities and the support activities are exploited will be important. These linkages may be considered, most crudely, in terms of costs. Investigating where economies of scale and economies of scope (*see* Chapter 8) may be derived and returns maximised is one aspect of making cost savings. Another aspect is to look at where the organisation may make actual cost reductions. Specialisation on the part of employees was the fundamental form of cost savings, as identified by Adam Smith in *The Wealth of Nations* in 1776. Further cost savings may be derived as a result of the organisation's experience and its relative position on the learning curve (as discussed in Chapter 10).

Cost savings may also be derived via the manner in which the organisation manages its work in progress and the associated supply costs. By operating a system of just-in-time (JIT) management with suppliers, the organisation can minimise its stocks of raw materials and manage its cash flow more effectively. Many organisations do operate a JIT policy and also see the advantages of maintaining very close links with their suppliers. The importance of good relations with suppliers cannot be understated, or so management thinking of the mid-1990s would propose!

A final factor in internal analysis is comparison of the organisation's performance to with respect industry norms and also with respect to competitors. Reference to industry norms is relatively easy as statistics are readily available. For example, the OneSource UK and Europa Private Companies' financial databases, which are available on CD-ROM in some academic institutions and other organisations, are easy to use, accessible and provide relatively up-to-date information in terms of industry norms etc. The analyst or organisation may require some key performance indicators against which to measure itself. Benchmarks usually define separate, independent activities within the organisation which are easily measured, and are useful for an organisation which wishes to assess its relative position against competitors.

Up to this point, the mix of products and the markets in which the organisation is operating have not been considered. Obviously, the product and the associated market are of ultimate importance to any organisation wishing to succeed. The product analysis and also the organisation's strategy analysis will be discussed later in the chapter in the strategic choice section. This section is presented separately because it is of fundamental importance in its own right and does not only sit in the internal analysis section, but in other sections as well, such as strategic choice and strategic implementation.

## Stakeholder analysis

Stakeholder analysis provides a link between internal analysis and external analysis. **Stakeholders** are those individuals and organisations which have a vested interest in the activities of the organisation. Internal stakeholders are the management, the different departments within the organisation and its employees. The needs, wants and motivating factors for each of these groups are different. What may please management could cause unease among the workforce. On their own, no one group is able to completely influence the direction and activities of the organisation. There are groups, however, who possess greater power than others. Stakeholder analysis seeks to identify these.

External stakeholders cannot simply be identified or listed; they differ between organisations and industries. However, external stakeholders may be grouped into segments which are frequently involved in the organisation's activities: owners (shareholders), suppliers, customers and financiers. Other groups which could also have stakeholder status for an organisation are the government (central and local), guilds and associations, and pressure groups who may or may not have an interest in the success of an organisation with its present or future activities.

There are various ways in which stakeholder analysis is performed to measure the relative power of different groups and individuals. These techniques typically utilise a mapping or matrix approach. For example, in Figure 14.4(a), the relative interests on the part of each group in the organisation's proposed activity are given numerical values. The total for each group is then analysed to assess their power. In Figure 14.4(b), a 'hi–lo' type of matrix analysis is given. Each group is placed in its relative position on the matrix. Therefore, the 'safe' and 'danger' groups are easily identified. 'Safe' groups may be those with a lo–lo position; they are easy to manage and have relatively little power. A 'danger' group could be, depending on circumstances, a hi–hi positioned group, since it is powerful (able to influence decisions of others) and requires high levels of management. Obviously, these examples are only for

**Figure 14.4 Stakeholder analysis**

| Proposed change | Overall | Dept 1 | Dept 2 | Dept 3 | Management | Shopfloor employees | Owners | Suppliers | Customers | Financial backers |
|---|---|---|---|---|---|---|---|---|---|---|
| New market entry | 4 | 2 | 3 | 4 | 4 | 3 | 4 | 4 | 4 | 3 |
| New technology | 3 | 5 | 5 | 3 | 3 | 2 | 2 | 3 | 3 | 2 |
| Customer products | 3 | 1 | 4 | 2 | 4 | 2 | 3 | 2 | 5 | 3 |
| Divest from market | 2 | 1 | 1 | 4 | 4 | 1 | 4 | 1 | 3 | 4 |

**(a)**

Level of intervention

|  | | Low | High |
|---|---|---|---|
| **Power** | Low | Not a problem, manageable | Manageable, but time consuming |
|  | High | Opportunities/free hand | Can enable certain changes to take place |

**(b)**

(a) Relative power matrix. The reactions by each group to certain changes in the organisation are given a relative numerical value (1 = strongly opposed, 5 = in strong agreement). The overall position may then be considered with reference to each group. As can be seen, there is a strong positive reaction to the proposal to move into a new market, while the proposal to divest from an existing market faces opposition. There is no clear balance of feeling for the adoption of new technology or to provide buyers with customised products.

(b) Positional matrix. The relative position of each group of stakeholders is mapped, thus it is easy to identify both relative threats and friends and to make moves to maintain/change the relationship.

guidance: different circumstances and proposals or projects could change the observations made. The organisation is then able to identify who to win over and who to maintain good relations with.

By analysing certain stakeholders' attitudes and reactions to given events, the analyst can build up a picture of the likely reactions or the power of the various groups in supporting a change/activity. Remember that stakeholder analysis provides a link between internal and external analyses. It is therefore important to attempt to consider all stakeholder groups or individuals. Stakeholder power can change over time and so can attitudes. The relative power of stakeholders and even who is regarded as a stakeholder particularly liable to change.

## External analysis

External analysis means analysis of the environment in which the organisation is operating. There are numerous acronyms which describe the factors which constitute the environment: 'LE PEST C', 'STEEPL', 'PESTLE' etc. As can be seen by comparing these acronyms, there are certain letters common to each. The main constituents of external analysis are:

Sociological
Technological
Political
Economic
Environmental
Legal
Competitive

Each of these factors will now be considered and explained in turn.

## Sociological factors

The social changes in the environment. Quantitatively, the different demographic trends which affect the organisation are often considered. Changes in the rate of births, deaths, people over the age of 18 etc. and many other categories may be of use when attempting to calculate the potential buying population for products. On a qualitative level, social differences and changes may also affect an organisation. Attitude shifts by large proportions of the population with respect to, for example, the use of private transport versus public transport will affect the demand for both. Thus an organisation producing accessories for private motor vehicles will be able to assess the changes in demand for its product or to identify potential markets for new products.

## Economic factors

The economic changes likely in the economy need to be identified. These may be economic indicators which are recognised as leading changes in the economy, indicators which change at the same time as the economy and other indicators which follow changes in the economy. Also important is consideration of the Economic Trends statistics, which in the UK are published by the Office for National Statistics (previously the CSO). These give details of the numbers and the changes in numbers of employed, unemployed, interest rates, inflation rates, productivity, GDP, GNP etc. Manufacturing and retail sales indices are also published. Analysts should in addition be aware of the effects of changes in exchange rates (and the likelihood of change).

It may be simplistic to separate sociological factors: the social and economic environments are closely linked, hence the term 'socio-economic'. Changes in the earnings of the population and in sections of the population will affect demand for products, but cannot be categorised as purely sociological or economic. These are usually termed socio-economic factors.

---

◆ **Exercise 14.1**

What are the likely effects on employers of a predicted ageing of the population within the EU, with over half of the working population predicted as being over 50 years of age by the year 2010?

---

## Technological factors

Improvements and changes in technology cannot easily be quantified. However, they can have significant effects on organisations. In the mid-1990s, the major technological change facing many organisations, one which is becoming increasingly important, is the adoption and use of the information superhighway: the Internet and electronic data-transfer systems.

A recent example of technological change might be the utilisation by many organisations of computer-aided design and computer-aided manufacturing systems. These have tended to increase production levels, improve efficiency and reduce wastage rates. Many car manufacturers now utilise such technology: in the 1980s Fiat began to have its cars built entirely by robots.

## Political factors

Although a change in central government in any economy is likely to lead to major changes for many organisations, the change could be exaggerated where elected officials were previously sympathetic to the organisation's needs or aspirations. A lack of understanding, or lower priorities to certain issues, may cause a threat to the organisation. Changes in central government objectives as a result of changes in priorities may also be threatening. Local government changes may have an impact; they may lead to different attitudes to town and country planning, road building etc. Support for local industry may be withdrawn or increased.

## Environmental factors

The growing awareness of environmental issues has a twofold implication for organisations. At a customer level, the organisation must be aware of opinion and act to ensure that its products and processes are in line with such feeling. On a wider level, the organisation must stay abreast of changes in legislation. New guidelines controlling waste management, emissions in to the atmosphere etc. may require the organisation to make additional expenditure in order to comply.

### Legal factors

Legislation changes frequently. Any organisation must be aware of and comply with its obligations to employees and customers and with health and safety practices. Organisations exist to sell their products to customers. They must therefore ensure that they are in line with legislation on the sale of goods and services. The safety of the product must also be monitored.

### Competitive factors

Identification of the factors affecting the environment in which the organisation is operating cannot be complete without analysis of its competition. Local and potential competitors must be identified. The relative importance of competitors should also be recognised. *Competitive posture* of others is as much a factor of an organisation as its own aspirations and strategy/capabilities.

Remember that each of the different factors should be investigated and analysed with reference to the appropriate context. If an organisation is concerned with its strategic capability in the European market, a purely domestic analysis would be short-sighted, naïve and incomplete. Any analysis is only as effective as the way in which it is used.

Analysts need to be aware of the levels of change in both the internal and external environment. Predicting change and analysing factors is easiest when the environment is static and less liable to change. The more dynamic and volatile the environment, the more complex the analyst's job becomes. It stands to reason that a 'same as before' analysis is much easier to perform than an analysis where all factors are liable to change.

Collecting masses of information and data relating to the STEEPL C factors is worthless if it is not processed. There are elements of subjectivity to any analysis, but the more detailed the analysis, the more informative it will be to the organisation. This does not mean that there needs to be masses of information presented. Quite the opposite: key points and an executive summary with appendices are the usual way in which such work is presented. The SWOT analysis (*see* next section) is an ideal way of doing this.

## SWOT analysis

**SWOT analysis** is an extremely flexible and powerful tool. It is used in marketing, personal development planning and other disciplines, not only strategic analysis. SWOT is another acronym. It stands for Strengths, Weaknesses, Opportunities and Threats. Strengths and weaknesses are factors of the internal environment, opportunities and threats factors of the external environment. There are undoubtedly links between the effort put into the SWOT analysis and the results forthcoming. After performing the internal and external analyses, the key strengths and weaknesses of the organisation can be summarised, as can the opportunities and threats facing the organisation. Methodologies differ, but diagrammatic formats are popular. A relative value analysis may be used, or a simple four-segment summary matrix (*see* Figure 14.5). From the summary diagram, it becomes obvious where there may be crossover points between strengths and opportunities, or between weaknesses and threats. Other crossovers may also become obvious. Analysts should not be

**Figure 14.5 SWOT analysis**

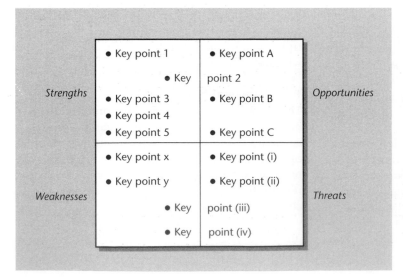

Simply placing summary key or bullet points on to the matrix gives instant and simple recognition of the key factors relating to the organisation. There do not need to be equal numbers of strengths, weaknesses, opportunities and threats.

There are times when a strength may also be seen as an opportunity, or a weakness could also be a threat. This is obvious in the case of key points 2 and (iii).

constrained by the axes of the matrix, rather they may be used for positional purposes to highlight unique points.

## STRATEGIC CAPABILITY

The outcomes of the internal and external analysis, which may be summarised as a SWOT analysis, may be formulated to give the organisation's strategic capability. The overall results of the strategic analysis may therefore be used as a kind of strategic health check. Strategic capability describes the organisation's fitness for purpose with reference to the variety of actions it may take. Once the organisation knows how fit it is, and where its particular capabilities lie, it can make strategic choices. That is, it can decide what its strategies will be and the manner in which it will implement these. Additionally, it may make decisions about its product portfolio and the markets in which it will operate.

Within the concept of strategic capability, the organisation may define its 'core competence' (Prahalad and Hamel (1990)), that is, a specific activity or product which it has particular knowledge and competitive advantage in producing or supplying. Among the core competencies acknowledged by Prahalad and Hamel are Sony's for miniaturisation, 3M's for sticky-tape products and Black and Decker's for small electrical motors.

## STRATEGIC CHOICE

Strategic choices must be made on many levels. On a corporate level, choices must be made about which markets to enter and how to do so, that is, the strategic direction the organisation wishes to take. The methods to be used to achieve the organisation's goals and direction – the strategies – must also be defined. This may be decided at a corporate or business unit level. Again, at either level, decisions must be made about the product markets and indeed the product range to produce.

Before the organisation can decide which markets it finds attractive and wishes to enter and how it may do so, it must make choices about what it will include in its product range. This decision has to bear in mind many factors, which include the general strategic direction, the core competencies of the organisation and its ability to adapt to different markets in the future.

The choice about products and product range represents the debate between those who believe in the importance of the *generic strategies* used by the organisation and those who are more interested in the actual markets and product portfolio.

### Generic strategies

Michael Porter first published the idea of generic strategies in his 1980 text. Here, he differentiates between and defines types of strategy followed by successful organisations. Generic strategies are strategies which may be applied to any organisational context. Porter identified three generic strategies:

- low-cost leadership
- product differentiation
- focus.

Porter believed that, to be successful, an organisation must exclusively follow one of these strategies. Success is measured by the organisation's ability to achieve and to maintain **competitive advantage** over its competitors. Competitive advantage enables the organisation to compete for longer, more effectively and efficiently, and to derive greater profits than competitors. Writers and academics, such as those identified with the Design School (Mintzberg is one) have since debated the validity of the need for organisations to make such an exclusive decision. They argue that an organisation can be successful and follow both a low-cost and a differentiation strategy. This will be discussed in greater depth later in the section.

## ◆ CASE STUDY 14.2

### Bus exports keep growing: the IMF would approve  [FT]

On the outskirts of Cairo, along the road to Alexandria, there is a large privately-owned industrial complex where a team of designers are creating the next generation of Egyptian-made buses. Coloured drawings of luxury coaches line the office walls and computerised prototypes are tested for aerodynamics and stress patterns.

▶

Case study 14.2 *continued*

Outside, noisy factory workers manufacture and assemble a range of vehicles from 15-seat micro-buses to 50-seat touring coaches. In a nearby building sit the sales staff who communicate by telephone and fax with markets across the Arab world and in Europe.

Such a scene should quicken the pulse of any International Monetary Fund or World Bank official working on the Egypt desk, since this is exactly the kind of business they think is needed to widen the country's private sector manufacturing base and help reduce its big trade deficit. Ghabbour Brothers is Egypt's largest manufacturer of buses and an increasingly successful exporter. Last year it made 650 coaches – of which 50 per cent were exported to the Gulf countries – and more than 1000 mini-buses for the domestic market. Although the group began exporting only in 1990, its buses can already be found in Saudi Arabia, Kuwait, Bahrain, Syria, Malta and Romania; it is currently negotiating contracts in China, Hong Kong, Russia and Ukraine.

Founded in 1946 by Mr Kamel Ghabbour, its president and owner, the company began as a general trading company and later became the agent for Sweden's Scania, Germany's Mercedes and Japan's Isuzu trucks and buses. It has since grown organically into an employer of 1500 people with an annual turnover of E£450m and operating profits last year of about E£70m. The group won a licence to manufacture buses in 1982 and two years later it broke the state's monopoly on vehicle manufacturing when its first bus was assembled, using imported parts from Scania. 'Looking back, it was quite a risky move because everything was dominated by the government but at the time we had no choice because the customs duties were so high and our domestic sales were at best flat,' says Mr Ghabbour.

From the outset, the group's manufacturing strategy capitalised on Egypt's cheap but skilled labour force. According to Mr Ghabbour, one coach takes 3000 hours to build. With Egyptian labourers working for as little as E£10 an hour, he says the costs saved in the payroll helped reduce today's retail price on the local market to 45 per cent below the equivalent imported vehicle.

Further cost savings were made by increasing the percentage of local content in the finished vehicle.

This rose from next to nothing in 1984 to a sustained 70 per cent of local content in each vehicle by 1991. Parts were made either within the factory, such as the bodywork and seats, or contracted out to other manufacturers in the country.

Not only did this reduce costs in terms of labour, but the duties paid on imported parts went down as part of a government incentive to promote the use of local content. The group pays 15 per cent customs duties on essential parts such as the axle, engine and power transmission compared to a 60 per cent tariff on finished vehicles.

Mr Ghabbour argues that the cost of technology required to achieve 100 per cent local content would not be economical for his business. 'The manufacture of the other parts is too capital intensive for us. We've reached our peak in local content and now need to further improve our design and quality until it is faultless,' he says.

By 1990 the company had captured about 75 per cent of the local market but sales of coaches were slowing down as the threat of terrorism was keeping tourists away. It was then the management decided to expand by selling its buses overseas.

When competing in overseas markets Mr Ghabbour says that his Egyptian-made buses can undercut European manufacturers by as much as 30 per cent on price. He admits that the group can still improve the quality of its vehicles, although this year it expects to receive recognition from the International Standards Organisation. However, he says some foreign buyers have been surprised how good the buses are.

'When we started exporting it was very, very difficult to convince our customers that Egypt could produce good quality vehicles but now in Saudi Arabia they don't buy from anyone else,' he says.

Mr Ghabbour says that while the group has benefited from government protection and high tariffs on imports, it has succeeded in avoiding the inefficiencies usually associated with protected industries. He is confident that with the gradual improvement in the regulatory environment, local exporters will benefit from Egypt's low labour costs and good geographical position.

(E£ = Egyptian pound)
*Source*: *Financial Times*, 15 May 1995. Reprinted with permission.

### Comment on the case study

It is clear in this case study that Ghabbour Brothers, manufacturers and exporters of buses, have achieved Porter's low-cost leadership within their market. This is due to their low labour costs and also the fact that they are paying less to the government in terms of import duties because they utilise locally made components. As a result of the low cost involved in making the buses, Ghabbour Brothers are able to charge a low market price. This fits in perfectly with Porter's concept.

By keeping costs low, they are charging a lower price than their competitors, but (probably) achieving a similar profit margin. As a result, they have captured 75 per cent of local market sales and moved to exports as a way of further increasing their volume of sales. In overseas markets, Ghabbour Brothers are still able to charge a lower price than European manufacturers. The lack of sales in such markets, according to Mr Ghabbour, is related to the quality of their buses and to the fact that they are not yet ISO (the international quality standard) recognised. Such recognition would assist the organisation in its desire for consumers to appreciate the level of perceived quality of the buses.

## Profit maximisation and competitive advantage

Pearson contends that the three generic strategies are based on the single goal of profit maximisation, as discussed by economists. He further holds that there are two ways of gaining competitive advantage – by price leadership and differentiation – thus implying that focus as an autonomous strategy does not exist.

> The analysis of profitability starts from the very basic assumption that:
>
> Profit = Revenue – Costs
>
> This relationship is both a statement of the obvious and also the starting point for the profit-maximizing model of classical microeconomics which only requires the assumptions of perfect competition for it to be amenable to solution by calculus. It may not look too promising as the foundations of a practically useful strategic model but that is how Porter used it.
>
> The question is: 'How can a business maximize its profitability, or at least become the most profitable performer in its industry?' Maximum profitability can, in principle, only be achieved in one of two ways: either by minimizing costs or by maximizing prices. Thus, any effective business strategy must aim to pursue one or other of these aims: to be the lowest cost producer or the highest price seller. It would be convenient to refer to these two strategies as cost leadership and price leadership except that 'price leadership' is used by economists to mean something rather different. Consequently, the terms initially used by Porter were 'cost leadership' and 'differentiation', referring to the means by which a premium price is earned. These two were referred to as 'generic' strategies because they are the only two ways, in this model, in which profitability can be maximised, i.e. the only two sources of competitive advantage. (Pearson (1992) p 36)

Porter advocates that organisations should pursue one of the above strategies in order to gain a position as the leader in their given industry (or group)

or to bring about changes in the shape of the industry. It is not possible, according to Porter, except in exceptional circumstances which are not explicitly outlined, to follow more than one generic strategy simultaneously. Doing so would strategically place the organisation in a 'stuck in the middle' position. This means that the organisation is unable to gain a sustainable competitive advantage from any of its activities. Instead of following one of the generic strategies fully, it follows a mixture in a satisficing manner.

### Cost leadership

The rationale for an organisation to follow a strategy of overall cost leadership is that having a low-cost position will yield above-average returns in its industry, despite the presence of strong competitive forces. By maintaining a low-cost position the firm builds a defence against rivalry from competitors; its lower costs mean that it can still earn profits after its competitors have competed their profits away through rivalry.

The low-cost leader, then, is able to maintain activity in the marketplace after its competitors have reached their own lower-limit price to be able to remain active for the long term (see Chapter 9: the firm's shutdown price and production decision). The low-cost leader is able to derive greater margins from its activities day to day than its competitors because its costs at the same market price are lower. This strategy is distinguished, according to Porter, by a large market share for the leader. Such a large market share means that the organisation is able to derive advantage through economies of scale, market power and through savings on learning and experience curves.

The risk that the low-cost leader faces is that its competitors may gain knowledge of its processes, utilise them, reduce their costs and thus reduce the leader's profit margins. It is also the case that inflationary price pressure can cause problems for the low-cost leader, especially if new technology is introduced into the industry which again erodes the margin derived with reference to competitors. Changes in the economy can also affect the low-cost leadership position: changes in import duties, tariffs etc. which give advantage to competitors will reduce the competitive advantage of the low-cost leader.

### Differentiation

The rationale for the organisation to strive for differentiation is given by Porter as follows:

The second generic strategy is one of differentiating the product or the service offering of the firm, creating something that is perceived industry-wide as being unique. Approaches to differentiating can take many forms: design or brand image. . . technology. . . customer service.dealer network.or other dimensions. Ideally the firm differentiates itself along several dimensions. . . It should be stressed that the differentiation strategy does not allow the firm to ignore costs, but rather they are not the primary strategic target. (Porter (1980) p 37)

Therefore the organisation is recognised for its product. Sales will be reliant on the consumer's recognition of, and preference for, the product's differences compared to others offering similar attributes in the marketplace. The organisation has thus made its product or product range distinctive in the eyes of the consumer and distinct from its competitors. Differentiation may be achieved, according to Porter, by making the product unique. Uniqueness may be derived as a result of product characteristics or design, or via the service offered to the consumer.

As an industry or product market matures, differentiation between products becomes increasingly important to the consumer. This concept will be discussed in the next chapter.

The risks inherent in differentiation are that the cost of differentiating may make the product uncompetitive. Consumers may thus reject it on these grounds, or on the grounds that they do not like the differentiated product. Alternatively, if it is accepted, the product becomes open to imitation. The case then arises that the differentiator may have borne part of the development costs and part of the risks of the differentiated product launch for the imitators; a saving for which they would doubtless be grateful!

◆ **CASE STUDY 14.3**

## Brand name of the hotel game: creation of a strong brand image is vital    FT

Last year senior executives at a UK hotel company spent four successive Saturdays looking at pictures of thistles. The task was part of a rebranding strategy aimed at promoting Mount Charlotte Thistle hotels. What emerged was a new thistle design for the chain and a subtle change of name to Thistle and Mount Charlotte hotels.

Peter Bates, former sales and marketing director and brand enthusiast, says market research showed that Mount Charlotte was correctly perceived as a three-star hotel chain and Thistle as a four-star business. 'But the research also showed that because the company was called Mount Charlotte Thistle, some people thought that Thistle hotels were turning into 3-star hotels. We decided to separate the names and to put Thistle first.' Branding is the current buzzword among hotel groups which are now trying to emulate the success of brands in other sectors, notably in consumer industries. Building up a brand, though, is not simply a matter of putting the same name above many hotel doors. Crispian Tarrant, managing-director of Business Development Research Consultants, a London-based marketing research company, says that a 'brand promises to the customer certain things he can expect'.

He explains: 'More business travellers attach importance to brands than to star ratings and 66 per cent of business travellers say that recognition of a hotel brand either has a great deal or fair amount of influence on their decision to use a hotel.'

Hotel branding began in the 1950s in North America with the evolution of Holiday Inn, Quality International and Marriott hotels mirroring the growth of inter-state highways and travel. In Europe, Accor has led the way in branding with its Sofitel, Novotel, Ibis and Formule 1 brands, reflecting the 4-star to 1-star spectrum. . .

Well-established and mature brands such as Holiday Inn try to grow their market through 'product segmentation' by adding new types of hotels to appeal to different customers, such as the mainly 4-star Crowne Plaza hotels for business travellers and Holiday Inn Express for the more budget conscious.

For the many chains using franchising or management contracts as a way of expanding business, a strong brand is all-important. Robert Peel, chief executive of Thistle and Mount Charlotte hotels, believes that the value of repositioning Thistle hotels lies in gaining new management contracts or franchises.

Because of the high costs of global distribution and central reservation systems, independent companies are increasingly being pushed into the arms of the branded chains.

Frank Croston, managing-director of PKF, the hotels consultancy, says: 'If I have a hotel which is unbranded, do I employ 20 people in sales and marketing or do I franchise from an existing brand? Increasingly the choice is to seek the shelter of the brand. The big are getting bigger and the battle is on for pan-European brand strength.'

*Source: Financial Times,* 8 June 1995. Reprinted with permission.

## Comment on the case study

Although this article may be more 'at home' in Chapter 11, it does serve to illustrate how careful an organisation must be in differentiating its product or products within a range! Consider the problem in which Thistle and Mount Charlotte has found itself. Its consumers, who, it has been established, choose hotels mainly on the brand name, are confused about the status of Thistle 4-star hotels and Mount Charlotte 3-star hotels. As a result, management is concerned with differentiating between the two chains in the marketplace for the consumer. This, it is hoped, will clarify the difference for the consumer and attract them into staying at the hotels. A vague brand, as the Mount Charlotte Thistle had become, serves only to confuse consumers. Confusion can lead to consumer frustration or indifference as a result of an ill-informed purchase (or in this case, booking) and at worst may mean that the consumer does not purchase again in the future. If the consumer understands the brand and the differentiation, they will make purchases (bookings) in line with their expectations and hopefully therefore remain consumers into the future.

## Focus

The third generic strategy identified by Porter is that of focus, where the organisation strives best to serve a particular market segment. This involves the identification of a suitable target segment and the consequent attention to its given needs and expectations.

The organisation will therefore focus on a particular group of consumers, or a particular segment of the product line or geographical market. Usually, low-cost and differentiation strategies are designed to assist the organisation in achieving its objectives on an industry-wide basis, while a focus strategy is generally built around serving a particular target to the smallest detail. Focus strategy is based on the premise that the organisation is able to serve its narrow strategic target more effectively or efficiently than competitors who are competing more broadly. As a result, the organisation achieves either differentiation from better meeting the needs of the particular target, or lower costs in serving this target, or both. Even if the focus strategy does not achieve low cost or differentiation from an industry perspective, it achieves one or both of these positions with reference to its narrow market target.

The risks involved in following a strategy of focus are that the segment chosen may be too narrow, with differences which are not broad enough

to derive any real advantage from them. Also, it is possible that the competitors are able to 'outfocus' the focuser.

Porter is often criticised for putting forward focus as a third alternative strategy. To many writers, especially economists, focus is simply a special (microcosmic) case of the two preceding strategy types. Pearson, it has already been noted, ignored it. Others have done similarly. Some writers claim that it is possible to achieve both cost-leadership and differentiation strategies simultaneously. Indeed, the group of writers identified as the Contingency School maintains that focus is simply a special case of cost-leadership and differentiation strategies, not worthy of explicit treatment in itself.

Hill (1988) proposed the idea that differentiation can be used to achieve low-cost leadership. He claims that the differentiator loses advantage as the industry matures: a result of learning, experience and imitation. He puts forward the idea that differentiation is the only manner in which low-cost advantage may be maintained in an older market setting. At the very least, Hill claims that there are three conditions necessary to succeed: the product must be differentiable; switching costs must be minimal; and there must be a source for cost savings to be made, through learning effects, economies of scale or economies of scope. Hill also claims that the price sensitivity of consumers (that is, their price elasticity of demand) is related to the organisation's ability to differentiate products. This is justified, he claims, by the fact that when price sensitivity is low, successful differentiation can occur and the extra price charged without jeopardising the organisation's low-cost position. To any economist, then, it should be clear that Hill is including price differentiation within his definition of product differentiation.

◆ **Exercise 14.2**

Analyse and criticise the concept of generic strategy and its detractors from an economist's perspective.

Diagrammatically, the generic strategy choices open to an organisation may be easily seen on a matrix. In Figure 14.6, the competitive advantage achieved by the organisation is measured against the competitive scope (or range) of the organisation. If advantage is gained via a lower cost base than competitors on an industry-wide basis, the organisation can be seen to have a cost-leadership strategy. Compare this to the situation where the organisation gains its advantage through differentiation of its product on an industry-wide basis. In such a situation, it is obviously following a differentiation strategy.

Where the competitive scope is more narrow than the industry-wide basis, concentrating on a particular market segment, and either cost leadership or differentiation is achieved, the organisation may be seen to be following either a cost-focus or differentiation-focus strategy.

The generic strategy concept is based on a structured, formal, S–C–P-type approach to analysis. It is therefore based on factors exogenous to the organisation. There are other approaches which are also based on a structural approach, for instance the Wheelan model of situational analysis, which involves three stages of analysis leading to strategic choice:

■ Identification of the distinctive competence of the organisation.
■ A TOWS matrix configuration (TOWS: similar approach to SWOT).
■ A portfolio analysis within the organisation.

It can be argued that Wheelan's approach provides more foresight than the generic strategy approach because it incorporates consideration of the organisation's abilities, resources, core competences etc. There are other approaches to strategic choice (which could also be considered as methods of internal analysis) which also consider the internal capabilities and current state of the organisation. Competitive posture analysis and portfolio analysis are commonly used. Such analysis is important because organisations are rarely only producing one product or providing only one service. Management of the portfolio, or range, is therefore important.

## Competitive posture analysis

Ansoff's product portfolio analysis, as mentioned in Chapter 11, was developed from Ansoff's competitive posture flowchart where the stages of strategic analysis are outlined. Ansoff (1987) clearly points out that organisations should avoid the tendency to 'see the future through the eyes of the firm's traditionally successful products, technologies and marketing strategies'. Ansoff's approach is for the organisation to find a preferred competitive posture, that is, the competitive position which will be occupied by the organisation in any given number of strategic business areas (SBAs) in the future with reference to current position and likely future changes in the market. However, Ansoff found that his original approach was 'too crude to permit realistic business decisions' and did not take account of the turbulent nature of 70 per cent of businesses, so he has now developed a new strategic paradigm, to accommodate the varying levels of turbulence within the environment of business organisations, as shown in Figure 14.7.

In Figure 14.7, the attractiveness of strategic business areas, SBAs, both present and potential, are matched against products, both present and potential. For example, within the present SBA, the organisation could stay with its existing product, or use product innovation, or look for new forms of technology. The resulting actions would be those shown in the first column. It is also clear from the matrix that the organisation could alter market situation as well as product. This would lead to the other scenarios depicted.

Ansoff's original matrix was concerned with market growth and market share. A development

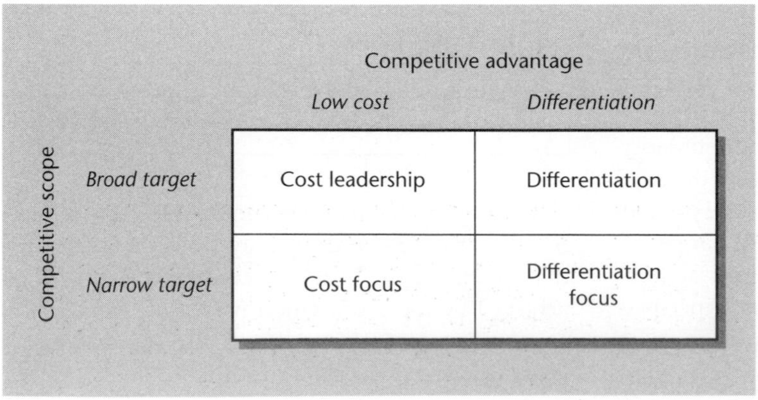

**Figure 14.6 Generic strategy matrix**

The generic strategy matrix clearly shows the combinations of the ways in which competitive advantage may be derived with reference to a given competitive scope. The combination of these factors gives the generic strategy which the organisation follows.

| Product \ Market | Present SBA | New SBA | Novel domestic SBA | Transnational SBA |
|---|---|---|---|---|
| Present | Competition | Market innovation | Novel domestic SBA + Present product | Transnational SBA + Present product |
| New | Product innovation | Product innovation + Market innovation | Novel domestic SBA + Product innovation | Transnational SBA + Product innovation |
| Novel | Present market + Technology substitution | New market + Technology substitution | Novel domestic SBA + Technology substitution | Transnational SBA + Technology substitution |

*Source*: Copyright © H I Ansoff 1995.

**Figure 14.7 The firm's strategic action alternatives**

Ansoff's matrix matches the attractiveness of strategic business areas, both present and potential, against existing and potential products.

of this approach is the General Electric Company's (GEC's) business screen. This combines product market attractiveness with business strength in the future and so provides the organisation with a snapshot of the markets which should be entered and those from which it should divest, as well as those which will provide earnings in the future. Other developments have also been made. Lifecycle analysis and business strength are used as the axes for another, alternative matrix developed for similar purposes.

The point of all such approaches is that the organisation is easily able to see the areas or products into which it should be entering and those from which it should be moving. The organisation is therefore able to make strategic choices with reference to its portfolio and its strategic capabilities. The portfolio approach therefore offers a different insight to the generic strategy approach by considering an overview of the product ranges available, their attractiveness in the market and the interlinkages between them. Generic strategy approaches tend to consider each product or range individually

and could be claimed to be more myopic than portfolio approaches.

Both of the approaches suffer from the same problem, however. They are subjective, based on the bias(es) of the analysts involved. Additionally, both approaches are snapshot approaches, relevant at the time of analysis, but dated beyond that, particularly if the markets are dynamic and changing rapidly. No model details how the organisation should enter or move between markets.

If the movement is into a new, yet related market, the organisation is likely to fund and manage the movement via its internal activities. It will already have some level of expertise with reference to the new market and will therefore be capable of managing the movement itself. However, for completely new markets, the organisation may wish to purchase expertise in the new market, or to collaborate with incumbent organisations. The amounts of money and immediate expertise required to enter some markets mean that without such collaborative enterprises, entry would not be possible.

## ◆ CASE STUDY 14.4

## The odd couple

Bill Gates has always assured those alarmed by Microsoft's voracious appetite for new markets that no matter how big the firm got it would stick to software. It now seems he was using a rather broad definition of the word. Mr Gates is talking to Ted Turner about buying a minority share (worth $1 billion-2 billion) of Turner Broadcasting, the parent company of CNN and several other cable channels.

The attraction for Mr Turner is clear: he needs money to buy the broadcast TV network he has always lusted after – and for which his desire has become still more ardent now that Disney has snapped up Capital Cities/ABC. For Mr Gates the main appeal is content – Turner Broadcasting's news and entertainment programmes. He needs compelling material to lift the Microsoft Network, his new on-line service which

Case study 14.4 *continued*

starts next week, above the competition and eventually into an interactive TV future.

The Microsoft money could allow Turner Broadcasting to buy back the 18% of its shares owned by Time Warner, a stake it valued at $1.6 billion earlier this year. Time Warner has been the main voice on the Turner Broadcasting board blocking Mr Turner's pursuit of a television network. Westinghouse, a diversified conglomerate, has already made a $5.4 billion bid for Mr Turner's chosen target, CBS, but, providing he can arrange outside financing, Mr Turner could challenge it. Mr Turner wants not only CBS's programming but also the clout that comes with a broadcast network (it pains him that CNN was not allowed to bid to cover the Olympics in Atlanta, its home town).

Like Mr Turner, Mr Gates wants to be a media mogul of sorts, but he is in a very different world from the TV business, where a finite number of channels ensure that a few companies grab most of the viewers. In the world of computer networks there is a limitless number of channels. Owning your own commercial on-line service once guaranteed exclusive access to content that would draw viewers. But now the explosively growing Internet (which is owned by no one) lets any content provider reach on-line viewers without a middleman.

This leaves Mr Gates with a problem: the Microsoft Network risks feeling like a glossy cinema without any films. Granted, he has endowed the network with all sorts of other advantages. Everyone who starts up Microsoft's new operating system, Windows 95, will be invited to sign up for the service. And the price, starting at $4.99 a month, is half that of competitors. But other big fish are coming into this pond: on August 15th AT&T announced that it would soon begin marketing a consumer Internet service to its 90m customers, priced 'competitively' with Microsoft's.

With only 7% of Americans subscribing to any on-line service today, there is still plenty of room for competitors. But Microsoft is hoping for more than just

subscribers. The real money is not in those who will use the Microsoft Network as an entry to the Internet, but those who pay for content that is only on the Microsoft Network itself (and for which they are charged extra). Mr Gates, in other words, must find some compelling content before he can win the best customers.

Hence the talks with Mr Turner. If content is the aim, then CNN's news-gathering power is an obvious lure; if Mr Turner's bid for CBS is successful, some of its programming could go to the Microsoft Network too. (Earlier this year Mr Gates paid $4m to sign up NBC.) The putative marriage has a best man: Telecommunications Inc, a cable TV giant, owns 20% of both Turner Broadcasting and the Microsoft Network. And there might even be a bit of chemistry. Bill Bluestein of Forrester Research, a consultancy, notes that of all the media tycoons, Mr Turner is 'the most tuned into the computer world. He viewed himself as a cable pioneer and he sees on-line networks as the next thing.'

Although CNN and the networks have plenty of programming to offer a television audience, none has yet shown much aptitude for the sort of interactive content that works on a computer screen. And even if television firms can move into the on-line world, they will not be alone. MCI, America's second largest long-distance telephone company, is investing up to $2 billion in Rupert Murdoch's News Corp, which owns Fox, the fourth American TV network, and a big Hollywood film studio. The familiar aim: to use News Corp's content for their joint Internet service.

These sort of deals are the baffling reality of 'convergence': odd couples from media, computers and telecoms getting into bed together and looking for a spark. At best, these deals may reveal some real synergy; at worst, they can be costly experiments. But if the usually level-headed Mr Gates is willing to even consider a deal with a mercurial figure like Mr Turner, they have surely become irresistible.

*Source*: © *The Economist*, London, 19 August 1995. Reprinted with permission.

### Comment on the case study

The case study describes a technically complex relationship being built up between Bill Gates' software company Microsoft and the Turner Broadcasting organisation. The relationship is synergistic, Gates needs Turner and Turner needs Gates. Both are concerned to be main players in the future TV and multimedia industries (industry?). As a result, they are forming an alliance which not only offers entry opportunities into new markets, but which also means that there are opportunities to share technologies.

Such alliances are not new. In the heyday of video game sales, Sega and Nintendo were the market leaders, but collaborative partnerships by organisations such as Sony and Philips were also made in an attempt to compete.

Gates and Turner stand to profit from sharing technology and also content in what are currently different sections of the multimedia market. In time, Gates believes that the TV, rather than the computer terminal, will be the focal point for the Internet. Until then, he is attempting to boost the Microsoft on-line network by offering content provided by

Turner's news broadcaster, CNN. The results of such a venture remain to be seen. The cast claims that Gates' interest displays his belief in such success. Gates had been looking around for a partner for quite a while before settling on discussions with Turner.

### Mergers and acquisitions

Mergers and acquisitions are another way in which organisations are able to move into completely new markets. Merger and acquisition activity tends to go in cycles. Evidence in the UK (Griffiths and Wall, 1993) shows that merger activity is highly concentrated in terms of horizontal integration, while only 4 per cent is between organisations at different stages of the production process (vertical integration). The reason for such activity, it has been suggested, is that organisations are rationalising their activities, integrating technology and expertise and generally attempting to gain economies of scale. Merger activity is regulated in all domestic European economies. Additionally, the EU has legislation to regulate cross-border mergers and takeovers.

## STRATEGIC IMPLEMENTATION

The manner in which the organisation's strategy is implemented is as important as the strategy itself. A poorly implemented strategy can be as disastrous as a poorly designed strategy. Inevitably, implementation requires change within the organisation: change in previous behaviour, culture, the key players etc. Such changes will induce resistance. Even though individuals have an input into the planning stages relating to strategic change, they may be resistant when the time comes to implement such change. The ways in which strategic analysis, choice and planning are done will affect the implementation process. Some people may feel alienated, while others will be empowered, enthused and ready to go.

Resistance to change can occur in many ways. Typically, it manifests itself in the following forms:

- *Delay* – in initiating the change process and during the process.
- *Sabotage* – either conscious or unconscious by individuals not fully committed to the change process.
- *Rejection* – claims and actions which imply that the individual does not believe that there is any need for change.

- *Performance deterioration* – it is unlikely that the productivity and performance of the organisation will improve immediately the new strategy is implemented. Time to adapt to new processes and systems is required.
- *Competition* – there will be a time period where the organisation is running two systems, the new and the old. Therefore these two will be in competition for resources of all kinds.
- *Lack of ownership, leadership and control* – successful implementation requires a key figure to lead the process and regular measurement to ensure that it is progressing adequately.

Resistance to change occurs because individuals feel threatened by aspects of its implementation. As human beings, individuals feel most threatened when there is likely to be a change to the culture of the organisation or the distribution of power within it. When change affects both culture and power, it is most likely to be resisted.

Obviously, if change is carefully planned and communicated, resistance can be reduced or avoided. Communication and 'selling' of the change so that all individuals understand their role in the process can be beneficial. Allowing individuals to give their input regarding the manner in which things should be implemented can also assist the process.

If the organisation's leaders exhibit visible reactions to the process, change may be more effective. Other individuals will see them leading by example and therefore have a greater propensity for acceptance of the process themselves. There are various models which exist to assist the change process. These mainly deal with the manner in which the workforce is won over by management, motivated and enthused with reference to the changes ahead of them.

Lewin's model (1958) of strategic change is a three-phase model. It deals with the 'people' aspect of the change process and requires understanding of the manner in which people learn and behave. Its usefulness in assisting a complicated change process may be limited, although its simplicity makes it attractive. Quite simply, the three stages in the model are:

- *Unfreeze* – assist people to 'unlearn' their behaviour; the more dramatic the unfreezing action or activity, the more effect it is likely to have.
- *Relearn* – teach people the new way of doing things.
- *Refreeze* – make the change stick by putting in reinforcements such as rewards.

There must be a period of stabilisation between the relearn and refreeze stages, so that people are able to get used to the change and also so that any defects or flaws may be eliminated.

A more complicated model is that based on a process-oriented approach, which offers a flow-chart for successful management. The process is:

- Diagnose the present condition, including the need for change by defining what the driver for change is.
- Develop a picture of the future in qualitative and quantitative terms. Include definition of management roles, culture, reward systems etc.
- Set goals and define the state of the organisation after a successful change process.
- Define the transition stage between the present and future, giving a time frame, measurement criteria, manner in which transition will occur. (Change is never instantaneous or painless.)
- Develop specific strategies and action plans to manage the transition.
- Evaluate the change effort required, appoint change agents and set up change networks.
- Stabilise the new condition and establish a flexible balance to allow monitoring and evaluation of the process.

This model is more complex than Lewin's, but it does offer a more detailed prescription for the management of change. It also takes into account the fact that successful change requires both 'hard' and 'soft' criteria for success.

There are other important factors for management to consider when implementing strategy. The readiness of the organisation to implement the strategy and its current ability to do so are very important. Without readiness or ability, the organisation is likely to fail in its new direction. Resource analysis, cultural and stakeholder analysis are useful tools to ascertain the organisation's current position. Formulation of new teams, or reorganisation of existing teams, may also be necessary.

Additionally, the implementation stage requires there to be key players and leaders with ownership of the new strategy and the workforce must also feel ownership. To monitor the ongoing success of the implementation at various stages, all those involved need to be aware of the key performance criteria, and the manner and timing of their measurement. In most instances, change is managed in stages across the organisation. There are times when it is more appropriate to pilot the process on a small scale before actually 'going live'. Depending on the situation, either methodology is valid.

## SUMMARY

◆ This chapter has introduced, explained and discussed a variety of introductory aspects of strategy and strategic management. The development of strategy was discussed as an introduction to the discipline.

◆ There are two identifiable levels of strategy: corporate level, dealing with the overall direction and goals of the organisation; and business unit level, concerned with a more operational implementation of the objectives.

◆ The strategic process may be identified as the strategic triangle of analysis, choice and implementation.

◆ Strategic analysis is performed in an internal and external context with reference to the organisation. Stakeholder analysis links internal and external analysis because it includes agents with interests relating to the activities of the organisation, some of which are within the organisation and some external.

◆ For internal analysis, many models exist. Specifically, ratio analysis and the value chain differ in their quantitative and qualitative approaches.

◆ External analysis is usually based on the LE PEST C, STEEPL or PESTLE framework of analysis.

◆ SWOT analysis is used to analyse and summarise the positive and negative aspects of an organisation's internal and external analysis. From the SWOT analysis, the analyst is able to derive the strategic capability of the organisation.

◆ Strategic choice is represented by Porter's generic strategies of low-cost leadership, differentiation and focus.

◆ Ansoff's and other approaches which offer an alternative to generic strategies are concerned with the organisation's portfolio of product offerings and its competitive posture within its chosen markets.

◆ Strategic implementation is a process which must be planned and managed carefully in order to generate success. There is frequently resistance to and sabotage of such operations on both conscious and subconscious levels by employees, management and others involved in the process.

## REVIEW QUESTIONS

1 Give definitions for the following:
   a mission
   b strategy
   c competitive advantage
   d internal analysis
   e external analysis
   f strategic capability
   g portfolio analysis.

2 Outline the main components of the strategy process.

3 Differentiate between levels of strategy and give examples of the main considerations appropriate to the different levels of strategy.

4 If Ghabbour Brothers (*see* Case study 14.2) wish to continue to expand their operations overseas, give a brief outline of the process they should invoke to do so successfully.

5 Show how consistency in management style, culture and strategy is important for any organisation. Illustrate your answer with reference to an organisation which has demonstrated this via its success or failure.

## Appendix 14.1

## RATIO ANALYSIS

With reference to the organisation's accounts for previous years' trading, ratio analysis can provide insight into its financial health.

### PROFITABILITY

**Gross profit margin**

Sales – cost of goods sold/sales

**Net profit margin**

Profits after tax/sales

**Return on assets**

EBIT/total assets (EBIT = earnings before interest and tax)

**Return on equity**

Profits after tax/total equity

*For each of the sections below, calculate the ratios given. For an overview of the results of the section, compare the results with those of a close competitor, or with those for the previous year, by placing the relative performances (very low – very high) in the boxes.*

*Repeat this for all sections and consider the overall results for the organisation.*

Profitability profile

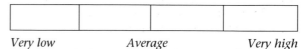

*Very low*        *Average*        *Very high*

### LIQUIDITY

**Current ratio**

Current assets/current liabilities

**Quick ratio**

(Current assets – inventory)/current liabilities

**Inventory to net working capital**

Inventory/(current assets – current liabilities)

Liquidity profile

| | | | |
|---|---|---|---|
| | | | |

*Very tight*　　　*About right*　　　*Too much slack*

## LEVERAGE

**Debt-to-assets ratio**

Total debt/total assets

**Debt-to-equity ratio**

Total debt/total equity

**Long-term debt to equity ratio**

Long-term debt/total equity

Leverage profile

| | | | |
|---|---|---|---|
| | | | |

*Too much debt*　　　*Balanced*　　　*Too much equity*

## ACTIVITY

**Inventory turnover**

Sales/inventory

**Fixed-asset turnover**

Sales/fixed assets

**Average collection period**

Accounts receivable/average daily sales

Activity profile

| | | | |
|---|---|---|---|
| | | | |

*Too slow*　　　*About right*　　　*Too fast*

*Source*: Adapted from Rowe, Mason, and Dickel (1985) *Strategic Management: A Methodological Approach*, Addison Wesley, Harlow.

## GLOSSARY OF NEW TERMS

**Business strategy:** The manner in which organisations intend to compete in order to achieve their goals.

**Competitive advantage:** The 'edge' which organisations have over others in their market or industry.

**Mission:** The overall aim or goal of the organisation, frequently detailed in the mission statement.

**Strategic business unit (SBU):** An autonomous subsection (in terms of management and operation) of the organisation which may operate within more than one business area.

**Stakeholders:** Individuals and agencies who possess some interest in the activities of an organisation.

**SWOT analysis:** Combined internal and external analysis of the organisation based on its internal Strengths and Weaknesses and external Opportunities and Threats.

**Value chain:** A way of looking at the structure of organisations which breaks it down into 'primary' activities and 'support' activities. If any of the processes fails to add value to the organisation or its product, further analysis and perhaps reorganisation are required.

## READING

Bowman, C and Asch, D (1987) *Strategic Management*, Macmillan, Basingstoke.

Griffiths, A and Wall, S (1993) *Applied Economics*, 5th edn Longman, New York.

Johnson, G and Scholes, K (1993) *Exploring Corporate Strategy: Text and Cases*, 3rd edn, Prentice Hall, Hemel Hempstead. (*See also* 4th edn, 1997.)

Levitt, T (1960) 'Marketing Myopia', *Harvard Business Review*, July–August, pp 45–56.

Lewin, K (1957) *Field Theory in Social Science*, Harper & Row, New York.

Morden, T (1993) *Business Strategy and Planning: Text and Cases*, McGraw-Hill, Maidenhead.

Shrivastava, P (1994) *Strategic Management: Concepts and Practices*, Southwestern, Cincinatti, Ohio.

Stacey, R D (1996) *Strategic Management and Organisational Dynamics*, 2nd edn, Pitman Publishing, London.

### Further reading

Ansoff, I (1987) *Corporate Strategy*, Penguin Business, Harmondsworth.
*Offers a unique insight into strategic analysis, choice and implementation based on portfolio analysis.*

Christopher, M (1992) *Logistics and Supply Chain Management*, Financial Times/Pitman Publishing, London.
*Provides a link between the logistics function of the organisation and its strategic direction. Christopher sees the competitive advantage of organisations as coming from the effective management of their complete production process – from 'goods in' to 'goods out'. The better the processes within the organisation and the interactions with suppliers and buyers, the better its performance.*

Handy, C (1993) *Understanding Organisations,* 4th edn, Penguin Business, Harmondsworth.
*Gives an outline of the manner in which organisations operate and the manner in which people interact within them.*

Hill, C (1988) 'Differentiation versus low cost: or differentiation and low cost: a contingency framework', *Academy of Management Review*, Vol 13, No 3, pp 410–12.
*A critique of Porter's generic strategies, offering the view that organisations can be both low cost and differentiating with reference to their strategy choices.*

Mintzberg, H (1987) 'Crafting strategy', *Harvard Business Review*, July–August.
*An alternative approach to strategy formulation and implementation which advocates involvement of the whole workforce, rather than management alone. Additionally, Mintzberg claims that strategy should be flexible: changing with the environmental context of the organisation, reacting to it and evolving as a result.*

Ohmae, K (1983) *The Mind of the Strategist*, Penguin, London.

Pearson, G (1992) *The Competitive Organisation*, McGraw-Hill, Maidenhead.
*An up-to-date analysis of the techniques used within the successful organisation, including a critique of the profit-maximisation model and assumptions, on which Porter's texts can be seen to rest.*

Peters, T and Waterman, R (1982) *In Search of Excellence*, HarperCollins, New York.

Porter, M (1980) *Competitive Strategy*, Macmillan Free Press, New York.
*Generic strategies were introduced in this text.*

Porter, M (1985) *Competitive Advantage*, Macmillan Free Press, New York.
*The value chain as a method of achieving competitive advantage was introduced in this book.*
*Both the Porter texts are very readable, although a little dated.*

Porter, M and Montgomery, C (eds) (1991) *Strategy*, Harvard Business School Press, Boston, MA.
*A useful collection of seminal articles regarding strategy from the 1980s.*

Prahalad, C K and Hamel, G (1990) 'The core competence of the corporation', *Harvard Business Review*, May–June.
*The seminal article discussing the core competence of the organisation: its identification, exploitation and development.*

CHAPTER **15**

# ANALYSING THE STRUCTURE OF COMPETITION

## KEY ISSUES

Business issues

Business strategy

Decision-making techniques

Economic concepts

Management decision issues

Optimal outcomes to management issues

## OBJECTIVES

◆ To introduced the various stages of competitive analysis: at an industry level, intra-industry and individual competitors within the industry.

◆ To explain the Five Forces of Competitive Rivalry and its use as a framework for the analysis of industry and market situations.

◆ To provide an insight into the difficulties for the analyst in defining the industry in which an organisation may be competing. The proposition that it is better to ignore industry boundaries will also be examined.

◆ To discuss the manner in which strategic groups analysis may be undertaken and how this gives insight into which organisations are close competitors to the organisation in question and which are not really in competition, although they are within the same industry.

◆ To highlight the key points and questions to consider when analysing the strength of, or danger posed by, close competitors via competitor response profiling.

◆ To criticise the staged approach to the analysis of competitors, as put forward by writers such as Porter. One of the more fundamental critiques is that this is based on the S–C–P approach of the neoclassical economists, an approach which many economists consider to be invalid given contemporary market conditions and the simplistic assumptions on which it is built.

## CHAPTER OUTLINE

## KEY TERMS

## BUSINESS APPLICATION

# Reinventing the bicycle

Long a humble means of transport, the bicycle suddenly became a fashion accessory with the advent of the mountain bike a decade ago. Most may never so much as climb a molehill, but two out of three bikes sold in Western Europe and America are now of the 'mountain' kind; demand for these machines in America grew from 1m in 1985 to 8.7m in 1994, adding at least 2m to the overall bike market, according to Mike Kershow of the Bicycle Manufacturers Association of America. But now demand for mountain bikes has peaked, leaving bike makers scrabbling for a new trick.

In America, bike sales are stagnant at 16m a year; the German market, Europe's biggest, shrank by 10% last year, while British sales are static. Bike manufacturers in these countries must also compete with cheap Asian imports that are driving down prices and squeezing

margins. The share of imports in the American market has grown from 36.7% in 1992 to 46% this year. Imports from China alone took 23.7% of the market last year, up from 14.6% two years earlier. This has benefited consumers: some mountain bikes now retail for $79 in some outlets, about $10–20 down on 1994. But producers are screaming: Huffy Corporation, owner of one of America's biggest bike makers, posted a third quarter net loss of $4.5m. On November 1st, America's Commerce Department slapped preliminary tariffs of 62% on Chinese bikes.

European bike makers face similar problems. In Western Europe, with sales of over 18m bikes, local producer's share of the market fell to a third in 1993, down from 42% in 1990. In 1993 the European Commission introduced an anti-dumping duty of

▶

30.6% on Chinese bikes, and in October this year it announced provisional duties of up to 48.8% on imports of bikes from Indonesia, Malaysia and Thailand. This may help flagging British firms such as Casket, the second-biggest British bike maker, which in October announced a merger with EFG, a horticultural-products group.

But the best answer to Asian imports is innovation. For that, America must look to the designers who invented the mountain bike. Britain's boffins are also busy trying to reinvent the bike. Clive Sinclair (infa-

mous for the C5, an electric tricycle which flopped) recently promoted his Zeta, a battery-powered motor for bikes, as 'the next major breakthrough'. However, it failed to propel enough grannies up hills to electrify the market. Still, Mr Sinclair is undaunted: he is working on a foldable bike which he hopes will be 'as convenient as an umbrella' and weigh less than 3.5lbs (1.6 kilos). It may (or perhaps may not) end up as the bike for the 21st century.

*Source*: © *The Economist*, London, 18 November 1995. Reprinted with permission.

### Comment

In the Netherlands there are more bicycles than people. Germany, Europe's largest bicycle market, shrank in terms of volume last year. In the UK and the USA, most sales are of the mountain bike (MTB: mountainbike, VTT: velo tout terrain) variety. In France, the entry-level specification of sports bicycles available in hypermarkets would necessitate a visit to a specialist shop in other countries of Europe. There is diversity of tastes and requirements in all of the markets mentioned above. Given these differences and also the changes outlined in the case study, how can component manufacturers such as Shimano, Mavic, Sachs and Campagnolo continue to maintain their dominance in the industry? These manufacturers make and sell bicycle brakes, gear changers, brake levels, chainsets and pedals.

The component market is dominated by the Japanese manufacturer Shimano at present, especially at the lower end of the price spectrum. The other manufacturers, however, manage to stake and maintain their market-share claims and to profit from them. The industry, far from being *the* bicycle industry, is fragmented. The different component manufacturers compete in different segments of the industry. They share out the industry with reference to their particular market strengths and interests. All of the component makers are aware of what their rivals are developing and what they are likely to launch at the annual trade shows, and they are usually in a position to react or launch something of their own.

The component manufacturers are competing in a volatile and fickle market (who had heard of MTB/VTT in 1985?). Currency fluctuations and shifting tariff levels can exacerbate losses or reduce profits. Despite all these negative points, the manufacturers continue to operate. Apart from the fact that they are all good at what they do, the reason that they are able to cope with such developments is knowledge. They are aware of their competitor's movements and developments. They are aware of who their nearest competitors are. They also know how quickly (or whether) their competitors are likely to react to new product launches. Such knowledge comes from analysis: of the market, of the key players within market segments and by developing profiles of those competitors.

The manner in which such analysis should be undertaken will be outlined in this chapter. Market knowledge about competitors is as important as consumer and product knowledge for an organisation which wants to be successful in the 1990s.

## INTRODUCTION

Chapter 14 concentrated on the basic concepts of business strategy and the strategic process. This chapter will concentrate on the way in which markets and competitors may be identified and analysed. One of the best recognised authors in this area of business strategy is Michael Porter.

His 1980s texts, *Competitive Strategy* (1980) and *Competitive Advantage* (1985), may be considered as among the books which began the debate about how markets and competitors should be analysed. There have subsequently been many protagonists in the debate; a number will be recognised and their ideas discussed throughout this chapter.

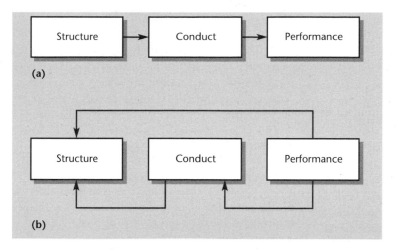

**Figure 15.1 S–C–P**

(a) The simple deterministic relationship. Mason and Bain are commonly associated with this simple model.

(b) With Scherer's feedback loops. These recognise that there is more to the relationship than simple one-way cause and effect.

# THE ECONOMIC PERSPECTIVE: THE NEOCLASSICAL PARADIGM (S–C–P)

The structure of competition may be taken as an analogy, or an indicator of the likely managerial conduct and corporate performances within an industry. Such thinking is based on the S–C–P paradigm of the neoclassical economists. S–C–P stands for **Structure–Conduct–Performance**.

S–C–P describes a deterministic relationship, where the structure of the industry or market is taken to affect and determine managerial conduct, which in turn has an effect on corporate performance. This relationship was first developed by an economist called Mason; however, Bain and Scherer are perhaps more readily recognised as proponents of the framework. The initial model was a simple, linear model, as has already been described. This may be seen in Figure 15.1(a).

Scherer is credited with adding feedback loops to the model. These feedback loops were an attempt to recognise and include the effects that conduct and performance may have on the structure of an industry or market over time; *see* Figure 15.1(b). Even in such a model, however, there is, for many critics, an overemphasis of the role played by structural aspects. They do not believe that the conduct and performance of organisations within a market or industry are so primarily dependent on the structure within which the organisations are operating.

Such a counter argument may be valid. Under S–C–P analysis, an organisation operating within a monopoly market structure would be expected to act to maintain higher than competitive prices, artificially to restrict quantities produced and sold and

thus to make supernormal profits. Such a development is logical. However, there are monopolists who do not act in such a manner. Indeed, there may be times when a monopolist has to change its conduct and performance in order to maintain its position as such. New entrants may be in a position to enter and transform the market into a competitive oligopoly. In such a case, the prudent reaction of the monopolist would be to lower prices (to a limit level; *see* Chapter 9) and to increase the supply of goods or services in the marketplace. Obviously, in this case, the conduct and performance of the monopolist are not dictated by the market structure. Conduct and performance have been dictated by the conduct (in proposing to enter markets) of other organisations.

The S–C–P paradigm is mentioned in this chapter, which is concerned with structural and environmental analysis, because many of the frameworks developed by strategists are based on the assumptions of S–C–P. This will become clearer as the appropriate frameworks are introduced. Remember that the S–C–P paradigm has its detractors. Many economists are extremely critical of this neoclassically and mechanistically based framework. Although there is a case for attempting to analyse industries and competitors in order to gain strategic insight, the cautions provided by the critics of the framework should be borne in mind.

# PORTER'S FIVE FORCES MODEL OF COMPETITIVE RIVALRY

The first stage in the analysis of the industry and its incumbent and potential competitors is an analysis of the forces causing the rivalry within the industry itself. Porter holds that there are five forces existing within any industry at any one time, found in different combinations and causing different levels of competitive rivalry in that industry, depending on the type of industry under analysis, the time of the analysis etc.

In setting up the model, Porter defines the industry as any group of firms which are in competition with each other, regardless of recognised or standard industrial classifications (SIC as they are known in the UK). The definition of competition is based on the substitutability (or cross-price elasticity of demand) between products. This is useful because it is notoriously difficult to define the boundaries of the industry or market. Even the cross-price elasticity of demand which measures the substitutability between products requires precise definition. For example, the cross-price elasticity of demand for butter and margarine is likely to be higher than the cross-price elasticity of demand for two products within a 'spreads' market.

As a result of his definition, Porter negates the need to consider geographic boundaries, similarities in manufacturing processes and so on. For the purposes of making a **Five Forces Analysis**, it is assumed that the industry boundaries are already defined. (This can actually be used as a criticism and will be developed later on in this chapter.)

Identification of the major components relating to each of the five forces can lead to an assessment of the relative strengths and weaknesses of the players, as a group within the industry, and thus highlight the possibilities for an organisation to exploit the possible changes within the industry over time. The organisations' ability to defend their position or to influence an attack on potential entrants or competitors will depend on the extent of the competitive rivalry within the industry.

The Porter model of industry analysis which uses the five forces is outlined in Figure 15.2.

The main consideration of the analysis is identifying the key issues relating to:

■ threat of entry
■ threat of substitution
■ power of suppliers
■ power of buyers.

The combination or the manner of interaction of these forces will determine the intensity of rivalry within the market or industry.

The fact that all industries will have different profiles will mean that each industry will have different factors contributing to competitive rivalry, both compared to other industries and over time.

## Threat of entry

The threat of entry exists when potential competitors to incumbents are interested in entering, or look likely to enter, the market by placing their goods or services for sale. Threat of entry is consid-

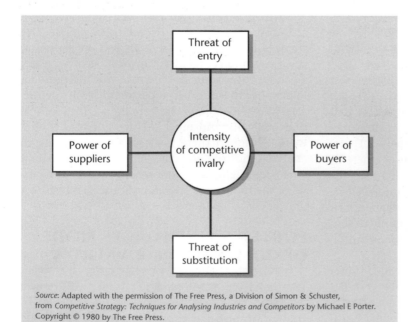

**Figure 15.2 Porter's Five Forces of Competitive Rivalry**

*Source*: Adapted with the permission of The Free Press, a Division of Simon & Schuster, from *Competitive Strategy: Techniques for Analysing Industries and Competitors* by Michael E Porter. Copyright © 1980 by The Free Press.

ered to be those actions which are likely to evoke retaliation from the incumbents. The incumbents' ability to set up or exploit barriers to entry is defined as the 'height' of the entry barriers. The barriers typically recognised are listed and (where necessary) explained below:

■ Economies of scale, savings arising from operation at high volumes of production.
■ Product differentiation, which induces advertising expenditure to develop brand loyalty for entrant's products.
■ Large levels of capital requirements, relating to the set-up and entry costs which an entrant would incur.
■ Switching costs for customers, between the product of the existing organisation(s) and that of the entrant. The higher the switching costs, the harder the entrant will have to work to convince customers to change products.
■ Distribution channels, to get the product to the point of sale. These are possibly already exploited and may be well developed. The more this is the case, the harder it will be for the entrant to develop their own channels.
■ Cost disadvantages which are independent of scale, in addition to the above.

There also exist other non-cost savings which may be made, such as learning curve effects, acquirement of subsidies and technology (all of these would have the effect of moving the whole LRAC curve downwards). It is possible for experience and learning curve effects to be reduced or negated as a result of purchase of such expertise by competitors and entrants. Such purchases may be made by takeover, merger or as a result of buying expertise possessed by consultants. Consequently, the height of barriers to entry may be eroded over time.

The relevance of economies of scale should not be ignored, however. The propensity for putting an entrant at a permanent cost disadvantage can be explored with reference to both cost and experience. If economies of scale gained by the incumbent are large enough relative to total market demand, an early move to restrict entrants' capacity will not leave enough residual demand for them to be competitive. In such cases, competitors who wish to enter must invest heavily and still risk entering a competition to fill the left-over market

capacity. Otherwise, they will face higher costs which will prevent them from competing if they enter on a smaller scale. Therefore they will either enter at an immediate disadvantage, or they will be deterred from investing at all.

## Threat of substitution

Substitutes to the product or service of the industry under analysis are considered to be those products which perform the same function. The same function may be confirmed by investigation of the cross-price elasticities of demand between products and services considered to be within the same market or industry. Although other markets or industries could also potentially provide substitutes, the beauty of the cross-price elasticity measure is that boundaries and industry definitions do not matter, merely the substitutability between products or services.

When analysing the level of the threat of substitution for an industry's product, it is quite possible that the substitute offers superior price performance compared to the incumbents' product due to a tradeoff with input development costs. Therefore the threat of substitution may well be increased for the incumbents as a result of previous expenditure on developments in experience or knowledge. Competitors will enter and exploit the knowledge of processes, products or the marketing efforts made by the incumbent without the related costs. In many economies, to protect such developments, developers of both products and processes are able to patent their inventions. Patents allow the developers to exploit profits on their product for a given period of time. After patent expiry, the market is open to all-comers. In such situations, if the market is attractive, then substitute products may become available. Competition usually pushes the market price level down.

---

◆ **Exercise 15.1**

The threats of substitution and entry increase when patents expire or when technological developments spread to other firms. Why does an increased threat of entry or substitution lower the price charged by incumbents? Are there any examples of such events which readily spring to mind?

---

◆ **CASE STUDY 15.1**

# Fast food: hunting the Big Mac in Africa

Zulu dancers and a visual feast of Africana were due on November 11th to greet the opening in Johannesburg of the first McDonald's hamburger restaurant in sub-Saharan Africa. But there was one tiny hitch. South Africa's supreme court ruled last month that the American restaurant chain does not own its trademarks in the country, and that it could not stop local rivals from themselves trading under the same (or a similar) name.

This Big Mac affair began when McDonald's tried to stop two South African companies, Dax Prop (which operates a restaurant called MacDonalds in Durban) and Joburgers Drive-Inn Restaurant from using the same name. Indignant, these firms applied two years ago to have McDonald's removed from South Africa's trademark register. They argued that in the five years since McDonald's had last registered its name, the firm had neither used it nor intended to do so, and by law had thus forfeited its trademark rights. Last month, the supreme court upheld their argument, and struck McDonald's from the books.

McDonald's had by then already picked and trained two South Africans, one black, one white, as franchisees of its first two restaurants. It was enraged. Under the law as it stood when the South Africans lodged their case, a company would indeed lose its ownership of a trademark if it did not use it within five years – unless it was prevented by 'special circumstances'. McDonald's, which first registered its name in the 1960s and had renewed it regularly until the mid-1980s, argued that it had faced 'special circumstances' in the form of sanctions against apartheid.

The court disagreed. It was not convinced that McDonald's failure to open up, even after America's sanction against South Africa were lifted in 1991, was

an anti-apartheid gesture, as the firm claimed. Instead, declared the judge, it was because 'South Africa simply did not rank on McDonald's list of priorities'. The judge also rejected a separate application made by McDonald's to prevent South Africans imitating its name, under a new law which protects 'well-known trademarks'. The judge told a stunned audience that McDonald's was not well-known in South Africa – among rich whites, perhaps, but not in the black, television-less majority.

This complex legal battle has not daunted McDonald's. It has been granted the right to an appeal, which will probably take place next year; until then, the supreme court judgment is suspended. 'In the meantime', says Carter Drew, head of McDonald's South Africa, 'McDonald's is entitled in law to use its marks and to legitimately operate in South Africa.'

But the South Africans also use the same argument. This week, days before the American McDonald's, Dax opened its own new MacDonalds restaurant in Johannesburg. 'There is no registered proprietor of the trademark as far as we're concerned,' says Shaun Ryan, Dax's lawyer.

Some among those South Africans who do recognise McDonald's as a famous American cultural icon seem delighted by what they see as its failure to trample all over Africans. But the affair has left the government, which begs Americans to invest in its country, red-faced. That may be why Trevor Manuel, the trade minister, said he would ask the justice minister to try to speed up the appeal. The golden arches may yet march across the veldt.

*Source*: © *The Economist*, London, 11 November 1995. Reprinted with permission.

### Comment on the case study

The ability of incumbents to prevent or discourage entry by creating barriers to entry is essential to their success in maintaining power within a market. This article shows clearly that McDonald's has been unable to protect its market position and to use its name as a barrier to entry/to reduce the threat of substitution within the fast-food industry. Because it is not begun operating a restaurant within the required time period, claiming special circumstances, it is no longer the registered holders of the trademark (name) in South Africa.

As a result, another fast-food outlet will be able to use the MacDonald's name to operate under in

South Africa. It will therefore be able to take advantage of the US chain's globally recognised reputation and even advertising campaigns to boost its own sales levels. The other restaurant will be exploiting the promotional experience and expenditure of McDonald's for its own benefit. It will therefore be hoping that it does not have to spend as much on advertising as it would have to if it was (a) building up recognition of its own name, (b) competing for custom with McDonald's.

There are costs involved here, however. The South African government has been embarrassed by the issue. Also, as (the original) McDonald's fights against the ruling which has given rise to this situation, both sides will undoubtedly run up huge legal bills.

## Buyer power

There are a number of factors which can add to the power of the buyer, or consumer, of the industry's product. These are listed and explained below:

■ Volume purchased relative to the number of supplier organisations within the industry; the greater the volume bought from a supplier, the greater the potential power of the buyer.
■ Significance of the purchase to the buyer; the greater the significance, the greater the authority the buyer will desire over the purchases made.
■ Level of standardisation or differentiation of the product; the greater the standardisation, the easier it is for the buyer to move between suppliers and the more likely they are to gain power.
■ Low switching costs mean that the penalty to the buyer of moving between suppliers within the industry is reduced, thus improving the chances of such actions taking place. This is particularly true where there is a change in prices or relations between the supplier and the buyer.
■ Low buyer profits will induce the buyer to pressure suppliers to gain the best possible deal from them; again, demanding greater power.

■ Threat of backward integration increases the potential power of the buyer.
■ If the buyer is not reliant on the product to maintain the quality of its own production, then again the buyer is in a much stronger position relative to the supplier.

## Supplier power

If suppliers to organisations within an industry possess high levels of power over those organisations, they are in a better position to demand better deals with reference to the sales of the raw materials or intermediate products they provide. The power of the suppliers to the organisations within an industry can be seen to increase/improve as certain conditions exist:

■ Low numbers of suppliers relative to receivers means that the suppliers are able to choose the organisations they supply to.
■ Fewer substitutes for the supplier's product increase the power of the supplier, as switching costs increase and opportunities decrease.
■ Increasing levels of importance placed on the supplier's product by the producer will increase the power of the supplier.
■ Increasing importance to the supplier of the product being supplied will also increase the power of the supplier.

## ◆ CASE STUDY 15.2

## Paternalistic relations: increasing buyer power

The late 1980s and early 1990s saw great increases in buyer power as a result of the trend for working closely with established suppliers to set up **just-in-time (JIT)** supply chains. JIT contracts are often long term and involve training and accreditation supplied by the buyer. The buyer will often enter into JIT contracts with many different intermediate product suppliers. The suppliers may then become dependent on the buyer for business, but the buyer has several purchase options for the same product, should any supplier attempt to exploit their position. The power gained by the buyer can be considerable. The larger the buyer, obviously, the more power they are able to wield, even to the extent that they demand exclusive product contracts with their suppliers. It is frequently argued that such agreements increase the backward vertical integration of the buyers without increasing the level of risk they face.

In the UK examples of such agreements may be seen in the automotive industry. Nissan and other Japanese car manufacturers operate widely on a paternalistic, JIT basis with their suppliers. Similarly, retailer Marks & Spencer is famous for selling only own-brand products. It sources and contracts products from a variety of suppliers in the UK and Europe. Each supplier tends to be dependent on Marks & Spencer for their business, while Marks & Spencer dictates quality, personnel practices and other internal processes to these suppliers. It also requires that its products are exclusive and that the suppliers do not supply them elsewhere. To maintain power, Marks & Spencer does not buy any range exclusively from any one supplier; the risk is spread over several suppliers. Thus, strike, dispute or mutiny on the part of suppliers or their employees will not have a drastic effect on Marks & Spencer.

*Source*: Authors.

- As switching costs for the consumer increase, so too does the power of the supplier.
- Threat of forward integration: as this becomes more viable the supplier gains greater power relative to the buyer due to the threat imposed.

---

◆ **Exercise 15.2**

JIT contracts can increase the power of either buyers or suppliers, depending on industry conditions. Under what conditions will the supplier benefit? When will the buyer benefit?

---

## Intensity of rivalry

The combination of the factors above, and the interdependence of the competitors in the industry itself, together produce the intensity of rivalry within the industry. For example, high supplier power, matched with a high threat of entry, high buyer power and a very real threat of substitution for the incumbent's product, puts the incumbent in a weak bargaining position and is likely to make the industry in question highly competitive.

If the industry in question is also dominated by a few organisations, the analysis and discussion from Chapters 9, 10 and 11 with reference to oligopolies may be applied.

Porter outlines several situations in which the competitive rivalry of an industry will increase. These are listed and explained below:

- As competitors in the industry increase, so too does the competitive rivalry in that industry.
- Slow industry growth means that the organisations within it have to compete more fiercely to capture for themselves the growth available.
- Increasing fixed and capital costs induce an organisation to compete for greater market share/business in order to recoup the outlay.
- A lack of differentiation in the industry means that consumers will, and are easily able to, purchase from any of the competitors, and activity to capture the marginal consumer therefore increases.
- When an organisation's capacity increases are dependent on large capital resources, competitors will be anxious to sell each unit of the extra production.
- Increasing diversity of competitors' products will mean that each competitor will have to compete more fiercely in order to gain and maintain a niche in the marketplace.
- The greater the strategic stakes within an industry, the greater the competitive rivalry in that industry.
- High exit barriers mean that firms have a heightened interest in remaining in the market/industry – competitive rivalry thus increases in line with increases in/or greater barriers to exit.

---

## ◆ CASE STUDY 15.3

# Iberia faces bumpy landing   FT

Spain's big state-controlled monopolies, such as Repsol, the energy consortium, and the telecommunications group Telefonica have adapted well to liberalisation, are profitable and tap the markets regularly. But Iberia is an exception to the rule.

The national airline has been a casualty of aggressive price strategies spearheaded in Europe by British Airways and of increasing internal competition. Two private sector companies, Spanair and Air Europa, have begun to fly routes that were once Iberia's preserve. Travellers, now enjoying choice and cheaper fares, have been the main beneficiaries of liberalisation.

The creation of small regional airlines, such as the Valencia-based Air Nostrum which expects to transport 250 000 passengers by December in its first full year of operations, point to the potential buoyancy of the domestic air travel sector following the removal of its protectionist wraps. Air Nostrum, which flies Fokker

50s, was one of the first ventures to be undertaken by the wealthy Serratosa family after it sold a large cement business that it controlled to Mexico's Cemex group in 1992.

If the growth in new companies illustrates domestic entrepreneurial initiative at its best, Iberia, which lost Pta44.1bn ($358.8m) last year and Pta69.5bn in 1993, represents Spain's state sector at its worst. A succession of chairmen – four in little more than five years – has contributed towards an erratic business strategy and the company's strongly entrenched unions have hindered management efforts to reduce its high cost base.

Iberia is not the only European carrier that is struggling to adapt to competition but it faces one of the bumpiest landings in the industry as it approaches the deregulated runways. The company's losses and its mounting debt burden have virtually wiped out a

Pta120bn emergency injection of public funds three years ago and the Madrid government is currently lobbying Brussels for authorisation to plough a further Pta130bn into the airline to stave off bankruptcy.

Part of the debt burden has been incurred by an ambitious strategy to buy into Latin American airlines, including Aerolineas Argentinas. The acquisitions have now become an embarrassment because an Iberia alliance with United Airlines that would have linked its Latin American network with the US has proved still-born. The company says that its search for an international partner is even more pressing than its need for funds. The planned recapitalisation follows an agreement at the end of last year between Iberia's management and unions to cut wages by 8.3 per cent and to shed 3500 of the 25 000 labour force by 1998. This is the first serious attempt to cut Iberia's cost base but already questions have been raised over the legality of the funds and the plan's effectiveness.

An EU ruling on the funding request is expected within weeks and Mr Juan Manuel Eguiagaray, the industry minister, says a Brussels ban would be 'unacceptable' because the subsidy is to be used solely to scale down Iberia's size. But the request will be strongly contested by rival European companies, and also by AECA, the association that groups Spain's private airlines, on the grounds that it flouts the EU's 'one time, last time' policy on subsidies.

Mr Felipe Navio, AECA's chairman, argues that the viability plan will not succeed in salvaging the airline. 'The only solution for Iberia is to adjust its costs to those of its competitors and to concentrate on certain routes.' The plan falls well short of the cost-cutting measures that Iberia's management had sought. Faced with strike action, the company abandoned its bid to reduce wages by 15 per cent, agreed to make up back-pay that it had previously said it was in no position to honour, raised incentives for voluntary redundancies and increased union representation on the company's board.

One of the more ominous aspects of the agreement was that the management bowed to pressure from the powerful pilots' union and wound up regular routes flown by its small and profitable Viva Air unit. Productivity at Viva Air, a former charter operator, is far higher than Iberia's and it began to compete directly with the flag carrier three years ago precisely in order to reduce the parent airline's cost base.

Iberia's management is now seeking to cut costs radically at Aviaco, its domestic subsidiary airline which is particularly vulnerable to the deregulation of internal routes. A strike by Aviaco pilots this month suggests that a new climbdown may occur.

Improved productivity is vital for Iberia because in addition to the increased competition prompted by deregulation, the airline has to battle against the charter carriers which account for some 80 per cent of Spain's air traffic.

The charter business plays havoc with Iberia's revenues and is the downside of Spain's lucrative tourism industry as far as the national carrier is concerned. Although Iberia has comparable unit costs to Lufthansa, its revenue increased by a mere 7 per cent between 1990 and 1993 against a 22 per cent rise posted by the German airline over the same period.

Iberia's costs, measured in available seat kilometres, stand at US11.5c and are at a middle ranking level but the airline has to slash them to about the US8c level registered by British Airways, the best performer among the big European carriers, if it is to compete effectively with the charter companies.

Unless the government-carrier forcefully addresses its unsustainable costs base, new public funding will only buy it time for a while. Iberia risks being elbowed out of the international market and relinquishing its own Spanish skies to the private sector.

*Source: Financial Times,* 30 June 1995. Reprinted with permission.

## Comment on the case study

The impact of competition, the need to sell extra units of capacity in order to remain competitive and the need to understand the industry may be clearly seen in this case study. Iberia, Spain's national airline, is suffering problems because it is facing domestic competition from new/start-up airlines which are operating on a regional basis. There is also a danger that Iberia will not be able to purchase landing slots and thus protect its current timetable as the market is deregulated.

Further problems have arisen for Iberia as it has attempted to break into other international markets by forming alliances with other airlines. These have not materialised and so Iberia is now left without international links.

Overall, the intensity of rivalry in Iberia's operating industry is great. There are pressures from the domestic operators and also from international competitors. Iberia is not in a strong position to fight off such competition. The airline is looking for government subsidy (which it may not receive as a result of EU rules) to help with its debt. Confidence is not boosted when it is noted that Iberia is a high-cost airline with reference to the industry standard cost per passenger kilometre benchmark.

Iberia, it would seem, is indeed in line for a bumpy landing. This has been the fate of many of Europe's state-owned or newly privatised airlines in the volatile European air-passenger industry.

## Changes and developments

The intensity of rivalry will change over time within any market in line with its lifecycle. A more mature industry will see greater rivalry, due to the fact that competitors are trying to make ever-increasing gains from what is essentially an environment which is increasingly stable and less dynamic than it will have been in the growth stages. This effect will be heightened in the decline stage of the industry lifecycle or, as it gains a new lease of life, an extension.

This will be the case in 1997 for the European airline industry, when any airline will be able to enter and operate flights between European cities. Such a change in the industry will undoubtedly make it more competitive as potential entrants battle to gain the right to operate on profitable routes against the incumbents.

By analysis of the Five Forces of Competitive Rivalry, Porter claims that the position and situation of the industry in question may be derived. By highlighting the major factors within each of the five forces, the potential opportunities and threats pertaining to the industry may be extrapolated.

By further analysis and examination of the forces in detail, a strategy for longevity and success within the industry may be developed which will be coherent with the findings. The factors highlighted in the Five Forces Analysis will either be defended against or attacked.

In other words, once the forces affecting competition in an industry and their underlying causes have been diagnosed, the organisation is in a position to identify its strengths and weaknesses relative to the industry. From a strategic standpoint, the crucial strengths and weaknesses are the firm's posture with relation to the underlying causes of each competitive force. Where does the organisation stand:

- Against substitutes?
- Against the sources of entry barriers?
- In coping with rivalry from established competitors?

Furthermore, the analysis gives a vital picture of the industry in which the organisation is operating, or wishes to enter. By undertaking the Five Forces Analysis, an understanding of the industry, its quirks and its main characteristics becomes apparent. From this, a definition of the industry may be developed and also a guide to its dimensions: the geographical boundaries, the key barriers to entry and also the height of those barriers. Additionally, it may be possible to ascertain which are the key factors within the industry; details which can assist and provide a context for intra-industry analysis. The Five Forces Analysis is therefore a useful tool in the initial stages of analysing the strategy of other incumbent competitors in an industry.

One fault of this analysis is that it only provides a snapshot of the current state of the industry. Future potential movements are very much ignored. The implication of this criticism is that the model is a general tool which could be applied to numerous situations, and as such the results are of a general nature. To be used effectively, the framework needs to be customised by the analyst concerned to make it appropriate and relevant to the context of the case in question.

However, Porter's intention was not to provide an all-encompassing analytical framework. The fact that the analysis is performed and that the analyst becomes aware of the players within the industry, the rivalry between the players and the key factors within, it provides the insights that Porter was advocating. By going through the processes outlined by Porter, the analyst will gain that information and identify competitors and key competitive factors within the industry.

Once the five forces have been identified and analysed and the definition and dimensions decided on, strategic groups analysis, or competitive analysis of groups, may be performed.

## COMPETITIVE ANALYSIS OF GROUPS

The next stage in making a structural analysis is the **competitive analysis of groups**, operating within the industry or market identified in the five-forces analysis. Competitive analysis of groups may be an analysis of intra-industry and inter-group rivalry. Consequently, the reason for the superior performance of any one competitor over others may be identified.

There are a number of strategic options open to any competitor in any group. Examples of such options are: the level of specialisation; the manner/nature of product development, by organisational push or consumer pull; the quality of the product; the level of integration utilised by the organisation; the cost position of the product etc. By placing together competitors with similar profiles in terms of what are considered the key characteristics or strategic options, groups of competitors may be derived. These groups will contain firms which have more in common with each other than mere membership of the same industry.

It should be noted that an industry could contain any number of groups, depending on the factors at work there. It is possible for all individual competitors within an industry to be individual groups, or for all competitors to be members of a given group.

In order to carry out an analysis within the industry, for example to revel the particular reasons for the superior profitability and performance of one organisation over another within the same group, a **strategic groups** analysis may be performed.

Such analysis is useful for all organisations which seek to understand their competition. It is likely to yield a better understanding of the competitive characteristics of competitors and the reasons for their successes. It also allows the analyst to ask how likely, or possible, it is for the organisation to move from one strategic group to another – rather than from industry to industry, which is probably more difficult.

When considering a strategic groups analysis, it is necessary first to identify the strategic groupings to be considered. Subsequently, these groups can be 'mapped' with reference to given parameters of major areas of competition or the key mobility barriers (as derived from the industry analysis). The final stage is to investigate each of these groups, as mapped with reference again to a competitive-type analysis, such as an *intra-group* Porter's five forces, or the competitor response profile (*see* later section).

Strategic groups analysis may be preferable to portfolio analysis because it provides a clearer overview of the nature of the competition. For the purposes of providing a diagnostic snapshot, the considerations of portfolio analysis as outlined by Ansoff are:

■ It is not concerned with the current position. The analysis put forward is in fact concerned with the attractiveness of diversification strategies etc. This is something that can surely only be performed after the current situation has been determined.

■ It is a tool more appropriate to internal rather than external analysis of the portfolio and portfolio mix, due to the fact that the analysis is concerned with forming the future intentions of the organisation.

Portfolio analysis is therefore something which is more appropriate for consideration once the current position has been defined, the current strategy examined and recommendations for the future have been made. In contrast, strategic groups analysis provides an insight into the current position of the organisation and its competitors on both a local and industry basis.

Strategic groupings of firms should be considered when there is a need to be able to analyse the reasons for the greater success of one firm over another within that group. The analysis is therefore based on a generic strategy approach which leads to an identification of the developed distinctive competencies of a given member of the group. As Wright, Pringle and Kroll (1992) state:

> Most industries are comprised of a number of business units that compete more directly with certain businesses in the industry than others. Groups of direct competitors are identified by the similarity of their strategic profiles, and each collection of direct competitors is termed a strategic group. . . . In most cases, each business unit attempts to develop a distinctive competence relative to its competitors in the same strategic group. This distinctive competence can come from an organisation's particular strengths in any functional area.

In most industries, organisations will adopt very different competitive strategies about the range of products they produce or sell, their organisational structure and scope (including vertical integration). They are therefore likely to achieve different levels of market share. Some organisations will also persistently outperform others in terms of the rate of return on invested capital. The first step in structural analysis within industries is to identify and characterise the strategies of the significant competitors with reference to these critical, or major, strategic factors. Usually, within any industry, there are a small number of strategic groups which may be identified as representative of the structure of the industry as a whole.

The first stage in performing a strategic groups analysis is to identify the similarities between firms in the same groups in terms of strategy. The second stage is to identify the key dimensions or mobility barriers common to the firms within each group, so that the parameters or boundaries of the group may be identified. This done, the barriers to entry or exit to each group and those affecting movement between groups will assist identification of the common strategic (and other) characteristics which cause groups of organisations to cluster together within the industry.

Strategic groups may be mapped, to give a pictorial representation of the strategic position and posture of the competitors within the industry. The strategic groups are considered on two dimensions. The axes are found by identification of the two main differentiating factors between groups. These are called the mobility barriers. The rationale behind this is that barriers to movement between groups is a valid dimension on which to measure and map a set of groups within the boundaries of any industry. Movement between groups is commonly considered to be unlikely, due to differences in the expectations and objectives of the organisations within different groups and the similarity of the expectations and objectives inside the group.

An example of group mapping may be seen in Figure 15.3. Here the case of the aircraft manufacturing industry is explored. The main manufacturers in each of the identified groups have been named. It is clear that Cessna, for example, does not compete directly with Boeing.

---

◆ **Exercise 15.3**

In the case of the aircraft manufacturing industry, including such manufacturers as Boeing and Cessna, what do you consider to be the main mobility barriers or dimensions? That is, if you were mapping the competitors within the industry by placing them in groups with their close competitors, which labels for the axes would you use?

---

The industry has been grouped in this case with reference to the key dimensions of 'size of aircraft manufactured' and 'sales coverage', where sales coverage refers to the extent of geographical sales made: domestic or international.

The resultant mapping is one which sees four groups emerge. In keeping with the logic behind groupings, it is unlikely that Boeing and Astra target sales to the same market segment. They are therefore not directly in competition with each other, despite operating in the same industry.

Group mapping can highlight the fact that there are marginal groups which exist within any

industry. It can also highlight the likely trends and reactions of groups to changes in the environment as a result of their posture. The directions and trends of movement of groups may also be highlighted by the mapping exercise.

Porter recognises that industry rivalry may be mapped in terms of the strategic groups identified. The intensity of rivalry may be defined by the number of groups, the degree of product differentiation, etc. Thus, a mapping of intensity of rivalry may also be derived. This will assist, or clarify, the analyst's understandings of the Five Forces Analysis findings.

## Changing group boundaries

Finally, with reference to the process of strategic groups analysis, it is within the ability of firms to change the boundaries of their particular groups and hence the industry, and thus influence the industry evolution. The propensity for this to occur may be derived from analysis of the trends within the industry, the activities of the groups in that industry at any point in time and the existing competitive rivalry.

Such findings must be linked in and related to the stages of industry evolution: the industry lifecycle. It is necessary, but not sufficient, to be able to identify the major competitors, their likely future actions and reactions, etc. It is also necessary to identify the stage of evolution, as this will give an indication of the constraints and opportunities within the industry context.

### Emerging industries

An emerging industry, for instance, will contain 'embryonic' companies and their spinoffs. There will be a variety of opportunities for entry and action within the industry. At the same time, however, there are likely to be high levels of customer confusion, due to the new nature of the industry and a lack of information about it. An emerging industry can be a completely new industry, or one evolving from the decline or split of another.

Emerging industries are newly formed or reformed industries that have been created by technological innovations, shifts in relative cost relationships, emergence of new customer needs, or other economic and sociological changes that elevate a new product or service to the level of a potentially viable business opportunity. However, there may be problems for competitors within emerging industries, as a result of consumer confusion. The multitude of similar products, made

**Figure 15.3 Strategic groups in the aircraft manufacturing industry**

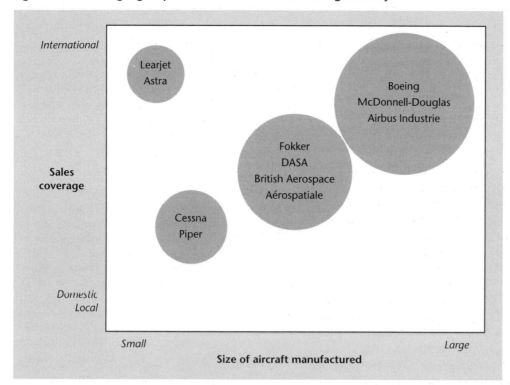

Using the dimensions for the mapping of 'size of aircraft manufactured' against 'sales coverage', it may be seen that the smaller jet manufacturers, Learjet and Astra, are in a relatively small group which serve an international customer base. A larger group of small, non-jet manufacturers exists, where the likes of Cessna operate.

The other two groups illustrated are jet manufacturers. The more localised in terms of sales coverage, 'minibus' manufacturers Fokker, DASA and British Aerospace, may be seen as incumbent in one group. In the other group are the major players in aircraft manufacture, Boeing, McDonnell-Douglas and Airbus Industrie.

Clearly, the largest volume (money value) is this latter group. This is represented on the mapping by the size of the encompassing circle. The smallest group would appear to be the small jet manufacturers' group; note the size of the circle here.

available by the competing organisations, differing in terms of quality, different brand names and specification attributes, increases complexity for the consumer. Until the industry is more stable, products are standardised and industry norms established, the industry is extremely competitive and volatile. Consumers may defer purchases until the product norms are established, to reduce the risk of purchasing a product with technological attributes which become obsolete in the medium term, when they will have to purchase another, 'normalised' product.

## ◆ CASE STUDY 15.4

## Not perfect enough

There was a time, not long ago, when a personal computer and WordPerfect were virtually synonymous. If you used a word processor (and who didn't?) you probably saw visions of 'F7' keys in your sleep, along with the rest of WordPerfect's perversely arbitrary key commands. Microsoft may have owned the operating system (whatever that was), but for most users WordPerfect owned the desktop. No more: today,

Case study 15.4 *continued*

Microsoft's World and its other software programs dominate this market. And WordPerfect has become an ailing orphan.

Just 19 months ago Novell, a rival software firm, brought WordPerfect (the company that made the eponymous program) in order, it said, to compete head-to-head with Microsoft. On October 30th, Novell raised the white flag: it said it wants to get out of this sort of software and is seeking a buyer for WordPerfect.

It is easy to see why Novell has lost heart. Since WordPerfect's heyday in the late 1980s, when it had nearly 70% of the word-processor market, its share has fallen to less than 20%. In the fast-growing market for software 'suites' – generally, a packaged word processor, spreadsheet and database from the same manufacturer – WordPerfect has a share of just 5%, compared to Microsoft's 90%. Novell will not bring out a new version of WordPerfect for Microsoft's new Windows 95 operating system until next year; analysts reckon it will pay heavily for this mistake in the peak Christmas buying season.

Things looked different early last year, when Novell's then-chairman, Ray Noorda traded $855m worth of his firm's shares for Wordperfect. Novell was the world's second-largest PC software company, with an enviable 66% of the fast-growing market in networking software.

But as it has struggled to absorb the fading WordPerfect, Novell has been slow in launching new products in its core networking market; this delay has allowed Microsoft to get a foot in this market (its share climbed to 22%, to Novell's 35%, in the second quarter of this year, according to International Data, a consultancy). And in the booming market for Internet software, where Novell's networking experience gave it a natural advantage, it has been overtaken by more nimble competitors. In early October, Novell warned that its latest quarterly earnings would be less than half last year's figures.

For the rest of the software industry, the lesson is all too clear: take on Microsoft at your peril. Novell is

a deep-pocketed giant and WordPerfect, much improved from its 'F7' days, is still an excellent word-processing program with many loyal users. It didn't matter. Neither does it matter that many in the industry think that Word Pro, a word processor made by Lotus (a firm acquired by IBM earlier this year) is technically superior to Microsoft Word. Most software customers find it better to have the industry standard than any fringe candidate, however technically accomplished it may be.

Because Novell's announcement was unexpected (at least in timing), no potential buyers rushed forward. The unpredictable Mr Noorda might just be tempted to buy WordPerfect back. Analysts, casting around for more plausible candidates, have proposed Oracle, the second-largest software firm after Microsoft; Computer Associates, a mainframe software giant; and IBM itself, which has hinted that it is on the look out for further acquisitions. But Oracle, which is concentrating on databases and network software, has quietly indicated that it is not interested in word processors and the like. So has Computer Associates. And IBM is not officially commenting, although sources say it has not ruled out a bid.

Of all of these, IBM is the most plausible. Buying WordPerfect would give it both of Microsoft's main desktop software competitors; it might be able to mix and match its own software with that of WordPerfect to put together a more compelling package. If IBM was willing to pay $3.2 billion for Lotus, surely it can afford to buy WordPerfect for what analysts think will be a bargain price of between $200m and $300m? But IBM may have a bigger target in mind: Novell itself. Despite the firm's problems, Novell's software still runs most office networks. IBM could use that as a platform to do battle with Microsoft. IBM has tried for Novell before, and been foiled in part by the steep asking price. It may not be long before Novell becomes too cheap to pass up.

*Source*: © *The Economist*, London, 4 November 1995. Reprinted with permission.

### Comment on the case study

Consideration of the case will show that the software industry is maturing and changing direction in response to consumer requirements. In the late 1980s, possessing and using individual word-processing software was *de rigueur*. Organisations were happy to purchase multiple copies of *WordPerfect* (bought recently by Novell) and to also purchase copies of databases and spreadsheets for installation as required.

Since 1993, however, the market has changed. Many more organisations now operate software from a 'Windows' base, rather than directly through the Microsoft operating system (DOS). This, and the increased trend for local networks within organisations, has led to a reduced demand for standalone software packages such as *WordPerfect*. Instead, buyers require integrated packages which contain wordprocessing, spreadsheet, database and other facilities. The advantage of such integration is that the files created may be successfully imported, exported and merged between the different applications.

As a result of the change, *WordPerfect* has lost its dominant position as *the* wordprocessing package to run. Novell, its owner is keen to leave this market and is looking for buyers. It is more interested in maintaining its core market operations in network software.

Thus, the maturing market outlined has undergone changes in industry norms. This makes it clear that even norms are open to change and that markets may change direction as technology improves and different competitors become dominant.

### Fragmented industries

Later on in the lifecycle, after the growth stages, there is a possibility of fragmentation. This occurs in an older industry which for any of a variety of reasons has experienced a split. Typically, fragmented industries contain large numbers of small and medium-sized organisations serving a variety of consumer segments.

It is not possible to define a fragmented industry precisely. However, these may be identified in many areas of the economy. Typically, primary- and tertiary-sector activities are representative of fragmented industries.

### Mature industries

Further along the lifecycle there is a transition to maturity. Typically, this will be an industry's critical period. At this stage, growth is in decline, inducing increased competition for market share.

Consumers are more experienced, and costs and service become important considerations for consumers as they make their purchase decisions. Thus, the industry is much more competitive and consumers are more difficult to please. This could well mean that organisations will implement changes in their system of marketing, selling, management, distribution etc. *See* Figure 15.4 for the stages of the industry lifecycle.

## Mapping groupings

Returning to the competitive analysis of groups, once the major barriers to movement have been identified, it becomes possible to map the groupings and diagrammatically identify the various groups, their magnitude and dimensions with reference to the industry.

A strategic groups analysis will lead to identification of the opportunities and threats to the organisation now and in the future, but it is not without inaccuracies or faults.

First, any inaccuracies in the industry analysis will be perpetuated here, since it is based on and therefore includes the previous preconceptions about the industry.

Second, the changing nature of competition is also relevant. This can cause inaccuracies if not forecast/considered in the groups analysis.

Third, the definition of the key mobility barriers is important to the direction which the analysis takes. Thus, the analysis throughout provides only a general direction – not the complete answer to the question of strategy now and into the future.

**Figure 15.4 Stages of the industry lifecycle**

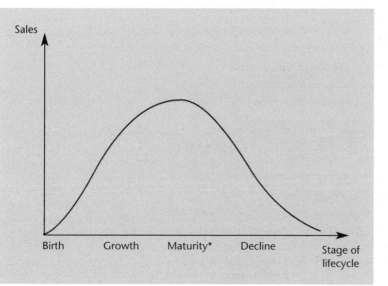

Very similar to the product lifecycle diagram, this is a simple way of representing the changes through which an industry goes as it develops and matures. Note that the industry is likely to fragment as it stabilises, or matures.*

In order to gain further insight into the analysis of the industry's competitors and their likely actions and reactions to activities and events, it is necessary to analyse the major or key competitors in more depth.

## COMPETITOR ANALYSIS: COMPETITOR RESPONSE PROFILING

The **competitor response profile** outlined by Porter offers a framework for the analyst to use when considering the position and capabilities of the major competitors in relation to those of the organisation under consideration. The outcome of the analysis will be a profile of competitors which either defines them as 'defensive' in their current strategies and actions and future likely movements, or 'offensive' (proactive in determining the future state of group and its competitive rivalry).

Such findings will allow the strategist to make an inference about the best 'battleground' for the future, based on the likely actions of competitors. Hence, situations or activities may be identified

where changes may be implemented in order to make gains.

Competitor analysis will identify the various strengths and weaknesses of the organisation's competitors in each of the strategic groups. Potential opportunities or threats within each strategic group will be highlighted or identified. These may be further utilised once the organisation's strategy, strengths and weaknesses have been examined and recommendations for future areas for expansion or divestment are identified.

The analysis considers in detail the propensity of competitors to move into new or different groups, the possibilities for forward and backward integration, and also the likelihood of growth or change in the current strategy. This may be done by considering the competitor's 'response profile' as a staged and logical analysis of its future goals, current strategy, assumptions about itself and the industry and its capabilities.

This type of analysis is not dissimilar to that described by Pearson (1992). In a chapter on 'Analysing the competitor', he claims that competitor analysis should concentrate on the assessment of competitors' relative strengths and weaknesses in terms of certain key strategic characteristics. That is,

**Figure 15.5 Pearson's framework for competitor analysis**

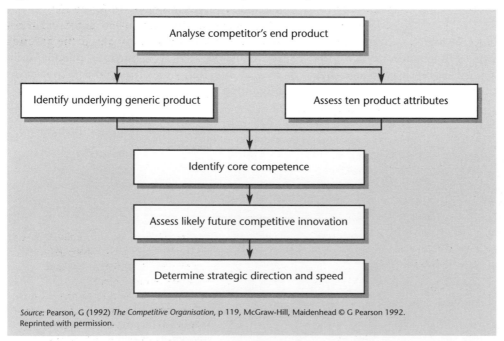

Source: Pearson, G (1992) *The Competitive Organisation*, p 119, McGraw-Hill, Maidenhead © G Pearson 1992. Reprinted with permission.

Here, the competitor's product is analysed in order to make assumptions about the competitor. The flowchart requires an identification and statement of the competitor's core competence in order to assess its potential for movement in the future. Additionally, the analyst is required to make a judgement about the speed at which the competitor is likely to be able to make any moves.

each competitor organisation's general position and level of activity in the market should be found by considering relative market shares, pricing policies and other competitive practices, such as the introduction of new products and new technologies. This relationship may be seen in Figure 15.5, Pearson's framework for competitor analysis.

Pearson criticises the Porter competitive response approach (or, as he calls it, the generic strategy) for its requirement of an infinitely detailed analysis of all areas – information which could not possibly be known to an observer. However, the model Pearson advocates, analysing the competitor's product at first hand, is also impossible in this respect.

◆ **Exercise 15.4**

What are the main characteristics of products which are easily analysed at first hand? What are the main characteristics of products which cannot easily be analysed at first hand?

In the case of manufactured products which are readily available and cheap enough to purchase, the analyst may relatively easily make such an analysis. However, does the purchase and use of a product actually give any insight onto a competitor's particular strengths, weaknesses and distinctive or unique abilities? Many critics would argue that they do not. Similarly, there are many products and services which cannot simply be purchased or sampled for the purposes of research and analysis. Pearson's approach has as many limitations as Porter's!

Bearing the above drawback in mind, however, each competitor response profile will give some indication of the competitor's level of satisfaction at present, potential movements in the future, vulnerabilities and possible retaliation to movements made by others in the group. The overall outcome, then, will be a summary of each competitor's likely response to changes in the group with reference to the concepts of 'offensive' or 'defensive' reactions.

Offensive refers to the competitor initiating action within the group or groups. This may be determined by considering the competitor's current level of satisfaction within the group, its likely movements and its capabilities or propensity for movement and proactivity relating to the current group or change of groups.

Defensive refers to the competitor reacting to movements by others within the group or groups. This may be determined by considering its weaknesses or vulnerabilities, likely provocations, propensity to and effectiveness of retaliation within a group, its reactive capabilities to actions by other group members and its abilities to maintain its position within the group given an offensive action by other members or an external instigator. Porter's competitive response profile is outlined in Figure 15.6.

Once such profiles have been constructed for competitors, it is possible to investigate the preferred

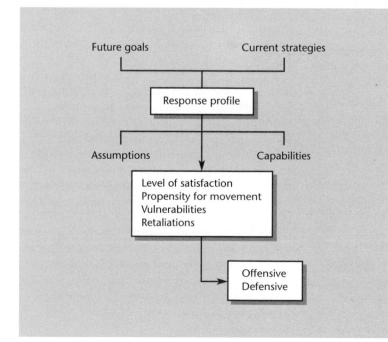

**Figure 15.6 Porter's competitor response profiling**

By identifying the key competitors' current strategies, future goals, capabilities and assumptions about the market, their individual response profiles may be constructed. These take into account and outline their attitudes to the market in terms of their level of satisfaction, propensity for movements and so on. In turn, this information may be used to classify the competitors as likely to be defensive/reactionary to actions or as offensive/proactive competitors.

position of the analyst's own organisation regarding its current strategy, future strategy and best moves for the future, if indeed the future strategy does not include these. It should be stressed at this point, however, that competitive analysis and competitor response profiles are limited in terms of actual (and not perceived) knowledge about various competitors because primary research is not possible or available.

When analysing competitors, it is possible to identify actions which will upset them and which may spark off bitter competition. It is also possible to identify actions which will give advantage without provoking retaliation. By being aware of and sensitive to competitors' key goals, such actions may be identified. The organisation will therefore be in a position to gauge the likely reaction and make contingency plans. A likely aggressive reaction requires more resources than a passive or defensive reaction.

For example, if analysis can identify a competitor's cash cows and harvest businesses on which the parent is trying to build, it may be possible to gain a position against such a cash cow if the actions do not threaten the competitor's cash flow. On the other hand, it would be more dangerous to attempt to make gains against a business which the competitor is attempting to build up or to which it has emotional attachments, such as strong brand identity or recognition.

Similarly, where a competitor relies on an aspect of its business to achieve stable sales, it may fight aggressively to protect that business. Such reactions even occur at the expense of profits.

The competitive response profile highlights four areas for analysis: the competitor's current strategies, its future goals, its assumptions about itself and the industry and its capabilities in the light of the preceding concerns. It should be noted again that it is difficult to gain insight into a competitor's strategies, goals and assumptions without first-hand knowledge. Taking messages from the marketplace, as proponents of such analysis advocate, can be misleading.

Information which has reached the marketplace is usually information which organisations wish to be there. Such information can be misleading and can lead analysts to the wrong assumptions. When a competitor is undertaking strategic development, or potentially groundbreaking activity, secrecy will be of the utmost importance. The marketplace will not contain such information.

## Current strategy

The current strategy of the firm may be investigated by analysis the markets in which it is operating at present, the signals it is sending into the marketplace etc. Strategy statements are also included in the organisation's published accounts, or annual report, as well as in press releases or articles. However, such information will be limited in detail. Current strategy is difficult to gauge, unless the analyst has direct links within the organisation.

## Assumptions

Each competitor will have assumptions about its industry and its own position within that industry. Competitors' assumptions are available by considering their history and performance. Their activities and the markets in which they have operated in the past will give information and insight about their view of the other competitors, likely developments in the future etc.

The accuracy of the assumptions may be measured by considering the competitor's relative position within the group or industry, likely future demand for its products and 'conventional wisdom'.

## Future goals

The factors to be taken into consideration when analysing the future goals of an organisation are listed and explained below:

- The goals of the SBU (strategic business unit), as opposed to those of the organisation, will give a clearer picture of what the direct competitor, the SBU, wishes to achieve.
- The competitor's attitudes to risk: the more risk averse, the greater the likelihood that future goals will be conservative and along current lines.
- The competitor's values and opinions will guide the manner in which it moves in the future.
- Organisational structure and culture are suited to particular environments. Knowledge of the given structure will give insight into likely activities in the future. Changes in structure may give warning of likely future intent.
- Control and incentives within the organisation will guide the culture and the ability of the organisation to operate or be active in given areas.
- Accounting systems will also influence the organisation's ability to move into new areas or to maintain activity in current areas.

- The management style and personality will affect future abilities.
- Constraints imposed by the government, the changing nature of the environment etc. will also have an effect on the organisation's ability to maintain its current levels of activity and to expand or divest etc. in the future.

The organisation's current portfolio is important to know, as this will give an indication of its future goals and also its assumptions about itself and the industry. Areas in which it is investing will be an indication of its perception of rising stars, promising products and activities. Moves to divest from a product area or activity similarly give insight into the attitudes and assumptions about markets in which the organisation is operating.

## Capabilities

Capabilities are the competitor's abilities in relation to its core competencies and activities and to its potential to undertake growth. The rate of response to changes and market developments, flexibility or ability to change and 'staying power' will all provide indications of a competitor's capabilities. These should be analysed with reference to strengths and weaknesses, which, along with the other areas, will lead to an overall profile when considered in full.

Note, however, that it is very difficult to build up a comprehensive and informative strengths and weaknesses profile which can be used effectively without first-hand insider knowledge of the organisation under consideration. It is once more the case that internal knowledge of the organisation may only be derived with confidence by gaining that information at first hand.

## Overall competitive profiles

The analyst and the organisation should be able to recognise and react to a variety of market signals. The types of signal range from prior announcements of intent, to information passed on by customers etc. There are reasons for the competitor wanting to issue information and for when this is released. The nature and source(s) of market and competitor information must be considered. Typical information sources and the reason for issue or announcement are listed below:

- Prior announcements of an action, launch, change in direction etc. – to make threats to competitors, to communicate sentiments to competitors, to minimise provocation, to avoid simultaneous moves by others within the competitive grouping and to gain internal support for the action to be taken.
- Post-action announcements – to verify the reasons for the action, to detail results etc.
- Public discussion of results and outcomes – to verify them and to communicate to the competition and the public.
- Discussions with customers – these will inevitably lead to a 'leak' to competitors, especially if related to an innovation of some kind.

These are not just statements of current or future strategy relating to the topic of the communication. A broader and more in-depth analysis can be carried out by considering whether or not changes in direction have been outlined, whether the strategic implications are in line with previous activities, whether the results communicated are superior or inferior to those noted historically etc.

However, the signals and reasons for issuing them are, it would seem, more validly applied to the manufacturing and retail industries and private-sector services than to those industries comprised of public-sector or publicly owned organisations providing a service, such as those traditionally provided by councils, local authorities etc. Nevertheless, it is the case that where competitive rivalry within the group or industry is intense, the assessment may also be true of public-sector service organisations.

For instance, since the change in UK legislation which allowed private firms to tender for contracts in competition with council organisations for provision of services such as meals, cleaning services and rubbish collection, this analysis may be equally as applicable to the organisations concerned.

The frameworks used for the purpose of such analysis, as outlined above, are essentially tools for the analysis of competitive situations. There is a question concerning the appropriateness of using a competitive model in industries which are not competitive, or are only emerging as competitive. This is the case in many industries in Europe as privatisation and deregulation increase. Again, the doubt over validity could possibly be a result of the fact that the model is based on the S–C–P paradigm.

A criticism of S–C–P is that it is deterministic, in that current structure is claimed to determine/ influence current conduct, which in turn determines/influences current performance. The interactions between time periods and between past and present industry structure and past and present organisational performance are very much ignored. To follow that argument through, it would therefore be the case that the frameworks outlined do not make any consideration of the changes in the structure and regulation of industries and the effects that these may have on the organisations within that industry.

## CRITICISM OF FIVE FORCES ANALYSIS

The first major intellectual hurdle in the analysis is to decide on the broad definition of the industry. The implication is that, if strict attention is paid to the industry as defined, the results could exclude other, relevant competitors from alternative geographical or competitive sectors when considering overall strategy and competition.

Such a bias could lead to a myopic view of the nature and configuration of the defined competition, ignoring potentially dangerous competitors elsewhere. Additionally, the definition of the industry under consideration leads to a 'follow-through error', unless care is taken to relax or change the definition at later stages in the analysis. Flexibility to change the scope of the investigation is required for an effective analysis.

## CRITICISM OF STRATEGIC GROUPS ANALYSIS

In a similar context, the strategic groups analysis must be examined critically. The obvious difficulty with the manner in which the analysis is done, that is, mappings, is that the axes for the maps must be decided carefully.

There is an additional point for consideration relating to the strategic groups analysis: the grouping itself is also subjective. The diversity and breadth of the group are again subjective. Different observers could formulate different groupings purely because their perceptions differ of which organisations are similar in strategic profile. At the extreme, each organisation could be placed in its own group. This would be futile, as there would be no basis for comparison between members of a group. It does highlight, however, the fact that the groupings included for analysis may be subjective.

## CRITICISM OF COMPETITOR RESPONSE PROFILING

When competitor response profiling is being done, the assumptions made for the purposes of analysis are based purely on market knowledge which is commonly available. In reality, however, this typically causes problems. Analysts may attempt to reduce the error and ambiguity in their analyses by increasing the number of sources of data used to construct profiles. Porter (1980) dedicates a chapter to the manner in which it is possible to use market signals to analyse competitors.

## CONCLUDING REMARKS

In conclusion, it can be seen that there exist several points of concern about the staged analysis of Porter and other frameworks, although none of the problems faced is insurmountable. Assumptions have to be made in order to resolve the sticking points and difficulties encountered, therefore there will be inaccuracies and biases within the analysis. An inaccuracy in the definition of the industry would then have to be carried on through the project. Thus, there is the potential for high levels of inaccuracy to be perpetuated due to the shortcomings of the framework and of the information available.

The ideas and concepts inherent in the Five Forces Analysis are not dissimilar to the S–C–P paradigm as developed by neoclassical economists. The S–C–P concept is, like the Porter framework, a deterministic model, where, as Lawler (1986) notes (from an economist's perspective), the characteristics of industrial markets are:

- The degree of seller concentration.
- The degree of buyer concentration.
- The degree of product differentiation.
- The conditions of entry/exit.
- Scale economies.
- Merger and acquisition activity.

These characteristics, he claims, are influential in determining the relationships between buyers and sellers within markets. This relationship then determines the patterns of conduct adopted by the organisations within the market. Finally, the conduct will have an effect on organisations' performance.

Therefore the characteristics of the markets will determine the structure that the market/industry takes. This depends on the interactions between each of the six characteristics listed. The size of the activity in each will combine to determine the level of competitive activity within the industry. Thus, the Porter framework of the five-forces of competitive rivalry is essentially derived from the neoclassical school of economic thought.

It is not surprising, therefore, that the criticisms of the neoclassical model may be applied to Porter's work. Much of the debate surrounding his writing is, in fact, concerned with the mechanical nature of the framework put forward, similar to the recognised drawbacks of the S–C–P paradigm and its use for the analysis of industries.

Approaches such as the portfolio analysis of competitors (Ansoff, Boston Consulting Group) have the advantage that they are not constrained by the need to define the organisation in its industrial context. Instead, they consider the organisation's products or businesses with reference to those are identified as competitors. Thus, it is not an S–C–P-type technique, but a more fluid, flexible approach which allows the analyst to look outside what might typically be defined as the industry or market. Therefore, organisations with a core competence or market interest which could make them potential competitors could be included in the analysis.

## SUMMARY

◆ This chapter has introduced the various stages of competitive analysis: at an industry level, intra-industry and individual competitors within the industry.

◆ The five forces of competitive rivalry were introduced and discussed as a framework for the analysis of industry and market situations. The five forces are:

– threat of entry;
– threat of substitution;
– power of suppliers;
– power of buyers; all of which combine to give
– intensity of competitive rivalry.

◆ From the Five Forces Analysis, it is possible to derive a definition and dimensions for the industry in question. These can be considered in terms of key barriers to entry, or target market segments.

◆ Intra-industry analysis may be performed by using competitive group analysis to consider the relative strengths, weaknesses and competencies of key players within the groups defined.

◆ Major competitors, or organisations of interest, may be profiled with reference to their likely reaction to market changes. Thus, it is possible to classify competitors within groups and to identify those which may cause strategic problems for any incumbents or potential entrants.

◆ There are criticisms of such a staged approach to the analysis of competitors. One of the more fundamental criticisms is that it is based on the S–C–P approach of the neoclassical economists. Many economists consider this approach to be invalid given contemporary market conditions and the simplistic assumptions on which it is built.

## REVIEW QUESTIONS

1 Outline the main stages to be undertaken in making a complete analysis of competitors within an existing industry.

2 For each of the stages outlined above, detail the key potential blockages or problems which an analyst may encounter in trying to carry out the analysis.

3 For an industry with which you are familiar:
   a Make a Five Forces Analysis in order to identify the definition and dimensions of that industry.
   b Choose an organisation from within the industry and identify its key competitors and their appropriate profiles from a competitive analysis of groups and individuals.

c Discuss the problems you encountered in making your analysis. Were these consistent with those detailed in (2). Discuss.

4 There are reasons which lead economists to reject the frameworks for strategic analysis outlined in this chapter. Discuss these reasons and comment on the validity of such criticism.

5 Make an analysis of the Five Forces of Competitive Rivalry in your own country's pharmaceutical market. What effect would reductions in the lifespan of a new drug patent have on the five forces?

## GLOSSARY OF NEW TERMS

**Competitive analysis of groups:** The process of identifying strategic groups with reference to key industry dimensions. Usually also involves a diagrammatical representation (known as a mapping).

**Competitor response profiling:** Analysis of the main competitors within a strategic group. The outcome is a profile where the competitor is considered to be either offensive/proactive in the marketplace or defensive/reactive.

**Five Forces of Competitive Rivalry:** A term used to describe the factors affecting and causing competition in any market or industry. The five forces are: threat of entry, threat of substitution, power of buyers, power of suppliers, all of the preceding combined to make the intensity of competition.

**Just-in-time (JIT):** Supply chain relations where the supplier is contracted to deliver customers' intermediate product requirements on an 'on-demand' basis. Such systems benefit the customer, who is able to reduce work in progress and stock levels and thus improve their cash flow situation.

**S–C–P:** Structure–Conduct–Performance – an economic framework which outlines the deterministic relationship between an industry's structure, the managerial conduct of organisations within it and their subsequent performance.

**Strategic groups:** Subsets of organisations within industries. Members of a strategic group possess similar characteristics and compete in similar market subsections.

## READING

Johnson, G and Scholes, K (1997) *Exploring Corporate Strategy: Text and Cases*, 4th edn, Prentice Hall, Hemel Hempstead.

Morden, T (1993) *Business Strategy and Planning: Text and Cases*, McGraw-Hill, Maidenhead.

Shrivastava, P (1994) *Strategic Management: Concepts and Practices*, Southwestern, Cincinatti, Ohio.

Stacey, R D (1996) *Strategic Management and Organisational Dynamics*, 2nd edn, Pitman Publishing, London.

Wright, P, Pringle, C D and Kroll, M J (1992) *Strategic Management: Text and Cases*, Allyn & Bacon, Needham Heights, Mass.

### Further reading

Ansoff, I (1987) *Corporate Strategy*, Penguin Business, Harmondsworth.
*Offers a unique insight into strategic analysis, choice and implementation based on portfolio analysis; an alternative approach to the one outlined in this chapter.*

Handy, C (1993) *Understanding Organisations*, 4th edn, Penguin Business, Harmondsworth.
*Gives an outline of the manner in which organisations operate and how people interact within them.*

Lawler, K (1986) *The Firm and Industrial Analysis*, Peter Andrew Publishing, Droitwich, Worcs.
*A microeconomics textbook for specialist economics students, which considers alternatives to the neoclassical approach as its basis. Empirical studies undertaken by the author are also outlined and discussed within the text.*

Lynch, R (1997) *Corporate Strategy*, Pitman Publishing, London.

Pearson, G (1992) *The Competitive Organisation*, McGraw-Hill, Maidenhead.
*An analysis of the techniques used within the successful organisation, including a critique of the profit-maximisation model and assumptions, on which Porter's texts can be seen to rest.*

Porter, M E (1980) *Competitive Strategy: Techniques for Analyzing Industries and Competitors*, Macmillan/Free Press, New York.
*A text devoted to Porter's framework for competitive and strategic analysis.*

Porter, M E (1985) *Competitive Advantage: Creating and Sustaining Superior Performance*, Macmillan/Free Press, New York.
*Readable, and offering a framework for the manner in which organisations may gain and maintain their position in their given market. This text develops the generic strategies introduced in the 1980 text.*

Porter, M and Montgomery, C (eds) (1991) *Strategy*, Harvard Business School Press, Boston, MA.
*A useful collection of seminal articles on strategy from the 1980s.*

CHAPTER **16**

# COMPETITIVE WEAPONS: SCALE, SCOPE AND CORE COMPETENCES

## KEY ISSUES

Business issues

Business strategy

Decision-making techniques

Economic concepts

Management decision issues

Optimal outcomes to management issues

## OBJECTIVES

◆ Introduce and differentiate between different stages in the innovational process (namely invention, innovation and diffusion).

◆ Consider the decisions facing organisations developing an invention into a market product, including:
  – likely payoff measured against risk
  – the timing of the launch of a new product to the market
  – the threat of imitation and the manner in which it can be delayed/prevented.

◆ Discuss the effect of operating in given market structures on the incentive to innovate.

◆ Outline theoretical thinking about the rate of adoption by organisations of inventions and innovations.

◆ Introduce and discuss the analysis of core competences within organisations.

◆ Examine the concept of synergy and how organisations may gain advantages from it.

◆ Investigate how benchmarking is being used by European organisations to measure their performance against others and to achieve strategic superiority.

◆ Give insight into the processes required and emanating from the identification of core competences and core products.

◆ Discuss the constraints on expansion and diversification of the organisation with reference to core competences and economies of scale.

## KEY TERMS

Benchmarking
Core competence
Diffusion
Innovation
Invention
Outsourcing
Synergy

## CHAPTER OUTLINE

Business application

Introduction

Exploitation of innovations for competitive advantage

Imitation

Monopolists are most likely to innovate

Organisations in competition are most likely to innovate

The time/cost tradeoff

The nature of the innovational process

Strategically exploited economies of scale and barriers to entry as sources of competitive advantage

Using advertising to gain barriers to entry and economies of scale

Synergy and economies of scope

Case study 16.1 Markets approach saturation

Core competences as a competitive weapon

Case study 16.2 Office work for benchmarkers

Core competence, core businesses and diversification

Case study 16.3 And then there were two

Case study 16.4 The outing of outsourcing

Concluding remarks

Summary

Review questions

Glossary of new terms

Reading

# Microsoft in multimedia alliance with NBC

**FT**

Microsoft, the world's largest computer software company, has formed a strategic alliance with General Electric's NBC television network to create and market multimedia products including on-line services, CD-ROM and interactive television programmes.

The move reflects growing ties between traditional media interests and the high-tech sector for the development of new forms of digital media.

The agreement is expected to provide a lift for MSN, Microsoft's planned on-line service, which is scheduled to be launched in August.

As part of the alliance, NBC will create on-line information services for MSN. NBC said that it would put together 'an extensive full-time staff' to draw material from its entertainment, sports, news and other programming divisions to create the new on-line services. NBC's advertisers and 214 television station affiliates in the US will be invited and encouraged to participate.

NBC and Microsoft would work together on the development, marketing and production of interactive television and other new digital products, the companies said. By combining new and traditional media, the alliance aims 'to create an integrated media experience that continually moves consumers from one media to another,' they said.

Financial terms were not disclosed.

'Success in multimedia takes a combination of technology, creative resources and core competencies that no one company currently possesses,' said Mr Bob Wright, president and chief executive of NBC.

NBC was the first US television network to establish an on-line information service, via America Online, a competitor to the planned Microsoft network. NBC is expected to abandon its on-line ventures when MSN is launched.

The Microsoft–NBC alliance follows MCI's $2bn investment in News Corporation last week.

*Source*: *Financial Times*, 17 May 1995. Reprinted with permission.

*Comment*

Why is it that Microsoft wants to be involved with television? Isn't it enough that Bill Gates (Microsoft's owner) has made it one of the most famous names in the computing world?

Although there are considerable gains to be made in the computing software industry, Microsoft is far from resting on its laurels. It is concentrating on its ability to develop and sell computer programs and collaborating with the US television broadcasting giant NBC in the latter's area of expertise: television.

The two intend to work together to produce an interactive television service to paying viewers. The project will require collaboration to develop the technology required and the content to be delivered. NBC will provide the news and Microsoft the technical delivery to the marketplace. Neither could have done this alone. They are working together by necessity. There have obviously been developments in terms of trust and sharing information between the two organisations in beginning to work on this project.

The reasons for the project are logical: to continue to gain competitive edge, or advantage, in the future, both organisations feel that it will be necessary to be leaders in this area of the telecommunications industry. Neither is likely to be acting out of a sense of charity; they will be looking forward to the stream of profits which the project will accrue. As a result, the two are willing to invest money now. NBC and Microsoft are among the first to come together in the race to develop multimedia and interactive television. They are no doubt also hoping that this will give them advantages over competitors in terms of learning and experience and possibly even setting industry standards for the future. If this were to transpire, they would be guaranteed even greater streams of income as their competitors struggled to catch up.

## INTRODUCTION

This chapter will provide an overview and outline of the weapons open to the organisation in seeking to maintain its competitive position. One of the most basic of such weapons consists in economies of scale, introduced in Chapter 8. The manner in which organisations may derive or exploit such economies was outlined and examples given there. Refer back to Chapter 8 if a reminder of the concept is required. In this chapter, however, examination will be made of the manner in which economies of scale may be exploited in order to gain or maintain competitive advantage. In this context, the idea that organisations may use economies of scale as entry barriers will be examined. Additionally, the role of economies of scale in defining the boundaries of the organisation, or the market, will also be examined.

Economies of scale are not the only competitive weapons open to an organisation. Much time is devoted to discussion and investigation of organisations' 'core competences'. These come from the activity at the heart of their business which provides the key for their success – the one key element which provides survival at worst, or a leading market position at best.

Exploitation of invention and innovation can also provide organisations with competitive advantage. Breakthroughs in either productive processes or products can give an organisation a time advantage or financial advantage in its particular marketplace. The nature of invention and innovation will be explored first in this chapter to give a context for the activity which may be observed in markets in economies worldwide.

# EXPLOITATION OF INNOVATIONS FOR COMPETITIVE ADVANTAGE

Before **innovations** may be exploited, they need to be invented! **Invention** can occur for any of a variety of reasons, three of which are: to provide for latent demand; to exploit potential financial reward; or spontaneously, to satisfy the inventor's quest for knowledge and self-development (or fame).

The chain (for ease, call it the innovational process) from idea or concept to market sale or use has been identified by economists as including three distinct stages:

- *Invention* – the initial idea, usually at the stage where it is a tangible product or prototype.
- *Innovation* – acceptance and introduction of the invention into a valid or acceptable marketplace proposition; that is, it is put into production.
- *Diffusion* – acceptance of the innovation in the market context by competitors to such an extent that they buy the product or imitate it.

Within the innovational process, there are five types of innovation. These were initially identified by Schumpeter in 1934, who recognised that there is more to innovation than merely bringing a new product to the market:

- The introduction of a new product (or service), or an improvement in the quality of an existing one.
- The introduction of a new method of production; that is, the process by which a current product or service is brought to the marketplace.
- The development of a new market.
- The development or capitalisation of a new source of supply in the marketplace.
- A change to methods of operation within the industry.

It is widely accepted that different industries (at different stages in their lifecycles) will possess different rates of change in their innovational process(es). The invention and innovation stages of the process possess two major characteristics. Between invention and innovation, there is often a requirement for additional research and development expenditure and improvement. Organisations often require some level of guarantee that the invention will be commercially successful for them. By undertaking research and development expenditure and projects, the organisation can affect the outcome, to the extent that maximum benefits or revenue will accrue. Additionally, the second characteristic is that the organisation is able to protect its investment from imitation via patent regulations.

In the neoclassical framework there would be no need for innovation. Remember that perfect information is assumed to exist. If there is perfect information, then organisations will already be producing the optimal product via the optimal processes and no further improvement can be made. Thus, the neoclassical assumption that perfect knowledge exists must be relaxed for investigation of the invention, innovation and diffusion process. That is, *uncertainty* exists; there are continuous frictions constraining the flow and development of information and ideas. Uncertainty in the innovational process thus gives rise to a number of constraints. These help to define what may or may not arrive in the marketplace. Chapter 13 gives an overview of decision-making processes when uncertainty and risk exist.

◆ **Exercise 16.1**

Why is it important for organisations to invest in research and development?

Why should they attempt to innovate? Wouldn't it be better to invest the funds elsewhere? (*See* the section below for an answer.)

## IMITATION

In order to optimise the innovational process, organisations need to be able to protect against imitation by rivals. This is particularly true if the market is attractive for some reason, as is the case when large profits are declared. As has already been mentioned, the use of patents can particularly assist in protecting against imitation.

However, patents are a short-term protection measure. They do not prevent rivals from developing similar products; rather, they prevent rivals from selling their alternative(s). Therefore, once a patent expires, competitors are able to offer to the market their version of the previously protected product.

The pharmaceutical industry is often quoted as one which develops and markets new products so voraciously that it is a process of innovative destruction. However, various sources, including the UK press, claim that the rate of patenting and new product development is so great because of the short lifespan and low payback of innovative products once patents expire. Indeed, Ferguson and Ferguson (1994) make the point that, although pharmaceutical organisations are able to protect their innovations by patent *to the level of the individual molecule and its analogs*, the life expectancy of products is only five years!

## MONOPOLISTS ARE MOST LIKELY TO INNOVATE

Monopolists, it is claimed, are in the best position to innovate. They are able to exploit (or even develop) new technology which may lead to further innovation. Furthermore, they have the funds available to purchase and exploit experience in the market and expertise. Additionally monopolists, by their very nature, are more likely to be able to innovate and produce on such a scale that they gain positive economies of scale. Also, they are able to adopt and internalise any process developments they make, further strengthening their monopoly position.

However, consider the counter argument that monopolists have little incentive to innovate, since they are already in a strong market position and any expenditure on research and development will detract from profits. It makes sense that an organisation which is in control of its marketplace is loath to incur cost which will not necessarily give it any benefits.

It could be argued that such a stance is short-termist. Any monopolist in an attractive market which stagnates or 'rests on its laurels' will undoubtedly find itself in a position of competition in the future. Therefore, any expenditure now could be seen by the monopolist as an investment in its own future and longevity. The incentive to innovate is usually driven by the promise of future profit streams, that is, private benefit for the innovator. Such promises of private benefits may be devalued, but not made obsolete, by the fact that the organisation is a monopoly.

## ORGANISATIONS IN COMPETITION ARE MOST LIKELY TO INNOVATE

An alternative view is that organisations in competitive industries are innovators. Such thinking arises if one considers that the innovator will be striving to convert the innovation into additional profits or some other private benefit.

In competitive situations, it is recognised that there may be a drastic development or innovation, or there may be non-drastic developments or innovations – which are improvements to existing products or processes. A differentiation is usually made between product or process improvements. This will be discussed later. Given the nature of the arguments surrounding incentive to innovate, the opportunities within the competitive situation are far wider and far more widely discussed. It is easier to see which benefits may accrue to the competitive organisation in the present and into the future. This is not to say that the perspective of monopolist as innovator is wrong, just that further theoretical advances have been made since that view was published.

◆ **Exercise 16.2**

Who do you think is more likely to innovate, an organisation in a competitive market or a monopolist? Give reasons for your answer.

## THE TIME/COST TRADEOFF

In a competitive situation, there is a tradeoff between the time to innovate and the cost of innovation. Intuitively, the more quickly an invention can be transformed into a viable market product, the lower the costs to the innovator and the greater the stream of income. However, this is not necessarily the case, since there are a number of other factors to be taken into account.

First, although the time to market may be shorter, the final product may not have gone through such rigorous testing as it otherwise would have and so the likelihood of errors or faults in the product is increased. Second, greater resources are required to develop sequentially a range of related products than to manage the process such that optimum resource use (and, where possible, economies of scale) is achieved in developing a range or cluster of products in parallel. This is particularly true if, third, there is any requirement within the process for experiments or tests which are relevant to all products.

Thus, there is a carefully balanced tradeoff between time and cost in new product development and the nature of learning effects and benefits. The tradeoff cannot be stated exactly, but must be reached by experimentation and careful management.

This has to be balanced against the fact that there is the prospect of increased payback and profit when the development time is reduced. Furthermore, the leadtime stolen from competitors is increased; it will take them longer to innovate and the subsequent market share is also increased if the organisation is able to minimise development time and capitalise on a market as a monopoly in the first instance. There are other advantages accompanying such a position, for example brand loyalty and increased economies in advertising.

## THE NATURE OF THE INNOVATIONAL PROCESS

The innovational process differs in each situation in which it occurs. Broadly, however, two key distinctions may be made. First, the innovational process may lead to either a product or a process improvement. This was discussed above in the context of the improvements identified by Schumpeter. Given that the innovational process does lead to a product or process improvement, a further distinction may be made. The innovational process may lead to either an entirely new product or process development, or to an improvement or alteration to existing products or processes, that is, 'drastic' or 'non-drastic' innovation. Thus, the key differences which are observable are between:

■ product or process development, and
■ drastic or non-drastic innovational processes.

## STRATEGICALLY EXPLOITED ECONOMIES OF SCALE AND BARRIERS TO ENTRY AS SOURCES OF COMPETITIVE ADVANTAGE

Chapter 8 dealt with the basics relating to economies of scale and the manner in which they may be derived. There are, however, certain actions which organisations may take in order to derive an advantage strategically by exploiting existing economies of scale or creating new ones.

This section will concentrate on the economies of scale which may be derived by organisations consciously wishing to create or exploit economies of scale (or barriers to entry) for the market or industry particular to their newly adopted product (process etc.). A distinction is therefore being made here between what may be termed 'innocent' economies of scale – those which the organisation gains passively, as a result of its day-to-day activities and processes – and 'strategic' economies of scale. Strategic economies of scale are derived by organisations as a result of a conscious effort to gain competitive advantage through manipulation, exploitation or alteration of processes which give economies of scale. As a result of such exploitation, the organisation may gain further competitive advantage, or may be able to build up barriers to entry to the industry or market for potential competitors.

## USING ADVERTISING TO GAIN BARRIERS TO ENTRY AND ECONOMIES OF SCALE

Advertising can be used in a number of ways strategically to increase the barriers to entry for potential entrants. The advantages applicable to advertising for an organisation's product are:

- *Loyalty* – Increased advertising benefits the organisation with increased loyalty. Enhancing loyalty also increases the obstacles to any potential competitor in terms of market entry.
- *Increased absolute costs* – The finance required to enter a market or industry increases as the standard (or normal) requirement for advertising to remain competitive within that market or industry increases.
- *Increased pecuniary expenses* – The amount required to remain in the market or industry will increase as a result of increased advertising expenditure by competitors. Also, the marginal effect of advertising expenditure decreases on a financial basis. (Note, however, that the greater the number of units over which a given advertising spend may be spread, the lower the average cost of advertising.)

For a new product, when an organisation wishes to enter a new market, the organisation can make gains and set up entry barriers to others from advertising when it uses this to launch the product. There are several reasons for this:

- Launching new products requires an increase in advertising expenditure on the part of the organisation. The greater the intensity of effort on the launch, the more likely potential customers are to become aware of the product and therefore the better the chances of achieving sales.
- The holder of the greatest market share in terms of sales in an existing market does not necessarily spend the most on advertising. An intensive advertising campaign can be used to steal market share from the market share leader. This might, however, provoke a reaction from that leader and give rise to an expensive advertising war, and so on.
- Brand loyalty decreases on the part of the consumer as advertising expenditure and competition within a market or industry increase. Thus, an intensive campaign on the part of a new market entrant may attract consumers, particularly those who are marginal, or impulsive decision makers with respect to the nature of the product in question.

Exploiting economies of scale resulting from advertising can be particularly lucrative. Of specific interest is the fact that the greater the product range related to a given brand name, the more products an advertising campaign will promote.

Thus, the organisation is able to derive economies because it does not have to develop and buy advertising campaigns for individual products, only for the range.

Additionally, there are economies of scale to an advertiser able to enter into anything more than a minimal advertising campaign. The set-up costs for a campaign in terms of the design, typesetting, recording and other processes involved in creating an advertisement are the same whether the advertisement is run once or several times. Thus, it should be obvious that there is an optimal level of advertising. Organisations should be able to ascertain the level of least cost per unit of advertising associated with any campaign (or media within that campaign) and purchase that quantity.

## SYNERGY AND ECONOMIES OF SCOPE

The economies of scale which may be earned by advertising a complete product range under a given brand name, rather than individual products, could also be thought of as economies of scope derived through synergies. **Synergy** has many definitions, but the easiest and perhaps most popularly used is:

$$2 + 2 = 5$$

That is, the sum of the parts is greater than the whole. By using a brand name for a number of products rather than a series of different and unconnected names, the organisation is able to make economies in many different contexts:

- Economies of advertising: the name of the brand can be spread more broadly for the same budget than a series of different advertising campaigns for different brands (*ceteris paribus*).
- As a product within a range, the organisation may be able to make production economies of scale if any of the production processes used to make products within the range can be shared.
- Managerial economies are possible, where the skills of the various specialist functions within an organisation are available to a number of different products, rather than one product. (This does not only apply to a product within a range, but to any similarities between products.) This is particularly true in cases where managerial skills are not fully utilised before additional products are introduced.

For example, Heinz decided to put a halt on TV advertising for individual products in the UK in 1995/6. Instead, it promoted those products using direct marketing techniques. TV advertising, on the other hand, was used to instil and cement the brand name in the minds of consumers. Thus Heinz as a whole, as opposed to individual product managers, was responsible for the TV campaigns. The rationale was that there is more to be gained by advertising products elsewhere once the public is familiar with the company producing them. In some of the advertisements, more than one product was shown at a time. What was distinctive about these advertisements is that they concentrated on the Heinz name, rather than the product name.

Savings through synergy are of particular interest to an organisation considering taking over or merging with another. The economies available from sharing complementary activities and skills may be particularly effectively exploited in the case of a horizontal merger or takeover. Vertical takeover or merger is not likely to gain such economies because similarities between activities and processes used at different stages in the production process are fewer and these are less likely to be transferable.

To gain economies of scope, the organisation is able to operate from a reduced cost base as a result of an extended product range, that is, by operating multiproduct production lines with similar inputs in terms of materials and on machinery which requires minimal adjustment or tool changes. Product similarities, of whatever type, mean that the average costs incurred in producing more than one product are less than the average costs incurred in producing one product alone. It is obvious, here, that the two concepts are basically the same. However, synergy typically relates to savings as a result of introducing complementary activities and skills, whereas economies of scope typically relate to the savings possible as a result of extending the product range.

As can be seen in Table 16.1, the higher the ranking, the more likely is the sector to use common raw materials or parts and common production facilities.

**Table 16.1 Economies of scope in EU manufacturing**

| Sector | Economies of scope* |
|---|---|
| Motor vehicles | 8 |
| Pharmaceutical products | 5 |
| Electrical machinery | 5 |
| Office machinery | 5 |
| Domestic-type appliances | 5 |
| Manmade fibres | 3 |
| Carpets | 3 |
| Machine tools | 1 |
| Cement, lime and plaster | 0 |

*Source*: *European Economy*, No 35, March 1988. The Office for Official Publications of the European Communities, Luxembourg.

* Percentage increase in average costs at half the number of models.

## ◆ CASE STUDY 16.1

## Markets approach saturation

The recent downgrading of Daimler-Benz's long-term debt by the Standard & Poor's ratings agency came as an unnecessary but timely reminder for the German automotive industry that this year's expected recovery in profits, however welcome, has yet to be underpinned by an enduring improvement in competitiveness.

As S & P said, despite a 6.8 per cent increase in European car registrations in the first half, long-term demand growth was likely to slow as markets approached saturation. At the same time, increasing economic integration within the region, the erosion of world trade barriers and intensifying price competition would probably heighten the impact of future ups and downs in the economic cycle.

Profits are set to increase across the board this year after last year's slump into losses by all but BMW, and most analysts expect further improvements as the end of the decade approaches and the savings wrought by rationalisation in the past two years show up.

The most striking change in German factories has been on the shop floor, where automotive company's workforces have been slashed and reorganised. From a peak of 788 000 employees in July 1991, the industry had reduced its headcount by 150 000 in July this year, and a further 50 000 jobs are scheduled to go. Team working and continuous improvement processes have become commonplace methods of increasing productivity.

BMW, earliest into restructuring and the most advanced down the road to modern production methods, has managed a job-cutting programme which started in 1989 through natural wastage and limited early retirement.

Flexible working times, short-term contracts for production workers and weekend shifts have been introduced to cope with fluctuations in demand. This policy reflects BMW's determination to establish a new order in its domestic manufacturing processes. In short, long-term investments in domestic fixed plant will be based on long-term prospects and plans, while short-term demand shifts will be countered by the flexible use of manpower.

But even the most bright-eyed optimists recognise that the savings to be gained from cutting and shuffling staff and reordering working methods are not enough to compensate for Germany's ingrained labour cost disadvantages. In the most extreme instances, each DM1 in basic pay is supplemented by a further 80 pfennigs in tax, health, and statutory and voluntary welfare and social benefit contributions.

One common response has been an increase in foreign components sourcing – a possibility enhanced by the development of market economies in relatively low-wage countries such as Poland and the Czech Republic – which has increased the estimated average proportion of non-German parts built into German-made vehicles from 25 per cent in 1992 to about 35 per cent this year.

There is also an accelerating trend towards outsourcing of components formerly made within car manufacturers' works to specialist suppliers which can increase their economies of scale and reduce unit costs. Hence, for example, Mercedes-Benz's recent decision to hand over seat construction at its Bremen works to Leister Recaro.

Even more significant is the emergence of new partnerships between vehicle makers and their suppliers which is creating a new hierarchical structure among components makers. Accordingly, Mercedes has in the past two months set up two trend-setting joint ventures dedicated to supplying Mercedes and outside customers with key component modules.

Accordingly, its future supplies of complete power steering units will be supplied from an operation set up with and to be operated by ZF. Volkswagen has said it may join in later. Mercedes has also bundled its engine valve systems manufacture, currently focused in a factory in Bad Homburg, into a separate arrangement with two parts suppliers in a three-sided operation to be known as MWP. . .

Announcements of joint ventures in assembly and to a lesser extent full-scale manufacturing are becoming regular occurrences. Although over-shadowed in terms of scale by such investments as BMW's and Mercedes' first US manufacturing plants, due to open shortly, the trend is now clearly set.

Mercedes, targeting the Chinese bus market, has three joint manufacturing ventures under development or study. In India it has a majority stake in a new concern to manufacture E-Class executive saloons. Volkswagen was early into the Chinese car market and is now enjoying rapid sales growth. But it has had less luck elsewhere as continuing shake-outs at its ventures in Spain's Seat and Skoda demonstrate. Autolatina, a collaborative venture between VW and Ford in Brazil is also on the verge of restructuring.

Meanwhile, its arch rival in the German market, Adam Opel, is stretching its wings into every accessible corner of the emerging global market for passenger cars. A network of Opel assembly plants stretching from Poland to Indonesia is being established around a central hub at the company's Russelsheim technical development centre near Frankfurt.

While other German manufacturers' plans appear less clearly defined, they share the same logical basis as Opel's: while their high domestic costs and the expensive D-Mark militate fiercely against exports, Germany's high reputation for technical excellence is the passport which will give them a fighting chance in the new markets needed to secure their long-term future.

*Source: Financial Times*, 4 October 1994. Reprinted with permission.

## Comment on the case study

It is clear in this case study that the German automotive industry is suffering from reduced volume of sales. It is also true, however, that it is taking measures to improve its position. There have been considerable reductions in the number of employees: 150 000 jobs were lost in 1994. But these have not been sufficient to boost the industry. The case study claims that one of the main sources of advantage has been gained through the nature of the supply contracts enjoyed by the German manufacturers. The close link between Mercedes-Benz and its seat constructor is quoted as one

such example. Additionally, there is the claim that Mercedes's close collaboration with its component suppliers is making a difference to costs. The company is able to gain economies of scale because its component makers are producing on a greater scale than for Mercedes alone.

The joint ventures into which automobile manufacturers are entering are also proof that they are unwilling, or unable, to finance such schemes individually. These ventures are similar to that discussed at the beginning of this chapter between Microsoft and NBC.

# CORE COMPETENCES AS A COMPETITIVE WEAPON

This kind of development in markets has led to organisations turning their attention to identifying their **core competence** (competences) and to reorganising their core activities in order to build up business based on exploitation of such strength(s).

The identification of these strengths was first advocated by Selznick, who used the term 'distinctive competence' in 1957 to describe the process of identifying the organisation's 'key success factors'. These are defined as the distinctive competence which should be borne in mind when formulating, evaluating and implementing strategy.

The concept of distinctive competence did not, however, achieve universal recognition. Core competences were introduced once more and brought into popular use as a result of the work of Prahalad and Hamel. These authors advocate the identification of core competences within an organisation to gain competitive advantage. This was proposed in opposition to the then popular policy of organisations building up and managing a portfolio of products for success.

Core competences, Prahalad and Hamel claim, are 'the collective learning in the organisation, especially how to coordinate diverse production skills and integrate multiple streams of technologies'. That is, identifying and concentrating on the organisation's strengths in productive organisation and ability and applying these strengths to other areas. The key to such success is the harmonisation of such activities in order to optimise production and maximise returns. A core competence is not therefore a simple definition of what the organisation does well. It is a list of what the organisation can do well and an analysis of the way in which it does this. The organisation must ask itself the following questions:

■ What is it that is done well?
■ Why is this done so well?
■ How can these techniques be applied to other aspects of the organisation?

Identification of core competences is therefore an analysis of the systems, knowledge and techniques used by the organisation. Such systems add to the success of the organisation and enable it to gain competitive advantage. By remaining aware of such competence and working to maintaining or even improving in these areas, organisations may sustain competitive advantage.

Identification of core competences leads to the organisation identifying of its core product. The core product is not necessarily a market-ready product, but possibly an intermediate one. A corporate example of this is the Japanese Honda company: its core competence involves the production of motors and engines, and its core product is engines. The core product is the one which gives the organisation its major market share(s) and contributes to the success of market-ready products.

Without the identification of its core competence and product, the organisation is said to be operating with 'bounded innovation'. It is not working within a context of complete knowledge about the contributors to its own success. The organisation is not aware, therefore, of what is required for success and longevity. Core competences and core products need to be both identified *and* deployed in order to gain success.

This is not to say that the organisation has to constrain its product range. Indeed, the greater the range of products into which the organisation is able to build its core product, the more the risk is spread. The more markets in which the organisation operates, the less likely it is to be severely affected by recession or downturn in any individual market. To continue with the Honda example, it is operating in many different markets: motorcycles, cars, even lawnmowers. What it has brought to each of these markets is an expertise with reference to the engine contained by the products listed. Recently, Honda was involved in the UK auto market as a result of its ownership stake in the (then) British Rover company. It was able to bring expertise which the UK firm did not have and turn Rover from a struggling, recently privatised auto manufacturing company to a more successful European competitor.

Once the core competence has been identified, it would seem logical that there is a place for analysis of the portfolio of products held by the business. The balance of products and product markets is therefore still important, but only once the core competence and product are understood.

Core competences and core products, if used successfully, can provide the following benefits:

■ Increased potential for access to new markets as a competitive force within that market.
■ Conscious exploitation of the core competence can obviously lead the organisation to an improved competitive position.

■ Expertise and learning curve effects mean that even the most basic core competences and core products are not easily imitated by others. First-mover advantage and market leadership are extended in such circumstances.

■ The benefits are not restricted to the organisation: the consumer may also benefit from lower prices, or additional attributes in the product at the same price.

However, over time, the organisation must be aware of the increased threat of imitation and competition inherent in maturing industries and therefore develop a range of products for the future in order to protect the competitive position gained.

## Benchmarking

**Benchmarking** is a tool frequently used to identify, assess and evaluate the success of a core competence. Benchmarking as a concept is easy. Organisations measure their key performance indicators against those of an organisation considered to be an industry leader, or global competitor. In practice, it is much more difficult. Identification of the industry leader can prove difficult, gaining information about its internal activities and quantifying these even more so. It is also true that if an organisation only identifies its 'best' competitors as desirable to benchmark against, it may fail to identify organisations with desirable operating practices or technologies.

The process of benchmarking is widely used. In the UK, the management consultancy Coopers and Lybrand has been actively involved in setting standards for the processes involved in benchmarking. It is also one of the main exponents of benchmarking on behalf of clients. Benchmarking involves the organisation making performance comparisons internally and externally in order to gain new insights into business practices and to identify where there may be situations or areas for making improvements. Essentially, then, it is a type of 'gap analysis'. The benchmarking organisation investigates where it falls behind others and quantifies this gap in performance compared to preferred levels. Once steps have been taken to close the gap, the organisation is able to measure its success in doing so.

Coopers and Lybrand has realised that competitor information can be difficult to obtain and that it is frequently incomplete. In order to improve the process of benchmarking, it is beginning to advocate what it calls 'best in class process' comparisons. Here, organisations group and work together, sharing learning which results in gains in competitive advantage. There are problems, however. Benchmarking clubs and consortia are not well established in the UK, although they do exist. Efforts have to be made to encourage organisations to work together for mutual gain. Late in 1995, for example, it was announced that chartered accountants (in the UK) would have free access to a worldwide database which would provide financial information relating to 650 organisations. The database is owned and maintained by the Hackett Group.

## ◆ CASE STUDY 16.2

### Office work for benchmarkers

**FT**

Property accounts for about 40 per cent of company assets and, typically, about 10 per cent of operating costs. Organisations using their buildings efficiently should, therefore, have a competitive edge.

The snag is that managers have had no way of knowing whether they are using property more or less efficiently than their peers. The practice of comparing property performance between companies – benchmarking – has often foundered on the lack of reliable data.

Companies such as Rank Xerox have tackled the problem by sharing information on property costs with a select group of competitors. Similar benchmarking 'clubs' exist in industries such as food retailing and information technology.

Big firms of surveyors such as Hillier Parker and DTZ Debenham Thorpe have also set up clubs, collecting and analysing information from their clients across a range of industries.

Hillier Parker's benchmarking club was set up at the end of last year. The firm collects data from nine club members, concentrating on office property. 'Rents, rates and facilities costs are much higher for office property than for industrial space. Benchmarking offices will lead to the greatest potential savings,' says Chris Boulton of Hillier Parker.

The first batch of data collected by Hillier Parker has produced some telling comparisons. Members of the club pay, on average, £2.50 to £3.25 per sq ft in rates. Yet one of the members has an average rates bill of £6.50.

▶

Case study 16.2 *continued*

'Looking at the location of their properties there is no obvious reason for such a large difference. This is clearly an area for potential savings,' comments Boulton.

However, most benchmarking clubs are relatively small. Plans for a new Occupational Property Databank, collecting data on thousands of properties from dozens of occupiers, could lead to benchmarks based on a much wider spread of data.

'There are lots of clubs collecting bits and pieces of data but nothing standardised across the property market. We are hoping to rectify that,' says Christopher Hedley, who is setting up the project for the Investment Property Databank, which already runs performance measurement services for institutional investors in property.

Fourteen companies, including Barclays, National Westminster, Eagle Star, Sears, BT and British Gas, have agreed to supply information on 25,000 properties to the occupational databank.

IPD hopes that companies from sectors which are not represented, such as food retailing, will join in as the project gains credibility.

Initially, the new databank will collect 50 variables from the companies, delivered by electronic transfer. The plan is to evolve benchmarks covering four main areas:

Property costs, including space and detailed information on rents and rates.

Utilisation of property: space per employee and broad measures of efficiency such as turnover or transactions per square metre.

Estate management costs: how much it costs companies to manage their property.

Asset performance, the rate of return companies achieve on property investment and the capital value of occupational properties over time.

The biggest danger in property benchmarking is that companies will focus on numerical measures, such as cost per square foot, without considering the impact on productivity or staff morale or asking why variations in performance arise.

For this reason, many of the companies joining the new databank hope it will lead to greater informal communication between the participants as well as quantitative benchmarks.

'We are looking for information on best practice as well as costs. I hope the IPD will bring opportunities to network with other companies,' says Mark Smith, group premises manager at Eagle Star, the insurance company.

Hedley would eventually like to run standardised staff satisfaction surveys among databank members as a proxy for productivity.

'It has never really been possible to tell a good building from a bad building. This is a particular problem for developers who would like to charge more for what they believe to be a better product,' he says.

In the meantime he believes the databank will stimulate debate and discussion, helping companies to arrive at the best way of organising their property management.

*Source*: *Financial Times*, 7 April 1995. Reprinted with permission.

### Comment on the case study

Notable examples seen in the case are those of Hillier Parker and the soon-to-come Occupational Property Databank which specifically concentrate on property benchmark performance measures. These clubs have agreements from prospective members to supply data relating to their office spaces. This will then be used to calculate best in class standards such as payments per square unit of area rented. The standards and other information will then be made available to the members of the club. The clubs mentioned are also collecting information relating to the manner in which such space is used, the human factors, in order to identify best practice in management of all resources with reference to the monetary cost.

### Benchmarking in Europe

In Europe, the percentage of companies using benchmarking differs between countries. However, overall it is claimed that over 80 per cent of all companies in Europe use benchmarking to compare their performance against competitors. Coopers and Lybrand states that 70 per cent of benchmarking projects lead to success (measured in terms of improvements in performance). Percentages of utilisation of benchmarking projects in various European countries are:

- Netherlands – 72 per cent
- Switzerland – 68 per cent
- UK – 78 per cent.

Nevertheless, it should be noted that there are different definitions of benchmarking. Therefore, although the analytical and learning processes may be similar, one organisation's idea of benchmarking may be another's idea of search for best practices which may be emulated, or another's of comparing functions within organisations.

# CORE COMPETENCE, CORE BUSINESSES AND DIVERSIFICATION

Once best practices have been identified, measured and utilised, organisations are able to operate more effectively within their traditional market areas and also in other, unconnected areas. Such expansionary actions frequently lead organisations to diversify into activities within several seemingly unrelated industries. This can lead to the organisation's key resources being overstretched and require a return to its core business. In some circumstances, the organisation may decide not to return to its core business, but to enter new market areas which it considers to be more attractive at the expense of core business activities.

◆ **CASE STUDY 16.3**

## And then there were two

Like St Paul, the capital of Minnesota, which it dominates, Minnesota Mining and Manufacturing (3M) is conservative at heart. It hardly ever sacks workers, it avoids acquisitions and it rarely hits the headlines. So when, on November 14th, the conglomerate said it would spin off its data-storage and imaging division, and shut down its audio- and video-tape unit, Minnesotans knew that things must be bad.

3M has prospered by mixing conservatism with creativity. It has awed management gurus with its ability to come up with an unending stream of new inventions: in all, it sells more than 60,000 different products, ranging from Post-It notes and pan scourers to surgical supplies and road signs. Spurred on by Livio DeSimone, who took over as chairman and chief executive four years ago, 3M last year registered an astonishing 543 patents – 40% more than in 1991. About $1 billion of 3M's 1994 sales of $15.1 billion were earned on products launched during the year; 30% of revenues came from products less than four years old – a goal originally set by Mr DeSimone. The firm spent 7% of its revenues on research and development during the year – double the American average.

But 3M's obsession with inventiveness has its drawbacks. For every blockbuster such as Post-It and Scotch adhesive tape, there have been costly flops such as the Floptical disk, a high-tech memory device that 3M hoped would become the next standard for personal computers (it didn't). Since Mr DeSimone took command, around $1.2 billion – over a third of the firm's total capital budget – has been sunk into the information, imaging and electronics (II&E) division (responsible for the Floptical), but with little to show for it. Last year the division, which accounts for 31% of 3M's sales, made an operating-profit margin of 6.3%. Margins at 3M's two other divisions – industrial and consumer products, and life sciences – were three times that.

One of the biggest drags on 3M's II&E unit has been its audio- and video-tape business, which has sales of about $650m a year. 3M discovered the hard way that price, rather than innovation, is what matters in the tape business – and competition in the market has been fierce. At the same time, the cost of the raw materials for tapes has soared: the price of cobalt has almost tripled in the past two years. The tape business is being shut down, says Mr DeSimone, because 'we don't see the prospect for significant improvement'.

With the tape business closed, and the electronics unit of II&E being kept by 3M, the (as yet unnamed) company being spun off to shareholders next year will focus on imaging and data storage, and will have annual revenues of around $2.3 billion. In theory, the newly independent group, which will have about 11,000 employees, should be more profitable without the audio- and video-tape millstone: its operating margins could hit double figures in its first year. The unit also has a strong portfolio of new products. But if it hopes to approach the profitability of the remainder of 3M, it will have to cut its costs when it wins its freedom.

All told, 3M's restructuring will cost it a $600m pre-tax charge in the fourth quarter of this year; it will also cost around 5,000 jobs from its total workforce of 85,000. Most of the job losses will be voluntary; but coming on top of a 5% reduction in the firm's payroll since 1990, they amount to the most severe shrinkage in 3M's history. Mr DeSimone notes that the businesses retained by 3M 'hold leading global market positions, have very good profit margins and generate strong cash flow'. But under pressure from raw-material costs (up 8% in the past year), stagnant selling prices and sluggish sales volumes, how can he ensure that the newly slim 3M will not one day head the way of its dismal II&E division?

Part of the answer, claims Mr DeSimone, is to concentrate 3M's inventive powers on churning out more blockbusters. To do that, the firm will specialise in about two dozen core technologies (such as microreplication, a promising surface-texturing technique). A company-wide database links scientists in varying

397

Case study 16.3 *continued*

disciplines, giving them access to each other's expertise. Product development is now following a more 'market-centred' approach: scientists work more closely with marketers, and marketers work more closely with customers. To cut the bureaucracy, Mr DeSimone has reduced the number of managers in 3M by a fifth since he took charge.

Couple all this with tough financial goals (3m's overall 21% return on capital employed last year fell well short of its stiff 27% target) and cost-cutting drives,

and 3M is now well-placed 'to outpace the growth of the markets we serve', says Mr DeSimone. But managing innovation is a notoriously hit-and-miss business – and the hits are often happy accidents. After all, who could have predicted that Art Fry, a 3M researcher, would invent the Post-It note while trying to come up with a better bookmark for his hymn-book?

*Source*: © *The Economist*, London, 18 November 1995. Reprinted with permission.

### Comment on the case study

Examination of the 3M case clearly shows that the organisation is involved in industrial areas as diverse as data storage and imaging (as in computer diskettes), audio- and videotape (although this is the area which it intends to shut down or sell off), surgical supplies, road signs and the ubiquitous sticky-tape products and Post-It notes. However, there comes a time where even organisations such as 3M are not able to sustain their competitive advantage in all areas. At such times, as 3M has found, businesses begin to sell off less profitable areas and to divest some of their business involvements.

Core competencies and core products do not diminish with use. There is not a point at which there are negative returns to use. However, the manner in which they are used may contribute to an organisation's demise. In this case, 3M has expanded into so many market areas that it is not

able to sustain them all. Its core competence is in plastic products (particularly adhesive plastic products and glues). It has entered many markets by creating and adapting products to make them large-volume sellers. As a result, 3M has been very successful. Although it has remained true to its core competence, the size to which the corporation has grown means that more and more products have been unsuccessful. It may be that there have been less effective channels of communication and less sharing of ideas between research and development departments within the different divisions into which 3M has become split.

In the future, 3M intends to concentrate on new product development; much of its revenue comes from products less than four years old. It does, however, intend to spread itself less thinly, and to concentrate on a smaller (but still considerable) number of core technologies, where it has a proven ability.

## ◆ CASE STUDY 16.4

## The outing of outsourcing

There can be few companies whose **outsourcing** strategy is as well-coiffed as that of TopsyTail. This small Texan company has sold $100m-worth of its hairstyling gadgets since 1991. And yet it has virtually no permanent employees of its own. Almost everything the company does – design, manufacturing, marketing, distribution and packaging – is handled by subcontractors. Tomima Edmark, TopsyTail's boss, says her company could not have grown so swiftly in any other way.

Outsourcing, as this reliance on subcontractors is known, used to be a last resort for big companies in trouble. Now, says Frank Casale, executive director of the Outsourcing Institute in New York, it is part and

parcel of the way American companies of all sizes do their business. Having shrunk and reorganised themselves to focus on their 'core competences', big firms turn to specialists to supply them with everything from janitors and guards to salesmen and machine operators. Small firms, meanwhile, see the use of outsourcers as a way to reduce risk and grow rapidly without taking on extra fixed costs.

The outsourcing boom has transformed American business into a daisy-chain of arm's-length alliances, and brought a host of new firms selling services that others no longer want to perform for themselves. No task seems too specialised or humble to have become the 'core competence' of some such outsourcer. Typical of the new breed are Matrixx Marketing, a telephone-sales firm in Cincinnati whose 9000 workers handle up to 140m phone calls a year for a stable of clients, and Milwaukee's Johnson Controls, which specialises in maintaining buildings and in making car seats.

The outsourcers, moreover, subcontract for one another. Thus one of the clients of Octel Network Services, a firm in Dallas that operates more than 1m electronic voice 'mailboxes', is Electronic Data Systems, a big computer-services company. EDS, in turn, all but invented information-technology (IT) outsourcing. It has a $3.2 billion contract to run Xerox's computer and telecoms network, a deal that involves some 1700 of Xerox's employees transferring to EDS. And Xerox itself provides invoicing and billing services for Motorola, which in turn designs and makes parts of Octel's voice-messaging systems.

In principle there is nothing wrong, and indeed much that is right, with this circularity. It is simply the latest manifestation of the efficiency-creating division of labour that Adam Smith observed with such delight in an English pin factory two centuries ago. Mr Casale forecasts that firms in America will spend $100 billion on outsourcing in 1996, and by so doing will cut their costs by 10–15%. But can the division of labour sometimes go too far? In their scramble to outsource, some American firms are in danger of tripping themselves up.

When Compaq Computer, a leading personal-computer maker, outsourced some of its laptop-PC production to Japan's Citizen, it hit all kinds of difficulties, in design, manufacturing, cost and quality. The problem, says Greg Petsch, head of corporate operations at Compaq, was that 'there was nobody in command.' The American firm eventually put two of its people in Citizen's factory to oversee operations. This year booming demand encouraged Compaq to try again, with Taiwan's Inventec making a new range of laptops. Though Mr Petsch says he is pleased with the results, he concedes that it would have been cheaper to make the computers in-house.

One reason why outsourcing may not live up to expectations is that American firms have already cut costs to the bone, leaving subcontractors little leeway to turn a profit. Compaq has reduced its unit costs by 70% since 1991. A combination of new production techniques and just-in-time stock control has made Harley-Davidson, a motor-cycle maker, so efficient that many of the components it formerly subcontracted are now once again made in-house. And when Chrysler recently thought of outsourcing its data-processing centres, it found that its own IT division could easily undercut the bids of big subcontractors. Tongue in cheek, the car maker offered to help one of the bidders run its own systems.

## A long-term relationship

A second drawback is that American firms have traditionally taken a piecemeal approach to outsourcing: in deciding what to contract out, they have tended to look at short-term savings in overheads, rather than at long-term strategy. By contrast, Japanese companies, which pioneered outsourcing, use it to improve long-term quality and efficiency rather than to cut overheads. This, paradoxically, has resulted in bigger savings. Outsourcing now accounts for more than a third of Japanese companies' total manufacturing costs, and routinely reduces those costs by over 20%. Some American firms have started to follow suit: Chrysler, in particular, has cut the number of its subcontractors, but is working closely in long-term relationships with those that remain.

By contrast, Vikas Kapoor and Arnab Gupta of Mitchell Madison, a New York management consultancy, see such cosy, long-term relationships between firms and subcontractors as 'almost un-American', on the grounds that they abandon the discipline of the marketplace. Messrs Kapoor and Gupta would prefer to see companies setting up more red-blooded competition between suppliers. Some firms taking that line have indeed seen dramatic results: American Express cut its supply costs by about a fifth in two years. 'We also strengthened our relationships with outsources,' says Jim Cracchiolo, the firm's head of reengineering.

American firms can also seem woefully inept at managing their relationships with outsources. Lynda Applegate, a professor at Harvard Business School, points out that many see outsourcing as a way of washing their hands of a problem. 'It isn't,' she says. After years of frustration, Compaq this year formed a separate management group to oversee its outsourcing ventures. Moreover, says Mr Petsch, the company's subcontractors must now supply daily quality data and undertake 'product-integrity audits'. He thinks too many firms run into trouble because they fail to change their management structure when they decide to outsource. For companies that rely heavily on outsourcing, he advocates the appointment of a 'chief resource officer' to oversee their supply strategy.

But even a well-managed outsourcing venture can sometimes work against a firm, especially when what is being bought in from outside is information technology. Big computer-services firms such as EDS and IBM's Integrated Systems Solutions Corporation (ISSC) make money mostly by selling tailored versions of their off-the-shelf IT sevices. This can leave clients locked into old technology (EDS was slow to move from mainframes to PCs), or into proprietary and inflexible systems (some analysts have criticised ISSC for pushing IBM's big computers too hard). And within the cost of IT tumbling,

Case study 16.4 *continued*

long-term contracts that seem cheap today may look exorbitant next year.

**May the source be with you**
Other firms fear that outsourcing may weaken their relationship with customers. Ken Hodge of Mercer Management Consulting says that several of his utility-industry clients have drawn back from outsourcing everything from fleet management to communications because they feared alienating customers. Harvard's Ms Applegate points out that 'customers can't separate out who's done what when things go wrong.' When several big American and Japanese car manufacturers were forced to recall 8m vehicles earlier this year, it was the car makers who took the flak. Few customers blamed Japan's Takata, the outsourcer that supplied the rogue seat-belt assemblies.

The difficulties of outsourcing have been compounded by the increasing resistance of trade unions. Last month Ford narrowly avoided a strike by 3600 workers protesting at the car maker's decision to sub-contract seat-making work to Johnson Controls. John Sweeney, who last month was elected head of the AFL-CIO labour confederation, has hinted that he will encourage more direct action when jobs are under threat from outside contractors.

Ironically, however, it may be the need for extra speed – the very factor which first drove many companies into the arms of outsourcers – that will force many managers to reconsider. High-tech products as diverse as pagers and PCs are increasingly being built to order, offering consumers swifter delivery of custom designs and cutting manufacturers' inventory costs, too. But if Compaq is to build its PCs to order, says Mr Petsch, it will have to rely less on outsourcing. Only by taking key operations back in-house will it achieve the flexibility and speed that building to order requires. The choice of what to do in-house, and what to outsource, should be the result of careful thought, rather than fad or fashion.

*Source*: © *The Economist*, London, 25 November 1995. Reprinted with permission.

*Comment on the case study*
As can be seen in this case study, there are organisations which, by concentrating on what they do best and **outsourcing** other activities, have been very successful. The case identifies TopsyTail as an example of success. TopsyTail has very few permanent employees of its own. Many of the activities which bring the organisation's hair-styling products to the market are subcontracted. This may be an extreme example, but it is claimed that outsourcing and subcontracting are entered into by most US organisations.

Further examples given in the case describe how companies such as Motorola (for Octel Network Services) subcontract to Xerox. Such outsourcing 'pyramids', it would seem, are commonplace in many areas of the economy. There are, however, potentially great problems for the organisation at the top of the pile. Compaq, for instance, failed to outsource effectively with respect to its laptop personal computers (to Japan). There are problems associated with quality standards, control mechanisms and, perhaps most importantly, business objectives.

The case claims that Japanese outsourcing is more successful because the organisations involved are more agreeable to longer-term contracts and to working closely with suppliers. The Japanese are well known for their long-termist attitude to business. Other organisations, such as those in the USA and Europe, are typically seen as interested in activities and projects which result in short-term, high-level gains. This means that there is less willingness in many cases to work closely with suppliers and more of a desire to cut costs and make gains at the expense of another company. Such objectives are linked to the idea that unless there is competition in the supply market, the best deal may not have been struck. Suppliers are regularly asked to bid for contracts which might generate better payoffs if lengthened, rather than shortened, to give both parties time to work together more effectively.

The case concludes not that outsourcing is an undesirable activity, but that it is not being managed effectively in many instances. Therefore, by taking more time to set up the agreements and establishing working practices and standards, outsourcing may be made mutually beneficial. The 'quick kill' which many perceive outsourcing as giving seems to be increasingly a myth or fantasy rather than reality.

# CONCLUDING REMARKS

Overall, several observations may be drawn from this chapter. The identification of core competence and the desire to exploit that competence encourage organisations to outsource many more non-core activities. As a result of exploiting core competences, organisations seem to be heavily involved in research and development activity (resulting in innovation); 3M and Honda are examples. This means that they do not confine themselves only to traditional businesses and markets, but operate wherever they are able to sell their products.

Benchmarking has enabled organisations to compare their performances against 'best in class' and also against their own historical records. For this information to become available, levels of trust and collaboration must exist. In some cases, organisations are joining clubs to share this kind of information.

Other situations which exhibit trust and collaboration between organisations are the many joint ventures which have arisen in recent years. Partly these share funds and partly they share expertise. One of the factors leading to the need to share both is the increase in barriers to entry into new markets. Advertising, technology and experience requirements mean that one organisation alone is not willing or able to finance the risk involved. Additionally, the time taken to acquire the expertise from scratch might be prohibitive in terms of gaining successful results.

# SUMMARY

◆ There are three stages in the innovational process: invention, innovation and diffusion. There are different incentives for innovation for individuals, competitive organisations and monopolies.

◆ Before developing an innovation into a market-place product or process, the organisation will consider the likely payoff it will make against the risk associated with success of the project. Additionally, the timing of the launch and threat of imitation by competitors will affect the innovator's decision.

◆ Imitation can be delayed or prevented by patenting products. If a product or process has a particularly steep learning curve for others to follow, then the time before it is imitated may be lengthened.

◆ Core competences within organisations are the key processes or systems which can be identified and reproduced to gain competitive advantage over competitors.

◆ Constraints on expansion and diversification with reference to core competence and economies of scale arise where the organisation attempts to control too many markets simultaneously, or where it grows so large that it begins to attract diseconomies of scale as a result of its size and scope.

# REVIEW QUESTIONS

1 Discuss the view that a monopolist is more likely to innovate than an organisation in a competitive position.

2 Identify five organisations which are well known in your region or country. With reference to each, what is the organisation's core competence, what is its core product and how does it use these across a variety of product market types?

3 Give a brief exposition of the manner in which economies of scope and synergy may theoretically be used for strategic advantage. Offer examples of organisations which may be seen to be exploiting such economies of scope and synergy.

4 Outline the changes which occur in a market or industry as it matures. What are the implications of such changes for the strategic choices and competitive weaponry typically used by organisations?

**5** Discuss the problems arising for any organisation wishing to embark on a benchmarking survey of its activities. Are there any ways in which these problems may be alleviated?

**6** Outsourcing remains popular, although some organisations can be seen to be moving away from it. Give arguments for and against outsourcing, with reference to examples from the business world.

## GLOSSARY OF NEW TERMS

**Benchmarking:** Measuring aspects of an organisation's performance against other organisations (normally from the same industry or market). Usually, key performance indicators are quantified to enable the organisation to gauge its own performance against that of others.

**Core competence:** A key activity, process or system possessed by an organisation which allows it to gain competitive advantage over competitors.

**Diffusion:** Acceptance and use of an innovation by other organisations, by imitation, licence agreements or sale.

**Innovation:** The process of developing an invention to such a state that it may be launched in the marketplace.

**Invention:** The physical (tangible) output resulting from an idea.

**Outsourcing:** Contracting out/subcontracting activities, where an organisation enters into agreements with its suppliers to establish formal standards for delivery times, quality of product and so on.

**Synergy:** Quite simply: 2 + 2 = 5! That is, the sum of the parts is greater than the whole. Exploiting synergy means that the organisation (or its departments) is able to organise and share knowledge and skills in such a way that the whole organisation benefits.

## READING

Brozen, Y (1983) *Concentration, Mergers and Public Policy*, Collier Macmillan, Oxford.

Carlton, D W and Perloff, J M (1994) *Modern Industrial Organization*, 2nd edn, HarperCollins, New York.
*A very readable text with illustrative cases, which has sections and chapters relating to the economics discussed in this chapter.*

Davies, S and Lyons, B (1998) *The Economics of Industrial Organisation*, Addison Wesley Longman, Harlow.
*A more involved economics text, giving more in-depth discussion of the theory and empirical evidence relating to the innovative process, economies of scale, entry barriers and strategic behaviour. Mathematical proofs and discussion of theoretical points are included.*

Ferguson, P R and Ferguson, G J (1994) *Industrial Economics: Issues and Perspectives*, 2nd edn, Macmillan, Basingstoke.
*An economics text which has some useful sections relating to the role of advertising and economies of scale, and which gives an in-depth exposition of the rationale and process for invention, innovation and diffusion.*

Mintzberg, H (1990) 'The design school: reconsidering the premises of strategic management,' *Strategic Management Journal*, Vol 11, pp 171–95.
*Offers an insight into the Design School criticism of Porter's 1980s texts. Included here as a result of its discussion of distinctive competences.*

Prahalad, C K and Hamel, G (1990) 'The core competence of the corporation,' *Harvard Business Review*, May–June.

Schumpeter, J A (1934) *The Theory of Economic Development*, Harvard University Press, Boston, MA.

Timmerman, A (1995) *Benchmarking International Survey*, Coopers and Lybrand Internal Working Paper, London.
*An internal report which makes comparisons between the use of benchmarking techniques across Europe. The report is based on empirical data provided by organisations and includes a survey of attitudes about benchmarking.*

### Further reading
Bowman, C and Asch, D (1987) *Strategic Management*, Macmillan, Basingstoke.

Griffiths, A and Wall, S (1997) *Applied Economics*, 7th edn, Addison Wesley Longman, Harlow.

Johnson, G and Scholes, K (1997) *Exploring Corporate Strategy: Text and Cases*, 4th edn, Prentice Hall, Hemel Hempstead.

Morden, T (1993) *Business Strategy and Planning: Text and Cases*, McGraw-Hill, Maidenhead.

Selznick, P (1957) *Leadership in Administration*, Harper & Row, Scranton, Penn.

Shrivastava, P (1994) *Strategic Management: Concepts and Practices*, Southwestern, Cincinnati, Ohio.

CHAPTER **17**

# TRANSACTION COST ECONOMICS

## OBJECTIVES

◆ To examine the role of transaction costs as a catalyst to organisational growth, both horizontally, vertically and in a diversified manner.

◆ To consider how transaction costs may be reduced if economic coordination takes place within an organisation.

◆ To explain the specialisation or asset specificity of resources as a factor behind the growth of organisations.

◆ To examine the role of market failure and the means by which governments may or may not take action dependent on the size of the transaction cost/benefit ratio.

◆ To explain labour market skill ratios and the role of productivity in determining the appropriate control mechanisms.

## KEY TERMS

Asset specificity

Backward vertical integration

Bounded rationality

Externality

Forward vertical integration

Free-rider

Impacted information

Opportunism

Perfect information

Strategic business alliance

Transaction cost

## CHAPTER OUTLINE

Business application

Definition of transaction costs

Transaction costs and economic coordination

Case study 17.1 Taking the paper out of trade

Williamson's development of transaction cost analysis

Asset specificity

Market failures and transaction costs

Case study 17.2 Dutch cartel loses appeal

Case study 17.3 US insurers face a bill for toxic waste fund

Transaction costs and vertical integration

The transaction cost approach to labour

Case study 17.4 Regulation blamed for stifling new EU jobs

Strategic business alliances

Case study 17.5 The good and the bad of bigness

Summary

Review questions

Glossary of new terms

Reading

# Trust: the basis of market economy

Can the market economy be the panacea for the problems within an economy? Well, almost. Francis Fukuyama believes that neoclassical free-market economics is about 80 per cent right, but the other 20 per cent is crucial. Culture, he argues, comes before economics. By culture he means the way in which groups combine into teams, as in darts clubs, parent–teacher associations and in companies. The reason why these clubs work is trust, and this is the foundation of individuals' ability to work productively together.

Most economic activity is carried out by organisations and this requires a high degree of social cooperation. Property rights, contracts and commercial law are all indispensable institutions behind the successful working of a market-oriented system. However, it is possible to economise substantially on transaction costs (the cost of specifying and policing contracts) if such institutions are supplemented by social capital and trust. High trust is, therefore, synonymous with low cost.

High-trust societies such as Germany and Japan find it easy to establish large, impersonally managed companies which last for generations, such as Toyota and BMW. Low-trust societies either need state help to form large companies (Thomson, France; ENI, Italy) or are limited to sectors which thrive on entrepreneurial family firms (Hong Kong, China).

However, trust is frustratingly difficult to measure. Nonetheless, as an advert indicated in January 1996, 'the loyalty and commitment of customers, workers, suppliers, regulators, the public at large . . . is a company's most valuable asset'. Thus, although many companies during the 1980s have downsized, outsourced, hived off less profitable parts, demerged or set up internal markets according to economic theory, they may have lost the strength of firm-wide relations. For example, if we take the internal markets that have been set up in the British Broadcasting Company (BBC) or the National Health Service (NHS) in the UK, these may reveal the cost of internal services but they also have increased transaction costs as they undermine the integrity of the institution as a whole. While the first law of the market is that it always does things cheaper, the second is that it is never as cheap as you think, the apparent gain being eaten up by transaction and agency costs.

Enormous management effort is spent rebuilding the dismantled trust through the market mechanism such as supplier partnerships, thereby removing and protecting the relationship from the very market that was invoked to sharpen the business up.

*Source*: Simon Caulkin, *The Observer*, 21 January 1996. Reprinted with permission.

## Comment

The notion of trust, or lack of trust, outlined in the case indicates the costs to an organisation of monitoring relationships. The organisation may have to protect itself from **opportunism** by suppliers, or opportunism by its workers which have specific skills which only this organisation uses. The monitoring may be replaced by contractual arrangements between both parties. But if these transaction costs, or costs of the market, are too high, then the organisation may seek to subsume these costs within the organisation. Here, the costs of the market are replaced by the costs of monitoring the product and individual actions by management. It is possible that monitoring can be undertaken by peer groups, and such an approach is developed in this chapter. On occasions, peer-group monitoring will be replaced by hierarchical monitoring as the organisation grows and the processes of production become more complex.

This chapter, therefore, seeks to develop and analyse the different transaction costs that can affect the performance of the organisation, and considers further how transaction costs can be used to explain the growth of the organisation through horizontal, vertical and multinational activity.

# DEFINITION OF TRANSACTION COSTS

**Transaction cost** means the cost of using the market. Organisations are active in the marketplace for a variety of reasons. They are there to transform scarce resources into products or services, which are then sold in markets, and in doing so expect to gain from these activities. But this participation is not a costless activity and is accompanied by a variety of costs that cannot be avoided if the market transaction is to occur. Any purchaser requires information on the product, and for some products this acquisition of information can involve substantial costs. Furthermore, there may have to be substantial negotiations between buyer and seller, for example between the government and the companies purchasing television franchises. After the transaction has taken place, still more costs will be incurred to ensure that both parties to the transaction live up to their side of any bargain – contract costs. These costs of taking part in trade and exchange are the transaction costs. It is these transaction costs that cause organisations to be developed. If an interaction in the open market leads to high transaction costs, then it may be possible to perform the activity more efficiently inside the organisation. Thus if organisations are more efficient at undertaking transactions than relying on trade and exchange between individuals, there is an economic reason for the development of the organisation.

As an example of this process, consider an individual who has purchased a brand new house. Externally this may require a lawn to be laid, borders to be dug, borders to be stocked and a paved area developed. It is possible that the purchaser of the property can do all these things themselves. For most people the transaction costs of developing the garden would be extensive as they seek to find out information and monitor the contractual arrangements between garden suppliers, builders, garden designers etc. Garden development firms can economise on the transaction costs and more efficiently carry out the tasks.

Of course, although there are lower transaction costs for the garden development firms, these transaction costs are not zero since the information possessed by the firms is partial, but they are likely to have greater knowledge than the home owner. Although it is well known to applied economists that transaction costs are not zero and information is not free, this is in contrast to the traditional theoretical view of economic agents, in which optimal decisions are made on the basis of complete information. Because in practice more information is known by some than by others, information is **impacted**. In addition, there is said to be **bounded rationality** in the transaction cost approach. That is, individuals are limited in their ability to handle intricate information. This diverges from the traditional approach in which individuals are assumed to process unlimited amounts of information.

# TRANSACTION COSTS AND ECONOMIC COORDINATION

Transaction costs may be avoided if economic coordination takes place within the organisation. Thus the importance of transaction cost analysis is that it can explain why the organisation itself comes into existence. For example, suppose that an individual wishes to buy a shrub from a garden centre. If this garden centre saves seeds or cuttings, grows them on and then sells the fully grown shrub through its outlet, the process is vertically integrated. Such a scenario is not always the case. Seed merchants exist who only sell seed. This can be purchased by nurseries who plant the seed and begin the growing process. Finally the fully grown plant is sold to a garden centre for sale to the general public. In the first case of the vertically integrated organisation, it has to undertake the tasks of policing and organising which would have been undertaken by the market. This process of coordination would involve management costs, such as making sure the correct amount of plants come through the growing process and monitoring heat in the greenhouses. If the process from seed to shrub is undertaken by a number of independent organisations, there will be transaction costs, such as adhering to the contractual arrangements for delivery and for quality. Thus management costs are the organisation's equivalent of transaction costs in using the market.

Management's role is to find out as much information as possible about the technical processes involved with plant production, to consider ways in which the costs of production can be reduced, and to estimate ways in which staff can be motivated. Where management does not possess these skills, coordination becomes expensive.

Thus there is a need for both organisations and the market to coordinate economic activities. Whether the organisation does all the arrangements itself or uses the market depends on comparing the transaction costs of the market with the management costs of the organisation.

Therefore in most markets there may exist both types of institution. Of course, transaction costs are not limited to garden centres: they occur in a wide variety of markets, as the case above indicates.

## ◆ CASE STUDY 17.1

# Taking the paper out of trade

**FT**

The General Agreement on Tariffs and Trade recently put the global gains from the Uruguay Round trade liberalising accords at an eventual $500 bn a year. This could be boosted by another $100 bn, by cutting the costs of doing business abroad.

The United Nations International Symposium on Trade Efficiency is focusing on ways of making trade cheaper and easier, so enabling small companies and poorer nations to exploit the global market on more equal terms with established traders.

According to the UN Conference on Trade and Development the costs of voluminous paperwork, complex formalities and associated delays and errors amount to about 10 per cent of the final value of goods. A typical transaction may involve 30 different parties, 60 original documents and 360 document copies, all of which have to be checked, transmitted, re-entered into various information systems, processed and filed. For small companies this can be daunting, even without the additional handicaps faced by many Third World exporters such as poor infrastructure and cumbersome, sometimes corrupt, bureaucracies.

However, transaction costs – totalling perhaps $400 bn a year by the end of the decade – could be sliced by 25 per cent by streamlining procedures and extending use of paperless trading, Unctad argues.

The symposium is expected to adopt recommendations for tackling problems encountered by exporters in the areas of transport trade information, telecommunications, business practices, and customs and finance, with special emphasis on the difficulties confronting smaller companies and developing countries.

One example is computerisation to speed up customs clearance, increase government revenues and reduce opportunities for corruption. Unctad's Automated System for Customs Data, used by more than 60 developing countries, enabled Ghana and Mauritius, for example, to cut clearance times from a week to half a day, and Sri Lanka boosted revenues by $25 m or 10 per cent in the first three months of operation, despite lower tariff rates. Although more than 100 companies operate fully automated customs clearing systems, most trade transactions are still paper based. Errors and delays in paperwork cost companies business and customers. With the growing trend towards purchasing 'just-in-time', delays increasingly imply lost business. If local suppliers can produce and deliver inputs within a given deadline, remote suppliers must be able to do likewise or they will lose market share.

Similar problems apply to the other essential of successful trading – business information. This is increasingly available in electronic form but many companies, especially in the Third World, could find themselves excluded from trade if they cannot adequately exploit the new technologies.

*Source: Financial Times, 13 October 1994. Reprinted with permission.*

*Comment on the case study*

Paperless trading therefore provides one way in which the proportionately heavier costs of trading by small organisations or by weaker trading nations can be reduced. For these smaller countries the chances that errors will occur are far greater and, in a world where set delivery times are playing an increasingly important role in international trading agreements, the transaction costs of monitoring contracts are reduced by moving away from a paper-based system. This benefits both large companies in developed countries and those companies in the Third World. The former are now finding that transaction costs have been reduced with the companies in the Third World.

## ◆ Exercise 17.1

1 Suppose that there is a company in France which is trading with a supplier in Nigeria. What transaction costs are likely to be involved in any trading agreements?

2 How could transaction costs damage the export potential of small organisations?

3 How could reductions in transaction costs enhance or harm the competitive positions of companies?

## Governance costs

The level of competition could influence the choice of organisation or market from which to buy. If there are few suppliers, then an organisation may face higher prices for its inputs and may proceed to consider developing these in-house, thereby reducing transaction costs. Such a scenario was considered in the discussion of Porter's five forces in Chapter 14.

Although governance costs were considered in Chapter 3, these impose transaction costs on both the market and the organisation to encourage individuals to behave in the appropriate manner. Both the market and the organisation can provide the conditions under which individuals will be motivated or given incentives to achieve optimal production. On occasion the market offers conditions of great efficiency. There is the profit motive, and this pursuit of profits provides the incentive to drive down costs as well as developing tight contractual arrangements. This process, however, does not rule out the problems of **opportunism** in the case where a contract is unlikely to be renewed. Within the organisation it may not be possible to organise a close substitute for the market. Incentives for employees may come from various different reward systems, such as profit-related pay or through promotion if particular targets are met. The extent to which opportunism can be reduced in the workplace may depend on how effective sanctions are at limiting opportunism and thereby reducing governance costs.

As the organisation grows, governance costs may rise and it may be difficult to control opportunism. In addition, as the organisation grows there may be an increase in the type of assets which are related solely to one purpose – asset specificity – and this again gives rise to an increased chance for opportunism. The increase in governance costs may lead to cost disadvantages for some organisations compared to others, particularly where the organisations come from different cultures with different ethical backgrounds. Thus organisations in cultures which have less ethical behaviours may find themselves becoming less competitive, particularly where they rely on contractual relationships outside the organisation. Thus a way of reducing their governance costs may be to make greater use of coordination within their organisation.

## WILLIAMSON'S DEVELOPMENT OF TRANSACTION COST ANALYSIS

Coase's (1937) contention was that efficiency was the motivating force behind the emergence of organisations. Coase saw the organisation as a series of relationships that came into being when resources needed to be directed by an entrepreneur. This system of relationships develops from the cooperation of a number of factors of production. Given that the world is uncertain and dynamic, it is essential for the organisation to be able to enforce contracts and settle any disputes. It is the contractual relationship and its enforcement that distinguish the organisation or entrepreneur from a set of contractual exchanges that exist in the market. Of course, some of the contractual exchanges can be undertaken by the operation of the market mechanism, but the organisation has emerged as a means of economising on transaction costs. This does not suggest that the organisation will always supersede market transacting, since internal transacting within the organisation may provide no cost saving. If there is no cost saving by the organisation undertaking a number of tasks within its organisational structure, then the organisation may purchase these services at no greater cost from the market. This would suggest that there would be many units undertaking contractual relationships with one another and that these units themselves would not need to change their functional expertise, since they too can purchase what they need as effectively from the market. This could provide one of the reasons for the existence of a large market for the self-employed. In addition, if there are decreasing returns to the entrepreneurial function, this may explain why some organisations remain small and some grow. In this case, the organisation expands up to the point at which the marginal cost of an extra transaction equals the marginal cost of the same transaction carried out in the market or by another organisation. Overall, Coase believed that it was transaction costs which were responsible for the emergence of organisations and were a determinant of their size.

Nonetheless, it has been pointed out that it may be working together as a team that creates organisations rather than the transaction cost savings. Williamson (1975), while conceding that team working can provide benefits, is more inclined to agree with the view expressed by Coase that the development of organisations is due to economising on transaction costs. Williamson's view is that business activity is carried out in a complex environment and one in which uncertainty exists. Because individuals are limited in their use of information, they may not be perfectly rational in their behaviour. The interaction of imperfectly rational individuals with environmental attributes can lead to substantial transaction costs. Attempts to reduce these transaction costs result in the types of business organisation that we see today. For example, suppose that the market is made up of many highly competitive organisations. If one of these behaves in a manner which takes advantage of the customer, this deceit will soon be noticed by the market and the organisation may be forced to leave the industry in the long run. Suppose, however, that the deceit occurs in a market where there is a single organisation. In this case, a great deal of time and energy may need to be involved in establishing a contractual relationship between buyer and seller. This contract will need to be monitored closely. It may well be that a party may feel that they can undertake the task at less cost themselves rather than experience the transaction costs associated with dealing with the deceitful organisation. What Williamson suggested was that efficiency in reducing these transaction costs was the reason for the organisation emerging and this may influence whether it makes decisions to expand horizontally or vertically, looks towards joint ventures, mergers or the development of multinational activity.

## ASSET SPECIFICITY

**Asset specificity** refers to the extent to which a resource is specific to its current use. Assets which are highly specific are likely to have almost zero other usage. This concept will be seen again in terms of contestable markets and sunk costs in Chapter 18.

For example, a footballer who can do nothing else but play football is asset specific. This may seem odd and suggests ranges of human asset specificity. A footballer can switch from one club to another, therefore it might be suggested that their human asset specificity is low. However, suppose that this highly skilled footballer has received a large amount of the skill training at one club – for the sake of this example let us use Liverpool FC. This person's skills fit within a highly effective passing game. These type of skills may not be required

if the player was to move to Wimbledon FC, which is more renowned for its 'long ball' game. Because the footballer's skills are more specific for Liverpool they may not be fully transferable. The presence of organisation-specific skills or human asset specificity implies transactional problems, since the footballer acquires monopolistic powers but may lose some of their passing skills if dismissed. In addition, if the footballer quits or is dismissed, Liverpool FC will need to incur extra expenses to train their replacement. It is a noticeable phenomenon at Liverpool FC that when any new player is bought from another football club there is a time lag before the new purchase enters the side. This time delay is usually so that the new player can learn to play in the Liverpool style. Although human asset specificity may be relatively high in the football example, for many occupations, such as engineers or architects, who are relatively mobile, the asset specificity is low and for street cleaners and refuse collectors almost insignificant.

However, an additional source of transaction cost in the case of human resources relates to monitoring individuals to make sure that they are putting in sufficient effort. It may be difficult to monitor footballers without getting them to repeat the task and, given these substantial monitoring costs, what may follow is vertical integration between football club and footballer, that is, employee ownership. For some occupations, such as lawyers or solicitors, this measurement of productivity may not be a problem, since it can be easily quantified in terms of the revenue they bring in. Thus the transaction costs for labour will vary depending on the occupation.

Capital may also have asset specificity. If there is a complex piece of machinery that can only be used in one type of production process, this is asset specific.

There are other forms of asset specificity to consider. A whisky distillery associated with a particular brand of whisky requiring water from a particular Scottish river next to the distillery may have site specificity. The distillery could be elsewhere, but there would be transportation costs involved. The distillery could be placed close to another river, but there may be a loss in the unique taste of this Scottish whisky. Similarly, site specificity can be seen with the Cognac area of France and the types of grapes grown there.

Some machinery may only be able to undertake a particular task, and this type of resource is said to have physical asset specificity. All the types of asset specificity above are likely to be associated with a limited range of buyers or sellers. Suppose that we have an organisation in the second stage of production which purchases items from a company in the first stage of production. If the primary producer finds that asset specificity is increasing, it becomes increasingly likely that the organisation in the second stage of production will find its costs rising. Why? The reason for this is that, as asset specificity increases, the primary organisation may be placed in a position where their output is very narrowly focused. Before, when they had less asset specificity, their output may have served a number of organisations. Thus as asset specificity rises the primary producer may lose economies of scale. This will be associated with higher average costs per unit of output and thus the organisation in the second stage of production may find it beneficial to purchase the organisation in the earlier stage. That is, it may vertically integrate backwards. What is being said here is that if governance costs are greater than the costs of buying in the market, the organisation will continue to buy in the market, but once the growth in asset specificity reaches a particular point, the actual costs of buying externally may exceed the governance costs of controlling the production of the primary product in-house and it is now worth the organisation vertically integrating.

## MARKET FAILURES AND TRANSACTION COSTS

In Chapter 9 a number of features of the behaviour of monopolistic firms were developed. In equilibrium, the profit-maximising monopolist, by equating marginal revenue to marginal cost, creates a deadweight loss to society and a reduction in consumer surplus. It was also shown that if a monopolist could separate its markets price discrimination was possible, which would yield a higher level of profits. For complete price discrimination the monopolist would like to charge a separate price to each of its customers. This is known as first-order price discrimination. This approach is possible where products are sold to the highest bidders through sealed auction bids. The auction approach is more appropriate for situations where the volume of sales is low, where there are many potential buyers who are unable to cooperate among each other, but who all have the same information about the product. Therefore, first-order price discrimination is possible for products such as art objects, antique furniture, the rights to mining or exploration or to television franchises. For less expensive goods and services, such as hairdressing or medical care, it may also be possible to use first-order price discrimination, particularly at exclusive hair salons or upmarket private medical practices. However, in practice the costs that are incurred by trying to bargain with each customer may be prohibitive. In other words, the transaction costs may be sufficiently large that the best solution for the monopolist may be to charge all customers the same price or different prices for different bundles of the commodity. This would be the price that equates to the monopolist's marginal revenue/marginal cost equilibrium. Of course, there may also be transaction costs involved in obtaining the true position of the marginal revenue/marginal cost curves.

The costs of trying to bargain with customers separately are not limited to the monopoly situation. If a number of competitive organisations can form a cartel, it may be possible to reduce the transaction costs of dealing with the market by charging a single price.

◆ CASE STUDY 17.2

## Dutch cartel loses appeal

The European Court of First Instance (CFI) has rejected an appeal by 29 Dutch building contractor associates. The association had appealed against a 1992 European Commission decision that refused them an exemption from EC competition rules and imposed fines totalling ECU22.5 million.

The Commission decision concerned the constitution and certain rules on tendering procedures and prices of the member of the Dutch national builders association.

The rules of the Dutch builders association (SPO) provided that, when several members tender for a building contract, the SPO must hold a meeting to determine the lowest competitive tender. The tenderer chosen (the entitled) is then protected in various ways from competition from the other members, thus reducing the freedom of choice of the customers awarding the construction contract.

The regulations also required certain price increases to be added to the tender price to cover reimbursement by the entitled undertaking of tender costs incurred by the unsuccessful members (calculation costs).

The CFI confirmed the Commission's findings that the rules in question restricted competition in breach of the treaty, since there was an unlawful exchange of price information and concerted action by the would-be tenderers on the terms and prices of their tenders which limited the parties' freedom to negotiate.

The CFI rejected the association's criticism of the Commission's micro-economic analysis of their rules, which they claimed were intended to remedy macro-economic structural imbalances between supply and demand. These resulted from the characteristics of the sector and from the Dutch legislation, which favoured the consumer and did not facilitate counteraction to the 'playing-off' of tenders by the contract awarders.

The Court also found that the restrictions of competition were not indispensable to achieve their alleged aims, namely improvement of the market balance between supply and demand by limiting transaction costs and to counteract 'play-offs' which could lead to ruinous competition between tenders. In particular, the contractor awarders who knew their requirements best were excluded from the system.

*Source. Financial Times, 7 March 1995. Reprinted with permission.*

### ◆ Exercise 17.2

1 Why did the Dutch building contractors want to be exempted from EU competition rules?

2 Suppose that a cartel fixes the price of its output. How can this save on transaction costs?

### *Comment on the case study*

Both in the case of a monopolists and where a cartel is formed, organisations have argued that this is one way of reducing their transaction costs. In the case of the Dutch cartel, since they do not have to deal with a highly competitive market, one in which they would have to consider very carefully the prices that could be charged for a contract by their competitors, there are savings in transaction costs. If these savings had been passed on to the consumer or the awarder of the contract, then their case might have been stronger. In fact, the reverse appears to be the case as a markup on price occurred to reimburse those building firms which were not successful in gaining the contract.

## Analysis of externalities

A similar type of analysis as described above can be applied to externalities. An **externality** occurs when the market fails to reflect all the economic costs and/or benefits resulting from an operation or when the economic agent fails to take account of its own activities on others. For example, an externality occurs when a factory discharges pollution into the atmosphere and does not take account of its effect on individuals who live nearby. If this is the case, there are a number of ways in which the pollutant can be encouraged to produce an output which is closer to the socially optimal level. The polluter could face legal action from the individuals who live nearby. In this case the polluter could offer monetary compensation to the individuals and continue to pollute, it could reduce pollution altogether, or it could reduce pollution by a certain amount and offer limited compensation to the individuals. Suppose, however, that the polluter has the right to pollute. In this case the individual may be willing to pay the polluter not to produce. Whichever method is adopted, the polluter is now moved to an output level that corresponds more closely to the socially optimal level. However, this result depends on the assumptions of **perfect information** and zero transaction costs. If the individuals wish to take legal action against the polluter, it is possible that the transaction costs of taking legal action outweigh the potential gains from reduced pollution. In addition, it cannot be assumed that everyone will pay their part of the costs of undertaking the legal action. Some individuals may **free-ride** on the fact that others are more likely to pay. In other words, they hope to benefit from the legal action but at no extra cost. In both these cases, the legal action may not take place and the externalities may stay in existence.

◆ CASE STUDY 17.3

## US insurers face a bill for toxic waste fund    **FT**

The Clinton administration is proposing to set up a $3 bn fund paid for by the insurance industry as part of its overhaul of the controversial Superfund laws governing the clean-up of toxic waste sites. The new fund, to be built up by a levy on the industry starting at $500 million a year, would help settle insurance claims arising from waste dumped before 1986, when the Superfund law was revised, and cut down on lawsuits.

The administration's draft legislation would also set up a new form of arbitration process for allocating responsibility for cleaning up waste sites, under the auspices of an independent expert, and make other changes that it hopes would resolve some of the law's current problems in assigning liability.

Superfund legislation was first passed in 1980 amid public outcry over notorious dumps such as Love Canal, near the Niagara Falls, or Kentucky's Valley of the Drums. Its operation, however, has been widely criticised for the unfairness with which liability is distributed, the slowness of clean-ups – only 217 of the 1280 sites

listed as national priorities have been declared clean – and the amount of time and money spent on litigation. A study by the Rand Corporation, a California-based think-tank, estimated that transaction costs ate up 27 per cent of the money spent on clean-ups.

The administration's proposals would make clean-ups quicker and cheaper. The proposals are estimated to cut the length of clean-up by 10 to 20 per cent and the cost of the clean-up by up to 25 per cent. The draft legislation aims to introduce some consistency by setting up national standards for clean-ups, although these standards will vary according to the future use of land.

One of the most controversial aspects of Superfund has been the application of joint and several liability, in which companies which contributed only a little to the pollution of a site may end up being saddled with most of the bill because other polluters have gone out of business. The new bill retains this principle of joint and several liability, but now allows businesses to settle their share and not worry about being sued by others.

*Source: Financial Times, 4 February 1994. Reprinted with permission.*

---

◆ **Exercise 17.3**

Would a fixed fee for legal costs increase the clean-up of environmental pollution?

---

*Comment on the case study*

Although the Europeans have an equivalent, the Superfund legislation reinforces the problem that the actual cost of undertaking the control of pollution, and in this case the litigation costs, may outweigh the benefits that are to be gained. On a case-by-case basis some areas of pollution may not be economic to put right, although this is very much dependent on the value placed on the environment once returned to its former usage. Herein may lie a weakness: to what extent is it possible to predict the future usage of land?

## Regional policy

Other areas where market failure can take place can be seen in the context of regional policy. It is acknowledged that some regions in Europe and the UK are more prosperous than others. For example, in the European Union the triangle encompassing London, Hamburg and Turin contains regions

where the gross national product *per capita* greatly exceeds that of the rest of the EU. If information is perfect and capital and labour are perfectly mobile, organisations should move to the regions of Europe with higher unemployment because costs are lower. In reality this is not the case. Labour costs do not always fall quickly in high unemployment areas, labour is not perfectly mobile because of social ties and cultural factors, and organisations may not move to high unemployment areas because the infrastructure and the various skills required are not there. Conversely, the more prosperous regions tend to continue to attract the better organisations and the better-skilled individuals. This adds to the cost of housing, journey-to-work times and pollution costs. These are externalities that occur because the market fails to achieve an efficient allocation of resources and this process is only taking account of the costs and benefits to the individuals and not the costs and benefits to society.

Transaction costs also play their part. Organisations and individuals may have limited knowledge of the market elsewhere and obtaining this information may be costly. If the anticipated benefits do not exceed the transaction and migration costs, the individual may well remain in an area of high unemployment. A similar argument has been developed for organisations. The costs of finding out about potential sites to which the organisation could consider moving may exceed the reduction in costs that it can achieve by moving to a lower-cost location.

## TRANSACTION COSTS AND VERTICAL INTEGRATION

Vertical integration occurs when one organisation merges with another organisation, either in an earlier stage of production (**backward vertical integration**) or with another organisation further forward in the production process (**forward vertical integration**). Many reasons have been put forward to explain why organisations grow in a vertically integrative fashion. These include the desire to increase monopoly power, to safeguard supplies, to monitor the quality of retail outlets, to reduce competition and to raise barriers to entry. For an organisation which is only in one of the stages of production, there are transaction costs of using the market. These would include searching for prices of inputs and making sure, once a price is agreed, that the quality of the input matches specification, closing contracts, collecting payments, making sure delivery occurs at specified times and the like. Vertical integration may provide one way of avoiding these costs. Technology may provide a case for organisations to be linked together vertically, but transaction costs are the decisive factor. However, after vertical integration activities which were previously external to the organisation become internalised. Workers will need to be supervised to prevent opportunism, operations must be carried out in an efficient manner and need to be coordinated.

The process of vertical integration may also save on information costs, as the process of production can be more closely monitored within the organisation and this provides consistent quality and delivery.

It is possible that specific externalities which occur in the market can be internalised by reducing transaction costs. Suppose that an organisation is dealing with a number of other organisations in different stages of production. Contracts may be signed with these. If there are changes in the external environment that result in a number of revisions of these contracts, these will

prove to be costly and in particular may require close monitoring. Where the organisation is vertically integrated contract revisions may not need to be undertaken continuously in response to outside events. Furthermore, organisations which are in different stages of production may need to pass on to each other quite technical information resulting from the specifications of the product. This exchange of information can be costly and is reduced in the vertically integrated organisation.

Once again, one of the problems that can be experienced with separate organisations is the opportunistic or undesirable behaviour of some organisations in the production process. For example, suppose that a car producer signs contracts with a body-part maker. The body-part maker produces the part to the car producer's specification. Suppose now that the car producer is not happy with the quality of the parts produced and the body-part maker feels that the specifications set for the body parts are too intricate, so that production runs do not match those needed by the car producer. Both organisations may now want to renegotiate the contract between them. In particular, the body-part maker may want to negotiate a higher price because of the intricacy involved, while the car producer would want to negotiate a lower price because the body parts are specific to this car producer. The result of these protracted negotiations and revision in the contracts may result in the car producer purchasing the body-part maker, thus reducing many of the problems experienced.

An example of opportunistic behaviour which led to organisations growing backwards has been noted in California's electricity industry during the 1980s. The electricity generators charged different prices for commercial and domestic electricity. The price of commercial electricity was set above the cost of production and the difference used to subsidise the domestic market. Industrial users, noting that the difference between actual cost of electricity generation and the prices they were being asked to pay was growing, began to look at their own manufacturing processes to generate their own electricity and by-pass the electricity-generating companies. Similarly in the UK, since the privatisation of the electricity-generating industry, there has been greater scope for large organisations to generate some of their own electricity needs.

A factor that may be important in the decision to integrate vertically or not is the degree to which assets may be specialised in particular tasks. This concept of asset specificity has been discussed earlier. In this context, where asset specificity is substantial an organisation may indulge in opportunistic behaviour and the contractual governance over opportunism may become very costly in the latter stages of production. Internal control of this exchange through vertical integration may be a more efficient governance structure. It is acknowledged that the organisation's structure may itself give rise to bureaucratic distortions. Thus the degree of asset specificity and the relative cost of governance prescribe the choice between contractual exchange and vertical integration. If asset specificity is weak, contractual exchange is likely to be the preferred option; whereas if asset specificity is strong, vertical integration is preferable.

In addition to asset specificity, externalities and uncertainty of both product and raw material quality may lead to transaction costs that provide the impetus for vertical integration. If the purchaser of an intermediate product is uncertain about the quality, and this uncertainty cannot be reduced through any contractual arrangements, backward vertical integration may follow. Increasingly, quality provides an important characteristic behind the demand for an organisation's product or service. If this quality can be delivered consistently then high premiums may be paid for the product. In addition, an organisation which achieves a poor quality rating in one area of its production process may find that this taints its other products/services. One way of redeeming the situation may be to integrate vertically, strengthening its product range.

## THE TRANSACTION COST APPROACH TO LABOUR

Labour transactions are similar to other transactions in that they involve uncertainty, can be complex and are sometimes asset specific. Thus to get the best out of the labour resource requires reductions in transaction costs. This means considering the asset specificity of labour and how to evaluate the performance of this labour. As workers become more asset specific there are increased transactional difficulties, since on the one hand they are acquiring monopolistic power within the organisation, while on the other hand there may be little use for their skills elsewhere. Moreover, if the organisation loses highly-skilled workers there will be high costs of training, since employers will not be able to transfer these skills readily to other

workers. This will impose costs on the employer. Since these costs increase with the asset specificity of the workers, the organisation needs to consider ways of retaining these workers, controlling them and getting maximum productivity from them.

A problem arises with measuring the productivity of each worker. It might be possible to measure the productivity of a group of workers or team, but allocating different productivity ratios to each worker is problematic. A number of possible scenarios could be considered, from the low skill/ease of measuring individual productivity combination to high skill/difficult to measure individual productivity. The more relevant ones for transaction costs will be discussed below.

## Low skill/difficulty in measuring individual productivity

Since group or team output can be observed, but not individual output, there is an incentive for each member of the team to avoid work. The costs of shirking are therefore not borne by the individual but by the group as a whole. To overcome this opportunistic behaviour it may be possible to monitor each individual to improve the work effort. To be effective the monitor must be able to discipline the workers and go so far as dismissing them. Since labour is not asset specific, there should be an abundance of this type on the market and total team productivity should not be greatly disrupted. For example, suppose that an educational organisation is setting up a business studies degree course which mirrors those of many other institutions that are currently available, in that it is based on general business studies skills without any specific subject specialisms, such as 'entrepreneurship' or 'doing business in China'. There may be a temptation for some individuals in the team to free-ride, allowing others to undertake most of the new course development. If one individual refuses to do anything it may be possible to dismiss this person and replace them easily with someone else who has general business experience. If, on the other hand, the institution wished to offer a specialism in an area that one member of the current staff could deliver, and that person did not wish to take part in the course development, it may prove more difficult for the institution to find a substitute if they dismissed the reluctant person.

Suppose, however, that the output of the whole group is difficult to measure. In this case organisations may attempt to pay workers less than their perceived average productivity. Because workers do not have organisation-specific skills, they may be able to find employment elsewhere if they believe that their pay is not sufficient to cover their average productivity levels. The threat of such a proposal is reduced when general levels of unemployment arise. However, the employers may not act opportunistically if they get the reputation of paying their workers less than their average productivity levels.

## High skill/ease of measuring productivity

In this case the asset-specific skills of the employees make it more difficult for them to move to other jobs. Conversely, there may be few alternative employees to which the employer can turn if one or more of their employees leaves. In this case of bilateral monopoly, there may be a large amount of bargaining over pay and other non-monetary rewards. What both parties require is continuance of employment. This can be achieved through procedures which review any problems with employment rather than institute instant dismissal, and contracts could also incorporate enhanced non-pay packages to retain employees.

## High skill/difficulty in measuring individual productivity

Efficiency here requires that the employees are dedicated to the mission of the organisation. There may be provision for almost absolute job security, as has been argued to exist in some Japanese firms

such as Sony, and this job security obtains full dedication from the employees. Therefore, what the organisation requires is a structure which encourages efficiency, reduces opportunism and bounded rationality (the inability of individuals to handle complex pieces of information). This would then reduce transaction costs. A complex structure which requires high levels of monitoring for work which is relatively simple would prove to be costly, while a simple monitoring approach for complex work would be ineffective.

Organisations which have horizontal or vertical hierarchies can reduce transaction costs through performance review and evaluation. Where the work is more complex, a structure needs to be developed which prevents both employees and employers from behaving opportunistically. Here internal labour markets are required where individuals earn relatively high rates of pay, where there exists a promotional ladder, and where it is difficult for outsiders to enter this market, that is, the ports of entry are reduced. These are all features of what is called the primary labour market, an example of which can be seen in the administration classes of the civil service in many economies. If this is contrasted with the secondary labour market, where there is low skill, low pay and relative employment instability, then there would be expected to be high turnover in the latter.

Thus the degree to which assets are specific in the labour market and the difficulty of measuring individual labour productivity can lead to high transaction costs for the organisation, which can be reduced through appropriate incentive and monitoring schemes.

## ◆ CASE STUDY 17.4

## Regulation blamed for stifling new EU jobs    FT

Government barriers to competition rather than labour market rigidities explain why recent employment creation has been lower in the European Union than in the US and Japan, according to a study on comparative employment performance published in November 1994, by McKinsey Global Institute.

The report asserts: 'If European countries had matched the job creation performance of Japan and the US over the 1980s without suffering a productivity penalty, their gross domestic products would be 5 to 15 per cent higher and their unemployment problems would have gone away'. The study urges European

policy-makers to 'abstain from regulations limiting competition even if they are intended to preserve jobs'. Strengthening general anti-trust regulations and removing barriers to market access 'are important instruments for increasing competitive intensity and overcoming vested instruments'.

The report examines employment performance in a number of industries, ranging from cars, furniture and banking to film/video/television and construction. It covers the US, Japan, France, Germany, Italy and Spain and concludes that 'product market barriers play an important part in determining employment levels'.

►

### Case study 17.4 continued

The report says restrictions in Europe have 'inhibited the emergence of new labour-intensive segments' in the film/video/television industry while in European construction 'the myriad rules and regulations' of land use, building quality, safety, rent and taxes stifled the product market.

McKinsey also questions a number of widely held assumptions about the alleged inflexibilities of the western European labour market. It suggests job protection regulations do not 'play a major role' in creating rigidities. 'While many employers complained about inflexibility in interviews, the evidence showed that when companies were forced to react to dramatic changes in the market place, they were able to overcome these barriers. The transaction costs of hiring and firing play a relatively minor role compared with total labour costs.'

*Source*: *Financial Times*, 18 November 1994. Reprinted with permission.

---

### ◆ Exercise 17.4

1 What are the transaction costs of hiring and firing labour?

2 Are these transaction costs greater for more highly skilled workers?

---

### Comment on the case study

Case study 17.4 gives a non-European perspective on the workings of the European labour market. The UK government has often suggested that UK labour markets are more flexible, and in this sense their transaction costs are lower. French, and in particular German, labour markets, when seen from a UK perspective, appear to be guided by a higher degree of regulation, thus making transaction costs higher. Work by Beatson (1995) appears to confirm this view. When manufacturing employers in Europe were questioned about whether there was insufficient flexibility in hiring and shedding labour, over 40 per cent of Italian and Dutch manufacturing employers felt it was a very important reason compared to 20 to 30 per cent of other EU member manufacturers. The UK, at 9 per cent, felt that its markets were very flexible. The McKinsey study sheds doubt on the importance of labour flexibility. However, it must be noted that within any sector there are different types of labour asset specificity and the report does not tell us whether we are dealing with high-skill or low-skill individuals in any of the sectors discussed. Moreover, the report is sector specific and it is quite possible that a different outcome could have been achieved if they had looked at biotechnology, nuclear power and clinical research.

## STRATEGIC BUSINESS ALLIANCES

Transaction cost theory has also been used to explain the development of **strategic business alliances**. These often involve large set-up and monitoring transaction costs. Included here would be the possibility that the partner in the strategic alliance may behave in a way that is detrimental to the other company's interests, and this problem may be more acute if the other company has historically been one of the organisation's main rivals. Thus the other company may be in a position to improve its competitive position.

Whether a joint venture takes place requires a comparison of the levels of uncertainty about the behaviour of the contracting partners, when both may be specialising in one area of production, with the production and acquisition costs of sole ownership. In other words, if the sole ownership route is more expensive than setting up a joint venture, with all its inherent costs, then the joint venture will take place. In the case of R&D alliances, organisations may opt for joint ventures as a way of eliminating the control costs of R&D development in-house or where the costs involved with merger or acquisition are high.

◆ **CASE STUDY 17.5**

# The good and the bad of bigness

**FT**

Bigness used to be considered a virtue in business. But it has had a decidedly bad press of late. For more than a decade, pundit after pundit, from Tom Peters to Harvard economist Michael Jensen, has sounded the death knell for large companies.

The real world has appeared to bear them out: action by governments, shareholders and management themselves has broken up all sorts of established dynasties, both sensible and unwieldy business monoliths such as AT&T, and illogical conglomerates such as ITT. Other big companies have reacted by stripping themselves 'back to basics': concentrating on their core businesses, and divesting or outsourcing the remainder. A fashion has developed for the voluntary demerger.

In the marketplace, lumbering giants, from IBM, Sears Roebuck and General Motors to the American TV networks, have been overtaken by more sprightly upstarts – Microsoft, WalMart, Toyota, CNN – and been attacked by hordes of smaller innovators. Small is now beautiful, it seems. However, is it true that we have moved from bigger is better to bigger is inefficient, costly, wastefully bureaucratic, inflexible and now, disastrous? This blanket judgement is at best misleading and at worst dangerous.

IBM appears to have reversed its strategy of breaking up the company to focusing on leveraging its economies of scale across research, development, manufacturing, distribution and services. Ford appears to be integrating the motor company's design, engineering, and manufacturing operations across the globe. Why has BMW bought Rover? Why is British Airways seeking closer integration with US Air,

Qantas and BA Deutsche? What this suggests is that in its right form, bigness can mean the organisation is vibrant, powerful and agile. What people confused was economies of scale and economies of scope. That is, some large companies were just too diverse to be managed correctly.

Nor is big necessarily fat. For example, Hewlett-Packard and 3M are big in their chosen markets but exceedingly lean in the way they are managed. The same applies to a growing number of large multinationals, both in the US and Europe.

Stripped of their superfluous businesses and activities, they are managed increasingly like a collection of small businesses – but with the difference that they also exploit scale economies in selected parts of their value chain. For many this means sharing various degrees of research, design, development and purchasing across their businesses, and also aspects of distribution and service. It also means sharing managerial skills, in particular through the common development of people. In each case, bigness brings benefits.

The trick in this process is twofold. First, to recognise that the required level of bigness varies not only between industries, but also between the various businesses and value-adding activities within each industry. The second, far harder, challenge is to achieve the requisite degree of co-ordination or integration without falling foul of what management professors call 'the cost of complexity' – what economists prefer to term 'unacceptable high transaction costs'.

*Source: Financial Times, 8 April 1994. Reprinted with permission.*

---

◆ **Exercise 17.5**

1  How does diversification increase transaction costs?

2  In the light of the case study, why might splitting up an organisation not lead to increased transaction costs?

*Comment on the case study*

Although there was a trend through the 1970s and 1980s for many organisations to grow to enhance their market position, achieve economies of scale and reduce their transaction costs, the process appears to have been reversed throughout the 1990s. On the one hand, this must have suggested that the governance costs of the diversified organisation were now becoming greater than the transac-

tion costs that had to be overcome before growth took place. On the other hand, managers may have become converted to the need for their companies to grow, irrespective of the difference between management costs and transaction costs. As the case study suggests, once the organisations are reduced in size there is a requirement for better coordination between the parts. If this is not achieved, the future could see a return to larger organisations.

The use of transaction costs to explain the activities of organisations is becoming increasingly popular. Transaction costs can explain why companies exist in the first place. If there are high transaction costs of dealing with the market, these costs may be absorbed by being internalised within the organisation. Transaction cost analysis can also explain why, once organisations come into existence, they seek to grow vertically and horizontally and some become multinational companies. Transaction costs are therefore characterised by a world in which there is a lack of complete knowledge and where the operators show self-interest and are less than perfectly rational in their decision making. Thus it is lack of trust, together with opportunism, the divergence of interest between parties, and the difficulties of undertaking contractual arrangements, that provide the basis for this relatively new approach to the theory of organisations, a theory which places the organisation at centre stage.

## SUMMARY

◆ Transaction costs, which are the cost of using the market, occur when there are conditions of uncertainty, lack of complete information and individuals are able to follow opportunistic paths. Because of high transaction costs in dealing with the market, organisations may attempt to internalise these by seeking to undertake the tasks in-house.

◆ Transaction costs can be used to explain why the organisation comes into existence. Where bounded rationality and opportunistic behaviour can be internalised at lower costs than the market, an organisation will be formed, but the degree to which the opportunistic behaviour is reduced may depend on the structure that exists within the organisation.

◆ Resources may be put to a number of uses, but it is possible that some resources have almost zero other usage. Here, the resources are asset specific. When asset specificity increases, there is a greater chance for opportunistic behaviour and the monitoring of these assets and the contracts signed may be costly, thereby increasing the transaction costs. This problem may lead to organisations integrating vertically.

◆ Transaction costs can explain why a monopolist may not use first-order price discrimination. First-order price discrimination means charging each customer a different price up to the point at which they are willing to pay. To find this information out may be too costly, thus a monopolist may adopt a pricing regime of charging different prices for different blocks or units of commodities.

◆ In the case of an externality, such as pollution, the transaction costs of taking legal action and monitoring any arrangements may exceed the benefits of reducing the pollution. Market failure also occurs in the area of regional differences. If markets were perfect then high unemployment in one region should lead to lower relative wages and this should attract new organisations. However, organisations and individuals may have limited knowledge of some markets and obtaining full information is costly. Thus if anticipated benefits do not exceed transaction and migration costs an individual may remain in a high unemployment area. For organisations the cost of finding information about high unemployment sites may exceed any reductions in cost they obtain from a potential move there.

◆ Because there are transaction costs in using the market, such as searching for prices, closing contracts, collecting payments or communicating job specifications, vertical integration may provide a way of avoiding these transaction costs. Once these costs are internalised into the organisation, the transaction cost savings need to be compared with the internal cost of monitoring any arrangements.

◆ Transaction costs may provide an explanation of the arrangements that are set up with employees. Employees may have different levels of skill and different levels of productivity. Measuring individual productivity levels may be difficult, particularly where teamwork is involved, and an approach to this problem may be through peer-group pressure or monitoring and evaluation techniques that attempt to reduce the opportunistic or free-rider behaviour of individuals.

◆ Transaction cost theory can also be used to explain the development of strategic business alliances, rather than growth through mergers, takeovers or multinational activity. There are costs involved in joint ventures such as the continual monitoring of contractual agreements, but where these are lower than the sole-ownership route, then the joint venture will be preferable.

## REVIEW QUESTIONS

1  Transaction costs should not be confused with marketing costs. Discuss.

2  Your line manager is concerned that the output from your team has been falling back over the last six months in relation to other teams within the group. She has recently finished a

managerial economics course which covered the area of transaction cost analysis. She asks you to consider which areas of transaction cost analysis could be used to explain why the output of your team has fallen back, and asks you to recommend ways in which productivity might be improved.

**3** The most important result of the growth of multinational enterprises is not the possible abuse of monopoly power that may follow, but the potential gains that can be made from inter-organisation planning and the replacement of the market mechanism by the organisation's internal machinery. Discuss.

**4** What may be the role of transaction cost analysis in determining the future shape of the tourism industry?

**5** Joint ventures have become increasingly common among organisations in the EU and Eastern Europe. Examine their likely merits and demerits. Do you think that joint ventures are more likely to be short-term arrangements than other forms of business arrangements? Explain your answers.

## GLOSSARY OF NEW TERMS

**Asset specificity**: The extent to which a resource is specific to its current use.

**Backward vertical integration**: The growth of an organisation from one stage of production as it takes over an organisation in the preceding stage of production.

**Bounded rationality**: The limit in an individual's ability to handle intricate information.

**Externality**: A situation in which the market fails to reflect all the economic costs and/or benefits resulting from a particular operation.

**Forward vertical integration**: The growth of an organisation that exists in one stage of production as it absorbs an organisation in the next stage of production.

**Free-rider**: One member of a group who benefits from the actions of others.

**Impacted information**: The degree to which information is known to some individuals/groups but not known to others.

**Opportunism**: A situation in which one party in a contracted arrangement is able to take advantage of another.

**Perfect information**: All decision makers know every piece of information that is available.

**Strategic business alliance**: Alliances or joint ventures which enable an organisation to gain access to an external market without having to expand its operations there.

**Transaction cost**: The cost of using the market.

## READING

Ferguson, P R and Ferguson, G J (1994) *Industrial Economics: Issues and Perspectives*, Macmillan, Basingstoke.
*A very user-friendly text which discusses the role of externalities and transaction costs in some detail.*

Moschandreas, M (1994) *Business Economics*, Routledge, London.
*This text provides a fairly extensive account of transaction cost analysis, although the information is not always collected in one area.*

Schmalensee, R and Willig, R (1991) *Handbook of Industrial Organisation*, North-Holland, Amsterdam.
*This handbook has almost 30 chapters covering a wide variety of industrial economic issues. There is a chapter on transaction costs written by Williamson and a further chapter on vertical integration which also includes a section on transaction cost analysis.*

### Further reading
Beatson, M (1995) 'Progress towards a flexible labour market', *Labour Market Quarterly*, February, pp 55–65.

Coase, R H (1937) 'The nature of the firm', *Economica* (New Series), Vol 4, pp 386–405.

Hymer, S (1976) 'The efficiency (contradictions) of multinational corporations', *American Economic Review, Papers and Proceedings*, Vol 60, No 2, pp 441–8.

Williamson, O E (1975) '*Markets and Hierarchies: Analysis and Antitrust Implications: A Study in the Economics of Internal Organisation*, Free Press, New York.

CHAPTER **18**

# DETERRENCE AND REPUTATION AS STRATEGIC TOOLS

## OBJECTIVES

◆ To consider how pricing strategies can be used to deter entry into markets.

◆ To discuss the role of reputation and production processes in erecting barriers to entry.

◆ To evaluate how governments can support existing organisations and in so doing impede the inflow of other organisations into markets.

◆ To explain how organisations' ability to deter entry into their market can be determined by the credibility of their actions.

◆ To discuss how new product launches may be used as a weapon to deter entry to markets by prospective competitors.

◆ To explain how the use of new products can be considered as an entry barrier with respect to use of brands and brand names.

◆ To assess how the availability of a range of products across the complete spectrum can increase the sales potential of an organisation.

◆ To explain how a product may be used as a strategic weapon; for example, concentration on core competences can improve an organisation's long-term position in its market.

◆ To consider the advantages associated with being the first to make a strategic move in a market situation and demonstrate that there are circumstances when it is best to follow another's movement.

◆ To discuss how organisations can use a variety of actions to circumvent entry barriers set up by incumbents in markets and industries.

# CHAPTER OUTLINE

Business application

Pricing strategies as an entry barrier

Reputation as a barrier to entry

Case study 18.1 Volvo shifts onto the fast track

Choice of production process as a deterrent to entry

Case study 18.2 The drive to reduce costs and improve North Sea performance is not without its victims

Use of new products as an entry barrier

Case study 18.3 SmithKline seeks to limit generic rivalry

Government assistance as an entry barrier

Placing competitors at strategic disadvantage

Case study 18.4 Takeover fills gaps in core markets

First-mover advantage

Second-mover advantage

Case study 18.5 Sainsbury alters cola packaging to avoid legal action

The credibility of deterrence

Commitment to deter entry

Undertakings to customers

Strategic investment as a barrier

Overcoming barriers to entry

Case study 18.6 Flying in formation

Concluding remarks

Summary

Review questions

Glossary of new terms

Reading

## KEY TERMS

Credible threat

First-mover advantage

Non-tariff barrier

Privatisation

Quota

Reputation

Second-mover advantage

Sunk costs

Tariff barrier

> **BUSINESS APPLICATION**
>
> **FT**
>
> # Familiarity breeds respect
>
> How does a company achieve such a strong corporate reputation that it succeeds in receiving recognition for its superiority right across Europe? A study by the *FT* and Price Waterhouse suggests that to be ranked in the top six of overall winners by peer group companies – as was achieved by ABB, Nestlé, British Airways, BMW, Shell and Marks and Spencer – takes more than outstanding business performance.
>
> This lack of emphasis on performance is less surprising if it is accepted that corporate reputation or image is 'the net result of the interaction of all experiences, impressions, beliefs, feelings and knowledge people have about a company.'. . .
>
> Being large and well-known, as all the top six companies are, will, of itself, play a large part in the achievement of a top ranking for reputation. . .
>
> As Professor Worcester (chairman of Mori) told an audience early in 1995, 'Companies get to be well known, most of them anyway, by doing good things for people, and by doing so, gain esteem. This in turn aids their recruitment and retention of staff, share purchase and its retention, the ear of editor and journalist, consideration by the customer and potential customer.'. . .
>
> Apart from doing good things for people, what are the other means companies can use to become familiar? There is corporate advertising and . . . corporate brands, with the company name equating to the name of the goods or services which constitute the company's main output. Any individual product advertising, therefore, will strengthen the corporate name. . .
>
> Finally, also at work are a host of other, more informal, factors which feed into the experiences, impressions, beliefs, feelings and knowledge that senior executives will have of their fellows across Europe.
>
> With increasing proportions of executives now in their forties and early fifties more likely to have gone to university and business school, future generations of chief executives will be more used to using business school case studies.
>
> A 'different mindset', together with the increased use of benchmarking to measure company performance against the best in the field, will help the business community to arrive at an even clearer consenus about Europe's most respected companies.
>
> *Source*: *Financial Times,* 19 September 1995. Reprinted with permission.
>
> *Comment*
>
> This business application provides evidence of the role of **reputation**, advertising and branding as means of erecting entry barriers to other potential entrants into markets. The products provide the companies with an image which would require extensive advertising by a new entrant to surmount. Politicians too will reinforce these barriers by using these companies as benchmarks and inviting them as part of trade delegations, further enhancing performance. At the same time, this may allow these companies to achieve further economies of scale which provide additional barriers to entry.
>
> In this chapter, therefore, the role of barriers to entry, such as reputation, R&D and government legislation, will be developed as a means of explaining why these barriers exist and then considering suitable ways of overcoming them.

## PRICING STRATEGIES AS AN ENTRY BARRIER

In Chapter 9, a number of pricing strategies were developed, some of which can be used to strengthen the barriers to entry into a market. Limit pricing is one of these. In order to practise limit pricing, the incumbent organisation must have a cost advantage over potential entrants into the market. The limit price is then the lowest price which will not induce the entry of new organisations into the market. The entrant into the market may, however, be willing to face short-run losses in the hope that in the long run it will make profits. In this case the limit price will be the highest price that can be set without making the new entrant's present value of future profits positive.

But what of the characteristics of the new entrant? It is possible to investigate two cases, the high-cost organisation and the low-cost organisation. In the case of the former, the existing organisation sets a price that is below the short-run average cost curve at all levels of output for the new entrant.

**Figure 18.1**
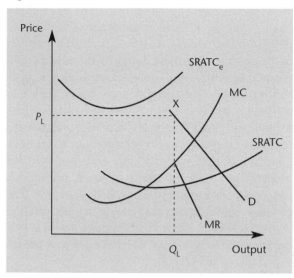

The demand curve, D, is that for one of the organisations already in the industry. The organisation will not want to set a price above $P_L$. Given this price, at all output levels the new organisation has $SRATC_e$ greater than $P_L$. Up to output $Q_L$, the price faced by the existing organisation is $P_L$ and after this point the price follows the demand curve D. For existing organisations, the demand curve is $P_LXD$.

In Figure 18.1 the limit price is $P_L$. At all levels of output the new entrant is not in a position where $P_L > SRATC_e$. For the existing organisations, the price that will be charged is $P_L$ up to output level $Q_L$; thereafter the price follows the demand curve. In other words, for the existing organisation its demand curve is $P_LXD$, that is, a kinked demand curve with the kink at X. Where a demand curve is downward sloping its marginal revenue curve lies below it and for the profit-maximising organisation the level of output chosen is where marginal revenue equals marginal cost. This gives the output level $Q_L$. The scenario above provides a necessary condition for deterring entry, but not a sufficient condition. It is still possible for the new entrant to enter the market if the existing organisations have not predicted accurately the SRATC curve of the new entrant, and for some part of its range it lies below the limit price. In addition, the new entrant could gain entry if it invests to better levels of technology before the existing organisations, or if it is willing to face short-term losses.

Suppose, however, that the new entrant is a low-cost organisation, that is, it has the same cost curves as the existing organisations. Can limit pricing still be used to deter entry? In this case there is no reason to set the limit price below the new entrant's costs, since all organisations would make losses. What the existing organisations will do is set the price such that any additional supply by the new entrant will push prices down below the level of costs for all organisations. Thus the outlook facing the new entrant is one of losses in the short term unless there are changes in the demand conditions facing the whole of the market. Thus when the new organisation enters the market the existing organisations continue to supply the same level of output.

In order to pursue such strategies and successfully set limit prices, the incumbent must possess accurate quantitative knowledge with respect to the supply and demand conditions for its own situation and that of the industry. The implication of this is accurate knowledge on the part of the organisation of its costs and revenue position. Similar knowledge on the part of the entrant is also desirable, but not always possible if industry information is not freely available.

## REPUTATION AS A BARRIER TO ENTRY

**Reputation** can be viewed from a number of perspectives. Kay (1993) sees reputation as providing the business with a competitive edge, adding value to it and providing it with a distinctive capability. In this respect, if a potential entrant does not have the same reputation as the incumbent organisation(s) then this acts as a barrier to entry. This view of reputation enables the company to charge higher prices, above those that would normally limit entry into the market. Alternatively, reputation enables the organisation to gain a larger market share at a competitive price for a functionally equivalent product. Kay's view is that reputation plays an important part in industries such as food retailing and in the banking sector. However, the business application at the beginning of this chapter shows that reputation can also assist organisations in the motor manufacturing and airline industries. Being large and well known in its chosen market helps an organisation to succeed. Knowledge and positive experiences encourage consumers to use the organisation's products or services; that is, its reputation helps.

Reputation can also be viewed in terms of consistent action and the **credible threat**. Although the idea of credible threats will be considered more

423

closely later in the chapter, it is possible for the incumbent organisation in the industry to act aggressively, cutting prices and sustaining short-term losses which can be recovered later as long as the monopoly or above-normal profit position is retained. Thus if a number of organisations are potentially seeking entry into the incumbents' market, aggressive behaviour to the first of the entrants may give the other potential entrants some knowledge of the reputation of the incumbent organisation and could possibly deter entry into the incumbent's market. The practical significance of the role of predatory pricing – *see* Chapter 9 – as a means to build reputation, and for an existing company to use such measures, has been seen by some as a reason for the existence of legislation to curb such action.

In Chapter 24, labour and human resource issues are discussed fully, but reputation plays an important part in the way in which employees and potential employees view the company. If an organisation is seen to act aggressively or opportunistically against its workforce, it might obtain such a bad reputation that productivity falls, costs rise and the organisation begins to lose its cost-competitive edge. It may also not be able to indulge in limit pricing to its normal degree and potential entrants may therefore begin to find it much easier to enter the market. In addition, a company which has a poor reputation with its employees may find it difficult to recruit additional staff and may lose current good-quality staff because

their motivation is low. This problem increases the work pressure on the remaining staff. Since high-quality staff are often a key to the use of better technology, this company may find itself in a position of seeing its market share decline because of the better-quality, enhanced value-added products of its competitors. Potential competitors, which have better-quality staff and have invested in higher levels of technology, could then move in on the incumbent's market. In other words, an organisation which has a good reputation with its staff and retains them probably has higher productivity levels and finds it easier to attract the best staff. All three factors lead to lower per unit costs and enable the organisation to erect a further barrier to possible entry of a new organisation which may not have these relationships with its workforce.

The reputation of an aggressive responder to new entrants may come about from the manager, leader or owner of the company. An individual who has particular characteristics can endow the organisation with these. It is possible, therefore, that a potential new entrant which knows the characteristics of the manager may expect a certain response from the incumbent company in the case of an attempted market entry. Thus it can be argued that a manager with a particular reputation can be of significant value to the organisation as a means of enhancing its own reputation as a quality provider and as a clear indication of the organisation's response to any potential new market entrant.

◆ CASE STUDY 18.1

## Volvo shifts onto the fast track

**FT**

A Volvo that goes faster than a Ferrari. Even the most unabashed executives might balk at making such a startling claim in an international campaign.

Under the heading 'The Porsche will be along in a couple of seconds', the advertisement showed a Volvo 850 estate car outpacing a Ferrari. The small print made clear this occurs only when accelerating in top gear, but the image was none the less striking for that explanation.

Nor was this advertisement any sort of aberration. Lately, Volvo has been marketing a flashy version of the 850 model called the T5R in extravagant yellow livery, with a high-performance engine and racy, low-profile tyres, which is the antithesis of the traditional, staid Volvo family car.

For the past three seasons the company has been competing on the popular and highly competitive

British Touring Car circuit and in 1995 was one of the leading contenders for the championship.

What is going on at a company that for years produced some of the world's most conservative cars, whose most touted qualities were safety, reliability and, recently, environmental friendliness?

The answer is . . . 'a paradigm change' which seeks to shift the public's perception of Volvo cars and thereby spread their appeal well beyond the family segment that has been the company's core market. The image change could be summed up as a move from 'boxy and boring' to 'safe but sexy'. . .

The trick is to achieve this expansion of market appeal – the 'paradigm change' – without eroding the core reputation of Volvo. Mr Mohlin (the company's head) thinks that Volvo is attempting this at an auspicious time, when factors such as safety and environmental friendliness in cars have become highly valued qualities which can be married to other, racier qualities, such as driving pleasure. 'I firmly believe we are lucky in the core values that we have. It's not so much a question of change but more a question of building on what we have.' . . . Mr Horbury (the company's design director)

says it is important to preserve the Scandinavian element in the design of Volvo cars – 'good materials used in a clear way'. He compares Volvo's aim with that of Ikea, the furniture retailer, which uses its Scandinavian character as a worldwide selling point.

*Source: Financial Times, 21 July 1995. Reprinted with permission.*

---

♦ **Exercise 18.1**

1 Suppose that Volvo is successful in adapting its reputation. Are there any dangers with its approach?

2 Why does Volvo wish to enhance its reputation?

---

# CHOICE OF PRODUCTION PROCESS AS A DETERRENT TO ENTRY

Although price may be used quite often as a mechanism to bar entry into a market, it is possible for the existing organisation to discourage entry into its market by the use of excess capacity. This excess capacity can be used to pose a credible threat to new entrants. The excess capacity clearly signals that, if a new entrant seeks to enter the market, the incumbent organisation will increase its output levels and reduce its price. This can be a powerful tool to restrict entry, since it is highly likely that the incumbent organisation can increase its output more quickly than the new organisation can build new productive capacity. Thus by the time the new entrant is ready for the market, output will be higher and prices lower than before it sought to enter the market.

Holding excess capacity is going to be more costly for the incumbent organisation, but when compared to a low-cost pricing strategy it may be less costly. It is also possible for the incumbent organisation to consider and commit itself to investment projects which reduce the marginal cost of production since, on cost grounds alone, the new entrant may be deterred from entering the market. If entry does occur then the incumbent organisation can increase output very rapidly or, if there is cooperation between the incumbent organisation and the new entrant, the lower cost base of the incumbent would place it in a much stronger position in terms of initial market share.

Scope economies, as discussed in Chapters 8 and 16, can also provide a useful source of barrier to entry. Economies of scope are gained when producing two or more related goods together is less costly than producing these goods separately. It follows, therefore, that if an organisation is a multi-product producer and these two goods are produced together, it may well have a cost advantage over any organisation that produces the goods separately. Such an approach may not lead to the new entrant being discouraged from all the two or more markets since it is possible for the new entrant to concentrate on the production of one product. However, since raising finance may be more problematic for the new entrant, the scope economies achieved by the incumbent may be sufficient for it to bar entry into some of its markets.

Other sources of production advantages that might deter entry are those associated with lower per unit costs. The incumbent organisation may have a highly skilled management team or access to much better-quality raw materials. Lyons (1988) suggests that unpatented expertise which newcomers could not imitate is a barrier to entry in the UK for sophisticated machinery, mass-produced components and bulk chemical processes. The production costs of incumbent organisations may be lower because of the impact of vertical integration. Industries like the petroleum sector are backwardly integrated, thus when a new entrant seeks to enter the market they may also need to be backwardly integrated to match the cost or production advantages of the incumbent organisation. This process of vertical integration can create barriers to entry which are either strategic or structural. They are strategic when the vertically integrated organisation consciously controls a resource, thus preventing a potential competitor from entering the intermediate stage of the market. That is, the organisation is consciously trying to gain a competitive advantage, perhaps even by buying backwards or forwards into the complete production process. If entry is influenced by efficiency considerations, potential entrants need to enter when fully integrated so that they can be on a comparative cost footing.

◆ CASE STUDY 18.2

## The drive to reduce costs and improve North Sea performance is not without its victims

Against a background of gently declining oil prices, the growth in alliance contracting and 'risk and reward' contracts, in which any cost savings or over-runs are shared, is a key element in the continuing drive to reduce costs and enhance business performance in the North Sea. The starting point was around 1990 when operators became aware that the high cost of North Sea operations compared with the rest of the world was untenable. The process has accelerated over the past two to three years with the off-shore industry's Crine (cost-reduction initiative for the new era) initiative looking to take 25–30 per cent of costs out of both the capital expenditure and operating expenditure ends of the system. Oil companies are handing over greater responsibility to the large integrated engineering companies such as Amec, Brown and Root, Trafalgar John Brown and the Wood Group. But there is a risk that under the new contractual relationships smaller companies are being squeezed out, which could lead to less cost-reducing innovation.

The small service and supply companies are known as SMEs (small to medium-sized enterprises); typically they have a turnover of £1m to £2m and employ 10–12 people. Because of the change in the system, small companies do not always have the expertise required and have a higher cost base.

However, Scottish Enterprise, funded by the Scottish Office, is trying to encourage the participation of small companies in alliance contracting. If the small companies can get the experience of integrated contracting, this may be a skill that can be marketed elsewhere. One of Scottish Enterprise's main thrusts is to assist small companies to internationalise in markets where there are high entry barriers, but also high potential for doing business. The focus is on Western Siberia, Azerbaijan, Malaysia, Vietnam, Venezuela and Colombia.

For some small companies the omens are not good. Small companies no longer have direct access to the oil companies in the way they had before. The slightly harsh message is that there may not be room for everybody.

This new arrangement in the North Sea has been suggested as mainly a win for the oil companies, with little in it for contractors. The oil companies counter that without the cost-reduction initiatives many of the projects currently under development would not have been commercially viable. The contractors, meanwhile, particularly the larger ones, are adapting well to the new ways of working. However, the small firms, because of differences in expertise and production processes, may be the losers.

*Source: Financial Times*, 4 September 1995. Reprinted with permission.

◆ **Exercise 18.2**

Does the presence of better levels of technology in general enable or prevent small organisations competing with larger organisations?

### Comment on the case study

Case study 18.2 suggests that some organisations, perhaps larger ones, have a distinct advantage when it comes to alliance contracting with the large oil companies. They may possess different ways of working and have different expertise which enables them to be more suitable in any integrated arrangement. This way of behaviour and production constitutes a barrier to entry for smaller organisations. If these can partake in the alliance-contracting arrangement then the expertise they pick up will allow them to have a comparative advantage elsewhere in the world and this will enable them to erect entry barriers to other organisations.

## USE OF NEW PRODUCTS AS AN ENTRY BARRIER

There are various ways in which new products may be used as a barrier to entry. Their exploitation depends on factors such as the following:

■ Level of competition/market structure in the market where the new product will be competing.
■ Whether the product is unique, or an entrant competitor to an existing market situation.
■ The stage of the lifecycle at which the market or industry currently is.
■ Whether the product is one of a range or will be associated with a brand name.

## Market structure

It may be seen that both the product type and the competitive market in which the organisation finds itself are important. Where the competition in the market or industry is fierce, it is obviously very difficult to successfully introduce and maintain a new product. This is particularly true of an oligopolistic market, where non-price factors are as important as price competition (if not more so). Therefore, a new entrant would be required to enter into heavy advertising or other promotional activities in order to succeed. Such actions are likely to be very expensive and can deter entry without further actions on the part of the incumbent. If, in addition to this, the incumbent was to launch new product(s) on to the market, the expenditure required of any prospective competitor would increase further. There would be a greater number of products to compete against and it is also likely that any new product launch on the part of an incumbent would have a promotional budget associated with it. Finally, it is possible that the new product(s) launched by the incumbent are strategically launched so as to fill gaps in the range of products available. This argument will be extended in the following section.

Where there is less competition in the market, perhaps because there is a monopolist, new entrants will not find it so difficult to enter and compete on a product basis. The lack of competition in the market means that the level of advertising is theoretically lower than in the case of oligopoly. Additionally, new product development by the monopolist will merely increase the pressure on its own existing product, detracting from demand for that product. Alternatively, however, if the monopolist possesses a strong corporate or product identity, it may be difficult to enter the market to compete against any products it has on the market. A new product would, under such circumstances, therefore serve to increase such a reputation.

## Unique products used as a deterrent

As was discussed above, the monopolist can be at an advantage in terms of its capability for deterring entry if its product or corporate identity is high, i.e. their reputation is recognised by consumers. This is also true if the product is unique, giving the organisation a local, or market segment, monopoly. Therefore, additions to the product range in such situations will add to the potential coverage

and size of the segment, leading to an increase in 'local' power. Where there is a monopolist in a given market with high levels of corporate identity, the price elasticity of demand will be lower, that is, more inelastic, than would be the case in a competitive market situation. Consumers will exhibit greater brand loyalty and levels of price insensitivity than would be the case where there is not a controlling incumbent and thus recognised leader in the market or industry.

Where the incumbent's new product is not unique, a different analysis may be made. In such circumstances, the incumbent is able to use the new product to fill the gaps in any range of products available to the consumer; the organisation is therefore increasing its own chances of capturing the sales appropriate to the marginal (undecided) consumer. Recall from Chapter 9 that products are differentiated on a horizontal basis in order to capture the marginal, or random, consumer who may be unsure of their consumption preferences with reference to brands or brand names associated with a given product type. The greater the number of different products within a range that any organisation has in the marketplace, the more likely theirs is to capture the random choice made. Price elasticity in such cases is relatively high or elastic. Consumers are less sensitive to changes in price and exhibit low levels of loyalty. This is particularly true of those consumers who are unsure of their preferences for products in terms of product attributes.

## New products and the stage of the industry or market lifecycle

The manner in which new products may be used by incumbents to deter entry to a market or industry depends on the factors above. However, consideration of the stage of the lifecycle which the market or industry is at is also important. New product launch during the growth stage of the market or industry can prevent the entry of prospective competitors and can assist the organisation in line with the product range argument discussed above.

New product launch at the mature or decline stage of a market or industry lifecycle may attract more competitors than it discourages. Maturity in markets is exhibited by lack of growth in terms of sales. That is, the market is as large as it will ever get. In declining markets, the volume of sales may be observed to be decreasing. Any new product launch takes place with the intention of increasing the number of potential sales. Therefore, it can be

## SmithKline seeks to limit generic rivalry

SmithKline Beecham, the Anglo-US drugs company, is to launch an unbranded version of its former best-selling ulcer drug Tagamet in the US in an attempt to stave off competition from makers of cut-price generic products after Tagamet's US patent expires on May 17. SB has said that as many as 10 generics manufacturers could enter the market after the patent expired. The US accounted for two-thirds of Tagamet's global sales of £673m in 1993.

From next week, SB will sell Tagamet under its generic name cimetidine directly to US hospitals and the health management organisations, which run healthcare services for employers and insurance companies. Customers could include Diversified Pharmaceuticals Services which SB bought for $2.3bn last week.

SB has also signed a distribution agreement with Lederle, part of American Cyanamid, known for its aggressive selling of generics. The generics will be made at Tagamet's Puerto Rican site but sold by SB's subsidiary Penn Labs. No pricing details were revealed, but Mr Jerry Karabelas, president of SB's North American pharmaceuticals business, acknowledged that previous patent expiries have seen prices fall by more than 80 per cent within 18 months. . .

SB is likely to reveal further parts of its strategy to limit the damage of the patent expiry. They have already included legal action against US generics company Mylan, which has US Food and Drug Administration approval to sell cimetidine. That action alleges trademark infringements: Mylan's cimetidine is the same pale green colour as Tagamet and could confuse patients, said Mr Karabelas.

*Source: Financial Times, 11 May 1994. Reprinted with permission.*

argued that the new product launch will result in an extension to the lifecycle. Any successful extension will obviously make the market more attractive than it previously may have been. There will be increased opportunities for potential competitors to exploit. Thus, the new product launch could be damaging to the incumbents rather than consolidating their position(s).

## New product launch within a range or in association with a brand name

Where a new product can be launched as a new addition to a range, or in association with a brand name, the deterrent effects can be greater than those accruing to an individual product. The argument relating to the benefits of new products introduced within an existing range has already been covered in terms of capturing marginal consumers. Additions to a range can benefit from positive association in the consumer's mind with the organisation's other products. If these other products are popular, or possess a reputation for value for money, high quality or other positive attributes, these may spill over to the new product, or be associated in the consumer's mind with it. Thus the position of the incumbent will be improved in the market. Prospective entrants would be deterred from competing with such a consolidated/improved position on the part of incumbent(s).

*Comment on the case study*

Case study 18.3 clearly illustrates the real-life strategies used to beat the lifecycle effects of the expiry of patents and also product launch in association with a known brand name. When the patent expires, the market will be open to all-comers. It will essentially have undergone a lifecycle extension as a result of the patent expiry. Increased competition and the likelihood of lower prices will represent a threat to Tagamet's continued sales. SmithKline Beecham is launching an unbranded (generic) version of its Tagamet product so that it will be able to gain sales to US hospitals and health services. It will also continue to sell Tagamet. The hoped-for result is that, when the patent expires and (up to 10) competitors enter the market to sell the generic drug, SmithKline Beecham will be able to sell its own generic product as well as its branded product. If events go as planned, it will be able to sell the generic product at a lower price and crowd out the other non-branded competition, while maintaining branded sales as much as possible.

## GOVERNMENT ASSISTANCE AS AN ENTRY BARRIER

The issue of competition policy and government intervention will be considered in Chapter 22. This will discuss the reasons put forward for governments needing to be actively involved in markets. Nonetheless, government activity directly and through legislation can act as a barrier to entry for new organisations. In the case of a monopoly, the granting of patents and copyrights protects the organisation in two ways: in terms of a cost differential and protection from imitation. As far as consumer welfare is concerned, patents may encourage further development of R&D in the knowledge that future profits from this will be guaranteed for the organisation. However, patents can be used for strategic purposes. A biotechnology organisation which has patented a particular product may look for slight variations on the product and patent these as well. Such a blanket approach may prevent other organisations from developing practical substitutes.

Essentially, governments have a choice here. They may choose to protect the organisation or industry in question from competition, perhaps in its research and growth stages so that it is able to compete on a larger scale in the future. Alternatively, the government may decide that protection is not necessary and that the organisation or industry will benefit from operating in a competitive market. However, if the decision is to protect, then one way is to impose barriers to entry.

Governments may impose barriers to entry in the way that they award charters or franchises to particular companies. For many countries nationalised industries are monopolies because they have been granted the sole rights to provide a service, for example the post office in the UK and many other European countries. Nonetheless, these barriers have become more surmountable as governments have attempted to reduce these constraints through **privatisation**. In such cases, however, governments have often erected other barriers, as enterprises which are state owned or publicly owned have tended to offer contracts to organisations within their own country. Sometimes this is couched in the strategic industry argument.

Many governments have powers to restrict the monopoly behaviour of organisations. However, this power may not be the same in all countries. A country which is more tolerant with respect to monopolies is likely to see the development of national companies which by their size can achieve economies of scale and thus provide an increased barrier to entry.

The government can ostensibly operate on grounds to protect the consumer, but this will lead to entry barriers being increased. For example, a government can use health and safety regulations to limit the entry of some products into its market. It could endorse a policy for consumers to buy domestic manufactured goods. It can set up environmental and pollution controls that prevent an organisation, with its current level of technology and production processes, from entering a market. It can offer various forms of state aid to its domestic organisations, such as low-cost finance, lower levels of taxation, government subsidies and competitive land prices that reduce their costs of production and thus raise the barriers of entry.

On a macroeconomic level, governments can use various forms of **tariff** and **non-tariff barriers** to protect their home industries. In the case of non-tariff barriers the health and safety argument above would be included, together with factors that affect the size or dimension of the product. Tax regimes can lead to a barrier to trade. The French domestic tax on cars is positively related to a car's horsepower; as such, it raises the prices of US cars since these, until recently, had more horsepower than their French contemporaries. The UK and Italian governments have sometimes required importers to deposit, at their government's treasury, a sum equal to half the value of the import of a commodity for six months at no interest. In the case of other forms of trade barriers that can assist domestic organisations, included here would be tariffs, **quotas**, voluntary export restraints and the like.

## PLACING COMPETITORS AT STRATEGIC DISADVANTAGE

New product launches are just one weapon among many which may be used by organisations to place new and existing competitors at a disadvantage. Chapter 16 considered the manner in which the organisation may utilise and exploit economies of scale, core competencies, outsourcing agreements and other techniques to gain competitive advantage. Although organisations which pay such attention to their activities may be looking for short-term gain, more frequently the expenditure associated with such activities means that organisations are likely to gain longer-term advantages. Large investments and the changes associated with projects designed to improve competitive advantage mean that organisations are actually searching for *sustainable* competitive advantage, that is, advantage which will give both short-term and longer-term benefits to the organisation.

Sustainable competitive advantage is not gained merely as a result of a one-off investment, whatever form it takes. Such investment begins the process of gaining and maintaining sustainable competitive advantage. Unless this process is maintained, the benefits will be short lived and non-sustainable. Organisations must therefore enter into a cycle in which they identify and assess their position of current strategic advantage, investigate and consider changes which may maintain or add to this position, implement those changes, review the advantages connected to the changes and then monitor the ongoing situation by further identifying and assessing the source(s) of competitive advantage possessed, and so on through the cycle.

Exploitation of core competencies and entering into outsourcing contracts with other organisations are sources of sustainable competitive advantage. There are arguments surrounding the benefits of outsourcing, some of which were considered in Chapter 16. What was not discussed in any depth there, however, was the possibility of suppliers and buyers gaining sustainable competitive advantage by entering into long-term contractual arrangements. Arguments against outsourcing are based on the fact that organisations use such arrangements to cut costs and pass responsibility for activities, with potential losses, to other members of the supply and production chain for any product. There is also a danger, according to some critics, that suppliers will enter into agreements with buyers, supply their needs satisfactorily for a given period of time and then begin to sell any knowledge or process improvements gained to the buyer's competitors via a supply agreement with those competitors as well as with the original buyer. Thus, a supplier is in a strong market position because it gains knowledge not available in the marketplace which may be transferred between buyers for large sums of money!

It is also claimed that outsourcing is based on suppression of competition. That is, by entering into medium- and long-term contractual arrangements, the partner organisations are stifling free-market mechanisms. These contracts, it is argued, are signed at a given time and for a given price in the circumstances dictated by the market at that time. By entering into such agreements, both parties are removing themselves from the competitive process for an agreed period of time, although perhaps not completely with reference to all of their activities. The result is that they are not therefore in a position to negotiate better terms for themselves for the duration of the contract. Such an

argument may be particularly attractive for the buyer in market-specific or general economic situations where average price levels are changing. Overall, it is claimed that the partner organisations are potentially losing out on market opportunities by entering into such agreements.

---

### ◆ Exercise 18.3

Are the potential gains through outsourcing mutually beneficial for all parties concerned, or does one party make gains at the cost of the other?

---

There is a counter argument, however, that long-term relationships, such as outsourcing, between suppliers and buyers can be mutually beneficial and lead to benefits on both sides which might not normally be available to either party. There may be improvements in processes and understanding of needs. The organisations will spend their time cooperating and collaborating on improvements which may be made to the processes and products involved in the relationship which has been invoked as a result of the contractual agreements. This situation may be improved further if both parties are encouraged by the progress made and look to extend contract periods. Longer-term relationships therefore allow the partners to concern themselves with improving the processes and products which contribute to their success, rather than concentrating on making or deciding between tenders and bids for business. A greater proportion of the organisation's time is therefore spent in core, productive, value-adding activities, rather than in support and search activities, which do not add value to organisations unless successful.

In addition to the stability benefits which long-term relations between organisations bring, there are other benefits which might be achieved. Economies of scale and scope may be realised which otherwise would be unachievable. When organisations concentrate on their core competencies or core businesses and outsource complementary and support processes, they are able to improve their expertise in these areas. They may also be able to extend or increase the volume of production, because space and resources are released from other, less efficient activities or activities in which the organisation possesses less expertise.

Successful exploitation of such activities can lead to sustainable competitive advantage. It can also lead to the partner organisations entering and competing in markets or industries which would otherwise be inaccessible to them. The fact that they are specialising means that they are more efficient as a result of the division of labour – the allocation of tasks and processes to contractors who are able to perform the function at lower cost and/or higher quality than the contractees.

Inevitably, such arrangements can also lead to increased potential for business. Possible sources are:

■ An increased network of other organisations with which the partner organisations come into contact. That is, the greater the variety of organisations that any individual organisation partners, the greater the chances that different business opportunities will present themselves. Invitations to conferences, trade fairs and other networking possibilities will arise and provide the organisation with the opportunity to network with other potential customers or buyers.

■ A different spectrum of opportunity presents itself to the partners via formal, existing contracts. This may be through the formalised channels which the contractual agreements require: say, when a buyer diversifies from desktop personal computer manufacture to include laptop manufacture. A component supplier may be invited to increase its portfolio of supplied products to include a unique (but related) laptop component.

■ Different opportunities present themselves informally as a result of expertise gained via current contracts. It is possible that the component suppliers or buyers will encounter new or alternative chances to develop business links with others or in other markets. For example, the offshoot of a development programme for the laptop component may be the development of a component which may be competitively placed in the television manufacture market. Thus, the supplier will be able to enter into negotiations with television manufacturers as a result of its related activities.

Overall, the boundaries of the organisation, the scale of operations and the scope of those operations are increased as a result of the contractual outsourcing relationships developed. As a result, individual organisations may seek to redefine their own core competencies, or to involve themselves in reformulating strategy. Thus, a complete internal and external analysis is required in order for the organisation to understand and recognise its resources and how these present themselves in the different marketplace(s) it is aiming to enter. An example of such a reorganisation may be seen in the Scandinavian SCA paper group which took control of the German PWA pulp and paper group in early 1995.

## ◆ CASE STUDY 18.4

# Takeover fills gap in core markets

While most Scandinavians were enjoying the Christmas and New Year holiday that comes as a welcome break in the darkest days of the cold Nordic winter, executives at the SCA group were hard at work putting together the biggest deal of the year in Europe's pulp and paper business.

If they regretted missing the spiced wine and succulent hams that are the traditional seasonal fare, they made it worthwhile when they announced on January 5 that SCA was taking control of the PWA, Germany's largest quoted pulp and paper group.

The deal, initially for 60 per cent of PWA, but later extended to a 75 per cent shareholding, transformed SCA into Europe's biggest forestry industry company with annual combined turnover last year of SKr56bn, overtaking Stora, its Swedish rival. SCA's turnover in 1994 was SKr34bn.

Reaction from analysts and investors was largely positive to an acquisition which cost SCA some $1.02bn because PWA's businesses are mostly complementary to those of SCA and, crucially, they filled a gaping German gap in SCA's core European markets . . .

What does the addition of PWA do to SCA's structure? At first sight, it adds further width to a group that already spans most of the full range of forestry-derived products, from timber to tampons. It takes SCA, for example, into fine and decorative papers. At a time when many companies in the industry are narrowing their focus to core areas of competence, this diversity could be seen as a weakness.

But Mr Martin-Lof (SCA president and chief executive) stresses that the addition of PWA strengthens SCA in its three key product areas of transport packaging, fibre-based hygiene products and graphic papers. It consolidates SCA's intention that each of these areas should have integrated control over all processing stages from raw materials to end products. It also entrenches SCA's position in Europe, which the group wants to keep as its long-term core market.

▶

### Case study 18.4 *continued*

'You can always question whether we should be in two main areas, not three. But we have the resources to grow in all three areas. We have managed to create critical mass in all three areas,' says Mr Martin-Lof. 'If we were to give up one of the three, we would be under pressure to go outside Europe and we don't want to do that.'

In the packaging sector, SCA is now the biggest European producer of corrugated products and container board, ahead of Ireland's Jefferson-Smurfit.

Most importantly, PWA extended SCA's penetration into Germany where previously it had been weak.

At a stroke, the acquisition of PWA lifted the proportion of packaging sales in Germany from about 2 per cent to 30 per cent of divisional sales. In a business where multinational industrial buyers of packaging materials increasingly want a Europe-wide service, this was of considerable importance.

*Source*: *Financial Times*, 28 June 1995. Reprinted with permission.

### Comment on the case study

SCA gained 75 per cent of PWA in early 1995. The takeover made SCA Europe's largest company in the forestry industry. The unique aspect of this case is that the activities of SCA and PWA when they were separate were complementary. SCA has now moved into a position where its range of operations within the forestry-derived industry is wider than ever before. It produces a variety of items ranging from tampons to wallpaper. It is also now involved in operations in three core areas: packaging, hygiene products and graphic papers. In each, it controls highly vertically integrated processes.

The move to expand or diversify into three areas, rather than to concentrate on building up only two, as critics have proposed, is strategically based. If SCA was to concentrate on two areas, in order to maintain scale and volume of sales, it would be forced to look to markets outside Europe. With the concentration on three areas, it will be in a better position to break into the German market and to achieve its desired magnitude of operations while remaining within Europe. Thus, by reorganising, SCA is redefining itself as a European force to be reckoned with, rather than as an expert in specialised market areas.

# FIRST-MOVER ADVANTAGE

In addition to the identification and exploitation of core competencies, entering into outsourcing agreements, achieving expertise and economies of scale and related activities, the organisation may be able to exploit sources of competitive advantage which are less fundamental and extreme in terms of the changes associated. One such possibility is the short-term, enhanced payoff which it is possible to earn as the first mover in a given market situation. From an economist's perspective, a possible source of **first-mover advantage** is the advantage of being the first to change quantity available in the market.

According to Cournot's oligopoly model, first-mover advantage is gained by an organisation making changes to the quantities available in the marketplace. Cournot's model is based on the actions and reactions in terms of quantities and a fixed price level. In the initial period under analysis, there will be an initial equilibrium position, E, as seen in Figure 18.2. Assume that Firm A leads with an increased quantity being released on to the market, in order to increase profits and market share. It could increase to point e in Figure 18.2. If the leader's isoprofit line is given by $\pi^{Leader}$, it can be seen that it would be more rational to increase to point E' rather than point e. B's isoprofit line is given by $\pi^{Follower}$ and the rational point for it to settle at will be at the position $E^{Follower}$.

As a result of the move instigated by the leader, A, the first mover, the follower must *ceteris paribus* accept a decrease in quantity of the same amount as the increase gained by A. The consequence of this leader/follower movement is that the leader's profit increases to greater than the original equilibrium level and the follower's to lower than the original level ($\pi^{Leader} > \pi^{Original} > \pi^{Follower}$). Thus, as a result of being the first to increase quantity supplied to the market, Firm A has gained a first-mover advantage.

There are other sources of first-mover advantage that are not associated so closely with economic

**Figure 18.2**

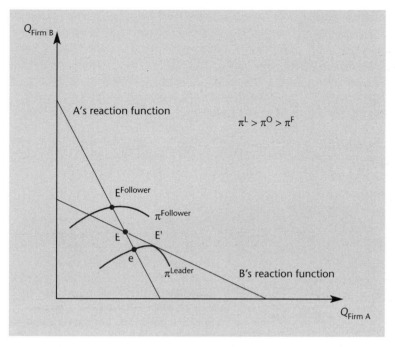

Initially, equilibrium is found at E: the intersection of the reaction functions for A and B. Firm A is the first mover: the leader in the market. A increases quantity to point E' on B's reaction function, causing a reduction in B's quantity by exactly the same amount. (This is a symmetrical model with a zero sum. That is, every action has an equal and opposite reaction.) Therefore, B will see a reduction in quantity from E to E$^{Follower}$. A could have increased to e but, given that it lies on the same isoprofit line as E', as a rational firm A would prefer to increase to E'.

theory. Innovations and the introduction of unique products can give access to new or extended markets, which could otherwise be unavailable to organisations. This is particularly true when the product is technically unique, or requires high levels of research and development on the part of any imitating prospective competitors. That is, the learning curve will be steep for any imitators and therefore require large investments on the part of any imitating organisation in order to join the original in the marketplace. New product advantage can be short lived if the product is easily imitated and the organisation does not take steps to protect its investment. Patents can be applied for and protect products from imitation for given periods of time – usually 15 years. To augment patent protection and to maintain the first-mover advantage, organisations may also enter into advertising and promotional campaigns. The intention in such circumstances is to create a brand awareness and loyalty which will exist beyond the time of entry by any competitors.

## SECOND-MOVER ADVANTAGE

In some cases, it is advantageous to wait and be a follower with respect to market changes, that is, to take **second-mover advantage**. Again, this relates to oligopoly theory, particularly Bertrand's model. In such cases, followers are able to exploit the advantage of being the second to change prices.

In this model, the organisations, Firm A and Firm B, are competing on price of their products. The quantity which they are willing to supply to the market will change accordingly, while prices are the exogenous, or determining, variable. In such cases, it is better to wait and see what the extent of the competitor's price change will be and to beat it, rather than to instigate the round of price changes. According to accepted knowledge, the higher a competitor's prices, the greater the level of own profits. Thus, the higher the prices charged by Firm B, the greater the level of profits for Firm A; *see* Figure 18.3.

Initially, equilibrium is at E. If Firm A increases its prices, it will gain an increased profit from that at point E to the profit at E$^{Leader}$. Firm B will then be in a position to undercut the increase in prices and to gain extra volume of sales by increasing prices by less than the leader's increase. Firm B will move from E to E$^{Follower}$ – a greater increase than that experienced by A. In this model, both firms do gain by the increase in prices, but the gain is greater for the second mover, the follower.

**Figure 18.3**

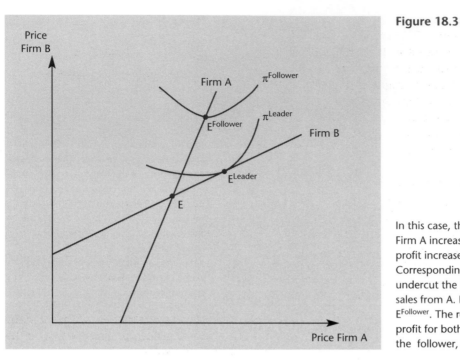

In this case, the equilibrium position is E. Firm A increases its prices and gains a profit increase from E to $E^{Leader}$. Correspondingly, Firm B will wait, undercut the increase made by A and steal sales from A. Firm B will move from E to $E^{Follower}$. The result will be an improved profit for both firms, but a better payoff for the follower, B.

◆ **CASE STUDY 18.5**

## Sainsbury alters cola packaging to avoid legal action          **FT**

J Sainsbury, the supermarket group, is making minor changes to the packaging of its look-alike cola to ward off the threat of legal action from Coca-Cola, in a dispute which exemplifies the growing row between brand manufacturers and retailers over shops' own-label products.

Sainsbury, however, will retain the 'Classic' name, which Coca-Cola uses in the US, and all the core elements of the design and the colour.

Mr Tom Vyner, Sainsbury's deputy chairman, said customers would not notice the difference in the packaging. 'What we have agreed to do is minor,' he said. Sainsbury is modifying the type face of the vertically printed 'cola' inscription and removing the squiggle underneath it.

Mr Vyner said there had been a 'gi-normous' upsurge in sales in the three weeks since the cola was launched.

A survey by market research group AGB shows that in the third week since it appeared in the stores, Sainsbury's Classic has captured approximately 15 per cent by value of all cola sales through UK retail outlets, compared with the 2.5 to 3 per cent share held by Sainsbury's previous own-brand cola before the launch.

The dominant shares of Coca-Cola and PepsiCola have both been squeezed but there has also been an 8 per cent increase in overall sales of cola through grocery outlets, following the Sainsbury initiative.

Mr Vyner said the rapid surge in Sainsbury's sales in part reflected the great media attention the product has received. A TV advertising campaign is likely within two months, he said.

Coca-Cola has taken the Sainsbury threat so seriously that negotiations have been led by its Atlanta head office, largely bypassing UK-based executives. The dispute has been keenly watched by other manufacturers, increasingly angry at the damage to sales of market leading brands by supermarkets' own-label look-alikes. Under existing UK law, it is difficult for them to take legal action for 'passing off'.

Sainsbury has consistently denied that its product could ever be mistaken by customers for Coke's. However, Mr Peter Stokes of Coca-Cola said it had carried out surveys which showed customers were 'readily confused' about which product was which.

Sainsbury said it disputed the findings but was happy to make the changes. Mr Vyner said: 'What we have achieved is the elimination of any danger of confusion.'

The design changes are believed to have eliminated any possibility of Coca-Cola's taking legal action for alleged passing off. This will disappoint other brand manufacturers.

*Source: Financial Times, 11 May 1994. Reprinted with permission.*

### Comment on the case study

Sainsbury avoided legal action due to the similarity of its cola's packaging compared to that of Coca-Cola by changing the can design. What it has achieved, despite Coca-Cola's attempts to protect its design and colours, is to steal market share from Coke. It was claimed that the can design was so similar that consumers could become confused and pick up the Sainsbury version, believing it to be Coke.

If the claims about sales are true, then Sainsbury will have benefited from the years of publicity invested by Coke. Coke's brand building and constant advertising has made the general public aware of the drink. Sainsbury is therefore gaining a second-mover advantage of sorts by attempting to compete with Coke in the UK. This example is simplified; Sainsbury is already a household name in the UK and has a guaranteed distribution for Classic Cola via its UK supermarkets. However, the fact that it is benefiting from Coke's advertising efforts seems clear.

## THE CREDIBILITY OF DETERRENCE

If a firm enters a market where there is an incumbent, is it possible for the existing organisation to match the price-cutting behaviour of the new organisation in the former's best interests? Perhaps it is better to start the other way. Suppose that an organisation wishes to enter a market in which, even if the existing organisation follows the price fall, its position in terms of profits is worse than if it did not follow the price fall. In this case for the new entrant the threat that the existing organisation will follow the price cut is not conceivable, that is, not credible.

Using Figure 18.4, which is presented in a 'prisoner's dilemma' payoff matrix, suppose that the new entrant into the market has a low-price strategy. Given the payoff in the table, the incumbent organisation may threaten to reduce prices too. The resultant situation would be 'low–low', with a negative payoff (loss of 2 units) for the incumbent and a small profit of 2 units for the entrant. However, the new entrant realises that the incumbent is better off if it charges a high price following the new entrant's low-price strategy. Here the existing organisation will make zero profits and the new entrant 10 units

**Figure 18.4**

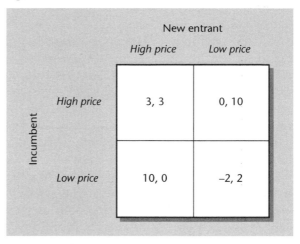

A threat to the new entrant which is not credible

of profit. Thus the threat from the existing organisation that it will follow the low-price strategy of the new entrant is not credible.

Such a strategy by the existing organisation does not seem logical business behaviour. In Chapter 9 it was noted, using the kinked demand curve theory of oligopoly behaviour, that this would not be the scenario adopted. Organisations tend to follow a price reduction by one of their major competitors. But the kinked demand curve theory would also suggest that, if all organisations in an oligopoly make a price reduction, individual companies are unlikely to have obtained increased market share from their rivals. There may have been some new customers attracted into the market who could not buy at the old market price but can afford the lower price. It would be expected that any new customers would be distributed equally among the existing organisations in the market.

However, all the organisations in the oligopoly are receiving a lower price for their output and profit margins will have been reduced. If profit margins are reduced sufficiently, it is possible that some of the existing organisations which have followed the price fall could be making losses. This is the scenario that appears in the bottom right-hand cell of Figure 18.5. This suggests what might be the best position for some of the oligopoly organisations: not to reduce their prices. In this scenario those organisations which do not reduce their prices will find themselves losing customers, but perhaps not all their customers. The ones that remain will continue to pay the higher price, and although these organisations may be facing reduced profits they may still be in a profit-making position, a better outcome than if they were to follow the price fall.

It is possible to alter the outcomes shown in Figure 18.4 to those in Figure 18.5 so that the threat by the existing organisation(s) in the market will be undertaken, that is, a credible threat. In this scenario, the most profitable position for the incumbent is the low-price one. For the new entrant which enters the market on the back of a low-price strategy, the threat of a response by the incumbent to copy the strategy is credible, since this is their smallest loss position. In this case both organisations will make losses and both the new entrant and existing organisation in the oligopoly will be deterred from making price cuts.

## COMMITMENT TO DETER ENTRY

If the incumbent is to deter entry into its market it must show to any potential entrant that it is committed to responding to the threat of the new entrant. In fact, the incumbent must show that it is in its interest to engage in any battle with the new entrant. If this is not made clear, the new entrant will belittle any possible threat. For example, it is possible that a market-sharing position with the new entrant, where the incumbent still has a greater share of the market, yields a better level of profits than one in which the incumbent has to fight the new entrant. In this case, the com-

mitment to deter entry is not credible. For there to be a credible commitment to deter entry, the incumbent needs to be in a position where fighting the new entrant brings it more profit than some form of market-sharing arrangement. Such a situation could occur if the incumbent has excess capacity. The threat of entry into the incumbent's market would be responded to by bringing this excess capacity into production. Prices would be forced down and the new entrant could be faced with a situation of making losses and be forced to leave the market in the long term. In this case the commitment to deter entry is credible.

## UNDERTAKINGS TO CUSTOMERS

Customers may be loyal up to a point, but the entry of a competitor which is charging lower prices for a product may stretch customer loyalty too far. For example, in the telecoms market in the UK, British Telecom has become increasingly customer focused with a whole range of deals to customers which lower the actual charges for a telephone call. It has offered 10 per cent off customers' ten most used numbers, for example. All this comes as BT's markets are being threatened by Mercury Telecommunications and the cable companies. Similarly, the supermarket chains of Tesco and Sainsbury in the UK have responded to the entry of discounters Costco, Netto and Aldi by introducing a range of 'value' products sold under their own names to infer that they are still quality products, and by reducing the prices on some of their other products.

Some organisations have responded to an increase in the level of competition by putting up signs that they will refund money to the customer if they can find the same product at a lower price elsewhere. A number of electrical good outlets do this, as does the John Lewis Partnership. In this respect they are encouraging their competitors to set a high price so that a cosy market relationship can be developed. For example, suppose that two Spanish shoe shops have this arrangement. Shop $S_1$ has a notice saying that it will refund the difference between its shoes and the equivalent shoes elsewhere if they are priced more cheaply. Suppose that the customer purchases shoes from shop $S_1$ and subsequently finds they are cheaper elsewhere, at shop $S_2$. The customer will now go back to $S_1$ and request a rebate. The customer will not buy

**Figure 18.5**

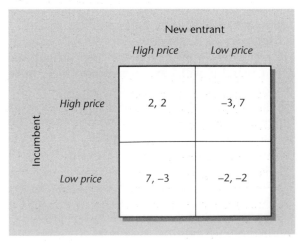

A threat to the new entrant which is credible

from shop $S_2$. Shop $S_2$ does not benefit from setting a price below $S_1$ for this particular type of customer and therefore prices will gradually move towards those set by $S_1$.

Currently a number of supermarket chains in the UK are using a points system to encourage shoppers to stay with them. These points can be redeemed against goods within the store once certain quantities have been accumulated. Suppose that one of the supermarkets now agrees to accept other companies' points along with its own. There will be much reduced customer loyalty at the other food shops, since consumers can now shop around using their accumulated points at the one supermarket which accepts any of them. At present this scenario is not in existence, as the technology behind the electronic card readers prevents a customer from accumulating different stores' points on the same card. Nevertheless, in the future one of the supermarket chains may break ranks in a conscious decision to undermine its rivals' customer base.

## STRATEGIC INVESTMENT AS A BARRIER

Expenditure on new product development, advertising, increasing entry barriers and other such actions may be considered to be investments on the part of the organisation. The distinction should be made, however, between 'innocent' and 'strategic' investment:

- *Innocent investment* – The investment in resources, capital stock and other expenditure which is normally required to maintain the organisation's position in the market. Innocent investment is required to maintain the status quo.
- *Strategic investment* – Investment in resources, capital stock and development of processes which will further develop the organisation's position in the market. Strategic investment is undertaken by organisations when they have decided on the requirements for achieving a planned goal.

Strategic investment relates not only to the organisation's goals in terms of production, but also to any expenditure which is required in order to achieve success. Such expenditure can include investment in advertising, improving reputation and in furthering research and development. Also, investment in infrastructure and support activities

and roles may be considered strategic if it is required for the organisation to achieve its goal.

There are two stages to the strategic investment process according to Lyons (1988). The first stage is the strategic stage, in which the organisation increases its capital stock base. Such increases allow it to make an analysis of its new cost position and thus set the price and quantity which it will be able to offer to the marketplace. This second, 'market' stage is the point at which competitors become aware of the changes made by the organisation. This is the stage at which any signals are first communicated to the marketplace in general.

## OVERCOMING BARRIERS TO ENTRY

There are strategic responses to barriers to entry, be the barriers innocent or strategic, which organisations can utilise in order to gain access to their sought-after market or industry. That is, organisations are able to circumvent barriers to entry if they so desire. Of course, there may be financial or other resource penalties associated with such activities.

The most direct method of overcoming barriers to entry is to spend enough money to ensure that they are no longer a problem. Finance may be raised internally, such as via share issues, use of retained profits and funds and freezing of dividends. Additionally, the organisation may decide to divert a proportion of existing resources from current activities to new market entry. Externally, the organisation may apply for bank loans or make itself available for takeover.

An alternative, and increasingly fashionable, activity which organisations undertake in order to gain the scale of operations, funding or expertise to enter new markets or industries is to enter into collaborative agreements (or joint ventures; *see* Chapter 17) with other organisations with the same desire. Such undertakings are not entered into lightly. The legal and other contractual arrangements can be very complicated. Additionally, when organisations collaborate, they share information and other potentially sensitive internal secrets with each other. They are therefore placing themselves in a potentially vulnerable position with respect to the undesirable release of such information on to the marketplace. Examples of collaborative projects such as this may be observed in a range of different markets. From the discussion below, it would seem that typically they occur in finance or knowledge-intensive industries.

◆ **CASE STUDY 18.6**

# Flying in formation

British Airways has made agreements with other airlines to ensure that passengers embarking in London are able to purchase a 'straight-through' ticket to destinations in the United States and Australia. It has made alliances with USAir and Qantas. These alliances mean that passengers experience British Airways' quality of service throughout their flight(s), even though they change planes at international 'hub' airports to smaller planes which will take them on to their destination.

The alliances mean, therefore, that British Airways is able to offer flights to towns and cities which would not usually be routes open to them. Internal and domestic routes in many countries are awarded only to domestic airlines. Alliances are one way around this.

Another example of European airline alliances is Swissair's 49.5 per cent ownership of Sabena (Belgium's national airline). Swissair also has an alliance with Delta Airlines. KLM has an alliance with the American airline Northwest, and Lufthansa, the German national, with United Airlines.

The number of alliances has grown throughout the 1990s. Increasingly, passengers are offered a service which does not distinguish between the partner airlines. For example, cabin staff wear the same uniforms and internal decor and seating is the same. Alliances are expensive to maintain, however, and even British Airways has expressed doubts about its willingness to maintain long-term arrangements with USAir.

*Source:* © *The Economist*, London, 22 July 1995. Reprinted with permission.

## Entering an unknown market

Attempting entry to a completely new and unknown market is recognised to have greater risks associated with it compared to the risk of entry to a market where an organisation may already possess some knowledge or experience. It is intuitive, therefore, that organisations seek to move sideways into related markets, rather than diversifying into completely new ones. Where there are aspects of the market which are known, there may be greater potential for spotting new opportunities than when there is uncertainty, or ignorance. Organisations are therefore able to gain entry into markets without facing the full effect of barriers to entry as a result of their experience or knowledge *and* they are more likely to be recognised by the consumers in the new market. As a result, the immediate prospective consumer base is larger than it would be in the case of an anonymous market entry.

Anonymity need not be a barrier to entry if an organisation possesses considerable reputation or standing in general. An organisation which is able to move successfully between markets can literally jump between attractive markets as seems appropriate. Such activity obviously requires considerable financial support, especially if there is low potential for transfer of skills and resources between those markets.

An example of such market-hopping may be seen in the case of Richard Branson's Virgin company. Virgin began as a music publishing and retail organisation in the 1980s. By the early 1990s, Branson had sold his stake in Virgin Music to EMI.

The funds which the sale raised were used to expand Virgin Airways, which was, at the time, operating a much smaller transatlantic service between the UK and US compared to the mid-1990s situation. Indeed, Virgin Airlines is now attempting to install itself on other routes, such as the lucrative London to Johannesburg route. Additionally, Virgin has diversified (successfully) into the sale of condoms (under the Mates brand name) and also into the soft drinks market. Since the launch of Virgin Cola in 1995, considerable market share has been captured in the UK domestic market. More recently, Branson has been involved (unsuccessfully) as the driving force behind bids to operate the UK National Lottery and the fifth terrestrial television channel, Channel 5. A more successful venture recently has been Virgin's movement into personal financial management, offering personal equity plans (PEPs) to UK investors.

---

◆ **Exercise 18.4**

Are there any other instances you are aware of which have involved transfer of resources or collaborative agreements to overcome otherwise unsurmountable entry barriers?

---

Finally, it should be noted that the theory relating to barriers to entry is based on the assumption that the entrant is a small competitor with low levels of financial backing, reputation and other resources.

Such a theory is less easy to defend now than when it was developed in the 1930s and 1940s. It was been implied in the discussion above that the better prepared the organisation is prior to attempting entry, the more likely entry is to be successful. This implication may be observed to be true if you consider the proposition that it is more difficult to deter entry by well-resourced competitors (whatever the relevant 'resource' may be). The Petroleum company Q8 found this to be true when it attempted to enter the UK market on a scale to match the established companies such as BP, Esso, Shell and Texaco. Therefore, the Virgin story and other documented stories of successful entry into markets should not come as a surprise; indeed, they should come as proof of the fact that such entry is both feasible, rational and likely to succeed. Indeed, given the growth in pan-European companies, such entry may be more prevalent in the future, although the more recent move towards de-merger by Hanson may militate against this. It may be the case in the late 1990s that events show organisations which grew through merger are beginning to specialise through demerger.

## CONCLUDING REMARKS

Overall, it has been seen that there are a variety of tools which may be used by organisations for strategic reasons. Incumbent organisations may deter entry by erecting barriers to entry to their market. Within markets, it is possible to gain advantage over competitors by manipulation of product availability or price. Bertrand's model suggests that the largest payoffs accrue to the second mover, rather than the first. Whatever change is made in the market, or threatened, the organisation must be capable of following it through, that is, the threat must be credible.

Many of the actions and tools discussed in this chapter require large levels of financial backing to implement or to overcome. The reputation of organisations can also play a part in their success, however. Attracting customers and employees can be easier if the organisation has a good reputation. Similarly, a well-known brand name can put the owner at an advantage compared to its rivals.

## SUMMARY

◆ This chapter has considered a range of strategies that organisations can use to deter entry into their markets. Limit pricing, as seen in oligopolistic market structures, provides one approach. Here the price is placed at a level which does not encourage entry into the market.

◆ Reputation may also provide a competitive edge. This may be viewed in terms of consistent behaviour of the incumbent organisation, as a measure of its relationship with its workforce, and can be linked with the characteristics of the owner/manager of the organisation.

◆ The incumbent organisation can use excess capacity to deter entry, flooding the market and thereby pushing down prices. Alternatively, the incumbent could use economies of scope to lower the costs of production. Management expertise may also be an advantageous characteristic for the incumbent, as well as its ability to integrate vertically to create both strategic and structural barriers to entry.

◆ Governments often operate in markets to reduce the failure of the market mechanism. Yet governments can also provide barriers that favour their own domestic organisations. They can issue

patents, use trade barriers to reduce competition, offer contracts to domestic organisations and support their industries through lower costs of finance and other state aid.

◆ Deterring entry into a market may be related to whether the response of the incumbent organisation is credible or not. The incumbent must show that being committed to an entry deterrence strategy is its most profitable strategy. If it is not, the new entrant will realise that the incumbent's best position is a market-sharing one, and thus entry by the new organisation will follow.

◆ Products may be used as a weapon in the marketplace to deter entry and to gain market share. Organisations which differentiate horizontally between products, with a wide product range, are able to attract and capture greater numbers of random consumers than others with a narrower portfolio.

◆ Outsourcing, long-term agreements and other contractual arrangements can lead to benefits for both parties. Increased market coverage and a greater network of potential other partners are examples of such benefits.

# REVIEW QUESTIONS

**1** Consider the breakfast cereal market in your country. What are the top five brands? How do these brands deter new entrants into their market?

**2** In what ways is the European Commission reducing the barriers to entry into EU markets? Do you consider this will harm or benefit your own country's organisations?

**3** Are strategic alliances in the airline industry a one-minute wonder, or sustainable sources of competitive advantage?

**4** New product launch at the mature or decline stage of an industry lifecycle is potentially dangerous due to the entrants it attracts. Strategically, why might an organisation believe it necessary to launch a new product at such a critical stage?

**5** Comment on the trend for joint ventures and collaborative agreements in some industries rather than merger or takeover. Is there an identifiable trend? What are the advantages of joint ventures and agreements over merger or takeover (and vice versa)?

## GLOSSARY OF NEW TERMS

**Credible threat:** A possible behavioural scenario of the incumbent organisation which will be carried out.

**First-mover advantage:** Enhanced profit, market share or other payoffs which are gained as a result of an organisation being the first to launch a product, expand market quantity, change price, extend advertising and so on. In time, others will imitate and the enhanced payoff will return to the 'normal' level.

**Non-tariff barrier:** Any barrier to trade which is not a tariff, such as a quota, or health and safety restrictions.

**Privatisation:** The process by which state-owned enterprises are moved from public ownership to the private sector.

**Quota:** A limit on the quantity of goods allowed into a country in any one period.

**Reputation:** A factor that provides the organisation with a competitive edge, adding value to it and providing it with a distinctive capability.

**Second-mover advantage:** Enhanced profit, market share or other payoffs which are gained as a result of following another organisation's new product launch or advertising campaign or similar market movement. The advantage accrues to the second mover because it is able to use technology, learning or experience developed by and paid for by the first mover.

**Tariff barrier:** A tax placed on an import arriving in a country so that its price becomes less competitive with domestically produced goods.

## READING

Bertrand, J (1883) Théorie Mathématique de la Richesse Sociale, *Journal des Savants*, Paris.

Cournot, A (1838) *Recherches sur les Principes Mathématiques de la Théorie des Richesses*, Paris.

Ferguson, P R, Ferguson, G J and Rothschild, R (1993) *Business Economics*, Macmillan, Basingstoke.
*This text covers some of the areas of barriers to entry in a chapter on oligopoly, and also provides some useful applied analysis in the case study section.*

Hay, D A and Morris, D J (1991) *Industrial Economics and Organisation: Theory and Evidence*, 2nd edn, Oxford University Press, Oxford.
*This text provides a useful background to barriers to entry in the chapter on market structure and performance.*

Moschandreas, M (1994) *Business Economics*, Routledge London.

*A slightly more advanced text than Ferguson et al. above, providing good analytical tools and a strong mathematical examination of the issues.*

The Economist (1995) 'Holding the hand that feeds', 9 September, p 87.
*An interesting article which gives an informed argument for and against the practice of outsourcing. Reference is made to actual companies' experiences.*

**Further reading**

Bain, J S (1968) *Industrial Organisation*, 2nd edn, John Wiley, New York.

Kay, J (1993) *Foundations of Corporate Success: How Business Strategies Add Value*, Oxford University Press, Oxford.

Lyons, B (1988) 'Barriers to entry' in Davies, S and Lyons, B with Dixon, H and Geroski, P (eds), *Economics in Industrial Organisation: Surveys in Economics*, Longman, Harlow.

CHAPTER **19**

# QUALITY AND THE ECONOMICS OF THE ORGANISATION

## KEY ISSUES

Business issues

Business strategy

Decision-making techniques

Economic concepts

Management decision issues

Optimal outcomes to management issues

## OBJECTIVES

◆ To consider what quality standards are and the benefits they can bring to accredited organisations.

◆ To assess the costs and benefits of adopting a company-wide quality programme.

◆ To discuss how design and quality have been used as differential strategies for an organisation's product.

◆ To evaluate the importance of service excellence as a differential strategy for an organisation.

◆ To explain brand name advantages as a means to deliver a strategic advantage.

◆ To consider the threats to companies who have differentiated their product through a brand name.

## KEY TERMS

Brand name
Costs of quality
Credence goods
Differentiation strategy
Experience goods
Kaizen
Product proliferation
Quality circle
Quality focus
Quality leadership
Quality standards
Search costs
TQM
Zero defects

## CHAPTER OUTLINE

Business application

The definition of quality

Why choose quality?

Quality standards

Case study 19.1 Quality shows a profit

Costs and benefits of quality

Quality leadership

Case study 19.2 Adidas has been shaping up

Beyond quality leadership

Case study 19.3 What's the score?

Differentiation and type of product

Case study 19.4 The global solution to cutting costs

Quality focus strategy

Case study 19.5 Learning to run faster in order to stand still

Case study 19.6 Survey of Europe's most respected companies: BMW

Summary

Review questions

Glossary of new terms

Reading

# When it's all in the label

**FT**

*Vorsprung durch Technik*. The sound of the words alone, even if their precise meaning is obscure to many customers, tells you all you need to know: it's made in Germany, and therefore soundly engineered.

A 'Made in Germany' label is associated the world over by consumers, and particularly strongly by those in Europe, with positive images of quality. However, a new study suggests that at an international corporate level the label also has negative associations, including lack of top-notch design and innovation, little emotional appeal and poor value for money.

The issue of the national badge is clearly of importance to those attempting to build global brands.

As far as 'Made in Germany' is concerned, a Wolff Olins study found: '90 per cent of companies surveyed associated German manufacturing with durability; all recognised the technical prowess of German-made goods; 98 per cent expected goods to be high quality; and 91 per cent considered the goods would be environmentally friendly'.

But 90 per cent of companies commented on lack of top-quality design and innovation; none felt that German goods had emotional appeal; 84 per cent said the goods were expensive; and 60 per cent criticised the poor flexibility of German product offers.

Wolff Olins points out that the risk for German manufacturers is that 'as other producers improve their reputation for producing technologically advanced and reliable goods, there will be little reason to choose German goods.

Two other recent international studies of the worth of national badges have concentrated on individual consumer, rather than corporate views of what it means for goods to be made in a particular country. Both these surveys underline national differences in perceptions of country brands and attitudes to the home market.

For example, Americans have a considerably higher opinion of American products than consumers in the rest of the world . . . When asked who makes the best movies, 81 per cent of Americans said the US, compared with 53 per cent of those questioned around the world. The same was true for a range of other goods, including blue jeans (78 per cent, compared with 59 per cent); moderately priced cars (61 per cent, compared with 16 per cent); and beer (40 per cent, compared with 11 per cent).

A similar survey . . . found the Japanese even more confident than Americans about their national produce.

Self-perception of quality appeared lowest among UK and Taiwanese consumers in this survey. Just 27 per cent of those questioned in the UK rated domestically produced manufactured goods as 'excellent' or 'very good', while the figure in Taiwan was 16 per cent.

While Japan, Germany and the US are universally acknowledged quality leaders, their exact ranking among consumers in any one country depends on proximity . . . Japan has the highest ranking in Asia, Germany leads in Europe, while the US tops the list in the Americas.

To lower further the UK consumer's lack of self-esteem, in 1995, the UK was overtaken by France and now ranks fifth for quality in the world, compared with fourth in 1994.

*Source: Financial Times, 3 August 1995. Reprinted with permission.*

## Comment

Quality and the image it gives, both to consumers and other companies, can be linked to the country of origin. This provides some organisations with a competitive advantage in both domestic and foreign markets. Thus a UK organisation which wishes to compete with a German or Japanese firm may face an uphill struggle to compete with them on quality. Even if it matches quality levels, the perception may still be that the Japanese or German product is superior. In trying to compete in foreign markets with German and Japanese firms, the problems may be further exacerbated by the proximity condition outlined above. Therefore, although a UK firm may wish to compete using a strategy of quality leadership, a better approach may be one of **low-cost leadership**, particularly in the light of what the survey of international companies is telling us.

This does not mean that a quality leadership strategy should not be followed by UK organisations, since in earlier decades Japanese products, in particular, were viewed as inferior. It probably means that at this stage, UK firms in a number of sectors just need to try harder. With regard to appropriate strategies that organisations can use to gain entry into markets or to strengthen their dominant positions, this chapter considers a range of possible strategic scenarios.

# THE DEFINITION OF QUALITY

Most people would feel that they are able to give a definition for what is meant by 'quality'. However, many of those people, unless they have worked in an organisation which has adopted a programme of quality enhancement or improvement, will probably possess a misconception of the term. Typical incorrect definitions of quality within a product tend to include reference to the high price, good reputation, high esteem or level of specification/attributes associated with it.

In truth, even low-priced, low-cost and low-specification products can be of 'high' quality. The definition of quality focuses not on quantities of attributes or financial values of products, but on how well the product performs the function it is designed for. Therefore, quality may be broadly defined as:

> *Production which consistently meets the requirements of timescale, market price, availability and cost to the organisation and with **zero errors** or **defects** with appropriate specification and performance of a product within the consumer context.*

Or, more simply:

> *The right product in the right place at the right time for the right price every time.*

## Total quality management (TQM) and quality circles

**TQM** and **quality circles** are attributed to Japanese management techniques and working practices. TQM requires an organisational focus on the quality of products and services at all stages of production. Quality circles are used when organisations set up groups of employees responsible for the complete production process. In extreme cases, the members of a group have input into the recruitment of further members and all future training. In most cases, the quality circle will operate on a system where any member unhappy about the standard of a part or even completed product is able to 'stop the line', that is, halt work until the source of the defect or error is found and put right.

## Benchmarking

Benchmarking was discussed in Chapter 16, as a technique for identifying core competences and measuring performance in key areas against major competitors. Benchmarking may also be used as a quality measure. Benchmarking is the process of comparing performances with those of other companies in order to gain insights into better (or best) practices used by others with a view to adopting these.

## Kaizen

**Kaizen** is a further development of the concept of quality implementation. Broadly translated from the Japanese as 'continuous improvement', its foundations may be clearly seen in the works of Deming and others. *Kaizen*-oriented organisations communicate to and involve their workforce in quality production assurance techniques. Empowerment of all members of the workforce to take responsibility for defects or errors which occur at their stage of the productive process is an important part of *Kaizen*.

# WHY CHOOSE QUALITY?

It is common for organisations to announce proudly that they have 'adopted a quality programme'. What does this mean and why do they do it?

Both in the UK and Europe, there are measurable potential benefits to adopting a quality approach or programme throughout the organisation. That is, there are potential benefits to those organisations which adopt a programme to ensure that their complete operation is consistent in terms of performance and that the resultant product or service is also consistently delivered in the marketplace with the correct specification and zero errors or defects.

Strategic decisions to implement quality programmes tend to have synergistic relations. The organisation, as it develops a quality ethos, frequently also develops a customer focus. Thus the organisation, at all levels, develops an awareness of what the customer requires. This enables many organisations to serve those customers better. For example, many organisations, once they develop a quality approach to production and a customer focus, redesign the manner in which their employees interact with customers. That is, all employees (rather than just the sales team) are trained in dealing with customers. As a result, anyone who comes into contact with a customer is able to assist them with their problem or query. Additionally, organisations expect their employees to take the initiative and act to resolve any customer issues that arise.

# QUALITY STANDARDS

Other benefits of adopting quality are to be found in respect to the recognised **quality standards** with

◆ **CASE STUDY 19.1**

## Quality shows a profit

One of the biggest questions facing managements who take their companies through quality standard certification is knowing how much impact it has on profits.

While the experience usually seems positive sceptics may doubt the programme's worth, particularly since it often involves a significant increase in the training budget.

Researchers at Surrey University have produced a report which shows that companies which have won approval of ISO 9000, the international quality standard, deliver above average performance when comparing profitability and capital employed with industry averages.

The research does not prove that ISO 9000 gives companies a distinct advantage – it may be that the best organisations tend to seek certification – but, say the researchers, it does show that there are financially measurable benefits to be gained.

The study compared the performance of 225 mechanical engineering manufacturing companies

certified to ISO 9000 by Lloyd's Register Quality Assurance, an international certification body, against the industry average for the sector between 1990 and 1992. It looked at profitability and return on capital employed.

The study found that companies certified to the standard recorded profits that were double those of the industry average. Smaller certified companies performed even better, returning profits three times the industry average.

The report also showed that companies which had achieved the standard were investing twice as much on each employee as the industry average but the capital employed was paying off in sales and profits.

Ron Turner, LRQA's managing director, said: 'The research shows that the benefits associated with gaining approval to ISO 9000 are applicable to all sizes of company.'

*Source: Financial Times, 26 July 1995. Reprinted with permission.*

which organisations may be accredited. In the UK, in the late 1980s and early 1990s, many organisations were working towards, or had achieved, British Standard 5750 (BS 5750). Achievement of BS 5750 provides certification that an organisation has ensured its quality systems and other operations, resulting in a company-wide quality approach.

Although BS 5750 is still a worthy accreditation for organisations to gain, much attention in the UK and Europe has turned to the ISO 9000 (International Organisation for Standardisation) quality award. ISO 9000 is an internationally recognised quality standard which 'opens doors' for accredited organisations; buyers choosing between an accredited supplier and a non-accredited supplier are more likely to choose the accredited supplier. Quality accreditation therefore provides an opportunity for organisations to gain an advantage over their competitors when bidding for contracts if those competitors are not accredited.

### Comment on the case study

It is expensive to gain BS 5750 or ISO 9000 accreditation. For smaller organisations, it is sometimes difficult to make the decision about whether to begin the process or not. However, recent research shows that accreditation can be beneficial to organisations where it counts – on the bottom line. Smaller engineering manufacturers studied

even recorded profit levels three times the industry average. Larger organisations can also be seen to gain: their profits were up to twice the industry average. Profits are not necessarily increased by the fact that they have gained quality accreditation, but the research does seem to highlight enhanced results for those organisations studied.

## COSTS AND BENEFITS OF QUALITY

Implementation and adoption of a quality programme require a financial and also a resource investment. In order to assess the savings accruing through any such programme, an organisation must be able to quantify:

■ The cost of errors and defects prior to implementation.
■ The cost of implementing the programme.
■ Savings made with respect to the previous two factors.

That is, would the organisation be better off by not implementing a quality programme at all? (What is the opportunity cost?) The objective of any quality programme must be to enhance organisational profits. If the **total costs of quality** (TCQ) detract from this, the programme is not worth implementing. It is also worth noting that TCQ should also be pushed as low as possible in order to have an optimum effect on profits.

## Categories of costs

Information relating to costs allows quality programmes to be assessed. Identifiable quality cost categories are:

- *Prevention* – Costs associated with preventing any errors or defects. Included here are the administration and planning of the quality programme, quality data collection and analysis, training and also any consumer surveys which are carried out in order to elicit customer opinion of the product(s).
- *Appraisal* – Costs associated with the inspection, test and set-up of the quality standards which will be applied in the quality programme. Also included are the costs of any materials and field tests which are a part of the quality programme.
- *Internal failure* – Costs associated with the analysis of defects and failures which are detected in intermediate or completed products. Included within this category are also the costs of any repair, rework, scrap and retesting of repaired/reworked products.
- *External failure* – Costs associated with the failure or test of any products once purchased. Within this category are repair, rework, replacement and any other 'field activities' required to maintain customer satisfaction.

The four categories proposed above may be condensed into the categories of 'assurance' (prevention and appraisal) and 'defects and failures' (internal and external failures). By considering defects and failure costs against appraisal costs and prevention costs, with TCQ also given, as in Figure 19.1, it may be seen that there is an optimum level of quality costs.

TCQ fall from an infinite level to a minimum level and then begin to rise once more towards infinity. The minimum TCQ level is at the zero-defect level. As defects increase, failure costs increase. More and more units of production require rework, with associated administration costs. Appraisal costs may be assumed to be constant, while prevention costs are at their greatest level when defects are minimised. Prevention costs quickly diminish as the level of defects increase.

A 'normal' level of TCQ is usually found to the right of the minimum point and also beyond the level of defects which may be found when failure costs and appraisal costs are equal. An absolute level of 'normal' TCQ may not be stated because this will differ for various organisations within various industries, at various stages of their lifecycle.

## Benefits

There are benefits to be gained from quality programmes. In terms of costs, in Figure 19.1, it may be seen that there is a tradeoff between prevention/appraisal and failure costs. The relationship

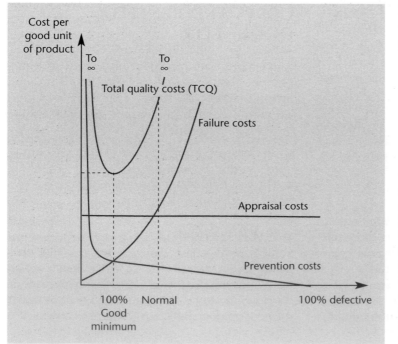

**Figure 19.1 Total costs of quality (TCQ) and the relationship between prevention and repair costs**

TCQ fall from an infinite level to a minimum level and then begin to rise once more towards infinity. The minimum TCQ level is at the zero-defect level. As defects increase, failure costs increase. More and more units of production require rework, with associated administration costs. Appraisal costs may be assumed to be constant, while prevention costs are at their greatest level when defects are minimised. Prevention costs quickly diminish as the level of defects increase.

between cost increase and the production cycle shows that there are benefits in early detection of errors and defects. Additionally, in terms of lost custom, cancelled repeat business and poor reputation, the costs are far greater as the level of defects increases. In short, the tradeoff between costs and production is emphasised if non-tangible factors such as those discussed above could also be measured.

Other benefits from the adoption of a quality programme may be considered in terms of the effects on production and profits. A direct result of the implementation of a successful programme will be an enhanced, positive image for the product or the organisation in the marketplace. Therefore, opportunities to increase the price of the product will arise, as the consumer associates the product or reputation with value for money. At the same time, as reputation improves, it follows that units sold will also increase. The organisation will be required to increase production and will be able to explore the benefits accruing from increased scale: economies of scale.

Reduced costs, increased profit margins (possibly also increased prices), a greater volume of sales and possibly even greater market share are all advantages which may be measured against the quality programme. However, recall what the quality programme is really meant to do: to decrease the quantity of errors and defaults which occur during the production process. There is a measurement which may be placed on this as well. If a product's production run contains fewer errors and defaults, then fewer substandard products will reach consumers. There are several benefits which may be associated with such an effect, two of which are:

■ Lower external failure costs for the organisation in terms of repairs and rework or replacement of faulty products.

■ A lower level of product liability costs: communication with the complainant, reduced likelihood of legal action, opportunity to reduce the size of the consumer relations and legal teams.

---

◆ **Exercise 19.1**

1  What is the overall objective of any quality enhancement programme?

2  Why is it so essential that the benefits of any quality programme adopted should outweigh the costs?

---

As a whole, the benefits of adopting a quality programme are multifaceted and synergistic. All areas of the organisation are affected and costs savings and improvements to working practices may be observed across the organisation. In the marketplace, reputation improves, sales increase and greater profits are available. The overall effect *must* be that the organisation's profit levels are improved. A programme which costs more than the benefits associated with it will detract from profits.

For any programme adopted, and the method of implementation will be as individual as the number of adoptees, the key point is that there is commitment on the part of the organisation. Once this commitment is gained, communication can be made, changes to processes invoked, training implemented and employees can be given responsibility for their part of the operation. The adoption of a programme, whatever form it takes, requires a shift in culture and thinking within the organisation. Such change cannot take place immediately, but can be dramatic if managed effectively.

## QUALITY LEADERSHIP

**Differential strategies** can be associated with achieving a competitive advantage through quality. One of the approaches to demand in Chapter 5 indicated that consumers selected products on the basis of their desired attributes. Here quality is being used as a proxy for the desired attributes in a product or service. To be successful any organisation must be able to offer better quality at the going price than its rivals. Different customers, or groups of customers, may have a reservation price at which they are seeking to purchase the commodity and the organisation seeks to pull the consumer to the top of their reservation price. In fact, it could be argued that a successful quality-oriented organisation may seek to pull the consumer past their original reservation price.

Quality can be associated with a number of characteristics of the organisation and the product. For example, this could be enhanced after-sales service, superior customer service, continual innovation of the product so that the consumer feels that they are getting the 'state of the art' and bold design and artwork. The organisation, by adopting a **quality leadership strategy**, is therefore able to keep ahead of its rivals. Given the consumers' reservation price, it would be expected that there would be different quality leader products in different segments of the market. Sometimes these may be made by different producers, sometimes the different market segments are dominated, in quality terms, by the same producer. As an example of quality leadership consumers may feel that Porsche, Ferrari or Mercedes dominate the top-of-the-range car market, but because consumers' reservation prices may be set much lower they may need to settle for a make of car which fits the more middle-income groups, such as VW or Toyota. Alternatively, in the hi-fi market it is possible to argue that quality, in terms of large-scale production at a number of income points, is dominated by Sony.

Therefore, to stay ahead of the market on quality terms organisations need to listen to what consumers are saying about current products. Such information can come from direct contact with the customer at point of sale, through consumer surveys or via questionnaires. Once this information is gathered it is important that, whatever definition of quality the organisation is using, it is disseminated throughout the workforce.

Using quality leadership as a differential strategy does not mean that the organisation will stay as the market leader. The business environment is not static and it would be expected that competitors would attempt to incorporate many of the quality advantages of their rivals. Therefore, unless the quality leader keeps enhancing its quality, it may begin to lose share to its competitors.

## ◆ CASE STUDY 19.2

### Adidas has been shaping up

**FT**

Adidas, the German sports equipment maker, in October 1995 announced its share price for its forthcoming floatation. [Many observers felt that the company would never be in this position.]

Founded by Adi Dassler just after the second world war, Adidas presents a familiar story of a company that ran into trouble after the death of its owner (or in this case, after the death of the patriarch's son, Mr Horst Dassler, in 1987).

The late 1980s and early 1990s were marred by internal family feuds and a changed strategy.

The floatation prospectus asserts that in the early 1990s the group changed from being an authentic sports goods maker to a follower of fashion, lost its leadership in product innovation and quality, failed to exploit marketing and kept manufacturing in high cost locations at a time when competitors had moved to low wage countries.

There has been a radical change since the company was bought by the French investment company Sogedim. Adidas has gone back to a strong focus on technological innovations and quality, but with the added ingredient of aggressive advertising to compete with the sportswear market leaders – Nike and Reebok of the US.

The company has also virtually abandoned Germany as a production base in favour of Asia, especially China, Indonesia and Thailand.

*Source: Financial Times, 27 October 1995. Reprinted with permission.*

### ◆ Exercise 19.2

1 What are the key qualities brought to the market by Adidas footwear and clothing? Do Nike and Reebok have different characteristics?

2 How important is quality leadership in the sports footwear industry?

#### *Comment on the case study*

Adidas therefore provides an example of a company which had followed a strategy of quality leadership which was then lost as the organisation was sold by the originating family and whose new owners sought to change the direction of the company. In addition, in Adidas's case it could not become the low-cost leader since it continued to make its sports equipment in high-cost areas. The improved success of the company in recent years is due to a return to quality leadership and a greater ability to compete on costs, as the organisation has switched the majority of its production to South-East Asia.

## BEYOND QUALITY LEADERSHIP

During the 1970s and 1980s, it could be argued that many Japanese companies have seized the position of quality leaders in their markets. Japanese manufacturers have been in a position to match most of the developments in rivals' products and rivals, seeing the success of Japanese companies and their use of quality via *kaizen*, have dramatically altered their approaches to their products, so that consumers may believe that quality *per se* is not a major distinguishing factor. They are therefore expecting quality as of right. As a response, some manufacturing companies have now moved towards service excellence; that is, meeting and exceeding customer expectations. This may involve, for example, offering the installation and monitoring of equipment at no extra cost, or improving delivery times.

This move towards improving customer service and customer expectations can be brought about by a number of approaches: making customer commitment a high priority of senior management; selecting employees who have a high commitment to customer satisfaction, training and retraining managers – this might go as far as encouraging managers to partake in the customer–organisation interface; investing time and effort in the initial meeting between the customer/organisation/service staff (overall consumer focus strategy) – often the opening minutes of any meeting between parties determines how customers feel about the organisation; using technology to deal with customer queries as soon as possible; and using policies which greatly exceed customer expectations. Toyota, for example, has a policy of providing the customer with their new car within one week of receiving the order. On the basis of this behaviour and others, customer loyalty to Toyota is

65 per cent, while for most other manufacturers it is 50 per cent.

Such concentration on factors beyond the actual quality of the product can propel an organisation which is not the dominant player in the market to outperform the market leader in the eyes of the customer. Therefore, although many Western companies have caught up with their Japanese rivals in terms of quality, Japanese customers have moved on towards supplying **zero defects** in customer service. Western companies, of course, are also customer focused, but the difference may lie in the way employees at all levels in the organisation attempt to enhance customer satisfaction as a means to gain competitive advantage. In terms of cost–benefit analysis, the move by some companies towards customer service quality may not appear to be worthwhile, since this is perceived to play a marginal role in customer decision making. Nonetheless, if many companies are now producing outputs which are similar in quality, then the move towards a customer expectation focus may be sufficient to provide a competitive edge. As stated in Chapter 15, it is cheaper to retain customers than to attract new ones.

## ◆ CASE STUDY 19.3

# What's the score?                                    FT

When Michael Heseltine, the trade and industry secretary, launched the government's white paper on Britain's competitiveness in 1994, the Chartered Institute of Marketing (CIM), the marketing professional body in the UK, was left fuming.

Nowhere in the 163-page document, which ranged over areas as diverse as training, export promotion and prompt payment of bills, was there reference to the need for companies to market their goods and services effectively . . .

Part of the difficulty for the CIM and other proponents of marketing has been lack of factual evidence, there have been few attempts systematically to benchmark the marketing performance of companies and even fewer efforts to link marketing excellence with competitive advantage . . .

However, a study by Bradford University's management centre may have the answer. In a survey of 44 UK manufacturing companies and their senior managers, scores on a framework for evaluating companies' marketing operations were matched against companies' financial performance, as measured by the ratio of pre-tax profits to sales turnover.

The results of the first part of the exercise are startlingly bad: on average, companies in the sample scored poor marks under all of the seven headings of

the framework – marketing strategy, quality strategy, innovation, customer development, branding, supply chain management and manufacturing strategy.

Just six, including SmithKline Beecham, Amersham International and Lucas Aerospace, qualified as marketing 'professionals', having already developed the best practice in their sector and scoring high marks under all headings . . .

As for the link between marketing and the bottom line, the authors are convinced there is strong evidence 'to argue that investment in critical processes can be repaid in terms of superior business performance'.

The study highlights particular weaknesses in UK manufacturing . . . For example, much product development work was considered by the authors to be reactive . . . 'Only a few companies were deliberately extending technology beyond customers' current requirements to focus on future opportunities which the customer was not yet aware of.'

Many companies were found to emphasise product and price but to neglect distribution and most of the sample scored badly on branding. 'There was no awareness of the strategic role of branding as a device to communicate the company's unique and distinctive position to internal and external markets.'

*Source: Financial Times, 4 May 1995. Reprinted with permission.*

### ◆ Exercise 19.3

From your understanding of the case study, why, for UK firms, may there not be a link between investment in quality and improved business performance?

#### Comment on the case study

Quality strategy, which includes such things as top management commitment, culture which underpins quality and quality control, appears to be poorly developed once we go outside of the top UK manufacturing companies. It could be argued that even if UK companies can become price competitive, the failure to develop a quality strategy fully may hamper their overall performance. Moreover, even if the quality is there, if consumers still believe that UK quality is inferior to that of other organisations, sales may still be constrained.

# DIFFERENTIATION AND TYPE OF PRODUCT

Although organisations may have progressed along a route to provide practically similar-quality products in different market segments, differentiation between products may still exist. These differences can be real or imagined, tangible or intangible. How these differences are perceived by the purchaser distinguishes one product from another.

There are costs in sampling a market for information; consumers do not have perfect information and the **search costs** can be high. If consumer search costs are low, however, and the organisation's product has distinct advantages over other competing products, buyers will realise that they cannot do better and will move towards buying the organisation's product. If the characteristics of the favoured product can be reproduced by competing organisations, the advantages which one organisation has over others are relatively short lived. Nonetheless, as described earlier, if the market leader also changes the characteristics of its product to be even more in line with what the consumer desires, even where search attributes are relatively easy to copy, the market leader may stay one step ahead of its rivals.

Where the product or service is defined as either an experience or credence product, differentiation provides an opportunity for the market leader to remain in that position for longer without having

continually to innovate or change. In the case of goods which have **experience attributes**, such as taste, sound quality and product durability, these attributes cannot be evaluated before purchase. Only once the product has been purchased is the consumer able to evaluate the quality of the product and decide whether it is worth purchasing it again. **Credence products**, such as restaurant service, hotel service, the competence of lecturers or the taste of some food, are products whose attributes cannot be evaluated even if the product has been purchased before, because the product's attributes might change the next time, or because the product's attributes cannot be easily identified. The consumer must show faith or belief in the product.

In these cases the organisation has much more scope concerning the product's quality. Due to individual preferences, one person may prefer one product over another but this may be completely the opposite of another consumer's opinion. Examples of this behaviour can be found in detergents, beers and soft drinks. From the organisation's point of view the task is to try to emphasise the preference differences as a way of enlarging market share. This is easily done in the food and drink sectors, where product attributes may be changed in the product to suit consumers' demands. Also, it is possible to advertise the inclusion of these attributes to increase awareness of the product in the marketplace. Of course, the argument also holds true for other categories of product, from a diverse list including cars, toothpaste, stereos, watches.

## Brand name advantages

Where the product has credence or experience attributes which require the customer to purchase the product, consumers may consider the **brand name** as a means of conferring quality on the product. This image or feel of quality may come from other products produced by the organisation which the consumer has bought in the past, from advertising campaigns, or from promotions that the organisation runs, such as support for sporting activities. Some brand names are more successful at this process and others have tarnished their image in the past. For example, some of the Benetton adverts were disliked by individuals in the UK, although there were few problems with the same adverts in France and Italy.

◆ CASE STUDY 19.4

## The global solution to cutting costs   FT

Far less well known than its brand name opposition and also less understood, the world's generics industry, with sales of $14 bn in 1993, has had an upsurge over the last two years. The drive by government health departments worldwide to cut costs and reduce healthcare budgets has put considerable pressure on the drugs bill.

In many countries the generic solution has been seen as a way to assist this cost-cutting exercise. The US is the biggest generic market followed by Europe, which is dominated by Germany, the UK, Denmark and the Netherlands. But it is noticeable that the generics market is spreading on a global scale with the Australian and New Zealand governments indicating the preferred use of generics . . .

However, it seems that it is the brand name companies, rather than the independents with their far greater resources, overseas experience, and new-found familiarity with generics, that appear to be taking the lead in global expansion.

The cost containment measures have cause a batch of acquisitions with the drive being led by German

companies. Hoechst purchased 51 per cent of US-based Copley Pharmaceuticals, Bayer took 28.3 per cent of another US company, Schein Pharmaceutical, and BASF set up its own generics unit by taking a share in the US company Ivax.

[One of the reasons put forward for the move into generics by some of the big brand name companies is that developing a product through R&D gives the branded organisation the flexibility or strategic advantage of developing it in the generics market.]

Many industry observers firmly believe that there will be further consolidation and integration in the generic industry. Generic companies need the large ethical manufacturers to provide the funding for research in order to develop the big selling drugs for their new opportunities.

The once cut-throat traditional rivalry between the two groups is rapidly declining as both groups seek to explore new kinds of relationships.

*Source: Financial Times, 25 April 1995. Reprinted with permission.*

### ◆ Exercise 19.4

Are brand name advantages always short lived, as Case study 19.4 suggests, or are there products whose brand name still dominates the market?

### Comment on the case study

Case study 19.4 outlines one way of dealing with the growth of generics in the pharmaceutical industry, that is, either takeover or merge with an organisation which sells generics or develop your own generics company. In many ways the brand name companies are responding to a threat to their products because of the changing nature and power of purchasers. In this way the threat can be turned into an opportunity for improved profits. In addition, the case also notes something outlined earlier: that the powerful position established by brand names is under threat and companies cannot take for granted that consumers will search out their product solely because of the brand names. Brand named manufacturers may just have to try harder in the future.

These observations are emphasised in the pharmaceuticals industry, where monopoly revenues await the original manufacturer of branded prod-

uct, but only until the patent expires. At that stage, the market is open to all and the monopoly position is lost. If the branded product has been successful, the original manufacturer will obviously want to protect its position, especially if research and development costs have been high. However, at the same time, entrants will also be attempting to gain a share of the lucrative market. One way of competing for the original manufacturer is to launch a generic version of its branded product. This was seen in Chapter 18, in Case study 18.4.

## QUALITY FOCUS STRATEGY

Quality leadership of a market is one way of securing competitive advantage. However, in the longer term, in order to maintain any captured advantage, an organisation must decide on and sell to a target group of consumers within its given market segment, that is, it must focus. The decision to undertake a **quality focus** strategy involves the organisation in a decision to concentrate on supplying the wants and needs of a small part of the market on which it concentrates its selling efforts. Thus the organisation essentially takes the decision to serve a select part of the market.

Quality focus strategy usually relates to situations where the organisation offers an upmarket product. The product attributes and specification will be superior to other products available in the marketplace. The organisation is, as was stated in the section on quality leadership, aiming to exploit the consumer by providing a product which possesses the desired attributes and yet which tempts the consumer to spend beyond their reservation price. There is a risk that the organisation is unable to provide the desired attributes at the correct price, or that competitors will, through experience, surpass the level of specification package offered for sale at the market price. Thus, in order to maintain competitive advantage via quality focus, the organisation cannot remain static, it must continually develop and improve its product offering.

## ◆ CASE STUDY 19.5

# Learning to run faster in order to stand still

**FT**

All it takes is a glance at the recent share price performance of Sony, Philips and Matsushita to realise that all is not well in the consumer electronics industry.

Philips' shares fell last week when the Dutch group announced a steep decline in consumer electronics profits, shortly after Japan's Matsushita disclosed a substantial reduction in audio-visual sales. Sony's share price has faltered on fears that it will report a net loss in next week's second-quarter results.

Optimists argue that the industry will recover when the next hot new product – the digital video disc (DVD) system which combines the functions of audio CDs, video cassettes and computer discs – arrives next autumn. Pessimists suspect that the difficulties mark the start of a long-term decline when personal computers will steadily replace conventional electronics products.

'Consumer electronics has had decades of growth as a leading edge industry,' says Mr Edward Hadas, electronics analyst at NatWest Securities in London. 'These companies have got to focus on the fact that growth will be much slower in the future and they're now a lagging industry behind PCs.'

The PC phenomenon could scarcely have been worse timed for the leading electronics groups, which include France's Thomson and Japan's Hitachi and Sharp.

Low-cost competitors from South Korea, Taiwan and China have locked them out of the emerging Asian economies. They have imposed intense pressure on prices in North America, Japan and Europe at a time when VCRs and CD players, the products that fuelled the industry's growth in the 1980s, have hit maturity.

Japanese and European manufacturers have cut costs to improve competitiveness. Philips and Thomson have also, somewhat belatedly, increased investment in design to try to achieve the premium status of Sony. But competitive pressures are so intense that the large groups have, according to one Sony executive, had 'to run faster just to stand still' . . .

The only product that seems capable of revitalising the electronics market is DVD. But its launch has been haunted by industry rows over technical specifications. The threat of a DVD format war was averted this summer when Sony and Philips agreed to thrash out a common format with their rivals, but the talks are dragging on. Unless they are concluded within the next few weeks, DVD's launch may have to be delayed from next autumn.

Sceptics suspect that DVD may not fulfil the industry's sales expectations. One worry is that it will not be tempting enough for consumers. The new discs offer a similar improvement in the visual quality of films, compared with video cassette, as audio-CD did against tapes and vinyl. But the first DVD systems will not have a recording facility, one of VCR's main selling points.

However, the chief concern is that no new electronics products will have the same impact on sales as colour TVs or audio-CDs, because they no longer hold the same allure for consumers compared with innovations in related sectors such as PCs and mobile phones.

These products are challenging the share of consumer expenditure commanded by electronics . . .

There are opportunities for consumer electronics companies to diversify into the multimedia PC market. Mr Yoshiharu Izumi, electronics analyst at UBS Securities in Tokyo, believes that the company which invents the industry standard for enhancing the television and video functions of PCs will 'gain a huge advantage over its rivals'.

Japanese groups have been diversifying into new areas such as this for some time. Sharp has had great success with its liquid crystal display technology. Sony is one of the world's largest manufacturers of CD-Rom drives. Matsushita managed to compensate for the decline in audio-visual sales in the first half with a healthy increase from electronic components. The electronics groups are expanding into computing and telecommunications. They have had some success with mobile phones and Sony's first foray into video games has been a triumph. It has sold over 1m of its PlayStation systems since its launch in Japan last Christmas and has virtually sold out in the US and UK.

But the consumer electronics companies did not move quickly or aggressively enough into telecommunications and computing, as Finland's Nokia did with mobile phones. The thrust of their early 1990s expansion was entertainment. Sony has since incurred heavy losses on its film interests. Matsushita sold control of MCA, its entertainment group, last winter.

*Source: Financial Times, 3 November 1995. Reprinted with permission.*

### Comment on the case study

In Case study 19.5 it is clear that, although Philips, Sony and Matsushita are well-known names within the consumer electronics industry, continuous development is required in order to maintain competitive edge. Sony, the case implies, possesses the position of industry leader in terms of status. This is due to its edge in terms of product design and attributes. Although Sony is also feeling the pressure, Philips, Matsushita and other recognised names are suffering as a result of low-cost competitors based in the Far East, who are able to produce reasonable quality products at much lower prices. The reaction on the part of the recognised names has been to develop new products and to improve the quality of their existing products. For example, the picture quality of televisions was drastically improved in the late 1980s by Toshiba's 'flatter, squarer tube'. Other innovations since include minidiscs and the compact cassette, improvements to established product types. In the future, consumers can look forward to improvements in computer monitor technology which will give picture quality equivalent to a television's and also digital video discs (DVD), combining audio, video and computer technology.

These products are developed by larger organisations and offered to consumers at the higher end of the market (quality focus). Initially, prices are high and availability restricted. As imitation occurs and technology spreads, more organisations are able to supply the product, consumers can afford the product and eventually, what was a new, improved, product becomes the norm. In order to stay ahead, further improvements are required and so the cycle continues.

It is feared by some that the development of DVD will not be sufficient to prop up the flagging consumer electronics industry. Quite simply, it is feared that the development is not drastic enough. Although there are perceptible differences between DVD and its forebears, the price and also the lack of recording ability will deter many consumers. Organisations such as Sony have given credence to such fears recently, by its divergence into the electronics games industry with PlayStation. The case suggests that other organisations will also have to diversify to survive.

## Quality focus in car manufacture

Quality focus may also be seen on the part of auto manufacturers. There are recognised leaders in the auto business: Mercedes-Benz, Rolls-Royce, Jaguar and so on. However, further down the price range, there is a cluster of organisations competing for the executive car market. Here, traditionally, Audi and BMW have been market leaders, with very little competition. However, Japanese manufacturers successfully entered the market in the early to mid-1980s and offered specifications equal to those of BMW and Audi, but at much lower prices. Obviously, such developments caused increased competition in the market and Lexus (the quality division of Toyota) gained considerable market share in Europe and the USA. The incumbent manufacturers responded in two ways: by attempting to drive down costs and to convince consumers of the worth and even 'snob value' of their cars. This was largely unsuccessful, however. The prevailing economic climate did not help; the recession caused organisations and individuals to become more conscious of price and value for money.

The resulting market structure in Europe has been one of far larger and all-encompassing manufacturers. Each of the major manufacturers now possesses a small, medium and large car division and also a luxury division. These are owned under the same name (for example, General Motors and Ford) or under various names which have previously been known as separate entities, such as the Skoda, Volkswagen, Audi group, or BMW's ownership of Rover. Thus motor manufacturers are able to use transferable knowledge and skills in the design and production of their cars. Such transferability can help to push down costs and improve competitive positions. At the same time, the maintenance of different names enables exploitation of consumer's beliefs with reference to the names with which they are familiar. The motor manufacturers are using focus strategies in each of the small, medium, large and luxury car markets in which they operate, and quality focus is just one of the focus segments used.

◆ **CASE STUDY 19.6**

# Survey of Europe's most respected companies: BMW  [FT]

When social historians look back on the closing years of the 20th century, the blue and white quartered circle of Bayerische Motoren Werke (BMW) will go down as one of the icons of the period.

No other car maker has managed to capture the yuppie niche as effectively as BMW, and none has defended its territory so adroitly.

While arch-rival Mercedes-Benz still dominates the market for prestige transport for chairmen and ambassadors, BMW's hegemony over slightly smaller executive vehicles has turned out to be a distinct advantage.

Although BMW also produces large gas-guzzlers, it remains best known for smaller cars for up-and-coming bosses rather than vehicles for those who have already arrived. That has proved vital in making its cars desirable without being unattainable . . .

Its product success has been based on steady, but cautious, expansion of the range. With Mercedes-Benz having staked out the high ground for executive transport, BMW's earliest pitch was at a lower level.

Good quality and performance gradually allowed the company to move up-market. The range was expanded in the 1970s, with bigger and smaller models to complement the group's mainstream 2-litre saloons.

It was the smaller cars which provided the breakthrough. Now in its third generation, the 3-series combined comfort, quality and performance in an exclusive, but affordable, package.

BMW also set its sights at the top end. The flagship 7-series, now in its second generation, has become a direct competitor to Mercedes's big S-Class.

Good products are, however, a necessary, but not a sufficient, condition for financial success. BMW's marketing has been as adroit as its product strategy. The company has created an aura of desirability achieved by few other manufacturers. Although output is now around 600,000 units a year, BMWs remain special in the mind of the public . . .

High quality manufacturing and technical innovation have been combined with impressive agility in identifying market niches and spotting trends. That has left rivals stalled at the lights.

Such agility has been translated to the bottom line. Profits have risen steadily while BMW's margins are the envy of its German counterparts. In 1994, the company claimed to be the only car manufacturer in Europe making profits at the operating level, before the contribution of financial or other subsidiaries. Nonetheless, since 1989, BMW has managed an average annual increase of only 0.4 per cent in earnings per share.

But BMW's management can hardly relax.

The strength of the D-Mark and continuing high German pay rises mean they must constantly review their production strategy.

The company has already reacted more boldly than most by building a US plant and buying Rover in the UK. The US project will free the group from unpredictable dollar–D–Mark exchange rate swings, which can play havoc with earnings.

But while the US risk is calculable, buying Rover has been a much bigger shot in the dark. For a modest £900m, BMW gained control of a medium-volume car manufacturer with a desirable and profitable specialist division (Land Rover) and an improving, but still loss-making, volume cars operation.

Although Land Rover was the bait, even the volume car side had its attractions. Rover's expertise in making small front-wheel-drive cars complements BMW's skills building larger rear-wheel-drive vehicles. And while Rover's rupture with Honda, with which it has an ambitious collaborative pact, was messy, BMW is now firmly in the driver's seat.

The question is how it will manage Rover. Broader issues of cultural compatibility between BMW in Munich and Rover takes second place to the more pressing worries – the problem of the high volume, loss-making aspect of the production of the smaller Rover car.

*Source*: *Financial Times*, 19 September 1995. Reprinted with permission.

*Comment on the case study*

BMW is a recognised quality auto manufacturer. Its products are desired by aspiring executives throughout Europe. The reputation is enhanced by the high prices which BMW manages to demand for its cars and the relatively high resale/secondhand values they attract. BMW has therefore for many years maintained a successful quality focus strategy. More recently it has, in order to maintain productivity levels and profitability, decided to build and operate a manufacturing plant in the US. Even more dramatically, it has bought the Rover Group in the UK. These additions to BMW's assets provide instant access to highly skilled workforces and also, in the case of Rover, a range of products which extends from small cars to luxury to four-wheel-drive vehicles. BMW's interests are clearly now in many markets. Yet the case clearly explains that the knowledge and technology transfers between these different markets may be shared between divisions and companies in the future: continuous development of the quality focus strategy.

# SUMMARY

◆ 'Quality' refers not to the price or 'snob value' of a product, but to the consistency with which it can be produced with reference to given standards – even if these are minimal and low cost.

◆ Developments in thinking on quality during the twentieth century involve and empower all members of the workforce. TQM, quality circles, benchmarking and *kaizen* have all become popular since 1980.

◆ BS 5750 and ISO 9000 are recognised quality standards, for which organisations can gain accreditation. Quality standards are concerned with the production process and also with other, associated and administrative operations.

◆ Quality costs may be classified as either assurance of quality costs or the costs of defects. For any organisation, the optimum, minimal costs of quality may be obtained by considering the tradeoff between assurance and defects.

◆ The quality advantages possessed by some organisations have been eroded by competition. These quality leaders are looking towards refocusing their efforts on customer service or customer excellence.

◆ A differentiation strategy can only work so long as customers recognise that one company's product is different from another. This actual or perceived difference is related to whether the product is a search, credence or experience good.

◆ A brand name often confers quality on a product, although some brands are better at this than others. A brand name advantage allows an organisation to charge a premium price and other organisations, which do not have such a strong brand image, may be forced to charge a lower price to compete.

◆ The strength of the brand name as a differential strategy may be under threat as markets become internationalised, retailers in Europe grow in strength and the media becomes increasingly fragmented.

◆ Quality focus strategies are followed by organisations targeting a small target sector within their market. The product is usually of additional specification to those in the mainstream market, thereby offering the opportunity for higher profit margins.

# REVIEW QUESTIONS

1 In deciding whether or not to adopt a quality enhancement programme, which factors should an organisation take into consideration?

2 With examples, discuss whether product quality is more important in commodity or consumer goods markets.

3 Outline the potential advantages and disadvantages for an organisation of gaining quality accreditation with a body such as ISO.

4 At which stages along the value chain is it possible to work more closely with customers and suppliers? How else might the relationship between organisations and customers be strengthened?

5 Your organisation has a number of relatively weak brands which sell in your domestic market. Given the growth in the strength of retailers, how might you encourage retailers to purchase your brands?

6 What are the implications of quality leadership for product design? Use examples to illustrate your answer.

## GLOSSARY OF NEW TERMS

**Brand name:** The development of the name of an organisation or its products to provide the customer with an image of the characteristics the products provide.

**Costs of quality:** The categories into which costs associated with quality may be put. Assurance (prevention) and defects (repairs) are two broad categories.

**Credence goods:** Products which are imperfectly evaluated even after purchase.

**Differentiation strategy:** A strategy used by organisations to differentiate their products from a rival's.

**Experience goods:** Goods which the consumer can only evaluate after purchase.

**Kaizen:** Continuous improvement by doing.

**Product proliferation:** The production of a number of similar products, made by the same organisation, but sold under different brand names.

**Quality circle:** A development of TQM, where groups of employees take full responsibility for their product, from goods inwards to complete product.

**Quality focus:** The decision to concentrate on supplying the wants and needs of a small part of the market.

**Quality leadership:** A strategy which attempts to suggest that product, service and all elements of the organisation are of high quality. Purchasing an item from this organisation will therefore lead to a high level of satisfaction.

**Quality programme:** A process or programme adopted by organisations in order to achieve consistent specifications for products with reference to customer requirements.

**Quality standards:** Awards and accreditation for organisations who are consistently able to work to defined specifications for products and processes. British Standard and ISO are recognised awarding bodies.

**Search costs:** The cost of finding out information, both in monetary terms and in time.

**TQM:** Total quality management – a quality programme involving the whole organisation and requiring employees to take responsibility for their own work and areas of work.

**Zero defects:** A strategy to supply products, now including services, which cannot be faulted.

## READING

Certo, S C (1992) *Modern Management: Quality, Ethics and the Global Environment*, 5th edn, Allyn and Bacon, London.
*The area of quality permeates a number of the chapters, but Chapter 21 provides a detailed analysis of the area.*

Johnson, G and Scholes, K (1997) *Exploring Corporate Strategy*, 4th edn, Prentice-Hall, New York.
*A useful chapter in this book is 'Strategic options' which considers the work of Porter and the associated literature, discussing its merits and demerits.*

Porter, M E (1980) *Competitive Strategy: Techniques for Analysing Industries and Competitors*, Free Press, New York.
*This book provides much of the seminal material on strategic options and provides an excellent starting point.*

Timmerman, A (1995) *Benchmarking International Survey*, Coopers and Lybrand Internal Working Paper, London.
*A report comparing attitudes to benchmarking and use of benchmarking across Europe.*

### Further reading

Connell, D (1980) 'The UK's Performance in Export Markets – Some Evidence from International Trade Data', NEDO, Discussion Paper No 6.

Daly, A and Jones, D J (1980) 'The machine tool industry in Britain, Germany and the United States', *National Institute Economic Review*, No 92, pp 53–63.

Davies, H (1989) 'The designers' perspective: managing design in the UK', *Journal of General Management*, Vol 14, No 4, pp 77–87.

Design Council (1993) *UK Product Development Survey*, Design Council, London.

Krause, L B (1968) 'British trade performance', in Caves, R E (ed), *Britain's Economic Prospects*, George Allen and Unwin, London.

CHAPTER **20**

# BUSINESS ISSUES AND THE ENVIRONMENT

## KEY ISSUES

Business issues

Business strategy

Decision-making techniques

Economic concepts

Management decision issues

Optimal outcomes to management issues

## OBJECTIVES

◆ To consider the relationship between business and its impact on the environment.

◆ To examine the methods by which environmental damage can be controlled.

◆ To explore how company image and environmental protection are interrelated.

◆ To indicate the reasons that organisations undertake environmental auditing.

◆ To consider the role of both the international community and the European Union in forging rules and regulations to protect the environment.

◆ To show how environmental management can lead to a competitive advantage for organisations.

◆ To illustrate how eco-labelling has been used to provide organisations with a means to indicate the environmental friendliness of their products.

◆ To consider the conflict that may exist between free trade and the environment.

## KEY TERMS

Ambient-based systems

Contingent evaluation method

Cradle-to-grave management

Eco-labelling

Emission-based systems

Environmental auditing

Environmental impact assessments

Environmental management and auditing system

Environmental management system

Environmental standards

Environmental taxes

Ethical portfolios

Negative externality

Polluter pays

Property rights

Sustainable development

Total economic value

Tradeable emission permits

## CHAPTER OUTLINE

Business application

Developing interest in the environment

Environmental issues and business

Direct approaches

Indirect methods of valuation

Hedonic pricing model

Total economic value

Controlling pollution through taxation

Pollution control through tradeable permits

Property rights and pollution control

Environmental standards and the level playing field

Company image and environmental protection

Environmental auditing

Case study 20.1 Green reporting takes on a perennial quality

Environmental management and total quality management

Environmental management and competitive advantage

Global policies towards the environment

EU policies towards the environment

Policies to protect the EU environment

Eco-labelling

Case study 20.2 The EU eco-label has irked some manufacturers

Green trade issues

Summary

Review questions

Glossary of new terms

Reading

# Business and the environment: antagonists clear the air

FT

Business and the environment are fundamentally at odds with each other – that seems to be a fact of life. Business makes money by exploiting the environment, the environment fights back by curbing business. Much of the environmental debate is about trying to find some common ground: a point in the middle where motivations that drive business can be harnessed to minimise environmental damage and even do some good.

At a meeting in Cambridge, UK, in September 1995 both businesses and environmentalists met to discuss some of the issues. The main purpose of the meeting was to inspire rather than depress the delegates, and they were treated over four days to a parade of reasons why some of the world's largest companies take the environment seriously.

National Westminster Bank thinks an understanding of environmental issues helps it to reduce losses on bad loans. Munich Re, the large German insurance company, sees a 'healthy' environment as a way of controlling claims from pollution and changing weather patterns.

Procter & Gamble of the US uses environmental concerns to push through tighter management controls on waste: 'more from less' is the watchword. National Power, Britain's largest power generator, has little choice: unless it cleans up it could lose its operating license. Thorn-EMI admitted that one reason it started publishing an environmental audit was pressure from its pop artists who wanted to be sure they were signing up with a 'clean' company.

As one delegate noted, 'You're looking at less than 1 per cent here.' Of the world's thousands of multina-tional companies, only 110 have published environmental reports. Fear of loss is probably the biggest motivator: loss of business, customers or licenses. But even these potential losses have to outweigh the considerable costs associated with cleaning up a company and implanting genuinely green attitudes.

In one sense, environmentalism is only another word for better waste management. Reduce waste or, better still, stop producing it in the first place.

The environment is also a good way, companies have found, to strengthen line management and motivate staff. A well-managed environmental programme can do a lot more than simply clean a company up: it boosts morale and profits. Environmental audits are probably little read, but the process that goes into their preparation provides further incentive to good housekeeping.

The external situation is something else. Business feels bested – unfairly of course – by unsympathetic regulators and public opinion, and by a financial system that wants quick results. Even customers are fickle: they demand 'green' products and then refuse to pay for them.

What businesses need to do is involve themselves more with stakeholders. Shareholders are the most obvious, but others are employees, customers, suppliers, government, regulators, non-government organisations and even the media. The purpose of this contact should be to raise understanding and find areas where companies can do something to satisfy demands that they make their operations more sustainable.

*Source: Financial Times, 27 September 1995. Reprinted with permission.*

### Comment

Can businesses and the environment live happily with one another? There will be tensions, as organisations have historically paid little attention to the effect their operations were having on the environment. Yet during the 1980s there were forces in play which encouraged them to take a more proactive stance. Consumers began to demand more environment-friendly products, governments began the process of controlling emissions and waste and stressed the need for recycling, and organisations perceived that producing products in a more environment-friendly manner was not only cost-effective but gave them a competitive advantage.

In the light of these changes, this chapter considers the ways in which environmental factors affect organisations, the means by which legislation has sought to control pollution and the ways in which organisations have responded to changes in the environment.

# DEVELOPING INTEREST IN THE ENVIRONMENT

Growth, both at a macroeconomic level and through the behaviour of organisations, can bring enormous benefits to societies, but correspondingly a number of potential costs. In particular, growth may cause negative externalities such as pollution, noise and increased congestion. Many of these costs are likely to be understated, since accurate measurement of externalities is not always possible.

The main upsurge in interest in the care of the environment took place in the 1960s and 1970s. However, the notion that progress results in unintended, detrimental consequences was featured earlier, in Rachel Carson's *Silent Spring* (1962). The 'Club of Rome' in 1972 put forward the argument that, if growth rates proceeded exponentially and resources were finite, at some time in the future there would be a point where all these resources were used up and economic growth would grind to a halt. The catastrophe, if it came, would be such that even if individuals realised it was coming, the structure of economies would not be able to be altered quickly enough.

A number of the foreseen problems did not in fact arise during the latter part of the 1970s: the population rate began to slow and the depletion of natural resources did not occur as quickly as predicted, as most of the world economies began to slow down. Critics also suggested that the price mechanism would prevent the doomsday scenario happening. They argued that as a resource is depleted so its price will rise and consumers will reduce their demand. At the same time, however, there will be a switch to suitable substitute goods. As this substitution takes place, the price of these substitute goods will rise. It is also possible that resources which were not profitable to use at the old price levels will now come into use, for example gas turbine electricity generators. These marginal resources may be used effectively and efficiently if technology can provide the means of increasing capacity usage. Thus technology enables society to obtain, from marginal resources, a level of output which keeps consumers happy.

By the end of the 1980s and during the 1990s, this view was to change. Evidence was being gathered about growing threats to the environment via the depletion of the ozone layer, global warming, atmospheric pollution and drinking water contamination. These threats to society were embraced in the Earth Summit conference in Rio de Janiero in May 1992, where the call was for sustainable development much along the lines expressed by the Bruntland Report in 1987.

For **sustainable development**, the environment was not to be considered as a free good. It needed to be protected, especially where demands were being made on non-renewable resources and where eco-systems were being disrupted. Thus sustainable development stressed the interdependence between economic growth and the use of resources. The preoccupation with economic growth has resulted in a mass-consumption society which behaves as if all economic resources are infinite. In addition, there needs to be a more equitable use of resources by all countries and a recognition that, if developed nations seek to emulate the First World and make the same mistakes with resources, the environment will be even more severely damaged. In this respect equity requires the problems of poverty and low income to be addressed by all nations. Finally, both governments and organisations need to move away from short-term, profit-maximising scenarios to long-term environmental considerations, with an emphasis on proactive rather than reactive policy decision making.

# ENVIRONMENTAL ISSUES AND BUSINESS

There are few organisations in any industry which are not aware of, and under pressure to consider, environmental issues. Government regulation, competitive advances through innovation and the growth in consumer awareness have moved environmental issues from an area which organisations only gave a cursory glance to one which has taken centre stage.

Organisations therefore need to change to reflect consumers' views of the natural environment, treating the threats to their organisations from government regulations as opportunities for product development and market enhancement. Parallel to this change, there is an increasing need for tools that allow proper and quantifiable measurement of the performance of organisations with respect to the environment. James (1994) has identified five main driving forces in the pressure for business environmental performance measurement: the biosphere, financial stakeholders, non-financial stakeholders, buyers and the public.

Haines (1993) added a further factor: 'to attain leadership in defining industry-wide environmental excellence'.

For those organisations involved with capital budgeting and investment appraisal, project projection often needs to take account of environmental liability or **environmental impact assessments** (EIA) in project financing. This approach enables management to make more informed estimates as to the economic and environmental feasibility of a new investment proposal. The European Union's EIA Directive of 1988 required an assessment to be undertaken for all environmentally sensitive investments, such as oil refineries and major road-building programmes. This approach has not yet been extended to all investments taken by the private and public sectors. If such an approach is adopted, it will provide a more accurate measure of the social costs associated with a project and therefore a more accurate decision about whether a project should go ahead. The project would then have to assess the costs and means of disposal of extra waste generated during the production phase and the production process, environmental degradation through the destruction of flora and fauna and the like. As part of the process, the project proposal should consider the ecological characteristics of buildings in terms of their energy consumption, how well they integrate into the surrounding countryside (for example, many of food retailer Tesco's superstores are very similar in design, suggesting a medieval barn structure which integrates well into many of its greenfield sites; nonetheless, such buildings are not appropriate for developments in towns and the company has used a whole range of designs to integrate its stores with local buildings), and how the site will deal with the destruction of badger setts or pools for great crested newts, for example.

This whole process of EIA needs to ensure that all parties to the proposal have a chance to provide evidence about the possible impacts of any new development. The EIA may also include suggestions and remedies to offset the effects of environmental impacts, such as the erection of noise-reduction barriers along the side of roads to limit noise for nearby residents. In this respect, the development of a new international rail-freight terminal in Daventry, Northamptonshire, will result in the construction of major earthworks to reduced noise, the use of light gantries only up to a certain height and the use of tiling techniques for buildings so that they merge well into the rolling landscape.

The use of EIAs can lead to great controversy, as occurred in the building of the M3 extension at Twyford Down. Of the three routes possible, the one causing the least environmental damage was a tunnel under St Catherine's Hill. Although this was the most expensive, the two other routes took the motorway either to the west of St Catherine's Hill – a route favoured by the environmentalists – or to the east – a route favoured by the Department of Transport. For the chosen eastern route, two kilometres passed through an area of outstanding natural beauty and took away two hectares of St Catherine's Hill. However, the government argued, that although the scheme was environmentally damaging, there would be positive environmental benefits, including the removal and landscaping of the existing A33 road on the eastern side of St Catherine's hill. Although environmentalists and other groups tried to get the motorway stopped, and the Commissioner for the EU in 1991 even ruled that the British government was acting illegally by failing to inform the public of the true environmental impact of the scheme, the government defied EU law and went ahead with the construction work. By 1992, the EU, with a new Environment Commissioner, had done an about-turn and agreed that the government had undertaken satisfactory consultation with the relevant groups concerned. But this may have been an occasion where cost factors overruled environmental considerations.

There is no doubt that EIA adds to monetary costs, but the tradeoff can be greater acceptance of a project by all parties concerned.

EIAs have brought a change to the way projects are assessed, but generally these sea changes in environmental considerations have not been proceeding quickly, but have tended to take place in a slow but iterative manner. This has allowed organisations more time to meet the environmental challenges.

The policy instruments that governments have used to control environmental pressures have changed over the decades. During the 1970s governments were very active in commanding and controlling resources as a means to protect the environment. However, the general view was that the costs of pollution were becoming onerous, that regulation was getting more and more complex, and that government control was not efficient enough to provide the incentive for technological innovation. Thus alternative tools for environmental control were sought.

During the late 1970s and early 1980s, many countries adopted a more market-oriented approach to environmental protection. These approaches included the use of **environmental taxes** and charges, deposit-refund schemes and **tradeable emission permits.** The 1990s have seen a further change towards using a set of hybrid policies under which different sectors of the economy in the EU have been set long-term performance standards, such as the quality of drinking water or cleanliness of rivers, while at the same time further control is coming about through the use of market-based instruments.

In addition, there has been a move to consider the utilisation of more comprehensive approaches to pollution rather than dealing with one issue at a time. For example, if regulations are developed to control waste, organisations may respond to this by incinerating the waste. This may reduce the environmental damage from the waste itself, but the gases and pollutants which result from the incineration process may, in themselves, have important environmental consequences. Thus, broader approaches to pollution control have been adopted via the use of integrated pollution and prevention control, **cradle-to-grave management** and multimedia management.

Therefore, approaches to counteract the problems of environmental damage have varied over time and have been tailored to meet specific problems.

# DIRECT APPROACHES

## Contingent valuation method

The **contingent valuation method** (CVM) for evaluating environmental goods was first used by Davies (1963). Since then it has become one of the most widely used techniques for evaluating environmental goods. Work by Hanley and Spash (1993) and Bateman and Willis (1995) provides extensive accounts of this process, and also points to some of its weaknesses.

The CVM process can be split into a number of stages:

- Setting up the hypothetical market.
- Obtaining bids.
- Estimating mean willingness to pay (WTP) and/ or willingness to accept compensation (WTAC).
- Estimating bid curves.
- Aggregating the data.

In stage one the hypothetical market for the environmental service flow is set up. For example, respondents might be told that the local authority is looking to expand one of its country parks and this operation can only go ahead if more money is available. How the funds will be raised should also be described – the bid vehicle – that is, should the funding come from increased council tax/local tax, entry fees or income tax.

The second stage consists of administrating the questionnaire. Here the individual could be asked to state their maximum WTP and/or minimum WTAC for the increase or decrease in environmental provision.

In stage three the mean of the WTP or WTAC is found. It may be expected that the median WTP is less than the mean WTP, since a few large bids given for WTP will raise the overall average.

Stage four considers the determinants of WTP/WTAC. Here regression equations are set up – *see* Chapter 7 – with WTP/WTAC as the dependent variables regressed against a number of independent variables, such as income, education and age of respondents.

Stage five consists of converting the mean bid or bids of the sample to find the population figure.

The CVM, however, is subject to a number of problems. Biases can occur, such as overstating or understating the true WTP or WTAC. These biases can be the result of overstating or understating the true costs of the funds to be raised. In addition, there could be strategic bias, where respondents understate their WTP, hoping to 'free-ride' on the fact that others will state a willingness to pay higher bills for a resource which is non-excludable. An example could be improvements in river purity by improving sewerage treatment works. Here individuals can have the incentive to reduce their WTP, since they may estimate that others would be willing to pay a higher price for improved river purity and they cannot be excluded from the benefits. Mitchell and Carson (1989) provide an extensive account of other possible biases.

A second problem for CVM is that of embedding. Many people appear to want to do something about the environment and this 'warm glow' effect leads them to drop this into the first commodity/scenario they are asked about in a CVM. For example, suppose an individual is asked in their first question about their willingness to pay for expanding all parkland or just one specific park. If embedding occurs then the answer to both could be very similar.

A third issue is the difference between WTP and WTAC. It would be expected that the difference would be small, but in studies by Kahneman *et al* (1991), for example, when it comes to environmental goods/services, people value losses more highly than equivalent gains.

## Stated preference methods

While it may be argued that the CVM approach is a stated preference method, it is only one possible technique. It is possible that individuals could be asked to rank a series of environmental options or choose between pairs, such as cost of provision and access. Adamowicz *et al* (1994) provide some of the more useful tools for this approach.

## INDIRECT METHODS OF VALUATION

An alternative approach to the direct methods of valuation to environmental services/amenities is to consider complementary goods for which a price is paid. In the case of a 'free' countryside park, the prices charged for a similar private country park could be used.

## Travel cost model

This method, popularised by Clawson and Knetsch (1966), uses travel costs as a proxy for the price of visiting outdoor recreational sites. The simplest version of the travel cost method (TCM) collects data on visits to a site from different parts of the country. The costs of travelling to the site are related to both distance and the time spent travelling. What can now be calculated is the number of visits per head from each area of the surrounding country. It would be expected that visits per head will fall as travel costs rise and a demand curve can be constructed for each area from which the individual sets out, up to the cost at which visits become equal to zero. There are a number of weaknesses with this approach, not least of which is that of multipurpose trips. A visitor to a site may come specifically only to this site in the area; others, however, come to visit the amenity as one part only of a package. For them, clearly some of the travel costs to this site are not independent of the travel costs to other sites in their package. The problem concerns how the overall travel costs for

these people should be apportioned between the various sites they visit.

## HEDONIC PRICING MODEL

The hedonic pricing model approach uses a characteristics approach similar to that developed by Lancaster (1966); *see* Chapter 5. This estimates the value that individuals would be willing to pay to live closer to an environmental amenity. One approach to this valuation method is to consider the differences in house prices for a similar house closer to the amenity compared with one further away from an environmental site. In other words, environmental characteristics such as pleasant views, distance from toxic waste sites or offensive smells from factories or farms can be included in the characteristics bundle.

Once again there are weaknesses with this approach and Hanley and Spash (1993) discuss these in detail. Briefly the problems that may arise are: omitted variable bias where a variable which is significant in affecting house prices is omitted from the equation, multicollinearity – *see* Chapter 7 – attitudes to risk, and the failure to appreciate that house prices may be related to future environmental conditions as well as current ones.

## TOTAL ECONOMIC VALUE

From an economic perspective, the value of all environmental assets can be measured by the preferences of individuals for the conservation/utilisation of these assets. If it is assumed that individuals, given their existing preferences/tastes, hold a number of values, then these can be assigned to objects. To enable us to obtain an aggregate measure of these values (total economic value), we must start by distinguishing between user values and non-user values.

There has been much debate as to whether is it possible to find the **total economic value** of an environmental asset. The following equation has been put forward as providing one form of explanation:

Total economic value (TEV) = use value + option value + existence value

The use value is the current use made of the environmental resource. This would include the actual use of the environmental resource, plus an estimate of the opportunity costs of using it in the current mode.

The option value is the value placed on the use of the asset now compared with the value that might be placed on the asset at some future date. As can be imagined, valuing this precisely will prove difficult. The option value can then be considered as expressions of preference (willingness to pay) for the conservation of environmental systems or components of systems against some probability that the individual will make use of the asset at a later date. A related form of value would be bequest value, a willingness to pay to retain the environment for our descendants.

The existence value is the value placed on an environmental asset as it exists currently, independent of any current use for the asset or any future use for the asset. This is a measure of the willingness to pay for an asset to keep it in its current use.

As can be appreciated, getting a precise figure for the TEV can prove to be difficult. Nonetheless, this concept has been used with regard to recreational

beaches in the EU and an assessment of the existence value compared with the use value of the Grand Canyon in the US. Gren *et al* (1994) provide one approach to assessing these values in terms of wetland eco-systems, while Figure 20.1 provides a way of assessing total economic value for woodland.

At this stage it may be possible to make a fairly good attempt at evaluating the costs and benefits associated with an environmental asset. But how can either the market mechanism or regulation be used to determine the optimal level of pollution?

## CONTROLLING POLLUTION THROUGH TAXATION

Figure 20.2 illustrates the case for a pollution tax. A per unit tax has been applied which raises the MPC curve to $MPC_{tax}$. Here the organisation itself must pay a price (the tax) for the pollution it imposes on society. The tax is shown as the distance $P_s$ minus $P_t$. In this case the profit-maximising output level

**Figure 20.1  The total economic value of woodland**

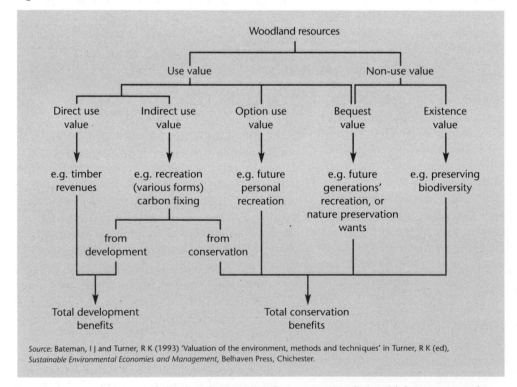

*Source*: Bateman, I J and Turner, R K (1993) 'Valuation of the environment, methods and techniques' in Turner, R K (ed), *Sustainable Environmental Economies and Management*, Belhaven Press, Chichester.

To arrive at an aggregate measure of total economic value, economists distinguish between use values and non-use values. In the woodland example, use values derive from the actual use of the environment. Option values are expressions of willingness to pay for the conservation of environmental systems against some probability that the individual will make use of it at a later date. A bequest value is a willingness to pay to preserve the environment for the benefit of one's descendants.

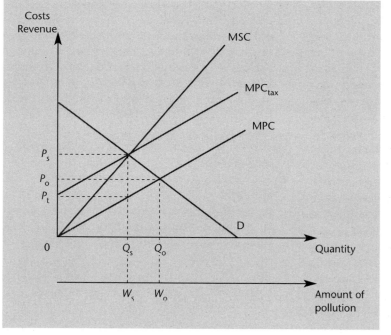

**Figure 20.2 Using taxes to reduce pollution**

The socially optimum level of output is to be found from the intersection of MSC and demand (marginal social benefit). The organisation would prefer to produce at the point at which demand is equated to its marginal private cost (MPC). Taxes can be used to encourage the organisation to produce at the socially optimum level of pollution, and in this Figure a per unit tax of $P_s - P_t$ is imposed on the organisation. This shifts the MPC curve upwards to $MPC_{tax}$ and the organisation is forced to produce at the socially optimum level.

of the organisation now coincides with the social optimum level $OQ_s$. An environmental tax used in this way is said to internalise the externality, that is, the organisation now has to take the externality into account in its decision making. The environmental tax follows the concept of **'polluter pays'**, a principle adopted by the OECD in 1972. This suggests that the producer of the pollution should bear the costs of the measures being used by the authorities to reduce the level of pollution. If all countries adopted such an approach, it would remove the competitive advantages some countries have had by controlling pollution through less rigorous and less costly methods.

There are a number of problems to consider, however, with the use of pollution taxes. The tax, although a per unit one in Figure 20.2, may have to vary if the level of pollution changes for each unit of output. Moreover, what is the level of taxation needed to move towards the socially optimum level of output? To develop a tax rate requires knowledge of the MPC curve and the socially optimum level of output. The government may require organisations to provide information about their marginal private costs of production, and it is possible that organisations may attempt to disguise some of the information so that any level of tax imposed is not as onerous as the true tax rate. It may be easier for the government to base its pollution tax rate on the level of output rather than on the level of emissions. This poses a number of problems, in that not

all organisations emit the same level of pollution per unit of output and it fails to provide incentives for organisations to adopt new production technologies as a means of reducing pollution per unit of output. In addition, it has been suggested that the level of fines has not had a detrimental effect on pollution for some larger organisations.

## POLLUTION CONTROL THROUGH TRADEABLE PERMITS

It is possible that pollution may be controlled through the use of tradeable permits. These permits can be bought by organisations from the government and allow the organisation the right to pollute up to a specific level. Each organisation can buy (or be given) and sell permits. For example, it is possible that some organisations can easily meet the pollution standards set by the government. If this is the case, they can sell their permits to other organisations who currently find it too difficult or too expensive to meet the current level of standards for pollution. If the government decides that the current level of pollution is undesirable, it can withdraw permits completely or ration them. For each organisation a decision must be made between the costs incurred in curbing pollution and the cost of buying a permit.

There are a number of perceived advantages that can be gained from using permits. Unlike pollution-control schemes based on taxes or subsidies, permits do not require adjustment for changes in the level of inflation. In comparison with **environmental standards**, a pollution-control mechanism that will be examined shortly, they allow organisations to have greater flexibility and to improve economic efficiency. Costs of production will be lower, since it may be cheaper to buy the tradeable permit rather than undertake costly methods of pollution control. However, the advantages that lie with permits depend on the type of scheme used. Under **ambient-based systems** (ABS) the method is to control the total amount of pollution in specific areas or zones. For example, a UK power station which produces acid rain that falls on Norway would need to obtain sufficient permits from the Norwegian government to satisfy Norway's requirements. This can be administratively costly. Moreover, it is possible that the acid rain affects a number of countries and, therefore, a wide range of permits may be required from different organisations/governments, all at different prices.

An alternative approach is to use aggregate **emissions-based systems** (EBS) which seek to control the origin of the pollution. Administratively this is much easier to operate and in addition there would be only one price for the permits. Nonetheless, it is often the case that pollution which emanates from a particular source is not evenly distributed over an area due to topological or geographical distortions. It follows that some areas may be subject to much higher levels of pollution than others. The difficulties of EBSs may be partially overcome by reducing the size of the emitting zone, but this would remove one of advantages of an EBS over an ABS approach. EBS, however, may work better where pollution is more evenly distributed, localised or where the pollution is quickly dispersed into the broad environment.

Although marketable permits have been used in domestic economies to control pollution (for example the Clean Air Act of 1990 in the US fully endorses the use of pollution permits for sulphur dioxide emissions) can such permits be used to control international pollution, as suggested by the United Nations Conference on Trade and Development? Tomkins and Twomey (1994) make a strong case to support this. However, Collins (1994) suggests that their work overstates some of the issues and neglects a number of important points. His main areas of criticism are:

- Once a market is set up for tradeable permits, anyone could theoretically buy into it. Thus if environmental groups buy up permits the 'permission to pollute' by organisations is reduced. While this procedure has some appeal in industrialised countries, suppose that foreign pressure groups were to do this in developing countries. It would only add to the tension that already exists if they are further prevented from producing an output which they perceive as being a major source of foreign exchange.

- The view that marketable permit systems (MPS) are likely to deliver least-cost solutions is open to question. Because of potential market failure in actual emission trading, it is possible that alternative pollution instruments may be more comparable.

- There are issues to be raised about whether a true global permit system to address the problems of greenhouse gases is possible. It is a more likely scenario that developments will occur on a subglobal or regional level, such as a customs union.

- If we are to consider the international market in permits, this requires a global-wide body to supply them. Such a global body can lead to problems for organisations which may wish to buy these permits, since organisations' investments and strategic plans may differ. Moreover, given that many markets are globally oligopolistic, there are questions about the degree to which price fixing and collusion may occur.

- Finally, the work by Tomkins and Twomey (1994) relates to the particular case of single pollutants affecting the environment. They do not discuss the possibility of synergistic pollutants where the joint effect of two or more pollutants differs from the sum of their individual effects. Examples of this are hydrocarbon/nitrogen oxide combinations and water discharges of cyanide/metals combinations.

# PROPERTY RIGHTS AND POLLUTION CONTROL

What we have come to realise is that many markets are subject to market failure. To avoid market failure we would require markets to be complete, that is, enough markets should exist to cover each and every possible transaction or eventuality so that resources can move to their highest valued use. Markets will be complete if traders can costlessly create a well-defined property rights system such that a market will exist to cover any exchange needed. The characteristics required of this property rights system are that:

- All assets or resources must be either privately or collectively owned, and all entitlements must be known and enforced effectively.
- All benefits and costs from use of a resource should accrue to the owners, and only to the owner, either directly or by sale to others.
- All property rights must be transferable from one owner to another in a voluntary exchange, thus providing the owner with the incentive to conserve the resource.
- Property rights to natural resources should be protected from involuntary seizure or encroachment by other individuals, organisations or the government. This provides the owner with the stimulus to improve and preserve the resource rather than exploit the assets.

It is possible that **property rights** to pollute could be assigned to either the polluters or the people who are being polluted. If the property rights are assigned to the polluters, then those who are suffering from the pollution may be willing to pay the polluter not to pollute. The individuals suffering from the pollution will only agree to this course of action as long as the compensation they are paying is less than the benefits from reduced pollution. On the other hand, if the property rights are assigned to the sufferers of pollution, then the polluters may compensate the sufferers for the pollution they are producing so that they can continue to pollute. The polluters will only pay as long as the compensation offered to the sufferers is less than the benefits the polluters can receive from selling the output which causes the pollution emission.

In environmental matters there is often market failure, since well-defined property rights have not always been established. When dealing with a piece of agricultural land, property rights exist, but what about the rivers or air that travel through and over the land? Here there is a lack of property rights. Thus the lack of property rights for clean air prevents individuals who are downwind of a fossil fuel power station from halting the damage from poor air quality which the power station is causing them. From the point of view of the power station, the owner does not bear the downwind costs, therefore these are ignored. Similarly, farmers who pollute rivers through adding nitrates to the soil do not have any incentive to compensate those people who live further downstream who may suffer from poorer fishing and contaminated drinking water.

However, even though property rights are difficult to assign, this has not prevented some countries from operating such a system.

The principle of the sufferer pays is in evidence in Europe, where Sweden provides the Polish economy with money so that Poland will reduce its output of acid rain which is damaging its forests and lakes. This type of policy also lies behind some of the proposals at the Earth Summit at Rio de Janiero, where as a consequence of trying to encourage some of the developing nations to reduce their outputs from some of their worst-polluting industries, which would subsequently reduce their overall growth rates, the industrialised countries agreed to compensate these nations with increased financial aid.

## ENVIRONMENTAL STANDARDS AND THE LEVEL PLAYING FIELD

Earlier it was shown that environmental standards, if applied equally to all companies in a country, could lead to some level of unfairness, as some companies were able to achieve the required reduction in the environmental externality more easily than others. When individual countries are examined, there is no reason to believe that the standards set in each country will be the same. In general standards are often set higher in developed countries than in less developed countries. Moreover, within the developed countries the standards can also vary greatly. For example, environmental standards in Norway, Sweden, the Netherlands and Germany tend to be higher than those in the Mediterranean countries of the EU. Because different countries pursue different environmental standards, this can impose increased costs on those organisations which are situated in countries where standards are high and thereby makes their products less competitive compared with those produced by organisations where the environmental standards are lower. Conversely, a country which sets high standards for the production of a particular product may prevent other companies from setting up in its home market. In addition, by advocating regulations with regard, say, to packaging, countries with higher environmental standards can use these as barriers to entry to prevent the sale of products produced in other countries which do not match these standards. Therefore, movements towards freeing trade within a trading zone may be hampered by the use of environmental legislation. Examples of environmental factors which may restrict trade within the EU are the legislation on minimum sizes for fish and the extent to which drink containers are recyclable.

Variations in environmental standards between countries can lead to a redistribution of production sites from countries which have high levels of environmental standards to those countries, like those in Eastern Europe, South America and Africa, where environmental standards are less strict. Thus what the EU has attempted to do is to set its environmental standards fairly high, ratcheting up member states' environmental care towards a level playing field rather than downwards to the lowest common denominator. This may suggest that, although companies within the EU are more equally competitive, they can still be undercut by companies producing outside the EU. For those countries in the EU which were originally producing at the higher level of environmental standards, there is, however, an advantage in that they are now in a position to sell to companies in other EU countries and elsewhere, whose environmental standards are lower, the equipment they need to make their production processes match new higher environmental standards. For example, German companies are market leaders in equipment that deals with the treatment of water effluent because the standards have existed for a longer period and been set at a higher level. Dutch and US companies, however, have a comparative advantage in equipment for cleaning contaminated soil and hazardous wastes.

## COMPANY IMAGE AND ENVIRONMENTAL PROTECTION

Increasingly companies have come to realise that environmental issues are becoming more important and can affect company strategy. Companies are considering both how products can be produced in a more environment-friendly manner and how products can be recycled. Currently car manufacturers, such as Nissan, BMW and Vauxhall, are advertising the fact that a growing proportion of the parts of their cars are recyclable.

Consumers are also demanding that organisations take more care of the environment. In this respect the growth in consumer awareness and the subsequent impact on companies have been dramatic in some economies. Products which appeared to be rejected by consumers a few years earlier, such as recyclable toilet paper, suddenly became extremely popular and companies needed to respond to the change in consumer choice fairly quickly.

Companies found that if they were to produce environment-friendly products then they needed not just to consider the end product but also the processes by which the product was made or sold. For example, a company that makes bottles that can be recycled may go further to provide a bottle bank. Other companies, such as Gateway, a UK supermarket chain, are now more committed to developing new shops in urban areas rather than developing greenfield sites.

Retailers are in a powerful position in the environmental chain and once they became conscious of the growth in consumer awareness with regard to the environment this message was transmitted back to suppliers. In the interim, however, other companies in other more environmentally aware countries were able to take advantage of the demand for 'green' products. For example, in the UK the German company Varta was able to increase its market share of the UK battery market since it produced mercury-free and cadmium-free batteries, while more traditional battery makers were slower in adapting their products.

The move towards environmentalism has provided both opportunities and threats to companies. Opportunities are available for companies which can reposition their products in markets where demand is growing and which can change their product's characteristics to match the changes in customer preferences. Successful companies here would be those which changed the chemical composition of their products, changed the raw materials used in the production process and modified the packaging of the product. These changes in consumer needs pose a threat for branded products whose characteristics are seen to be things other than environmental factors. Thus a new entrant can gain a substantial market share if it targets these environmental issues successfully.

Company image can also have an impact on other stakeholders within the organisation. Individual shareholders may require an organisation to follow a more responsible approach to business, although whether individual shareholders can achieve this through their diffuse holdings of shares is debatable. Nonetheless, this has not stopped the development of **ethical portfolios** of green investments.

From a consumer's perspective, green issues alone can lead to changes in particular purchasing decisions, for example consumers boycotted aerosols which contained CFCs. For other products environmental factors can be seen as playing an important part in the overall characteristics that make up the product's image. Thus a company which can state some credible environmental reasons for buying its particular product may place itself at an advantage compared with similar products which do not present a strong environmental image.

Some organisations are not at the end of the chain in supplying to consumers and may feel that environmental factors will have little impact on the way consumers perceive their products. However, organisations further forward in the supply chain may influence those producing intermediate products, since they need to respond to consumers who are demanding environmentally friendly products from organisations which supply final outputs. Increasingly companies are aware of being involved with other organisations which have a strong environmental image and can use this to their competitive advantage. Environmentally responsive companies can also have an impact on their workforces. Ethical and responsible companies may attract, retain and in turn motivate a high-quality workforce, as both Laura Ashley and Marks & Spencer can confirm.

It follows, therefore, that companies need to understand more about their impact on the environment and market themselves as environment-friendly companies. Organisations may need to formulate strategies which can give them a competitive advantage. Such strategies would include how they are currently meeting environmental standards and how well they are placed to meet potential changes. Consideration of competitors' responses to environmental changes is also important, as are the financial constraints which may prevent the organisation from achieving its full potential in the production of environment-friendly products, the company's image, and whether the organisation could easily produce products which will enhance its environmental image.

# ENVIRONMENTAL AUDITING

**Environmental auditing** was first developed in the United States in the early 1970s as a means of assessing whether a company was complying with environmental legislation. The Bhopal disaster led to US companies which had subsidiaries abroad using the same kind of approach. Thus environmental auditing was brought to Europe via US multinationals, but it took on a different role. Companies saw environmental auditing as a means by which they could improve their environmental account and at the same time demonstrate to the rest of the world that they were taking environmental issues seriously. In particular, the auditing process focused not only on processes but also the sources from which organisations obtained their raw materials.

The environmental audit should be seen not as a one-off approach but as a continuous requirement, monitoring and assessing the organisation's performance in a number of areas. The key aspects of the environmental audit are:

- To consider the degree to which environmental management systems are working at a satisfactory level within the organisation.
- To consider how the organisation complies with 'local' health and safety legislation.
- To cultivate internal policies so that the organisation's environmental objectives can be achieved.
- To ensure that the organisation meets adequate health and safety legislation.
- To recognise and assess the risk to the organisation which might result from environmental failure.
- To assess the impact on the natural environment of particular production processes through the appropriate measurement techniques.
- To determine where improvements can be made to the organisation's environmental policy/behaviour.

The advantages that an environmental audit can bring to the organisation can be seen in reductions in costs through improved energy usage, waste minimisation and recycling; the reduced probability of facing legal action over its environmental behaviour; improved public image; and improved quality of products and services.

Along with these benefits there are a number of disadvantages. There is the cost of the audit itself and the costs that may arise through complying with the results of the audit. Moreover, if the audit is undertaken by outside auditors, there may be some reluctance to accept some of the findings by internal stakeholders, especially where these are seen as threatening. Nonetheless, the process can often lead to benefits which outweigh the difficulties.

The triggers for an environmental audit can come from a number of sources. It can be influenced by the costs of insurance; by the behaviour of consumers switching to purchase more environment-friendly products; through the actions of competitors who are producing 'green' products; through the process of acquisitions and mergers as companies need to assess the complete impact of taking over another company; and through the process of legislation itself, both within the domestic economy and within a trading bloc such as the EU.

It is obviously important once the environmental audit has been undertaken that it is implemented and that the scope of the audit is defined. The boundary can be specified in terms of the geography of a particular site, it may be defined in terms of the subject area of the environmental audit, such as transportation safety, product safety or occupational health, or in terms of different segments within the organisation, such as by business unit. Finally, since the audits are not to be singular acts, subsequent audits can be judged against a set of past criteria allowing for problems to be rectified. In addition, the initial audit may concentrate on a fairly narrow area of the company and subsequent ones can develop so that they encompass wider areas of the organisation's behaviour.

## ◆ CASE STUDY 20.1

## Green reporting takes on a perennial quality

Yorkshire Water Services pleaded guilty and was fined £17 000 on three charges relating to discharges from waste water treatment plants.

CV Home Furnishings at Stockport in the UK has developed a system to greatly reduce the water consumption when washing out colour supply pipes.

ICI requires all its new plants to be built to standards that will meet the regulations it can reasonably anticipate in the most environmentally demanding country in which it operates that process.

These disclosures from the annual report and accounts illustrate the growing quantity and quality of so-called green reporting by UK-based companies.

Environmental reporting has a history of allowing form to outweigh content. 'Green glossies', attached to the annual report and accounts, have often in the past been comprised largely of pious intentions. Quantitative information has been scarce.

However, this appears to be changing. *Company Reporting*, the Edinburgh-based financial reporting journal, noted that of 540 companies reviewed, including all the FTSE 100, 32 per cent had made some form of environmental disclosure in their annual report and accounts or an accompanying special environmental report published at the same time. That compares with 27 per cent in 1994.

Of those disclosing this kind of information only 4 per cent quantified their environmental targets – compared to 9 per cent in 1994. Among the quantifiers were ICI, Norweb, Grand Metropolitan and T&N. *Company Reporting* sees in this an encouraging shift from forecasts to quantifying actual environmental achievements.

Some 12 per cent of those disclosing data on their environmental activities revealed achievements by monetary value, including Anglian Water, BAA, Marks & Spencer, Scottish Power and Unilever. Another 16 per cent reported achievements against other criteria. In 1994, a total of 25 per cent covered both categories – as against 28 per cent in 1995.

The results of environmental audits were disclosed by 7 per cent – compared with 2 per cent in the 1994 survey. Companies in this category include Bowater, British Gas, Coats Viyella, Courtaulds Textiles, HP Bulmer, Laporte, Redland, Rexam and Thames Water.

Although these companies provide examples of good practice, green reporting is still patchy. While it is common in some sectors, such as chemicals, food and drink, transport and the utilities, there are numerous inconsistencies. Many companies have complained that they have had to drop environmental information in the crowded annual report in favour of data on research and development, or internal controls.

For many companies, especially those outside the manufacturing sectors, environmental reporting will always be a side-show – although laudable forays are often made by companies such as Reuters. But the *Company Reporting* survey reveals that where it is relevant there is a perceptible drift towards bringing environmental reporting more into the heart of the report and accounts – a development enhanced by the inherent value of the information to the business itself, as well as to the shareholders and society at large. If gathering such data is seen as contributing to profits the trend will continue.

*Source: Financial Times*, 14 September 1995. Reprinted with permission.

---

◆ **Exercise 20.1**

What factors lie behind different companies' requirements to undertake environmental audits?

---

### Comment on the case study

Case study 20.1 indicates that only a small proportion of UK companies are undertaking environmental audits and that these are likely to be concentrated in the manufacturing sector. Moreover, the type of information revealed in the company accounts can vary markedly – a few are quantifying the impact of the organisation on the environment, more are noting their environmental performance in terms of its monetary impact. By undertaking a 'green' audit, organisations are providing shareholders and other possible stakeholders with information about their environmental attitudes. The process of quantifying environmental targets provides goals on which the company will subsequently need to report, which may put the organisation under pressure. However, at the same time a company can report on its success in managing to reach its objectives. For example, ICI set itself building standards targets and the company is able to report that all plants designed and built since 1994 have met this objective. ICI's policies are far from pure altruism. The highly visible impact of this multinational's activities on the local environment makes it imperative that it is seen to be maintaining the highest standards. Nonetheless, few companies will report on quantifiable environmental targets – only 4 per cent of UK companies had done so in their 1995 reports. It waits to be seen whether either national government or EU pressure or the behaviour of competitors leads to a wider variety of firms undertaking quantifiable environmental audits.

### Environmental audits and the EU

Although various aspects of environmental legislation had been developed both across the EU and within the separate nation states, the EU only really became interested in the process of environmental audits during the early 1990s. EU directives have stressed the need for companies:

■ To carry out periodic environmental audits of their industrial activities which have potentially the greatest impact on the environment.

■ To have their audits assessed by independent external advisers.

■ To notify the relevant authorities and the public about audit information.

To overcome the problem of different countries developing different systems, the European Commission has developed a voluntary **Environmental management and auditing system** (EMAS), which is basically a comprehensive management system rather than a technical measure for compliance. Its emphasis is on the need for integration through clear corporate goals, policy and programmes developed by the organisation. It stresses reporting requirements and these are verified through an independent agency. In order to join the eco-management and audit scheme an organisation has to adhere to an eco-audit cycle.

# ENVIRONMENTAL MANAGEMENT AND TOTAL QUALITY MANAGEMENT

There are strong links between total quality management (TQM) and environmental management systems (EMS). The former is concerned with an all-pervasive view of improving quality developed in the US by Deming; *see* Chapter 19. This will lead to a reduction in defects and lower costs, since there will be less waste. The TQM process requires commitment at all levels within the organisation. Figure 20.3 indicates the process of TQM and just-in-time (JIT) management, with its links to reductions in material waste, quality control, higher-quality products and the competitive advantage that can be gained through these procedures.

The EMS is also about being more integrated and committed, but with an emphasis towards the environment. Thus under EMS we would be concerned about energy conservation, reductions in pollution and ways to reduce waste. The TQM process which reduces waste also makes the organisation more environment friendly. TQM is also about commitment and this is an important feature of EMS. An EMS requires all levels of the organisation to be signed up to managing resources more efficiently, considering all aspects of health and safety and linking this process into the way stakeholder and consumers perceive the workings of the organisation. In this respect Kleiner (1991) identified a number of key components for the 'green' organisation:

■ The need to record and publish environmental data. This might enable the organisation to

**Figure 20.3  Just-in-time/total quality management production**

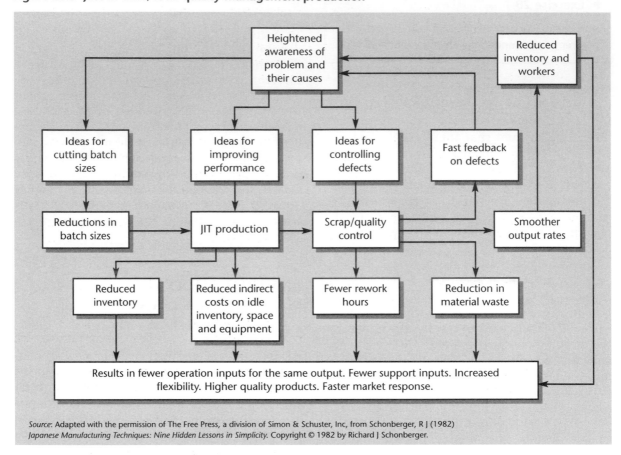

*Source*: Adapted with the permission of The Free Press, a division of Simon & Schuster, Inc, from Schonberger, R J (1982) *Japanese Manufacturing Techniques: Nine Hidden Lessons in Simplicity.* Copyright © 1982 by Richard J Schonberger.

The interrelationships between JIT and TQM indicates not only how the two techniques reduce costs, but shows how their interrelatedness improves quality and enhances the organisation's competitive position. In addition the two techniques rely on quality control, a reduction in material waste and commitment. All three factors are important in environmental management systems.

avert future environmental disasters and at the same time improves the relationship of the organisation with its stakeholders.

■ By being committed to reducing waste at source, that is, through some form of TQM programme.

Exxon was an organisation which failed on some aspects of TQM and which was involved with subsequent environmental problems. When the *Exxon Valdez* ran aground in Alaska in March 1989, Exxon faced a £1.3 billion cost in terms of fines and cleanup charges for its oil spillage. Cannon (1994), however, has estimated that this was not the full cost, since Exxon's loss of market share, the disruptions to its supplies, the compliance with new regulations and the effect on its share price resulted in a cost to the organisation of between £5.2 and £9.7 billion. This does not include the bad publicity and loss in consumer confidence.

Roome (1992) has also noted that adopting commercial and environmental excellence is a strategy which can create opportunities for the organisation. An organisation should attempt to ensure that its core managerial values always take account of environmental management issues, while leading-edge businesses set standards for a particular industry through the adoption of state-of-the-art environmental management systems.

Organisations which have attempted to integrate waste-management systems, both as a way of improving their environmental position and as a means to enhance their TQM processes, are those in the titanium oxide industry. SCM Chemicals, the US-based Hanson subsidiary and the world's third-largest titanium oxide producer, estimates its environmental spending over the last 20 years to be more than £65 million. Similarly, Rhône-

Poulenc of France, the fourth largest producer in Europe, has invested FFr600 million (£79 million) since 1990. These companies also incur annual operating costs to run neutralisation and recycling plants. They are now trying to offset these costs by selling by-products made from their waste. Thus a liability is being turned into an opportunity, and extending the lifespan of landfills where the waste would otherwise have been dumped.

The approach adopted by the titanium oxide producers is more of an 'end-of-the-pipe' strategy, which involves pollution control at the end of the process. There is an argument that an effective pollution-prevention policy throughout the process is cheaper in the long run. 3M, whose expertise is based on substrates, coatings and adhesives and which produces adhesive tape and 'Post-it' notes, has adopted a policy of 'pollution prevention pays' designed to cut pollution at source. The programme can be represented as a number of stages:

■ *Product reformulation* – that is, can the product be made using fewer raw materials or fewer toxic materials?
■ *Process modification* – that is, can the product be produced with less waste?
■ *Equipment redesign* – that is, can equipment be altered to reduce waste?
■ *Resource recovery* – that is, can waste be salvaged, reused or sold?

Each product produced must also meet the criteria of eliminating or reducing pollution, save on energy and resources, provide evidence of technological innovation and save money.

By following these procedures, 3M noted that waste per unit of output fell, although not by as much as it envisaged. This resulted in the adoption of 'pollution prevention plus' in 1989.

Thus, as with the overall approach to quality shown in Chapter 19, EMS can provide similar competitive advantages to organisations.

## ENVIRONMENTAL MANAGEMENT AND COMPETITIVE ADVANTAGE

Environmental management should be an all-pervasive culture and way of working within an organisation and not be left to a distinct group of individuals. Thus groups within the organisation need to think environmentally as well as in the now more traditional ways of quality.

In terms of production, waste needs to be reduced, treated or avoided altogether. Rather than considering what they do with the waste at the end of the production process, organisations find it more beneficial to deal with it during production. Alternatively an organisation may put pressure on its suppliers to provide it with less hazardous material. For a number of products it has been possible to replace oil-based products with water-based products, such as in the painting industry. In addition, it is possible to recirculate some of the waste to provide energy for other processes within the organisation. This provides cost savings as well as being more environment friendly.

In terms of product development, designers have now had to take into account both legislation and other market requirements, such as the reuse of packaging, recyclable products, and emission standards. In other words, the attribute space of products has widened.

How should companies sign up to the importance of thinking environmentally across the whole of the organisation? This may be undertaken in terms of a 'big-bang' process where the whole of the organisation moves rapidly towards embracing environmental management techniques, environmental products and the like. However, positive incrementalism may be a more appropriate approach. This may require a whole range of reward systems to be in place to encourage employee suggestions and increased training to improve environmental effectiveness.

Because the organisation is often only one part of a chain in bringing the product to the market, it requires close cooperation with other producers in a 'cradle-to-grave' approach. An example of this is the development of returnable containers or recyclable bottles which are part of the recycling loop within a production process. This requires the organisation to consider details such as the design of the product and its efficiency, the amount of energy used to make the product and whether there are any alternatives which are more environment friendly. It needs to look at how the production process itself can save on energy, reexamine the disposal of the product and its packaging. In the light of this a number of schemes to recycle waste paper, glass and plastic bottles have been developed. The degree to which recycling occurs varies between countries, although in the UK many district and local councils have set themselves recycling targets.

Finally, management has to be able to deliver on 'green' issues. It is no use having a well-established policy within the organisation if it cannot provide the environment-friendly products required both by other organisations and by consumers. If organisations wish to build up the trust of their various stakeholders, they need to be honest in what they are saying and doing. This transparency is important and actual reporting is one way of disclosing, rather than hiding, environmental factors. In the past one of the reasons for refraining from open disclosure has been that it might help competitors. Public disclosure can also lead to action by environmental pressure groups. The 1986 Superfund Amendment and Reauthorisation Act (SARA) in the United States required organisations to report, publicly, all emissions. This had the result that companies began to act more sensibly with regard to the environment and incorporated pollution-saving devices in the production processes or altered such processes in the manner outlined in earlier sections.

## GLOBAL POLICIES TOWARDS THE ENVIRONMENT

At a global level the main focus of regulation has been the agreement by the various nation states to environmental-protection initiatives through international summit meetings. The Rio Earth Summit of 1992, which set standards for environmental protection, might be thought of as having had only secondary effects on businesses. However, the International Treaty on Ozone-Depleting Substances – the Montreal Protocol – had a more direct effect in that it set a programme for the phased withdrawal and elimination of CFCs by the year 2010.

However, progress on a global scale has been slow. At the Climate Change Conference in Berlin in 1995 it became apparent that little progress had been made towards achieving the targets agreed at the 1992 Earth Summit. Environmental groups and the 36 small nations that form AOSIS – the Alliance of Small Island States – accused the European Commission in particular of abandoning its commitment to stabilising carbon dioxide emissions. Evidence submitted to the Commission in early 1995 indicated that carbon dioxide emissions in the EU will not be stabilised, but will actually rise by over 6 per cent between 1990 and 2000 and could possibly rise by a further 15 per cent between 2000 and 2015. As an indication of further concern for the environment, figures produced by the Worldwatch Institute of Washington for 1995 indicated that the earth's average temperature rose to 15.39°C and its emissions of carbon dioxide to 6.06 billion tonnes. Similarly, a report by the intergovernmental panel on climate change, submitted to a UN conference held in Geneva in July 1996, forecasts that by the year 2100 temperatures will probably have increased on average by a further 2°C and sea levels raised by an average 50 cm. Given that these environmental effects herald changes both in flooding and drought, particularly in the southern part of the EU, this has resulted in agriculture ministers reducing by half the land set aside so that grain production can be increased.

## EU POLICIES TOWARDS THE ENVIRONMENT

The EU is a major generator of atmospheric pollution, besides both industrial and domestic waste, such as non-biodegradable packaging, scrap and domestic refuse. Historically this has been disposed of in landfill sites or by incineration, sewage treatment or dumping untreated into rivers and seas. The result of this has been to make some seas and beaches unfit to use and has led to the death of marine life. The extent of these emissions per capita is shown in Table 20.1.

Although the original Treaty of Rome made no specific mention of environmental issues, in 1972 the EU heads of government noted that economic growth, although improving living standards and the quality of life of EU citizens, had implications for the environment and natural resources. What followed was a series of environmental action programmes, the first beginning in 1973 and lasting until 1977, leading through to the fifth (called Towards Sustainability) which commenced in 1993 and runs until 2000. Through these programmes over 200 pieces of environmental legislation have been put in place within the EU, covering such areas as air and water quality, noise pollution, waste, environmental impact assessment, industrial accidents and wildlife protection. Directorate General DG XI has responsibility for initiating and implementing EU policies on the environment set out in the EAPs (Environmental Action Programmes). However, enforcing the legislation has not always been easy. A fundamental problem is that most of the legislation is by means of direc-

**Table 20.1 Per capita emissions by EU countries, 1993**

| Country | Carbon dioxide emissions | Sulphur dioxide emissions | Nitrous dioxide emissions | Municipal waste |
|---------|------|------|------|------|
| Belgium | 11.6 | 42 | 32 | 343 |
| Denmark | 12.1 | 35 | 55 | 475 |
| France | 6.7 | 23 | 26 | 360 |
| Germany | 12.1 | 72 | 41 | 333 |
| Greece | 7.2 | — | 15 | 296 |
| Ireland | 9.0 | 50 | — | 312 |
| Italy | 6.9 | 34 | 35 | 348 |
| Luxembourg | 33.8 | 26 | — | 445 |
| Netherlands | 10.7 | 14 | 37 | 497 |
| Portugal | 4.2 | 21 | 12 | 257 |
| Spain | 5.7 | — | — | 322 |
| UK | 10.2 | 62 | 48 | 348 |
| EU12 | 8.9 | — | — | 350 |

*Source: Eurostat (1994) Facts Through Figures: A Statistical Portrait of the European Union*, European Commission, Brussels.
*Notes:*
(i)   Where data is missing it is not available.
(ii)  Carbon dioxide emissions from fossil fuel – measured in tonnes.
(iii) Sulphur dioxide emissions from all sources – measured in kilograms.
(iv)  Nitrous dioxide emissions from all sources – measured in kilograms.
(v)   Municipal waste – kilograms per inhabitant.

tives. Individual members are supposed to transpose the spirit and intention of the directive into their own domestic law. Some countries fail to do this quickly and effectively. The northern European countries have tended to be more successful in pushing ahead in the environmental protection field, while the southern European countries have been more concerned with bridging the gap between themselves and their wealthier northern neighbours.

Nonetheless, although it has also been recognised that legislation has not always been complied with, the European Court has come to take a much harder line with individual countries. In January 1992 the Advocate General suggested that the UK was failing to meet EU purity standards for drinking water and more specifically had failed to implement a 1980 directive setting standards to be met by 1982. This was a result of excessive nitrate levels in 28 water supply areas in the UK. It was not only the UK that was singled out: the Commission proposed taking similar action against all member states except Denmark, Greece and Portugal.

Over the life of these five environmental action programmes (EAP), the emphasis has changed. In the first two programmes through to 1982 the emphasis was largely reactive to problems which already existed. The third EAP, which began in 1983, switched the accent to the need to prevent problems before they occur. It also stressed the constraints imposed on future economic and social growth by finite resources and the need for future EU policies to have an environmental dimension. Its weakness was in treating each sector, such as air, water etc., separately, rather than considering an integrated policy. As each of the EAPs has come into existence previous EAPs have been reviewed to see if targets have been met.

The Single European Act in 1986 strengthened the EU's position on the environment, stressing that environmental legislation should meet a number of principal objectives:

- To preserve, protect and improve the quality of the environment.
- To safeguard human health.
- To make more efficient use of natural resources.

Until 1987, EU environmental policy consisted of a number of command-and-control directives covering a wide variety of areas. The problem, however, was one of enforcement. Thus EU policy switched in the late 1980s towards improving enforcement and there was a noticeable shift in emphasis towards market-based instruments such as eco-labelling, environmental auditing and taxation principles such as the carbon tax.

These views, and the need to plan industrial growth in the light of possible environmental impacts, lay behind the EU's Fifth Environmental Action Programme in 1992. This set out the EU's stance on the environment in the future and included a number of specific measures relating to industry.

If the EU is successful in moving down the environmental protection route, this could enhance the performance of a number of EU companies, but not necessarily all companies in all countries. Therefore, what is needed is full enactment of current legislation and for the member states of the EU to work together rather than one member state or another trying to obtain some financial advantage from not enacting some parts of EU environmental policy.

## POLICIES TO PROTECT THE EU ENVIRONMENT

It is possible that incentives could be used to encourage businesses and consumers to adopt environment-friendly practices. Tax concessions could be given for green production processes and goods. Financial support could be given to promote R&D into energy-saving or environment-friendly products. The EU hopes to double its use of renewable energy resources from 4 per cent to 8 per cent by 2005. It could increase its campaigns on the issues of global warming and encourage domestic governments to provide grants to improve home insulation. Since it tends to be the poorer regions which have the worst environmental record, EU regional, social and Agricultural Guidance and Guarantee Funding can be used to improve the GDP of these regions and thereby ameliorate their environmental records. Training programmes can also be used to heighten consumer awareness of renewable energy sources. For businesses and consumers one approach that has been used is the development of the eco-label; *see* below.

In terms of disincentives to pollute, the direction of EU policy has moved towards the 'polluter pays' principle. This frequently means that it is the consumer who pays in the form of higher prices. Environmental policy instruments may be classified into two types – market-based instruments such as taxes on emissions or the issuing of a limited number of permits to emit noxious gases, and non-market-based policy instruments such as regulations and directives.

Taxes appear to be one of the main weapons for reducing environmental damage. Changing the duties on unleaded fuel compared with leaded petrol has led to a major shift in the use of unleaded fuel. In 1986 only 1 per cent of petrol purchased in the 15 member states was unleaded, by 1994 this had risen to 54 per cent, and it was over 90 per cent in Germany.

## ECO-LABELLING

**Eco-labelling** was devised as a means of establishing the use by organisations of environment-friendly production methods and as a process to reduce the spurious claims by some companies about the extent to which their products were environment friendly. The first schemes of this type were introduced in West Germany in 1978 and followed by similar schemes in Canada, Japan and Norway during the late 1980s. In the UK the Advertising Standards Authority (ASA) has established a set of guidelines on the use of environmental claims by organisations for their products.

The forerunner to the EU's eco-labelling scheme was the Blue Angel eco-label developed in Germany, currently covering around 4000 products and available on both domestic and foreign-manufactured goods that are for sale in Germany. Given the importance placed on the environment in the German economy, possession of a Blue Angel award is paramount if products are going to be bought by the various sections of the German community.

The EU eco-labelling regulation was agreed in 1991 and has been developed, first, to promote products which have reduced environmental impact through the whole of their lifecycle, and second, to provide consumers with better information about the environmental impacts of products. These two overarching goals should not lead to any other environmental costs, such as a detrimental effect on health and safety. Products awarded an eco-label may still cause environmental damage, but they will be the least costly, environmentally, in any group of products. Because the eco-label emphasises the lifecycle of the product, then all component suppliers will have to be more environmentally conscious, since they are listed in the detailed information on the final product.

In terms of products which can seek an eco-label, some are excluded such as food, drink and pharmaceuticals, as well as those which are classified as dangerous or cause significant direct harm to people or the environment.

The process under which a product can achieve an eco-label is as follows. A manufacturer or importer applies to one of the bodies in a member state for an eco-label. This costs the manufacturer or importer an administration charge and if the eco-labelling is successful a fee will subsequently be charged for its use. The verifying body in the member states decides whether an eco-label can be awarded and informs the Commission and other member states. These two groups now have 30 days to object. If there are objections, the outcome is referred to a further regulatory committee made up of national experts. If there are no objections, however, a contract is issued by the validating body in the member state to the importer or manufacturer which has applied and a list of products able to use the eco-label is then published.

A number of criticisms have been raised about this process. First, the EU stressed the idea that eco-labelling was to be related to the environmental impact of the product over its whole lifecycle. Obtaining the information required to study the impact of a given product over all stages of its life-cycle – resource extraction, energy use, production, distribution, use and ultimate disposal – rather than the impact of a given plant or organisation can prove to be very expensive, and complete knowledge of the full environmental impact may not be available. The lifecycle analysis mainly aims at identifying the impacts and quantifying them in 'natural' units such as physical, chemical and biological. Although lifecycle assessment methodologies are well established for the first level – the impact – at the second level of quantifying the effects of a product no standard methodology exists, although efforts are being made by Sullivan and Ehrenfeld (1993) and others. Some authors suggest, Arnold (1993) for example, that lifecycle analysis is impractical and very expensive. However, these could provide the organisation with the definitive tools for the study and monitoring of its activities on the environment. As such they should be considered from the start and could provide a useful means of getting the price system

to reflect properly the true impact of products in financial and monetary terms; *see* Portney (1994).

If eco-labelling is granted to products where life-cycle analysis has not taken place, the environmentalists feel that it is their due to criticise the process. In addition, eco-labelling is product group specific in that any manufacturer only needs to satisfy the criteria laid down for that specific product group. Thus environmentalists suggest that what will happen is not a true lifecycle analysis. Nonetheless, organisations may benefit from obtaining an eco-label, which is equivalent to a kind of starring system for products based on environmental impacts.

---

◆ **Exercise 20.2**

**1** To what extent can the eco-labelling system be criticised for not being stringent enough?

**2** Does eco-labelling favour higher-quality manufacturers?

---

## ◆ CASE STUDY 20.2

# The EU Eco-label has irked some manufacturers

All products are green, but some are greener than others: that might well be the observation of today's shopper wondering at the variety of claims to environmental friendliness splashed across everything from shampoo to dishwashers. To remove this confusion the EU has produced the Eco-label which aims to be the objective mark of an ecologically sensitive product.

Since Hoover attached a European Eco-label to a range of washing machines in 1994, it has increased market share in Germany and at the top end of the UK market.

For washing machines, the EU's standard for labelling limits the consumption of energy, water and detergent. It also sets basic performance criteria and stipulates that manufacturers identify water and energy-saving programmes. In 1994, less than 15 per cent of the washing machine industry fulfilled the Eco-label criteria. In 1995, nearly 30 per cent do so.

However, a number of producers argue that the Eco-label is not necessarily a mark of distinction. For products at the top end of the market which surpass the label's environmental requirements, there is no way of indicating their superior performance. A row of washing machines all carrying the sticker could mislead shoppers into thinking that all the products' env-

ironmental records were the same, say some producers. It may blur the distinction between a luxury machine carrying the Eco-label and a cheaper model which also has an Eco-label.

Another disincentive is the cost. The cost of the initial application for the label is minimal, but companies must pay the board 0.15 per cent of their annual European turnover at ex-factory gate prices once the label is awarded.

The biggest problem, and one that is echoed by a number of environmentalists, is that the conditions for winning an Eco-label are not stringent enough.

In the case of washing machines, it is only efficiency in usage rather than production materials or the ecological record of the company that is assessed. For many white goods producers that means the label is neither distinctive enough to give exceptional environmental kudos nor a benchmark to show adequate standards. In addition the Eco-label system does not suppress labels that manufacturers and shops give their own products and that is confusing to buyers who find it difficult to distinguish between official and unofficial marks.

*Source: Financial Times*, 29 March 1995. Reprinted with permission.

## Eco-labelling – advantages and disadvantages

Possession of an eco-label can give organisations a competitive advantage. Nonetheless, manufacturers have provided other methods or badges which have suggested that their products are environment friendly. This has added to the confusion for consumer groups. In addition, the eco-label was meant to promote products which had minimised their environmental impacts throughout their life-cycle, yet the criteria being used for some products does not necessarily stress this. At present there are a limited number of product groups which use the eco-labelling system and the speed with which agreement is taking place elsewhere suggests that a system covering a wide range of products will not be EU-wide in the short term.

As organisations enter the second part of the 1990s, it will be interesting to note how far they go down the eco-labelling route. During periods of slower growth, as a number of EU economies attempt to satisfy the criteria for monetary union, eco-labelling may prove to be too expensive. Nonetheless, it may prove to be the competitive advantage which companies are looking for.

# GREEN TRADE ISSUES

As will be seen in Chapter 21, markets and organisations have become increasingly globalised. This has been helped by the move towards free trade since the Second World War. But what is the relationship between international trade and the environment? Proponents of free trade argue that environmental regulations often lead to unnecessary barriers to trade, reducing the efficiency of the global economy and slowing down the process of technological change. Those who support the protectionist view of limiting trade argue that free trade enables multinational enterprises to shift their polluting activities to less well-regulated countries, thereby perpetuating the use of inefficient technologies and harming the world's poor.

For example, take the European eco-label discussed above. The eco-label for tissue paper is intended as a means of informing European consumers which tissue products are environment friendly. It sets standards for air and water emissions and for resource use. These standards are consistent with the conditions that exist within Europe, but they are not consistent with the condi-

tions in Brazil, the USA and Canada. In other words, this eco-label discriminates against products from the Americas. As Morris (1996) notes, since governments are beginning to include environmental considerations in their procurement policies, eco-labels are a new form of protectionism.

However, there are other regulations that clearly impede free trade, such as the Convention on International Trade in Endangered Species (CITES) and the Basel convention on Transboundary Movements of Hazardous Wastes and their Disposal, which both rule out trade in certain substances. The Montreal Protocol was concerned with ozone depletion and initiated the phasing out of CFCs. The treaty, however, also allowed member countries to implement trade sanctions against non-member countries. In addition, the convention prohibits imports of all products which use CFCs in their production processes, such as computer components cleaned with CFC-based solvents.

Some countries, such as the Asian tiger economies and Chile, which have been spoken of as successful growth economies during the last decade are themselves creating major environmental problems. Chile's economic recovery has depended on the exploitation of non-renewable natural resources such as forests and fish. In the tiger economies rapid economic expansion has resulted in rising air and water pollution. In Thailand, for example, government planners are seeking to decentralise pollution by decentralising industry. Having used a great deal of their own timber resources, Thai entrepreneurs are helping to do the same in Burma, Laos and Cambodia.

The trade rules of the General Agreement on Tariffs and Trade (GATT), the World Trade Organisation (WTO), the North American Free Trade Association (NAFTA) and the EU have been used to curb efforts to protect the environment. These have included US efforts to protect dolphins by banning Mexican tuna, which tended to be caught in nets which also caught dolphins; Denmark's efforts to protect its refillable bottle system by requiring all beer and soft drinks to be sold in refillable bottles; and Sweden's attempts before joining the EU to introduce a ban on imports of products containing or produced with ozone destroyers.

The problem for the WTO is that multilateral environmental agreements such as the Basel Convention or the Montreal Protocol state that countries can restrict trade on environmental grounds, whereas the WTO is trying to remove all trade restrictions. Therefore there is a conflict between the two. Efforts, however, are under way to try to 'green' the WTO. The pressure groups come from environmentalists and from business. A coalition of 120 international companies called the World Business Council for Sustainable Development (WBCSD) has been set up by environmentalists to 'green' the WTO.

The WBCSD endorses a variety of management techniques such as lifecycle assessment, environmental management standards, eco-labelling and recycling laws. Environmental criteria would be applied internationally through the International Organisation for Standardisation (ISO).

The eco-labelling issue has received considerable attention because many industries see that it can be used as a disguised form of protectionism. Interpretation of the Agreement on Technical Barriers to Trade of the Uruguay Round of GATT talks will be crucial for determining the status of eco-labelling in the WTO. The tension between MNEs and free trade therefore needs to be reconciled, and at the first Ministerial Conference of the WTO in December 1996 the WTO Committee on Trade and the Environment attempted to move this issue forward, though there are still further issues to be considered.

But are free trade and the environment in conflict? It is possible that free trade is not a threat but a prerequisite for environmental quality. Free trade can improve economic growth and wealth, and Grossman and Krueger (1991) have shown that economic growth begins to alleviate air pollution when per capita income reaches $4000 – $5000 per year. Material poverty, not economic exchange, is the single greatest threat to environmental quality. In other words, green protectionism will be particularly damaging to those countries where per capita incomes are low and which cannot undertake sufficient economic growth to reach the threshold per capita income suggested by Grossman and Krueger.

The notion of free trade within the EU following the Single European Market (SEM) also may be in conflict with further progress on European integration. Member states often regard taxation as a national prerogative, levying national eco-taxes at a level which are the least possible impediment to the free movement of goods within the internal market. During 1997 the DG XI is due to draft documentation to make a start at attempting to distinguish between those taxes which are in accordance with EU law and those which are not. Although the Fifth Environmental Action Programme encourages environmental taxation, the problem has been that individual states want control over fiscal matters. Thus differences in taxation have resulted in barriers to the free flow of goods. What DG XI would like is for the individual states to describe the timing and the manner of their plans for environmental taxation, so as to promote transparency and avoid future problems. In addition, the EU countries are being asked to specify the environmental objective being pursued and the manner in which it would be promoted by the tax or levy, the impact on the internal market and selection of the instrument which achieves the environmental goal with the least limitation on the free movement of goods. The environmental objectives which are being pursued under the proposed treaty are to modify the behaviour of consumers or businesses in such a way as to benefit the environment; to generate income which will be used for environmental protection; and to internalise pollution costs by the application of the 'polluter pays' principle.

What really appears to be the problem is that individual countries still want control over their own fiscal policies and in this respect can use the various forms of taxation to restrict the flow of goods.

## SUMMARY

◆ Environmental issues particularly came to the fore in the 1970s with the publication of the *Limits to Growth* by the Club of Rome, with its view that since resources were finite and economic growth rates were growing exponentially there would be insufficient resources in the future.

◆ Environmental problems can be controlled through the market mechanism but governments have used a number of policy instruments, such as pollution taxes, tradeable permits, subsidies and property rights, as their main approaches to pollution control.

◆ Increasingly organisations have come to realise that environmental issues are playing an important part in corporate strategy. This has provided both opportunities and threats to organisations.

Companies need to formulate environmental strategies that will give them a competitive advantage in the market.

◆ Environmental auditing can provide benefits to organisations through improved energy usage, waste minimisation and recycling. There can be an improved public image, a reduction in litigation costs and improved quality. Set against this are the costs of the audit itself, its compliance costs, and the need to trust external auditors if they are used.

◆ Within the EU some argue that differing environmental standards in the member states can provide a competitive advantage for those companies in countries with lower standards. Nonetheless, countries which set high standards can use these as barriers to entry into their markets, and because they have usually developed the environmental protection technology earlier than other countries have a competitive advantage in selling this to other companies.

◆ The EU countries are responsible for a fairly large proportion of the environmental damage in the world. The Treaty of Rome made no specific mention of environmental issues, yet by the mid-1990s there were around 200 pieces of environmental legislation in place to reduce the environmental damage by EU companies and its citizens. The EU has been most active in reducing $CO_2$ emissions, eliminating the use of CFCs and curbing other greenhouse gases.

◆ The EU's approach to the environment during the 1990s can be seen in its Fifth Environmental Action Programme relating to its stance on the environment in the future. It stressed that sectors which are under the most environmental pressure should be tackled first and that existing regulations should be better enforced rather than new legislation being developed. There was emphasis on the need for all member states to work together.

◆ Eco-labelling was devised to establish a standard which indicted those products within Europe which used environment-friendly production techniques and to reduce the spurious claims of some organisations. Its accent is on the promotion of products which have reduced environmental impact throughout the whole of their lifecycle and to provide consumers with better information about the environmental impacts of products.

◆ There appears to be some conflict between agreements to free trade under both GATT and the WTO and the role of multilateral environmental agreements which permit countries to impose trade restrictions against other nations whom they believe are damaging the environment in some way. Some see environmental factors as being used as a new form of non-tariff barriers to trade. The conflict between environmentalism and free trade has still to be resolved under the WTO.

◆ Environmental protection may also conflict with the freeing of markets that followed the SEM. The nation states in the EU may be required to state how their tax regimes not only are being used to protect the environment but can influence the free flow of goods within the union.

## REVIEW QUESTIONS

1 What are the implications for developing countries of the development of environmental management standards by the industrialised countries?

2 To what extent does European integration help the development of environmental policies within the EU?

3 What advantages can an organisation obtain by becoming more environmentally aware? What might be the disadvantages of such a policy?

4 Given the slowdown in the world economies during the 1990s, environmental issues will become less important. Discuss.

5 For organisations there is no one best method of controlling the level of pollution. Discuss.

6 What methods can organisations use to improve the environment?

**7** Is sustainable development a practical solution or just a theoretical explanation of a means to safeguard the environment?

**8** Can industries be left to their own devices to introduce environmental management systems?

## GLOSSARY OF NEW TERMS

**Ambient-based systems:** A method of controlling the total amount of pollution in specific areas or zones.

**Contingent valuation method:** Method of evaluating environmental goods, based on willingness to pay or willingness to accept compensation.

**Cradle-to-grave management:** The environmental impact of a product through its lifecycle from raw material usage to disposal.

**Eco-labelling:** An EU system which has been developed to promote products which have reduced environmental impact throughout the whole of their lifecycle.

**Emission-based systems:** A procedure which attempts to control the origin of pollution.

**Environmental auditing:** A check on both the environmental performance of the company and on the performance of the management system designed to bring about improved performance.

**Environmental impact assessments:** Assessment of the impact of an investment decision on the environment.

**Environmental management and auditing system:** A comprehensive management system rather than a technical measure for compliance to improve environmental management.

**Environmental management system:** A process by which the organisation manages resources more efficiently, considers all aspects of health and safety and links this to the way stakeholders and consumers perceive how the organisation works.

**Environmental standards:** A limit set on the amount of pollution permitted by each organisation.

**Environmental taxes:** A tax which when applied successfully pushes the output of organisations to the socially optimum level.

**Ethical portfolios:** A portfolio of investment shares or unit trusts made up of organisations which behave in an ethical or environment-friendly manner.

**Negative externality:** This is the pollution that arises where the market fails to achieve the optimum allocation of resources.

**Polluter pays:** The polluter should pay for the cost of clearing up pollution rather than using public money.

**Property rights:** For a good to have property rights it means that an individual or group has the exclusive right of use, the exclusive right to receive income generated and the full right to transfer ownership.

**Sustainable development:** Stresses the interdependence between economic growth and environmental quality, where economic growth needs to be 'managed'.

**Total economic value:** The sum of the use vale, option value and existence value of a resource.

**Tradeable emission permits:** Permits which allow organisations to pollute up to a particular level and which can be bought or sold.

## READING

Ferguson, P R and Ferguson, G J (1993) *Business Economics*, Macmillan, Basingstoke.
This book covers a wide range of issues, but there is a chapter on the economics of the environment.

Griffiths, A and Wall, S (1997) *Applied Economics: An Introductory Course*, 7th edn, Addison Wesley Longman, Harlow.
Chapter 10 covers the economics of the environment and provides a wide range of up-to-date statistics on environmental pollution and emissions.

Hanley, N, Shogren, J F and White, B (1997) *Environmental Economics: In Theory and Practice*, Macmillan, Basingstoke.
This text provides an up-to-date theoretical exposition of environmental economics with some useful cases.

Welford, R and Gouldson, A (1993) *Environmental Management and Business Strategy*, Pitman Publishing, London.
The text covers a very wide range of environmental issues and their effects on business.

Welford, R and Prescott, K (1996) *European Business: An Issue Based Approach*, 3rd edn, Pitman Publishing, London.
Chapter 10 covers many of the important developments in environmental management and EU environmental policies.

**Further reading**
Adamowicz, W, Louviere, J and Williams, M (1994) 'Combining stated and revealed preference methods for valuing environmental amenities', *Journal of Environmental Economics and Management*, Vol 26, No 2, pp 271–92.

Arnold, F (1993) 'Life cycle doesn't work', *The Environmental Forum*, September/October, pp 19–23.

Bateman, I and Willis, K (eds) (1995) *Valuing Environmental Preferences: Theory and Practice of the Contingent Valuation Method*, Oxford University Press, Oxford.

Cairncross, F (1993) *Costing the Earth: The Challenge for Governments and the Opportunities for Business*, Harvard Business School Press, Boston, MA.

Cannon, T (1994) *Corporate Responsibility: A Textbook on Business Ethics, Governance, Environment: Roles and Responsibilities*, Pitman Publishing, London.

Carson, R (1962) *The Silent Spring*, Fawcett-crest, New York.

Clawson, M and Knetsch, J (1966) *Economics of Outdoor Recreation*, John Hopkins University Press, Baltimore.

Collins, A (1994) 'International pollution control: a review of marketable permits – a comment', *Journal of Environmental Management*, No 43, pp 185–8.

Cook, M and Healey, N M (1995) *Economic Growth and Structural Change*, Macmillan, Basingstoke.

Davies, R (1963) 'Recreation planning as an economic problem', *Natural Resources Journal*, Vol 3, No 2, pp 239–49.

Gren, I-M, Folke, K, Turner, K and Bateman, I (1994) 'Primary and secondary values of wetland eco-systems', *Environmental and Resource Economics*, No 4, pp 55–74.

Grossman, G and Kreuger, A (1991) 'Environmental impacts of a North American Free Trade Agreement', Princeton University, Princeton, November.

Haines, R W (1993) 'Environmental performance indicators: balancing compliance with business economics', *Total Quality Management*, Vol 2, No 3, pp 367–72.

Hanley, N and Spash, C (1993) *Cost–Benefit Analysis and the Environment*, Edward Elgar, Aldershot.

Hopfenbeck, W (1993) *The Green Management Revolution: Lessons in Environmental Excellence*, Prentice Hall, Hemel Hempstead.

James, P (1994) 'Business environmental performance measurement', *Business Strategy and the Environment*, Vol 3, No 2, pp 59–67.

Kahneman, D, Knetsch, J and Thaler, R (1991), 'The endowment effect, loss aversion and *status quo* bias', *Journal of Economic Perspectives*, Vol 5, No 2, pp 193–206.

Kerry Turner, R, Pearce, D and Bateman, I (1994) *Environmental Economics,* Harvester Wheatsheaf, Hemel Hempstead.

Kleiner, A (1991) 'What does it mean to be green', *Harvard Business Review*, July–August, pp 38–47.

Lancaster, K (1966) 'A new approach to consumer theory', *Journal of Political Economy*, Vol 74, No 1, pp 132–57.

Mansfield, E (1993) *Managerial Economics: Theory, Applications and Cases*, 2nd edn, Norton, New York.

Meadows, D H (1972) *Limits to Growth*, Earth Island, London.

Mitchell, R and Carson, R (1989) *Using Surveys to Value Public Goods: The Contingent Valuation Method*, Resources for the Future, Washington.

Morris, J (1996) *Green Goods? Consumers, Product Label and the Environment*, Institute of Economic Affairs, London.

Pearce, D (ed) (1991) *Blueprint 2*, Earthscan, London.

Pearce, D W and Turner, R K (1990) *Economics of Natural Resources and the Environment*, Harvester Wheatsheaf, Hemel Hempstead.

Portney, P R (1994) 'The price is right: making use of life cycle analyses', *Issues in Science and Technology*, Winter, pp 69–75.

Roome, N (1992) 'Developing environmental management systems', *Business Strategy and the Environment*, Spring, Part 1.

Sullivan, M S and Ehrenfeld, J R (1993) 'Reducing life-cycle environmental impacts: an industry survey of emerging tools and programs', *Total Quality Environmental Management*, No 2, pp 143–57.

Tomkins, J M and Twomey, J (1994) 'International pollution control: a review of marketable permits', *Journal of Environmental Management*, No 41, pp 39–47.

Wheeler, D (1992) 'Environmental management as an opportunity of sustainability in business – economic forces as a constraint', *Business Strategy and the Environment*, Vol 1, No 4, pp 37–40.

CHAPTER 21

# THE GLOBALISATION OF BUSINESS ACTIVITIES

## OBJECTIVES

◆ To consider the role of international trade and trading agreements in stimulating international business.

◆ To develop relevant theories of trade and indicate how useful they have been to the development of globalisation.

◆ To show how GATT has helped stimulate international trade.

◆ To explain how trading blocs provide both opportunities and threats for organisations.

◆ To reveal how deregulation has stimulated international business.

◆ To consider how technology has influenced the process of globalisation.

◆ To illustrate the impact of multinational enterprises on both the home and the host economies.

◆ To consider how globalisation has influenced corporate strategy.

◆ To investigate the role of governments and multinational enterprises.

## KEY TERMS

Absolute advantage

Comparative advantage

Demonstration effects

Deregulation

Global triad

Internalisation-specific advantages

International division of labour

Intra-industry trade

Location-specific advantages

Multinational/ transnational/ international organisation

Non-tariff barriers

Ownership-specific advantages

Screwdriver operations

Structural market distortions

Theory of appropriability

Trade creation

Trade diversion

Voluntary export restraint

## CHAPTER OUTLINE

Business application

The role of international trade and trading agreements in stimulating international business

The Heckscher–Ohlin theorem

Alternative theories of trade

Intra-industry trade

The importance of trade

General Agreement on Tariffs and Trade (GATT)

Trading blocs

Case study 21.1 Move towards NAFTA raises fears for Caricom

The global triad

Deregulation and international business

Case study 21.2 Telecom Eireann's prospects of forming an international strategic alliance

The impact of technology on globalisation

Case study 21.3 Advances in information technology are bringing entire industrial sectors into financial services

Why do companies become multinationals?

The impact of multinationals on the host economy

Multinational activity within Europe

Effect on the home economy

Global competition and corporate strategy

Global shift theory

MNE regulation

Summary

Review questions

Glossary of new terms

Reading

## BUSINESS APPLICATION

# New alliances for a new era

Telecommunications markets and the economic and regulatory factors surrounding them are in fundamental global transition. Their world is in the throes of a revolution, the extent and significance of which has yet to be determined in terms of economic, political and social consequences . . . New markets are evolving with previously unseen speed.

Inextricably linked to this global development, is the end of the monopoly era. Very few companies will have adequate staff levels, technology and finance to handle the new market volume and the requirements of the specific target groups. Modern corporate strategy . . . must hinge on elements such as internationalisation and the formation of alliances.

Deutsche Telekom AG must follow these lines in order to do justice to its economic significance for Germany and Europe as a whole. Its strategic alliance with France Telecom – and now with the US carrier, Sprint – represents a promising way of assuring its future as a global player in an ever intensifying competitive environment . . .

Alliances such as Unisource, British Telecom/MCI or AT&T/McCaw are already showing the way towards globalisation. For this reason, Deutsche Telekom must reposition itself in many areas.

The repositioning is based on three main strategic objectives:

■ Safeguarding key business activities.
■ Opening up new markets for the future, such as multimedia.
■ Internationalisation of the company's business activities.

To realise the necessary level of flexibility, the process of outsourcing complete business segments is being systematically pushed forward; furthermore, Deutsche Telekom is forging links with highly competent business partners, such as Intel and Microsoft.

Markets do not just need to be occupied geographically; they must also be penetrated with new, innovative and customer-orientated products. In this respect, the field of multimedia and the much talked about information highway play a key role. Home-shopping, home-banking, video-on-demand, telemedicine and other services, the visions of today, but the reality of tomorrow, will contribute to the expansion of Deutsche Telekom's market share.

By the end of 1995, the first multimedia trials will be put into operation with video-on-demand services in Berlin. Deutsche Telekom will be building on already existing technology, which will then be adapted to the demands of the future . . .

Safeguarding the home market is just as important as the internationalisation of the company. However, they must both be achieved together. In its efforts to do this, Deutsche Telekom was quick in laying the foundations for successful international business operations. Numerous foreign representative offices were set up, for example, in Asia and the US, Russia and Britain . . .

The transatlantic alliance between Deutsche Telekom, France Telecom and Sprint represents an important step towards the provision of comprehensive telecommunications services. However, there is one thing nobody must lose sight of: a global presence can only really be achieved by successfully conquering the fastest growing market in the world – the Asian-Pacific region.

*Source: Financial Times*, 3 October 1995. Reprinted with permission.

### Comment

Deutsche Telekom is a good example of a company which has become increasingly globalised in its focus. This is a response to changes in technology, increases in competition and alterations in both German and European legislation over deregulation. It requires a different approach to strategy: the corporation must think internationally rather than nationally while at the same time protecting its home market. Part of the reason for the growth in telecommunications has been the changes in technology that have merged markets together, thus increasing competition but also allowing existing organisations to access new markets. In addition, the growth in international trade and more comprehensive trading agreements have also enhanced the development of global corporations.

# THE ROLE OF INTERNATIONAL TRADE AND TRADING AGREEMENTS IN STIMULATING INTERNATIONAL BUSINESS

There are many reasons for international trade developing and for countries trading. One reason for trade taking place stems from economic advantage. Trade creates value by increasing the efficiency to which resources are used worldwide. It reduces production costs through economies of scale and therefore lowers input costs. This has a knock-on effect in terms of lower prices paid by consumers and increases product variety. Trade also flows from the prospect of mutual benefit. Organisations and governments are unlikely to engage in international trade if they cannot enhance their economic situation or achieve any material gain. Differences in costs of production can also lead to international trade taking place. For example, the democratisation of Eastern Europe has led to a number of organisations establishing production platforms in Eastern Europe and using these lower-cost facilities as sources from which to export to other countries in Europe. International trade also provides organisations with the benefits of large-scale production and allows them to produce at levels which they might not be able to achieve if they concentrated solely on their domestic markets.

Of great importance in the trade debate are the changes that have taken place in international markets. Many markets have recently become deregulated, with reductions in barriers to trade, and this has enhanced trading opportunities. New patterns of organisation and business location have emerged. These include foreign suppliers, foreign direct investments, joint ventures and international cooperation. These have arisen to obtain better access to markets and to improve competitiveness by exploiting specific local production factors such as favourable labour costs, labour skills or tax situations. With the growth in exports and imports, competition has intensified in both foreign and domestic markets.

From a theoretical perspective, the theories of **absolute advantage** (Adam Smith) and **comparative advantage** (David Ricardo) suggest that in a perfectly competitive world of constant returns to scale, where there is an absence of externalities and where the level of technology is fixed, countries should specialise in the production of goods for which they have either a comparative or an absolute advantage. If specialisation takes place, total world output may increase. This does not mean that on every occasion each country benefits from trade. There will be winners and losers in terms of individual industries and countries. But the world will benefit in terms of increased output.

It should be fairly obvious that the conditions under which the theories of comparative and absolute advantage were developed are open to question. First, the theories suggest that countries should specialise in products for which they have either a comparative and/or an absolute advantage. This may lead to the danger of overspecialisation in a small range of products or services. Therefore, countries may consider producing items for which they are not the most efficient producer. In order for them to do this they need either to subsidise the products produced in the domestic market, reducing their prices down to world levels, push up the prices of imports into the domestic economy, or somehow limit the supply of imports into the domestic economy. Thus countries have used a variety of tools, such as subsidies, tariffs, quotas or **voluntary export restraints** (VERs), to prevent the free flow of goods between countries. Second, the assumptions on which the theories of absolute and comparative advantage are based do not appear to be appropriate for countries in the twentieth century. For example, many markets are not highly competitive: there is a tendency for markets to be more oligopolistic. Factors of production are also not highly mobile. From the model of comparative advantage, it can be concluded that the full benefits of international trade can only be found if there are no barriers to trade. A movement towards this scenario has been established through the GATT trade talks, the development of trading blocs and, in the European Union (EU), the establishment of the Single Market.

However, what we also realise is that markets are not made up of a large number of firms competing with one another. Multinational organisations, through their very nature, may be located in inappropriate locations but ones which still offer cost advantages compared to more favourable locations which should in theory have a comparative advantage.

Although comparative advantage suggests that trade is based on different costs, it does not explain what leads to these differences in costs. A suggested solution to this issue arose during the first part of the twentieth century in the Heckscher-Ohlin theorem.

# THE HECKSCHER-OHLIN THEOREM

The Heckscher-Ohlin theorem assumed that not only was there more than one factor of production, but also that different goods required different proportions of the various factors of production. This means that to produce some goods would require more labour-intensive means of production, others would be more capital intensive and so on.

The definition of intensity used here is to do with the proportions in which labour and capital are used, in other words, the capital:labour ratio. For example, if the manufacture of CD players is more capital intensive than pine furniture production, it follows that furniture making is more labour intensive than CD player production.

In addition to these differences in intensity, different countries have different amounts of the factors of production (factor endowments) and these lead to the different relative prices of factors. If a country has a large amount of land, agricultural goods – that is, land-intensive goods – should be relatively cheap to produce and that country will have a comparative advantage in land-intensive goods. According to this theory, countries such as Australia, Canada and New Zealand should export land-intensive goods such as meat, wheat and wool. Similarly, labour-intensive countries, such as India and Taiwan, should export labour-intensive products, such as footwear and textiles. Capital-intensive countries like Germany and Japan should export capital-intensive products such as computers, cameras and CD players.

If demand conditions are the same in the two countries, then the prices of the factors are determined by their supply as reflected by their abundance – factor endowment. In the capital-abundant country, capital becomes relatively cheaper, while in the labour-abundant country, labour is relatively cheaper. Neoclassical theory states therefore that the goods produced in the capital-intensive country will be produced at lower cost in the relatively capital-abundant country. The labour-intensive country will produce labour-intensive products more cheaply. Capital-intensive countries will, therefore, export capital-intensive goods and labour-intensive countries will export labour-intensive goods.

Samuelson expanded the Heckscher-Ohlin model through his notion of factor price equalisation. The trade that takes place between labour-intensive countries and capital-intensive countries continues until a common price ratio is established between capital-intensive commodities and labour-intensive commodities.

In reality, factor prices are obviously not equalised among nations – neither a factory worker nor a doctor earns the same in India and Germany. Factor price equalisation theorem emphasises free trade in commodities as an imperfect substitute for factor movements between countries, but to gain real-world efficiency free trade in both commodities and factors is needed.

When the Heckscher-Ohlin model was tested empirically some doubts were cast on the validity of its assumptions. Leontief (1954), in his study of the US, found that, while it was a capital-intensive country, the US's exports were labour-intensive while its imports were capital intensive.

A number of reasons were put forward for this seemingly anomalous result. Leontief proposed that US labour was approximately three times more productive than foreign labour as a result of superior management, training, skills and better motivation, and by taking these factors into account he showed that the US was a labour-abundant country. It was also possible that labour-intensive industries in the US had been protected by trade barriers and this biased imports in favour of capital-intensive goods. These are just two among a whole raft of arguments put forward to explain the apparent paradox in US exports and imports.

# ALTERNATIVE THEORIES OF TRADE

Modern industries tend to be dominated by large industrial units and thereby gain various economies of scale. This suggests that modern industry is characterised by increasing, not constant, returns to scale – the assumption of both the Ricardo and the Heckscher-Ohlin theories.

If organisations concentrate on their domestic market there may be limited economies of scale. Trade encourages specialisation in a narrower range of products, and production can exceed that necessary for the domestic market, thereby allowing further economies of scale to be gained through larger plants and larger production runs. As a result, large countries would be expected to benefit over small countries in the production of goods whose methods of production allow them to reap the benefits of scale economies.

The presence of scale economies could suggest that trading patterns could be determined by which country's organisations had established an early lead over its rivals. Getting this early lead and thus gaining scale advantages may make it potentially difficult for rival countries (organisations) to compete successfully. Countries could therefore be exporting goods which are contrary to those related to its factor endowments.

Technology has also been suggested as providing an explanation of export potential. The argument, put forward by Posner (1961) and others, is that as new products are developed by industrially advanced countries they are able to gain both static and dynamic economies of scale. Developing new products gives organisations a temporary monopoly and leads to access into foreign markets. High profits both at home and abroad lead to imitation of the product and the short-lived comparative advantage will be lost. Once this has been lost the organisation may seek another new product and so a new cycle of innovation and imitation ensues. Posner's theorem fails, however, to explain why this technological gap exists or the size of the gap.

Linder's (1961) view of trade is that income similarity explains the increasing volume of trade between industrialised countries with similar factor endowments. Countries will concentrate on their domestic markets first before exploring similar markets abroad. There are a number of factors behind this conclusion:

- Selling the product in the domestic market first gives producers a greater awareness of the opportunities for profit from their product.
- Any research and development undertaken by organisations is aimed at satisfying obvious needs – often made clearer through sales in the domestic market.
- Once a product has been developed for the domestic market it may be cheaper to sell a similar type of product in foreign markets, even though the organisation recognises that there may be other profitable opportunities. This is simply due to the cost of adapting or developing a new product.

Thus the range of products which a country exports will be a subset of the products produced and consumed in the domestic market. Similarly, the products which a country imports will closely resemble products it already consumes. Whether these products are imported or produced domestically depends on the relative price of imports compared to domestic goods. This leads to the conclusion – one that appears opposed to 'tradi-

tional' theory – that the closer the overlap between two countries' consumption patterns, the more potential there is for trade to exist.

Linder's theory therefore explains intra-industry trade from the point of view of the demand side. However, it has difficulty explaining the fact that a country such as South Korea exports Christmas articles to the UK when there is little demand for these at home. One suggestion is that foreign importers in the UK, aware of demand at home, seek low-cost suppliers of the product. If this argument is accepted, then the reason for this type of trade taking place is down to cost differentials, not Linder's view.

## INTRA-INDUSTRY TRADE

Greenaway and Miller (1986) have estimated that 60 per cent of world trade is in manufactured goods and half of this is accounted for by intra-industry trade, that is, between the same industries in different countries but where the products are differentiated. If we categorise trade in manufactures as **intra-industry trade**, this would include the trade in bicycles in return for cars. Defining intra-industry trade this way is far too wide. If, on the other hand, we disaggregate manufactured goods too narrowly, such as the trade in Italian shoes, and define these as being different to British shoes, then no intra-industry trade takes place. Therefore, when considering intra-industry trade we mean such things as the trade in cars between countries, that is, France selling Citroëns to Germany while Germany sells Mercedes models to France.

Grubel and Lloyd (1975) saw product differentiation and economies of scale as reasons for intra-industry trade. However, there are other factors that could explain differentiated intra-industry trade, as we shall see later. Intra-industry trade can also exist for homogenous products. For these products three factors are important in intra-industry trade:

- The existence of entrepôts or the re-export of trade. One country may import a product in bulk, break it down into smaller quantities and export this to neighbouring countries. This would indicate the simultaneous importing and exporting of the same commodity.
- Due to seasonality of products, one country might import a commodity at one time of the

year but export that commodity during another period of the year.

■ The cost of transport may mean that it is cheaper for a country to import a commodity from a close neighbour rather than transport the commodity from the far reaches of the country. Similarly, the domestic producer might export this commodity to a near neighbour. This type of trade is quite common for land-locked European countries.

Other suggestions have been put forward for differentiated products. As incomes rise, domestic consumers can overcome some of the barriers to trade that might exist to prevent them from purchasing a slightly different product. For example, suppose that a UK consumer wishes to buy a new Japanese computer since computers made in the UK do not completely satisfy their needs. Although the consumer knows that the type of computer they desire exists in Japan, high transport costs do not make the product attractive to buy. As incomes grow, however, consumers may be able to afford to pay the transport costs and so import a Japanese computer.

The economies-of-scale argument has also been put forward as an explanation of differentiated intra-industry trade. Suppose that trade barriers exist between countries. Domestic suppliers may concentrate on a small range of varieties. Once trade barriers are reduced, sufficient demand may be created for more varieties, and the producer which gets the lead in production may be able to achieve economies of scale by producing a commodity for their own domestic market and the export market which is a different variety to that which had previously existed. Chance may dictate which firm gets the lead in this race. Krugman (1979) suggests that it is possible for a government to undertake a strategic trade policy so that it, rather than another country, can reap the benefits from trade.

If markets are imperfectly competitive due to the economies-of-scale argument, we have moved a long way from the trade theories of absolute and comparative advantage. What now needs to be established is that free trade in an imperfectly competitive world is better that an imperfectly competitive world with high barriers to trade. Krugman (1987) notes that, 'The presence of increasing returns increases rather than reduces the gains from international trade' and 'by creating larger, more competitive markets, trade may reduce the distortions that would have been associated with imperfect competition in a closed economy'. Thus free trade is best even in a second-best world.

## THE IMPORTANCE OF TRADE

International trade continues to increase. Trade in goods from European OECD countries increased from 14.3 per cent of GDP in 1962 to 23.2 per cent of GDP in 1994. However, there is increasing evidence of the Europeanisation of international trade, with trade between European countries taking an ever greater proportion of total European trade. This intra-European trade rose from 61.5 per cent in 1962 to 73.1 per cent in 1994.

Since the 1950s the 'openness' of all European Union member states has increased. However, openness is inversely related to size, with the smaller countries within the EU being more open. This has implications for small and medium-sized enterprises (SMEs) in the various EU countries, where the more open the economy the more likely SMEs are to be involved in export markets.

As Table 21.1 indicates, the main target markets for EU exporters are intra-EU markets, in particular those of neighbouring countries. This is especially true for smaller countries such as the Netherlands. Larger EU members are more likely to possess a greater number of large-scale enterprises which can

**Table 21.1 Destination of exports by EU-12 and EFTA-4, 1992 (%)**

| Country | Intra EU-12 | Extra EU-12 |
| --- | --- | --- |
| Belgium/Luxembourg | 75 | 25 |
| Denmark | 55 | 45 |
| France | 63 | 37 |
| Germany | 54 | 46 |
| Greece | 64 | 36 |
| Ireland | 74 | 25 |
| Italy | 58 | 42 |
| Netherlands | 75 | 24 |
| Portugal | 75 | 24 |
| Spain | 66 | 33 |
| United Kingdom | 55 | 44 |
| EU-12 | 61 | 38 |
| Austria | 64 | 36 |
| Finland | 53 | 47 |
| Norway | 67 | 33 |
| Sweden | 56 | 44 |
| EFTA-4 | 61 | 39 |

*Source*: Eurostat. Reprinted by permission of The Office for Official Publications of the European Communities, Luxembourg.

address global markets. Thus their proportion of intra-EU trade will be lower. Other smaller EU countries, such as Denmark, on the periphery of the EU, have a greater proportion of their trade directed to countries fringing the EU. During recent years countries situated closer to Central and Eastern Europe, such as Germany, have also seen an increasing proportion of their trade directed towards Hungary, Poland and the Czech and Slovak Republics.

Outside the EU it is still true that a high proportion of trade takes place between industrial countries. This has been a feature of trade which has been increasing since the Second World War. The growth and impact of world trade have led to domestic markets being subsumed into regional and now international markets. Thus a key feature of economic activity since the 1960s in particular has been the internationalisation of markets. Ohmae (1991) refers to this as the interlinked economies of the **global triad**: Europe, the US and Japan together with the newly industrialised economies (NICs) of Hong Kong, Singapore and Taiwan. In the twenty-first century this relationship will expand to include mainland China. This interlinking of markets has meant that organisations which saw themselves in monopoly positions serving their own domestic market now find themselves facing new challenges in regional or global markets.

In addition, two other factors which on first inspection appear contradictory have helped to enhance trading opportunities for organisations. First, trade has been liberalised through the various General Agreement on Tariffs and Trade (GATT) talks; and second, there has also been a growth of economic integration through the development of trading blocs.

## GENERAL AGREEMENT ON TARIFFS AND TRADE (GATT)

Because countries want to produce products in which they possess neither a comparative nor an absolute advantage, there used to be a tendency for many developed nations, for a whole variety of reasons, to introduce barriers to trade. GATT was set up in 1946 as an attempt to reduce the main form of barrier to trade, the tariff, which had been gradually ratcheted upwards during the two world wars.

Although GATT may not appear to affect individual countries directly, it has a number of indir-

ect effects. In particular, encouraging countries to lower their trade restrictions with other member countries of GATT enables some organisations to achieve greater cost competitiveness and widens their markets. In addition, it provides companies with consistency, since they realise that they can undertake longer-term trading contracts without these being disrupted on the whim of a country's government.

GATT's charter contains 38 articles with three overriding aims:

- To provide a framework for the conduct of orderly trading relations.
- To encourage free trade and reduce the possibility of countries taking unilateral action against others.
- To reduce tariffs and quantitative restrictions.

GATT agreements embody three main principles: non-discrimination, reciprocity and transparency:

- *Non-discrimination* – Countries should treat all their trading partners in the same way. For example, if the UK places a 10 per cent tariff on Japanese CD players, it should not impose a 20 per cent tariff on similar CD players from South Korea.
- *Reciprocity* – If country A makes a 10 per cent reduction in tariffs on an import from country B, country B should make a corresponding reduction in tariffs on imports from country A.
- *Transparency* – Countries should replace disguised and less quantifiable protectionism with more visible tariffs.

In addition, under GATT rules customs unions and free-trade areas are permitted. It was realised that the existence of such arrangements could discriminate against non-member countries, but this was more likely to be offset by the development of trade within the trading bloc.

While GATT has been successful in reducing tariffs generally, countries have still sought to limit the free flow of trade via other means. In particular, barriers such as quotas and voluntary export restraints, and **non-tariff barriers** such as the use of 'red tape', government legislation and health and safety factors, have increasingly come into play. Thus one of the reasons for the protracted last GATT round of trade talks (1985–93) was because the trade talks sought to address these issues seriously for the first time. A key factor behind the change in emphasis was the fact that the developed nations' economies are becoming more and more skewed to providing services, and the developing nations, which are now a larger and more powerful bloc, have agriculture as a relatively important source of income.

A final conclusion to the Uruguay Round was agreed in December 1993 and involved 28 separate accords devised to extend fair-trade rules to agriculture, services, textiles, intellectual property rights and foreign investment. Tariffs on industrial products were cut by more than one-third and were eliminated entirely in 11 sectors. Many non-tariff barriers were to be converted into tariff barriers and these would subsequently be removed. At the same time, the members of GATT agreed to establish a new trade body, the World Trade Organisation (WTO), which came into operation on January 1995. This body is in charge of administering the new global trade rules agreed in the Uruguay Round and reflects a widespread desire to operate in a fairer and more open multilateral trading system for the benefit and welfare of all countries.

WTO's objectives are to oversee the tariff cuts (averaging 40 per cent) and the reduction of non-tariff measures agreed at the Uruguay Round. It will be the guardian of international trade, examining on a regular basis the trade regimes of individual members. In this respect it will examine proposed trade measures and proposals by countries which could lead to trade conflicts. Members of WTO are also required to supply a range of trade statistics which will be kept on the WTO database.

It is recognised that issues will arise that could lead to trade disputes. Thus WTO provides a whole range of conciliation services and also a dispute mechanism for finding an amicable solution to problems. If trade disputes cannot be solved through bilateral talks, then the dispute will be adjudicated through the WTO dispute settlement 'court'. Here panels of independent experts are established to examine disputes in the light of WTO rules and provide rulings. This tougher, streamlined procedure ensures equal treatment for all trading partners and encourages members to live up to their obligations. The whole programme of dispute settlements is far more streamlined than the old GATT system and will encourage parties to seek independent jurisdiction of their case rather than resorting to individual pieces of domestic legislation. In addition, WTO is a forum in which countries can continuously negotiate exchanges of trade concessions to lower trade barriers further.

# TRADING BLOCS

The GATT rounds were a series of multilateral trading agreements, but these have been paralleled by regional trade agreements. There are a number of ways in which these trading agreements can be formed. They can involve reducing tariffs, quotas and non-tariff barriers between member countries while retaining their own trade barriers with external countries. This is known as a free-trade area, examples of which are EFTA (European Free Trade Association) and ASEAN (Association of South East Asian Nations). It could involve the formation of a customs union, of which the European Union (EU) is a good example; and as a further development of the second type regional trade agreements can attempt to promote much more than commonality in trading arrangements and can cover other rules and regulations, such as common currencies and common defence/social policies. This would be the establishment of a full economic union. The pursuit of a single currency within the EU will see the EU15 become a fully fledged economic union. Table 21.2 indicates the regional trading agreements operating as at January 1995.

From a European perspective the European Union is one of the oldest and best-known trading blocs. Originally this was founded as the European Economic Community (EEC) under the Treaty of Rome signed in 1957, with signatories being Belgium, the Netherlands, Luxembourg, France, West Germany and Italy. In July 1967, as a result of the merger of a variety of treaties, the EEC became the European Community (EC) and this name was used until November 1993, when it became the European Union (EU).

Since the early 1970s membership has expanded. In 1973 Denmark, Eire and the UK joined, while Norway, which had negotiated its membership, voted to stay out following a national referendum. In 1981 Greece joined. Greenland, which had become part of the EC in 1973 when Denmark joined, left in 1982. Membership expanded once again in 1986 with the entry of Spain and Portugal and in 1991 with the reunification of Germany. Enlargement occurred once again in 1995 with the entry of Austria, Finland and Sweden. For the second time the people of Norway voted not to join. The EU's growth and development have seen greater focus on intra-bloc trade, rising from 34.5 per cent in 1957 to over 65 per cent in 1995. There are now plans to include Poland, Estonia, the Czech Republic, Hungary, Slovenia and Cyprus by 2010.

## Table 21.2 Reciprocal regional integration arrangements notified to GATT and in force as of January 1995

*Europe*
- European Community (EC): Austria, Germany, Netherlands, Belgium, Greece, Portugal, Denmark, Ireland, Spain, Finland, Italy, Sweden, France, Luxembourg, United Kingdom
- EC Free Trade Agreements with Estonia, Latvia, Norway, Iceland, Liechtenstein, Switzerland, Israel, Lithuania
- EC Association Agreements with Bulgaria, Hungary, Romania, Cyprus, Malta, Slovak Republic, Czech Republic, Poland, Turkey
- European Free Trade Association (EFTA) Iceland, Norway, Switzerland, Liechtenstein
- EFTA Free Trade Agreements with Bulgaria, Israel, Slovak Republic, Czech Republic, Poland, Turkey, Hungary, Romania.
- Norway Free Trade Agreements with Estonia, Latvia, Lithuania
- Switzerland Free Trade Agreements with Estonia, Latvia, Lithuania
- Czech Republic and Slovak Republic Customs Union
- Central European Free Trade Area: Czech Republic, Poland, Slovak Republic, Hungary
- Czech Republic and Slovenia Free Trade Agreement

*North America*
- Canada-United States Free Trade Agreement (CUFTA)
- North American Free Trade Agreement (NAFTA)

*Latin America and the Caribbean*
- Caribbean Community and Common Market (CARICOM)
- Central American Common Market (CACM)
- Latin American Integration Association (LAIA)
- Andean Pact
- Southern Common Market (MERCOSUR)

*Middle East*
- Economic Cooperation Organization (ECO)
- Gulf Cooperation Council (GCC)

*Asia*
- Australia-New Zealand Closer Economic Relations Trade Agreement (CER)
- Bangkok Agreement
- Common Effective Preferential Scheme for the ASEAN Free Trade Area
- Lao People's Democratic Republic and Thailand Trade Agreement

*Other*
- Israel-United States Free Trade Agreement

*Source*: WTO (1995) *Focus* Newsletter, May–June, No 3, p 9.

During the 1980s and 1990s the United States has become more focused on the issue of regional trading relations. The development of the North American Free Trade Agreement (NAFTA), which took effect on 1 January 1994, after two years of negotiations between the United States, Canada and Mexico, provides the US with a much more liberalised set of trading arrangements between the three countries. For all three countries the reasons for joining NAFTA were largely economic, although their dependence on the newly forged agreement differed. Almost 80 per cent of Canada's exports go to the US, constituting 23 per cent of its GDP. While 70 per cent of Mexico's export go to the US, only 25 per cent of US exports go to Canada and only a small fraction of this to Mexico.

From the US's perspective NAFTA linked it into a more fully coordinated area of economic development. It gave it access to raw materials, such as Mexican crude oil, and to a larger market into which it could sell its cars and electronic goods, and enabled it to switch production to low-cost labour areas which enhances its competitiveness. In addition, the increased demand for its products also leads to domestic job creation. NAFTA also provided regional control over intellectual property rights and patents, as well as being a better bargaining arrangement with other trading blocs over trade arrangements.

For Canada's part, NAFTA was seen as a way of securing the benefits of the 1988 Free Trade Agreement with the US. In particular, Canada also saw Mexico as an important market for its exports.

Mexico has had a very fast level of export growth since the early 1990s and saw membership of NAFTA as a way of furthering its penetration of the North American market and as a safeguard against sometimes hostile US trade policies in the Americas. Mexico has also undertaken a wide variety of policies to liberalise its factor and labour markets and signing up to NAFTA eases foreign direct investment into its country and thereby widens its industrial base.

In the six months after NAFTA was set up US exports to Mexico and Canada increased by 16.7 per cent and 9.6 per cent respectively. Imports into the US from Mexico increased by 20.3 per cent and from Canada they rose by 10.2 per cent. One estimate was that US employment grew by 100 000 jobs in this period. However, for Mexico the adjustment costs were high: by the middle of 1994, unemployment had risen by 3.7 per cent and inflation to 45 per cent. Because interest rates also rose, purchasing power in Mexico fell rapidly. To overcome these difficulties Mexico received a loan of $50 billion on condition that it undertook structural reforms to its economy and pledged its oil revenues as collateral. At the same time Mexico invoked NAFTA emergency clauses to impose special duties on imports in its most sensitive areas. The result of this was a 53 per cent fall in the value of the peso and the $1.5 billion trade surplus in favour of the US during the first eight months of 1994 had turned into a $10 billion deficit during the same period in 1995. This led to a loss of jobs in the US.

At the same time, all three countries are involved with each other concerning disputes on protective duties and subsidies in industries ranging from agriculture to car parts. Because NAFTA does not have a supranational institution to supervise dispute settlement, only a binational panel whose decisions are enforceable by domestic laws, this process is very time consuming. Moreover, the panel's jurisdiction is limited to anti-dumping and countervailing duty proceedings. Thus any major issues are forced to use the GATT or WTO dispute mechanisms.

Overall, NAFTA offers a number of opportunities to all three members, encouraging competition, permitting scale economies and furthering efficiency. Through special duties and taxes there has been a growth in multinational development, particularly in Mexico. However, non-American multinationals can now gain access to all three markets. Perhaps the biggest problem is for Canada. Since US companies do not now need to have branch plants in Canada, a number of these have been closed and there has been a greater focus of US investment towards Mexico.

Given the relative success of NAFTA, Chile has also opened negotiations with the United States in an attempt to gain membership. At present such negotiations are on hold. The idea that by the year 2010 a free-trade area will exist which covers the whole of the Americas appears somewhat optimistic at this stage.

A further ambitious project is also under way to create a free-trade area, the Asia-Pacific Economic Co-operation Forum (APEC) to include the USA, Japan, China, Taiwan, Malaysia, Australia and other countries with Pacific coastlines. At present this is a loose grouping of countries, rather than a trading bloc. Asian-Pacific interdependence has led countries there to adopt a more flexible approach to development and trade. This relies on interregional transfer of industries from early starters to latecomers, which has helped to promote regional trade and enhance political stability, but has not led to economic integration. The Association of South

East Asian Nations (ASEAN), of which Brunei, Indonesia, Malaysia, Singapore, the Philippines and Thailand are members, has not really succeeded in bridging the gap between the economic philosophies of export-promoting countries such as Malaysia and Singapore and the poorer, import-substituting countries around Indonesia. Thus internal tariff walls have remained relatively high. Over the past few decades ASEAN's main concern has been to encourage inward flows of investment rather than concentrating on expanding exports. ASEAN has not always been successful in channelling regional investment from Australia, Japan and the US, nor has it been able to link itself strongly enough with large growth regions such as the Greater South China Economic Zone.

APEC was set up to confront these issues. Although a number of study groups were set up to consider phased trade liberalisation and development as a move towards global, multilateral liberalisation, problems soon emerged. Issues arose over labour regulations in some countries and problems over human rights. Thus establishing a fully liberalised set of trading relations between these countries is still a long way off.

At the same time as the US was becoming more focused on its closer neighbours, the European Union began looking for even closer ties with Eastern European countries and there has even been talk of a free-trade area being set up between the EU and North America. But to what extent do these free-trade areas affect organisations?

Here the concepts of trade creation and trade diversion need to be considered. When a free trade area is set up it encourages trade between member countries (**trade creation**), but countries outside the free-trade area may find it more difficult to sell their products in the free-trade area since they may face external tariffs. Thus external countries' exports may no longer be price competitive and they are forced to seek other markets into which they can sell their products (**trade diversion**). In addition, consideration needs to be given to any differences in the tariff regimes in existence before countries enter a trading bloc. If one country has imposed high tariffs on another before any trading agreement, then after the establishment of the free-trade area and the removal of tariffs, the country with the high-tariff regime will lose tax revenue and the organisations in the lower-tariff country will gain from lower prices in their export markets.

◆ **CASE STUDY 21.1**

## Move towards NAFTA raises fears for Caricom

**FT**

Plans by Jamaica and Trinidad and Tobago to seek membership of the North American Free Trade Agreement (NAFTA) have raised questions about the future of the Caribbean Community (Caricom) of which both countries are members . . .

However, a recent report by the Commonwealth Secretariat on the impact of NAFTA on Caricom says if Caribbean states remain outside the North American trade bloc, their interests will be adversely affected by the policies of NAFTA members, as well as by trade and investment diversion.

The report supports the arguments of economists, trade ministers and the regions' lobbyists in Washington that a regional approach to NAFTA would be better received by the US, Canada and Mexico than separate discussions with several small countries . . .

'If the Caribbean countries do not become members of NAFTA, they will be denied tariff and non-tariff free access to the regional bloc as it expands and deepens,' according to the report . . .

While Jamaica and Trinidad and Tobago have sought to strengthen their cases by signing bilateral investment treaties and intellectual property rights accords with the US, smaller Caricom countries are likely to balk at suggestions that they should deregulate their trade and open their markets. This would destroy fledgling industries, cut government revenues and increase unemployment, say some officials.

However, the Commonwealth Secretariat's report suggests that important economic sectors in Caricom will suffer unless there is some accommodation with NAFTA. Arrangements for Mexico to increase sugar exports to the US could affect Caribbean exporters with US quotas. Also, the Caribbean's growing and increasingly important apparel industry will suffer from trade diversion to Mexico . . .

The report highlights the growing tendency towards the division of the world into large trading blocs. Joining NAFTA would give the Caribbean countries access to such a bloc.

*Source: Financial Times,* 21 June 1995. Reprinted with permission.

---

It has been argued that for some countries and, therefore, for some organisations, the development of trading blocs may lead to their being barred from traditional markets. However, the development of trading blocs might lead to significant reductions in trade barriers between member countries and the lower barriers may then be transmitted throughout the world in a kind of domino effect. The result of this is that many countries outside the trading bloc could benefit.

---

◆ **Exercise 21.1**

What benefits and losses are expected to arise through developing closer ties between Caricom and NAFTA?

---

*Comment on the case study*

In the case of Caricom, some familiar arguments are raised about membership of NAFTA. The case also notes the long-term development and domination of world trade by trading blocs and the danger of being excluded from such blocs. Although damaging to small economies, trading blocs may enhance their position in the long run through the strength of the bloc to negotiate on

members' behalf with third parties or with other trading blocs.

## THE GLOBAL TRIAD

The growth in the number and significance of trading blocs – between 1947 and 1994, a total of 108 regional agreements were notified to GATT – has led to questions regarding whether there is complementarily between regional integration and the multilateral trading system. A report to GATT (*WTO Focus,* May–June 1995) concluded that the co-existence of regional integration agreements and the world trading system has been at least satisfactory, if not broadly positive. However, this is not a view shared by everyone. Ohmae (1985) has suggested that the world has become dominated by three major trading markets, Japan and the newly industrialised countries (NICs) of South-East Asia, Europe and the European Free Trade Association (EFTA) countries, and North America (US and Canada). These three trading blocs account for over 60 per cent of world trade. However, the Europeans have often felt that one of the advantages that US companies have in their trading bloc is freedom of movement and economies of scale. Moreover, as Japanese companies improved their overall position in the world compared to other regions, there has been increased pressure by some trading blocs both to further reduce the barriers that exist within the blocs – this was one of the reasons for the development of the Single European Market (SEM) – and for regions or blocs to strengthen their external barriers to organisations.

One response to this growing threat is for multinational enterprises to have operations in all three triad regions. This strategy has a number of advantages for organisations:

- Organisations avoid surprises from foreign organisations and/or from domestic competitors by forming alliances with foreign companies.
- By knowing the basic needs of the triad consumers, the multinational can develop a universal product. In this way it can tailor its basic product to fit the needs of local tastes, for example Ford and the Mondeo, the company's first attempt at a truly global car.
- With a presence in all three regions the company can get its products to the market in a very short space of time.
- If a local competitor develops a new product which has great potential, then a company which is involved in all three regions will be able to copy it and deprive the developer of the opportunity for sales in the other two markets.

This need to be in all three trading blocs has led to a growth in foreign direct investment (FDI). Approximately 98 per cent of all FDI flows are within triad member regions. Thus the development of the global triad has resulted in a greater shift of FDI to the triad members. Some countries have sought to control this through the use of local-content rules. For example, Japanese cars must have at least 90 per cent of their parts manufactured in EU member states. However, not all countries have tried to control FDI and some countries, such as the UK, have actively encouraged the process. In fact, over 30 per cent of Japanese FDI has come to the UK. The degree to which multinationals will continue to grow in importance within the triad depends very much on the relationships between triad members. If there is greater concentration on the relationship between members, agreements may bar non-triad members. For less developed countries a way forward would be to seek agreements with at least one of the triad regions. For the regions themselves there may be

moves to widen their regional bases. The future looks interesting for the WTO and its relationship with the changing economic order.

# DEREGULATION AND INTERNATIONAL BUSINESS

During the 1930s and 1940s and through to the 1960s many governments followed a path of increased state ownership or regulation of specific sectors with their economies. This process was undertaken because governments believed that there was market failure, that is, the 'correct' amount of the product would not arrive on the market if left to market forces. In addition, there was a view that certain areas of the economy should by their very nature be in state ownership and this was one way in which the benefits of economic performance could be shared out more equally between the various stakeholders.

By the late 1970s, this view of state ownership was to change. In the UK, the Conservative administration under Margaret Thatcher believed that state ownership was in itself inefficient and that the market mechanism should be allowed to prevail in many areas. Thus in the early 1980s the process of privatisation began in the UK. This process is discussed in more detail in Chapter 22.

However, selling off state enterprises to the private sector, a feature that has become a worldwide phenomenon, is only one method by which state enterprises can feel the full effect of private-sector forces. One alternative approach is **deregulation**. Deregulation is a method by which state involvement in an industry can be reduced, allowing other companies to compete with either a state or private monopoly that currently provides a particular good or service. Deregulation also has the effect of reducing differences between national regulatory systems, and thus previously regulated national markets become more international, deregulated ones. Therefore, how do deregulation and privatisation affect the globalisation of business activities?

The most notable of the deregulations that took place in the UK was that affecting the telecoms market. In 1981 British Telecom's monopoly of the telecommunications market in the UK was ended. The result was the establishment of a number of small new entrants into the telecoms market, but these organisations have slowly grown over the past 16 years gradually to threaten British

Telecom's dominant position. A number of the new entrants have been US-owned companies. Moreover, the response by British Telecom to the growing threat of competition was to seek products which provided greater variety at a lower cost, e.g. it offered a much wider variety of telephones, many of which were made outside the UK.

Liberalisation in continental Europe has been slower to take place. However, a number of countries have had to respond to changes that have come into being through the deregulation principles embodied in the Single European Act (SEA) and to the problems of losing business to countries which had deregulated earlier.

One noticeable fact in the EU during the 1980s was the general slowdown in its economic growth and one approach to improving the overall growth performances of the member states was through the development of the Single European Market (SEM). Apart from reducing various barriers to trade and encouraging the free movement of labour, the Single European Act (SEA) freed capital markets within Europe. The Banking Coordination Directive, adopted in 1989 and implemented in January 1993, permitted any banking organisation established in one member state to open operations in another member state. In addition, the directive provided for reciprocal access to the single market for institutions from non-EU countries.

In the area of telecommunications, the EU's aim is to liberalise the provision of telecommunications services and technical equipment both within and between member states. For some countries, such as the UK and France, this has been relatively easy since this sector has been privatised. In other countries the state is still in control of telecommunications. However, by 1997, the whole of this sector is expected to be deregulated.

Japan has also not been immune from the move to deregulate markets. In the main this has been in the sectors described elsewhere and above. Thus Japan has attempted to liberalise its financial and telecommunications sectors. Foreign banks have made significant inroads into the Japanese banking sector, and as a result of deregulation there has been increased penetration of the Japanese market by foreign firms. The deregulation of the telecoms sector in 1985 allowed both new organisations and foreign companies to enter the market, which up to then had been controlled monopolistically by Nippon Telephone and Telegraph.

Deregulation has therefore been important for international organisations which have been able to penetrate previously protected markets and has had important implications for the erstwhile protected monopoly providers, which have had to respond by improving efficiency.

◆ CASE STUDY 21.2

## Telecom Eireann's prospects of forming an international strategic alliance  FT

Telecom Eireann, the state-owned telecommunications monolith, is due shortly to start negotiations in earnest on the formation of a strategic alliance with one of a number of international telecommunications companies . . . These developments are inevitable because of the opening up of the Irish telecommunications market to competition, as required by the European Union.

Although the republic can avail itself of the option to postpone deregulation in 1998, the market must be opened up by 2003 at the latest. The government may decide to bite the bullet and open up the Irish market ahead of 1998, as other EU countries have done.

At the moment, Telecom competes only with other providers of international services and in a few other areas. It has no competitors in the domestic market, and operates the only mobile phone system.

However, even in these limited areas it is feeling the pressure. A number of high profile companies have shifted over to other providers for their international requirements. [It has been estimated that] £1.2bn will have to be invested in Telecom over the next five years in order to make sure Ireland's competitiveness is maintained.

[If the government cannot find a partner it] will be left with an inefficient, debt-laden state telecommunications company that is being hammered in the profitable sectors of its business by 'cherry picking' international giants.

Companies that have expressed an initial interest in a strategic alliance include BT, Cable and Wireless, AT&T, Telia of Sweden and PTT Netherlands.

*Source: Financial Times, 26 May 1995. Reprinted with permission.*

> **◆ Exercise 21.2**
>
> What factors lie behind the need to deregulate the telecoms market in the Republic of Ireland?

### Comment on the case study

Without the need to deregulate, the telecommunications market would remain, on the whole, as a state monopoly. This would prevent new organisations entering the market in a big way. This in itself may not be a problem for the Irish telecommunications industry if Telecom Eireann operated efficiently and had sufficient resources to carry out its investment programme. However, in a globalised environment, the quality of telecommunications can give organisations a competitive advantage, particularly in the area of telesales. Deregulation may therefore encourage new organisations to set up in a country, improve the competitive position of existing organisations and provide enhanced job opportunities.

## THE IMPACT OF TECHNOLOGY ON GLOBALISATION

Technology can affect international business in a number of ways. It allows countries/companies to obtain comparative advantages in products. This means that they are the most efficient producers of a commodity through lower costs, and on the back of these cost advantages previously unprofitable markets are now worth considering. As a result, organisations may export to new markets or expand into these markets via indigenous growth or through mergers/takeovers/joint ventures. In addition, however, technology may provide organisations with products which are completely new and this allows them to expand into new external markets. Technology also allows markets to be interconnected. Product markets which were once believed to be separate are now joined together and competition is increased.

Posner (1961), in his technological gap theory, suggested that innovation and imitation are particularly important for exports. Having a new product gives an organisation a comparative advantage and allows it access into foreign markets. The new product is soon imitated by rivals and the comparative advantage is eroded. Thus the organisation will search for another new product and so a new cycle of innovation and imitation begins. Vernon (1970) further developed the work by Posner in terms of the product lifecycle; see Figure 21.1.

In the new product stage the product is produced, marketed and tested in the domestic market. In the mature stage, the product gradually becomes standardised and mass production begins to take place. At this stage the product would be marketed internationally and producers will look for similar markets in other similar countries. As exports increase, producers will start to look at the possibility of locating nearer, or in, these markets. The final stage is one of more advanced standardisation. Factors such as production and location costs are more important in location decisions and it is more likely that the product will be made in other countries and imported into the original producing country. Gradually production in, and export from, the original market ceases and production is shifted elsewhere.

An example of Vernon's theory can be seen in the market for colour TV receivers. The market began in 1954 in the US and in the early years it was dominated by domestic producers. In 1967 imports were 6 per cent of the market, but only three years later these amounted to 19 per cent (the great majority of which were from Japan). Later, as the technology spread to other countries, imports from Taiwan and South Korea began to challenge Japanese imports, which subsequently fell. A similar scenario could also be recognised within the UK, but here the domestic producers were gradually crowded out of the market, and although the UK is now a net exporter of televisions none of the organisations producing them in the UK is domestically owned.

However, the usefulness of Vernon's theory has been questioned. The role and development of multinational companies has meant that products are not tested solely in the domestic market, but are able to be brought to a range of markets almost simultaneously. Thus the theory may have more relevance for small and medium-sized enterprises.

The activity of multinationals can also lead to technological changes that affect host economy organisations and make it possible for them to compete in other external markets. For example, the establishment of Japanese car manufacturers in the UK has resulted in car component suppliers providing products of a much higher quality. The result has been to create a strong positive externality, improving the international competitiveness of the UK car-supply industry and improving the quality of these suppliers for domestic car producers.

**Figure 21.1  Phases in the product lifecycle and changes in production location**

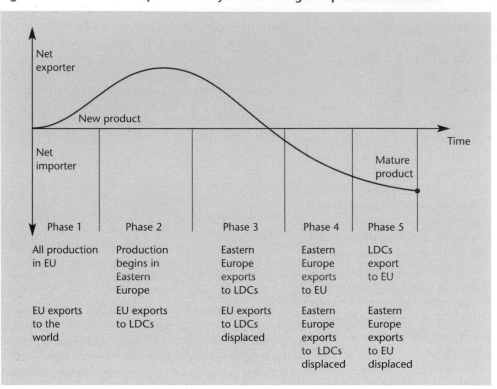

This relates to Vernon's product lifecycle. The EU begins production and exports to the rest of the world (phase 1). As the EU market matures, production starts in Eastern Europe, which begins to replace exports from the EU (phase 2). Eastern European countries begin to export to LDCs, displacing EU exports to LDCs (phase 3). Eastern European companies begin to export to the EU while the LDCs begin production, displacing imports from Eastern Europe (phase 4). As technology gradually spreads, the LDCs become the low-cost producers and export to the EU.

This improved quality specification now enhances the performance of UK car makers in external markets.

However, there are also positive indirect **demonstration effects** to consider which may encourage technological transfer. Here the domestic company, the less efficient organisation, attempts to imitate the superior processes and organisational advantages of the foreign company. This process of technological transfer may be diluted, however, by a multinational company keeping under control its 'best' levels of technology, and where a foreign company moving into a host economy retains its links with previous suppliers rather than setting up new arrangements with the host economy's suppliers.

In sectors such as pharmaceuticals, semiconductors and telecommunications, R&D costs are increasing rapidly while at the same time product lifecycles are shrinking. Since often national markets are too small to support R&D costs, companies

have been forced to expand internationally to support their technological developments.

In terms of technological change, breakthroughs in basic science or the discovery of new innovations open large new markets. These new markets attract new investments and the entry of established and new companies. For example, in the semiconductor industry the breakthrough in logic and memory devices caused the rapid development of new applications to computers, telecommunications and other markets. These breakthroughs acted as structural breaks in the market and led to the development of new companies, the expansion of incumbent companies and the decline of others.

Technological developments have also played an important part in linking and integrating markets while leading to increased heterogeneity and market fragmentation. Technology also heightens the pace of competition. A company with a technological lead can no longer expect to maintain this over a competitor in introducing a new product. It is quite likely that fast followers may be able to leapfrog their competitors as technology evolves, introducing a superior product incorporating the latest technology.

Technological advances in communications have also revolutionised business operations, permitting then to be managed on a wider geographical range. Global information systems have rapidly improved and expanded the coordination of global production and distribution logistics. Similarly, advances in communications enable the organisa-

tion to monitor changes in customer demand and in competitors' behaviour, allowing a more rapid adaptation and response. Organisations have therefore become increasingly aware of potential opportunities as well as alternative production and distribution techniques, and of technology and equipment that their competitors are using elsewhere in the world. For example, the expansion of satellite TV means that large areas of the world are now exposed to Western and European products and this therefore increases market penetration and the growth of globalised companies.

◆ CASE STUDY 21.3

## Advances in information technology are bringing entire industrial sectors into financial services

**FT**

The fate of many financial institutions may well depend on the successful deployment of data processing and telecom systems. From electronic trading rooms and risk management systems to automatic teller machines and multimedia kiosks, the future of the global financial services industry is extricably linked with information technology . . .

Indeed, the fate of many financial institutions, as they gear up to face new competition, both from within the financial services industry and from outside, may well depend on the successful deployment of data processing and telecommunications software.

The intensification of competition reflects several factors including the deregulation of the industry which has attracted new entrants, including overseas-based institutions and non-banks. Ironically, it is technology which has helped make this challenge possible . . .

In the US companies such as Ford, General Motors and Shell Oil could come to dominate the credit card business. [Banks therefore,] will have to demand ever more of their IT resource if they are to keep pace with, if not see off, this new competition . . .

[It is seen to be a principal business driver, whether core business executives like it or not.] The key shift

facing bankers is the move from transaction to relationship banking – [banks need to] start dealing with customers as individuals.

There is little doubt the recent rapid changes in the financial services sector present both risks and opportunities . . . Globalisation and the parallel and massive trends of securitisation which began during the mid-1980s are still in force. The emergence of so-called new financial instruments, such as derivatives, have offered to the larger and international-orientated banks a new niche and playground for high risk–high reward margin trading opportunities.

Used effectively, IT can help financial institutions including banks, insurance companies and equity traders develop new products, respond quickly to market changes and improve the quality of customer service . . .

Breakthroughs in telecoms, such as asynchronous transfer mode and other high speed technologies, are enabling banks to interact with customers in a variety of locations and different times – the capacity to transmit integrated data, video, voice, and image files has opened up a new world of customer-contact strategies.

*Source: Financial Times,* 5 July 1995. Reprinted with permission.

---

◆ **Exercise 21.3**

1  How has technology changed the competitive markets for financial institutions?

2  How can technology make financial institutions more customer focused?

*Comment on the case study*

Finance is only one of many sectors that have had to respond to the changes in the level of technology. IT provides a wealth of information which financial institutions previously could not obtain. This allows them to focus better on customers. However, this information is available to other companies in other sectors too and enables them to both reach and move into markets with which they were not normally associated. Technology also provides a global network, enabling financial institutions to target customers worldwide. Because of competition raised through improvements in technology, financial institutions have had to become more global. In particular, they have been involved in a number of global joint ventures and the integrated financial institution is likely to become pre-eminent.

## WHY DO COMPANIES BECOME MULTINATIONALS?

The neoclassical theory of factor location predicts that productive capital will move towards capital-scarce centres. Yet multinational growth has mainly been into capital-rich countries. Nevertheless, the discussion of multinational behaviour brings together a number of elements of economic theory. Because **multinationals** exist in more than one country the theory of international trade is relevant. Market structure analysis is important, since multinationals may face different competitive conditions in each market. Furthermore, the multinational, because it coordinates transactions across national borders, raises the question of internationalisation or markets versus hierarchies. In addition, there are other macroeconomic factors which may encourage multinational activity to take place:

- The increase in world trade and the opening up of new markets.
- The development and impact of new technologies.
- The development of trading blocs with common external tariffs.

However, there may be specific advantages that the organisation possesses which encourage it to become a multinational. **Ownership-specific advantages** (OSAs) refer to the types of knowledge and privileges which an organisation possesses but which are not available to its competitors. These arise because of imperfections in commodity markets, such as product differentiation, collusion and special marketing skills. In addition, imperfections in factor markets, such as special managerial skills, ease of access to capital, technology protected by patents, can also provide OSAs. Imperfect markets may also arise from government policies regarding taxes, interest rates and exchange rates.

**Location-specific advantages** (LSAs) refer to certain advantages which the organisation possesses because it locates its production activities in a particular area. These would include access to raw materials or minerals; imperfections in the labour market which encourage firms to locate to low-cost labour areas – an example of this being electronics component firms using South-East Asian locations for assembly production; and trade barriers which provide an incentive for the organisation to set up within the trading area.

**Internalisation-specific advantages** (ISAs) occur when international market imperfections render market solutions too costly. Thus it is because of transaction costs that multinational activity arises; *see* Chapter 17.

Hymer (1976) was one of the first authors who brought together both LSAs and OSAs as an explanation of multinational activity. He saw the multinational as a monopolist/oligopolist in product markets, investing in foreign enterprises as a means to eliminate competition. The multinational is able to compete in a foreign market because it possesses an advantage over the domestic organisations. The multinational chooses to be involved in foreign markets because of tariff barriers and transport costs. Establishing franchising arrangements is an alternative approach, but it has its costs since the franchisee is a potential competitor and because the franchiser loses some control over the product. Hymer's approach is useful in explaining defensive foreign investment, in that if the company does not expand into a foreign market its major competitor may do so.

Another theory relating to multinational growth is that of Vernon (1966), discussed earlier. This is related to the lifecycle of a product. However, the weakness with this approach is that multinationals are capable of developing, maturing and standardising products almost simultaneously.

A further interpretation of the internalisation process of multinational behaviour can be seen in work by Buckley and Casson (1985). The incentive to internalise depends on the relationship between four groups of factors:

- Industry-specific factors, for example economies of scale, external market structure etc.
- Region-specific factors, for example geographical distance and cultural distance.
- Nation-specific factors, for example political and fiscal conditions.
- Firm-specific factors, for example management expertise.

An additional theory which makes use of the concept of internalisation is the **theory of appropriability**. Once an organisation develops a product or has particular management expertise that gives it advantages in the market, the best way of appropriating the potential gains from this advantage is to keep control and ownership of the advantage itself. Partners are seen as potential competitors and therefore sharing knowledge with them is risky. This theory explains, perhaps, why there is a strong presence of high-technology industries among multinationals.

Dunning's (1981, 1992) eclectic theory attempted to integrate the view expressed by Hymer with the process of internalisation, suggesting that all three types of advantages, LSAs, OSAs and ISAs, are required for multinationals to exist. However, are all three conditions necessary? The answer to this question appears to be no. LSAs and ISAs appear to be sufficient to explain multinational behaviour by themselves, thus rendering OSAs redundant. In fact, some people claim that the concept of internalisation alone is sufficient for multinational activity to take place.

The theory of the **international division of labour** developed by Frobel *et al* (1980) can also be used to explain multinational activities. It is acknowledged that organisations in their domestic markets can reduce their production costs by minimising their labour input costs, and Frobel similarly argues that in the pursuit of global profits the multinational will search for cheap, controllable labour on a global scale. In this respect production will be relocated to low-cost areas such as Eastern Europe and the Third World as a means to minimise production costs.

There are a number of conditions which are necessary for the international division of labour to take place according to this theory:

■ There need to have been developments in transport and communication technology.
■ Technology must be able to break production down into specific tasks which could then utilise unskilled labour.
■ Unskilled labour needs to be available in the global economy.

If the international division of labour theory is to be believed, jobs should be continually moved by multinational organisations from high-cost countries to low-cost areas. However, such a process does not take account of improvements in technology and different ways of working in the developed economies which have led to some of the jobs being transferred back to industrialised countries, nor does it take account of the role of governments.

Domestic governments in the industrial world may use incentives to discourage higher-cost jobs from leaving their economies, and some developed countries may take a dim view of foreign-owned sweatshop labour. Nonetheless, the advantage of this theory is that it signals the ways in which the organisation and structure of the global political economy can and do affect the decisions and strategies of individual organisations.

Many economists view internalisation as a prime factor behind multinational activity. Coase (1937) suggested that any transactions subject to market costs would eventually be internalised – that is, brought under one administrative head to eliminate the market.

The nature of the market failure which gives rise to multinational activity depends on the ownership advantage whose sale is impeded, but examples would include the costs of negotiation, opportunism, uncertainty and the need for control.

Faced with imperfect external markets, firms may choose to internalise by using backward and forward integration. For example, suppose that an organisation develops a new product or process. Where there are time lags, uncertainty and high investment expenditure, and where success may depend on coordination, the rapid exchange of information and detailed planning, some potential advantage for the organisation may be lost. Internalisation, that is, reductions in transaction costs, may increase the efficiency with which each of these is done. Where this internalisation involves operations across national boundaries, a multinational may be created.

Barriers to trade may also provide some explanation of MNE (multinational enterprise) activity. If transport costs are sufficiently high, they may make the expansion of production in domestic plants and the export of that increased production less profitable than production within the putative importing country. In some respect problems with the cost of transport form a 'natural' barrier. The same cannot be said of tariffs, import quotas and the like. The imposition of such barriers to trade may as a consequence increase MNE activity. This is because of a number of factors. Import barriers raise the price of the good within the protected market, thereby leading to increased profits for those organisations which produce within the protected market. Import barriers reduce the exports of organisations in other countries and these may be provoked to invest in the protected country as a way of retaining market share. It has been suggested

503

that the inward investment of Japanese car producers into both the US and the UK is an example of this. However, it is possible that increased barriers to trade actually lead to a reduction in MNE activity. For example, suppose that protection is given to industries producing intermediate products to such an extent that the effective protection for those producing final products is reduced: this will discourage MNE activity in the latter.

Much of the current theory of the MNE has developed independently of orthodox trade theory. Attempts to develop a theory of MNE behaviour by adding capital movements on to the Heckscher-Ohlin theory have failed, since there are no transaction costs in the Heckscher-Ohlin model. However, Casson (1979) notes that it is possible to integrate internalisation theory with the Heckscher-Ohlin model if we consider the relative and not the absolute costs of transacting. If the cheapest method of transacting is always a costless one, the Heckscher-Ohlin model approach to the location of production remains valid. However, the approach outlined above still runs into the problems with the basic assumption of the Heckscher-Ohlin model.

Suppose that the Heckscher-Ohlin model is modified to allow for technology gaps. Then the export of technology through foreign direct investment substitutes for the export of high-technology products, as occurs in the maturing product phase of the product lifecycle; *see* Vernon (1966). Thus the modified Heckscher-Ohlin model can shed light on the global implications of import-substituting high-technology investment.

The main issues with attempting to synthesise transaction cost theory and neoclassical theory is still that too much is conceded to the neoclassical position. The problem occurs because neoclassical theory focuses on markets and on the functional specification that markets permit: the organisation is really of no intrinsic interest.

**Structural market distortions** are also relevant to MNE behaviour. These may occur for a number of reasons. They can arise due to the anti-competitive nature of participants in the market, or by governments intervening in the market to achieve objectives which the market is unable to achieve. The common feature of many of these structural market distortions is that they confer some degree of monopoly power on the sellers of factor or intermediate products. The origin of this power may be in a reduced number of sellers, some barriers to market contestability, or the ability of the seller to differentiate its product from that of its competitors. The power may lead to prices being above competitive market levels, reductions in the quality of the output or increased variability of output, and increased negotiation costs over wages or working conditions. Thus these structural imperfections can lead to an MNE being formed to reduce the uncertainties in supply, but at the same time the MNE may be able to wield sufficient market power of its own to enable it to prevent the entry of new organisations into its market and to charge a price above the competitive level.

The choice between licensing and the organisation becoming international may be related to the nature of the advantage. Where this is a patent, the advantage is easier to identify. However, in some cases the organisation might not know what its competitive advantage is. Also it may be too expensive to transfer the advantage outside the originating organisations or local entrepreneurs may not have sufficient know-how.

Porter (1985) notes that, where there is uncertainty about whether giving information to a competitor might provide it with an advantage in the future, the organisation may expand abroad itself. In other words, where transactions between two organisations are made more difficult by distance, culture, politics and the legal framework, the organisation itself may choose to become international. Casson (1982) notes yet another feature of multinational behaviour. If buyers are internationally mobile, they will prefer to buy from a single market-maker rather than a different organisation in each country – so long as the market-maker offers a good-quality product in each location. The incentive to become a multinational is, therefore, enhanced.

The process by which multinationals are formed, that is, the reasons for becoming a horizontal multinational or a vertically oriented company, can vary. In the case of horizontal multinationals, the internationalisation process may be motivated by the development of new markets and greater sales. In this respect, it would be expected that market-oriented multinationals would have grown horizontally into the developed economies of the richest industrial nations such as the US, Japan, Germany, France, Italy and the UK. During the twenty-first century, however, it is highly likely that these types of multinationals will be increasingly drawn to China, India and the South-East Asian economies.

In the case of vertical integration by multinationals, the driving force has been to secure natural resources at as low a price as possible, the approach adopted by a number of the major oil companies such as Exxon and BP. Forward vertical integration has also been a motivating factor, as multinationals have sought to keep the quality of their products high and tap into cheaper assembly facilities with high-quality labour. This has been a process operated by a number of manufacturing companies. It was the fear that the UK would fall into this type of position that has led to the EU adopting local-content rules for products made by foreign multinationals in the EU.

Technology must also play its part in the expansion of multinational activity. This includes improved communications such as cheaper air travel, growth of the Internet, improved satellite and fax facilities; the globalisation of consumer markets, enhanced by television, music and video, which makes it easier for organisations to penetrate foreign markets; and new organisational technologies, such as the growth of divisional organisational structures based on product or geographical divisions which make managing organisations more practical.

Although this section has concentrated on more micro reasons for the organisation wishing to internationalise, within Europe one feature has intensified multinational activity: the Single European Market. The Single European Act (SEA) sought to reduce barriers between the various member states of the EU, particularly non-tariff barriers to trade. Within the EU member states previously protected markets therefore became less protected, leading to an increase in multinational activity between the member countries. However, some non-EU countries felt that the SEA had been set up to exclude

them from the EU market – the fortress Europe view. As a consequence of this, Japanese, American and South-East Asian multinationals sought to gain a foothold in Europe, and the whole SEA triggered off a massive merger/takeover boom within Europe, as shown in Table 21.3

It is important to recognise that the theory of MNEs seeks to explain the existence and growth of MNEs, while the theory of the activities of MNEs aims to identify and evaluate the determinants of these organisations' foreign-owned production. Although the areas are similar, the former is more micro based and concentrates on the reasons for the existence of MNEs, while the latter is more oriented towards explaining the factors influencing the ability and willingness of organisations or countries to engage in foreign value-added activities. Thus, as Dunning (1992) notes, 'No one model of the MNE is likely to be adequate.'

## THE IMPACT OF MULTINATIONALS ON THE HOST ECONOMY

The impact of MNEs on economies can be viewed in terms of their individual behaviour in markets and their effects on the macroeconomic environment in which they exist.

In the area of pricing in particular, MNEs can have an important impact. Organisations which operate transnationally may be able to increase their profits by taking advantage of differences in tax rates among countries by using transfer prices. The concept of transfer prices has already been

**Table 21.3  Cross-border acquisitions of EU companies, £ million**

| Bidder country | 1989 value | 1990 value | 1991 value | 1992 value | 1993 value |
|---|---|---|---|---|---|
| US | 10 040 | 2 257 | 2 755 | 3 592 | 3 094 |
| UK | 2 651 | 4 894 | 1 536 | 4 435 | 2 676 |
| Germany | 3 152 | 1 085 | 1 635 | 1 061 | 1 693 |
| France | 5 470 | 6 270 | 3 328 | 3 658 | 1 528 |
| Sweden | 680 | 6 486 | 683 | 986 | 956 |
| Switzerland | 1 337 | 516 | 902 | 350 | 620 |
| Netherlands | 458 | 603 | 1 217 | 3 273 | 406 |
| Italy | 762 | 886 | 1 153 | 2 207 | 400 |
| Luxembourg | n/a | 114 | 1 007 | 367 | 185 |
| Japan | 515 | 1 768 | 559 | 229 | 83 |
| Others | 4 787 | 9 986 | 4 539 | 8 949 | 3 785 |
| Total | 29 816 | 34 865 | 19 314 | 29 107 | 15 426 |

*Source*: Peat Marwick

considered in Chapter 9, but we can develop the points further in the context of MNE activity. Transfer prices are those that the various divisions of an MNE charge each other, for example the price that Ford UK charges Ford Italy for its cylinder heads. Because tax regimes differ between countries, Ford would prefer to declare as much of its profits as possible in the country with the lower tax level. Suppose that company tax rates are lower in Italy than in the UK. Ford could lower its tax bill by declaring more of its tax in Italy, through increasing the transfer price on cylinder heads imported into the UK. The Italian subsidiary will now obtain higher profits, since each cylinder head is sold at a higher price, and the UK branch of Ford will declare lower profits, since its costs of each cylinder head have increased. Such behaviour can undermine the ability of governments to fashion their own tax systems, particularly those in developing countries. Of course, what may constrain Ford from doing this is the price it may charge outside customers for cylinder heads. But suppose that there is no external market or that the transfer price concerns a licensing fee for a patent whose true value can only be approximated.

Abuse of transfer pricing, whether real or imagined, has been one of the major criticisms of MNEs and has led to extensive friction with national governments. It can be argued that there is little incentive for organisations to use transfer pricing, since using false prices can cause managers in the different parts of the corporation to make inefficient decisions. Moreover, shifting profits from one company to another makes it difficult to analyse individual managers' performance.

The entry of an MNE into an economy can also alter the competitive nature of the market. It could leave the MNE in a dominant position, the result of which is that a competitive price regime is replaced by one in which there is a market leader, which sets a price above the competitive level, or can lead to the establishment of oligopolistic pricing arrangements with other domestic organisations. It is possible that the MNE which has subsidiaries in other countries also indulges in 'non-export' activities to the markets in which its other subsidiaries exist, thus setting itself up in a monopolistic position in a number of external markets. In this way the MNE can also indulge in discriminatory pricing methods; see Chapter 9.

On a macroeconomic level the impact of multinationals on the host economy may well differ, depending on the size of the host economy in GDP terms relative to the size of the multinational and whether the host country is a developed or developing one. The case in favour of multinationals is really a development of the case in favour of free trade. If multinationals are able to move capital around the globe to the areas in which they will get the best return, then global economic welfare will increase. Therefore German multinationals will earn higher returns abroad than they would have done if they had invested in Germany; and workers in foreign multinationals in Germany will be more productive than they otherwise would have been and earn higher salaries. There is some evidence, particularly in relation to multinationals in the UK, to show that they are 10 per cent more productive and earn 20 per cent more than their contemporaries in similar, domestic organisations. In general, the impact on the host economy is believed to relate to the following.

## Filling the savings, foreign exchange and revenue gaps

One of the most often cited positive contributions of MNE activity is that foreign private investment is a way of filling the gaps between domestically available supplies of savings, foreign exchange, government revenue and human capital skills, and the desired level of these resources required to achieve growth and development targets. In addition, the MNE not only brings with it foreign exchange which can reduce balance of payments problems, but can also provide a net positive flow of export earnings. However, some less developed countries (LDCs) have found that allowing MNEs to establish subsidiaries behind protective tariff and quota walls leads to a net worsening of both the current and capital account balances. This is due to the importation of capital equipment and intermediate products, perhaps at inflated prices, and the outflow of foreign exchange through repatriated profits, management fees, royalty payments and interest on private loans.

The tax revenue gap can be reduced by taxing MNE profits, although, as we have seen, transfer price practices may reduce the level of profits in the host economy.

## Transfer of resources and technology

The multinational may cause an inflow of capital and technology into the host economy. An inflow of capital leads to increased resources for the host economy as domestic savings can be mobilised. In LDCs this may stimulate aid from the multinational's home economy in support of its trading activities. Multinationals may raise finance locally, or reinvest the profits made by local subsidiaries, and this may crowd out funds for local organisations. From the host's perspective there may still be advantages if the multinational is a more efficient user of capital resources than domestic organisations. A problem may arise if the multinational is a less efficient user of these resources.

There may be a transference of managerial skills, patents and product designs to the host economy. But in the case of technology, is the level appropriate for the developing nation? Multinationals have been criticised for not exporting the 'best' technology abroad, but keeping this at home to be used as a further competitive advantage. Perhaps this is an unfair criticism, since an LDC may prefer to have exported to it a more labour-intensive technique. If multinationals do not do this then they are criticised for not accommodating the wishes of the host economy. For the more developed economy a multinational may bring new technologies and management techniques which may disperse through the host economy. For example, the influx of Japanese multinationals into the UK has resulted in closer links with suppliers for many organisations, improvements in quality, and changes in industrial relations through single- or no-union agreements. The level of technology transfer is maximised where there are direct links between multinationals and suppliers, as has been the case between Nissan, Toyota and Sony in the UK.

Managerial skills may allow managers in a multinational to take a global perspective through internalised flows of knowledge and thereby increase the effectiveness of indigenous managers. Running counter to this argument is the fact that multinationals may use managers trained in the home economy who may not mix with the host economy managers. Nonetheless, the changes that they bring about will still be felt by the workforce, who may pass on good practice as they change employment. Furthermore, local managers may seek to emulate the practices of the incoming multinational organisation.

## Effects on trade and the balance of payments

If there is a capital inflow into the host economy, this will improve the capital account in the short term, although capital outflows are likely to occur in the future as the repatriation of profits and dividends occurs. A rational multinational would seek to have long-term capital outflows at least equal to short-term capital inflows into the host economy. The UK, which is both a high outward investor of capital and a high receiver of capital, has, with the exception of one or two years, had an excess of outward capital over inward. Thus it has been able to reap the benefits of strong positive contributions on net overseas earnings.

If the multinational produces goods for export or goods which are import substitutes, the current account of the host economy will improve. However, such benefits depend on the amount of value added in the host economy. Some multinationals have been accused of setting up plants in the host economy which are merely **screwdriver operations**, which often do not leave much room for manoeuvre in terms of added value. It was this fear that resulted in the EU countries specifying local-content rules for Japanese and South Korean organisations within the EU.

## Competitive and structural effects

Not only might multinational behaviour in the host economy affect competition through its influence on the rate of technological change and the adoption of new management techniques, but it might also affect the conduct and performance of indigenous organisations. Casson (1987) suggests that any organisation which develops a new technology can only recover its costs through the use of its monopoly power. The multinational may be able to strengthen the barriers to entry into its market through the process of internationalisation.

Multinationals have also been criticised for their impact on industrial structure if their use of labour does not coincide with that desired by the host government. If their move into the host economy is simply to develop assembly plants, then this may not equate with the host economy's expectations for improving the skill base and the level of technology of their workers and organisations. Some multinationals have also been reproached for keeping their research and development plants in the home economy and limiting the host economy to lower levels of technological expertise.

## Employment effects

A multinational will bring employment opportunities to the host economy, but the fear must always be that the multinational could rationalise production facilities in the future and in doing so close down some of the host economy's plants, leading to an increase in unemployment. In this respect it is also possible that an MNE can play off one subsidiary against another to get improved performance, with the threat of job losses if this does not occur.

On the other hand, foreign multinationals which are attracted into expanding sectors can provide the capital and know-how that is required to increase the productive capacity of the domestic economy, thereby improving employment in growth industries.

The overall impact of multinationals on employment is really made up of three effects: direct job creation, indirect job creation (linkages with suppliers) and displacement as indigenous firms lose out to the more efficient multinational. The overall net effect is difficult to estimate. Nonetheless, the direct effect can be seen as positive, and the enforcement of local-content rules within the EU in particular suggests that the indirect effect will also be positive. The displacement effect is more difficult to estimate since it may not be on host country suppliers but on exports from third countries, both inside and outside of the EU, into the host economy. France has expressed concern over this effect, suggesting that the Japanese-led recovery in some industrial sectors of the UK economy is damaging employment in France, Germany and Italy.

For LDCs the overall impact may not be so positive, or perhaps a better way of looking at the issue is that things are becoming less negative.

Some examples of the control that some MNEs have over their costs and operations may help at this stage. Some MNEs use cheap labour under conditions which would not be condoned in the developed economies to produce items which have very large markups. For example, Nike sells its training shoes at anywhere from around £50–£100. The actual price for these is under £5 per pair and they are produced in South-East Asian countries such as Indonesia using a workforce chiefly made up of women who are paid 10 pence an hour for a minimum 12 hours per week.

There are also ethical and health concerns over some MNE actions. In the Philippines, as in many other developing countries, bananas need to be sprayed with insecticides. In order to refill the tank that they carry on their backs to spray the bananas, workers may scoop up chemicals with

their bare hands. The result of this can be skin rashes and other health damage. Dangerous chemicals that are banned in developed countries are still in use in some LDCs. It is also not unusual to find that aeroplanes which are supposed to dust the banana plantations with chemicals also dust workers, their homes and water supplies. In the Philippines most of these plantations are owned by large MNEs which have been encouraged to make use of cheap labour. For many of these people there may be no alternative but to accept the low wages and dangerous working conditions on the plantations.

## MULTINATIONAL ACTIVITY WITHIN EUROPE

The first main source of foreign direct investment or multinational activity within Europe came from the US, particularly in the early post-war period. This was partially triggered by the development of the EC, but even then Europe was not the main focus of US multinational activity. In 1960, for example, 54.7 per cent of US direct investment in industrial countries went to Canada and only 34.2 per cent to Europe (Sleuwagen (1988)). By 1985, 55 per cent of US investment was going to Europe, but at the same time the US was a net recipient of European investment. Geographically the UK has been the most important recipient of both US and Japanese investment in Europe. Behind the UK, the US has favoured Germany, while Japan has favoured Luxembourg, the Netherlands and to a lesser extent Germany. Of the smaller countries within the EU, Ireland has been a significant recipient of foreign investment, particularly from the US.

There has also been an appreciable level of multinational activity between member states of the EU. Molle and Morsink (1991) found that four EU countries (Greece, Portugal, Spain and Ireland) were net recipients of FDI activity, the Netherlands and Germany were net donors, while the remaining countries had an almost balanced flow of FDI.

The general impact of this FDI and multinational activity in Europe can really be seen in the context of the host economy effects outlined earlier. That is, it has improved the balance of payments, although it has been noted in terms of multinational car firms that the luxury models still appear to be made outside of the host European economy. In terms of technological change, in innovative and competitive industries, foreign investors established local R&D facilities to gain access to local expertise, which further increased the rate of innovation. In declining sectors, however, investment tended to be in assembly production, with R&D located abroad. FDI production then competed with domestic producers which had to cut back their R&D as a cost-saving measure even further and entered a vicious circle of decline.

## EFFECT ON THE HOME ECONOMY

Much of the debate about the impact of multinationals on the home economy centres around areas similar to those investigated within the context of the host economy.

### Balance of payments effects

Capital movements to the host economy from the home economy initially worsen the home economy's capital account. Repatriated profits will improve the home economy's current account at a later date. Goods produced in the host economy could provide import substitutes for similar products produced in the home economy. But the general growth stimulated in the host economy may encourage more, but different, goods to be bought from the home economy. The overall impact is therefore uncertain.

### Employment effects

Multinationals have been accused of exporting jobs away from the home economy – especially where operations are later transferred to an overseas location – and in addition this could have contributed to reducing the balance of trade. However, jobs created abroad may be in addition to those and of a type which are not economic in the home country.

### Loss of technological lead

It has been argued that home countries lose their technological advantage by transferring production to an overseas company. Even if the technology is kept within the host country's organisation, some developing countries have flouted patent rules. Such problems were one of the reasons that the developed nations wanted patents, technology,

intellectual property and the like included in the Uruguay Round of GATT talks.

What has been noted is that multinationals are increasingly becoming more global, undertaking different stages of the integrated productive process in different countries as a means of exploiting their natural advantages. Given that multinational activity is not expected to wane, what will become evident is that increasingly companies in different countries are not owned or controlled by the sovereign state. What this means for the control of these companies is another matter.

## GLOBAL COMPETITION AND CORPORATE STRATEGY

The concept of business strategy has been developed in Chapter 14. How applicable is this to the behaviour of multinational or global companies? Porter (1986) defines an industry as global if it has or can achieve a competitive advantage by becoming global. Downstream activities such as marketing, sales and service need to be placed close to the consumer, but upstream activities such as the manufacturing of a product are less dependent on proximity to the purchaser. Porter suggests two fundamental dimensions which may explain why the organisation competes globally:

- configuration
- coordination.

Configuration refers to the locations in which activities are placed, while coordination is the extent to which the different sites work together. In terms of configuration, it is possible to have locations and activities concentrated or dispersed. In the former the R&D facility only occurs in a single location, whereas in the latter the activity takes place at a number of sites. With regard to coordination, it is possible to have each plant operating differently or conversely for each plant to follow the systems and practices set out at head office. For example, the traditional view of the Japanese car industry is that it keeps a tight geographical concentration within the home economy, retaining production and many of the other activities close to home, while foreign-owned plants are all highly coordinated. Compare this to General Motors, which has highly dispersed activities with low levels of coordination between them.

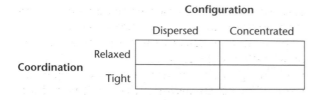

The problem for organisations can be envisaged in a two-by-two matrix with tight and relaxed coordination on one axis and concentrated and dispersed configuration on the other. What the global organisation requires is to select the combination of coordination and configuration that allows it to achieve its particular goals. This type of analysis needs to be undertaken for each activity in the value chain.

Such a process may be very time consuming and at each stage a cost–benefit approach may need to be undertaken. It is possible that such an approach, combined with Porter's generic strategies, value chain and scope economies, may lead to global organisations having distinct competitive advantages.

As much as Porter has outlined how to undertake a more globalised strategy, it may require a change in the organisation's thinking. Purchasing plants in other countries which may traditionally have served local markets, which may have produced a whole range of different products and which may be relatively small given their national market, pose some reorganisation questions for a multinational. The multinational may have to follow a more product-based strategy rather than one based on geography. Thus each plant may now concentrate on producing a small range of products which are shipped around the multinational's markets. This poses some interesting questions, since plants may have to be redesigned and there may be a need for better materials handling, new investment and increased specialisation. There may also be savings to be made in terms of economies of scale and the chance to delayer some parts of the organisation.

Successful companies are those that have become used to managing operations in a multicultural, multilingual environment and in coping with differences in economic performance and national political agendas. For European multinationals Brazil is currently in a situation similar to Spain and Portugal before they entered the EU. Thus EU multinationals can use their experience in the Iberian countries to penetrate further into the Brazilian market. Similarly, South-East Asia, with its high growth rates and expanding markets, provides a similar scenario to the high-growth countries in the more developed world.

To be successful in global markets means thinking globally rather than nationally, which may mean specialisation of production sites, producing products which can be customised to fit different cultural markets, standardising the product and packaging and identifying the obstacles to global strategy, such as constraints applied by governments, environmental regulations and cultural differences.

## GLOBAL SHIFT THEORY

Dicken (1992) suggests that not only has the world become more internationalised, but it has also become increasingly globalised. That is, businesses no longer operate internationally with reference to their domestic capital markets, culture, etc, but in a truly global sense, using global capital markets, sometimes global labour, and with reference to other cultural and political factors. Dicken argues that the globalisation of business activity is primarily due to the internationalisation of capital organised through transnational or multinational companies. Globalisation is seen to be related to three major phenomena:

■ The impact of technology, since this can overcome geographical distance through standardisation and the possibility of fragmentation of the production process.
■ The ability of governments or regions to regulate and control international business.
■ The desire for global profits.

Dicken acknowledges that global corporations still have the objectives of increasing market share or being a market leader, but envisages that the desire for global profit is a dominant motive. Globalised firms are now not just competing for profits in their own domestic markets or regions but are likely to face other major transnational companies in similar worldwide markets. Thus they need to think globally and to pursue global profits. This process of internationalisation of business must be seen and understood in the framework of the internationalisation of capital and capital accumulation. The extent to which these global companies can expand, imposing their strategies and going across boundaries – thereby improving their profits, also depends on the way governments behave.

Governments can be supportive of their actions or try to make conditions not so conducive to the globalisation and enhancement of profits. Thus in the search for global profits both the behaviour of governments and multinational organisations influences the globalisation process.

Ohmae (1990) has sought to expand on this relationship between multinationals and governments. To his strategic diamond of the three Cs – customers, competitors and company – he adds country and currency. Because exchange rates are volatile, organisations need to be in regions to neutralise their effects. The old theory of trade – see earlier in this chapter – i.e. that the prosperity of a country depends on its abundance, or lack, of natural resources, is no longer true. For example, countries such as Switzerland, Japan and Singapore are all characterised by few natural resources. Their economic development and prosperity are related not to the conservation of natural resources but to developing a well-educated, hard-working labour force (Ohmae (1990)).

A further approach to the internationalisation process has been developed by Stopford *et al* (1991). Because of the globalisation of business, governments on their own are no longer able to negotiate among themselves but face increasing pressure to negotiate with foreign organisations. In other words, multinational organisations are behaving like states, seeking international alliances to improve their market shares.

Activity is therefore increasingly being carried out on a triangular basis. Globalised companies do not recognise national boundaries. Negotiations take place between executives of companies, governments and other government ministries. This blurs the distinctions between politics and economics, the state and the organisation, and public and private sectors. A good example of this blurring and the operation of triangularity can be seen in the El Yamamah contract signed between the UK, Saudi Arabia and British Aerospace.

Stopford *et al* further indicate how global structural changes in finance, technology, knowledge and politics often lead to governments being forced to seek the help of managers of multinational organisations.

The process of global shift highlights both the beneficial and detrimental effects that MNEs can have on the deindustrialisation process outlined in Chapter 2. Once large organisations appear to have lost their competitiveness in the domestic economy, they may shift some of their operations over-

seas. This may be the case particularly where a foreign government in a less developed economy imposes trade barriers to imports, or where the organisation seeks to retain control of any products and processes which it has developed. In terms of deindustrialisation, there will be a direct loss in jobs as the MNE transfers production abroad. For example, Stopford and Turner (1985) noted that between 1972 and 1983 almost a third of all manufacturing jobs lost in the UK could be attributed to 58 British multinationals which during the same period added 200 000 jobs overseas. However, it is also possible that establishing plants overseas leads to increased administrative jobs at head office in the source country and can improve the export of component parts to the host economy as sales of the finished product rise there.

It is also possible that MNEs tend to be more footloose than domestic companies and are more likely to change the home of their operations when the right conditions occur. For example, it has been suggested that Ford, by having operations in a variety of European countries, has been able to shift production of engines, transmissions etc. around to take advantage of lower labour costs and greater labour flexibility in European countries. Some European countries, notably France in this instance, have complained that lower wage costs and the failure of the UK to sign up to that social chapter has led to Hoover switching production from France to Scotland.

MNEs can also lead to deindustrialisation by displacing domestic producers. By being dominant players in some markets they can use their size to undercut local competition, leading to job losses. In addition, they may wish to retain their existing supply chains so that domestic companies may further experience job losses.

However, it is also possible to argue that MNEs lead to the rejuvenation of domestic organisations and industries. Their presence in the economy stimulates both competitors and suppliers. They can add to the skill base of the workforce and bring with them higher levels of technology and better ways of working. These are often copied by the indigenous organisations which also improve their productivity levels. MNEs also bring with them a direct improvement in employment and can alter sectoral deficits in the balance of payments to surpluses, as is the case for the UK car and television industries. As competitors in the domestic economy also copy the techniques and procedures of MNEs, they too become more competitive, further enhancing employment opportunities.

If domestic organisations fail to meet the strict quality and delivery targets of the MNE, however, the impact on the domestic economy in terms of job losses can be heightened further.

# MNE REGULATION

Once we move away from perfectly competitive markets and enter the world of oligopoly or monopoly, the question of government intervention and regulation becomes more important. Organisations have choices about where and how they conduct their business and their decisions can have important influences on their economic environment. When organisations become MNEs, not only do governments have to worry about their behaviour, but there are issues about the impact of MNEs on national power and national autonomy.

Policy responses to MNEs are far from uniform. Some countries, perceiving that the costs outweigh the benefits, have sought to restrict MNE activity. Others, like the UK, have encouraged foreign organisations to enter their economy. Still others have sought ways to redistribute any economic rents that might arise. The relationship between MNEs and host economies may best be viewed in terms of whether the host economy is an LDC or a developed economy.

## MNEs and governments in developing countries

Some developing countries, such as Mexico, require 50 per cent of ownership and directorship to be in domestic hands. Although wholly foreign-owned investment is permitted in the export sector, all foreign investment is screened, as is also the case in India, by a Foreign Investment Commission, which lays down criteria for the investment. The requirements include items such as the sector and the location of the investment, the extent of local participation, the transfer of technology, and the disclosure of company information. Other LDCS have attempted to improve their control over MNEs by means of equity participation and joint ventures.

In terms of the LDC–MNE relationship, an important theoretical model was the obsolescing bargaining model suggested by Vernon (1993), whereby investment contracts that are initially favourable to the foreign organisation, reflecting risk and uncertainty, may be renegotiated on terms more favourable to the host country, as risk and uncertainty reduce. In this way Third World governments would gradually move to majority ownership of projects or completely towards nationalisation. For example, in 1975 the assets of 83 MNEs were confiscated; Madden (1992). But can this obsolescing bargaining model be used in manufacturing? Here the problem becomes more complex. The project may have much more diverse characteristics, such as the size of the initial investment, the stability of technology, the extent of product differentiation, the level of competition and the like, which can strengthen the hand of one side or the other in negotiations over the lifecycle of the product. In addition, host country objectives in manufacturing have changed over the past two decades, shifting from a focus on tax revenues and joint ownership to local value-added, domestic R&D, job creation and exports, and therefore studies which highlight local ownership as a measure of the success of the obsolescing bargaining model are considering the wrong factors. For example, Bennett and Sharp's (1985) study of the Mexican car industry noted that the progressive imposition of performance requirements, in terms of domestic content, and export requirement on GM, Ford, VW, Nissan and Chrysler, with the goal of encouraging them to establish worldscale production and supplier industries, was estimated to have created more than 100 000 jobs and exports of $5 billion per year. These outcomes could have been missed if the focus had been on the recovery of tax revenue and ownership factors.

However, this does not mean that things appear to be shifting to the advantage of LDC governments. It is possible that LDC governments are constrained in what they can do by their own political elites and indigenous business groups, who may seek to shape host policies towards MNEs. In addition, it is possible that a host economy government may intervene on behalf of its own MNEs.

Thus providing an overall policy to consider the activities of MNEs may not be possible – their activities may need to be considered on a case-by-case basis.

## Developed countries and MNEs

Here the debate concerns whether developed countries should nurture or protect domestic organisations in particular industries as a means of serving national needs, rather than becoming dependent on foreign companies. If there is an answer to this question, does the answer alter if the MNEs dominate a market in which there are only a few suppliers in sensitive sectors, such as high-technology sectors?

In terms of controlling MNEs so that national champions can be developed, how much should governments intervene in the market? A mechanism often used to encourage national champions is trade restrictions. However, these also lead to higher prices for products produced by MNEs currently in the domestic economy. Moreover, even when successful national champions have been developed, they have had a tendency to behave like MNEs themselves. For example, Fiat rejected directives from the Italian government to develop the Mezzogiorno region and expanded production in Brazil, and Michelin reacted to French indicative planning by building plants outside France in a ratio of three-to-one to those built within its domestic economy. In other words, national champions can be seen to behave in the same way as foreign-controlled MNEs when their own objectives conflict with those of national governments. If policies are used to inhibit indigenous organisations from expanding abroad while their international rivals have greater flexibility, then it tends to weaken domestic organisations, making them less competitive.

However, do MNEs provide different quality jobs to those provided by indigenous organisations? In terms of the quality of jobs, it is difficult to find systematic evidence in either the US or Europe that value added per worker is different between indigenous firms and MNEs when industry type is held constant; Graham and Krugman (1993). These researchers showed that R&D experience was also very similar, although MNEs had a greater tendency to import.

In terms of the developed economies, it might be asked why MNEs should be regulated any differently. Given the globalisation of business, if a foreign MNE is providing employment in the domestic economy, it should be given equal treatment to all competitors in the local market.

However, if we consider high-tech or sensitive defence markets, then the answer may not be so clear cut. Countries are wary when it comes to high-tech or defence industries where there is a strong tendency for a few suppliers to exist, many of which could be under the control of foreign-owned organisations. Given that many of these industries are subject to large economies of scale and that there can be dynamic gains from learning by doing and significant first-mover advantages, there is an argument that a domestic company should be one of these global players. As a way around the problem of being shut out of domestic markets, MNEs have responded by developing strategic alliances. For example, Boeing and Airbus have sourced as much as 50 per cent of their components and technology abroad as a part of a strategy to neutralise opposition in external markets.

Raines (1993) sees some promising signs in regulating MNEs. The EU, for example, persuaded IBM to change its basic way of operating to meet Union competition standards, treating product information in a less restrictive manner, and preparing the way for incorporating the MNE into the EU research programme (ESPRIT).

But what of the case where the government in the home economy orders the MNE not to provide the host economy, or research programmes in the host economy, with high levels of technology? For example, Japan's MITI ordered the Kyocera company in the US not to provide its high-technology ceramic products for use in the Tomahawk cruise missile programme. Such a policy will only work where suppliers are few and the leadtime to develop an alternative product is long.

It might be inferred from the above that the relationship between MNEs and governments has been rather strained. However, the 1980s and 1990s have seen governments adopt a much more positive stance to MNEs. The basic challenge for policy makers is therefore to pursue policies that attract MNEs, but to use them for the development of domestic organisations and at the same time not to offer MNEs any protection from competition from both domestic companies and other MNEs.

For some countries the carrot to attract MNEs has been the development of export processing zones (EPZs). These are zones which offer a range of privileges for MNEs, such as the absence of import controls so long as imported intermediate goods are turned into finished goods for exports. For developing countries the carrot for MNEs has increased through their aggressive use of locational grants and subsidies. This can result in the MNE playing one country off against another. What might be needed here is a multilateral agreement that covers all locational policies. But to what extent is there a need for a global police force? As markets become more globalised, domestic and regional MNEs are being replaced by global MNEs. National or even regional governments may not be in a position to prevent these global MNEs dividing economic rent in their favour. Somewhere along the way a global body may be required to oversee the behaviour of global corporations.

# SUMMARY

◆ Both in a perfectly competitive and imperfectly competitive world, trade is seen to enhance world economic welfare. The move towards freer trade since the 1940s has enhanced trading opportunities and encouraged many organisations to become global in their activities.

◆ The theories of absolute and comparative advantage, together with the Heckscher-Ohlin theorem, indicate the type of products which countries, and by definition their organisations, should produce. However, their assumptions do not always match the requirements of global markets. Thus we need to turn towards alternative theories such as those provided by Posner, Linder, Krugman and the theories of intra-industry trade, to provide us with more appropriate reasons for trade taking place.

◆ GATT, and its replacement the WTO, have been important in the move towards free trade. They have not only reduced the tariffs on manufactured goods but also widened their scope to consider trade in services, intellectual property rights and agriculture. Reducing these barriers to trade enhances business opportunities.

◆ Parallel to the work of GATT/WTO has been the development of trading blocs. Because many of these have reduced barriers to trade between member countries within the trading bloc, but raised external barriers against countries outside the bloc, they have important implications for the regions in which organisations can do business. The key factors here are trade creation and trade diversion. The development of these trading blocs has led to the growth of a global triad – the North American bloc, EFTA and the EU, and South-East Asia and Japan bloc. These three blocs have come to dominate both trade and foreign direct investment flows.

◆ Markets may be protected through national legislation, giving advantages to domestic organisations. The 1980s has seen a major shift in deregulating a whole range of markets, including telecommunications, transport and finance. This has led to increased competition between organisations, improved efficiency and enhancement of business opportunities for global organisations.

◆ Technology has also been a major factor in the globalisation process. It improves an organisation's comparative advantage and opens up new markets. Vernon explained the importance of technology through a product lifecycle approach, although this theory is open to question. The role of multinational companies can partially explain how technology is transmitted throughout the world.

◆ Multinational companies arise for a variety of reasons. They may have ownership-specific advantages, location-specific advantages and/or internalisation-specific advantages. Reasons such as securing resources, ability to purchase from one supplier, the role of technology and external factors such as the SEM are also important factors behind the growth of the global organisation.

◆ The international division of labour provides an alternative approach to MNE behaviour as organisations seek on a global scale to locate in lower-cost labour areas which can specialise in the production of items. Structural market distortions play their part too in the growth of MNEs, as organisations seek to take advantage of monopolistic or oligopolistic positions in global markets.

◆ Multinationals are seen as bringing both benefits and costs to both the home and host economy. Their impact on the host economy depends on the relative size of the multinational in relation to that of the host economy, and their general impact can be seen in terms of balance of trade effects, employment opportunities and resource transference effects.

◆ Corporate strategy developed in the context of local market needs to be altered as the organisation develops globally. The multinational may need to follow a more product-based strategy rather than a geographically oriented one. Successful companies are those that can manage operations in a multicultural, multilingual environment, coping with differences in economic performance and national political agendas.

◆ Dicken has argued that not only has the world become more internationalised, but it has also become more globalised. This globalisation is seen to be generated by the impacts of technology, the desire for global profits and the behaviour of governments.

◆ The globalisation of business raises questions about the relationship between government and business. Governments may no longer be able to conduct relationships between themselves without involving MNEs. Nonetheless, the relationship between MNEs and governments is not a static one. In the 1970s it was generally one of governments trying to control and extract from MNEs their share of economic rent. The 1980s and 1990s have seen a greater partnership being established between MNEs and governments, although not one that is always comfortable.

## REVIEW QUESTIONS

**1** To what extent do multinational enterprises benefit (harm) the host economy?

**2** Can you apply Vernon's product lifecycle theory to a particular product?

**3** Which sectors of the economy are important to which EU countries?

**4** 'The 1992 legislation has not led to "Fortress Europe" being established, therefore the upsurge in repositioning and mergers has not been worthwhile.' Critically assess this statement.

**5** How could the future development of trading blocs influence business activity?

**6** How important is technology in influencing the locational behaviour of international business?

**7** To what extent do you think Japanese foreign investment will change the character of British and European business activity? Do you think these changes will be for the better?

**8** Do you think that global corporations need to be regulated? If so, how?

## GLOSSARY OF NEW TERMS

**Absolute advantage:** When a country is able to produce more cheaply in absolute terms than another country.

**Comparative advantage:** When a country is able to produce a good more cheaply relative to other goods produced domestically than another country.

**Demonstration effects:** The advantages to an organisation of copying the processes of more efficient foreign competitors which have located in the domestic market.

**Deregulation:** A process under which government restrictions on markets are reduced.

**Global triad:** The increasing role of three trading regions, the North Americas, Europe, and South-East Asia and Japan, to account for world trade and FDI flows.

**Internalisation-specific advantages:** Reductions in external costs of the market that can arise through internalising these costs.

**International division of labour:** The desire for multinational organisations to seek low-cost labour which specialises in a task on a global rather than a regional or domestic level.

**Intra-industry trade:** Trade between similar industries in different countries.

**Location-specific advantages:** The advantages which the organisation possesses because it locates its production to a particular area, such as access to raw materials.

**Multinational/transnational/international organisation:** A company which owns or controls production or service facilities in more than one country.

**Non-tariff barrier:** Barrier to trade such as 'red tape' or health and safety factors.

**Ownership-specific advantages:** The types of knowledge and privileges which an organisation possesses but which are not available to its competitors.

**Screwdriver operations:** An organisation in a foreign country which simply combines the parts delivered to it by the parent company from its host economy.

**Structural market distortions:** Conditions in a market caused by organisations/governments which move it away from the competitive condition. This often leads to some aspect of market failure.

**Theory of appropriability:** Obtaining the maximum returns from a product through control and ownership of the advantages that this product may bring.

**Trade creation:** The development of trade between member countries within a trading bloc.

**Trade diversion:** The reduction in trade between two countries following one country's membership of a trading bloc.

**Voluntary export restraint:** An exporting country agrees to limit the amount of a product it will export to another country or region.

# READING

Cleeve, E (1994) 'Transnational corporation and internationalisation: a critical review', *British Review of Economic Issues*, Vol 16, No 40.

Davies, H (1998) *Managerial Economics*, 3rd edn, Pitman Publishing, London.
*This text has a useful chapter on multinational enterprises.*

Dunning, J (1981) *International Production and the MNE*, George Allen and Unwin, London.

Dunning, J (1992) *Multinational Enterprises and the Global Economy*, Addison-Wesley, Harlow.
*These texts provide a well-written and in-depth approach to the activities of multinational enterprises.*

Piggott, J and Cook, M (1997) *International Business Economics: A European Perspective*, 2nd edn, Addison Wesley Longman, Harlow.
*This text covers the areas of international trade, trading agreements and multinational activity both from a theoretical and applied perspective.*

## Further reading

Bennett, R (1996) *International Business*, Pitman Publishing, London.

Bennett, D C and Sharp, K E (1985) *Transnational Corporations Versus the State: The Political Economy of the Mexican Auto Industry*, Princeton University Press, Princeton.

Buckley, P and Casson, M (1985) *The Economic Theory of Multinational Enterprises*, Macmillan, Basingstoke.

Casson, M (1979) *Alternatives to the Multinational Enterprise*, Macmillan, Basingstoke.

Casson, M (1982) 'Transaction costs and the theory of multinational enterprises' in Rugman, A M (ed), *New Theories of the Multinational Enterprise*, Croom Helm, Beckenham, Kent.

Casson, M (1987) 'Multinational Firms' in Clarke, R and McGuiness, T (eds), *The Economics of the Firm*, Blackwell, Oxford.

Coase, R H (1937) 'The nature of the firm', *Economica* (New Series), 4, pp 386–405.

Dicken, P (1992) *Global Shift: Industrial Change in a Turbulent World*, 2nd edn, Paul Chapman, London.

Frobel, F, Heinricks, J and Kreye, O (1980) *The New International Division of Labour*, Cambridge University Press, Cambridge.

Graham, E M and Krugman, P R (1993) 'Foreign direct investment in the United States' in Moran T H (ed), *Governments and Transnational Corporations*, Vol 7, pp 252–80, Routledge, London.

Greenaway, D and Miller, C R (1986) *The Economics of Intra Industry Trade*, Blackwell, Oxford.

Grubel, H G and Lloyd, P S (1975) *Intra industry Trade: The Theory and Measurement of Trade in Differentiated Markets*, Macmillan, London.

Hymer, S (1976) *The International Operations of National Firms: A Study in DFI*, MIT Press, Cambridge, Mass.

Krugman, P R (1979) 'Increasing returns, monopolistic competition and international trade', *Journal of International Economics*, Vol 9, No 4, pp 469–79.

Krugman, P R (1987) 'Is free trade passé?', *Economic Perspectives*, Vol 1, No 2, pp 131–3.

Leontief, W (1954) 'Domestic production and foreign trade: The American capital position re-examined', *Proceedings of the American Philosophical Society*, 97, pp 331–49.

Levitt, T (1983) The Globalisation of Markets, *Harvard Business Review*, May–June.

Linder, S B (1961) *An Essay on Trade and Transformation*, John Wiley, New York.

Madden, P (1992) *A Raw Deal: Trade and the World's Poor*, Christian Aid, London.

Molle, W and Morsink, R (1991) 'Intra-European direct investment' in Burgenmeier, B and Mucchielli, J L (eds), *Multinationals and Europe*, Routledge, London.

Ohmae, K (1985) *Triad Power*, Free Trade Press, New York.

Ohmae, K (1990) *The Borderless World: Power and Strategy in the Interlinked Economy*, Collins, London.

Ohmae, K (1991) *The Borderless World*, Fontana, London.

Porter, M (1985) *Competitive Advantage*, Free Press, New York.

Porter, M (1986) 'Competition in global industries: a conceptual framework' in Porter, M (ed), *Competition in Global Industries*, Harvard Business School Press, Boston, Mass.

Posner, M V (1961) 'International trade and technical change', *Oxford Economic Papers*, Vol 13, pp 323–48.

Raines, J P (1993) 'Common market competition policy: the EC–IBM settlement' in Moran, T H (ed), *Governments and Transnational Corporations*, Vol 7, pp 189–99, Routledge, London.

Samuelson, P: papers now available in (1966) Stiglitz, J E (ed) *The Collected Scientific Works of Paul A Samuelson*, Vol 2, MIT Press, Cambridge, Mass.

Sleuwagen, L (1988) 'Multinationals, the European Community and Belgium: the small country case' in Dunning, J and Robson, P (eds), *Multinationals and the European Community*, Blackwell, Oxford.

Stopford, J, Strange, S and Henley, J S (1991) *Rival States, Rival Firms: Competition for World Market Shares*, Cambridge University Press, Cambridge.

Stopford, J M and Turner, L (1985) *Britain and the Multinationals*, Wiley, Chichester.

Vernon, R (1966) 'International investment and international trade in the product cycle', *Quarterly Journal of Economics*, Vol 80, May, pp 190–207.

Vernon, R (1970) *The Technology Factor in International Trade*, Columbia University Press.

Vernon, R (1993) 'The multinational enterprise: power versus soverignty' in Moran, T H (ed), *Governments and Transnational Corporations*, Vol 7, pp 37–50, Routledge, London.

Walters, J (1997) 'Halewood plant faces new crisis', *Observer Business*, 12 January, p 1.

World Trade Organisation (1995) *Focus*, May–June, p 6.

CHAPTER 22

# GOVERNMENT INTERVENTION: COMPETITION AND REGULATION

## KEY ISSUES

Business issues

Business strategy

Decision-making techniques

Economic concepts

Management decision issues

Optimal outcomes to management issues

## OBJECTIVES

◆ To consider the economic basis on which competition policy is founded.

◆ To outline and discuss the reasons for alternatives to, and arguments against, competition policy based on the neoclassical paradigm.

◆ To differentiate between levels of competition policy and place these in different schools of economic thought.

◆ To develop the criteria on which both UK and EU competition policy is created.

◆ To consider the role of state aid to industry in the EU.

◆ To outline the role of restrictive practices in both the UK and EU.

# CHAPTER OUTLINE

Business application

The economic basis of competition policy

The case against monopolies

Production efficiency

The case for monopoly

What sort of competition policy?

Alternative levels of competition policy

S–C–P failure

Alternatives to the S–C–P paradigm as a classification of markets to inform competition policy

UK competition policy

An overview of EU competition policy

Case study 22.1 Unilever offer on Irish ice cream

State aid and subsidies

Case study 22.2 Ailing state airlines

Restrictive practices in the UK and EU

Breaking down state monopolies

Case study 22.3 The UK privatisation experience

The role of regulation

Summary

Review questions

Glossary of new terms

Reading

# KEY TERMS

Allocative efficiency

Austrian approach

Block exemption

Competition policy

Compulsory competitive tendering

Concentration ratio $(CR_x)$

Full line enforcement

Liberalisation

Parallel imports

Public interest

Public procurement

Regulatory body

State aid

# Probe into packaging merger

The European Commission began an investigation into a merger between Anglo-French and American packaging manufacturers in the summer of 1995. Their concern was that the proposed deal would lead to reduced competition in a number of markets, especially in tinplate aerosol and food cans.

The proposed merger, if permitted, would create the world's largest packaging company, with an estimated European market share of 60 per cent. As a result, the new company would be able to control the marketplace for cans. Additionally, it would be in a position to dictate terms to its tinplate suppliers. As a result, it would be able to negotiate such low prices that existing competitors would not be able to produce their cans at the same cost levels.

Brussels has signalled that the merger may be permitted, but on the condition that some areas of the resultant business are sold off. For example, if the new company were to sell off its aerosol production interests, that market would remain competitive and the present incumbents would be able to compete.

*Source: Financial Times, 26 July 1995. Reprinted with permission.*

## Comment

This chapter will outline and explain the rationale for restricting such merger activity. The processes and formulae which are used to measure competition and the decisions which lead to investigation of mergers will also be discussed. The basis for policy formulation in the UK and Europe has largely been the neoclassical paradigm. Neoclassical failings have been highlighted previously in this text; the possible inaccuracies arising in competition policy will be put forward in the context of the neoclassical assumptions made.

# THE ECONOMIC BASIS OF COMPETITION POLICY

**Competition policies** are means for controlling the competitive environment in which organisations exist. For a government to intervene in a market implies that there may be some form of market failure and that resources may be better allocated among the stakeholders. Competition policy could therefore be examined from a number of perspectives. Its role may be to improve the competitive environment in which organisations exist by prohibiting anti-competitive practices or through breaking up monopolies. In addition, the government may seek to promote the level of competition through its merger and takeover policies. To achieve their aims, different governments may adopt different policies. Some governments place greater emphasis on the encouragement of competition, while others are more inclined to remove or control monopolies.

One of the driving forces behind the development of competition policy has been the structure–conduct–performance (S–C–P) paradigm,

developed by Bain (1951), Caves (1974) and Scherer and Ross (1990). This suggests that the more competitive a market, the more efficient are resources used, the more prices tend towards marginal cost, and the lower is each company's level of profit. It follows that the more monopolistic a market becomes the less efficient are resources, the less incentive organisations have to produce at their lowest-cost positions and the greater the level of profits made by each of the organisations, since price exceeds the marginal cost of production. This S–C–P paradigm has been a key factor in driving the development of competition policy. However, although competitive forces may encourage organisations to operate more efficiently, a free market is not a sufficient condition for there to be the most suitable use of resources. Market failure may occur. This may arise when information is imperfect and transactions costly. It is these market failures that may lead to the growth of organisations, both horizontally and vertically, as managers attempt to reduce transaction costs.

Nonetheless, it can be recognised that where an organisation dominates a market, both its price and non-price decisions can cause a social welfare loss to society. In this situation, advertising may be wasteful, innovation and R&D slow and the structure of the organisation may not encourage efficiency. However, this position should be compared with that of perfect competition, which for all intents and purposes is a theoretical 'best' position. What really ought to be encouraged is the behaviour of the market and other organisations to encourage existing dominant organisations to behave efficiently, that is, to reduce entry barriers and encourage firms to move further down their long-run average total cost curves. Therefore, competition should stress more efficient behaviour rather than encouraging markets to be perfectly competitive. Thus any organisation needs to be clear as to what any regulating body means by competition policy, since this will have a direct impact on the organisation's behaviour. Although the above has developed the practical aspects of formulating competition policy, it will be useful also to consider the theoretical position.

## THE CASE AGAINST MONOPOLIES

In theory the main arguments against monopolies are the welfare losses when compared with a perfectly competitive market.

A diagram similar to Figure 22.1 has been seen before in Chapter 9, but here it has been simplified with the assumption of constant costs, from which it follows that the marginal cost curve (MC) and average cost curve (AC) are drawn as the same horizontal line. It is now possible to determine the price/output combinations under perfect competition and monopoly. The profit-maximising monopolist equates marginal revenue to marginal cost and produces output $Q_m$ and charges price $P_m$. Profit maximisation under perfect competition is where marginal cost, which is the industry supply curve, intersects with the market demand curve (D). Under perfect competition, therefore, price is $P_{Pc}$ and output $Q_{Pc}$. In the case of the perfectly competitive position, each of the individual organisations is producing at the minimum point on its average cost curve: they are said to be **allocatively efficient**.

Using Figure 22.1 it is now possible to compare the gains and losses to society of the two equilibrium positions. The area under the demand curve but above the price line is called consumers' sur-

### Figure 22.1 The welfare losses under monopoly

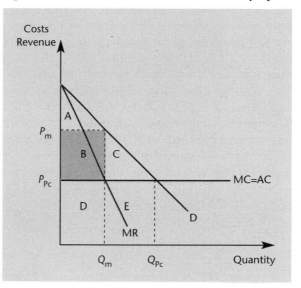

This shows the price and output decisions under monopoly and perfect competition. The monopolist produces at $Q_m$ and charges a price $P_m$, while under perfect competition price is $P_{Pc}$ and output $Q_{Pc}$. Under perfect competition consumers' surplus is shown as A+B+C; under monopoly consumers' surplus is reduced to area A.

plus. Consumers' surplus is the price which each of the individual consumers would have been willing to pay but did not have to pay. In the case of perfect competition, this is shown as the area A+B+C. Under monopoly this is shown as area A. In the perfectly competitive case, areas D and E represent consumers' expenditure on the commodity, that is, price times quantity. Therefore, the total value which society places on the commodity under perfect competition is the sum of the areas A to E. To calculate the effect on society's welfare, the costs of the resources used to produce the commodity should also be considered; these are shown as areas D+E. Therefore, the net benefit accruing to society from the perfectly competitive output/price decision is A+B+C+D+E minus D+E, in other words, area A+B+C, the consumers' surplus.

In the case of a monopolist, consumers' surplus is reduced to area A. Area B is transferred from the consumers to the monopolist as part of supernormal profits. Since the monopolist chooses to produce $Q_m$ rather than $Q_{Pc}$, area C, which was previously part of the consumers' surplus, is lost: this is called the allocative or deadweight loss. This is a measure of the extent to which monopoly price/output is allocatively inefficient when compared to perfect competition.

Thus the notion of allocative inefficiency and the fact that monopolists tend to charge a higher price than under perfectly competitive conditions are just two reasons for competition policy being developed. Nonetheless, it should be noted that there are only a few occasions where an organisation controls the whole of a market. Therefore what should be considered are markets which become less competitive against those which are more competitive. However, even under oligopolistic market conditions the organisations which make up this market structure are able to raise prices almost to the levels that could exist under monopoly conditions. Therefore, as market concentration increases there is a trend towards a reduction in consumers' welfare.

Figure 22.1 also shows that the welfare loss of monopoly depends on the size of the monopoly and on the price elasticity of demand. If the demand curve was drawn with a steeper slope, then area C would be larger. Thus the extent to which competition policy could rectify any problems will depend on the size of the monopoly and the degree to which the product is essential.

## PRODUCTION EFFICIENCY

The degree to which monopolies lead to a welfare loss, as shown in Figure 22.1, depends on the monopolist facing the same demand and cost conditions as those under perfect competition. It is possible to hypothesise that a monopolist may have more power in the market and is thus able to achieve economies of scale. This would be seen in a downward shift of both average and marginal cost curves.

In Figure 22.2, given an initial marginal cost curve $MC_0$ and average cost curve $AC_0$, under perfect competition the price charged is shown as $P_{Pc}$ and quantity of output is $Q_{Pc}$. Suppose, on this occasion, that the monopolist is able to achieve economies of scale which shift the marginal/average cost line down to $MC_1/AC_1$. Area 2 shows that part of consumers' surplus which the monopolist obtains. Area 1 is the deadweight loss to society following the shift from production under perfect competition to production under monopoly conditions. Area 3 indicates the advantages to producers (the monopolist in this case) of producing at lower average costs. To assess whether monopoly is beneficial to society requires, therefore, an assessment

**Figure 22.2 Comparison of monopoly and perfect competition where cost savings are possible**

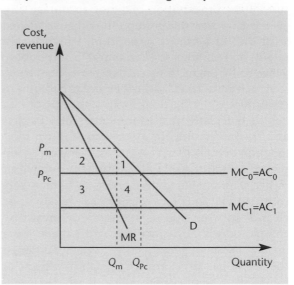

This shows the output and pricing decisions under perfect competition with marginal cost $MC_0$ and average cost $AC_0$. These are shown as $Q_{Pc}$ and $P_{Pc}$ respectively. Where the monopolist can achieve economies of scale, the monopolist's average/marginal cost curve is shown as $MC_1/AC_1$. The monopolist gains area 2 from consumers via a reduction in consumers' surplus. The welfare gain for society centres on a comparison of the deadweight loss, area 1, and the cost savings to monopolists, area 3.

of areas 1 and 3. Social welfare remains the same, is enhanced or deteriorates as the deadweight loss is equal to, is smaller than or is larger than, the production cost savings shown by area 3. It might be believed that if area 3 was greater than area 1, then social welfare will be increased. However, whether there are cost savings or not as production shifts from perfect competition to monopoly, there will always be allocative inefficiency since the monopoly charges consumers a higher price than that which was charged under perfect competition. Even though area 3 could be greater than area 1, a monopoly position may be prevented under competition policy because consumers' surplus is being reduced. Therefore, decisions about the level of competition in a market are not just economic but may be influenced by political considerations and notions of fairness.

It is also possible that the economies of scale achieved by the monopolist are sufficiently large that the monopolist could produce a greater output and charge a lower price than under perfectly competitive conditions.

In Figure 22.3 the perfectly competitive industry output is shown as $Q_{Pc}$ and the price charged is $P_{Pc}$. Consumers' surplus is shown as area $P_{Pc}AB$. A monopolist which achieves sufficient economies of scale could find that its marginal/average cost curve is shown as $MC_1/AC_1$. A profit-maximising monopolist will now produce at output level $Q_m$ and charge price $P_m$. Output is greater under monopoly and price lower than in the perfectly competitive position. In addition, consumers' surplus is now larger at $P_mCB$. Thus it needs to be recognised that policies designed to counteract the perceived problems created by monopolists could lead to reduced benefits for consumers.

## THE CASE FOR MONOPOLY

Although the preceding sections have concentrated on the detrimental effects of monopolies in terms of price, output and efficiency losses, there may be factors which encourage monopolies to come into existence and cause them to have positive effects on society.

**Figure 22.3 Production under monopoly where output is greater and price lower than under perfect competition**

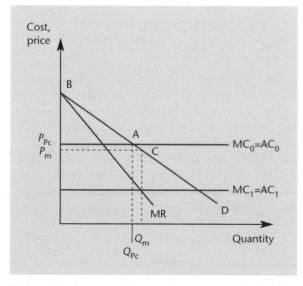

Under perfectly competitive conditions, output will be $Q_{Pc}$ and price $P_{Pc}$. Consumer surplus is shown as area $P_{Pc}AB$. Suppose that economies of scale are sufficient to push the monopolists' average/marginal cost curve down to $MC_1/AC_1$. The profit-maximising monopolist will produce $Q_m$ at price $P_m$. Here output is greater than under perfect competition and price lower. Consumers' surplus increases to $P_mCB$.

A monopoly may come into existence because of efficiency gains. In the earlier section it was noted that monopolies could achieve economies of scale through growth (due to high transaction costs in the market) and this expansion may lead to market dominance. Once they have reached a dominant position inefficiencies may occur, thus competition policy needs to account for periods where market domination can lead both to gains and perhaps to subsequent losses in efficiency. A similar argument could be developed for the natural monopoly case, where a tradeoff needs to be developed between production efficiency and the desire for greater competition.

Market dominance may arrive through patent provisions. Patents have been developed to provide organisations with the rewards for past R&D. Once again, a balance needs to be struck between granting patents for a certain period of time, which encourages R&D, and a patent which runs for too long and acts to stifle competition in the long term.

In Chapters 9 and 11 collusive behaviour was developed. Collusion enables the participating companies to act against the public's interest. However, there may be occasions when collusion is supported, particularly where investment expenditure is very high and there would be averse effects from the duplication of this research.

Mergers and acquisitions are sometimes used to enable market domination to take place. Should competition policy be used to prevent this type of behaviour? Again, the answer is unclear. Mergers may lead to improvements in efficiency. Moreover, the threat of being taken over is one means by which the potential victim organisation can be 'forced' to manage its affairs efficiently.

It is also possible to argue that access to patents encourages other organisations, through a process of creative destruction to try to get round any patent legislation. Finally, a monopoly may arise through an organisation bringing a new innovation to the market. This may enable it to obtain monopoly profits, but this dynamic efficiency through innovation and a more cost-effective use of resources can benefit consumers who now have a new product. If this product is successful, it is highly likely that other organisations will attempt to duplicate the innovation. In doing so, supply is increased and the price level will fall so that only competitive profits are made.

# WHAT SORT OF COMPETITION POLICY?

The preceding discussion suggests that there are no hard and fast rules about the type of competition policy that might be developed. However, there may be some useful starting points. Differences in market structure may affect the competitive behaviour of organisations. Markets that are highly competitive are unlikely to lead to organisations whose performance could reduce market welfare. On the other hand, it is not possible always to say that markets which are oligopolistic or where there is a single provider will lead to reductions in economic welfare. Where there exists an oligopolistic market structure, a number of scenarios have been put forward to explain the behaviour of the organisations there. In Chapters 9 and 11 oligopolies were seen to behave both competitively and cooperatively. In theory, organisations may be said to behave in a number of ways, but proving that they do so in practice is another matter. Cartels, although illegal in the EU, are notoriously difficult to prove. Nonetheless, the recent cases of cement manufacturers in the UK, building organisations in the Netherlands and steel manufacturers in the EU indicate that proving their existence is not impossible. In the case of uncompetitive behaviour by other organisations, it may be possible to consider an organisation's performance against some industry norm, or against a similar-sized organisation. However, it must be recognised that organisations which make high levels of profits may be doing so because they are very efficient at controlling costs, rather than by charging high prices because they can abuse their monopolistic position in the market. In addition, it is also important to consider what happens to these profits over time. Are they short term or have they been in existence over longer periods? Are current levels of profits acceptable as a return on previous research and development, and will profits be eroded in the future as new organisations seek to enter the market?

Consideration should also be given to the contestability of markets. Evidence which shows the movement of organisations into and out of an industry may suggest that the market is contestable and that economic welfare is not being harmed. Conversely, where markets do not appear to be contestable, entry barriers may be being used and competition policy needs to consider how these entry barriers can be reduced.

Competition policy should therefore be designed either to promote more competition or to prevent a reduction in competition. The problem, however, is that economists differ as to the market conditions necessary to best promote competition, that is, either market forces or government involvement, and it therefore follows that the type of competition policy advocated differs. If the S–C–P approach is taken, competition policy should attempt to change market structure and impose constraints on the behaviour of organisations. That is, barriers to entry should be reduced, monopolies should be broken up or regulated, and there should be attempts to stop organisations reaching a dominant position through a merger policy. Competition policy should actively prevent organisations from abusing their dominant market position via resale price maintenance, using restrictive practices or through the process of **full line enforcement**, where customers cannot decide to take one item out of a portfolio supplied by an organisation but must take all or nothing.

Conversely, the Austrian view is that competition policy is required to ease entry into markets. These barriers to entry may be erected by the private sector, but from the Austrian School perspective are likely to be government-imposed barriers.

## ALTERNATIVE LEVELS OF COMPETITION POLICY

Alternative approaches may be taken with respect to competition policy. Which type of policy individual governments may subscribe to is determined by their ideological viewpoint. Governments influenced by the **Austrian economics approach** are more likely to accept a free-market approach to competition policy. Keynesian-influenced governments will be more likely to adopt a policy position which utilises interventionist approaches to promote or maintain competition.

The range of alternative approaches is as follows:

■ *Laissez-faire/free-market approach* – This would be adopted by Austrian-influenced governments. Intervention in the market is rejected because it is assumed that intervention will distort the market process. Further, Austrians would argue that no one organisation has the power to distort the competition within a market in any case. If monopoly power exists, it is because that is the most efficient system for that market.

■ *Supportive* – Under a supportive market regime, there is recognition that markets function with imperfect knowledge and that transaction costs are involved. Policies in such cases are designed to improve the efficiency of markets. Over time, however, it is recognised that a supportive policy will be removed and the market will continue to function efficiently. Therefore, a supportive policy is one which allows a market to achieve its own equilibrium after a period of time.

■ *Active* – Active policy is more involved in markets than a supportive policy. Here there is direct government involvement – which is necessary to maintain the desired position within the market. Active policy is not likely to be withdrawn because the market in question would not be self-sustaining in its desired state after withdrawal was made.

Most government policy provides a mixture of active and supportive policies. The UK and European experiences, as discussed later in this chapter, clearly demonstrate this. For both, the policies used to maintain and encourage competition are designed to remove any obstacles to competitive processes. Modifications to market structure and regulatory behaviour are actions which may be classed as supportive, while the legislation and practices used by governments to prevent further anti-competitive processes are more supportive in nature.

# S–C–P FAILURE

The fact that the S–C–P paradigm is not a sufficient explanation of markets and industries has been explained previously (*see* Chapter 15). A linear and causal relationship between structure of markets, conduct of organisations and their overall performance has been criticised for many years. Scherer *et al*'s (1990) addition of a feedback loop to the linear models of Mason (1939) and Bain (1951) confirms this.

In addition to the failure of the S–C–P paradigm to assist in an in-depth and dynamic understanding of markets, iteratively it may be concluded that the S–C–P paradigm is not sufficient to guide policy decisions with reference to competition in those markets. Recall that the main criticisms of the S–C–P paradigm are based on the assumptions made:

■ Perfect knowledge is assumed. However, it is commonly accepted that perfect knowledge

does not exist. Individuals, organisations and markets are seen to operate in conditions of bounded rationality.

■ The structure of the industry does not necessarily dictate the conduct and performance therein. This point was discussed in Chapter 15 with reference to the fact that not all monopolists seek to restrict output and maintain artificially high prices. This is despite the fact that a deterministic link may be observed between structure, conduct and performance.

Additional arguments exist against the S–C–P paradigm specifically in guiding competition policy. Overall, S–C–P causes problems for those wishing to gain insight into policy arguments because of the danger of erroneous or misleading resultant analyses.

S–C–P's detractors argue that it focuses on the fact that there is a greater danger of exploitation when the concentration of an industry increases.

## Concentration ratios

Discussion of the advantages and disadvantages of different types of concentration measures could constitute a chapter on its own. Here, the objective is to outline a simple measure of concentration which may be used throughout this book for illustrative purposes. This is the **concentration ratio**, usually abbreviated to $CR_x$. The '$x$' refers to the number of organisations considered within the concentration ratio. For example, if the concentration ratio considers the top three organisations within the market, the '$x$' will be replaced by '$_3$'. Similarly, the $CR_5$ considers the top five organisations within the market, $CR_{10}$ the top 10 organisations within the market, and so on.

Concentration ratios are created by calculating the cumulative market share of the largest $x$ organisations in descending order of share. Mathematically:

$$CR_x = \sum_{i=1}^{x} S_i$$

where,

$CR_x$ = the $x$ organisation concentration ratio

$S_i$ = the percentage market share of the $i^{th}$ organisation.

Thus, if concentration increases, one (or a small number of colluding) organisation(s) will gain increased power within the industry and begin to increase prices. The effect of such exploitation will be social welfare losses (*see* Chapter 9). Government intervention will be enacted to reinstate competition and aim to force prices back down to a competitive level and to recapture the lost social welfare.

There is a danger that overemphasis on the price levels in an industry will lead to welfare losses. Governments typically intervene in markets to regain welfare when they become overpriced. Overpriced products are judged to be those priced at greater than the marginal costs of production. That is, if $P > MC$, there is an exploitation of consumer welfare. However, this is a blinkered stance, since there are situations when an artificially high price may lead to welfare gains in the future. Two possible sources of welfare gains exist:

■ Retained profits and other gains made by maintaining an artificially high price may lead to reduced welfare in the current period. If these are used, however, for research and development and other product improvements, it may be argued that there is a potential for long-term welfare gains and increased consumer surplus. Such a situation requires that the savings or improvements are passed on to the consumer.

■ Where an organisation is using funds to gain scale increases and possibly even economies of scale, it is possible to make cost savings. As long as any such efficiencies are passed on to the consumer, the current welfare loss may be traded off against welfare gains in the future as a result of the cost savings.

In many cases, analysis of the structure of an industry provides government agencies with a benchmark. This benchmark provides a critical market-share point at which intervention and/or regulation should occur. However, the constitution of concentration within the industry should also be considered.

Compare two industries, A and B (Table 22.1), both with a concentration ratio ($CR_5$) of 60. Industry A is dominated by one large organisation, with 35 per cent market share; 78 others share the remaining 65 per cent with varying degrees of size. Industry B, on the other hand, is relatively evenly distributed. The top five organisations in terms of market share are all equal, with 12 per cent each. The smallest organisation even possesses 7 per cent market share – not insignificant!

Simply looking at the concentration ratios would lead to the assumption that both industries are highly concentrated and that the opportunity to control the market is great in both. However, the opportunity to collude and control is far greater in the more evenly distributed Industry B, although conversely it could be argued that industry B is more competitive on the grounds that with a greater equality of market share there is more jostling between equals. A competition policy based purely on concentration, without considering the detail, would overlook these differences.

---

◆ **Exercise 22.1**

Calculate the $CR_3$ and $CR_4$ for Markets A and B. Explain why further information than merely the concentration ratio is required in order to differentiate between markets when considering the existing concentration or equity.

---

In addition to considering concentration ratios and constitution of the industry, the S–C–P paradigm fails to consider the internal activities of organisations. Performance, the P in S–C–P, tends to lead to a consideration of the exogenous, easily identifiable, external performance of organisations. Internal performance and factors are ignored and therefore the roles and aspirations of the organisation are ignored. Non-price factors, for example, are ignored and signposts to likely future changes in the industry may not be identified.

# ALTERNATIVES TO THE S–C–P PARADIGM AS A CLASSIFICATION OF MARKETS TO INFORM COMPETITION POLICY

Alternative benchmarks to the S–C–P concentration-measure approach have been put forward. These provide analysts with key values which will give an indicator of when mergers and growth of organisations may lead to exploitative or costly actions against consumers.

**Table 22.1 Concentration in different industries**

| Market | A | B |
|---|---|---|
| Firm 1 | 35 | 12 |
| Firm 2 | 10 | 12 |
| Firm 3 | 8 | 12 |
| Firm 4 | 5 | 12 |
| Firm 5 | 4 | 12 |
| Other firms | +76*0.5 | +4*10 |
| $CR_5$ | 60 | 60 |

Although there are no absolute figures for specific industries, economists now recognise that there are different stages to the industry lifecycle *and* that these affect its 'critical concentration'. A distinction is made in such cases between rising and falling concentration. As the industry becomes more concentrated, the critical value of concentration attracting governmental attention will be lower than that for an industry which is becoming more competitive, although this figure still requires the nature of the concentration to be considered.

As an example, consider traditional, heavy engineering (steel/steel fabrication) or mining industries. These have suffered structural decline in many European countries, as the industries reach and pass the mature lifecycle stage. As a result of the decline, competitors have left the industry and closed factories, works or mines. The remaining competitors are obviously smaller in number and likely to decline further. However, the concentration ratio will increase once organisations leave the industry. That is, the industry becomes more concentrated among the remaining incumbents. Such a situation is not a worry for the government concerned, since natural selection has evoked the change and is likely to ensure that the incumbents are performing to optimum efficiency in order to survive.

The nature of the concentration is partly considered in cases where a distinction is made between cooperative and competitive industries. When industries are cooperative, a far lower concentration value will define an exploitative position than if industries are competitive.

Overall, then, it should be obvious that there are many criticisms of the S–C–P approach to industry analysis, leading to problems with its recommendations for competition policy. However, there are relatively few alternatives and even fewer which are not based on a form of concentration measure.

The overriding message here, nevertheless, is that, due to the assumptions of the S–C–P paradigm and the commonly accepted knowledge and measures associated with S–C–P, there are fundamental errors of judgement and analysis which may arise if it is used to identify organisations and industries which may not be competitive or in the public interest.

## UK COMPETITION POLICY

The UK's competition policy was established approximately 50 years ago with the creation of the Monopolies and Restrictive Practices Commission (MRPC) in 1948, under the Monopolies and Restrictive Practices Act. This defined a monopoly as an organisation or group of organisations which act together to control a third or more of a market. The 1956 Restrictive Practices Act separated unitary monopoly investigations from restrictive practices operated by groups of organisations. The 1965 Monopolies and Mergers Act provided for the investigation of mergers and acquisitions which might produce or strengthen a monopoly, if they involved a takeover of assets in excess of £5 million.

A major piece of legislation for competition policy in the UK was the 1973 Fair Trading Act. This act created an Office of Fair Trading with a Director General and cases selected for investigation were referred to the newly named Monopolies and Mergers Commission (MMC). The Act also altered the definition of a unitary monopoly to one where a single organisation controlled 25 per cent of more of the market and where these sales can be defined at a national, regional or local level. Mergers could also be investigated where they involve 25 per cent or more market share or where at least £30 million worth of assets were taken over.

The 1973 Act implied that there was a cut-off point: a company which perhaps controlled 24 per cent of the market probably would not be investigated, whereas one which controlled 25 per cent or more of the market was more likely to be investigated. The figures chosen were a little at odds with the economists' view of a monopoly, and would indicate that oligopolies were more likely to be investigated. However, the policies adopted did suggest that vertical and conglomerate mergers could be investigated.

It should be noted that the MMC has to prove that a monopoly or proposed merger operates against the public interest. If this situation occurs, the MMC can recommend that appropriate action should be taken, but it cannot enforce this action; only the Secretary of State can enforce changes in the behaviour and operation of organisations. The 1973 Act did, however, define the **public interest** as including the desirability of maintaining and promoting competition. Nonetheless, an exact definition of what was meant by 'against the public interest' was difficult to pin down. Some obvious features of this definition would be encouraging cost reductions, promoting competition and improving quality, yet the MMC is able to take into account any factors which it considers relevant.

Although it considers some monopolies and mergers to be against the public interest, the MMC could also see the benefits from allowing monopolies to exist. Thus each case brought for investigation is considered in terms of its costs and benefits, and the case judged on its own merits rather than having blanket considerations.

The Competition Act 1980, although concerned with anti-competitive practices – an area that will be considered later in this chapter – also extended monopoly control and provision to the nationalised industries and other public-sector bodies. Finally, the Companies Act of 1989 modified merger legislation in three ways. First, the companies involved must provide a formal pre-notification of their activity. Second, even if the Director of Fair Trading has recommended that the Secretary of State should refer the merger to the MMC, if the organisations agree to sell off some of their assets to decrease their excess power, the merger may still be allowed to take place. Third, once the merger has been referred to the MMC, the companies are prohibited from acquiring each other's shares.

## AN OVERVIEW OF EU COMPETITION POLICY

Organisations within the EU are increasingly subject not only to their national policies on monopolies, mergers or takeovers, but also to EU policies in these areas. EU competition policy runs parallel to policies that abolish institutional obstacles to trade between countries. Its main aim is to prevent organisations frustrating trade between countries and therefore its emphasis is on the promotion of constructive competition. Thus the main purpose of competition policy within the EU is to prevent price fixing, collusion, cartels and other collaborative anti-competitive behaviour; to control the size to which organisations grow through the process of acquisition and merger, thereby ensuring that competition is not removed from the marketplace; to free up competition, particularly in the area of **public procurement**; and to restrict **state aid** to indigenous firms.

The EU has no power where the effects of a monopoly or takeover are confined to one member state, but if there is a difference between national and EU law the latter takes precedence. Organisations which are based outside the EU can also be affected by its policy on competition. If the EU considers that foreign-owned firms are damaging competition within the EU, it can restrict or ban the sale of their goods and services.

The main provisions of EU competition policy are Articles 85 and 86 of the Treaty of Rome. Article 85 prohibits restrictive agreements and practices between companies affecting trade or leading to distortion of competition within the Union. Such agreements could include price fixing, market sharing and exclusive purchase. Article 85 does grant **block exemptions** in some cases where restrictions that may result from the behaviour of an organisation are compensated for by benefits that are in the public's interest.

Article 86 prohibits the use of a dominant position within the Union. A dominant market position is said to be in existence if an organisation can affect the outcome of a market by exercising monopoly power. It is not the monopoly position that is the problem but its abuse. Article 86, therefore, can rarely be used to prohibit mergers and acquisitions. It is for the European Commission and the European Court of Justice to assess and define the terms 'abuse' and 'dominant position' for individual cases, and their assessment will depend on the market, type of product, market structure etc.

Articles 92–94 ban national government aid to domestic industries which distorts or threatens to distort competition between firms within the Union. However, some exceptions are made, notably in the areas of development subsidies and regional aid.

In addition to the Treaty of Rome, regulations with respect to mergers and acquisitions have been developed separately. The Merger Control Regulation (1989) allows the European Commission to inspect a merger or takeover involving organisations with a combined annual turnover of ECU 5 billion or more or where the aggregate EU turnover of each of at least two of the enterprises concerned is more than ECU250 million. If each of the organisations has more than two-thirds of its total turnover from sales within any one member state, then the proposed merger is subject to national merger policy even if the first two conditions outlined above are satisfied. Smaller mergers are usually subject to national mergers and acquisitions regulations, but the Commission may intervene at the request of national governments.

◆ **CASE STUDY 22.1**

## Unilever offer on Irish ice cream

**FT**

The European Commission (in March 1995) is close to winding up its case against Unilever for breach of competition rules in the sale of 'impulse' ice cream in Ireland after undertakings by the Anglo-Dutch consumer group to open up the market.

Unilever's offer centres on changes to its distribution arrangements, including the introduction of non-discriminatory pricing schemes in all the 14 other European Union member states during 1995.

The Commission said yesterday that it welcomed Unilever's undertakings, which appeared on first view to meet the conditions required for granting an exemption from EU competition rules under Article 85 (3) of the treaty of Rome.

Mr Karel Van Miert, EU competition policy commissioner, said the original distribution arrangements infringed competition rules. . .

The case goes back to 1991 when Masterfoods Ireland, a subsidiary of the Mars group, and Valley Ice Cream complained about distribution arrangements relating to the sale of impulse ice cream – single wrapped items which are sold for immediate consumption.

The distributor was HB Ice Cream, a subsidiary of the Unilever group, now trading as Van den Bergh Foods

operating in Ireland where Unilever enjoyed a market share of 70 per cent in 1993. Unilever challenged the Commission's view of the legality of the original arrangements which fell into two parts. First, Unilever provided freezer cabinets to retailers subject to an exclusive provision which allowed only Unilever products to be stored. Second, the cost of providing a cabinet was included in the price of ice cream itself, and this price was charged to all retailers, irrespective of whether they had a Unilever cabinet.

Unilever has now offered to introduce a differential pricing scheme immediately. This would provide a lump sum to retailers stocking Unilever ice cream but not taking a Unilever freezer, on condition that the retailer achieves a minimum turnover of I£650 (£645). The lump sum is currently set at I£78 a year.

The Commission's preliminary conclusion that Unilever's distribution practices for impulse ice creams in Ireland was anti-competitive was in direct contrast to the findings of the UK competition authorities which examined the issue in 1993.

(I£: Irish pounds.)
*Source: Financial Times*, 11 March 1995. Reprinted with permission.

---

◆ **Exercise 22.2**

1 Before the Commission's action, why were other ice-cream manufacturers upset with Unilever's behaviour?

2 Why do you think that other ice-cream manufacturers did not operate in the same way as Unilever?

---

*Comment on the case study*

Case study 22.1 indicates the use of restrictive agreements by a dominant organisation which therefore comes under the jurisdiction of Article 85. Unilever was attempting to restrict the sale of other ice cream by preventing other ice creams being stored in 'their' freezers. It was further penalising retailers if they turned down Unilever's offer of a freezer so that they could sell ice creams from other manufacturers. This is not the first instance of this type of behaviour; *see* Monopolies and Mergers Commission (1979). The Unilever case highlights, however, the different interpretations of restrictive practices at a national and

European level. Mars, in bringing the action, noted that Unilever's behaviour in the rest of Europe was similar to that which it was following in Ireland.

## ASSESSING EU COMPETITION POLICY

Compared with the UK position, the EU's approach to what constitutes a dominant market position is less clear. With regard to market definition, the Commission takes account of all closely substitutable products and the potential for new organisations and new products to enter the market. A dominant market position has never been clearly defined, but it would appear according to the judgments that have been made that a market share of around 40 per cent may suggest that dominance could be taking place, whereas a market share of 80 per cent is sufficient proof of a dominant position. By using scales of this type the Commission's definition is less demanding than the criteria set out in the UK. Abuse of the dominant position has been increasingly judged on the existence of organisations whose position depends very much on their interrelationship with another organisation.

With regard to merger policy, the 1990 Merger Control Regulation set out the guidelines for mergers within the EU; *see* earlier. Some saw these threshold levels as being set too high and thus the majority of mergers between European companies would not be investigated. Moreover, given the high thresholds, the majority of mergers that would come under the scrutiny of the Commission would be conglomerate rather than vertical or horizontal mergers. The problem is that EU regulation of mergers is in terms of monetary size rather than in terms of market size or industry size. Often vertical and horizontal mergers are more likely to lead to actions which may reduce consumer welfare, yet these types of mergers are not likely to be looked at by the Commission.

It is also the case that the majority of mergers which take place within the Union are between organisations from the same member state, as Table 22.2 indicates. The data reveal that merger activity is cyclical, and although mergers between companies in different member states are a much smaller part of total merger activity, their relative percentage has grown.

The legislation within the EU sought to make it clear that either a merger would be administered by national governments, although national policies towards mergers could differ, or the proposed merger would come under the jurisdiction of the Commission. However, member states could prevent a merger that has been agreed by the Commission if it involved public security, some aspect of the media or where competition in local markets is threatened. It is also not clear how far the Commission would pursue its rules if a merger involved two organisations which were non-EU

companies. In addition, where joint ventures are concerned, those which lead to less competition are covered by the 1990 Act but those which involve cooperation will still need to be cleared through Articles 85 and 86.

What appears to have come out of the Commission's policy towards mergers and takeovers is flexibility. For example, before the bid made by Nestlé for Pérrier, the French bottled water market was made up of three providers: Nestlé, Pérrier and BSN. The bid by Nestlé for Pérrier would have put the newly merged company in a strong position in the French market, with by value and volume twice the market of BSN. If Nestlé sold Volvic to BSN, a scenario that was supported by BSN in Nestlé's bid for Pérrier, then the French market would be a duopoly, with Nestlé and BSN holding 94 per cent. The Commission rejected this idea and suggested that Nestlé sell two of its bottled water companies to the Castel Group, thereby improving the competitive nature of the French market.

Although this is an example of the flexibility of the Commission, it has left unanswered the problem of differences in national law for mergers. The Edinburgh Summit in 1992 did attempt to rectify this issue and a number of countries, including Belgium, Spain, Italy and France, adopted new takeover laws or modified their existing ones.

In comparison to the UK's behaviour with regard to mergers, the time limits for investigations are shorter. The decision to undertake an investigation must occur within a month and the results must be given within four months. Whatever decision is reached is the result of the majority vote of the EU Commissioners and it is possible that some form of tradeoff could take place. It was noticeable in the first year of EU policies being in place that, of the 50 cases considered, all were approved except for the takeover of de Havilland by Aérospatiale of France and Alenia of Italy, the

**Table 22.2 Mergers and acquisitions in Europe**

| | National | EU | EU/International | International/EU |
|---|---|---|---|---|
| 1987–88 | 2110 (69.9) | 252 (0.3) | 499 (16.5) | 160 (5.3) |
| 1988–89 | 3187 (63.1) | 761 (15.1) | 659 (13.0) | 447 (8.8) |
| 1989–90 | 3853 (60.2) | 1121 (17.6) | 655 (10.2) | 768 (12.0) |
| 1990–91 | 3638 (62.0) | 947 (16.2) | 550 (9.4) | 729 (12.4) |
| 1991–92 | 3720 (66.6) | 760 (13.6) | 497 (8.9) | 605 (10.9) |
| 1992–93 | 3004 (62.2) | 634 (13.1) | 537 (11.1) | 656 (13.6) |

*Source*: Commission for the European Communities (1994) *23rd Competition Report for the Commission*, Com (94) 161 Final. Reprinted with the permission of The Office for Official Publications of the European Communities, Luxembourg.

reason being that the newly merged company would have had 50 per cent of the world market in 20–70-seater commuter aircraft and 67 per cent of the EU market. In addition, the Commission's view was that there would be no cost savings in the merger. In fact, the de Havilland case highlights a further feature of merger policy within the EU, in that mergers and takeovers may be viewed separately in terms of the definitions of their product markets. Sometimes they are narrowly defined, which suggests that the merger is unlikely to take place; sometimes they are defined as pan-European markets; while at other times they are viewed as more domestically based.

There has also been tension between the various national governments and the Commission. The French and southern European countries see mergers as one way of establishing national champions, which conflicts with the view of establishing a high level of competition. The Germans would like the ability to scrutinise the decisions of the Commission via their own cartel office, but cannot do so apart from the exceptions outlined earlier. In addition, although the EU legislation has operated only for a short time, there is a view that it is difficult to measure improvements in the way mergers perform since a number of them, historically, have been financially disappointing.

## STATE AID AND SUBSIDIES

One of the basic principles on which the EU was built was the creation and maintenance of a system of free and undistorted competition. Subsidies risk threatening the efficient functioning of this system, as they tend to reduce efficiency and distort trade in a manner similar to protectionist measures. Within the EU these state aids or subsidies are used, for example, to encourage the use of public transportation, the intensification of R&D and the support of declining industries. Not only do the subsidies distort the market, but the taxes raised to provide the subsidies add a further problem in reducing international welfare. Moreover, the effort to obtain subsidies and retaliate against others who have them uses up resources and further incurs a welfare loss.

The level of these subsidies in the EU is difficult to establish. A survey undertaken by the Commission in 1990 revealed that there were on average ECU82 billion of state aid in the member states between 1986 and 1988, amounting to 2.2 per cent of EU GDP and 4.5 per cent of total general government expenditure in the Union. There were also major differences by state, with the UK and Belgium spending approximately 1 per cent of GDP on state aid, while Italy, the Netherlands and France spent 3 per cent or more, as Table 22.3 indicates.

Furthermore, the subsidies are industry specific; around 60 per cent went on three sectors: transport (30 per cent), coal (16 per cent) and agriculture/fisheries (13 per cent). The remaining 40 per cent went mainly to manufacturing, with the principal sectors being cars, electronics and aviation. The subsidisation of these sectors is particularly high in Greece, Spain, France and Portugal. Concerning horizontal aid which has no sectoral or regional specificity, there is heavy subsidisation of general investment in Portugal, Belgium, the Netherlands and Luxembourg; and of small and medium-sized enterprises in the Netherlands, Belgium, Greece, Italy and Luxembourg. While this state aid is in existence, a number of countries and their industries cannot be said to be operating on a 'level playing field'.

Article 92 says that all state aid to industry is illegal. This state aid can take many forms and includes not only direct government grants and cheap loans, but also tax concessions and the provision of goods and services on favourable terms. Some types of state aid are allowed, however. These include aid which supports social improvement, or aid to support a project which has EU-wide implications.

Within the EU, the real extent of state aid is difficult to assess since it includes more that just direct loans to organisations and can include such items as favouring domestic organisations with contracts and the like. In terms of direct support, the

**Table 22.3  Subsidies as a percentage of GDP**

| Country | 1960 | 1975–9 | 1985–9 |
|---|---|---|---|
| Austria | 0.5 | 3.0 | 3.0 |
| Belgium | 1.3 | 1.4 | 1.3 |
| Denmark | 0.7 | 3.1 | 3.1 |
| France | 1.6 | 2.5 | 3.0 |
| Germany | 0.8 | 2.1 | 2.2 |
| Italy | 1.4 | 3.2 | 3.3 |
| Japan | 0.4 | 1.3 | 1.1 |
| Netherlands | 1.2 | 2.4 | 3.7 |
| Sweden | 1.0 | 3.9 | 4.7 |
| UK | 1.9 | 2.7 | 1.7 |

*Source*: Adapted from Crafts, N (1992) 'Productivity growth reconsidered', *Economic Policy*, Vol 15, October, p 411. Reprinted with permission of the Oxford University Press.

Commission has investigated several sectors and ordered the repayment of a number of loans, for example in the British Aerospace takeover of the Rover Group and Fiat's purchase of Alfa-Romeo. In fact, the overarching direction of policy appears to be that state aid should not be given to organisations which need it but which have little chance of recovery, but it can be given to those that perhaps do not need it but are in growth or profitable sectors of the economy. To some extent the Commission's view clashes with that of national governments which wish to develop national or pan-European champions and which have heavily supported their inefficient, often publicly owned, industries. The air carrier industry in the EU provides a suitable example of a sector supported by a number of national governments for which the Commission appears to have drawn a line and said 'enough is enough'. A number of national industries that have received high levels of both direct and indirect state aid in the past are those likely to

be large employers, and the harsher reality of a system without state aid, coupled with low growth conditions within the EU, may lead to conflict between national and EU policies on state aid.

---

◆ **Exercise 22.2** (*see Case study 22.2*)

**1** How might non-state-owned airlines respond to the greater competitiveness of Iberia?

**2** Suppose that Iberia and other state-run airlines do not become profitable by the year 2000. What is likely to be the competitive position of the airline industry in Europe?

---

*Comment on Case study 22.2*

The airline industry provides a good example of a sector where there is a mix of both private and state-run enterprises. The private carriers see the state aid provided to state-run enterprises as an

## ◆ CASE STUDY 22.2

# Ailing state airlines

In theory Europe's airlines have been free to charge more or less whatever they like for flights within the European Union, and to fly wherever they want, for the past three years. Why then, in this supposedly competitive market, has no overmanned, loss-making state airline ever gone out of business?

The short answer is that most of the flag-carriers – Air France, Belgium's Sabena, Ireland's Aer Lingus, Greece's Olympic – have been kept aloft by government subsidies; and by political pressure to have those subsidies approved by the European Commission. . . In early February 1996 it was the turn of Spain's Iberia, beneficiary of a capital injection of Ptas 87 billion ($690m), with another Ptas 20 billion potentially available in 1997. Yet in 1992 Iberia received state aid of Ptas 120 billion, approved by the commission as a 'one time, last time' bail-out. How does Neil Kinnock, the transport commissioner, justify this apparent second bite of the cherry?

The answer: by invoking what the commission calls 'the market investor principle'. Teneo, the Spanish state holding company that controls Iberia, is alleged to be acting as a private investor would in similar circumstances. This principle has been accepted by the EU's Court of Justice. [It says that if the state-run company is restructuring itself and operating as though it was in the private sector, it can receive further state aid.]

When Iberia, reeling from peseta devaluations and European recession, came knocking on the commission's door in late 1994, it was seeking permission for Ptas 130 billion in state aid. Now it is getting less, and has had to abandon its past ambitions, by selling off its holdings in Argentina's national airline and part of its holdings in Chile's Ladeco airline.

Add a requirement for a rate of return of at least 30 per cent on the capital (the Spanish government had originally asked for 23 per cent), a reduction in Iberia's fleet from 120 aircraft in 1993 to 104 in 1997, a salary freeze and another 3,500 redundancies (on top of 5,000 already made between 1991 and 1993). By the reckoning of Mr Kinnock, all this is evidence then there is a view that the commission is not cosseting Iberia – and that rival airlines and other governments should have few complaints.

But Britain, with its unsubsidised and profitable airline industry, certainly should. Indeed, its Conservative government ministers are already – and predictably – denouncing Mr Kinnock, and threatening to challenge his decision in the European Court. The real complaints, however, should come from the passengers. Whatever the liberal theory of Europe's aviation policy, the reality is that airfares in Europe are roughly twice as high as America's; and that only 7 per cent of international routes within Europe are served by more than two airlines.

*Source*: © *The Economist*, London, 3 February 1996. Reprinted with permission.

unfair advantage. It allows them to remain competitive in areas of the market which they should, in terms of market forces, be exiting. Like a country's currency, the state airline is seen as an element of national pride and this has resulted in high levels of support; moreover, airlines are good employers. The state-aid question, however, is only one element of the protection that is provided to state airlines. The market is not truly competitive in terms of landing rights and licences for different air routes. It appears that it will take some time before the airline industry in Europe is more than just partially competitive.

## RESTRICTIVE PRACTICES IN THE UK AND EU

Restrictive practices in the UK fall under the Restrictive Practices Act 1956 and the Restrictive Trade Practices Act 1976. Restrictive practices refer to fixing the prices that are charged and the conditions of supply. Any agreement that is registered as restricting price is against the public interest, and will be referred to the Restrictive Practices Court where it is the responsibility of the organisations to prove otherwise. In assembling their defence companies are limited to eight gateways which are allowed under restrictive practices legislation, so a restrictive practice is deemed to be against the public interest unless an organisation can satisfy one of the gateways. These gateways are that the restrictive practice:

- Protects the public against injury.
- Bestows specific benefits on consumers.
- Prevents local unemployment.
- Counters current restrictions on competition.
- Maintains exports.
- Supports other acceptable restrictions.
- Assists the negotiation of fair trading terms for suppliers and buyers.
- Neither restricts nor deters competition.

The eighth gateway was added in 1968.

If organisations satisfy one or more of the gateways, they must still show that the overall benefits from the restrictive practice are clearly greater than the costs incurred. This 'tailpiece' is the final stumbling block for many restrictive practices.

These gateways can come into play where the restrictive practice is registered, but it is possible that a number of restrictive pricing practices go unregistered. In addition, it is possible to internalise price restrictions through merger or takeover, although this might lead to the newly merged organisation being investigated under monopolies and merger legislation.

Since 1956 almost 10 000 agreements have been registered, although only a small proportion of these have been referred to the courts. The majority have been abandoned. ABTA (Association of British Travel Agents) was successful, however, in defending its restrictive practice arrangement whereby ABTA members only deal with other ABTA members, on the grounds that it protected the consumer, and this type of protection was not obtainable in any other way.

A main issue with restrictive practices legislation in the UK has been that there were no financial penalties for failing to register a restrictive agreement. For example, in 1991 three major suppliers of steel roofing supports were found to have operated a market-sharing cartel. Because the restrictive practices legislation cannot deal with restrictions which are not registered, there is a need to bring it into line with the more effective EU Article 85 on restrictive practices.

Article 85 is concerned with restrictive practices. It considers 'agreements between undertakings, decisions by associations of undertakings and concerted practices which may affect trade between Member States and which have as their object the prevention, restriction, or distortion of competition within the Common Market'.

In the main, whereas UK legislation is concerned with market structures that are oligopolistic, the EU legislation simply deals with collusive behaviour. It is much easier to obtain a prosecution under EU law, with the result that a number of both domestic and European organisations/industries have received bans and heavy fines. Notorious examples of price fixing within the EU have been seen in the steel industry, cement and Dutch building industry.

As with UK legislation, exemptions are made where the restrictive practice agreement improves social welfare, for example where an agreement improves production and distribution or augments innovation and technical progress.

The Competition Directorate can also grant block exemptions as a way around the restrictive practice. A good example of this is the block exemption provided for car franchises to sell a particular maker's car and no other. This block exemption is allowed so that consumers benefit from better-quality service and stockholding. It is also argued that the policy enables smaller manufacturers to arrange distribution rather than having to compete with larger manufacturers for space through a distribution outlet that sells many makes of car.

It is possible that this process could also lead to price differentials between EU countries for the same make of car. In an attempt to reduce this discrepancy, the organisations which have been granted block exemptions should not be in a position to ban parallel imports. Thus a block exemption ceases to be in existence when **parallel imports** are constrained. In reality it has been difficult for the Commission to stop this process taking place.

Exclusive purchasing agreements can also be granted block exemptions. For example, these exist between a petrol station and a petrol supplier, where the agreement can last no longer than 10 years provided that the supplier does not own the site. In the case of beer, there are also special provisions. Purchasers must be able to buy drinks other than beer from any supplier which offers the most reasonable terms. Block exemptions can also be allowed for licensing agreements, specialisation, research and development and franchises.

# BREAKING DOWN STATE MONOPOLIES

Most governments now agree that the most efficient way of improving the effectiveness of markets is to increase competition. By breaking down monopoly power and encouraging market entry, competition increases, prices fall and quantities made available increase. That is, the market is freed to competitive forces. Such arguments have been put forward with reference to the private sector in preceding sections. Should there be a different argument with reference to the public sector?

Contemporary popular thinking suggests that it is logical to install competitive forces in the public sector in order to improve efficiency, in the same way as happens in the private sector. The UK experience and model of the 1980s is often quoted as a role model for other governments. In that period, the UK government, under then prime minister Margaret Thatcher, used a variety of measures to open markets to competitive forces. These measures were as follows.

## CCT – compulsory competitive tendering

This largely involved local government organisations providing services within the community. Typical services were refuse collection, hospital cleaning and catering and school meals provision. Local authorities were required to put provision of the service out to tender for an initial five-year contract. In many cases, the local authority was able to set up companies which successfully tendered for the contracts, thus maintaining employment for those involved in the original service provision.

**Competitive tendering** means that, unless revoked, the successful organisation gained a five-year monopoly of provision. That is, the market is only opened up to competitive forces every five years.

## Liberalisation and deregulation

Typically used in services or markets such as on bus routes in the UK and air routes in the United States. Here, additional licences and permission to operate are granted to entrants in the market. Deregulation is similar, but usually occurs where the industry has previously been privatised.

In the case of buses, the change meant that instead of one, national provider, many, mostly local, operators began to compete on routes. The danger of **liberalisation/deregulation** in such cases is that no profitable routes are left in the hands of the incumbent, while profitable routes are subject to heavy competition. A way round this is to require entrants to run buses on both attractive and less attractive routes as a condition of their permission to operate.

## Selling off

This is perhaps the best recognised form of opening markets to competition. It involves selling publicly owned (usually) monopolies to private shareholders in a share issue open to all members of the general public. This process is known as privatisation.

Some analysts and economists claim that the increased competition and efficiency associated with privatised markets could be gained without selling publicly held assets. These critics claim that alternatives such as liberalisation and deregulation would be more effective catalysts to competition. The structure, line of command and control and traditions of nationalised (publicly owned) industries, it is argued, could be changed to accept additional competition, without selling off nationally owned and recognised organisations.

◆ **CASE STUDY 22.3**

## The UK privatisation experience

The first privatisations in the UK were low key. As time has passed and experience has been gained, the process has become more sophisticated. One of the first privatisations was that of Sealink – a passenger ferry company operating in the Channel and the Irish Sea. By its very nature, this was an easy sale, of just one company which did not in fact hold a natural monopoly as such.

One of the most famous privatisations was the later issue of British Gas shares. British Gas was a more difficult sale because of its status as a natural monopoly. Selling off the regional gas companies separately was a step towards promoting competition. For some time now, business customers have been able to choose their supplying gas company. Since late 1995, domestic customers in the southwest of the UK have also been able to choose their supplier. The regional British Gas company has been joined in the domestic market by a competitor, offering gas supplies to customers at a lower price per unit than the regional British Gas's price.

The main British privatisations are shown in Table 22.4.

**Table 22.4 Major British privatisations**

| Enterprise privatised | Years(s) |
| --- | --- |
| British Aerospace | 1980–86 |
| Cable and Wireless | 1981–5 |
| Associated British Ports | 1983–4 |
| Austin-Rover | 1984–8 |
| British Telecom | 1984–91 |
| Sealink | 1984 |
| National Bus Company | 1986 |
| British Gas | 1986 |
| Rolls Royce | 1987 |
| British Airports Authority | 1987 |
| British Airways | 1987 |
| British steel | 1988–9 |
| Water Boards | 1989–90 |
| Electricity Distributors | 1990 |
| Electricity Generators | 1991 |
| British Coal | 1994 |
| Railtrack (British Rail) | 1995–6 |
| British Energy | 1996 |

*Source*: HM Treasury, *Financial Statistics*, Office for National Statistics. Crown Copyright 1996. Reproduced by the permission of the Controller of HMSO and the Office for National Statistics.

In total the UK government sold almost £50 billion of state assets over the period 1979–96.

Although there were important supply-side arguments advanced in defence of privatisation, there is little doubt that other considerations played a supporting role:

◆ Privatisation fitted in with the broader political objective of widening private share ownership.
◆ Under British public-sector accounting conventions, privatisation proceeds reduce public spending. The logic is that, since capital spending in nationalised industries adds to the public expenditure totals, the sale of such public investments should reduce spending totals in a mirror-image fashion.

A further reason for the privatisation programme was that under public control, nationalised industries had no incentive to reduce costs and respond to changing patterns of consumer demand. Since many nationalised industries enjoyed considerable monopoly power, they could easily achieve the crude financial objects placed on them by successive governments – such as achieving a specified rate of return on capital investment – by manipulating their prices, rather than by cutting over-manning and producing more efficiently.

Nationalised industries in the 1970s were characterised by considerable *X*-inefficiency (that is, bureaucratic waste), overstaffing and ill-directed investment. Productivity growth lagged well behind that of the private sector, and many enterprises made heavy financial losses which absorbed huge amounts of taxpayers' money. To the general public both at home and abroad, British nationalised industries were synonymous with overpriced, poor-quality service.

However, given that many privatised industries continued to enjoy a significant degree of monopoly power after their transfer into the private sector, it is not immediately clear precisely how privatisation was intended to spur incumbent management to greater efficiency. The neoclassical economists argued that the impetus to greater competition and efficiency lay in the new vulnerability of privatised enterprises to hostile takeover bids on the stock market.

*Source*: Authors.

## Natural monopolies

Many of the enterprises that have been privatised are natural monopolies; *see* Figure 22.4. A natural monopoly occurs where the minimum efficient size of the organisation is at least as large as the total market demand. Thus an organisation can meet current market demand while it is still on the downward portion of its long-run average total cost curve.

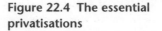

Figure 22.4 The essential privatisations

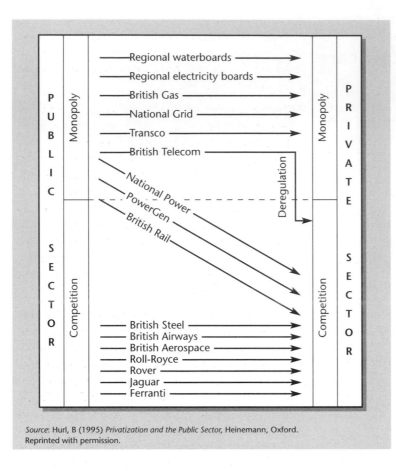

Source: Hurl, B (1995) *Privatization and the Public Sector*, Heinemann, Oxford. Reprinted with permission.

A profit-seeking natural monopolist will produce at the point at which marginal revenue (MR) equals marginal cost (MC); *see* Figure 22.5. Thus the natural monopolist produces output $Q_m$ charging price $P_m$. The perfectly competitive industry price and output level are shown as $P_{Pc}$ and $Q_{Pc}$ respectively. A regulator who wishes to control the price charged by a natural monopolist will be able to push prices down to $P_1$. This is the price at which the natural monopolist will cover its costs, including normal profit. If a price is set below $P_1$ then the natural monopolist will not earn normal profits and in the long run will exit the industry. At the price level $P_1$ there is a welfare loss to society shown by the shaded area.

The transfer of ownership of natural monopolies such as electricity, gas and water not only risks consumer exploitation, but it may also result in the industries becoming less, rather than more, efficient in terms of average production costs. That is, as output increases, costs continuously decline, so that as one organisation grows slightly larger than its rivals, it enjoys a self-reinforcing cost advantage which allows it to grow and cut costs until it has captured the whole market.

Figure 22.5 Price and output under a natural monopoly

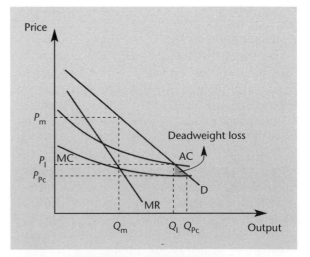

A profit-maximising natural monopolist faces a downward-sloping average cost curve, with marginal cost below it, and produces at the point at which MR=MC, that is, output $Q_m$ at price $P_m$. A perfectly competitive industry would produce at output level $Q_{Pc}$ and charge $P_{Pc}$. The lowest price at which the regulator can set the price is price=AC, which results in a deadweight loss to society.

Given that, by definition, it is counter-productive to break up a natural monopoly, the task facing the government was some form of regulation on the transfer of ownership.

## THE ROLE OF REGULATION

The privatised monopolies are regulated by terms laid down in their privatisation legislation and their operating licences. For example, British Telecom, which was the first major utility to be privatised, has an operating licence which runs for 25 years in the first instance. This sets out the terms under which the utility must operate, including the supply of rural services, telephone boxes and emergency calls.

Such a privatisation requires technical and regulatory sophistication. Obviously, the government does not wish to create a scenario where all entrants to the market have to create their own infrastructure – gas supply pipes to people's homes, for example. Other strategies are required. Privatisations are therefore carefully thought out. Further indication of the difficulty of selling off natural monopolies is given by the privatisation of the regional electricity supply companies and their separation from the electricity generators. Similarly, the privatisation of British Rail and the series of alterations to the proposed privatised structure illustrate that planning and accepted thinking with reference to the issues change over time.

Overseeing the results of any privatisation are **regulatory bodies**, known as watchdogs, established at the time of privatisation. Each body's terms of reference are to act in the public's interest. Each is known by an acronym beginning with the letters 'Of', referring to 'Office', and followed by the industry in question. For example, Ofgas is the gas industry watchdog and Ofwat is the water industry watchdog. The watchdogs are given the task of liaising with consumer groups to ensure that standards and service are maintained, watching over price levels to ensure that any price rises are fair – largely regulated by a predetermined formula – and so on.

The impact of the regulatory system depends on its influence on managerial behaviour. In the US, where private monopoly suppliers of electricity, gas and water have existed for many years, the regulatory system has variously controlled service, environmental considerations and pricing, much as in the UK. Three broad problems have been experienced in the US:

- The system gives too many opportunities to lobbyists and lawyers, who waste resources in lengthy, so-called rent-seeking activities.
- The regulatory agencies in the US have been criticised for siding with the supplier against the consumer – so-called **regulatory capture**.
- Prices have been regulated with a view to achieving a 'satisfactory' rate of return on capital, which tends to reduce the incentive for management to control costs, encouraging them to pursue growth and output targets instead of maximising efficiency.

The method of control introduced in the UK was designed to overcome the main disadvantages of the US system. The retail price index (RPI) minus $X$ formula, as it is known, was intended to control prices while permitting increased profits resulting from lower costs. The regulators would fix the $X$-factor on the basis of forecast productivity gains in comparable industries (e.g. 3 per cent). If the privatised industry achieved productivity growth in line with the sectoral average, it could then raise its prices each year by 3 per cent less than the inflation rate. In this way it should maintain a broadly constant rate of return. If productivity improvements exceeded 3 per cent, this would allow the industry to increase its rate of return for the same permitted price rise.

However, the RPI – $X$ formula does contain a major flaw which can lead to precisely the same inefficiencies as the US-style regulatory system. It appears that the $X$-factor is periodically reassessed, in the light of what the regulatory body considers to be a satisfactory rate of profit. For example, when BT reported a spectacular rise in its profits in 1991, largely because it had managed to exceed the productivity gains implicit in the $X$-factor by a very large margin, Oftel responded to mounting public resentment by threatening to increase the size of the $X$-factor. Such adjustments, however apparently reasonable on social grounds, may destroy managerial incentives to reduce costs and become more efficient.

# SUMMARY

◆ There is a distinction between the interventionist and the Austrian view of competition policy. In the former market failure may exist in terms of abuse by monopolies and therefore competition policy is required to reduce this failure. In the latter, organisations grow, not to abuse their position, but as a means of improving the efficiency to which resources are put. Large/dominant organisations should therefore be encouraged.

◆ There are a number of ways in which competition policy could be developed. Should it prevent dominant organisations being in existence? Should it control dominant firms? Should dominant organisations be encouraged as cost savers or as a way to establish pan-European organisations which find it much easier to compete on a world stage? The problem is that economists differ as to the market conditions necessary to promote competition and therefore the policy advocated differs.

◆ The S–C–P paradigm does not necessarily provide a solid basis for the development of competition policy. S–C–P is based on a linear, deterministic relationship which places undue emphasis on the structure (particularly the concentration) of industries. Therefore the benefits of highly concentrated industries are ignored.

◆ UK competition policy was established in 1948 with a definition of the monopoly position as a firm that controlled 33 per cent of more of the market. This was altered in 1973 to 25 per cent. UK policy is founded on establishing that a monopoly or merger is against the public interest. On each occasion the MMC considers the whole range of current and future costs and benefits from the monopoly or merger.

◆ EU competition policy was established in the Treaty of Rome under Article 85, which prohibits restrictive agreements and practices between companies affecting trade or leading to distortion of competition within the Union, and Article 86, which prohibits the use of a dominant position within the Union by organisations. In addition, Articles 92–94 ban national government aid to domestic industries which distorts or threatens to distort competition between firms within the Union. Finally, the Merger Control Regulation (1989) allows the EU Commission to consider both national and cross-border mergers within the Union.

◆ State aid has played an important part in distorting trading patterns within the EU. These are viewed as unfair by the Commission, which has sought to reduce the level of state aid paid by national governments. This state aid appears to be industry specific, being associated in the main with the car, electronics and aviation industries. National state-aid policy may conflict with both the Commission's and national governments' attempts to develop national or pan-European champions.

◆ Restrictive practices within the UK and EU, that is, the ability of organisations to set prices and behave as a cartel, are frowned on within Europe. UK legislation is more concerned with oligopolistic market structures, while EU legislation simply deals with any collusive behaviour. EU legislation does allow for block exemptions, so long as parallel imports are not restricted, where the block exemption has a finite life and where other, associated areas of the market are open to competition.

# REVIEW QUESTIONS

1 What factors lie behind merger cycles?

2 Outline UK and EU policy towards restrictive trade practices. How might the control of cartels be improved?

3 One way to resolve the issue of state aid to industry is to let all countries offer state aid. What are the problems with this approach?

4  Should we encourage the merger of EU organisations so that they can compete more effectively in world markets?

5  In which circumstances could the S–C–P concentration ratio approach to analysis of markets potentially lead to welfare losses after application of the policy, rather than the intended welfare gains?

6  Table 22.5 shows national newspaper circulation in the UK. Calculate the $CR_5$ ratio for each of the three years. Is the national newspaper market becoming more concentrated? Give reasons for your answer.

**Table 22.5  National newspaper circulation in the UK**

| Title of newspaper | Owned by | Daily circulation 1992 | 1993 | 1994 |
|---|---|---|---|---|
| Sun | News Corporation | 3 588 077 | 3 513 591 | 4 007 520 |
| Daily Mirror | Headington Investment | 2 868 263 | 2 676 015 | 2 484 436 |
| Daily Mail | Daily Mail | 1 688 808 | 1 769 253 | 1 784 030 |
| Daily Express | United Newspapers | 1 537 726 | 1 409 323 | 1 369 266 |
| Daily Telegraph | Ravelston Corporation | 1 043 703 | 1 024 340 | 1 007 944 |
| Daily Star | United Newspapers | 808 486 | 773 908 | 746 412 |
| Today | News Corporation | 495 405 | 533 332 | 579 910 |
| Guardian | Guardian Newspapers | 418 026 | 416 207 | 400 399 |
| Times | News Corporation | 390 323 | 368 219 | 471 847 |
| Independent | Newspaper Publishing | 376 532 | 348 692 | 284 440 |
| Financial Times | Pearson | 291 915 | 290 139 | 296 984 |
| Totals | | 13 507 264 | 13 204 019 | 13 433 188 |

Source: Audit Bureau of Circulation

7  Calculate $CR_3$, $CR_4$ and $CR_5$ for the markets given in Table 22.6. Briefly describe the markets given.

**Table 22.6**

| Relative market share (%) | Market A | B | C | D |
|---|---|---|---|---|
| Firm 1 | 25 | 15 | 35 | 20 |
| Firm 2 | 25 | 15 | 4 | 10 |
| Firm 3 | 25 | 15 | 0.5 | 8 |
| Firm 4 | 25 | 15 | 0.45 | 6 |
| Firm 5 | – | 15 | 0.4 | 5 |
| Others in market | – | 1 firm with 15% and 1 firm with 10% | 100 firms with less than 0.4% each | 35 progressively smaller firms with less than 5% each |

# GLOSSARY OF NEW TERMS

**Allocative efficiency:** Production levels at which price is equal to marginal cost.

**Austrian approach:** A group of economic theorists who believe that the most efficient way for the market to work is based on market forces without the involvement of government.

**Block exemption:** An exemption to competition rules allowed by the European Commission where consumers can appear to benefit from the uncompetitive behaviour of organisations.

**Competition policy:** A policy designed to encourage competition between organisations or reduce the dominance of organisations.

**Compulsory competitive tendering:** Legislation introduced by the UK government requiring certain local authority services to be put out to tender.

**Concentration ratio (CR$_x$):** The percentage of the total market controlled by the five largest firms.

**Full line enforcement:** An arrangement under which a supplier agrees either to sell the whole portfolio of its products to a retailer where the alternative is no supply.

**Liberalisation:** The granting of additional licences or permits to allow organisations to compete in previously state-monopolised industries

**Parallel imports:** Imports of competitive products to those supplied in the domestic economy.

**Public interest:** A term used in monopoly and merger control in the UK to suggest that a monopoly or merger should at least maintain or promote competition.

**Public procurement:** The purchase of products and services by the state.

**Regulatory body:** In the UK, known by the prefix 'Of-', regulatory bodies ensure on the government's behalf that newly privatised industries act in the public interest. Pricing policies are a primary concern. Oftel, for example, is the body which oversees the activties of British Telecom, privatised in the 1980s.

**State aid:** The provision of public monies as a means to sustain ailing industries.

# READING

Cable, J (ed) (1994) *Current Issues in Industrial Economics*, Macmillan, Basingstoke.
  *There is a discussion of policies concerning competition and monopoly legislation in the UK and the US in Chapter 5.*

Cook, M and Healey, N M (1995) *Growth and Structural Change*, Macmillan, Basingstoke.
  *Chapter 10 considers the role of the EU and its influence on business. It provides a clear account of the issue of state aid and competition policy.*

Davies, S and Lyons, B (1992) *The Economics of Industrial Organisation*, Longman, Harlow.
  *Chapter 5 contains an in-depth discussion of the problems and issues surrounding the use of S–C–P as a guide to competition policy.*

Griffiths, A and Wall, S (1997) *Applied Economics: An Introductory Course*, 7th edn, Addison Wesley Longman, Harlow.
  *Chapter 5 gives a development of both UK and EU competition policy and provides some useful data on merger activity. The HHI is also investigated in depth, with particular reference to the US Justice Department's position.*

Mason, E S (1939) 'Price and production policies of large-scale enterprises', *American Economic Review*, Supplement No 29, pp 61–74.

Parker, D and Martin, S (1994) 'The impact of UK privatisation on employment, profits and distribution of business income', Occasional Papers in Industrial Strategy, No 18, Centre for Industrial Strategy, Birmingham Business School, University of Birmingham.

Parker, D and Martin, S (1995) 'The impact of UK privatisation on labour and total factor productivity', *Scottish*

*Journal of Political Economy*, Vol 42, May, pp 201–20.
  *Both these articles provide a good assessment of the privatisation experience in the UK.*

Welford, R and Prescott, K (1996) *European Business: An Issue Based Approach*, 3rd edn, Pitman Publishing, London.
  *This text provides a good background to competition policy in the EU as well as supplying a useful set of examples of EU organisations' behaviour and the way the European Commission has dealt with this.*

## Further reading

Bain, J S (1951) 'Relation of profit rate to industrial concentration: American manufacturing 1936–40', *Quarterly Journal of Economics*, Vol 65, pp 293–324.

Bishop, M and Kay, J (1988) *Does Privatisation Work? Lessons from the UK*, London Business School, London.

Caves, R E (1974) 'Industrial organisation' in Dunning, J H (ed), *Economic Analysis and the Multinational Enterprise*, Allen and Unwin, London.

Cook, M and Meredith, C (1994) 'European mergers and takeovers', *Business Studies*, Vol 7, No 2, December, pp 29–33.

Curwen, P (1994) *Understanding the UK Economy*, 3rd edn, Macmillan, Basingstoke.

Ferguson, P R and Ferguson, G J (1994) *Industrial Economics: Issues and Perspectives*, 2nd edn, Macmillan, Basingstoke.

Ferguson, P R, Ferguson, G J and Rothschild, R (1993) *Business Economics*, Macmillan, Basingstoke.

Harberger, A (1954) 'Monopoly and resource allocation', *American Economic Review Papers and Proceedings*, Vol 44, No 1, pp 77–87.

Hirschey, M, Pappas, J and Whigham, D (1995) *Managerial Economics (European Edition)*, Dryden Press, London.

Miller, R L and Meiners, R E (1986) *Intermediate Microeconomics*, McGraw-Hill, New York.

Monopolies and Mergers Commission (1979) *Ice-cream and Water Ices: A Report on the Supply in the United Kingdom of Ice-cream and Water Ices*, Cmnd 7632, HMSO, London.

Parker, D (1992) 'Agency status, privatisation, and improved performance: some evidence from the UK', *International Journal of Public Sector Management*, Vol 5, No 1.

Scherer, F M and Ross, D (1990) *Industrial Market Structure and Economic Performance*, 3rd edn, Houghton Mifflin, Boston.

Schwartzman, D (1960) 'The burden of monopoly', *Journal of Political Economy*, Vol 68, December, pp 627–30.

CHAPTER 23

# THE CHANGING BOUNDARIES OF THE ORGANISATION

## KEY ISSUES

Business issues

Business strategy

Decision-making techniques

Economic concepts

Management decision issues

Optimal outcomes to management issues

## OBJECTIVES

- ◆ To examine the reasons for organisations changing in size, that is, alter their boundaries.

- ◆ To consider the macroeconomic factors which lead organisations to grow.

- ◆ To explore the factors which lead to organisations reaching an optimal size.

- ◆ To discuss the success or otherwise of merger activity.

- ◆ To consider the role of joint ventures in altering the boundary of the organisation.

- ◆ To examine the impact of core competencies on boundary size.

- ◆ To explore how the process of organisational shrinkage takes place.

- ◆ To consider how downsizing and reengineering have affected organisational size.

## CHAPTER OUTLINE

Business application

The scope of the organisation

The linkage approach

Merger behaviour

Joint ventures

Case study 23.1 Joint ventures in the heavy machinery industry

The shrinking boundaries of the organisation

Case study 23.2 Trelleborg divestment was a reluctant decision

Divestment

Management buyouts

Case study 23.3 Nothing ventured, nothing . . .?

Downsizing and all that

Demergers

Case study 23.64 Demergers

Summary

Review questions

Glossary of new terms

Reading

## KEY TERMS

Conglomerate diversification

Core business

Corporate reengineering

Demerger

Divestment

Downsizing (right-sizing)

Fixed input proportions

Fordism

Horizontal integration

Joint venture

Linkage approach

Management buyin

Management buyout

Merger

Upsizing

Variable input proportions

Vertical integration

FT

# International telecommunications

The three big long-distance carriers, American Telegraph and Telephones (AT&T), Microwave Communications International (MCI) and Sprint, have each adopted a slightly different approach to global competition.

MCI has formed an alliance with British Telecom; Sprint has tied up arrangements with Deutsche Telekom and France Telecom; AT&T – depending on one's viewpoint – is either operating through a looser series of alliances in Europe and the Far East, or going it alone. The logic of these groupings is derived not only from the strategy of the US companies but – perhaps more importantly – from that of foreign companies which are seeking access to the US market. Whereas there are only three big US long-distance companies, Europe has far more players. So who would the European companies choose?

AT&T it was argued was ruled out because of its size. In revenue terms, AT&T is bigger than Deutsche Telekom and France Telecom together and almost four times the size of BT. Even after the divestment of its computing arm and equipment manufacturing operations, it is still a behemoth among carriers. No European company could enter an alliance with AT&T and be assured of equality.

That made MCI the most attractive target, as the next biggest but of manageable size. BT has linked up with them purchasing a 20 per cent stake – the maximum allowed under US regulations. By 1994, a 20 per cent stake in Sprint had been purchased by Deutsche Telekom and France Telecom.

AT&T's own arrangements include Uniworld, a joint venture with Unisource, which is in turn a venture formed by the telephone companies of Switzerland, Sweden and the Netherlands. It also formed World-Partners, a loose alliance with Singapore Telecoms and KDD, the Japanese long-distance company.

How remunerative these global alliances will prove is perhaps another matter. Multinationals, such as Unilever or General Motors, which need to communicate across a myriad of international subsidiaries, are already highly experienced in telecoms. The ability to offer them a single compatible world-wide system for voice and data is, of course, attractive but equally, these companies can drive a hard bargain, especially among active competitors.

There is one further imponderable. At some point, the Internet will presumably become sufficiently global – and sufficiently secure – to form the basis of a communications network for some corporations, or at least for some of their traffic. In that case, the telephone companies need to differentiate their own services enough to make sure they are not reduced to commodity status, and above all, they need to work out how to collect a more respectable toll for Internet traffic passing over their wires.

*Source: Financial Times, 3 October 1995. Reprinted with permission.*

## Comment

The telecommunications industry is just one of a number of industries which are having to respond to changes in global competition by altering their boundaries. But what is the optimal size of industries in the telecommunications sector? The organisations themselves may not know, and even if they do today's optimal size may be tomorrow's wrong size. Nonetheless, it might be expected that one factor that would cause the boundaries of the organisations in this sector to change would be the role of regulatory bodies, which may dictate maximum sizes or suggest cost structures which encourage the organisation not to grow. In addition changes in technology, as the case study suggests, and the role of competition will also affect the size of the organisation. The case study illustrates widening the boundaries of the organisations involved through more formal joint ventures and other looser alliances, but also indicates how organisations reduce their boundaries through divestment. Thus many organisations change their boundaries over time.

It should be realised that there will be organisations whose boundaries may be fairly static, and a group that would fit this category are some of the small and medium-sized firms discussed in Chapter 2. In the light of these boundary changes and the factors that lead to them, the approach of this chapter is to consider the factors that lead to organisations extending their boundaries first, before developing and considering the factors that result in organisations contracting their boundaries.

# THE SCOPE OF THE ORGANISATION

As Chapter 17 showed, transaction costs provide one explanation not only for organisations existing but also for organisations altering their boundaries and seeking to grow or diminish in size. The substitution of internal organisations for market exchange permits the internalisation of transaction costs and a subsequent reduction in contracting and monitoring. As Williamson (1985) notes, an advantage of the organisation is that intra-organisation activities are more easily and sensitively enforced than inter-organisation activities. An organisation is more able to evaluate performance than is a buyer, and an organisation's reward and penalty instruments may be more refined than those that exist in the marketplace. At some point, however, it is quite possible that the increased marginal costs of coordination outweigh the gains from additional evaluation of performance and resolution of conflicts, and thus this might imply limits for the size of the organisation. Similarly, Williamson (1985) proposes that there are limits to internalising transactions in **vertical integration** – for example, the tendency of internal supply sources to distort procurement decisions and the distortion of communications along management lines.

The advantages and disadvantages that flow from the transaction cost approach can be seen in both the public and private sectors in the UK. During the 1980s and 1990s organisations which had grown over many years in order to internalise transaction costs began to return to the market by way of outsourcing. This was particularly prevalent in the public sector, such as in the contracting out of services in the NHS and local government. Conversely, it is clear that some organisations will continue to grow beyond efficient limits for various reasons, including competitive pressures, managerial aspirations and external expectations.

External supply effects may limit the scope or size of the organisation. As it expands difficulties may arise from the use of inferior inputs, from paying increased costs of transportation and materials, perhaps also from the exhaustion of particular sectors of the labour market. A single organisation may not be able to affect supply by itself, but if it is in an industry where all other organisations are also attempting to expand, this can lead to external diseconomies of scale. These external diseconomies first affect the industry through increased supply prices and are then translated into increased costs on an individual organisational basis. For the individual organisation, therefore, there will be an increase in its marginal costs for each unit of output, as Figure 23.1 indicates.

Organisations may alter their boundaries through economies of scale and through economies of scope. Both give unit cost reductions as output increases, the former through the advantages of buying in bulk, having cheaper access to finance etc., while the latter are achieved through changes in average costs as a result of alterations in the mix of production between two or more products. Chapter 16 considers economies of both scope and scale. Economies of scope are the benefits to be obtained from the joint production of two or more products. For unrelated products scope economies can come about through the sharing of inputs in the production process, such as management, administration or storage facilities. For related products there may be cost advantages through complementarity of production, such as for cars and trucks. Environmental factors may also provide the conditions for economies of scope through by-products from one process being used in the production of another product.

**Figure 23.1 External diseconomies of scale**

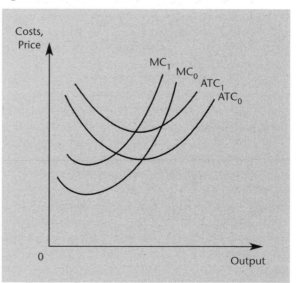

The individual organisation initially faces marginal cost and average total cost, $MC_0$ and $ATC_0$ respectively. External diseconomies of scale increase marginal costs for each unit of output, causing both marginal cost and average total cost to shift upwards to $MC_1$ and $ATC_1$.

Once again, there may be limitations to both scale and scope economies which place limits on the boundary of the organisation. In the case of scale economies, diseconomies may arise through the process of bureaucracy, conflicting objectives among the organisation's stakeholders or a loss of control or lack of motivation of the workforce. In the case of economies of scope, consider the following formula:

$$S = \frac{C(Q_1) + C(Q_2) - C(Q_1, Q_2)}{C(Q_1, Q_2)}$$

where,

$C(Q_1)$ = the cost of producing output $Q_1$ by itself

$C(Q_2)$ = the cost of producing output $Q_2$ by itself

$C(Q_1, Q_2)$ = the cost of producing both outputs jointly

When there are economies of scope, the cost of producing both items jointly is less than the cost of producing each item separately, so S will be positive. If S is zero there are no economies of scope and if S is negative there are diseconomies of scope. The latter indicates that it would be better if the multiproduct output was produced separately in two different plants or organisations.

Scope economies can be seen in large car companies such as Ford and Toyota, which produce many different models using common assembly and production equipment. Where the cost of one output falls as the output of another product increases, scope economies are available. Pharmaceutical companies are able to achieve scope economies where, using the same raw materials, a whole range of dyes and pharmaceutical products could be produced from the same production process. A study of the US publications industry in the 1970s found that the cost per journal declined as the number of journals published increased (Baumol and Braunstein (1977)). It found that the cost per journal for a publisher producing 36 different scientific journals was 80 per cent of the cost for the publisher which produced only one scientific journal. Thus these scope economies allowed the publisher to increase the size of its business.

Many other features can affect the boundaries of the organisation, encouraging both growth and **downsizing**. Porter (1980), in Chapter 15, identified five forces influencing the state of competition in an industry: power of buyers, power of suppliers, threat of new entrants, the threat of substitutes and current competitors in the marketplace. Porter suggests that if the organisation grows, widens its boundaries, then this is one way by which it can attempt to mitigate the effects of increasingly competitive markets, particularly as markets and products mature. However, markets are themselves interdependent and every player is itself a supplier, buyer, substitute or potential new entrant somewhere else. Therefore, altering the boundary of the organisation must take a wider perspective than the market into which the organisation sells.

Porter's assertion that companies alter their boundaries to mitigate against competitive market situations can be illustrated by a number of examples, including British Airways' merger with British Caledonian in 1987. British Airways wished to gain access to airport rights held by British Caledonian, particularly the landing and takeoff rights in the congested facilities at the London airports. The merger enabled British Airways to reduce competition on these routes. For example, after the merger British Airways had a nearly 100 per cent monopoly on the London–Manchester route, and almost 50 per cent of the London–Hong Kong route. It also allowed British Airways to generate economies of scale, particularly marketing, which in the longer term also allowed it to compete even more vigorously in other markets, further increasing the size of the company.

However, it is questionable how far organisations are free to alter their boundaries to exploit market power due to the regulation of their activity through monopolies and merger policy.

As markets mature and product lifecycles reduce, companies need a portfolio of products, preferably at different stages of the lifecycle, to ensure current as well as future earnings. This concept can be illustrated by the BCG matrix (*see* Chapters 15 and 16), which classifies products as cash cows, stars, question marks or dogs. Companies may try to acquire elements missing from their own portfolios, especially if they lack stars or potential new products; take as an example, the takeover of Rowntree by Nestlé, which, having identified chocolate confectionery as a gap in its existing portfolio, elected to fill it by acquisition rather than by direct entry into a highly competitive market.

Many other factors can cause the boundaries of the organisation to change. There may be a greater desire to gain the cheaper access to finance which arises through being a larger organisation. Organisations may increase in size by expanding into low-cost areas. For example, Fiat's entry into Eastern Europe and the formation of Ford Europe has enabled both organisations to exploit lower-cost areas. However, cost reductions do not always lead to expansion; they may simply lead to relocation. There may be a desire to reach a critical size in order to compete with international contemporaries that leads to boundary change. In Europe this has been seen through the establishment of pan-European champions. Boundary changes may also be triggered by changes in the macroeconomic environment, such as the upsurge in merger activity that followed the passing of the Single European Act.

Organisations may seek to change their boundaries to gain synergy. This is commonly expressed as the inequality $(a + b)^2 > a^2 + b^2$ (or $2 + 2 = 5$), and describes the advantages allegedly gained by combining operations rather than operating alone. Various synergies have been identified:

- *Sales synergy* – gains from combining marketing and promotional activities.
- *Operating synergy* – the gains to be made from spreading fixed costs, or through discounts on bulk purchases.
- *Investment synergy* – particularly the joint use of technology and equipment.
- *Management synergy* – transferring skills between operations.

However, synergies are not always easily gained and barriers to achieving full advantage may include the vested interests of the parties or stakeholders as well as insufficient management skills. If such negative synergies occur, over the longer term it is likely that the boundary of the organisation will change once again as it seeks to **demerge** and move back to what it sees as its **core business**.

As has already been noted in Chapter 4, the differing objectives of organisations may themselves have an impact in terms of more rapid growth in some organisations, compared with declining or more static positions for others. Organisations seeking to maximise profits may see their boundaries change disproportionately to those which are satisficing or seeking to maximise sales.

External motives are also important in altering the boundaries of the organisation. The formation of major trading blocs such as the North American Free Trade Agreement (NAFTA), the European Union (EU) and the Association of South East Asian Nations (ASEAN) has had a profound effect on the way in which organisations view world markets

and plan international investment. The rise in trading blocs in particular has changed the nature of direct foreign investment, promoting cross-border mergers and acquisitions for immediate competitive advantage. The same could be said for the development of the Single European Market.

The conclusion of the last round of the General Agreement on Tariffs and Trade (GATT) – the Uruguay Round in 1993 – has improved the prospects for world trade and is expected to benefit organisations that operate internationally. The fall of the communist bloc and the opening up of China to Western European countries both continue to influence the growth policy of many organisations, particularly transnational companies. Much of the direct foreign investment (DFI) into China takes the form of **joint ventures**. For example, in April 1994, Hoechst announced plans to transfer masterbatch dye production to China in the form of a joint venture with Guangzhou synthetic fibre plant. Such arrangements have advantages for the external organisation, such as a local partner which understands the economy, while the multinational will often provide the capital and technology.

Worldwide economic cycles have always had a profound effect on altering the boundaries of the organisation. In times of recession, markets become intensely competitive, with organisations looking to more international expansion to reduce their exposure at home. At the same time, some organisations realise that they are not in a position to carry any of their less profitable products or companies and may seek to divest themselves of these. Conversely, when economies move into boom phases, organisations have sufficient profits to grow. Such activity in the UK can be reconciled with the merger booms of 1969, 1973 and 1989/90. This is not to suggest that there are not other factors that partly explain the merger cycle, such as the growth in international markets, the rapid growth of financial intermediaries such as insurance companies and investment trusts, which began investing heavily in company equity, and the increase in the gearing ratio of companies which provide much of the funding for merger activity.

Labour costs can also provide the stimulus for boundary changes. The growth in unemployment in the EU has partially been blamed on EU organisations being handicapped by high labour and social security costs as well as state intervention in environmental affairs. World manufacturing costs vary markedly between countries, as Table 23.1

**Table 23.1 World manufacturing labour costs 1993 (dollars per hour)**

| | | | |
|---|---|---|---|
| West Germany | 24.9 | Singapore | 5.1 |
| East Germany | 17.3 | South Korea | 4.9 |
| Japan | 16.9 | Hong Kong | 4.2 |
| US | 16.4 | Hungary | 1.8 |
| France | 16.3 | Czech & Slovak Republics | 1.1 |
| UK | 12.4 | China | 0.5 |

*Source*: *Financial Times*, 7 March 1994.

indicates, and it is not surprising, therefore, that multinationals are prepared to move to locations with low labour costs.

Of course, whether labour costs do cause organisations to grow into different locations not only depends on the price of labour but also on the productivity of labour and other cost factors, such as raw materials, transportation costs and financial risks.

The term 'new international division of labour' (NIDL) has been used to explain the shift of production from the 'core' industrialised economies to less developed countries, as transnationals seek cheap, controllable labour on a global scale. There are a number of preconditions which cause organisations to seek these alternative sources of labour:

- developments in transport and communications
- developments in production processes permitting the use of unskilled labour
- the emergence of a worldwide reservoir of potential labour power.

Further, there may be push factors which, in the industrialised economies, combine to encourage organisations to look for new locations, such as falling profits and increasingly militant labour forces. However, concentrating on labour as a motive for altering the boundary of the organisation may be taking a one-dimensional perspective. For example, other cost factors may be of equal, if not greater, importance, such as government grants to attract an organisation to a particular location.

The impact of industry on the environment has been a major source of public concern in recent years, especially in Europe and the US; *see* Chapter 20. Over the last 20 years, the EU has passed more than 200 pieces of environmental regulations. Although these have received enthusiastic public support, some organisations are finding compliance increasingly costly and are looking for alternative sites and technologies, sometimes taking the opportunity to relocate outside the EU. Examples include ICI, for which the need to com-

ply with mercury emission standards from its chlorine plant at Hillhouse, Scotland, resulted in the plant's closure.

Finally, technological factors play an important role in altering the boundaries of the organisation. Advances in technology make previously restricted markets profitable to enter. Organisations may expand into these markets by locating there or expand their provision in the domestic market and export goods/services. As Dicken (1992) notes, 'technology is, without doubt, one of the most important contributory factors underlying the internationalisation and globalisation of economic activity'. He identifies advances in communications and transport as fundamental 'space-shrinking' technologies which have facilitated the development of the global organisation. Other technologies which have formed the basis of boundary changes are:

- information technology
- biotechnology
- materials technology
- energy technology
- space technology.

Escalating R&D costs can provide a strong incentive for boundary change, particularly in rapidly moving technological sectors. Industries such as pharmaceuticals and aerospace often require expansion to finance investment, while at the same time continuing to provide returns for shareholders. This encourages them to look for exports and growth overseas. High R&D costs also encourage firms to collaborate, reducing investment costs and risk. This often leads to the establishment of joint ventures, although where collaboration is out of the question acquisition may be pursued in an attempt to reach a critical mass.

For example, in semiconductors, the discovery of logic and memory devices led to rapid development of new applications to computers, telecommunications and other specialised markets. A similar structural break can also be seen in biotechnology. In both sectors new organisations were set up, incumbent companies entered the markets and some were forced to retire. However, the difference between the two sectors is the way in which the boundaries were changed. In biotechnology alliances were frequently formed, involving a licensing arrangement between the startup company for distribution access controlled by the larger company. For large pharmaceutical companies this arrangement may be the most appropriate, since the problem is that biotechnology could destroy competence and render their current skills and talents obsolete. Semiconductor alliances, on the other hand, have been more oriented towards technology sharing, licensing or co-development.

The impacts of technology are manifold and can alter both the domestic and international allocation of economic activity in a number of ways:

- It may affect the productivity and costs of individual factor inputs.
- It may introduce completely new products with different spatial needs to those it replaces.
- It can have consequences for natural and created factor endowments.
- It can affect transport and communication costs.
- It may affect the advantages of assembling activities close to one another.
- It may affect the dynamics of market structure and the level of competition.

Thus technology provides conditions for organisations to grow internally and for organisations to seek closer alliances as a means of market access and to reduce risks. At the same time it poses challenges for some organisations in terms of market obsolescence which could lead to their demise.

Therefore, there are many reasons for organisations seeking to alter their boundaries. As external factors change, is there an 'optimal' boundary for the organisation?

## THE LINKAGE APPROACH

The **linkage approach** considers the skills and expertise possessed by the different parts of the organisation, such as its managers and workforce. A competitive advantage can be obtained if the organisation makes use of the information which each part of the organisation has and is able to link these together in a way that improves its competitive advantage. A review of the organisation's current activities facilitates identification of current linkage strengths and weaknesses. This may help to explain the current boundaries of the organisation. Where weaknesses are found linkages can be strengthened, enabling the organisation to expand its boundary. However, sometimes the absence of some linkages explains why the organisation does not perform a particular task itself. In other words, the organisation does not expand its boundary in that direction.

For example, airlines do not manufacture aircraft. Manufacturing aircraft requires knowledge of manufacturing, engineering, production and the development of relationships with component suppliers and other airlines. Since these are outside the experience of airline managers, whose expertise lies in the field of services, the airline organisation stays within its knowledge frame. However, the links to other service areas of the travel industry do provide airlines with the opportunity to expand. So instead of just taking passengers from one destination to another, an airline may move into the areas of ticket sales, selling holidays and freight transportation. For instance Air 2000, whose main routes are to holiday destinations, is owned by the package holiday company Owners Abroad. Strangely, the Japanese airline JAL has moved into supplying school uniforms and into a Western-style family restaurant chain. On first inspection there may appear to be very little connection. However, both were used as a way of advertising the brand name JAL, and the restaurant chain was used as a resource through which potential airline managers could receive training and as a location for airline managers which JAL wished to redeploy.

By building on linkages with its strategic core the organisation can improve its competitive advantage. The way in which these linkages are developed can be through vertical integration, joint ventures or alliances. Whichever approach is adopted, Kanter (1990) suggests that the success of a strategic linkage depends on the following factors, or six 'Is':

- The relationship is important, that is, it should receive adequate resources and management attention.
- Investment should be seen as long term to equalise the benefits to both parties.
- Both sides of the linkage are interdependent.
- Each party is well informed about the plans of the other.
- The organisations are integrated, allowing for good communication and contact.
- The relationship is institutionalised through supporting mechanisms, social ties and values.

These linkages between one organisation and another can take on a number of forms and sometimes it may be more profitable for a company to take control of these within one organisation. It is to the ways in which organisations grow that we now turn.

# MERGER BEHAVIOUR

A **merger** is defined as a situation in which two or more enterprises (business activities of any kind) cease to be distinct. This can occur in two ways:

■ They are brought under common ownership and control.

■ There is an arrangement between the enterprises so that one of them ceases to be carried on. For example, Company X may agree with Company Y that the latter will close down operations which compete with Company X.

Mergers can be made in a number of ways: through vertical integration, or through horizontal integration, or through the formation of conglomerates.

## Vertical integration

Vertical integration occurs through an organisation, say in the manufacturing stage of production, purchasing market outlets (forward vertical integration) or a company providing raw materials that are used in the manufacturing stage (backward vertical integration). The purchase of Texas Eastern, an oil exploration company, by Enterprise Oil in 1989 is an example of growth by backward vertical integration, as is British Gas's stake in offshore gas field developments in the North Sea. The expansion by brewing companies into public houses and other outlets is an example of forward vertical integration. Brewing group Bass is the owner of thousands of pubs, which gives it control of the brands of beer and lager which these outlets offer. Currently, Bass is able to sell some of the UK's best brands through these outlets, such as Carling Black Label lager, Bass ale, Caffrey's Irish ale, Tennant's lager, Worthington's beer and Hooper's Hooch. Bass is also involved in horizontal boundary changes with the proposed acquisition (November 1996) of Allied Domecq's half share of Carlsberg-Tetley, another brewing company. Although this is subject to inquiry by the Monopolies and Mergers Commission, it has been estimated that permission for the takeover by Bass will be given as long as Bass sells around 200 pubs to Cannon. Thus Bass can widen its boundaries with the proposed takeover of Domecq's share of Carlsberg-Tetley to achieve around 38 per cent of the UK beer market, while at the same time there will be some boundary shrinkage through the sale of the 200 pubs to Cannon.

The extent of vertical integration varies not only among industries but also among firms. It is common in the aluminium industry but not in the tin industry. In the brewing industry it has been noted that many of the major brewers have integrated in this way, yet at the same time small brewing companies have tended to remain as brewers.

Why do organisations seek to grow through the process of vertical integration? When two stages of production are technologically interdependent, vertical integration may reduce production costs. Such a situation occurs in the production of iron and steel, where there are substantial advantages of integrating production. In addition to these technological cost savings, vertical integration may lead to savings in advertising, and managerial and R&D economies.

Vertical integration may arise because of the need to save on transaction costs. In situations where transactions become increasingly costly, perhaps because of contractual problems, common ownership economises on transaction costs and integration becomes the most efficient way to proceed. For example, Monteverde and Teece (1982) found that, if the level of engineering investment required to develop a component was high, vertical integration was more likely to take place. The reason put forward was that, if a product was technologically complex, and a manufacturer was dependent on a supplier for one part, there was always the chance that the supplier could hold a manufacturer to ransom. In this case a manufacturer may vertically integrate backwards to overcome such risks.

Although market power is not viewed as a major driving force behind vertical integration – usually being associated with horizontal growth – market power can be enhanced if there are no available substitutes for the monopolised input or resource that can come under the control of an organisation through vertical integration. In fact, the degree of market power may be related to whether the production technology consists of **fixed input proportions** (FIP) or **variable input proportions** (VIP). Where there are fixed input proportions organisations further forward in the production chain may not be able to substitute for the output produced by the monopolist. For example, suppose that both firms B and C purchase inputs from firm A, where firm A is the sole provider of a particular input. If Firm B vertically integrates backward, purchasing firm A, then through the vertical integration process the new organisation may have market power over firm C, since its production process used a fixed amount of input from the newly integrated firm. Where the production technology is produced using variable input proportions because technology allows for the substitutability of factors, any use by newly integrated monopolist of their price/output muscle may cause firm C, further down the production chain, to substitute for the monopolist's input. In this case the integrated monopolist's market power is reduced.

In most countries it is illegal to use vertical integration to monopolise a market. In the 1990s a US federal court ruled against Eastman-Kodak for attempting to monopolise the service and parts markets for its photocopiers and business machines by refusing to sell parts to independent service operators that were competing against Kodak's own network of service operators. What Kodak was doing was raising entry barriers in its market for the supply of parts and servicing by vertically integrating into the provision of this service.

These entry barriers can not only be through the control of supply, but through the control of distributive outlets which refuse to stock a competitor's product, or through cost advantages that the vertically integrated organisation possesses which forces any new entrant to have to enter the market in a big way.

## Horizontal mergers

Horizontal mergers occur when one organisation combines with another in the same stage of production. This type of boundary change is the most common, with over 80 per cent of mergers being ascribed to horizontal growth. Examples of this process have been shown earlier and would include British Airways, takeover of British Caledonian, Ford's purchase of Jaguar, BMW's purchase of the Rover Group, and the acquisition process in the building society industry in the UK.

**Horizontal integration** occurs for a variety of reasons. The chief one may be to obtain economies of scale such as managerial economies, financial economies, the chance to purchase in bulk and the like. Horizontal growth also leads to increased market share or new market segments, which organisations hope will have a positive, synergistic effect on profits. Horizontal growth can be used as a method to defend current market share against a larger rival, but at the same time can be a process by which national champions can be developed. It

might be argued that in the international business environment in which organisations operate size is all important if organisations want to have a global presence. Boundary changes through horizontal growth can also enhance market power, and the recognition of this has led to many governments having legislation to curb this market power; *see* Chapter 22.

## Conglomerate growth

Between 10 and 15 per cent of company growth in the UK during the 1960s was of this type; *see* Griffiths and Wall (1997). It is possible to categorise diversification in a number of ways:

- Product extension diversification, reflecting the expansion of a range of products which are related somehow to current demand or through common technology.
- Market extension, expanding sales of existing products but in different geographical areas.
- **Conglomerate diversification**, where expansion is into unrelated products.

By the 1980s this type of growth represented around 30 per cent of merger activity in the UK; *see* Geroski and Vlassopoulos (1990). The attractiveness of this type of boundary change can be seen as reducing an organisation's risk from changes in demand for different products, differences in the economic cycle, changes in the lifecycle of products etc. For example, a company such as Unilever has interests which include animal feeds, toiletries, chemicals, paper and plastics, and sells its products in over 80 countries.

There are some other notable conglomerates, such as Hanson, whose behaviour has been to expand in this manner and then 'asset strip' their victim corporation, i.e. selling off the less profitable parts and keeping the core enterprise. In this way the conglomerate hopes to make a level of profit in excess of the original outlay on the whole company.

Table 23.2 provides some indication of the motives for European merger behaviour, based on public statements made by the organisations about their motives for growth. It suggests that merger due to rationalisation, synergies and diversification is waning and mergers for expansion and strengthening market position are increasingly important.

Economies of scope provide another reason for diversification. For example, an organisation may find that in the production of one good it has

**Table 23.2 Motives for European mergers and acquisitions**

|  | 1985–86 | 1986–87 | 1987–88 | 1988–89 | 1989–90 | 1990–91 | 1991–92 |
|---|---|---|---|---|---|---|---|
| Expansion | 17.1 | 22.1 | 19.6 | 31.1 | 26.9 | 27.7 | 32.4 |
| Diversification | 17.6 | 5.8 | 8.3 | 7.1 | 3.0 | 2.8 | 2.1 |
| Strengthening market position | 10.6 | 11.5 | 25.4 | 42.2 | 45.3 | 48.2 | 44.4 |
| Rationalisation and synergies | 46.5 | 42.0 | 34.4 | 14.4 | 17.7 | 13.3 | 16.2 |
| R&D | 2.4 | 5.3 | 0.7 | 0.0 | 0.6 | 0.0 | 0.0 |
| Other | 5.9 | 13.3 | 11.6 | 4.9 | 6.4 | 8.0 | 5.0 |

*Source*: European Commission (1994) 'Competition and integration', *European Economy*, Vol 57.

spare capacity that could be used in the production of another. In this case, if the organisation produces two goods, X and Y, then the minimum cost of producing a combined unit of X and Y will be lower than the cost of producing each item separately. It may be technological interdependencies that lead to such economies, as is the case with wool and mutton. If an organisation possesses spare capacity and there are uncertainties in the market so that the associated transaction costs are very high, then diversification may be the most efficient way of producing the new product.

Economies of scope may be interlinked with transaction costs and, as has been noted above, can lead to diversification to ameliorate the problems of using the market. This is not to suggest that scope economies will always lead to diversification. Suppose that an organisation has the opportunity to sell or lease any excess resource or service, but this is surrounded by complexity, uncertainty or opportunism, so that any transaction costs associated with this activity are large. Diversification may be the more efficient route. Therefore, if selling the excess resource is not practical, economies of scope will lead to multiproduct operations. Economising on transaction costs may lead to diversification even if there are no economies of scope, thus economies of scope are neither a necessary nor a sufficient condition for diversification. For example, suppose that a manufacturing organisation has a machine which makes parts for cars, but it does not reach the minimum point on its average total cost curve just by producing car parts. The same machine could be used for producing parts for the freight industry. In other words, there are economies of scope in jointly producing parts for cars and for freight. This does not mean that the same organisation must produce the parts for both cars and freight. It is possible that such a machine could be owned by a car producer which contracts its use to the freight industry, or vice versa.

Alternatively, a third organisation could own the machine and contract its services to both the freight and car industries. Thus the existence of economies of scope does not necessarily imply diversification.

Diversification may also be a route to follow because of its revenue-raising ability. First, diversification may make it possible for an organisation to differentiate its products so that it can undertake price discrimination. Second, there may be interdependencies in demand for an organisation's products which enable it to make higher revenue when it produces a range of products than if these same products were produced by a number of separate organisations. This arises from the fact that, where the products are not made by the diversified organisation, each of the individual organisations needs to consider and predict the pricing behaviour of the others and there is less certainty. It is this reduced level of certainty that leads to reduced revenue.

Extending the boundaries of the organisation can also arise through managerial objectives and behaviour. As has been alluded to earlier, the growth of the organisation may be a managerial objective since it could link to managers' salaries.

Reducing the level of competition in the market may again be a factor in the diversification process. Diversification may allow the organisation to practise the pricing process of tie-in sales and thereby reduce the sales of a competitor's product. It may be possible for the diversified organisation to cross-subsidise one or more of its products, again squeezing a competitor's profit margins. Diversification may eliminate a potential entrant from the market, especially where the organisation taken over was believed to be a potential entrant.

If there were only advantages to be gained from being a conglomerate, then we would increasingly see the development of diversified mega-companies. In fact, with increasing diversification come problems with controlling the organisation, together with other diseconomies of scale. Profits may not be as large as the organisations had hoped for and demands made by shareholders may result in companies examining whether they have overstretched themselves. During the 1990s, the advantages that might have been perceived through the diversification process appeared to have been outweighed by the costs and there has been a return to 'core businesses' for a number of organisations – a process which will be discussed later in this chapter.

## Drivers of the merger process

Despite the fact that many mergers are not successful and profit margins are not enhanced, business leaders seem undaunted by the merger and acquisition process. It appears to be an important component of corporate strategy, as evidenced by the increasing amount of activity in the UK and in Europe in recent years.

Various theories have been put forward to explain this trend; the intense pressure on companies to boost earnings per share, and the advent of the Single European Market with its perceived opportunities and threats, are just two. In addition, it is possible that the market sometimes undervalues companies, and high real interest rates in the early 1990s (particularly in the UK) have meant that profits have been heavily discounted, thus making it cheaper to buy other companies than to expand the current business through internal growth. In addition, Young (1989) proposed the following arguments for expanding the boundaries of the organisation:

■ Acquisitions allow established companies to change direction quickly and reposition them-

selves in the market when their traditional activities are no longer capable of producing the desired growth rate.

■ Acquisitions may be necessary to fill gaps in the organisation's product/market profile or as a way to acquire new skills and expertise.

■ Mergers may act as a means to integrate businesses with converging technologies, for example the erstwhile merger of British Aerospace and the Rover Group.

Moreover, de Jonquieres (1990) suggests that the growth of global competition has led more and more organisations to use acquisitions as a way of achieving a substantial presence in the world's main developed markets, for example the Nestlé–Rowntree merger. Other external factors can also play a part, such as the deregulation of capital markets, moves towards privatisation, and advances in technology which enable instantaneous communication between the world's main business centres. In fact, in the EU the five main motives for merger are:

■ strengthening market position
■ expansion
■ complementarity
■ diversification
■ rationalisation/restructuring.

## Are mergers successful?

One advantage that can come from merger behaviour is economies of scale. A number of studies, such as that by Mueller (1989), have concluded that it is difficult to distinguish economies of scale after the merger takes place. One reason could be that the

**Table 23.3 Cross-border acquisitions of EU companies, £million**

| Bidder country | 1989 value | 1990 value | 1991 value | 1992 value | 1993 value |
|---|---|---|---|---|---|
| US | 10 040 | 2 257 | 2 755 | 3 592 | 3 094 |
| UK | 2 651 | 4 894 | 1 536 | 4 435 | 2 676 |
| Germany | 3 152 | 1 085 | 1 653 | 1 061 | 1 693 |
| France | 5 470 | 6 270 | 3 328 | 3 658 | 1 528 |
| Sweden | 680 | 6 486 | 683 | 968 | 956 |
| Switzerland | 1 337 | 516 | 902 | 350 | 620 |
| Netherlands | 458 | 603 | 1 217 | 3 273 | 406 |
| Italy | 762 | 886 | 1 153 | 2 207 | 400 |
| Luxembourg | n/a | 114 | 1 007 | 367 | 185 |
| Japan | 515 | 1 768 | 559 | 229 | 83 |
| Others | 4 787 | 9 986 | 4 539 | 8 949 | 3 785 |
| Total | 29 816 | 34 865 | 19 314 | 29 107 | 15 426 |

*Source*: Peat Marwick.

motive of scale economies is not that high up on the list of factors for merger. Nonetheless, problems with different organisational cultures, accounting practices and the like can contribute to disappointing performance from the newly merged organisation. Whittington (1980) and Kumar (1985) also found that profitability was independent of organisation size. Therefore, although synergies may not result from the merger of two or more organisations, this does not imply that the hoped-for synergies do not play their part in encouraging mergers to take place.

There is some evidence to suggest that it is the faster-growing companies which are more likely to be the acquirers in a merger process. In terms of other managerial theories of the organisation, studies by Firth (1979) and Conyon and Gregg (1994) suggest that there is a link between managerial rewards and mergers, with managers receiving salary increases above the going rate after merger, related to the improved sales performance of the company. Growth of the organisation also appeared to be related to takeover. The larger the organisation, the less likely it was to be taken over. Thus growth of the organisation enhances the security of the manager. However, once an optimum size is reached the growth of the organisation may slow down. The deregulation of capital markets has now altered the rules of the game and during the late 1980s and 1990s even some of the largest organisations became part of the merger boom as victims themselves, such as Hong Kong and Shanghai Banking Corporation's acquisition of Midland Bank for £3.9 billion in 1992, and the purchase of UK pharmaceutical firm Beecham in 1989 by SmithKline of the US for £4.5 billion.

An organisation can shift its boundaries via a number of routes, such as internal growth or external growth. But why do some organisations only grow within their domestic markets while others seek and achieve multinational status? Moreover, why even grow in this way: why not consider other methods of boundary change, such as a joint venture?

## JOINT VENTURES

A joint venture is an arrangement under which organisations remain independent but set up a newly created organisation jointly owned by the parents. Commitment to participation in a joint venture represents a strong statement of trust and cooperation by both partners. Independence is maintained, *de facto* and *de jure*, and is only seriously threatened if

one partner is larger than the other. Why should a joint venture be established rather than a subsidiary? Several explanations have been proffered, such as:

- economies of scale
- a desire to overcome barriers to entry
- the pooling of complementary pieces of knowledge
- a means of reducing the xenophobia that arises when entering a foreign market
- a way for organisations to diversify
- to strengthen an organisation's market position
- to reduce the costs that may arise through R&D, production and marketing
- a process to develop complementary products.

However, the main reason for setting up a joint venture may be that this form of approach is preferred when the transaction costs are lower than those faced when establishing a wholly owned subsidiary.

Dicken (1992) subdivides joint ventures, first into 'alliance joint ventures' which involve the creation of a separate legal entity in which each partner has a share, such as Interox formed between Solvay and Laporte. On the other hand there are alliances which have no legal status but which are formed for specific types of collaboration, notably R&D, which he calls 'functional specific alliances', such as the European Airbus consortium.

Joint ventures have become a popular form of growth in the 1990s, often used as a method to serve rapid expansion while at the same time reducing the financial risk for the partners. They may currently be the prime way of moving into the Chinese economy, where the government is keen to attract investment but wants to retain some element of state control. Joint ventures are also frequently used as a means of achieving critical mass without the risks of acquisition, such as was the case in the car industry with the alliance between the Rover Group and Honda during the 1980s. Similarly, a successful joint venture can be seen in that established by Renault and Matra to produce the Espace minivan. Renault benefited from Matra's knowledge of product concepts, design capability and its manufacturing competence, while Matra gained access to Renault's marketing, distribution and service resources.

Johnson and Scholes (1997) view joint ventures as a potential growth strategy for 'market followers', giving advantages of size and increased market power without acquisition cost or risk. Certainly, joint ventures may be the only form of significant rapid growth open to small organisations without large capital reserves or financing opportunities.

## ◆ CASE STUDY 23.1

# Joint ventures in the heavy machinery industry [FT]

From Siberia to Latin America, the mining industry thinks big when it comes to using machinery. The bucket on the world's biggest mining shovel, built by Germany's Mannesmann Demag, is big enough to scoop up a small house. But the forces bringing equipment suppliers together are as powerful as the machines they produce. That is why, in November 1995, Demag and Komatsu of Japan said they would join forces to build and market heavy excavators, used mainly by the mining and natural resources industries. The venture, which will have annual sales of about DM300m (£136m), is the latest cross-border link-up to reshape the heavy end of the construction equipment industry.

Although the market is relatively small, margins are high – it is not unusual to pay well over $1.5m dollars for a machine. But the price associated with developing and marketing the machines, and keeping them operational during their service life, is also high. These costs, coupled with the need to offer a full package of machinery, have forced other plant manufacturers into

marriages of convenience. In 1993, Hitachi Construction Machinery, Komatsu's Japanese rival, forged an agreement with Belgian-based VME (now called Volvo Construction Equipment) to form a joint venture, Euclid-Hitachi Equipment, to make rigid-type dumptrucks in North America. Both parties market and service Hitachi's big hydraulic mining shovels and Volvo's dumptrucks and large-wheeled loaders.

Demag and Komatsu argue that their alliance, which is to be equally owned, reflects the consolidation taking place among the companies' clients. The client it seems wants to buy from one dealer – they do not want to run around to a dozen different places.

For Demag, an important element in the alliance is improved distribution. The German company is an acknowledged master at designing and building mining shovels. Komatsu's strength lies in its service and distribution network.

*Source: Financial Times, 28 November 1995. Reprinted with permission.*

## ◆ Exercise 23.1

1 Why has there been a move towards strategic alliances in the heavy machinery industry?

2 Do the two companies offer each other distinct advantages?

## Risks and benefits of joint ventures

As Case study 23.1 shows, the main attractions of a joint venture are increased size and market power while sharing risks relative to acquisition or internal growth. In addition there are advantages of complementarity, as each organisation in the joint venture gains the other's superior competence. However, there are a number of risks. Porter (1980) suggests that, however attractive the business proposition, any divergence in the partners' objectives in terms of goals, expectations or managerial style can make sound business propositions fail. He recommends that as much effort be put into examining the intended partner(s) as is put into analysing the business opportunity itself. Kotler (1996) identifies disagreements between parties about policies, investments etc. as a common problem in joint ventures, bringing with it increased

'strategic risk' through divergent aims and objectives. Further, he suggests that joint ownership can prevent a multinational enterprise from carrying out specific manufacturing and marketing plans on a worldwide basis.

Dicken (1992) is also critical of US–Japanese joint ventures, asserting that they will severely damage the long-term competitiveness of US organisations through the loss of key technologies and insufficient R&D. He also suggests that they are difficult to manage, with particular reference to problems created by culture and differing national accounting standards and tax rules. Thus many joint ventures are not long lived. Management of the joint venture may also be problematic, with alternating chairmen and boards creating instability and uncertainty which sometimes alienates the workforce and reduces company productivity and loyalty.

Do these problems outweigh the benefits? Joint ventures provide organisations with ways to implement changes in their strategic positions or to defend current strategic positions. They allow companies to concentrate on what they are good at, while allowing diversification into unfamiliar business areas.

Although joint ventures were perhaps not high on many managers' lists of strategic developments, the growth in global competition, the increase in the size and riskiness of projects and the cost of some technologies mean that many managers have had to appraise their positions, particularly in the home market.

It may well be the case that not only do some organisations not possess the resources and technological knowledge they require, but in addition they cannot purchase this on the open market. Thus a joint venture provides a useful arrangement. It may also provide access to a higher level of technology, the means to utilise a by-product from one process or to enhance the performance of an organisation which is located in an older global sector, such as farm equipment or chemicals.

Joint ventures also provide a competitive edge in business. Some projects would never be undertaken without a joint venture being in place to share financial costs and reduce risks. In terms of first-mover advantages, a joint venture can give organisations a competitive edge, because the first movers can gain access to the better partners. It may also be possible, by binding a company into joint venture, to make a competitor a future ally. Therefore the process of joint ventures can be seen from two perspectives. For those in the joint venture it may provide technical know-how, be market protective and a way of surmounting trade barriers. For those outside the joint venture, the process may be seen as denying access to markets, and in the long term denying the organisation access to higher and competitive levels of technology and products.

Joint ventures may, by reducing competition, pose a threat to competition regulation. Furthermore, they can be problematic if the reasons for joining the joint venture were poorly conceived, if the partners were not chosen carefully or if the agreements and systems to manage the venture were inadequate. What seems to be the case in terms of altering the boundaries of the organisation is that joint ventures need to change. Sometimes a change in managers will result in the parent company reappraising the joint venture. This may lead to its termination or the refocusing of the joint venture.

Joint ventures may be fragile, proving that today's partner is tomorrow's competitor, and organisations need to be aware of losing what they perceive as their competitive advantage in the joint venture process. Kay (1993) draws attention to three further difficulties with joint ventures:

- Joint ventures involve significant bargaining costs in negotiating and policing agreements.
- Because there are two parents controlling the child there will be duplication in monitoring and potential for confusion and conflict in directing the venture.

- Intellectual property and other intangible assets may be appropriated by partners.

Thus, although joint ventures provide a number of opportunities for the organisation as a means to stretch its boundary, they also provide a number of important threats.

# THE SHRINKING BOUNDARY OF THE ORGANISATION

As the section on joint ventures indicates, a joint venture may provide many reasons for extending the boundary of the organisation, yet at the same time some joint ventures will fail and the organisation will see its boundary shrink. Yet the failure of a joint venture is only one reason for company size changing. Organisations may seek to divest themselves of less profitable or loss-making sections of their business. They may do this through selling the company to another organisation or through a process such as a management buyout. Increasingly during the 1980s organisations sought to alter their structure through downsizing or rightsizing, and towards the end of the 1980s and during the 1990s organisations have become more focused on what they call their core businesses, concentrating on what they are good at. Downsizing should not be considered in terms of the company getting smaller in terms of turnover, profits etc., since the whole point of undertaking the downsizing is to enhance these. Only in the case of demergers will the size of the company change. Downsizing is usually about shedding more and more labour, using existing labour more efficiently, replacing some of it with capital and hence improving profits. In the short term we might expect the downsizing process to be costly in terms of redundancy payments, new ways of production and the like. In the light of the argument as to whether organisations have been shrinking in the size of their market or in terms of employment, Table 23.4 may provide some answers.

Table 23.4 considers the concentration ratios for various industries, based on the net employment or output under the control of the five largest organisations. Overall industrial concentration continues to grow in some sectors, but this trend is less evident in employment. Thus some firms may be widening their boundaries but at the same time shrinking their workforces.

Perhaps a better way to consider boundary changes is to look at the 100-firm concentration ratio for the manufacturing sector in the UK (see Table 23.5).

**Table 23.4 Five-firm concentration ratio for selected industrial groups, UK, 1984 and 1991**

|  | Net output (%) 1984 | Net output (%) 1991 | Employment (%) 1984 | Employment (%) 1991 |
|---|---|---|---|---|
| Tobacco | 99 | 99 | 99 | 98 |
| Cement, lime and plaster | 88 | 82 | 87 | 83 |
| Motor vehicles and their engines | — | 82 | — | 82 |
| Aerospace equipment manufacture and repair | 63 | 77 | 64 | 70 |
| Ice cream, cocoa, chocolate and sugar confectionery | 65 | 74 | 59 | 63 |
| Insulated wire and cable | 70 | 66 | 64 | 62 |
| Domestic-type electrical appliances | — | 56 | — | 54 |
| Glass and glassware | 53 | 50 | 44 | 44 |
| Pharmaceutical products | 39 | 48 | 38 | 32 |
| Footwear | 37 | 46 | 31 | 44 |
| Brewing and malting | 51 | 41 | 46 | 50 |
| Textile finishing | 24 | 23 | 26 | 22 |
| Printing and publishing | 22 | 17 | 19 | 14 |
| Leather goods | 14 | 15 | 14 | 12 |

Source: *Business Monitor* (1993) Office for National Statistics. Crown Copyright 1993. Reproduced by the permission of the Controller of HMSO and the Office for National Statistics.

Although the manufacturing sector has increasingly been dominated by the 100 largest private firms in manufacturing since 1981, this domination has been on a downward trend, possibly due to the pulling in of the organisations, boundaries and the resurgence of small and medium-sized organisations.

For a number of organisations, the 1990s have not been about managing growth but investigating how they can use their resources more efficiently through the process of boundary shrinkage. Downsizing, as mentioned above, is only one of the ways in which organisations seek to alter their boundaries and it is to this and other aspects of boundary changes that the chapter now turns.

**Table 23.5 Share of 100 largest private firms in manufacturing: net output by output size**

| Year | Percentage |
|---|---|
| 1949 | 22.0 |
| 1958 | 32.0 |
| 1963 | 37.0 |
| 1968 | 41.0 |
| 1975 | 41.7 |
| 1981 | 41.0 |
| 1983 | 38.8 |
| 1984 | 38.8 |
| 1987 | 38.1 |
| 1989 | 36.6 |
| 1991 | 36.2 |

Source: Sawyer, M C (1981) *The Economics of Industries and Firms*, Croom Helm, Beckenham, Kent, and *Business Monitor* (1993). Crown Copyright 1993.

# DIVESTMENT

During the later part of the 1980s and early 1990s there appeared to be growing evidence that much of the growth by large conglomerates was not yielding the profits expected. Companies began to consider **divesting** themselves of their non-core areas, for both defensive and offensive reasons. The offensive reasons would include:

- Refocusing the total business and selling areas no longer required, even though they may be profitable.
- The need to raise extra money, for example British Aerospace's sale of the Rover Group to BMW.
- To improve the return on investment.
- The sale of a family company where there is no obvious succession.

In terms of defensive reasons for divestment, the following are felt to be important:

- A part of the organisation does not and is unable to meet profitability requirements.
- As a means to avoid acquisition (BAT divested itself of a number of businesses to avoid the unwanted attention of a predator).
- Because the organisation requires the money to prevent it from going under.
- Because the organisation may be risk averse and future projects in some areas of its business may be quite risky.
- It has become too difficult to manage a wide range of diverse industries.

◆ **CASE STUDY 23.2**

## Trelleborg divestment was a reluctant decision [FT]

Trelleborg, the Swedish mining, metals and rubber group, said that its decision to divest itself of its 28 per cent share in Falconbridge, the profitable Canadian mining concern in July 1995, was to free resources for investment in its core operations, and had only been taken reluctantly.

'We really liked Falconbridge, which has great potential. But in the long term we cannot afford to have 40 to 50 per cent of our earnings coming from a company where we don't control the cash flow.'

The Falconbridge sale was the latest – and one of the last – steps taken by Trelleborg in a radical restructuring undertaken over the last two years to rescue the group from deep losses and a heavy debt burden. Trelleborg's strategy is to focus on its core 100 per cent-owned mining, metals, rubber and trading activities. Two years ago, the group was carrying debts of SKr10bn. It has since sold a series of holdings in companies such as Munksjo, a forestry group, Svedala, a materials handling company, and Phoenix, a German rubber concern.

Trelleborg, originally a rubber products maker, expanded rapidly into mining and metals through acquisitions in the 1980s but ran into problems during the recession. It is now concentrated in three divisions: mining and metals, rubber and distribution operations.

*Source: Financial Times,* 28 July 1995. Reprinted with permission.

---

◆ **Exercise 23.2**

What advantages are there for companies which return to their core businesses? Are there any disadvantages?

---

Selling off the businesses may be problematic. The organisation may be able to sell them at a profit, especially if the business unit is profitable or can be expected to make profits. Nonetheless, it is possible that the subsidiary will be sold off for a price less than it was purchased for. This may be especially true if buyers are aware that the parent company wishes to get rid of the subsidiary as quick as possible, or where the parent company was forced to pay a price for the subsidiary above its true value because of the competition from a previous round of bidding. The Trelleborg case also shows a further reason for divestment: not being in control of a major source of earnings which could easily be lost in the future.

## MANAGEMENT BUYOUTS

**Management buyouts** are not new and are particularly popular in the US, but in the 1980s they became a significant part of the overall mergers and acquisitions market in the UK. A buyout occurs when the ownership of an organisation is transferred to a new range of shareholders, of which the current management team make up a significant element and are often the ones who initiated such an arrangement. The organisation now becomes a private independent company, financed through a mixture of equity, provided by a number of development capital firms, and debt, provided by the banks. Similar to the concept of buyouts is that of **buyins**, where an external management team, sometimes with the help of the current internal managers, executes a transfer of ownership with a similar pattern of institutional support. In the UK buyouts and buyins appeared to be reaching a new high in the first quarter of 1995, totalling a value of £1.35 billion – up by 42 per cent on the same period of 1994 (*Financial Times*, 18 May 1995).

The reasons for buyouts and buyins having proved popular are numerous and would include the desire of the existing owners to restructure their business, the desire to retire, the growth in entrepreneurial spirit that was engendered in the UK during the 1980s, and the growth in venture capital firms following the Wilson Committee report. In addition, the 1980s saw a large rise in receiverships and buyouts offered a way of saving some, if not all, of the jobs involved. Sometimes the incumbent management were the only group to show any interest in saving the organisation. In addition, there were a number of important public sector buyouts as the Conservative government rolled back the control of the state. In this case the sale of state-owned enterprises involved either the sale of the whole organisation (National Freight Corporation), the complete break-up of the organisation into many buyouts (National Bus) or the divestment of parts while the core of the business remains in public ownership (British Rail until fully privatised). Thus both supply- and demand-side factors can lead to the development of buyouts.

◆ **CASE STUDY 23.3**

## Nothing ventured, nothing . . . ?

In September 1995 the awards were announced for the sixth Venturer of the Year award, and it is now possible not only to congratulate the winners but also to assess some of the previous recipients of these awards.

One aim of the venturer awards is to give a higher profile to entrepreneurs and to managers in buy-out teams. When the awards were launched, the economy was coming to the end of the Lawson boom and heading into the recession of the early 1990s. Yet most award winners are not only surviving but are also in good health.

Award-winners in the large buy-outs category – funding up to £10m – appear to have been highly successful. Compass group, which was bought out from Grand Metropolitan, is now one of the world's largest catering companies. But the record of companies in the small buy-out category has been mixed. Jeyes Group, the cleaning products business which won the 1990 award, went temporarily into loss in 1994. The 1993 winner, Metrotect, a piping coatings supplier, announced falling profits and a cut in its dividends in 1995.

Three of the entrepreneurs who headed companies that had won awards in the small buy-outs categories have resigned. But most of the award-winners have stayed with their businesses, which remain independent or have floated.

So would many of the buy-out managers do it again? There was a certain level of reluctance and this is perhaps less encouraging for the future of UK business.

*Source: Financial Times*, 23 September 1995. Reprinted with permission.

---

◆ **Exercise 23.3**

1 What factors can lead to a buyout taking place?

2 Why are some buyouts successful while others are not?

---

Buyouts and buyins in continental Europe have tended to lag behind the level of activity in both the US and the UK. The reasons for this have been the initial lack of highly developed capital markets, the greater proportion of family-owned firms, national industrial structures and the legal and taxation frameworks. However, by 1987, significant buyout and buyin activity had been registered in Ireland, the Netherlands, Sweden and France. The sources of the deals in these countries are of interest. In Ireland, a high proportion were divestments, a third of which were by foreign organisations exiting the country, the next most important factor was receivership, while few were due to retirements. Moreover, the buyout process in Ireland was influenced by the structures already in place in the UK. In both Sweden and the Netherlands the main reason for buyouts was again divestment by foreign firms. In addition, the Netherlands had a legal framework conducive to buyouts and Sweden had a relatively active mergers and acquisitions market.

In France the buyout process has grown rapidly due to the reduced role of the state in industry and changes in tax regimes for family-owned businesses. Thus a high proportion of buyouts were of family-owned firms. In Germany buyouts have been less noticeable. This can be partly explained by the underdeveloped venture capital market and secondly by regional stock markets. However, there were still problems with succession in family-owned businesses and changes in tax breaks towards the end of the 1980s saw a growth in the buyout process in this country too.

The extent of the growth in buyouts in continental Europe can be seen with the purchase of Saunier Duval from Saint Gobain in 1988 (France), Rimoldi from Rockwell Inc (Italy) and Juvena from Beecham (Switzerland). It is interesting to note that most of these buyouts were divestments by foreign investors.

Stock market buyouts, although concentrated in the UK, have become increasingly frequent in France. In many cases these have been out of a desire by family shareholders, which are often in the majority, to liquidate their holdings while retaining a minority shareholding interest in the organisation.

## DOWNSIZING AND ALL THAT

During the 1980s and the early 1990s one of the main ways of influencing both the size and boundary of the organisation was **corporate reengineering**. Businesses have been downsized and rightsized while processes have been investigated which will enhance the organisation's productivity. In doing so portfolios have been rationalised with greater emphasis on the core business. For example, Scott Paper of the US was downsized. Its non-core business was sold off and the remainder was sold to Kimberly-Clark, leading to sizeable returns for the Scott Paper shareholders.

Although the process of rightsizing or downsizing has often been associated with reductions in employment, the process of reengineering is somewhat different. In the past productivity was increased by specialisation. Tasks were repetitive, using standardised parts, with management compartmentalised into different functional areas. Although this 'Fordist' approach to production yielded large increases in productivity, it also caused problems with workers' alienation and the inability to respond to changing customers' demands for variety. Such requests resulted in each of the business units needing to be adaptable, and led to a large amount of the organisation's time and cost being devoted to monitoring the internal business units. Reengineering an organisation ceases to consider it as a number of vertical but separate units and instead considers it as a collection of horizontal processes. Multifunctional, multiskilled teams handle an order from initial enquiry to final product. In doing so some tasks are merged or removed altogether. If this is done successfully, leadtimes are reduced and payments for labour and materials are more easy to collect.

Although reengineering has proved popular in organisations such as Rover, ICL and Rank-Xerox, why have all companies not done the same? Almost three-quarters of reengineering attempts fail. This is because of intransigence in the organisation, management not completely 'taking the bull by the horns' etc. In addition, it has been argued that in the long term, if all companies reengineered successfully, there would be no competitive advantage. Furthermore, if reengineering is successful and enhances productivity by an amount that increases supply and drives down prices, it is possible that total revenue will fall by so much that the organisation fails to make sufficient profits to stay in the industry. For some companies that are reengineered their sales have fallen faster than their costs. So too has the ability to stay at the leading edge of technology and innovation. Thus, reengineering may provide short-term gains but it may not provide long-term benefits to either the organisation or its shareholders.

For organisations which downsized or rightsized as a means to reduce costs, questions are also being raised about whether this is an appropriate long-term strategy. In a study by Mercer Management Consulting (*The Economist*, 10 February 1996) based on 1000 large US firms, confirmed by a later study into German and UK firms, organisations which downsized or reengineered as a means to cut costs and to reposition found that it was diffi-

cult to restart growth. In Mercer's study only 24 per cent of firms were able to make the transition to growth. Two-thirds of organisations which downsized did so again. By concentrating on internal structures and processes, downsizers take their eye off the customer, leaving no alternative but to cut costs again.

For those who have downsized successfully only 45 per cent found that their profits improved, which was one of the main reasons for downsizing in the first place. Moreover, one of the main problems with downsizing is the slump in morale, which can lead to reduced productivity and profits.

Management theorists are beginning to return once more to corporate growth or **upsizing**. Downsizing may, however, have been important for some businesses, especially if they can concentrate on their core business. J P Morgan, an investment bank in the US, found that those companies which are highly focused have produced the best results (*The Economist*, 1996). Gertz and Baptista (1996) suggested that three strategies are important for growth:

■ Customer franchise management, carefully defining customers so that the organisation can offer better products than its competitors.
■ Produce a stream of new products.
■ Channel management, selling products through channels which established companies have previously overlooked.

Therefore, although downsizing or reengineering may have worked for some organisations, altering boundaries in this way has not always proved successful for others. It may be possible that there were short-term advantages in the process, but if there has been no vision of where the company would like to be, then both downsizing and reengineering can cause more problems in the longer term. In other words, if downsizing is combined with revitalisation of the business, this may prove to be a more optimal scenario for longer-term survival.

It is also important to note, once again, that for many companies downsizing is not about becoming smaller but about reducing the workforce. It gives the opportunity for organisations to remove middle tiers of management, introduce different working practices, slimming down core staff and supplementing them by a range of other employees on temporary contracts, all in an effort to improve profits, reduce costs or raise sales revenue so that shareholders can be kept happy.

In the UK, KwikSave, the discount food retailer, and the changes in car dealership arrangements by

Ford, Vauxhall, Rover and Nissan show the contrasting face of downsizing. For KwikSave, a reported fall in profits from £125 million in 1994/5 to £80 million in 1995/6 was followed by a reduction in its outlets and a loss of jobs. At least 100 stores are likely to close, and the restructuring process that is to take place will cost around £65 million. The reason for KwikSave's demise is that it has been squeezed between the 'hard' discount food retailers such as Aldi, Netto and Lidl – which offer little-known brands at rock-bottom prices – and the mainstream superstores such as Tesco, Sainsbury, Asda and Safeway, which have all introduced own-brand budget lines.

In the case of the car dealerships run by Rover, Vauxhall, Ford and Nissan, it is estimated that more than 50 000 jobs will be lost over the next five years. However, the total number of customer outlets will remain about the same. The four large car makers wish to introduce a system where one main dealer will be selected for each town or area and they will then be expected to organise a lower tier of smaller 'satellite' showrooms and service centres. Sales will then be channelled through the high-value top-tier dealers.

Thus KwikSave faces boundary and employment changes, whereas, if the car manufacturers are to be believed, outlets will remain the same but employment will fall.

# DEMERGERS

Mergers and takeovers come in cycles and it has been argued that not all mergers are successful. In this case divestment or demerger takes place. This sometimes provides a range of suitable victims that leads to a further round of mergers. Demergers may also take place as a way of deflecting a hostile takeover bid: first, the organisation may not be so attractive if it is leaner, and second, the money raised from a demerger may enable the company to fight off a takeover bid.

However, demergers can arise through the organisations initiative rather than as a means of fending off a takeover bid. Both Hanson and Courtaulds have gone down this route. The argument here is that a demerger can lead to improved efficiency. Hanson is a large conglomerate which had interests in a variety of areas. In 1996 it chose to break itself up into more discrete parts. Courtaulds has turned its textile division into an independent business, concentrating management effort on its chemical and industrial activities. In the original business the combination of poorly linked activities drew on disparate and unrelated management skills, leading to management problems and conflicts. In changing its boundaries, Courtaulds had a number of options open to it. It could sell one of the areas as a management buy-out, it could sell some of the areas to another organisation, or it could float off the other company on the stock market and allow existing Courtaulds shareholders to retain a controlling interest. It chose to do the latter. The problem with any of the three approaches, and one which Thorn-EMI faced, was that demerging leads to smaller core business units which make the new companies vulnerable to predators.

Further impetus to the demerger process can be found in the work by Buzzel and Gale (1987) which indicated an inverse relationship between market size and the rate of return on investment in the US. They found that organisations attempted to reduce the disadvantage of size by restructuring, either by demerging or through establishing smaller strategic business units.

## ◆ CASE STUDY 23.4

### Demergers  FT

Investment banks should rename their mergers and acquisitions departments. Demergers and disposals have become more lucrative. Even before AT&T unveiled its plans to split, demergers valued at about $60bn had been announced in the US in 1995. In Europe the demerger wave is less pronounced, but companies ranging from Sandoz to Volvo are spinning off businesses to focus on core activities.

So which other companies look as if they may head towards demerger? The clearest sign is the marriage within a single group of mature growth businesses, which the equity market struggles to value. On that definition, the German chemicals giants – BASF, Bayer and Hoechst – should be tempted to follow ICI by demerging their pharmaceuticals interests. The separation of mobile telephone and industrial interests, already practised by Racal and Vodafone, could be usefully copied by Mannesmann. In the UK, groups such as Lonrho and Ladbroke encompass such a range of activities that, in theory, value could be released by demerger. For the investment banks whilst mergers and acquisitions remove potential clients from the market, demergers create new ones.

*Source: Financial Times*, 22 September 1995. Reprinted with permission.

◆ **Exercise 23.4**

Apart from mature businesses, what other factors could lead to a demerger?

## Looking to the future

Demergers are likely to become more popular as the stigma associated with failed merger policy wanes.

Having delayered, reengineered and downsized, demergers now offer the scope for competitive advantage in the future. Of course, demerging different sectors of the market may not always be to the organisation's advantage, especially where both sectors use the organisation's core competence. Nonetheless, as markets continue to become more competitive, there may be increased emphasis on this route as a means of staying ahead of competitors.

## SUMMARY

◆ There are many factors that can lead to organisations changing their boundaries. One possible explanation is transaction costs. If using the market is too expensive then organisations may expand their activities by growing horizontally, vertically or in a diversified manner to reduce these costs.

◆ Organisations may expand to achieve economies of both scale and scope. The latter is a means to reduce costs from the joint production of two or more products, the former is a means to increase output via a reduction in per-unit costs.

◆ Porter suggests that organisations grow because they attempt to mitigate the effects of competition. This may come about through the internationalisation of trade via the development of new trading blocs or the signing of trading agreements.

◆ Dicken suggests that technology underlies the internationalisation or globalisation of business activities. In addition, changes in environmental regulations may lead to organisations opening up in less well-regulated markets. The cost of labour is also seen as a driving force as organisations expand in one area, perhaps being balanced by contraction elsewhere as they seek to take advantage of low-cost labour.

◆ Mergers have been one of the most popular ways of expanding organisations. Mergers come in cycles and they can be thought of as being of three types. First, mergers may be vertical, where organisation merges with organisation either closer to the market or in an earlier stage of production. Second, mergers can be horizontal, where an organisation takes over another in the same stage of production. Finally, growth may be through conglomerate mergers, that is, where the takeover of another company may be in a sector or product which appears to be unrelated to the predator's experience.

◆ The drivers of the merger process include pressure by shareholders to improve earnings per share, external environmental factors such as the development of the Single European Market which increased the competitive pressures organisations were facing, to fill a weakness in an organisation's portfolio of products, a means to change the direction and reposition the organisation, and as a way of strengthening its market position.

◆ Organisations may expand their boundaries through setting up a joint venture. The reasons for this type of approach rather than using a subsidiary would include a desire to overcome barriers to entry, the ability to pool complementary pieces of knowledge for the parties involved, achieving lower transaction costs than with a subsidiary, and where developing a product on their own becomes too great. Joint ventures may, however, pose a threat to competition regulation, can be problematic if the partner is chosen unwisely, and may be fragile, allowing a partner access to information and know-how that allows them to become a threat in the future.

◆ Organisations do not always extend their boundaries by increasing in size or by looking for different forms of contractual relationships. There are occasions when organisations will seek to shrink. They may seek to divest themselves of unprofitable sections of their business, may be forced to sell a profitable area as a means to raise cash, or may seek to restructure themselves to enhance future competitiveness.

◆ An organisation can divest its non-core activities through management buyouts or buyins, contracting out or demerger. Buyouts have become increasingly popular in both the UK and continental Europe over the past decade. Shrinkage has also occurred through organisational down-sizing or rightsizing, and through reengineering. Downsizing was believed to make the organisation leaner and fitter, but there is now evidence to suggest that post-downsizing performance has been disappointing. A number of organisations which have downsized to enhance profits have noted that profits have actually fallen and have been forced to downsize once again. Thus the message for the mid-1990s and beyond is that downsizing may not always work and the organisation might benefit from upsizing.

## REVIEW QUESTIONS

1  The current boundaries of the organisation are as much an explanation of where it is planning to go as of where it has been. Discuss.

2  What criticisms can be levelled at the process of reengineering?

3  Using a joint venture of your choice, examine what each of its parents hoped to get out of its formation. Have these expectations proved to be well founded?

4  What are the likely impacts of vertical integration on a firm's price and output level?

5  On the whole conglomerate growth is not well thought through, profits appear to be disappointing and the move towards demergers appears to confirm this. Discuss.

6  Although management buyouts appear to be successful in the short to medium term, their long-term prospects are not good. Critically analyse this statement.

7  What is the difference between a buyout and a buyin? When is one preferable to the other?

8  The Astrax company has noticed that its profits have been steadily falling over the last three years. Recommend ways in which the company can alter its boundaries to improve its profits.

## GLOSSARY OF NEW TERMS

**Conglomerate diversification:** The growth of the organisation through merger and takeover into new products and new markets not related to current business activities.

**Core business:** The set of markets in which the organisa-tion's distinctive capability is likely to yield comparative advantage.

**Corporate reengineering:** The movement away from considering a business as a set of vertical but separate units to considering it as a collection of horizontal processes.

**Demerger:** The break-up of a previously merged organi-sation into separate parts.

**Divestment:** The sale of non-core parts of the organisation.

**Downsizing (rightsizing):** The reduction in the size of the organisation as a means to reduce costs and enhance prof-its. Often associated with reductions in the labour force.

**Fixed input proportions:** As the quantity of inputs to a production process rises, the ratio of the various inputs required stays constant.

**Fordism:** A way of increasing output per head, begun by Henry Ford using automated production lines for the mass production of standard consumer goods.

**Horizontal integration:** The growth of the organisa-tion by takeover or merger with other organisations in the same stage of production.

**Joint venture:** A relationship between two organisa-tions which set up a new organisation producing a good or service.

**Linkage approach:** A practical means for deciding whether or not it is efficient to integrate an activity within the organisation.

**Management buyin:** When the ownership of an organisation is transferred to a new set of share-holders who are a management team external to the organisation.

**Management buyout:** When the ownership of the organisation is transferred to a new set of shareholders, among whom the incumbent management is a significant element.

**Merger:** A situation where two or more enterprises cease to be distinct but come under the control of a new organisation or one of the parties in the merger.

**Upsizing:** Expanding the size of the organisation.

**Variable input proportions:** Where increases in inputs do not require fixed proportions of the factors of production.

**Vertical integration:** Entry by an organisation into the markets served by either its suppliers or distributors.

## READING

Gertz, D and Baptista, J (1996) *Merger Management Consulting: Grow to be Great*, The Free Press, New York. *The authors provide results of a study which suggests that corporate growth is better than downsizing.*

Johnson, G and Scholes, K (1997) *Exploring Corporate Strategy*, 4th edn, Prentice Hall, Hemel Hempstead. *Chapter 6 provides a management overview of the strategic decisions which may influence the boundaries of the organisation.*

Williamson, O E (1985) *The Economic Institutions of Capitalism*, Free Press, New York. *This text provides much of the background for the development of the transactions cost of organisational growth.*

**Further reading**

Baumol, W J and Braunstein, Y M (1977) 'Empirical study of scale economies and production complementarities: the case of journal publication', *Journal of Political Economy*, Vol 85, No 4, August, pp 1037–48.

Buzzel, R and Gale, B (1987) *The PIMS Principle*, Strategic Planning Institute, London.

Conyon, M J and Gregg, P (1994) 'Pat at the top: a study of the sensitivity of top director remuneration to company specific shocks', *National Institute Economic Review*, August, No 149, pp 83–92.

De Jonquieres, G (1990) 'Wave reflects wider trends', *Financial Times*, 18 October.

Dicken, P (1992) *Global Shift: Industrial Change in a Turbulent World*, 2nd edn, Paul Chapman, London.

Dunning, J H (1992) *Multinational Enterprises and the Global Economy*, Addison-Wesley, Harlow.

Dunning, J H (1993) *The Globalization of Business*, Routledge, London.

*Economist, The* (1996) 'Upsizing', *Management Focus*, 10 February, p 81.

Firth, M (1979) 'Takeovers, shareholders' return and the theory of the firm', *Economic Journal*, Vol 89, June, pp 316–28.

Geroski, P A and Vlassopoulos, A (1990) 'Recent patterns of European merger activity', *Business Strategy Review*, Vol 1, No 2, Summer, pp 17–27.

Gourlay, R (1995) Survey of management buyouts (1), *Financial Times*, 18 May, pp 29–20.

Griffiths, A and Wall, S (1997) *Applied Economics: An Introductory Course*, 7th edn, Addison Wesley Longman, Harlow.

Kanter, R M (1990) *When Giants Learn to Dance*, Unwin, London.

Kay, J (1993) *Foundations of Corporate Success: How Business Strategies Add Value*, Oxford University Press, Oxford.

Kotler, P (1996) *Marketing Management*, 9th edn, Prentice Hall, Hemel Hempstead.

Kumar, M S (1985) 'Growth, acquisition and firm size: evidence from the United Kingdom', *Journal of Industrial Economics*, Vol 33, March, pp 327–38.

Laurance, B (1996) 'Fiddling with edges while the core burns', *Observer*, 27 October, p 7.

Monteverde, K and Teece, D J (1982) 'Supplier switching costs and vertical integration in the automobile industry', *Bell Journal of Economics*, Vol 13, No 2, pp 206–13.

Mueller, D C (1989) 'Mergers – causes, effects and policies', *International Journal of Industrial Organisation*, Vol 7, Part I, pp 1–10.

Peters, T J and Waterman, R H (1982) *In Search of Excellence*, Harper and Row, New York.

Porter, M (1980) *Competitive Strategy*, Free Press, New York.

Prahalad, C K and Hamel, G (1994) 'The core competence of the corporation' in *Strategy: Process, Content, Context*, De Wit, R and Meyer, R (eds), West, St Paul, Minn.

Vernon, R (1965) 'International investment and international trade in the product cycle', *Quarterly Journal of Economics*, Vol 80, May, pp 190–207.

Whittington, G (1980) 'The profitability and size of UK companies', *Journal of Industrial Economics*, Vol 28, No 4, June, pp 335–52.

Young, B (1989) 'Acquisitions and corporate strategy', *Management Accounting*, Vol 67, No 8, September, pp 23–6.

CHAPTER **24**

# THE LABOUR MARKET

## OBJECTIVES

◆ To develop the theory of both the supply of, and demand for, labour.

◆ To consider the impact on the labour market of minimum wage legislation.

◆ To explore the changes in employment trends within the international economy.

◆ To show how different economies have attempted to make their labour markets more flexible.

◆ To consider the skill deficiencies and skill needs of the European economies throughout the 1980s and 1990s.

◆ To explore the role of older workers in the labour market and the response by organisations to the ageing demographic profile of the working population.

◆ To appraise the role of women in the labour market.

◆ To consider the role of both the social charter and social chapter in safeguarding workers' rights and encouraging flexibility in the labour market.

## KEY TERMS

Collective bargaining

Diminishing returns

External labour market

Indifference curve

Marginal productivity
of labour

Market failure

Minimum wage

Production function

Social charter

Sticky-downwards
wages

Supply-side policies

Tax wedge

Wages council

## CHAPTER OUTLINE

Business application

Introduction

Supply of labour

Demand for labour

Equilibrium in the labour market

Minimum wages

Other labour costs

Employment trends

Flexibility in the labour market

Case study 24.1 Are European companies becoming more sceptical about social legislation?

Skill deficiencies and skill needs

Older workers

Case study 24.2 The cost of employing older workers

Women in the labour market

Case study 24.3 Women's work

The social charter

Summary

Review questions

Glossary of new terms

Reading

# Flexible labour markets and the skilled labour force

**FT**

Are deregulated and flexible labour markets much more efficient and competitive than those that are not? A formidable array of reports from international organisations, including the International Monetary Fund, the Organisation for Economic Co-operation and Development and the World Bank, during 1994/95 have argued that they are and this assertion has hardened what is almost an unquestionable orthodoxy.

The credibility of this argument has drawn undeniable strength from the starkly drawn contrast in recent years between the achievement of employment creation in the European Union compared with that of the US. In the former, jobs grew by fewer than 6m between 1970 and 1992 while in the latter nearly 40m jobs were created over the same period.

The alleged inflexibility of European labour markets was identified by many as the primary cause of mass unemployment and poor record in job growth since the 1970s. The UK government has emphasised the main characteristics of efficient and flexible labour markets. This included the maximising of employment and labour productivity by an 'efficient matching of supply and demand', the removal of constraints affecting working practices and patterns, ensuring that wages reflect local labour market conditions and are based on performance rather than a going rate, and creating a welfare benefit system that provides people with an incentive to work. This, it says, is why unemployment fell sooner in the UK during the current recovery.

But why does de-regulation work now when the most successful economies throughout the 1970s and 1980s were those like Sweden, West Germany and Austria, which, it might be asserted, had some of the highest levels of regulation in their labour markets? Indeed it is possible to argue those societies were efficient because of, not in spite of, their commitment to social protection in the workplace. Moreover, the more recent publication of a number of international comparative studies does not suggest flexible labour markets and economic efficiency are necessarily synonymous even today in more difficult circumstances. It is true the US topped the league table for competitiveness produced by the Geneva-based World Economic Forum, but that country was followed by a range of others who are not renowned for the deregulated character of their labour markets – Japan, Switzerland, Germany, the Netherlands, Denmark and Norway. The UK – for all its commitment to employment flexibility – staggered in in 18th place, mainly because of its poor levels of skills and training. Such reports indicate a diversity of factors help to explain why one labour market turns out to be more efficient than another which has little to do with the degree of regulation.

*Source: Financial Times, 6 October 1995. Reprinted with permission.*

# INTRODUCTION

As markets are becoming increasingly global, organisations and governments are considering a whole raft of policies and arrangements that can enhance their performance. On the one hand are those that believe in deregulation of labour markets, making it easier to hire and fire people, wanting workers to be more flexible, and organising the labour input to respond to changes in demand through the use of temporary and part-time staff. On the other hand, there are those that consider that such policies reduce the protection offered to labour and do not encourage employers to undertake sufficient training to improve the skills of their workforce.

There are many ways of approaching a discussion of labour issues and their effects on the organisation. This chapter considers an environmental approach to labour. It appraises the changes that are occurring in the demographic makeup of the workforce and how organisations are responding to this. There is discussion of the minimum wage debate and the social charter and their influence on the competitiveness of organisations, both within and outside the EU. Further, the changing nature of jobs is considered in the context of the growth of part-time employment and the greater participation of women in the labour market. Finally, in the context of improved competitiveness, the role of skills and qualifications is discussed. In choosing this approach little is said about wage competitiveness, the role of trade unions or the more human resource management angle of labour rewards and motivation. Given the wide array of labour matters that could be discussed, we will adopt the more traditional starting point of labour issues by considering the supply of, and demand for, labour.

# SUPPLY OF LABOUR

The neoclassical model of the supply of labour can be considered within a framework developed earlier, that of consumer behaviour; *see* Chapter 5. In this case individuals are assumed to divide their time between two activities, work and leisure. The individual maximises their utility by choosing different balances in a composite good made up of income and leisure hours, subject to both time and income constraints.

The individual's utility function can be written as:

$$U = f(Y, L)$$

where,

$Y$ = total income received during the period
$L$ = total leisure received during the period
$U$ = utility (satisfaction) obtained from consuming different quantities of work and leisure.

The individual's hours of work ($H$) are related to both $L$ and $T$ (the total time available for the individual, which can vary depending on how much sleep they require!) through a time constraint.

$$H = T - L$$

As can be deduced from the above:

$$T = H + L$$

That is, the total time available for the individual is made up of leisure time and work time.

It is also possible to define the individual's income:

$$Y = W(T - L) + V \text{ or } Y = WH + V$$

where,

$W$ = a constant wage rate
$V$ = non-earned income which is not related to hours worked, and
$WT + V$ = the individual's full income, that is the maximum amount of income which the individual can receive without taking any leisure time.

Therefore, if non-earned income, $V$, is £60, the hours worked, $H$, 35 and the wage rate is £5, then the individual's income is;

$$Y = 60 + 5(35)$$

or,

$$Y = £235$$

The individual's optimisation problem may be stated as:

$$\text{Maximise } U = f(Y, L)$$

subject to,

$$Y = V + W(T - L)$$

It is now possible to use the indifference curve analysis and budget lines which were introduced in Chapter 5 to illustrate the individual's tradeoff between work and leisure (*see* Figure 24.1).

Income from hours supplied to the labour market and non-earned income is measured on the vertical axis and the amount of leisure is measured along the horizontal axis. It is possible for the individual to choose to consume no hours of leisure. All the hours, therefore, would be devoted to work and the individual would earn their maximum amount. This is shown as point B. On the other hand, it is possible that the individual does not offer any hours of work to the labour market but devotes all their time to leisure. Here income would be non-earned income only and the individual would be at point A. The line joining B to A shows all the combination of hours worked and time devoted to leisure. The equation of this line is:

$$Y = W(T - L) + V \text{ or } Y = W(H) + V$$

**Figure 24.1 Individual tradeoff between work and leisure**

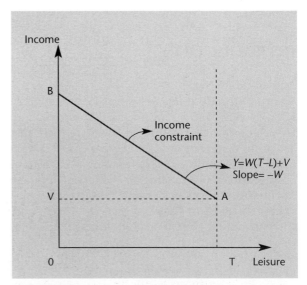

At the extreme the individual can choose to take no hours of leisure point B, with total income being $WH+V$, or devote all their time to leisure point A, receiving only non-earned income. The budget constraint is the line connecting A and B and is given by $Y = W(T - L) + V$, whose slope is $-W$.

If the individual chooses to be at B, then there is no leisure, $L = 0$, and total time available is equal to the hours worked, $T = H$. So $Y = V + WT$ or $WH$. If the individual chooses to be at A, that is, spend all their time, $T$, devoted to leisure, then the equation becomes $Y = W(L - L) + V$, that is, $Y = V$.

The equation $Y = W(T - L) + V$ is the equation of straight line, with intercept $WT + V$, on the vertical axis, and slope, $Y/L = -W$.

Where the individual chooses to be on their income line depends on the particular point that maximises their utility. That is, the individual will choose to be at the point on their budget line which just enables them to reach their highest **indifference curve**. Suppose such an indifference curve is that shown as $I_0$ which just touches the income (budget) line at C. If there was any other indifference curve which was just tangential to the budget line which would yield a greater level of satisfaction for the individual, then the person would be at that point.

At C, the individual will be choosing to take $0L_1$ amount of leisure and $L_1T$ amount of work hours.

Suppose that the individual now receives an increase in their wage rate. If the individual con-tinues not to offer any hours of work to the labour market, then the maximum amount of leisure time is still shown at A. However, because the wage rate has increased, then for each hour of time offered to the labour market there will be an increase in income. In terms of the diagram, the budget line pivots upward at A giving a new budget line $AB^1$. Because the budget line has pivoted outwards, the utility-maximising individual can now reach a higher indifference curve. This is shown as indifference curve $I_2$. In Figure 24.2 this new indifference curve is tangential to the new budget line ($AB^1$) at D, and indicates that an increase in the wage rate leads to the individual supplying fewer hours of work to the labour market. It is quite possible that an increase in the wage rate could lead to the individual supplying the same or even more hours to the labour market. Why?

The movement from C to D is made up of two effects – the income and substitution effects. These can be found in the following way. Suppose that the individual is at their final position after an increase in the wage rate, that is, point D. Now suppose that income is removed from this individual so that they are forced back to the original indifference curve, $I_0$. The individual will not be at point C since removal of income is represented by a parallel shift to the left of the income restraint line (budget line). The budget line, which is now tangential to the original indifference curve $I_0$ at G, is shown as EF. Therefore, the movement from C to D is made up of two parts: the movement from C to G (the substitution effect) and the movement from G to D (the income effect).

Notice that following an increase in the wage rate the substitution effect is away from leisure. This is due to the fact that an increase in the wage increases the opportunity cost of taking each hour of leisure in terms of income forgone. That is, each hour of leisure has increased in price. It is normally expected that when the price of a commodity increases individuals will substitute away from that commodity. Thus the increase in the wage rate leads to the individual substituting away from leisure, each hour of which has become more expensive in terms of income forgone. In moving from G to D the income that was taken away from the individual is restored. If leisure is assumed to be a normal good, then an increase in income will lead to an increase in the demand for leisure. Whether D, therefore, lies to the right of C depends on whether the income effect of taking on more leisure hours exceeds the substitution

**Figure 24.2**

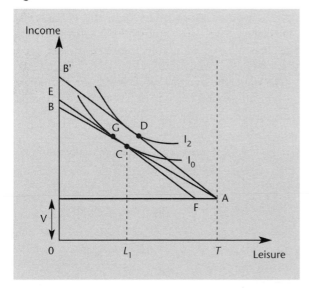

With budget line AB, the utility-maximising individual will choose to be at C, the point at which the budget line is just tangential to the highest indifference curve. An increase in the wage rate causes the budget line to pivot outwards at A to AB'. The individual can now reach a higher indifference curve, $I_2$. The new point of tangency is shown as D. The movement from C to D can be broken down into two parts: the substitution effect C to G and the income effect G to D.

effect, which is encouraging a reduction in leisure hours since the price of leisure has increased. In Figure 24.2 the positive income effect is greater than the negative substitution effect.

If the substitution effect outweighs the income effect then, as the wage rate increases, the individual worker is willing to offer more hours to the labour market (take less leisure). That is, the individual supply-of-labour curve slopes upward and to the right. If the income effect outweighs the substitution effect then, following a wage increase, fewer hours of work are offered and the individual supply-of-labour curve begins to bend backwards to the left.

Of course, the reality of the situation is that very often individuals do not have complete control over their decision to supply hours to the labour market. Their contractual arrangements are for a specific number of hours or else they will be offered no hours at all. Moreover, some individuals will face a backward-bending supply curve of labour. As the wage rate rises these individuals take on more leisure time rather than offer more hours of work. Other individuals will not enter the labour market at all at lower wage levels, perhaps because the benefits they receive exceed the value of any income they could obtain at the current wage rates. In addition, should the discussion actually be about an individual's supply of labour to the labour market, or should it be about a household's decision to supply labour? It is possible to pursue all these routes individually, but it is sufficient for the analysis here to consider the aggregate supply of labour (that is, everybody's supply of labour added together) as being upward sloping and to the right. For those who wish to pursue

this area, the works by Pencavel (1986) and Killingsworth and Heckman (1986) provide excellent surveys of the literature.

Within Europe there is clear evidence that real wages have increased over time while at the same time hours worked by full-time employees have fallen (*see* Figure 24.3). By 1993 this had reached an average of 39.6 hours across the EU, a fall in working hours which has continued uninterrupted since 1988 and which dropped under the 40-hours-a-week level in 1990. However, it is important to consider not only the *actual* hours worked, that is, a respondent's figure for hours worked in the week that the data is collected, but also hours *usually* worked. For actual hours the number of hours worked by employees in the UK was slightly higher than that in both France and Italy. Until 1988 UK employees worked fewer hours than their German contemporaries, but since then the picture has been reversed. Since 1992 the gap between the UK and the other large EU countries has narrowed.

If the hours usually worked are considered (*see* Figure 24.4), the average for the EU was 40.2 hours in 1993, higher than the hours actually worked. The fall in hours worked is once again confirmed, but it is less significant than for actual hours worked and came to a halt in 1991. Of the 'big four' countries within the EU only employees in the UK worked more hours than the EU average. Not only is the UK's figure higher than the average, it is also considerably higher than the other three large EU countries.

For men, the average work week, the retirement age and in general the rate of labour-force participation have fallen since 1900. For women, labour-

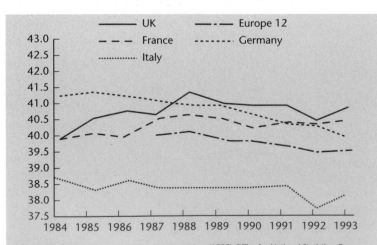

**Figure 24.3 Hours actually worked per week**

Source: UK Business in Europe: A Statistical Comparison (1995) Office for National Statistics. Crown Copyright 1995. Reproduced by the permission of the Controller of HMSO and the Office for National Statistics.

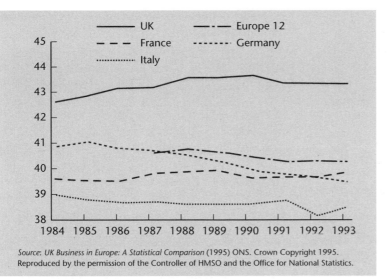

**Figure 24.4  Hours usually worked per week**

Source: *UK Business in Europe: A Statistical Comparison* (1995) ONS. Crown Copyright 1995. Reproduced by the permission of the Controller of HMSO and the Office for National Statistics.

force participation and hours worked per week have in fact increased. Thus it would appear to be the case that for men the income effect dominates the substitution effect, while for women the substitution effect dominates. The works by Pencavel (1986) and Killingsworth and Heckman (1986), who examined empirical studies over the previous 20 years, appear to confirm this view. In addition, the elasticity of labour supply was larger for women than for men, so taken together the results suggest that, for the population as a whole, the aggregate labour curve is positively sloped both in the US and UK. However, Elliot (1991) claims that 'more recent evidence on the slope of the women's labour supply curve appears to suggest that it is no longer as positively sloped as was once suggested'.

## DEMAND FOR LABOUR

There are a number of ways of approaching this area, but the following may suffice. Suppose that an organisation has two factors of production, labour (*L*) and capital (*K*), and can combine these in a manner which produces an output. What has been described here is a **production function**. This can be shown as:

$$Y = f(L, K)$$

where,

> *Y* = output
> *L* = amount of labour input
> *K* = amount of capital stock

In the short run it is possible that labour is the only factor of production that can be varied. Additional units of output can be obtained by increasing the labour input while in the short run the capital stock is held constant. However, due to the law of **diminishing returns**, increasing one factor of production while holding the other factors constant increases output but at a diminishing rate. Figure 24.5 shows this in detail.

Output is drawn on the vertical axis and the amount of labour on the horizontal. The production function, *Y* = f(*L*, *K*), is drawn as a curve whose gradient is becoming less and less. That is, because of diminishing returns it requires more and more units of labour to produce an additional unit of output. This additional output that is produced by each extra unit of labour is called the **marginal productivity of labour** (MPL) or the slope of the production function. Suppose that in the same diagram is placed a line which shows the wage rate earned by each unit of labour. This is the line OS, whose slope is the wage rate (*W*). At this wage rate there must be one point on the production function where the slope of the production function just equals the wage rate. This is shown as point A. Point A shows the maximum difference between the production function and the cost-of-labour line. In other words, this is the position at which the organisation will make the greatest profit. Thus the maximum profit for the organisation will occur at the point at which MPL = *W*.

Suppose that to the left of A, MPL>*W*. The organisation is able to obtain from its last unit of labour a level of output which exceeds the wage

## Figure 24.5 The production function

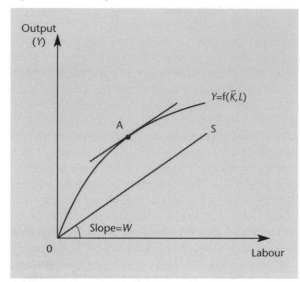

The production function is shown as $Y = f(\bar{K},L)$. It is a curve because increasing the labour input ($L$) with a fixed quantity of capital ($K$) leads to diminishing returns. The wage rate is shown as line OS. At point A on the production function, the slope of the production function equals the slope of the wage line, that is, MPL = $W$. To the left of A, MPL > $W$ and the organisation has the incentive to increase the labour input. To the right of A, MPL<$W$ and the organisation will reduce its demand for labour.

rate. There is an incentive, therefore, for the organisation to employ additional workers. As it does so, because of the law of diminishing returns, the marginal productivity labour will fall and at some time will come to the point at which MPL = $W$. If, on the other hand, to the right of A we have MPL<$W$, this implies that the organisation is paying a wage level to its employees which exceeds their level of output. The organisation will reduce the quantity of employment and as it does so, because of diminishing returns, the marginal productivity of labour will rise and the organisation will once again find itself in a position where MPL = $W$. Therefore, the optimal position for the organisation is where MPL = $W$.

Because the slope of the production function declines as the labour input is increased, the MPL declines as the labour input increases. If the wage rate were to increase, the organisation would not come to rest at A since, as Figure 24.6 indicates, the slope of the production function at A does not match the slope of the wage line. Given the wage line OT, point B is the position at which the MPL equals the wage line. Since line OT is steeper than OS, this must mean that the wage rate has increased. Thus an increase in the wage rate

## Figure 24.6 Impact of an increase in wages on the demand for labour

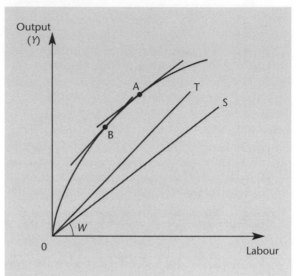

At wage rate $W$, the marginal productivity of labour equals the wage rate at A. With an increased wage the wage line becomes steeper, OT, and the slope of the production equals the slope of the new wage line OT, at B. At B less labour is demanded than at A, so an increase in the wage level reduces the demand for labour.

implies that the demand for labour falls. Conversely, if the wage rate falls the demand for labour rises. Thus the demand-for-labour line is downward sloping to the right.

## EQUILIBRIUM IN THE LABOUR MARKET

As Figure 24.7 indicates, equilibrium in the labour market is obtained at the point at which the supply of labour curve intersects with the demand for labour curve. Here the real wage is $W_0$ and quantity of labour is $L_0$. If the real wage is higher than $W_0$, say $W_1$, then the demand for labour is $L_{d1}$ and the supply of labour is $L_{s1}$. At the wage rate $W_1$ there is excess supply of labour and some individuals are unemployed. In a pure market system without friction, the excess supply of labour should cause the real wage to fall. As it does so, there is increased demand for labour and the supply of labour is reduced so that once again equilibrium is established at $W_0$, $L_0$. Similarly, if the real wage is below $W_0$, there will be excess demand for labour and the real wage will be 'bid up'. As the real wage rises the demand for labour falls and the supply of

## Figure 24.7 Equilibrium in the labour market

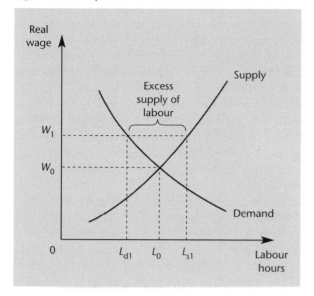

Equilibrium in the labour market is achieved where the demand for labour equals the supply of labour. This is shown as $W_0$, $L_0$. If the wage rate is set above the equilibrium, say $W_1$, then the demand for labour falls to $L_{d1}$ and supply of labour rises to $L_{s1}$. There is no excess supply of labour $L_{s1} - L_{d1}$. If labour markets are flexible the wage rate should be bid downwards, thus clearing the market.

labour increases so that equilibrium is once again restored at $W_0$, $L_0$. To enable this equilibrium condition to prevail requires flexibility in the labour market, particularly with the supply of labour and with the wage rate. In fact, it has been suggested that complete flexibility in the labour market does not exist and that the real wage is **sticky downwards**. In this case there will always be some individuals who wish to offer themselves to the labour market but are unable to find employment.

An important feature that has been noticeable in EU labour markets in particular has been the gradual rise in unemployment, especially in comparison with the US. Both economies have been subject to massive external changes such as the rise of the newly industrialised countries (NICs), rapid changes in technology, changes in the way production is organised, structural reforms and the like. However, while the US has reduced its unemployment rate to around 6 per cent, a number of EU countries have a rate in double figures. This is not to say that some EU countries are not more successful than others at keeping unemployment relatively low, but that on average EU unemployment rates are some 4 percentage points higher than those in the US. One factor that has recently exacerbated

the EU problem is monetary union. Governments seeking to achieve targets set by the Maastricht Treaty for their level of government expenditure as a proportion of GDP have resorted to demand-dampening policies which have resulted in higher levels of unemployment. Some governments have also resorted to reducing their social packages and this may in the long term improve the flexibility of the labour market.

One feature that appears to be similar in the US and the EU is wage rigidity (Griffiths and Wall (1995)). However, once short-term unemployment rates rise in the US they appear to fall back, which is different to the effect in Europe. To try to explain this a number of hypotheses have been postulated. One of these is the insider–outsider hypothesis proposed by Blanchard and Summers (1986), among others. Insiders are unionised employees who pay little regard to the outsiders, the unemployed. When a downturn in demand occurs some insiders will lose their jobs, but when demand picks up the unionised insiders use their position to gain higher pay awards, rather than showing restraint in order to enhance the job-creation prospects for others. The economy therefore settles at a new equilibrium but at a higher wage and with less employment. Alternatively, the problem can be seen as being related to the outsiders. Once they have been out of employment for some time their skills may become redundant and the wage they could now earn if they participated in the labour market might fall below their non-labour income. Thus it is beneficial to them not to participate in the labour market. In addition, it may well be that, the longer individuals are out of the labour market, the more reticent employers are at taking them on. In other words, the long-term unemployed become discouraged and effectively give up searching for jobs.

A third factor that may explain the fact that some employers do not take on more labour are the high costs of firing their existing workforce. If firing costs are high then employers may be reluctant to take on new employees unless demand is seen to be long term; *see* Bean (1994). Until recently, Spain was used as an example where high firing costs and high unemployment have gone hand in hand. Bean also puts forward a hypothesis that the level of capital stock in a number of EU countries, such as France, Germany and the UK, is not the optimal amount, thus lowering the marginal productivity of labour in these countries. When demand picks up then the unemployment level will only fall as capital stock is built up.

# MINIMUM WAGES

The effect of a **minimum wage** on a competitive labour market, where workers are assumed to be homogenous (in skill and effort), where all workers in the market are covered by the minimum wage and where there are no obstacles to the interaction of labour supply with labour demand, can be seen in Figure 24.8.

A minimum wage level, $W_{min}$, has been set above the equilibrium wage, $W_0$. The impact is to reduce the demand for labour from $L_0$ to $L_d$ and to increase the supply of labour to $L_s$. The excess supply of workers ($L_s - L_d$) will contain some who were previously employed ($L_0 - L_d$) and therefore can be viewed as those made jobless by the wage increase. The analysis can be expanded to include the role of trade unions and where the employer is a monopsonist (a single purchaser of labour), but it suffices here to use competitive market conditions.

It has been argued that, if the setting of a minimum wage leads to increases in unemployment, the way to reduce unemployment is, naturally, to reduce or scrap the minimum wage. However, there has been a growing amount of evidence to suggest that setting a minimum wage does not always lead to higher unemployment. Before

**Figure 24.8 Impact of minimum wages on employment in a competitive market**

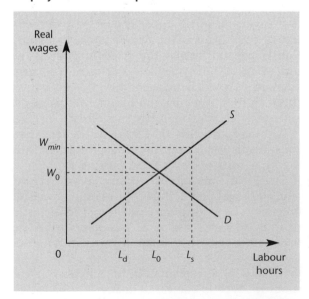

Setting a minimum wage in a competitive market above the market-clearing rate, $W_0$, causes the demand for labour to fall from $L_0$ to $L_d$ and the supply of labour to rise, leading to an excess supply of labour ($L_s - L_d$).

exploring this debate it is worth considering why minimum wages were introduced in the first place. Minimum wages have been in place for a considerable period in many countries, mostly to protect younger people from exploitation. Paradoxically, the imposition of a minimum wage may itself lead to higher youth unemployment. Organisations are deterred from hiring young people because their marginal productivities are perceived as being below the minimum wage level. This may also apply to older workers who possess obsolete skills.

Within the EU, France, the Netherlands, Portugal, Spain and Luxembourg have statutory minimum wages, while in Belgium and Greece a national minimum wage is set by collective bargaining. In Germany, Italy and Denmark, pay minima for individual sectors are set by binding collective agreements covering a large proportion of the workforce, while in Ireland legal minimum rates are set for certain low-wage sectors such as hotels and catering. Of the EU countries only the UK has no minimum wage protection at either national, regional or sectoral level, having abandoned minimum wages set by wage councils in 1993. Table 24.1 sets out the systems of minimum wages that have operated in most European countries. It might be expected that the minimum wage would be related to labour productivity. The most common measure is therefore the minimum wage as a percentage of average earnings, known as the Kaitz index. Using this index the minimum wages in most European countries are about 50–70 per cent of average earnings compared with around 39 per cent in the US, which has had a federal minimum wage for many decades. It has been argued that the lack of a minimum wage in the UK explains its unemployment level during the 1990s which is lower than that of many of its partners in Europe. Moreover, because the US minimum wage is set lower than those in Europe, this explains the US unemployment rate which is 50 per cent less than those in the EU.

So is it true that minimum wages lead to higher unemployment? In June 1996, the UK's Competition and Consumers Affairs Minister, John Taylor, estimated that a minimum wage of £4 or £4.15 per hour would cost around one million jobs in the UK, even if higher-paid workers were only able to renegotiate 50 per cent of their wages to restore differentials (*Observer*, 27 October 1996). The majority of jobs destroyed would be those of the lower paid. It has also been argued that the UK would lose some elements of price competitiveness

**Table 24.1 Minimum wage systems in Europe and the USA**

| Country | Determination | Variation by: | Kaitz index (year) | % of workers at or near minimum | Youth minimum as % of adult minimum |
|---|---|---|---|---|---|
| Austria | Legally binding collective agreement at industry level | Industry, region, dependants, age, job tenure | 0.62 (1993) | 4% | Embodied in industry agreements |
| Belgium | Negotiated by unions and employers as part of national agreement | Age, job tenure | 0.60 (1992) | 4% | Small reduction for <23 (lower rates for short job tenure) |
| Denmark | Negotiated as part of collective agreements | Industry, age | 0.54 (1994) | 6% | 40% (<18) |
| Finland | Negotiated as part of collective agreements | Age, occupation, industry, region | 0.52 (1995) | | Embodied in industry agreements |
| France | Set by government constrained by formula | Age, training | 0.50 (1995) | 11% | 80% (age 16); 90% (age 17) + schemes + 30–70% for trainers |
| Germany | Part of collective agreements, then extended | Age, qualification, trainee status, region | 0.55 (1991) | | Embodied in industry agreements |
| Greece | Part of national collective agreement | Manual/non-manual, job tenure, marital status, qualifications | 0.62 (1995) | 20% | Lower rates for short job tenure |
| Ireland | Joint Labour Committees in 16 low-paying industries | Age, industry, region, occupation, job tenure | 0.55 (1995) | | Varies; 63% (<18); 81% (<21) in hotels |
| Italy | Extension of collective agreements | Age, industry, job tenure | 0.71 (1991) | | Embodied in industry agreements |
| Luxembourg | Statutory minimum wage | Age, skill, family characteristics | 0.56 (1993) | 11% | 70% (<21) |
| Netherlands | Statutory minimum wage | Age | 0.55 (1993) | 3.2% | 34.5% (age 16) rising to 84% (age 22) |
| Norway | Negotiated as part of collective agreements | Industry, age, job tenure, job | 0.64 (1993) | | |
| Portugal | Statutory minimum wage | Age, trainee status, industry | 0.45 (1993) | 8% | 75% (<18) |
| Spain | Statutory minimum wage | Age, homeworkers, casual workers | 0.32 (1994) | 6.5% | 66% (<18) |
| Sweden | Negotiated as part of collective agreements | Age, industry, job tenure, occupation | 0.52 (1992) | 0% | 85% (<24) |
| Switzerland | Industry-level collective agreements (coverage 30%) | Age, industry | 0.52 (1993) | | Embodied in industry agreements |
| United Kingdom | Pre-1993 set by Wages Councils by industry; now only agriculture | Age, industry (more complex pre-1986) | 0.40 (1993) | | 0% (<21) (1986–93) |
| United States | Federal minimum wage (higher in some states) | Limited youth sub-minimum | 0.39 (1993) | 4% | No reduction |

*Source:* Dolando, J, Kramarz, F, Machin, S, Manning, A, Morgolis, D and Teulings, C (1996) 'Minimum wages: the European experience', *Economic Policy: A European Forum*, October (Centre for Economic Policy Research).

in external markets, as it has often put forward its low wage costs as a reason for attracting foreign direct investment but also as a means to keep overall costs lower. Moreover, it has also been argued that the UK needs to maintain a flexible labour market, that is, to allow employers freedom to pay low wages if employees will accept them and to make it easy to hire and fire employees as circumstances change. As plausible as these arguments appear, it is possible that any minimum wage would not be a national minimum wage but would have regional variations, higher in the South of England and lower in the North, for example. Minimum wages are also industry specific, in that they are likely to have a greater impact in some sectors of the economy than in others. Five areas of the UK economy stand out in terms of low pay: industrial cleaning; healthcare, such as attendants for older persons, nurses and the like; hairdressing; textiles; and catering. In almost all cases it is women who are likely to be earning low wages and, with the exception of textiles, low-pay industries are mainly in the service sector. Since most of the low-pay sectors are in the service sector of the economy, often undertaken only in the domestic economy, the international-competitiveness argument is difficult to sustain. It is also possible to suggest that some organisations in these sectors only exist because their inefficiencies are disguised by low wages. Thus a minimum wage would either see these organisations go out of business, to be replaced by their more efficient rivals, or eat into their profit margins.

There have also been a number of empirical studies which appear to suggest that raising the minimum wage does not always lead to less employment; *see* Card (1992) and Card and Kreuger (1994). The Card and Kreuger study considered the effects of an 18 per cent rise in minimum wages in New Jersey, from $4.25 to $5.05 in April 1992, on employment change in the fast-food industry. Restaurants in neighbouring Pennsylvania were used for comparison, as their minimum wages stayed at $4.25. The researchers found that there was no evidence that employment fell in restaurants in New Jersey because of the higher minimum wage. In fact, they found the reverse to be true. Although some have expressed doubts as to the validity of these results, Machin and Manning (1994) found similar results in the UK in areas that previously had been controlled by **wages councils**. In their survey of wages councils

between 1979 to 1990, the authors found that the decline in the level of the minimum wage relative to the average wage did not increase employment; on the contrary, adult employment appeared to have declined as the effectiveness of wages councils diminished. Some sectors which had been controlled by wages councils were low-growth sectors which would have been subject to decline anyway, with or without a wages council in operation. However, in the UK the issue is further confused by the fact that, although the wages councils were wound up, any individual employed prior to 30 August 1993 has a right to the same terms and conditions of employment after that date if they remain with the same employer. So the minimum wage is still operating for many existing workers and it is only the wages of new employees that employers can reduce.

In other words, labour markets cannot be treated in the same way as those for goods or services. Notions of fairness, commitment to particular jobs and information about available alternatives make people a more complicated commodity. In fact, the classical assumptions about the labour market – that employers can easily hire workers and that they can without cost obtain all the information they need about available jobs and wage rates – are almost never met in practice. When staff turnover is rapid and workers are young and inexperienced, it is quite possible for different workers of the same age and the same skills to be paid different wage rates, even in the same organisation.

Coming back to the issue of whether higher minimum wages in Europe relative to those in the US can be blamed for the greater job losses in Europe, the answer is 'perhaps'. Minimum wages do appear to be higher for adults in Europe, but the reverse is true if we examine young workers. As Dolando *et al* (1996) note, 'It is surprisingly hard to find strong evidence of any adverse employment effects of minimum wages'. Further, they suggest, 'The presence or absence of a minimum wage will not be the difference between economic success and failure'.

## OTHER LABOUR COSTS

The cost of labour to businesses is substantially greater than the take-home pay of employees in many EU member states. A distinguishing feature of most EU economies is the high level of social protection provided by the state. To fund this social protection charges are made on businesses and, as international competitiveness in markets has grown, there has been concern that these effects on labour costs are putting European organisations at a competitive disadvantage and discouraging them from employing people. In addition, these charges differ between countries and it has been suggested that those countries with the higher charges are losing business and employment to those where the requirements are lower. One question that needs to be addressed is how any charges on the organisation are borne. It could be that the organisation absorbs these increased costs and thereby profits are reduced. It is possible that it passes the labour charges on to the consumer by raising prices, or the costs may be borne by the employee through reduced wages. For those at the minimum wage level, their wages cannot be reduced to compensate for higher social protection charges and they may simply lose their jobs. It would be expected that the impact of these labour charges will depend on the market in which organisations find themselves, but it could also lead organisations, irrespective of the markets in which they operate, to substitute capital for labour.

It is also important to recognise when making comparisons between the EU, Japan and the US that a number of large companies make considerable contributions to private schemes for their employees' social protection. These may not always be considered as social contributions but as part of a salary package offered to their employees.

Suppose that employers were able to have their social-protection costs lowered, the impact on employment may not be as clear as expected since the government would have to raise its revenue from elsewhere. Nonetheless, in the long run it is expected that a reduction in social contributions would provide the incentive for job creation. This is particularly so because of the **tax wedge** between what employees receive in net earnings and what employers pay to employ people, implying both a possible deterrent to employment and an incentive to avoid or evade paying taxes and contributions.

Figure 24.9 provides a theoretical perspective of the tax wedge. The demand for, and supply of, labour are shown as lines $D_L$ and $S_L$ respectively. Equilibrium in the labour market occurs at $L^*$, $(W/P)^*$. The introduction of a tax on employers for each worker they employ (to go to the government

**Figure 24.9 Taxes and unemployment**

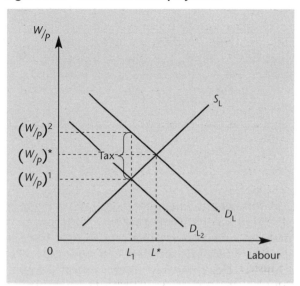

Equilibrium in the labour market without taxes is shown as $(W/P)^*$, $L^*$. The imposition of a tax on employers shifts the demand-for-labour curve to $DL_2$ and the real wage falls for employees to $(W/P)^1$ and demand for labour is reduced to $L_1$. Employers will pay a tax on labour shown as the difference between $(W/P)^2 - (W/P)^1$.

for social contributions) means that organisations will no longer regard the marginal productivity of labour as being equal to the value of labour. They will regard labour as being worth its marginal productivity minus the tax that has to be paid on each worker employed. The demand curve for labour shifts down to the left, to $D_{L2}$. A new equilibrium is established at $L_1$ and $(W/P)^1$. Here the level of employment is lower, as is the real wage rate. The tax paid to the government when $L_1$ units of labour are employed is shown as the vertical difference between $D_L$ and $D_{L2}$. Thus if this tax was reduced employment would increase.

Before considering a number of other aspects of the labour market both in Europe and elsewhere, it is worth considering the state of employment and unemployment in Europe.

## EMPLOYMENT TRENDS

After a period of high employment growth in the second half of the 1980s, the European Union has experienced a number of years in which the numbers of people in work have progressively declined; *see* Table 24.2.

**Table 24.2 Comparative unemployment rates (%) standardised**

|  | 1960–68 | 1969–73 | 1974–79 | 1980–85 | 1986 | 1988 | 1990 | 1992 | 1996* |
|---|---|---|---|---|---|---|---|---|---|
| UK | 2.6 | 3.4 | 5.0 | 10.5 | 11.2 | 8.3 | 5.8 | 9.9 | 8.4 |
| USA | 4.7 | 4.0 | 6.7 | 8.0 | 6.9 | 5.4 | 5.4 | 7.3 | 5.6 |
| France | 1.7 | 2.5 | 4.5 | 8.3 | 10.4 | 10.0 | 8.9 | 10.3 | 11.9 |
| Germany (FR) | 0.7 | 0.8 | 3.2 | 5.9 | 6.5 | 6.1 | 4.9 | 4.6 | 9.0 |
| Japan | 1.4 | 1.2 | 1.9 | 2.4 | 2.8 | 2.5 | 2.1 | 2.2 | 3.1 |
| Sweden | 1.6 | 2.2 | 1.9 | 2.8 | 2.7 | 1.6 | 1.5 | 4.8 | 9.2 |

* At March 1996.
*Source: OECD Economic Outlook* (1992) OECD, Paris; *Labour Market Trends* (1996). Office for National Statistics. Crown Copyright 1996. Reproduced by the permission of the Controller of HMSO and the Office for National Statistics.

Although the unemployment rates have been standardised to compensate for differences in national definitions, further care must be taken in making comparisons between countries. For example, the countries' figures reflect different labour-market practices. Although the job-for-life agreements between employers and employees in Japan have now come under strain, the fact that they are still very much in evidence means that the low unemployment figures for that country will contain a certain element of disguised unemployment. Thus comparability of unemployment rates between countries is a complex issue, and we must bear this in mind when discussing particular areas or countries.

In Central and Eastern European countries (CEECs) unemployment measures have had to be started from scratch, because unemployment was not considered as existing in centrally planned, communist economies.

As Table 24.3 indicates, there was a rapid increase in the number unemployed in CEECs between 1990 and 1991. This may be explained by the way in which unemployment was measured, since the earliest measures of unemployment in the region were based either on registrations for work, or on claims for unemployment-related benefits. However, since unemployment had not been a recognised phenomenon, the benefits systems that had existed were very basic. After 1990 new benefit regimes were introduced which were very generous compared with other international schemes and led to a large rise in claims. Subsequently, the CEECs began to operate schemes which were closer to those operating internationally. However, there was also a problem of data accuracy, since the CEECs were not experienced in keeping track of the unemployed. Therefore, although accuracy has been improved, this caveat must be borne in mind.

Although output in Europe is recovering during 1996, the unemployment rate is proving to be difficult to reduce in many EU countries and it has been made more problematic as countries attempt to achieve the Maastricht criteria for entry into a single currency in January 1999. The problems for the EU15 have been described in the Commission White Paper on growth, competitiveness and employment (1994) as:

■ Lack of sufficient coordination of economic policy within the member states, which has resulted in inadequate economic growth.

**Table 24.3 Evolution of registered unemployed as a percentage of the labour force in CEECs**

| Country | 1990 | 1991 | 1992 | 1993 | 1994 | 1995 |
|---|---|---|---|---|---|---|
| Bulgaria | 1.7 | 11.1 | 13.2 | 16.3 | 13.3 | 12.5 |
| Croatia | 8.0 | 14.0 | 15.0 | 13.8 | 13.4 | 13.2 |
| Czech Republic | 0.7 | 4.1 | 3.1 | 3.0 | 3.3 | 3.4 |
| Hungary | 1.7 | 8.5 | 10.7 | 12.8 | 11.3 | 11.2 |
| Poland | 3.5 | 9.7 | 12.9 | 14.9 | 16.4 | 15.5 |
| Romania | – | 3.0 | 6.2 | 9.2 | 11.0 | 10.5 |
| Slovakia | 0.58 | 6.6 | 11.3 | 12.9 | 14.6 | 15.0 |
| Slovenia | 4.7 | 8.2 | 11.5 | 14.4 | 14.5 | 14.0 |

*Source: Eastern Europe Monitor.*

- The failure to achieve a sufficiently employment-intensive pattern of growth, which has led not only to higher levels of unemployment but also to a rise in hidden unemployment, such as in that part of the female workforce which has been discouraged from looking for work.
- Insufficient flexibility of labour markets, which has slowed down the structural change in economic activity needed to maintain competitiveness and thus employment opportunities.
- Inadequate investment in education and training to improve the skills and capabilities of the labour force, which reduces overall competitiveness.

In addition, these problems have been accompanied by a widening of the gap between those who have skills and a certain degree of market power and those individuals in weaker positions. Moreover, there has been limited progress in convergence between living standards and job opportunities for people living in different EU regions.

So how have some of these problems been addressed?

## FLEXIBILITY IN THE LABOUR MARKET

Flexible working can mean different things in different countries. But what is meant by flexibility? It has been used to encompass a great many ideas.

- *Wage or earnings flexibility* – the responsiveness of wages to market pressures. At the micro level it is about matching pay with productivity, e.g. performance-related pay, bonus-related productivity, performance or profits. At the macro level this is the degree to which payment responds to changes in the demand and supply of labour.
- *Labour mobility* – the ability of individuals to move between regions, occupations and jobs and includes the level of movement within a company.
- *Functional flexibility* – reducing the demarcation lines between different occupations. This has sometimes been linked to 'core:periphery' models of the flexible organisation, where the core workforce (full-time permanent staff) may receive different levels of training with the view that they adopt working practices based on greater task flexibility, thus enabling them to undertake a variety of tasks.
- *Flexibility in the pattern and organisation of work* – including flexibility in the place of work, so covering both traditional working at home and tele-working. Numerical flexibility concerns the ways in which organisations change the numbers of staff or the number of hours in response to changes in demand. In other words, it concerns the use of part-time, temporary and self-employed (subcontracted) workers. A further subset of the above would include working-time flexibility, that is, being able to offer different amounts of time per week or per quarter to coincide with peak demand pressures.

So what is the evidence about whether labour markets have become more flexible? Table 24.4 shows changes in the flexibility of the labour market within the UK.

The data suggest that the UK labour market has become more flexible over the past 20 years. In particular, there has been a major growth in both part-time and self-employment, working patterns have also become more diverse, and many barriers to flexibility within the workplace have been removed. Wages have also become more flexible, with a growth in decentralisation of wage negotiations. By 1990 under half of all employees were covered by **collective bargaining** agreements. The pay–performance link appears to have been strengthened during the 1980s: three-quarters or more of medium/large organisations may now use some form of performance-related pay. At a macroeconomic level employment levels also appear to respond more quickly to changing economic conditions. However, there is less evidence at this level of greater wage flexibility, although during the 1993–5 period average earnings growth has been very low relative to the 1980s. In addition there appears to be a gender dimension to labour-market flexibility: women are more likely than men to work in part-time or temporary jobs (often by choice). They are also more likely to move between jobs.

The breakdown of the labour market into core full-time staff and part-time or temporary staff may enhance flexibility for employers, but increases the strain on full-time staff who may feel threatened in losing their status and may have to take on greater responsibilities.

There are some significant differences between flexibility in the UK and in other countries. Labour-market regulation is much less harsh in the UK than in most other EU member states and this gives the former greater perceived labour-market flexibility, as Figure 24.10 indicates. Less regulation

**Table 24.4 Summary assessment of whether the labour market has become more flexible**

| Indicator | Evidence of greater flexibility since the end of the 1970s |
|---|---|
| **1 Microeconomic flexibility indicators: employment and hours worked** | |
| Part-time, temporary and self-employment | Yes |
| Engagements and dismissals | *Probably* yes |
| Working time | *Probably* yes |
| Functional flexibility | Yes |
| Labour mobility | Uncertain |
| **2 Microeconomic flexibility indicators: wages** | |
| Wage determination | Yes |
| Relative wage flexibility: | |
|     Regions | Yes |
|     Industries | Yes |
|     Human capital | Yes |
| **3 Macroeconomic flexibility indicators: employment and hours worked** | |
| Relationship between employment, hours worked and output | Yes |
| **4 Macroeconomic flexibility indicators: wages** | |
| Real wage flexibility | Uncertain |

*Source*: Beatson, M (1995) 'Progress towards a flexible labour market', *Employment Gazette*, February, pp 55–65. Office for National Statistics. Crown Copyright 1995. Reproduced by the permission of the Controller of HMSO and the Office for National Statistics.

**Figure 24.10 EU employers' perceptions of labour-market inflexibility[a] in 1989**

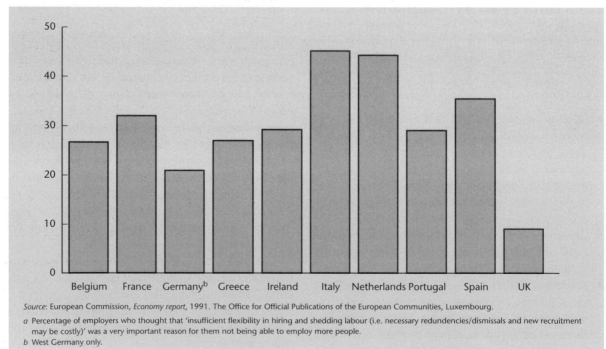

*Source*: European Commission, *Economy report*, 1991. The Office for Official Publications of the European Communities, Luxembourg.

a Percentage of employers who thought that 'insufficient flexibility in hiring and shedding labour (i.e. necessary redundencies/dismissals and new recruitment may be costly)' was a very important reason for them not being able to employ more people.
b West Germany only.

may also explain why the UK has a more diverse pattern of working hours than any other EU member state.

In the US, the absence of labour-market regulation has produced a high degree of external flexibility. Labour is also highly mobile, thus there is less of a requirement for internal flexibility. Wages tend to be more flexible at the micro level than in other countries, although like the UK this is not necessarily the case at the macro level.

In both Germany and Japan there appears to be a high level of aggregate wage flexibility. At the micro level the emphasis is on internal rather than external flexibility and, as a result, employment tends to be relatively stable over the business cycle. In the Nordic economies there appears to be little wage flexibility. However, this has been compensated for by aggregate wage flexibility and high rates of mobility out of unemployment. In other EU countries flexibility appears to be limited at the micro level and labour-market regulations may be an important factor here.

## ◆ CASE STUDY 24.1

### Are European companies becoming more sceptical about social legislation? FT

At a time of increasing global competition, the European Union persists with social policies which the US has rejected as an affordable luxury. European policy makers have so far resisted copying the US system, arguing that it has produced in-work poverty and provides little social protection for the vulnerable. There are signs, however, that, individually, many European countries are beginning to share the UK's scepticism towards social legislation.

The European Commission itself recently noted trends towards deregulation and greater labour market flexibility across all member states. France and Spain, for example, are beginning to use more temporary and fixed-term contracts. In Germany's most important economic sector, the metalworking industry, working time flexibility is dominating the industrial relations agenda, partly because of the 35-hour week introduced across the industry in October 1995.

If nothing is done, the alternative is large-scale redundancies, often leaving fewer people to work longer hours while those who have been laid-off place an increasing social burden on the state. Some European countries have introduced restrictions on the number of hours that can be worked. In the Netherlands, for example, there is a limit of 2500 hours annually and a maximum of eight hours per day. In Spain, the maximum working week is 40 hours. While some European countries, including the Netherlands, Spain and France, have a statutory minimum wage, there are signs of greater acceptance of lower wages in order to encourage the unemployed back into work. The Netherlands has introduced exemptions such as particular sectors and age variations and Spain and Italy have introduced initiatives to encourage young people and the long-term unemployed to take low-paid jobs.

Italy and the Netherlands have both introduced tax breaks and incentives for employers to assist recruitment. Some countries are also introducing measures to help people leave the labour market through early retirement.

In addition, some countries are looking to reduce non-wage labour costs. Companies in Belgium, for example, are being given exemptions from social security contributions for hiring young unemployed people.

Source: *Financial Times*, 24 October 1995. Reprinted with permission.

---

### ◆ Exercise 24.1

1 What reductions in non-wage costs will lower the cost of labour?

2 What other factors may lead to employers increasing the demand for labour?

---

### Comment on the case study

While there still seems to be no uniform consensus about tackling European unemployment, there does appear to be increasing appreciation at government level of organisations' employment needs. The way of approaching these needs differs between countries. The UK lies in an intermediate position between the US and its EU partners in terms of labour-market flexibility: this has been due to a whole raft of **supply-side policies** introduced over the past two decades. These policies in the UK include:

- reform of the tax and social security system to increase incentives to work and invest
- improvements in the skills and training of the labour force
- reductions in red tape and other impediments to investment and risk-taking
- the abolition of wage councils
- improvements in the geographical and occupational mobility of labour
- a whole range of trade union legislation to curb the powers of the trade unions.

The question that is always raised is what has been the cost of this improved flexibility? It may be seen that a larger proportion of the workforce does not have full-time permanent work, that they remain less skilled, that certain groups are more likely to be barred from the workplace, and that many of the social costs of employment have been shifted from the employer to the employee. It is to some of these areas that the chapter now turns.

# SKILL DEFICIENCIES AND SKILL NEEDS

One reason that the supply side of the market is constrained is that some workers do not have the appropriate qualifications currently demanded by the labour market. In the area of training, one of the biggest problems for UK industry is a lack of vocational skills at the intermediate level, as indicated in Table 24.5.

The UK falls behind its major competitors not only at the intermediate level, but also in some areas of higher education where the number of graduates in engineering and technology per million of the population is only 73 per cent of the US and German level and only 45 per cent that of Japan (Trade and Industry Committee, 1994). As a means to address some of these problems, the UK government set up Training and Enterprise Councils (TECs) in the early 1990s to provide a range of training, education and enterprise initiatives. Organisations' low level of training is believed to stem from the nature of the British labour market, in which workers expect to move jobs frequently – in contrast to Japan, for example, where workers often stay with the same employer throughout their working lives. This mobility reduces the incentive to train staff. Rather than expensively training workers who may then move to rival organisations, it is more cost-effective for each organisation to 'free ride', waiting for others to pay for the training and then 'poaching' trained staff by paying marginally higher wages.

A more recent skills audit called 'Forging Ahead' (1995) suggested that Britain's skills gap with the rest of continental Europe is narrowing. On basic skills (literacy and numeracy) Britain's performance is similar to that of the US and Singapore but lags behind that of France and Germany. At level 2 (the standard tested at the end of compulsory schooling), the UK has fewer entrants and a smaller proportion of the total population qualified than both France and Germany and is close to the level of Singapore. Germany appears to have a significant lead in vocational level 2 qualifications.

At level 3 (intermediate skills) Germany has a clear lead over France, UK, US and Singapore in vocational qualifications; the UK is approximately level with France and the USA and a little ahead of Singapore in the total stock of qualifications at this level.

At the higher skills level (subdegree, degree and postgraduate), the UK has a stock of qualifications which is similar to that of the US, slightly higher than those of France and Germany and higher than that of Singapore. However, although the report suggests that the UK is not that far behind in the skills profile of its workforce, a worrying feature is not so much the UK catching up, but the speed with which countries such as France and Singapore are improving their rates of qualifications and drawing ahead of the UK. In addition, when comparing equivalent-level qualifications between countries, it is important to establish whether like is being compared with like. It would appear that what stands for general-level education in, say, France can be very different from that in the UK. For example, it is not unusual for prospective craft workers to study calculus in France. In the UK (General) National Vocational Qualifications (G)NVQs (qualifications which are aimed at industry-based skills) rarely include a foreign language or advanced maths.

## Remedying skills shortages

For some organisations in the UK the skills shortage exists not because there are the wrong number of people with the right skills, but because the working population is not geographically mobile. This problem can be reduced by encouraging increased labour mobility. If the problem for employers is on a national scale, then the harmonisation of educational awards throughout the EU should see skilled labour coming in from abroad. This is becoming more of an issue: the 1994 Skills Survey of the UK (Ward, 1994) found 63 per cent of employers reporting that the skill needs of their workforce were increasing, up from 60 per cent in 1993.

If unemployment is not set to fall in the near future and employers are considering or requiring

**Table 24.5**

|  | Britain | France | Germany |
|---|---|---|---|
| University degrees | 11 | 7 | 11 |
| Intermediate vocational qualifications | 25 | 40 | 63 |
| Of which: technician | 7 | 7 | 7 |
| craft | 18 | 33 | 56 |
| No vocational qualifications | 64 | 53 | 26 |

Source: Trade and Industry Committee (1994) Table 9, *Competitiveness of UK Manufacturing Industry, Second Report*, House of Commons, April. Parliamentary copyright material is reproduced with the permission of the Controller of Her Majesty's Stationery Office on behalf of Parliament.

their labour force to have more skills, then those currently unemployed with few skills or redundant skills would benefit from training courses. Robinson (1996) suggests that this may not be the best approach. For the UK the proportion of the unemployed who are not qualified has declined significantly: 70 per cent of unemployed men in 1979 had no qualifications, but by 1994 only 30 per cent were in this position; 40 per cent of unemployed men in 1994 had A-level or equivalent qualifications or some form of higher education.

However, skill shortages are often confused with shortages in educational qualifications. In the 1994 Skills Survey, when employers were asked the specific causes for recruitment difficulties they cited 'shortage of skills' as the main factor; the least common response was 'lack of qualifications'. But which skills? For lower-level occupations employers tended to favour an individual's personal skills, such as motivation, honesty and the ability to get on with others. Thus programmes which improve the employer's knowledge of personal skills may be quite effective. In fact, work by Riccio (1995) in the US found that, of three groups of unemployed individuals, those receiving help with their job search, those receiving job search assistance plus access to training programmes and those receiving no additional experience, only the first group experienced a significant effect on their employment opportunities. These studies have been replicated in Sweden and similar effects were found for the Restart programme in the UK. Robinson's overall view is that more intense training should be given to fewer people, and that programmes designed to show the skills which individuals already possess appear to be worthwhile instruments in reducing unemployment.

Finally, the problem of **market failure** in the area of skills training appears to be exacerbated by the UK government's efforts to reduce the power of trade unions and thereby improve the flexibility of the labour market. By market failure here we mean that, without government involvement, organisations tend to underinvest in skills training for their employees. Trade union reforms, along with other employment measures, have made it easier to hire and fire workers and in this respect have strengthened the external labour market. It is now easier for organisations to release unwanted labour into, and draw needed workers out of, the pool of unemployed labour. In the past getting rid of unwanted staff was difficult and costly, so that many organisations were chronically overmanned for extended periods and others preferred (inefficiently) to use their existing workforces more intensively in boom periods, in preference to taking on extra workers whom they might find it hard to sack in the future.

But the side-effect of a stronger **external labour market** is a natural tendency for firms to look outside for skilled labour whenever their requirements change. In contrast, labour regulations in Germany make the firing of workers very difficult, and in Japan many workers still have jobs for life with the same company. In both these countries the external labour market is weak. One consequence of this is that organisations may be overstaffed during recessions. The positive dimension, however, is that when the nature of the demand for labour changes (e.g. due to the introduction of a new production process), the onus is on German and Japanese organisations to retrain their existing labour forces, rather than simply bidding for previously trained workers in the external labour market. Because of the weakness in the external labour market there is little chance that staff will be poached by 'free-riders'. Thus one unintended consequence of the government's labour union reforms may have been to exacerbate the skills market failure by strengthening the external labour market.

## OLDER WORKERS

Organisations need to consider the optimal age structure of their workforces. One perception is that younger workers are cheaper, more adaptable in terms of taking on new training and skills and more highly productive. Yet older workers may provide a wealth of experience, may also wish to be trained but are often overlooked, and their work ethic is very different. In other words, organisations need to consider both the costs and benefits of having an older workforce.

Work by Dibden and Hibbett (1993) has established that although older workers (those aged 50 or more) are increasing in number, their participation rates are declining. Interest in older workers has been engendered by increasingly older populations. For example, in the EU by the year 2020, approximately 25 per cent of the population will be over 60. The equivalent figures for 1960 were 15 per cent, and for 1990 20 per cent. Although their participation rates are falling, there is considerable variation between member states and between the sexes. A similar trend can also be seen across OECD countries, with again wide variations between countries. In Japan the participation rate was 44 per cent in

1990, the highest among OECD countries, declining from 52 per cent in 1965. At the opposite end is Italy, where participation rates among those aged 55 and over were 10 per cent both in 1965 and 1990.

In the UK the number of older people in the population has remained relatively unchanged over recent years (17 million people aged 50 and over); but the proportion of economically active older women has increased, while that of men has decreased (*see* Dibden and Hibbett (1993)).

There have been a number of policies and practices affecting this older group of people. The main effects can be viewed as follows:

- Policies relating to exit strategies adopted by older workers, e.g. the incentives in place for retirement.
- Policies relating to incentives for the recruitment or retention of older workers, such as wage subsidies, targeted training schemes or placement services for older workers. The existence of anti-discrimination legislation was also viewed as a recruitment strategy.
- Measures in support of older workers, such as health-at-work initiatives, job assessment and the like.

With regard to retirement arrangements, there have been moves in Japan, France, Australia, New Zealand and the US to raise the retirement age. The main reason is that it will reduce the overall amount of public expenditure required to support them.

In some countries pension entitlements are flexible, that is, the individual can decide when to retire within certain age bands. For example, in Belgium individuals can choose to retire between the ages of 60 and 65; in Greece they can choose to retire and take their pension up to five years before the official retirement date, depending on conditions. Where pensions are based on a certain number of years of contributions, the individual can also apply for early retirement. Such systems are in existence in Italy, Greece, Germany and Austria. Sometimes it is also possible to defer taking pension entitlements. This is possible in Germany where workers can stay on after the official retirement age of 65, but such a procedure is discouraged in Belgium and Luxembourg because of the desire to open up the market to younger people.

Only a small number of countries have enacted age-related anti-discrimination legislation. These include the US, Canada, France, Spain, Australia and New Zealand.

### ◆ Exercise 24.2

1 Is government legislation required either at a national or EU level to resolve the issue of age discrimination in the labour market?

2 Why do some British firms discriminate against people in terms of their age?

For both questions you may find it useful to consult Dibden and Hibbett (1993) and Whitting *et al* (1995).

### ◆ CASE STUDY 24.2

## The cost of employing older workers

The announcement in August 1995, by nearly 100 leading British companies, that they would no longer use age limits in their recruitment advertising looks impressive.

The 100 companies which have signed the declaration amounted to only about one in five of those employers approached by the Carnegie Third Age Programme. This suggests either indifference or outright opposition by many companies to any move towards eradicating age limits from job applications.

It is possible to understand why companies should insist on age barriers in some jobs. For example, driving a train or piloting a plane, working in jobs with a high level of physical stress on a building site, or down a mine are clearly jobs done by younger rather than older workers. Many companies are also keen to stimulate young talent and not become top-heavy with old or even middle-aged staff. And it is obvious that younger employees are less expensive to recruit than older ones.

Moreover, merely removing an age-limit stipulation from a recruitment advertisement does not solve the problem. Most employers have a clear idea of the kind of person they want to fill a particular vacancy, and age, as much as qualification, is bound to affect their attitudes – whatever they say in the job description. However, sensible companies are starting to realise they need 'a good mix' of ages among their staff.

There is something artificial about associating a particular age with a particular job. This is especially true as labour markets become more flexible and deregulated, with workers being urged to adopt a pattern of employment throughout their lifetime that involves different skills and occupations.

*Source: Financial Times*, 30 August 1995. Reprinted with permission.

# The costs of early retirement

Whether organisations like it or not, stereotyping of people by age can be very shortsighted, particularly in the light of the demographic shift in the population. However, given the increased stress some people find in their working lives, some older workers will leave as early as possible.

Where an early retirement scheme exists, such schemes have tended to lower the average retirement age. For example, in Finland the retirement age is 65, but the average pension age is approximately 58. The take-up of early retirement schemes also depends on the proportion of the full pension an individual will receive by retiring early.

However, organisations are becoming more aware of the problems they may face through encouraging early retirement. On the one hand they see it as a saving on their wage bill. For example, in the UK many locally managed schools have offered fairly attractive early retirement packages for some of their senior staff and have replaced them with cheaper, junior staff. Furthermore, they have tried to increase productivity by appointing flexible, enthusiastic, adaptable individuals.

On the other hand, the early retirement of older staff is ultimately costly as it represents a waste of human capital. For example, in 1993 the German chemical company Heinkel attributed a fall in profits to the extraordinary expenses incurred to pay for the early retirement of workers. In fact, the costs to Heinkel were both the early retirement packages and the costs of training younger people to replace those who had been persuaded to retire early.

So what of employers' attitudes to older workers? Can a case be built that suggests that older workers offer many more advantages than disadvantages?

Given that the average age of the economic population is rising (in the UK it will be over 40 by the year 2005) and that older workers are less economically active, this poses problems, both at the macroeconomic level and at the level of individual organisations. The case for older workers, therefore, should include such issues as the following:

■ Employers need to protect their human assets, both to ensure a full return on their investment and to prevent skill shortages arising in the future. Allowing early retirement to take place may mean a loss of important skills. For example, Aérospatiale in France suffered a loss of skills and know-how as a result of the early retirement of some of its skilled key workers in the 1980s and this gave rise to concern within the company that it would not be able to sustain its 'knowledge pool'. In the UK it is these same older workers who are least likely to receive training. Employers often argue that a lack of appropriate skills is one of the main factors in discouraging the recruitment and employment of older workers, yet they give the lowest priority to this age group. However, research by Barth *et al* (1993) suggests that older workers are better endowed with the qualities needed for a high-quality, trainable and flexible workforce. Thus an important issue is the transference of skills and knowledge from older to younger people, which in itself can reduce skill shortages.

■ As individuals grow older does their performance deteriorate? Work by Belbin (1965) and Warr (1994) suggests that age is a very poor proxy for performance in employment and training. Therefore, organisations which discriminate against older workers are denying themselves access to the widest pool of talent. Such arguments may have had more validity when there were a large number of younger workers to choose from, but this policy may be less appropriate when the working population is ageing.

■ Since the working population is ageing, so must be consumers. Organisations will need to tailor their products more to the demands of this ageing population. Thus they will need to consider employing people who are more familiar with older consumers. In the UK, B & Q, a do-it-yourself retail chain, has found its policy of employing older people to be very effective.

■ Successful companies in the future may well be those which can draw on a wide variety of skills and knowledge. Such a pool of information and experience may be better obtained from a workforce which is more evenly balanced in its age profile.

What have been organisations' responses to older workers? First, the definition of an older worker may well differ and may be a reflection of the sector in which the organisation operates. For example, a person may be deemed old at 40 in the information technology sector. Generally, employers associate different characteristics with older and young people:

■ *Younger workers* – ambition, trainability, flexibility, health, IT skills, qualifications and mobility.
■ *Older workers* – stability, reliability, work commitment, responsibility, maturity, and managerial skills.

Although some employers view age and productivity to be inversely related, this is not true for all and many of the prejudices about older workers are often dispelled when employers come into contact with them.

Metcalf and Thomson (1990) found that employers considered particular types of jobs to be associated with different age ranges. Employers consider older people to be more appropriate for jobs which demand low skill, little responsibility and are repetitive in nature. Examples are routine clerical jobs, selling jobs, counselling/caring jobs and tedious jobs. The younger age group was favoured for jobs which were IT related, heavy manual jobs and stressful office jobs.

Overall, staff turnover is lower for older workers. There is consistent evidence that older workers are more likely than younger ones to stay with the same employer and that age is not a sound basis on which to judge ability to work or learn. It is therefore hard to justify why there is still discrimination against older people in the labour market. If organisations are to improve their competitive advantage in the future, they may well have to examine closely their policies on the recruitment of older people.

# WOMEN IN THE LABOUR MARKET

Many EU countries have seen changes in the participation of women in the labour market. Part of this may have been supply led, but it could also be linked to changes in the demand for labour. Organisations may see women as more likely to fill the growing number of part-time jobs, which has enabled them to improve their flexibility and competitive position. They may also see the move towards employing more women as a way of replacing full-time, unionised male employees with more 'flexible' female employees. At the same time, many organisations have realised that by not providing jobs for women they are losing out on a very important resource. The reduction in discrimination against women in the workforce has improved women's role models, encouraging more women not only to increase their participation in the labour market but also to seek higher positions. Thus for a variety of reasons the labour market for women is changing and organisations appear to be more keen to tap into this important resource.

In terms of Europe, on an aggregate level, the participation of prime working-age women (25–49 age category) in the EU rose from 34 per cent in 1960 to 67 per cent in 1992, slightly less than in the EFTA countries and the US, in both of which it was 75 per cent in 1992. The present rates of participation by women in the labour force vary substantially between countries. In Ireland the rate was around 50 per cent in 1992, in Spain and Greece below 55 per cent, whereas in Portugal and the UK it was over 70 per cent and in Denmark almost 90 per cent. This implies that in the future, apart from in Denmark, further increases in the participation rate for women can be expected, particularly in Spain, Ireland and Southern Italy, posing a considerable challenge for job creation in the future (European Commission (1994)).

In the UK the unemployment rate for women is lower than that for men. In this respect the country stands out from the rest of the EU and to a lesser extent the US; *see* Table 24.6.

This is not to suggest that a smaller proportion of women are unemployed in the UK: it may well be that they do not register themselves as unemployed. One reason could be that British women are less able than women in other countries to say that they are available for work in the next two weeks (the definition used to register as unemployed) because of the low availability of subsidised childcare. Another reason for UK women having lower unemployment than men is the high rate of part-time women's employment in the UK. Britain

**Table 24.6 Standardised unemployment rates by sex (per cent of employed + unemployed)**

| Country | 1984 M | 1984 F | 1987 M | 1987 F | 1993 M | 1993 F |
|---|---|---|---|---|---|---|
| Belgium | 8.0 | 18.3 | 7.0 | 17.4 | 6.9 | 12.7 |
| Denmark | 7.7 | 10.0 | 5.3 | 8.0 | 11.3 | 13.7 |
| France | 8.0 | 12.6 | 8.6 | 13.7 | 9.9 | 13.8 |
| Germany | 6.8 | 9.3 | 6.3 | 9.3 | 8.0 | 8.4 |
| Greece | 6.0 | 12.1 | 5.1 | 11.5 | 5.4 | 14.2 |
| Ireland | 15.9 | 17.0 | 18.1 | 22.1 | 18.8 | 19.5 |
| Italy | NA | NA | NA | NA | 8.1 | 17.3 |
| Luxembourg | 2.4 | 4.7 | 3.1 | 2.7 | NA | NA |
| Netherlands | 10.7 | 13.5 | 7.7 | 12.2 | 5.7 | 10.5 |
| Portugal | 6.6 | 12.5 | 4.9 | 9.0 | 4.6 | 6.5 |
| Spain | 19.7 | 24.9 | 15.6 | 27.9 | 12.3 | 23.9 |
| UK | 11.6 | 10.3 | 10.8 | 9.6 | 12.4 | 7.5 |
| USA | 7.4 | 7.6 | 6.2 | 6.2 | 7.0 | 6.5 |

NA = not available

*Sources:* OECD, *Employment Outlook*, September 1988, Table 5.2 for 1984 and 1987. Figures for 1993 taken from *ILO International Year Book 1994.*

has one of the highest rates of part-time employment in Europe, and women fill almost 90 per cent of the part-time jobs. British women employed part-time have also been less likely to be eligible to receive unemployment benefit when made redundant than is the case in some countries.

Labour turnover among women in the EU is significantly greater than among men. Between 1984 and 1992, an average of 15 per cent of women working in a sector had entered since the previous year, while the average figure for men was 10 per cent. This was especially the case for Ireland, the UK and Luxembourg.

Women tended to work fewer hours than men: 49 per cent worked less than 38 hours per week and 4 per cent had a normal working week of under 10 hours in 1992. Although part-time working predominantly involves women, who fill 85 per cent of all part-time jobs, what is meant by a part-time job varies across the EU. The problem arises in how individuals define their jobs: some consider that, although they are working part-time hours, they are full-time employees.

In a survey of the UK women's labour market (Sly (1996)), although women dominated part-time working, this was not simply because the flexible labour force was supplying more part-time jobs but was also demand led, with 80 per cent of women working part-time not wanting full-time employment, although this varied with the number of dependants. The occupations or subgroups in which most women worked were clerical/secretarial, personal services such as nursing/care assistants, catering and hairdressing and sales. These were also the occupations in which there were more part-time jobs. Women were also to be found predominantly in the service sector of the economy. Teleworking is one of the growth sectors which improves the flexibility of the labour market and it may lead to a greater involvement of women. However, although this may conjure up a picture of a high-tech employee working from a rural idyll, the greatest use of teleworking is associated with information processing, telephone enquiries and sales work. Women predominate in this area partly because the jobs involve routine secretarial and administrative work. The European Commission estimates that there could be 10 million teleworkers in Europe by the year 2000, and because they have few labour rights they will need protecting.

◆ **CASE STUDY 24.3**

## Women's work

By rights, women ought now to be receiving hefty consultancy fees advising companies on the trials of the modern UK labour market. After all, for more than 20 years they have experienced first-hand the most often-remarked recent trends in UK employment practices. They have benefited disproportionately from the steady rise in 'flexible' working practices. By the same token, they have also experienced a larger share of the insecurities and/or low pay which non-traditional employment patterns imply.

Yet far from learning from women's experience at the cutting edge of these changes, society continues rather to exploit it, by paying female workers less than male ones and promoting them less often.

Women's continued lower earnings come partly from the continued segregation of occupations along gender lines. But even in sectors where women predominate they tend not to hold the senior positions. As ever, the biggest obstacles to a lucrative and long-lasting career are motherhood-related. Many companies have introduced flexible working hours in order to attract – and retain – female employees who have chosen to have children. But insufficient, and costly, childcare provision tends to mean that opting to have a child means opting-out too, for a long career break and much lower promotion chances thereafter.

*Source: Financial Times, 9 August 1995. Reprinted with permission.*

◆ **Exercise 24.3**

1  How might organisations improve the problems women face in lack of childcare?

2  Why do women continue to earn lower salaries than men in many comparative occupations?

*Comment on the case study*

For their part employers have found that flexible working patterns have helped them remain competitive in markets. Yet as Case study 24.4 indicates, this flexibility could be further enhanced if both employers and organisations tried harder to stop not only full-time but also part-time women leaving the labour market for long periods.

# THE SOCIAL CHARTER

For those who believe in the free-market system, the Social Charter, which guaranteed a whole range of rights to workers, was seen as a mechanism to reduce the flexibility of the workforce and make industry less competitive. The **Social Charter** of 1989 – more precisely, the Community Charter of Fundamental Social Rights – was developed as a parallel set of actions to safeguard social rights for EU citizens that might be threatened by the increased competition that would ensue from the development of the Single European Market. The Social Charter therefore established a list of minimum conditions which all countries should implement to ensure that social dumping did not occur. Table 24.7 indicates the main areas.

Although the Social Charter was approved by 11 of the 12 EU states at the Strasbourg summit in December 1989, the UK felt unable to accept its provisions since it contradicted its own beliefs in free labour markets. Table 24.8 shows the beliefs of the more social-minded EU states and those that tend to favour the UK's position.

The free-marketeer's view is that the Social Charter imposes increased costs on organisations, raising prices therefore leading to reduced market shares. Conversely, those who believe in the workings of the Social Charter see the social provisions as raising the working and living conditions of labour, enabling it to provide better-quality goods and improving productivity. In fact, they argue further that currently there is no way in which the EU can compete with the Pacific Rim countries on a price basis, particularly without competitive currency devaluations.

## The Social Chapter

Under the Maastricht Agreement, the Social Charter was put forward as the Social Chapter. However, because of the UK's opposition, it was appended as a separate protocol between the 11 members excluding the UK. What this means is

## Table 24.7 The twelve rights of the Social Charter, 1989

1 *Freedom of movement*: the right of citizens of any EU country to work anywhere in the EU and on equal terms of employment with nationals of the country where the work is.

2 *Employment and remuneration*: the right to employment and to receive a fair wage (however defined) for that work.

3 *Improved living and working conditions*: with emphasis on upward harmonisation, e.g. introduction of maximum permitted hours of working week; rights to annual paid leave; and the extension of this to all modes of employment including, in recognition of changing labour markets, part-time and fixed contract workers.

4 *Adequate social protection*: this guarantees all EU workers a minimum wage (although not the same one) regardless of status, and social assistance for citizens excluded from the labour market or who lack adequate subsistence.

5 *Freedom of association*: any worker or employer may belong to any trade union or professional organisation of his or her choice. This also recognises, implicitly, freedom to bargain and conclude collective agreements and, if necessary, collective action including strikes.

6 *Vocational training*: recognising the changing nature of the labour market and the end of jobs for life, every worker shall have the right to vocational training. This should be provided by the public sector, companies and trade unions and other workers' organisations.

7 *Equal treatment for men and women*: specifically equal pay for equal work. Article 119 of the Treaty of Rome also stressed this same point. The fact that it had to be addressed again after thirty years shows how little progress has been made on this issue.

8 *Worker information, consultation and participation*: this refers to the rights of workers to be informed and consulted and even have the right to participate in management decisions of the business they work for, where these affect working conditions and job security. The recent introduction of European Works Councils is a consequence of this.

9 *Health and safety at work*: every worker has the right to satisfactory health and safety conditions at work. Emphasis is placed on upward harmonisation of these conditions.

10 *Protection of children and adolescents*: among other things this gives school-leavers the right to two years' vocational training, defines sixteen as the minimum working age and guarantees fair wages for those who do work.

11 *The rights of the elderly*: this guarantees the right to a pension for those who have retired to afford decent living standards. If he or she does not have a pension then minimum social protection and medical assistance is to be provided.

12 *Disabled persons*: are to be entitled to training and occupational and social integration and rehabilitation.

*Source*: Harris, N (1996) *European Business*, Macmillan, Basingstoke. Reprinted with permission.

**Table 24.8 The contrasting views of the EU and the UK regarding the labour market**

| The EU position | The UK position |
| --- | --- |
| Markets are imperfect and fail occasionally. | Markets should be allowed to work efficiently without the intervention of governments. |
| Governments need to intervene to protect the labour force from the problems that competitive conditions may provide. | Government intervention in the labour market prevents this market working efficiently. |
| The benefits of the SEM need to be disseminated throughout the EU. | Imposing extra cost on employers via social welfare payments leads to higher production costs. |
| By raising standards to those of the highest providers (upward harmonisation) social dumping will be prevented. | EU firms now become less competitive, less labour is employed. |
| | The EU state experience greater social provision as unemployment rises. |
| The EU needs to compete less on price and more on quality and value added. | If the EU reduced its overprotective social welfare provision it would be able to be more price competitive. |

that, when a social policy proposal is made which the UK cannot accept, the other countries opt into the Social Chapter. For some areas of social provision qualified majority voting is permitted, such as in health and safety, equal working opportunities and working conditions. Other areas require unanimous voting, such as social security and the collective bargaining rights of employers and employees.

Opting into the Social Chapter has arisen with regard to a number of directives since 1993:

- *Posted workers* – This relates to the minimum pay and conditions for workers from one member state working in another member country. It is to prevent posted workers from being employed at lower salaries and with lower conditions than domestic workers.
- *Acquired Rights Directive* – This attempts to give employees some protection and involves them in consultation when a business is transferred elsewhere within the Union or changes to a new owner.
- *Parental Leave Directive* – Both parents would be entitled to three months' leave after the birth or adoption of a dependant and be entitled to return to work on the same pay scale.
- ◆ *Works Council Directive* – Although opted out of by the UK, this requires companies employing more than 1000 people, or more than 150 in two European countries, to establish workers' representative committees after September 1996. This enables employees to gain more rights in developing and enacting the strategy of the organisation.

- *Part-Time Workers Directive* – Part-time workers who are employed for more than eight hours per week have the same rights pro rata as their full-time colleagues, including pay, holidays and entitlement to company pension schemes. These pension entitlements can be backdated to 1977 for those employees who have been employed by the same employer since that time.
- *Maximum Working Week Directive* – Adopted in 1993, this directive limited the maximum working week to 48 hours. However, because of opposition this was diluted to include the provision 'unless they wish to [work more than 48 hours]'.

The extent to which social policy affects the workforce therefore depends on which countries have opted in to the various parts of the package; how far policies have been watered down; the difficulties of setting levels, e.g. a fair wage in Germany is a very good wage in Greece or Portugal; and whether issues such as the fact that over 45 per cent of EU unemployed have been out of work for more than one year influence decisions.

In addition, the ageing population in the EU and the increased pressure from the Pacific Rim countries in both traditional and domestic markets has meant that the Commission has had to re-examine the whole area of social provision and its impact on labour costs and the labour market itself. Strangely, although the British government appears to be an arch critic of EU social policy, it was the only country to have adopted all of the EU social legislation to which it had signed up by 1995. The laggards in Europe appeared to be Belgium and Greece with 83 per cent, with Spain bottom of the list at 70 per cent.

From a UK perspective the fact that it has not opted in to the Social Chapter as a means of maintaining its flexible and competitive workforce does not mean that legislation will not affect its companies. The works council directive gives a good example of this. In February 1995 the TUC noted that at least 20 European-owned multinational companies – predominantly French and German – had established works councils for all their employees, including those employed in the UK. These included Elf Aquitaine, Renault, Thomson, Bull, Nestlé, Volkswagen and Crédit Lyonnaise. However, there have also been a growing number of UK-owned companies which have established work councils, not only for their continental European employees but also for their domestic workforces. These include SmithKline Beecham, National Westminster Bank, Barclays Bank, Cadbury Schweppes, Coats Viyella, ICI, Courtaulds and British Telecom. Thus it has been argued that the British economy is opting in to the Social Chapter even if the British government is not.

The labour market is likely to play an even bigger part in EU and national government policies during the next millennium. Currently employment may not be a priority issue as the EU member states attempt to achieve the criteria for monetary union. In fact, in these criteria there is no target for unemployment. Once policy on the labour market takes a more central position, the EU will need to address issues about job creation – it is suggested that the small and medium-sized firm sector looks a promising source of this – and improved competitiveness. This may require consideration of minimum wage laws and the whole raft of social legislation that prevents the labour market, as the UK perceives it, from working efficiently. At the same time the labour market itself is changing: there are problems regarding the long-term unemployed, there will continue to be higher participation rates for women, and there is the question of an ageing workforce. In addition, both organisations and governments need to consider improving the participation of ethnic groups and disabled people in the labour market. If forecasts are correct there will also be increasing numbers of people working from home. Thus the future of the labour market is likely to be one of major change, and also throws up major opportunities for both governments and organisations.

## SUMMARY

◆ The aggregate supply curve for labour is upward sloping to the right. Individual supply curves can bend backwards as the wage rate rises, due to the tradeoff of leisure for work at the higher wage rate. The shape of the individual supply curve of labour is dependent on the strength of income and substitution effects.

◆ Using a short-run production function where capital stock is fixed and labour is the only variable, the demand for labour is obtained from the point at which the marginal productivity of labour is equal to the wage rate. The demand-for-labour curve slopes down to the right because of the eventual declining marginal productivity of labour. Equilibrium in the labour market is established at the point at which the demand for labour equals the supply of labour.

◆ It has been argued that setting a minimum wage in a competitive market leads to higher unemployment, not only because some individuals are priced out of the market but because other workers increase their wage demands to keep relative differentials intact. Minimum wage levels have been used in Europe and the US as a means by which younger workers can be protected from exploitation. More recent research work in both the US and the UK appears to suggest that minimum wages may not lead to higher unemployment. On the contrary, these studies suggest minimum wages can have a beneficial effect.

◆ Many EU labour markets have a high element of social protection which is often funded through charges on businesses. These higher charges are reducing the competitiveness of some European organisations, and this could partly explain why the number of jobs created in the EU over the past decade is rather disappointing when compared with the US.

◆ Neoclassical economists have advocated the development of free markets – markets which are flexible to the conditions of supply and demand. This flexibility includes wage or earnings flexibility, labour mobility, functional flexibility and flexibility in the pattern and organisation of work. The UK labour market is viewed as being one of the most flexible in the EU. This flexibility, it has been argued, has resulted in the UK having a lower level of unemployment than its continental EU rivals. However, the tradeoff has been less security for workers, possibly less productivity, and a greater numbers of individuals working on part-time or flexible contracts.

◆ One of the weaknesses of the UK economy has been its skill and educational deficiencies. The improvement in the staying-on rate at school and in higher education has alleviated some of the shortfall in the proportion of people with educational qualifications. Nonetheless, the UK still lags behind in the skills level. Employers may not wish to undertake skills training if they believe that competitors will poach their newly trained workers. Both in Germany and Japan there is evidence of less mobility between jobs, thus leading to greater training in skills.

◆ Although skills training is seen as an important aspect of providing the higher-value-added goods of the future, demographic changes in the labour market are also affecting organisations' labour resources. The working population is getting older and older workers' participation rates are declining. During the 1980s and early 1990s some organisations encouraged older workers to leave employment. However, there are costs and benefits in this approach. The benefits include lower wage bills, perceived

improved productivity, use of younger, flexible, enthusiastic and adaptable individuals. The costs are seen in terms of the high financial costs of retirement packages, loss of the 'knowledge pool', loss of committed staff, and the failure to have staff who are aware of the demands of the ageing consumer market.

◆ Over the last three decades there has been a large increase in the participation rate of women in the labour market. This differs markedly within the EU, from over 75 per cent in the UK and Denmark to less than 55 per cent in Spain, Greece and Ireland. Women are more likely to be in part-time employment and part of the flexible labour market, often through choice. There is still a stereotyping of the occupations into which women gravitate.

◆ The Social Charter of 1989 was developed as a parallel set of actions to safeguard social rights for the EU's citizens that might be threatened by the increased competition that would develop from the Single European Market. It implemented minimum conditions for EU member states so that social dumping did not occur. Neoclassical economists saw this as adding to the costs faced by organisations. The Social Charter became the Social Chapter under the Maastricht Treaty. The UK did not sign up to this. However, there is evidence that the UK has been affected by a number of elements of the Social Chapter as UK organisations have offered the same rights to their workforces as those in continental Europe.

## REVIEW QUESTIONS

1 Suppose that an individual faces a wage level of £10 per hour, can work up to eight hours per day, and can negotiate the number of hours they wish to work.
   Construct the individual's budget line. Suppose that the individual now faces a reduction in their wage to £8 per hour: construct the new budget line.
   What will be the impact on the original budget line of a reduction in income tax of £2 per hour?

2 Using Figure 24.2, show what might happen if leisure is viewed as an inferior good.

3 Consider what might be the impact on the labour market of minimum wage legislation if the employer is a monopsonist (sole purchaser of labour) or where labour supplied is unionised.

4 If the labour market in the EU requires more highly skilled labour, where does this leave those individuals who are:

a long-term unemployed?

b without qualifications?

5 Consider the advantages and disadvantages of encouraging older individuals back into the labour market.

6 'The rest of the EU has a lot to learn from the UK's deregulated labour market.' How far do you agree with this statement?

7 How can you explain the UK's lower level of unemployment compared to its main continental European rivals in 1996, while at the same time it has one of the least well-educated workforces?

## GLOSSARY OF NEW TERMS

**Collective bargaining:** A procedure where a union or occupation agrees to negotiate wages for all its members which will be the same throughout the country.

**Diminishing returns:** A concept which describes the fact that with two factors of production, of which only one can be varied, output rises but at a diminishing rate.

**External labour market:** The labour market outside the organisation.

**Indifference curve:** A curve which is convex to the origin and describes the combinations of outputs/products which yield the same level of satisfaction.

**Marginal productivity of labour:** The extent to which output increases when there are one-unit changes in the labour input.

**Market failure:** A case where, when left to market forces, the market does not provide the optimal output of a good or service.

**Minimum wage:** A wage often set above the equilibrium or market-clearing wage, which guarantees a minimum payment per hour.

**Production function:** Describes the way in which the output of an organisation is related to the factors of production it has at its disposal.

**Social charter:** A group of policies set up in 1989 to safeguard social rights the EU citizens.

**Sticky-downwards wages:** A process where, given an excess supply of labour, the wage rate does not fall due to rigidities in the labour market, such as the impact of trade unions.

**Supply-side policies:** Policies that can be used to reduce the frictions in the supply side of the economy, such as lower taxes or ways to reduce trade union power.

**Tax wedge:** The difference between what an employee receives in net earnings and the additional charges which employers pay for employing that person.

**Wages council:** Councils set up to administer the wages of different sectors of the UK economy, e.g. agriculture.

## READING

*Department of Employment Gazette* (now called *Labour Market Trends*) Office for National Statistics, London.
*This is a monthly publication which provides in-depth research and analysis of both UK and European labour market issues.*

Dolando, J, Kramarz, F, Machin, S, Manning, A, Margolis, D and Teulings, C (1996) 'Minimum wages: the European experience', *Economic Policy: A European Forum*, October, pp 319–72 (Centre for Economic Policy Research).
*This article brings together the latest research on both sides of the minimum wage debate.*

European Commission (1989–94) *Employment in Europe*, European Commission, Brussels.
*This is an annual publication which deals in great detail with many aspects of the European labour market.*

European Commission (1994) *Growth, Competitiveness, Employment: The Challenges and Ways Forward into the*

*21st Century*, European Commission, Brussels.
*This document provides a good analysis of the current state of the labour market in the EU.*

Killingsworth, M R and Heckman, J J (1986) 'Female labour supply: a survey' in *The Handbook of Labour Economics*, Ashenfelter, O and Layard, P R G (eds), Vol 1, North-Holland, New York and Amsterdam.

Pencavel, J H (1986) 'Labour supply of men: a survey' in *The Handbook of Labour Economics*, Ashenfelter, O and Layard, P R G (eds), Vol 1, North-Holland, New York and Amsterdam.
*Both these articles provide excellent surveys of the male and female labour supply.*

Sapsford, D and Tzannatos, Z (1993) *The Economics of the Labour Market*, Macmillan, Basingstoke.
*This text provides a very good overview of the demand and supply of labour.*

## Further reading

Barth, M C, McNaught, W and Rizzi, P (1993) 'Corporations and the ageing workforce' in Mirvis, P (ed), *Building the Competitive Workforce*, pp 156–200, John Wiley, New York.

Bean, C (1994) 'European unemployment: a survey', *Journal of Economic Literature*, Vol XXXII, No 2, June, pp 573–619.

Belbin, R M (1965) *Training Methods for Older Workers*, OECD, Paris.

Blanchard, D and Summers, I (1986) 'Hysteresis and the European unemployment problem', *NBER Macroeconomic Annual*.

Card, C (1992) 'Do minimum wages reduce unemployment? A case study of California, 1987–89', *Industrial and Labour Relations Review*, Vol 46, No 1, pp 38–54.

Card, C and Kreuger, A (1994) 'Minimum wages and unemployment: a case study of the fast food industry in New Jersey and Pennsylvania', *American Economic Review*, Vol 84, No 4, pp 772–93.

Department for Education and Employment (1995) 'Forging Ahead', *The Skills Audit: A Report from an Interdepartmental Group*, DFEE Publications, London.

Dibden, J and Hibbett, A (1993) 'Older workers – an overview of recent research', *Employment Gazette*, June, pp 237–50.

Elliot, R F (1991) *Labour Economics: A Comparative Text*, McGraw-Hill, Maidenhead.

Griffiths, A and Wall, S (1995) *Applied Economics: An Introductory Text*, 6th edn, Longman, Harlow.

Laurance, B (1996) 'Free the £3.50-an-hour wage slaves', *Observer Business Section*, 30 June, p 4.

Laurance, B (1996) 'Fiddling with edges while the core burns, *Observer*, 27 October, p 7.

Machin, S and Manning, A (1994) 'The effects of minimum wages on wage dispersion and employment: evidence from the UK wages councils', *Industrial and Labour Relations Review*, Vol 47, No 2, pp 319–29.

Metcalf, H and Thompson, H (1990) 'Older workers: employers' attitudes and practices', *Institute of Manpower Studies Report*, No 194.

Riccio, J (1995) *Welfare to Work: What Works? Lessons from California*, Manpower Demonstration Research/Policy Studies Institute, New York.

Robinson, P (1996) 'Skills, Qualifications and Unemployment', *Economic Affairs*, Spring, pp 25–30.

Sly, F (1996) 'Women in the labour market: results from the spring 1995 Labour Force Survey', *Labour Market Trends*, March, pp 91–101.

Trade and Industry Committee (1994) *Competitiveness of UK Manufacturing Industry, Second Report*, House of Commons, London.

Ward, H (1994) 'Skill needs in Britain 1994', *Employment Gazette*, December, pp 485–90.

Warr, P (1994) 'Age and employment' in Dunnette, M D et al (eds), *Handbook of Industrial Organisational Psychology*, Vol 4, Consulting Psychologists Press, Palo Alto, CA.

Whitting, G, Moore, J and Tilson, B (1995) 'Employment policies and practices towards older workers: an international overview', *Employment Gazette*, April, pp 147–52.

# INDEX

## A

ABC (activity based costing)  35
ABM (activity based management)  35
absolute advantage  488, 515
acid rain  190, 468, 469
Adidas  448
advertising  63, 260, 264–5, 278, 422, 521
  barriers to entry and economies of scale
    390–1
  benefits of  276
  effect upon retail sales and retailers  276
  information and  274–5
  market structure and  277
  oligopoly where mutual dependence is
    recognised  272
  persuasion and  274
advertising elasticity  130, 138
Advertising Standards Authority
  (ASA UK)  478
aerospace  16, 548
Aérospatiale  11, 375, 530
Air 2000  549
Air France  67–8
Airbus Industrie  194, 251, 513
aircraft manufacturing industry  374, 375
Aldi  436, 561
Alenia  530
Alliance of Small Island States
  (AOSIS)  476
allocative efficiency  41–2, 53, 206, 521
alternative investment criteria  295–6
Amato Law (Italy 1990)  52
ambient-based systems  468, 483
analysis of demand trends  151–2
Ansoff, Igor,  268–9, 278, 336, 338, 354–5,
  358, 383
appraisal costs  446
arbitrage selling  219
arc elasticity of demand  125, 138
Asda  561
Asia Pacific Economic Co-operation group
  (APEC)  12, 495
Asian tigers  20, 480
assessment of different projects  7
asset specificity  409–10, 413–14, 418–19
Association of British Travel Agents
  (ABTA)  533
attitude to risk  309–10, 326, 329
attribute approach to consumer
  behaviour  103
audits  49
augmented products  262
Australia  287, 335, 489, 495, 584
Austria  13, 51, 538, 540, 584
autocorrelation  163, 164–6, 170, 173
automatic washing machine pricing  240
average book value of investment  295

## B

B&Q  43, 585
backward vertical integration  413–14,
  419
'bad' products  116, 190
Bain, J S  217–18, 520, 525
balance of trade  6, 9
Bank of Scotland  247
Banking Coordination Directive
  (1989)  498
barometric forecasting  152–3, 170
barriers to market entry
  choice of production process  425
  government assistance as  428–9
  overcoming  437–8
  pricing strategies  422–3
  reputation  423–4
  strategic investment and  437
  use of new products  426–8
Bass  550
Bata Shoe Company  343–4
Baumol, W J  62–4, 67, 68, 219, 546
BCCI  49
Bean, C  13, 573
behavioural models of the organisation
  74
behavioural perspectives, decision making
  and  102
behavioural theories  62, 74, 76
behaviourist views, consumer behaviour
  81
Belgium  24, 40, 250, 530–1, 574,
  584, 589
benchmarking  20, 342, 345, 386, 395,
  401, 402, 422, 444, 455
Bertrand, J  433, 439
'best in class process'  395, 401
best response  211
beta coefficient  304
beyond quality leadership  448–9
Bhopal disaster  471
Black and Decker  349
bliss point  81, 85, 105
block exemption  528, 533–4, 540
Blue Angel eco-label (Germany)  478
BMW  241, 392–3, 422, 453–4, 470, 557
The Body Shop  43–4
Boeing  24, 374, 513
bonus schemes  47, 264
Boston Consulting Group (BCG) (see also
  McKinsey Consulting Company)
  268–9, 278, 336, 355, 383, 546
  Boston matrix, see McKinsey matrix
'bounded innovation'  394
bounded rationality  58–9, 76, 525
BP Oil International  25, 439, 505
brand name  422, 450, 455, 456

Brazil  287, 510, 513
break-even analysis  181–3, 195, 296
Brent Spar oil platform  37–8
British Aerospace  292, 511, 557
British Airways  244, 422, 438, 546
British Caledonian  546
British Telecom  436, 497–8, 537, 590
Brooks Brothers  147–8
Brylcreem  147
BS 5750 (British Standard)  445, 455
budget constraint  85–7
budget line  81, 86, 87–8, 95, 105
Burger King  261
business application (see also case studies)
  business and the environment:
    antagonists clear the air  461
  Caterpillar plans to buy back 20m
    shares and raise dividend  57
  demise of the Net Book Agreement  108
  drug companies face anti-trust review
    229
  Europe reaches for its cereal  259
  European restructuring  11
  familiarity breeds respect  422
  Ford: Jac the Knife  335–6
  flexible labour markets and the skilled
    labour force  567
  guessing the cost  176
  international telecommunications  544
  management: drawing a line under
    corporate strategy  4
  management: the ethical way to
    profitability  31
  Microsoft in multimedia alliance with
    NBC  387
  new alliances for a new era  487
  Nintendo and Sega attacked by MMC
    for 'inflated prices'  203
  Porsche sees sharp expansion in output
    141–2
  probe into packaging merger  520
  reinventing the bicycle  363–4
  switch without a timetable – digital
    terrestial television  307–8
  trust: the basis of market economy  405
  tunnel vision  282
  when it comes to the crunch  80
  when it's all in the label  443
Business Cooperation Network (BC-NET)
  23
business economics defined  5, 7, 9
business ethics  13, 44
business policy  360
business strategy  6–9, 336–7, 360
business-unit-level strategy  337

595